THE TRIBES AND CASTES OF THE NORTH-WESTERN PROVINCES AND OUDH

THE TRIBES AND CASTES OF THE NORTH-WESTERN PROVINCES AND OUDH

W. CROOKE

IN FOUR VOLUMES
VOL. IV

GYAN

Published by

GYAN

Gyan Publishing House
5, Ansari Road
Daryaganj, New Delhi-110002
Phone: 011-47034999, 9811692060
E-mail: books@gyanbooks.com

Distribution Network
gyanbooks.com
India, USA, Canada, UK, Australia, France

ISBN : 978-81-212-4170-0 (Set)
ISBN : 978-81-212-4714-6 (HB)
First Published, Calcutta, 1896

2nd Impression 2020

Printed at: Gyan Press, Delhi.

The
Tribes and Castes of the North-Western Provinces and Oudh Vol. IV
Author: W. Crooke

THE TRIBES AND CASTES OF THE NORTH-WESTERN PROVINCES AND OUDH.

VOLUME IV.

M

Monas, Maunas.—A sept of Râjputs found almost exclusively in the Benares Division. According to their own account they take their name from their eponymous ancestor Maunas or Monas Rishi. Their original home is said to have been Amber or Jaypur, and the legend goes that a party of them, coming to bathe at Benares, envied the fertile plain, which is now the Bhadohi Pargana of the Mirzapur District, and conquered it from the Bhars, from whom it took its name. Their immigration from their home in Rajputâna is fixed by the tribal legend at some six or seven hundred years ago. The enquiries, however, of Mr. Duthoit go to show that the Bhar rule in Bhadohi survived the Muhammadan conquest of Kanauj by some two centuries, during which it was in dependence on the Kantit Gaharwârs, and the rise of the Maunas power in Bhadohi cannot be fixed with certainty before the time of Sâgar Râê, whose descendant Jodh Râê, in the third generation, obtained a grant of the pargana from the Emperor Shâhjahân. At one time they enjoyed considerable property, and used, it is said, to give their daughters in marriage to the ruling families of Mânda and Kantit; but in the general anarchy which ensued on the downfall of the Mughal Empire, they suffered from the aggressions of more powerful neighbours, in particular the famous Balwant Sinh of Benares. The Maunas say that their Râja, Siu Bakhsh Sinh, was fraudulently induced to give up to Balwant Sinh the royal grant (*Shâhi farmân*) by which he held the pargana from the Mughal Government. At any rate, whether this be true or not, the greater part of the Maunas territory was absorbed into the Benares Râj, and forms a considerable portion of the domains of His Highness the Mahârâja of Benares. Naturally in the Mutiny the sept gave much trouble. They are now, as a rule, in great poverty, and till as tenants the lands their forefathers used to own. They are held in little estimation, and now-a-days give and take girls from the septs of the Gaharwâr, Bais, and Bisen of Mirzapur and Benares. In Jaunpur they are reported to take brides from the Bisen, Raghubansi, and Chaupat Khamb septs, and to give brides to the Raghubansi, RâjKumâr, Durgbansi, and Bais.

2. In Bhadohi of Mirzapur, which is one of the chief seats of the sept, the Maunas say that their original seat was Amber in Rajputâna, and some fifty generations ago some of them started on a pilgrimage to Gaya. Bhadohi was then ruled by the Bhars, and one of their Râjas ordered a Brâhman, named Siva Man, to give his daughter in marriage to the son of the Râja. The Brâhman appealed to many of the neighbouring Râjas for protection: but they failed him, until the party of Maunas Râjputs took up his cause and finally captured Chauthâr, which was the chief stronghold of the Bhars. Thus they gained the country. Their last Râja was Takht Sinh, who was overcome by the first Râja of Benares. Their *gotra* is Maun. They take brides from the Bisen, Bais, Bachgoti, BhatKariya, Bhanwag, Rikhbansi, Raghubansi, Saunakh, and Tisahiya septs; and give girls to the Gaharwâr of Mânda and Bijaypur, Bachgoti, and Sombansi. The Maunas of Bhadohi do not intermarry with Baghels, as some of their brethren do. There are two grades in the sept—one the real Maunas, and beneath them others, who were introduced by being allowed to eat with the genuine Maunas. The latter marry in inferior septs and families.

Distribution of the Maunas Râjputs by Census, 1891.

Districts.	Number.	Districts.	Number.
Agra	16	Ballia	287
Bânda	2	Gorakhpur	24
Allahâbâd	1,938	Azamgarh	401
Benares	582	Faizâbâd	1
Mirzapur	9,144	Sultânpur	1
Jaunpur	1,721	Bârabanki	52
Ghazipur	60		
		Total	14,229

Mongil.[1]—A sept of Râjputs in Oudh. They are said to have preceded the Bhars. One family of them is found in Sujanpur Ta'aluqa Adharganj.

Mughul, Mughal.—One of the four great Muhammadan sub-divisions known in Europe under the form Mongol. Mr. Ibbetson,[2] writing of the Panjâb, does not attempt to touch upon "the much debated question of the distinction between the Turks and Mughuls. In the Delhi territory, indeed, the villagers accustomed to describe the Mughuls of the Empire as Turks, used the word as synonymous with 'official,' and I have heard my Hindu clerks of Kâyasth class described as Turks, merely because they were in Government employ. On the Biloch frontier the word Turk is commonly used as synonymous with Mughul. The Mughuls proper probably either entered the Panjâb with Bâbar, or were attracted thither under the dynasty of his successors; and I believe that the great majority of those who have returned themselves as Mughuls in the Eastern Panjâb really belong to that race." In these Provinces they say that they take their name from their ancestor Mughul Khân.

2. In the last Census they are classed under three sub-divisions: Chaghtai, Qazalbâsh, and Turkmân. Writing of Afghânistân Dr. Bellew [3] says:—"What the origin of these new clans was, whether they were conquered and converted Pathâns, who became absorbed into the dominant tribe, and thus, by the mere force of numbers and other favouring circumstances of the period, gave them both their language and social code of laws; or whether they were kindred tribes of Turks imported by Sabaktakîn (that is, 'the one called Sabak;' as Alaptakîn, 'the one called Alap,' *takîn* being the distinctive affix of the names of Turk slaves), the founder of the Turk Tâtar (as distinguished from the Mongal or Mughul Tâtar) dynasty at Ghazni, is not clearly ascertained. Without excluding the possibility of their increase by the occasional immigration of other kindred Turk clans from across the Oxus, it may be considered more probable that the increase in the clans of the Ghilji took place mostly by the absorption and adoption of subjugated native tribes; for we find several instances of Chaghatai Turk clans living in close proximity to the Ghilji, yet quite distinct from them, and entirely ignor-

---

[1] *Partâbgarh Settlement Report*, 1888.
[2] *Panjâb Ethnography*, paras. 506, 507.
[3] *The Races of Afghânistân*, 101.

ant of any kindred connection with them. Such Turk clans are the Bayât about Ghazni and Herât, the Cârlûgh, Chûng, and Mughal Turk (Yaka, Chirikcha, etc.) of Balkh, etc. Such also are the Mongol and Chaghatai Turk clans of Mangal, Jâji, Jadrân, Khitâi, etc., who are settled about the Pewâr and the head-waters of the Kurram river and who were brought to these situations on the invasions of Changhis and Tymûr—the Tâtar scourges of the world during the thirteenth and fifteenth centuries. These clans, with the exception of the Jadrân, though they have almost entirely lost the typical physiognomy of their race, their mother tongue, and, indeed, everything else, but their names, which would connect them with their original stock, hold themselves entirely distinct, political relations always excepted, from the Ghilji, who are their neighbours."

3. Other clans in these Provinces are the Qazalbâsh or Qizilbâsh, "red heads," Uzbak, Turk, Kai, Chak, Tâjîk. In the Panjâb the main tribes are the Chaghtai and Barla. Some of these, especially the Chaghtai, are claimed by the Bhatti Jâdons to have descended from them when they were rulers of Ghazni and Zabalistân. The last Imperial family was drawn from the Chaghtai. The Jhojha also call themselves Mughul, but they are supposed to be slaves of Mughul or low caste Hindus converted to Islâm by some Mughul nobleman. They are not suffered to intermarry with the Râjput Musulmâns, or with any of the pure Muhammadan tribes.[1]

Distribution of the Mughuls according to the Census of 1891.

Districts.	Chaghtai.	Qazalbâsh.	Turkmân.	Others.	Total.
Dehra Dûn	108	...	...	93	201
Sahâranpur	477	1	30	1,916	2,424
Muzaffarnagar	305	16	832	578	1,731
Meerut	880	5	40	1,181	2,106
Bulandshahr	780	17	9	1,657	2,463
Aligarh	16	...	101	785	902
Mathura	112	56	15	215	398

[1] Williams, *Oudh Census Report*, 76; Râja Lachhman Sinh, *Bulandshahr Memo.*, 191. *sq.*

Distribution of the Mughuls according to the Census of 1891—contd.

DISTRICTS.	Chaghtai.	Qazalbâsh.	Turkmân.	Others.	TOTAL.
Agra	520	26	76	1,400	2,022
Farrukhâbâd	375	...	27	673	1,075
Mainpuri	100	...	...	117	217
Etâwah	162	...	9	460	631
Etah	264	2	15	415	696
Bareilly	1,162	...	1	2,040	3,203
Bijnor	1,341	7	...	489	1,837
Budâun	809	26	3	618	1,456
Morâdâbâd	713	77	2,015	9,629	12,434
Shâhjahânpur	721	2	39	561	1,323
Pilibhît	338	...	...	406	744
Fatehpur	708	...	...	594	1,302
Bânda	103	2	10	299	414
Hamîrpur	...	...	...	468	468
Allahâbâd	42	...	...	487	529
Jhânsi	65	...	...	213	278
Jâlaun	122	...	218	317	657
Lalitpur	10	...	1	53	64
Benares	123	...	...	997	1,120
Mirzapur	55	...	...	265	320
Jaunpur	...	...	...	548	548
Ghâzipur	227	...	18	319	564
Ballia	17	...	...	193	210
Gorakhpur	332	3	11	943	1,289
Basti	81	...	...	1,696	1,777
Azamgarh	139	...	256	1,632	2,027
Kumaun	...	...	...	10	10

Distribution of the Mughuls according to the Census of 1891—concld.

DISTRICTS.	Chaghtai.	Qazalbâsh.	Turkmân.	Others.	TOTAL.
Garhwâl	...	...	...	40	40
Tarâi	1	...	...	143	144
Lucknow	1,370	673	37	11,143	13,223
Unâo	249	6	6	646	907
Râê Bareli	211	27	...	362	600
Sîtapur	1,084	69	50	1,225	2,428
Hardoi	...	1	...	427	725
Kheri	864	...	...	520	1,384
Faizâbâd	1,102	190	...	1,378	2,670
Gonda	780	...	86	527	1,393
Bahrâich	429	15	20	883	1,347
Sultânpur	118	...	...	784	902
Partâbgarh	38	...	5	348	391
Bârabanki	721	...	...	466	1,187
TOTAL	19,038	1,237	3,982	52,416	76,683

Mukeri.—A Muhammadan tribe, which was separately enumerated at the last Census, but which is usually treated as a sub-caste of the Banjâra, under which head some account of them will be found.

Distribution of the Mukeri according to the Census of 1891.

DISTRICTS.	Number.	DISTRICTS.	Number.
Mathura	1	Bânda	18
Farrukhâbâd	79	Hamîrpur	75
Shâhjahânpur	201	Allahâbâd	140
Pilibhît	18	Jhânsi	38
Cawnpur	14	Jâlaun	74

Distribution of the Mukeri according to the Census of 1891—concld.

DISTRICTS.	Number.	DISTRICTS.	Number.
Ghâzipur . . .	140	Sîtapur . . .	41
Ballia	69	Kheri	6
Gorakhpur . . .	361	Faizâbâd . . .	9
Basti	868	Bahrâich . . .	535
Azamgarh . . .	1,834	Sultânpur . . .	1,032
Lucknow . . .	273	Partâbgarh . .	150
Unâo	13	Bârabanki . . .	174
Râê Bareli . . .	80	TOTAL .	6,243

Murâo [1] (Sanskrit *mûla*, "a root," Hindi *mûli*, "a radish").—A tribe of cultivators and gardeners. They are really the same as the Koeri and Kâchhi, with whom they agree in manners and customs.

Internal structure.

2. At the last Census they were recorded in nine sub-castes:—Bhadauriya, who take their name from the Pargana of Bhadâwar, South of Agra, which also gives its name to a well known Râjput sept; Bhagta from Bhagat, a vegetarian; Hardiya or growers of turmeric (*haldi*); Kâchhi, the name of a distinct tribe; Kachhwâha, which is also the title of a famous Râjput sept; Kanaujiya from Kanauj; Saksena from the old town of Sankisa in the Farrukhâbâd District; Sakta or worshippers of the female energies of nature (*sâkti*); and Thâkuriya or the Thâkur sub-caste. In Faizâbâd we find the Hardiya or Hardiha, who are again sub-divided into the Bhaktiya or Bhaktiha and the Saktiya or Saktiha; the Kanaujiya and the Tanraha. In Farrukhâbâd they divide themselves into the Saksena, Haldiya, and Bâghwân, or keepers of gardens (*bâgh*). The Murâo sub divisions, according to the Census returns, are 232 in number. Those most important locally are the Bakandar and Mîtha of Bareilly; the Bhukarwâl of Morâdâbâd;

[1] Partly based on notes by M. Râm Saran Dâs, Faizâbâd, and the Deputy Inspector of Schools, Farrukhâbâd.

the Purabiya of Shâhjahânpur and Pilibhît; the Bâhman of Basti; the Dhakuliya of Lucknow, who take their name from the water-lift (*dhenkli*) which they use; the Mewâr of Sîtapur, Hardoi, and Kheri; the Pachhwahân of Kheri; the Malikpuri of Gonda; and the Kalaphartor of Bârabanki.

Religion, customs, and occupation.

3. The Murâos are orthodox Hindus. In Faizâbâd the Bhaktihas put a necklace (*kanthi*) on every child immediately after birth; this is done by the Saktihas immediately after initiation. Their chief deities in Faizâbâd are Mahâbîr, Pârvati, Mahâdeva, Sîtala, and Phûlmati. The Saktihas worship Kâli, and two tribal godlings, Karai and Gorai. There the Saktihas and Tanrahas eat goats, sheep, and pork, which the Bhaktihas, Hardihas, and Kanaujiyas refuse. Their occupation throughout the Province is gardening, cultivation, and, in particular, the growing of the more valuable crops, such as opium, tobacco, sugarcane, vegetables, etc. They are a most industrious, hardworking, quiet people, and about the most thriving class of agriculturists in the Province.

Distribution of Muráos according to the Census of 1891.

Districts.	Bhadauriya.	Bhagta.	Hardiya.	Káchhi.	Kachhwáha.	Kanaujiya.	Saksena.	Sákta.	Thakuriya.	Others.	Total.
Dehra Dûn	...	...	560	...	...	94	...	...	...	52	706
Sahâranpur	...	...	...	1	...	10	...	...	...	29	40
Muzaffarnagar	...	...	...	...	...	3	...	...	...	6	9
Meerut	...	...	...	...	...	...	...	...	...	13	13
Bulandshahr	...	...	...	...	...	...	...	...	...	614	614
Aligarh	...	...	35	...	...	...	...	...	...	1,326	1,361
Agra	...	...	...	...	...	...	...	...	...	5	5
Bareilly	784	...	10,823	1,412	1,234	...	54,634	...	...	2,838	71,725
Bijnor	...	...	...	...	...	...	...	...	...	30	30
Budâun	...	...	6,839	5,843	776	...	74,463	...	...	573	88,494
Morâdâbâd	...	...	1,739	1,224	8	11	894	...	...	9,974	13,850
Shâhjahânpur	1,429	...	4,347	...	7,672	251	13,491	...	...	1,160	28,350

Distribution of Murâos according to the Census of 1891—concld.

Districts.	Bhadauriya.	Bhagta.	Hardiya.	Kâchhi.	Kachhwâha.	Kanaujiya.	Saksena.	Sâkta.	Thakuriya.	Others.	Total.
Pilibhît	1,870	...	3,066	2,191	3,386	8	11,270	...	...	4,343	26,134
Cawnpur	...	...	9	...	...	215	...	...	...	26	250
Fatehpur	...	...	4,293	4	...	11,255	...	...	...	2,150	17,702
Bânda	...	9	669	...	22	901	...	49	38	455	2,143
Hamîrpur	...	...	...	...	...	1	...	...	...	97	98
Allahâbâd	...	959	72	...	...	10,028	...	1,428	...	748	13,235
Jhânsi	...	...	...	...	...	...	...	...	...	14	14
Jaunpur	...	...	...	...	...	...	...	...	...	82	82
Gorakhpur	...	105	260	...	...	145	...	...	...	142	652
Basti	...	4,650	24,478	...	...	1,960	...	...	...	1,860	32,948
Tarâi	...	...	541	6	...	...	2,133	...	...	40	2,720
Lucknow	...	...	687	169	55	4,460	...	...	10,044	981	16,396
Unâo	...	1	60	...	...	3,843	...	...	356	274	4,534

Râê Bareli	...	44	40,373	134	1	8,964	...	...	...	1,075	50,591
Sîtapur	...	...	212	644	...	5,717	...	..	16,582	15,656	38,811
Hardoi	...	15,233	...	...	...	2	...	...	...	666	15,901
Kheri	3	...	1,207	54	491	11,842	...	...	6,039	16,227	35,863
Faizâbâd	...	4,713	25,654	...	...	4,410	...	570	...	361	35,708
Gonda	...	...	32,278	...	...	11,472	1,818	...	...	1,192	46,760
Bahrâich	...	...	16,644	33	...	8,384	...	...	339	535	25,935
Sultânpur	...	1,759	35,354	242	32	2,799	...	1,274	...	2,016	43,473
Partâbgarh	...	651	3,818	52	...	17,599	...	3,180	...	1,533	26,833
BâraBanki	...	...	6,540	...	...	15,220	...	...	573	600	22,933
TOTAL .	4,086	28,124	220,558	12,009	13,677	119,594	158,703	6,501	33,971	67,693	664,916

Muriya, Muriyari.—An endogamous sub-caste of Mallâh. Dr. Buchanan[1] calls them Muriyâri Mâlas, and says they came from the upper banks of the Ganges. Their only tradition is that their progenitor was a certain Kaldâs, who came from the South country. Their social position is much the same as that of Kurmis and Koeris, and Brâhmans will take water and certain kinds of sweetmeats from their hands. Those in Bhâgalpur, who have taken to cultivation, call themselves Maghaiya or men of Magadha, and profess to look down on the boating and fishing members of the caste, whom they represent as having come from the North-West Provinces.[2]

Musahar.—A Dravidian jungle tribe found in the Eastern districts of the Province.[3] Mr. Nesfield, in his elaborate monograph on the tribe contained in Volume LXXXVI of the *Calcutta Review*, prefers to call them Mushera, and remarks that the ordinary derivation of the word, as meaning "rat-catcher," is probably incorrect, as "rat-catching" or "rat-eating" is by no means the peculiar, or even a permanent, characteristic of the tribe; and the name in Upper India at least is pronounced by the natives of the country as Mushera and not as Musahar ("rat-taker") or Musaha ("rat-killer"). "In an old folk tale, which has recently come to my knowledge, the name is made to signify 'flesh-seeker' or 'hunter' (being derived from *mâsa*, 'flesh,' and *hera*, 'seeker'), and a legend is told as to the event which led to the tribe being driven to maintain itself by hunting wild animals. Probably, however, both derivations are fanciful Hindi versions of a name which is not of Hindi origin.[4]" Mr. Nesfield's account of the Musahars, however interesting and complete, must be accepted so far with caution, as he seems to have included among them the aggregate of the Dravidian tribes who inhabit the Vindhya-Kaimûr plateau and the valley of the Son with the hill country to the South of that river. Mr. Risley[5] rightly prefers to call them Musahar. The Mirzapur tribe have the following legend to explain their origin: When

---

[1] *Eastern India*, I, 172.

[2] Risley, *Tribes and Castes* II, 109, *sq.*

[3] These, or some of the kindred Dravidian races of the Vindhya range, are probably those referred to in the *Ain i Akbari* (Jarrett's Translation, II, 159) as people in the vicinity of Chunâr "who go naked, living in the wilds, and subsist by their bows and arrows and the game they kill."

[4] *Calcutta Review*, LXXXVI, 2.

[5] *Tribes and Castes*, II, 113.

Paramesar created the first man of each caste, he gave each a horse to ride on, and a tool to work with. The others took each his tool and mounted his horse; but the Musahar began to dig a pair of holes in the belly of his horse in which he might fix his feet as he rode. Paramesar saw his folly and ordered that his descendants should live on rats, which they should dig out of the earth. When Paramesar had finished eating, the Musahar began to lick his leaf platter (*patari*). Seeing this, Paramesar said: "These are low people. They shall always lick the platter;" and so they have been degraded ever since. In connection with this Mr. Nesfield notes that the horse is a tabooed animal to the genuine Musahar, as the ass is to the Dom, the dog to the Bâwariya, the sheep to the Kharriyas of Manbhûm, and the pig to the Musalmân.[1]

Traditions of origin.

2. Mr. Nesfield quotes several interesting legends to explain the origin of the tribe. They are called Banmânush or "man of the forest;" Deosiya, from their great ancestor Deosi; Banrâj or "king of the forest;" Maskhân or "eater of meat." Sometimes a Musahar will say that his is a sub-division of the Ahîr tribe, but, in point of fact, they are the hereditary enemies of Ahîrs, as all their legends testify, and many are the petty raids they have made against them for the possession of cattle and forest.[2] One legend traces their origin to the Chero tribe: "At the foot of the Pipri wood lived a Chero warrior and king named Makara Durga Râê. He levied tribute from the peasantry on the Ganges plain near Chunâr. At a distance of twenty or thirty miles on the North bank of the river lived, in the fort of Gaura, an Ahîr, named Lorik,[3] who possessed large herds of cattle. Between the two princes there had been a long-standing friendship: the bond of union was a man named Sânwar, who, with his twin-brother Subchan, had been deserted by his mother immediately after their birth. Sânwar was reared by Lorik's mother as her own child; and Subchan, the other orphan, was similarly adopted by Birmi, the wife of Makara, the Chero king. But the friendship was broken when Lorik in search of adventures left Gaura and went on a distant expedition to Hardi, a city much further East,

---

[1] *Loc. cit.*, 26.

[2] Nesfield, *loc. cit.*, 3.

[3] For the regular Lorik legend, see under *Ahîr*.

with his mistress whose husband was still alive.[1] Meanwhile, Sânwar remained in charge of the cattle at a pasturage called Boha.

3. "When Lorik had been absent for twelve years, the mother of the woman who had eloped with him presented herself before Makara, and, throwing a basketful of gold before his feet, implored him to avenge the insult. She showed him how easy it would be to make a sudden descent on Boha and catch Sânwar unawares, and how he could then cut off the head of Sânwar as a substitute for that of Lorik, and capture the deserted wife of Lorik in revenge for the capture of her own daughter. The Chero king hesitated to incur the resentment of Lorik, but yielding to the solicitations of his wife Birmi, and after sacrificing five boys to his guardian goddess, he set out against Sânwar, taking with him Deosi, the bravest and most warlike of his seven sons. But Sânwar, as it happened, had left Boha for Gaura immediately before Makara arrived there with his forces. So the watchmen and keepers of the cows were left defenceless, and were without a leader when Makara commenced his attack. These were soon defeated, and the cows were about to be seized and driven to Pipri as booty, when the bulls turned round and, making a joint attack against the enemy, drove him back to his own side of the river.

4. "After sacrificing seven more boys, and thus making sure of the help of his goddess, Makara made a second attack on Boha, and, after killing Sânwar in single combat, carried off his head as a trophy. The cattle and Gaura, the stronghold of Lorik, fell into the hands of Makara. On learning this news, Lorik determined to revenge himself on the Chero king, and attacked Pipri, which he was unable to capture until one of his men entered the fort in disguise and drugged the liquor of the Cheros at the Holi festival, on which Lorik entered the place and massacred Makara and all his subjects. At the time of this disaster, Deosi, son of Makara, happened to be absent, and being taunted by his elder brother, Shyâmjît, with deserting his father in his extremity, he was expelled by his family and driven to become a flesh seeker or hunter in the jungle, and was known as Musahar. Hence his descendants are called Deosiya, and, to the end of his life, he continued to attack the Ahîrs: hence the traditional enmity between the castes, and the

---

[1] Hardi also appears in the Bengal legend, and the woman is called Chanâyin.—Cunningham, *Archæological Reports*, XVI, 28.

proverb *Jab tak jīwē Deosiya, Ahīr na chajē gāē*: 'As long as a Deosiya is alive, the Ahîr will get no good out of his cows.'

5. "Then he invented the digging instrument (*gahdāla, gadhāla*), characteristic of the tribe, and with this he one day slew Lorik, but was himself killed by Shyâmjît, son of Sânwar. Near the ruins of Pipri, at the confluence of two rivers, and in the very middle of the stream, there is an image carved out of a natural monolith of the goddess Behiya, to whom Makara sacrificed—first five and afterwards seven boys,—and who was once the guardian goddess of Pipri. In her right hand she holds a dagger, sword, and in her left the half of a human skull for holding charcoal. All this is carved out of stone: a long red tongue projects from her mouth, smeared with the blood of human victims. According to the Musahar legend, she was originally the guardian goddess of Sânwar, the elder brother of Lorik; but when Makara, the Chero, had won her over to his own side by the sacrifice of so many boys, and when Sânwar had been slain, she left Gaura, the house and stronghold of the Ahîrs, and took up her residence in Pipri under the patronage of the Cheros." [1]

6. The legend further relates "that when Pipri, in its turn, was captured by Lorik and ploughed up with asses, she fled out of the fort to escape the threatened indignity, and posted herself in mid-stream in the confluence of the two rivers, where she still remains, nursing her wounded pride. The natives round Pipri now call her by the name of Nikundi, and she is doubtless one of the numerous forms of the death goddess Kâli. Pipri is now uninhabited, and has been so ever since it was ploughed up with asses by Lorik, the Ahîr. No Ahîr, or other Hindu, will live in it. But to Musahars it is sacred, as Gaya to a Buddhist, or Mount Athos to a Greek. Every Musahar (unless long separation by time and place has made him forget the place in which his ancestors were born, and from which they were banished) would see Pipri if he could before he dies, and would like to have his corpse thrown into the river by which the fort is surrounded. Meetings of the tribe are stealthily held here at midnight, and the imagination is left to guess at the orgies celebrated at such gatherings. Musahars attempt even to live there. But the Ahîrs of the neighbourhood combine together to expel them, and thus the old traditions are kept alive." [2]

---

[1] Nesfield, *loc. cit.*, 12, *sq.*
[2] Nesfield, *loc. cit.*, 7 *sq.*

7. By another legend, "Musahars are a rejected offshoot from Chhatris, as, by the previous one, they are a rejected offshoot from Ahîrs. Between Chandels[1] (as the story runs, and so far the story is correct) there was deadly and unceasing warfare. At last all the Chandels were slain except a single woman, who escaped and fled into the forest. Her son became the founder of the tribe called after him Banmânush or Musahar. But, as he could not prove his origin from the Chandel Chhatri, neither he nor his descendants have been admitted into the Chhatri fraternity."[2]

8. Another legend again is told by the Brâhmans: "Arjuna, one of the five heroes of the Mahâbharata, had retired temporarily into the forest to meditate on the 108 names of Siva. In order to test the steadfastness of his devotion and tempt him to break the current of his thoughts, the god caused a wild boar to run in front of him. But Arjuna, notwithstanding his passion for hunting wild game, was proof against the temptation, and completed his devotions before he got up to seize his bow and arrow. The boar, on being chased by Arjuna, led him on through the bushes till he reached a hermit's hut, where Siva and his wife Pârvati had already seated themselves in bodily form, in the disguise of a Savar and Savari: he holding a *gahdâla* (the Musahar implement) and she supporting a basket on her head. Arjuna and the Savar both commenced pursuing the boar, and when the animal had been hunted down and killed, a contention arose as to who had the right claim to it. It was agreed that the matter should be decided next day by a wrestling match.[3] Arjuna wrestled with the disguised god all the day till sundown, when he pleaded that he must go and repeat his evening devotions: to which his antagonist consented. Through the intensity of these devotions it dawned on him that he had been wrestling, not with a Savar, but with the divine being himself disguised as a Savar, on which he was now meditating. Returning to the hermit's hut, where the disguised Siva still was, he threw himself at the feet of his divine antagonist, received a blessing, and returned to his four brethren. Now, in the hermi-

---

[1] Whom Mr. Nesfield would identify with the Chero.

[2] Nesfield, *loc. cit.*, 14.

[3] These wrestling matches with divine beings are common in folklore; *e.g.*, Jacob.—See Conway, *Demonology*, I, 239; II, 134.

tage where these events took place, there was a maiden of unknown parentage, who used to wait on the hermit and prepare his food; and whom the hermit loved and cherished as a daughter. The maiden had just completed her period, and had gone, as the custom is, to bathe and purify herself in the waters of the adjoining river. On her return to the hermitage she found Siva seated there in the disguise of a Savar, with Pârvati by his side in the disguise of a Savari. The eye of the god fell on her. From the glance of that eye she became pregnant, and gave birth in due course to twins, one a male and the other a female, who bore an exact resemblance to the Savar and Savari whom she had seen in the hermitage. The hermit, judging from the uncouth features and dark complexion of the babes that she had been guilty of unchastity with some wild man of the woods, sent her out of his hermitage. From the two children whom she had borne, one a male and the other a female, sprang the Musahar tribe, the men of which are still noted for using the *gahdâla* and the women for carrying baskets."[1]

9. These legends are interesting as illustrating the connection between the Musahar, Chero, and Savar or Seori tribes. It is also curious to mark the survival of the custom of human sacrifice to the aboriginal gods: and the traditional descent of the caste from a female ancestress, with which Mr. Nesfield compares the descent of the Kanjar tribe from Nathaiya, the husbandless mother of their deified hero Mâna, and of the Aryas themselves from Aditi, the great mother of gods and men.[2] We may also note the tolerance of intercourse between brother and sister which marks a very early social stage.[3]

Tribal organization.

10. Mr. Nesfield divides the tribe into three sub-tribes, which do not intermarry or eat with each other. These are the Jangali or Pahâri, "men of the forests and mountains," who have maintained the largest share of their primitive speech and customs and who stand entirely aloof from their descendants in the open plain, whom they regard as degenerate; the Dehâti or Dehi, who have become partially Hinduised and live within reach of settled and semi-civilized communi-

---

[1] Nesfield, *loc. cit.*, 15, *sq.*

[2] Lubbock, *Origin of Civilization*, 146, *sq.*

[3] See instances collected in Westermarck, *History of Human Marriage*, 290, *sqq.*

ties ; the Dolkârha, who have a peculiar occupation, for which they are disowned and condemned by their brethren, *viz.*, that of carrying palanquins (*doli*) for hire, whence they obtain their name. But at present the tribe is clearly in a state of flux, and the more Hinduised branch of the tribe in Mirzapur have now the following occupational exogamous septs—the Khadiha, who work at carrying manure (*khad*) ; the Bhenriha, who say they take their name from living together in the jungles like sheep (*bhenr*) in their pen ; the Kharwâra, who say they are so called because they collect grass (*khar*) and make platters (*dauna, patari*) of leaves ; the Kuchbandhua, who make the brush (*kûncha*, Sanskrit *kuncha*) used by weavers in cleaning thread ; and the Rakhiha, who are said to derive their name because they cower in the ashes (*râkh*) during cold weather. Again, among the Musahars who live near towns, we find in Mirzapur two endogamous sub-divisions : Dhuriya, "men of the dust ;" and Jaiswâr, a name common to many low castes, and said to be a local term derived from their supposed connection with the town of Jais in the Râê Bareli District of Oudh.

11. As regards the division of the tribe into palanquin-bearers and men of the jungle, Mr. Nesfield quotes a legend that a Musahar, named Anseri, who lived on the Kantit estates in Mirzapur, used to work as a field watchman, but he and his sons, in the absence of the regular bearers (*Kahâr*), were once forced to carry a litter in a marriage procession, and were expelled by his brethren. Ansâri, the reputed founder of this sub-caste, is now beginning to supersede Deosiya, the eponymous leader, and this branch is beginning to take to fishing. Mr. Nesfield assumes that Ansâri means the divider (*ansa* meaning "half"), and hence he was the man who broke up the tribe into two halves—the Dolkârha, on one side, and the Bindrabani or Banmânush, on the other.[1] In Bengal, the organization of sub-castes and sections is much more elaborate, but there appear to be only two real sub-castes which are of local origin : the Tirhutiya and Maghaiya, who take their name from Tirhût and Magadha. According to Mr. Nesfield, the Dolkârha eat the flesh or carrion of horses and rear fowl, whereas the Bindrabanis whether of the hills or plains, do not touch either. The complete

---

[1] *Loc. cit.*, 236, *sq.*

Census returns show 137 sub-divisions. Many are borrowed from Râjput and other tribes, such as Ahîr, Bachgoti, Baghel, Bais, Chandel, Chauhân, Dabgar, Donwâr, Dor, Gaharwâr, Gusâin, Gwâl, Gwâlbans, Kewatiya, Kharbind, Kharwâr, Khatri, Lodh, Palwâr, Raghubansi, Râwat. With these are other local groups, such as Bijaypuriya, Bindrabâsi, Bishnpuriya, Ghâzipuriya, Jaiswâr, Kanaujiya, Purabiya, Sarwariya. Those of most local importance are the Bankhadwa, Chauhân, Jangali, Jaiswâr, and Mughra of Jaunpur, and the Baghochhiya of Gorakhpur.

Law of exogamy.

12. In Mirzapur, though the internal organization of the tribe seems to be very unsettled, it appears that the Khadiha, Kharwâra, and KuchBandhua are exogamous and intermary on equal terms. Similarly, the Bhenriha and Rakhiha intermarry. This rule of exogamy is reinforced by the prohibition against marrying the daughter of the maternal uncle, sister, or father's sister.

Mr. Nesfield [1] states the rule of exogamy as follows:—"On the mother's side, a girl cannot be given in marriage to the son of her mother's sister, or of her mother's brother. On the father's side, she cannot be given to the son of her father's sister or of her father's brother, or to the son or grandson of any of her father's aunts or uncles. Thus, on the mother's side, the prohibition goes back to only one generation, and on the father's to two." On the other hand, among the more Hinduised endogamous sub-castes, the Dhuriya and Jaiswâr in Mirzapur, the rule appears to be that the descendants of the maternal grandfather (*nâna*) and that of the father's sister's husband (*phûpha*) are barred. At the same time they say that they intermarry with agnates or cognates after five or six generations, or when all remembrance of relationship has been lost. They have a tribal council (*panchâyat*), presided over by a hereditary president (*chaudhari*). The offences enquired into are charges of adultery and fornication. Inter-tribal infidelity is punished by both parties being fined. The fine is heavy—liquor, pork, rice, and pulse to the value of R30; eight annas worth of tobacco; and one rupee's worth of hemp (*gânja*). Connection with a man or woman outside the tribe involves excommunication, and such persons are called "those outside the tribal mat" (*tât bâhar*).

---

[1] *Loc. cit.*, 232.

Widow marriage and divorce.

13. Among some of the Mirzapur Musahars, the rule appears to be that, if husband or wife indulge in habitual adultery, either can divorce the other with permission of the council. According to Mr. Nesfield, "Divorce, except for the one offence of infidelity, is not practised or tolerated. Such an offence very rarely occurs; and the habitual chastity of one partner ensures that of the other. If, however, a wife is accused of unchastity by her husband, and has been declared guilty by the assembly, her position is one of great difficulty. No married man can take her in addition to his own wife, for bigamy is disallowed. No unmarried man, or widower, can take her of his own free will, without incurring the penalty of excommunication. A man cohabiting with such a woman could, of course, retire with her and live in a state of isolation in the corner of some jungle, as some couples do from choice; but if he sought to ally himself to one or two other households for mutual aid and protection, he would for some time be rejected altogether, and could only obtain admission at last by incurring what is to him the heavy penalty of banqueting the other households for several days in succession. The separation of man and wife is so much disliked and discouraged by tribal opinion that a wife cannot be divorced, except on the most direct proof of guilt, or by a successful appeal to some ordeal, if the accuser is rash enough to expose himself to such an uncertain test. Frivolous charges, or improbable suspicions, if the husband is so imprudent as to bring them before an assembly, are dismissed with contempt, and the accuser is hooted for his pains. Supposing, however, that unchastity is proved, and a sentence of divorce is pronounced by the assembly, the ceremony by which divorce is effected is as follows: An earthen pot is placed between the husband and wife, and an assembly is called to witness it. After it has been lying there for some time, the man gets up and breaks it with the tribal tool, indicating thereby that the union between them is broken beyond repair. This ceremony is called *khapparkuchi* or breaking the pot."[1] There appears to be a difference of practice as regards the levirate. Among some of the Mirzapur Musahars the younger brother of the deceased husband can claim the widow. If he abandons his claim and she marries an outsider, the late

[1] *Loc. cit.*, 236, *sq.*

husband's brother has the right to the custody of the male children while the female children go with the mother. According to Mr. Nesfield, however, the widow, while she is still young enough to re-marry, has no claim upon the younger brother of the deceased husband, nor has he upon her. If she comes to terms with some widower who desires to re-marry, the union is sealed by them by simply eating and drinking together in the presence of witnesses who are invited to share in the repast.[1]

Customs of marriage.

14. Among some of the Mirzapur Musahars, the marriage is arranged by the brother-in-law of the boy. The father of the bride then comes to the bridegroom's house with three or four relatives with a rupee and a quarter and a dish to perform the betrothal (*barrekhi karna*), a square (*chauk*) is made in front of the hut, and five platters (*dauna*) are filled with liquor and placed in the square. The two fathers sit in the square opposite each other. The fathers change platters five times and drink the contents. The clansmen are then treated to liquor, and get a feast of pork and rice. Some of the more Hinduised Musahars pay a Pandit four annas for fixing a lucky day before the wedding. Five days before the wedding day, they have the ceremony of the lucky earth (*matmangara*).[2] On the same day the marriage shed (*mânro*) is put up. It consists of a bamboo at each of the four corners, and in the middle a bamboo near which is placed a representation of some parrots (*suga*) sitting on a branch. Near this is fixed, on a platform made of the lucky earth, the sacred jar (*kalsa*), which is decorated with mango leaves, and over it is placed a saucerful of pulse (*urad*) and a lighted lamp. The bride is bathed in a mixture of curds and water in which the bridegroom has been first bathed. At the bride's door, her father worships the feet of the bridegroom (*pair pûja*). Some curds and treacle are sent from the bride's house for the bridegroom, but he only touches it with his tongue. The bridegroom at the actual service marks the ploughshare fixed in the middle of the marriage shed with red lead, and then applies it to the parting of the bride's hair. They, then, with their garments tied, walk five times round the ploughshare, while the bride's brother pours a little parched rice into a winnowing fan which the bridegroom holds.

---

[1] *Loc. cit.*, 237.

[2] For this ceremony, see *Bhuiya*, para 14.

15. Next morning his father shakes the pole of the marriage shed, and the bride's father has to give him a present (*mânro hildi*). One special portion of the ceremony is that the bride's mother takes the pair away into a field at some distance, and warns the husband to treat his wife for the future with consideration. During this exhortation, the bride is supposed to weep violently. This and the shaking of the pole of the pavilion are probably survivals of marriage by capture. When the bride comes home, her entrance is blocked by her husband's sister, and then she has to cook for all the relatives. Next day, as is usual with these tribes, the marriage jar (*kalsa*) and festoons (*bandanwâr*) are thrown into a neighbouring stream. The jar is taken out, refilled with water, and brought home. With this water the bride makes some mud plaster and constructs a little shrine, at which she offers a small sacrifice to the evil spirits which live in the old trees about the village. The ordinary ceremony thus described is called *charhauwa*. Besides this are the *dola*, which is done by poor people, where there is no ceremony at the bride's house and the girl is merely brought home and the clansmen fed, and *gurâwat*, when two people exchange sisters.

16. The ceremony which Mr. Nesfield [1] describes is a rude form of the *dola* marriage above described : "The girl sets out to the house of the affianced bridegroom, accompanied by her parents, or by any other male or female relatives who may be invited to go with her. Previous to their arrival at the bridegroom's hut, a fowl's egg is placed at the entrance. The youth to whom she is to be married then comes out to receive her. The girl is presented to him by her mother. Taking her by the hand, and holding her hand firmly in his own, he leads her up to the mouth of the hut, and breaks the egg with his foot. On his completing this act (which he can only perform when holding her hand, so that it may be considered a joint action), the company present raise a simultaneous shout of *ku!* which means 'hurrah!' By holding her hand firmly in his own, he signifies that he has accepted her. The Hindu ceremony of *pani grahana*, usully regarded as a purely Aryan rite, may perhaps after all be of non-Aryan origin. By breaking the fowl's egg with his foot while he is in the act of hold-

---

[1] *Loc. cit.*, 226.

ing her hand, he signifies that he has renounced all desire for any other woman: and she, by allowing him to hold her hand while he performs this act, signifies to him and to the company that she, on her part, has renounced all desire for any other man; for the fowl, it will be remembered, is an animal which Musahars do not rear, and which they avoid almost as scrupulously as the horse. The girl is then made to enter the hut, the youth directing her to the door. On entering the hut she takes hold of the feet of the youth's mother and touches them with her forehead, signifying by this that she intends to do honour to her son as his wedded wife. The mother-in-law then gives her blessing in the following words (some of which are of Hindu and others of the Musahar language): *Bhū magnū maharin hilo sohāgin ramali kanto rasa kio*: 'Remaining in the blissful state of marriage, do thou give delight to thy husband.' The youth then leaves the hut, the bride remaining with her newly made mother-in-law. This closes the first part of the ceremony.

17. "The next part begins with the cooking of a kind of rice (which, in the Musahar language, is called *kutki*) [1] into a paste or gruel thin enough to be drunk. This decoction is poured into cups made of the leaves of the *Mahul* tree, one cup being provided for each adult present, including the bride and bridegroom. Here it should be understood that rice is the sacred grain among several of the Kol tribes, a sanctity which it shares with barley in Hindu or Brâhmanical marriages.[2] When the rice paste or gruel is ready, and each *Mahul* cup has been filled, the company are made to sit round in a ring, and the bride is brought out of the hut and made to take her seat in the middle with the bridegroom. The bridegroom then kisses her on the mouth in token that he is to be her husband: and she in turn kisses his feet, and strokes his back up and down with her hand, in token that she is to be his and will tend him as a dutiful wife. This ceremony is called *mukhra chumba*

---

[1] *Kutki* is really a millet (*panicum miliare*).

[2] "No sanctity attaches to wheat in Hindu marriages: but rice and barley are indispensable in such ceremonies, and little branches of mango. Wheat is nowhere, nor are any other grains, but rice and barley, recognised at such times. Barley is frequently alluded to in the Vedas as the food of the Aryas. Rice and mango are indigenous to India. The most natural inference to be drawn from this is that wheat found its way into India at a later date, but was unable to deprive the older grain (rice) of its already acquired sanctity." On the sacrificial use of barley, see Schrader, *Prehistoric Anti uities*, 292.

('kissing the mouth'), or *munh dekhna* ('seeing the face'), or *kar pherna* ('moving the hand up and down'). When the pair have given this public token that each has accepted and appropriated the other, the cups are distributed, one to each person, and every person present, including the bride and bridegroom, swallows the contents of his own cup. Immediately after this, the following couplet is repeated in unison by all the company, excepting only the bride and bridegroom themselves, to whom the words are addressed: *Kutki ki pīch bandi, māhul kā dauna, Bodi boda byāh bhyau lena na dena*: 'The rice paste has been prepared in the *Mahul* cup; the maid and the youth are married—no giving or taking.' Then there is a general shout of *ku!* or 'hurrah!' which means that the ceremony is completed.

18. "It seems most probable that each of the two rites described above was originally a complete marriage ceremony by itself, but they have now been so long associated in practice that neither could be safely omitted. The blessing pronounced by the bridegroom's mother on the bride at the close of the first rite implies that she (the bride) is now fully married. 'Do thou give delight to thy husband.' Similarly the words spoken by the witnesses at the close of the second ceremony imply that there is nothing left to complete the validity of the marriage. 'The rice paste has been eaten; the youth and girl are married; hurrah!' What gives the binding force in the first ceremony is the joining of hands, while the groom breaking the eggs, and the formal reception inside the bridegroom's house or hut, the *deductio in domum,* as the Romans would have called it, form a parallel ceremony of their own. What gives the binding force in the second ceremony is the fact of the bride and bridegroom eating together some rice paste or gruel cooked in the bridegroom's own fire: and this the Romans would have identified with a marriage rite of their own, known as *confarreatio.*" The prominent part taken by the mother on both sides is taken by Mr. Nesfield to be a survival of the matriarchy.[1] At marriages, Musahars pay worship to Deosi, the male ancestor and founder of the tribe, and sometimes a piece of cloth with some sweetmeats is set aside in honour of Savari, their more remote female ancestor, or to Mother Bansapti, their great goddess and pro-

[1] He quotes similar customs among the Kurs of Sarguja from Dalton, *Ethnology,* 234.

tector. In the worship of Devi it is, again, the mother of the bridegroom who acts as priestess and sacrificer: and, again, it is rice which is used as the sacred grain. The first act in this worship is to take some unhusked rice, remove the husk with her own hand, grind the grain, mix it with water, knead it, and cook it into a pancake. All this and whatever follows must be done with the right hand only. The pancake so cooked is then besmeared with honey, the wild honey which Musahars are so clever in collecting from the woods, and which is, therefore, a fit offering to the deified ancestor from whom they learnt the art. Taking this pancake with her, together with some rice beer, a piece of yellow cloth, some more honey, some wild fruits and flowers, some *dúb* grass, and a live kid or lamb, she proceeds to the clay figure or mound intended to represent Deosi. Then, after sprinkling some river water in front of the figure or mound in order to purify the spot (for Musahars, like Hindus, are worshippers of rivers, and believe in the purifying influence of their water), she deposits all her offerings, except the kid or ram, on a plate or plates made of *Mahul* leaves. She then strikes pure and new fire by the sacred process of rubbing one stick on another,[1] and with this fire she cooks the offerings. Her object in thus cooking the offerings is to enable the deified Deosi to inhale the scented smoke, a vaporous invisible being like Deosi, being not fit to inhale any but vaporous substances.[2] She then decapitates the goat with a single blow of the axe, and places the bleeding, uncooked head as an offering of blood and life before the image. Then, touching the earth with the forehead, she repeats or sings the following four lines (every word of which, except the second, is in the Musahar language) :—

Deosi bába hit timro magnu maharin Indra hadariya potis ri.
Boglo pokpa dudhali chimla niberi hit timri boglo pokpari,
Popaki imiriya chimla chimli thammo ri,
Kemali Indra hadariya hutmu chimlo teplis kero ri :

'Come into the world, O Father Deosi! from the palace of Indra.
Eat food cooked by the mother of the bridegroom : come and eat the food.
Having eaten these offerings, bestow thy blessing on the bride and bridegroom ;

[1] For this, see *Korwa*, para. 13.
[2] This is exactly the idea of the Homeric sacrifices—*Iliad*, I, 317 : " High rose to heaven the savoury steam and the curls of wreathed smoke."—Blackie's translation.

Then return to the palace of Indra! O ancestor! and behold again the dances of the dancing-girls.'

"The singing or intonation of these words completes the ceremony. The carcase of the victim is then carried back to the hut, where it is cooked in the evening for the marriage feast, with which the day is brought to a close. The bride and bridegroom are the most honoured guests in this banquet, and the festivities of the day generally close with some singing and music after Musahar fashion. Next morning the newly-wedded pair quit the paternal hut or cave and go out into the forest to seek their fortunes together and found an independent home.[1]"

Birth ceremonies.

20. Unlike many of the kindred tribes, the Musahars have protective ceremonies during pregnancy. When the pregnancy is announced, a sacrifice of pork and liquor is offered to Mahâbali, a sort of ill-defined tribal god, who may perhaps be identical with Deosi. A cock and spirits are offered to Pahlwân, "the wrestler," who is considered an evil spirit (*bhût*), some betel and sweetmeats to the goddess Phûlmati, and a young ram to the Baghaut, or shrine of a person killed by a tiger. The customs, as in the case of marriage, differ in the two divisions of the tribe. Among the Musahars of the plains the mother, during delivery, sits on two bricks or stones, and it is immaterial what direction she faces. The cord is cut by the Chamârin midwife and buried on the spot where the child was born, a fire being lighted over it. They have the sixth and twelfth day ceremonies (*chhathi*, *barahi*) performed in the usual way. Among the more primitive branch of the tribe, as described by Mr. Nesfield,[2] "As soon as labour commences, a fire is lighted near the woman and kept burning till the labour is over. Into this fire, rice, grain, and rice straw are immediately thrown; and as soon as the child is born, its body is gently rubbed over with the ashes by the woman who acts as midwife — the child's paternal aunt. The cord, as soon as it is cut, is put with the after-birth into another fire kept burning at the door of the hut or cave: a curious analogy to which is furnished in certain Irish folk-sayings current at the present day, in one of which it is said that 'an after-birth must be burned to preserve the child from the fairies,' the fairies being, in this instance, evil-hearted goblins whose propensities are the same as those of the Indian *bhûts*. The hair of

[1] Nesfield, *loc. cit.*, 229.
[2] *Loc. cit.*, 246.

a bear and a slip of wood torn from an *âsan* or *deodâr* tree are kept inside the hut, so long as the woman and child remain there. For one whole day and night at least a peacock's feather is dropped occasionally into the fire, which is still kept burning at the mouth of the hut. From the second to the tenth day, if the child is a male, or to the fifteenth, if it is a female, some powder of the burnt *chiraunji* nut is rubbed occasionally on its body: the longer period being deemed necessary for the female on account of its power of resistance to malignant spirits being considered less. When all these ceremonies are completed, the mother and child have a final purifying bath in water mixed with the ashes of rice straw."

21. According to Mr. Nesfield,[1] the plain Musahars place much reliance on the protective power of peacock feathers. They do not keep a bear's bone in the hut, and sometimes wash the bodies of the mother and child with liquor. It may be noted that the parturition impurity extends to all the women of the house; for the men, during eleven days after the birth, cook for themselves outside the house, and keep apart from the women. The husband does not cohabit with his wife for three months after her confinement. Mr. Nesfield [2] describes the custom at naming a child: "On the day fixed for the naming, a sacrifice is offered to Barkê Bâba, the 'grandfather,' *viz.* Deosi, the founder of the tribe. Two names are given—one being the name of some Devi, or rather a name selected from among the numerous titles by which the Devi or indigenous goddess is known, such as Bangari, Nikundi, Bahiya, Britiya, Mohani, Rânkini, etc. The other name is taken from the tree near or under which the child was born, or from some hill near which or on which the family reside. Thus if a male child is born under a *Jigan* tree, it is called Jignu. Possibly in this custom we may see the germ of totemism on the male side, which, though undeveloped among Musahars, so far as I can discover, is found among certain other Kol tribes in Chutia Nâgpur. The name given to a daughter is fixed by the mother according to her own fancy. There is no ceremony of any kind attending the giving of the name, and no rule regulating the selection. The following are among the names commonly given to females: Birmi, Mughni, Ghanni, Kumâni, Jajiya, but I am unable to trace their meaning." The plain Musahars have the usual custom of

---

[1] *Loc. cit.*, 248.

[2] *Loc. cit.*, 248, *sq.*

boring children's ears, which is done at the age of five or six by a Sunnâr. This is called among them "the distribution of betel" (*pân bakheri*), and is accompanied by a tribal feast of pork, rice, and liquor, and songs to the music of their drum (*huruka*). After this the child must conform to caste regulations in the matter of food.

Death ceremonies.

22. The plain division of the tribe burn their dead in the usual way on the edge of a stream, into which the ashes are thrown. When they return home they chew a leaf of the bitter *nîm*, as a mark of mourning, and the chief mourner throws a piece of lighted charcoal behind him to bar the ghost. Like the kindred tribes, they fix up a bunch of reed grass (*jurai*) near the water's edge, which the chief mourner waters every morning as an abiding place for the spirit. On the tenth day, the clansmen shave their heads, and the brother-in-law (*bahnoi*) of the dead man, who officiates as priest, offers a lump of flour to the dead man's spirit. When he comes home, he takes an earthen-potful of food and lays it out in the jungle for the use of the dead. Then a hog is sacrificed, and, being cooked with rice, is eaten by the clansmen. The death impurity lasts ten days. According to Mr. Nesfield,[1] the tribe in Singrauli, south of the Son,[2] simply leave the corpse in the place where the man or woman died. If he or she died in the jungle, or in the open air, they cover the body with leaves and bushes and go away. If he died inside the cave or hut, no other covering is considered necessary. The place is thenceforth abandoned by the survivors, who take no relic of the dead with them when they migrate to another part of their hill or jungle. There is safety, as they believe, in this precaution. For if they took with them a limb or bone from the dead man's body, the ghost would probably follow, and they cannot be sure that its company would be more to their benefit than to their injury. Their safest course is, then, to leave the corpse intact on the spot where the departed breathed his last, trusting that the ghost will not forsake the vicinity of the body in which it lately resided: *tumulum circumvolat umbra.* Musahars of the Son valley have a ceremony almost as rude. They simply throw the corpse into the river or its nearest tributary. The body floats in the water and is carried out of sight, until at last,

---

[1] *Loc. cit.*, 237.

[2] There are, apparently, no people in Singrauli who called themselves Musahars, and Mr. Nesfield is, probably, referring to tribes like the Korwas and Parahiyas, who practise these customs, but are very unwilling to give any information on the subject.

perhaps, it may reach the Ganges : which river is regarded by many of the Kol tribes with a respect equal to that paid to the Son. The custom of river burial is exemplified in what Dr. Oldham has recorded of a Savari woman whom he accidentally met with in the Ghâzipur District. Her husband had died on the march and she had carried his bones in a sack for over a hundred miles in order to throw them into the Ganges.[1] Water burial must be a very ancient custom in the Musahar tribe; for this, according to the legend, was the way in which the corpse of Deosi himself, the reputed founder of the tribe, was disposed of.

23. "Other Musahars have retained the water ceremony, but have made some approach towards cremation also. They carry the body to the river bank, and, having washed it in river water, tie a cloth made of cotton or of *deodâr* bark fibre round the loins. The corpse is then laid on the ground, with its face upwards, and the head towards the north, the region of Indra, to which it is hoped the soul will take its flight. The spot on which the head and feet were laid is marked off for the purpose of paying future obsequies. The son of the deceased, or, if there is no son, his brother or brother's son or other male relative next of kin, takes a handful of straw, (rice straw, if possible), and, placing it on the face of the dead body, sets fire to it. The face is merely singed : but it has had the contact of fire, the great purifying element, so much used in all parts of the world in lustral ceremonies. The chief mourner then takes the body by the feet, and, using all his strength, throws it into the river. In this simple rite we see the germ of the Hindu ceremony of cremation followed by that of immersion—a rite in which the Vedic custom of cremation and the indigenous custom of water burial appear to have met each other from opposite directions, thus giving rise to the composite ceremony which Hindus now practise. Among Musahars, as among Hindus, the contact of fire is interdicted to persons who have died of small-pox; for small-pox is believed to be of the same substance with Sîtala, the goddess who presides over the dreaded malady, and it is thought that by burning such a corpse, they will be burning or otherwise offending the goddess herself. The same interdict applies to persons who have died of cholera and for similar reasons Other Musahars practise a rite in which earth sepulture is the leading characteristic, but qualified by some show of water

[1] *Memoir of the Ghâzipur District*, 50.

burial and cremation, and this composite rite appears to be of frequent practice among Dehâti or village Musahars wherever they may be found. The body, as above mentioned, is washed in river water, and the loins are bound round with a cloth of cotton or *deodâr* fibre, and fire fed with rice straw is put on the face. The corpse, however, instead of being thrown into the water, as in the preceding rite, is deposited by the chief mourner in a tomb about two yards long and one broad, the earth having been excavated for this purpose with the tribal tool, the *gahdâla*. The face, as above, is placed towards the North. If the deceased was a man, the body is placed on the right side of the tomb; if a woman, on the left.

24. The explanation given of this is that man and woman were originally a single body, just as now man and wife are one flesh, and that the right or stronger half belonged to the male and the left or inferior to the female. It was further explained that when the two halves split asunder, each half became a whole and perfect body, one a complete man and the other a complete woman, and that the primeval pair thus formed were the first ancestors of mankind."[1] Some of the village Musahars leave the corpse in the groud for six months after sepulture, committing it to the care of their guardian goddess, Bansapti: at the close of the six months the remains are taken out of the earth and burnt, and the ashes are thrown into the river. The cremation ceremony that is now performed is called *lakhâri*. Some of the lowest caste of Hindus, those that are halting between the custom of earth sepulture, handed down from their ancestors, and the rite of cremation as taught and practised by Brâhmans, adopt a similar compromise, burying the corpse in the earth for the first six months, and then disinterring and burning what remains of it. Those tribes, or families, who practise this ambiguous rite, commit the body during the six months of sepulture to the care of the earth goddess, Bhuiyân (so commonly worshipped by the lower castes); just as Musahars commit it to the forest goddess, Bansapti, Bansatti, Bânsuri, or Bandevi.[2]

---

[1] These aboriginal burial grounds are scattered over all the hill country of Mirzapur. From some excavations made, it appears as if the body was partially cremated and then buried. These graves have the sides and tops covered with flagstones. On this, see Lubbock, *Prehistoric Times*, 103. Mr. Nesfield compares this with the Eve legend.—*Loc. cit.*, 239.

[2] Nesfield, *loc. cit.*, 240.

25. The method in which the dead are propitiated varies according to the manner the corpse is disposed of. Some avoid the ghost by leaving the place and conveying no relic away with them. Those who dispose of the dead by simply throwing them into a river, make an offering of food and water every day for some nine days in succession at the foot of a *deodār* tree, the nearest one they can find to the spot from which the body was thrown. The soul of the dead is believed to reside in this tree as long as the obsequies are continued : and from this tree the ghost descends to receive the offerings.[1] The offerings are usually made at midday, and are presented by the chief mourner, that is, by the man who threw the corpse into the river. They consist generally of cooked rice mixed with honey, the flesh and eggs of the tortoise, the flesh of the lizard (*goh*), the porcupine (*sahi*) the boar, the crab (*kekra*)—all kinds of flesh in fact which the man or woman while living considered a luxury. Different offerings are presented on different days, not all at once. Those who before throwing the corpse into the river lay it decently out, place the head towards the North, and put fire on the face, perform the same kind of obsequies as the preceding, but with more system and formality. Instead of presenting the offerings at the foot of a *deodār* tree, they present them at the spot were the body was laid out before it was thrown into the river. For the first four days the offerings are laid at the South end of the spot—that at which the feet of the deceased were laid—and the offerings during those days consist of rice beer, rice pancakes mixed with honey, the flesh and eggs of the tortoise. At the time of presenting the offerings, the mourner repeats the following words (all in the Musahar language) :—

The propitiation of the dead.

Timro hutmu, Indra, hadaria potis !
Boglo magno pokha bahru bal :
"Come, O dead one, from the palace of Indra !
Come and eat the food of the world.
Take it and return to thy palace ! "

26. The offerings remain for some time at the spot where they were laid : after which the mourner removes them to his own cave or resting place (in which he is forced to live apart during the continuance of these rites, cooks the flesh and rice, throws one mouthful on the fire for the dead, addressing him again in the same words, and

[1] On these tree spirits, see Tylor, *Primitive Culture*, II, 215, and II, 10.

then takes his own meal of what remains. From the fifth to the eighth day the same process is repeated; but the offerings during these days are placed on the West side of the spot, the diet remaining the same as during the four days preceding. On the ninth day, the offerings are placed on the North side, that is, the part where the head of the deceased was laid, and the flesh diet is now changed from tortoise to crab. This is continued till the twelfth day. On the thirteenth day, the offerings are placed on the East side and the flesh diet is changed from crab to porcupine. This is continued for one day more. On the fifteenth, the mourner goes no more to the spot, but, after being shaved, re-visits his family, who then, with the Patâri or tribal priest, solemnize a feast of the dead, consisting chiefly of rice beer and hog's flesh.[1] Then follows the shaving of the head and face of the chief mourner, which is done not by the mourner himself, but by the brother of his mother or by some son of that brother, or by the husband of his mother's sister or by some son of his mother's sister. When the shaving has been completed, the shaved man and his shaver boil some strips of bark torn from an *ásan* or *deodár* tree, and, after straining off the fibre, wash their face and body in the sacred water. He is then at last fit to enter the family cave or hut." [2] Last comes the general tribal feast of the dead. For a woman the offerings are made for nine instead of fourteen days, as in the case of a man.

27. The explanation given is that the woman carries the child for nine months before it is born, whereas the father keeps his son with him for fourteen or fifteen years, that is, till he is old enough to marry and go out and maintain himself independently in the forest. In some parts, the period of mourning is extended for a married woman from nine days to twelve, and the explanation, then, is that three more days are added in recognition of three days of weakness and suffering attending child-birth. Thus, in the case of the married woman, the final feast of the dead, which closes the days of mourning, takes place either on the tenth or the thir-

---

[1] Here Mr. Nesfield is mistaken. The Pathâri or Patâri is certainly the tribal priest only of the Majhwârs or Mânjhis, who are quite distinct from Musahars. In fact, Mr. Nesfield seems, in regard to the latter, to have combined information, some of doubtful accuracy, regarding the mass of more primitive aboriginal population along the valley of the Son.

[2] Here, again, Mr. Nesfield must be incorrect. According to Watt, *Dictionary of Economic Products* S. V. *cedrus*, the *deodár*, is purely a Himalayan tree. Ther is plenty of the *ásan* (*terminalia glabra*) in the jungles of South Mirzapur.

teenth day: while that for a man takes place on the fifteenth day. Again, there is a distinction as to the amount of hair to be shorn off before the mourner can be considered pure enough to be readmitted into his family. If the deceased was a man, it is necessary that he should be relieved of his beard and whiskers as well as of the hair of his head. If the deceased was a woman, it is enough that he should part company with the hair of his head only: for, as a woman has no beard or whiskers, there is no need (they think) to have such appendages shorn off on her account." [1]

Religion.

28. The ordinary Musahars, in Mirzapur, do not worship any Hindu gods. They worship, with prayers and sacrifices, one Sadalu Lâl, about whom it is not known exactly whether he was one of their ancestors or not. He is worshipped in Sâwan with the sacrifice of a hog and the oblation of liquor. In connection with him, ancestors generally are worshipped. They also worship the village deities (*dih*) with a hog, liquor, flowers, and a piece of cloth. Disease and death are attributed to evil spirits (*bhût*), to whom hogs and liquor are offered under a banyan or *pîpal* tree, in which they are believed to reside. They recognise five different kinds of ghosts: Nat and Pahlwân, who are supposed to belong to the Nat tribe; Daitya, the spirit of a Brâhman or Chhatri; Ahîr of an Ahîr; and Teliya Masân of a Teli. In Bârabanki, according to Mr. Nesfield,[2] they worship one Maganpâl under the title of Banrâj or "forest king." As before described, they worship the tribal ancestors, Deosi and Ansâri, the latter "under the name of Dûla Deo," which is now understood to signify the "dooly god." The offerings paid to this divinity consist of the head of a ram or goat, the eggs of the lizard (*goh*), and a piece of yellow cloth. These are presented to him on a large plate made of *dhâk* leaves. Treacle and butter are offered to him through fire. The month in which these offerings are chiefly made is Baisâkh (April), the commencement of the marriage season amongst Hindus, when litters are in much request, and when the god is, therefore, especially propitious." [3] Like all jungle tribes, they worship Baghaut (whom Mr. Nesfield's inform-

---

[1] Nesfield, *loc. cit.*, 244, *sq.*

[2] *Loc. cit.*, 258.

[3] The conversion of Dulha Deo, the Gond god of marriages (*Central Province Gazetteer*, 106, 275) into Dûla Deo, the god of the litter, is curious, if correct. For Dulha Deo, see *Introduction to Popular Religion and Folklore*, 75.

ants converted into Bhâgwat Deo), the ghost of a person killed by a tiger. They also have in their villages images of Mahâbir or Hanumân, the god-monkey in his phallic form. "The great active power in the universe, according to Musahar belief, is Bansapati, Bansatti, or Bânsuri, the goddess who (as her name implies) personifies and presides over forests. By her command the trees bear fruit, the bulbs grow in the earth, the bees make honey, the tussar worm fattens on the *âsan* leaf, and lizards, wolves, and jackals (useful for food to man) multiply their kind. She is the goddess of child-birth. To her the childless wife makes prayers for the grant of offspring. In her name and by her aid, the medicine man or sorcerer expels devils from the bodies of the possessed. In her name and to her honour, the village man kindles a new fire for lighting a brick kiln. Woe to the man who takes a false oath in the name of Bansatti."[1]

29. "Bansapti is worshipped by Musahars in their own houses or huts. They make a platform (*chauri*) in the corner of the hut, about one inch in height, above the level of the floor, and nine inches in breadth and length. This little square is made of clay, and the sacrifice is smeared with river water or cowdung. This is the altar on which the offerings to her are placed—an altar without an idol; for there is no mound, idol, or other visible symbol under which Bansatti is worshipped. On ordinary occasions, the offerings consist of flowers, fruits, grasses, roots, &c., brought fresh from the jungles : and the days on which the offerings are made are Monday and Friday. If the worshipper has any special favour to ask, he cuts the ball of his finger with some blades of the sacred *kusa* grass, and lets four or five drops of blood fall on the altar, a survival, as we may readily infer, from the now obsolete custom of human sacrifice."[2] Her special festival is in the second half of the month of Baisâkh. On that day it is supposed that Bansapti is married to Gansâm (whom Mr. Nesfield takes to be derived from Ghanasyâma one of the titles of Krishna),[3] whom Musahars call Dâu

---

[1] Nesfield, *loc. cit.*, 264.

[2] Nesfield, *loc. cit.*, 265, *sq.*

[3] This, however, is more than doubtful, and it looks much more as if Gansâm, the local god of the Kols, was introduced into the Hindu pantheon as Ghanasyâma, "the thick, dark rain cloud," a title of Krishna.

Gansâm, or "uncle Gansâm," or Bansgopâl. To him, in his phallic manifestation, a cone-shaped pillar of mud is erected.

30. Among the village Musahars the phallic deity Gansâm is replaced by Bhairon, whose vehicle is a dog. A little mud pillar, in the shape of a lingam, is erected in his honour, and among the plains men of the Gangetic valley he has become a sort of village guardian deity. He is probably of aboriginal origin, and has been introduced into the Hindu pantheon in the form of Bhairava, "the terrible one," who, like his Dravidian prototype, in this form, rides on a dog, and is called Swaswa, "whose horse is a dog." Some of the village Musahars, in Mirzapur, consult for their marriage ceremonies Upâdhya Brâhmans, who are held in contempt by their brethren. Four festivals are observed by the tribe in addition to the special tribal festival in Baisâkh: the Phagua or Holi; the Khichari or Khicharwâr, in the end of Mâgh (January—February); the Pancheinyân, generally taken as equivalent to the Nâgpanchami, or snake feast, on the 5th of the light half of Sâwan; and the Kajari or women's festival in the rains.

General superstitions.

31. Their ideas, as regards omens, do not differ from those of the kindred tribes. Friday and the number five are lucky. To meet a fox on the road is lucky, and a jackal the reverse. They swear on Bansapti and the tiger, and on liquor poured on the ground in honour of Parihâr, who is really a member of the Pânchonpîr or Ghâzi Miyân cycle, but who, according to Mr. Nesfield,[1] has become a god of wine in the hill tracts, and is represented in the plains by Madain, the deity of liquor (*mada*). They have a water ordeal, in which the two disputants dive, and the man who comes up first is considered to have been discarded by the pure element, and loses his case. They have the common oath by swearing on the head of a son. When the oldest woman in a Hindu household drives out poverty (*Daridr khedna*) on 15th Kârttik by beating a sieve in the house, and then throwing it away, Musahars, who wish to obtain the powers of a sorcerer (*ojha*), lurk about, and, when the woman comes out, rush at her with loud cries and snatch her sieve from her. She is supposed to be a witch (*tona*), and the man who can first seize her fan inherits the powers. The man thus affected has to rush off and propitiate the offended deity by a sacrifice to Sadalu.

---

[1] *Loc. cit.*, 280.

To cure a person affected with witchcraft, the *ojha* makes three marks on the ground with a piece of iron, which he then waves five times round the head of the patient with a prayer to Sadalu to make the exorcism effective. Witches generally attack young children, and the result is that they are seized with vomiting.

Social customs.

32. Women are tattooed on the wrists, cheeks, and nose. They believe that Paramesar will brand a woman in heaven who desires to enter without these protective marks. Men wear earrings (*pagara*), bracelets (*dharkaua*), and arm ornaments (*bijayath*). The women wear two kinds of nose rings—the *nathiya*, in the side of the nose, and the *bulâq*, in the septum. They have ear ornaments (*karanphûl*), bead necklaces, and glass bangles (*chûri*). The village Musahars have now begun to abstain from beef, and will not touch a Dom or Dhobi, or eat with Chamârs, Doms, or Dharkârs. They will not touch the wife of the younger brother, the wife of the elder brother-in-law, or the mother of the son's wife. The hill Musahar eats the flesh of the cow and buffalo, and was, as the legends show, until lately, a professional cow-lifter. Their clothes are of the coarsest and scantiest description. The use of the bark fibre, as described by Mr. Nesfield,[1] seems now totally abandoned, and careful enquiry in the Mirzapur hill tracts has failed to verify the assertion that any one of them now lives the life of the cave troglodyte. Their houses are generally low huts or booths of branches. According to Mr. Nesfield,[2] they have a prejudice against living under a thatch, but this hardly prevails now among the tribe in Mirzapur. They generally live in small scattered communities like other savages.[3]

Industries.

33. Mr. Nesfield has prepared an elaborate account of their industries.[4] These he classifies into the collection and sale of medicinal roots and herbs, wild honey, manufacture and sale of leaf plates, sale of wood for fuel, collection and sale of gum, the sale of the live lizard (*goh*) used by burglars in fixing their rope on the roofs of houses,[5] the lighting of brick kilns, the watching of fields

---

[1] *Loc. cit.*, 38.

[2] *Loc. cit.*, 34.

[3] Spencer, *Principles of Sociology*, I, 452.

[4] *Loc. cit.*, 40, *sqq.*

[5] It is said that the lizard is thrown up, attached to the rope, and, clinging to the roof enables the burglar to climb up.—Nesfield, *loc. cit.*, 46.

and crops by night, field labour, making of catechu, rearing the tussar silk worm. Now-a-days, in Mirzapur, their chief occupation is that of carrying palanquins. They are short, stout, hardy, little fellows, and make excellent bearers.

Distribution of the Musahars according to the Census of 1891.

Districts.	Banmânush.	Kharêbind.	Kharwâr.	Other sub-castes.	Total.
Allahâbâd	...	361	...	1,142	1,503
Benares	...	...	2,560	322	2,882
Mirzapur	...	...	4,506	891	5,397
Jaunpur	1,010	253	1,660	1,989	4,912
Ghâzipur	...	...	1,535	723	2,258
Ballia	...	...	8	192	200
Gorakhpur	...	...	...	14,993	14,993
Basti	227	...	...	...	227
Azamgarh	...	...	...	1,877	1,877
Râê Bareli	412	...	...	...	412
Faizâbâd	2,140	...	...	76	2,216
Gonda	12	...	...	...	12
Sultânpur	2,011	...	...	394	2,405
Partabgarh	242	...	...	978	1,220
Bârabanki	68	...	...	80	148
Total	6,122	614	10,269	23,657	40,662

N

Nâgbansi.—A sept of Râjputs in Gorakhpur, of whom Dr. Buchanan[1] writes :—"There are in this District a good many Nâgbansis, some of whom call themselves merely by that name, while others call themselves Vayasas, a name which in the account of Shâhâbâd has been written Vais. The Vayasas or Vais, however, universally admit that they are Nâgbansis, and that they assumed the name of Vayasa from Vayaswara, a town between Lucknow and the Ganges, where they were long settled, and from whence they came to this District, some generations ago, in consequence of a famine. Some of these, with whom I conversed, agreed with the account which I received at Shâhâbâd, and looked upon themselves as descended of the great dragon (*nâg*), and, as such, claimed a superiority over all other Râjputs, the great dragon being a personage of a good deal more consequence than the Rishis, from whom the others claim a descent. They said, and perhaps believed, that should a serpent from ignorance or mistake bite one of them, the poison would do them no injury. But I had no opportunity of putting their faith to the trial, that was proposed by the chief of Nâgpur. Other Vayasas, however, altogether disclaimed this extraction and gave one as fully difficult of belief. There was, they say, a certain very holy personage named Vasishtha, well known to all Hindu scholars, who had a cow known to all, and named Kâmdhenu. This was a very precious animal, which was coveted by Viswamitra, king of Gadhipur, who threatened to take her by force. Vasishtha was much afflicted at this, and Kâmdhenu seeing his grief, asked him if he meant to part with her. To this he replied that he had no wish of this kind, but had no power to resist the king; on which a number of warriors sprung from the cow, overthrew Viswamitra and, having killed most of his armies and children, reduced him to become a Brâhman, in which character he became an eminent saint. On this occasion the Singhâr Râjputs sprang from the horns of the cow, the Hâras from her bones, the Kachhoyas from her thighs, the Chandels from between her horns, and the Tilokchandras from the root of her nose. The great king Sâlivâhana was of this tribe, and having had three hundred and sixty wives, was ancestor of many Râjputs, among whom are the

---

[1] *Eastern India*, II, 461.

Vayasas who derive their name from Vayaswara, as already mentioned. Those who claim descent from the cow, account in this way for their being called Nâgbansi; they say that a child of a Tilokchandra was in habit of feeding daily with milk a serpent which he found in a wood. After some time the serpent was highly pleased and told the child to call his descendants Nâgbansi; and that he would make him a great Râja, which accordingly happened. Bhîma was one day poisoned by his cousin Duryodhana and the body thrown into the river. It so happened that in that vicinity the daughter of a dragon had long been in the habit of praying to Siva, and was a great favourite; but on that day she had offered flowers which were rather decayed, on which the irascible god cursed her, and declared that she should have a corpse for a husband. The afflicted damsel (for the dragons of the lower world, both male and female, have human shape whenever they please) went to Siva's spouse and told her the hard sentence. On this the goddess upbraided her husband for bestowing so severe a punishment for so trifling an offence. It was, therefore, agreed that Bhîma should be restored to life after the fair dragon had married his body and he had by her a numerous offspring. The Nâgbansi Râjputs in the female line are thus descended of the devil, and if Bhîma's mother had been what she ought, might by the father's side be descended of the Moon; but the good man Pandu had nothing to do in the matter, and the lady, his wife, had Bhîma to the god of wind. This, I am told, is the story which the Nâgpur Râja wishes to be believed, and he probably thinks that the bar of bastardy so long ago and in such circumstances is no great blot on his scutcheon. In this District the tribe is very numerous, but have chiefly come lately from the West, and possess no considerable estates, so that no family can be traced to the time when the Cheros, their real ancestors, held the country."

2. This local account of the connection between the Nâgbansi Râjputs and the Tilokchandi Bais of Oudh is interesting. The Oudh legends will be found under the head *Bais*.

Nâi,[1] Nâo, Nâu.—(Sanskrit *nápita*, according to some a corruption of *snápitri*, "one who bathes") the Hindu barber caste. In

---

[1] Based on enquiries at Mirzapur and notes by Pandit Baldeo Prasâd, Deputy Collector, Cawnpur; Mr. W. Cockburn, Jâlaun; M. Chhotê Lâl, Archæological Survey, Lucknow; Mr. W. H. O. N. Seagrave, District Superintendent of Police, Basti, and the Deputy Inspector of Schools, Bareilly and Agra.

NÂI.

Bundelkhand he is also known as Khawâs which was a title for the attendant on a grandee; and Birtiya or "he that gets his maintenance (*vritti*) from his constituents." When he is a Muhammadan he usually calls himself Hajjâm, which means in Arabic "a scarifier." It is curious that the Nâi, who is the great gossipmonger of the country side, has so little in the way of traditions about his own caste. According to one account they are descended from a Kshatriya father and a Sûdra mother; according to Parâsara from a Kuveri father and a Pattikâra mother. Another tradition is that Siva created them to cut the nails of Pârvati. The tribal saint of barbers is Sen or Sain Bhagat, whose name according to Muhammadan tradition was really Husain. He is said to have been a resident of Partâbpura, a village in the Phillaur Tahsîl of Jalandhar District. According to Prof. Wilson, whose authority was the Bhaktimâla, he was a devout worshipper of Vishnu and his descendants were for some time the family Gurus of the Râjas of Bandhugarh. One day he was so entranced in his devotion that he forgot to attend the Râja to shave him; when he came later on in the day to apologise he found to his amazement that the Râja had been shaved as usual. It then became clear that the deity had really come in person and officiated for his absent votary. His votaries are mostly barbers and are found in the Western Panjâb.

Internal structure.

2. At the last Census the barbers were enumerated in a Hindu and Muhammadan branch. Of the Hindus the following sub-castes were recorded: Banbheru, which is said to mean "quarrelsome;" Bâri, which is the name of a caste who have been separately described; Golê, which is also a sub-caste of Kumhârs; Kanaujiya and Mathuriya, "residents of Kanauj and Mathura" respectively; Sainbhagat, who take their name from the tribal saint; Sribâstab from the city of Srâvasti, and Ummara, which is the name of one of the Banya tribes. But besides these there are many others. Thus to the east of the Province we find the Sribâstab, Kanaujiya, Bhojpuriya, or "residents of Western Bengal;" Audhiya or Awadhiya from Ajudhya; Magahiya from Magadha or Bihâr; Byâhta who pride themselves on prohibiting widow-marriage and taking only virgin brides (*byâhta*), and Musalmâni which is another term for the Hajjâm. In Lucknow we have the Sribâstab; Chamarmunda or "those who shave Chamârs;" the Kumhra who do the same service for Kumhârs, and the Usarha. In Jâlaun are the Sribâstab; Ummarê; Husrentê; Bawar, and Bhe-

niya. In Bijnor are the Golê, Pachhâhi or "Western" and the Purbiya or "Eastern;" and the Bhimbru who are apparently the same as the Banbheru. In Basti are found the Sarwariya, which is the name of a well-known Brâhman tribe and means "a resident of Sarjupâr or the land beyond the river Sarju:" the Kanaujiya and the Turkiya or Turkish Muhammadan branch. Lastly, in Cawnpur we find the Sribâstab; Ummar and Râthaur, the name of a famous Râjput sept. Here the barbers refer their origin to Srinagar or Kashmîr. In the Hills again they are reported to have regular *gotras* like the higher classes, such as Chanwal, Kasyapa and Bhâradwâjâ. The complete returns of the last Census show 888 sub-divisions of the Hindu and 197 of the Musalmân branch of the tribe. Those of most local importance are the Bahlîmi, Deswâla and Gaur of Sahâranpur, the Bulehra and Deswâla of Muzaffarnagar; the Turkiya of Bareilly and Gorakhpur; the Golê of Bijnor; the Bais, Sulaimâni and Turkiya of Basti; the Purabiya and Turkiya of Kheri, and the Pîrzâda of Gonda.

Marriage rules.

3. The Nâis generally observe the usual rule of exogamy which bars marriages in their own family, and those of the maternal uncle and father's sister as long as relationship is remembered. To the East of the province the marriage age is ten or eleven, and a man may marry as many wives as he can afford to keep. They have the usual triple form of marriage—*Charhaua, dola,* and *sagâi*; the last for widows. In the first two the binding part of the ceremony is the worshipping of the feet of the bridegroom (*pânwpûja, pair pûja*) by the father of the bride and the *Sendurdân* or marking of the forehead of the bride by the bridegroom with red lead. The *dola* form is adopted only by poor people. Widows are re-married by all the sub-castes except the Byâhta. The ceremony merely consists in dressing the woman in a suit of new clothes provided by her lover who also gives her a set of jewelry. From Jâlaun it is reported that Nâis will not marry in their own village because they consider residents of the same village brothers and sisters. One origin of this feeling may be the desire so strongly felt by barbers to keep the constituents or persons they serve (*jajmân*) in the same family; but at the same time it illustrates an important principle which is at the bottom of one plausible theory of the origin of exogamy. Thus Dr. Westermarck[1] maintains "that there is an innate aversion to sexual intercourse between people living very closely together from early

[1] *History of Human Marriage*, 320.

youth, and that, as such people are in most cases related, this feeling displays itself chiefly as a horror of intercourse between near kin."

Religion.

4. Nâis belong to all the recognised Hindu sects—some being Vaishnavas, some Saivas and some Sâktas. As we have seen, to the West of the province their tribal saint is Sain Bhagat. To the East their clan deities are Phûlmati, a form of Devi, Bhairon Bâba, who is a genuine village godling and has been adopted, as has been shown elsewhere,[1] into the Brâhmanical pantheon as Bhairava, one of the most terrible forms of Siva, and Birtiya or Birtiha. These deities are worshipped on any lucky day in the month of Chait:—Phûlmati with the sacrifice of a ram or chicken and the offering of a piece of cloth dyed with turmeric; Bhairon Bâba with only a ram; Birtiha, who is a low class godling, with a young pig and an oblation of spirits. Their marriage and other domestic ceremonies are regulated by Brâhmans, who to the West are drawn from the Kanaujiya or Sanâdh tribes and to the East from the Sarwariya. In Basti they worship Mahâbîr and Bhâgawati and to the West Sain Bhagat and some Muhammadan saints like the Miyân of Amroha or Jalesar and Zâhirpîr. They cremate their married dead and dispose of the ashes in the Ganges or one of its tributaries. The unmarried dead are either buried or thrown into a river after a sort of perfunctory cremation (*jal pravâh*). They perform the usual *srâddha*, but in a less complete way than as is usual among the higher and more orthodox castes.

Occupation and social status.

5. The barber's trade is undoubtedly of great antiquity. In the Veda[2] we read—"Sharpen us like the razor in the hands of the barber;" and again, "Driven by the wind, Agni shaves the hair of the earth like a barber shaving a beard." In early times they must have enjoyed considerable dignity; Upâli the barber was the first propounder of the law of the Buddhist Church.[3]

6. A village song from Bundelkhand gives a very graphic description of his functions. *Sabsê Nâi bara khilâri; Lekar sil naharni, chhura kari tayyâr churâuri; Choti pakar sabon komûnda, baghal, mochh aur dârhi; Gola phirva sir men rakhkar*

[1] *Introduction to Popular Religion and Folklore*, 67.

[2] Wilson, *Rig Veda*, IV, 233: X, 142-4: Rajendra Lâla Mitra, *Indo Aryans*, I, 219.

[3] Oldenberg, *Life of Buddha*, 159. Spence Hardy, *Eastern Monarchism*, 238.

kalam nukîli kârhi; Mûnd mûnd kar pet chalâvai, kheti karê na bâri; Peti baghal dabâkar lota hâth liyê rujgâri.

"Of all men the barber is the greatest trickster. With his whetstone, nail parer and razor he gets ready his tool wallet. He catches people by the topknot and clean shaves them, armpit, moustache and beard. Leaving a round tonsure on the head, he points off the side-locks. By clean shaving he fills his belly. Neither field nor garden has he. With his wallet under his arm and his brass water pot in his hand, he makes his living." This, however, describes only one and perhaps not the most important function of the barber. Besides shaving and shampooing his constituents, he acts as a village menial; prepares the tobacco at the *chaupâl* or village rest-house and waits on strangers and guests. As we have seen in dealing with various castes, his duties in connection with marriages and other similar functions are numerous and important. He acts as the general village match-maker, a duty which his wandering habits of life and his admittance into respectable households admirably fit him to discharge. He is always on the look-out for a suitable match for the children of his employers, and his powers of lying and exaggerating the beauty of a girl and the qualities of a marriageable youth are highly developed. He also acts as confidential envoy and carries announcements of marriages, invitations and congratulations at pregnancy and child-birth. In the absence of a Brâhman he takes up the duties of a hedge priest and can bring a wedding or a funeral to a successful issue. But he will not bear news which is inauspicious, such as that of a death. This is carried by the Bhangi, Chamâr, Balâhar, Dusâdh or other village drudge. Besides this he is the rural leech, bone setter, tooth drawer and performer of petty operations, such as lancing boils and the like. For this business he takes the name of Jarrâh who is usually a Nâi. If a Muhammadan he usually performs circumcision; but some Hindu Nâis perform this operation for their Musalmân neighbours. Akin to him are the Jonkâra or leech applier, which is the name of one of the Kori sub-castes, the Kânmailiya or ear cleaner and the Mahâwat who is a Nat and does cupping with a cow's horn and carries some rude lancets and a bamboo pipe with which he sucks the matter out of abscesses and sore ears. The functions of these craftsmen all more or less closely trench upon those of the Nâi.

7. It is rather surprising then, that with all these important

and confidential duties intrusted to him, his social position is not higher than it is. We have seen that menial tribes have their own Nâis and most of the barbers who serve Europeans are Muhammadans, because this employment would offend his high caste Hindu clients. The Nâi is not much higher in the social scale than one of the minor grades of handicraftsmen. The reason of this is that his duty of surgery brings him in contact with blood, and he has not only to cut the first hair of the child and thus contracts some of the parturition impurity, but he also has to shave and cut the nails of the corpse before cremation. He also shaves the heads of the mourners, and his wife, as we have seen in dealing with the birth customs of various castes, succeeds the Chamârin midwife and acts as a sort of monthly nurse. She also brings out the bride at the marriage ceremony where she is very much in evidence. All this tends to procure for her a somewhat doubtful reputation.

8. Nâis drink spirits and eat the flesh of goats, sheep and deer. They eat the leavings of Brâhmans, Kshatriyas, Vaisyas and Kâyasths. All Hindus will drink water at their hands, and part of their trade is to attend feasts, wash the feet of the guests, hand round the dishes and remove the leavings. Chamârs and other outcaste tribes will eat *kachchi* cooked by them and many high castes will eat *pakki* prepared by them.

9. The barber is one of the most important members of the village community. His wandering habits and his right of entry into households give him great facilities for the collection of gossip, and the place where he carries on his business, usually in the open air, becomes, like the Roman *tonstrina* or the Florentine barber's shop immortalised in "Romola," the centre of village talk and intrigue. He is a prosperous craftsman, receiving not only annual dues from his constituents, but special fees for marriages, confinements, circumcisions, and so on. The wit and wisdom of the country side is much devoted to the Nâi. "These four are always foul—the barber, the midwife, the leech and the butcher" (*Nâi, dâi, baid, quassâi, in ka sutak kadhi na jâê*). "In a barber's wedding every one is a Thâkur." (*Nâu kê bârât men Thakurê Thâkur*). Hence he gets the mock honorific title of Thâkurji. "The barber washes others' feet but is ashamed to wash his own" (*Ân kâ gorva dhoê naunya, âpan dhovat lajâê*), and lastly, "Every one must bow his head to the barber" (*Hajjâm ke âgê sab kâ sir jhukta hai*).

Distribution of the Nâis according to the Census of 1891.

Districts.	Banbheru.	Bâri.	Golê.	Kanaujiya.	Mathuriya.	Sainbhagat.	Sribâstab.	Umrê.	Others.	Hajjâm (Musalman).	Total.
Dehra Dûn	204	43	36	...	...	...	77	...	631	272	1,263
Sahâranpur	4,118	302	32	...	...	...	28	...	3,577	11,088	19,145
Muzaffarnagar	5,324	579	2,089	...	...	1	50	...	619	5,567	14,229
Meerut	6,894	...	12,990	...	...	...	3	...	1,400	8,710	29,997
Bulandshahr	1,741	...	6,684	...	1	...	...	...	6,663	3,570	18,659
Aligarh	...	...	6,660	...	535	...	236	...	13,529	893	21,853
Mathura	18	...	5,360	...	3,069	2	43	...	5,517	286	14,295
Agra	20	...	112	...	16,423	...	548	...	3,948	281	21,332
Farrukhâbâd	...	...	...	8	250	...	14,648	...	879	616	16,401
Mainpuri	...	...	82	...	4,294	...	7,146	...	3,561	77	15,160
Etâwah	...	...	...	...	467	...	12,626	87	2,137	94	15,411
Etah	...	...	203	...	9,463	...	1,411	...	2,062	813	13,952

Bareilly	...	...	2,532	...	13	...	10,261	...	1,638	4,026	18,470
Bijnor	8,501	...	127	...	...	...	54	...	55	10,585	19,322
Budâun	...	...	4,447	...	5,059	9	2,880	...	759	3,196	16,350
Morâdâbâd	2,183	6	6,739	...	1	...	31	...	1,090	12,729	22,779
Shâhjahânpur	...	...	...	...	199	...	13,478	...	1,217	2,883	17,777
Pilibhît	16	...	17	...	30	...	5,908	...	1,459	1,411	8,841
Cawnpur	6	...	30	48	11	...	22,469	...	1,151	328	24,043
Fatehpur	...	...	...	1	...	...	13,727	1,922	272	1,754	17,676
Bânda	...	...	...	2	...	...	9,867	...	209	183	10,261
Hamîrpur	...	...	...	...	3	...	916	2,267	1,328	108	4,622
Allahâbâd	...	...	9	98	...	486	15,334	8,769	2,581	3,793	31,070
Jhânsi	...	...	...	...	...	284	5,433	...	2,094	25	7,836
Jâlaun	...	...	...	...	33	...	7,053	...	854	16	7,956
Lalitpur	...	...	...	...	...	...	53	1,381	6,651	...	8,091
Benares	...	...	...	2,906	...	45	6,126	3	1,824	3,513	14,417
Mirzapur	...	...	...	4,043	...	...	11,900	...	595	2,397	18,935
Jaunpur	...	...	...	...	...	852	13,747	...	513	6,402	21,514

Distribution of the Nâis according to the Census of 1891—contd.

DISTRICTS.	Banbheru.	Bâri.	Golâ.	Kanaujiya.	Mathuriya.	Sainbhagat.	Sribâstab.	Umrê.	Others.	Hajjâm (Musalman).	TOTAL.
Ghâzipur	...	...	...	8,348	...	12	200	...	543	4,905	14,008
Ballia	...	...	...	11,843	...	...	7	...	277	1,871	13,998
Gorakhpur	...	...	...	30,306	...	22	794	...	10,969	8,665	50,783
Basti	...	...	...	2,559	...	...	7,028	...	12,513	13,002	35,102
Azamgarh	...	...	...	8,357	...	19	3,967	...	1,145	9,173	22,661
Kumaun	...	...	...	...	...	...	...	...	117	...	117
Garhwâl	...	...	...	...	...	...	...	...	18	...	18
Tarâi	519	...	454	...	6	...	326	...	20	2,314	3,639
Lucknow	1	...	...	176	4	...	10,149	...	1,084	3,217	14,631
Unâo	300	...	...	14	...	...	19,107	...	2,220	585	22,226
Râê Bareli	...	...	...	147	105	14	17,632	...	1,877	1,853	21,628
Sîtapur	...	...	...	...	...	...	11,201	...	752	11,280	23,233

Hardoi	...	...	...	...	129	...	16,945	...	245	1,419	18,738
Kheri	...	...	...	...	121	...	9,601	...	555	6,092	17,269
Faizâbâd . . .	...	...	...	...	...	1,495	13,196	...	1,114	4,777	20,582
Gonda	...	...	...	...	...	...	14,353	...	3,330	10,953	28,636
Bahrâich	...	...	...	5	...	...	5,467	...	6,347	9,601	21,420
Sultânpur . . .	...	...	6	34	...	2,245	10,620	...	3,395	4,525	20,825
Partâbgarh . . .	...	...	...	35	5	464	11,450	5	1,976	2,478	16,413
Bârabanki . . .	...	...	...	...	...	5	12,966	...	758	10,711	24,440
GRAND TOTAL .	29,845	930	48,609	68,930	40,221	5,955	341,062	14,434	118,101	193,937	862,024

HINDUS	668,087
MUHAMMADANS	193,937
TOTAL .	862,024

Naithâna.—A class of Hill Brâhmans who belong to the middle class and Bhâradwâja *gotra*. "They ascribe their origin to Jwâlapur near Hardwâr in the Sahâranpur District, whence they came some thirty generations ago and took service with Râja Sona Pâla. They belong to the Gaur Division and owe their name to the village of Naithâna. They are distinct from both Sarola and Gangâri, but the better class of Naithâna Brâhmans intermarry with the former and the poorer with the latter. They affect service especially."[1]

Nakhi.—A Saiva order, so called because they allow their nails (*nakh*) to grow long. This appears to be the only difference between them and Atîts or Sannyâsis. Most of them live by begging, but some have a private income from trade. They are very vain of their austerity (*tapasya*).

Na'lband.—(*Na'l* "a horse shoe," *band*, "fastening") the farrier and horse shoer. They are Muhammadans, some calling themselves Shaikh and others Pathân. These divisions are endogamous. They observe the usual Muhammadan customs. Those who are well-to-do marry their daughters as infants; some defer marriage till 15 or 16. Widows re-marry by the Nikâh form which is equivalent to the Hindu *sagâi*. Among lower class Muhammadans the term Nikâh, which properly means the orthodox ceremony of marriage,[2] has been appropriated in this degraded sense. Widow-marriage does not appear to be common, but a widow may marry the younger brother of her late husband or a stranger to the family. Infidelity in the wife warrants divorce, but the fact must be proved to the satisfaction of the tribal council. They belong to the Sunni sect, and specially revere, like many of the inferior Muhammadan tribes, the Pânchonpîr and Shaikh Saddu, the latter of whom is propitiated by the offering of a he-goat and sweet cakes fried in butter (*gulgula*) with garlands of flowers. They also burn incense (*lobân*) in his honour. They so far follow Hindu usage as to offer sweetmeats (*halwa*) and cakes to the sainted dead at the Shabibarât and on Friday when there is sickness in the family.

Occupation.

2. Their occupation is farriery and treatment of horses and is thus equivalent to the Hindu Sâlotari (Sanskrit, *Sâlihotra*[3] "one who receives oblations of rice or corn," and hence a horse).

---

[1] Atkinson, *Himalayan Gazetteer*, III, 269.

[2] See Hughes *Dictionary of Islâm*, 318

[3] On this see Max Müller, *Lectures on the Science of Language*, I, 167, note.

Nânakpanthi, Nânakshâhi.—A general term which seems to be used in rather an uncertain way to denote various kinds of Sikh Faqîrs. They all take their name and derive their doctrine from Nânak, a Khatri of Talwandi, in the Lahore District, who was born in 1469 A.D. and died in 1538-9 A.D. "Nânak combined the excellencies of preceding reformers and he avoided the more grave errors into which they had fallen. Instead of the circumscribed divinity, the anthropomorphous god of Râmanand and Kabîr, he loftily invoked the Lord as the one, the sole, the timeless Being; the Creator, the Self-existent, the Incomprehensible, and the Everlasting. He likens the Deity to Truth, which was before the world began, which is and shall endure for ever, as the ultimate cause and idea of all we know or behold. He addresses equally the Mula and the Pandit, the Darvesh and the Sannyâsi, and tells them to remember that Lord of Lords who had seen come and go numerous Muhammads, Vishnus, and Sivas. He tells them that virtues and charities, heroic acts and gathered wisdom are nought of themselves; that the only knowledge that availeth is the knowledge of God, and then as if to rebuke those vain men who saw eternal life in their own act of faith, he declares that they can only find the Lord on whom the Lord looks with favour. Yet the extension of grace is linked with the exercise of our will, and the beneficent use of our faculties. God, said Nânak, places salvation in good works and uprightness of conduct; the Lord will require of man what he has done, and the teacher further required timely repentance of men, saying "If not until the day of judgment the sinner abaseth himself, a punishment shall overtake him." [1]

2. And yet Mr. Maclagan [2] says: "There is nothing in his doctrine to distinguish it in any marked way from that of the other saints who taught the higher form of Hinduism in Northern India. The unity of God, the absence of any real distinction between Hindus and Musalmâns, the uselessness of ceremonial, the vanity of human wishes, even the equality of castes are topics common to Nânak and the Bhagats; and the Adi-granth or sacred book, compiled by Nânak, is full of quotations from elder or contemporary teachers, who taught essentially the same doctrines as

---

[1] Cunningham, *History of Sikhs*, 44.

[2] *Panjáb Census Report*, 148.

Nânak himself. Nor in spite of the legends relating to him, does he appear to have had any very remarkable following during his lifetime. And yet the persons now returning themselves as his special adherents very largely outnumber the followers of any of the Bhagats or reformers of the same period. The particular success of Nânak's teaching, as compared with that of the other reforming teachers, had its foundation in a variety of circumstances, of which not the least important were the character of his successors and the nature of the people who listened to him. Most of the other Bhagats were men of the south-east, teachers from Benares, Rajputâna and Delhi. Nânak alone had his origin in the Panjâb proper, removed equally from the centre of the Empire and of Hinduism, and found his following among castes who possessed such sterling qualities as the Panjâb Khatris and Jats. But if Nânak had no successors, or successors of no moment, his following would doubtless have remained a trifling one; and it must not be supposed that the large number of Nânakpanthis shown in our tables would have been so returned if Sikhism had not had subsequently a political history."

3. "The Nânakpanthis of the sixteenth and seventeenth centuries were a sect much as the Kabîrpanthis and Dâdupanthis are sects,—a sect with certain wide opinions differing from the ordinary Hindu orthodoxy and distinguished from other sects more by the character of its Gurus and the organisation of their adherents than by any remarkable differences of doctrine. The Nânakpanthis of to-day are known roughly as Sikhs who are Sinhs, followers of the earlier Gurus, who do not think it necessary to follow the ceremonial and social observances inculcated by Guru Govind Sinh. Their characteristics are, therefore, mainly negative; they do not forbid smoking; they do not insist on long hair, or the other four *kakkas*; they are not baptized with the *pâhul*; they do not look on the Brâhman as superfluity, and so forth. The chief external difference between the Nânakpanthi Sikh and the followers of Guru Govind Sinh is the disposal of the hair; the former, like the Hindu, shaves all but the scalp lock (*bodi, choti*) and hence is often known as a Muna or Munda ("shaven") or Bodiwâla Sikh, while the Sikh proper wears long hair. They are also known as Sajhdâri. The only form of baptism known among the Nânakpanthis is the ordinary Hindu practice of drinking the footnectar of the Guru and this is not very common. It is known as *Charankâ*

pâhul or "foot baptism" as opposed to *Khandé ká pâhul* or "sword baptism" of the Govindi Sikhs. It will thus be seen that from one point of view there is very little difference between a Nânakpanthi and an ordinary lax Hindu."

The Nânakpanthis of the North-Western Provinces and Oudh.

4. In these Provinces also the term Nânakshâhi seems to be a general term applied to all followers of Nânak, and includes six sections: Udâsi, Nirmala, Kûkapanthi, Akâli, Sutharashâhi and Ragreti. Some are said to be initiated by shaving the hair and washing the body with curds and water; others do not shave the hair and let it grow all their lives. Their body is bathed in Ganges water which the initiate has to drink, and he also washes the feet of the Guru and drinks the water (*charanamrita*). After this the *mantra* or formula *satya nâma* is whispered into his ear, and when he reaches a higher stage he receives the *mantra-tatwa masi mâha vâkya*. Any of the four great divisions (*varna*) may join the order and there is no condition of age. The habits and guise of the various sections differ.

(1) Among Udâsis some have the hair shaved, some let it grow long. They wear a narrow waistcloth (*kopin*) dyed with red ochre (*geru*) and an *anchala* or cloth round the waist. They carry a water vessel (*kamandal*) like Sannyâsis. Those who are heads (*mahant*) of a monastery wear a head dress (*sâfa*) dyed with vermilion.

(2) The Nirmalas dress like the Udâsis, but keep their hair long and sometimes wear white clothes.

(3) The Kûkapanthis wear the hair uncut and wear a turban and ordinary clothes. They live a family life (*grihasth*) and carry a white rosary.

(4) The Akâlis wear the hair long and wear a waist band (*jân-ghiya*) and a black, and sometimes a white, turban. They are sometimes family men and sometimes wandering ascetics. They wear an iron ring (*chakra*) in the turban and an iron rosary. To the Brâhmanical thread (*janeu*) they tie a small knife and wear an iron ring (*kara*) on the waist.

(5) The Suthrashâhis are both house-keepers and mendicants. They beat two sticks together and sing the praises of Guru Nânak or some other worthy of the sect. They wear a white dress with a strip of black cloth round the neck and a turban of the same colour. This cloth is usually of wool.

(6) The Ragretis are said to be the lowest of all and to be like Chamârs. They are followers of Guru Govind Sinh. They are apparently the same as the Rangretas of the Panjâb where they are classed as a sub-division of the Chûhra sweepers.

Occupation.

5. Udâsis and Nirmalas live on cooked food which they beg both at houses and at regular alms-houses (*kshetra*). Many of them have an income of their own or are maintained by rich disciples. They ask for alms with the cry *Nârâyan!* They will eat *kachchi* prepared by a Brâhman, Kshatriya or Vaisya and will take *pakki* from a Sûdra. They will drink water from the hands of any of the four classes. The ascetic class do not marry; those who adopt a family life marry in their own sect. Some keep concubines and those who are of Sûdra origin allow widow marriage. Ascetics eat only once a day; the others twice. The use of tobacco, spirits and meat is prohibited. But some of the Udâsis smoke and use snuff. Those who have adopted a family life eat and drink according to the custom of the caste from which they originally sprang. They have cooking vessels like ordinary Hindus. They do not officiate as priests in Hindu temples. Their own temple is known as *sangat*, and the *granth* or sacred book of Nânak is worshipped there. Their chief place of pilgrimage is Amritsar, but they also go to Jaggannâth, Badrikâsrama, Setbandh Rameswar and Dwârika, where they worship the idols of the shrine. They salute each other with the phrase "*Jay Guru ki fateh!*" "Victory to the Teacher." Udâsis in saluting each other use the word *Dandwat* "obeisance." The Grihasthas and Mathdhâris, the family men and abbots are cremated; the bodies of the ascetic class are thrown into a river. Besides the Granth they revere the five deities (*Panchdeva*), Brahma, Vishnu, Siva and the Sâkti. The duties of those who act as Gurus are to read the Scriptures, to ponder over the Vedanta philosophy, to give religious instruction according to the Upanishads, to give advice to their disciples. Whatever their disciples offer the Gurus take and in all religious matters they are consulted.

Nânbâi, Nânbâ, Nânpaz.—(Persian *Nân* "bread") the baker caste. In the cities they call themselves Rotiwâla or Biskutwâla "biscuit maker." He either purchases flour himself, and sells English bread (*dabbal roti*) or he cooks dishes prepared by his customers. All those recorded at the last census were Muhammadans. The caste is, of course, entirely occupational and they intermarry freely with other Muhammadans.

Distribution of Nânbâis according to the Census of 1891.

Districts.	Numbers.	Districts.	Numbers.
Meerut	89	Ghâzipur . . .	64
Mathura . . .	3	Gorakhpur . . .	743
Agra	120	Azamgarh . . .	58
Farrukhâbâd . . .	135	Lucknow . . .	243
Mainpuri . . .	19	Unâo	48
Etâwah	71	Râê Bareli . . .	12
Etah	10	Sîtapur	33
Budâun	21	Hardoi	56
Morâdâbâd . . .	55	Kheri	13
Shahjahânpur . . .	290	Bahrâich . . .	32
Cawnpur . - .	25	Sultânpur . . .	22
Fatehpur . .	3	Partâbgarh . . .	11
Lalitpur . . .	1	Total .	2,177

Nandwâni.[1]—A sept of Oudh Râjputs, who were, in Sîtapur, the predecessors of the Gaur Râjputs.

Naqshbandi, Naqshbandiya.—An order of Muhammadan Faqîrs which was founded by Khwâja Pîr Muhammad Naqshband, whose tomb is in the Kasar-i-Urfân at Bukhâra. "This man and his father were both manufacturers of brocade, hence the name Naqshband or the 'pattern maker.' The sect was introduced into India by Shaikh Ahmad Sirbandi, whose priestly genealogy is traced back to Abu-Bakr, the first Khalîfa. The Naqshbandis worship entirely by the *zikr-i-khafi* or the 'silent process,' sitting perfectly calm and quiet, and repeating the Kalima under their breath. They often sit immersed in meditation (*murâqabah*), quite motionless, with the head bent, and the eye closed or fixed on the ground. All singing and music they utterly repudiate, and are

[1] *Sîtapur Settlement Report*, 39.

extremely strict adherents of the institutes and traditions of orthodox Muhammadanism. The spiritual guides of the order do not sit apart from their disciples, but, ranging them in a circle, seat themselves by their sides, with a view of communicating their own mystic virtues to the minds of their followers by some sort of hidden magnetism.[1]" They have a practice of going about begging with a lamp in their hands, whence the proverb *Chirâgh raushan murâd hâsil,* "The lamp is lighted and the wishes fulfilled."

Distribution of the Naqshbandis according to the Census of 1891.

Districts.	Numbers.	Districts.	Numbers.
Sahâranpur . . .	7	Gorakhpur . . .	6
Muzaffarnagar . . .	1	Azamgarh . .	491
Mainpuri	92	Lucknow . . .	5
Etâwah	13	Faizâbâd . . .	27
Pilibhît	1		
Allahâbâd . . .	15	Total .	658

Narauliya.—An influential Râjput sept in Ghâzipur, who claim to be a branch of the Parihâr, and to take their name from Narwar in Gwâlior. They are among the earlier settlers and say that their ancestors killed the Chero Râja, while he was in a state of intoxication, and occupied his dominions. They are inordinately proud, passionate, and extravagant, and have lost a large part of their ancestral property. They claim to belong to the Kasyapa *gotra*.[2]

Nat[3] (Sanskrit *nata,* "a dancer,") a tribe of so-called gypsy dancers, acrobats, and prostitutes who are found scattered all over the Province. The problem of the origin and ethnological affinities of the Nats is perhaps the most perplexing within the whole range of the ethnography of Northern India, and the enquiries, of which

[1] *Panjâb Census Report,* 196.
[2] Oldham, *Ghâzipur Memo.*, I, 61.
[3] Based on information collected at Mirzapur and notes by Bâbu Badri-nâth, Deputy Collector, Kheri; M. Niyâz Ahmad, Fatehpur; A. B. Bruce, Esq., C. S., Ghâzipur; Bâbu Sânwal Dâs, Deputy Collector, Hardoi; M. Gopâl Prasâd, Nâib Tahsîldar, Etâwah; the Deputy Inspectors of Schools, Shâhjahânpur, Budâun, Bijnor.

the result is given here, leave its solution almost as uncertain as ever. The real fact seems to be that the name Nat is an occupational term which includes a number of different clans who have been grouped together merely on account of their common occupation of dancing, prostitution, and performance of various primitive industries.

2. The same people are found also beyond the boundaries of these Provinces. Thus they appear to be identical, at least in occupation, with the Kolhâtis of Bombay, who are also known as Dombari, and are "rope dancers and tumblers, as well as makers of the small buffalo horn pulleys which are used with cart ropes in fastening loads. They also make hide combs and gunpowder flasks. When a girl comes of age, she is called to choose between marriage and prostitution. If, with her parents' consent, she wishes to lead a married life, she is well taken care of and carefully watched. If she chooses to be a tumbler and a prostitute, she is taken before the caste council, a feast is given, and with the consent of the council she is declared a prostitute. The prostitutes are not allowed to eat with other Kolhâtis, except with their own children. Still, when they grow old, their caste-fellows support them. They worship Amba Bhawâni, Hanumân, Khandoba, and the cholera goddess Mariâi; but their favourite and, as they say, their only living gods are the bread-winners or hunger-scarers, the drum, the rope, and the balancing pole."[1]

3. Of the same people in the Dakkhin, Major Gunthorpe[2] writes:—"The Kolhâtis belong to the great Sânsya family of robbers and claim their descent from Mallanûr, the brother of Sânsmal. There are two tribes, Dukar Kolhâtis and Kam or Pâl Kolhâtis. The former are a non-wandering criminal tribe, whereas the latter are a non-wandering criminal class. Depraved in morals, the males of both tribes subsist to a great extent by the prostitution of some of their females, though let it be said to the credit of the former that they are not so bad as the latter. They labour for themselves by cultivating land, by taking service as village watchmen, or by hiring themselves to villages to destroy that pest of Indian farmers, the wild hog, and above all they are professional robbers.

---

[1] *Bombay Gazetteer*, XX, 186, *sq*.

[2] *Notes on Criminal Tribes*, 46, *sqq*. The Kolhâtis take their name from *Kolhât*, the bamboo on which they perform.—*Bombay Gazetteer*, XII, 123, *sq*.

Kam Kolhâtis, on the other hand, are a lazy, good-for-nothing class of men who, beyond making a few combs and shuttles of bone, will set their hands to no class of labour, but subsist mainly by the immoral pursuits of their women. At every large fair may be seen some of the portable huts of this tribe, made of grass, the women decked in jewels and gaudy attire sitting at each door, whilst the men are lounging lazily at the back. The males of the Dukar Kolhâti tribe are a fine manly set of fellows, and obtain the distinction of Dukar, 'hog' from the fact of their hunting the wild, and breeding the domesticated pig."

4. Again we have in Bengal[1] a people known as Nar, Nat, Nartak or Nâtak, who form the dancing and musician class of Eastern Bengal; on the other hand many of the people whom in these Provinces we class as Nats, such as the Bâzigar, Sapera, and Kabûtri, are classed in Western Bengal with the Bediya, who in Northern India are undoubted kinsfolk of the Sânsya, Hâbûra, and similar vagrant races.

5. Lastly, of the same people in the Panjâb, Mr. Ibbetson[2] writes :—"The Nat, with whom I include the Bâzigar, form a gypsy tribe of vagrant habits, who wander about with their families, settling for a few days or weeks at a time in the vicinity of large villages or towns, and constructing temporary shelters of grass. In addition to practising acrobatic feats and conjuring of a low class, they make articles of grass, straw, and reeds for sale; and in the centre of the Panjâb are said to act as Mirâsis, though this is perhaps doubtful. They often practise surgery and physic in a small way, and are not free from suspicion of sorcery. They are said to be divided into two main classes, those whose males only perform as acrobats and those whose women, called Kabûtri, perform and prostitute themselves. About three-quarters of their number returned themselves as Hindus, and most of the rest as Musalmâns. They mostly marry by circumambulation (*phera*) and burn their dead; but they are really outcastes, keeping many dogs, with which they hunt and eat the vermin of the jungles. They are said especially to reverence the goddess Devi, Guru Tegh Bahâdur, the Guru of the Sikh scavengers, and Hanumân, or the monkey god, the last because of the acrobatic powers of monkeys. They very generally

[1] Risley, *Tribes and Castes*, II 129.
[2] *Panjâb Ethnography*, section 588.

trace their origin to Mârwâr; and they are found all over the Province, except on the frontier, where they are almost unknown."

6. There seems, then, very little doubt that under the general name Nat are included various tribes; some of whom are closely allied to the vagrant, criminal races, like the Sânsyas, Beriyas, and Hâbûras; and as we shall find a well pronounced totemistic section system among some of the so-called sub-castes, it seems possible that they have decided Dravidian relationship.

Tribal organisation.

7. As has been already stated, the tribal organization of the Nats is most complex. Everywhere they merge with the regular vagrant tribes, and where to draw the line is practically impossible. In the last Census, about two-thirds of the Nats in these Provinces declared themselves as Hindus and one-third as Muhammadans. Of the Hindus we find ten main sub-castes:—The Brijbâsi, who take their name from their supposed country of origin, Braj or Mathura, and its neighbourhood. Next come the Guâl or "cowherds," some of whom claim a Jât and others an Ahîr origin. The Jogila seem to be connected in name with the vagrant, criminal Jogis. The Kabûtara, who take their name from the pigeon (*kabûtar*), are prostitutes so-called from characteristic wooing of the bird. The Kalabâz is literally "a tumbler or juggler." The Karnâtak is supposed to come from the Karnâta country, the modern Karnâtic in Madras. The Mahâwat is so called from the Sanskrit *Mahâmâtra*, "a great officer of state" or an "elephant driver," an occupation to which the word is now generally applied. The Mîrdaha is literally "a village ruler" (Persian, *mîrdah*), and now-a-days the word is usually applied to a man who carries a chain for a surveyor. The Râthaur is the name of a famous Râjput sept; and Sapera (Sanskrit, *sarpahâraka*) is literally "a snake catcher."

8. But this is far from exhausting the tribal organization of the Nats. Thus Mr. Carnegy [1] divides the Oudh Nats into eight sub-castes:—First, the Gwâliyâri Nats or those of Gwâlior, with three sections, Kapûri, Bhâtu and Sarwâni. Of these the Kapûri appear to take their name from the Sanskrit *karpura*, "camphor;" the Bhâtu are seemingly the same as the Bhâtu or Bhântu, a sub-

[1] *Notes*, 17.

caste of the Sânsyas. The men of this sub-caste buy cattle for butchers, while the women are cuppers, dentists, and aurists. They are Hindus, bury their dead, and drink inordinately. Secondly, the Sânwat, who are Muhammadans. They also supply butchers, and sing the praises of Alha and Udal, the heroic Banâphar warriors, who were afterwards subject to the Râthaurs, from whom this sub-caste claims descent. Thirdly, Brijbâsi, who are Hindus. The men walk on high stilts and the women show their confidence by dancing and singing under them. They eat pork, drink spirits and bury their dead. They say that they came to Braj or Mathura after the capture of Chithor, which is the starting point of the traditions of so many other castes. Fourthly, the Bachgoti, who are Hindus and connected by Mr. Carnegy with the Râjput sept of the same name. The men wrestle and play single stick; the women are depraved. They bury their dead. Fifthly, the Bijaniya or Bajaniya, who seem to take their name from the music (*bâja*) accompanying their performances. They are Hindus and dance on the tight rope. They are addicted to drinking; they bury their dead in an upright position. Sixthly, the Bariya, who are Hindus. They do not perform, but attend feasts and eat scraps. The women are depraved and all are addicted to drinking. They bury their dead. Seventhly, the Mahâwat, who are Musalmâns by religion. They are said to be expert in treating rheumatism and deal in cattle. Drinking is confined to the seniors on the occasion of deaths. Lastly come the Bâzigar, or common conjurers, who are given to drinking. They bury their dead.

9. In addition to this enumeration the present survey has produced a long set of diverse lists from different districts. The confusion, as already indicated, seems to have sprung from the practical impossibility of distinguishing the Nat from his allies, the Sânsyas and similar tribes. Thus, in Mirzapur we find the Bajaniya, Byâdha, Karnâtak, Kashmîri, Kalabâz, Mahâwat, Bâdi and Malâr. From Shâhjahânpur comes a list of Hindu sub-castes, including the Bhântu, who are Sânsyas, with the Guâl, Ghara, Kalabâz, Kabûtariya, and Lakarbâz, or performers on stilts. From Kheri we find the Bhatiya, who are perhaps the Bhâtu of Shâhjahânpur; the Kingariya, who are discussed in a separate article; the Kanjar, who, of course, forms a tribe of his own; the Gulahla, Kalabâz, Râjnat, and Dhârhi, who again are usually classed as a quite different group. The list from Budâon gives Guâl and

Brajbâsi, with, as sections, the Kakhera or Kanghigar, "comb makers," and the Banjâra, where we meet a distinct group. In Hardoi we find the Kalabâz, Karnâtak, Brijbâsi, and Bâgula; in Bijnor, the Bâdi, Guâl, and Keutâr, the last of whom are possibly connected with the Kewats. The sub-castes of the Muhammadan Nats are much less well established. In Ghâzipur we find the Panjâbi, Goriya, and Hagiya; in Fatehpur, the Meghiya, Dariya, Chhijariya, and Krîm or Karîm.

10. The complete Census returns show 386 sections of the Hindu and 205 of the Musalmân Nats. They have, as might have been expected, largely adopted the names belonging to other castes and septs, such as Bhântu, Chamargautam, Chamarmangta, Chamarnat, Chamar Sangla, Chamarwa, Chandel, Chauhân, Chhatri, Dhîmar, Dhobi, Dom, Ghosi, Gond, Gûjar, Guâl, Guâlbans, Jâdon, Kâbuli, Kanchan, Kâyasth, Khatri, Kori, Korwa, Kormangta, Mainpuri Chauhân, Panwâr, Paturiya, Râjput, Râthaur, Sakarwâr, Teli. With these are the usual local groups: Brijbâsi, Chithauriya, Daryâbâdi, Gangapâri, Indauriya, Jaiswâr, Jaypuriya, Kanaujiya, Kâshipuri, Lâhauri, Mathuriya, Panjâbi, Râmpuriya, Sribâstam. The Musalmân branch show an equally curious mixture of names. We have many distinctively Hindu titles as Bâhman, Bais, Bhadauriya, Chauhân, Gaur, Gûjar, Râthaur, and Tomar; regular Musalmân names like Chisti, Ghori, Khwâja Mansûri, Khwâja Miyân, Lodi, Mughal, Nawâb, Naumuslim, Pathân, Sadîqi, Shaikh, Turkiya, and Yûsufzai; occupational terms and those connecting them with other gypsy tribes, such as Bâzigar, Beriya, Bûchar, ("Butcher"), Dom, Fîlwân ("elephant driver"), Kanchan, Mangta ("beggar"), Pahlwân ("wrestler"), Randi ("prostitute"), Sânpwâla and Sapera ("snake men"), and Tawâif.

The Eastern Nats.

11. The information at present available is much more complete for the Eastern Nats, and it may be well to describe some of their sub-castes with more or less detail.

The Bajaniya Nats.

12. The Bajaniya Nats of Mirzapur have seven sections, which are obviously of totemistic origin. These are Makriyâna which take their name from *makri*, "a spider," which no member of the section will kill; Gauharna, which are called from *goh* the Gangetic alligator or lizard known as the *goh sânp*, which none of them will harm; Deodinâik or "leader given by God," the members of this section are generally

headmen (*chaudhari*) of the tribe; Bahunaina or "the fly," which takes its name from having many eyes; this insect none of them will injure; Gagoliya of which they are unable to give any explanation; Sânpaneriya, none of whom will kill the snake (*sânp*); and Sûganâik, none of whom will injure the parrot (*suga*). These sections are exogamous, but there is no other prohibition against intermarriage, and it is notorious that Nats marry very close blood relations. They say that they were originally residents of Mârwâr, and passed into Mirzapur through Bundelkhand. The migration is said to have occurred about a century ago. They have no other tribal tradition, except that they were created by Parameswar, whose pleasure it was that they should be acrobats and rope-dancers.

13. They have their own council known as Panth, presided over by a head man (*mutâna*), who is assisted by a messenger (*harkâra*), whose business is to collect the elders for meetings. No woman can be divorced for simple adultery. Her paramour is merely fined five rupees, which is spent on drinking. They cannot marry again while the first wife is alive. They purchase brides, the price according to tribal custom being twenty-five rupees in cash, four rupees worth of sugar, one rupee worth of pulse (*dâl*), one rupee worth of *ghi*, two rupees worth of wheat, some turmeric and cakes.

14. Concubinage is not allowed. Widows can marry by the ordinary form, which they call *ghughuna*. When the connection is sanctioned by the headman, the future husband goes to the house of the widow, puts bangles and a nose-ring of silver on the woman. Her friends then take the pair into a closed room, where they are left some time to themselves, and in the meantime wine is served round to the brethren. Next morning the husband takes his wife home, and the business is over. The levirate is allowed on the usual conditions; if she marry a stranger, she loses all right to the goods of her first husband.

15. A Chamârin midwife attends the mother only for one day. The mother is kept secluded for six days with a fire and a box of iron for holding lamp-black (*kajranta*) near her. The ceremony on the sixth day is known as *huabar*. The mother bathes and then goes to the nearest well with the bosom of her sheet full of parched grain, with four pice, some powdered sugar and ginger, and two roots of turmeric. When she comes to the well, she lights a lamp, and collecting the lamp-black in her iron box, marks several lines

with it and some vermilion on an earthen pot, and puts red lead on the parting of the hair of the women who go with her. She bows in obeisance to the well and returns home, where the parched grain is distributed among her women friends. At the same time the father serves round wine to his male friends, and after that the mother is considered pure.

16. The betrothal is settled by the father of the boy paying five rupees to the girl's father, which is spent on wine for the brethren. A feast is given and the father of the bride sends a bead necklace and a handkerchief for his future son-in-law.

17. When the wedding day is fixed, the bride-price is sent in advance. This is usually five days before the wedding, and during that time the pair are kept at their own houses in a thatched shed in the courtyard. This shed, contrary to the usual Hindu custom, is surrounded with screens. We have here probably a survival of the custom of seclusion at puberty. Every day the pair are anointed with turmeric and oil. A friend takes the bridegroom on his shoulder to the house of the bride, and when they reach her door her relatives make a square, in each corner of which a brass *lota* is placed. A pice is put into each *lota*, and the four vessels are joined with a string. Into this enclosure the pair are led, and inside it they make five circuits. This is the binding part of the ceremony. The bride returns to the house and the bridegroom to his friends. That night is spent in eating and drinking, and next morning the bride puts on a dress purchased out of the bride price. The pair stand at the door, and the bride's mother waves a plough yoke (*jūa*) over their heads for good luck. Then the bride and bridegroom are taken home on the shoulders of two male friends. At the door the boy's mother again waves a plough yoke over them, and the boy, seizing the yoke, runs and demolishes with it the nuptial shed (*mānro*) in the courtyard. This concludes the marriage.

18. They bury their dead in their own cemetery. When a person dies they put a copper coin in his mouth as a viaticum. The corpse is taken on a bier and buried with the head to the north and the feet to the south. When the grave is filled, they pour some wine on the ground, and they do the same at the house of the deceased, where wine is served round when they return after the burial. The ceremonies for the repose of the soul are done some months later, when they can afford to do so. They go to the river side and cook cakes, rice, and pulse. Then they spread a cloth

on the ground, on which the ghost is supposed to sit, and the nearest relative taking an earthen cup (*purwa*) and a knife in his hand plunges into the water. He puts the knife on the cup and sits down till the cup, which is placed on his head, gets full of water. This cup full of water he brings out and places under the cloth on which the ghost is supposed to be sitting. Again he places four cups of water, one at each corner of the cloth, and connects them with a thread so as to form a square. In the enclosure thus formed they place a little of each kind of food for the refreshment of the ghost, and pray to it to partake of the food. They then wait for a few minutes while it is supposed to be eating, and then they address it: "Go and join those who have departed before you." Until this ceremony is performed, the ghost will not pass quietly to the world of the dead. They have no idea of ceremonial impurity, resulting from death.

19. Their tribal deities are Hulki Mâi, the goddess of cholera, the Vindhyabâsini Devi, Durga-Kâli, and Parameswar. They worship these collectively every year when they return from their annual wanderings. This worship is done in the family kitchen and the only sacrifice is a he-goat with sweet bread and wine. This is their chief festival, and is done either on the tenth (*dasmîn*) of Kârttik or at the *Holi*. Whenever, during the year, any trouble comes upon them, they make a special offering of sweet bread and wine to the deified ancestors, all of which, after presentation, they consume themselves.

20. They regard the Dom and the Hela with special dislike. They do not eat beef or vermin, such as rats; but they eat fowls, fish of every kind, crocodiles, tortoises, and the *nîlgâê* deer. They drink spirits and use *gânja*, *bhang*, and palm wine (*târi*), but not opium. No respectable Hindu will take food or drink from their hands. They will eat food prepared by any one except a Dhobi, Pâsi, Dharkâr, Dom, or Chamâr. The men wear short drawers (*janghiya*) turban (*pagri*), a necklace of white beads (*guriya*), and earrings (*bâli*). The women wear a petticoat (*lahnga*), boddice (*choli*), a black and white bead necklace and ear-rings.

21. The men are rope-dancers and acrobats. The women beg and prostitute themselves. They usually live in out-of-the-way hamlets away from the village, and during the cold and hot weather they wander about from fair to fair and to the houses of rich people, usually sleeping under trees in the course of their journeys.

22. The Byâdha are another tribe of these vagrants. They take their name from the Sanskrit *Vyâdha*. "a hunter." They are a short, black race, with very large dark eyes, very black hair, which they keep long and unkempt, short beard, whiskers and mustache, and a short, rather broad, nose. Those of Mirzapur are unable to name any of their exogamous sections, and their rules of intermarriage are very vague. They do not even maintain the ordinary formula that the line of the paternal uncle (*chacha*), maternal uncle (*mâmu*), paternal aunt (*phûphu*), and maternal aunt (*mâosi*) are to be avoided. In short, they have practically no prohibited degrees Thus a man will marry his son to his own sister's daughter, to his maternal aunt's daughter, and so on.

The Byâdha Nats.

23. The marriage negotiations are carried on by the maternal uncle (*mâmu*) of the boy, a custom which may be a survival of the matriarchate. Sometimes one of the meaner Brâhmans goes with the envoy. When the match is settled the boy's maternal uncle, brother-in-law, and some of his female relations go to the house of the bride and pay the bride-price, which consists of twenty rupees in cash, a set of glass bangles (*chûri*), a cocoanut, a betel-nut, and a suit of clothes. These things are given to the mother of the bride. They return after fixing the marriage day. A pavilion (*mânro*) is erected at the boy's house, and next day he starts for the bride's house. They have no regular Purohit or family priest, but the lucky dates for these events are ascertained from some village Brâhman. All the relations, including the women, which is absolutely opposed to all Hindu usage, accompany the procession. On that day the bride's father entertains the whole party with goat's flesh and rice.

24. When the time comes for the marriage, the bridegroom takes his seat in the pavilion with the bride seated beside him, her mother shading her face with the end of her sheet. Then the bride's female relations rub the pair vigorously with a mixture of oil and turmeric. This is done three times while the ceremony goes on. The binding part of the rite is the rubbing of the parting of the bride's hair with red lead, which is done by the brother-in-law of the bridegroom, the husband of his sister. This is, of course, contrary to all Hindu usage; the boy usually does this rite himself. During the marriage the girl's father performs no rite, which again is very unorthodox. They have no retiring-room

(*kohabar*) ceremony as among low Hindu castes. When the marriage is over, her father dresses the bride in new clothes, gives her a *lota*, and sends her off at once with her husband. The age for marriage is fifteen for boys and ten or twelve for girls: as a rule it takes place immediately when the pair have attained puberty.

25. Widows are married by the *sagâi* form and the levirate prevails under the usual condition that she marry the younger, not the elder, brother of her late husband. If the younger brother do not claim her, she may marry an outsider with leave of the tribal council. Nothing is paid to the parents of the widow. Her lover is expected to give a goat to the council. When this is done, he puts some oil on the widow's head, while her sister's husband (*bahnoi*) rubs red lead on the parting of her hair. He then takes her off to his house.

26. At child-birth the mother is isolated and attended by the Chamârin midwife. After the fifth day is the *chhathi* or sixth-day rite when the brethren (*âtma*), men and women, are fed. The Chamârin, who is known as *soin*, bathes the mother and baby, and gives their clothes and those of the other members of the household to a Dhobi. All the men have their hair shaved. The birth pollution ceases on the twelfth day (*barahi*), when the mother and child are bathed again. The husband keeps away from his wife for twenty days after her confinement. The Chamârin among these people plasters the delivery-room,—a duty which, among other Hindus, is usually done by the husband's sister (*nanad*). The menstrual pollution lasts for five days, during which the woman is isolated, and her husband cooks for her.

27. These Nats say that they came originally from Ratanpur and Bilâspur in the Central Provinces. They bury their dead, not in a regular cemetery, but in any convenient place north of the village. The grave lies North and South, and they profess not to care in which direction the corpse is laid. A woman is buried face upwards and a man face downwards. After the burial, they all bathe and return to the house of the deceased, where they sit for a while in the courtyard, wash their hands, and then go home. No food is cooked in the house that day; the family are fed by a neighbour. On the tenth day the brethren assemble at some tank or stream and have their heads shaved. No sacred balls (*pinda*) are offered. They return to the house of mourning and there they are feasted. If the son of the deceased can afford it, he gives a cup

and plate (*lota, thâli*) and a female calf to a Brâhman. This concludes the death rite.

28. All who can afford it have an annual propitiation of the dead (*barsi*). They do not on this occasion feed the brethren, but give a Brâhman some brass vessels. Then he stands up and raising his hands says :—" Children of the dead man! Live in happiness!" They have no regular fortnight of the dead (*pitrapaksha*), and no *srâddha*.

29. In the month of Sâwan, they worship Hariyâli Devi, " the goddess of greenery," who watches the crops. To her a fire offering (*hom*) is made in the field with sugar and *ghi*. In Phâlgun they burn the old year (*sambat jalâna*) when they drink and eat good food. They observe no other Hindu festival except the Phagua or Holi. On some day in the light fortnight of Asârh, they worship their deceased ancestors (*purakh log*). They make a fire offering with sugar and *ghi*, and sprinkle a little spirits on the ground. This worship is done by the head of the family at home. Their tribal deity is Bhawâni Devi, who is worshipped every third year in the light fortnight of Phâlgun. To her is offered a black goat, which is fed on rice before being sacrificed. The worshipper does the sacrifice himself. When sickness or other trouble comes upon them they sometimes get the Baiga to sacrifice a goat to the village gods (*deohâr*). Men and women both eat the flesh of the victims to Bhawâni. She has no temple, but most people make a stone or mud platform near their houses, where she is supposed to dwell. When they eat, they throw a little food and water on the ground for the ancestral ghosts, and say—" If any of you are hungry, come and eat."

30. The women of this tribe do not tattoo; this is done by the Bâdi Nats. The women get themselves tattooed with little spots on both wrists: but the custom is not well defined. If an unmarried woman is caught in an intrigue with a member of the caste, the council order him to pay twenty rupees to her father, and she is then made over to him by a sort of informal marriage. In the same way, if a married woman is caught with a man her paramour pays the husband twenty rupees and takes over the lady. If her lover be of another caste she is permanently expelled. They profess to have stringent rules to enforce chastity among their women, but they are not free from the suspicion of occasionally prostituting their girls. They have no occupation but begging, and do not dance, play, sing,

or perform acrobatic feats. Their women wear glass bangles (*chûri*), bead necklaces (*nuriya*) of all colours, anklets (*pairi*) and arm ornaments (*churla*). They do not wear nose-rings. They will eat all ordinary meat except beef, monkeys, horses, tame pigs, and snakes They swear by the words : "If I lie, may I eat beef," or on their sons' heads; or they fill a *lota* of water and swear by Kansâsur Deota, "the godling of brass." Until a child is five or six years old they do not care what he eats ; but when he arrives at that age he is obliged to conform to caste custom, and to commemorate this event, if they can afford it, they put a silver bangle on his wrist.

The Karnâtak Nats.

31. This sub-caste of Nats is quite distinct from the Bajaniya, but they have the same sections, Gohna or Gouharna, Makriyâna, Suganâik, Deodinâik, Gagoliya, Sânpaneriya and Waniawaraha. These are exogamous ; but like all Nats they are very careless about prohibited degrees, and first cousins are allowed to marry. The highest section is the Deodinâik, and then follow the Suganâik, Gohna, Gagoliya and Sânpaneriya. Some of them are Hindus and some Muhammadans. Those who are Hindus worship the Vindhyabâsini Devi of Bindhâchal or Durga. They will eat the leavings of all high castes and are hence known as Khushhâliya or "those in prosperous circumstances." They dance on ropes and with cow horns tied to their feet ; their women do not tattoo other women. Some of the better looking girls are reserved for prostitution, and these are never married in the tribe. One condition of marriage among them is that both parties should be of the same age. The Muhammadan branch in Etâwah allow the levirate, and a widow can marry either the elder or younger brother of her late husband. There, it is said, they will admit any one into the tribe except a Bhangi, Dhânuk, Chamâr, Teli, Dhobi or Bâri. When the initiate is not a Muhammadan they send for the Qâzi, who recites the *Kalima* over him. A girl who is seduced, whether her paramour be a tribesman or not, can be restored to caste rights on payment of a fine ; but if her lover be a low caste man, like a Dom or Dharkâr, she is permanently expelled. If her lover be a Brâhman or Râjput, she is admitted back, and can be married in the caste.

Kashmîri Nats.

32. These people have no occupation except loafing, begging, and prostituting their women. Very few of the women are married in the tribe, and even the married women are sometimes prostituted. Most of their

real wives are girls of other castes, who are bought by them or kidnapped. This is a costly and dangerous business; hence the number of old bachelors among them is very large. When they do marry in the tribe they observe no prohibited degrees and marry cousins. No regard is paid to the paternity of their children. Some of them are Hindus and some Muhammadans. The Hindus employ low Brâhmans as their priests, and burn their dead. The Muhammadans bury. Hindus worship their ancestors in the month of Kuâr, and to the east of the Province their favourite deities are the Vindhyabâsini Devi of Bindhâchal and Garbara Devi. These are worshipped in the month of Aghan with the sacrifice of a goat and an offering of cakes and sweetmeats. The Hindu branch do not eat beef and pork. They eat mutton, goat's flesh, venison, and the like. They will not eat the flesh of the horse, camel, jackal or rats. The Muhammadans do not eat pork, but use beef and drink spirits. They eat the camel and fowls and the other animals which the Hindu branch of the tribe eat.

The Kalabâz or Gara Nats.

33. This branch of the Nats has exogamous sections, but few of them are able to give a list of them. In Hardoi their sections are Savâi, Ghughasiya, Panchhiya, Jimichhiya. Their tradition is that they were once Kshatriyas, and were forced to deny their caste when Alâ-ud-dîn conquered Chithor in 1303 A.D. Another account of them is that their first ancestor was a Dhînwar, and that they were begotten by him from a Teli woman. They wander about the country in rude huts (*sirki*) made of reeds. To the east of the Province they appear to conduct their marriages in one of these huts with a rude form of the circumambulation (*bhanwari*) ceremony. They have a strange legend that Parameswar was once incarnated as a Nat at Sambhal in the Morâdâbâd District, and became such an accomplished acrobat that in one bound he fixed a cart and in a second some mill stones in a tree which no Kalabâz has been since able to take down. Their occupation is rope-dancing and other acrobatic feats. They are fairly strict Hindus, and are said not to prostitute their women In Oudh their favourite deity seems to be Hardeo or Hardaur Lâla, the godling of cholera. From Etah it is reported that a distinction is drawn between the Baghaliya Nats, who dance on ropes, and the Kalabâz, who do somersaults and other athletic feats. They are very fond of singing the Alha song to the accompaniment of the drum. During the rains these people move about from vil-

lage to village. It is understood that only one party encamps in the village at a time, and no other party is allowed to intrude on them until the performance is over. Wilful intrusion of this kind is severely punished by the tribal council. Even if any other body of Nats perform there, the fees go to the party which is first in possession of the place. The women do not perform or dance, sing or beg. They have regular circles within each of which the bones of the dead of the tribe are buried under a masonry platform, as is the rule among the Hâbûras, and to these the tribal worship is performed.

The Mahâwat Nats.

34. The Mahâwat Nats take their name from the Sanskrit *Mahâmâtra* "a high officer of state" or "an elephant driver." They say themselves that keeping elephants was their original occupation, and that from this they derive their name. They are also known as Baid, "physician;" (Sanskrit *Vaidya*) and Lohângi, because they use surgical instruments of iron (*loha*) in treating their patients. They say that they are divided into four endogamous sub-castes; Turkata Pahlwân, Kapariya, Chamarmangta and Lohângi Nats. Of these the first and fourth are Muhammadans and the second and third Hindus. The Turkata Pahlwâns teach wrestling and athletic exercises and their women tattoo. The Kapariyas are dealt with in a separate article. The Chamarmangta are so called because they beg (*mângna*) from Chamârs. In Mirzapur the true Lohângi Nats marry second cousins. They fix their earliest settlement at Kara Mânikpur on the Ganges. They say that they are descended from Hathîla who has now been deified as one of the Pânchon Pîr. They worship him with prayers and the sacrifice of a fowl in the month of Jeth. This worship is done by Dafâlis, who, while they make the offering sing songs in honour of Hathîla. The proper offering to him is a red cock. This sacrifice is offered only by married men, and they alone are allowed to consume the offering.

35. Their domestic ceremonies are of much the usual Nat type. They pay as a bride-price twenty or some multiple of twenty rupees. Infidelity in women is punished by a compulsory feast, and similarly a man is put out of caste if he cohabit or eat with a Domin or women of the menial tribes. They have a tribal council, the chairman of which is appointed at each sitting. The levirate and widow marriage are allowed under the usual conditions. Even when they profess to be Muhammadans, it is alleged that they perform no rite

of circumcision (*musalmáni*). They have practically no marriage ceremony. The girl's father attires her in a new dress, puts bangles and ear-ornaments (*tarki*) on her and then she is sent into the hut where her husband receives her. If he can afford it, he feeds the brethren. They bury their dead in any convenient place. When they bury a corpse, they put his tools with him, so that he may be able to support himself in the next world. When any one falls sick, they sacrifice fowls at the graves of their ancestors and make an offering of spirits and tobacco.

36. They are nominally Muhammadans, but carry out hardly any of the rules of the faith. They worship the goddess known as Bhîtari and Sâyari, and their deified ancestor Hathîla. Bhîtari is worshipped on a Monday or Tuesday in the fields with a sacrifice of goats, which only the married males are allowed to eat. She is the protectress of their camp and children. Sâyari is the patroness of their trade and is worshipped in the tent or hut with an offering of a black cock and some spirits. The Devi of Bindhâchal also receives the sacrifice of a goat. The only festival which they observe is the Kajari, when they sing, drink, and practise a good deal of rude licentiousness. They have the usual fear of ghosts and demons. When a child suffers from the Evil Eye, they get a handful of dust from an exorcisor, and wave it over the child's head. They drink spirits, eat beef, goat's flesh, mutton, fowls, camels, venison, etc. They abstain from pork. They will not eat from the hands of a Dom, Dhobi, Musahar, Kol, or similar low castes, and no one will eat their food.

37. The Mahâwat has all the appearance of a degraded outcaste. He wears dirty clothes and a filthy rag as a turban, keeps his hair long and unkempt, and has round his neck strings of coral beads or *ghumri* seeds. In his ears he wears iron rings. The women wear a petticoat (*lahnga*), sheet (*sári*), with strings of beads round their necks, bracelets, and thick anklets. The men carry in a wallet rude lances (*nashtar*), a cupping horn (*singhi*), and some hollow bamboo pipes, with which he extracts by suction the matter out of abscesses and sore ears. It need hardly be said that he is quite ignorant of cleanness and antiseptics, and his instruments must be responsible for much horrible infection. He takes the "worm" out of carious teeth, bleeds and lances abscesses, and cleans the wax out of ears, in which department of his business he is known as Kânmailiya (*Kán* "ear," *mailiya*, "filth"), Khutkarha or Khuntkarha, "the man of

the spike" (*khúnta*) or Singhiwâla. He wanders about the villages calling out *Baid! Baid!* "Who wants a doctor?" He is altogether rather a loathsome vagrant. Some of them are skilled fishermen and trap hares.

The Bâdi Nats.

38. The Bâdi sub-caste of Nats are said to take their name from the Sanskrit *vâdya*, "a musical instrument." They are also known as Pâras Bâdi (*pâras*, "the philosopher's stone") and Tumriwâla Madâri (*tumri*, "a hollow gourd"). In Mirzapur they specially beg among the Mânjhis. They profess to have seven exogamous sections. These, when compared with those of the Mânjhi-Majhwârs, are, in many cases, identical, and they explain that like the Patâris they were priests of the Majhwârs. It will be seen that the Patâris also follow the section organization of the Majhwârs, and there must apparently have been some ancient connection between the tribes. As might have been expected, the explanation given of these section names is in some respect different from that of either the Mânjhis or Patâris, but there seems little doubt that they are in the main of totemistic origin. The names of the sections, as given by the Mirzapur Bâdis, are Jaghat, which they say is a kind of snake; Urê, which they say means "a pig"; Marai, "a kind of tree;" Neta, which they say means "the mucus of the nose," in which form they came out of the nose of their first ancestor. The Neshtri was one of the Vedic priests, and the name may represent their ancient office, but is more probably some totem which has now been forgotten. The next section is Netâm, which is found among the Majhwârs. Of its meaning the Bâdis can give no explanation. Jhinjhariya is said by them to mean "a kind of bamboo." Next comes the Oika section. This is also found among the Majhwârs. The Bâdis have an absurd story that a Bâdi woman had a son by a Muhammadan, and after they had admitted him to tribal rights, they called him Oika "What? Who?" because they could not admit him to any regular section.

39. Their account of themselves is that they came from Garh Mandla, in the Central Provinces, with the Majhwârs, and there is nothing in their appearance and manners which makes it improbable that they may really be of Gond descent, and may have been beggar priests who accompanied the Majhwârs when they emigrated along the hills towards the East.

40. The legend of their connection with the Majhwârs they

tell in this way :—Mahâdeva Bâba once created four men. To one he gave the musical instrument known as *nâgdaman* or "snake pipe," with which serpents are expelled, and his own drum, the *damaru*, whereby they might earn their living by playing and begging; to the second, he gave the musical instrument known as the *kikari*, by playing which he might support himself; to the third, he gave a loom, and he became a Panka; to the fourth, he gave the means of smelting iron, and he became an Agariya. This legend thus brings the Bâdis into contact with the Agariyas and Pankas who are certainly of Dravidian origin. The first man, according to the story, came to the Majhwârs, who fed him and appointed him to be the receiver of their alms. These sections are divided into three groups, of whom the Jaghat, Marai, and Jinjhariya intermarry; so do the Urê and Neti, and, lastly, the Netâm and the Oika.

41. They have a tribal council under a hereditary chairman (*mahto*), who arranges marriages, sanctions divorces and fines those who offend against caste rules. The fine ranges, according to the means of the offenders, from one and quarter to twenty rupees. If he fail to pay the fine, he is excommunicated for twelve years. The intermarriage of first-cousins is allowed, and they marry by preference their cousins on the mother's side.

42. Widow marriage and the levirate are allowed. There is no ceremony in widow marriage, except that the Mahto admonishes them in the presence of the brethren to behave well to each other. In the marriage ceremony there is nothing peculiar, except that the father or mother of the bride washes the feet of the bridegroom, a rite which is known as *nah chhorwa*. When the bridegroom goes to fetch his bride, he carries a bow and arrows, and most part of the rite is done at the house of the bridegroom, possibly a survival of marriage by capture.

43. The Bâdis of Mirzapur cremate their dead, unless they are unmarried, in which case they are buried The ritual is practically the same as that in force among the Majhwârs.

44. The religion of the Bâdis is largely made up of ancestor worship. They offer to them, at the Holi, goats, cakes, and sweetmeats, as a propitiation. They say that formerly the Patâris officiated as their priests, but now do so no longer. They accept no services from Brâhmans. Their chief objects of worship, except their deceased ancestors, are Juâlamukhi, Bûrhi Mâta "the old mother" and Masân, the deity of the cremation-ground. Juâlamu-

khi and Bûrhi Mâta are worshipped on the seventh day of Sâwan Juâlamukhi receives a she-goat and cakes; Bûrhi Mâta, a libation of milk and treacle mixed together. This worship is performed in the court-yard of the house. They worship Masân at any time when trouble overtakes the household. At the last Census 1,929 persons recorded themselves as worshippers of Masân.[1] They also regard their snake pipe (*nâgdaman*) as a fetish. A piece of ground is plastered, the instrument laid within it, and a white cock is sacrificed. Some spirits is also poured on the ground. Mari is worshipped when cholera appears in the village. She receives the sacrifice of a hog and a libation of spirits. When snakes appear in considerable numbers, they lay milk and parched rice at their holes. They observe only three festivals, the Sâwani, when they worship Juâlamukhi and Bûrhi Mâta; the ninth (*naumi*) of Chait, when there is a worship of Bûrhi Mâta, and the Holi, when they worship the sainted dead. They particularly respect the cotton tree (*semal*) which is the abode of Bhûts. They swear on the head of their sons or by holding a pig's tail at the shrine of their deity. They have a special detestation for the Dom. They will not eat beef, but they use all the animals, birds, and fish which are eaten by the Majhwârs and similar Dravidian races. They will not eat meat while the funeral rites of a member of the sub-caste are being performed. Wine is the only intoxicant they habitually use. They salute one another by the *pâêlagi* form, and seniors give a blessing to their juniors. Only Korwas and Doms will eat from their hands. They will eat *Kachhi* cooked by Ahîrs and Majhwârs. The women wear a sheet (*sâri*) nose-rings, ear ornaments (*tarki*) and arm ornaments, known as *lahsaniya churla* and heavy anklets (*pairi.*)

45. The Bâdi is a loafing beggar, who wanders about among the Majhwârs and begs alms, playing on the *nâgdaman* pipe, the drum (*damaru*) and the cymbals (*jhânjh*). The special business of the women is tattooing girls, and when marching through villages you will often hear a girl shrieking, and, on enquiring the cause you will find her tied down on a bed, while her friends sing to encourage her to bear the pain, and a Bâdi woman operates on her arms, breasts or legs, with two or three English needles tied together with thread. The punctures are rubbed with a mixture of lampblack and milk. The best lampblack is produced from the smoke of the wood of the *salai* tree.

---

[1] *For Masân see Introduction to Popular Religion and Folklore, 84.*

46. This sub-caste is said to take its name from the Sanskrit, *mallaka-kâra*, "the maker of a cocoanut-oil vessel." Those in Mirzapur refer their origin to Lohârdaga in Chota Nâgpur, and say that they were originally Sunârs. They even now procure Brâhmans and barbers from that part of the country whence they say they emigrated some two generations ago. They have their own tribal council known as *Kutumb bhâi* or "the family of the brethren," with a president (*mahto*). Offences against caste discipline are punished by fines usually amounting to twelve or thirteen rupees. This is spent in food and drink for members.

The Malâr Nats.

47. The prohibited degrees are first-cousins on both sides. The usual age for marriage is twelve, or when the pair attain puberty. Marriages are arranged by the friends on both sides, but runaway matches appear not to be uncommon. The price of the bride is fixed by tribal custom at sixteen rupees. Polygamy is allowed, and the only privilege of the senior wife is that she alone is allowed to perform the worship of the family gods. Infidelity in women is forgiven on a fine being paid to the council. The council has the power of ordering divorce and a divorced woman can be remarried in the caste by the *sagâi* form, after she provides a dinner for the brethren. Widow marriage and the levirate are permitted under the usual conditions. Their domestic ceremonies are much the same as those of the Majhwârs, among whom they live.

48. They are Hindus by religion and their tribal deities are Kâli, Bûrhi Mâi and Bhairon. They worship Kâli at the Naurâtra of Chait in the house chapel (*deoghar*) with an offering of a goat, and cakes, milk, and wine. Bhairon receives the same offering, but to him a blood offering is very seldom made. The women have no gods peculiar to themselves. They fast on Sundays and offer to the sun godling, Sûraj Nârâyan, rice boiled with milk in a new earthen pot. They bow to him as he rises in the morning. They also bow to the new moon, but have no special form of worship. They occasionally consult a Sakadwîpi Brâhman, but the real tribal priest is the Mahto or headman. He acts for them at marriages and deaths. Most houses have a chapel (*deoghar*) with a mound of earth, on which are rude representatives of the tribal gods. They swear on the feet of Brâhmans, on a leaf of the *pîpal* tree or *tulasi* leaf, by holding a cow's tail or a piece of copper. They worship Hariyâri Devi, "the goddess of greenery," as the protectress of crops.

49. They eat pork, mutton, goat's flesh, venison, fowls, and fish.

Before they eat, they offer a little food to Devi. No one but a Dom will eat food cooked by them, and they will eat and drink from the hands of Kharwârs and Majhwârs.

50. Their chief occupation is making brass or pewter rings, boxes to hold the lime used in chewing betel (*chunauti*), and various ornaments used by women.

51. From Etah it is reported that among the Guâl Nats, when a child is born, the clansmen are invited to be present at the naming rite. Food is distributed, but the attendance of a Brâhman is unnecessary. Among the Kalabâz Nats, a Brâhman is sent for on the tenth day after birth, and he names the child, receiving in return a ration of uncooked grain (*sîdha*).

Patois of the Nats.

52. There is a class of Nats known as Tasmabâz, who are so called because they practise one of the numerous games played by thimble-riggers in England, which was taught to them in 1802 by a British soldier.[1] The game is played thus:—A strap is doubled and folded up in different shapes. The art is to put the stick in such a place that the strap (*tasma*), whence they derive their name, when unfolded, comes out double. They have an argot of their own of which the following are examples:—When they are sitting on the road side and see a yokel coming, they say *Dhurayi*; *Taradê* means "to begin to play;" *Asradê*, "give back the money to this fellow or he will make a row;" *Hakeri*, "a European;" *banriwâla* "a policeman;" *Hanswâla*, "a mounted officer;" *Thoa*, "an official;" *Beli* means "one of the gang informing." In one of the earliest accounts of the Bâzigar Nats, Captain Richardson[2] gives some specimens of their patois, most of which consist of mere inversions of syllables. Thus, *Kâg* (*âg*), "fire;" *nâns* (*bâns*), "bamboo;" *koâd* (*yâd*), "remembrance;" *komar* (*umr*), "age;" *nalâsh* (*talâsh*), "search;" *Kindustân* (*Hindustân*), "India;" *nagîr* (*faqîr*) "beggar;" and so on. The Bajaniya Nats of Mirzapur call mother *jâ*; son, *dikaro*; wife, *biari*; brother-in-law, *bauhewi*; father-in-law, *hâro*; mother-in-law, *kau*; elder brother's wife, *bhadai*; father's sister, *phoi*. Their numerals are—one *ek*, two *baidna*, three *tâna*, four *syarna*, five *pân*, six *sad*, seven *hât*, eight *âth*, nine *nau*, ten *dahad*.

---

[1] *Selection, Records of Government, North-Western Provinces*, I, 312, *sq*.

[2] *Asiatic Researches*, VII, 451, *sq*.

Distribution of Nats according to the Census of 1891.

Districts.	Brijbâsi.	Gual.	Jogila.	Kabûtra.	Kalabâz.	Karnâtak.	Mahâwat.	Mirdah.	Râthaur.	Sapera.	Others.	Muhammadans.	Total.
Dehra Dûn	...	...	...	...	...	...	...	...	...	...	...	28	28
Sahâranpur	...	...	...	...	...	...	...	...	...	...	266	468	734
Muzaffarnagar	...	...	...	...	...	...	...	...	...	...	251	354	605
Meerut	...	442	...	...	...	...	...	...	...	37	1,046	461	1,986
Bulandshahr	...	64	...	...	...	...	...	37	226	15	556	702	1,600
Aligarh	...	...	...	...	...	...	...	...	...	...	244	193	437
Mathura	...	...	...	...	...	...	...	5	...	42	279	57	383
Agra	15	...	...	6	...	88	...	77	249	2	480	198	1,115
Farrukhâbâd	378	25	...	...	207	4	...	2	39	..	710	136	1,501
Mainpuri	98	...	..	29	63	96	...	2	148	127	788	62	1.413
Etâwah	16	189	...	26	32	145	...	7	134	211	737	198	1,695
Etah	105	...	...	...	112	7	...	...	97	...	564	91	976

Distribution of Nats according to the Census of 1891—continued.

Districts.	Brijbâsi.	Guâl.	Jogila.	Kabûtra.	Kalabâz.	Karnâtak.	Mahâwat.	Mirdah.	Râthaur.	Sapera.	Others.	Muhammadans.	Total.
Bareilly	1,244	398	49	81	40	141	...	...	...	...	555	25	2,533
Bijnor	...	...	...	306	...	...	...	...	...	...	1,210	154	1,670
Budâun	71	816	285	15	169	8	...	...	92	...	987	382	2,825
Morâdâbâd	40	699	...	47	40	30	...	..	19	18	321	304	1,518
Shâhjahânpur	551	2	52	...	359	...	...	...	89	...	1,406	49	2,508
Pilibhît	302	...	31	...	155	...	...	...	73	...	565	303	1,429
Cawnpur	129	...	...	...	2	45	10	...	10	...	724	102	1,022
Fatehpur	101	...	...	...	...	...	...	...	...	...	270	486	857
Bânda	...	...	...	...	...	...	...	...	...	...	105	195	300
Hamîrpur	...	...	...	...	...	...	...	...	...	...	83	352	435
Allahâbâd	61	..	...	...	...	33	...	...	20	...	1,648	636	2,398
Jhânsi	...	...	...	...	...	...	...	19	...	...	33	282	334

Jâlaun	...	...	...	...	...	...	...	...	...	...	3	518	521
Lalitpur	...	...	...	...	...	6	...	...	...	...	...	321	327
Benares	42	...	...	...	...	...	...	...	107	...	291	235	675
Mirzapur	...	...	...	...	...	429	...	...	...	...	310	323	1,062
Jaunpur	44	...	...	...	...	128	...	...	...	...	394	772	1,338
Ghâzipur	54	...	...	...	...	...	...	...	243	...	322	1,100	1,719
Ballia	8	...	...	...	...	...	...	...	...	...	310	157	475
Gorakhpur	186	...	...	433	...	...	...	...	376	...	104	2,826	3,925
Basti	180	...	...	...	...	...	...	...	309	...	208	3,013	3,710
Azamgarh	142	...	...	...	77	...	...	...	176	...	201	1,327	1,923
Tarâi	5	75	...	108	6	...	...	...	...	...	77	53	324
Lucknow	13	...	12	39	...	...	...	...	...	...	497	324	885
Unâo	461	...	...	138	154	227	...	...	...	...	627	96	1,703
Râê Bareli	127	...	...	...	...	...	...	...	...	...	436	456	1,019
Sîtapur	59	...	206	281	1	56	38	...	344	...	811	461	2,257
Hardoi	586	50	587	...	354	64	...	...	...	...	714	1	2,356
Kheri	659	...	...	421	...	...	118	...	142	...	424	67	1,831

Distribution of Nats according to the Census of 1891—concluded.

DISTRICTS.	Brijbâsi.	Guâl.	Jogila.	Kabûtra.	Kalabâz.	Karnâtak.	Mahâwat.	Mirdah.	Râthaur.	Sapera.	Others.	Muhammadans.	TOTAL.
Faizâbâd	98	...	...	...	...	44	126	...	91	...	383	567	1,309
Gonda	63	...	...	...	...	6	...	...	457	...	622	178	1,326
Bahrâich	459	...	...	...	...	...	40	...	66	...	695	376	1,636
Sultânpur	...	...	...	...	...	...	...	...	...	...	441	292	733
Partâbgarh	22	...	...	...	...	2	2	...	...	...	5	392	423
Bârabanki	...	83	...	...	...	...	...	...	271	...	520	629	1,503
TOTAL	6,319	2,843	1,222	1.930	1,771	1,559	334	149	3,778	452	22,223	20,702	63,282

Naumuslim (*Nau*, "new" *Muslim*—"Muhammadan").—A term applied to recent converts to Islâm. It is often particularly selected by fresh Râjput converts. These, however, in the lists of the last Census, are given under the head Râjput, such as the Lâlkhâni and similar tribes, who have been separately discussed. Many of them have only imperfectly adopted Islâm, and still retain several of their own tribal customs in connection with birth, death, marriage, inheritance, etc.

Distribution of the Naumuslim according to the Census of 1891.

DISTRICTS.	Ahîr.	Banya.	Brâhman.	Chamâr.	Kâyasth.	Kori.	Mâli.	Others.	TOTAL.
Dehra Dûn	...	...	...	...	...	...	...	147	147
Sahâranpur	...	...	...	...	...	...	...	1,886	1,886
Muzaffarnagar	3	...	1	1	1	...	794	1,010	1,810
Meerut	2	...	...	...	...	...	4	28,960	28,966
Bulandshahr	...	...	...	...	...	...	1	821	822
Aligarh	...	...	...	...	...	...	...	12,357	12,357
Mathura	...	...	...	1	...	...	...	61	62
Agra	3	...	2	6	...	1	...	98	110
Farrukhâbâd	...	...	1	...	6	20	...	860	887
Mainpuri	...	8	...	...	...	...	...	101	109
Etâwah	1	7	16	8	...	...	...	165	197
Etah	18	299	30	...	...	5	...	2,045	2,397
Bareilly	...	...	...	...	...	...	...	406	406

Bijnor	...	...	...	...	...	...	...	1,277	1,277
Budâun	15	1	2	2	2	...	77	2,896	2,995
Morâdâbâd	100	...	1,323	223	12	...	239	14,645	16,542
Shâhjahânpur	136	...	...	11	3	28	1	797	976
Pilibhît	1	...	...	...	7	7	...	269	284
Cawnpur	...	...	...	2	...	...	...	496	498
Fatehpur	...	...	32	3	4	...	50	6	95
Bânda	...	...	40	...	...	...	...	1,576	1,616
Hamîrpur	...	...	...	...	...	...	...	16	16
Allahâbâd	...	...	...	1	454	...	267	395	1,117
Jhânsi	1	1	...	4	...	...	...	25	31
Jâlaun	...	...	...	...	...	...	...	20	20
Benares	...	...	...	...	...	...	64	...	64
Mirzapur	...	...	...	...	...	...	68	...	68
Jaunpur	555	...	...	...	...	1	147	46	749
Ghâzipur	3	...	...	27	...	...	15	358	403
Ballia	...	...	...	...	...	...	...	184	184

Distribution of the Naumuslim according to the Census of 1891—concluded.

Districts.	Ahîr.	Banya.	Brâhman.	Chamâr.	Kâyasth.	Kori.	Mâli.	Others.	Total.
Gorakhpur	3	3	...	2	1	...	92	262	363
Basti	1,766	...	...	...	...	...	662	19	2,447
Azamgarh	...	27	...	...	...	...	71	117	215
Tarâi	...	...	...	...	...	...	57	95	152
Lucknow	2	...	...	...	...	...	157	201	360
Unâo	56	...	...	1	...	2	...	29	88
Râê Bareli	...	4	...	...	19	...	...	137	160
Sîtapur	...	4	...	...	...	...	155	266	425
Hardoi	...	...	...	...	...	...	...	945	945
Kheri	...	...	10	1	...	2	...	80	93
Faizâbâd	...	...	...	...	...	...	273	23	296
Gonda	1,145	...	...	...	...	...	1,374	...	2,519
Bahrâich	2	...	...	...	...	...	1,826	4	1,832

Sultânpur	...	...	...	...	...	...	119	108	227
Partâbgarh	...	...	...	...	801	...	5	34	840
Bârabanki	3	...	3	2	8	26	97	252	391
TOTAL	3,815	354	1,460	295	1,318	92	6,615	74,495	88,444

Nikumbh.—A sept of Râjputs chiefly found in the Eastern districts. The word *nikumbha* in Sanskrit means the plant *Croton Polyandrum,* and is perhaps connected with *kumbha,* "a jar." They are, according to General Cunningham,[1] of the race of the Kings of Ajudhya "from which sprang Mândhâtri, Sâgara, Bhâgîratha, and Râma. Kuvalayaswa, the great-grandfather of Nikumbha, having conquered the demon Dhundhu, acquired the title of Dhundhumâra, "slayer of Dhundhu," and gave his name to the country which is now known as Dhundhâr or Jaypur. Here his descendants remained under the name of Nikumbhas, and to them is ascribed the foundation of most of the old forts and cities in Alwar and Northern Jaypur. Under Mândhâtri and Sâgara they came in collision with the Haihayas and Talajangas on the Narbada, where a branch of their race still held territory in the tenth century. Two inscriptions have been found in Khândes,—one, dated A.D. 1153; and the other, in 1216 A.D.,—in the latter of which the reigning king is said to have been of the great Solar race from which "the King Nikúmbha, best of princes, sprang; in whose line Mândhâta was famous, as well as Sâgara, Bhâgiratha and others." In the former, the reigning prince is said to be "celebrated in the race—the illustrious Solar race, in which the Nikumbha was born whose descendant was Râma." Of this race, as Colonel Tod[2] says, "to which celebrity attaches in all the genealogies, we can only discover that they were proprietors of the district of Mandalgarh prior to the Gahlots, that is, they preceded the Sisodiyas in Mewâr." But a writer in the *Rajputâna Gazetteer*[3] adds that "had his enquiries extended to Alwar, he would have discovered that local tradition declares the Nikumbhas to have been the earliest possessors of the fort and town of Alwar, and of the surrounding territory." General Cunningham concludes from these data that "it would seem that the Nikumbhas were among the earliest Aryan settlers in Râjputâna. During the lapse of many centuries they lost their central provinces, and at the time of the Muhammadan conquest only the two out-lying districts of Khândes on the South and Alwar on the North remained to them. The name of Nikumbha has been supplanted in Northern India by that of the Raghuvansa or "descendant of Raghu," one of the ancestors

---

[1] *Archæological Reports,* XX, 8, *sqq.*
[2] *Annals* I, 28,
[3] III., 172.

of Dasaratha and Râma. The Nikumbhas, who settled in this region, retained their early tribal name, while their brethren of Ayodhya assumed the name of Raghuvansi."

The Nikumbhas of the North-Western Provinces and Oudh.

2. In Hardoi[1] the Nikumbhas say that they came from Alwar about 1450 A.D. Another account makes them out to be a Kachhwâha or Sûrajbans clan which left Aral or Arwal in Jaypur and alternately served the Tomar Râja of Delhi and the Râthaur of Kanauj. They derive their name from the good work (*nek kâm*) they did in the service of these monarchs. Others say that the name means "low caste" or "illegitimate." They were the original Thâkur settlers in Farrukhâbâd[2] in the old Pargana of Pipargâon, now included in Muhammadâbâd. The Azamgarh[3] branch are said to have come from Jaunpur, sixteen or seventeen generations ago, being called in by a Brâhman to save his daughter from marriage with a Râjbhar. The family became Muhammadan under the Sultâns of Jaunpur. Those in Gorakhpur have the title of Sirnet, which they gained in the time of one of the Emperors of Delhi. Then, as now, they only raised the hand to the head, and never bowed, when making obeisance. The Emperor, annoyed at this apparent want of respect, had a sword placed across the doorway, and some of them, maintaining their position, were decapitated.[4] The Râjas of Basti, Unwal, and Rudrapur, in the Gorakhpur District belong to this sept. Those in Ghâzipur trace their descent from Vikrama Deva, brother of Akhraj Deva, Râja of Unwal, in Gorakhpur, who, when he came to bathe at the confluence of the Sarju and the Ganges, founded a colony there. They endeavour to keep up their connection with Gorakhpur, and nearly a hundred years ago their headman, Bâbu Râghunâth Sinh, visited Unwal and planted groves and dug wells at his own expense.

3. In Farrukhâbâd they claim to belong to the Garga *gotra*, give girls to the Chandel, Bhadauriya, Kachhwâha, Chauhân, and Pramar septs: and marry brides from the Chamargaur, Râthaur, Gaharwâr, Sombansi, and Ujjaini. In Unâo they say they belong to the Bhâradwâja *gotra*; take wives from the Gaur, Dhâkrê, Bais, and Janwâr; and give girls to the Sombansi, Râthaur and Chauhân.

---

1 *Settlement Report*, 74.
2 *Settlement Report*, 13.
3 *Settlement Report*, 63.
4 For a similar story *see* Bernier, *Travels*, 151.

Distribution of Nikumbh Rájputs according to the Census of 1891.

District.	Number.	District.	Number.
Farrukhâbâd . .	898	Mirzapur . . .	53
Mainpuri . . .	57	Jaunpur . . .	2,279
Etâwah . . .	19	Ghâzipur . . .	560
Etah	32	Ballia	3,896
Bareilly . . .	35	Gorakhpur . . .	50
Budâun . . .	44	Basti	40
Morâdâbâd . . .	6	Azamgarh . . .	4,433
Shâhjahânpur . .	755	Lucknow . . .	427
Pilibhît . . .	114	Sîtapur . . .	158
Bânda	9	Hardoi . . .	3,698
Allahâbâd . . .	34	Kheri	1,051
Jâlaun	46	Partabgarh . . .	3
Benares . . .	216	Total .	18,904

Nimbârak.—A Vaishnava order who have not been separately recorded at the last Census. The word means "the sun in a *nîm* tree," a curious designation, which is thus explained, "The founder of the sect, an ascetic by name Bhaskarâcharya, had invited a Bairâgi to dine with him, but unfortunately delayed to go and fetch his guest till after sunset. Now the holy man was forbidden by the rules of his order to eat except in the day-time, and was greatly afraid that he would be compelled to practise an unwilling abstinence; but at the solicitation of his host the Sun god, Sûraj Nârâyan, descended upon the *nîm* tree, under which the repast was spread, and continued beaming upon them till the claims of hunger were fully satisfied. Henceforth the saint was known by the name of Nîmbârka or Nîmbaditya. Their doctrines, so far as they are known, are of a very enlightened character. Thus their doctrine of salvation by faith is thought by many scholars to have been directly borrowed from the Gospel; while another article in their creed, which is less known but equally striking in its divergence from ordinary Hindu sentiment, is the continuance of conscious individual existence in a future world, when the highest reward of the good will be, not extinction, but in the enjoyment of the visible presence of the Divinity whom they have served upon earth; a state, therefore, absolutely identical with Heaven, as our theologians define it. The one infinite and invisible God, who is the only real existence, is, they maintain, the only proper object of man's devout contemplation. But as the incomprehensible is utterly beyond the reach of human faculties, he is partially manifested for our behoof in the book of creation, in which natural objects are the letters of the universal alphabet, and express the sentiments of the Divine Author. A printed page, however, conveys no meaning to any one but a scholar, and is liable to be misunderstood even by him; so too with the book of the world. And thus it matters little whether Râdha and Krishna were ever real personages; the mysteries of divine love which they symbolise remain though the symbols disappear."[1]

2. From enquiries made at Benares it appears that initiates are accepted from among Brâhmans, Kshatriyas, Vaisyas, and all Sûdras from whose hands high caste Hindus can take water. No regard is paid to social status, but no one is accepted who is addicted to drunkenness or incontinency, or who eats and drinks from the hands of persons of other creeds. The formula of initiation is *Sri Krishna sarnam mama*, "I seek refuge in Sri Krishna;" or *Sri mukund charanamsarnam prapadye*, "O Sri Krishna! give me refuge at thy feet;" or *Sri Krishanaynamah*, "I salute thee, Sri Krishna." When the candidate is initiated he is taught to be truthful, to abide by the rules of the order, to be peaceful, to fast on the eleventh (*ekâdashi*) of the month, to trust in Sri Krishna for all earthly and heavenly blessings, to avoid slandering and backbiting, to abstain from flesh and spirituous liquor, and to instruct the disciples.

3. They have a great respect for the Guru, whom they constantly visit; but he does not come to them unless specially invited. When a disciple visits his Guru, he brings a money present, and receives in return some consecrated food (*prasâd*). Those of the sect who are family men live at home; the ascetic class in monasteries. The latter are supplied with food and other necessaries of life by the Guru.

---

[1] Growse, *Mathura*, 181 *sq*.

Niranjani.—Classed in the last Census as an order of the Gusâîns and found only in very small numbers in these Provinces. They are apparently a Panjâb order, founded by Handâl, the cook of Guru Amar Dâs (A.D. 1552-1574). Bâba Handâl worshipped God under the title of Niranjana, "without collyrium or ointment, pure." According to Mr. Maclagan[1] their chief claim to notice is their rejection of the ordinary burial customs of the Sikhs and Hindus. The memorial ceremony (*kirya karam*) is not observed and the bones are not taken to the Ganges. They have special marriage rites of their own, and do not reverence the Brâhmans. There is a Gurudwâra or Darbâr Sâhib of Bâba Handâl at Jandiyâla in the Amritsar District, where the Niranjanis chiefly resort.

Distribution of the Niranjanis according to the Census of 1891.

Districts.	Numbers.	Districts.	Numbers.
Dehra Dûn . . .	7	Jhânsi . . .	2
Hamîrpur . . .	5	Jâlaun . . .	13
Allahâbâd . . .	1	Bahrâich . . .	1
		Total .	29

Males 18
Females 11

Nirola.—A class of Hill Brâhmans who are considered to be somewhat lower in the social scale than the Sarolas and contain in themselves in a separate class a number of sub-divisions known generically as Dubhâgi; for they neither eat from the hands of Sarola or Gangâri, nor intermarry with them. They have several *gotras*, such as Kasyapa, Angiras, etc., and hence the name Nanagotri given to them. Their principal subdivisions are Dhûsâli, Jamlogi, Batanwâl, Kandhâri, Baramwâl, Silwâl, Poldi, Bilwâl, Garsâra, Thalwâl, Gugleta, Kimoti, Maikota, Darmwâra, Dyolki, Kandyâl, Thalâsi, Phalâta, Gatyâl, Dhumakwâl, Sanwâl, Managwâl, Bamola, Binjâl, and Ganai. Most

[1] *Panjâb Census Report*, 158.

of these names are derived from some village. All intermarry with each other, and now follow agriculture, service, peddling, and providing for the wants of the pilgrims to Kedârnâth, who are regarded as their legitimate prey and shorn accordingly.[1]

Niyâriya.—(Hindi *niyâra*, *nirâla* "separate, distinct").—A refiner of precious metals, who washes the sweeping of the shops of goldsmiths and similar craftsmen, and extracts the gold and silver. The caste, such as it is, is purely professional and though some families have made it their hereditary occupation and call themselves Pathân or Shaikh Niyâriyas, many outsiders, such as weavers and others, practise the trade. Those to the east of the Province ascribe their origin to Kota and Bûndi, from whence they say they emigrated about a century or so ago. They are Muhammadans and practise the usual Musalmân ceremonies at birth, marriage, and death.

Occupation.

Mr. Hoey[2] thus describes the way the trade is carried on in Lucknow. "Having his *aqua fortis* ready the Niyâriya takes the melted mixture of gold and silver filings or clippings (*rawa*) and melts it in a crucible (*ghariya*), and when it is in a liquid state, he pours it from a height into a vessel containing water. This fall into water makes each large drop of liquid metal remain separate. Then all those pieces of metal are placed in a glass phial (*âtish shîshi*) prepared to resist the action of fire. These phials are like balloons covered with a coating of mud so as to leave only a circular portion of the glass exposed at one side for the use of the operator watching the action of the acid. The narrow neck of the balloon is of course turned up vertically to prevent the contents from spilling, and it is not closed up in any way. The mud used to cover the glass is called *pîlimatti*. Having placed one hundred *tolas* of metal drops in the phial the Niyâriya pours upon it two hundred *tolas* of acid. He then places the phial on a charcoal fire, and when the action of the *aqua fortis* and fire has become complete, the liquid is poured off. The gold lies in the bottom of the phial and the silver passes off with the acid, which is poured into a mud vessel in which there are pieces of copper. The silver adheres to the copper and is scraped off and thrown again with the acid into

[1] Atkinson, *Himalayan Gazetteer*, III, 28.

[2] *Monograph on trades and manufactures*, 156 *sq*.

another mud vessel in which there is no copper. The Niyâriya then places a cloth-strainer over an empty mud vessel and lays over the cloth a sheet of bamboo paper. He pours the silver and acid into this strainer, and the silver settles on the paper, the acid passing through the cloth into the vessel below. The silver is then further cleared by burning in an earthenware pan containing cold charcoal ashes ground to powder. In these ashes a lead is made about the size of the hollow of the hand. The silver is laid in this hollow with a piece of lead and covered over; charcoal fire is laid above the ashes and blown with a pair of bellows. This clears the silver completely." He also melts down old ornaments for silversmiths.

Distribution of the Niyâriya according to the Census of 1891.

Districts.	Hindus	Muhammadans.	Total.
Sahâranpur	2	...	2
Muzaffarnagar	6	2	11
Meerut	18	...	18
Aligarh	3	...	3
Etâwah	...	1	1
Bijnor	...	7	7
Fatehpur	...	12	12
Hamîrpur	...	35	35
Jâlaun	...	2	2
Benares	33	15	15
Ballia	...	...	33
Gorakhpur	...	33	33
Basti	...	2	2
Azamgarh	...	9	9
Tarâi	...	2	2
Lucknow	...	18	18
Sîtapur	...	31	31
Faizâbâd	...	9	9
Gonda	...	4	4
Bahrâich	...	9	9
Sultânpur	...	2	2
Total	65	193	258

O

Ojha.—A word commonly derived from the Hindi *ojh*, "entrails," in the sense that this class of exorcisor, like the Roman Haruspex, inspects the entrails of the victim. This, it is hardly necessary to say, the Indian diviner never does. It is almost certainly a corruption of the Sanskrit *upâdhyaya*, "a teacher." The term is used in various senses. In the first place it is used to designate the devil priest, or diviner of the aboriginal races, such as those of Dravidian origin. Some account of the position and practices of this functionary has been given in another place.[1] Next, it is appplied to a special class of inferior Brâhmans who perform the same duties for the more Hinduised races. Thirdly, it is used as a title of the Maithila Brâhmans of the Eastern Districts. Mr. Sherring[2] is obviously in error in saying that "formerly the Ojha was always a Brâhman; but his profession has become so lucrative that sharp, clever, shrewd men in all the Hindu castes have taken to it." The process has certainly been quite the reverse of this, and the Ojha Brâhman is, without any doubt, a direct importation into Hinduism from the demonolatry of the aboriginal races, from which much of the coarse worship of Mahâdeva and the Sâktas has been probably derived.

2. The Ojha Brâhman is a follower of the Tantras, the most debased form of modern Hinduism. "Whole Tantras," writes Sir M. Monier Williams,[3] "teach nothing but various methods of making use of spells for acquiring magical power. Some give collections of charms for making people enamoured, for destroying enemies and rivals, for producing or preventing diseases, for curing blindness, for injuring crops. Others simply describe the most effectual modes of worshipping the Sâktis, Mahâvidyas, Mâtris, Yoginis, Vatukas, or by whatever name the innumerable manifestations of Siva and his wife may be called. Others confine themselves to an explanation of the Yantras, Bijas, and Mudras (intertwining of the fingers) belonging to each manifestation, the places suited for the worship of each, the names of trees and plants sacred to each, or permeated by each, and the days of the year allotted to each. Some few touch on nearly every conceivable topic of human knowledge, and

---

[1] *Introduction to Popular Religion and Folklore*, 96.
[2] *Hindu Castes*, I, 37.
[3] *Brâhmanism and Hinduism*, 206.

contain, here and there, really interesting matter." On account of these functions the Ojha is often known as Panchamakâri, because the conditions under which he performs the rites are represented in five words, each of which begins with *ma-madya*, "wine," *mánsa* "meat," *matsya*, "fish," *mudra*, "mystic intertwining of the fingers," and *maithuna*, "sexual intercourse."

Distribution of Ojha Bráhmans according to the Census of 1891.

DISTRICTS.	Numbers.	DISTRICTS.	Numbers.
Dehra Dûn . . .	16	Morâdâbâd . . .	57
Sahâranpur . . .	18	Pilibhît . . .	4
Bulandshahr . . .	6	Cawnpur . .	23
Aligarh . . .	403	Allahâbâd . . .	1
Agra . . .	371	Jhânsi . . .	12
Farukhâbâd . . .	41	Jâlaun . . .	1
Mainpuri . . .	6	Tarâi . . .	5
Etah . . .	89	Bahrâich . . .	5
Budâun . . .	103	TOTAL .	1,161

Orh.—A tribe recorded in the recent Census as a sub-caste of Koris and almost entirely confined to Bulandshahr and Aligarh. They appear to have their origin in Central India. "The Ods in Kâthiâwâr are professional pond diggers. The yclaim to be Kshatriyas, the descendants of Bhâgîratha, son of Sâgara. According to the *Rás Mála*, Sindh Râj sent for a number of Ods from Mâlwa to dig the Sahasraling Lake at Pâtan. He fell in love with one of them, called Jasma, and wished to take her to his palace. She declined and tried to make her escape. He pursued her, and, on overtaking her, slew several of the Ods. Jasma committed suicide, cursing the king, and declaring that the lake should never hold water. The curse was removed by the sacrifice of Mayo Dhed. The Ods lead a wandering life, coming to Kâthiâwâr for work, and returning to their houses in Mârwâr and Central India during the rains."[1] In the Dakkhin they are known as Vadar.[2] Of the Ods in the

[1] *Bombay Gazetteer*, VIII, 158, *sq*.
[2] *Ibid*, XV, 347; XVI. 64: *Indian Antiquary*, III, 155.

Panjâb Mr. Ibbetson writes:[1] "The Od or Odh is a wandering tribe, whose proper home appears to be Western Hindustân and Rajputâna; at least the Ods of the Panjâb usually hail from those parts. They will not, as a rule, take petty jobs; but prefer small contracts on roads, canals, railways and the like, or will build a house of abode and dig a tank or even a well. They are vagrants, wandering about with their families in search of employment on earthwork. They settle down in temporary reed huts on the edge of the work; the men dig, the women carry the earth to the donkeys, which they always have with them, and the children drive the donkeys to the spoil bank. In the salt range tract they also quarry and carry stone; and in parts of the North-West Provinces they are said to be wandering pedlars. They eat anything and everything, and though not unfrequently Musalmâns, especially in the West, are always out-caste. They have a speech of their own, called Odki, of which I know nothing, but which is very probably nothing more than the ordinary dialect of their place of origin. They wear woollen clothes or at least one woollen garment. They claim descent from one Bhâgîratha, who vowed never to drink twice out of the same well, and so dug a fresh one every day till one day he dug down and down and never came up again. It is in mourning for him that they wear wool, and in imitation of him they bury their dead even when Hindu, though they marry by the Hindu ceremony. Till the re-appearance of Bhâgîratha they will, they say, remain out-caste. They are said to claim Râjput or Kshatriya origin and to come from Mârwâr. They worship Râma and Siva. They are, for a vagrant tribe, singularly free from all imputation of crime." In Bihâr they are described as a sub-caste of Luniyas.[2]

The North-Western Provinces Branch.[3]

2. There can be little doubt that the Orhs of these Provinces are of the same race as those already described. They have the same tradition of descent from Bhâgîratha, son of Râja Sâgara, and a woman named Gandharani. They are not allowed to marry in their own *gotra* or that of their mother or grandmother. They lead a settled life, and do not admit outsiders. Marriage is both infant and adult, and sexual license before marriage is neither recognised nor tolerated. Polyandry is

---

[1] *Panjâb Ethnography*, para. 573.
[2] Risley, *Tribes and Castes*, II, 150.
[3] Mainly based on notes by M. Âtma Râm, Head Master, High School, Mathura.

not permitted, but polygamy is allowed. They marry in the way common to all respectable Hindu castes, and the binding part of it is the perambulation (*bhanwar*) of the pair round the sacred fire. Widow marriage is allowed, and the ceremony is known as *dharaicha*. The widow is allowed full freedom of choice ; but she can marry by the levirate any of the younger brothers of her late husband. A wife can be divorced for infidelity, and such a woman can be married again by the *dharaicha* form.

Religion.

3. They are usually Hindus of the Vaishnava sect. Their special godlings are the Miyân Sâhib of Amroha in the Morâdâbâd District, whom they worship in any month except Muharram ; Devi in Chait and Kuâr ; Masâni of Karanbâs and Zâhir Pîr in Sâwan and Bhâdon ; Kuânwâla, "the god of the well," in Sâwan, and the ordinary Hindu gods. The offering to these godlings consists of sweetmeats (*batâsha*) and cocoanuts, which the priests receive. They employ Brâhmans as their priests, and these are received on terms of equality with other Brâhmans. They burn their dead and leave their ashes on the burning ground. No ceremony, except the ordinary *srâddha* in the month of Kuâr, is performed.

Occupation.

4. Their occupation in Mathura is the weaving of coarse cloth (*dobra*), and most of them still follow this trade. But some of them have taken to agriculture and landholding and are dealers in grain, and lend money and grain usually on very usurious rates in the villages.

Social rules.

5. They eat meat, fish, and fowls, and drink spirits. They abstain from the flesh of monkeys, cows, pork, and uncloven-footed animals, crocodiles, snakes, vermin, and the leavings of other people. They are thus in these Provinces in a far higher grade than their vagrant brethren in the Panjâb.

Distribution of Orhs according to the Census of 1891.

Districts.	Numbers.	Districts.	Numbers.
Dehra Dûn . . .	41	Farrukhâbâd . .	5
Meerut	936	Etâwah . . .	1
Bulandshahr . . .	5,876	Etah	86
Aligarh . . .	2,966	Morâdâbâd . . .	60
Mathura . . .	763	Jhânsi	2
Agra	15		
		Total .	10,751

Oswâl.[1]—A wealthy and respectable trading class found in small numbers in these Provinces. They derive their name from the town of Ossa, Osi, Osiya or Osanagar, in Mârwâr.

Traditional origin.

2. The tribal legend runs as follows: About Sambat 222 (165 A.D.) there was a Râja in Osanagar who had no issue. He heard that an ascetic named Sri Ratan Sûri was practising austerities in a jungle near the town, and he went to pay his respects to him. The ascetic told him that he would obtain his desires within a year; and accordingly within a year a son was born to him. The people of the town, fearing that the success of this prophecy would induce the Râja to become a Jaina, excluded the disciples of Sri Ratan Sûri from the town. Then Osadevi, the guardian goddess of the place, told the saint to convince the Râja by a miracle. So she took a small hank (*pûni*) of cotton and passed it along the back of the saint, when it immediately became a snake and bit Jaychand, the son of the Râja, in the toe, while he was asleep beside his wife. Every means was tried to save his life, but he died. As his corpse was about to be burnt, Sri Ratan Sûri sent one of his disciples and stopped the cremation. Then the Râja came with the body of his son and stood with hands clasped before the saint. He ordered that it was to be taken back to the place where the prince had been bitten, and that the princess was to lie down beside it as before. At midnight the snake returned and licked the bite, when the prince was restored to life. Then the Râja, with all his court and people, became a Jaina. He and his family became the *gotra* now known as Srisrimâl; his servants that of Srimâl, and the Kshatriyas Oswâl. When the Brâhmans of the place heard of these conversions, they asked the saint how they were to live, as all their clients had become Jainas. The saint directed that they should remain as their family priests and be known as Bhojak or "eaters." The Kshatriyas, who were thus converted, consisted of eighteen *gotras*. Subsequently other Kshatriyas were converted to Jainism by the Jaina priests, and in order to distinguish them from the original Oswâls, who were converted by Sri Ratan Sûri, they were called Khara Oswâl. In Sambat 1167 (1110 A.D.) Sri Jiudat Sûri, now known throughout the Jaina world as Dâdaji, converted about a lakh of people into Oswâls,

---

[1] Based on enquiries at Mirzapur, and notes by Bâbu Vishnu Chandra, Deputy Collector, a member of the tribe.

and no addition has been made to the caste since then. The Kachh tradition is somewhat different from this. "The Oswâls from Os, Parinagar and Budhesar in Pârkar say, that forced to leave Pârkar on account of the misconduct of their chief, they went to Sindh, and finding the Musalmân element too strong, came to Kachh. They are of three sub-divisions Vîsa, Dasa, and Pâncha. The Dasas separated about three hundred years ago, wishing to introduce widow marriage. They afterwards gave up the practice, and within the last few years a small off-shoot introduced it and were named Pânchas. Another story is that the Srimâl King Desal allowed none but millionaires to live inside his city walls. One of the lucky citizens, a Srimâli Vânya, named Ruâd, had a brother named Sâad, whose fortune did not come up to the chief's standard of wealth. Forced to live outside, he asked his brother to help him to make up the required million, but meeting with no encouragement, he and Jay Chand, a discontented son of the king of Srimâl, and many Srimâlis, Râjputs, and others, left Srimâl, and settling in the town of Mandavad called it Osa or 'the frontier.' Among the settlers were Srimâli Vânyas, Bhatti, Chauhân, Gahlot, God, Gohil, Hâda, Jâdav, Makwâna, Parmâr, Râthaur, and Thâr Râjputs, all devout worshippers of Siva. Ratan Sûri, a Jaina, by working miracles, converted Jay Chand, then king, and all the settlers to the faith, and calling them Oswâls formed them into one caste. This is said to have happened in 166 A. D. Tod gives a different account of their origin, claiming them as descendants of the Solanki kings of Anhilvâda (942—1240) who gave up the sword for the till. Chiefly image worshipping Jainas in religion, their family goddess is Satya in Pârkar."[1]

Tribal organization.

3. The annexed list gives the names of the exogamous *gotras* of the Oswâls as found in the Eastern Districts of these Provinces. The Bombay tradition as to the division into Dasa and Bîsa is as follows:—"An Oswâl widow, contrary to the rule against widow marriage, lived with a Jaina priest and had two sons by him. The sons grew rich and hit upon the following plan to force their caste fellows to overlook their illegitimate descent. At the town of Raya, where there was a large number of Oswâls, they made grand preparations for a dinner, and asked the Oswâls, who, not knowing that the hosts were of illegitimate descent, attended the party in large numbers. A widow told

[1] *Bombay Gazetteer*, V, 52.

her son the history of the men who were giving the feast, and he went before the assembled Oswâls and begged of them to allow his mother to re-marry. They asked him why he had come there to make this request, and he told them the story of the birth of the two brothers who had invited them to dinner. On hearing that their hosts were out-caste, there was a sudden confusion among the guests. Those who had touched the food joined the two brothers, and were called Dasa, while those who had not touched the food remained pure or Bîsa. The terms seem to mean Bîsa or 'twenty to the score,' that is pure blood, and Dasa or 'ten in the score,' or half caste."[1]

Exogamy.

4. As already stated, the *gotras* or sections are exogamous. As stated from Benares the rule is that a man cannot marry in his own *gotra*; he cannot marry a girl whose father's or maternal grandfather's *gotra* is the same as that of his father or maternal grandfather. He cannot marry the elder sister of his deceased wife; but can marry her younger sister. There is no formula defining the prohibited degrees. Difference of religion or sect is no bar to marriage, as, for example, a Digambari Oswâl, or worshipper of the naked idols, can marry a Swetambari girl, or one who worshipped the clothed idols, or a Jaina Oswâl boy can marry a Vaishnava Oswâl girl or *vice versâ*. It is said that in South Western India an Oswâl can marry in the Khandêwâl, Porwâl, and other similar tribes, the only condition being that both parties should be Jainas.

Marriage ceremonies.

5. In these Provinces the ceremony of betrothal is performed by sending the *tîka*, one or two rupees, with a cocoanut and sweetmeats. The betrothal generally takes place when the girl is between seven and eleven years of age. The consent of the parents of the boy and girl is invariably necessary, and the girl is not allowed any freedom before marriage. A betrothal can be annulled, but there is no rule for the repayment of the expenses incurred. With the seventh circuit round the sacred fire, the marriage is complete. As the Oswâls are foreigners to these Provinces, the customs followed in Bombay may be quoted: "Boys are married between fifteen and twenty-five and girls between eight and fifteen. The boy's father, with from ten to fifty castemen, visits the girl and presents her with a silver

[1] *Bombay Gazetteer*, XVI, 45.

ring worth four annas or one rupee. The girl's father treats the company to betel and her priest puts the silver ring on the girl's finger. The girl's father returns the visit, presenting the boy's younger brother with one or three rupees, and treats the guests to betel. Cocoanuts are served in the presence of both fathers, the priest fixes a lucky day for the marriage. Some days before the marriage, the boy's father presents the girl with ornaments, invitation cards are sent round, and the boy and the girl are rubbed with turmeric paste. The turmeric rubbing takes place, at least, a month before the marriage. A thread tinged with turmeric powder is cut in two and each of the pieces is passed through an iron ring and tied round a piece of lac bangle, and one of the threads is fastened to the girl's right foot and the other to the boy's right hand. The month between the turmeric rubbing and the marriage is a time of gaiety. The friends and relations of the boy and girl in turn send one of their household to the boy's or the girl's house. The messenger places a cocoanut and silver coin in the boy's and girl's hand and asks him or her to come to their house in the evening. After sunset the boy or girl is seated on horse-back with music, and a band of friends is taken to the entertainer's house, the procession being known as *gadganer* or 'entertaining the bridegroom or bride.' The house is brightly lighted, and carpets are spread in front on which the guests are seated. The women of the house and the guests take their seats in the verandah and sing Mârwâri songs. The women go on singing till the sister of the boy or the girl waves a light, and is presented with a cocoanut and a silver coin. On the marriage day the girl's priest goes to the boy's, and formally asks his family to the wedding. The bridegroom is seated on horse-back, and with music in front and a band of friends behind is taken to the temple of the bride's village Mâruti. The marriage party leave the bridegroom at the temple and go to the bride's house, where her father welcomes them, and betel is served. The Brâhman priest tells the bridegroom's father the lucky moment for the wedding, and the party return to the temple with music. When the lucky hour draws near, it generally falls when it is growing dusk, the bridegroom lays a packet of betel leaves, a nut, and a copper before the village Mâruti, bows and starts on horse-back to the bride's house. On reaching the bride's booth, a stick is handed to the bridegroom, and he strikes with it at the entrance of the porch (a survival of marriage by capture), bows to the pictures of

Ganpati, is presented by the bride's father with a turban worth from one to twenty-five rupees, and dismounts.

"6. Until the lucky hour for the marriage the guests amuse themselves, watching dancing-girls in the marriage hall, or return home to take their food, while the bridegroom, with five or six of his men, steps into the house and bows to a betel-nut Ganpati, lays before it sandal paste, rice, flowers, red powder, vermilion, and scented powder (*abîr*), burns frankincense before it, waves lamps filled with clarified butter round it, and offers sugar. The pair are seated in a booth on a soft cushion laid on a carpet, and a Brâhman priest makes an altar of black earth, kindles the sacred fire (*hom*) on the altar, and drops into the fire clarified butter, grains of barley, and bits of sandal-wood. The pair look on in silence and are not allowed to move from the place until the fire worship is done. When the fire worship is over, the priest tells the pair to walk four times round the altar. Then comes the daughter-giving (*kanyâdân*), when the bride's father pours water on the bridegroom's hands with a money gift varying from one to one hundred rupees. The Brâhman priest is paid five to one hundred rupees, and the bridegroom takes the girl to his house with music and friends. At the boy's house, the pair again sit before the betel-nut Ganpati, which is set on a heap of rice, and their priest lays flowers and red powder before it. When the Ganpati worship is over, the bride's women take her home, and the first wedding day is ended. The bride's parents, who have fasted all day, dine with the bride when she comes back from her husband's house. No caste feast is given this day. Next morning, in the bride's house, a list is made of households to be asked to dine, and the list is given to the priest, who goes round to the houses named, ending at the bridegroom's. At noon the invitations are again sent through the priest as in the morning, and the bridegroom's party goes to the bride's, and is treated to a sumptuous dinner, with a party of the bride's friends and relations. The Brâhman priests cook and serve the guests with food, not allowing any of the guests to touch them, and themselves eating when the others are done. At night the guests are treated to a rich supper, and the party retire after betel is served. The third day passes like the second. On the fourth comes the cloth-presenting ceremony (*phal*), when the marriage party goes with music to the bride's. The bridegroom is seated on a seat somewhat higher than the rest, and the bride's friends and relations arrive. A low wooden stool is set before the bridegroom, and on the stool a bell-metal dining dish marked with upright and crossed lines of vermilion. A metal cup is set in the dish, and a silver coin is dropped in the dish in the name of the family gods. The bride's father presents the bridegroom with as rich a dress and ornaments as he can afford, or at least with a cocoanut, and turbans are handed to his male friends. The bride's party throws red powder at the bridegroom's, who depart taking the pair with them." [1]

Birth ceremonies.

7. No ceremony is performed during pregnancy except for the first child, when the *satmâsa* or seventh month ceremony is performed. The mother goes to her father's house, where she is presented with a dress and sweetmeats and a feast is given. The midwife and servants attend the mother for twelve days after her accouchement. After the child is born, its astrological horoscope (*janampatri*) is prepared on the sixth day (*chhathi*), the mother and child bathe before sunrise, the child is for the first time dressed and decorated with ornaments, and the mother and child worship the Sun. On the twelfth day (*barahi*), mother and child bathe before sunrise and a feast is given. On the *maswân*, after a month, the mother and child visit her father and receive dresses and ornaments for the mother and clothes and toys for the child. The father is unclean during the twelve days after his wife's delivery, and is not permitted to worship the gods. In Bombay when a "child is born, a little cold water is poured over it, and close to it a metal plate is beaten with a rod (to scare off evil spirits). The navel cord is cut, and the woman is bathed in warm water. Some of them dig, and others of them do not dig, the bath water hole in the lying-in room. Those who do not dig the hole, bathe the child in a large and deep metal tray. The mother and child are laid on a cot under which an earthen jar with burning cow-dung cakes is placed. On the first and three following days the child is given a rag soaked in castor oil to suck. From the fourth the mother suckles the child, and is given to eat a pounded mixture of cummin seed and molasses mixed with clarified butter. During the first three days, her diet is wheat flour boiled in clarified butter mixed with sugar, and from the fourth she eats rice and pulse with clarified butter. On the fifth day, a few among them worship the image of Satvâi placed on a stone

---

[1] *Bombay Gazetteer*, XV, 79, *sqq.*

slab, as among the Kunbis of the district, while, as a rule, all of them place sandal paste flowers, turmeric powder, vermilion and fruit with sweet food cooked in the house before an inkstand, reed pen and paper with or without an image of the goddess Satvâi. They say that the worship of the image of Satvâi is not a Mârwâr custom, and the habit has been adopted by their women since they settled in Ahmadnagar. Lamps of dough filled with clarified butter are lighted and set before the goddess, or the pen, ink and paper, and in the place where the mother and child are bathed. These lamps are placed so that the child may not see them; if the child see the light, it is likely to fall sick. Unlike local castes they do not worship Satvâi on the twelfth day, nor do the child's aunts name it. A Brâhman priest generally attends the naming on the thirteenth, and fixes the name after consulting his almanac. A cradle is hung in the lying-in room, and the mother's female friends and kinswomen are called and formally cradle and name the child."[1]

Disposal of the dead.

8. The adult dead are cremated; bodies of children are thrown into a river, and, where this is not possible, are buried. The ashes are thrown into a river, and, where it is not possible to do this, they are left on the place where the body was burnt. When the corpse is placed on the pyre, the nearest relative of the deceased, who acts as chief mourner, puts five pieces of firewood on the corpse and with fire in his left hand goes three times round the pyre and then sets it alight. When the burning progresses, he cracks the skull to allow the soul to escape (*kapâlkriya*). No ceremonies are performed for the propitiation of ancestors in general,-childless ancestors or those who die by a violent death. They do not perform the *srâddha*; no person officiates as priest at the cremation, nor are any prayers repeated. In Bombay "after death the body is placed on a low stool, bathed and dressed in new clothes. A woman who dies before her husband is dressed in a new robe, her hair is decked with flowers and her body with ornaments. These honours are not shown to a widow's body. Poor Oswâls lay their dead on a bamboo ladder-like bier, like that used by Brâhmans. The rich use a raised bamboo seat with a bamboo covering like an English umbrella, fastened to it, and ornamented with small parti-coloured flags decked with tinsel. When the bier is used, the body is laid on

---

[1] *Bombay Gazetteer*, XVII, 59.

the back with the face to the sky. If the canopied chair (*mád*) is used, the body is kept in a sitting position. Two dough balls with a copper coin in each are tied in a piece of cloth, which is put in a bell-metal cup and tied on the bosom of the dead. The funeral party starts for the burial ground with the bier on their shoulders, the barber going before, carrying a fire-pot, and the chief mourner following with the others who are all men. Unlike local Brâhmanic Hindus, they have no rule against the fire-pot carrier turning round and looking back. This rule is intended to bar the return of the ghost from the burial ground. As they draw near the burning ground they halt, lay down the body, and throw the dough balls to the left and right. They go to the nearest water, strip the body of its ornaments, and hand them to the next of kin, when he returns home. The pile is made ready and the body is laid on it, and the fire is kindled by the son or nearest relation. When the body is burnt, they bathe in the nearest water and go home. Neither the bearers nor the mourners are held to be impure, and nothing is done to clean the house or the spot where the death took place. Next day the mourning family, both men and women, visit Pârasnâth's temple, and lay one *ser* of Indian millet before the god, bow to him, and go home. They do not gather the ashes of the dead, nor do they perform any mind-rites, nor keep the yearly death day. Their only observance is that, on some day between the twelfth day after the death and at the end of a year, the caste people are treated to a dinner of sweetmeats and the dead are forgotten "[1]

9. Some Oswâls are Swetambari and others Digambari Jainas. Swetambari Oswâls worship Sri Jiudat Sûrji, Sri Kusal Sûrji, Sri Chand Sûrji, who were Achâryas or high priests of Kartargachha and famous by the name of Dâdaji. Their footprints are generally worshipped, and the offering is taken by the Bhojak already described, or in their absence, by any Brâhman. The offering consists of fruits, sweetmeats, uncooked rice, and money. Some also, in imitation of the Hindus, amongst whom they live, worship snakes and trees like the *pípal*. They all worship the sun and fire, particularly at marriage. The chief places of pilgrimage are Sikharji, the Pârasnâth Hill in Hazâribâgh District, Champapur in the Bhâgalpur District, Pavapur in Bihâr, Benares, Ajudhya, Sidhachâl in Bhav-

Religion.

---

[1] *Bombay Gazetteer*, XVII, 81.

nagar, Girvar Hill in Jûnagarh, Kesariyaji in Udaypur, and Mount Abu. Such pilgrimages are usually undertaken in the cold season. For ceremonial purposes Bhojaks are employed, and, in their absence, Brâhmans of any tribe. The real priests are the Jaina Jatis. In temples are worshipped the twenty-four Arhat or Tirthankara: Adinâtha or Rishabhanâtha, Ajitanâtha, Sambhunâtha, Abhinandananâtha, Sumatinâtha, Padmaprabhunâtha, Suparswânatha, Chandraprabha, Suvidhanâtha or Pushpadanta, Sîtalanâtha, Sri Ansanâtha, Vasupadya, Vimalanâtha, Anantanâtha, Dharmanâtha, Santanâtha, Kunthunâtha, Aranâtha, Mallinâtha, Munisuvrata, Neminâtha, Naminâtha, Pârasnâtha, Vardhamana or Mâhavîra. Of course no animal sacrifice of any kind is allowed in the Jaina temples. The Swetambari Oswâls read the Kalpa Sûtra and pray and fast during the eight days of Parjûshana, which commences on the twelfth or thirteenth of Bhâdon. The Digambari Oswâls observe the Parjûshana for ten days, commencing from the twentieth of Bhâdon. This is their greatest religious festival. Nine days in Chait and Kuâr are set apart for the *navakâra mantra* or the Jaina *gâyatri*, beginning from the twenty-first of each of these months. During this time prayer and fasting are performed. On the twenty-first of Kârttik in each year, they fast and worship Gyân or true knowledge; on thirtieth Kârttik, tenth of Pûs, and eighteenth Baisâkh, the deities are carried about on cars. On the nineteenth and twentieth of Chait, women, whose husbands are alive, worship Gangaur, as Hindus do, and entertain their friends. Similar feasts of joy are held on the eighteenth of Sâwan. This is known as Tîj. Like Hindus they observe the Holi, Rakshabandhan, Dasmi, Divâli, Basantpanchmi. The winter solstice, Makar Sânkrant, commonly known as the Khicharwâr, is also observed. There is no regular propitiation of the dead, but those who have long lived under Hindu influence believe in ghosts and use the ordinary means of repelling them.

Social rules.

10. Animal food is universally prohibited. Like other respectable Hindus, they will not touch Doms, Bhangis, and similar menial castes. They follow the usual Hindu taboos regarding food and family intercourse. When they salute each other, they raise the right hand. Brâhmans and Jatis are saluted with joined hands. Elders and Brâhmans return the salute with the *asîs* and Jatis say in return *Dharma lâbh*. In Bombay "they neither eat flesh nor drink liquor on pain of loss of caste. On the second, fifth, eighth, and eleventh of each lunar

fortnight, they do not eat vegetable. Even on other days few eat onions or garlic. Most men take a pill of opium in the morning and at noon after food. They shave the head except three knots, one on the crown, and one above each ear, a practice which has given them the name of Trishendi, or "three knotted."[1]

The eighty-four sections of the Oswâls.

Thatha.	Bachhâwat.	Vaid.	Sikhâwat.
Barhiya.	Chhorâwat.	Bora.	Mirich.
Sethiya.	Darhiwâl.	Bothara.	Palecha.
Lorha.	Kumât.	Jhâvag.	Ulencha.
Dâga.	Rampuriya.	Rawâni.	Jhovarh.
Kojar.	Daftari.	Bhandâri.	Lembu.
Pârakh.	Sekhâni.	Bhansâli.	Tâuk.
Kodhâri.	Bhâtera.	Sihâni.	Tikuliya.
Dugarh.	Monot.	Chaurariya.	Dosi.
Nuniya.	Guguliya.	Sânr.	Brahmachiya.
Nunâwat.	Lokar.	Katâri.	Kachhab.
Seth.	Khater.	Srimâl.	Gandhi.
Palâwat.	Birar.	Srisrimâl.	Jhajlani.
Sucheti.	Bhuteriya.	Singi.	Chauthâliya.
Hirâwat.	Picha.	Pitaliya.	Bhurant.
Surâna.	Vinayakiya.	Tugaliya.	Rauswâsi.
Thajer.	Kochar.	Mauhata.	Marori.
Kukara.	Goriya.	Parsâni.	Dadha.
Dhapaiya.	Syâmsukh.	Modi.	Ranka.
Dhamâwat.	Pagariya.	Nâpharani.	Phophariya.
Barariya.	Dudheriya.	Râêdâsani.	Dugar.

Distribution of the Oswâls according to the Census of 1891.

DISTRICTS.	Numbers.	DISTRICTS.	Numbers.
Debra Dûn . . .	6	Aligarh	19
Sahâranpur . . .	16	Mathura . . .	21
Muzaffarnagar . . .	4	Agra	102
Meerut	1	Farrukhâbâd . . .	2
Bulandshahr . . .	16	Etâwah	34

[1] *Bombay Gazetteer*, XV, 77.

Distribution of the Oswâls according to the Census of 1891—concld.

DISTRICTS.	Numbers.	DISTRICTS.	Numbers.
Etah	1	Jâlaun	12
Budâun . . .	113	Lalitpur . . .	17
Cawnpur . . .	14	Benares	67
Fatehpur . . .	1	Mirzapur . . .	3
Bânda	4	Kheri . . .	2
Allahâbâd . . .	37		
Jhânsi	12	TOTAL .	504

P

Pachhtoriya.—A sept of Râjputs found in the eastern districts who claim to be of Dikshit origin and take their name from Pachhotar in the Ghâzipur District. They hold a fairly respectable rank. One branch of them has been converted to Islâm.[1]

Pahâri (*pahâr*=a hill).—A general term for the hillmen of the higher and lower Himâlayas. The name is applied to a considerable sept of Râjputs in Dehra Dûn, who are probably allied to the Khasiya (*q.v.*).

Pahriya.—A caste of messengers and village watchmen so called because they do watch and ward (*pahra*). In the hills they are a branch of the Doms. In the plains they are probably an occupational offshoot from some of the menial tribes.

Distribution of the Pahriya according to the Census of 1891.

Districts.	Numbers.
Gorakhpur	344
Basti	19
Gonda	88
Bahrâich	44
Total	495

Palliwâl.—A sub-caste of Banyas who take their name from the town of Palli or Pâli in Mârwâr. According to Mr. Sherring they are supposed not to be true Vaisyas and to have Bargûjar blood in their veins. They emigrated westward in the time of Alâ-ud-dîn Ghori.

[1] *Census Report*, 1865: *Appendix B*, 122: Elliott, *Chronicles of Unao*, 35, *note*.

Distribution of Palliwâl Banyas according to the Census of 1891.

Districts.	Hindus.	Jainas.	Total.
Meerut	...	2	2
Bulandshahr	1	5	6
Aligarh	156	399	555
Mathura	154	281	435
Agra	98	1,609	1,707
Farrukhâbâd	29	351	380
Etah	...	33	33
Cawnpur	...	114	114
Jâlaun	8	...	8
Lalitpur	3	...	3
Gorakhpur	405	...	405
Lucknow	...	4	4
Bârabanki	...	57	57
Total	854	2,855	3,709

Palliwâl.—A local tribe of Brâhmans who, like the Banya sub-caste of the same name, take their title from Pâli, the commercial city of Mârwâr. They belong to the Kanaujiya division of the Pâncha Gauda. Colonel Tod had a theory that as they worshipped, among other things, the bridle of a horse, they were survivors of the priests of the Palli Scythian race. They are said to give a bride-price at marriage. They appear all over Upper India as money-lenders, merchants and cultivators. A great misfortune fell upon them in 1156 A. D. when Sivaji, the founder of the Râthaur dynasty and son of the King of Kanauj, passed Pâli on his return from a pilgrimage to Dwârika. The Brâhmans of Pâli sent a deputation to him asking for protection from the two evils which prevailed—the Mînas of the Aravalli range and the lions. Sivaji relieved them from both; but the opportunity to acquire land was too good to be lost, and on the festival of the Holi he put the leading Brâhmans to death and seized Pâli.[1]

[1] *Annals of Râjasthân*, II, 15.

Distribution of Palliwâl Brâhmans according to the Census of 1891.

DISTRICTS.	Numbers.	DISTRICTS.	Numbers.
Sahâranpur . .	1	Farrukhâbâd . .	3
Muzaffarnagar . .	61	Etah . . .	48
Meerut . . .	397	Cawnpur . . .	67
Bulandshahr . .	213	Jâlaun . . .	102
Aligarh . . .	154	Lalitpur . . .	6
Mathura . . .	343	Jaunpur . . .	122
Agra . . .	114	TOTAL .	1,634

Palwâr, Paliwâr.—A sept of Râjputs confined almost altogether to the Gorakhpur Division and the Faizâbâd District. According to the Faizâbâd tradition,[1] one Prithivirâj Deo, Sombansi, known also as Mûr Deo or Bhûr Deo, came from the village of Pâli in the district of Hardoi in 1248 A. D. and took up his residence in the village of Rannupur, where he accepted service under the Bhars. From his native place he and his descendants gave up the name of Sombansi and adopted that of Palwâr. He is said to have formed a connection with a fairy (*deokanya*) or a witch (*dâin*), and by her he had a son Harihar Deo, who formed attachments with an Ahîrin and a Bharin, of whom there are multitudinous descendants in the Azamgarh District. These descendants have become known as Dainiyas or "children of the witch" and Bantariyas or "dwellers in the woods." Tradition says that on one occasion, soon after the birth of her son, this lady of the woods was engaged in the homely office of baking cakes, when her infant, which lay some paces off, began to cry. She had either to neglect the baby or the cakes; when, as her husband arrived, he saw his fairy wife assume supernatural and gigantic proportions, so as to allow of the baking and nursing to go on together. When she saw she was discovered she disappeared for ever, leaving the child as a legacy to her astonished husband.

2. According to another version of the legend the founder of the sept was one Patrâj of the Sombansi tribe, who is said to have

[1] *Settlement Report*, 153.

migrated from the neighbourhood of Delhi to Bandipur in Faizâbâd, where he made himself famous in his contests with the Râjbhars. He had four wives of different castes—a Râjput, an Ahîr, a Bhar and one whose caste is unknown. Their descendants were the Palwârs, Ahiriniya, Bhariniya and Dainiya.[1]

3. In a third version they claim a connection with Sandi-Pâli, which the Sombansis of that place deny. On this the Palwârs change ground and refer their origin to Pâli near Delhi, or to a village of that name in the Partâbgarh District, which is likely enough, as that is one of the chief seats of the Sombansi sept in the present day.[2]

4. Some interest has been taken in the tribe on account of the Chaurâsi or group of eighty-four villages which Sir H. M. Elliot attributed to them in the Gorakhpur District. On this Mr. Carnegy writes[3]:—"Sir H. M. Elliot, in his extraordinary article in his Supplemental Glossary on Chaurâsi, speaks of a collection of eighty-four villages in Pargana Anaula (should be Bhawapâr) in the Gorakhpur District, where their possessions, which have been mostly confiscated for their proceedings in 1857, are said by the tribe to have commenced with eighty-four *bíghas* of land and soon to have swelled into eighty-four full villages. But the fact is the whole of the Gorakhpur, Faizâbâd and Azamgarh Palwârs spring from one common ancestor. The system of reckoning by Chaurâsi and Biyâlisi, so much dwelt on by Sir H. M. Elliot, is uncommon in this part of Oudh—in fact few natives understand it; but the number 49 seems with these very Palwârs to have a special charm. For instance, they talk of *unchâs kos kâ bhât*, which means that on the occasion of ceremonial gatherings of the tribe to commemorate a birth, marriage or death, all the members inhabiting a circle of 49 *kos*, which area is supposed to represent their proprietary possessions, are invited to attend and eat the bread of sociability. Of these, however, the Surhurpur (Bandipur) branches are debarred from eating and drinking with the tribe by reason of illegitimacy; and Atrauliya branch because it is stained with blood. Members of these branches on such occasions are obliged to content themselves with having dry rations served out to them in lieu of cooked viands. The absurdity of the former of these exclusions, and of the system

[1] *Census Report, N.-W. P.*, 1865, II, 112, *sq*.
[2] *Census Report*, 200.
[3] *Faizâbâd Settlement Report*, 206, *sq*.

PANKA.

of caste generally, is forcibly illustrated by the following instance: A female of the Surhurpur illegitimate branch and another of the Birhar legitimate branch both married into the orthodox Râjkumâr family of the Râja of Dera, and thereafter both branches were alike admitted to the Râja's social board. Both parties then eat and drink with the Râja, but they still will not eat and drink with each other; and they thus remain a living confutation of the mathematical axiom that things that are equal to the same thing are equal to each other. *Unchâs kos ki kumak* is another common expression with these people, which means that the proprietors within an area of 49 *kos* were wont in the king's time to make common cause in opposing the aggressions of the Meopur faction of the Râjkumârs and all others."

5. The turbulence of the sept in Gorakhpur during the Mutiny led to the confiscation of nearly all their possessions, and they have now fallen on evil days and possess little rank or influence.

6. In Faizâbâd the Palwârs give brides to the Gargbansi, Sûrajbansi, Chandel, Bachgoti, Bais and Chauhân septs. In Azamgarh they claim to belong to the Bhârgava *gotra*; take brides from the Bais, Râthaur, Bisen, Chauhân, Raghubansi, Donwâr and Chandel septs; and marry their daughters to members of the Sûrajbans, Kalhans, Râjkumâr, Raghubansi, Sirnet and Chandrabansi septs.

Distribution of Palwâr Râjputs according to the Census of 1891.

DISTRICTS.	Number.	DISTRICTS.	Number.
Agra . . .	29	Azamgarh . .	7,664
Jâlaun . . .	5	Kheri . . .	1,206
Jaunpur . . .	11	Faizâbâd . . .	5,587
Ghâzipur . . .	80	Sultânpur . .	177
Gorakhpur . . .	3,376	Bârabanki . .	14
Basti . . .	231		
		TOTAL .	18,380

Panka, Panika.—A low weaving and watchman tribe in South Mirzapur. They are the same people who are known in Bengal as Pân, Panwa, Paur, Pâb, Panika, Chik, Chik Baraik, Ganda, Mahato, Sawâsi or Tânti. In Mirzapur they are known as Panka,

Panika or Pankiya and Kotwâr, the last of which, in relation to their occupation as village watchmen, means "keeper or porter of a castle" (Sanskrit *kota* or *koshtha pâla*). The name Panka or Panika is usually taken from *panik,* which means the elastic bow which the weaver uses to extend the cloth as it is woven; but the Bengali synonyms for the caste make this uncertain. Colonel Dalton was disposed from their appearance to believe them of Aryan or Hindu, rather than Dravidian origin, and describes them as "in all probability remnants of the Aryan colonies that the Hos subjugated.[1]" This is disputed by Mr. Risley,[2] who remarks that "the most cursory examination of the exogamous divisions of the Pâns affords convincing evidence of their Dravidian origin." Though they have lost in Mirzapur their totemistic septs, still their appearance clearly indicates their connection with the Dravidian races like the Majhwârs. They say that Parameswar created the first man of the caste out of water (*pâni*) and appointed him his water-carrier. One day Parameswar sent him to bring fire. He went in search of fire to a place where the Majhwârs were eating, and they gave him a share of their food. He returned to Parameswar, who taxed him with eating with such degraded people. He denied the charge, but Parameswar gave him a blow on his back and he immediately vomited up a quantity of rice and pulse. So Parameswar turned him out of Heaven, and the Pankas have since then gone down in the world and eat with Majhwârs. The Mirzapur Pankas describe themselves as emigrants from Bâhmandeva in Rîwa, and fix the date of their arrival some eight or ten generations ago.

Tribal organization and exogamy.

2. They have lost, if they ever possessed, the elaborate scheme of totemistic septs which are found among the Pâns of Bengal. Their rules of exogamy prohibit marriage with the daughter of the maternal uncle or of their father's sister, and they also do not marry in their own family as long as the members are united and live together, no matter how distant relatives may reside under the same roof. This abhorrence of marriage between persons residing closely together from early youth is, according to one theory, the basis of the rule of exogamy.[3] They have a tribal council known as

---

[1] *Descriptive Ethnology,* 185.
[2] *Tribes and Castes,* II, 156.
[3] See Westermarck, *History of Human Marriage,* 320, *sqq.*

kutumâyat or kabildâri.[1] There is no permanent president, but at each meeting the most respectable person present takes the chair.

Rules of marriage.

3. Differences of wealth or social position (except the practice of degrading employments, such as shoe-making) are not a bar to marriage. Polygamy is permitted, but they can seldom afford more than one wife. If there are more wives than one, the head wife alone is mistress of the household and shares in the family worship. If an unmarried girl is detected in an intrigue with a clansman, her parents have to give a tribal feast and she is then restored to caste: but if her lover be an outsider, she is permanently expelled. The bride price amounts to five rupees in cash and two maunds of rice and pulse. The rules as to physical defects in bride and bridegroom agree with those of the allied tribes.

Divorce.

4. Divorce is permitted in case of adultery in either party or if either eat with a low caste person like a Dom, Chamâr or Dusâdh. But the intention to divorce must be announced before, and sanctioned by, the tribal council.

Widow marriage and the levirate.

5. Widow marriage and the levirate are permitted on the usual conditions.

Succession, adoption and relationship.

6. The rules on these subjects correspond in every way with those of the Majhwârs.

Birth customs.

7. The woman is delivered on a cot and is attended by a Chamâin midwife, who cuts the cord and buries it under the cot. The woman receives no food for two days: on the third she gets rice and cakes made of pulse and pumpkin (*konkrauri*). They have the usual sixth day (*chhathi*) and twelfth day (*barahi*) ceremonies, after which the woman is clean and resumes her household work. A husband does not cohabit with his wife for three or four months after her confinement.

Adoption ceremony.

8. The only ceremony in adoption is the announcement of the fact and the exchange of mutual promises before the leader of the council.

Marriage ceremonies.

9. The marriage ceremonies do not appreciably differ from those of the cognate tribes. The betrothal is clenched by the boy's father sending to the bride's

---

[1] The first name means "family council," Sanskrit *kutumba*=the household; the latter an importation from the Arabic *qabîl*=kindred.

house five rupees and three or five sers of coarse sugar (*gur*). This is called *neg bharna.* Three days before marriage is the *matmangar* ceremony (see *Bhuiya*[1]). When the procession reaches the door of the bride, the relatives of the bridegroom distribute betel-nut among those of the bride, who return the compliment. After the procession returns to the reception place (*janwánsa*), the bride's mother goes there with five sers of coarse sugar and three tooth brushes (*datuan*): with these the bridegroom has to clean his teeth and she makes him smell the sugar. His father then sends the "offering" (*charhaua*) to the bride—two sheets (*sári*) and five sers of sugar. At the actual ceremony the bride's sister fills the hands of the bride and bridegroom with rice and dried mangoes. Then the bridegroom rubs some red lead (*sendur*) on the branch of the cotton tree (*semal*) fixed up in the marriage shed (*mánro*) and then smears it over the nose, forehead and parting of the bride's hair. This is the binding part of the ceremony. After this they are taken into the retiring room (*kohabar*) (for the significance of which, see *Majhwár.*[2]) There the bridegroom has again to smell some sugar. On returning home there is the usual feast, and a day or two afterwards the bride and bridegroom go to "drown the nuptial jars" (*kalsa*) in a neighbouring stream, and on their way home they worship every *pípal* and banyan tree they meet, and rub red lead on their trunks. This form of marriage is called *charhauwa.*

Marriage by sagâi.

10. The form of marrying a widow by *sagái* is very simple. The man has to pay three rupees as the bride price to her relations, then he brings her home, and as she enters the house he rubs red lead on the parting of her hair and puts palm leaf ornaments (*tarki*) in her ears. On that day he feasts the clansmen.

Death ceremonies.

11. Unmarried children and people who die of epidemic disease are buried: others are cremated.[3] When the mourners return home they pour a little oil on the ground and sit down and console the chief mourner. He goes to the riverside and fixes a bundle of reed grass into the ground, which he and the women of the household water every day at noon

---

[1] *Para.* 14.
[2] *Para.* 18.
[3] This is the custom also in Bengal; Ball, *Jungle Life* 322, *note*; Risley, *Tribes and Castes*, II, 159.

until the obsequies are completed.[1] The death impurity lasts ten days, when the obsequies are concluded by a tribal feast.

12. They profess a sort of bastard Hinduism. They are much afraid of evil spirits (*bhût*) which commonly reside in *mahua*, *pîpal* or banyan trees. These are periodically propitiated by offerings of goats and fowls performed by the Baiga. They do not employ Brâhmans in any of their religious ceremonies. Their two great festivals are the Holi and Dasami (Dasahra); but they in no way follow Hindu usage on these festivals, and offer a burnt offering to the marriage god Dulha Deva, who is represented by a piece of rudely cut stone on a mud platform. His worship is performed by the Baiga. They observe the Nâgpanchami festival, but do not appear to have as is the case in Bengal, any special worship of the snake as the ancestor of the tribe.[2]

Religion.

13. They believe that old wells, streams and trees are haunted by evil spirits. The Baiga raises a regular yearly subscription to provide for their worship; and offers to them young pigs, fowls and goats, with a burnt offering (*hom*) of sugar and butter. The tenth day of the second half of the month of Kuâr is devoted to the worship of the dead, to whom food and a burnt sacrifice are offered. On the tenth day after a man or woman dies a young pig is sacrificed. At the end of the proceedings they invoke the spirits of the dead in a low voice in these words—"Now live for ever in this house and do not trouble our children." Every day till the tenth day they lay out food at night for the dead along the road by which the corpse was taken to cremation or burial. They are constantly in the fear of the spirits of the dead, and whenever they have a bad dream or a nightmare they offer a burnt sacrifice (*hom*) to them.

Demonology and ancestor worship.

14. Women tattoo themselves on the arms in some conventional pattern. If they fail to do this, a woman in the next life is reborn as a Turkin or the wife of a Muhammadan, on whom they look with special abhorrence. They have the usual omens. They swear by putting a piece of iron in a drinking vessel of water which is held in the hand. No

Various superstitions.

[1] On the significance of this ceremony, see *Biyâr*, para. 14.

[2] Risley, *Tribes and Castes*, II., 159,

Panka will violate such an oath. They have a firm belief in witchcraft, and think that a witch can kill a man by looking at him; hence old women suspected of witchcraft are carefully avoided. They also believe that a witch can turn meat into a mass of blood and maggots merely by looking at it. Most diseases are due to demoniacal influence, which is treated by the Baiga. They have a firm belief in the Evil Eye which is avoided by the use of sundry amulets.

Social customs.

15. They regard the cow as Lakshmi, the goddess of wealth, and will not eat beef. Any one eating it is put out of caste. Besides the flesh of the cow and buffalo, they will not eat the horse, ass, camel, jackal, lizard or crocodile. They eat pigs, fowls, fish and all kinds of jungle game. The men eat first and women after them. Some men wear a special religious necklace (*kanthi*), and these, when they eat, throw a little bread and water on the ground as an offering to the earth goddess Dharti Mâta. They use liquor and tobacco freely. They salute elders in the form *pâêlagi*, and the reply is *asîs*, or a blessing. They respect their women, who work at spinning thread which the men weave. They are very hospitable to clansmen but fear strangers. They will not touch a Chamâr or Dharkâr, nor the wife of the younger brother. The father-in-law and mother-in-law of a married couple do not touch or speak to each other.[1] They will eat food cooked by a Brâhman and no one else. None but a Dom or Ghasiya will touch their leavings.

Occupation.

16. They work as weavers and village watchmen. The loom is known as *dongi*. The main kinds of cloth which they make are the *darap*, *charas* and *bhagua*. The *darap* is a woman's thick sheet worth about two rupees. The *charas* is a loin cloth for men like the Hindu *dhoti*: the *bhagua* a small cloth worn under the loin cloth only by Majhwâr women, for which they get a fancy price.[2] They often work up cotton into cloth for their customers, and for weaving a *dhoti* receive three sers of *kodo* or *sânwân* millet. Their dress presents no peculiarities. The women wear pewter anklets (*pairi*), glass wrist bangles (*chûri*), a wristlet (*berawa*) and a nose-ring (*nath*). As may be anticipated from their customs, they are regarded as pure village menials and their social status is very low.

---

[1] See Lubbock, *Origin of Civilisation*, 11, *sqq.*

[2] See *Majhwâr, para.* 60.

Pankhiya.—A peculiar class of Muhammadans who are found in the low lands (*khâdir*) of the Ganges in Shâhjahânpur and some of the neighbouring districts. They profess to be strict Muhammadans, but transgress the law of Islâm by eating turtles, crocodiles and other animals usually regarded as forbidden food. They appear to be a fairly well-to-do cultivating class, and their hamlets show a stock of cattle, goats and poultry much larger than that possessed by ordinary Hindu cultivators.[1]

Distribution of the Pankhiyas according to the Census of 1891.

DISTRICTS.	Number.	DISTRICTS.	Number.
Cawnpur . . .	65	Ghâzipur . . .	6
Allâhâbâd . . .	41	Basti	550
Benares . .	8	Azamgarh . . .	111
Jaunpur . . .	132		
		TOTAL .	913

Pant, Panth—(Sanskrit *pathin*, "a path in morals or religion") a class of Hill Brâhmans, who ascribe their origin to Mahârâshtra or the Marhâta country. They belong to the Bhâradwâja, Parâsara and Vasishtha *gotras* and the Madhyandinya *sâkha*. They say that some twenty-one generations ago their ancestor Jayadeva came to Kumaun. In the tenth generation his descendants divided into four branches, named after Sarma, Srinâtha, Nathu and Bhaudâs. Sarma became a physician, Srinâtha, the spiritual preceptor of the Râja, Nathu, a teacher of Paurânik theology, and Bhaudâs, a soldier. The last-mentioned acquired in camp and court a habit of eating flesh like his Khasiya soldiers, and his descendants retained the custom. But the others confined themselves to vegetable food, as their present representatives do, and even oblige their wives, who come from flesh-eating clans like the Tiwâris and Joshis, to do the same. The Bhâradwâja Pants intermarry with Tripâthis or Tiwâris, Joshis and Pâures. They rarely marry Pants of the two other *gotras*, and their customs and habits and manner of eating and drinking resemble those of other

[1] *Imperial Gazetteer*, XII, 317, *sq*.

Hill Brâhmans. Their favourite object of worship is the Vaishnava Sâkti.[1]

Panwâr.—A noted sept of Râjputs who in name represent the ancient Pramâra race. Colonel Tod[2] calls them the "most potent of the Agnikula or fire races." "The world is the Pramâr's" is an ancient saying, and Naukot Marusthali signifies the nine divisions into which the country from the Satlaj to the ocean was divided among them. By another theory they represent the Pauravas, the famous race which, after the time of Alexander, was predominant in Râjasthân under the name of Pramâra. They are mentioned in the Veda and Mahâbhârata, where the first kings of the Lunar race are represented as being Pauravas who reigned over the realms included between the Upper Ganges and the Jumna. They are the Porouaroi or Poruaroi of Ptolemy.[3] General Cunningham,[4] on the contrary, would identify these last with the Parihâr sept. The popular account of them is that they were the third in order of creation from the Agnikunda, and were hence called Pramâra or "first strikers."

2. In Bombay the Pramâras, who are called a detachment from the Agnikula tribes of Mount Abu, like the others under the same fictional appellation, are, according to Dr. J Wilson,[5] descendants of Kulis. Their traditions centre round the State of Dhâr, the Râja of which is still a member of the sept. In remembrance of their heroic defence of the capital they repeat the verse—

Jahân Puâr tahân Dhâr hai;
Aur Dhâr jahân Puâr;
Dhâr bina Puâr nahîn;
Aur nahîn Puâr bina Dhâr.[6]

"Where the Puâr is there is Dhâr; and Dhâr is where the Puâr is; there is no Dhâr without the Puâr and no Puâr without Dhâr." They claim that the great Râjas Bhoja and Vikramaditya of Ujjain were members of their sept, and allege that they were kings of Mâlwa for ten generations after Râja Vikramaditya. The Puâr dynasty of Mâlwa ended with Jaychand; then Jîtpâl estab-

---

[1] Atkinson, *Himalayan Gazetteer*, III, 421.
[2] *Annals*, I, 98, 102.
[3] McCrindle, *Indian Antiquary*, XIII, 362.
[4] *Archæological Reports*, IX, 55, *sq.*
[5] *Indian Antiquary*, III, 227.
[6] Tod, *loc. cit.*, II, 263.

lished the Tomar dynasty which lasted one hundred and forty-two years and was succeeded by the Chauhâns for one hundred and sixty-seven years.[1] They have now a poor reputation in Central India, because they are said to have intermarried with Marhatta Sûdras and the poorest Râjput chief would disdain to eat with them or give them his daughter in marriage.[2] Colonel Tod asserts that the famous Mauryas were the Mori, a branch of the Pramâra clan, which occupied Chithor in the eighth century. Their *gotras* or sections in Râjputâna are Delât; Kalât; Doding; Kheyât and Pokhariya, of which the Delât is the most numerous.[3] The men of the Pokhariya section like to be called Râwat, but are generally called Mer. The chief men are called Gameti. They are an industrious race, generally taller and better built than the Chauhân Mînas. The Kalâts will not give their daughters in marriage to this section, but will take wives from them, and they intermarry freely with the Hindu Chîtas and Barârs and the other Mer clans. Their customs are the same as the Chauhân Mînas.

The Panwârs of the North-Western Provinces and Oudh.

3. In these provinces their expulsion from Ujjain under their leader Mitra Sen is ascribed to the attack of the Muhammadans under Shahâb-ud-dîn Ghori. The story[4] runs that Râja Bijaypâl of Bayâna wished to bring about an alliance between his daughter and the son of Râja Sindpâl of Ujjain, and with this view sent an embassy with presents. Sindpâl, however, objecting to the proposed marriage, ordered the ambassadors to return, but his son Lakhansi meeting them on his own account accepted the proposal, and in spite of his father's objections, brought back the party to Bayâna and there the marriage took place. Villages were then assigned to the prince and princess for maintenance. These, however, proving insufficient, the daughter was sent back to her father some little time after to solicit a further grant. But all that Sindpâl gave his daughter was a sword, which she was instructed to deliver to her husband Lakhansi. He then interpreting the gift, whether rightly or wrongly, to mean that he should extend his possessions by its means, seized and added to his territories fourteen hundred villages, giving them over to his followers. At various times they moved northwards, their first halting-place being the Pargana of

[1] Malcolm, *Central India*, I, 26.
[2] *Ibid.*, I, 130.
[3] *Râjputâna Gazetteer*, II, 45.
[4] *Census Report, North-Western Provinces*, 1865, B, Appendix 67, *sq.*

Khairagarh, where they are landlords and cultivators. They have in course of time become dispossessed of many of their estates, bartering them for less substantial wealth to Gûjars and Brâhmans.

4. In Farrukhâbâd[1] they trace their colonization to Râja Sindpâl Sinh, who is said to have settled the Pargana of Amritpur by the favour of the Râja of Khor. His sons quarrelled with, and were expelled by, Partit Râê, the Kâyasth minister of the Râja, but one son Basant Sâh returned and recovered his estate. The Bulandshahr[2] branch say that they came from Nâgpur and Ujjain after their expulsion by Shahâb-ud-dîn Ghori.

5. The Khidmatiya, Barwâr, or Chobdâr are said to be an inferior branch of them, descended from a low-caste woman. No high-caste Hindu eats food or drinks water touched by them. According to the Aîn-i-Akbari[3] a thousand men of the sept guarded the environs of the palace of Akbar, and Abul Fazl says of them:—"The caste to which they belong was notorious for highway robbery and former rulers were not able to keep them in check. The effective orders of His Majesty have led them to honesty; they are now famous for their trustworthiness. They were formerly called Mâwis. Their chief has received the title of Khidmat Râê. Being near the person of His Majesty, he lives in affluence. His men are called Khidmatiyas."

6. In Unâo[4] the Panwârs have two colonies in different parts of the district. In the Morâwan Pargana they occupy about thirty villages. They say that their ancestor, Narhar Sinh Panwâr, distinguished himself in the siege of Chithor under Akbar Shâh and received a grant of this tract of land as a reward for his services. He founded the village of Narhai Chak, which is called after his name. These Panwârs must have been once a powerful clan; but the great encroachment of the Bais reduced them to complete insignificance, and deprived them of a large portion of their land. In Sîtapur,[5] also, they fix the time of their emigration in the time of Akbar. In Gorakhpur[6] they are said to have driven the Bisens out of Bhâgalpur, whence the latter retired to Majhauli. In Ghâzipur they trace their origin to Jhânsi and they

---

[1] *Settlement Report*, 13.
[2] *Census Report*, 1865, I, Appendix 17.
[3] Blochmann, I, 252.
[4] Elliott, *Chronicles*, 55.
[5] *Settlement Report*, 57.
[6] Buchanan, *Eastern India*, II, 365.

are known by the name of Ujjaini. The head of the sept in that part of the country is the Râja of Dumrâon who traces his descent in eighty-six generations from Vikramaditya. The great Râja Sâladitya, who at the beginning of the seventh century overcame the Gupta dynasty, was king of Mâlwa and no doubt belonged to this clan.[1] In Jhânsi they are regarded as a shade higher than the Bundelas and in consequence all powerful chiefs take their daughters in marriage. "They are needy and as proud as Lucifer and will always eke out their living by robbery if they can."[2] In Mahona of the Lucknow District they have, from their connection with the Delhi Court, adopted some Musalmân practices, such as fastening their coats to the left and paying reverence to the *tâziahs* emblematical of the martyrs Hasan and Husain, which are carried about at the Muharram, and they have before their residence a large stone which they hold in almost sacred reverence. They say that they brought it from Delhi and that it is their symbol of right to their estates which were granted to them by the Delhi Emperor; he is said to have enjoined them to take it as the foundation for their future settlement. Whenever a new Râja succeeds, he places upon it an offering of flowers, sweetmeats, and a few rupees.[3]

7. In Jâlaun the Panwârs give brides to the Bais, Bhâlê Sultân, Nikumbh, and Ahhan, and marry girls of the Chauhân, Kachhwâha, Parihâr, Sengar, Bhadauriya, Râthaur, and Chandel septs. In Unâo they marry their daughters to Dikhits beyond the Ganges, Gaurs, Chandels, Kachhwâhas, Chauhâns, Hâras, and Râthaurs; and their sons to Chauhân and Dikhit girls.

Distribution of the Panwâr Râjputs according to the Census of 1891.

DISTRICTS.	Hindus.	Muhammadans.	TOTAL.
Dehra Dûn	2,265	...	2,265
Sahâranpur	251	313	564
Muzaffarnagar	136	486	622
Meerut	1,794	...	1,794

[1] Oldham, *Memorandum*, 1, 56, *sq*.
[2] Sleeman, *Journey through Oudh*, I, L V.
[3] *Settlement Report*, LXI.

Distribution of the Panwâr Râjputs according to the Census of 1891—contd.

DISTRICTS.	Hindus.	Muhammadans.	TOTAL.
Bulandshahr	1,513	553	2,066
Aligarh	817	...	817
Mathura	683	2,686	3,369
Agra	7,366	12	7,378
Farrukhâbâd	2,994	8	3,002
Mainpuri	819	...	819
Etâwah	504	...	504
Etah	624	5	629
Bareilly	243	...	243
Bijnor	233	...	233
Budâun	778	123	901
Morâdâbâd	2,035	...	2,035
Shâhjahânpur	4,699	...	4,669
Pilibhît	310	...	310
Cawnpur	4,609	41	4,650
Fatehpur	1,263	...	1,263
Bânda	2,299	28	2,327
Hamîrpur	1,240	10	1,250
Allahâbâd	517	...	517
Jhânsi	1,045	5	1,050
Jâlaun	671	...	671
Lalitpur	3,241	1	3,242
Benares	465	88	553
Mirzapur	126	...	126
Jaunpur	4,105	7	4,112
Ghâzipur	691	783	1,474
Ballia	2,248	191	2,439

PARAHIYA.

Distribution of the Panwâr Râjputs according to the Census of 1891 —concld.

DISTRICTS.	Hindus.	Muhammadans.	TOTAL.
Gorakhpur	3,267	125	3,392
Basti	1,370	7,366	8,736
Azamgarh	1,465	1,417	2,882
Tarâi	3,214	...	3,214
Lucknow	2,664	1	2,665
Unâo	2,140	95	2,235
Râê Bareli	1,097	61	1,158
Sîtapur	2,845	587	3,432
Hardoi	6,143	...	6,143
Kheri	9	348	357
Faizâbâd	3,265	343	3,608
Gonda	336	...	336
Bahrâich	91	25	116
Sultânpur	705	73	778
Partâbgarh	190	...	190
Bârabanki	1,108	22	1,130
TOTAL	80,563	15,803	96,366

Parahiya, Parhaiya.—A Dravidian tribe found in small numbers in Pargana Dudhi in Mirzapur. The word is said to mean, in Gondi, "burners of the jungle." Bishop Caldwell[1] writes :—"It has been said that the name Pareiya or Pariah is synonymous with that of the Pahariyas (from *pahâr*, 'a hill') a race of mountaineers, properly called Malers, inhabiting the Râjmahâl Hills in Bengal : and hence it is argued that the Pareiyas may be considered, like the Pahariyas, as a race of non-Aryan, non-Dravidian aborigines. It is an error, however, to

[1] *Comparative Grammar*, 549.

suppose that there is any connection between these two names. The word Pariah, properly Pareiya, denotes not a mountaineer, but a drummer, a word regularly derived from *parei*, 'a drum,' especially the great drum used at funerals. The name Pareiya is, in fact, the name of a hereditary occupation, the Pareiyas being the people who are generally employed at festivals, and especially at funerals, as drummers." Dr. Oppert[1] considers it means a mountaineer, from the Dravidian root *para*, "a hill."

Appearance.

1. Those I have seen in Dudhi are a very wild looking set of men, about five feet three inches in height: not as robust as the Korwas, but still a strong, active race. Some have very scanty beards and moustaches. Some shave the front of the head, while others keep all their hair and leave it entirely unkempt. Colonel Dalton noticed considerable variety of features among them. Some, he thinks, might be classed as Negro, others as Mongolian. The former were dark and prognathous; the latter bright copper coloured, with flat, broad faces, and slightly oblique eyes.[2] He thinks that they are closely akin to the Bhuiyârs.[3] Mr. Forbes also notices the variety of type among them, and remarks that they are so athletic and powerful, that "as strong as a Parahiya" has passed into a proverb.[4] In Mirzapur they are renowned for their swiftness in running.

Traditions of origin.

2. The members of the tribe in Mirzapur fix their head-quarters in the villages of Jhânsi and Uspar, in Sarguja, close to the British frontier. They have emigrated from there in quite recent times, and the emigration is still going on. They still go to their original home at the festivals of the Râmnaumi and Dasahra. There is no temple there, but in one of the chief men's houses there is a shrine to Devi called "the House of God" (*deoghar*). There they worship the goddess, by each man throwing a little butter and resin (*dhûp*) on the fire as a burnt offering (*hom*). After that, butter cakes (*pûri*) are offered and consumed by the worshippers.

---

[1] *Original Inhabitants of Bharatavarsa*, 32, *sq.*

[2] *Descriptive Ethnology*, 131.

[3] *Ibid.*, 284, note.

[4] *Settlement Report on Palamau*, quoted in Hunter, *Statistical Account of Bengal*, XVI., 297.

Tribal organisation and rules of exogamy.

3. The Mirzapur people profess ignorance of the totemistic septs recorded by Mr. Risley.[1] They must marry within the tribe and the only prohibited degrees are that a man cannot marry his daughter to the son of his brother or cannot marry himself into the family of his children. These are perhaps about the most simple rules of exogamy to be found in any tribe in these Provinces. They have a tribal council called "the brotherhood" (*bhaiyári*). The rules do not differ from those in the allied tribes. The usual punishment is a two days' feast to the brethren. Adultery, or fornication with a person of another caste, is punished with excommunication for five years. The president (*Mahto*) is a hereditary permanent official. If any one disobeys his orders, he is tied up and beaten with rods. Polygamy is recognized, but as a rule a man does not take a second wife unless the first is barren.[2] The senior wife rules the household and shares in the family worship: if she is not treated with respect, they believe that the family goes to ruin. The wives live apart in separate huts. Polyandry is forbidden. Intertribal incontinence in women is easily condoned, but young women are kept shut up at night and not allowed to go about alone. In the case of intrigues in the tribe, the offenders are brought before the council, and are not allowed to sit on the tribal mat (*tát*) until they feed the clansmen. Men or women found misbehaving themselves with a stranger to the tribe are permanently expelled. The marriage age is 12 for both boys and girls. The marriage is arranged by the boy's father under the advice of the Mahto. The bride-price is one measure (*paseri*) of *sánwán* millet, five rupees in cash, and five cakes. This is the invariable rate fixed by tribal custom.

Divorce.

4. Divorce is easily managed. Either husband or wife can leave the other whenever they please. If the wife leaves her husband without due cause shown to the satisfaction of the Mahto, her relations are obliged to refund the bride-price. In ordinary cases of divorce, all that is necessary is to inform the Mahto. A divorced man or woman can re-marry.. In the case of illicit connections, the children follow the

---

[1] *Tribes and Castes*, II., App., 118.

[2] Westermarck, *History of Human Marriage*, 488

caste of the father, but a son of a Parahiya by a strange woman will not be admitted to full caste rights.

Widow marriage and the levirate. Adoption.

5. Widow marriage and the levirate are permitted as among Bhuînhârs (para. 8). The same is the case with adoption, (*ibid.*, para. 9).

Beena marriage.

6. The custom of Beena marriage (*gharjaiyân*) prevails. In this case the man who serves for his bride acquires no rights from his father-in-law but inherits his father's estate.

Succession.

7. All they know about succession is that a man's sons are his heirs, and that the eldest son gets somewhat in excess of the others, as the Mahto directs. If there are no sons, the nearest agnates inherit.

Relationship.

8. No Parahiya can name more than three generations in the ascending line—father, paternal grandfather, and maternal grandfather,—and sons and daughters and grand children in the descending line.

Birth ceremonies.

9. The birth ceremonies agree closely with those of the allied tribes like the Bhuînhârs (para. 12), but they are attended by the Chamâin midwife, who buries the cord under a tree in the jungle. On the third day at the exact time the child was born, the Dhobi comes and carries off the dirty clothes to the wash, and the baby is washed by the midwife. Then the mother is bathed and dressed in clean clothes by the husband's sister (*nanad*), who also re-plasters the delivery-room. Though this is done on the third day, they know it as the sixth-day ceremony (*chhathi*). A month after the Dhobi again takes away the mother's clothes and washes them. The mother bathes, throws away all the earthen vessels, which were in the delivery-room (*saur*), and changes the water pots in the house. Then she cooks for the family and is pure. The extension of the period of impurity, as compared with those in the cognate tribes, marks the strong dread felt by primitive races of the menstrual and parturition discharges.[1]

Puberty ceremony.

10. There is no actual ceremony at puberty, but the initiation of the child into caste is represented by the ear-boring (*kanchhedan*), which takes place in

---

[1] On this question, see *Majhwâr*, para. 35.

the fifth year, and after which the child must conform to caste regulations in the matter of food.

Marriage ceremony.

11. The marriage ceremony closely follows that of the Bhuînhârs, and there is a clear survival of marriage by capture in the custom by which, when he comes to be married, the bridegroom marches straight into the inner room and drags out the bride to the marriage shed, while she carries on a pretended struggle with him. The binding portion of the ceremony is the marking of the forehead of the pair by the bride's father with a mixture of curds and rice. There appears to be no trace of the Palamau custom by which oil or *ghi* is poured over the head and allowed to run down the face.[1] If the betrothal is annulled by either side the bride-price must be returned.

Death ceremonies.

12. Unmarried persons and those who die of small-pox or cholera are buried: all others are cremated. As among all the other Dravidian races, the dead are buried with the head to the South.[2] When a corpse is burnt, the feet are placed to the South. The ashes are floated away (*serwa dena*) by being thrown into a running stream on the day of cremation. The final ceremony, the "tenth" (*daswân*), is done on any day which may be convenient. On that day all shave and wash their clothes, and when they come to the house of the dead man, each one touches with his finger a mixture of oil and turmeric; after which they eat together, and the death impurity ceases.

Ancestor worship.

13. At this "tenth day" ceremony they kill and eat a goat in the name of the deceased, that he may not return and trouble them. When the dead are neglected, they return in evil dreams and bring death and disease. They are propitiated by offering a sacrifice under a *sâl* (*shorea robusta*) tree. In the month of Aghan, there is a special worship of the dead, when a cock and goat are sacrificed in their honour. The worshippers cower down in abject terror and murmur "Fathers! protect our children and our cattle."

Religion and festivals.

14. They pretend to be Hindus, but their worship is of a non-Aryan type. They worship the Dih, or collective village gods, and a female deity, Sairi

---

[1] Forbes, *Settlement Report*, quoted in the *Statistical Account of Bengal*, XVI., 297.
[2] Dalton, *Descriptive Ethnology*, 158.

Devi[1] with offerings of fowls, goats, and a burnt sacrifice (*hom*). The time for this worship is on a Monday in the months of Sâwan or Baisâkh. They have no temple, but offer the sacrifice under a *sâl* (*shorea robusta*) tree. At the same time they worship deceased ancestors and propitiate Mother Earth (*Dharti Mâta*) by pouring a little milk or liquor on the ground. They do not seem to have any knowledge of Gohet, which is one of their local gods in Lohârdaga.[2] Any one may make this offering. In each house there is a small mud platform dedicated to the sainted dead. The village gods and Sairi Devi are worshipped at the ordinary village shrine under a tree in the jungle. In all cases of sacrifice, the worshippers consume the offering. They have three festivals—the Sâwani, Baisâkhi, and Phagua or Holi. On the two first, so called from the months in which they take place, they offer a burnt sacrifice (*hom*), a goat, and a fowl to the local gods and Sairi Devi. These festivals are held in the light fortnight of the month and usually on a Monday or Friday: but Monday is more usual. At the Phagua, they do not burn the Holi, but, as at the other festivals, drink and practise rude debauchery. They believe that evil spirits (*bhût, pret*) live in the *mahua, sâl,* and *pîpal* trees: at such trees they make offerings and will not cut them or climb their branches. They also believe in a vague way that Devi lives in certain hills and mountains where they occasionally offer a goat. For this animal they have a peculiar respect.[3] Before they sacrifice a goat, they feed the animal on a few grains of rice, and then pour water on its head before sacrifice. This is called "the worship of the goat" (*bakra pûjan*). Sometimes, after worship, the goat is released in the jungles as a scape-goat, and this is particularly done when they worship Devi during an epidemic of small-pox.

Omens, oaths, ordeals.

15. Their omens, oaths, and ordeals are the same as those of cognate tribes like the Bhuiyârs and Bhuiyas. Dreams are interpreted by the senior man of

---

[1] The common explanation of her name is because "she moves about" (Arabic *sair*); but this is very improbable. She may be connected with Sewanriya, who appears to be a deity of boundaries; see *Bhuînhâr*, para. 16.

[2] Risley, *Tribes and Castes*, II., 164.

[3] It is curious that the Bengal Parahiyas have a tradition that their tribe formerly held sheep and deer sacred, and used the dung of these animals to smear floors with, as they now use cowdung.—Dalton, *Descriptive Ethnology*, 131, note.

They were possibly the tribal totems. The Mirzapur Parahiyas seem to have transferred this feeling of respect to the goat.

the family, and always imply the displeasure of the sainted dead. Disease always comes from them, and in such cases an Ojha is consulted. Of the Evil Eye, they assert they have no knowledge.

Taboos.

16. Beef is not eaten, but they admit that this rule is of modern growth and in imitation of their Hindu neighbours. They will not touch a Dom, Chamâr, Ghasiya, or Dharkâr. They will not eat food cooked by any one but a clansman. Women are not allowed to eat pork or to join in worship. A man cannot touch his younger brother's wife, and connection with her is considered the worst form of incest. They will not mention by name the dead, nor their fathers, nor the headman of the tribe.

Social customs.

17. They will not eat beef or the flesh of the horse, camel, ass, alligator, monkey, lizard, or snake. Any other kind of meat is allowed. Women are not allowed to eat pork. The men eat before the women, and they have no ceremony at meals. They do not smoke the water-pipe (*huqqa*), but use those made of leaves known as *chungi*,[1] and chew the dry tobacco (*surti*). They use *bhang* and liquor freely, which are believed to keep off malaria, but habitual drunkenness is considered discreditable. They salute each other in the form known as *pāēlagi*, but they are now beginning to do the ordinary *salám* to strangers and superiors. Generally, in the presence of a superior, they stand on one leg, take off what answers to a turban, and bow the head to the ground. They speak a sort of broken Hindi much intermixed with Mundâri and Gondi. They rank fairly high among these jungle tribes, having much the same status as the Chero. Chamârs, Dharkârs, and Doms will eat food cooked by them, and they pride themselves on their abstinence from beef as a mark of respectability. Kalwârs drink with them, but will not take water from their hands. The men wear earrings of gold or brass in both ears: the women pewter anklets (*pairi*) and brass wristlets (*churla*). They now do a little cultivation, but quite recently they never stored any grain, plucking and parching the crop as it got ripe. They usually pay about three rupees per annum for as much land (*tora*) as they can cultivate with a single plough. They make a living by cutting and selling wood and bamboos, and by collecting and exchanging forest produce, such as lac, silk-cocoons, and various dyes, fibres, etc. But they are

---

[1] See *Korwa*, para. 13.

a miserable people, living in little huts, apart from each other, along the hills, and with little clan feeling or effective tribal organization.

18. The following account of their brethren just across the border in Palamau may be quoted:—"In their habits and customs they present a curious mixture of the Hindu and the Aborigines: they are certainly not pure Mundas: they may be Kurkus, who are a branch of the Munda family. They differ so much in personal appearance, that it is difficult to assign them any distinct physiological features. I have seen many of them that might almost be mistaken for Korwas, while others are a tall, fair, handsome race of men, with features rather Aryan than otherwise, and so athletic and powerful, that the expression 'as strong as a Parhaiya' has almost passed into a proverb: these last have none of the Negrito stamp about them. Many of them are to be found residing in the plains, but they generally choose the more jungly villages, and reside in a separate hamlet (*tola*): some are good cultivators, but the majority, like the Brijiyas, live in the hill ranges, and roam about from spur to spur, clearing small patches of ground, and cultivating a few hardy crops: they also bring down to the plains honey, bees-wax, resin, lac, and other jungle products, which they barter for grain, salt, tobacco, and cloth. Most of them have Brâhmans as priests, and employ the barber at marriages. Hindus of every class will drink water from their hands, and eat any food, but rice, that has been cooked by them: and, strange to say, they carry their Hindu prejudices so far that they will not eat *ghi* that has been kept in a jar (*kuppa*) made of cow hide. They always smear the cooking-places with cowdung, and eat barefooted like the Hindus. They know nothing whatever of their former history: in fact the only ancient custom of the tribe that I have been able to discover is that they formerly held deer and sheep sacred, and used the manure of these animals, where we now use cowdung. Notwithstanding their affectation of Hinduism, they still adhere to many of their old customs, which decidedly point to their origin. Marriage rarely takes place before the age of puberty. In their wedded life they are chaste and moral: before this takes place, the intercourse between the sexes is unrestricted. They never marry out of their tribe, and any woman found misbehaving with a male of an alien tribe is at once outcasted; and so with the males. Notwithstanding the employment of Brâhmans and barbers, their marriage ceremony is

The Palamau Parahiyas.

simple and decidedly aboriginal. I have never witnessed one of their marriages, and am unable, therefore, to describe all that takes place: but the principal part of the ceremony consists in pouring *ghi* or oil upon the forehead of the bride, and allowing it to run down the face. If it trickles from the centre of the forehead straight down the ridge of the nose, the fates are propitious and the marriage will be a happy one: if, on the contrary, the *ghi* or oil trickles down to the right or left, it is a sign either that the girl will shortly die or prove unfaithful: and very often in this case the marriage is broken off, and the maiden has to wait till another seeks her hand." [1]

Paramahansa.—A general term for any notable ascetic, more especially one of the higher order of Sannyâsis and more particularly Dandi Sannyâsis. "He is the ascetic who is solely occupied with the investigation of Brahma, or spirit, and who is equally indifferent to pleasure or pain, insensible to heat or cold, and incapable of satiety or want. Agreeably to this definition, individuals are sometimes met with who pretend to have attained such a degree of perfection; in proof of it, they go naked in all weathers, never speak, and never indicate any natural want. What is brought to them as alms or food by any person is received by the attendants, whom their supposed sanctity or confederation of interest attaches to them, and by these attendants they are fed and served on all occasions as if they were as helpless as infants. They are usually included among the Saiva ascetics, but it may be doubted whether the classification is correct." [2]

Pardesi (Literally "foreigners").—A class of thieves and swindlers who, in the old Criminal reports, are classed with the Jogis of Aligarh and the Daleras of Bareilly. In 1868, a gang of them was captured and convicted in Gorakhpur, since when nothing more has been recorded of them. But recent enquiries show that there are still twenty-five families of them in Gorakhpur and about as many in the adjoining district of Champâran, where, however, they do not appear under that name in Mr. Risley's lists. The Gorakhpur Pardesis are still suspected of swindling in the disguise of *faqîrs* or pilgrims. They are not shown separately in the returns of the last Census.

Parihâr.—(Sanskrit *parihâra* "repelling") A sept of Râjputs

---

[1] W. L. R. Forbes, *Report*, p. 45.
[2] Wilson, *Essays*, I., 231 *sq.*

whose name is popularly derived from the fact that, when the first of the race issued from the *Agnikunda* or "fire-pit," he was placed as guardian of the gate (*prithahdwára*). The story how they supplanted the Kachhwâhas is given in connection with that sept. The Parihâr dynasty of Gwâlior [1] lasted for seven generations from 1129 to 1211 A.D. Kutab-ud-dîn Aibeg took the city in 1196; during the short reign of Azam it was re-taken by the Hindus, who held it till 1232 A.D., when the Parihâr dynasty became extinct. To the south of the Bolingæ Ptolemy places the Porvaroi with their three towns, named Bridama, Tholobana, and Malaita. They were probably either the Parihâr or Panwâr Râjputs, who occupied this part of the country from a very early date. The Parihâr Râja of Uchahara traces his lineage to a very remote date. As the Parihârs are said to have been subjected by the Kalachûris they were probably in possession of the country before the Kalachûri conquest of Kalinjar and the establishment of the Kalachûri or Chedi era in 249 A.D. They claim to have preceded the Chandels and Baghels in Bundelkhand and Rîwa. The Mahoba Khand [2] mentions the Parihâr minister of Parmâl, the Chandel, in the twelfth century and must therefore, be at least contemporary with the Chandels. The head of the family now lives in the Native State of Jagni. They call themselves descendants of Govind Deva, and Sârang Deva grandson of the celebrated Parihâr Râja Jhajhâr Singh of Hamîrpur who emigrated there from Mârwâr. According to Colonel Tod [3] the capital city of the Parihârs was Mandâwar, from which they were treacherously expelled by Chondu, the leader of the Râthaur exiles from Kanauj. He notes that there is a considerable colony of them at the confluence of the Chambal with the Sindh and the Kuâri, "who are the most notorious body of thieves in the annals of Thag history."

The Parihârs of the North-Western Provinces and Oudh.

2. They have maintained this evil reputation as inhabiting in Etâwah [4] "that intricate and inaccessible net-work of ravines that abuts on the Pachnadi as the confluence of the Jumna, Chambal, Sindh, Kuâri, and Pâhuj is here called. They have been a particularly lawless and desperate community." They here fix their rise after the defeat of Anangpâl of Delhi. Some of them have

---

[1] Cunningham, *Archæological Reports*, II., 376, *sq.*
[2] *North-Western Provinces Gazetteer*, I., 267.
[3] *Annals*, I., 108, *sq.*
[4] *Census Report, N.-W. P., 1865* I., *App.* 85.

recently raised their importance by marriages with Chauhân and Sengar families. The sept in the Unâo[1] District inhabit the Pargana of Sikandarpur and possess a Chaurâsi or estate of eighty-four villages. According to their tradition they came from Jigini or Srinagar in Kashmîr. "About three hundred years ago, in the time of the Emperor Humayun, a Dikshit girl from Parenda was married to the son of the Parihâr Râja, who lived in Jigini across the Jumna. The bridegroom came with a large escort of his friends and brotherhood to celebrate the marriage and the party on their journey passed through Sarosi. As they sat round a well (the locality of which is still shown, though the well has fallen) they asked who were the lords of the fort which stood not far off. They were told that it was held by Dhobis and other Sûdras who held the neighbouring country. The procession then went on to Parenda and, returning, conducted the bride to her home. Just before the Holi festival, a party headed by Bhâgê Sinh returned, waited for the evening of that riotous feast, and then, when the guards of the fort were heavy with wine, and no danger was looked for, suddenly attacked and slaughtered them and made themselves masters of the surrounding country." Their property became reduced because the law of primogeniture did not apply in the sept, and it gradually became divided among the heirs. They intermarry with the Kachhwâhas and Chauhâns of the West, but have to pay heavily for their brides. They seem to have disputed with the Gautams for the territory on the Jumna below Kâlpi, but were both finally overcome by the Chandels. Dr. Buchanan[2] asserts a connection between the Eastern branch and the Bhars; but in Gorakhpur they are held in good repute. In Azamgarh[3] they say that they came from Narwan and settled in Pargana Muhammadâbâd, whence they were driven out by the Gaharwârs. In Jâlaun they give brides to the Bais and Gautam septs; and take girls in marriage from the Kachhwâha, Bhadauriya, Chandel and Râthaur. In Hamîrpur they marry their girls to the Mainpuri Chauhâns, Bhadauriyas, Jâdons and Râthaurs; and their sons to girls of the Dikshit, Bais, Chandel, Gautam, Sengar, Gaur and Chauhân of the Cawnpur District. Their *Gotra* is said in Agra to be Kasyapa.

---

[1] Elliott, *Chronicles*, 58, *sqq*.

[2] *Eastern India, II.*, 463, Dr. Oppert (*Original Inhabitants of Bharatvarsa*, 93) would connect their names with the Dravidian Pâradas.

[3] *Settlement Report*, 62.

Distribution of the Parihâr Râjputs according to the Census of 1891.

Districts.	Number.	Districts.	Number.
Meerut . . .	20	Jâlaun . . .	2,410
Aligarh . . .	8	Lalitpur . . .	428
Mathura . . .	34	Benares . . .	5
Agra	2,772	Mirzapur . . .	126
Farrukhâbâd . .	996	Ballia	407
Mainpuri . . .	685	Gorakhpur . . .	93
Etâwah . . .	3,324	Azamgarh . . .	1,146
Etah	93	Tarâi	8
Bijnor	37	Lucknow . . .	68
Budâun . . .	58	Unâo	2,498
Morâdâbâd . . .	22	Râê Bareli . . .	721
Shâhjahânpur . .	52	Sîtapur . . .	191
Pilibhît . . .	11	Hardoi . . .	223
Cawnpur . . .	3,162	Kheri	84
Fatehpur . . .	1,646	Faizâbâd . . .	1
Bânda	732	Bahrâich . . .	134
Hamîrpur . . .	3,277	Sultânpur . . .	292
Allahâbâd . . .	1,346	Partâbgarh . . .	189
Jhânsi	4,162	Bârabanki . . .	419
		Total .	31,880

Parwâl; Parwâr, a sub caste of Banyas, enumerated in the former Census in Bundelkhand, Cawnpur and Agra, but who are not found in the returns of the Census of 1891. To the east of the Province they have two endogamous sub-divisions—Samaiya and Parwâl and twelve *gotras* with twelve sections (*mûl*). These *gotras* with their sections are thus given in Mirzapur:—

(1) Bachhalya with sections—Nârd; Pachlori; Dhumsar; Chharir; Rakari; Kadua; Barê Sareri; Ahari; Kathari; Jageswar; Nagâich; Tahari.

(2) Goil with sections—Bâr; Nagari; Kharo; Bhuri; Lubâich; Chhola; Baisâkhiya; Karkach; Godhu; Sara; Gâgero; Barahad.

(3) Bâsil with sections—Deda; Deriya; Bala; Haidam; Doha; Raka; Râvandim; Chhalkar; Sakheswar; Sadravad; Chandari; Pahu.

(4) Khohil with sections—Setsâgar; Kahala; Rathiya; Chhorari; Rohrairi, Kharhat; Sonharu; Lagait; Bagari; Khadhari; Birâri; Dhokhadari.

(5) Gohil with sections—Chhatra; Gaha; Mamala; Mahâdim; Baromaro; Indradhar; Baru; Kharahat; Punhara; Gabari; Papihad; Khalasi.

(6) Mâthil with sections—Mar; Rodo; Bâhil; Kathahai; Sakahman; Mandlari; Kharaich; Jhulari; Idoha; Gausil; Bhariwaro; Bharhuri.

(7) Kausil with sections—Bahuriya; Masta; Richa; Osil; Kochhichar; Gagwâro; Suchaha; Sirerê; Pabubarê; Chachâri; Basawalo; Sarbsola.

(8) Bharil with sections—Bharu; Big; Khona; Iga; Kuba; Pâbub; Kuchari; Bhagwant; Harari; Bagari; Horir; Gahori.

(9) Kâsil with sections—Ujiya; Divkar; Sarbchhâi; Sola; Digaya; Puthwar; Dhana; Lata; Dhodhara; Dogar; Sanga; Indmur.

(10) Phâgil with sections—Sobar; Gaghari; Phâgil; Buhrerê; Chhirari; Baresara; Mangala; Balaichrê; Jajarê.

(11) Kohil with sections—Padmâwat; Bebaro; Ghachi; Chhagati; Dahari; Horari.

(12) Bâchhil with sections—Irari; Bibikuttam; Basil; Gaha; Gâjaro.

This list is imperfect in the names of some of the sections, but it illustrates the fertility of invention exercised in establishing this tribal organisation.

Rule of exogamy.

2. A man cannot marry in his own *gotra* or in any of its sections; in the section of his maternal uncle, father's maternal uncle, grandmother's maternal uncle, maternal grandfather's maternal uncle, maternal grandmother's maternal uncle.

3. In their marriage ceremonies the Parwâls agree with those of the Mârwâris up to the stage where the procession goes to the house of the bride. But when the bridegroom reaches the door one peculiar ceremony is performed. They do not at this time worship Gauri and Ganesa as other Hindu castes do, which is known as the *duârpûja*. Among the Parwâls the bridegroom is there decorated with bangles and ear-rings and then joins his party at the reception place (*janwânsa*). Another special ceremony, known as *bol*, is also performed. In this the bride's father returns to the bridegroom Rs. 2-8 out of the sum paid by his father at the betrothal. Then the bride in a litter and the bridegroom on a horse walk round the nuptial shed—a ceremony called *binâyaki*. On this day the father of the boy feeds his relatives and friends on sweetmeats which is known as the *chabeni* or "giving of parched grain." On the fourth day the ceremony of *ganauna* is done. The bride and bridegroom, dressed in new clothes, stand under the marriage shed and the bride takes some rice and sugar in her hands and walks seven times round the shed. When she finishes the seventh circuit she puts the rice and sugar in the hands of her husband. On the fifth day is the *palaka upachâr*. The pair sit on a cot and on it is laid the dowry. After this the pair go to the place where the wedding party is being entertained and distribute sweets among them. Then the bride's brother takes her home. Next is the *keura* when the women of the bride's family go to where the bridegroom's party are halting and sing songs of abuse directed against the father of the bridegroom—a survival of marriage by capture. After this is the *phâg*. It consists in the relatives of the bride throwing coloured water on the friends of the bridegroom, as is done at the Phagua or Holi. They receive fresh clothes from the girl's father to replace those that have been soiled. Last comes the ceremony of *kahas bandhâi*. The father of the bridegroom distributes presents to dependents, such as the barber, washerman, etc., and the bridegroom comes to the bride's house and opens one of the fastenings of the marriage shed (*mânro*) and receives some money or ornaments from his wife's father.

Marriage ceremonies.

Pâsi; Passi [1] (Sanskrit *pâshika*, "one who uses a noose") a Dravidian tribe principally found in the Eastern Districts of the

[1] Based on enquiries at Mirzapur and notes by M. Sayyid Ali Bahâdur, Deputy Collector, Partâbgarh; Mr. E. J. Kitts, C. S.; M. Mahâdeo Prasâd, Head Master, High School, Pilibhit.

PÂSI.

Province and in Oudh. Their original occupation appears to have been tapping various kinds of the date tree for its sap, which is fermented into târi. Mr. Nesfield's idea that the name implies that they have recently emerged from the savage state of noosing birds does not seem to be justified by actual facts.

Traditions of origin.

2. The Mirzapur tradition of the origin of the tribe runs thus:— One day a man was going to kill a number of cows. Parasurâma was at that time practising austerities in the jungle. Hearing the cries of the sacred animals he rushed to their assistance, but the cow-killer was aided by his friends. So Parasurâma made five men out of *kusa* grass and brought them to life by letting drops of his perspiration fall upon them. Hence arose the name Pâsi from the Hindi *pasîna* "sweat" (Sanskrit *prasvinna*, "covered with perspiration"). The men thus created rescued the cows. Then they returned to Parasurâma and asked him to provide them with a wife. Just at that moment a Kâyasth girl was passing by and her Parasurâma seized and made over to the Pâsis—a remarkable survival of a tradition of primitive polyandry. From them sprang the Kaithwâs sub-caste.

3. In parts of Oudh they have a tradition which professes to explain their connection with other possibly allied tribes on the basis of a series of ridiculous folk etymologies. Thus the Râjpâsis say that they are a branch of the Pâsis and originally came from Gujarât. Tilok Chand, instead of being the eponymous hero of the Bais Râjputs, was according to them a Bhar king and called his family Râjbansi or "those of royal lineage" and from this came the name Râjpâsi. After a time they fell out and some took to their beds (*khatya*) and were called Khatîks; others took to the trees in a grove (*bâgh*) and were called Bâchhal; while the remnant were called Râjpâsi or "royal" Pâsis. It is said that the Pâsis and Arakhs there always claim kindred with the Bhars.[1] All through Oudh the Pâsis have traditions that they were lords of the country and that their kings reigned at Sandîla, Dhaurahra, Mitauli and Râmkot in the Districts of Kheri, Hardoi and Unâo.[2] Râmkot, where the town of Bângarmau in Unâo now stands, is said to have been one of their chief strongholds. The last of the lords of Râmkot, Râja Santhar, threw off his allegiance to Kanauj and

---

[1] *Lucknow Settlement Report*, XXIV.
[2] *Oudh Gazetteer*, II., 207.

refused to pay tribute. On this Râja Jaychand gave the Gânjer country to the Banâphar heroes, Alha and Udal and they attacked and destroyed Râmkot, leaving it the shapeless mass of ruins which we now find it.[1] Similar traditions prevail in other parts of Oudh. In the Kheri District the Pâsis, Râjpâsis, Arakhs, Mothis and Khatîks are looked on as kindred castes. The Râjpâsis of that part of Oudh say that they are descended from Ratan Dat Sinh, a Thâkur of Pataungarh, near Nîmkhâr, and a Pâsi woman who bore him several children. His descendants went so far as to claim a marriage alliance with the Ahban Râjputs. The head of the clan is said to have yielded consent on the ground of the Râjput paternity of the Râjpâsis, and to have invited the whole of the tribe to the betrothal feast. He plied them well with wine to which the tribe is to this day much addicted, and while they were in a state of drunken insensibility, some seven or eight hundred of them were put to death and their estates seized by the victors. Those who escaped are said to have fled and settled in Bângar, Mahmûdi and the northern part of Sîtapur.[2]

4. Another legend tells that during the time Parasurâma was incarnate there was an austere devotee called Kuphal who was asked by Brahma to demand of him a boon, whereupon he requested that he might be perfected in the art of thieving. His request was granted and there is a well-known verse regarding the devotions of Kuphal, the pith of which is that the mention of the name of Kuphal, who received a boon from Brahma, removes all fear of thieves; and the mention of his three wives—Mâya (illusion), Nidra (sleep) and Mohani (enchantment) deprives thieves of success in their attempts against the property of those who repeat these names.

5. There is also a tradition that a descendant of Kuphal, named Karan, who dwelt in the jungle and is now deified by his race, had two wives, the one a Chhatri and the other an Ahîrin. From the former of these, it is asserted, sprang the Râjpâsis and Bhîls and from the latter the Khatîks.

6. Still another tradition runs that the Pâsis came originally from Kacchh and settled in Kanauj. According to this form of the tribal legend there were four brothers who were called out to

---

[1] Elliott, *Chronicles of Unâo*, 24.

[2] Carnegy, *Notes*, 61 *sq.* *Sîtapur Settlement Report*, 88.

fight, and of these Mohan alone responded to the summons. He was killed and of him were sprung the Râjpâsis, while the descendants of the other brothers, who lived to fight another day, are known as Arakhs, Marghas and Thothos. A heroic Pâsi, named Siu of Barniya figures prominently in the legend of Alha and Udal.

7. In the Partâbgarh form of the story the Pâsis, Arakhs, Khatîks and Pachhars are all one. The original Pâsis had a great fight with the Râja of Newâr. Some of them were cowards and hid under a cot (*khatya*) whence they came to be called Khatîks; others behind an *Arka* plant (*Calotropis gigantea*) whence they came to be named Arakhs. Again it is said that there was a Pâsi, named Mahiyan, who was in the service of the Râja of Newâri, and he was the Râja's watchman. One day his pigs trespassed into the fields of a Murâo, named Koeli. He preferred a complaint to that Râja and demanded nine lakhs of rupees as damages. The Râja offered to give him four lakhs, but he insisted, in addition, that Mahiyan should be banished from the kingdom. When Mahiyan was ordered to go into banishment he refused and, summoning his castemen, defeated the army of the Râja; but he spared his life and compelled him to pay a fourth (*chauth*) of his revenue to the Pâsis. This is said to have happened just before the wars of Alha and Udal.

8. Another story current in Partâbgarh is that the ancestor of the tribe was one Ratan Daksha. When Parasurâma destroyed the Kshatriyas he killed Râja Vena as well as the others, and then the Râni kept the corpse of her husband and implored Parasurâma to create from it a man to continue the race. Parasurâma touched the head of Râja Vena and out of it sprung a man of dark complexion with a bow and arrows in his hand. He was the first Râjpâsi and to him was entrusted the duty of watchman of the kingdom. In the form of the story current in Pilibhît the Rishis were offended with Râja Vena for his impiety and killed him; but at the prayer of his Râni they formed a man out of his sweat (*pasîna*) and he was the first Pâsi.

9. From all this mass of tradition it may be gathered that there is a close connection between the Pâsis, Arakhs, Mothis and Khatîks, which from their appearance and manners is not antecedently improbable. Mr. Carnegy tries to make out a closer connection between the Pâsis and other Râjput tribes of Oudh, such as the Bais, than is perhaps warranted by the facts.

10. As might have been anticipated from the discrepant legends of their origin and connection with other tribes, the internal organisation of the caste cannot be ascertained with absolute certainty. At the recent Census they were enumerated in six sub castes—Arakh, Baurâsi, Kaithwâns, Mothi and Râjpâsi. In Mirzapur the Pâsis name five endogamous sub-castes—Kaithwâs who, as already stated, claim Kâyasth origin; Bhar, a tribe which though perhaps allied to the Pâsis it is more convenient to discuss separately; Pasmangta who are said to be begging Pâsis (*Pâsi mângna,* "to beg") and to be so called because they receive alms from other Pâsis at marriages; Baurâsi said to be so called because one of the five original Pâsis created by Parasurâma or Parameswar once ran amuck (*baurâna*). To the east of the Province Pâsis are often designated by the general term Pâsi-Baurâsi. Last come the Pahri who are said to take their name from their duty of keeping guard (*pahra*); they are often classed as a distinct tribe. Mr. Sherring[1] from Benares gives another list—Jaiswâra, who like the Banya and other clans of the same name take their title from the old town of Jais; Kainswât or Kaithwân, who correspond to the Kaithwâns or Kaithwâs of the other lists; Gûjar, who, of course, are a distinct tribe; Tirsuliya, who take their name from the *trisûla* or three-bladed knife with which they pierce the stem of the palm tree. Dr. Buchanan[2] makes a curious mistake in connecting the name of this sub-caste with the sacred *tulasi,* because they have planted the sacred *Ocymum,* called *tirsûli* in the vulgar tongue, and have thus become a sort of Hindus. Next in Mr. Sherring's list follow the Pasiwân; Chiryamâr or "bird-killers" (*chirya-mârna*) who are more properly included among Baheliyas, a possibly allied tribe; Byâdha (Sanskrit *vyâdha,* "a hunter") who also come more properly under Baheliyas; Bihâri or "residents of Bihâr" and Bhar which it is advisable to treat separately. In Bihâr[3] there are four sub-castes—Byâdha, Gaiduha, a word which seems to mean "milkers of cows" (*gâé-duhna*);—Kamâni and Tirsuliya, of whom the Byâdha say that their original occupation was cultivating the water chestnut (*singhâra*); but they now tap date trees like the other sub-castes. A list from Partâb-

Tribal organisation.

---

[1] *Hindu Tribes and Castes,* I., 389.
[2] *Eastern India,* I., 175.
[3] Risley, *Tribes and Castes,* II., 166.

garh, again, gives, Râjpâsi, Gûjar, Kaithwâns, Guâl, who are really Ahîrs, Mangta, Baurâsi, Arakh, Khatîk and Pachhar. From all this it seems obvious that the term Pâsi is merely occupational and includes a number of distinct tribes, whose only connection is the common occupation of extracting the juice of the date palm. The complete Census returns show 305 Pâsi sub-divisions of the familiar type. Those of the greatest local importance are the Baheliya and Bhîl of Budâun, the Aheriya and Bhîl of Morâdâbâd; the Parasarâmi of Allahâbâd and Fatehpur, the Boriya of Fatehpur; the Rewâs of Bânda; the Baheliya and Bharê of Mirzapur; the Baheliya, Manwâs and Tarmâli of Ghâzipur; the Chaurâsi of Basti, Sultânpur and Bârabanki; the Bhadauriya of the Tarâi; the Banya of Lucknow; the Boriya, Mahtiya and Parasarâmi of Unâo; the Boriya of Râê Bareli; the Bachar, Dhânuk and Khatîk of Sîtapur; the Banya of Gonda; the Bachar, Chunarha, Dhânuk and Khatîk of Bahrâich.

Marriage rules.

11. It does not appear that Pâsis actually introduce outsiders into the caste, but it is reported from Partâbgarh that if a woman of the tribe become pregnant by a stranger to the tribe and her child be born in the house of her father or husband it will be accepted as a Pâsi of pure blood and admitted to all tribal privileges. The rule of exogamy prevailing in the endogamous sub-castes is not very rigidly fixed. Many Pâsis say that they bar all near relations generally. In Mirzapur they fix the prohibited degrees as the families of the maternal uncle, paternal uncle, maternal and paternal aunts for seven generations in the descending line. Marriage questions are decided by the tribal council (*panchâyat*) which is presided over by a chairman (*chaudhari*) selected at each meeting from among the most influential adult males present. The council deals specially with cases of immorality and pollution caused by journeys across "the black water" (*kâlapâni*) which the criminal pursuits of the tribe occasionally necessitate. When a woman is detected in an intrigue with a clansman the relations on both sides have to give a tribal feast and the offenders are then admitted to caste. In the same way if a man offend with a strange woman he has to purchase his re-admission; but if a woman intrigue with a stranger she is permanently expelled. Concubinage, even with a woman of the tribe, is in Mirzapur punished by expulsion. Immorality in both sexes, provided it be inter-tribal, is lightly regarded. Marriage

takes place from the age of five or seven to sixteen; but infant marriage is the rule. No bride or bridegroom price is taken; out the friends of the girl are expected to give something to the relations of the bridegroom by way of dowry. If either party become blind or leprous after marriage a separation can be procured with the leave of the council. Widow marriage and the levirate both prevail. If the deceased husband leave a brother, who is of age to marry and is not already married, he is expected to take over the widow. The regular *sagâi* marriage is performed only in the case of virgin widows and they are as a rule married to widowers. In the case of widows whose marriage has been consummated there is practically no ceremonial of any kind and such a woman can with the permission of the tribal council live with a man as his acknowledged mistress (*rakhui*). This form of union is recognised after a tribal feast. In the ordinary *sagâi* the only ceremony is that the intended husband goes to the widow's house with a few friends taking with him some jewelry (generally five articles for luck) and a suit of clothes. The friends on both sides eat together and during the night in a dark room the man marks the parting of the woman's hair with red lead and next morning she is dressed in her new clothes and taken home. In the case of the levirate there is no fiction of ascribing the children of the subsequent union to the elder brother. If the widow marry an outsider she loses all rights in the property of her late husband. If she marry her husband's brother he has the usufruct of the property of his late brother and manages it until the sons of the first marriage come of age, when they succeed.

Adoption and succession.

12. The Pâsis of Mirzapur profess to be able to state elaborate rules on the subject of adoption in imitation of those prevailing among the higher Hindu castes; but practically a man only adopts his brother's son with leave of the council and there is no recognised religious element in the transaction. The same is the case with succession. A man's heirs are his sons or in default of sons his associated brethren. Primogeniture is so far recognised that the eldest son gets a quarter share in excess as compared with his younger brothers. Widows have a life interest, but this depends on their continuing chaste and not marrying by *sagâi*. In default of a daughter or a daughter's son the inheritance devolves on him who performs the funeral ceremonies of the deceased.

Birth ceremonies.

13. During pregnancy the Eastern Pâsis make vows and a sacrifice to Birtiya, the village pantheon (*dih*) and to Phûlmati Devi. If the mother has an easy delivery these deities are honoured with an offering of spirits (*khappar*) and a hog (*mâl*). They have no ceremony on the sixth day (*chhathi*). The Chamârin midwife attends for six days and receives as her remuneration four sers of grain and four pice, if the baby be a boy, and half that amount if it be a girl. On the twelfth day is the *barahi* ceremony when the house is cleaned and the earthen pots replaced. Mother and child are bathed by the barber's wife, her hand and toe nails are cut and her feet stained with lac dye (*mahâwar*). Then the father of the child sacrifices a young hog to Birtiya and pours a libation of spirits on the ground. After this he invites a few of the tribesmen and feeds them on the pork and boiled rice. By this dinner the birth impurity is finally removed. When the mother goes first to draw water from the well after her confinement she places a handful of rice on the platform and bows down to it. The husband does not cohabit with his wife for six months after her delivery. The only ceremony of initiation is the ear-boring (*kanchhedan*, *kanbedha*) which is done by the village goldsmith when the child is five or six years old. His fee for doing this is one pice. The family feed on choice food that day and from that time the child has to conform to caste rules in the matter of eating and drinking.

Marriage ceremonies.

14. The marriage is of the usual low caste type. The negotiations are commenced by the father of the bride who goes to the boy's house with the salutation *Râm ! Râm !* as he enters. The boy is sent for and approved. The Pandit is called in and approves the horoscopes of the pair (*râsbarg*). His future father-in-law gives the boy a rupee and this completes the betrothal (*mangni*). Then follows the *tilak* or marking of the boy's forehead by his father-in-law. This is known to the east of the Province as the "water drinking" (*pâni pîna*) and the bride's Brâhman and barber take with them a betrothal gift consisting of a tray (*thâli*), a cocoanut (*nâriyal*), one or two pieces of cloth, some sweetmeats and one rupee or eight annas in cash. A feast of rice and pork follows and on that day the wedding day is fixed. Then comes the rite of *matmangara* or collection of the sacred earth (for which see *Bhuiya*, paragraph 14) and the erection of the nuptial shed (*mânro*), which is made of four bamboos

and contains in the centre a plough beam (*haris*) and some wooden images of parrots (*suga*). On that day the Pandit binds round the wrist of the boy a bracelet (*kankan*) consisting of iron surrounding a mango leaf and some mustard seed to keep off ill-luck. Next follows the anointing of the bride and bridegroom with oil and turmeric, and on the day before the procession starts the boy's father sacrifices a hog and pours a libation of spirits on the ground in honour of Agwân Deva, the herald deity who presides over enterprises, the Pânchon Pîr and the goddess Phûlmati. The other ceremonies are of the usual type. The binding part of the marriage ceremony is the bridegroom rubbing some red lead on the ploughshare set up in the nuptial hut and smearing some on the parting of the bride's hair, after which they revolve five times round the ploughshare. Next follows the *kohabar* ceremony when the married pair retire into an inner room. The significance of this rite is explained in paragraph 18 of the account of the Majhwârs. Five days after the return of the bride with her husband, the bridegroom's sister flings the marriage festoons (*bandarwâr*) into running water with the sacred water pots, (*kalsa*), and on her way back she worships every banyan and *pîpal* tree she comes across with an offering of rice and water.

Death ceremonies.

15. The dead are disposed of in the usual Hindu fashion. They usually cremate their dead, but sometimes bury them when epidemic disease prevails. When they bury, the head of the corpse is usually laid towards the north and the feet to the south, while the face is slightly turned to the east. Immediately after death a little sugar is put into the mouth of the corpse. After cremation the relatives chew a leaf of bitter *nîm* as a sign of mourning and then eat a little sugar as a protection against demoniacal influence. The cremation is generally followed by a drunken revel at the village grog-shop. Next morning the chief mourner arranges a habitation for the vagrant spirit (*pret*) by fixing some blades of *kusa* grass on the bank of a tank. On this he regularly pours water during the ten days of mourning, and food is left out every night for the use of the ghost along the road by which the body was removed for cremation or burial. The ashes are usually left on the site of the pyre, but some who are more careful collect them for ultimate disposal in the Ganges or some other sacred river.

16. To the east of the Province some of the more advanced Pâsis are often members of the Sâkta sect, but few ever become regularly initiated. Many of them in Mirzapur worship Bandi Mâi, a form of Devi. She has no regular temple, but nearly every house has a platform (*chauri*) in her name and an image of brass or silver is placed upon it. This image is adorned with a necklace (*mâla*) and at every marriage in the family a fresh bead is added to the necklace, of gold for a boy and of silver for a girl. She is worshipped specially at marriages with the sacrifice of a castrated goat (*khassi*) cakes (*pûri laddu*), sweetmeats, rice, milk, flowers and betel leaves. There is no holiday in her honour but she is specially worshipped whenever a vow is made or any particular blessing craved. Others worship Agwân Deva, Phûlmati or the Pânchon Pîr. To these deities pigs and liquor are offered. The household worship of the Pânchon Pîr is often represented by an iron spear (*sâng*) with three points or by five wooden pegs buried in the floor of the court yard. In Partâbgarh they have a large collection of local gods, such as Kâradeva, Miyân, Kambîra, Kshetrpâl or Bhûmiya and Bahirwâr. To the last two pigs and liquor are offered which are consumed by the worshippers. These offerings are made on a Wednesday or a Saturday. In Pilibhît Bhûmiya, or the godling of the soil, is known as Bhûmsen. But Pâsis, like all the lower Hindu castes, are very catholic in their worship and will visit the tomb of any saint (*pîr*) or martyr (*sayyid, shahîd*) which is convenient. They offer water every day to the souls of their deceased ancestors in the first fortnight of Kuâr. In the east of the Province some Pâsis again have quite another set of deities, such as Râm Thâkur, who perhaps represents Râma, Mahâbîr and Bhaironnâth. Râm Thâkur is honoured with the sacrifice of a castrated goat at weddings. Mahâbîr and Bhairon receive a bloodless offering, the former *laddu* sweetmeats and the latter cakes (*bara*) made of the flour of the *urad* pulse. When small-pox breaks out Sîtala Mâi is specially worshipped by women. When the time comes for tapping the date palms they collect a few friends and burn some incense over the sickle (*hansuli*) used for the purpose, and over the wooden strop on which it is sharpened. All classes of Brâhmans will officiate at their marriages and other ceremonies, and do anything for them which does not involve touching them or anything in their houses. Their festivals are those ordinarily observed by Hindus, the Phagua or Holi, Dasami, Diwâli, Kajari, Khichari and Tîj.

Religion.

17. Their demonolatry is that common to the lower class of Hindus. They believe that old trees are occupied by evil spirits (*bhût*) or demons (*deo, bîr*) and to these collectively a pig is offered in the month of Aghan and a little spirits poured on the ground. They generally perform the *srâddha* rite, and some of the wealthier of them go even as far as Gaya for that purpose. They will not cut down or injure the *pîpal* tree which they believe to be the abode of Vasudeva.

Social status and occupation.

18. To the east of the Province the women wear bracelets of glass or lac (*chûri*) on their wrists, necklaces (*guriya*), nose-rings (*nathiya*), ear ornaments (*karanphûl*), heavy pewter anklets (*pairi*). The men wear an ear ornament (*lurka*) and round the neck a gold coin or bead or an image of Sîtala, if the wearer have escaped a severe attack of small-pox. If he has lost his first wife and married another he will hang an image of the dead woman round his neck. This is also very commonly worn as a protective by the second wife and is known as "the co-wife" (*sautin*). Any present made to the new wife is always first offered to this image in order to avoid any jealousy on the part of the ghost. They swear on water or on the head of their eldest son. They believe strongly in witchcraft, possession by evil spirits, the demoniacal theory of disease and the Evil Eye. In such cases the Ojha or Syâna is consulted. They will not eat the flesh of the cow, buffalo, alligator, monkey, horse, jackal or lizard; most of them eat pork, fowls and field rats, sheep, goats and deer, but no meat is eaten in the fortnight in Kuẫr sacred to the dead. Women eat apart from and after the male members of the family. They use tobacco and spirits and the latter often to excess. They salute castemen by the form *pâẽlagi* and their seniors by *Râm! Râm!* Low castes like Chamârs and Bhangis will take water from their hands. As a rule they will eat *kachchi* cooked by their own castemen or by Brâhmans, and *pakki* cooked by a Brâhman, a Râjput, respectable Banyas such as Agarwalâs or Rastâogis or by a Halwâi.

19. A few are landowners, but most of them are day labourers, collectors of palm-juice, or makers of grindstones or curry stones. They bear on the whole an indifferent reputation and in the east of the Province many of them are noted thieves and burglars, who often make long journeys and commit serious crime.

General Sleeman says that in his time it was supposed that there were one hundred thousand families of Pâsis in Oudh, who were skilful thieves and robbers by profession and were formerly Thags and poisoners as well. They generally formed the worst part of the gangs kept up by refractory landowners "who keep Pâsis to fight for them, as they pay themselves out of the plunder and cost little to their employers. They are all armed with bows and arrows and are very formidable at night. They and their refractory employés keep the country in a perpetual state of disorder." Things, of course, have much improved since the British occupation of the Province but "even now in the Bângar the Pâsis pride themselves on taking some evidence of their prowess—a penknife, a handkerchief, from the tents of the English officers who visit their jungles for sport, and with whom they are generally on the best of terms".[1]

---

[1] *Journey through Oudh*, 25.
Sîtapur Settlement Report, 87.
Hardoi Settlement Report, 5.

Distribution of Pâsis according to the Census of 1891.

DISTRICTS.	Arakh.	Baurâsi.	Gûjar	Kaithwân.	Mothi.	Râjpâsi.	Others.	TOTAL.
Dehra Dûn	...	648	231	92	...	69	244	1,284
Sahâranpur	...	122	78	7	...	6	529	742
Muzaffarnagar	...	12	...	9	...	...	6	27
Meerut	...	...	...	...	...	...	699	699
Mathura	...	...	...	...	...	...	14	14
Agra	...	...	...	...	...	...	11	11
Farrukhâbâd	...	8	4	...	...	9	15	36
Mainpuri	...	3	...	...	...	1	32	36
Etâwah	...	...	...	3	...	...	31	34
Etah	...	...	...	...	...	...	3	3
Bareilly	...	...	...	156	...	...	184	340
Bijnor	...	...	...	...	...	...	8	8
Budâun	...	...	8	...	...	...	6,738	6,746
Morâdâbâd	...	...	...	...	...	...	7,199	7,199

Shâhjahânpur	4	59	1,330	95	72	14,218	3,166	18,944
Pilibhît	18	5,826	2,742	183	...	2,657	348	11,744
Cawnpur	...	...	193	96	...	15	889	1,193
Fatehpur	...	2	9	29,552	...	88	1,206	30,857
Bânda	...	14	5	1,623	125	...	437	2,204
Hamîrpur	...	4	...	14	...	...	5	23
Allahâbâd	...	...	52	109,242	...	...	3,098	112,392
Jhânsi	...	...	...	13	...	...	98	111
Jâlaun	...	...	...	...	...	...	12	12
Lalitpur	...	...	...	10	...	...	2	12
Benares	...	...	...	3,283	...	...	1,641	4,924
Mirzapur	...	...	...	19,139	782	2,138	475	22,534
Jaunpur	...	...	...	29,456	...	...	1,070	30,526
Ghâzipur	...	...	...	37	...	...	4,785	4,822
Ballia	...	...	...	...	...	...	677	677
Gorakhpur	...	14,155	7,109	10,145	...	...	17,267	48,682
Basti	...	10,413	6,909	,098	...	...	324	18,744

Distribution of Pâsis according to the Census of 1891—concld.

Districts.	Arakh.	Baurâsi.	Gûjar.	Kaithwân.	Mothi.	Râjpâsi.	Others.	Total.
Azamgarh	...	...	...	22,421	...	...	65	22,484
Tarâi	...	...	1	1	...	7	912	921
Lucknow	102	169	29,971	67	4,638	39,107	1,602	75,656
Unâo	68	1,270	29,848	129	...	19,314	31,792	82,421
Râê Bareli	...	50,049	10,434	26,243	...	17	14,325	101,248
Sîtapur	3,020	14	13	...	1,043	95,653	5,157	104,900
Hardoi	...	8	22	...	74	85,308	627	86,039
Kheri	8,567	242	49	...	1,218	63,880	559	74,515
Faizâbâd	...	2,786	34,623	...	...	...	337	37,746
Gonda	...	14,061	22,011	...	315	168	1,110	37,665
Bahrâich	117	8,623	21,470	29	...	4,221	15,635	50,095
Sultânpur	...	23,455	2,687	6,598	...	...	1,973	34,722
Partâbgarh	...	...	127	61,993	...	...	239	62,459
Bârabanki	4,314	75,615	5,931	...	...	26,653	10,315	122,828
Total	16,210	207,558	175,857	321,914	8,267	353,535	135,961	1,219,311

PATHÂRI.

Patâri.—A branch of the Majhwâr tribe, who have now become their family priests. Two explanations of the name have been given: one connects it with the Sanskrit *patravârnika* in the sense of "a scribe" or "recorder," in which case they may have been originally priests and genealogists of the Gond Majhwârs. Another theory connects the word with *pât* which in Gondi appears to mean "a sacred place". Thus in Mandla to propitiate evil spirits the Gonds set up rude shrines (*pât*) which are "sometimes merely a bamboo with a piece of rag tied to the end, a heap of stones, or perhaps only a few pieces of rag tied to the branches of a tree. However, the spirit is supposed to have taken up his abode there, and in consequence on the occasion of any event of importance happening in the Gond's family, the spirit has his share of the good things going, in the shape of a little spirit, and possibly a fowl sacrificed to him."[1] The same word apparently originates Pât who is a mountain deity of the Kurs, and Mainpât which is the holy plateau of Sarguja, looked upon with reverence by these Dravidian tribes.[2] The word Patâri or Pathâri with synonyms Pradhân and Gugya appears as a sept of the Gonds of Mandla.[3] Of the Gond Pradhân Mr. Hislop writes: "The Pâdâl also named Pathâdi, Pardhân and Desâi is a numerous class found in the same locality as the Râj Gonds, to whom its members act as religious counsellors (*Pradhâna*). They are in fact the Bhâts of the upper classes, repeating their genealogics and the exploits of their ancestors, explaining their religious system and assisting at festivals on which occasions they play on two sorts of stringed instruments (*kingri* and *jantar, yantra*). For their services they receive presents of cows and bullocks, cloth, food and money."[4] This is pretty much the position of the Patâri among the Mirzapur Majhwârs.

Tribal organisation.

2. The Mirzapur Patâris are divided into four exogamous groups (*jund*) which each contain a number of septs (*kuri*) mostly totemistic. These septs are practically analogous with those of the Majhwârs (*q.v.*). In the first exogamous group we have six septs—Markâm, Poiya, Kusro, Soi, Neti and Serlo: in the second twelve—Tekâm, Marpachi, Netâm, Pusâm, Kariyâm, Sindrâm, Kerâm, Oima,

---

[1] *Central Provinces Gazetteer*, 275.
[2] Dalton, *Descriptive Ethnology*, 231, 135, 223.
[3] *Central Provinces Gazetteer*, 273.
[4] Hislop, *Papers*, 6.

Dadâichi, Koâchi, Ulagwati, Kargati : in the third Marâi, Sarota, Soiyâm, Sarotiya, Bandaru, Karbê, Kursenga, Purkela, Masrâm, Armor, Ârpati and Karpati : in the fourth Korâm, Poika, Armon, Pâwalê, Chichâm, Balariya, Otê, Urich, Salâm. Most of these are analogous to the Majhwâr septs and, as there shown, many of them are totemistic. A closer analysis of the Central Provinces' septs of Gonds will probably show that this is generally the case.

Tradition of origin.

3. The Patâris say that they were originally Majhwârs : the whole tribe was descended from seven brothers. When they could find no one else to act as family priest (*purohit*) they compelled the youngest of the seven to undertake the duties. The curious part of the arrangement is however that a Majhwâr must be attended as his priest by a Patâri of the same sept as his own. Thus a Markâm Patâri acts as priest to a Majhwâr of the Markâm sub-division and so throughout the tribe. The result is that the parishioners or constituents of a Patâri are scattered over a large area and he has to undertake long journeys in order to pay his periodical visits. The system under which, by a specialisation of function this class of aboriginal local priests was formed, is very instructive in its analogies to what was probably the method by which the tribe of Brâhmans with its numerous local sub-divisions was organised.

Tribal council.

4. Their tribal council is exactly on the same system as among the Majhwârs.

Marriage rules.

5. The rules of marriage agree with those of the Majhwârs, but there appears to be no hypergamy. They marry rather earlier than Majhwârs—at the age of ten for boys and nine for girls. The bride price fixed by invariable tribal custom is ten sers of sesamum (*tili*), ten sers of the *urdi* pulse, twelve measures (*panseri*) of rice, four measures of coarse sugar, three rupees in cash and a cloth (*dhoti*) for the bride. Formerly part of the bride price used to consist of liquor but this gave rise to such an amount of quarrelling that about four years ago the tribal council decided that coarse sugar (*gur*) was to take the place of liquor. A wife, who makes a practice of adultery, who wastes the family property or thieves, may be discarded with leave of the council. If a man does not support or ill-treats his wife she can leave him, and such divorced women can marry again by the *sagâi* form. Polygyny is allowed and the children of all the

wives rank equally as heirs. Concubines are not allowed: illegitimate children follow the caste of the fathers, but the clansmen will not eat with or intermarry with them.[1]

Widow marriage.

6. When a man dies the council marry his widow to some widower in the tribe. The consent of the parties and the kindred of the first husband is essential. On a day fixed the man eats at the widow's house. Next day he takes her home and puts on her a set of bangles and ear ornaments (*chûri, tarki*) and pays to the husband's younger brother, who accompanies her, twelve rupees, a turban and a loin cloth which are regarded as the equivalent of the bride price. The levirate is allowed on the usual conditions. They practise Beena marriage in the usual *gharjaiyân* form.

Domestic ceremonies.

7. The domestic ceremonies are practically the same as those of the Majhwârs.

Social position.

8. The position of the Patâri is decidedly low. He is looked upon with contempt as a beggar, and he is discredited because, like the Hindu Mahâbrâhman, he takes the clothes, utensils, etc., of the dead man which are given to him in the belief that he will pass them on for the use of the deceased in the next world. And although they are the family priests of the Majhwârs, the latter show their contempt for them by refusing to eat with them or drink water from their hands.

Pâthak.—(Sanskrit *pâthaka*, "a reciter, teacher") a functional division of Brâhmans, who like the Upâdhyâya, are devoted to the instruction of youths in religious knowledge and the manner of performing rites and ceremonies. The term *pâtha* is technically applied to the modes of recitation of the Vedic texts, of which there are five—Samhita, Pada, Krama, Jata and Ghana.

Pathân.—One of the chief Muhammadan tribes. There has been much controversy on the origin of the term. To quote Dr. Bellew, the latest and best authority on the ethnology of these races, "The origin of the name Pathân, and the nationalitics originally represented by it, carries us back to very early times. The term Pathân is not a native word at all. It is the Hindustâni form of

[1] This was exactly the position of the same class (*spurii*) under Roman law. "These children irregularly conceived, have a mother, but no legal father: they do not come under the paternal power of the father, like the child of lawful marriage and cannot be legitimated." Letourneau, *Evolution of Marriage*, 202.

the native word Pukhtâna, which is the plural of Pukhtûn or Pakhtun (the *a* as in our *pack*) as it is pronounced by the Afrîdi. And Pukhtûn is the proper patronymic of the people inhabiting the country called Pukhtûnkhwa, and speaking the language called Pukhta or Pukhto. What the meaning of the word Pukhta, from which Pukhtûn and its derivatives are held to come, may be a matter of speculation. By some it is supposed to be the same word as the native Pukhta, "a ridge" or "hill" in distinction to Ghar, "a mountain chain" or "peak"; the two words corresponding respectively to the Persian Pushta and Koh. Be this as it may, and there is no denying the fact that the name PukhtûnKhwa, "the Pukhtûn coast or quarter", is very well in accordance with the character of the country in its physical aspect; there is also the fact that in the time of Herodotus, four centuries before our era, this very country was called Pactiya or Pactiyaca, and its natives Pactiyans. In Western Afghânistân the harsh *kh* is changed into the soft *sh*, and Pukhtûn becomes Pushtûn, Pukhtu becomes Pushtu, and so on. By some Pukhtûn tribes, the Afrîdi notably, Pukhtûn, Pukhtu, etc., are pronounced Pakhtûn, Pakhtu, etc., and this brings the words nearer to the Pakhtues of Herodotus. In short, the Pakhtûn or Pukhtûn of to-day, we may take it, is identical in race and position with the Pactiyan of the Greek historian."[1]

2. The popular account is, it is almost needless to say, different. Modern genealogists trace the descent of Afghâns, Pathâns and Ghilzais from Kais or Kish, the father of Saul, and they say that the Prophet, pleased with the services of Kais named after his forefather, gave him the title of Pathân, the Syrian word for "rudder" and bade him direct his people in the true path. By one authority the name Afghân is said to mean "wailing";[2] but another explanation is more probable. Ashvaka, a name of Sanskrit origin was used as a territorial appellation of Gandhâra. This word, derived from *asva*, "a horse," signifies merely the "cavaliers." It was less an ethnic, in the rigorous acceptation of the word, than a general appellation applied by the Hindus of the Panjâb to the tribes of the region of the Kophes, renowned in antiquity for the excellence of its horses. In the popular dialects the Sanskrit word took the usual form Assaka, which reappears

---

[1] *The Races of Afghânistân*, 56, sq.
[2] Benjamin, *Persia*, 112.

scarcely modified in Assakâni or Assakeni in the first historians of the expedition of Alexander and subsequent writers. It is impossible here not to recognise the name Avghân or Afghân.[1] The theory which has been proposed by which Pathân is connected with the Hindi *pâtha*, "the top of a hill" is as untenable as that which derives their title Khân from the Dravidian tribe of Khândhs.[2] The latter word has been by others derived from the Sanskrit *asu* or *swâmin*, meaning "lord."

Tribal traditions.

3. To quote Dr. Bellew, again: "The traditions of the Afghâns refer them to Syria as the country of their residence at the time they were carried away into captivity by Bukhtanasar (Nebuchadnezzar) and planted as colonists in differents parts of Persia and Media. From these positions they, at some subsequent period, emigrated eastward into the mountainous country of Ghor, where they were called by the neighbouring people Bani Afghân and Bani Isrâîl, or "children of Afghân" or "children of Israel." In corroboration of this we have the testimony of the Prophet Esdras to the effect that the ten tribes of Israel, who were taken into captivity, subsequently escaped and found refuge in the country of Arsareth, which is supposed to be identical with the Hazârah country of the present day, and of which Ghor forms a part. It is also stated in the Tabaqât-i-Nâsiri, a detailed account of the conquest of this country by Changhiz Khân, that in the time of the native Shansabi dynasty there was a people called Bani Isrâîl living in that country, and that some of them were extensively engaged in trade in the countries around." Mr. Thorburn[3] quotes in support of their Jewish extraction, some peculiar customs obtaining among the tribes of purest blood, for instance the Passover-like practice of sacrificing an animal and smearing the doorway with its blood in order to avert calamity, the offering up of sacrifices, the stoning to death of blasphemers, the periodical distribution of land and so forth, and he points out that most of the learned men who reject the tradition of Jewish descent have no personal acquaintance with the Afghân people.

Tribal organisation.

4. Though the tribal organisation of the Pathâns in these Provinces is much less closely defined than along the Panjâb frontier, Mr. Ibbetson's

[1] St. Martin quoted by McCrindle, *Indian Antiquary*, VI., 343, *sq.*

[2] Râja Lachhman Sinh, *Bulandshahr Memorandum*, 192.

[3] Quoted by Ibbetson, *Panjâb Ethnography*, paragraph 390, *sqq.*

remarks on this subject deserve quotation: "The tribe is probably far more homogeneous in its constitution among the Pathâns than among the Biloches. Sayyid, Turk and other clans have occasionally been affiliated to it, but as a rule people of foreign descent preserve their tribal individuality, become merely associated, and not intermingled, with the tribes, among whom they have settled. Even then they generally claim Pathân origin on the female side, and the tribe is usually descended in theory at least from a common ancestor. The *hamsáyah* custom by which strangers are protected by the tribe with which they dwell is in full force among the Pathâns as among the Biloches. But with the former, though it does protect in many cases families of one tribe who have settled with another, it seldom accounts for any considerable portion of the tribe; and its action is chiefly confined to traders, menials and other dependants of foreign extraction who are protected by, but not received into, the tribe. Thus a blacksmith living in an Utmanzai village will give his clan as Utmanzai; but his caste will, of course, remain Lohâr. The nation is divided genealogically into a few great sections which have no corporate existence, and the tribe is now the practical unit, though the common name and traditions of common descent are still carefully preserved in the memory of the people. Each section of tribe, however small, has its leading man who is known as Malik, a specially Pathân title. In many, but by no means in all, the tribes, there is a Khân Khel or chief house, usually the branch of the tribe, whose Malik is known as Khân, and acts as chief of the whole tribe. But he is seldom more than their leader in war and their agent in dealing with others; he possesses influence rather than power; and the real authority rests with the Jirgah, a democratic council composed of all the Maliks. The tribe, clan and sept are alike distinguished by patronymics formed from the name of the common ancestor by the addition of the word *zai* or *khel*, *zai* being the corruption of the Pashto *zoe*, meaning "son," while *khel* is an Arabic word meaning "association" or "company." Both terms are used indifferently for both the larger and smaller divisions. The stock of names being limited, the nomenclature is exceedingly puzzling, certain names recurring in very different tribes in the most maddening manner. Moreover, the title which genealogical accuracy would allot to a tribe or clan is often very different from that by which it is known for practical purposes, the people having preferred to be called by the name of a junior ancestor who had acquired local renown. The frontier tribe, whether within or beyond our border, has almost without exception a very distinct corporate existence, each tribe, and within the tribe each clan, occupying a clearly defined tract of country, though they are in the Indus valley often the owners merely rather than the occupiers of the country, the land and smaller villages being largely in the hands of a mixed population of Hindu origin who cultivate subject to the superior rights of the Pathâns. These people are included by the Pathâns under the generic and semi-contemptuous name of Hindki; a term very analogous to the Jat of the Biloch frontier, and which includes all Muhammadans who, being of Hindu origin, have been converted to Islam in comparatively recent times."

Tribes of the Pathâns of North-Western Provinces.

5. At the last Census the Pathâns of these Provinces were classified under the following chief tribes:—Afrîdi, Bagarzai, Bangash, Barech, Bunerwâl, Daûdzai, Dilazâk, Durrâni, Ghilzai, Ghorgashti, Ghori, Kâkar, Qizilbâsh, Khalîl, Khatak, Lodi, Mehmad, Muhammadzai, Rohilla, Tarîn, Urmuz, Ushturyâni, Warakzai, Wazîri, Yâqûbzai and Yûsufzai. The following notes are mainly taken from the writings of Dr. Bellew and Mr. Ibbetson.

The Afrîdi Pathâns.

6. They represent in name and position the Aparytæ of Herodotus. One of the four great divisions of the Pactiyæ of Herodotus was that of the Gandhâri, the other three were the Aparytæ or Afrîdi, the Satragyddæ or Khatak, and the Dadicæ or Dadi, all alike of Indian origin. "The original limits of the Afrîdi country probably comprised the whole of the Safed Koh range and the country on the base of it on the north and south sides, to the Kâbul and Kurrum rivers respectively; whilst its extent from east to west was from the Pewâr ridge or the head waters of the Kurrum further west to the Indus, between the points of junction with it of the Kâbul and Kurrum rivers, in the former direction." Of the character of the tribe Dr. Bellew writes: "Looking at the Afrîdi as we find him to-day, it is difficult to imagine him the descendant of the mild, industrious, peace-loving, and contemplative Buddhist, abhorrent of the shedding of blood or the destruction of life of even the minutest of God's creatures; or even to imagine him descended from fire-worshipping ancestors, whose tender care for life was

almost equal to that of the Buddhist, and whose sincere and punctilious devotion to the observances of the minute ceremonies and ordinances of their religion was surpassed by none. The Afrîdi of to-day, though professedly a Muhammadan, has really no religion at all. He is to a great extent ignorant of the tenets and doctrines of the religion he professes, and even if he knew them, would in no way be restrained by them in the pursuit of his purpose.

7 "Whatever he may have been as a Buddhist or as a fire-worshipper, he has now sunk to the lowest grade of civilisation, and borders upon the savage. Entirely illiterate, under no acknowledged control, each man has his own king, the nation has dwindled down to a small community of less than three hundred thousand souls, mostly robbers and cut-throats, without principles of conduct of any kind, and with nothing but the incentive of the moment as the prompter to immediate action. Even among his own nationality (the Pathân), he is accounted the faithless of the faithless, and is held on all sides to be the most fierce and stealthy of all enemies. As we know him merely in the character of an independent neighbour, he is a wily, mistrusting, wolfish, and wilful savage, with no object in life but the pursuit of robbery and murder and the feuds they give rise to."

The Bangash Pathâns.

8. The Bangash Pathâns are regarded by Dr. Bellew as perhaps of Scythic descent, and are supposed to have come into their present positions with the Scythic irruption. They originally lived about Gurdez in Zurmat, but in the latter part of the fourteenth century they increased in numbers, and being pressed upon by the Ghilzai, emigrated eastward *en masse* and settled in Kurram. They are descended from Luqmân, and have absorbed several tribes of doubtful origin. Their chief settlement in these Provinces is at Farrukhâbâd, and a very complete account of them has been given by Mr. R. S. Whiteway.[1]

The Bunerwâl Pathâns.

9. The Bunerwâl tribe take their name from the Buner country, north-east of Peshâwar.

The Daûdzai Pathâns.

10. The Daûdzai occupy the left bank of the Kâbul river as far down as the junction of the Bara.

---

[1] *Calcutta Review*, 1865.

11. The Dilazâk Pathâns were the inhabitants of the Peshâwar valley before the Pathân invasion, and are apparently of Scythic origin, and came into the Panjâb with the Jâts and Katti in the fifth and sixth centuries. "They soon became powerful and important, and ruled the whole valley as far as the Indus and the foot of the northern hills. In the first half of the thirteenth century the Yûsufzai and Momand drove them across the Indus into Chach-Pakhli. But their efforts to regain their lost territories were such a perpetual source of disturbance that at length Jahângîr deported them *en masse* and distributed them over Hindustân and the Dakkhin. Scattered families of them are still to be found along the left bank of the Indus in Hazâra and Râwalpindi." [1]

The Dilazâk Pathâns.

12. The name Durrâni is derived either from *durr-i-daurân*, "pearl of the age," or from *durr-i-durrân*, "pearl of pearls." The title was adopted by Ahmad Shâh Abdâli, when he ascended the throne, in allusion to the Abdâli custom of wearing a pearl stud in the right ear. According to Dr. Bellew [2] :—"The special Afghân tribe is called Abdâli, and is more commonly known since the time of Ahmad Shah, the first independent sovereign of Afghânistân of this race, by the name Durrâni. The Durrâni comprise the following chief divisions or clans: Saddozai, Populzai, Barakzai, Halakozai, Achakzai, Nurzai, Ishâqzai, and Khagwâni. Their home and fixed seat is in Kandahâr Province, the former country of the Gandhâra, who, at an early period of our era, spread into the present Hazâra country along the courses of the Helmand and Arghandâb rivers. Members of each clan, however, are found in small societies scattered all over the plain country up to Kâbul and Jalâlâbâd, and they are there settled mostly as lords of the soil or military feoffees, the people of the country, so far as concerns the agricultural community, being their tenants or serfs."

The Durrâni Pathâns.

13. According to Mr. Ibbetson, "the Ghilzai are a race probably of Turkish origin, their name being another form of Khilchi, the Turkish word for 'swordsman,' who early settled, perhaps, as mercenaries rather than as a corporate tribe, in the Siahband range of the Ghor mountains,

The Ghilzai Pathâns.

[1] Ibbetson, *loc. cit.*, para. 415.
[2] *Loc. cit.*, 20.

where they received a large admixture of Persian blood. The official spelling of the name is still Ghaleji at Kâbul and Kandahâr. They first rose into notice in the time of Mahmûd Ghaznavi, whom they accompanied in his invasions of India. Not long afterwards they conquered the tract between Jalâlâbâd and Kelât-i-Ghilzai, and spread east and west over the country they now hold. In the beginning of the eighteenth century they revolted against their Persian rulers, established themselves under Mîr Wais as independent rulers at Kandahâr, and overran Persia. But a quarter of a century later they were reduced by Nâdir Shâh, and their rule disappeared, to be succeeded not long after by that of the Durrâni." Dr. Bellew tells the romantic legend of Bîbi Matto and Shâh Husain, whose son was called Ghalzœ, "son of a thief," the father having stolen his daughter's honour, whence the name Ghilzai.

14. He adds: "As a race the Ghilji mix little with their neighbours, and indeed differ in many respects, both as to internal government and domestic customs, from the other races of Afghânistân. Those small sections of the people who are settled in the plain live in villages and follow agricultural pursuits, but the great majority of the tribe are pastoral in their habits of life, and migrate with the seasons from the lowlands to the highlands with their families and flocks and easily portable black hair tents. They never settle in the cities, nor do they engage in the ordinary handicraft trades, but they manufacture carpets, felts, etc., for domestic use, from the wool and hair of their cattle. The pastoral clans are notoriously predatory in their habits, and continually at feud amongst themselves and with their neighbours. Physically they are a remarkably fine race, and in stature, courage, and strength of body, are second to none in Afghânistân. But they are very barbarous people, the pastoral clans especially, and in their wars excessively savage and vindictive. Several of the Ghilji or Ghilzai clans are almost wholly engaged in the carrying trade between India and Afghânistân and the northern states of Central Asia, and have been so for many centuries, to the exclusion almost of all the other tribes of the country. The principal clans employed in this great carrying trade are the Niâzi, Nâsar, Kharoti, and to some extent the Sulaimân Khel. From the nature of their occupation they are collectively styled, or individually so far as that goes, Povinda and Lawâni or Lohâni. These terms, it appears, are derived from the Persian word *parwinda*, 'a bale of merchandise,' and *rawâni*, 'a traveller.'"

15. The term Ghorgusht is a corruption of Ghirgisht or Ghurgusht, the third son of Kais. The word is only an altered form of Girgis or Ghirghis, "wanderer on the steppe," and indicates the country whence this people originally came, namely, Northern Turkistân.

The Ghorgushti Pathâns.

16. The Ghori Pathâns, who are very numerous in the Provinces, appear to take their name from the Ghor country to the east of Herât. They are usually classed as a sub-division of the Kand, one of the septs of the Bani Isrâîl, or pure Afghâns.

The Ghori Pathâns.

17. Of the Kâkar Pathâns Dr. Bellew writes[1]:—"The Kâkar of Afghânistân are a people of Scythian origin, and of kindred race with the Gokkar or Ghokhar, who are settled in Chach and Râwalpindi on the other side of the Indus, and other parts of India. According to the Afghân account, Kâkar was the grandson of Ghurghusht or Ghirghisht, by his second son, Dani. And this Ghirgh was the youngest of the three sons of Kais or Kish, the great ancestral progenitor of the Afghân nationality of modern times. It has already been shown how the name of the first son, Saraban, was merely the adoption of the race name of the people whom the Afghân genealogists classified together as one set of the descendants of Kais, and the fact of their Râjput origin might then have been made clearer by tracing up the descent to more recent times. Saraban had two sons, Sharjyûn and Krishyûn, which are evidently transformations of the commor Râjput names, Surjan and Krishna, and they have been still more altered by transformation into Muhammadan names, Sharjyûn being changed into Sharffuddîn and Krishyûn into Khyruddîn. Similar traces of Indian affinity are to be found in almost all the Afghân genealogical tables, and it is only what we might expect when we remember the tradition that the five Pândava brothers about the time of the Mahâbhârat emigrated to the Panjâb and Afghânistân as far as Ghazni and Kandahâr, and there established independent kingdoms which lasted for several centuries."

The Kâkar Pathâns.

18. Mr. Ibbetson calls the Qizilbâsh Pathâns "a tribe of Tartar horsemen from the Eastern Caucasus, who formed the backbone of the old Persian army and of the force with which Nâdir Shâh

The Qizilbâsh or Qazalbâsh Pathâns.

[1] *Loc. cit.*, 91.

invaded India. Many of the great Mughal ministers have been Qizilbâsh, and notably Mîr Júmlah, the famous minister of Aurangzeb. They are said to take their name from a red cap of peculiar shape which they wear, and which was invented by the founder of the Sophi dynasty of Persia, an intolerant Shiah, as the distinguishing mark of that sect, and which his son, Shâh Tumasp, compelled Humayun to wear when a refugee at the Persian Court. There are some twelve hundred families of Qizilbâsh in the city of Kâbul alone, where they were located by Nâdir Shâh and exercise considerable influence in local politics."

The Khalîl Pathâns.

19. The Khalîl occupy the left bank of the Bara river and the country along the front of the Khibar Pass. They have four main clans: Matuzai, Barozai, Ishâqzai and Tilarzai, of whom the Barozai is most powerful.

The Khatak Pathâns.

20. To quote Mr. Ibbetson again: "The Khataks are descended from Luqmân, surnamed Khatak. He had two sons, Turqmân and Bulâq. The descendants of the latter are still known as the Bulâqi section; while Tarai, son of Turqmân, rose to such distinction that the whole section, including two main clans, the Tari proper and the Tarkai, is called by his name. The Khatak are a fine, manly race, and differ from all other Pathâns in features, general appearance, and many of their customs. They are the northernmost of all the Pathâns settled on our frontier who speak the soft or Western dialect of Pushto. They are of a warlike nature, and have been for centuries at feud with all their neighbours and with one another. They are active, industrious, and a favourable specimen of Pathân, and are good cultivators, though their country is stony and unfertile. They are great carriers and traders, and especially hold all the salt trade with Swât and Buner in their hands. They are all Sunnis. The Marwat, the hereditary enemy of the Khatak, says: 'Friendship is good with any one but a Khatak; may the Devil take a Khatak,' and 'a Khatak is a hen, if you seize him slowly, he lies down: and if suddenly, he clucks.' Another proverb runs thus:—'Though the Khatak is a horseman, still he is a man of but one charge.'"

The Lodi Pathâns.

21. "To the Ghilzai and Lodi, the latter of whom gave a dynasty to Upper India," according to Mr. Ibbetson, "and especially to the former, belong almost all the tribes of warrior traders who are included under the term

Pawinda, from *parwinda* the Persian word for 'a bale of goods,' or perhaps more probably from the same root as *powal*, a Pushto word for 'to graze.' They are almost wholly engaged in the carrying trade between India and Afghânistân and the Northern States of Central Asia, a trade which is almost entirely in their hands. They assemble every autumn in the plains east of Ghazni, with their families, flocks, herds, and long strings of camels laden with the goods of Bukhâra and Kandahâr, and forming enormous caravans, numbering many thousands, march in military order through the Kâkar and Wazîri country to the Gomal and Zhob passes through the Sulaimâns. Entering the Dera Ismâîl Khân District, they leave their families, flocks, and some two-thirds of their fighting men in the great grazing grounds which lie on either side of the Indus, and while some wander off in search of employment, others pass on with their laden camels and merchandise to Multân, Rajputâna, Lahore, Amritsar, Delhi, Cawnpur, Benares, and even Patna. In the spring they again assemble, and return by the same route to their homes in the Hills about Ghazni and Kelât-i-Ghilzai. When the hot weather begins, the men, leaving their belongings behind them, move off to Kandahâr, Herât, and Bukhâra, with the Indian and European merchandise which they have brought from Hindustân. In October they return and prepare once more to start for India."

The Muhammadzai.

22. The Muhammadzai of the Census returns are perhaps the same as the Muhammad Khel, the largest sept of the Daulatzai. The present rulers of Bhopâl belong to this tribe.

The Rohilla Pathâns.

23. The country known as Pukhtûn Khwa, to which reference has already been made, is called by outsiders and foreigners, on the side of India almost exclusively, by the name of Roh, which has the same meaning as Koh, "a mountain;" Rohilla hence means "a Highlander." Their occupation of the country called after them Rohilkhand is quite modern. After the death of Aurangzeb in A.D. 1707 the dissensions among the Hindus of Bareilly gave a chance to Ali Muhammad Khân, the leader of the Rohilla Pathâns, to obtain possession of the country. In A.D. 1744 he conquered Kumaun as far as Almorā, but two years after he was defeated by the Emperor Muhammad Shâh in the Bareilly District. He was succeeded by the famous Hâfiz Rahmat Khân, and in his latter days he came in contact

with Warren Hastings, when the name of the Rohillas for the first time attracted attention.[1] They assert that they are of Coptic origin, and say that, driven out of Egypt by one of the Pharaohs, they wandered westward till they arrived under that part of the mountains known as Sulaimâni Koh, or "the hill of Solomon," where they halted. The Rohilla has been always notorious for bravery and turbulence. Shore[2] says that in his time the Rohilla soldiers would submit to be flogged within an inch of their lives with a leathern martingale, but to be struck with a whip or cane would be an indelible disgrace and very likely to be resented by a stab or a bullet.

The Tarîn Pathâns.

24. Dr. Bellew[3] writes of these: "The tribal traditions are to the effect that about three or four hundred years ago the Yûsufzai or Mândar and Mohmand tribes of Afghâns were settled on the Gwara Margha and the headwaters of the Tarnak and Arghasan rivers, as neighbours and allies. Beyond them, lower down the course of these rivers, were the Tarîn, another tribe of Afghâns, who still occupy the same positions, and the valley of Peshîn. Their lands were in the summer subject to droughts, and were besides in great part waste, owing to the exhaustion at that season of the tributary streams and the diminished volume of the rivers. The consequence was a contest for the better lands, and the Tarîn tribes, being the stronger of the two parties, gradually encroached on the fat pastures of the Mândar and Mohmand tribes and finally dispossessed them of their lands."

The Ushturyâni Pathâns.

25. Of the Ushturyâni, whom Mr. Ibbetson[4] calls Ushturâni, he says:—"They are the descendants of Hannar, one of the sons of Ushtaryâni, a Sayyid, who settled among and married into the Shirâni section of Afghâns. They were settled with the Shirânis to the south of the Takht-i-Sulaimân, and till about a century ago were wholly pastoral and engaged in the carrying trade. But a quarrel with their neighbours, the Mûsa Khel, put a stop to their annual westward migration, and they were forced to take to agriculture. They still own a large tract of country, in

---

[1] For their history, see *Morâdâbâd Settlement Report*, 12, *sq*.

[2] *Notes*, II., 490.

[3] *Loc. cit.*, 63, *sq*.

[4] *Loc. cit.*, para. 400, *sq*.

which indeed most of them live, cultivating land immediately under the hills and pasturing their flocks beyond the border. Their territory only includes the eastern slopes of the Sulaimâns, the crest of the range being held by the Mûsa Khel and Zmari. They are divided into two main clans, the Ahmadzai and Gagalzai, and these again into numerous septs. They are a fine, manly race, many of them in our army and police, and they are quiet and well behaved, cultivating largely with their own hands. A few of them are still carriers. They are much harassed by the independent Bozdâr (Biloch). They are all Sunnis."

The Wazîri Pathâns.

26. Of the Wazîri Pathâns, Dr. Bellew says[1]:—"The Wazîri, who displaced the Khatak or Shattak, as it is pronounced in the Western dialect of Pushtu, from his ancient seat on the Sulaimân range from the Sattagydia of Herodotus, for he is the only one of the ancient authors who has mentioned this people, appear to be identical with the Wairsi or Vairsi of the early Muhammadan historians. The Wairsi were a division of the Sodha tribe, which itself was a branch of the Pramâra Râjput. The Wazîri appear to have made their first assault against the Khatak about five or six hundred years ago, at a time when the country was sorely afflicted with famine; and the route they took was across the Shâm plain into the adjoining valley and district of Barmal. Here they settled and remained for some time before making a further forward move. Hence they occupied the whole of the ancient Khatak country from the Shâm plain on the South to the Kohât Valley on the North. They are a powerful and entirely independent tribe, and mostly pastoral and nomad in their habits of life. In personal appearance they are very different from other Pathân tribes and retain many customs peculiar to themselves."

The Yûsufzai Pathâns.

27. The history of the Yûsufzai Pathâns is given in detail by Dr. Bellew and Mr. Ibbetson. They now hold Swât, Buner, and the Lundkhwâr and Rânizai Valleys in the North-West of Yûsufzai.

Character of the Pathâns.

28. Mr. Ibbetson's remarks again deserve reproduction:—"The true Pathân is perhaps the most barbaric of all the races with which we are brought in contact in the Panjâb. His life is not so

[1] *Loc. cit.*, 89.

primitive as that of the gypsy tribes, but he is cruel, bloodthirsty and vindictive in the highest degree; he does not know what truth and faith is, in so much that the saying *Afghân beîmân* has passed into a proverb among his neighbours, and though he is not without courage of a sort, and is often curiously reckless of his life, he would scorn to face an enemy whom he could stab from behind or to meet him on equal terms if it were possible to take advantage of him, however meanly. It is easy to convict him out of his own mouth. Here are some of his proverbs :—'A Pathân's enmity smoulders like a dung fire :' 'A cousin's tooth breaks upon a cousin :' 'Keep a cousin poor but use him ; when he is little, play with him ; when he is grown up, he is a cousin, fight him :' 'Speak good words to an enemy very softly ; gradually destroy him root and branch.' At the same time he has his code of honour which he observes strictly, and which he quotes with pride under the name of Pakhtûnwâli. It imposes upon him three chief obligations : *Nanawatai*, or the right of asylum, which compels him to shelter and protect even an enemy who comes as a suppliant ; *Badal*, or the necessity to revenge by retaliation ; and *Melmastia*, or open-handed hospitality to all who may demand it. Of these three, perhaps, the last is greatest. And there is a sort of charm about him, especially about the leading men, which almost makes one forget his treacherous nature. As the proverb says : 'The Pathân is at one moment a saint and the next a devil.' For centuries at least he has been on our frontier subject to no man. He leads a wild, free, active life in the rugged fastnesses of his mountains ; and there is an air of masculine independence about him which is refreshing in a country like India. He is a bigot of the most fanatical type, exceedingly proud, and extraordinarily superstitious. He is of stalwart make, and his features are often of a markedly Semitic type. His hair, plentifully oiled, hangs straight to his shoulder ; he wears a loose tunic, baggy drawers, a sheet or blanket, sandals, and a sheepskin coat with its wool inside ; his favourite colour is dark blue ; and his national arms the long, heavy Afghân knife and the matchlock or *jazail*. His women wear a loose shift, wide, wrinkled drawers down to their ankles, and a wrap over the head, and are, as a rule, jealously secluded. Both sexes are filthy in their persons.

29. "Such is the Pathân in his home among the fastnesses of the frontier ranges. But the Pathâns of our territory have been much softened by our rule and by the agricultural life of the plains,

so that they look down on the Pathâns of the hills, and their proverbs have it:—'A hillman is no man;' and again, 'Don't class burrs as grass or a hillman as a human being.' The nearer he is to the frontier, the more closely the Pathân assimilates to the original type; while on this side of the Indus, even in the riverain itself, there is little or nothing, not even language, to distinguish him from his neighbours of the same religion as himself. The Pathâns are extraordinarily jealous of female honour, and most of the blood feuds for which they are so famous originate in quarrels about women. As a race they strictly seclude their females, but the poorer tribes and the poorer members of all tribes are prevented from doing so by their poverty. Among the tribes of our territory a woman's nose is cut off if she be detected in adultery; and it is a favourite joke to induce a Pathân woman to unveil by saying to her suddenly 'You have no nose.' The Pathân pretends to be purely endogamous, and beyond the border he probably is so; while even in British territory the first wife will generally be a Pathân, except among the poorest classes. At the same time Pathân women are beyond the Indus seldom, if ever, married to any but Pathâns. They intermarry very closely, avoiding only the prohibited degrees of Islâm. Their rules of inheritance are tribal and not Muhammadan, and tend to keep property within the agnatic society, though some few of the more educated families have lately begun to follow the Musalmân law. Their social customs differ much from tribe to tribe, or rather perhaps from the wilder to the more civilised sections of the nation."

30. In these Provinces, perhaps, the best class of Pathâns are those from Rohilkhand, who are active, intelligent, and good rulers of men; many of them hold appointments in the Revenue, Police, and other Government Departments.

Distribution of the Pathâns

Districts.	Afrîdî.	Bakarzai.	Bangash.	Barech.	Bunerwâl.	Dâudzai.	Dilazâk.	Durrâni.	Ghilzai.	Ghorgashti.	Ghori.	Kâkar.	Qazalbâsh.
Dehra Dûn .	63	...	44	...	...	...	...	...	42	...	115	218	...
Sahâraopur .	131	11	92	31	7	1	95	3	83	19	334	3,787	...
Muzaffarnagar .	593	5	6	1	18	4	4	18	12	...	262	2,630	...
Meerut . .	95	188	202	...	1	2	966	8	8	...	3,006	997	11
Bulandshahr .	33	...	12	3	...	49	3	182	404	...	1,867	81	...
Aligarh . .	96	...	169	...	...	...	1	8	123	...	5,529	8	...
Mathura . .	32	...	44	...	1	...	4	...	21	...	1,574	19	...
Agra . .	499	1	195	...	5	37	75	9	56	...	3,961	49	9
Farrukhâbâd .	3,658	15	4,043	...	...	25	403	11	309	...	3,292	1,240	...
Mainpuri . .	401	27	172	...	...	...	12	...	72	...	2,369	78	...
Etâwah . .	88	...	207	...	...	...	...	...	17	...	1,781	33	...
Etah . .	253	...	761	...	...	19	101	2	86	...	...	279	...
Bareilly . .	1,104	517	...	1,432	31	...	172	65	630	138	3,850	71	...
Bijnor . .	24	...	...	...	...	...	65	...	57	...	199	502	...
Budâun . .	153	19	593	741	206	9	607	7	65	40	6,232	5	...
Morâdâbâd .	186	2	178	578	943	36	755	11	125	...	2,740	262	...
Shâjahâopur .	609	1,070	1,117	23	1	524	2,668	62	126	...	3,807	486	...
Pilibhit . .	160	281	82	...	...	...	...	...	212	...	1,254	...	...
Cawnpur . .	196	...	611	8	...	4	74	29	35	...	1,879	...	...
Fatehpur . .	141	...	24	...	...	...	11	35	47	...	2,314	16	...
Bânda . .	27	5	28	...	...	...	10	2	88	...	6,162	148	...
Hamîrpur .	11	5	59	...	1	...	1	...	36	...	1,605	64	...
Allahâbâd .	80	9	4	...	...	..	596	105	...	...	722	14	...
Jhânsi . .	13	...	52	...	...	...	4	11	41	...	1,166	44	...
Jâlaun . .	21	...	124	...	...	...	4	11	68	...	1,823	...	.
Lalitpur . .	18	1	...	...	...	...	3	2	...	...	346	7	...
Benares . .	66	...	32	...	...	...	...	59	26	...	207	79	...
Mîrzapur . .	...	...	...	...	...	...	20	...	411	..	...	...	...
Jaunpur . .	14	...	...	...	...	...	483	41	34	...	1,499	...	...
Ghâzipur . .	4	...	...	...	...	...	34	...	15	...	29	70	...
Ballia . .	...	...	...	...	...	...	...	...	...	...	41	...	...
Gorakhpur .	27	...	11	...	...	...	233	21	75	..	715	1,605	...
Basti . .	...	28	...	...	...	19	...	...	74	...	912	16,539	...
Azamgarh .	6	...	...	...	...	...	79	...	...	...	2,479	372	...
Kumaun . .	...	...	...	...	...	...	...	...	...	...	...	...	...
Garhwâl . .	...	...	...	...	...	...	...	...	...	...	68	...	...
Tarâi . .	29	...	87	...	515	...	...	1	...	1	671	...	...
Lucknow .	1,421	18	180	9	...	...	102	55	91	...	1,788	215	16
Unâo . .	356	48	62	...	...	...	129	129	90	...	5,672	263	...
Râê Bareli .	431	...	87	...	...	...	...	25	202	...	768	540	...
Sîtapur . .	233	23	119	...	...	5	22	80	20	...	2,515	1,235	...
Hardoi . .	600	1,163	121	...	...	...	43	69	5	...	5,780	1,534	...
Kheri . .	140	340	56	...	...	622	86	7	68	...	3,369	697	...
Faizâbâd . .	24	...	...	...	...	...	...	4	40	...	523	1,210	53
Gonda . .	6	...	5	...	...	6	...	...	2	...	410	10,057	...
Bahrâich . .	317	...	91	3	20	16	...	40	52	...	2,315	2,909	...
Sultânpur .	72	...	8	...	...	...	423	2	59	...	414	286	...
Partâbgarh .	107	4	6	...	...	...	33	8	8	...	1,266	82	...
Bârabanki .	302	...	58	...	...	...	...	...	...	...	85	327	...
TOTAL .	12,840	3,780	9,742	2,828	1,749	1,378	8,321	1,116	4,035	198	89,712	49,049	89

according to the Census of 1891.

Khalil.	Khatak.	Lodi.	Mehmad.	Muham-madzai.	Rohilla.	Tarin.	'Urmuz.	Ushturyâni.	Warakzai.	Wazîri.	Yaqûbzai.	Yûsufzai.	Others.	TOTAL.
...	12	248	...	95	140	...	...	...	20	...	...	672	1,346	3,015
259	45	1,172	3	220	1,009	134	...	...	67	101	...	5,608	1,870	15,082
7	16	1,719	4	121	627	104	...	...	448	1	...	2,680	2,152	11,432
...	233	770	...	78	609	24	...	...	5	...	...	6,612	4,294	18,009
207	46	641	36	42	15	53	...	...	5	...	...	2,262	4,174	10,110
...	79	3,636	...	33	123	...	...	...	118	109	...	2,064	4,242	16,338
...	56	737	23	2	42	...	...	...	4	...	...	822	1,790	5,171
3	66	3,469	...	30	371	72	...	...	46	2	...	2,899	6,425	18,270
68	2,109	1,281	50	718	108	46	...	...	1,487	...	...	2,956	11,274	33,086
...	2	890	...	48	22	5	...	...	78	7	...	718	4,059	8,860
...	4	1,118	...	41	109	9	...	...	58	8	...	872	4,091	8,436
53	181	2,120	9	994	47	48	...	...	386	38	4	1,291	3,922	10,594
25	335	1,144	...	980	546	388	...	...	144	...	43	5,185	24,338	41,138
58	75	707	...	1,086	527	565	...	...	9	...	...	2,641	2,539	9,054
...	692	1,131	21	716	264	102	183	...	45	..	9	2,160	10,668	24,668
23	710	1,435	358	645	490	529	...	...	76	20	78	4,527	6,325	21,032
780	182	549	3,460	842	1,601	2,099	...	...	1,083	...	...	4,221	14,084	39,394
20	355	849	88	756	444	73	53	...	319	...	18	2,113	6,408	13,489
25	5	2,455	2	6	171	52	...	...	23	51	...	4,101	7,067	16,794
16	31	1,578	26	208	95	...	...	...	27	1	...	1,696	2,796	9,062
1	...	618	...	18	65	...	...	...	17	6	...	630	3,125	10,950
...	...	266	...	17	16	11	...	...	5	1	...	871	2,248	5,226
...	16	6,381	...	10	153	51	...	9	...	...	...	4,689	6,844	19,664
...	...	291	5	29	76	...	...	...	...	...	...	611	2,610	4,953
...	...	548	23	...	23	...	...	...	75	...	...	527	2,683	9,430
...	...	74	...	8	7	...	...	...	...	...	...	91	1,334	1,891
...	11	1,741	...	66	117	2	...	...	...	...	..	2,346	3,976	8,728
...	...	3,529	...	5	45	104	...	...	6	...	...	2,437	2,220	8,777
...	...	4,159	...	...	...	37	...	...	...	...	...	2,121	5,138	13,516
7	199	2,045	...	2	58	18	78	...	...	1	...	2,499	3,451	8,510
...	...	1,333	...	...	206	...	...	...	49	...	...	774	2,427	4,833
1	...	6,037	...	11	642	1	...	...	...	12	...	3,995	7,732	21,118
...	...	6,237	...	...	264	...	...	...	...	...	...	1,731	4,003	29,807
3	...	2,058	...	66	14	3	...	...	...	...	...	4,482	10,542	20,104
...	...	...	...	...	...	...	...	...	...	...	...	...	7	7
...	...	101	...	...	...	...	...	...	...	...	...	...	281	450
...	...	73	...	337	18	13	...	...	117	...	...	810	1,663	4,335
38	41	2,678	123	158	197	199	...	...	131	59	...	7,172	10,375	25,066
24	25	2,175	34	61	75	76	...	...	412	...	...	959	3,387	13,977
27	15	3,609	...	33	42	31	21	...	250	...	...	641	2,280	9,002
48	8	3,306	...	216	109	8	...	...	53	...	...	2,525	5,018	15,543
129	20	1,538	307	487	386	370	1	...	12	...	...	1,173	5,677	19,415
5	...	2,812	38	246	237	185	...	...	...	29	...	2,116	3,549	14,602
...	...	2,800	...	...	57	...	...	...	...	...	...	4,025	5,099	13,335
...	...	8,080	...	6	101	...	...	...	...	...	...	3,121	5,818	27,612
11	6	4,427	7	447	139	24	...	...	29	...	6	3,821	6,251	21,353
...	73	2,621	...	9	32	...	...	...	...	...	...	1,193	1,904	6,705
...	164	6,028	2	...	65	42	...	...	...	...	...	1,170	10,378	19,330
16	17	3,778	...	7	28	10	...	...	6	...	...	2,164	5,321	12,120
1,854	5,819	106,992	4,619	9,900	10,532	5,488	336	9	5,610	446	158	114,693	249,210	700,393

Patwa, Patua[1]—(Sanskrit *pata*, "woven cloth;" Hindi *pât*, "silk").—The caste of braid and silk fringe makers. They are also generally known by the name of 'Ilâqêband or 'Alâqêband (*'ilâqa*, *'alâqa*, "connection"), who are usually Muhammadans practising the same occupation: Pathâr, Patahra, Pathera.

Tribal traditions.

2. One tradition states that when Mahâdeva was about to be married to Pârvati, a goldsmith brought the wedding jewelry for the bride, and as there was no one to string them, Mahâdeva formed the "silkman" to do the duty. The Eastern Patwas trace their origin to Baretha in the Faizâbâd District and to Balrâmpur in Gonda. In Ahraura, in the Mirzapur District, there is a small community of them who make silk cloth from the cocoons collected in the jungles south of the river Son. They take the title of Sinh, and say that they are emigrants from Kot Kângra, where they were originally Katauj Râjputs, a sept which does not appear in Mr. Ibbetson's lists. In the Panjâb they say they are Khatris. In Hamîrpur they claim descent from Gokul in the Mathura District, and say that their ancestor was one Biha, a Pânrê Brâhman; they separated from the Brâhman stock on account of some quarrel about eating, and their brethren are now called Patiya Brâhmans and act as their family priests. They also assert that the Gahoi Banyas are a branch of the same stock. In Farrukhâbâd they claim their origin from Ujjain. They are apparently a purely occupational caste, and are probably composed of many different elements.

Tribal organization.

3. At the last Census they were recorded under the sub-tribes of Agarwâla; Deobansi, or "the race of a god;" and Kharwâr, which is the name of an undoubtedly Dravidian tribe. In Benares, according to Mr. Sherring, their divisions are Khârêwâl or Khandêwâl, which is the name of one of the Banya tribes; Khara, or "genuine," Deobansi; Lahera, or makers of ornaments in lac (Sanskrit *laksha-kâra*); and Jogi Patwa. In Mirzapur there is a sub-caste known as Khanrawa, who are said to take their name for some unexplained reason from *khânr*, or coarse sugar, and to be out-castes. In Lucknow their sub-castes are Gauriya, Rewar, and Tânti. In Hamîrpur they have a

---

[1] Based on enquiries at Mirzapur and notes by M. Râm Sahây, Teacher, Tahsîli School, Mahoba, Hamîrpur; M. Jamunadîn, Teacher, Sumerpur School, Hamîrpur; M. Chhote Lâl, Archæological Survey, Lucknow; and the Deputy Inspector of Schools, Ballia and Farrukhâbâd.

number of local sections which take their name from the villages in which they originally settled. These are Chhâniyân, who are named from the village of Chhâni; Ratha from Râth; Tarela; Barauniya; Sikarwâr; Kariya; Nasâniyân; and Jeorahiya. Here it is said that the sub-castes are exogamous, which is certainly a mistake. But these local divisions or sections practise hypergamy among themselves. Thus the Chhâniyân, Nasâniyân, and Barauniya give their daughters in marriage to the Tarela, Ratha, and Jeorahiya, but will not marry their sons in these groups.

Marriage rules.

4. The sub-castes are endogamous and follow the usual formula of exogamy, which prohibits intermarriage in the family of the paternal and maternal uncles and aunts for two or three generations, or as long as any relationship is remembered.

Domestic ceremonies.

5. The domestic ceremonies are of the normal type practised by respectable natives of the same social standing.

Religion.

6. Patwas are generally Vaishnavas of the Kabîrpanthi or Satyanâmi sect. To the east of the Province their clan deities are Mahâbîr, the Pânchonpîr, and Hardiha or Hardaul Lâla, who is the household godling. On the tenth of the light half of Kuâr they offer flowers and sweetmeats to Mahâbîr, Mahâdeva, Narsinha, and Nârâyana. At the Nâgpanchami festival, in the month of Sâwan, they let a ram loose in the name of Devi, and throw over it a mixture of sugar and pepper dissolved in water. Some are Nânakpanthis, and these at the Khichari festival, at the end of the month of Mâgh, worship the scriptures (*granth*) with an offering of the Halwa sweetmeat. This is known as *karâhprasâd*, or "the offering from the boiler." In Ballia some worship Durga and Bhairon and some a local saint known as Ganinâth. These deities are worshipped on the tenth day of the waxing moon in the month of Kuâr. Unmarried girls are excluded from this worship, and only women married by the regular ceremony, and not women married by the *sagâi* or *kâj* form, are allowed to attend. In Hamîrpur they specially worship Hardaul Lâla, prayer to whom averts danger at marriage and pregnancy, and brings good rain and keeps off storms. In addition to these they worship a crowd of godlings, such as Sati, Dhyân Dâs, Gharîb Dâs, Goswâmi, to whom worship is done by making a fire-sacrifice (*hom*) and burning some incense (*dhûp*). To the east of the

Province they have no shaving ceremony (*múnran*) for children and never cut their hair. At death they only cut their nails as a sign of mourning, rub their bodies with mustard oil (*karua tel*), and their heads with oil-cake. Their priests are Tiwâri Brâhmans of the Sarwariya tribe.

Occupation.

7. Some of the Patwas weave silk from the indigenous cocoons. The 'Ilâqêband, who, as already stated, is usually a Muhammadan, makes coloured cords of silk or cotton thread used for the threading of beads and the binding together of ornaments such as the *bázuband* or armlet, which consists of several pieces joined together in an elastic band, and he also makes braid, fringe, petticoat strings (*nára*), and girdles for drawers (*izárband*). The Patwa does pretty much the same work; but the Musalmân occasionally adds to this whip-making as part of his business, which the Hindu does not. He buys up plain cotton and silk thread and dyes it himself, not, however, usually employing fast colours. The Lahera sub-caste is said to be so called because they chiefly use the lac dye (*láh-lákh*) for this purpose. In Lucknow some are wealthy traders, selling lac trimming (*lachka*), *kalabatún*, or gold and silver thread, false gems and pearls, and they make up embroidery, presentation robes (*khil'at*) and necklaces for entertainments (*hár*), etc.[1] The country Patwa very commonly deals in women's spangles and forehead ornaments (*tikuli*), and he sells various kinds of cosmetics, substances for making caste-marks, and common medicines.

Distribution of Patwas according to the Census of 1891.

DISTRICTS.	Agarwâla.	Deobansi.	Kharwâr.	Others	Muhammadans.	TOTAL.
Dehra Dûn . .	...	...	...	8	...	8
Sahâranpur . .	...	...	...	343	15	358
Muzaffarnagar .	...	22	...	202	1	225
Meerut . .	...	...	...	202	10	212
Aligarh . .	...	...	...	33	...	33
Mathura . .	...	3	35	136	...	174

[1] Hoey, *Monograph*, 118, *sq.*

Distribution of Patwas according to the Census of 1891—contd.

DISTRICTS.	Agar-wâla.	Deobansi.	Kharwâr.	Others.	Muham-madans.	TOTAL.
Agra	...	...	...	528	...	528
Farrukhâbâd	...	175	...	217	...	392
Mainpuri	55	3	...	64	...	122
Etâwah	19	...	...	278	...	297
Etah	37	3	...	105	...	145
Bareilly	...	...	...	824	...	824
Bijnor	...	93	...	325	...	418
Budâun	...	101	...	404	...	505
Morâdâbâd	...	70	...	257	5	332
Shâhjahânpur	...	837	...	103	...	940
Pilibhît	...	366	...	42	...	408
Cawnpur	...	246	...	410	...	656
Fatehpur	...	407	...	171	...	578
Bânda	...	88	...	894	...	982
Hamîrpur	...	18	...	543	...	561
Allahâbâd	...	745	...	449	27	1,221
Jhânsi	...	...	...	163	...	163
Jâlaun	...	...	...	286	...	286
Lalitpur	...	...	...	315	...	315
Benares	...	58	...	819	...	877
Mirzapur	...	975	...	196	2	1,173
Jaunpur	...	651	...	...	...	651
Ghâzipur	...	166	9	352	...	527
Ballia	...	1,902	3	373	...	2,278
Gorakhpur	...	121	75	2,044	4	2,244
Basti	...	118	1,281	160	...	1,559

Distribution of Patwas according to the Census of 1891—concld.

DISTRICTS.	Agar-wâla.	Deobansi.	Kharwâr.	Others.	Muham-madans.	TOTAL.
Azamgarh	...	342	48	312	44	746
Tarâi	...	43	...	35	...	78
Lucknow	...	466	...	219	...	685
Unâo	...	464	...	118	...	582
Râê Bareli	...	763	...	100	...	863
Sîtapur	...	729	...	194	...	923
Hardoi	...	945	...	13	...	958
Kheri	...	760	...	202	...	962
Faizâbâd	...	48	359	337	12	756
Gonda	...	...	1,525	65	...	1,590
Bahrâich	...	113	...	703	...	816
Sultânpur	...	136	193	483	8	820
Partâbgarh	...	453	135	57	...	645
Bârabanki	...	356	...	168	37	561
TOTAL	111	12,786	3,663	14,252	165	30,977

Pauhâri.—A variety of Bairâgis, who are said to derive their name from the Sanskrit *payas*, "milk," *ahâra*, "food," in reference to their rule of abstinence. The Pauhâriji of Paikauli in the Gorakhpur District is a notable personage, who wanders over that and the neighbouring Bihâr Districts with a large train of followers. He has branch establishments at Baikunthpur, Ajudhya, Allahâbâd, and other places.

Pâwariya, Pânwariya.—A tribe of Muhammadan singers and dancers who take their name from *pânwara* (*pânw*, foot), the mat or carpet on which they sing and play. They are apparently very closely akin to the Dhârhi and Kingariya, under which heads some account of these people has been given.

Distribution of the Pâwariya according to the Census of 1891.

Districts.	Numbers.
Gorakhpur	147
Azamgarh	365
Total .	512

Pokharna.—A division of Brâhmans of whom only a few scattered families are found in these Provinces. According to the account generally received they take their name from the sacred lake of Pokhar or Pushkar, and by one legend they were the navvies who dug the lake, and who were raised to the rank of Brâhmans for their services. By their own story they were named Pushpakarna, "having a flower in the ear," because they offered flowers to Lakshmi, and, being cursed by Pârvati for refusing to eat flesh, migrated from Jaysalmer to Sindh, Cutch, Multân, and the Panjâb. Other castes affirm that the Pokharna is the illegitimate offspring of a Brâhman devotee and a Mohani fisherwoman, who independently undertook to ferry the holy man across the stream.[1] They wear the sacred thread, putting it on with little ceremony, generally at a relation's marriage, or at some place of pilgrimage. High caste Brâhmans do not eat with them. Among members of the same *gotra*, marriage is not allowed. On the sixth day after childbirth, the women of the family, singing as at a marriage, bring a clay horse from the house of the mother's father to the husband's house. At marriages the men dance in the procession and the women sing immodest songs.[2]

2. In the Panjâb they still worship the pickaxe with which they excavated the Pushkar Lake. They are the hereditary Brâhmans of the Bhâtiyas of Rajputâna, and are more strict in caste matters than the Sarasvatas. They are found in some numbers in the Western Districts of the Panjâb.[3]

Potgar[4]—(Hindi *pot*, "a bead;" Sanskrit *protakâra*).—A small caste of bead-makers found only in the village of Naurera, Tahsîl Patti, in the Partâbgarh District, and numbering only 92 persons. They say that they were originally Kshatriyas, but have

[1] Burton, *Sindh*, 310.
[2] *Bombay Gazetteer*, V, 44.
[3] Ibbetson, *Panjâb Ethnography*, para. 513.
[4] From a note by Mr. D. Calnan, C. S.

no tradition as to how they came to adopt their present occupation. They wear the Brâhmanical cord. They do not admit outsiders into the caste. They follow the customs of high caste Hindus. They will not touch liquor or eat any kind of flesh, and are strict vegetarians. They will not eat or smoke with any caste other than their own. A full account of the bead manufacture has been given by Dr. Watt.[1]

Prânnâthi.—A Hindu religious order which takes its name from one Prânnâth, a Kshatriya, who, being versed in Muhammadan as well as Hindu learning, composed a book called the Mahitâriyal, in which the Qurân is reconciled with the Vedas. He lived in the latter period of the reign of Aurangzeb, and is said to have acquired great reputation with Chhattrasâl, Râja of Bundelkhand, for whom he discovered a diamond mine. They appear in the Census returns chiefly in the Gorakhpur Division; but Professor Wilson says that Bundelkhand is the chief seat of the order, and at Panna is a building dedicated to the use of the sect, in one apartment of which, on a-table covered with gold cloth, lies the volume of the founder.[2]

2. "As a test of the disciple's consent to the real identity of the Hindu and Muhammadan creeds, the ceremony of initiation consists of eating in the society of members of both communions; with this exception, and the admission of the general principle, it does not appear that the two classes confound their civil or even religious distinctions; they continue to observe the practices and ritual of their forefathers, whether Musalmân or Hindu, and the union, beyond that of the community of eating, is no more than any rational individual of either sect is fully prepared for, or the admission that the God of both and of all religions is one and the same."

Distribution of the Prânnâthis according to the Census of 1891.

Districts.	Numbers.
Pilibhit	7
Lalitpur	13
Gorakhpur	26
Basti	23
Total	69

[1] *Dictionary of Economic Products*, I, 426, *sqq.*

[2] *Essays*, I, 351. For an account of the religious books of this sect, see Growse, *Mathura*, 230, *sqq.*

Pundîr.—A sept of Rajputs who appear to belong to the Dahîma, one of the thirty-six royal tribes, of whom Colonel Tod[1] writes:—"The Dahîma has left but the wreck of a great name. Seven centuries have swept away all recollection of a tribe who once afforded one of the proudest themes for the song of the bard. The Dahîma was the lord of Bayâna and one of the most powerful vassals of the Chauhân Emperor, Prithivi Râja. Three brothers of this house held the highest offices under this monarch, and the period during which the elder, Kaunas, was his minister, was the brightest in the history of the Chauhân. But he fell a victim to blind jealousy. Pundîr, the second brother, commanded the frontier at Lahore. The third, Châond Râê, was the principal leader in the last battle, where Prithivi Râja fell, with the whole of his chivalry, on the banks of the Kâgar. Even the historians of Shahâb-ud-dîn have preserved the name of the gallant Dahîma, Châond Râê, whom they style Khandê Râê; and to whose valour, they relate, Shahâb-ud-dîn himself nearly fell a sacrifice. With the Chauhân, the race seems to have been extinguished." The original seat of the Panjâb[2] Pundîrs was Thanesar and the Kurukshetra of Karnâl and Ambâla, with local capitals at Pûndri, Ramba, Hâbri and Pûndrak; but they were dispossessed by the Chauhân under Râna Har Râê, and for the most part fled beyond the Jumna. From this event most probably their settlement in these Provinces dates. In the Duâb they say that they came from Hardwâr in the Sahâranpur District. Their leader is said to have been Râja Damar Sinh, who established himself at Gambhîra in Pargana Akrâbâd of the Aligarh District. Their fort was Bijaygarh, which took its name from Bijay, brother of Damar Sinh. It was captured in 1803 at the cost of the lives of Colonel Gordon and other British officers. It has now passed into the hands of the Râja of Awa. These Duâb Pundîrs hold a respectable rank and intermarry with the higher Râjput septs.

2. In the Upper Duâb they are reported to give girls to the Bargûjar, Chauhân, Gahlot, Kathiya, Tomar, Chhokar, and Bhatti; and to take brides from the Bargûjar, Chauhân, Gahlot, Tomar, Bais, and Bhatti septs.

---

[1] *Annals*, I, 128.
[2] Ibbetson, *Panjâb Ethnography*, section 445.

Distribution of the Pundîr Râjputs according to the Census of 1891.

Districts.	Hindus.	Muhammadans.	Total.
Dehra Dûn	...	1	1
Sahâranpur	18,120	7,267	25,387
Muzaffarnagar	7,128	3,875	11,003
Meerut	...	15,680	15,680
Bulandshahr	991	122	11,113
Mathura	285	5	290
Agra	98	1	99
Mainpuri	29	7	36
Etâwah	1	...	1
Etah	1,693	22	1,715
Budâun	247	...	247
Morâdâbâd	54	...	54
Bânda	438	...	438
Allahâbâd	12	...	12
Gorakhpur	7	...	7
Basti	4	...	4
Râê Bareli	2	...	2
Bahrâich	...	24	24
Sultânpur	31	...	31
Total	29,140	27,004	56,144

Purohit—(Sanskrit *purohita*, "one placed foremost or in front").—One of the functional divisions of the Brâhman caste. In Vedic times the Purohit was regarded as a confidential and virtuous minister of state; but in Manu he is placed in a lower class than other Brâhmans. At the same time the institution of the Purohit, who was not only a mere house priest but a political functionary, goes back to that early period of history when the Turanians and Indians lived peaceably as one nation. His high position in early times is shown by the assertion that the gods do not accept the food offered by a king who has no house priest, and by the fierce contest for the office which arose between the families of Vasishtha and Visvamitra.[1]

2. The functions of the Purohit in modern times are confined to the performance of the less intricate rites, those of more ceremonial intricacy and importance being left to the Achârya, Hotri, Bidua, and other priests of higher rank. He helps his master to perform the annual *Srâddha*, acts the part of a Brâhman, who must be fed before his employer breaks his fast, officiates at the family-shrine of the household gods, helps the barber to find a husband for his master's daughter, cooks for him on a journey, and arranges for the feeding of Brâhmans. He sometimes does a vicarious pilgrimage for his employer, and the extension of these functions to the richer members of the lower castes is the chief method by which they are brought within the fold of Brâhmanism.

3. Of these Brâhman priests Sir Monier-Williams writes:[2] "His anger is as terrible as that of the gods. His blessing makes rich, his curse withers. Nay, more, he is himself actually worshipped as god. No marvel, no prodigy in nature, is believed to be beyond the limits of his power to accomplish. If the priest were to threaten to bring down the sun from the sky or arrest it in its daily course in the heavens, no villager would for a moment doubt his power to do so. And indeed the priests of India, in their character of Brâhmans, claim to have worked a few notable miracles at different times and on various occasions. One of their number once swallowed the ocean in three sips, another manufactured fire, another created animals, and another turned the moon into a cinder. The priest confers incalculable benefits on the community of which he is a member by merely receiving their presents. A cow given to him secures heaven of a certainty to the lucky donor. The consequences of injuring him are terrific. A man who does him the smallest harm, must make up his mind to be whirled about after death, for at least a century, in a hell of total darkness."

Purwâl, Purwâr.—A sub-caste of Banyas who are believed to take their name from Puri or Jagannâth. According to Mr. Sherring[3] they live in large houses in Benares and are persons of conse-

---

[1] Muir, *Ancient Sanskrit Texts*, I, 128. Note: Manu, *Institutes*, XII, 46. Haug, *Aitareya Brâhmanam*, I, 67: II, 528. Max Müller, *Ancient Sanskrit Literature*, 485, *sqq*.

[2] Monier-Williams, *Brâhmanism* and *Hinduism*, 457.

[3] *Hindu Castes*, I, 283.

quence. The sub-caste is divided into twenty branches. Some are Vaishnavas and some Jainas.

Distribution of Purwâl Banyas according to the Census of 1891.

DISTRICTS.	Hindus.	Jainas.	TOTAL.
Sahâranpur	1	7	8
Bulandshahr	...	5	5
Mathura	9	86	95
Agra	434	4,048	4,482
Farrukhâbâd	664	15	679
Mainpuri	336	237	573
Etâwah	9,621	7	9,628
Etah	...	3,159	3,159
Bareilly	519	...	519
Budâun	41	...	41
Pilibhît	42	...	42
Cawnpur	1,859	20	...
Fatehpur	40	...	40
Bânda	189	164	353
Hamîrpur	512	64	576
Allahâbâd	36	...	36
Jhânsi	189	1,504	1,693
Jâlaun	1,167	...	1,167
Lalitpur	...	6,694	6,694
Ballia	25	...	25
Gorakhpur	6,183	...	6,183
Lucknow	13	...	13
Sîtapur	4,078	...	4,078
Kheri	685	...	685
Gonda	156	..	156
Bahrâich	3,063	...	3,063
Bârabanki	1,041	...	1,041
TOTAL .	30,903	16,010	46,913

Q

Qâdiri, Qâdiriya.—An order of Muhammadan Faqîrs, who are the followers of Abdul Qâdir Jilâni, who is buried in Bâghdâd. The Arabs, who have no hard *g* letter, alter to Jilân the name of his birth-place Gilân, a tract between the Caspian and the Black Sea. He is also known as Pîran-i-Pîr and Pîr Dastgîr, "the saint of saints, the helper of the helpless," and as Ghaus-ul-Azam, Ghaus-ul-Sumdâni, Mahbûb Subhâni, and so on. He was born in 1078 A.D., and died in 1166 A.D., and was buried at Bâghdâd, where he held the post of guardian of Abu Hanîfa's tomb.[1] Mr. Maclagan writes:[2]—"Most of the Sunni Maulavis of the Panjâb belong to this order, as does also the Akhund of Swât. They practise both the silent and the loud form of service (the *zikr-i-khafi* as well as the *zikr-i-jalli*). In youth they shout the *Kalima* with a particular intonation of the words *illah 'illâhu*, but afterwards articulate it with suppressed breath. They reject musical accompaniments, and seldom indulge in songs, even unaccompanied by music, in their religious devotions. They wear green turbans, and one of their garments must be of ochre, a colour first used by the saint Hasan Basri. The repetition of the Darûd, or salutation to the Prophet, bears a conspicuous part in the ceremonial of this order. Their chief places of sanctity in the Panjâb are the Khânqâh of Maulâna Muhammad Fâzil in Batâla; the Mausoleum in Lahore of Shâh Muhammad Ghaus, whose disciples are found as far as Kâbul, Ghazni, and Jalâlâbâd; the shrine of Tâhir Bandagi in Lahore, and that of Shâh Kamâl at Hujra Shâh Muqîm in the Montgomery District. There is also a shrine of his between the fort and the city at Ludhiâna, where the saint is said to have left his tooth-brush. A fair, called the Roshani Fair, is held here on the 14th of Rabi-us-Sâni; cattle are tied up at night at the shrine for good luck, and are said to keep watch (*chauki*) at the shrine, and women who desire offspring make offerings."

2. The order has a special interest, as it was into this that Sir R. Burton was initiated before his famous pilgrimage to Makka and Madîna. The curious may consult the record of the journey for a copy of the diploma investiture which he received[3]

---

[1] Beal, *Oriental Dictionary*, *s. v.*
[2] *Panjâb Census Report*, 194.
[3] *II*, 327.

Distribution of the Qâdiris according to the Census of 1891.

Districts.	Numbers.	Districts.	Numbers.
Dehra Dûn	71	Bânda	8
Sahâranpur	316	Hamîrpur	6
Muzaffarnagar	164	Allahâbâd	78
Bulandshahr	759	Jhânsi	1
Mathura	13	Lalitpur	14
Agra	2	Ghâzipur	129
Farrukhâbâd	21	Gorakhpur	21
Mainpuri	22	Tarâi	453
Etâwah	36	Lucknow	32
Etah	65	Râê Bareli	110
Bareilly	1,152	Sîtapur	2
Budâun	206	Faizâbâd	236
Morâdâbâd	294	Gonda	1
Shâhjahânpur	401	Bahrâich	15
Pilibhît	677	Bârabanki	129
Fatehpur	2	TOTAL	5,436

Qalâigar (Arabic *qalâi*, "tin").—The man who tins the copper cooking-vessels, which are so widely used both by Muhammadans and Christians. The caste, so-called, is purely occupational, and all who entered their names as such at the last Census were Muhammadans.

Distribution of the Qalâigars according to the Census of 1891.

Districts.	Numbers.	Districts.	Numbers.
Muzaffarnagar	4	Tarâi	12
Budâun	22	Lucknow	
Morâdâbâd	31	Gonda	1
Fatehpur	3	Bahrâich	1
Jhânsi	2	Sultânpur	2
Ghâzipur	10	TOTAL	89

Qalandar.—A caste of Muhammadan Faqîrs, bear and monkey leaders. According to Mr. Platts, the word is used for the original *kalandar*, "a rough, unshaped block or log." They trace their origin to the Saint Bo 'Ali Qalandar, who died in 1323-24. Of him many wondrous tales are told. He used to ride about on a wall, but at last settled down at Pânipat. "The Jamna then flowed under the town, and he prayed so continuously that he found it convenient to stand in the river and wash his hands without moving. After seven years of this he got stiff, and the fishes ate his legs; so he asked the river to step back seven paces and let him dry. In her hurry to oblige the saint, she retreated seven miles, and there she is now. He gave the people of Pânipat a charm which drove away all flies from the city. But they grumbled and said they rather liked flies, so he brought them back a thousandfold. The people have since repented. There was a good deal of trouble about his funeral. He died near Karnâl, and there they buried him. But the Pânipat people claimed his body, and came and opened his grave; on which he sat up and looked at them till they felt ashamed. They then took some bricks from his grave with which to found a shrine; but when they got to Pânipat and opened the box, they found his body in it; so he now lies buried both at Pânipat and Karnâl."[1]

Occupation.

2. The Qalandar of these Provinces is generally a lazy, swindling rascal, some of whom go about with snakes; others with tame bears and monkeys. He wears round his neck several strands of white stones or beads and glass. He also carries a bead rosary (*tabîsh*), and usually on his right wrist two or a single brass bangle. On his right leg he has an iron chain. He also has a vessel (*kishta*), made of cocoanut shell (*daryâi nâriyal*), and a brass *lota*. Sometimes he has an iron bar as well. He announces his approach by twanging the *damaru*, or little drum, shaped like an hour-glass. Those who have monkeys, the male being generally called Maula Bakhsh and the female Zahûran, make them dance to amuse children. Those who have bears, make them dance, and allow for a consideration little boys to ride on their backs, which is believed to be a charm against the small-pox. They also sell some of their hair, which is a favourite

[1] Ibbetson, *Panjâb Ethnography*, section 224: Lady Burton, *Arabian Nights*, I, 81; VI, 227.

amulet against the Evil Eye. Some go about as ordinary beggars. Though they wander about begging they are not absolute vagrants, as they have settled homes and families.

Domestic ceremonies.

3. Marriage among them takes place at the age of from ten to twenty. They follow in all their ceremonies the rules of the Sunni sect of Muhammadans, to which they belong. Some of them have taken to the trade of the Bisâti, and make tin frames for lanterns and small boxes (*dibiya*) out of tin. All Muhammadans will eat and smoke with them. No Hindu, except a Dom or a Dharkâr, will touch their food.

The Criminal Qalandar.

4. The Qalandar is our old friend the Calendar of the *Arabian Nights*. Most of them are merely loafing beggars; but in Rohilkhand there appears to be a branch of them known as the Langrê, or "lame," Qalandars, who are said to be Rohillas from Râmpur.[1] They were formerly residents of Hardoi, and devoted themselves to stealing horses and ponies, which were passed from Oudh to British territory and *vice versâ*. Shâhâbâd, in Hardoi, was regarded as their head-quarters, and there they had the name of Machhlê. On the annexation of Oudh, they divided into gangs, and nominated one Bânkê as their leader (*sargiroh*), with two assistants, known as the Bhandâri, or purveyor, and Kotwâl, or police officer. On the celebration of the marriage of any of their members they continue, if possible, to assemble together and distribute food and wine to the best of their ability; on the occasion of marriage ceremonies among the Khatris, when any of the gangs are present, gifts of food and money are given to them, which they designate their *birt*, or "maintenance." This is also the name given to what they receive on certain occasions when religious ceremonies are performed. They are very superstitious, and have their own omens and signs, some of which are considered lucky, and others the reverse. Thus the barking of a hyæna behind them or on their left is considered a bad omen.

Mode of thieving.

5. This tribe, or rather the numerous gangs composing it, proceed through districts disguised and call themselves Langrê Qalandar or Rohillas of

---

[1] Report of Mr. H. Ross, District Superintendent of Police, Pilibhît.

Râmpur. In Râmpur and the neighbourhood they use the former, and towards Lucknow the latter. They travel about in the cold and hot weather, but in the rains they settle down and occupy themselves in begging. Their wives and children accompany them, but they do not encumber their movements with any luxury, such as cattle, furniture, etc., having only one or two ponies for the transport of their personal effects, in addition to which, hidden among their quilts and blankets, are reins, ropes, and headstalls for the stolen ponies. This is undoubtedly the reason why they have hitherto never been classed as a criminal tribe, nor have raised suspicion as to their real character. They pass the night under trees or in the fields, or, if near a populous place, in a convenient grove. During the day, disguised as beggars, they mark down the horses and ponies which they purpose to steal. When they obtain a fair number of animals, they pass off as horse-merchants, and make their escape as rapidly as possible. Animals stolen near Lucknow are sold in the northern parts of Oudh and the North-West Provinces—their chief markets being Bilâspur in the Râmpur State, Durâo in the Tarâi, and Chichait in Bareilly. They chiefly frequent the districts of Pilibhît, Kheri, Bahrâich, and the Tarâi, as they are close to Nepâl, where ponies and fodder are plentiful.

Thieves' argot of the Langrê Qalandars.

6. These people have a regular thieves' argot of their own, of which the following are examples :—

Bidna	Man.
Bidni	Woman.
Basta	Rupee.
Bairgi	Cot.
Botay	Sheet, quilt.
Bajrin	Gun.
Bodi	Hair tuft.
Châl	Hair.
Chetha	Flour.
Chiki	Fire.
Chitya	Cat.
Chimmi	Fish.
Charya	Tree.
Chirma	Colt.
Dhaind	Burglary.

Dhun	Ear.
Dúdrín	Leg.
Dhurd	Grain.
Dhurcha	Red pepper.
Dhungara	The *Singhára* nut (water caltrop).
Dhingaila . . .	Bullock.
Dhingaili	Cow.
Dhúwar	Pig.
Dhung	Sheep.
Dhujja	Cock.
Dhuttar . . .	Camel.
Dhúhari	Sugarcane.
Dhulludár . . .	Police Officer.
Dhuddah	Duck.
Dhurangi	European.
Dhúsa	Mouse.
Ealakh	Oil.
Ghutrín	Eyes.
Ghummar	Elephant.
Ghuttani	Eight annas.
Ghurka	Water pot, jug.
Jurha	Pony.
Jurhi	Pony mare.
Khunji	Buffalo.
Kumdár	Comrade.
Khuranga . . .	Donkey.
Khurchna . . .	Pipe, *huqqah*.
Khunnay	House.
Khail	Wine.
Lilka	Butter, *ghi*.
Lung	Rope.
Morhay	Tooth.
Matláo	Tank, pond.
Maikrín	Goat.
Mogán	Jackal.
Mithkar	Sugarcane.
Mukki	Sheep.
Mohidár	Village Watchman.
Markni	Bludgeon.

Nudli	Village.
Niklu	Bread
Oi	A well.
Phirkni	Cart.
Pecha	Pice.
Patki	Grass.
Ráp	Foot.
Ratáila	Stomach.
Ratki	Wheat.
Rípún	Shoe.
Surpna	Nose.
Thunda	Boy.
Thundi	Girl.
Thúb	Hand.
Tena	Head.
Thum	Grain.
Tundul	Rice.
Theman	Salt.
Thimman	Coarse sugar (*gur*).
Thimjái	Sweatmeat.
Thubbák	Reins.
Thokay	Jungle.
Urkna	Grain.
Dhulludár áya hai, paté hoé.	The Sub-Inspector is coming, run away.
Khurchna tudlo	Smoke the *huqqah.*
Oi sé chayan marap láo	Fetch the water from the well.
Phirni par dhurrup lo	Get into the cart.
Dhurangi bakussa	A European approaches.
Khunnay men dhaind lagi	A burglary has been committed in the house.
Mohidár bakussa, jurhi thokay men khon áo.	A watchman is coming, take the pony into the jungle.
Nukka nudli men hurka	A dog is barking in the jungle.

Distribution of the Qalandars according to the Census of 1891.

Districts.	Numbers.	Districts.	Numbers.
Dehra Dûn . . .	13	Ghâzipur . . .	106
Meerut	317	Ballia	241
Bulandshahr . . .	644	Gorakhpur . . .	929
Aligarh . . .	36	Basti	3,833
Mathura . . .	23	Lucknow . . .	11
Agra	11	Unâo	8
Furrukhâbâd . .	19	Râê Bareli . . .	207
Bareilly . . .	157	Sîtapur . . .	62
Pilibhît . . .	73	Kheri	74
Cawnpur . . .	8	Faizâbâd . . .	316
Fatehpur . . .	12	Gonda	4
Allahâbâd . . .	265	Bahrâich . . .	10
Benares . . .	25	Sultânpur . . .	58
Mirzapur . . .	63	Bârabanki . . .	93
		Total .	7,628

Qassâb, Qassâi—(Arabic *qasab*, "to cut"), the butcher caste.—They are usually separated into two endogamous sub-castes: Gaû, Gawa or Gorû Qassâi, who kill cows and buffaloes, and Bakar Qassâi, who kill only goats. The latter is also known by the names Chik, Chikwa or Buzqassâb (Persian *buz*, "a goat"). The Chiks are all Hindus, and have various sub-castes, one of which is Khatîk. The Qassâbs are all Muhammadans of the Sunni sect, and follow the ordinary Muhammadan rules of exogamy and inheritance. Marriage usually takes place at the age of fifteen or sixteen, and when there are two or three marriageable youths in a family, they are generally married at the same time to save expense. Special reverence is paid in the east of the Province to the Pânchon Pîr, and in particular to Ghâzi Miyân, to whom fowls, cakes (*malîda*), sweetmeats, and garlands of flowers are offered. The food, after dedication, is consumed by the worshippers. At the Shab-i-bârât festival, they offer food to the sainted dead. The Gaû-qassâb, from his trade, is naturally an object of detestation to orthodox Hindus. A common proverb runs: *Jahân sagaré gâon qassâi, tahân ek Ramdâs ki kâ basâi?* "How can a single servant of God live in a village of butchers?" In effecting his purchases, he often has to assume disguises, and sometimes procures his supplies through the agency of Nats. In Lucknow [1] there are two classes of Qassâbs: Kameladâr and Ghair Kameladâr, *Kamela* meaning the "shambles;" the former are slaughtermen, who sell wholesale, and the latter are retailers of meat, who buy from them and sell at shops. The former always count the hide their profit, and the latter sell at a fixed charge of one anna per ser for meat with bone, and one and a half annas per ser for boneless meat. Chikwas sometimes combine in a partnership of three or more; one remains in charge of the cattle yard and the other two go to neighbouring villages and buy up sheep and goats. Both Qassâbs and Chikwas again deal in hides.[2] Some, again, add to their meat business a trade in cloth and stone: a few hold land as non-occupancy tenants. "The Indo-Europeans all make their appearance in history as meat-eating peoples, and only among the Hindus did animal food as early as Vedic times give way more and more to a vegetable diet, obviously because of the climate."[3] In Vedic times the Vaikarta was the butcher, who cut up and distributed the flesh of the sacrificial victim, and the custom is distinctly recognized and prescribed by Manu.[4] In Buddhist times, however, we learn that in Madhyadesa "they do not keep swine or fowls, they do not deal in living animals, nor are there shambles or wine shops round their markets."[5]

Distribution of Chiks and Qassâbs according to the Census of 1891.

Districts.	Chik.		Qassâb.	
	Khatik	Others.	Bakar-qassâb.	Others.
Dehra Dûn . . .	...	...	...	79
Sahâranpur . . .	...	...	...	11,751
Muzaffarnagar . . .	...	...	17	12,170

[1] Hoey, *Monograph*, 163.
[2] See Hoey, *ibid*, 90, *sqq*.
[3] Schrader, *Prehistoric Antiquities*, 315.
[4] *Institutes*, V, 32, *sqq*.
[5] Beal, *Fahhian*, 55.

Distribution of Chiks and Qassâbs according to the Census of 1891 —contd.

Districts.	Chik.		Qassâb.	
	Khatîk.	Others.	Bakar-qassâb.	Others.
Meerut	...	...	...	16,013
Bulandshahr	...	...	906	8,384
Aligarh	...	...	291	5,461
Mathura	...	...	...	5,418
Agra	...	...	...	4,300
Farrukhâbâd	...	1,936	403	1,245
Mainpuri	...	551	...	1,019
Etâwah	34	812	...	745
Etah	..	722	...	2,947
Bareilly	...	287	2,394	242
Bijnor	...	...	766	8,500
Budâun	...	532	341	1,746
Morâdâbâd	...	...	33	6,851
Shâhjahânpur	...	585	533	2,519
Pilibhît	...	43	146	2,404
Cawnpur	2	1,774	40	2,040
Fatehpur	...	95	10	2,554
Bânda	...	778	38	134
Hamîrpur	...	541	...	575
Allahâbâd	...	409	621	2,675
Jhânsi	...	15	48	293
Jâlaun	...	138	...	30
Benares	...	...	...	1,295
Mirzapur	...	74	40	552
Jaunpur	...	...	540	1,240
Ghâzipur	...	...	...	1,945

Distribution of Chiks and Qassâbs according to the Census of 1891—concld.

Districts.	Chik.		Qassâb.	
	Khatîk.	Others.	Bakar-qassâb.	Others.
Ballia . . .	...	...	8	385
Gorakhpur	...	...	19	1,524
Basti	...	...	1,256	248
Azamgarh	...	...	124	2,510
Târai	...	2	...	696
Garhwâl	...	...	8	...
Lucknow	...	25	2,954	2,161
Unâo	...	...	297	2,380
Râê Bareli	...	11	1,929	1,448
Sîtapur	...	...	1,183	1,388
Hardoi	13	50	1,559	892
Kheri	...	1	1,183	829
Faizâbâd	...	...	570	1,105
Gonda	...	...	231	1,909
Bahrâich	...	...	918	675
Sultânpur	...	...	1,191	520
Partâbgarh . . .	...	...	506	301
Bârabanki	...	...	1,962	1,263
Total .	49	9,381	23,155	1,25,361

R

Râdha : Bhagat.[1]—A tribe found chiefly in Rohilkhand and Oudh. The people returning themselves as Bhagat in the last Census returns are probably the same people. In Bareilly they have three endogamous sub-castes : the Bhatela, Khatiya, and Bichauri. The rule of exogamy is that common to all tribes of this grade. According to tribal usage polygamy is forbidden; but this regulation is violated by the chief men of the tribe. They know nothing of their origin except that they are in some way connected with Râdha, the mistress of Krishna. They are perhaps, like the Kingariyas, akin to the great Nat race. They have now settled down and do not admit outsiders to their tribe. Those who can afford it practise infant marriage ; the poor seldom marry till they are adult. The women are allowed no license either before or after marriage. Polyandry is prohibited as well as widow marriage. A wife detected in adultery is expelled from the house. They are Hindus and worship Parameswar, Devi, Mahâdeva, the Ganges, and the Miyân of Amroha, who is honoured with a sacrifice of sweet cakes (*gulgula*) and goats. These offerings are received by the Madâris who attend his shrine. Men and women both worship this godling. They engage Brâhmans for their religious and *quasi*-religious ceremonies. Such Brâhmans are received on equal terms with their brethren. They burn their adult dead and bury children. The ashes are consigned to the Ganges or any of its tributaries. They perform the usual *srâddha* in the month of Kuâr as a propitiation to the spirits of the dead.

Occupation.

2. Their profession, as is shown by their name, is singing and dancing, and it has been so from time immemorial. Their musical instruments are the *tabla*, or tambourine, and the *sârangi*, or guitar. Some of them have now turned to cultivation. They do not, like other similar tribes, prostitute their girls or married women. They abstain from intoxicating liquor, and eat no meat but that of goats.

---

[1] Based on notes by the Deputy Inspector of Schools, Bareilly.

Distribution of the Râdhas and Bhagats according to the Census of 1891.

DISTRICTS.	RÂDHA.		BHAGAT.	
	Males.	Females.	Males.	Females.
Sahâranpur . . .	1	...	1	...
Farrukhâbâd . . .	60	64	82	103
Mainpuri	4	6	5	2
Etâwah	...	...	2	10
Etah	...	...	76	51
Bareilly . . .	29	28	12	2
Budâun	8	5	6	5
Morâdâbâd . . .	1	...	...	...
Shâhjahânpur . . .	281	282	...	...
Pilibhît	64	74	...	...
Cawnpur	1	...	...	...
Bânda	3	1	1	3
Benares	67	57	...	...
Tarâi	7	4	...	...
Lucknow	8	10	...	...
Sîtapur	359	376	...	...
Hardoi	772	662	...	...
Kheri	313	304	...	...
Bahrâich	107	130	...	...
Râmpur	18	33	...	...
TOTAL .	2,036	2,029	252	233

Râdha Swâmi.—A small sect, containing at the last Census only 188 adherents, mostly residents of Mathura; is said to have been founded by Râê Sâlig Râm, late Postmaster General of these Provinces. The tenets of the sect seem to differ little from those of the modern reformed Vaishnavas.

Râdha Vallabhi.—A Gusâîn order founded by Hari Vans, of whom Mr. Growse[1] says:—"His father Vyâsa was a Gaur Brâhman of Devaban in the Sahâranpur District who had long been childless. He was in the service of the Emperor, and on one occasion was attending him on his march from Agra, when at last his wife Târa gave birth to a son at the little village of Bâd, near Mathura, in the Sambat year 1559. In grateful recognition of their answered prayers, the parents named the child after the god they had invoked and called him Hari Vans, *i.e.*, 'Hari's issue.' When he had grown up he took to himself a wife by name Rukmini, and had by her two sons and one daughter. After settling his daughter in marriage, he determined to abandon the world and live the life of an ascetic. With this resolution he set out alone on the road to Brindaban, and had reached Charthâwal near Hodal, when there met him a Brâhman, who presented him with his two daughters, and insisted on his marrying them, on the strength of a divine command which he said he had received in a vision. He further gave him an image of Krishna with the title of Râdha Vallabha, which, on his arrival at Brindaban, was set up by Hari Vans in a temple that he had erected between the Jugal and the Koliya Ghâts on the banks of the Jamuna. Originally he had belonged to the Mâdhvâcharya Sampradâya, and from them and the Nimbâraks, who also claim him, his doctrine and ritual were professedly derived. But in consequence of the mysterious incident by which he had been induced to forego his intention of leading a celibate life, and to take to himself two wives, or rather in consequence of his strong natural passions which he was unable to suppress and therefore invented a fiction to excuse, his devotion was all directed, not to Krishna himself, except in a very secondary degree, but to his fabled mistress Râdha, whom he deified as the goddess of lust."

2. After quoting some of his poems, Mr. Growse goes on to say: "If ever the language of the brothel was borrowed for temple use it has been so here. But, strange to say, the Gusâîns, who accept as their gospel these nauseous ravings of a diseased imagination, are for the most part highly respectable married men, who contrast rather favourably with the professors of rival sects that are based on more reputable authorities. Several of them have a

[1] *Mathura*, 185, *sqq.*

very good knowledge of literary Hindi; but their proficiency in Sanskrit is not very high.

3. "To indicate the fervour of his passionate love for his divine mistress, Hari Vans assumed the title of Hit Ji, and is popularly better known by this name than by the one which he received from his parents. His most famous disciple was Vyâs Ji of Orchha, of whom various legends are reported. On his first visit to the Swâmi he found him busy cooking, but at once propounded some knotty theological problems. The sage, without any hesitation, solved the difficulty, but first threw away the whole of the food which he had prepared, with the remark that no one could attend properly to two things at once. Vyâs was so struck with this procedure that he then and there enrolled himself as his disciple, and in a short space of time conceived such an affection for Brindaban that he was most reluctant to leave it, even to return to his wife and children. At last, however, he forced himslf to go, but he had not been with them long before he determined that they should themselves disown him, and accordingly he one day in their presence ate some food from a Bhangi's hand. After this act of social excommunication, he was allowed to return to Brindaban, where he spent the remainder of his life, and where his Samâdh or tomb is still to be seen."

Distribution of the Râdha Vallabhi Gusâins according to the Census of 1891.

Districts.	Numbers.	Districts.	Numbers.
Muzaffarnagar	30	Morâdâbâd	2
Agra	70	Lalitpur	5
Mainpuri	5	Gorakhpur	13
Etah	13	Gonda	111
Bijnor	3	Total	252

Males	160
Females	92

Raghubansi.—A sept of Râjputs connected with the Nikumbh (*q. v.*). Those in Sultânpur [1] profess to be lineally descended from Raghu, an ancestor of Râma, and claim to have been settled in

[1] *Settlement Report*, 135.

their present abode ever since the time of their eponymous ancestor. For centuries they resisted successfully the threatened encroachments of the Bachgotis; and maintained intact a frontier marked by a little nameless affluent of the Gumti. It was not till within the half century of disorder and misrule which preceded the annexation of the Province, that they succumbed, and even now, though only in a subordinate position, they retain no considerable portion of their ancient heritage In Sîtapur[1] they have suffered much in recent times, and are gradually dying out. In their estates a tradition exists that the cultivation of sugar is fatal to the farmer, and that the tiling of a house brings down divine displeasure upon the owner; hence to this day no sugar is grown and not a tiled house is to be seen.

2. In Sultânpur they marry girls of the Bilkhariya, Tashaiya, Chandauriya, Kath Bais, Bhâlê Sultân, Chandel, and Palwâr septs; and give brides to the Tilokchandi Bais, Mainpuri Chauhâns, Sûrajbansis of Mâhul, Gautams of Nâgar, Majhauli Bisens, Râjkumâr and Bachgoti. Their *gotra* is Kasyapa. In Jaunpur they take brides of the Nikumbh, Gaharwâr, Chaupat Khamb, Bais Bisen, Kâkan, Singhel, Sombansi, and Ujjaini.

Distribution of the Raghubansi Râjputs according to the Census of 1891.

DISTRICTS.	Numbers.	DISTRICTS.	Numbers.
Sahâranpur	9	Bareilly	59
Meerut	21	Budâun	342
Aligarh	46	Morâdâbâd	95
Mathura	19	Shâhjahânpur	1,396
Agra	83	Pilibhît	114
Farrukhâbâd	210	Cawnpur	261
Mainpuri	221	Fatehpur	479
Etâwah	294	Bânda	1,725
Êtah	414	Hamîrpur	614

[1] *Oudh Gazetteer*, III, 390.

Distribution of the Raghubansi Râjputs according to the Census of 1891—concld.

DISTRICTS.	Numbers.	DISTRICTS.	Numbers.
Allahâbâd . . .	403	Lucknow . . .	269
Jhânsi	57	Unâo	324
Jâlaun	33	Râê Bareli . . .	797
Lalitpur . . .	10	Sîtapur . . .	611
Benares . . .	15,197	Hardoi . . .	156
Mirzapur . . .	2,935	Kheri	431
Jaunpur . . .	17,412	Faizâbâd . . .	2,921
Ghâzipur . . .	2,956	Gonda . . .	11
Ballia	151	Bahrâich . . .	175
Gorakhpur . . .	1,445	Sultânpur . . .	3,687
Basti	997	Partâbgarh . . .	90
Azamgarh . . .	2,477	Bârabanki . . .	1,249
Tarâi	20	TOTAL .	61,216

Rahwâri[1] (*rahwâr*, "quickpaced, active").—A caste of camel owners and drivers, also known as Riwâri, Râêwâri. Of these people Abûl Fazl writes[2] :—"Raibâri is the name given to a class of Hindus who are acquainted with the habits of the camel. They teach the country-bred *lok* camel so to step as to pass over great distances in a short time. Although from the capital to the frontiers of the Empire, into every direction, relay horses are stationed, and swift runners have been posted at the distance of every five *kos*, a few of these camel riders are kept at the palace in readiness. Each Raibâri is put in charge of fifty stud *arwânahs*, to which, for the purpose of breeding, one *bughur* and two *loks* are attached." Colonel Tod,[3] writing of the Raibâris, says :—"This term is known throughout Hindustân only as denoting persons employed in rearing

[1] Largely based on a note by Bâbu Atma Râm, Head Master, High School Mathura.

[2] Blochmann, *Aîn-i-Akbari*, I, 147, *sq.* For a complete account of the camel, see Watt, *Economic Dictionary*, *s.v.*

[3] *Annals*, II, 357.

and tending camels, who are there always Muslims. Here they are a distinct tribe and Hindus, employed in rearing camels, or in stealing them, in which they evince a peculiar dexterity, uniting with the Bhattis in the practice as far as Dâûdputra. When they come upon a herd grazing, the boldest and most experienced strikes his lance into the first he reaches, then dips a cloth in the blood, which, at the end of his lance, he thrusts close to the nose of the next, and, wheeling about, sets off at speed, followed by the whole herd, lured by the scent of blood and the example of their leader." Of the Bombay branch of the tribe we are told that "in Kachchh they say they came from Mârwâr, and this is supported by the fact that the seat of their tribe goddess Sikotra is at Jodhpur. The story of their origin is that Siva, while performing religious penance (*tap*), created a camel and a man to graze it. This man had four daughters, who married Râjputs of the Chauhân, Gambhîr, Solanki, and Pramâr tribes. These and their offspring, were all camel drivers. Tall and strongly made, with high features and an oval face, the Rahwâri, like the Ahîr, takes flesh and spirits, and does not scruple to eat with Musalmâns. He lives for days solely on camel's milk. Except a black blanket over his shoulders, the Rahwâri wears cotton clothes. This waist cloth (*dhoti*) is worn tucked through his legs, and not wound round the hips like a Râjput's. They live much by themselves in small hamlets of six or eight grass huts. They are described as civil and obliging, honest, intelligent, contented, and kindly. They are very poor, living on the produce of their herds. Each family has a she-camel called Mâta Meri, which is never ridden, and whose milk is never given to any one but a Hindu." [1]

The Rahwâris of the North-West Provinces.

2. They pretend to possess a complete set of *gotras*; but no one can even attempt to give a full list of them. A man cannot marry in his mother's or grandmother's *gotra*. They claim to be Râjputs, but cannot designate any particular sept as that from which they have sprung. They do not admit outsiders into their tribe. Both infant and adult marriages are allowed, and no sexual license on the part of the girls is tolerated before marriage. Polyandry is prohibited, and polygamy allowed up to the extent of three wives at a time. The marriage is celebrated in the usual Hindu fashion, and the perambulations

[1] *Bombay Gazetteer*, V, 80; see also VII, 137, *sq.*

(*bhânwar phirna*) round the nuptial shed are the binding part of the ritual. A widow may marry again by the *dharîcha* form, and the levirate is permitted, but it is not compulsory on the widow to marry the younger brother of her late husband. A wife can be expelled from the house for infidelity, and for no other cause. Such a woman may marry again in the tribe by the *dharîcha* form.

Religion and customs.

3. The Rahwâris are Vaishnavas and worship Bhagwân. They worship Devi in the months of Chait and Kuâr, as well as Zâhir Pîr in Bhâdon. They eat the offerings themselves, which consist of sweetmeats and fruits. They employ Brâhmans as their family priests, and such Brâhmans are received on an equality with those who do the same service for other castes. They burn their dead. Poor people leave the ashes on the cremation ground; those who can afford it take them to the Ganges or Jumna. They do the *sráddha*, and some even go to Gaya for that purpose. Their primary occupation is rearing, tending, and letting out camels for hire. Some have purchased land, others cultivate as tenants, and others are landless labourers. They eat the flesh of cloven-footed animals, fowls, and fish; but not monkeys, pork, beef, flesh of whole footed animals, crocodiles, snakes, lizards, jackals, rats, or other vermin, or the leavings of other people. They can eat *pakki* in the same dish with Jâts, and can use their tobacco pipes, and they will also smoke with Gûjars; but they will eat *kachchi* only with their own caste. The Rahbâri, as he appears in these Provinces, has rather an evil reputation for high-handedness, and he is proverbially deceitful and untrustworthy.

Distribution of the Rahwâris according to the Census of 1891.

DISTRICTS.	Numbers.	DISTRICTS.	Numbers.
Muzaffarnagar . .	39	Mainpuri . . .	34
Meerut . . .	18	Etah	4
Bulandshahr . . .	89	Jhânsi . . .	2
Mathura . . .	454	Ghâzipur	4
Agra	254	TOTAL .	898

Raikwâr.—A sept of Râjputs who claim to be of Sûrajbansi origin. Their settlement in Bahrâich[1] dates from about 1414 A. D.,

[1] *Settlement Report*, 28, *sq*.

when, during the anarchy that prevailed through Hindustân on the decline of the house of Tughlaq, the two brothers, Pratâp Sâh and Dondi Sâh, Sûrajbans Râjputs, migrated from Raika in Kashmîr, whence they profess to take their name, and finally took up their abode at Râmnagar in the Bârabanki District. His sons overcame the Bhar Râja and acquired his estate about 1450 A.D., and since then the Raikwârs have been masters of the western part of the district. In the time of Akbar, Harihar Deva, fifth in descent from Pratâp Sâh, who had been summoned to court to explain a breach of good manners in levying toll from one of the Princesses as she passed through his estate on a pilgrimage to the shrine of Sayyid Sâlâr, rendered such assistance to the Emperor in his campaign against the rebellious Governor of Kashmîr, that he was granted nearly nine parganas. The connection of the Unâo [1] family with the great Râjas on the banks of the Ghâgra had been entirely broken off; but when they began to rise in political importance they sought to renew it, and Mitthu Sinh and Bakht Sinh went to Râmnagar and claimed brotherhood with the Râja. He heard their story and entertained them with hospitality, and sent them out food. Amongst other things he provided tooth-brushes made of the wood of the *nîm* tree. All other Râjputs place a special value on this wood; but the Raikwârs alone are forbidden to use it. The rejection of these tooth-brushes by his guests proved to him that they were truly of his own kin. The brother of the founders of the families of Baundi and Râmnagar [2] was Bhairwanand. His nephews concocted a prophecy that their uncle should be sacrificed to secure the future greatness of the family, and he gave up his life for their sake. A platform, erected in the village of Chanda Sihali, marks the tradition that Bhairwanand fell into a well and was allowed to drown there in the hope that the prophecy would be fulfilled and their rule continue for ever. To the present day Raikwârs make an annual pilgrimage to the platform of Bhairwanand.

2. In Râê Bareli [3] their sons marry girls of the Bisen and Trans-Ghâgra Bais; their daughters marry in the Bais, Panwâr, and Amethiya septs. In Bareilly they select brides from the Bâchhal

---

[1] Elliott *Chronicles*, 44, *sq*.

[2] *Manual of Titles in Oudh*, 10; *Oudh Gazetteer*, I, 117, 120 *sq*., 257, 285, 288.

[3] *Settlement Report*, Appendix C.

and Gautam septs; their sons marry Janghâra, Bhûr and Katheriya girls. In Farrukhâbâd they claim to belong to the Vasishtha *gotra;* their girls marry in the Sombansi, Râthaur, and Chauhân septs; their sons, in the Katheriya, Gaur, Baisgaur, Nikumbh, Jaiswâr, Chamâr Gaur, Ujjaini, and Parihâr. In Unâo their daughters marry Dikhits, Gaharwârs, Janwârs, Chauhâns, and Chandels; their sons, Mahrors and Gahlots. In Unâo they say they belong to the Bhâradvâja *gotra;* they take brides from the Bisen, Ahban, Katheriya, Gaur, and Chandel, and give brides to the Sombansi, Chandel, Gaur, Chauhân, Tomar, and Ahban. In Hardoi,[1] during the Mutiny, they were remarkable for their lawlessness, and it was in attacking their fort at Ruiya that the lamented Adrian Hope was killed.

Distribution of the Raikwâr Râjputs according to the Census of 1891.

DISTRICTS.	Hindus.	Muhammadans.	TOTAL.
Dehra Dûn	1	...	1
Sahâranpur	...	14	14
Muzaffarnagar	...	606	606
Mathura	2	...	2
Agra	1	...	1
Farrukhâbâd	623	32	655
Mainpuri	87	...	87
Etâwah	80	...	80
Etah	39	...	39
Bareilly	355	..	355
Budâun	760	...	760
Morâdâbâd	41	...	41
Shâhjahânpur	99	10	109
Pilibhît	2	10	12
Cawnpur	261	...	261
Fatehpur	116	...	116

[1] *Settlement Report*, 184.

Distribution of the Raikwar Rajputs according to the Census of 1891—concld.

Districts.	Hindus.	Muhammadans.	Total.
Bânda	28	...	28
Hamîrpur	63	...	63
Allahâbâd	401	45	446
Jhânsi	4	...	4
Jâlaun	462	1	463
Lalitpur	3	...	3
Benares	1	...	1
Jaunpur	95	...	95
Ghâzipur	228	...	228
Ballia	701	...	701
Gorakhpur	843	14	857
Basti	881	...	881
Azamgarh	1,025	...	1,025
Lucknow	407	...	407
Unâo	2,070	431	2,501
Râê Bareli	168	39	207
Sîtapur	1,165	62	1,227
Hardoi	2,073	...	2,073
Kheri	306	9	315
Faizâbâd	1,758	...	1,758
Gonda	737	...	737
Bahrâich	4,247	350	4,597
Sultânpur	282	42	324
Partâbgarh	916	116	1,032
Bârabanki	2,578	17	2,595
Total .	23,909	1,798	25,707

Râin.—A gardening and cultivating caste found in the Meerut and Rohilkhand Divisions, with both a Hindu and Muhammadan branch. They are the same as the Arâins of the Panjâb, of whom Mr. Purser writes[1]:—"The Arâins say they came from Sirsa, Raniya, and Delhi, and were originally Hindu Râjputs. They claim to be descended from Râê Jaj, the grandson of Lava, founder of Lahore. Jaj was the ruler of the Sirsa territory, and on that account was called Râê; and his descendants became subsequently known as Arâin. They became Muhammadans chiefly in the time of Shahâb-ud-din Ghori, or at the end of the twelfth century. Some three hundred years ago they came to this part of the country. Some of the Arâins of the Jâlandhar Tahsîl say they are the descendants of Râja Bhûta, fifth in descent from Râja Karan, and were settled in Uchh. They were forcibly converted by Mahmûd of Ghazni. They then migrated to Sirsa, and thence at various times came into the Panjâb. They had to leave Uchh because they refused to give a lady, called Basanti, to the king. This is clearly proved by this verse, which also shows the straits they were reduced to—

Uchh na dîtê Bhûtian chata Basanti nâr;
Dâna pâni chuk gaya; châban moti hâr.

'The Bhûtas neither gave Uchh nor the lady Basanti;
food and water were exhausted; they had to eat pearls.'

2. "One of the chief Arâin clans is called Bhutta. They are generally supposed to be converted Kambohs, and say they are legitimate, and the Kambohs the illegitimate, offspring of a common ancestor. In my enquiries they would admit no relationship. It would seem they were originally located on the lower Indus, and that one section of them settled on the Ghaggar. When this river dried up, they moved into the Jumna and Cis-Satlaj tracts; and perhaps spread along the foot of the hills and across the line of movement of their brethren, who were moving up the valleys of the great rivers. By some they are said to be the same stock as the Sainis; but this is certainly not a common tradition, and the assertion is probably based on the fact that the Arâins are called in Persian Bâghbânân, which is the translation of *Máli*, or gardener, and that Saini is only a local term for the *Mális*. It may be noted that Mahr is a title among the Arâins, and also among the Gûjars."

---

[1] *Jalandhar Settlement Report*, 82, *sq.*

3. From Hissâr Mr. Fagan writes:—"In Hissâr they are exclusively Musalmân and claim Râjput descent, their ancestor having lost caste by taking to agriculture. Their *gotras* appear to bear Râjput names, such as Siroha, Chauhân, and Bhâti. There is however one *gotra* called Katma, which is said to consist of the true Arâins, who are not Râjputs. The tradition of the Sirsa Râins is that they were expelled from Uchh, near Multân, by their enemies, and escaped by abandoning their military rank and taking to market gardening, the tribal occupation of their neighbours, the true Râins. They came and settled on the Ghaggar, and up to the famine of 1795 A.D. they are said to have held the whole of the Ghaggar valley from Bhatner up to Tohâna in Fatehâbâd. The famine, combined with the attacks of the marauding Bhatti Râjputs, weakened their hold on the land, and they finally broke before the Châlîsa famine of 1783 A.D. (*Sambat 1840*) and many of them emigrated to Bareilly, Pilibhît, and Râmpur in the North-West Provinces. On the advent of British power they again expanded, principally in Sirsa. One clan deny any connection with the Musalmân Kambohs, which the Sirsa Râins appear to admit."

4. Mr. Ibbetson says[1]:—"The Satlaj Arâins in Sirsa say that they are, like the Arâins of Lahore and Montgomery, connected by origin with the Hindu Kambohs. Mr. Wilson thinks it probable that both classes are really Kambohs who have become Musalmâns, and that the Ghaggar Arâins emigrated in a body from Multân, while the others moved gradually up the Satlaj into their present place. He describes the Arâins of the Ghaggar as the most advanced and civilised tribe in the Sirsa District, and he considers them at least equal in social status to the Jâts, over whom they themselves claim superiority."

Distribution of Râins according to the Census of 1891.

DISTRICTS.	Hindus.	Musalmâns.	TOTAL.
Dehra Dûn	...	135	135
Sahâranpur	131	1,168	1,299
Muzaffarnagar	12	2,099	2,111

[1] *Panjâb Ethnography*, 267.

Distribution of the Râins according to the Census of 1891—concld.

DISTRICTS.	Hindus.	Musalmâns.	TOTAL.
Mathura	...	1	1
Bareilly	...	1,918	1,918
Morâdâbâd	...	1	1
Pilibhît	...	5,197	5,197
Jhânsi	...	3	3
Gorakhpur	3	...	3
Tarâi	...	4,573	4,573
Bahrâich	...	2	2
TOTAL	146	15,097	15,243

Râj, Râj Mistri, Thawai (in Persian *Me'mâr*).—The mason and bricklayer caste. The word Râj means either a "head workman" (Hindi *râja*) or is a corruption of the Persian *râz*; Mistri is a corruption of the Portuguese *mestre*; Thawai of the Sanskrit *stha pati*. The caste is a purely occupational one, and is recruited from many of the lower castes, among whom Chamârs are very numerous.

Distribution of the Râj Mistris according to the Census of 1891.

DISTRICTS.	Hindus.	Musalmâns.	TOTAL.
Sahâranpur	318	166	484
Muzaffarnagar	390	166	556
Meerut	246	77	323
Bulandshahr	577	4	581
Aligarh	285	2	287
Mathura	54	...	54
Agra	8	56	64
Farrukhâbâd	16	189	205
Mainpuri	181	...	181

Distribution of the Râj Mistris according to the Census of 1891— contd.

DISTRICTS.	Hindus.	Musalmâns	TOTAL.
Etâwah	157	2	159
Etah	145	90	235
Bijnor	...	258	258
Budâun	41	327	368
Morâdâbâd	26	290	316
Shâhjahânpur	12	122	134
Pilibhît	...	3	3
Cawnpur	...	38	38
Fatehpur	...	158	158
Hamîrpur	26	1	27
Allahâbâd	21	35	56
Jhânsi	123	3	126
Jâlaun	10	...	10
Benares	...	98	98
Jaunpur	...	109	109
Ghâzipur	...	10	10
Gorakhpur	34	128	162
Basti	...	112	112
Azamgarh	...	12	12
Tarâi	...	5	5
Lucknow	2	5	7
Unâo	...	249	249
Râê Bareli	...	184	184
Sîtapur	...	4	4
Hardoi	4	4	8
Kheri	145	36	181
Faizâbâd	...	90	90

Distribution of the Râj Mistris according to the Census of 1891—concld.

DISTRICTS.	Hindus.	Musalmans.	TOTAL.
Gonda	...	28	28
Bahrâich	171	...	171
Sultânpur	...	238	238
Partâbgarh	...	21	21
Bârabanki	73	148	221
TOTAL .	3,165	3,468	6,633

Râji ("the royal people").—A tribe, apparently of non-Aryan affinities, found in Askot, in Kumaun, and in small numbers along the lower Himâlayan ranges.

Traditions of origin.

2. They have been identified with the Râjya Kirâtas, who, in early Sanskrit literature, are joined with the Sakas and Savaras as Dasyus, and are placed by the Varaha Sanhita between Amaravana and China, or between Jagesar and Tibet; and the title will mean either "the princely Kirâtas" or the "the Kirâtas of Râjya."[1] The Râjis have often been noticed by ethnographers whose speculations have been based on a few lines by Mr. Traill.[2] It is there said that the Râji represent themselves as descendants of one of the aboriginal princes of Kumaun, "who with his family fled to the jungle to escape the destruction threatened by an usurper. Under the pretension of royal orgin, the Râwats or Râjis abstain from offering to any individual, whatever his rank, the usual Eastern salutation." He also states that there is a total dissimilitude of language between the Râjis and Kumâunis, and that the Doms may have been descended from these Râjis, "the former being, for the most part, extremely dark, almost black, with crisp, curly hair, inclining to wool." This, until the present enquiries, is the only account that has been given on any authority regarding the Râjis; yet

[1] Muir, *Ancient Sanskrit Texts*, II, 365, 491; Wright, *Nepâl*, 89, 106, 110, 312; *Journal, Asiatic Society of Bengal*, 1849, pages 733, 766; 1858, page 446, quoted by Atkinson, *Himalayan Gazetteer*, II, 364, *sqq*.

[2] *Report, Kumaun*, 19, 57; *Asiatic Researches*, XVI, 150.

Professor Ritter found in it confirmation of the opinion that a Negro race may have been among the aboriginal inhabitants of the Himâlaya and Kuen-lun. There is no foundation for the statement that the Doms have curly hair inclining to wool. Out of hundreds that have come under notice, not a single one can be said to have any Negroid characteristic, though many are of an extremely dark complexion, like the other similar servile castes in the plains. Dr. Pritchard[1] conjectured that the Râjis would be found to resemble the other numerous aboriginal tribes found along the Himâlayan border, all "possessing the physical character of the Bhotiyas in general and very unlike the Doms." Dr. Latham[2] too expresses his conviction that the Râjis are "the equivalents to the Chepang of Nepâl." Captain Strachey noticed "nothing very remarkable about them, except an expression of alarm and stupidity in their faces, and they are perhaps darker and otherwise more like lowland Hindustânis than the average Kumaun *Pahâris*." They manufacture wooden bowls for sale and "live under temporary huts, frequently moving from place to place amidst the jungles of Chipula; their principal subsistence being certain edible sorts of wild plants and what game they can catch, and they occasionly get presents of cooked food from the villagers. They have a dialect of their own, but some of them can communicate with their civilized neighbours in *Pahâri* Hindi." The scanty vocabulary of the Râji languages that has been collected supports the connection with the tribes of Nepâl suggested by Dr. Latham.

Fresh enquiry.

3. The following more particular account of the Râjis has been prepared from notes by Bhawâni Singh, Teacher of the Deoliya Kot School in the Almora District:—

Traditions and marriage.

4. They are known by two names: Râji and Râwat. These names are used by the people themselves as well as by outsiders. They say that they are descended from the servants of the Râja of Kutpur, by whom they were expelled for some fault. Since then they have been wandering about in the hills and forests, living on jungle produce. At the time of their expulsion the Râja of Kutpur was Nîl Kapâl, but they cannot say how many

[1] *Researches*, IV, 206, 231.

[2] *Ethnology of the British Colonies*, 132; Atkinson, *loc. cit.*, 366.

years ago he lived. This Kutpur family, they say, reigned for thirty-eight generations—from Vikramaditya to Biram Deo. All the members of the tribe consider themselves equal and intermarry freely. Their appearance, in the opinion of this observer, suggests a doubt as to whether they are not the degraded descendants of one of the higher castes. Their tribal deity is Bâgh Nâth, "the tiger lord," who has a shrine at Kutpur, supported by an endowment of villages. They practise the ordinary Hindu law of exogamy; but they are not allowed to marry two sisters. They are monogamous, but can keep concubines. The bridegroom's father or, in default of him, some near relation, arranges the marriage. If the parties are minors, the consent of the parents is essential. Some small bride-price is usually paid. Part of this is paid a few days before the marriage, and the balance when the husband brings home his bride. The greater part of it becomes the special property of the bride, and if she be divorced, which can be done if she proves unfaithful or contracts leprosy, she takes away with her her own share of the bride-price. A divorced woman, can marry again, and the offspring of regular marriages, widow marriages, and those contracted with divorced women, all inherit equally the property of their father. The levirate is allowed with the usual restriction that it is only the younger brother of the husband that can marry his widow. If the widow marries an outsider, the guardianship of her children by her first husband falls to the brother of her late husband. They succeed to the whole estate of their father; if there be no sons, his brethren succeed.

Birth ceremonies.

5. The baby is named five days after birth, and on that day the family eat specially good food. There is no trace of the couvade and no custom of adoption.

Betrothal.

6. When a boy attains majority, his father goes and arranges the price of a bride for him. He pays over something in advance to close the bargain, and is then feasted, and remains there for the night. Then a date is fixed, and the boy's father comes with his friends and relations and takes the bride home. A betrothal cannot be annulled by the friends of the girl once they have received part of the bride-price in advance. The only ceremony at the reception of the bride into the family of her husband is that his mother rubs some yellow pigment on her forehead as she enters the house.

7. They bury their dead in any convenient place in the jungle. The clothes of the dead person and the sheet in which the corpse is wrapped are laid over the grave and not removed by the friends. It may be conjectured that the idea is to provide clothing for the naked spirit in the next world.

Disposal of the dead.

8. The children of the deceased and his younger brothers get their heads, beards, and moustaches shaved, and the hair is thrown on the grave as a sacrifice to the spirit of the dead man. They appear to perform no ceremony in the nature of the *srâddha*, and no loss of ceremonial purity results after death, childbirth, or menstruation.

Ancestor worship.

9. They call themselves Hindu by religion. They worship Devi in the month of October under a large tree with an offering of cooked food and animal sacrifice. When any one gets ill, they worship the gods, ghosts, and demons of the jungle; but they erect no temples in their honour, and make no pilgrimages. They appear to have no caste initiation ceremony, and no priests. Their religious duties are performed by the eldest male member of the family. The worship of Devi is performed publicly by day; but that of the ghosts and demons, secretly by night. The special offering to Devi consists of goats; the demon and ghosts are propitiated by a sacrifice of fowls. These offerings are made on the tops of hills or under some large trees. After the offering is made, the meat is consumed by the worshippers.

Religion.

10. Their festivals are the Kark Sankrânt, or "passage of the sun into the sign of Cancer;" and those of Aries and Capricornus, *Mekha, Makara ki Sankrânt;* marriage days and after childbirth. On these festivals they eat specially good food themselves and entertain their relations and friends. They believe that demons and ghosts inhabit the tops of mountains, rivers, wells, and wherever water accumulates. If, after a visit to the jungle, a person becomes ill, they attribute the attack to the wrath of the jungle demon. It is then necessary to propitiate him with appropriate sacrifices. The fields are haunted by a special demon known as Chhal, who is, as a rule, benignant. Though they keep no annual feasts in their honour, they live in excessive dread of the ghosts of their deceased relations. These ghosts are of two kinds: some are worshipped as

Festivals.

the protectors of the household; and others because, if neglected, they bring disease and death.

Omens.

11. Their chief omens are derived from throbbing of various parts of the body. Thus the throbbing of the left eye or of any member on the left side of the body forebodes evil; the opposite is the case with the throbbing of any member on the right side of the body.

Evil Eye.

12. They are much in dread of the Evil Eye, and of demoniacal influence generally: the favourite precaution is to bestow opprobrious names of their children.

Magic and witchcraft.

13. They are not skilled in any special form of magic or witchcraft, but certain persons occasionally fall under the influence of a demon, and in a state of ecstasy pour out incoherent expressions, which are regarded as oracles. In such cases the family guardian demon is invoked to expel the malignant intruder, and he instructs them which form of worship or sacrifice should be used to bring about this result. The name of this family demon is Baitâl, the Sanskrit Vetâla.

Social rules and occupation.

14. They are not allowed to eat food which has been touched by Doms, Dhobis, and similar foul castes. Their chief business is to act as the pioneers of civilization by clearing the jungle. In this occupation they believe themselves to be much exposed to the attacks of the demons of the jungle; and in order to ward them off, they bury in the earth some animal bones or hang them on a tree close to the spot where they are working. They eat the flesh of cloven-footed animals and fish. They drink spirits freely when procurable. There is no food or drink specially reserved for males. All members of the family eat together in the same plastered enclosure (*chauka*), within which they place the leaf vessels in which they take their food. They are said never to use any form of salutation, either to strangers or to relatives and friends; the reason of this is, that they pretend to be of royal blood, and consider themselves inferior to no man. They are very shy in their intercourse with strangers; but those who gain confidence are well received and hospitably entertained on the roots and fruits which form their ordinary food. Usually when they see a stranger approaching, they run away and hide in the jungle. They have a dialect of their own, which is not intelligible to outsiders, and this

language is always spoken by the women and children. Most of the adult males are able to communicate with strangers in rude *Pahâri* Hindi. They are constantly on the move in search of jungle produce of various kinds; and it is only recently that they have begun to settle down and have taken to a rude form of cultivation in which they burn down scrub jungle and sow the seed in the ashes. This is the *dahya* cultivation of the Central Indian Plateau. At present one of their chief industries is the making of rude vessels out of the wood of the *genti* tree; these they exchange in the villages bordering on the jungle for scraps of coarse cloth and grain. When they acquire any grain by barter in this way or by cultivation, they hide it away in caves or tie it up in leaves and hang it from the branches of trees. Meanwhile, they live on any roots and fruits they can secure, and return to their grain stores only when pressed by extreme hunger. Some roots and fruits they hide away in caves for use in time of need. Their cultivation has hitherto been of the most casual and careless kind; but in recent years they have been helped by Government to obtain cattle and implements, and the younger generation show signs of taking more steadily to cultivation than their forefathers. The bride-price is almost invariably paid in coarse earthen or wooden vessels and implements for digging jungle roots.

15. From this account they appear to be in about the same stage of culture as the Korwas of Mirzapur.

2. **Râjkumâr** (Sanskrit *râja kumâra,* "a prince").—A sept of Râjputs in Oudh and the Eastern Districts. The term Râjkumâr is commonly applied to the junior branches of all houses in which a Râj exists, and thus there are Râjkumâr Bais, Râjkumâr Kânhpuriya, and Râjkumâr Bachgoti. It is to the last of these that the term is most generally applied, and the only explanation suggested of their appropriation of the title is that it is to distinguish them from their brethren the Rajwârs, who could once pride themselves on their chief being a Râja. With them alone the distinction has superseded the broader appellation of the clan.[1] The clan to which Bariyâr Sinh, the common ancestor, belonged, has now five branches, from which circumstance it is likened to the five fingers of a man's hand; these are the Chauhân, the Râjkumâr, the Rajwâr, the

[1] *Sultânpur Settlement Report,* 152.

Bachgoti, and the Khânzâda.[1] The Râjkumârs, through Bariyâr Sinh, claim direct descent from Râja Kundh Râj, brother of Prithivi Râja of Delhi. Opinions are divided as to the birth-place of Bariyâr Sinh. Some fix it at Sambhal near Morâdâbâd; some at Sâmbhar in Ajmer. By one account his emigration was due to the defeat of the Delhi Chauhâns; by another story his father, who had already twenty-two sons, married a young bride and she insisted that her son should succeed to the title; so Bariyâr Sinh and his brothers were driven to go abroad and seek their fortunes. The chief families of the sept are Dera, Meopur, Nânau, and Pâras Patti. The history and traditions of the sept have been elaborately illustrated by Mr. Carnegy. One of the earliest accounts of Râjput infanticide referred to the Râjkumârs.[2]

2. In Sultânpur it is reported that they take brides from the Bilkhariya, Tashaiya, Chandauriya, Kath Bais, Bhâlê Sultân, Raghubansi, and Gargbansi; and give girls to the Tilokchandi Bais, Mainpuri Chauhâns, Sûrajbansi of Mâhul, Gautams of Nagar, Bisens of Majhauli, Kânhpuriya, Gahlot, and Sombansi. Their *gotra* is said to be Vatsya. In Jaunpur it is said that they take brides from the Raghubansi, Bais, Chaupat Khamb, Nikumbh, Dhanmast, Gautam, Gaharwâr, Bisen, Panwâr, Chandel, Saunak, Drigbansi; and give girls to the Kalhans, Sirnet, Gautam, Sûrajbansi, Bachgoti, Rajwâr, Bisen, Kânhpuriya, Gaharwâr, Baghel, and Bais.

Distribution of the Râjkumâr Râjputs according to the Census of 1891.

Districts.	Numbers.	Districts.	Numbers.
Mathura	199	Bânda	2
Agra	4	Allahâbâd	216
Farrukhâbâd	2	Jhânsi	11
Morâdâbâd	27	Benares	199
Pilibhît	1	Mirzapur	115
Cawnpur	12	Jaunpur	5,745
Fatehpur	4	Ghâzipur	38

[1] *Faizâbâd Settlement Report*, 129; Elliot, *Chronicles of Unâo*, 43.
[2] *Asiatic Researches*, IV, 340: *Calcutta Review*, I, 377.

Distribution of the Râjkumâr Râjputs according to the Census of 1891—concld.

Districts.	Numbers.	Districts.	Numbers.
Ballia	6	Sîtapur	2
Gorakhpur . . .	285	Faizâbâd	1,575
Basti	337	Gonda	10
Azamgarh . . .	212	Bahrâich	23
Lucknow	29	Sultânpur . . .	15,299
Unâo	8	Partâbgarh . . .	123
Râê Bareli . . .	219	Bârabanki . . .	61
		Total	24,764

Râjput (Sanskrit *râja-putra*, "son of a king").—The warrior and land owning race of Northern India, who are also known as Thâkur, "lord" (Sanskrit *thâkkura*), or Chhatri, the modern representative of the ancient Kshatriya. All or most of the Râjput tribes in these Provinces have legendary accounts of their origin from the country known as Rajwâra, Rajasthân or Rajputâna. As General Cunningham writes [1]:—"The term Rajputâna is at present restricted to the States lying between the Jumna and Narbada, of which the Jumna forms the eastern boundary; but previous to the Mahratta conquest it really extended from the Satlaj on the west to the Chhota Sindh River of Mârwâr on the east.

2. "Within these limits the old States of Rajputâna may be conveniently divided into three large groups according to their relative positions, as Western, Eastern, and Southern.

3. "Western Rajputâna including the Râthaur States of Bikâner and Mârwâr; the Jâdon-Bhatti State of Jâysalmer; the Kachhwâha States of Jaypur and Shaikhâwati; and the Chauhân State of Ajmer.

4. "Eastern Rajputâna would include the present Narûka-Kachhwâha State of Alwar; the Jât States of Bharatpur and Dholpur; the Jâdon State of Karauli; the British Districts of Gurgâon, Mathura, and Agra; and the whole of the Northern Districts of Gwâlior, which still bear the names of their old Râjput proprietors,

[1] *Archæological Reports*, XX, 1, *sqq*.

as Jâdonwati, Tomargâr, Kachhwâhagâr, Bhadaurgâr, and Khichiwâra.

5. "Southern Rajputâna including the two Chauhân States of Bundi and Kotah, with the whole of Mewâr and Mâlwa.

6. "In ancient times the whole country lying between the Arvali Hills of Alwar and the Jumna was divided between Matsya on the west and Surasena on the east, with Dasûrana on the south and south-west border. Matsya included the whole of the present Alwar territory, with portions of Jaypur and Bharatpur. Bairât and Muchâri were both in Matsyadesa; while Karnân, Mathura, and Bayâna were all in Surasena. To the east was Panchâla, including the Antarveda and Rohilkhand. The Surasenas were Yadavas or Yaduvansis. A large portion of their old country is still in the possession of the Jâdon Râja of Karauli. Their chief towns were Methora and Kleisobaras, Mathura and Krishnapura. The Yadavas first succumbed to the great Maurya dynasty of Magadha, and were afterwards overwhelmed by the Indo-Scythians under the Satrap Rajubul and his son Saudâsa. It next fell under the Gupta dynasty, the power of which was broken by the death of Skanda Gupta in 319 A.D. At the time of Hwen Thsang's visit in 635 A.D., the King of Mathura was a Sûdra, but a few centuries later the Jâdon Râjputs were in full possession of both Bayâna and Mathura. Nearly the whole of Eastern Rajputâna, therefore, belonged to the Yaduvansi or Jâdon Râjputs. They held one-half of Alwar with the whole of Bharatpur, Karauli, and Dholpur, besides the British Districts of Gurgâon, Mathura, and the greater part of Agra west of the Jumna. It seems possible also that they may have held some portions of the present Gwâlior territory, lying along the Chambal River, opposite Karauli."

7. It was on the death of Harsu Vardhhana, the famous king of Kanauj, who reigned from 607 to 650 A.D., that most of the Râjput families would seem to have risen to power. The Tomaras of Delhi, the Chandelas of Khajuraho, and Sisodiyas of Chithor, as well as the Kachhwâhas of Narwar and Gwâlior, all begin their genealogies from that time.[1] As far as the eastern part of the Province is concerned, Sir C. Elliott[2] suggests that the amount of pressure from the Muhammadan invaders determined the character of the Râjput colonisation.

---

[1] *Archæological Reports*, II, 311.

[2] *Chronicles of Unâo*, 28, *sq.*

The Chauhâns are scattered over a wide extent of country and broken up into many small estates, while the powerful Gahlots of Chithor and Kachhwâhas of Amber maintained their independence for three centuries more and threw out hardly any colonies. The Oudh Râjputs may be divided into three great classes : the Bisen, Gaharwâr, and Chandel were settled in the pre-historic period ; the Gautam, Janwâr, Chauhân, Raikwâr, Dikhit, and Sakarwâr emigrated after the incursion of Shahâb-ud-dîn Ghori at the close of the twelfth century ; the Gahlot, Sengar, Panwâr, Gaur, and Parihâr came after the establishment of the Muhammadan power ; the Râwat and Mahror are indigenous to Unâo and are not found elsewhere. According to the Ghâzipur traditions, only from fifteen to thirty generations have elapsed since the first advent of their forefathers. Except the Hayobans and Kinwâr septs, all the tribes name places in the north, north-west, or west as the homes of their race. Malwâ, Bundelkhand, the Ganges-Jumna Duâb, the country beyond the Jumna from Agra to Delhi, Oudh, and the country beyond the Ghâgra, all are named as the old home of tribes now found in Ghâzipur.[1] The Oudh septs which claim an extra-provincial origin, trace their descent to single Chhatri leaders and not to troops of Râjput invaders. Such are the Bais of Baiswâra, who claim descent from Tilokchand, who came from the Central Provinces, and the Râjkumârs, from Bariyâr Sinh Chauhân of Mainpuri, through whom they claim kindred with Prithivi Râja of Delhi. With these exceptions none of the clansmen of Eastern Oudh claim Western origin.[2]

8. The traditions of the septs, which have been separately referred to, exemplify the fact that many of them are probably connected closely with the aboriginal races, and that there are grave grounds for suspecting the purity of their descent. Thus the Kânhpuriya and Bandhilgoti septs are traditionally descended from misalliances between two Brâhman brothers and women of the Ahîr and Dharkâr castes. The Chamar Gaur are supposed to be descended from a Chamâr father and a Gaur woman. Within the memory of man an Amethiya chieftain has, according to General Sleeman, taken to wife the daughter of an *ex*-Pâsi village watchman and raised up orthodox seed unto himself. The Râotârs, another

---

[1] Oldham, *Memo.*, I, 45.

[2] Carnegy, *Journal, Asiatic Society of Bengal*, 1876.

numerous clan, have the same traditional parentage (Brâhman-Ahîr) as the Kânhpuriyas. They are said to take their name from Râwat, an Ahîr chief. The Palwârs are alleged to be descended from a common ancestor who had four wives, of whom only one was of his own status, the others being of the Bhar, Ahîr, or other lower castes. The Bhâlê Sultân are in some way akin to Ahîrs, and there is a lower grade of the Bais with whom the real Tilokchandi branch will not intermarry.[1] The same process of the adoption into the Râjput body is still going on in the case of the Khasiyas of the lower Himalayan range and along the Vindhyas, as in the case of the Singrauli Râja in South Mirzapur, who has in quite modern times developed from a Dravidian Kharwâr into a Benbans Chhatri. Under the head of Jât will be found some considerations which lead to the belief that they are ethnologically identical with the Râjputs.

9. This process of corruption is aided by the results of infanticide. The difficulty among some septs of procuring wives has led to the introduction of low caste girls in the guise of high-born brides into many Râjput families. In many places a regular trade has arisen with the object of supplying girls of this kind. In some cases doubtless the husband is the victim of a deliberate fraud on the part of the match-maker or go-between; but in numerous instances there seems little doubt that the arrangement has the sanction of tribal custom; and even when a man finds that he has been induced to receive a low-born girl as his wife, the dread of a scandal prevents him from giving publicity to the matter.

10. Râjputs are endogamous and the septs are exogamous. As will be seen from the rules of intermarriage given in the separate articles on these septs, they practice what Mr. Ibbetson calls hypergamy, by which he means the rule according to which a Râjput prefers, if possible, to marry his daughter in a sept of higher rank than his own, while he will take a bride for his son from a sept of inferior social status. One form of this is embodied in the formula—*Beti pûrab, larka pachchham,* that is to say, a girl may be married to the eastern or inferior septs, while the son must seek a bride among the blue-blooded septs of the west; like the Mainpuri Chauhâns or the Râthaurs. Many Râjput youths, owing to the scarcity of girls, the result of infanticide, do not marry at all, and

---

[1] Carnegy, *loc. cit.*

form temporary connections with women of the low wandering tribes, such as Nâts, Kanjars, Beriyas, and the like. There has thus grown up in many of the septs two classes of different social rank: one the offspring of wives of legitimate descent, married in the orthodox way; the other the descendants of irregular connections with low caste women. Such people, as a rule, if they marry at all, marry in their own grade, and, unless they are wealthy, find it impossible to procure brides of unequivocal ancestry. It is needless to say that this connection of Râjput youths with women of these criminal races is a fertile source of crime. Gypsy gangs hang round Râjput villages and are supported and protected. During recent epidemics of violent crime in these Provinces, it has always been found that the dacoit bands were largely recruited from these half-bred Râjputs and their criminal associates.

11. The country legends abound with instances of the conflict between the Râjput and the Brâhman in pre-historic times. As a survival of this it may be noted that, in Bundelkhand, Brâhmans will not allow the navel string (*nâra*) of Râjput children to be buried in their villages lest the latter tribe may some day supplant and dispossess them.[1]

Distribution of Râjputs according to the Census of 1891.

DISTRICTS.	Hindus.	Muhammadans.	Aryas.	Jainas	Sikhs.	TOTAL.
Dehra Dûn	46,065	677	131	...	3	46,876
Sahâranpur	37,806	21,089	59	...	56	59,010
Muzaffarnagar	21,911	20,526	82	...	...	42,519
Meerut	60,954	30,656	215	1	13	91,839
Bulandshahr	84,351	31,406	1,585	...	...	117,342
Aligarh	77,856	808	188	...	2	78,854
Mathura	59,005	8,040	31	355	14	67,445
Agra	93,232	5,501	82	73	67	98,955
Farrukhâbâd	58,802	1,697	92	...	...	59,591

[1] Elliot, *Supplemental Glossary, s.v. Athmana.*

Distribution of Râjputs according to the Census of 1891—contd.

Districts.	Hindus.	Muhammadans.	Aryas.	Jainas.	Sikhs.	Total.
Mainpuri . .	53,175	329	46	...	...	53,550
Etâwah . .	54,743	522	52	...	3	55,320
Etah . . .	60,036	4,911	236	...	...	65,183
Bareilly . .	35,013	6,358	5	...	24	41,400
Bijnor . .	84,183	3,265	79	...	...	87,527
Budâun . .	60,999	5,636	152	...	5	66,792
Morâdâbâd . .	59,065	8,194	182	...	6	77,447
Shâhjahânpur .	64,503	3,596	59	...	...	68,158
Pilibhît . .	10,078	950	159	...	...	111,187
Cawnpur . .	88,031	785	121	...	...	88,937
Fatehpur . .	44,830	6,141	...	...	...	50,971
Bânda . .	51,926	1,653	...	2	8	53,589
Hamîrpur . .	35,085	457	...	...	...	35,542
Allahâbâd . .	53,131	2,173	...	...	...	55,304
Jhânsi . .	18,075	146	23	...	18	18,262
Jâlaun . .	35,155	328	...	...	...	35,483
Lalitpur . .	15,887	39	...	...	...	15,926
Benares . .	51,203	1,446	...	...	...	52,649
Mirzapur . .	63,171	210	...	...	147	63,528
Jaunpur . .	112,242	3,903	...	...	...	116,145
Ghâzipur . .	85,406	13,746	43	...	2	99,197
Ballia . . .	139,194	1,385	...	...	...	140,579
Gorakhpur . .	97,487	10,833	...	...	1	98,321
Basti . . .	50,938	39,465	...	...	...	90,403
Azamgarh . .	130,168	15,405	...	...	...	145,573
Kumaun . .	255,536	...	...	...	...	255,536
Garhwâl . .	231,953	...	...	...	...	231,953

Distribution of Râjputs according to the Census of 1891—concld.

DISTRICTS.	Hindus.	Muhammadans.	Aryas.	Jainas.	Sikhs.	TOTAL.
Tarâi . . .	16,557	536	5	...	...	17,098
Lucknow . .	26,565	1,308	28	...	119	28,020
Unâo . . .	60,766	2,028	26	...	28	62,848
Râê Bareli . .	69,664	7,757	...	...	6	77,427
Sîtapur . .	37,693	9,057	...	...	10	37,760
Hardoi . .	79,365	2,283	...	...	...	81,648
Kheri . . .	26,361	11,887	23	...	...	38,271
Faizâbâd . .	68,880	11,662	...	...	10	80,552
Gonda . .	61,361	27,431	...	...	...	88,792
Bahrâich . .	23,462	11,812	6	...	290	35,570
Sultânpur . .	88,547	25,497	...	...	...	114,044
Partâbgarh . .	61,487	4,795	...	...	...	66,282
Bârabanki . .	40,515	7,504	...	...	17	48,036
TOTAL .	3,251,418	375,833	3,710	431	849	3,632,241

Ramaiya[1] (Sanskrit *ram*, Hindi *ramna*, "to wander").—A pedlar class found in small numbers to the west of the Province. The Ramaiya of the east of the Panjâb is the Bhâtra, under another name. "The Bhâtra claims Brâhman origin, and his claim would appear to be good, for he wears the sacred thread, applies the *tilak*, or forehead mark, and receives offerings at eclipses in that capacity. He is probably a low class of Gujarâti or Dakaut Brâhman, and, like them, practises as an astrologer in a small way. The Bhâtras of Gujarât are said to trace their origin to the south beyond Multân. The Bhâtras hawk small hardware for sale, tell fortunes, and play on the native guitar, but do not beg for alms."[2] The Ramaiya of these Provinces, who is a pedlar and beggar, is properly a Sikh; but he is now so thoroughly domiciled here that it is difficult to

[1] Mainly based on notes by Pandit Janardan Dat Joshi, Deputy Collector, Bareilly.

[2] Ibbetson, *Panjâb Ethnography*, para 552.

distinguish him from other Hindus. Begging is recognized by him as an honourable profession, and a Ramaiya who is rich will have no hesitation in marrying his daughter to another Ramaiya who gains his living by begging. They trace their origin to Amritsar, and say they first began to come into these Provinces about four generations ago. Some of the wealthier members of the caste in Bijnor still draw their Brâhmans, their priests, or barbers, from the Panjâb. Some of them say that they are the direct descendants of the Guru Govind Sinh.

Tribal organization.

2. Their sections, as given in the Census returns, indicate that they are a very mixed race and made up of elements foreign to the races of these Provinces. Of the Hindu branch we find Bamra, Bank, Barsari, Bhalira, Bhât, Bhatti, Bisâti, Dargal, Gajra, Gaur, Gûjar, Gujarân, Hardoiri, Kathak, Nomâin, Râdi, Râê, Rânipâri, Râthaur, Sinha, and Siphmatua; of the Muhammadan branch, Banjâra, Râjput, Ramai.

Tribal council.

3. The tribal council (*panchâyat*) includes representatives from every family in the village, and is under a headman (*chaudhari*). The office is permanent and is conferred on the richest and most influential man in the community.

Marriage rules.

4. The rule of exogamy is that a man must marry in a *gotra* different from his own, and avoid connections with near relatives on the female side, such as the daughter of his sister or aunt. He may not have two sisters to wife at the same time, but there is no rule against his marrying the younger sister of his late wife. They very seldom marry more than one wife, and then only with the object of getting an heir. Girls are married from five to ten years of age; it is exceptional for a girl not to be married till fifteen, and the richer the family is the greater tendency there is towards infant marriage. The bride gets presents of jewelry from both sides, but there is no bride price paid. There is no formal divorce, but a wife detected in adultery is turned out of the house. Widows are married by the form known as *kâj, kârao*, of which the feast to the clansmen is the most important part. The levirate is allowed if the younger brother of the late husband is himself unmarried. She has power to marry an outsider if her brother-in-law does not claim her.

Birth customs.

5. The woman is attended by some elderly woman of the family, or by a *dâi*, or professional midwife, if she be procurable. At the birth of a son,

charity is distributed to Brâhmans and to the poor, and the child is named by the Brâhman on the eleventh day.

Marriage ceremonies.

6. The betrothal is marked by the distribution of some coarse sugar to the clansmen by the father of the bridegroom, and then the engagement is announced. The binding portion of the marriage ceremony is the walking of the pair seven times round the sacred fire.

Death ceremonies.

7. They burn their dead. The ashes are thrown into some river and some of the fragments of the bone are kept to be consigned to the Ganges. The corpse is tied on a bier, a *pinda* is offered, some gold is put in the mouth, and with an appeal for aid to Guru Govind and the words *Râm! Râm!* it is cremated. They do not perform the regular *srâddha*; on the third day (*tîja*), the clansmen bathe and eat at the house of the deceased; they are regarded as impure by their neighbours until this ceremony is done. On the tenth day, the Brâhman is given food, clothes, bedding, and other necessaries for the use of the spirit in the other world. This ceremony is repeated on the first anniversary of the death, and after this nothing more is done. On the last day of the Kanâgat fortnight, they place food on the house roof for the use of the deceased ancestors. A little water is then sprinkled, and the Ramaiya with folded hands invokes the spirits of the departed, and first of all that of Guru Govind. Those who make the pilgrimage to Gaya, even once in their lives, omit this ceremony. The invocation and all the prayers are in Hindustâni. They call this the *srâddha*; but of course it does not conform to the regular ritual. They employ Brâhmans as their priests, but consider it more meritorious to give charity to the son of a sister or daughter than to a Brâhman.

Religion.

8. By religion they are Sikhs, and particularly respect the Guru and the Grantha. But they also worship the ordinary Hindu deities, such as Ganesa, Devi, Siva, and Bhûmiya. They visit the Sikh temples at Patna, Amritsar, Dehra Dûn, and Nânakmatha, of which the last is the favourite. The married pair after the ceremony go to the temple of Bhûmiya and make an obeisance. They also worship snakes, like ordinary Hindus, and respect the *pîpal* tree. Some visit the tomb of Guru Râm Râê in the fair during the month of Bhâdon. Their temple is known as Dharmsâla or Nânakshâhi Dharmsâla. It bears the flag of the Guru, and contains the holy book known as the Granth Sâhib. During the Dasahra they hold a festival known as

the Parva, when they assemble at the Dharmsâla to hear the Granth Sâhib read. The praises of the Guru are recited, and some *halwa* if purchased with the contributions of those present, is distributed. The most binding oath is by the Granth Sâhib, and then by the Guru; in ordinary cases the oath is taken by Ganesa or one of the ordinary Hindu deities. Women are not allowed to visit the Dharmsâla.

Social rules.

9. They eat no food forbidden to ordinary high caste Hindus. When they eat they throw a little food into the fire in the name of the Guru. Their salutation is *Wâh Guruji ki fateh,* "Victory to the Guru." When inferiors salute superiors, they say *Matha teko,* "I lay my forehead at your feet." They will not eat *kachchi* prepared by any one but a casteman, not even by a Brâhman. *Pakki* can be eaten if cooked by any Hindu of respectable caste.

Occupation.

10. They live by petty trading and begging. Those who are pedlars sell coral beads and medicines. Those who beg, have a sort of picture (*patta*) representing the gods and the various hells. One important part of it is a drawing of a miser dragging a chain in hell, which they show to people to stimulate them to give alms. They do not appear to rob or steal at home, but in more distant parts of the country their conduct is not free from suspicion, and some are notorious swindlers.

11. To this may be added the following account of the tribe by Mr. F. S. Bullock, C. S.:[1]—"The Ramaiyas have been for years past settled down in the Bijnor District in the Chândpur and Dhâmpur Tahsîls. Altogether they are found in thirty-five or forty villages, but chiefly in large groups in the villages of Nûrpur, Rohunagli, Nahilpur, and Harupur. I believe this to be the only district in India in which they have settled down in any number; but they live in a few villages in the Panjâb, *viz.*, in Delhi, Amritsar, and Patiyâla, one village (Chilkhâna) in Sahâranpur, two villages (Chând pur and Soron) in Aligarh, and Bettiah and Bhâgalpur in Bengal. They are pedlars by profession, and sell precious stones and *boxwâla* goods, such as mirrors, combs, soap, candles, and stones. They call themselves Sikhs by religion, and they worship Guru Nânak, and

---

[1] *North-West Provinces Census Report,* 1891, I, 322.

say they came from the Panjâb. Some shave their heads, and some do not. In fact they seem to have two sects, and account for it thus :—Guru Nânak had two sons : Srichand, who founded the Sâdhu Branch; and Lakshmi Dâs, who founded the Sikh Branch. The descendants of Srichand shave and look like Hindus, but they are a drunken lot, eat meat, but do not worship the cow. They travel all over India, chiefly in the Dakkhin, while the Sikhs travel chiefly in the Panjâb. The small number of males as compared with females in Bijnor is accounted for by the fact that the males travel about and earn their living, while the women stay at home. They do not cultivate, but are well off and earn large sums by peddling goods."

Distribution of the Ramaiyas according to the Census of 1891.

DISTRICTS.	Hindus.	Muhammadans.	TOTAL.
Dehra Dûn	4	...	4
Sahâranpur	156	...	156
Muzaffarnagar	95	158	253
Meerut	308	...	308
Bulandshahr	4	...	4
Bareilly	53	...	53
Bijnor	2,980	...	2,980
Morâdâbâd	58	...	58
Pilibhît	21	...	21
Târai	86	...	86
TOTAL	3,765	158	3,923

Males	1,372
Females	2,993

Rânghar, Rângar.—A sept of Muhammadan Râjputs principally found in the Upper Ganges-Jumna Duâb. According to Colonel Tod[1] the word is derived from *rana*, "strife," in the sense of "turbulent;" but this is very doubtful. Mr. Ibbetson[2] says :—

[1] *Annals*, I, 487.

[2] *Panjâb Ethnography*, para. 446; *Census Report, North-Western Provinces*, 1865, I, Appendix 8

" Rângar is a term sometimes contemptuously applied in the Eastern and South-Eastern Districts of the Panjâb to any Musalmân Râjput. I am told, however, that in Fîrozpur and Gurdâspur, there are small Râjput colonies known only by this name; and, if so, it is probable that they have emigrated from the Delhi territory. If a Hindu Chauhân Râjput become a Musalmân to-morrow, he would be called a Chauhân Râjput by both himself and his neighbours of both religions; but his Hindu brethren would call him Rânghar, which he would resent as only slightly less abusive than *chotikat*, a term of contempt applied to those who have, on conversion to Islâm, cut off the *choti* or Hindu scalp lock."

2. The Bhatti or Jaiswâr Râjputs of Bulandshahr claim descent from Râja Dalip, son of Jaswant Râo, of Nânamau near Bithûr in the Cawnpur District. He is said to have had two sons named Bhatti and Rânghar. The descendants of the latter were converted in the time of the Sultân Qutb-ud-dîn and Alâ-ud-dîn, and were called Rânghars after their eponymous ancestor.[1]

3. Again, according to Sir H. M. Elliot,[2] many of the Kankauriya and Naigâniya Ahîrs have been converted to Islâm and are known as Rânghars. In the Dûn they are said to be descendants of strangers of Pundîr extraction from Sahâranpur, who gained a footing during the decline of the Garhwâl kingdom. There are very few of them, and they are being gradually absorbed by marriage with hill women.[3] In Hariyâna their sections are said to be Jât, Satrola, and Raghu.[4] The sept, in fact, seems to be a sort of cave of Adullam for out-castes of various tribes.

4. The Rânghars have always borne an evil reputation for turbulence. This is shown by the many proverbs concerning them:—*Gujar, Ranghar, do; kutta, billi, do; ye chár na ho; to khulé kiwáré so*: "The Gûjar and the Rânghar are a pair; so are the dog and the cat; if it were not for these four, you might sleep with open doors." Another says:—*Yár Dom ne kiya Rángharya; aur-na dekha aisa harya:* " A minstrel made friends with a Rânghar and found no worse thief than he."

---

[1] *Census Report, North-Western Provinces*, 1865, I, Appendix 16.
[2] *Supplemental Glossary, s. v. Ahír.*
[3] Williams, *Memo.*, 27.
[4] *Indian, Antiquary*, VI, 341; *Journal Asiatic Society, Bengal*, 1868.

Distribution of the Rânghars according to the Census of 1891.

Districts.	Numbers.	Districts.	Numbers.
Dehra Dûn . . .	138	Bijnor . . .	2,256
Sahâranpur . . .	368	Pilibhît . . .	168
Muzaffarnagar . .	1,174	Cawnpur . . .	2
Meerut . . .	2	Jhânsi . . .	7
Bulandshahr . . .	21	Lalitpur . . .	5
Mathura . . .	5	Tarâi . . .	166
Agra . . .	44	Lucknow . . .	23
Mainpuri . . .	16	Unâo . . .	2
Etah . . .	4		
		Total .	4,401

Rangrez[1] (*Rang* = "colour;" *rez, rekhtan* = "pouring").—The dyer caste. The Census returns show in the Hindu Branch, which is very scantily represented in the Provinces, as one sub-caste—Haral. There are 81 sections of the Muhammadan Branch, which are of the usual type,—some territorial, like Desi, Deswâla, Gaur, Multâni; others occupational or connected with other tribes or castes, such as Bhât, Chandelwâl, Chauhân, Ghosi, Guâl Pathân, Kamângar, Khatri, Quraishi, Nîlgar, Pathân, Shaikh, Sadiqi, and Usmâni. In Mirzapur there are three endogamous sub-divisions: Rangrez, Mauâlê (who take their name from the town of Mau in Azamgarh), and Mârwâri Rangrez. Each of these again is broken up into a Pathân and Shaikh sept, which are also endogamous. They appear to aim at the full prohibited degree of Islâm,[2] but practically only sisters' daughters are excluded. Religious differences are so far regarded that a Sunni cannot marry a Shiah. All marriages are local, and are contracted with those families with which they have been accustomed to eat and smoke. They believe themselves to be descendants of one Khwâja Bali, who was a very pious man, about whom the following verse is current:—*Khwâja*

[1] It is really a Hindustâni corruption of Persian Rangraz—*Aîn-i-Akbari*, Blochmann, I, 307.
[2] *Qurân, Sûrah*, IV, 26, 27.

Bali Rangrez Rangé Khuda ki sez: "Khwâja Bali dyes the bed of God."

Marriage rules.

2. They do not admit outsiders into the caste; if any one happen to be admitted, he cannot be married in the caste. Marriage takes place at the age of ten or twelve; and polygamy is allowed. Marriage is by three forms: *Charhauwa,* when the bridegroom goes in procession and marries the bride at her house; *Dola,* used by poor people, when the bride is brought home quietly and married at the house of the bridegroom; *Sagâi,* for widows. The binding portion of the ceremony is, in all cases, the recital of the Sharah. A widow can marry her deceased husband's younger brother or an outsider: the levirate does not seem to be enforced. A man can divorce his wife for adultery, and a wife, her husband, if he is converted to another religion. All divorce is by leave of the tribal council. Divorced women can remarry, but there is a prejudice against it, and the friends of such a woman have to make it worth the man's while to take her over.

Religion.

3. They are mostly Sunni Muhammadans, and their tribal deities are Ghâzi Miyân and the Pânchon Pîr. They are worshipped jointly on the first Sunday in Jeth with offerings of parched barley flour (*sattu*), cucumber (*kakri*), melon (*kharbûza*), and sweetmeats. Ghâzi Miyân is also worshipped after marriages with an offering of boiled rice, curds, and a fowl. This offering is known as *kandûri.*[1] With Ghâzi Miyân the Pânchon Pîr are also worshipped with an offering of sweetmeats and garlands of flowers. They bury their dead in a graveyard in the usual Muhammadan fashion, and at the festivals of the 'Id and Shab-i-bârât make offerings of vermicelli (*siwaiyan, senwai*), milk, and *halwa* sweetmeats to the spirits of deceased ancestors. They also offer them bread and meat at the festival of the Baqar-'Id.

Occupation and social status.

4. Their trade is dyeing cloth; the process has been very fully described by Mr. Hoey.[2] Owing to foreign competition the trade has become much reduced in recent years, and many of them

---

[1] *Kandûri* or *sahnak* is properly the term used for a special worship of Fâtima, the daughter of the Prophet, by the most virtuous women. No male is ever allowed to see the food cooked as an offering on this occasion.

[2] *Monograph on Trades and Manufactures,* 165, *sqq.*

have now taken to agriculture and petty shopkeeping. Their women are reputed chaste. They indulge in liqour, but secretly, and the practice is reprobated. They eat the flesh of goats, sheep, cows, buffaloes, camels, and fowls, and all fish except the fresh water shark (*gúnch*). All Muhammadans eat and smoke with them. The women will not eat food touched by Hindus. Only Chamârs and Doms eat their leavings. Their social status is low, and they rank about on a level with Julâhas and other low Musalmân castes.

Distribution of the Rangrez according to the Census of 1891.

DISTRICTS.	Hindus.	Muhammadans.	TOTAL.
Dehra Dûn	...	48	48
Sahâranpur	...	1,581	1,581
Muzaffarnagar	...	4,239	4,239
Meerut	...	4,919	4,919
Bulandshahr	...	1,679	1,679
Aligarh	...	502	502
Mathura	...	616	616
Agra	...	878	878
Farrukhâbâd	...	667	667
Mainpuri	...	193	193
Etâwah	...	519	519
Etah	...	488	488
Bareilly	...	1,392	1,392
Bijnor	...	2,556	2,556
Budâun	...	515	515
Morâdâbâd	1	1,176	1,177
Shâhjahânpur	...	805	805
Pilibhît	...	495	495
Cawnpur	2	382	384
Fatehpur	...	356	356

Distribution of the Rangrez according to the Census of 1891—concld.

Districts.	Hindus.	Muhammadans.	Total.
Bânda	...	20	20
Hamîrpur	...	581	581
Allahâbâd	5	311	316
Jhânsi	...	133	133
Jâlaun	...	123	123
Lalitpur	...	81	81
Benares	...	304	304
Mirzapur	...	86	86
Jaunpur	...	481	481
Ghâzipur	...	543	543
Ballia	...	762	762
Gorakhpur	...	1,131	1,121
Basti	...	231	231
Azamgarh	...	1,136	1,136
Tarâi	...	573	573
Lucknow	...	467	467
Unâo	...	244	244
Râê Bareli	...	680	680
Sîtapur	...	136	136
Hardoi	...	193	193
Kheri	...	467	467
Faizâbâd	...	648	648
Gonda	...	320	320
Bahrâich	...	198	198
Sultânpur	...	531	531
Partâbgarh	...	163	163
Bârabanki	...	586	586
Total	8	35,135	35,143

Rangsâz (*Rang*, "colour," *sâz*, *sâkhtan*, "making").—The caste of painters and varnishers. With the almost entire disappearance of the palanquin their business has reduced; but there is a considerable trade in carriage painting and house painting in the larger cities and towns.

Distribution of the Rangsâz according to the Census of 1891.

DISTRICTS.	Hindus.	Muhammadans.	TOTAL.
Sahâranpur	...	245	245
Muzaffarnagar	1	240	241
Meerut	...	452	452
Bulandshahr	...	28	28
Mathura	...	1	1
Farrukhâbâd	17	...	17
Mainpuri	29	15	44
Etâwah	...	22	22
Etah	...	36	36
Budâun	...	6	6
Morâdâbâd	...	38	38
Shâhjahânpur	4	22	26
Cawnpur	1	12	13
Fatehpur	...	18	18
Hamîrpur	...	39	39
Allahâbâd	...	3	3
Jhânsi	...	11	11
Jâlaun	...	87	87
Gorakhpur	...	24	24
Azamgarh	7	14	21
Unâo	...	8	8
Râê Bareli	...	12	12
Sîtapur	...	7	7

Distribution of the Rangsâz according to the Census of 1891—concld.

Districts.	Hindus.	Muhammadans.	Total.
Hardoi	10	19	29
Gonda	...	15	15
Bahrâich	...	8	8
Sultânpur	17	18	35
Partâbgarh	1	...	1
Total .	87	1,400	1,487

Rastâogi, Rastaugi.—A sub-caste of Banyas found nearly all over the Province. Those in Oudh have, according to Mr. Carnegy, one peculiarity, that their women will not eat food cooked by their husbands. There they are said to have come originally from Amethi, and have three endogamous sub-divisions: Amethi, Indrapati, and Mauhariya. In Mirzapur they name two subdivisions: Purbiha or Purbiya, "Eastern," and Pachhiwâha, or "Western," which have their boundary at Allahâbâd. It has been found impossible to obtain a complete list of their *gotras* and sections at Mirzapur. Religious differences are a bar to marriage. Thus, those who worship Hardiha Deva or Hardaur Lâla, do not intermarry with the votaries of Mahâbîr or the Pâchón Pîr. The Mirzapur Rastaugis say they came here from Delhi about the time of the Mutiny. They marry between the ages of eight and twelve. Widow marriage is forbidden. They can marry two wives. They are generally initiated into the Râmanandi sect, and their priests are Gaur Brâhmans, who have come with them from the West. The use of meat and spirits is forbidden.

Occupation.

2. In Mirzapur they generally keep shops for the sale of cloth (*bazzâzi*) and brass vessels. "In Lucknow," according to Mr. Hoey,[1] "there are two special classes of money-lending by the account-book (*bahi*), practised chiefly by Rastaugis: *augahi* and *rozahi*. *Augahi* is lending of money to be repaid with interest at 20 per cent. in monthly instalments. Thus, if a Rastaugi lends on the 1st January R10, he receives one rupee on the first of each month for twelve months, and thereby realises R12, of which R2 are interest. A Ras-

[1] *Monograph*, 144.

taugi's *augahi bahi* is a curiosity. It is ruled like a chess-board, but has twelve columns. As each month's instalment is realized, it is entered in a square until the twelve squares are filled. He generally also keeps a separate *bahi* in which the principal is noted when lent. It may, however, be noted in the margin of his check-pattern account. *Rozahi* is money lent to be realized in daily instalments with interest at 25 per cent. Thus, if a rupee be lent, one half anna (*taka roz*) will be realized daily. The account of this money is kept in a similar way, but the account-book will be ruled in lines of forty squares. A Rastaugi keeps his accounts by locality; that is, he has several 'fields' (*khet*). Debtors are called *asâmi*, and the amount to be collected is 'rent' (*lagân*). A separate set of account-books is kept up for each *khet*, and a servant (generally a Brâhman) is employed to collect at each *khet*."

Distribution of Rastâogi Banyas according to the Census of 1891.

Districts.	Numbers.	Districts.	Numbers.
Sahâranpur	8	Jhânsi	1
Muzaffarnagar	107	Jâlaun	3
Meerut	3,109	Benares	888
Bulandshahr	799	Mirzapur	97
Agra	22	Ghâzipur	442
Farrukhâbâd	814	Ballia	1
Etâwah	1	Gorakhpur	167
Etah	37	Basti	496
Bijnor	554	Azamgarh	420
Budâun	892	Tarâi	100
Morâdâbâd	1,679	Lucknow	1,966
Pilibhît	9	Unâo	1
Cawnpur	292	Râê Bareli	35
Fatehpur	488	Faizâbâd	56
Bânda	91	Gonda	81
Hamîrpur	3	Bahrâich	21
Allahâbâd	453	Total	14,133

Râthaur (Sanskrit *râshtrakûta*, "royal house").—A famous sept of Râjputs. Besides that already given, which is probably correct, there are various explanations of their name. According to the tradition current in Mârwâr,[1] the family deity of its rulers was, in the Krita Yuga, or first epoch, Mansa Devi; in the Treta Yuga, Râshtra Sena; in the Dwapara Yuga, Pankhâni; and in the present or Kali Yuga, Nâganechi. The legend runs that the authors of the human race were Mâya and Brahma. In the first epoch the female deity was called Mansa as at her desire (*manas*) the world was formed. Then she successively took the names of Pankhâni, "the winged one," and Râshtra Sena, "the falcon of the State." The name arose because the goddess Râshtra Sena gave her blessing (*vara*) on the present Râthaur race. In the present epoch the name of the deity was again changed to Nâganechi, because when Duhâr, the grandson of Sivaji (the original founder of the Râthaur dynasty in Mârwâr), succeeded his father as ruler, he went to the Karnâtak, where the Râthaurs ruled previous to becoming kings of Mârwâr, for the purpose of bringing the image of the goddess to his own land. When the cart containing the image came to the village of Nâgana of Mârwâr, the vehicle came to a standstill. Upon this he built a temple for her there, and she took her present name, which means "resident of Nâgana." The same story is told at Mathura of the image of Kesava Deva.[2] Another derivation of the name of the sept is that they sprang from the spine (*raht*) of Indra. They are the Oraturæ of Pliny's lists. He notes of them that their king had only ten elephants, though he possessed a strong force of infantry.[3]

History of the clan.

2. The history of the sept begins in 1050 A.D., when they expelled the Tomars from Kanauj, which once more became a famous kingdom and the rival of Delhi both in extent and magnificence. Here Jay Chand, the last of the dynasty, celebrated the Aswamedha, or horse sacrifice, and here in open day did Prithivi Râja, the daring Chief of the Chauhâns, carry off the willing daughter of the Râthaur king in spite of the gallant resistance of the Banâphar heroes, Alha and Udal. The war that ensued between Delhi and Kanauj paved

---

[1] *Rajputâna Gazetteer*, II, 246.
[2] Growse, *Mathura*, 120.
[3] *Indian Antiquary*, VI, 341.

the way to the Muhammadan invasion ; until finally, in 1191 A.D., Muhammad Ghori, after the fall of Delhi, marched on Kanauj and defeated Jay Chand at Benares, where he was drowned in the Ganges. Thus ended the Râthaur kingdom in the Ganges-Jumna Duâb.[1]

3. Subsequent to these events, Sivaji, who was by one account the grandson, and by another the nephew, of Jay Chand, entered Mârwâr on a pilgrimage to Dwârika, and halting at the town of Pâli, displayed his valour by routing a body of marauders. The Brâhmans requested his protection, and he established himself there and became the founder of the Râthaur dynasty of Mârwâr. In less than three centuries after their migration from Kanauj the Râthaurs occupied an area of 80,000 square miles. Colonel Tod[2] estimated their numbers in his time, in spite of the ravages of war and pestilence, at half a million of souls. This estimate must have been much too high. The Census of 1891 shows the total Râthaur population of Rajputâna to be 173,909, of whom 86,858 are in Mârwâr. The Mughal Emperors owed half their conquests to the one hundred thousand Râthaurs (*lâkh talwâr Râthaurân*) who served under them. In Bikâner[3] they have fewer prejudices than their more Eastern brethren: they will eat food without enquiring by whom it was dressed, and will drink either wine or water without asking to whom the cup belonged. The opium draught (*piyâla*) is a favourite with every one who can afford it.

The Râthaurs of the North-Western Provinces and Oudh.

4. According to Dr. Hoernle[4] the so-called Râthaurs were a branch of the Gaharwârs, and it may well be that about the time of Mahipâla a separation occurred in the Gaharwâr clan, possibly on religious grounds. For the Pâlas professed Buddhism, while the Chandras were Brâhmanists. The secession was marked by the departure of the latter to Kanauj, and by a change in nomenclature —Chandra and Râthaur for Pâla and Gaharwâr. The contempt for the Gaharwârs, alluded to by Colonel Tod, may perhaps be accounted for by their heretical faith in the time of the Pâlas. The head of the family in these Provinces is the Râja of Râmpur in the Etah

---

[1] Cunningham, *Archæological Reports*, I, 283.
[2] *Annals*, II, 24.
[3] *Ibid*, II, 218.
[4] *Indian Antiquary*, XIV, 98,*sq*.

District, who claims to be thirty-ninth in descent from Jay Chand. Besides these there are two other families of the genuine Râthaurs in the Central Duâb, those known as the Dhir Sâh ki Sâkha and the Khimsipur Râo family; of the former the Râja of Kurâoli is the head, but he acknowledges fealty to the Chief of Râmpur. In Mathura they are represented by the Râja of Kishngarh, and the Farrukhâbâd branch claim descent from Parjan Pâl, and through him to Jay Chand. Of the same stock is the Usait family in Budâun. The Eastern branch is of much lower status. In Gorakhpur they do not marry in the higher tribes, and the Azamgarh family allege that they conquered the Râjbhars some nineteen or twenty generations ago.[1]

5. In Farrukhâbâd they claim to belong to the Kasyapa *gotra*. They give girls in marriage to the Bhadauriya, Kachhwâha, and Chauhân, and receive brides from the same septs. In Aligarh they marry Chauhân, Gahlot, Sakarwâr, Jangâra, Chandel, Bundela, Dhâkrê, Tomar, Pundîr, and Solankhi girls, and give brides to the Gahlot, Pundîr, Sakarwâr, Chauhân, and Jangâra septs.

Distribution of the Râthaur Râjputs according to the Census of 1891.

DISTRICTS.	Hindus.	Muhammadans.	TOTAL.
Dehra Dûn	9	...	9
Sahâranpur	195	16	211
Muzaffarnagar	89	213	302
Meerut	152	...	152
Bulandshahr	242	22	264
Aligarh	1,975	...	1,975
Mathura	339	1	340
Agra	1,529	2	1,531
Farrukhâbâd	6,815	3	6,818
Mainpuri	3,098	5	3,103
Etâwah	2,025	...	2,025

[1] *Mainpuri Settlement Report*, 20; *Mathura Settlement Report*, 35; *Farrukhâbâd Settlement Report*, 13; Buchanan, *Eastern India*, II, 458.

Distribution of the Râthaur Râjputs according to the Census of 1891—contd.

DISTRICTS.	Hindus.	Muhammadans.	TOTAL.
Etah	6,537	19	6,556
Bareilly	3,002	...	3,002
Bijnor	31	...	31
Budâun	4,215	101	4,316
Morâdâbâd	795	...	795
Shâhjahânpur	5,774	3	5,777
Pilibhît	928	...	928
Cawnpur	2,417	1	2,418
Fatehpur	328	31	359
Bânda	170	25	195
Hamîrpur	233	...	233
Allahâbâd	162	...	162
Jhânsi	143	...	143
Jâlaun	1,180	...	1,180
Lalitpur	181	...	181
Benares	46	14	60
Mirzapur	48	...	48
Jaunpur	1	...	1
Ghâzipur	121	4	125
Ballia	1,699	...	1,699
Gorakhpur	1,691	...	1,691
Basti	1,135	127	1,262
Azamgarh	3,137	82	3,219
Tarâi	129	...	129
Lucknow	204	3	207
Unâo	598	...	598
Râê Bareli	1,151	1	1,152

Distribution of the Râthaur Râjputs according to the Census of 1891—concld.

Districts.	Hindus.	Muhammadans.	Total.
Sîtapur	1,992	103	2,095
Hardoi	3,114	2	3,116
Kheri	3,117	222	3,339
Faizâbâd	50	...	50
Gonda	438	...	438
Bahrâich	395	38	433
Sultânpur	114	...	114
Partâbgarh	131	...	131
Bârabanki	682	...	682
Total	62,557	1,038	63,595

Rauniyâr, Roniyâr.—A sub-caste of Banyas confined to the Benares and Gorakhpur Divisions. Mr. Nesfield derives the word from *ravan* in the sense of "crying or hawking wares for sale." Others derive it from *rauna*, to "shout;" but having regard to the special occupation which they follow, the word may possibly be a corruption of *lavanakâra*, or "a person engaged in the salt trade."

Tribal organization.

2. In Mirzapur the Rauniyârs have two endogamous sub-divisions: Khariha and Samariha or Sambhariya. These they say are descended from two brothers, one of whom dealt in *khâra*, or alkaline salt, and the other in *Sâmbhar*, or the salt which comes from the lake of that name in Rajputâna. A man must marry in his own sub-division, and their rule of exogamy is that a man cannot marry in the family of his maternal uncle, father's sister, his own family or that of his sister, as long as any recollection of relationship exists. In Mirzapur they say that they are emigrants from Patna, whence they came some four or five centuries ago. On the contrary the Rauniyârs of Bihâr say that they have come from these Provinces.[1] In Champâran

[1] Risley, *Tribes and Castes*, II, 198.

they have broken up into two endogamous groups: Chhatri and Samri (who are probably akin to the Samarihas of Mirzapur): the former of whom claim to be Râjputs from the North-West Provinces, who were degarded for intermarrying with women of the Banya caste.

Marriage.

3. Rauniyârs marry at the age of nine or ten. They cannot take a second wife in the lifetime of the first unless she be barren. As in Bengal they make no concealment of the fact that they allow widow marriage.[1]

Religion.

4. Some of them are Saivas, but they appear to prefer the Vaishnava sect. In Mirzapur they employ Sarwariya Brâhmans as their priests, but in Bihâr they say that they are usually served by those of the Sâkadwîpi tribe.

Occupation.

5. In these Provinces they say that their real business was selling salt, whence they derive their own name and that of their two endogamous groups. But they are very often what is known as *pheriwâlas* or *ladahas* and wander about with bullocks from village to village, collecting grain and other country produce, which they exchange for salt, sugar, etc. They are generally men of small capital.

Social rules.

6. Those who are not initiated into any particular sect use meat and spirits; but there is no drinking allowed at meetings of the tribal council, and if a man is found drunk at such occasions, he is put out of caste. Brâhmans and Kshatriyas in Bihâr are said to eat *pakki* from their hands; but this is not the case in Mirzapur. They will eat *kachchi* cooked by Brâhmans and *pakki* cooked by Halwâis, Brâhmans, and Kshatriyas.

Distribution of the Rauniyâr Banyas according to the Census of 1891.

DISTRICTS.	Numbers.	DISTRICTS.	Numbers.
Farrukhâbâd . .	1	Gorakhpur . . .	4,321
Mirzapur . . .	649	Azamgarh . . .	14
Ghâzipur . . .	474	Gonda . . .	2
Ballia	2,703	TOTAL .	8,164

[1] O' Donnel, *Bengal Census Report*, 204.

Rawa.—A caste confined to the Western Districts, who call themselves low Râjputs, and say they came into this part of the country in the time of the Emperor Shâhjahân. The women of this caste procure divorce in a peculiar way. All they have to do is to throw a cowdung cake (*upla*) from outside into the house. Seeing this done, the husband separates finally from his wife without any further formality. They rarely rise above the grade of farm servants.

Distribution of the Rawas according to the Census of 1891.

DISTRICTS.	Numbers.
Muzaffarnagar	6,042
Meerut	8,270
Bijnor	11,139
TOTAL	25,451

Rohtaki.—A sub-caste of Banyas who claim descent from a certain Râja Rahat, the founder of Rohtâsgarh. The foundation of it is, however, more usually ascribed to Râja Rohitaswa, the son of Harischandra. They are more probably a local sub-caste deriving their name from the Rohtak District in the Panjâb. They are said to be very careful in religious observances. Râja Lachhman Sinh[1] says they are numerous in Sayâna in the Bulandshahr District; but the last Census shows none of them in that District.

Distribution of Rohtaki Banyas according to the Census of 1891.

DISTRICTS.	Numbers.	DISTRICTS.	Numbers.
Shâhjahânpur	1	Bijnor	835
Muzaffarnagar	118	Morâdâbâd	460
Meerut	4	Pilibhît	1
Agra	29	Lucknow	10
Bareilly	28	TOTAL	1,486

[1] *Memo. of Bulandshahr*, 168.

Ror.—A small caste of cultivators in the Western Districts. Of their kinsmen in the Panjâb Mr. Ibbetson writes:[1]—"The real seat of the Panjâb Rors is in the great *dhâk* jungles south of Thanesar on the borders of the Karnâl and Ambâla Districts, where they hold a *Chaurâsi*, nominally of eighty-four villages, of which the village of Amîn, where the Pândavas arranged their forces before their last fight with the Kauravas, is their head village. But the Rors have spread down the Western Jumna Canal into the lower parts of Karnâl and into Jînd in considerable numbers. They are fine stalwart men of very much the same type as the Jâts, whom they almost equal as husbandmen; their women also working in the fields. They are more peaceful and less grasping in their habits than the Jâts, and are consequently readily admitted as tenants, where the latter would be kept at arm's length. Of their origin I can say nothing certain. They have the same story as the Aroras, of their having been Râjputs, who escaped the fury of Parasurâma by stating that their caste was *aur*, or 'another.' The Aroras are often called Roras in the east of the Panjâb; yet I can hardly believe that the frank and stalwart Ror is of the same origin as the Arora. The Amîn men say that they came from Sambhal in Morâdâbâd; but this may be only to connect themselves with their neighbours the Chauhân Râjputs, who certainly came from there. But almost all the Rors seem alike to point to Badli in the Jhajjar Tahsîl of Rohtak as their immediate place of origin, though some of them say they came from Rajputâna. Their social status is identical with that of the Jâts; and they practise *karewa*, or 'widow marriage,' though only, they say, within the caste. Their divisions appear to be exceedingly numerous; some of them are Sagwâl, Maipla, Khichi, and Jogrân."

2. In Sahâranpur the Rors claim to have been created at Kaithal by Sri Krishna in the war of the Mahâbhârata. Their marriage ceremonies resemble those of Jâts and Gûjars; they permit widow marriage; and the levirate is practically compulsory. They eat mutton, fish, pork, and venison, and drink spirits. It is said that they will eat *kachchi* and *pakki* and drink and smoke with Jâts and Gûjars.

3. From an account of the Rors of Bijnor supplied by the District Officer, it appears that the tribal tradition of their origin

---

[1] *Panjâb Ethnography*, section 476.

is that when Râma Chandra severed his connection with Sîta, she was pregnant, and went into the jungle under the protection of the Rishi Vâlmîki. She bore a son there, who was named Lawa, and one day, when she was leaving the house, she put the child in charge of the Rishi. The child followed his mother, and the Rishi missing him, and supposing him to be dead, constructed another child out of a wisp of *kusa* grass. When Sîta returned and saw the other child, she asked what it all meant. The Rishi said, "*roraphora*" (apparently meaning 'this useless thing') "is also your son." Hence they were called Rors.

4. They are supposed to have emigrated to Bijnor some four centuries ago from a place called Fatehpur Pundri in the Karnâl District. Half this village was owned by the Rors, and half by a colony of Sayyids. The Sayyids quarrelled with the Rors, who were forced to emigrate under their leader Mahi Chand. By another story they were originally Tomar Râjputs of Delhi, which they were forced to leave after the conquest of their tribe. By a third account, their emigration from Delhi took place in the time of Aurangzeb.

5. They marry and perform their other family ceremonies in the usual manner common to respectable Hindus. Widows can marry again, and the levirate, though permissible, is not compulsory on the widow. There is no regular form of divorce, but a wife detected in adultery is expelled from the tribe by the decree of the tribal council, and cannot subsequently on payment of a penalty be readmitted to caste rights.

6. Their chief occupation is agriculture, to which they add the making of hemp matting and twine (*tât, sutli*).

7. They eat mutton, goats' flesh, and fowls. They will not eat beef, monkeys, or vermin. They will not eat *kachchi* cooked by any caste but their own. They will smoke with Jâts and Gûjars, and eat *pakki* cooked by them or any superior caste.

Distribution of Rors according to the Census of 1891.

DISTRICTS.	Numbers.	DISTRICTS.	Numbers.
Dehra Dûn . .	3	Etâwah . . .	5
Sahâranpur . .	3,320	Bijnor . . .	614
Muzaffarnagar . .	475	Benares . . .	41
Mathura . . .	1	TOTAL .	4,459

S

Sadgop, Satgop (also known as **Châsa**).—A cultivating caste of Bengal Proper, who are supposed to have separated themselves from the Guâlas by abandoning pastoral pursuits and taking exclusively to agriculture. Mr. Risley has given a full account of the tribe.[1] Those found in these Provinces are only Bengal pilgrims.

Distribution of the Sadgops according to the Census of 1891.

DISTRICTS.	Numbers.	DISTRICTS.	Numbers.
Sahâranpur . . .	6	Allahâbâd . . .	22
Mathura . . .	144	Gorakpur . . .	2
Etâwah . . .	3	TOTAL .	177

Sâdh—(Sanskrit *sâdhu*, "pure, saintlike").—The word Sâdh ordinarily means nothing more than a Hindu ascetic or devotee; but it is applied in a special sense to a sect of Hindu Unitarians, which had its origin in the Panjâb, but has now widely spread into these Provinces. In the Sambat year 1600 (1543 A.D.) Bîrbhân of Bijesar, near Narnaul, is said to have received a mysterious communication from Udho Dâs, who was a pupil of Râê Dâs, the founder of the Satnâmi sect, of which some account has been given in connection with the Chamârs. To Bîrbhân was communicated the present creed of the Sâdhs. Udho Dâs gave at the same time to Bîrbhân sundry marks by which he might know him at his re-appearance—*First*, that whatever he foretold should happen; *second*, that no shadow should be cast by his figure; *third*, that he would tell him the thoughts of his heart; *fourth*, that he would be suspended between heaven and earth; *fifth*, that he would bring the dead to life.

2. The Sâdhs of these Provinces are known by that name to outsiders, but they generally use the name Satnâmi among themselves. Adults are required to wear a white dress; and ornament and the use of rich apparel of every kind are prohibited. They never wear a cap, but use instead a turban of a peculiar shape. They are enjoined by their religion never to tell a lie and never to take an oath. They are in the same way prohibited from using

[1] *Tribes and Castes*, II, 212.

any kind of intoxicant or any article which borders upon luxury. Wine, opium, *gânja, bhang,* betel and tobacco are abominations to them. They have an intense respect for animal life, which extends to even the smallest insect, and the use of any kind of animal food is strictly denounced. They will salute no one but the Divine principle, which they term Sat or "The Truth;" and when they meet a European or any superior they salute merely by raising the hands to the level of the breast. They detest idolatry and all outward forms of religious belief. They are very reticent about their beliefs, and it is only with the greatest difficulty that it has been possible to obtain a copy, which is probably incomplete, of the book of religious songs (*bâni*) which embody the principles of their faith. All controversy or argument on religious matters with strangers to the sect is reprobated. Their religious books, known as *pothi,* are written in Bhâsha, or ordinary Hindi, and are not the work of any single author, but contain a number of songs, many of which are taken from the writings of Nânak and Kabîr. These books are read almost daily in their chapel or meeting-house, which is known as *jumlaghar,* or "house of assembly," or *chauki,* "station." The service takes place in the evening, when all members of the sect, male and female, attend. This is their only form of worship.

Regulations of the sect.

3. It has been held judicially that the ordinary Hindu law of succession applies to them. The principal seats of the sect in this part of India are Delhi, Agra, Jaypur, and Farrukhâbâd. There is a small colony of them in Mirzapur, who do not appear in the Census returns. They live by calico printing. They deny that there are any caste divisions among them. They are endogamous, and in arranging their marriages they pay no regard to wealth or station. To recognise any distinctions of rank is forbidden, and the only disqualification is the violation of the rules of the sect and the practising of any degrading or sinful occupation. They all eat and drink together, and any jealousy, hatred, or quarrels between the members are considered disgraceful. They appear to have no regular formula of exogamy; marriage with near relations is forbidden, and they will not marry in a family with which any previous connection by marriage is remembered. They all live together in the same *muhalla,* or "quarter," and are always ready to assist each other and provide for the poor, widows, and orphans of the sect. They are hard-working and industrious; it is considered disgraceful to be

dependent for support on another; beggary is unknown among them.

Marriage.

4. Children are betrothed in infancy, and marriage is solemnised at the age of twelve, fourteen, or sixteen. No bride-price is given, but the bride usually receives a dowry. Polygamy is not approved and polyandry is unknown, and the very idea of such an institution is most abhorrent to them. As they all live close together, their betrothals are arranged privately among themselves. When the father of the youth contemplates his marriage with a certain girl, he sends a man or woman of his family as an envoy to the father of the girl. As they have no horoscopes there is none of the almost endless bother which accompanies the preliminaries of a betrothal among respectable Hindus, in order to ascertain if the match is unobjectionable from the astrologer's point of view. If the father of the girl agrees to the proposal of the marriage, he feeds the envoy with sweetmeats or makes him drink some milk, and gives him money. This settles the engagement (*mangni pakki*).

5. When the pair reach puberty the marriage day is fixed. The notice of the appointed date is sent by the father of the girl, and on receipt of the message the father of the youth calls a meeting of the members of the sect, to whom the approaching marriage is announced. The envoy is fed and is given a present of a turban and a sheet. During all this time the songs known as Mangal or "rejoicing," of which examples are given below, are sung. From that day begins the usual anointing (*ubtauni*) of the bride and bridegroom. Every day the members of the sect assemble at the meeting-room (*chauki*), and the Mangal is recited. On the wedding day the father of the bride gives a feast to the members of the sect at noon. In the evening the bridegroom, accompanied by his father and friends, goes to the house of the bride, where they are all seated on a white floor-cloth. Opposite them the pair are seated on two cushions. After sitting in this way for a short time, the garments of the bride and bridegroom are knotted together, and both of them move four times round the cushions, while some member of the sect reads the Mangal verses. This constitutes the whole of the marriage service. The binding portion of the service is the revolutions round the cushions of the bride and bridegroom. All then return to the house of the bridegroom, and the bride stays for a short time at the

house of the bridegroom; she is then escorted home by her brother, and, when it is so arranged, she comes permanently to live with him; but there is no further ceremony like the Hindu *gauna*.

Divorce.

6. They divorce their wives only when they have committed some offence which renders them liable to excommunication from the sect. In this case all that is done is to announce the fact before a meeting of the members of the sect. They arrange most of their affairs before a council of the caste, and they very seldom have recourse to the Courts.

Religion.

7. As already stated, the Sâdhs are Unitarians and worship one God, the Author of the universe, under the name of Satya Guru or Satya Nâm. There is no material representation of Him of any kind. By meditation on Him, and the practice of virtue, they believe that they attain ultimately absorption into the Divinity. Their religion teaches them that they should give alms only in secret, and not to strive after riches or the hoarding of wealth. The following are the rules of the faith:—

(1) "Worship one God, Who is the Creator of all and has power to destroy. None is higher or loftier than He; and man should not in wantonness worship any stone, metal, wood or tree, or other created thing. Rather, all honour and renown are due to Him. He is the only God and His the only word. Whoever fixes his thoughts on anything near him, errs and sins; and whoever sins goes to Hell.

(2) Preserve a modest and humble demeanour and fix not your heart on things of this world; and perfectly carry out the principles of your faith. Do not practise what is contrary to your faith, and this some Sâdhus deny, saying that the order is—" First feed one's own people; feed no stranger."

(3) Never speak falsely, and curse not the earth, the water, the trees, nor the beasts. Use your tongue only in praise of God, and never spoil any one of his land, wealth, or beasts. Steal not their goods; be not critical of them or their possessions; and be content with what you have. Think not upon what is evil; and cast not your eye upon what is shameless or unlawful, be it man or woman, dance or pastime.

(4) Think not on evil words, but employ yourselves in the

praise and glory of God; and amuse not yourselves with stories, nor fables, nor singing, nor music, but only with hymns.

(5) Do not greedily desire anything, whether wealth or beauty, and take not what belongs to another. God is the giver of all; and as you put your trust in Him, so you will receive.

(6) When you are asked "Who are you?" say, "I am a Sâdh." Make no mention of caste, and enter not into controversy. Rely firmly on the strength of your religion; rest not your pride and hopes on man.

(7) Wear white clothes; use not antimony, nor belladonna, nor henna. Wear not caste marks, either on the body or forehead. Put on no chaplet, nor Ḅrâhmanical thṛead, nor jewels.

(8) Eat vegetables, not flesh, nor certain kinds of fish. Eat no betel. Snuff not up sweet perfumes, smoke not, and make no use of opium. Lift not up your hand and bow not your head before any idol or man.

(9) Slay not; tyrannise over no one; give no evidence on oath; take nothing by force.

(10) Let each man have one wife; and each wife have one husband. A married man should not eat the leavings of his wife; but a wife should eat what is saved from her husband's food, as is customary; and the wife should obey her husband.

(11) Assume not the guise of faqîrs and ask not for alms; take no presents; fear not magic; before you trust in anything, test it well. The assembly of good men is your place of pilgrimage. Recognise good people before they salute you.

(12) The Sâdh should observe no particular days. Pay no attention to the intercalary months, nor the months themselves. Do not look upon as your own the voice of any bird or beast. Seek only the word of God, and be content therewith."

Writing from Fatehgarh Mr. Steel says:—"In spite of the injunction to say, when asked who they are, 'I am Sâdh', there was a marked tendency in the recent Census operations to put down the Sâdhs as Hindus. Also the order to wear plain clothes is more honoured in the breach than the observance, the wealthy Sâdhs of Farrukhâbâd being very gorgeous in their attire. A story is told (perhaps by their enemies), but denied by the Sâdhs themselves, that in Nawâbi times their funeral ceremony consisted in tying the corpse in a standing position to a tree with its face to the wind and leaving it so. This used to take place north of the city of Farrukhâbâd. It is said that the practice was interdicted in consequence of the remonstrances of the English Officers at the Fatehgarh Cantonment. The whole story is probably a Brâhmanical invention."

8. Marriage songs of the Sâdhs:—

Darshan dé Guru! param sanehi!
Tum bina dukh páwai mori dehín!
Nínd na áwé, ann na bháwai!
Bar bár mohín birah satáwai;
Ghar angana mohín kachhu na suháé;
Fajar bhai par birah na jáé.
Nainan chhútai salhal dhára;
Nis din panth nihárún tumhára.
Jaíse mín marai binu níra,
Aisé tun bina dukhat sharíra.

"O most beloved preceptor! Let me see thee!
My frame aches without thee! I feel no desire for sleep or food!
Again and again, I grieve for separation from thee;
I feel no pleasure in my house or courtyard;
When the morn dawns the pain of separation does not leave me.
Floods of tears flow from mine eyes;
I consider thy doctrine night and day.
As a fish without water, so does my frame ache without thee."

Dukhat tum bina; rotat duáré; pargat darshan díjiyé.
Binti karún meré sániya bali jáún, bilam na kíjiyé!
Bibid bibid kar bhayáún byákul bina dekhen chit na rahai.
Tapat juála uthat tan men, kathin dukh mero ko sahái.
Augun aprádhi dáya kíjai augun kachhu na bicháriyo.
Patil pánwan rakhu pati ab pal chhin na bisáriyo.
Dáya kíjo, daras díjo, ab ki badi ko chhoriyo.
Bhar bhar nayanan nírkhi dekhon nij sanch na toriyo.

"My frame aches without thee! I am wailing at thy door! Now appear and let me see thee.
O my Lord! I pray thee make no delay!
I have become restless through weeping and wailing.
I cannot live without the sight of thee.
Flames rise within me and consume my frame. Who can endure my pain?

I am full of faults and sin; do thou have mercy upon me.
Take not my faults and failings into thy regard!
O thou that freest the soul from sin! maintain my honour!
Forget me not even for a moment, and have mercy upon me!
Show me thy form and forget my sins of the present!
Cast thine eyes full upon me, and sever not thy love from me!"

9. Death song of the Sâdhs:—

Tujhé bináná kiya pari tu apna niber?
Bájai tál bajantre man báwaré! Sutari na chher?
Par haqq chháro haqq pichháro. Samajhwála pher.
Jhútha bázi jagat ka, man báwaré! Sun shabd ki ter.
Káya to nagri sakal bhamari pánch jamen ser.
Guru gyán kharag sam bhal lé, man báwaré!
Yam karai na zer.
Tera jíwana chhin pal ek, jag men phir na aisi ber.
Tera para jaház samudra men, man báwaré! phir sakai pher.
Sabhi musáfir ráh ké sab kharé kamar kasé.
Lená hoé so líjiyé, man báwaré, bíti ját aber,
Kar sumaran Sát Guru chháro dund duhel.
Tíjé bhám milain Sát nám sé, man báwaré! man báwaré, jagat ki na zer.

"What hast thou to do with others? Guard against the danger that awaits thee!
Why needest thou awake the sleeper?
Abandon what is unreal. Recognise what is real.
This is only the perversion of the understanding.
O foolish mind! The things of this world are false; so saith the Voice of Truth.
The body is like a city; in it are five lions.
Gird on the sword of the knowledge of the Preceptor, and then, O foolish mind! thou needest not fear the Lord of Death!
Thou livest for a moment, yea for the twinkling of an eye.
Thou shalt never have such time at thy disposal.
Thy bark has sailed into the deep; O foolish mind! If thou canst steer it safe to the yonder shore:
All thy fellow-passenger stand ready with their loins girt.
Take what thou desirest to take, O foolish mind! The time is fast passing away.

Leave the noise and tumult of the world. Repeat the True Name.

Then shalt thou gain the third virtue (God) through the True Name; and then, O foolish heart! thou shalt have no longer to endure the labour of this world!"

Distribution of the Sâdhs according to the Census of 1891.

DISTRICTS.	Numbers.
Farrukhâbâd	1,866
Cawnpur	4
TOTAL	1,870

Sahariya.[1]—A tribe, which is apparently of Dravidian origin, found in Lalitpur and some of the adjoining parts of Bundelkhand. They do not appear in the returns of the last Census, having apparently been included with the Soiri. The name of the tribe is usually derived from the Arabic *sahara*, "a wilderness," which is familiar as the name of the great desert of Northern Africa; but this, of course, is out of the question. It may perhaps be conjectured that the name is connected with that of the Savaras, the name in Sanskrit writers of the aggregate of the Kolarian or Dravidian tribes who dwelt in the highlands of Central India, and included races like the Kols, Mundas, Kurkus, Bhîls, Bhuiyas, and their kinsfolk. Some account of them will be found in connection with the Soiris. Another name for these Sahariyas of Bundelkhand is Râwat, which comes from the Sanskrit *Râja-dûta*, "King's messenger," or *Râjaputra*, "King's Son."

Tribal organization.

2. The Sahariyas of Lalitpur are divided into a number of exogamous sections (*gotra*), such as the Sirausiya, Kodoriya, Thegotiya, Sanauliya, Rajauriya, Jachoriya, Kusmorwa, Sarosawa, Chakardiya, Chirauncha, Kurwariya, Bagauliya, Sanhauriya. Of the origin of these names the tribe can give no account. Further enquiry will probably show that some of them at least are of totemistic origin. These

[1] Principally based on a note by Mr. H. C. Ferard, C. S.

sections are, as has been already said, exogamous. But as is usual, the rule of exogamy is reinforced by the prohibition of intermarriage between at least first and second cousins. Of their origin and history they can give no account. In Lalitpur they profess to be indigenous to the district.

Marriage rules.

3. When the bride is admitted into the family of her husband, she has to perform the rite of *confarreatio*, which is known among them as *dudha bhâti*, or "the eating of boiled rice with milk." A man may marry as many wives as he pleases, but he cannot take a second wife in the lifetime of the first, unless she is barren or suffering from some serious disease. Concubinage, with the leave of the tribal council, is permitted. Unmarried girls are obliged to be chaste. If an unmarried girl is detected in an intrigue with a man of the tribe, she and her relations are put out of caste, until they feed the brethren; she can then be married, usually to her paramour. As far as possible infant marriage is the rule, and a girl should not remain unmarried after the age of ten. There is no regular bride-price, but by tribal custom the father of the bridegroom pays eight rupees to defray the expenses of the marriage. If a married woman is found intriguing with an outsider, she is permanently expelled, and this, being done with the sanction of the tribal council, operates as an absolute divorce, and such a woman cannot be remarried or taken as a concubine by a member of the tribe, on pain of the man she lives with being also excommunicated. But if her paramour be a member of the tribe, the matter is brought before the council, and on giving the necessary dinner to the brethren, her husband can take her back, if he be so disposed; if he refuse, she is made over as a concubine to the man who seduced her. Children, the offspring of an adulterous connection with a stranger to the tribe, are not admitted to full caste rights, and, being considered as of a lower grade, find husbands and wives for themselves as best they can among persons of their own rank. Widow marriage and the levirate are allowed under the usual restrictions. If the deceased husband leave a brother who has no wife, and is of the suitable age, he generally takes over the widow of his brother; but under no circumstances can an elder brother take the widow of his younger brother. If a widow marry an outsider, she loses all right to the custody of her children and to a share in the goods of her late husband. The heirs of a man are his sons, and

there is no trace of the fiction by which the children of the levir are attributed to his dead brother.

Birth rites.

4. There is no ceremony during pregnancy. The mother is attended by a midwife of the Basor tribe, and on the tenth day the birth impurity is removed by the *daswán* rite, when the brethren are feasted ; or, if the family is very poor, some boiled gram (*ghughuri*) is distributed among them. There is no trace of the couvade and no rule of adoption.

Marriage ceremonies.

5. When the match has been arranged by the parents of the parties and their friends, the father of the boy, accompanied by a few of his brethren, goes to the house of the bride, and taking her in his lap puts a rupee and some sweetmeats in her hand. The party are then entertained, and next morning, as he is going away, the father of the girl gives a rupee to the father of the boy, which fixes the betrothal. On the wedding day, the bridegroom and his relatives go to the house of the bride, and a mark (*tilak*) is made on his forehead. Next day the pair walk five times round the shed in the presence of the brethren, and this concludes the marriage. No Brâhman is employed, and the ceremony is carried out by an old man of the tribe or the brother-in-law of the bride.

Death rites.

6. The dead are cremated, except those who are unmarried or those who die of some epidemic disease. The ashes are thrown into some neighbouring stream, and the mourners have their heads shaved. There is no rite of the nature of the *Sráddha*, and no funeral priest is employed. The man who fires the pyre is impure for three days. A woman is impure for three days after her menses, and for ten days after her confinement. The impurity after the menstrual period is removed by bathing.

Religion.

7. They are chiefly worshippers of Bhawâni, but they also reverence Râma and Krishna. They have no special ancestor worship, and do not employ Brâhmans in any of their domestic rites, which are conducted by the sister's son or by some old man of the tribe. They propitiate demons and evil spirits with the sacrifice of a goat; sometimes the ear of the victim only is offered. When an animal is sacrificed, the worshippers consume the flesh themselves. They have also various local deities, such as Gonr, Narasinha, Sânwar, Goraiya, Katiya, Tholiya, Somiya, and Abay Pâl,—most of which appear to be deified

worthies of the tribe. They swear standing in water or with a piece of hot iron in the right hand. They have the usual belief in the demoniacal theory of disease, witchcraft, and the Evil Eye.

Social rules.

8. They eat mutton, goats' flesh, and pork, and drink spirits. They salute each other in the form—*Râm! Râm! Sitarâm! Râdha Krishna!* Their mode of life is the collection of various kinds of jungle produce and cultivating on the edge of the forest. They are classed generally as a criminal tribe, but it has not been as yet found necessary to take any special coercive measures against them. The chief offences to which they seem to be addicted resemble those of the Sanaurhiyas—burglary, petty theft, and an occasional robbery or dakâiti.

Sâîn, Sânîn, Sâni.—(Sanskrit *syâmika, svâmi,* "lord, master") —An order of Muhammadan ascetics. The term is very usually employed in a general sense to designate any religious Muhammadan mendicant. In the Panjâb, the Sâîns or Gulâbdâsis are a Sikh sect, who, according to Mr. Ibbetson,[1] are chiefly interesting in the near approach of their doctrines to Epicurianism. They disbelieve in the existence of God, and venerate only living persons of their own persuasion. They are profligate both in profession and practice—esteeming wine, women, and personal enjoyment, and all that life offers which is worth having, and seeing no wrong in adultery and incest. These have, of course, no connection with the Muhammadan order of the same name in these Provinces.

Distribution of the Sâîns according to the Census of 1891.

DISTRICTS.	Numbers.	DISTRICTS.	Numbers.
Sahâranpur	525	Bânda	12
Muzaffarnagar	1	Hamîrpur	3
Farrukhâbâd	2	Jhânsi	8
Bijnor	4,131	Ghâzipur	78
Pilibhît	68	Gorakhpur	167
Fatehpur	20	Fasti	92

[1] *Panjâb Ethnography,* para. 268.

Distribution of the Sâîns according to the Census of 1891—concld.

DISTRICTS.	Numbers.	DISTRICTS.	Numbers.
Tarâi	7	Gonda	34
Lucknow	34	Bahrâich	116
Unâo	19	Bârabanki	204
Sitapur	489		
Kheri	645	TOTAL .	6,655

Saini.—A gardening and cultivating tribe found only in the Meerut Division and Bijnor. As is shown by their sub-castes, they are very closely allied with the Mâli, if not identical. From Jâlandhar Mr. Purser writes [1]:—"According to their own account the Sainis were originally Mâlis and lived principally in the Mathura District. When Mahmûd of Ghazni invaded India, the ancestors of the Sainis came into these parts, and, finding the land suitable for cultivation, settled down here and went not back to their homes. The explanation of the name Saini is that they were such good agriculturists and did such wonders with the land that the natives called them the Rasaini tribe (from *rasâi*, "cleverness, skill"), and in course of time the first syllable was lost and the present name Saini left. They are admirable cultivators, and surpassed by none in industry and skill. They do more market gardening than the Jâts, and perhaps even than the Arâins, but this is in addition to, and not in place of, ordinary farming. They have no bad qualities to distinguish them which call for special notice. The Sikhs among them pay much respect to the Granth Sâhib, and in every village have a copy of it, which is read diligently in the audience of the people. Men of this tribe not seldom take service and especially in the cavalry." In Jâlandhar, according to another account,[2] they claim Râjput origin, and say they are connected with the Arâins, though the latter know nothing of the relationship. In Ambâla they are described as an ill-conditioned set, first-rate cultivators, but refractory and intriguing. Another derivation of their name current in these Provinces is that it is taken from *sânna*, which is the technical word for mixing up the chopped

[1] *Settlement Report*, 84.
[2] Ibbetson, *Panjâb Ethnography*, 267.

millet fodder with chaff and water for farm cattle. In their customs and manners they are identical with the Mâli.

2. In Sahâranpur many of them breed ducks for the markets in the adjoining hill stations.

Distribution of the Sainis according to the Census of 1891.

Districts.	Baheniya.	Bhâgirathi.	Golê.	Phûlmâli.	Others.	Total.
Dehra Dûn	...	...	...	...	97	97
Sahâranpur	2,265	2,898	7,191	...	7,910	20,264
Muzaffarnagar	1,816	19,022	578	47	1,714	23,177
Meerut	221	4,265	...	...	3,022	7,508
Agra	...	...	...	...	1	1
Bijnor	7,184	37,663	126	...	3,386	48,349
Benares	...	...	...	...	18	18
Tarâi	...	...	...	...	1	1
Total	11,486	63,848	7,895	47	16,149	99,425

Saiqalgar, Siqligar, Sikligar—(Arabic *saiqal*, "a polisher") —The caste of armourers and polishers of metals. They are also known as Bâriya (*bâr*, " the edge of a weapon", Sanskrit *pâli*) or Sânwâla, Sândhara (*sân*, " a grindstone"), but these are especially cutlers and razor setters. In Mirzapur some call themselves Shaikh and others Pathân, and these do not intermarry. In Benares they say that they were originally Râjputs from Mârwâr.[1] At Mirzapur they trace their origin to Partâbgarh, and call themselves the descendants of Dâud or David, probably in reference to the passage in the Qurân which says (*Surah* XXI, 79-80) : " We taught him (David) the arts of making coats of mail (for before his time plates of metal were used) for you among mankind in general, that they might defend you from your suffering in warring with your enemies." They follow the ordinary Musâlman rules of exogamy, marriage, and inheritance. Widow marriage and the levirate are recognised,

[1] Sherring, *Hindu Tribes and Castes*, I, 317.

Religion.

2. They pay special reference to the Pânchon Pîr, Shaikh Saddu, Kâli Bhawâni, and Ghâzi Miyân. To the Pânchon Pîr and Ghâzi Miyân the offerings consist of melons, mangoes, parched gram, pulse, cakes (*bari*), boiled rice, sugar, curds, and clarified butter. When cholera rages, they sacrifice a goat to Kâli Bhawâni. Shaikh Saddu is more specially venerated in Oudh. His visitations cause melancholy and hypochondria. He is worshipped by the distribution of sweets to the poor and the sacrifice of a black goat. He once found a magic lamp, the powers of which he abused, and was torn in pieces by the Jinn.[1] By the Saiqalgars he is worshipped with an offering of sweet cakes (*gulgula*) and the sacrifice of a goat.

Occupation and social status.

3. Since the disarming of the country the trade of the armourer and cutler has become depressed. The ordinary Siqligar seen in towns is a trader of no worth, and his whole stock-in-trade is a circular whetstone (*sân*) worked by a strap between two posts fixed in the ground. He sharpens a four-bladed knife, a pair of scissors or two razors for a pice (three pies). Their status is that of ordinary Muhammadans of the lower artizan class.

Distribution of the Saiqalgars according to the Census of 1891.

DISTRICTS.	Hindus.	Muhammadans.	TOTAL.
Dehra Dûn	45	...	45
Sahâranpur	12	312	324
Meerut	18	33	51
Bulandshahr	...	23	23
Aligarh	...	74	74
Mathura	8	42	50
Agra	49	43	92
Farrukhâbâd	8	...	8
Mainpuri	3	70	73

[1] For a full account of this worthy, see Mrs. Mir Hasan Ali's *Observations on the Muhammadans of India*, II, 324, *sqq*.

Distribution of the Saiqalgars according to the Census of 1891—continued.

Districts.	Hindus.	Muhammadans.	Total.
Etâwah	2	39	41
Etah	...	7	7
Bareilly	2	18	20
Budâun	23	9	32
Morâdâbâd	...	17	17
Shâhjahânpur	88	112	200
Pilibhît	23	11	34
Cawnpur	53	14	67
Fatehpur	...	4	4
Hamîrpur	...	12	12
Allahâbâd	...	65	65
Jhânsi	1	...	1
Jâlaun	...	53	53
Lalitpur	...	1	1
Jaunpur	...	103	103
Ghâzipur	...	72	72
Gorakhpur	...	305	305
Basti	...	107	107
Azamgarh	...	234	234
Tarâi	148	...	148
Lucknow	86	7	93
Unâo	1	...	1
Râê Bareli	...	89	89
Sitapur	12	230	242
Hardoi	1	116	117
Kheri	66	181	247
Faizâbâd	...	130	130

Distribution of the Saiqalgars according to the Census of 1891—concluded.

DISTRICTS.	Hindus.	Muhammadans.	TOTAL.
Gonda	...	265	265
Bahrâich	54	260	314
Sultânpur	...	190	190
Partâbgarh	1	85	86
Bârabanki	...	113	113
TOTAL	704	3,446	4,150

Sâkadwîpi, Sâkaldwîpi.—A tribe of Brâhmans who take their name from the land of Sâkadwîpa, which has been identified with the Kâbul Valley which was occupied by the Sâkas in the first century before Christ. In the Mahâbhârata the Sâkas are associated with the other Dasyu races of the North-Western Frontier, and we are told that Saineya, the charioteer of Krishna, "made the beautiful earth a mass of mud with the flesh and blood of thousands of Kambojas, Sâkas, Savaras, Kirâtas, Varvaras, destroying thy host;" and the same record affirms their connection with the Aryas in the verses:—"These tribes of Kshatriyas, *viz.*, Sâkas, Yavanas, Kambojas, and Drâviras have become Vrishalas from seeing no Brâhmans." How it came to pass that these Kshatriyas lost their Aryan status is thus related:—"Satyavrata was degraded to the condition of a Chandâla, or outcast, and called Trisanku on account of three sins (*tri sanku*),—of killing a cow, displeasing his father, and eating flesh not properly consecrated. But on his repentance and feeding the family of Visvamitra during a twelve years' drought, he was transported to Heaven. His descendant Bahu was vanquished by the tribes of Haihayas and Talajhangas and died in exile. To him a posthumous son, named Sâgara, was born, who nearly exterminated the Haihayas and would have also destroyed the Sâkas had they not applied to their family priest Vasishtha for protection. The priest desired Sâgara to refrain from the slaughter of those who were as good as dead; for he had compelled the tribes to abandon the duties of their caste and all association with the twice born, and Sâgara thereupon imposed upon them peculiar distinguishing marks. He made the Yavanas shave their heads completely, the Sâkas to shave the upper half of their heads, the Pâradas to wear their hair long, and the Pahlavas to let their beards grow. He deprived them of all religious rites, and thus, abandoned by Brâhmans, they became Mlechchhas.[1]" This notable instance of early ethnography shows that the writers of the early Paurânik periods believed that these Scythian races, some of whom like the Chinese shave the fronts of their heads, were of common origin with themselves. "They, at the same time," as Dr. Muir notes,[2] "erroneously imagined that these tribes had fallen away from Brâhmanical institutions; thus assigning to their own polity an antiquity to which it could in reality have no claim." What real connection there may be between these Indo-Scythian Sâkas and the Sâkadwîpi Brâhmans it is now impossible to ascertain.

Tribal legend.

2. The legend of their origin is thus told by themselves: Sûraj Nârâyan, the Sun god, married the daughter of Visvakarma, the craftsman of the gods. When she was incommoded by the heat of her spouse, she went and complained to her father; but he said that he could not interfere unless Sûraj Nârâyan himself asked him to come with her to Visvamitra. When he arrived, Visvakarma told him that the only way by which his heat could be diminished was by cutting him into twelve pieces. Sûraj Nârâyan agreed to have this operation performed, and thus came to existence the twelve units (*kala*). As Visvakarma was cutting the Sun's body with his file, eighteen fragments fell in Sâkadwîpa and from these sprang the eighteen divisions of Sâkadwîpi Brâhmans. It may be noted in passing that Sun worship prevailed largely among the Indo-Scythian tribes. The story goes on to say that Sri Krishna, by the advice of the Sun, summoned these Brâhmans from Sâkadwîpa to cure his son Samba, who had been stricken with leprosy. They came flying through the air on the back of Garuda and effected the cure, for which they would take no remuneration. Again they started on the back of Garuda for Gaya, where the Râja Suloma was afflicted with the same disease. Him they also cured, and the Râni was so pleased that she secretly made to some of them a gift (*dâna*) of five

[1] Professor Wilson's *Works*, VIII, 294.
[2] *Ancient Sanskrit Texts*, I, 488.

villages, the names of which she wrote on betel leaves, and made the Brâhmans chew. Seeing them degraded by thus accepting a reward for their services, Garuda refused to take them back again, so they were obliged to settle at Gaya. But four of them were so conscious of the disgrace which resulted from the treachery of the Râni, that they retired to the holy land of Badarinâth (*Badari ka âsrama*), and there died in the Himalayan snow. The four who thus lost their lives were Suratkrita, Sutaya, Sudhrama, and Sumati. The remaining fourteen founded the existing *gotras* of the Sâkadwîpis—Mihransu, Vasu, Parâsara, Kaudinya, Kasyapa, Garga, Bhrigu, Bhabhyamati, Sûryadatta, Nala,. Arkadatta, and Kausila. They have in these Provinces at least no division by local areas (*dih*) and their system of exogamy depends altogether on the *gotras.*

3. Their titles are Misra, Pâthak, and Pânrê. In Bengal, according to Mr. Risley[1] their tribal organization is different: "It is a curious fact that although the Sâkadwîpi have the standard eponymous *gotras* of the Brâhman caste, their marriages are regulated not by these, but by ninety-five divisions (*pur*) of the local or territorial type, that is to say, a Sâkadwîpi man may marry a woman of his own *gotra* who in theory is descended from the same mythical ancestor or Rishi as himself, but may not marry a woman whose forefathers are shown by the name of her *pur* to have come from the same village or the same tract of country as his own. To abandon the *gotra* altogether, and to substitute for it exogamous divisions based on a wholly different order of facts, involves so serious a departure from orthodox usage that one is inclined to doubt whether the Sâkadwîpi can never have been organised on the orthodox lines. This doubt is borne out by the statement made by Mr. Sherring that the test applied to a stranger pretending to be a Sâkadwîpi is to offer him what iscalled *jhûtha pâni*, or water from a vessel from which another person has drunk,—a custom prohibited by all strict sects of Hindus. Should the stranger not be a Sâkadwîpi, he will refuse the water, probably with some indignation, as by drinking it, his caste, whatever it was, would be broken. If a Sâkadwîpi, however, he will take it willingly."

4. Whatever may be the case in Bengal, there seems little doubt that in these Provinces the Sâkadwîpi follow the ordinary Brâhman formula of *gotra* exogamy; and it is perhaps possible that the

[1] *Tribes and Castes*, I, 159.

rule which, according to Mr. Risley, prevails in Bihâr, represents a falling off from the stricter rules of the Western Branch of the tribe. In these Provinces the Sâkadwîpi act as family priests and astrologers and seem to have a preference for the Tantrika rites.

Distribution of Sâkadwîpi Brâhmans according to the Census of 1891.

DISTRICTS.	Numbers.	DISTRICTS.	Numbers.
Sahâranpur . . .	7	Gorakhpur . .	12,272
Meerut	11	Basti	6,736
Bulandshahr . . .	1	Azamgarh . . .	2,697
Mathura . . .	2	Tarâi	1
Farrukhâbâd . . .	3	Lucknow . . .	121
Mainpuri	179	Râê Bareli . . .	471
Bareilly . . .	3	Sîtapur	1,313
Morâdâbâd . . .	15	Hardoi	5
Pilibhît	4	Kheri	495
Cawnpur	24	Faizâbâd . . .	4,545
Bânda	22	Gonda	8,263
Benares	1,773	Bahrâich . . .	14,526
Mirzapur	657	Sultânpur . . .	1,554
Jaunpur	47	Bârabanki . . .	7,121
Ghâzipur	1,938		
Ballia	2,381	TOTAL .	67,186

Sakarwâr.—A sept of Râjputs who take their name from some place named Sikri. This, by one account, is Fatehpur Sikri, where Akbar built his famous palace near Agra. "In Unâo [1] they are the

[1] Elliott, *Chronicles*, 43, *sq.*

least considerable of all the clans who figure in these chronicles, and their weakness has had the common effect of destroying their ancestral pride and effacing the memory of their old traditions. None of them can give a clear account of where they came from, or what their history has been. But there seems reason to believe that they are a portion of the same Sakarwârs, who, emigrating into Oudh from the West, settled in the Faizâbâd District, near Dostpur. These latter are certainly earlier colonists than the Bachgoti and Râjkumâr Râjas, who have now nearly succeeded in reducing them to servitude, and whose immigration was contemporaneous with that of the Chauhâns of Chauhâna. The latter probably colonised their present position in 1350 A. D., and belong to the first class of colonists; and, consequently, if the above line of reasoning be correct, the Sakarwârs, who are earlier than them, belong to the first class also."

2. They appear to have held North Gorakhpur[1] before the Sirnets. They are the strongest Hindu landowners in Ghâzipur,[2] except the Kinwâr Bhuînhârs. They claim to have been originally Misr Brâhmans from Fatehpur Sikri. They have split into a Râjput and Bhuînhâr branch, and some are Muhammadans. In Azamgarh[3] the Râjputs ignore the Bhûinhâr branch; but the latter assert that they are of the same stock, which is generally believed. They call themselves Gadiya, and derive the name from an ancestor named Gâd, or one who was afflicted with ringworm (*gâd*). Another story is that he was a Râja Gâdh, who was the founder of Ghâzipur and the ancestor of the Sakarwâr as well as the Kausik sept. In the Azamgarh story he lived at Sikrigarh, near Lahore, which was the home of the sept. Another branch moved into the hills and are known as Parbatiya. They settled in Pargana Nizâmâbad after expelling the Suiris. The Muhammadan branch in Sultânpur trace their origin to one Pûran Mal, who is said to have been converted to Islâm in the time of Tamerlane, or more probably of one of his successors.

3. It is reported that the Sakarwârs give and take brides to and from the Bhadauriya, Dhâkra, Gahlot, Kachhwâha, Panwâr, and Parihâr septs.

---

[1] Buchanan, *Eastern India*, II, 458.
[2] Oldham, *Memo.*, I, 64.
[3] *Settlement Report*, 30, 57.

Distribution of the Sakarwár Rájputs according to the Census of 1891.

DISTRICTS.	Hindus.	Muham-madans.	TOTAL.
Bulandshahr	31	17	48
Mathura	228	34	262
Agra	10,001	13	10,014
Farrukhâbâd	276	...	276
Mainpuri	384	3	387
Etâwah	340	...	340
Etah	405	3	408
Budâun	349	...	349
Morâdâbâd	506	...	506
Shâhjahânpur	35	...	35
Cawnpur	46	10	56
Fatehpur	112	...	112
Bânda	56	...	56
Allahâbâd	57	1	58
Jhânsi	24	...	24
Jâlaun	112	3	115
Benares	485	13	498
Mirzapur	5	...	5
Jaunpur	121	116	237
Ghâzipur	5,616	6,101	11,717
Ballia	1,776	31	1,807
Gorakhpur	2,702	141	2,843
Basti	585	103	688
Azamgarh	2,179	284	2,463
Lucknow	90	9	99
Unâo	222	...	222
Râê Bareli	444	...	444

Distribution of the Sakarwâr Râjputs according to the Census of 1891—concluded.

Districts.	Hindus.	Muhammadans.	Total.
Sîtapur	341	11	352
Hardoi	2,448	...	2,448
Kheri	128	11	139
Faizâbâd	618	1,473	2,091
Bahrâich	16	...	16
Sultânpur	897	1,194	2,091
Partâbgarh	234	23	257
Bârabanki	18	...	18
Total .	31,887	9,594	41,481

Saknyâni, Shaknyâni.—A class of Hill Brâhmans. Common report makes them the progenitors of both Sarolas and Gangâris, and the name is said to be derived from the great Sâka race. Others connect the name with a colony of ascetics who lived near Tapuban and Rikhikes; others again assign the name to a great grove of *sakin* trees, whose bluish flowers are used in worship, and which gave the name of Sakinyâni to the parent village and Saknyâni to the people. Those who remained on the banks of the Ganges became known as Gangâris. They intermarry with Ghildyâls, Unyâls, Ingwâls, Dâdais, and Naithâna and Bughâna Brâhmans.[1]

Sanâdh.—A tribe of Brâhmans most numerous in the Central and Lower Ganges-Jumna Duâb and Rohilkhand. Sir H. M. Elliot lays down the boundaries of the Sanâdh country as follows:[2]—"They touch the Kanaujiyas on the North-West, extending over Central Rohilkhand, and part of the Upper and Central Duâb, from Pilibhît to Gwâlior. The boundary line runs from the north-west angle of Rampur, through Richa, Jahânâbâd, Nawâbganj, Bareilly, Farîdpur, to the Râmganga; thence through Salîmpur and the borders of Mehrâbâd; thence down the Ganges to the borders of

[1] Atkinson, *Himalayan Gazetteer*, III, 271.
[2] *Supplemental Glossary*, S. V. *Kanaujiya*.

Kanauj; thence up the Kâlinadi to the western border of Alipur, Patto, through Bhongânw, Sij, Bibâmau, and down the Jumna to the junction of the Chambal. Instances, of course, occur of occupation by either party on the other line, but they are very rare. On the North-West the Sanâdh are met by the Gaur Brâhmans, whose boundary line is also sufficiently definite to admit of description. It runs through the Râmpur territory as far as the Râmganga, thence through Sarauli, Seondara, Narauli, Bahjoi, Râjpura, Dabhai, and the western border of Koil, Chandausi, Noh-Jhil, and Kosi."

2. There is much doubt as to the origin of the name. According to one authority [1] it is derived from *sana*, "austerity," and *adhya*, "wealth," a conjunction which applied to a Brâhman would imply "one possessed of the wealth of religious austerities." According to others, *sana-adhya* means "absorbed in asceticism." Mr. Nesfield, without much apparent reason, would connect the name with that of the criminal Bundelkhandi tribe known as Sanaurhiya. They claim to be a sub-branch of the Kanaujiya, and the tribal legend as given by themselves tells how Râma, on his return from Lanka, assembled a large number of Brâhmans at the great Rudâyan tank, near Shâhpur Tahla, in Pargana Azamgarh of the Etah District, to perform a *sanâha yuga*, or sacrifice. At the conclusion of the ceremony, he distributed among them grants of land and money, and hence the name Sanâdh, either from the ceremony in which they participated, or from the Sanskrit root *sana*, "to obtain as a gratuity." There is a curious resemblance between this story and the account given of themselves by the Tagas of Meerut and the Nâgars of Bulandshahr. Most of the Sanâdhs of Etah represent themselves as the descendants of the Brâhmans of Râma's days; a few belonging to the Dandotiya *al* say that they came from the Gwâlior territory, where the Emperor Akbar had given them a group of eighty-four villages (*chaurâsi*) on the banks of the Chambal. These villages, known as the Dandtoghar Chaurâsi, are said to be in the possession of the Sanâdhs to the present day. The Bhateli Brâhmans of Etah are an offshoot of the Sanâdhs. In Etâwah Sanâdh Brâhmans of the Singhiya and Merha *gotras*, the former with the title Chaubê, are found in Pargana Auraiya. They trace

---

[1] Râja Lachhman Sinh, *Bulandshahr Memo.*, 153.

their origin to one Vasudeva or Bâsdeo, and are said to have been among the earliest immigrants. According to their family traditions, Bâsdeo came and settled at Sahabda or Sabhad under the protection of the Sengar Râjputs, and then one of them went to Delhi as late as the reign of Shahâb-ud-dîn Ghori and obtained some service. In the reign of Akbar they obtained a grant of land near Auraiya, and assumed the title of Chaudhari, or were appointed to the office. Some of the family have since borne the title, and in the neighbourhood of Auraiya they still retain many villages. The Singiyas derive their name from Singiya, a tract near Delhi, from which they came into the Etâwah District. They say that Garga Achârya, the spiritual preceptor of Krishna, belonged to their family. The Merhas profess to have been the family priests of the Bhareh Râjas. Besides these, two other important *gotras* of the Sanâdhs are settled in Etâwah. In the fourteenth century, when Alâ-ud-dîn captured Rinthambor, Hari Pant, a famous Pandit, came to Etâwah, accompanied by Ugra Sen of the Mathuriya *gotra* of the Sanâdhs; similarly the Svarna *gotra* are said to have come with Sumer Sâh.[1]

3. The Sanâdhyas are not purely endogamous. It would appear that wherever their habitat, as shown above, joins that of the other tribes, intermarriage is not infrequent. Thus in Farrukhâbâd, where they meet the Kanaujiyas, both intermarry. In the same way in the Bulandshahr District they intermarry with the Gaur. But here, for some time, and perhaps in some cases even now, a sort of hypergamy prevailed, that is to say, the Gaur and Kanaujiya married Sanâdh girls, but did not give their own daughters to a Sanâdh in marriage. This distinction is, it appears, being obliterated by degrees.

Tribal organization.

4. One division among the Sanâdh Brâhmans is into the "three-and-a-half houses" (*sârhê-tîn ghar*) and the "ten houses" (*das ghar*). The former are considered superior, and a system of hypergamy prevails among them by which "the three-and-a-half houses," for a money consideration, take brides from the "ten houses," and do not give them girls in exchange. The result of this is that the former find no difficulty in marrying even at an advanced age.

5. The Rohilkhand legend tells that Adisur was Râja of the Pargana of Kot Satâsi in the Budâun District. He had four famous

---

[1] *Gazetteer, North-Western Provinces*, IV, 38, 274.

Pandits in his Court. To the four sons of the chief Pandit, known as Misraji, he gave four villages for their support, *viz.*, Sarâha, Rahariya, Târapur, and Bhatta. These originated four sections, the Misras of Sarâha, Rahariya, and Târapur, and the Pâthaks of Bhatta. These four, being descended from the same ancestor, cannot intermarry. The second Pandit was named Sankhadhâra. He had also four sons, and to them the Râja gave four villages : Auni, Dhamai, Reunai, and Parsara. Hence arose four sections, the members of which being of the same stock cannot intermarry : Auni kê Sankhdhâr, Dhamai kê Sankhdhâr, Reunai kê Sankhdhâr, and Parsara kê Sankhdhâr. The village of Auni is close to Budâun, and is still in the possession of these Brâhmans. The descendants of the third Pandit are called after him Parâsari, and from the villages held by his descendants spring four sections, *viz.*, Para, Chandâwali, Pipara, and Ubra. The section taking its name from Ubra is known as Trigorâyat, because their ancestor had mastered the three Vedas. The others are known as Parâsari. These four, being of the same stock, cannot intermarry. The fourth Pandit had only two sons to whom the Râja gave two villages : Dungarpur and Kataiya. These are known as the Misras of these two places. The fourteen families thus enumerated constitute the "three-and-a-half houses."

6. There is also some connection between the Sanâdh and the Kataha or Mahâbrâhman. The story runs that this same Râja Adisur was once going on a pilgrimage, when he became seriously ill. The Râja of Nâgadesa, where he was at the time, sent him a skilful physician, who restored Adisur to health. His patient was so pleased that he gave him the name of Kashtaha, or "remover of trouble," of which Kataha is without much probability said to be a corruption It is alleged that Râja Adisur compelled the "three-and-a-half houses" to intermarry with these Katahas, an assertion which clearly marks some fall in status of which the real explanation has been forgotten.

Domestic rites.

7. The domestic rites of the Sanâdhs are of the normal type. At marriage they have a ceremony which seems to be peculiar to them called *nitasuti*. The bridegroom is made to sit behind the bride, and behind him the eldest man of the family and the other relations sit in a line. The barber's wife moves a milk churner (*rai*) and a bundle of thread over the heads of all the men and women present. Then one or more vessels of sweetmeats are shown to the bride and she is asked

if they are full or empty. If she says that they are full, it is a good omen; if she says that they are empty, the marriage will not be prosperous. After this potter's wheel is worshipped. Some make an image of it on the wall of the house, others go to the potter's house and worship his wheel there.

8. The Sanâdh Brâhmans have, on the whole, a doubtful reputation, and are not much respected among the other Brâhmanical tribes. Many, in addition to some priestly functions, hold land and cultivate, but they will not hold the plough themselves.

9. The Sanaurhiya, a thieving tribe of Bundelkhand, claim kindred with the Sanâdh Brâhmans. According to one story they were excommunicated, because they attended the rite (*jag*) held by Râmchandra when he was defiled by the blood of the Brâhman Râvana. Others say that they were degraded, because they did not attend the sacrifice performed by Brahma at Brahmavartta or Bithûr.

Distribution of Sanâdh Brâhmans according to the Census of 1891.

Districts.	Numbers.	Districts.	Numbers.
Dehra Dûn	148	Budâun	41,817
Sahâranpur	222	Morâdâbâd	8,022
Muzaffarnagar	329	Shâhjahânpur	14,840
Meerut	1,051	Pilibhît	10,027
Bulandshahr	8,477	Cawnpur	759
Aligarh	76,209	Fatehpur	381
Mathura	63,345	Bânda	1,211
Agra	106,381	Hamîrpur	4,371
Farrukhâbâd	6,087	Allahâbâd	1,070
Mainpuri	42,691	Jhânsi	8,606
Etâwah	36,659	Jâlaun	15,155
Etah	44,070	Lalitpur	3,498
Bareilly	31,630	Benares	468
Bijnor	382	Mirzapur	704

Distribution of Sanâdh Brâhmans according to the Census of 1891—concluded.

Districts.	Numbers.	Districts.	Numbers.
Jaunpur	411	Sîtapur . . .	1,056
Ghâzipur . . .	149	Hardoi . . .	908
Ballia	69	Kheri . . .	1,844
Gorakhpur . . .	2,110	Faizâbâd . . .	610
Basti	1,429	Gonda . . .	2,320
Azamgarh . . .	474	Bahrâich . . .	1,306
Kumaun . . .	9	Sultânpur . . .	1,532
Tarâi	634	Partâbgarh . . .	399
Lucknow . . .	548	Bârabanki . . .	2,867
Unâo	113		
Râê Bareli . . .	814	Total .	548,261

Sanaurhiya, Sanorhiya.—A so-called caste of criminals in Bundelkhand. They seem to have escaped separate enumeration at the last Census by recording themselves as a tribe of Brâhmans, and, in fact, they claim to be akin to the Sanâdh Brâhmans of the Ganges-Jumna Duâb.[1] Attention was first distinctly called to their criminal propensities in 1851, when they were called Uthaigiras or Sanorhiyas, and were estimated to number 4,000 in Tehri State, 300 in Bânpur, and 300 in Datiya. The Râjas of Tehri and Bânpur gave them protection, receiving presents in return, and frankly admitted this when addressed by the Political Agent.

2. The Sanaurhiyas are not a caste but a confraternity recruited by the initiation of promising boys from all castes except sweepers and Chamârs. A census taken of them in 1882 showed that they then included Brâhmans, Lochans, Telis, Thâkurs, Kanjars, Ahîrs, Dhîmars, Sunârs, Kurmis, Lodhas, Nâis, and Dhobis. One account of their origin is that they are Sanâdh Brâhmans who were excommunicated, because they attended the feast given by Râm Chandra when he was defiled with the blood of Râvana. Another story is

[1] See Mr. D. T. Robert's note in connection with the Police Commission of 1890.

that they were degraded for not attending the sacrifice performed by Brâhma at Brahmavartta or Bithûr. A third account is that they came from Delhi about two centuries ago. It is quite obvious that they have no claim to rank as Brâhmans. They possess a slang vocabulary of their own, confine themselves to thefts by day, and are said entirely to abstain from nocturnal theft, house-breaking, and crimes of violence: so much so that members of the confraternity offending in this way are excommunicated. They never steal near home and begin their depredations at least a hundred miles away. But they visit all parts of India, including Calcutta, Bombay, and Madras. They assume the disguise of respectable merchants and travellers, and their favourite method of shop-lifting is by the agency of a boy, whilst one or two of the gang as customers engage the shop-keeper in conversation and lead him to display his goods. A gang will be absent on an expedition sometimes for a year at a time. The fascination of their profession is so great that they say "Once a Sanaurhiya, always a Sanaurhiya." In various distant cities one or more Sanaurhiyas used to reside, apparently carrying on an honest business, but really acting as receivers of stolen goods. The Criminal Tribes Act was extended to them in 1874, and Mr. Robert's note contains full details of the supervision exercised over them since that time. The result, as in so many cases, has been far from satisfactory.

Sanjogi—(Sanskrit *samyogi*, "joined").—Classed at the last Census as an order of Hindu ascetics. The word, or its equivalent *Grihasti*, "householder," appears to be equally applied to those who have so far abandoned the practices of the ascetic orders as to marry and lead a family life.

Distribution of the Sanjogis according to the Census of 1891.

Districts.	Numbers.	Districts.	Numbers.
Bulandshahr	31	Fatehpur	1
Agra	758	Bânda	22
Etah	6	Hamîrpur	66
Budâun	12	Allahâbâd	1
Cawnpur	4	Jhânsi	142

Distribution of the Sanjogis according to the Census of 1891—concluded.

DISTRICTS.	Numbers.	DISTRICTS.	Numbers.
Jâlaun . . .	178	Basti . . .	741
Lalitpur . . .	136	Hardoi . . .	67
Ghâzipur . . .	539	Gonda . . .	36
Ballia . . .	832		
Gorakhpur . . .	996	TOTAL .	4,538

Sannyâsi—(Sanskrit *sannyâsi*, "abandonment of the world,")—a term which is often used in very vague and uncertain senses.—It properly means the ascetic stage of life through which every Brâhman should pass. But the term is specially applied to the followers of the famous reformer Shankar Achârya. "The Saivas," writes Mr. Maclagan,[1] "have generally been defenders of the faith against innovation. The final struggles against Buddhism in the south and centre of the peninsula gave rise to one sect of Saivas, known henceforth as Sannyâsis, and the contest against the innovating Bhagats of Northern India in the fifteenth century gave rise to another sect now known as the Jogis." Some account from local sources of Shankar Achârya and his disciples has been already given under the head of the Gusâîns. Mr. Maclagan's account from the Panjâb tradition is somewhat different and may be given here: "Shankar Achârya, the well-known Sanskrit commentator, a very vigorous defender of orthodoxy, is supposed to have lived in the ninth or tenth, or, according to Professor Monier Williams, in the eighth century, and to have helped in the final extinction of Buddhism in India. Shankar Achârya is said to have had four pupils, from whom are derived the ten classes of Sannyâsis,—from Padman Achârya, the Tîratha and Âsrama classes; from Sarûpa Achârya, the Bana and Arana; from Tarnaka or Tânk Achârya, the Giri, Sâgara, and Parvata; and from Prithodar or Prithivi Achârya, the Puri, Bhârthi, and Sâraswati. According to others the order is divided into four Maths,—the Joshi Math containing the Giri, Puri, and Bhârthi; the Sangri Math containing the Bana, Arana, and Tîratha; the Narar-

[1] *Panjâb Census Report*, III, *sq*.

gini Math containing the Parvata and Asrama; the Brahmachâri Math containing the Sâraswati and Dandi. The fact that there are ten groups of Sannyâsis is well known, but different versions are given of the names. Of eight lists which I have before me from different parts of the Province the Giri, Puri, Arana, and Bhârthi appear in all, but one or other of the following names, Astâwar, Jati, Bodla, Dandi, Anandi, Datta, Achârya, Kar, Nirambhê, or Pari is often substituted for one or other of the remaining six class-names. According to some account only eight of the classes are really Sannyâsi, the Bhârthi being Jogis, and the Dandi, Vaishnavas. Three classes only—the Nirambh, Asrama, and Sâraswati—are allowed to wear or use arms. Five of the sub-divisions are said to be recruited from Brâhmans alone, *viz.*, the Sâraswati, Achârya, Arana, Bana, and Ananda; the other five being open to the public.

2. "A man of any caste may become a Sannyâsi, but in practice the order is made up of Brâhmans and Khatris mainly; and, according to some, the true Sannyâsi will partake of food only in the house of a Brâhman and a Khatri. The members of the sect are supposed to be strict celibates, but of late not a few of them have taken to marriage, and still continue to beg though married. They are, as a rule, of a higher class than the Jogis, and their morality is of a higher order, but scandals about their enticing away the wives of rich Hindus are said to be not infrequent, though generally hushed up. The whole order is in theory devoted to contemplation and abstracted from the cares of this world, and a large number of Sannyâsis are actually religious mendicants without wives and without money, who wear ochre-coloured clothes and distribute quack medicines, who refuse to touch a coin or to take in alms more food than will suffice for the day; but there are also many who work in business and are men of great wealth.

3. "In fact the order is sometimes divided into three groups called after the three philosophical qualities (*guna*): the Rajoguni, who are the principals of religious houses (*akhâra*) and live in the world; the Tamoguni, who are ascetics who live on charity, begging for the wants of the day; and the Satoguni, who do not even beg but trust to support from Heaven and their neighbour.

4. "The Sannyâsis are professedly followers of the Vedânta system of philosophy which was promulgated by their leader Shankar Achârya, and the books based in that philosophy are held specially sacred by them. They are, as has already been noticed, a

sect not indigenous in the Panjâb, and their chief places of pilgrimage, —Benares, Amarnâth, Narsinhnâth, etc.—are outside the Province. They are especially remarkable for some customs which are foreign to the Hindus of this and most parts of India. In the first place, they do not generally wear the scalp-lock (*choti*), but either wear all their hair or shave it all. Further, the true Sannyâsi does not, it is said, wear the sacred thread (*janeu*). And, again, their usual custom is not to burn their dead, but to bury them or throw them into rivers. When buried, the dead are placed in a sitting posture facing East or North-East, and the hands and arms are rested on crutch."

5. In these Provinces the rite of initiation takes, according to one account, three days. On the first day, his body is purified with milk, *ghi*, cow-dung, cow-urine, and curds, and all his hair, except the scalp-lock, is shaved off. On the third day, the *homa* and *srâddha* are performed and his scalp-lock and Brâhmanical cord are removed. Then the *mantras* of the order are recited into his ear by the Guru, and he receives a *dand* or bamboo stick with a piece of red cloth tied to one end of it. Then he is known as Dandi. Only Brâhmans can become proper Sannyâsis. There is no condition of age. Most become members of the order on account of trouble, as the verse runs —*Nari mûi, ghar sampatti nâsi; Mûnd murâi, bhâê Sannyâsi.* "When a man's wife dies and he loses his home and property, he shaves his head and becomes a Sannyâsi."

6. The sectarial mark is the *tripund*: three horizontal lines drawn on the forehead. Their dress is the *kopin* or small loin cloth with a broader piece of cloth rolled round the hips. They carry a water-pot known as *kamandal* and a rosary of the *rudrâksha* berry. They get their food either at alms-houses (*kshetra*) or from charitable Hindus. When they ask for alms they say *Nârâyan*, "Great God." The respectable title for them is Swâmi, "Lord." The proper Sannyâsi ought to eat a meal of only milk, fruits or vegetables once a day, and they are particular in abstaining from meat and other substances, such as garlic (*lahsan*), which are supposed to excite passion. They do not cook for themselves. They prefer to eat food cooked by a Brâhman or Kshatriya; but if such a person is not present, they can eat from the hand of a Vaisya or Ṣûdra. Their cooking vessels are of the usual Hindu pattern, and they are careful not to use the vessels belonging to a member of another religion. They do not enter Jaina temples, but visit all the ordinary Hindu

shrines. But they practise no form of idol worship, as they themselves have attained the rank of deities. They salute each other in the words *Namo Nârâyan.* They salute their religious guides and other eminent Sannyâsis by falling before them. They chiefly worship Nârâyana, but until they obtain the rank of complete saintship, they also revere Ganesa, Rudra, Bhâgawati, and Sûraj Nârâyan, the Sun godling.

7. Nizâm-ud-dîn Ahmad in the *Tabakât-i-Akbari* describes a terrible fight between a body of Jogis and Sannyâsis at Thânesar in the presence of the Emperor Akbar, when the Jogis were defeated.[1] General Goddard, in his march through Bundelkhand, was attacked by a body of two thousand Sannyâsis called Saiva Nâgas.[2]

Distribution of the Sannyâsis according to the Census of 1891.

Districts.	Numbers.	Districts.	Numbers.
Debra Dûn . .	37	Pilibhît . . .	34
Sahâranpur . .	137	Cawnpur . . .	6
Muzaffarnagar . .	101	Fatehpur . .	5
Meerut . . .	43	Bânda . . .	23
Bulandshahr . .	119	Hamîrpur . . .	40
Agra . .	35	Allahâbâd . . .	19
Farrukhâbâd . .	11	Jhânsi . . .	142
Mainpuri . .	3	Jâlaun . . .	17
Etâwah . . .	7	Lalitpur . . .	84
Etah . . .	25	Ghâzipur . . .	113
Bareilly . . .	82	Ballia . . .	651
Bijnor . . .	30	Gorakhpur . . .	1,069
Budâun . . .	14	Basti . . .	3
Morâdâbâd . .	38	Garhwâl . . .	1,077
Shâhjahânpur . .	19	Tarâi . . .	67

[1] Dowson's Elliot, *History*, V, 318.
[2] Pennant, *Hindustân*, II, 192.

Distribution of the Sannyâsis according to the Census of 1891—concluded.

Districts.	Numbers.	Districts.	Numbers.
Lucknow . . .	17	Faizâbâd . . .	218
Unâo . . .	1	Gonda . . .	13
Râê Bareli . . .	37	Bahrâich . . .	1
Sîtapur . . .	10		
Hardoi . . .	58	Total .	4,406

Males	2,668
Females	1,738

Sânsiya.[1]—A vagrant thieving tribe who were at the time of the last Census confined to the Western Districts of the Province. Of their name no satisfactory account has been given. Some derive it from the Sanskrit *svâsa*, "breathing," or *srasta*, "separated;" others with *svagânika*, "one who has to do with dogs," or *svapâka*, "dog-cooking," a person of a degraded and outcaste tribe, who, by the older law, was required to live outside towns, to eat his food in broken vessels, to wear the clothes of the dead, and to be excluded from all intercourse with other people; he could possess no other property than asses and dogs, and his office was to act as public executioner and to carry out the bodies of such as die without kindred. It is true that these are now-a-days the functions of the Dom, but the mode of life of the Sânsiya is sufficiently degraded to make it perhaps possible that he may have inherited the name. The Sânsiya is no doubt the near kinsman of the other degraded wandering races who occupy the same part of the country, such as the Kanjar, Beriya, Hâbûra, and Bhâtu. Their tribal legends, so far as they have been recorded, do not throw much light on their history of origin. Some of them allege that they are a sub-caste of Nats; but the Nats do not acknowledge kinship with them. Another of their legends appears in various forms. By one account when the Agnikula or fire-born races were created, the Chauhân Râjputs created the Sânsiyas to act as their bards and sing their

[1] Principally based on an excellent report by Mr. F. W Court, District Superintendent, Police, Aligarh; notes collected at Mirzapur and by the Deputy Inspector of Schools, Bijnor.

praises. Their first ancestor was, it is said, one Sâns Mal or Sahasman, who has given his name to the tribe. He is said to have had three sons: One was born early in the morning when these people take their morning draught of butter milk (*chhânchh*) and hence sprang the Chhânchhdih section. The second was born at midnight, which is said in their patois to be called *karkhand*, and hence the section known as Karkhand. The youngest was born at noon, and as this is the time they milk their buffaloes, he was called Bhains. Bhains, it may be noted, is a section of both the Beriyas and Kanjars, which tends to establish the connection between the tribes, and Kâra also means a "young buffalo." So the designation of these sections may be perhaps either totemistic or occupational. Another story makes out their ancestor to have been Sâns or Sahâns Sinh, a Râthaur Râjput. His house once fell down in the rainy season, and he could not afford to rebuild it; so he and his descendants took to living in wigwams. He is said to have had three sons—Chandu Sinh, Gaddu Sinh, and Beri Sinh,—all their descendants took to a jungle life and lived by collecting *khaskhas* grass and catching vermin. The women of Beri Sinh's family took to prostitution, and they are the present Beriyas; those of Chandu Sinh were called Chanduwâla; and those of Gaddu or Giddu Sinh, the present Gidiyas. These legends are of little value except to prove the identity of a number of castes of the same social standing and occupation, who are known in the Central Duâb as Beriyas, in the Upper Duâb as Gidiya, Hâbura or Bhâtu; in Mathura and Bhartpur as Radhiya or Radhua Kanjars; and in Rajputâna as Gharkhulo or "those who live with their doors open." According to another legend there were two brothers—Sâns Mal and Malanûr—from the former are descended the Sânsiyas and Kanjars; from the latter the Beriyas or Kolhâtis and the Doms and Mângs.[1]

Tribal organization.

2. As we have seen, the more degraded members of the tribe recognise three exogamous sections: Chhânchhdih, Karkhand, and Bhains. Those who are rather more advanced and lay stress on their alleged Râjput descent profess to have sections taken from the names of well-known Râjput clans, such as Chauhân, Khâgi, Pundîr, Gahlot, and Samhâr. There is again another endogamous division of them into

---

[1] Gunthorpe, *Notes on Criminal Tribes*, 46.

Kalka or those of pure Sânsiya blood and Malla, whose mothers were Sânsiya women and their fathers men of other castes. That the tribe is much mixed is quite certain. It is well known that they habitually kidnapped girls of other castes. Of the seven gangs in the Aligarh District it was recently ascertained that the women leaders of four were women of other tribes, who had been either kidnapped or introduced into the tribe. Even now it is admitted that they will take into the tribe men of almost any tribe except the lowest menials. The only ceremony is that the convert is made to eat and drink with members of the tribe.

The Sânsiyas as bards.

3. Another very curious fact about them is that they act as a sort of Bhâts or bard and genealogists to some tribes of Jâts and to some Chauhân Râjputs. Many of the Sânsiyas of these Provinces refer their origin to Bhartpur, where they allege they were bards to the original ruling family. So in the Panjâb we find that in Hoshiârpur [1] they receive an allowance from the Jâts known as *birt*. "Towards them they hold the same position as that of Mirâsis or Doms among other tribes. Each Jât family has its Sânsi; and among the Jâts of the Malwa and Mânjha, the Sânsi is supposed to be a better authority on genealogy than the Mirâsi; for this he takes a fee at marriages. If the fee is not paid, he retaliates effectually by damaging crops or burning ricks." This fact is corroborated by Mr. Ibbetson [2] in relation with various other Jât and Râjput tribes of the Panjâb. How this connection can have arisen it is impossible to say; but the case of the Patâris, the degraded priests of the Mânhis, is a case in point, and the relation between these tribes furnishes a possible analogy which may account for the creation of the degraded Brâhman tribes, like the Mahâbrâhman and Dakaut.

Marriage rules.

4. In addition to the prohibition of marriage within the section there is the additional prohibition against marrying in the families of first-cousins, until at least three generations have passed since the last connection by marriage. They generally marry in the same neighbourhood, but the feeling seems to be in favour of selecting a bride from another camp, which is perhaps one of the most primitive forms of

---

[1] *Settlement Report*, 106.

[2] *Panjâb Ethnography*, para. 577.

exogamy.[1] We have also probably a survival of the matriarchate in the rule by which the match is arranged by the *phúpha* or father's sister's husband of the bride or bridegroom. Besides this the marriage and funeral ceremonies are performed by the son-in-law (*dhiyána*) or by a connection through a female (*mán*). As among all nomadic tribes, owing to the comparative weakness of female infants, girls are in a deficiency. At the last Census there were only 1,955 women to 2,332 men; hence brides are in demand, and a heavy bride-price is charged for a suitable girl. In Aligarh it is reported that a bride sometimes costs as much as four or five hundred rupees, all of which is spent in drinking and debauchery during the ceremony. The marriage ceremony is analogous to that of the Kanjars. The bridegroom, after the match is arranged, arrives with a body of his friends, and there is a pretence of seizing the bride by force if she be not peaceably surrendered. He then seizes her in the presence of the assembled elders, drags her seven times round the marriage shed, and marks her forehead with red lead, and this makes them man and wife. Widow marriage does not need even this amount of ceremonial. The man is generally expected to repay to the relations of the first husband what they have spent on the first marriage; in the case of the levirate this compensation is, of course, not paid.

Death ceremonies.

5. The real vagrant Sânsiyas often merely expose their dead in the jungle. In Aligarh it is said that the Chanduwâla Sânsiyas cremate the corpse; with the others burial is the rule. Where they bury their dead they seem to have come under the influence of the example of their Muhammadan neighbours. Some members of the tribe, who were deported to Mirzapur after the proclamation, professed to adopt the following rules:—A pice is put in the mouth of the corpse immediately after death as a viaticum, when it is washed and wrapped in a piece of new cloth, which should be five yards long, and carried by four men to the burial ground on a cot. The corpse is buried with the head to the West and the feet to the East. After bathing the mourners return home. The chief mourner remains apart for four days and cooks for himself. At every meal he lays some food outside his hut for the spirit of the deceased. On the fourth day the brethren are fed on rice, pulse, sugar, and *ghi*, and on the twen-

---

[1] Westermarck, *History of Human Marriage*, 330, *sqq*.

tieth and fortieth day, the four men who carried the corpse to the grave are fed in the same way.

Religion.

6. The religion of the Sânsiyas is of a very elementary type. They have a vague idea of a great God, whom they call Bhagwân, or Parameswar, or Nârâyan; but of his character and functions they can give no satisfactory account. Some of them worship Devi or Kâli in the same vague way whenever they are sick or in trouble. They are, like all the allied races, continually in fear of the malignant ghosts of the dead, who, if not duly propitiated, turn into *Bhûts* or evil spirits and injure the survivors. They have nothing in the way of a *srâddha*, and one way of propitiating the *Purkha log* or "sainted dead" is by feeding some of the unmarried girls of the tribe in their honour. They also have a vague belief in a godling known as Miyân, who may be Ghâzi Miyân or the saint of Amroha and Jalesar. He is, they say, the king of the serpents, and when they do honour to him they and their families are safe from snake bite. They believe, of course, in the demoniacal theory of disease, and when they fall sick call in a Syâna or Ojha to mark down the ghost, which is causing the mischief, and suggest the appropriate sacrifice which should be made to him.

Oaths and ordeals.

7. They do not pay much regard to an oath on the Ganges or on the heads of their sons or daughters. They have three binding forms of oath: *First*, they kill a cock and pouring its blood on the ground swear over it; *secondly*, they throw some salt into a cup of spirits, and, throwing it on the ground, swear over it; *thirdly*, they crush a leaf of the *pîpal* tree in their hands and swear. When a woman is suspected of infidelity and denies the charge, she is made to undergo the following ordeal: Five leaves of the *pîpal* tree are placed on the palm of her hand, one over the other. She has then to take in her hand a red-hot *gadaila* or "spud," which is the national implement of the tribe, and used by them in digging out vermin, etc. With this she has to walk five steps, and if her hand shows no sign of burning, she is pronounced to be innocent. Similarly, of the Kolhâtis of the Dakkhin, Major Gunthorpe writes:—"The ordeals men and women of this race have to pass through to prove their innocence, if they deny an accusation, are curious. For a woman seven leaves of the *pîpal* tree are placed, one over the other, in the open palms of both hands. A wet thread is wound seven times round both hands and leaves. An axe

made red hot is then placed on the leaves, and she bears it seven paces forwards and throws it into a bundle of thorns. Should the metal have penetrated the leaves and burnt her hands, she is guilty ; but if not, she is considered innocent."[1]

Gang system.

8. The organization of these separate gangs, to which reference has already been made, as practising a sort of rule of exogamy among themselves, is curious, and may be illustrated by the condition of things which until recently prevailed in the Aligarh District. The Sânsiyas there used to be divided into seven gangs (*gol*), of which the leaders of five, *viz.*, those led by Roshaniya, Harro, Pâncho, Giyâso, and Kallo, were women; and two were led by men, Hariya and Lachiya. The reason that women so often command Sânsiya gangs is because so many of the males are habitually in jail. Of these the gangs of Roshaniya, Harro, Pâncho, Giyâso, and Hariya used to be all one gang, which was known in the Mathura District as the gang of Sewa. His brother Mathura separated from him and formed a separate gang. On Sewa's death his gang broke up into two parts—one called after Teja, nephew of Sewa, and the other after Hulâsi, son of Sewa. When Hulâsi was imprisoned, the gang was called after his wife Bela ; and when Teja was also sent to jail, his gang was named after Roshaniya, wife of Belha, son of Sewa; and when Mathura also got into trouble, his wife Pâncho took command of his gang. When the two sons of Harro, widow of Hulâsi, grew up, she started a separate gang of her own, and into this gang was absorbed the gang of Bela. Again, when Teja was released from jail, he formed a separate gang, which was known as that of his wife Giyâso. The gang known as that of Kallu sprang from a Nat woman who formed an amour with a Jât, and had a large family who followed the gypsy life of their mother and finally intermarried with Sânsiyas and became recognised members of the tribe. This gang is still known as Bânswâli, because its foundress used to dance on a bamboo (*bāns*). Finally, the gang known as Lachiya's, who were really Beriyas from Nohkhera in the Etah District, came to Aligarh in recent years and became amalgamated with the regular Sânsiya gangs. All these facts are very significant in considering the question of the origin of the present Hindus. If, as we have good rea-

---

[1] *Notes on Criminal Tribes*, 49.

son to suspect, the same process of amalgamation of castes owing to sexual intrigue and the formation of caves of Adullam, like these existing vagrant tribes, has been going on for ages, the anthropometrical evidence in favour of the practical unity of the existing races ceases to be surprising.

The Sânsiyas as criminals.

9. That the Sânsiyas are one of the most audacious criminal tribes in the Province is now admitted and formed the justification for the recent stringent proceedings which have been taken against them. In the year 1890, they were all simultaneously arrested; the younger members were removed to a reformatory, and the elders distributed throughout the Province in the hope that they would adopt an honest course of livelihood, an expectation which has certainly not been realised. In the Upper Duâb careful enquiry conclusively proved that they had no other means of livelihood except dakâiti, road robbery, thefts from vehicles, threshing floors and persons sleeping in the fields. In the course of their operations, unlike the Hâbûra or Beriya, they were always ready to commit violence, and have been known to cause serious bodily injury and even death with the heavy bludgeons, which in recent years thev had substituted for short clubs which they carried when they first came in contact with our Police, and which soon became an inconvenient means of identifying them and were consequently abandoned. When bent on highway robbery, their usual *modus operandi* was to hide by the side of the road and suddenly attack passengers or the drivers of vehicles with showers of stones. If this failed to compel them to abandon their property, they fell on them with their bludgeons. Another device was to disguise themselves as constables, and in the course of a mock search to rob travellers. They do not usually take the plundered property to their camp for a considerable time, but bury it at a distance. They use the railway freely in going to and returning from the scene of crime. On their journey they do not stay at *sarâis* or other recognised halting-places, but encamp outside a village or town, and, being well dressed, pretend to be Banjâras or merchants. Their operations extend to a very considerable distance, and some few years ago a series of dakâities in the Panjâb was traced to one of the Aligarh gangs.

10. They dispose of stolen property through Kalwârs and Sunârs; they will not take it with them to the shop, the intending purchaser has to accompany them to the jungle, and, strange to say, the Sânsiya is usually found very honest in such transactions. If

they take stolen property into their camp, the jewelry is deposited in the hollow legs of their beds, and the clothes hidden as stuffing of quilts, etc. The women sometimes appropriate some of the stolen jewelry for their own use, and when a search is made hide it in a way which cannot be described. Other jewelry is generally at once broken up. On arrest both men and women habitually give false names in order to conceal their identity, and hence the men greatly dread the punishment of flogging, as it marks them; for this reason they generally behave themselves well in jail so as to avoid corporal punishment. They are very averse to incriminating each other; if any of them turn approver, he is tried by the tribal council. The usual penalty is a fine of one hundred rupees for every person he has incriminated, and if he cannot pay the fine they will realize it by seizing his property or even a marriageable daughter. They never dare in such cases to complain to a Magistrate In fact all their disputes are settled by the council, and they are never seen in Court. When a member of a gang is arrested, his companions will provide for his wife and family, and when any stolen property has been acquired, the wife of a man arrested gets her husband's share.

The position of the women.

11. Owing to the constant absences of the men on thieving excursions and in jail, the women have gained a position of unusual influence in the tribe. Many of them, as we have seen, become leaders of gangs. They are, as a rule, affectionate, faithful wives, and the men are very much influenced by their advice. When a party of Police approaches a camp, the women all commence to call out at once *bhîtari! bhîtari!* "To your tents!" which is the signal for the men to escape. While search is being made, the women will resist to the utmost of their power, and they are in the habit of throwing all sorts of filth over the officers engaged, hence all Police dread the duty of searching a Sânsiya camp. Another plan is to take their babies in their arms and fling them round their heads in the hope that the search will be discontinued to save the lives of the children. They have a thieves' argot very like that of the Hâbûras. Of the corresponding dialect in the Panjâb it has been shown by Dr. Leitner[1] that it is not a real patois, but merely a perversion of Panjâbi according to a regular system. This is also certainly the case with the argot of these Provinces.

---

[1] *Analysis of Abdul Ghafûr's Dictionary*, 17.

12. There seems little doubt that the real vagrant Sânsiya will eat all kinds of meat, vermin and the leavings of almost any tribe except perhaps sweepers. In Aligarh it is reported that they will eat with sweepers when engaged with them in the commission of crime. Those who are beginning to settle down claim, however, a much greater degree of purity and pretend not to eat *kachchi* except from high castes like Brâhmans, Râjputs and Banyas. The vagrant branch of the tribe live under portable reed mats (*sirki*). The men, as a rule, sleep till 9 A. M., sleep again during the day, eat again at 5. P. M. and then spend the night on the prowl. The women help by going about begging and pretending to sell roots and other jungle medicine; they thus obtain entrance into respectable houses and obtain information which is of use to their male relations. They are very fond of dogs and keep a number of them to guard the camp. The camp is usually pitched on one of the high sandy ridges which are such a prominent feature in the landscape of the Upper Duâb. They are no doubt guided in this by sanitary considerations and the sand is a convenient hiding place for property and the meat and hides of stolen animals. They themselves keep numerous bullocks and donkeys which they use for the carriage of their huts and goods, as well as cows and goats for milk; these they habitually let loose in the fields adjoining their camp. Hence the Sânsiya is not by any means a favourite visitor to a respectable village, and they could not wander about with impunity, as they were in the habit of doing, were it not that they were protected by landowners and merchants who shared in their plunder. Every true Sânsiya woman must have her ears bored, and some time ago this fact was used in Court to prove the identity of a kidnapped girl.[1]

Social habits.

Distribution of the Sânsiyas according to the Census of 1891.[2]

DISTRICTS.	Hindus.	Muhammadans.	TOTAL.
Sahâranpur	3,043	...	3,043
Muzaffarnagar	71	3	74

[1] *Reports Nizâmat Adâlat; Mussammat Darbo*, 10th April 1852.

[2] This, of course, does not represent the present distribution of the caste since they were brought under the operations of the Criminal Tribes Act.

Distribution of the Sânsiyas according to the Census of 1891—concluded.

Districts.	Hindus.	Muhammadans.	Total.
Meerut	852	...	852
Bulandshahr	36	...	36
Agra	16	...	16
Etâwah	1	...	1
Bijnor	12	...	12
Budâun	5	...	5
Morâdâbâd	26	...	26
Cawnpur	49	...	49
Bânda	5	...	5
Hamîrpur	15	...	15
Tarâi	19	...	19
Lucknow	10	...	10
Kheri	20	...	20
Bahrâich	13	...	13
Sultânpur	91	...	91
Partâbgarh	3	...	3
Total	4,287	3	4,290

Sâraswati.—A tribe of Brâhmans who take their name from the river Sâraswati, the lost river of the Indian desert. It now loses itself in the sands near Bhatner in Rajputâna, and by devout Hindus is supposed to flow underground until it joins the Ganges and Jumna at the sacred confluence of Prayâg at Allahâbâd. One legend accounts for its disappearance in the sand by telling how Mahâdeva, the father of Sâraswati, in his drunken passion attempted to violate her modesty, and she dived under the earth to escape his attack. The river gained its name from Sâraswati, the goddess of learning, under whose auspices the sacred literature of the Hindus assumed shape and authority. This river appears to have been to the early Hindus what the Ganges, which is named only twice in the Veda, became to their descendants.[1]

Tribal organisation.

2. The Sâraswatis, who in these Provinces are found principally in Agra, Mathura, Aligarh and Morâdâbâd, are ranked among the Pancha Gauda and are the chief Brâhmans of the Panjâb proper. Dr. Wilson[2] gives a list of their sections which are said to number no less than four hundred and sixty-nine. Mr. Sherring,[3] on information received from Benares, divides them into four great classes, the Panjâti, who should by their name have five clans; the Ashthans, with eight clans; the Barahi, with twelve clans; and the Bâwanjâti, with fifty-two clans. It has, however, been found quite impossible to secure a complete and consistent account of these *gotras*. As Pandit Râdha Krishna, Dr. Wilson's authority, admitted, such a list could only be prepared by the collation of the registers kept by the Pandas of Hardwâr, Thânesar and Mathura, who keep genealogies of every family of note, any member of which has visited the holy place within the last three or four centuries.

Domestic rites: Birth.

3. After the bride has come to live with her husband the first period of menstruation which occurs is a season of rejoicing. The women of the household and their friends assemble and sing songs of joy; sweetmeats are sent to the houses of friends. On the fourth day when the bride is pure, she is bathed and dressed in her best clothes and jewelry, and in the evening her husband's sister leads her and her husband into a room where they are shut up together for the night. When pregnancy occurs, at the end of the third or fifth month, the tribal deities are worshipped and an offering of sweetmeats made of rice and sugar is made to them, which after dedication are distributed to the friends of the family. At the completion of the seventh or ninth month the same rite is performed on a more extensive scale. When the child is born the *nandi mukh srāddha* for the propitiation of the sainted dead of the household is done. A Chamârin is called in who cuts the umbilical cord, which she buries under the bed on which the mother lies. The mother and child are bathed and the eldest woman of the family plasters with

---

[1] Wilson, *Vishnu Purâna, Preface* LXVII; Muir, *Ancient Sanskrit Texts*, V, 338.

[2] *Indian Caste*, II, 124, sqq.

[3] *Hindu Castes*, I, 62, sqq.

cow-dung the place where the cord has been buried and scatters some washed rice over it. Then the friends assemble and each of them gives a pice or two to the Chamârin as a reward for cutting the cord (*nârkatâi*). Songs are sung on this occasion. The baby does not suck its mother's breast for three days after birth; in the interval it drinks cow's or goat's milk. On the fourth day one of the women friends washes the mother's breast and receives a present. Then the child begins to suck. The Chamâr midwife remains in attendance until the fifth day and is then succeeded by the barber's wife, who remains till the twelfth day. On the evening of the sixth day the women assemble and make images of men and women on the wall, which are worshipped by the mother. On that day, for the first time, she eats grain. Up to that time she is given fruit and milk. On the eleventh day she is bathed and puts on fresh clothes and then worships the tribal deities. This rite is done in the family kitchen In the evening she cooks *kachchi* and distributes it to the relatives and friends. After this, under the guidance of the family priest, she worships Ganesa and the Navagraha or nine planets. She sits down with her husband and their garments are knotted together as at the time of marriage. The baby is also dressed in fresh clothes. The mother again bathes on the twentieth, thirtieth and fortieth days, and on these occasions Ganesa is worshipped again with an offering of the *halwa* sweetmeat. This is distributed among the friends of the family. After the fortieth day the birth impurity is finally removed.

Childhood rites.

4. At the sixth month comes the "grain feeding" (*anna, prâsana*). This is done on the eighth or ninth day of the waxing moon. The eldest member of the family takes the child in his or her lap and makes the baby sip a little food, usually rice milk (*khîr*) off a rupee, which becomes the perquisite of the person who feeds him. After a year the rite of "the year knot" (*baras gânth*) is performed. Some *halwa* sweetmeat is cooked in a pot, in which is then placed some red powder (*rori*) and washed rice. A little *halwa* is offered to Ganesa and the rest is distributed to friends. This rite is done on every subsequent birth-day until the fifth. In the third or fifth year the ceremonial shaving (*múnran*) is done in the usual way. The women take the child to a shrine, worship the razor of the barber and the mother takes the child in her lap and gets him shaved. The

kanchhedan, kanbedha or ear piercing is often done at the same time. The child makes an offering to the family god, sweets are distributed and songs are sung.

Marriage rites.

5. The marriage rites are of the usual form. As a rule the bride does not live with her husband until after the *gauna* rite which takes place after one, three, five, or seven years from the marriage. During the first year certain gifts are sent to her from her house on festivals. The technical phrase is *teohâr bhejna.* Thus at the Kajari feast in the month of Sâwan, her husband's friends send her a coloured sheet (*chundari*), some henna (*mehndi*), fine clothes, cards and backgammon (*ganjifa, chausar*), sweetmeats and cakes, cowries and dice, red powder and coloured rice. The bride's family also send some clothes for the mother of the bridegroom. Similar gifts are sent at the Holi.

6. The *gauna* (Sanskrit *gamana* "going") generally takes place in Aghan or Phâlgun. The husband and his friends go to the bride's house and are entertained on choice food in a place (*janwâsa*) arranged for their reception. When the auspicious moment arrives, the bridegroom in his best clothes and with a sword in his hand, possibly a survival of marriage by capture, goes to the house of the bride. In the courtyard a platform is made on which a water jar (*kalas*) and images of Gauri and Ganesa are placed. The garments of the pair are knotted together and in the knot some betel-nut, turmeric, and money are placed. The bridegroom sits in a square (*chauk*) with the bride behind him and Gauri and Ganesa are worshipped. The bride's hand is placed on that of her husband and the Pandit repeats texts. Her mother comes up with a dish containing red powder (*rori*), sweetmeats, and money, and marking his forehead with the powder, puts the sweets and money in the corner of his sheet. The Pandit sprinkles water over the pair with a wisp of *Kusa* grass and the bride and bridegroom go to the *janwânsa.* The barber's wife carries a tray full of large *laddu* sweetmeats. The girl's father stands before the father of the boy and says:—"I place my daughter under your protection. I am to blame in everything. My daughter will serve you." The girl's mother says the same to the boy's mother and both of them accompany this appeal with a money present. Then the bride returns to her father's house and weeps and embraces each of her female relations. She is given a box containing the *sohâg* or paraphernalia of a married woman, sweets, bangles, red lead, etc., which are taken with her by a

woman. Half the dowry is paid in cash by the father of the bride who after blessing the pair dismisses them.

7. When the pair get home they are met at the door by a female servant with a pitcher of water into which they drop some copper coins. The bride's mother-in-law then looks at the bride's face and gives her a present, known as *mukh dikhâi*. The other female friends do the same. Two or three days after the pair worship the Ganges and the family deities and the rite is concluded.

Death ceremonies.

8. The corpses of the boys who have not been invested with the Brâhmanical cord and those of unmarried girls are wrapped in a clean sheet and thrown into a river. No rites are performed for the propitiation of their ghosts. The adult dead are cremated in the usual way. The younger brother usually fires the pyre of his elder brother; or this duty is performed by the father, which is the greatest misfortune which can befall him. The only difference between the customs of the Sâraswata and Sarwariya Brâhmans in this respect is that the former feed Brâhmans (*brahm bhoj*) on the seventeenth and the latter on the thirteenth day after death. It is also peculiar to them that when an old man dies they make rejoicings. The head of the corpse is smeared with red powder and sprinkled with red water. It is carried to the cremation ground to the sound of music, and from the date of death up to the tenth day the women sing, and sweetmeats and betel are distributed. For a year after on the day of death a Brâhman is fed.

The Shenavis of Bombay.

9. In Bombay the Sâraswati Brâhmans are known as Shenavi, which seems to be a corruption of Chhiânavê as they are supposed to have ninety-six sections. "In Gujarât, besides acting as family priests, they follow many callings, reading holy books, drawing horoscopes, teaching private schools, trading, and serving as accountants, soldiers and constables. Once the holders of high offices, they have long lost their special position, and are now degraded, eating with and serving as the family priests of Kshatriyas, Lohânas, and Bhansâlis, whom they say they saved from Parasurâma's persecutions. In religion Saivas and goddess worshippers, (their chief deities being Ambika, Asapurna, Bhawâni, Kumâri, and Mahâlakshmi) their family deity is Sâraswati, whose chief place of worship is on the river of the same name. Not careful to keep the ordinary Brâhman rules, they allow widow marriage, and freely

travel across the seas to collect payments for their patrons, Cutch Vânya traders settled in Mozambique and Africa.[1]

" Dr. Wilson says that they are Shukla Yajurvedis. In using animal food they abstain from that of the cow and tame fowls; but eat sheep, goats, deer, wild birds of most species, and fish killed for them by others. They also eat onions and other vegetables forbidden in the Smritis. They are generally inattentive to sectarian marks. They dress like the Hindu merchants and Amîns of Sindh, though using white turbans. They shave the crowns of their heads, but have two tufts of hair above their ears. Their physiognomy is supposed by some to be not so distinctly of the Aryan type as that of other Brâhmans. They are partial to the Gurmukhi written character used in the Panjâb."

10. In these Provinces they are the special family priests of the Khatris. They have in recent times commenced to intermarry with the Gaur.

Distribution of Sáraswati Bráhmans according to the Census of 1891.

Districts.	Number.	Districts.	Number.
Debra Dûn	8,261	Bijnor	714
Sahâranpur	1,278	Budâun	1,623
Muzaffarnagar	500	Morâdâbâd	3,901
Meerut	2,461	Shâhjahânpur	271
Bulandshahr	1,016	Pilibhît	89
Aligarh	8,136	Cawnpur	615
Mathura	7,419	Fatehpur	52
Agra	2,943	Bânda	31
Farrukhâbâd	386	Hamîrpur	20
Etâwah	290	Allahâbâd	259
Etah	230	Jhânsi	337
Bareilly	1,239	Jâlaun	22

[1] *Bombay Gazetteer*, V, 43.

Distribution of Saraswati Brâhmans according to the Census of 1891—concluded.

DISTRICTS.	Number.	DISTRICTS.	Number.
Lalitpur . . .	10	Sîtapur . . .	174
Benares . . .	2,586	Hardoi . . .	172
Jaunpur . . .	32	Kheri	124
Ghâzipur . . .	48	Faizâbâd . . .	306
Gorakhpur . . .	33	Gonda . . .	23
Kumaun . . .	1	Bahrâich . . .	150
Garhwâl . . .	26	Sultânpur . . .	16
Tarâi	102	Partâbgarh . . .	6
Lucknow . . .	1,069	Bârabanki . . .	46
Unâo	317		
Râê Bareli . . .	55	TOTAL .	47,389

Sarbhangi.—An order of Hindu ascetics who are said to take their name from their complete isolation (*sarva-bhanga*) from all others. There seems to be little or nothing to distinguish them from the ordinary Bairâgi.

Distribution of the Sarbhangis according to the Census of 1891.

DISTRICTS.	Number.	DISTRICTS.	Number.
Muzaffarnagar . .	29	Lucknow . . .	5
Shâhjahânpur. . .	1	Sîtapur . . .	1
Pilibhît . . .	1	Kheri . . .	3
Fatehpur . . .	1	Bahrâich . . .	2
Hamîrpur . . .	4		
Jhânsi . . .	9	TOTAL .	56

Males . 44
Females . 12

Sarpakarıya.—A Râjput sept found in Azamgarh who say they are descended from a serpent (*sarpa*). Some of them are Chhatris and some Bhuînhârs. They are of low standing among Râjputs, but rank high among Bhuînhârs.[1]

Sarwariya.—A division of the Kanaujiya Brâhmans, who take their name from living beyond the river Sarju (*Sarjupâr, Sarayu-pâra*). They say themselves that they settled on the east of the river Sarju in the time of Râja Aja, grand-father of Râma. Mr. Risley [2] gives from Bihâr a legend of their origin which as he says "throws light upon the part which misunderstood tradition may play in the growth of popular tradition. Once upon a time there were two brothers, Kanha and Kubja; they lived in Kanauj, and their descendants were called Kanaujiya Brâhmans. Now Râm Chandra, King of Ajudhya, wished to perform the great sacrifice of a horse, and sent for the Kanaujiya Brâhmans to help him. When they were starting, their father made them promise not to take any present for what they were going to do. But it seems that the sacrifice was of no effect unless the Brâhmans were duly rewarded. The Râja knew this, and caused diamonds to be hidden in the packets of betel which he gave to the Brâhmans. When they got home their father asked them if they had taken any presents, and they said they had not. But when the packets of betel were opened the diamonds were found, and these Brâhmans were at once turned out of their caste, so they went back to the king, ready to curse him for his treachery. But he appeased them with smooth words and with grants of land to dwell on, and the grants were made in this way. The king shot an arrow as far as he could, and the place where it fell was the boundary of the land. Now the name of an arrow is *sar* so these Brâhmans were called Sarwariya."

Tribal organisation.

2. The Sarwariya Brâhmans have the usual Brâhmanic organisation of sections (*gotra*) and local groups (*dih*); there are two superior sections in these Provinces:—

1. Garga *gotra*, called Sukla with the following groups (*dih*): Mâmkhor, Mehra, Bhenri, Bakrua, Kanail, Majhganwa.

---

[1] *Settlement Report*, 29.

[2] *Tribes and Castes*, I, 157.

2. Gautama *gotra*; title Tivâri; sections Sarya, Sohgaura, Dhatura, Deoriya, Sirjam, Chetiya. The last are properly speaking Tivâris of Burhiya Bâri, of Gorakhpur. Below these are thirteen inferior sections:—

1. Vatsya *gotra*; title Misra; *dih* Payâsi.
2. Vatsya; title Dûbê; *dih* Samadari, Sarari.
3. Kasyapa; title Dûbê; *dih* Brihatgrâma.
4. Kasyapa; title Misra; *dih* Dharmpura.
5. Gautama; title Gurdaban Dûbê; *dih* Kanchani.
6. Savarna; title Pânrê, Panreya; *dih* Itiya.
7. Savarna; title Pânrê, Panreya; *dih* Itâri.
8. Kasyapa; title Pânrê; *dih* Triphala.
9. Gard Mukha Sandilya; title Tivâri; *dih* Pinri, Nadâwali, Târa, Majauna.
10. Vatsya; title Pânrê; *dih* Nâga Chauri.
11. Vatsya; title Misra; *dih* Ratanmâla.
12. Vatsya; title Tivâri; *dih* Pâla.
13. Kasyapa; title Misra; *dih* Rârhi.

In addition to the above there are some whose claim to rank among the higher Sarwariya Brâhmans is not fully accepted. Such are the Parwa Dûbê of Kantit, the Pâthak of Sonaura, the Tiwâri of Bhargo, the Ojha of Karaili, the Pânrê of Thokawa, the Upâdhyâya of Khoriya, the Chaubê of Nepura, the Dûbê of Latihai. These Brâhmans, however, intermarry with the higher grade Sarwariya.

The Pantiha and Tutaha.

3. Sarwariya Brâhmans pay much regard to their *pânti* or rank which now hardly means anything more than a certain amount of prejudice in the matter of eating and drinking only with persons of equal or superior rank. The Pantiha Brâhmans will not eat *pakki* cooked by Kshatriyas; on the other hand those who are not Pantiha will eat *pakki* cooked by Kshatriyas whose lineage is undoubted. Pantiha Brâhmans will not allow their women to use the flour mill or rice pounder, and would rather die than get the work of preparing the grain done by their women. But the number of Pantihas is said now to be so rapidly diminishing that they find it difficult to marry without violating the prohibited degrees. All have fallen into the lower grade known as Tutaha or "broken," with a few exceptions. If a Pantiha marries the daughter of a Tutaha he falls into the status of the latter. Pantihas at present belong only to the higher sections, those of Garga, Gautama and Sandilya. These

three of the highest grade are exogamous and so are the thirteen lower divisions ; but a kind of hypergamy prevails, and while the higher three divisions give daughters to the lower, they do not take brides from them. The Pantihas of the lower grades exchange brides indiscriminately. But there is a constant effort to rise in the social scale on the part of those of inferior grade by contracting marriage alliances with those of higher status. When a man emigrates he takes his *dih* with him and the area of the group is thus constantly extending.

Domestic rites : Birth.

4. When a woman is five months gone in pregnancy she invites her mother-in-law and entertains her on cakes, sweetmeats and milk. Five Brâhmans are also fed at the same time. The woman gives her mother-in-law a present of a sheet (*sâri*), petticoat (*lahnga*) and boddice (*choliya*), accompanied with a present in cash varying with the wealth of the family. If her father-in-law be alive she gives the garments suitable to a married woman ; if he be dead, only two white sheets are presented. Up to the eighth month of her pregnancy the expectant mother wears a blue sheet as a protective against the Evil Eye. At the end of the eighth month eight sweet cakes (*pua*) are sent to the houses of each of the near relations. From that day the woman gives up wearing her blue garment, and the mother lays her head at the feet of her mother-in-law and makes her a present of two rupees, known as *pânw lagâi.*

5. When the baby is born, if it be a boy, the *nandi-mukh srâddha* is done as described in the case of other Brâhmans. The father, after this ancestor worship is over, binds the umbilical cord with his Brâhmanical thread and buries it in the confinement room. A fire is kept burning over it for six days ; during this time whoever wishes to enter the confinement room washes his feet and then dries them by holding them over fire. This repels the evil spirits which may have accompanied him from outside. This also keeps off the dreaded demon Jamhua, which represents the infantile lock-jaw resulting from the cutting of the cord with a blunt instrument and the neglect of sanitary precautions. On the sixth day the mother bathes at an auspicious moment selected by the Purohit. She bathes again on the tenth and twelfth day and then acquires a sufficient degree of purity to allow her to be touched by her relatives. But she cannot touch the drinking water of the family, or cook for them. On the day the child is born the mother-

in-law puts in an earthen pot the seeds of the Embelia ribes (*bâé birang*) and water, and in another *nîm* leaves and water. The former is drunk by the mother and she uses the second for bathing. On the third day the mother-in-law grinds some pepper (*pîpar*) and gets two rupees as a present. On the sixth day the mother dyes seven or nine sheets with turmeric; one is given to the Chamârin, Nâin, and Bârin, and the rest to the wives of Brâhmans. The Pandit who prepares the horoscope is also rewarded and a sheet is given to the Dhobin who washes the clothes used at the delivery. People of other castes will not drink water at the house of a man whose wife has been delivered for twelve days. On the twelfth day the house is cleaned, the old earthen vessels replaced and the birth impurity is removed.

6. When the baby is a month old it is bathed and a piece of red thread tied as an amulet round the wrists, feet, waist, and neck. Each thread has seven tassels, three yellow and four red. These threads are changed every month up to the sixth month when they are replaced by ornaments of gold or silver which are also regarded as protectives against demoniacal influence. The ornaments for a child consist of bangles (*kara*) on the wrist and feet, a waist chain (*kardhani*), and a necklace (*humel, kahula*) to which are attached seven charms (*yantra*). Then the child is dressed in a coat and cap and the *anna-prásana* rite or "feeding with grain" is performed as elsewhere described. At the first birthday what is known as the *varsha karm* is done. The child is made to drink a mixture of milk and sesamum which is first offered to the tribal goddess.

The shaving.

7. After the third year the ceremonial shaving (*múnran*) is done. For three days before the rite the women sing, a small silver razor is made costing a rupee and a quarter. The child is rubbed with the condiment known as *ubtan* during this time. On the third day the barber touches the child's head with the silver razor and then shaves the head with his own razor. The mother holds the child in her lap and receives the hair as it falls on a broad wheaten cake. She preserves the hair till she has occasion to go to Prayâg when she lets it float away in the sacred junction (*Triveni*) of the rivers. With the hair ten copper coins are also thrown into the stream. At the fifth year the ear-piercing (*kanchhedan*) is done at some favourite shrine.

8. The marriage and death rites are of the usual type as elsewhere described.

Other domestic rites.

9. Of the Sarwariya Brâhmans of Gorakhpur Dr. Buchanan[1] writes :—"The Sarwariya Brâhmans, and all the sacred order here imitate their example, do not eat rice cleaned by boiling, that is purchased in the market. What is cleaned without boiling may be anywhere purchased ; yet the distinction is very slight, for the Brâhman women never clean the rice themselves, and low women are employed to boil the rice before it is cleaned. The conscience is saved by this operation being performed in the Brâhman's house, and by the water used being drawn and carried home in his vessels, for this is done by the low women employed to clean the grain. The Brâhmans here in general decline to eat parched grain purchased from a shop, and sweetmeats consisting of grain and sugar fried in oil they altogether reject ; but they use the confections made of sugar and curds, and they carry grain to the parchers' shop, who prepare it before them, and this they eat without scruple. They never eat either of these refreshments without purifying the place on which they sit with cow-dung and water ; a ceremony which elsewhere is only considered necessary at regular meals. They eat goat's flesh both when sacrificed and when killed on purpose, but will not purchase a joint from the shop of a professed butcher. They also eat deer, porcupines and hares, partridges, quails, pigeons, turtle doves, and wild ducks of several kinds.

Social customs.

"It is admitted that according to the written law they might eat wild hog, lizards, turtles and wild pullets, but anyone who presumed to do so would infallibly lose caste. Two or three Pandits are shrewdly suspected of drinking in the worship of the goddess, but they keep it as secret as possible, as, if clearly proven, they would undoubtedly lose caste. The Brâhmans and all the women, except of the lowest dregs of impurity, never smoke tobacco except as a medicine ; but for this restraint they make up by chewing. Brâhmans may without loss of caste intoxicate themselves with hemp ; but it is only used to any considerable extent by those who have abandoned the pleasures of the world for a religious life."

---

[1] *Eastern India*, II, 472.

Distribution of Sarwariya Bráhmans according to the Census of 1891.

DISTRICTS.	Number.	DISTRICTS.	Number.
Dehra Dûn . . .	219	Pilibhît . . .	355
Sahâranpur . . .	273	Cawnpur . . .	835
Muzaffarnagar . .	108	Fatehpur . . .	6,436
Meerut . . .	255	Bânda . . .	57,392
Bulandshahr . . .	38	Hamîrpur . . .	237
Aligarh . . .	615	Allahâbâd . . .	177,975
Mathura . . .	200	Jhânsi . . .	251
Agra	111	Jâlaun . . .	28
Farrukhâbâd . . .	807	Lalitpur . . .	64
Mainpuri . . .	239	Benares . . .	77,196
Etâwah . . .	104	Mirzapur . . .	152,341
Etah	98	Jaunpur . . .	146,345
Bareilly . . .	235	Ghâzipur . . .	29,936
Bijnor	120	Ballia . . .	12,630
Budâun . . .	73	Gorakhpur . . .	241,791
Morâdâbâd . . .	79	Basti	185,086
Shâhjahânpur . .	218	Azamgarh . . .	103,728

Distribution of Sarwariya Brâhmans according to the Census of 1891 —concluded.

Districts.	Number.	Districts.	Number.
Tarâi	17	Faizâbâd . . .	194,937
Lucknow . . .	1,932	Gonda . . .	197,993
Unâo . .	303	Bahrâich . . .	41,322
Râê Bareli . . .	23,144	Sultânpur . . .	155,534
Sîtapur . . .	636	Partâbgarh . . .	123,039
Hardoi . . .	527	Bârabanki . . .	18,565
Kheri . . .	474	Total .	1,909,277

Satnâmi.[1]—A Hindu religious order who take their name from their invocation of Satyanâma, "The God of truth." There are at least two classes of people called by the same name.

2. There is first, the sect founded by Jag-Jîwan Dâs of Sardaha in the Bârabanki District, who was born in 1682 A.D. He was a Chandel Thâkur, and his chief disciples were Gusâîn Dâs, an Upâdhya Brâhman, Devi Dâs, a Chamar Gaur Thâkur, Dulam Dâs, a Sombansi Thâkur and Kheni Dâs, a Tiwâri Brâhman. He established some connection with Islâm; and two of his disciples were of that creed. They profess to adore the True Name alone, the one God, the Cause and Creator of all things, void of sensible qualities (*nirguna*), without beginning or end. They borrow, however, their notions of creation from the Vedânta philosophy, or rather from the modified form in which it is adapted to vulgar apprehension; worldly existence is illusion or the work of Mâya, the primitive

[1] *Indian Antiquary*, VIII, 289 sqq.; *Oudh Gazetteer*, I, 362; Wilson, *Essays*, I, 356; *Central Provinces Gazetteer*, 412.

character of Bhawâni, the consort of Siva. They recognise, accordingly, the whole Hindu pantheon, and although they profess to worship but one God, pay reverence to what they consider manifestations of his nature visible in the Avatâras, particularly Râma and Krishna. Their moral code is much the same as that of all Hindu ascetics, and enjoins indifference to the world, its pleasures and its pains; devotion to the spiritual guide; clemency and gentleness; rigid adherence to truth; the discharge of all ordinary social or religious obligations, and the hope of final absorption into the One Spirit with all things. There is thus but little difference between them and some of the Vaishnava sectaries. The sacred book of the sect is the Aghavinsa or "Sin remover." The Bâba died at Kotwa, five miles from Sardaha in 1761 A.D. Meat, *masûr* pulse and intoxicating liquors are prohibited, as well as the egg-plant (*baingan*) at least locally. The story goes that Râja Devi Bakhsh, late Ta'aluqdâr of Gonda, married in the family of the high priest, and on the occasion of his marriage he was entertained as a guest with his whole suite. But he declined their hospitality unless served with flesh. The Satnâmis at last prepared a curry of *baingan*, pronounced a prayer upon it, and when served out, it was found to be flesh. From thenceforth the Satnâmis renounced the eating of *baingan* as a thing convertible into meat. Smoking seems to be allowed.

3. Caste distinctions are not lost by profession. On the contrary its professors seem to be careful not to interfere with caste prejudice and family customs. Fasts are kept, at least to a partial extent on Tuesday, the day of Hanumân, and on Sunday, the day of the Sun. A good deal of liberality is shown towards local superstitions. Incense is weekly burnt to Hanumân under the title of Mahâbîr, whilst Râma Chandra seems to come in for a share of adoration. The water in which the Guru's feet have been washed is drunk only when the Guru is of equal or higher caste than the disciple. Satnâmis seem regularly to observe the festivals of their Hindu brethren. Their distinctive mark is the *andu*, or black and white twisted thread worn on the right wrist. The full-blown Mahant wears an *andu* on each wrist and each ankle. Their caste mark (*tilak*) is a black, perpendicular streak. The bodies of the dead are buried, not cremated. Marriage customs are those of the family to which the Satnâmi belongs.

4. The other class, known by the name of Satnâmi, are the Râê Dâsi Chamârs of parts of the Central Provinces. The creed preached by Râê Dâs seems to have been very similar to that of Ghâsi Dâs, the celebrated Satnâmi teacher, who started the revival among the Chamârs some seventy years ago. This seems hardly to have reached these Provinces.

Distribution of the Satnâmis according to the Census of 1891.

DISTRICTS.	Number.	DISTRICTS.	Number.
Muzaffarnagar . .	109	Moradâbâd	2
Meerut	2	Pilibhît . . .	21
Bulandshahr . . .	54	Mirzapur . . .	6
Farrukhâbâd . . .	1	Ghâzipur . . .	25
Mainpuri . . .	3	Faizabad . . .	26
Etah	1		
Bareilly	332	TOTAL .	583

Saun—A tribe recorded at last Census to the number of 1 in Morâdâbâd and 256 in the Tarâi. They represent in the hills the Kurmi of the plains and will do any kind of labourer's work except carrying palanquins. Their principal occupation is mining, and the reason they give for not carrying litters is that all castes will not drink water from their hands, though drinking it from the hand of the Kahâr.[1] In the Tarâi they show 63 sections. They claim to be a branch of the Khasiya Râjputs. They do not appear to be regularly domiciled in the Tarâi, but come in the cold weather for work and return in the hot season.

Sayyid; Sayyad—(said to be derived from *sûd*, "increase, gain") one of the four chief divisions of Muhammadans. They call themselves the descendants of the famous martyrs Hasan and Husain, the sons of Ali the fourth Khalîf, and Fâtima the daughter of the Prophet. How many of these are true Sayyids it is impossible to say. Many of them came with the early Muhammadan invaders and asserted some priestly pretensions which were in many

[1] Atkinson, *Himalayan Gazetteer*, III, 451.

cases rewarded by gifts of revenue-free land which their descendants still enjoy. Many of these now recorded as Sayyids have no real claim to the title. The common proverb quoted in the article on the Shaikhs says : "Last year I was a butcher, this year I am a Shaikh; next year if prices rise, I shall become a Sayyid." According to Mr. Ibbetson[1] the apostles who converted the Pathâns to Islâm were called Sayyids if they came from the West and Shaikhs if from the East. The characteristic qualities of a Sayyid as described by Farishta on the occasion of his dissipating the doubt whether Khizr Khân, the protégé of Taimûr, was really a Sayyid, were modesty, politeness, hospitality, compassion, charity, learning and bravery; but it is needless to say that few of the modern Sayyids reach this high ideal.

Tribal organisation.

2. The tribal organisation of the Sayyids is confusing because some of the divisions take their name from an eponymous ancestor and some are merely territorial. At the last Census they were enumerated in a large number of divisions—Abbâsi, which is also one of the Shaikh subdivisions and takes its name from Abbâs, the paternal uncle of the Prophet; Abidi, "worshippers of God;" Bani Fâtima, the descendants of Fâtima, the daughter of the Prophet. She married Ali the cousin of Muhammad and was the mother of the martyrs Hasan and Husain from whom the Sayyids generally are said to be sprung; Baqri (*baqar*, "an ox") Bâghdâdi, "residents of Bâghdâd"; Bukhâri, "residents of Bukhâra"; Chishti, followers of the Saint Salîm Chisti of Fatehpur Sikri; Hâshimi, also a Shaikh division, named after Hâshim, the great grandfather of the Prophet; Hasani, from the martyr Hasan; Hasani-ul-Husaini, from the two martyr brethren; Husaini from Husain; Ja'fari, also a Shaikh division, who take their name from Ja'far, one of the Imâms; Jalâli possibly from Al-Jalâl, a term used by the Sûfi mystics to express that state of the Almighty which places him beyond the understanding of His creatures; Qâdiriya, which is the name of a special sect who deny absolute predestination and believe in the power (*qadr*) of man's free-will; Kâzimi (*Kâzim*, "the restrainer of anger"); Naqwi; Pîrzâda, "descendants of some saint;" Riswi; Sabzawâri from Sabzwâr one of the chief cities of the Persian Province

[1] *Panjâb Ethnography*, para. 515.

Khurasân, between Mashad and the Caspian sea; Siddîqi, from As-Siddîq, "he who speaks the truth," a title given by the Prophet to the first Khalîf Abu Bakr; Taqwi, "the abstinent." Tirmîzi, residents of a place called Tirmîz in Persia; Ulwi or Ālawiya, who believe the Khalîf Ali to have been a prophet; Uskari and Zaidi.

3. Abul Fazl, Sayyid, of Wâsit in Irâq, is the ancestor of most of the renowned Muhammadan families in Upper India—the Bârha and Bilgrâmi Sayyids, and in Khairâbad, Fatehpur Haswa and many other places branches of the same stem are found. Sayyid Muhammad, the fourth in descent from him, was the ancestor of the Bilgrâm family.[1]

4. The Sayyids of Jais in Râê Bareli are another famous Oudh family who are said to have been settled since the thirteenth century. They are well known for learning and the Mujtahids of Lucknow, literally "one who strives" to attain a high position of scholarship and learning, the highest degree among Muhammadan divines, belong to the family. The Bilgrâm Sayyids are also famous for having produced many poets and learned men. They claim to have invaded Oudh in the time of Shamsuddîn and to have founded Bilgrâm on the site of a city named Srinagar.[2]

5. But perhaps more famous are the Sayyids of Bârha[3]; Sadat-i Bârha. They claim descent from Fâtima the daughter of the Prophet, and by one account came into these Provinces with Mahmûd of Ghazni. Their head-quarters are in the Muzaffarnagar District and a few colonies of them are found in Amroha of Morâdâbâd and Sikandra of the Allahâbâd District. There are various theories as to the origin of the name. Some say that, scandalised by the debaucheries of the Mîna Bâzâr of Delhi, which they considered unsuited to their sacred character, they obtained leave to reside outside (*bāhar*) of the town; others that it was the chief town of twelve (*bārah*) which belong to the clan. As Professor Blochmann remarks, whether the derivation from the Hindi numeral *bārah* be correct or not, there is no doubt that the etymology was believed to be correct in the time of Akbar and Jahângîr; for both the Tabaqât and the Tuzuk derive the name from the twelve

---

[1] *Hardoi Settlement Report*, 63; Elliot, *Chronicles of Unâo*, 93.

[2] Williams, *Oudh Census Report*, 74.

[3] Elliot, *Supplemental Glossary*; S. V. Blochmann, *Aîn-i-Akbari*, I, 390; *Census Report*, 1865; *N. W. P.*, I, 6, *Appendix*; Ibbetson, *Panjâb Ethnography*, para. 515.

villages in the Duâb of Muzaffarnagar, which the Sayyids held. Like the Sayyids of Bilgrâm, the Bârha family trace their origin to Sayyid Abul Farah of Wâsit; "but their *nasabnâma* or genealogical tree was sneered at, and even Jahângîr in the above-quoted passage from the Tuzuk, says that the personal courage of the Sayyids of Bârha, but nothing else, was the best proof that they were Sayyids. But they clung so firmly to this distinction, that some of them even placed the title of Sayyid before the titles which they received from the Mughul Emperors, as Sayyid Khân Jahân (Sayyid Abul Muzaffar) and others. But if their claim to be Sayyids was not firmly established, their bravery and valour has become a by-word. Their place in battle was the van (*harâwal*), they claimed to be the leaders of the onset, and every Emperor from the time of Akbar gladly availed himself of the prestige of their name. They delighted in looking on themselves as Hindustânis. Their military fame completely threw to the background the renown of the Sayyids of Amroha, of Mânikpur, the Khânzâdas of Mewât, and even families of royal blood as the Safawais."

6. They are divided into four branches—the Tihanpuri with Jânsath in the Muzaffarnagar District as their chief town; the Chatbanûri or Châtrauri of Sambalhara; the Kûndliwâl of Majhara and the Jagneri of Bidauli on the Jumna. Of these, the Muhammadan historians mention only the Kûndliwâl and the Tihanpuri. Besides these divisions they have private marks of recognition which they say have been very successful in excluding impostors from the tribe. Particular families have a sort of totemistic designations, such as "dog," "ass," "sweepers," etc., which are said to be derived from the menial offices which some of the Sayyids of this family are reported to have performed for the Emperor Humâyun when reduced to extremities in his flight from Shîr Shâh. As Sir H. M. Elliot remarks: "the improbability of men assuming such humiliating designations without a good cause, gives some colour to the story; particularly when we learn the devotion of the Emperor's attendants, which is so amusingly described by his right reverential Aftâlchi, Jauhar, in the Tazkirat-ul-Vikaya."

7. "The histories of India," writes Professor Blochmann, "do not appear to make mention of the Sayyids of Bârha before the times of Akbar; but they must have held posts of some importance under the Sûrs, because the arrival of Sayyid Mahmûd in Akbar's

camp is recorded by all historians as an event of importance. He and other Sayyids were, moreover, at once appointed to high *mansabs*. The family boasts also traditionally of services rendered to Humâyun; but this is at variance with Abul Fazl's statement that Sayyid Mahmûd was the first who served under a Timuride. The political importance of the Sayyids declined from the time of Muhammad Shâh (1131 to 1161) who deposed the brothers Sayyid Abdullah Khân, and Sayyid Husain Ali Khân, in whom the family reached the greatest height of their power. What a difference between the rustic and loyal Sayyid Mahmûd under Akbar, and the above two brothers, who made four Timurides Emperors, dethroned and killed two and blinded and imprisoned three. They made Farrukh Siyar, Rafi'uddarajât, Rafi'uddaula, and Muhammad Shâh Emperors; they dethroned and killed Jahândâr Shâh and Farrukh Siyar, whom they had moreover blinded; and they blinded and imprisoned Princes A'azzuddîn, Ali Tabâr, and Humâyun Bakht."

Distribution of the Sayyids

Districts.	Abbâsi.	Abidi.	Bani Fâtima.	Baqri.	Bâghdâdi.	Bukhâri.	Chishti.	Hashimi.	Husani.	Hasan-ul-Husaini.	Husaini.	Jáfri.
Dehra Dûn .	...	29	...	...	...	47	...	...	...	...	177	...
Sahâranpur .	3	4	2	2	3	1,598	...	271	...	...	1,899	58
Muzaffarnagar .	8	19	9	44	...	97	7	17	...	1	2,619	110
Meerut . .	8	17	8	9	12	902	...	8	...	22	1,883	306
Bulandshahr .	15	4	19	...	62	928	174	2	...	...	759	34
Aligarh . .	...	...	...	1	47	494	1	4	...	...	1,725	185
Mathura . .	3	3	...	...	...	120	...	4	...	...	240	66
Agra . .	54	126	18	2	4	111	16	40	...	...	1,056	278
Farrukhâbâd .	6	37	18	13	7	613	...	...	...	2	489	31
Mainpuri . .	1	...	...	...	...	17	146	33	...	...	188	156
Etâwah . .	14	19	8	2	7	19	...	...	...	21	169	38
Etah . .	1	33	2	...	7	178	...	1	...	...	762	28
Bareilly . .	203	14	66	...	256	1,392	105	82	...	9	2,273	113
Bijnor . .	...	...	...	...	...	715	2,273	100	...	...	1,948	32
Budâun . .	...	27	...	17	2	128	...	47	...	...	849	111
Morâdâbâd .	...	259	15	230	12	83	...	4	...	...	10,607	153
Shâhjahânpur .	...	1	...	...	21	501	28	16	...	656	710	36
Pilibhît . .	12	65	11	...	17	215	39	5	278	2	...	12
Cawnpur . .	40	205	1	4	2	312	...	36	...	14	827	420
Fatehpur . .	22	104	33	5	6	39	...	...	...	73	543	108
Bânda . .	19	75	16	4	1	59	...	9	...	...	9	50
Hamîrpur. .	5	50	3	1	14	46	...	82	...	26	240	38
Allahâbâd . .	42	289	7	1	13	137	9	104	...	26	1,491	362
Jhansi . .	54	...	...	...	31	31	26	...	...	...	113	16
Jâlaun . .	...	...	...	...	3	8	75	20	...	...	51	12
Lalitpur . .	...	...	...	...	...	10	...	...	...	...	14	10
Benares . .	3	158	...	40	...	3	...	...	...	...	609	265
Mirzapur . .	1	...	...	...	...	...	...	34	...	...	495	80
Jaunpur . .	...	...	...	...	...	14	...	122	...	...	1,048	281
Ghâzipur . .	7	...	...	...	7	13	...	...	...	...	874	32
Ballia . .	29	...	...	...	...	17	...	152	...	...	151	...
Gorakhpur .	1	231	31	1	...	72	4	...	...	7	474	49
Basti . .	...	67	71	...	771	11	...	...	...	...	1,304	9
Azamgarh. .	37	56	6	1	...	12	...	20	...	...	2,123	222
Kumâun . .	...	...	...	...	...	...	...	...	...	...	...	...
Garhwâl . .	...	...	...	...	...	...	...	...	...	...	...	...

according to the Census of 1891.

Jalâli.	Qâdiriya.	Kuzaimi.	Naqwi.	Pirzâda.	Qizwi.	Sabzwâri.	Siddiqi.	Taqwi.	Tirmizi.	Ulwi.	Askari.	Zaidi.	Others.	TOTAL.
2	...	4	...	56	7	7	10	...	...	...	...	...	292	631
19	125	160	47	8	150	180	6	...	658	78	15	127	1,133	6,546
5	107	766	108	35	46	302	25	...	234	110	95	5,236	2,659	12,659
80	57	296	...	...	2,801	220	...	41	51	37	...	500	2,798	10,056
2	9	8	633	...	1,430	29	29	915	14	23	...	57	727	5,873
...	28	4	...	103	294	79	10	35	...	88	...	...	1,492	4,595
4	...	...	138	...	213	...	20	...	19	...	...	18	1,381	2,229
122	20	32	7	...	890	...	71	54	13	59	2	12	3,307	6,294
68	2	51	4	55	255	...	43	493	582	414	67	106	2,744	6,100
61	1	75	...	28	346	10	165	75	1	67	...	25	2,517	2,912
2	11	36	107	...	224	...	...	...	3	43	...	...	1,805	2,528
3	4	4	26	14	55	18	23	...	5	17	8	50	1,383	2,622
557	5	10	...	...	178	70	...	...	2	...	46	1,037	2,184	8,602
19	...	1	...	11	344	238	...	345	476	1	...	3,342	2,162	12,007
122	...	1	119	...	117	62	...	...	...	...	...	25	1,877	3,504
201	14	54	2,313	...	909	10	...	...	20	49	...	523	2,327	17,783
106	43	15	...	9	134	...	...	20	163	16	...	...	1,324	3,799
137	...	17	...	...	2	9	3	29	41	1	...	73	957	1,915
...	63	64	10	18	1,089	...	110	83	57	60	3	53	3,456	6,927
54	21	39	264	...	430	102	...	715	31	95	5	368	1,969	5,026
26	24	28	118	...	483	4	42	...	8	8	...	47	1,177	2,597
640	12	61	13	...	72	...	39	...	...	17	...	28	1,096	2,483
156	...	546	...	31	4,141	230	42	1,152	12	190	1	394	4,131	13,507
20	21	10	...	...	88	...	33	32	39	5	...	87	1,085	1,691
3	22	26	...	...	85	5	24	28	15	24	...	17	1,093	1,511
1	2	...	..	...	36	4	11	4	6	1	...	...	268	367
...	...	56	...	...	429	...	...	...	...	26	...	...	1,334	2,973
...	...	35	...	...	229	...	...	...	...	...	...	...	1,325	2,209
4	...	53	...	...	1,005	2	40	...	...	142	96	561	1,445	4,818
6	...	284	...	...	336	216	23	22	271	24	...	189	976	3,280
...	...	...	...	...	122	...	1	...	...	...	...	...	279	751
13	4	73	...	1	131	1	1	15	5	24	...	17	2,178	3,323
...	31	...	...	...	1,314	...	...	51	...	14	...	...	2,647	6,290
7	...	334	...	3	940	19	...	...	137	629	137	473	1,680	6,836
...	...	...	...	...	...	...	...	...	...	...	...	...	36	36
...	...	...	...	...	...	...	...	...	...	...	...	...	41	41

Distribution of the Sayyids according

Districts.	Abbâsi.	Abidi.	Baui Fâtima.	Baqri.	Bâghdâdi.	Bukhâri.	Chishti.	Hashimi.	Husani.	Hasan-ul-Husaini.	Husaini.	Jâfri.
Tarâi	...	...	31	...	...	177	...	...	...	...	121	...
Lucknow	4	1,909	17	121	...	58	...	94	...	170	1,507	379
Unâo	...	...	3	29	...	41	...	66	...	112	169	119
Râê Bareli	...	73	53	...	...	5	1	6	...	132	261	228
Sîtapur	1	148	1	3	...	89	119	39	...	13	98	67
Hardoi	5	32	...	...	...	156	...	...	...	3	510	70
Kheri	...	54	1	...	...	84	...	19	...	...	211	131
Faizâbâd	4	103	11	...	...	1	...	73	...	...	1,148	53
Gonda	...	70	99	...	...	...	...	...	...	...	160	68
Bahrâich	2	102	18	47	19	11	40	27	...	...	230	175
Sultânpur	...	141	77	...	56	25	...	9	...	...	565	47
Partâbgarh	121	4	13	...	...	45	...	9	...	3	40	63
Bârabanki	...	...	18	39	77	71	...	...	...	...	833	...
TOTAL	725	4,518	691	716	1,457	9,705	3,063	1,555	278	1,292	44,962	5,111

to the Census of 1891—concluded.

Jalâli.	Qâdiriya.	Kuzaimi.	Naqwi.	Pirzâda.	Qizwi.	Sabzwâri.	Siddiqi.	Taqwi.	Tirmizi.	Ulwi.	Askari.	Zaidi.	Others.	TOTAL.
...	27	...	...	...	...	...	...	31	...	6	...	...	182	573
34	46	1,319	...	2	4,812	...	43	511	8	277	127	125	3,347	14,910
...	...	59	...	...	833	...	108	346	...	52	38	283	1,525	3,782
...	...	132	1,194	42	370	37	10	...	49	7	...	112	933	3,650
11	...	47	...	2	707	...	...	92	...	32	...	478	1,763	3,710
48	12	31	461	...	1,258	...	...	...	178	14	...	796	1,998	5,572
117	...	72	27	20	264	...	...	...	127	6	...	609	1,359	3,101
...	...	181	756	...	2,116	...	...	...	...	325	...	935	2,398	8,104
...	...	...	...	...	4,614	...	...	13	...	57	...	998	873	6,952
6	16	194	151	...	293	49	3	...	...	67	126	301	1,352	3,229
...	...	58	...	35	456	40	...	92	...	165	...	442	1,089	3,297
15	13	11	267	...	256	39	18	...	...	18	...	48	1,108	2,081
...	...	151	60	34	2,592	...	...	...	1	504	80	610	2,447	7,517
2,671	740	5,403	6,813	512	37,896	1,982	953	5,193	3,226	3,792	846	19,102	79,709	242,811

Sejwâri.[1]—A small caste found only in the Lalitpur District. The story told of their origin is that when Maharâja Devi Sinh, of Chanderi, went to attack Maler Kotla, he brought from there four boys, one of whom he appointed to arrange his bed (*sej*), whence their name. They enumerate fourteen exogamous sections :—Gadoi or Garoi; Hâra; Nachhniwâr; Bhâradwaj; Chobdâr; Sâni; Pachauri; Sikhaiya; Hardwâr; Gond; Kasâbka; Sawâr; Kachhwâr. They still regard Chanderi as their head quarters. They have a tribal council (*panchâyat*) of which the Panch or President is not hereditary, but is elected to act from time to time by the votes of the members.

Marriage rules.

2. A man may not marry in his own section nor the daughter of his maternal uncle or father's sister. He cannot marry or keep as a concubine a woman of another caste. He may marry two sisters. They generally marry their daughters in the sections from which they take their brides. Polygamy is allowed, and all the wives hold equal rank. Widows are allowed to marry. When a widow agrees to marry a man, she gives him her silver finger ring and he shows it to his brethren and informs them that he has arranged to marry such and such a widow. The giving of the ring is understood to mark the engagement and is known as *nânon*. After he brings home the widow he feeds his brethren. Girls have no liberty before marriage, and infidelity is punished by a fine on both parties. Until her parents pay the fine, the girl cannot be married in the tribe. Girls are married at the age of nine and boys at ten. The marriage is arranged by the girl's barber. A marriage is invalid without the consent of the girl and her parents. It is only widows who are allowed to select husbands for themselves. The girl's parents, if they can afford it, are expected to give her a dowry, the amount of which is fixed by the barber. A marriage cannot be annulled on account of any physical defects appearing in either party after the ceremony has been performed. A man can divorce his wife in the presence and with the sanction of the tribal council for habitual infidelity. Divorced women can marry again by the inferior form, and the children of divorced women who marry again, widows and regularly married brides rank equally for the purpose of inheritance. The levirate is allowed

---

[1] Mainly based on a note by Bâbu Bijay Bahâdur Sinh, Diwân, Lalitpur.

under the usual restriction; but the widow may, if she please, marry an outsider. When she does so, her husband's brother has the right of custody of the children of her first marriage, and they succeed to their father's goods, while their mother gets nothing. But if she marries the younger brother of her husband, she has a right to maintenance out of the estate of her first husband. There is no fiction whereby the children of the levir are affiliated to his late brother.

Domestic ceremonies.

3. While a woman is pregnant, they rub her head with powdered gram and water; but none of them can give an explanation of the custom. A woman of the Basor caste acts as midwife, and her place is then taken by the barber's wife. After the birth there are singing and dancing, and alms are distributed. When the child is a boy, the brethren are fed on the tenth day; if it be a girl, on the sixth day. There is no trace of the couvade. The mother remains secluded after her confinement for only three days. They have no rule of adoption. When boys arrive at puberty, the hair of their faces and heads is shaved with great solemnity.

4. The marriage arrangements are made by the family barber. When the matter is settled, the bridegroom gives the barber a rupee as his fee. Then the wedding day is fixed, and once that is done the match cannot be broken off. The various stages are:—the *abtauni* or anointing of the pair; the setting up of the marriage shed (*mânro*); the presentation of jewelry to the bride; the marking her forehead with red lead (*sendûrdân*); the giving away of the bride (*kanyâdân*) and the revolution round the central pole (*bhanwar*). The binding portions of the ceremony are the walking round the shed and the giving away of the bride.

Death rites.

5. They burn their dead and throw the ashes into the Ganges. At the time of cremation they are particular to perform the rite of *ara* or *kapâlkriya* by breaking the skull to allow the spirit to reach the other world. They do not perform the regular *srâddha*. But to remove his impurity, the officiating Brâhman makes the man who fired the pyre offer a sacred ball (*pinda*) to the manes of the dead. The death impurity lasts ten days, and that of a woman after her confinement for three days.

Religion.

6. The Sejwâris do not adopt the tenets of any particular sect. Their priests are Jhijhautiya Brâhmans and, like the Bundelas, whose servants

they are, they are worshippers of Râma and Krishna. The women worship snakes at the Nâgpanchami and the banyan tree at the Bársait festival. But they are not allowed to enter the temples of the higher Hindu gods. They are very much afraid of demons which they propitiate with offerings of cocoanuts and *athwâi* or a mixture of eight ingredients, of which treacle, cardamoms, and turmeric are the chief part. They believe in the Evil Eye which can be obviated by moving some mustard and salt over the head of the child.

Social rules.

7. They will not touch Doms or Mehtars. They eat pork, mutton, deer's flesh, and fish. They will eat only from the hands of Brâhmans and Râjputs and members of their own tribe. Their social rank is very low. They serve the Bundelas as menial servants, some serve as village watchmen and act as guards for bankers. A few cultivate lands as tenants without occupancy rights. At times of rejoicing, such as marriages and births, they get presents from their Bundela masters.

Distribution of the Sejwâri according to the Census of 1891.

District.	Number.
Lalitpur	386
Total	386

Sengar.—A sept of Râjputs who, like the Gautam, claim descent from Singhi or Siringhi Rishi, whose daughter Basantiya is said to have been married to Somapâla, King of Kanauj. They say that their ancestor Pûran Deva emigrated to the Dakkhin and thence to Dhâr. From thence they were forced to go to Bandhugarh in Rîwa, and thence to Kanâr in Jalaun, near Jagmohanpur in Etâwah. Their Râja Bisukh Deva or Sukh Deva founded the modern house. His date lies between 1065 and 1165 A.D. He married Deva Kula, daughter of Jay Chand Râthaur, of Kanauj, and after his defeat by Shahâb-ud-dîn Ghori the power of the Sengars increased and the river Basindh was renamed Sengar in their honour.[1]

[1] *Census Report, North-Western Provinces, I, Appendix* 81, *sqq.*

2. Their occupation of Oudh [1] dates from about 1527 A.D., when Shaikh Bayazîd, one of the Afghân generals of the Lodi Dynasty, submitted to Bâbar. This officer had in his service two Sengars from Jagmohanpur, across the Jumna, by name Jagat Sâh and Gopâl Sinh. They raised and commanded a cavalry regiment, which was cantoned near the village of Simri, in Pargana Asoha of the Unâo District, and after his defeat they settled quietly down in the Pargana, making Kantha their head-quarters. "For eleven generations they remained peaceably there, keeping the Lodhas, who had been the original proprietors, in subjection. During this time they were joined by another family of the same clan, who followed them from Jagmohanpur and settled in Parsandan. In the eleventh generation, the Lodhas, who had never thoroughly acquiesced in their loss of position, suddenly rose against the Sengars, and killed the majority of them, but allowed the women and children to escape. The fugitives did not think it safe to go to their brotherhood in Parsandan, but fled to Jagmohanpur, and returning thence with an accession of strength, the sons of the murdered Sengars, Askaran on Gopâl's side, and Garbu on Jagat Sinh's side, recovered their father's possessions in the country."

3. The Ghâzipur [2] branch trace their origin to Phaphûnd in Etâwah. They worship under the name of Nâth Bâba, a deified member of the tribe named Amar Sinh. Before the establishment of British authority they managed to secure for themselves an unrivalled reputation for courage, independence, and insubordination. They have now abandoned their old turbulent habits; they behaved well during the Mutiny, and are now loyal and peaceful citizens. In Jâlaun [3] they claim to have come from Lanka or Ceylon and to be descended from Singhi Rishi. They seem to have been originally Brâhmans who intermarried with Râjputs. According to General Sleeman,[4] the Sengars are almost the only class of Râjputs in Bundelkhand, Baghelkhand, Rîwa, and Sâgar, who used to put their female infants to death; in Oudh they are almost the only sept who do not.

4. There is a tribe in Gujarât called Sanghar who are on perhaps doubtful authority, connected with them. They are more pro-

---

[1] Elliott, *Chronicles of Undo*, 45, *sq.*
[2] Oldham, *Memo. I.* 575, *sq.*
[3] *Gazetteer North-Western Provinces, I.* 209.
[4] *Journey through Oudh*, *I*, *312*, note.

bably allied to the Panjâb Chhângars and perhaps to the Zingari of Europe.[1]

5. In Jâlaun they give brides to the Chandel, Bais, Bisen, and Parihâr septs, and marry their sons to the Kachhwâha, Bhadauriya, Râthaur, Sisodiya, and Hâra. In Ballia they take brides from the Karchhuliya, Bisen, Donwâr, Haihobans, Kâkan, Raghubansi, Kausik, Nikumbh, Sakarwâr, Udmatiya, and Pachhtoriya septs. They give their daughters to the Bais, Haihobans, Ujjaini, Kausik, Sirnet, Râjkumâr, Sûrajbans, Parihâr, Karchhuliya, Raghubansi, Sombansi, Udmatiya, Nikumbh, Barwâr, Kinwâr, Chauhân, Kâkan and Pachhtoriya. Their gotra is said to be Gautam.

Distribution of the Sengar Râjputs according to the Census of 1891.

DISTRICTS.	Numbers.	DISTRICTS.	Number.
Muzaffarnagar . .	2	Lalitpur	100
Bulandshahr . . .	56	Benares	79
Aligarh	74	Mirzapur . . .	42
Mathura	13	Jaunpur	8
Agra	171	Ghâzipur . .	1,913
Farrukhâbâd . . .	1,451	Ballia	32,189
Mainpuri	649	Gorakhpur . . .	1,553
Etâwah	11,164	Basti	213
Etah	28	Azamgarh . . .	282
Budâun	21	Lucknow . . .	73
Morâdâbâd . . .	43	Unâo	2,775
Shâhjahânpur . . .	31	Râê Bareli . . .	716
Pilibhît	43	Sîtapur	183
Cawnpur	5,233	Hardoi	198
Fatehpur	1,028	Kheri	75
Bânda	395	Faizâbâd . . .	163
Hamîrpur . . .	557	Gonda	15
Allahâbâd . . .	595	Bahrâich . . .	47
Jhânsi	601		
Jâlaun	6,656	TOTAL	59,425

Shaikh, Shekh (an Arabic word meaning an "elder," "chief," "a venerable old man").—The name should properly be applied to tribes of pure Arab descent; but it has now been applied to a much more vulgar use, and is adopted by converts from the

[1] *Bombay Gazetteer, V*, 95, *XIII*, 713.

meaner Hindu tribes to Islâm. This is marked in the common proverb—*Peshayîn Qassâb bûdem, badazân gashtem Shaikh ; ghalla chun arzân shawad, imsâl Sayyid meshawem*—"The first year I was a butcher, the next, a Shaikh ; this year, if prices rise, I shall be a Sayyid."

2. At the last Census the Shaikhs of these Provinces were enumerated in the following tribes :—Abbâsi, who take their name from Abbâs, the paternal uncle of Muhammad ; Ansâri from Al-' Ansâr, "the helpers," a term used for the early converts of Al-Madînah, but when all the citizens of Al-Madînah were ostensibly converted to Islâm, they were all named 'Ansâr, while those Muslims who accompanied the Prophet from Makkah to Al-Madînah were called Muhajirûn or "exiles"; Bahlîm; Bani Isrâîl or "children of Israel"; Farîdi or followers of the famous Saint Bâba Farîd Shakkarganj of Pâk Pattan in the Montgomery District.; Farûqi, who take their name from the Khalîf Umar, surnamed Farûq, "the discriminator between truth and falsehood"; Hâshimi, after Hâshim, the great-grandfather of Muhammad, who according to the tradition, was surnamed Hâshim on account of his liberality in distributing bread (*hashm,* "to break bread") to the pilgrims at Makkah; Ja'fari after Ja'far, a cousin of Muhammad, who from his charity was called Abul Masâkin, "the father of the poor"; or Ja'far, one of the twelve Imâms; Khurasâni, "residents of the land of Khurasân"; Kidwai; Qureshi, after the Arabic tribe to which the Prophet belonged; it is hence the favourite tribe to which persons of doubtful origin claim affinity, and many of them are probably not of genuine Arab descent; Milki, probably the same as the Maliks, who were originally a Persian tribe, though more recently the word has been used as a title, like Khân or Beg; Pîrzâda or "offspring of the saint"; a term of very wide meaning which may mean the descendants or followers of any spiritual guide; Siddîqi, who take their name from the first Khalîf, Abu Bakr, who received from the Prophet the title of As Siddîq or "one who speaks the truth"; Sulaimâni from Solomon; 'Ulwi or 'Alawîyah, who take their name from the Khalîf 'Ali Murtaza and 'Usmâni from 'Usmân, the fourth Khalîfa.

3. The Shaikhs, of course, follow, or pretend to follow, all the rules of Islâm. This the real Shaikhs do; but those who are recent converts from Hinduism, maintain many of the practices of the castes from which they have been drawn.

Distribution of Shaikhs according to the Census of 1891.

Districts.	Abbási.	Ansári.	Bahlim.	Bani Isráil.	Farídi.	Farúqi.	Háshimi.	Já'fari.	Khurasáni.	Kidwai.	Qureshi.	Milki.	Pirzáda.	Siddiqi.	Sulaimán.	'Ulwi.	'Usmáni.	Others.	Total.
Dehra Dûn	180	347	...	...	...	35	...	...	...	...	1,685	...	...	3,211	...	...	100	1,282	6,840
Sahâranpur	99	3,555	22	8	...	1,077	17	...	2	...	4,194	153	...	10,907	...	7	836	2,269	23,146
Muzaffarnagar	77	1,086	24	2	...	696	85	...	35	1	5,063	...	33	10,078	1	230	443	1,935	19,794
Meernt	23	562	311	1	1	551	...	...	6	...	11,778	...	...	12,281	66	5	88	5,491	31,164
Bulandshahr	302	2,426	29	155	...	122	11	...	92	...	7,509	...	7	9,701	2	9	97	2,352	22,814
Aligarh	30	933	...	410	25	971	...	...	134	...	8,080	...	17	3,202	...	...	290	3,029	17,121
Mathura	27	79	48	45	...	61	...	1	191	...	3,618	...	...	2,833	...	...	16	6,075	12,994
Agra	20	341	119	55	3	407	8	1	228	...	14,231	2	...	6,016	1	5	159	11,359	32,955
Farrukhâbâd	336	252	151	20	27	226	...	...	4	33	10,148	10	3	10,307	23	42	322	4,620	26,524
Mainpuri	121	96	18	2	...	63	...	...	30	...	2,607	4	...	2,690	...	...	23	7,652	13,306
Etâwah	127	143	...	1	...	73	11	...	...	...	2,075	3	...	3,563	...	35	23	4,664	10,718
Etah	20	203	137	997	44	210	1	...	6	...	4,788	3	...	1,988	1	...	44	5,587	14,029
Bareilly	158	1,017	25	895	...	177	90	...	...	...	26,689	...	...	12,718	419	7	309	11,453	53,957
Bijnor	...	4,84[illegible]	...	...	...	305	...	..	...	...	27,479	...	...	19,142	...	4	160	5,565	57,486
Budâun	101	1,636	16	467	27	811	...	...	...	...	10,670	...	...	14,732	15	50	338	11,541	40,404
Morâdâbâd	697	1,809	31	473	108	2,761	139	8	57	...	26,703	...	...	93,675	...	61	678	34,612	161,813
Shâhjahânpur	148	429	...	180	24	639	11	...	38	...	8,767	...	...	7,083	131	22	257	5,601	23,330

Pilibhit	4	16	67	91	2	26	5	...	1	...	4,792	...	...	2,579	...	...	61	4,005	11,646
Cawnpur	339	226	73	3	51	571	5	2	51	4	9,060	...	...	19,688	...	29	71	12,807	42,988
Fatehpur	...	254	5	4	103	889	2	234	...	...	2,595	...	52	18,523	65	26	976	5,488	29,216
Bânda	12	369	...	123	94	937	...	...	93	...	1,709	51	...	4,055	2	...	16	4,408	11,875
Hamirpur	18	49	23	2,855	1	27	...	19	25	...	699	...	...	1,526	4	45	291	3,582	9,264
Allahâbâd	1,764	1,552	...	5	...	976	460	165	...	...	4,783	1,146	1	43,484	34	150	1,856	9,687	66,063
Jhânsi	17	101	26	7	2	35	5	...	72	...	1,803	...	...	1,756	5	...	39	4,370	8,238
Jâlaun	37	79	136	...	...	34	...	...	...	...	1,705	...	...	1,621	...	3	48	5,413	9,076
Lalitpur	7	21	36	...	...	6	...	...	...	1	123	...	15	332	...	...	1	1,075	1,617
Benares	29	666	...	...	...	114	11	117	...	...	3,044	14	...	16,538	...	...	3	5,339	28,875
Mirzapur	41	483	...	...	...	191	...	...	...	...	2,067	122	...	12,995	...	...	35	11,494	27,428
Jaunpur	433	2,471	...	...	11	1,032	23	75	8	...	2,584	297	...	11,701	...	79	...	4,516	23,230
Ghâzipur	151	472	...	...	5	280	...	34	24	...	921	156	...	12,111	24	...	30	1,056	15,264
Ballia	560	1,714	...	...	...	206	...	1	...	...	1,269	34	...	4,242	...	...	86	870	8,982
Gorakhpur	63	4,151	...	3	...	248	8	...	70	824	6,061	180	24	16,137	...	...	542	4,444	32,755
Basti	432	1,045	1,126	...	...	1,733	...	...	...	...	10,106	728	...	26,260	...	...	1,811	13,339	56,580
Azamgarh	360	6,670	...	5	17	1,899	43	...	13	...	13,315	520	1	27,853	99	422	1,974	7,913	61,104
Kumaun	...	...	...	...	...	...	...	...	...	...	...	...	...	377	...	...	...	1,642	2,019
Garhwâl	...	...	...	...	...	...	...	...	...	...	...	...	...	47	...	...	...	2,570	2,617
Tarâi	...	55	549	...	...	...	...	...	...	...	2,404	...	...	8,857	...	...	20	2,996	14,881
Lucknow	201	1,345	...	19	...	584	35	...	18	95	9,529	81	...	24,267	1	371	285	15,498	52,329
Unâo	47	691	...	32	15	539	36	...	24	81	777	31	5	11,934	...	...	404	7,398	22,014
Râê Bareli	11	642	...	...	...	375	...	...	...	115	860	36	9	6,739	19	...	289	4,169	13,264
Sîtapur	15	352	...	123	...	188	22	...	...	210	2,356	447	...	10,419	...	1	138	3,774	18,045

Distribution of Shaikhs according to the Census of 1891—concluded.

Districts.	Abbâsi.	Ansâri.	Bahlîm.	Bani Isrâîl.	Farîdi.	Farûqi.	Hâshimi.	Jâ'fari.	Khurasâni.	Kidwai.	Qureshi.	Milki.	Pîrzâda.	Siddîqi.	Sulaimâni.	'Ulwi.	'Usmâni.	Others.	Total.
Hardoi	9	674	...	3	...	805	...	4	...	5	2,083	...	...	15,157	1	19	586	8,090	27,436
Kheri	2	496	...	...	20	199	...	...	30	...	1,748	67	...	4,976	...	12	154	2,347	10,050
Faizâbâd	231	1,508	...	...	...	781	...	2	172	...	4,313	288	...	14,074	...	...	208	7,246	28,818
Gonda	67	744	595	...	...	1,643	...	...	...	469	7,583	37	...	26,771	...	11	2,018	1,060	40,998
Bahrâich	6	2,077	11	1	8	412	15	...	23	524	2,766	174	8	10,040	44	...	58	2,287	18,454
Sultânpur	176	407	...	...	6	380	...	...	4	87	4,377	106	...	4,067	...	41	51	1,285	10,987
Partâbgarh	89	111	...	...	10	2,010	83	24	1	...	3,751	400	..	9,458	...	5	146	6,098	22,286
Bârabanki	130	5,896	...	242	...	520	1	...	...	1,222	1,328	325	9	17,876	...	16	386	7, 818	35,769
Total	7,817	55,192	3,578	7,232	604	26,825	1,127	687	1,452	3,671	286,595	5,416	185	610,586	957	1,707	16,756	302,171	1,332,566

Singraur.[1]—A tribe found only in the Fatehpur District to the number of 9,388. They claim to be Râjputs and descendants of one Sringi Rishi, who migrated from Ajudhya to Benares. They marry in the orthodox way, and widow-marriage is forbidden. They will eat *kachchi pakki* only with their own Brâhman family priest or members of their own tribe. Their claim to be Râjputs does not appear to be universally admitted, and by one account they are really Lodhas. Under their leader Daryâo Sinh they gave much trouble in the Fatehpur District during the Mutiny, and it is only in the Khâga and Khakhror Tahsîls that their pretensions to Râjput origin are to any extent recognised.

Sirnet.—A sept of Râjputs found principally in the Gorakhpur Division. There are various accounts of the origin of the name. According to one story they got the title from some Muhammadan king in whose service they were. Their chief was in the habit of wearing on his head a cloth of gold called *net*, and the king, not choosing to recollect the Hindu name, called him Sirnet or "the man with the golden cloth on his head" (*sir*). By another account they take their name from some place called Srinagar. A third legend is told in connection with the Nikumbh sept and tells how one of them allowed his head to be cut off on a sword placed across the door-way in preference to bowing his head before one of the Delhi Emperors. Dr. Oldham suggests that the name is derived from *sira* "head" and *neta* (*Sanskrit netri*, "a leader"[2]). All these are mere speculations and of little value.

2. The Oudh story[3] is that the Sirnet kingdom of Bânsi in the Basti District was founded by Banwâri, the third son of Jaswant Sinh, Dikshit; but the Sirnets of Bânsi claim a higher rank than this legend would give them, and do not acknowledge any connection with the Dikshits. The Unaula Râja told Dr. Buchanan that they came from Assam.[4] The Gorakhpur branch ascribed the origin of the Satâsi Raj to Chandra Sen, who was an emigrant from Lahore. He treacherously murdered the Domkatâr or Donwâr Râja and seized his dominions. In Basti they are said to allow their daughters to grow up to womanhood, and do not allow them to marry.[5] In

---

[1] Mainly based on a note by M. Hashmatulla, S. C. S.
[2] *Ghâzipur Memo.*, I, 59, sq.
[3] Elliott, *Chronicles of Undo*, 35.
[4] *Eastern India*, II. 353.
[5] *Selections of Records, North-Western Provinces*, I, 217.

Ghâzipur they call themselves Nikumbh and claim kinship with the Gorakhpur family, as represented by the Râjas of Unaula, Bânsi, and Rudrapur. "They are one of the most noble looking races in the District and are generally well disposed and on good terms with the District officials; but quite ready to join in a general rebellion to recover their estates."

Distribution of the Sirnet Râjputs according to the Census of 1891.

Districts.	Number.	Districts.	Number.
Fatehpur . . .	18	Azamgarh . . .	474
Bânda . . .	1,196	Lucknow . . .	6
Hamîrpur . . .	1	Râê Bareli . . .	153
Allahâbâd . . .	86	Faizâbâd . . .	56
Benares . . .	5	Bahrâich . . .	57
Ghâzipur . . .	5	Sultânpur . . .	338
Ballia . . .	495	Partâbgarh . . .	192
Gorakhpur . . .	11,810		
Basti . . .	459	Total . .	19,486

Soeri, Soiri, Suiri.—A small tribe found in parts of the Allahâbâd and Benares Divisions, about whom there has been much not very fruitful speculation. According to Mr. Risley [1] they are known by the names of Savar, Sabar, Saur, Sar, Sayar, Suir, Siwiri, and are "a Dravidian cultivating and servile tribe of Orissa, Chota Nâgpur, Western Bengal, Madras, and the Central Provinces. Colonel Dalton regards them as Dravidian, while Fredrick Muller, General Cunningham, and Mr. R. Cust place them on linguistic grounds in the Kolarian group of tribes. The evidence from language, however, is meagre and inconclusive; while, on the other hand, it is tolerably certain that the Savars, scattered and partially Hinduised as they are, represent the main body of an ancient race, an isolated fragment of which survives in the Malê or Saur of the Râjmahâl hills."

2. General Cunningham [2] identifies them with the Sauras about

[1] *Tribes and Castes*, II, 241, *sq*.

[2] *Archæological Reports*, XVII, 112, *sq*.

Dàmoh and Sâgar. The origin of the name Savara, he says, "must be sought for outside the language of the Aryans. In Sanskrit *Sàvara* simply means 'corpse.' From Herodotus, however, we learn the Scythian word for an axe was *sagaris* and as *g* and *v* are interchangeable letters, *savar* is the same word as *sagar*. It seems, therefore, not unreasonable to infer that the tribes who were so called took their name from their habit of carrying axes. Now it is one of the striking peculiarities of the Savaras that they are rarely seen without an axe in their hands. This peculiarity has been frequently noticed by all who have seen them." In opposition to this it may be urged that the word Savara, if it be, as some believe, derived from *sava* "a corpse," comes from the root *sav*, "to cause to decay," and need not necessarily be of non-Aryan origin, while, on the other hand, no distinct inference can be drawn from the use of the axe by the Savaras, when it is equally commonly used by various other Dravidian jungle tribes, such as Korwas, Bhuiyas and the like.

3. Of the Savaras, who are supposed to have been the ancestors of the existing race, not much is known. Of them Sir W. Hunter writes [1]—"The Savaras appear in very early Sanskrit writings and are spoken of with more than usual detestation. As the Sûdras or aboriginal tribes, who had been subdued into the servile caste of the Aryan Commonwealth, sprung from the feet of Brahma, so the Savaras and other forest races, who successfully withstood the invaders, proceeded from the sweat of a cow.[2] They were goblins, they were devils, they were raw eaters, they were man-eaters, and the Vishnu Purâna has concentrated the national antipathy towards them in its picture of a dwarfish race, with flat noses and a skin the colour of a charred stake. Another sacred text assures us that they were as black as crows, with tawny hair, red eyes, a chin jutting out, short arms and legs, and the typical flat nose. A third Sanskrit sage adds a protuberant belly, drooping ears and an ogre mouth. They seem to have made their individuality very strongly felt in ancient India. The beginning of their territory long marked the last point of the Aryan advance. They are often spoken of as border tribes, who resisted the Sanskrit invaders, scattered armies, and earned for themselves the name of the 'terrible Savaras.' Their

---

[1] *Orissa*, I, 176, *sq*.
[2] Muir, *Ancient Sanskrit Texts*, I, 391.

name even found its way into Greek geographies, and the ancient kingdom of Kalinga was known to the distant islands of the Indian Archipelago, while still a *terra incognita* to Northern India." On the whole it seems at least probable that the name Savara was a generic title for the aggregate of the Dravidian races who inhabited the line of hills which rise along the south of the valleys of the Jumna and the Ganges. It is thus that they appear in the Katha Sarit Sâgara of Somadeva and in one of these tales the Savara is described as running up "stained with dust, bow in hand, with his hair tied up in a knot behind with a creeper, black himself and wearing a loin-cincture of *vilva* leaves," in short very much like what the Juângs and similar tribes were almost to the present day.[1]

4. Modern observers give much the same account of them. Dr. Ball[2] describes the Savaras of Ganjam as small but wiry, often very dark in colour, and sometimes quite black, which agrees with Mr. Sterling's[3] account of the tribe in Orissa. "Their hair is generally tied in a top-knot, and sometimes it is cut short over the forehead, two long locks being permitted to hang over the ears. A few individuals have frizzled shocks, with which no such arrangement is attempted. Most of the men have small square beards. Of these races in Bengal, with whose appearance I am most familiar, they reminded me most strongly of the Bhumij, who belong to the Munda family; but I could also perceive in them some points of resemblance to the Dravidian Pahâriyas of the Râjmahâl hills. They have not, however, the manly bearing and good physique of the latter. Their manner of dancing resembles that of the Râjmahâl Pahâriyas, as I have on one occasion witnessed it, rather than that of either the Santâls or Kols."

5. Writing of Ghâzipur Dr. Oldham[4] says that the Soiri strongly resemble the gypsies of Europe; their women wear a tartan dress, and often have a kind of horn projecting from the forehead as an ornament. They live in light and easily moved booths, made of grass and reeds; are fond of intoxicating drinks, and eat the flesh of swine and oxen. They procure the wives for their young men by kidnapping female children, and live principally by jugglery, coin-

---

[1] Tawney, *Translation*, II, 384.

[2] *Jungle Life*, 267.

[3] *Orissa*, 42, quoted by Risley, *loc. cit.*

[4] *Memo.*, I, 57.

ing false money, and theft. They bring the bones of deceased relatives from long distances to the Ganges, which seemed to Dr. Oldham to indicate that the Ganges valley was once the home of the tribe. Another name of them is, he says, Sânsi, but they will seldom admit the name of either Sânsi or Soiri, and commonly say that they are Banjâras, Kanjars or Nats.

6. At the last Census the Soiris are found to have disappeared from the Districts of the Benares Division, except Benares itself. The fact is that within one decennial period the process of converting them into Râjputs has so far advanced that they now call themselves Sûrajbansis, and repudiate the name of Soiri. This is a very remarkable example, like that of the Kharwârs who have become Benbans Râjputs, of a process which has no doubt gone on extensively in former times, and by means of which there is no doubt that more than one of the Râjput septs has been formed. But in their appearance the so-called Sûrajbansi Râjputs of Mirzapur show unmistakeable signs of non-Aryan origin, and there cannot be any doubt that they belong to the Dravidian branch and are closely akin to the Kols and Cheros who live in their neighbourhood. They assert that they give daughters to respectable septs like the Raghubansi, Bais, and Chandel, and receive girls from the Bais. But there is good ground for believing this to be incorrect, and the real fact seems to be that, if they ever intermarry with Râjputs, it is only with bastard members of some sept which bars marriage with such people. There is in almost every Râjput sept a class of people who are in the Western Districts as Gaurua and to the East as Suraitwâl who are the result of connections of Râjput youths who find a difficulty, owing to infanticide or poverty, in finding respectable wives, with Natnis, Kanjarins or other prostitutes. Such children are, of course, excluded from full tribal privileges, and it is with them that tribes like the Soiri, who are on their promotion to become a regular Râjput sept, form marriage alliances.

7. These Mirzapur Soiri Sûrajbansis have no very distinct tradition of their origin. Some of them say that they were once rulers of the Majhwâr Pargana in the Benares District, whence they were expelled by the Barhauliya Râjputs. They allege that they still procure priests, who are Sarwariya Brâhmans, from the village of Keshopur in that Pargana.

Others say that, like the legitimate Sûrajbansis, they came from Ajudhya. Another account is that their first ancestor was a person named Garg, a Gautam Râjput, who settled at Bardiha near Mânda, in the Allahâbâd District, and kept as his mistress a Bhar girl, whose father he had treacherously killed. He is said to have lived in the time of Jay Chand of Kanauj. His descendants are alleged to be the present Soiri-Sûrajbansis.

8. However this may be, there is ample evidence from the customs of the tribe that they are not genuine Râjputs. Thus, they manage their tribal affairs by means of a tribal council (*panchâyat*) which no genuine Râjputs do. They permit widow marriage and the levirate, and they have, as might have been expected, to pay heavily for brides, and for this reason many of them are unable to contract a regular marriage. Only those who are married wear the Brâhmanical cord (*janeu*), and they have no regular rite of investiture, but merely hang it over their shoulders as they are going through the marriage ceremony. Again, they drive the plough with their own hands, which no real Râjput will do; and contrary to standard custom, when they are cremating the dead, they throw a handful of mustard seed (*sarson*) on the pyre. In other respects they follow the usual standard form in their domestic ceremonies. In fact, in their desire to be regarded as genuine Râjputs they are particularly careful to maintain a pretence of extreme orthodoxy.

9. They worship Mahâbîr, Mahâdeva, Sîtala Mâi, and Amina and Bandê, two of the deified quintette of the Pânchon Pîr. A special worship of these deities is performed at the Naurâtra of Kuâr. Mahâbîr and Mahâdeva receive an offering of sweetmeats, a Brâhmanical cord, a piece of cloth dyed in turmeric, a burnt offering (*hom*), and a lamp lighted with *ghi*. To Amina and Bandê they offer a plate of sweet cakes (*rot*), rice cooked with milk (*jaur*), and an image of Amina made of silver. To the Pânchon Pîr generally they present sweet cakes (*malîda*) and a sacrifice of a goat or fowl, which is done by a Dafâli. To Sîtala Mâi they present a goat, cakes, and some *halwa* sweetmeat in the months of Chait and Kuâr. Mahâbîr is usually worshipped on a Tuesday in the month of Sâwan. All these offerings are consumed by the worshippers themselves, except that to the Pânchon Pîr which is taken by the Dafâli officiant.

10. They do not eat beef or drink spirits. They eat goat's flesh, mutton, venison, and birds like pigeons. None of the higher castes will take food or water from their hands. They naturally hold a low social rank, and are not regarded with more respect than Koiris. They are, in the Mirzapur District, in poor circumstances. None of

them are landlords; a few cultivate as tenants, but the most of them are landless day labourers and serve as messengers or as stone cutters in the quarries about Chunâr. In Mirzapur, at least, they appear to have abandoned their old criminal habits, and are now a quiet, depressed race of people who very seldom come under the notice of the Courts.

Distribution of the Soiris according to the Census of 1891.

DISTRICTS.	Number.	DISTRICTS.	Number.
Allahâbâd . . .	468	Benares . . .	2,023
Jhânsi . . .	3,058		
Lalitpur . . .	12,273	TOTAL .	17,822

Solankhi, Solanki.—A sept of Râjputs. One derivation of the name is from the Sanskrit *sulakshana*, "having auspicious marks." They are supposed to have succeeded the Chavadas at Anhalwâda about 931 A. D.[1] The Bhâl and, according to others, the Baghel sept are an offshoot from them. Another name for them, Chalukiya, is said to be derived from the fact that when created out of the Agnikunda they were formed in the hollow of the hand (*chullu, challu*). Of them Colonel Tod writes:[2]—"Though we cannot trace the history of this branch of the Agnikulas to such periods of antiquity as the Pramâra or Chauhân, it is from the deficiency of materials, rather than any want of celebrity, that we are unable to place it in this respect on a level with them. The tradition of the Bard makes the Solankis important as princes of Suru on the Ganges, ere the Râthaurs obtained Kanauj. The genealogical tree claims Lokot said to be the ancient Lahore, as a residence, which makes them of the same branch (*sâkh*) Madwâni as the Chauhâns. Certain it is that in the eighth century we find the Langahas and Togras inhabiting Multân and the surrounding country, and the chief opponents of the Bhattis on their establishment in the desert. They were princes of Kalyân on the Malabâr coast, which city still exhibits vestiges of ancient grandeur. It was from Kalyân that a scion of the Solanki tree was taken and engrafted on the royal stem of the Chawaras of Anhalwâra Patan."

[1] Dr J. Wilson, *Indian Antiquary*, III, 227.
[2] *Annals*, I, 102.

In the reign of Chaond Râê, the son of this prince Bhojrâj, the kingdom of Anhalwâra was devastated by Mahmûd of Ghazni. Colonel Tod divides the Solankhis of Rajputâna into sixteen branches: Baghel, Bîrpur, Behila, Bhurta, Kalâcha, Langaha, Togra, Briku, Surki, Sirwariya, Raoka, Ranikiya, Kharâra, Tantiya, Almecha, Kalamor.

2. The Solankhis in these Provinces hold a respectable rank and give their daughters to Chauhâns, Bhadauriyas, and Jâdons; they take brides from the Katiyâr, Tomar, Râthaur, Bâchhal, Bais, Gaur, Pundîr, Bargûjar, and some Chauhân families.

Distribution of the Solankhi Râjputs according to the Census of 1891.

Districts.	Number.	Districts.	Number.
Sahâranpur	6	Jhânsi	88
Meerut	184	Jâlaun	104
Bulandshahr	375	Lalitpur	33
Aligarh	864	Benares	60
Mathura	154	Mirzapur	12
Agra	456	Jaunpur	39
Farrukhâbâd	864	Ballia	426
Mainpuri	773	Gorakhpur	842
Etâwah	57	Basti	237
Etah	5,636	Azamgarh	7
Bareilly	264	Lucknow	73
Budâun	1,553	Unâo	71
Morâdâbâd	131	Râê Bareli	10
Shâhjahânpur	359	Sîtapur	65
Pilibhît	75	Hardoi	115
Cawnpur	60	Kheri	109
Bânda	94	Sultânpur	4
Hamîrpur	78		
Allahâbâd	27	Total	14,305

Sombansi.—A sept of Râjputs who claim to be of the race of Soma or the moon. Of them Mr. Bennet[1] writes:—"This tribe are found at the beginning of connected history at the Fort of Jhûsi near Allahâbâd. They have no further traces of an immigration, and their tradition connects them for an indefinite period with their present dominions. The family worship is paid to five saints, four of them princes of the Sombansi blood, and the fifth a Gaharwâr Râja of Benares, who successfully abstracted themselves into nonentity during the Dwâpara Yuga. The principal of these, Ala Rikh or Rishi, gave his name to the town and Pargana of Alarikhpur, contracted into Aror, and since named Partâbgarh, and is perhaps identical with the Atap Rikh of Dalmau tradition, who resided in the Ganges forests, and whose teaching enabled Dal and Bal to attain their wide dominion." A reference to these worthies will be found in the article on the Bhars. "Two remarks may be made here: first, that the worship of the manes of their ancestors is common to all the Sombansis and several low castes in their neighbourhood. Barê Purukh ("the great old man") is one of the favourite local penates, and Kârê Deo, the snake, the chief object of home devotion which he shares with Siâu, the jackal. Another is that the most ancient tradition discovers the Sombansis on the northern, and the dawn of history on the southern, bank of the Ganges. An intermediate tradition, attested by the numerous remains of their peculiar forts, points to the existence of a Bhar Râj in the territory before and after occupied by the Chhatris. The commencement of the pedigree is, as usual, marked by some historical convulsion. Sakrâma Sinha had three sons—one of whom went to Nepâl, the second to Hardoi, while the third remained at Jhûsi. The son of the last was cursed by a Muhammadan Faqîr, Shaikh Taqi, and lost his kingdom. The usual posthumous son was born in exile, and, with the name of Lakhana Sena, founded the kingdom of Aror. One of his sons was a convert to Islâm, and in the eighth generation some subordinate centres of power began to branch off from the main Râj. No prince of this race attained distinction before Partâb Sinh, who, in the last quarter of the seventeenth century, consolidated the power of his clan, built a huge new fort at Aror, which has since been known by his name, and assumed all characteristics of independent sovereignty between the territories of the Bach-

---

[1] *Clans of Râé Bareli*, 34, *sq.*

gotis, the Râja of Mânikpur, and the Kânhpuriyas whom he subsequently defeated."

2. There is a section of the sept called Chauhâna,[1] said to be descended from Bhîm Sen, who fought the Râkshasa Handavi and married his daughter. In Farrukhâbâd[2] the Pargana of Khakatmau was entirely overspread by the Sombansis of the Baiyâgar (*Vyâgra*) *gotra*. They trace descent from Randhîr Sinh, who lived thirteen generations ago. They founded the Chând dynasty in Kumaun, and trace their descent, some to Jhûsi, and some to Nepâl. The Rautela of Kumaun are descendants of a junior branch.[3]

3. In Sultânpur they are reported to take brides from the Bilkhariya, Tashaiya, Chandauriya, Kath Bais, Bhâlê Sultân, Raghubansi, Gargbansi, Râj Kumâr, Bachgoti, and Bandhalgoti: and to give brides to the Tilokchandi Bais, Mainpuri Chauhâns, Mahal Sûrajbansis, and Bisens of Majhauli. They claim to belong to the Sûrya *gotra*. In Farrukhâbâd they are said to give brides to the Sûrajbansi, Râthaur, Chauhân, and Bhadauriya, and to receive girls from the Bamtelê, Chamar Gaur, Panwâr, and Gaharwâr. In Bareilly they take girls from the Salwant Gaur, Bargûjar, Tomar, Tânk, Bais, and Pundîr; and give girls to the Katheriya, Chauhân, Bhadauriya. In Hardoi they say that they belong to the Vyâgra *gotra*; take girls from the Chandel, Gaur, Gaharwâr, Pramâr, Bais, Ahban, and Nikumbh; while they give brides to the Chauhân, Râthaur, and Bhadauriya.

Distribution of the Sombansi Râjputs according to the Census of 1891.

DISTRICTS.	Hindus.	Muhammadans.	TOTAL.
Sahâranpur	1	...	1
Muzaffarnagar	2	...	2
Meerut	2	...	2
Bulandshahr	196	...	196
Mathura	16	...	16

[1] *Partâbgarh Settlement Report*, 112.
[2] *Settlement Report*, 13.
[3] Atkinson, *Himâlayan Gazetteer*, II, 497, *sq*. 504, 772, III, 432.

Distribution of the Sombansi Râjputs according to the Census of 1891—continued.

DISTRICTS.	Hindus.	Muhammadans.	TOTAL.
Agra	30	...	30
Farrukhâbâd	4,521	27	4,548
Mainpuri	366	...	366
Etâwah	126	...	126
Etah	83	7	90
Bareilly	2,488	197	2,685
Budâun	333	...	333
Morâdâbâd	133	386	519
Shâhjahânpur	2,200	8	2,208
Pilibhît	268	...	268
Cawnpur	1,214	...	1,214
Fatehpur	83	...	83
Banda	31	...	31
Hamîrpur	503	1	504
Allahâbâd	2,847	...	2,847
Jhânsi	115	...	115
Jâlaun	115	...	115
Lalitpur	2	...	2
Benares	394	51	445
Mirzapur	46	...	46
Jaunpur	2,515	32	2,547
Ghâzipur	2,006	...	2,006
Ballia	85	...	85
Gorakhpur	617	...	617
Basti	179	697	876
Azamgarh	8,891	153	9,044
Tarâi	126	...	126

Distribution of the Sombansi Râjputs according to the Census of 1891—concluded.

DISTRICTS.	Hindus.	Mahammadans.	TOTAL.
Lucknow	935	12	947
Unâo	501	...	501
Râê Bareli	2,770	89	2,859
Sîtapur	1,936	13	1,949
Hardoi	14,793	180	14,973
Kheri	1,910	604	2,514
Faizâbâd	1,300	...	1,300
Gonda	3,167	...	3,167
Bahrâich	1,002	67	1,069
Sultânpur	1,939	507	2,446
Partâbgarh	19,823	64	19,887
Bârabanki	377	269	646
TOTAL	80,987	3,364	84,351

Sorahiya, Surahiya, Surâya.—A tribe of boatmen, fishermen, and cultivators in the Eastern Districts. They are usually classed as a sub-caste of Mallâh. According to Mr. Risley "there is a shadowy connection between the Surahiya and the Châîn. The former use the water vessels and *huqqas* of the latter, but the Châîn assuming a higher rank, will smoke, but will neither eat nor intermarry with the Surahiya. The Surahiyas have no tradition of their own except the common one that their ancestors came from the West."

"They profess to be orthodox Hindus, and employ Maithil Brâhmans for religious and ceremonial purposes.

"In practice, however, the greater gods of the Hindu pantheon receive only occasional worship, and the working religion of the caste is concerned with the mysterious group known as the Pânch Pîr, Koil Bâba, the boatman's deity, and Amar Sinh, a canonised Surahiya, who seems to be their special patron. In his honour a part of the house is daubed with cowdung on stated days of every month in the year except Pûs (December-January) and Chait (March-April), and goats, rice, sweetmeats, *ghi*, etc., are offered, and incense burned, the worshippers afterwards partaking of the offerings themselves. In point of social standing the Surahiyas rank immediately below the group of castes from whose hands Brâhmans will take water. Thus Koiris, Barârs, Gangotas, who belong to that group, will accept sweetmeats from Surahiyas, but will not eat boiled rice in their houses. The characteristic occupation of the caste is boating and fishing.

"Dr. Wise describes them as enterprising and hardy sailors, often met with in Eastern Bengal during the cold season, in large trading vessels laden with grain pulse and fuller's earth, which is sold to Mahâjans, and a cargo of rice shipped for the return voyage. They are very muscular and large boned, and their physique offers a striking contrast to that of the average Bengali boatman. Some Surahiyas have taken to cultivation, and hold land as occupancy and non-occupancy tenants. Their number, however, is comparatively small, and there are at present no signs of their developing into a sub-caste : in fact, even cultivating Surahiyas are ready to engage themselves as boatmen."[1]

Sûd.—A Panjâbi tribe of whom only a very small number is found in these Provinces. Of them Mr. Ibbetson writes :[2]—"The Sûds are almost entirely confined to the lower hills and the districts that lie immediately under them as far west as Amritsar. Their head-quarters are at Ludhiâna and the neighbouring town of Machhiwâra. They are almost wholly mercantile in their pursuits, though occasionally taking service as clerks, and occupy a social position markedly inferior to that of either the Banya or the Khatri. They wear a sacred thread (*janeu*) made of three instead of six strands, and many of them practise widow marriage. With the exception of a few, who are Sikhs, they are almost all Hindus, but are, in comparison with the other mercantile classes, very lax in the observance of their religion. They indulge freely in meat and wine, and in habits, customs, and social position resemble very closely the Kâyasths. The tribe is apparently an ancient one, but I can obtain no definite information as to its origin. I attempted to make enquiries from some leading Sûds, but the result was the assembling of a

---

[1] Risley, *Tribes and Castes*, II, 283, *sq.*

[2] *Panjâb Ethnography*, section 537.

Panchâyat, the ransacking of the Sanskrit classics for proof of their Kshatriya origin, and a heated discussion in the Journal of the Anjuman.

2. They are divided into two main sections : the Uchandiya or Sûd of the Hills, and the Newandiya or Sûd of the Plains. I find, however, that some of the Sûds of Hoshyârpur trace their origin from Sirhind. They also distinguish the Sûds who do not practise widow marriage from those who do, calling the former Khara and their offspring Gola, Doghla (hybrid) or Chikân. These two sections, of which the latter corresponds exactly with the Dasa and Gola Banyas already described, do not intermarry. The Sûds forbid marriage in all four *gotras*, and here again show how much less their tribal customs have been affected by their religion than have those of the Banyas and Khatris. They are of good physique, and are an intelligent and enterprising caste, with great power of combination and self-restraint; and they have lately made what appears to be really successful effort to reduce their marriage expenses by general agreement. The extensive sugar trade of Ludhiâna and generally the agricultural money-lending of the richest part of that district are almost entirely in their hands. They are proverbially acute and prosperous men of business, and there is a saying:—'If a Sûd is across the river, leave your bundle on this side.' The husbandman of the villages is a mere child in their hands."

Distribution of the Sûd according to the Census of 1891.

DISTRICTS.	Number.	DISTRICTS.	Number.
Sahâranpur . . .	12	Jhânsi . . .	23
Muzaffarnagar . .	1	Gonda . . .	29
Mathura . . .	80		
Allahâbâd . . .	2	TOTAL . .	147

Sunâr, Sonâr;[1] in the Hills **Sona** (Sanskrit *Suvarna-kâra*, "a worker in gold"); in Persian Zargar—the gold and silver-smith, who also engages in money-lending, pawnbroking, and general trade. The internal organization and tradition of the tribe seem

[1] Based on enquiries at Mirzapur and notes by the Deputy Inspectors of Schools, Dehra Dûn, Pilibhît, Shâhjahânpur.

to indicate that it is probably originally occupational and may have been recruited from various sources.

Tradition of origin.

2. The tradition of their origin is thus told by the Sunârs of the Eastern Districts : There was in ancient times a Niyâriya, or purifier of gold, who lived near a jungle where Devi lived with the Râkshasa Sonwa Daitya, whose body was of pure gold. The goddess became tired of her demon lover and ordered the Niyâriya whose name was Mair, to destroy him. Mair approached the demon and offered to clean his body which had become very dirty. The demon allowed him to experiment on his little finger and was satisfied with the result. Then Mair told him that he could clean his whole body if he would agree to mount the fire. The Râkshasa consented, and Mair arranged a pyre, on which he placed the demon, and then laid pieces of lead on his head and breast, so the demon was consumed, and Devi blessed Mair with the promise that he and his descendants should always possess gold and silver and work in the precious metals.

3. The Bengal story adds that Mair was covetous and stole part of the demon's head, and, being detected with it by Devi, she cursed him and his descendants with poverty.[1]

4. According to the Bombay account : In the beginning of the world a pair were produced out of the fire : the male with a blow pipe, and the female with a burning hearth holding molten gold.[2]

5. By another legend current in Northern India, Devi created Mair out of the dirt (*mail*) of her body, and induced him to destroy her demon lover. In another form of the same story, Mair was created from the dirt scraped from the body of a Mâi or holy woman, and in return he rescued her from a golden demon by throwing him into the fire. In this version a Sarrâf seizes the golden ingot, and the Mair, who contented himself with the stray pieces of gold, received the Mâi's blessing, so that he does prosper to this day. Others again say that the gold demon was named Mâika Asura, and that from him was derived the name of Mair.

Tribal organization.

6. At the last Census the Sunârs were recorded under eight main sub-castes : Ajudhyabâsi, "residents of Ajudhya," Bâgri, which is also the name

---

[1] Risley, *Tribes and Castes*, II, 256.
[2] *Bombay Gazetteer*, XVII, 133.

of a well-known Râjput sept; Chhatri or Kshatriya, which are probably the same as the Tânk Sunârs of the Panjâb, who profess to be degenerate Kshatris or Aroras; Deswâli or "indigenous;" Kanaujiya or "residents of Kanauj;" Khatri, who are perhaps connected with the Chhatri sub-caste already referred to; Mair, who are apparently the original Sunârs of Upper India; and the Rastaogi, which is also the name of one of the Banya sub-tribes.

7. To the east of the Province the internal structure of the caste is very elaborate. There are three groups or sub-tribes, which, according to Mr. Sherring's[1] account from Benares, should contain respectively twelve (*bârah mûl*), fifty-two (*bâwan mûl*) and twenty-two (*bâîs mûl*) sections. It has been found practically impossible to procure a complete list of these sections. The following is the enumeration in Mirzapur. The names given by Mr. Sherring have been given in parenthesis where they apparently correspond—Tântê (Tâtê), Phankê (Phaphê), Thâkur (Thâkur), Rajghatiya (Rajghatiya), Anguriya (Anguriya), Sugawa Bair, Sinh Tarora (Tandora), Andhâri kâ khatanga, Râmtul (Râmtuli), Banwadhiya, Niyâriya, and Nawagiriha (Naugrahiya). Mr. Sherring adds three more —Phûl, Aldemaua, Nautakiya. He gives for the Sinh Tarora or Tandora sub-division thirteen minor clans: Sinh Tandora, Amlohiya, Jhanjhiya, Sugvahair, Naktunâik, Alona, Nujariya, Tahakhiya, Ghosiwâl, Khâspuri, Purhiya, Ghatkiya, and Pûrabi. Of these the Sugnahair is perhaps the same as the Sugawa Bair of the Mirzapur enumeration. Mr. Sherring does not give the sections of the other sub-tribes. The second group should, it is said, include ten sections, of which only nine are known in Mirzapur: Lâl, Mânik, Husainâbâdi, Tankiya, Teliya, Sergharlotiya, Agariya, Bilaiya, and Kuthawa. The third group, according to Mirzapur enumeration contains thirty sections: Dewaiya, Kataiya, Chûrihâra, Bahariyâbâdi, Naubariya, Narhaniha, Teraha, Mardaniya, Qâzipuriya, Badipuriya, Mânikpuriha, Bilâlapuriha, Hâjipuriha, Bigwa, Saharbâdiya, Kutmutiya, Sutaha, Thâna, Chikaniya, Charokoʻa, Mathaiwân, Kith, Panadaha, Bâbhan, Sunâra, Amawatiya Bilâra, Khatanga, Sarawaniya, and Lawaniya. Many of these sections appear to be of local origin; others, as the Chûrihâra and Bâbhan Sunâra, may indicate real or pretended connection with

[1] *Hindu Tribes and Castes*, I, 314, *sq*.

other castes. It is a good example of the extreme fertility with which castes like these produce their sections that there is no likeness between these lists and those given from Bengal and Bihâr by Mr. Risley.[1]

8. There is, again, another classification in parts of Mirzapur of Uttarâha, "Northern;" Dakkhinâha, "Southern;" Purabiya, "Eastern;" and Pachhainwa, or "Western." In Bhadohi, north of the Ganges, there is a section known as Bhatkhauwa, so called, it is said, because a Sunâr cohabited by force with a Kâyasth woman, and her descendants were afterwards admitted to the tribe after eating rice (*bhât khâna*). Another section is known as Kukar Khauwa or "dog-eaters," because once, when a house was burnt down, a dog was burnt, and they ate its flesh, believing it to be that of a goat.

9. In Rohilkhand the Chhatri sub-caste is said to be so called because, when Parasurâma was annihilating the Kshatriyas, one of them took refuge with some Sunârs and adopted their trade to save his life. They are said to have no less than four hundred and eighty-four sections, some of whom, according to a list from Pilibhît, are Amethi, Gonthi, Mangaiyân, Musarma, Haraihila, Karaihila, Tataila, Ugar, Bhuinganiya, Bhujwâr, Bachhrâjpuriya, Sûirajpuriya, Chandwariya, Nainhân, and Mediya,—all of which are said to be the names of their head-quarters. The complete census returns show 1,627 sub-divisions of Sunârs, of which those of most local importance are the Desi of Sahâranpur; the Pachhâdê of Meerut and Morâdâbâd; the Mahar of Agra; the Sundha of Fatehpur, Allahâbâd, and Bânda; the Deogayân of Benares; the Audhiya of Lalitpur; the Badhauliya and Ganga of Mirzapur; the Indauriya and Jalesariya of Jaunpur; the Bholiya of Ghâzipur; the Jaiswâr and Kanak of Ballia; the Fatehpuri and Sakarwâr of Gorakhpur, the Magahiya, Sarwariya, and Sikandarpuriya of Basti; the Deogayân of Azamgarh; the Syâmkrishna of Gonda.

10. Besides these there are other numerous sections, which are said to be merely occupational or recruited from menial tribes, and are not accepted by the genuine Sunârs for purposes of marriage. All Sunârs appear to practise hypergamy and marry, when possible, their daughters in a section of

---

[1] *Tribes and Castes,* II, 129.

rank superior to their own. The sub-castes are endogamous, and the sections exogamous. The strict rule is that a man cannot marry in his own, his mother's, his paternal grandmother's, his maternal grandmother's, his father's, paternal or maternal grandmother's section, or in that in which a brother or sister has been already married. In working out the connection the sections of both bride and bridegroom should be considered. They also do not marry within seven generations in the descending line. But it would seem that this rule is falling into abeyance, and the tendency appears, at least in the eastern part of these Provinces, for the sections to coalesce into larger groups, such as the Uttarâha, Dakkinâha, etc., which are becoming endogamous, and isolate themselves by some special observances, such as the maintenance or abolition of widow marriage, and then fall back on the ordinary exogamous formula, which bars intermarriage between the first cousins on both sides.

Tribal council.

11. The Sunârs have a tribal council (*panchâyat*) presided over by a permanent chairman (*mukhiya, chaudhari*). Offences against morality or caste usage are usually punished by two compulsory feasts,—one *pakki* and the other *kachchi*, at the expense of the offender. More serious offences are punished by compulsory pilgrimages, and by feeding and giving alms to Brâhmans, particularly to the tribal priests.

Marriage rules.

12. The Mair Sunârs admit widow marriage, which most of the others profess to prohibit; but the rule is not sufficiently precise to be defined. Polygamy is so far admitted that a man can marry again in the lifetime of his first wife with the approval of the council. As has been already noticed, there is so far a tendency towards hypergamy that parents desire to marry their daughters into a family of a higher rank than their own, while sons are married into families of the same or lower social rank. Concubinage is forbidden, and if a man keeps a strange woman he is put out of caste. Girls before marriage have a certain amount of freedom, but a girl detected in pre-nuptial infidelity is expelled from the family, and if her friends hesitate to take this step, they are put out of caste and not re-admitted until they pay a fine. Marriages are usually arranged by a Bhât. Girls are usually married at the age of ten or twelve; but the practice varies, the richer Sunârs having a preference for infant marriage. Those of higher rank give a dowry with their daughters; while those of a lower grade take money for their girls and often marry them to

the highest bidder. It seems to be understood, however, that the bride-price should be spent on the marriage ceremony and the feast which accompanies it. A man may, with the previous sanction of the council, repudiate an unfaithful wife; and a woman can, similarly, with the permission of the council, leave her husband if he be impotent, but, of course, she cannot be re-married by the regular form.

Birth ceremonies.

13. There is nothing peculiar in the birth ceremonies. There are the usual observances on the sixth (*chhathi*) and twelfth (*barahi*) day after confinement. The menstrual impurity lasts for three days; on the fourth the woman is purified by bathing. The time for the final ablution of the mother is fixed by the Pandit, who even decides what is the lucky direction in which she ought to sit while undergoing the final bath of purification. The Chamâr midwife receives as her fee, in addition to a money present, a sieve full of barley or rice which is known as *akhat* (Sanskrit *akshata*). On each of the two ceremonial bathings the barber's wife distributes, at the houses of the brethren, a preparation of ginger, molasses, and butter, known as *baina*, for which at each house she receives a present. They have the usual initiation into caste by means of the ear-boring (*kanchhedan, kanbedha*). They also wear the sacred cord (*janeu*); but this is not assumed with any special ceremony, and the investiture is done at marriage.

Marriage ceremonies.

14. The marriage ritual, on the whole, corresponds with that of the higher caste Hindus. Rich people marry their daughters by the respectable (*charhauwa*) form; poorer people use the *dola* rite, where the ceremony is performed at the house of the bridegroom.

Disposal of the dead.

15. The dead are cremated according to the standard form. They perform the annual *srâddha*, and some of the wealthier class go even to Gaya for this purpose.

Religion.

16. In Oudh a Sunâr, named Munna Dâs, who died nearly a century ago, established a sect the members of which have an annual fair at the tomb of their spiritual leader at Mandwa in the Kheri district.[1] Some of their special customs are to *salaam* with both hands, to abstain from flesh meat, and to worship an unlighted lamp. To the east of the Province, if they are regularly initiated into any sect, it is

---

[1] *Oudh Gazetteer*, II, 201.

the Râmanandi or Nânakpanthi. Their tribal deities are Mahâdeva, the Pânchon Pîr, Hardiha or Harda Lâla, Ambika and Phûlmati Devi. These deities are worshipped in the months of Jeth and Sâwan. The Pânchon Pîr receive an offering of cakes (*malîda*), *sharbat*, and garlands of flowers. The priests of the Pânchon Pîr are drawn from the Dafâli caste and receive a share of the offerings. They have also a special tribal Pîr, known as Mîran Sâhib, who is worshipped on Thursdays with an offering of sweets. Kâlika and the other deities receive cakes (*pûri*), pottage (*lapsi*), sacrifices of sheep and goats, and pieces of coloured cloth (*chunari*). Their priests are of the ordinary respectable Brâhman class. The meat offerings made by the worshippers are consumed by them after dedication. The family gods are worshipped in a special room in the house, where a platform (*chabûtra*) is erected in their honour.

Festivals.

17. They observe the ordinary Hindu holidays. On the full moon of Asârh, they mix various grains together, parch them, scatter them in the corners of the house, and make a sacred circle all round outside to guard the family from evil. Snakes are worshipped at the Nâgpanchami, trees on Saturday, the Sun on Sunday, and the Moon at full moon. The special women's holiday is the Tîj or third day of the light half of Bhâdon. Women fast the whole night and day and with singing go and bathe in a stream or tank. But on the previous evening they keep silence as they go to bathe. They worship Bâwan or Bâmana, the dwarf incarnation of Vishnu, on the twelfth of the light half of Bhâdon. They also fast at the Anant, and, on breaking their fast, they eat only wheat bread and milk. The special girl's holiday is the Dasahra or the tenth of the bright half of Jeth, when they throw dolls into the water. They respect the *nîm* tree as the abode of Sîtala and the *pîpal* as the home of the other gods. Dead people often become troublesome ghosts and are worshipped by their relations.

Social customs.

18. Women are tattooed on the wrists. If this be not done, they will be unable to find their mothers in the next world. They swear on Ganges water, on their own heads, on the heads of their sons, standing in water, or by putting *pîpal* leaves on their heads. They believe in magic and witchcraft, to relieve the effects of which they employ Ojhas or Syânas drawn from the lower castes. To obviate the effects of the Evil Eye, a child is usually taken to a mosque and

the Maulavi is asked to breathe over him when the service is over. They worship and protect the cow.

19. They will not touch a Chamâr, Dom or similar degraded castes. Some of them drink, but the habit is reprobated. As an intoxicant and tonic they use *bhang*. They eat the flesh of goats, sheep, and deer, but not beef or pork. Like all respectable Hindus, they will not eat onions, but use garlic instead, and they will not eat turnips or the *kaddu* pumpkin. They will eat the leavings of no one except those of their Guru. They salute their brethren in the forms *Râm! Râm!* or *Jay Râm! Sîtarâm!* They are said to respect women more than other castes of the same social level. They eat *pakki* cooked by Brâhmans and Râjputs, and *kachchi* cooked by clansmen or by their Guru.

20. The best account of the business of the goldsmith is that given by Mr. Maclagan for the Panjâb. Their business is making jewelry and money-lending and pawn-broking. They are very often "fences" and receive and dispose of stolen jewelry. They have a slang vocabulary of which a long list has been given by Sir H. M. Elliot.[1] There are, according to Mr. Hoey,[2] four classes of work in Lucknow: plain work (*sâda*) in which there is no ornamentation, such as ordinary gold and silver bangles; *chitâi* or mat-work, which includes all work in which there are cut or engraved designs of flowers, letters, inscriptions, etc.; *jarâo* or *murassa*, which includes all work involving the setting of stones and raised and joined work; *jaldâr*, which is of various classes, European goods, filigree, etc. Besides this there is a large business done by Sunârs in the manufacture of silver and silver-gilt vessels for the Indian market, and teapots, sugar-bowls, tumblers, etc, for English people. When manufacture of ornaments or vessels involves enamelling and gilding, these processes are not performed by the gold or silversmith, but by other artisans, known as the Mînasâz or Mulammasâz.

Occupation.

21. The occupation of the Sunâr is certainly very ancient, as the deities in the Rigveda are constantly represented as wearing gold jewelry. Gold was undoubtedly very extensively found and used in the earliest times in India.[3]

---

[1] *Supplemental Glossary*, 245.

[2] *Monograph*, 184.

[3] Rajendra Lala Mitra, *Indo Aryans*, I, 277: Schrader, *Prehistoric Antiquities*, 172, 185.

22. The Sunâr has a very indifferent reputation for honesty. "The ornament is the wearer's, but the gold remains with the goldsmith" (*Sona Sunâr kâ, abhran sansâr kâ*) is a common proverb. To the west of the Province they tell how a Sunâr made the gold of his own Guru disappear before his very eyes, and then complimented the Guru on his miraculous powers. Another tale describes how a Sunâr wasted away with regret because he made a nosering for his mother without alloying it, and a variant of the tale goes on to tell that he never stopped till he cut off his mother's nose to get the jewel back. So they say *Sunâr apni mâ ki nath men sê bhî churâta hai*—"A goldsmith will steal a piece of his own mother's nosering." Another Sunâr went to the temple of Badari Nârâyan in Garhwâl and finding that his iron ring on touching the statue became gold, cut off one of the god's fingers for his private use. But the stump began to ooze with unmistakable blood and from that day to this no Sunâr dares to come near the idol for fear of being struck blind.

Distribution of the Sunârs according to the Census of 1891.

Districts.	Ajudhya-bàsi.	Bâgri.	Chhatri.	Deswâlí.	Kanaujiya.	Khatri.	Mair.	Rastâogi.	Others.	Muhammadans.	Total.
Dehra Dûn	...	26	...	22	...	...	...	...	494	...	542
Sahâranpur	...	454	73	765	...	...	761	...	2,882	...	4,935
Muzaffarnagar	...	564	...	3,317	...	...	108	...	642	35	4,666
Meerut	...	22	...	4,632	...	...	1,312	...	2,461	...	8,427
Bulandshahr	...	...	...	479	...	...	1,033	...	2,679	113	4,304
Aligarh	...	...	...	...	...	...	1,466	...	3,139	...	4,605
Mathura	...	...	...	...	...	1	3,751	...	573	1	4,326
Agra	137	...	598	...	...	157	181	1	4,994	5	6,073
Farrukhâbâd	43	...	2,918	...	25	...	53	19	2,623	...	5,681
Mainpuri	...	...	2,315	...	...	...	...	...	1,900	...	4,215
Etâwah	551	33	1,426	...	199	240	249	53	2,031	...	4,782
Etah	...	...	1,608	...	8	...	72	7	1,773	...	3,468
Bareilly	21	...	1,857	...	...	...	122	3,996	1,320	...	7,316

Distribution of the Sunârs according to the Census of 1891—continued.

Districts.	Ajudhya-bâsi.	Bâgri.	Chhatri.	Deswâli.	Kanaujiya.	Khatri.	Mair.	Rastáogi.	Others.	Muhammadans.	Total.
Bijnor . . .	...	...	...	390	...	...	3,862	...	108	...	4,360
Budâun . . .	...	...	1,886	...	...	...	707	606	1,305	...	4,504
Morâdâbâd . . .	...	...	...	...	...	...	3,195	949	1,733	124	6,001
Shâhjahânpur . .	...	...	3,128	...	...	19	210	1,078	1,241	...	5,676
Pilibhît . . .	...	21	1,186	...	...	...	682	942	159	...	2,990
Cawnpur . . .	1,785	...	2,690	...	107	800	9	158	2,213	...	7,762
Fatehpur . . .	895	...	759	...	29	124	8	...	3,109	...	4,924
Bânda . . .	3,612	56	42	...	8	1,684	...	...	942	...	6,344
Hamîrpur . . .	5,201	...	...	...	...	1,065	...	...	143	...	6,409
Allahâbâd . . .	514	...	64	...	61	12	9	19	7,427	...	8,106
Jhânsi . . .	844	...	...	...	...	1,705	...	...	814	...	3,363
Jâlaun . . .	1,358	...	23	...	...	1,470	...	...	928	...	3,779
Lalitpur . . .	6	...	42	...	...	95	...	...	1,774	...	1,917
Benares . . .	124	...	...	...	...	2,091	303	...	4,795	...	7,313

Mirzapur	994	...	...	...	...	...	...	...	4,800	...	5,794
Jaunpur	258	...	...	...	...	...	...	...	5,959	...	6,217
Ghâzipur	474	...	...	...	19	282	...	...	7,895	...	8,670
Ballia	225	...	...	...	266	...	...	...	8,969	...	9,460
Gorakhpur	4,644	66	...	262	49	798	3	...	11,430	...	17,252
Basti	2,024	...	...	...	...	...	...	...	7,735	...	9,459
Azamgarh	2,290	93	...	...	128	444	...	...	5,414	...	8,369
Kumaun	...	...	...	...	...	...	...	...	681	...	681
Garhwâl	...	...	...	...	...	...	...	...	4	...	4
Tarâi	...	...	...	...	...	...	491	179	302	11	983
Lucknow	7	...	1,107	...	69	18	9	1,172	2,802	...	5,184
Unâo	223	...	824	...	4	...	...	139	2,833	...	4,023
Râê Bareli	120	...	497	...	14	42	16	239	3,935	...	4,863
Sîtapur	2	...	1,378	...	22	...	1	1,333	1,237	...	3,973
Hardoi	...	...	2,411	...	...	...	...	1,142	294	...	3,847
Kheri	...	...	1,328	...	...	...	406	1,207	334	...	3,275
Faizâbad	332	...	73	...	...	311	151	38	3,986	3	4,894

Distribution of the Sunârs according to the Census of 1891—concluded.

Districts.	Ajudhya-bâsi.	Bâgri.	Chhatri.	Deswâli.	Kanaujiya.	Khatri.	Mair.	Rastâogi.	Others.	Muhammadans.	Total.
Gonda . . .	...	175	40	...	28	...	...	1,374	3,532	...	5,149
Bahrâich . . .	7	...	789	14	...	...	1,483	301	1,400	2	3,996
Sultânpur . . .	...	...	...	7	36	...	...	...	3,956	24	4,023
Partâbgarh . .	....	...	6	...	17	...	...	...	2,663	2	2,688
Bârabanki . . .	...	846	53	5	17	...	...	1,175	3,340	...	5,436
Total .	26,691	2,356	29,121	9,893	1,106	11,358	20,653	16,127	137,703	320	255,328

Sunkar.[1]— A small caste of labourers entirely confined to Bundelkhand. They appear to have no traditions of origin. They have a number of exogamous *gotras*, some of which are Margiya, Gotiya and Jaraliya. A man cannot marry in his own *gotra* or in a family with which another marriage connection has been formed within the memory of man. Both infant and adult marriage is allowed. Neither polyandry nor polygamy is allowed. The marriage ceremony is by the usual form of *bhanwar* or revolutions round the marriage shed. Widows are allowed to marry and the levirate is preferred, but is not compulsory on the woman. In widow marriage the only observance is the feast to the brethren when the bride is brought home with her husband. A woman can be divorced for adultery with the consent of the tribal elders (*mukhiya*). A divorced wife may remarry in the caste according to the form allowed in the case of widow marriage.

2. They are Hindus and generally worship Devi. Their chief local god is Hardaul Lâla, who is worshipped at marriages. They burn their dead, and if a river be near the ashes are consigned to it; if not they are left on the burning ground. They offer the usual libations of water to the manes of the dead and feast the brethren.

3. Their chief occupation is dyeing cloth with the *âl* dye and making what is known as *khârua* cloth. Some of them burn lime and collect road metal (*kankar*) on the roads. They are allowed to eat goat's flesh and fish and drink spirits. They will not eat or drink with any of the menial castes, and no higher caste will take food or water from their hands.

Distribution of the Sunkar according to the Census of 1891.

Districts.	Number.	Districts.	Number.
Bânda . . .	1	Jâlaun . . .	497
Hamîrpur . . .	352		
Jhânsi . . .	546	Total .	1,396

Sûrajbans, Sûrajbansi (Sanskrit *Sûrya-vansa*, "the race of the sun").—A modern sept of Râjputs who claim to be the represen-

[1] Principally based on a note by M. Râdha Raman, Deputy Collector, Jhânsi.

tatives of the famous solar race of Ajudhya. The Malla Râjas of Nepâl assert that they are sprung from Ansuvarma, who, according to the Chinese pilgrim Hwen Thsang, belonged to the Sûrajbansi family of the Lichchhavis of Vaisali near Patna.[1] The famous tradition, accepted by Colonel Tod, represents that in 224 A. D., Kanak Sen left Ajudhya with a large following and migrated westward to Gujarât. "This tradition, however, is opposed to the widely received story that Vikramaditya, of Ujjain, visited Ajudhya about 50 B. C., and found it totally desolate and covered with forest, and, after discovering the sites of the ancient temples and palaces, rebuilt them in their original splendour. Granting, however, that this discrepancy is one of dates and not of facts, this migration of the Sûrajbansis from Ajudhya to Gujarât, and finally to Chithor, is the only tangible fact we have to lay hold on the early history of Oudh."[2] The Pahâri Chhatri Râja, who now holds the Pargana of Khairgarh, in the Kheri district, asserts[3] that his family governed at Sâraswati till the time of Râja Suthurot, whose son Marchhan Deva moved with his subjects to Ajudhya, where they reigned for one hundred and two generations till the time of Pitra Sen, who became King of Bhârat Khand or Northern India. There they reigned for eighteen generations, and then they moved to Kaphâr, in Kumaun, where forty-two more of them successively sat on the throne. The forty-second, Sârang Deva, emigrated to Kâthaur. The twentieth generation brings them down to Arjuva Pâla, who was a contemporary of the Emperor Akbar. "They claim then to have governed in different parts of India for more than two hundred and twenty generations prior to the sixteenth century. In spite of this long descent, it may be remarked that the family is hardly considered Chhatri at all; and even when they managed to marry their daughters to the Ahbans, Janwârs, and Raikwârs, they had to pay large sums as bribes. Further, none of these places or parganas appear on the map of Kumaun, and the whole story is probably one of those fictions in which the bards of India are so fertile."

2. According to the legend current in Faizâbâd,[4] their ancestor

---

[1] Atkinson, *Himalayan Gazetteer*, II, 514.

[2] Elliott, *Chronicles of Unâo*, 21.

[3] *Oudh Gazetteer*, II, 130.

[4] *Settlement Report*, 212.

came from Kumaun three hundred and fifty years ago and settled at Sultânpur, a suburb of Faizâbâd. He and his sons served a merchant named Dandâs Sahu, who had excavated a large tank in the neighbourhood, to which he gave his name. There dwelt hard by, in the village of Belahri Shâh Bhîkha, a hermit of great repute. On one occasion the merchant found the hermit washing his teeth at the edge of the tank, and admonished him for so doing. This so enraged the hermit that he vowed that in future not even donkeys should drink at the tank, and in consequence water is rarely found in it. The merchant died childless, and his property fell into the hands of his Sûrajbans servant, and thus the present family came to be founded. In Râê Bareli[1] their sons marry Chauhân and Bisen girls, and they give brides to the Amethiya and Bais. There is a flourishing branch in Ghâzipur, who claim to have expelled the Bhars.[2]

3. There is another sept of illegitimate Sûrajbansis who are probably included in the enumeration of the last census. They are described under the head of Soiris.

4. According to one account the Sûrajbansis take wives from the Bachgoti, Râjkumâr, Bandhalgoti, Sombansi, and Kalhans septs; and give girls to the Sirnet, Gautam, and Baghel. The poorer members of the sept are said to sell their daughters to rich Râjputs of any clan irrespective of social rank.

Distribution of the Sûrajbans Râjputs according to the Census of 1891.

Districts.	Number.	Districts.	Number.
Sahâranpur	110	Agra	211
Muzaffarnagar	13	Farrukhâbâd	30
Meerut	155	Mainpuri	2
Bulandshahr	2,294	Etâwah	4
Aligarh	11	Etah	134
Mathura	45	Bareilly	98

[1] *Settlement Report, Appendix* C.

[2] Oldham, *Memoir*, I, 65.

Distribution of the Sûrajbans Râjputs according to the Census of 1891—concluded.

DISTRICTS.	Number.	DISTRICTS.	Number.
Bijnor	185	Gorakhpur . . .	1,581
Budâun . . .	12	Basti	14,670
Morâdâbâd . . .	222	Azamgarh . . .	551
Shâhjahânpur . .	111	Kumaun . . .	184
Pilibhît . . .	56	Tarâi	49
Cawnpur . . .	166	Lucknow . . .	241
Fatehpur . . .	5	Unâo	9
Pânda	187	Râê Bareli . . .	55
Hamîrpur . . .	49	Sîtapur . . .	194
Allahâbâd . . .	429	Hardoi . . .	185
Jhânsi . . .	12	Kheri	458
Jâlaun	13	Faizâbâd . . .	4,124
Lalitpur . . .	2	Gonda . . .	826
Benares . . .	1,295	Bahrâich . . .	445
Mirzapur . . .	6,786	Sultânpur . . .	315
Jaunpur . . .	285	Partâbgarh . . .	172
Ghâzipur . . .	3,769	Bârabanki . . .	2,777
Ballia . . .	855	TOTAL .	44,382

Suthrashâhi.[1]—An order of Hindu mendicants who are found in very small numbers in these Provinces.

Of them Mr. Maclagan writes :—" The origin of this order is a little doubtful. According to one account, Suthra Shâh was a Budwâl Khatri of Bahrâmpur, in the Gurdâspur district, who became a disciple of Guru Arjan, and was called Suthra, " pure, " from his truthfulness. Another story is that he was a follower of Guru Har Govind, and various tales are told of the quarrelsomeness and somewhat coarse humour which he displayed in the days of that Guru. Professor Wilson, again, says that the Suthra-

[1] *Panjâb Census Report*, 154 ; Wilson, *Essays*, I, 272, *sq.* ; Ibbetson, *Panjâb Ethnography*, paragraph 522 ; Cunningham, *History of the Sikhs*, 65.

shâhis look to Guru Tegh Bahâdur as their founder. Dr. Trumpp, on the other hand, states that the founder of this sect was a Brâhman named Sucha, and that they took their origin under Guru Har Râê. His view is supported by a story, which says that when Guru Har Râê was summoned by Aurangzeb to Delhi, Suthra Shâh took his place and so pleased the Mughal by his wit and wisdom that he was given special permission to levy a *paisa* from every shop in the realm. On the strength of this his spiritual descendants are most importunate beggars and will seldom leave a shop till they get alms. They proceed along the bâzârs with black caste marks on their foreheads and black woollen ropes (*seli*) twisted round their heads and necks, clashing together a couple of short staves (*danda*) and shouting mystic Panjâbi songs indifferently in honour of Guru Nânak and the goddess Devi. They perform the funeral ceremonies of the Hindus, burn their dead, and throw the bones into the Ganges; but they neither wear the Brâhmanical thread nor keep the scalp-lock. They indulge freely in intoxicants and seldom cease from smoking. Their profligacy is notorious and they are said to be composed mainly of spendthrifts who have lost their wealth in gambling. They are recruited from all castes, and they always add the title Shâh to their names. "They have," says Trumpp, "a Guruship of their own, and receive novices (*chela*); but there is no order or regular discipline among them." They live chiefly in large towns, and their principal Gurudwâra is at Lahore. They are also said to have shrines at Nâgar Sain, near Benares, and at Patiâla; but as a rule they have no sacred places and spend their time in roving mendicancy."

2. Whenever they visit these Provinces they are regarded with extreme abhorrence, partly on account of the coarse way in which they demand alms and abuse and lampoon those who do not give in to their demands, and partly because they have the reputation of enticing away the sons of respectable people to join the order. Some of them say that they are the followers of one Jhakkar Shâh. Their distinctive mark is a straight line across the forehead made in black, and the ebony (*abnûs*) wood sticks which they beat together as they beg. A proverb current in the Eastern Districts says, in allusion to their rapacity,—*Kehu mûé, kehu jiyé, Suthra ghor batâsa piyé*: "Any one may live or die, but the Suthrashâhi must have his drink of sugar and water."

T

Taga.[1]—An important cultivating and land-owning tribe confined almost altogether to the Upper Ganges-Jumna Duâb and Rohilkhand. They are divided into a Hindu and Muhammadan branch.

Traditional origin.

2. The Tagas claim to be of Brâhmanical origin, as Sir H. M. Elliot writes:[2]—"They state that they were invited from Bengal to these parts by Râja Janamejaya for the purpose of exterminating snakes; which fable, though sufficiently ridiculous in itself, no doubt veils under an allegorical type a most important historical fact. The circumstances attending the sacrifice of the snakes by Janamejaya are preserved by local tradition in almost the same form as they are given in the Adi Parva of the Mahâbhârata. A garrulous old Taga, who has perhaps never read or even heard a line of that poem, will tell you how Râja Parichat (Parikshita) was bitten to death by a snake, notwithstanding all the precautions he took to avoid it by seating himself on a platform in the middle of the Ganges; how that Utang (Utanka), a Muni, persuaded Janamejaya, who had lately returned victorious from Takshasila, to avenge his father's death; how that they were all exterminated, except Takchak (Takshaka), brother of the Adityas, and Bâsuk (Vâsuki), sovereign of the Nâgas of Patâla; when, towards the end of the sacrifice, Astik, a holy man (of whose birth some marvellous paticulars are given), came forward and obtained the promise of Janamejaya to spare their lives, which promise he dare not break, as it was exacted by a Brâhman; and how that he was thus foiled in his object of sacrificing the chief offenders whom he had reserved for the close of the ceremony in order that none of their followers might come to their assistance.

"It was for the purpose of officiating at this serpent sacrifice that Janamejaya is said to have invited Brâhmans from Gaur. After they had performed all that he requested of them, he offered them remuneration, which some rejected, and others received in the shape of land; on which account they were called Tagas from having

---

[1] Based on notes by M. Muhammad Ali, Head Master, Zillah School, Bijnor; H. Frazer, Esq., C.S. Bijnor.

[2] *Supplementary Glossary: S.V. Gour Taga.*

consented to a relinquishment (*tyâg*) of their creed as Brâhmans, by pursuing agriculture, which they are forbidden by the Shâstras to practise.

3. "Those who continued to retain their titles and privileges as Brâhmans took up their abode chiefly in Hariyâna, while the Tagas remained in the neighbourhood of Hastinapur, within a circle of about one hundred miles round the ancient capital, where they are found to this day. This is the usual account.

"It is remarkable, however, that almost all the clans of Tagas state that they came from Hariyâna, not from Gaur, and even derive their names from places in that country, as, for instance, the Chûlat who say that their name is derived from Chûla in Bikanîr; and the Bikwâns, of Pur Châpar, who came from Bikanîr. It is, therefore, far more probable that the Brâhmans were already tenants of Hariyâna, that they must have settled there before Janamejaya's reign, and that the Tagas only, and not the Brâhmans, owe their residence to that powerful Râja; otherwise it is difficult to reconcile the apparent contradiction that he called Gaur Brâhmans from Bengal, and Gaur Tagas from Hariyâna; or it may be that the Brâhmans were invited from Gaur by Janamejaya, and afterwards settled in Hariyâna, and that the Tagas were invited by some succeeding Prince or Princes, after the Brâhmans had fully established themselves in Hariyâna; so that the occupation of the country round Hastinapur by the Tagas may be later than the occupation of Hariyâna by the Brâhmans. But what militates against this, and confirms the other hypothesis, is that it is expressly stated in the concluding section of the Mahâbhârata that Janamejaya, 'having concluded the ceremonies of the sacrifice on which he had been engaged, dismissed the multitude of Brâhmans and other pious mendicants who had thronged to the place, loaded with presents, to their several abodes.'"

4. It is of course dangerous to press the details of a legend like this too far. Mr. Ibbetson[1] attempts to explain the difficulty of their legendary connection with Hariyâna by the fact that they give Safîdon in Jhînd, on the border of Hariyâna, as the place where the holocaust took place, and the name of the town is not improbably connected with the snake (*sânp*). Whether, as Sir H. M. Elliot believed, their name was to be connected with the Takkas, who are

[1] *Panjâb Ethnography*, para. 477.

believed to have been a Scythian race, with the snake as their totem or not, there seems reason to believe that the Tagas are probably the earliest inhabitants of the Upper Jumna lowlands (*khâdir*), holding villages that have been untouched by the course of the stream for a longer period than most of their neighbours.

5. Lower down the Ganges-Jumna Duâb, the Tagas, Gaur Brâhmans, and Nâgars of Bulandshahr firmly believe that Ahâr in that district (said to be derived from *ahihâra*, "serpents destroyed") was the spot where their ancestors assisted Râja Janamejaya in the snake sacrifice and got largesses and assignments in return. Another legend gives a less respectable account of their origin. It is said that having been tempted by the munificent gifts offered by a certain Râja to married Brâhmans, a Gaur bachelor took in his company a common prostitute to the Râja's Court to pass as a married man and obtain the gift. The device succeeded, but was soon after discovered, and then to escape the Râja's displeasure the Brâhman kept the prostitute for good as his wife. The progeny of this pair imitated the pure Brâhmans by wearing the Brâhmanical cord (*tâga*), and hence they are called Tagas, or Brâhmans, in no other respect than that of wearing the cord. As an argument in support of the story, it is said that Taga women are still uncommonly fond of ornamenting their persons, a peculiarity supposed to be derived from their original ancestress.[1]

6. On the whole it seems not unreasonable to believe that, like the Bhuînhâr Brâhmans of the eastern part of the Province, the Tagas may have been originally Gaur Brâhmans, who lost status by abandoning priestly functions and taking to agriculture. At the same time their appearance, and the recognition of the Dasa or inferior grade, who allow widow marriage and are admittedly not of blue blood, leads to the inference that there has been at one time some admixture with other races. How far they really intermarry with other Brâhmans is not quite certain. In Gurgâon [2] it is said, that some thirty years ago one Gordhan, a Taga, was about to marry his daughter to a Gaur Brâhman; but a council of Gaurs forbade it. Sir H. M. Elliot says that in the Dehli territory the Gaur Brâhmans and the Tagas frequently intermarry; but that the practice is not observed by the Gaurs of the Duâb and Rohilkhand.

---

[1] Râja Lachhman Sinh, *Bulandshahr Memo.* 134, 159, *sq.*

[2] *Settlement Report*, 32.

7. The records of the last Census show no less than one hundred and fifty-five sections of the Hindu and fifty-five of the Muhammadan branch. Many of these are well known Râjput or Brâhman tribes, such as Bâchhal, Bais, Bargala, Chauhân, Chandel, Dikhit, Gaur, Sanâdh, Vasishtha. These appear to be exogamous groups framed on the Brâhman or Kshatriya model. But the really important division is into Dasa or Daswân, Bîsa or Biswân the "tens" and the "twenties," the former of whom allow widow marriage, which the latter prohibit. If a Bîsa allows this objectionable practice, he falls at once into the Dasa grade.

Tribal organization.

8. The Dasa and Bîsa form two endogamous groups, and within these groups they follow the usual rules of Brâhmanical exogamy. Polyandry and sexual license before marriage are strictly prohibited. Polygamy is allowed only when the first wife is barren. The age for marriage is from eight to fifteen. There is no legalised divorce; a faithless wife is simply expelled from the house. There is no bride-price; but it is usual to give a dowry with the bride. The domestic ceremonies are of the standard orthodox type.

Marriage.

9. The Hindu branch appear chiefly to worship Mahâdeva. They are very careful to propitiate the sainted dead of the household. One way of appeasing the spirit of the dead man is to make an unmarried boy drink milk under a *pîpal* tree on the death day in every fortnight for a year, and then on each succeeding anniversary. Their priests are generally Gaur Brâhmans of an inferior grade.

Religion.

10. The Tagas are a fine sturdy set of yeomen, all or nearly all occupied in agriculture. They are not as good farmers as the Jâts in their neighbourhood, but much more industrious and respectable than the Gûjars.

Occupation.

Distribution of the Tagas according to the Census of 1891.

District.	Hindus.	Muhammadans.	Total.
Dehra Dûn	12	...	12
Sahâranpur	15,961	2,855	18,816
Muzaffarnagar	12,792	6,637	19,429

Distribution of the Tagas according to the Census of 1891—concld.

DISTRICT.	Hindus.	Muhammadans.	TOTAL.
Meerut	43,290	12,049	55,339
Bulandshahr . . .	6,508	40	6,548
Bijnor	10,952	...	10,952
Budâun	21	...	21
Morâdâbâd . . .	9,822	6,537	16,359
Shâhjahânpur	1	...	1
Tarâi	49	...	49
Hardoi	1	...	1
TOTAL .	99,409	28,118	127,527

Tambâkugar, Tamkhera.—A dealer in tobacco (*tambâku*) This is hardly a caste, but was recorded as such in some of the Census schedules. One of the earliest references to tobacco in India is in the memoirs of the Emperor Jahângîr [1] where he writes:—"As the smoking of tobacco (*tambâku*) had taken very bad effect upon the health and mind of many persons, I ordered that no one should practise the habit. My brother Shâh Abbâs, also being aware of its evil effects, had issued a command against the use of it in Irân· But Khâni Alam was so much addicted to smoking that he could not abstain from it and often smoked."

Tamboli, Tamoli.[2]—(Sanscrit *tâmbûla,* the pungent and aromatic leaf of the *piper betel*).—The caste which is devoted to the cultivation and sale of *pân* (Sanskrit *parna,* "the leaf," *par excellence*). The man who cultivates the plant is properly called Barai (*q. v.*); but the respective functions of the Tamboli and Barai are not clearly defined. In Benares, according Mr. Sherring,[3] there is no real distinction between them. There the Tamboli sells betel-nut as well as *pân,* and appears to be more of a wholesale trader

[1] Dowson's Elliot, VI, 351; *Indian Antiquary,* I, 164.

[2] Based on enquiries at Mirzapur and notes by M. Chhotê Lâl, Archæological Survey, Lucknow; Mr. A. B. Bruce, C. S., Ghazipur.

[3] *Hindu Tribes and Castes,* I, 330.

than the Barai. The sub-castes of both Tambolis and Barais are very similar, and if there is any real distinction it is very ordinarily overlooked.

Internal structure.

2. At the last Census they were enumerated under the sub-castes of Chaurasiya, who seem to take their name from Pargana Chaurâsi in the Mirzapur District; Barai, Jaiswâr, from the town of Jais in the Râê Bareli District; and Kathyâr. In Agra we find the Barai, Chaurasiya, and Kathwâr, who are probably the Kathyâr of the Census enumeration and do not allow widow marriage. In Gorakhpur are the Tenduhâra, who are named from the *tendu* (Sanskrit *tinduka*) the tree *diospyros embryopteris*, the fruit of which is occasionally eaten, and the Jaiswâr. In Lucknow we find the Chaurasiya, Jaiswâr, Sribâstav, who are named from the town of Srâvasti, the present Sahet-Mahet of Gonda, and the Jaunpuriya. In Ghâzipur we have the Nâsarkhâni, Chaurasiya, Bhadesiya, and Mathesiya or Madhesiya, who are residents of Madhyadesa, "the middle land." Another enumeration from Ghâzipur gives the sub-castes as Nâsarkhâni, Kharwâra, and Turk or Muhammadan Tambolis. In Allahâbâd are the Chaurasiya, Jaiswâr, and Sribâstav. The complete Census lists show 244 sub-divisions of the usual type, many taken from well known castes and septs, such as Aheriya, Bagheli, Baiswâla, Chhatri, Gaur, Gaharwâr, Jâdon, Janwâr, Kahâr, Kâyasthwâr, Kalwâr, Luniya, Nâgbansi, Nandbansi, Raghubansi, Râjput, Râthaur, Râwat, Thâkur, with local sub-divisions, like Aharwâr, Ajudhyabâsi, Bindrabani, Chaurasiya, Gangapâri, Jaiswâr, Jamunapâri, Jaunpuriya, Kanaujiya, Mathuriya, and Sribâstavi. All these are endogamous, and the only regular rule of exogamy is that a man cannot intermarry with a family with which, during human memory, his family has been connected by marriage.

Domestic ceremonies.

3. Among the better classes marriage usually takes place in infancy, and the bride does not come to live with her husband until she is nubile, when there is a second ceremony (*gauna.*) All the Tambolis, except the Kathyâr sub-caste, appear to allow widow marriage and the levirate, but the latter is not compulsory on the widow. Polygamy is allowed, and a man can put away his wife by leave of the tribal council if she is guilty of adultery or of some other act which involves excommunication from the caste. In their domestic ceremonies the Tambolis follow the orthodox rules current among the

trading castes of the same social grade. They cremate their adult dead and perform the usual *sráddha*. At marriage the Tambolis of the east of the Province have a rite, which seems special to them' called *Ahorbahor*; the bride and bridegroom jointly pay five visits to the family of the other before they finally live together.

Religion.

4. By preference they seem to be usually Vaishnavas. But they have no special connection with any particular sect. In Lucknow some are said to be Saivas, Sâktas, Nânakshâhis or Kabîrpanthis. There some worship Brahm Gusâîn and Narsinha, and some affect the Vamachâri worship of Bhîtari Devi. Early in the morning, when they open their shops, they burn some incense before the little wooden box in which they keep their *pán*, with a view to propitiate Lakshmi, the goddess of wealth. In November the Tambolis of Ghâzipur go to a place called Magha, in the Patna District, where a particularly fine kind of *pán*, called *Magahi pán*, is grown. There is here a temple known as that of Sokha Bâba, containing a lingam of Mahâdeva, which they all worship and invoke prosperity in their trade. Some of the offerings are brought home and distributed among friends and relations. On their return, an offering of a bundle and a quarter of the leaves is made to Mahâbîr on a Tuesday, which is his day.

Occupation and social status.

5. The special occupation of the caste is the cultivation and sale of *pán*. The leaves are made up and sold in bundles of two hundred each, known as a *dholi* of *pán*. There are numerous varieties. Mr. Hoey [1] enumerates in Lucknow the *Kapúri*, *Kaker*, *Bangla* or Bengali, *Begami*, *Desáwari* or "foreign," and *Kalkatiya* or Calcutta *pán*. Abûl Fazl names six varieties.[2] "The leaf called Bilahri is white and shining, and does not make the tongue harsh and hard. It tastes best of all kinds. After it has been taken away from the creeper, it turns white with some care after a month, or even after twenty days, when greater efforts are made. The Kakar leaf is white, with spots, and full, and has hard veins. When much of it is eaten the tongue gets hard. The Jaiswâr leaf does not get white, and is profitably sold, mixed with other kinds. The Kapûri leaf is yellowish, hard, and full of veins, but has a good taste and smell. The Kapûrkant leaf is yellowish-green, and

---

[1] *Monograph*, 189.

[2] Blochmann, *Aîn i-Akbari*, 1, 72.

pungent like pepper; it smells like camphor. You could not eat more than ten leaves. It is to be had at Benares, but even there it does not thrive in every soil. The Banglah leaf is broad, full, hard, plushy, hot and pungent." The leaf is made up for sale with catechu (*katha*), lime (*chúna*), betel-nut (*supári*), and cardamoms (*iláchi*), and is then khown as *bíra* or *gilauri*.

6. The Tamboli, from his connection with the production and sale of what is almost a necessity in Indian life, holds a fairly respectable position. They observe a high degree of personal purity, and will eat *kachchi* only if cooked by a member of their own caste, and *pakki* cooked by a Brâhman or Halwâi. They will eat goat's flesh and fish, but not, of course, beef or pork. Many of them are Bhagats, and avoid the use of meat and spirituous liquor, the latter of which is permitted to those under no special vow. They have a special reverence for the conservatory (*bhít*) in which the creeper is raised, which is carefully protected from any kind of ceremonial pollution, and for the scissors (*sarauta*) used in preparing the leaf. *Pán* of course finds a place in the popular wisdom of the countryside:—

Suhbat achchhi baithê khâiyê Nágar pán. Buri suhbat baithkê kataiye nák aur kán—"Sit in good company and eat Nâgar betel: sit in bad company and you get your nose and ears cut off."

Bina vasílé chákari, bina dhál kê jwán, ye tínon phíke lagén, bina tamáku pán—"Service without a patron, a young man without a shield, and betel without tobacco are all four tasteless."

Distribution of the Tambolis according to the Census of 1891.

Districts.	Hindus.					Muhammadans	Total.
	Barai.	Chaurasiya.	Jaiswâr.	Kathyâr.	Others.		
Dehra Dûn . .	24	62	12	...	37	...	135
Sahâranpur . .	...	7	...	...	97	...	104
Muzaffarnagar . .	...	11	...	...	61	...	72
Meerut . . .	...	...	...	...	320	3	323
Bulandshahr . .	...	...	...	...	94	77	171
Aligarh . . .	...	...	...	5	429	8	442

Distribution of the Tambolis according to the Census of 1891—continued.

Districts.	Hindus.					Muhammadans	Total.
	Barai.	Chaurasiya.	Jaiswâr.	Kathyâr.	Others.		
Mathura	...	24	1	...	510	13	548
Agra	...	164	...	44	448	44	700
Farrukhâbâd	...	1,276	...	837	81	...	2,194
Mainpuri	...	178	12	404	241	...	835
Etâwah	25	721	...	34	162	...	942
Etah	...	2	...	218	106	29	355
Bareilly	18	305	...	579	20	...	922
Bijnor	...	...	...	20	73	...	93
Budâun	...	...	...	252	95	...	347
Morâdâbâd	...	...	...	...	222	40	262
Shâhjahânpur	36	197	...	1,533	160	...	1,926
Pilibhît	...	51	6	...	491	...	548
Cawnpur	56	5,261	52	6	363	...	5,738
Fatehpur	...	2,658	...	...	269	...	2,927
Bânda	22	912	6	9	337	...	1,286
Hamîrpur	17	702	...	...	172	...	891
Allahâbâd	...	183	...	...	...	...	183
Jhânsi	...	25	2	454	33	...	514
Jâlaun	...	440	...	...	509	...	949
Benares	...	1,146	172	...	1,117	...	2,435
Mirzapur	...	429	...	...	31	...	460
Jaunpur	...	11	...	...	...	...	11
Ghâzipur	...	2	...	...	...	39	41
Gorakhpur	41	146	559	...	325	...	1,071
Basti	...	...	...	...	217	11	228
Azamgarh	...	...	...	...	60	...	60

Distribution of the Tambolis according to the Census of 1891—concluded.

Districts.	Hindus.					Muhammadans	Total.
	Barai.	Chaurasiya.	Jaiswâr.	Kathyâr.	Others		
Kumaun . . .	...	...	...	...	35	...	35
Garhwâl . . .	...	...	...	...	...	...	...
Tarâi . . .	...	1	...	15	127	...	143
Lucknow . . .	...	5,307	492	50	749	...	6,598
Unâo . . .	105	8,500	2	1,029	340	...	9,976
Râê Bareli . . .	...	6,505	786	906	662	...	8,859
Sîtapur . . .	730	960	1,901	1,970	797	...	6,358
Hardoi . . .	...	483	...	...	14	...	497
Kheri . . .	183	...	1,163	...	24	...	1,370
Faizâbâd . . .	...	2	545	...	48	...	593
Gonda . . .	...	...	347	...	13	...	362
Bahrâich . . .	...	39	3,933	...	1,625	6	5,603
Sultânpur . . .	...	1	136	...	273	...	410
Bârabanki . .	...	2,517	1,993	...	884	...	5,394
Total .	1,257	39,228	12,120	8,365	12,671	270	73,911

Tânk.—A sept of Râjputs in the Western Districts. Regarding the Tak or Takshak Colonel Tod has various curious speculations.[1] General Cunningham[2] says that the Takkas of the hills are Turanians, "because they are certainly not Aryas." M. St. Martin identifies the Ganganoi or Tanganoi of Ptolemy with the Tangana of the Mahâbhârat and the Tânk Râjputs.[3]

2. The Tânk Râjputs in Mainpuri[4] say that they are Yaduvansis, and claim kinship with the Yâdava princes of Jaysalmir and Kurâoli. They originally settled in a cluster of twelve-and-half villages round Kosma, in the Ghiror Pargana, which still

[1] *Annals*, I, 111; Dowson's Elliot, *History*, I, 504, Appendix.
[2] *Archæological Report*, II, 6, 899.
[3] *Indian Antiquary*, XIII, 376.
[4] *Settlement Report*, 21.

remains the seat of the clan. In former times they were noted for their predatory habits, and even now the character of the heads of the clan is not above suspicion. During the reign of Akbar, the Kosma men, headed by the two sons of their late chief, attacked and plundered some imperial stores passing through the District, and as a punishment for this daring robbery, one of the brothers was carried off to the capital and there compelled to embrace the Muhammadan faith.

3. This accounts for the singular division even now existing of the Kosma family into two sections: Kosma Musalmân and Kosma Hindu. It is a curious fact that Ja'afar Khân, the head of the Muhammadan section, is, equally with Gulâb Sinh, the head of the Hindu branch, looked up to by the whole Tânk community, and his joint headship is fully recognised by every member in matters affecting the internal economy of the clan. The customs of the Muhammadan brotherhood still partake greatly of a Hindu character. At the ceremonies attendant on births, marriages, deaths, and at meetings of the tribal council amongst the Hindu brotherhood, Ja'afar Khân is always summoned and takes a prominent part.

Distribution of the Tânk Râjputs according to the Census of 1891.

DISTRICT.	Numbers.	DISTRICT.	Numbers.
Sahâranpur . . .	13	Budâun . . .	5
Meerut . .	58	Morâdâbâd . . .	43
Bulandshahr . . .	21	Shâhjahânpur . .	229
Mathura . . .	52	Pilibhît . . .	104
Agra . . .	147	Cawnpur . . .	159
Farrukhâbâd . .	128	Bânda . . .	1
Mainpuri . . .	1,104	Jhânsi . . .	647
Etâwah . . .	110	Jâlaun . . .	87
Etah . . .	52	Ghâzipur . . .	1
Bareilly . . .	4	Tarâi . . .	17
		TOTAL .	2,982

Tarkihâr [*tarki*, "a woman's earring," so called because originally made of the palm (*târ*) leaf; *kâra* maker].—The caste who make women's ear ornaments out of the palm leaf. They are a purely occupational caste. They call themselves in Mirzapur Bais Râjputs. In Gorakhpur they apparently pretend to be Brâhmans, as, according to Dr. Buchanan[1] "twenty-six houses of Brâhmans, but of what kind is not known, have suffered disgrace by making earrings of palm leaves, and are excluded from intermarriage with others; still, however, they are entitled to receive the whole Gâyatri, and should be exempt from capital punishment." The Census returns show 37 endogamous sections of the Hindu and two of the Musalmân branch, which are all of the type already familiar among these minor castes. They practise the ordinary rule of exogamy, which forbids marriage in the family of the paternal and maternal uncle and the paternal and maternal aunt for three generations. Girls are married between the ages of five and eleven. A man can marry a second time while his first wife is alive, only with the sanction of the tribal council (*panchâyat*), but this permission is given only on the condition that the applicant gives two feasts to the clansmen.

Marriage.

2. To the east of the Province marriage is conducted in the four standard forms: *charhauwa* for respectable people, *dola* for poor people, *sagâi* for widows, and *adala badala* or exchange when two families agree to exchange daughters, which Dr. Westermarck calls the simplest way of purchasing a wife.[2] In the regular forms of marriage the binding portion of the ceremony is the solemn giving away of the bride (*kanyâdân*) to the bridegroom by her father and the rubbing by the bridegroom of red lead on the parting of the bride's hair (*sendûrdân*). Widows can remarry by *Sagâi*, which they assert to be a practice of comparatively recent origin among them. The levirate is permitted under the usual conditions, but is not obligatory. The only ceremony in widow marriage is the bridegroom eating with the friends of his future wife, dressing her in a suit of clothes and ornaments provided by her future husband; and giving a feast to his clansmen when he introduces her into his family.

---

[1] *Eastern India*, II, 454.

[2] *History of Human Marriage*, 390.

3. They are orthodox Hindus and to the east of the Province employ Tiwâri Brâhmans of the Sarwariya tribe as their family priests. They usually worship Devi in her form as Bhâgawati, the Pânchon Pîr, and especially Ghâzi Miyân: to the south of Mirzapur, Hardiha Deva or Hardaur Lâla. These deities receive an offering of sweetmeats, cakes (*malída*), betel leaves, garlands of flowers, and occasionally a cock is sacrificed. This is not consumed by the worshippers but presented to a Muhammadan faqîr. Bhâgawati is sometimes worshipped by pouring a mixture of pepper, sugar, and water (*mirchwân*) at her shrine.

Religion.

4. Their primary occupation is making the *tarki*, a cylinder of folded palm leaves nearly an inch in diameter and with an outer boss decorated with beads, etc., which is worn by low caste Hindu women stuck through a hole in the lobe of the ear. They also go about to fairs and sell red lead (*sindur*), and forehead spangles (*tikuli*), which are worn by married women. They also sell various kinds of spices. They use liquor and eat the flesh of sheep, goats, deer, and fish. Brâhmans will drink water from their hands. Only Chamârs and menial tribes will eat *kachchi* or *pakki* cooked by them. They eat *pakki* cooked by all the Vaisya tribes, expect Kalwârs, Telis, and Bharbhûnjas.

Occupation.

Distribution of the Tarkihârs according to the Census of 1891.

DISTRICT.	Hindus.	Muhammadans.	TOTAL.
Cawnpur	59	...	59
Fatehpur	105	...	105
Bânda	309	8	317
Allahâbâd	347	6	353
Mirzapur	7	...	7
Jaunpur	48	...	48
Gorakhpur	13	...	13
Azamgarh	3	...	3

Distribution of the Tarkihars according to the Census of 1891—concluded.

District.	Hindus.	Muhammadans.	Total.
Lucknow	811	...	811
Unâo	123	...	123
Râê Bareli	361	...	361
Faizâbâd	33	...	33
Gonda	9	...	9
Bahrâich	96	...	96
Sultânpur	147	...	147
Partâbgarh	200	...	200
Bârabanki	62	...	62
Total	2,733	14	2,747

Tarmâli.—A sub-caste of Pâsis who have been separately enumerated at the last Census. They take their name from *târ-malna* "to press the toddy palm tree." They are recorded to the number of 27 only in Faizâbâd.

Tawâif (plural of *taifa*, "a troop or company of dancing-girls"[1]).—The caste of dancing-girls and prostitutes. The term is a general one, but is more generally applied to those who are of the Muhammadan faith. The Hindu branch is often called by the title Pâtar, Patoriva, Pâtur, Paturiya from the Sanskrit *pâtra*, "an actor." Kanchan, which is usually derived from the Sanskrit *kanchuna*, "gold" (but this is far from certain), is usually regarded as the equivalent of Tawâif and denotes the Muhammadan branch. The ordinary prostitute, of whatever religion she may be, is often known as Randi (*rânr*), Sanskrit *randa*, "mutilated," "a widow," from which class, where widow marriage is prohibited, the class is commonly recruited, or Kasbi (Arabic *Kasb*, harlotry). The large class who prostitute *sub rosâ* or live as kept mistresses

[1] Mainly based on enquiries at Mirzapur and notes by Chaudhari Dhyân Sinh, Moradâbâd ; M. Chhotê Lâl, Lucknow ; M. Sayyid Ali Bahâdur, Partâbgarh.

are generally known as Khânagi, "domestic" (*khâna*, "a house") or Harjâi, "a gadabout." The last Census classes most of the Hindu dancing-girls and prostitutes as Paturiya, and the Muhammadans as Tawâif. The lists of the so-called sub-castes of the Paturiya contain a number of names, no less than forty-nine in all, which it is impossible to class by any definite principle. Of these the best known are the Bharua (Sanskrit *bhâta*, "wages"), who is a pimp or pander; Gandharap, who represent, in name at least, the Gandharva of the old mythology, who lived in the sky, prepared the *soma* juice for the gods, were partial to women, over whom they exercised a mystic influence; Kanchan, Kasbi, Kashmîri, who are usually classed with Nats, the Râmjani (Sanskrit *râma-jani* "charming woman,") whose name the English sailor and soldier corrupts into Rummy Johnny; and the Râsdhâri, a name which means "singer," and is specially applied at Mathura to a set of Brâhmans who perform a sort of miracle play describing the loves of Krishna and his consort Râdha.[1]

2. Similarly the term Tawâif includes a number of distinct classes. Among these are the Gandharap, Kanchan, Kashmîri, Paturiya, and Râmjani, already mentioned, among the Hindu class, and the Baksariya or "those who come from Baksar" in Bengal; the Hurukiya, who take their name from the *huruk* (Sanskrit *hudduka*), the small drum, shaped like an hour glass, to which they dance; the Kabûtari, who is usually classed with the Nats, and is so called because she has the flirting ways of a pigeon (*kabûtar*); the Mangta or "beggars;" the Mirâsi, who is a Dom singer; the Miskâr or Mîrshikâr, "the chief huntsman," who is a Baheliya; and the Nâik or Nâika (Sanskrit *nayaka*, "leader"), a term specially applied to the mistress of a brothel. In addition to these is the Gaunhârin or "attendant" (Sanskrit *gamanadhâra*), who attends at festivals and occasions of rejoicing, and sings and dances to the music of the violin (*saringi*) and the drum (*tabla*); the Brajbâsi or "resident of the land of Braj," who, like the Râsdhâri, is associated with the dances in honour of Krishna and Râdha; and the Negpâtar, who receives dues (*neg*) for performances.

3. Of such a miscellaneous class as this it is impossible to give more than some notes of the more interesting sub-divisions.

---

[1] Growse, *Mathura*, 75, *sq.*

The Nâiks of Kumaun.

4. Of the Kumaun Nâiks Mr. Atkinson writes :[1] —" The Nâiks, whose pretty village in the Râmgarh valley and settlements at Haldwâni are so striking, owe their origin to the wars of Bharati Chand with Doti, when the first standing armies in Kumaun took the field, and the soldiers contracted temporary alliances with the women of the place, whose descendants became known as Khatakwâla, and eventually, Nâik The offspring of these professional prostitutes, if a male, is called Nâyak or Nâik; and if a female, Pâta. They soon became celebrated all over India, and in 1554 A.D. Shîr Shâh undertook the siege of Kalinjar to secure possession of a Pâta kept by Kirat Sinh. Notwithstanding their origin the Nâyaks contrive to belong to that well-abused *gotra*, the Bhâradvaja, and to the great mid-Hind *Sákha*. They even wear the sacred thread, though with only three strands, like the common Khasiya. They marry their sons into Râjput families on paying a considerable sum, but devote all their daughters to prostitution. Nâyaks live by cultivation and trade, and their villages in the Bhâbar are about the best. The son can succeed to the property of his uncle, and the daughters can leave their property to any relative. If a daughter has a son, he performs her funeral ceremonies; if not, her brother performs them. They are attached to the left hand *Sákta* ceremonial, and eat animal food, and are, strange to say, reported to be careful in ceremonial observances. They have a story of their own; of a brother and sister going on pilgrimage to Badarinâth, and the latter falling into evil ways; but the account first given is more probable, and has better evidence to support it."

5. According to another story one of the Kings of Kumaun had two slave girls: one of whom married a Râjput, and her descendants are known as Râjkanya; and the other, who married a Hill Chhatri, was the ancestress of the Pâtars. The Pâtars are Hindus and worship Devi, Bholanâth, Kallu Pîr, and Bhairon. Their girls are trained in singing and dancing and prostitute themselves. They are not married in their own tribe, which procures wives by purchase from other castes. When they are nubile the Pâtar girls marry a *pîpal* tree, and then commence their career of prostitution. The Râjkanyas dance in the temples of the Hindu gods, and among them prostitution is said to be rare.

---

[1] *Himalayan Gazetteer*, III, 448.

6. Of ten classes of prostitutes found ordinarily in the plains, two, the Râmjani and Gandharap, are practically all Hindus : the Magahiya, Chhâta, Janghariya Naurangi, Mirâsi, Gaunhârin, Domin and Akâshkâmini are nearly all Muhammadans. None of these marry their daughters. When their sons reach marriageable age they purchase a girl of some low Hindu or Muhammadan tribe and marry her to him. These married women are not allowed to prostitute. The sons, as they grow up, are supported by the earnings of the girls, and act as their pimps and attendant musicians (*bhanrua*). They wander about from one inn (*sarâi*) and town to another in search of business, and attend marriages and festivals, where they sing and dance. Hindus have, generally, as their personal god (*Ishtadevata*) Krishna, and as their guardian deity Mahâdeva. They employ the very lowest class of Brâhmans in their domestic ceremonies, and cremate their dead.

Other Hindu prostitutes.

7. Muhammadans admit any Musalmân girl to their society, and Hindus, after they have embraced Islâm. They are continually recruited from Hindu widows, and discarded or deserted wives. When a girl is seven or eight years old, she is put under the instruction of a Dhârhi or Kathak, who teaches her to dance and sing. At the commencement of her education, some sweetmeats are offered at a mosque, and then distributed among Muhammadan faqîrs. At the first lesson the master is given a present in money and some sweetmeats, and their fees are about four or five rupees *per mensem*. When the girl reaches puberty and the breast begins to develop the rite of *angiya* or the "assumption of the boddice" is performed. On this occasion some of the brethren are feasted. After this the girl is sold to some rich paramour. This is known as *Sir dhankâi* or "the covering of the head." When she returns after her first visit to her paramour, the brethren are feasted on sweetmeats. After this follows the rite of *missi*, which takes its name from the black powder used in colouring the teeth.

Muhammadan prostitutes.

She is dressed like a bride and is taken in procession through the streets and afterwards takes her seat at a party (*mahfil*), where the brethren assemble and sing and dance. Her teachers (*ustâd*) are remunerated, and the brethren are fed on *kachchi* and *pakki* according to the means of the family. This feast may be postponed ; but in that case she cannot stain her teeth until it is duly performed, and some sort of entertainment of the brotherhood is obligatory. This rule is said now at Lucknow to be gradually relaxed. The *missi* represents the final initiation into a life of harlotry. After the rite of *missi* the girl ceases to wear the nose-ring, and hence the ceremony is sometimes known as *nathni utarna*, the taking off of nose-ring.

Temporary marriage.

8. Some of these girls contract what are known as temporary or usufructuary marriages (*mut'ah*). In the *Aîn-i-Akbari* there is a curious account of a discussion in the presence of the Emperor Akbar as to the legality of such unions. The case was finally thus summed up by Badâoni. Imâm Malik, and the Shiahs are unanimous in looking upon *Mut'ah* marriages as legal; Imâm Ash-Shâfi' and the great Imâm Ali Hanîfah look on *mut'ah* marriages as illegal. But should at any time a Qâzi of the Malaki sect decide that *mut'ah* is legal, it is legal, according to the common belief, even for Shâfi's and Hanîfahs. Every other opinion on this subject is idle talk. This pleased the Emperor, and he at once appointed a Qâzi, who gave a decree which made *mut'ah* marriages legal.[1]

Social tolerance of prostitutes.

9. One curious point as regards Indian prostitutes is the tolerance with which they are received into even respectable houses, and the absence of that strong social disfavour in which this class is held in European countries. This feeling has prevailed for a lengthened period. We read in the Buddhist histories of Ambapâta, the famous courtesan of Visala, and of the Princess Salawati, who was appointed courtesan, and the price of her favours fixed at two thousand masurans.[2] The same feeling appears in the folk-tales and early records of Indian castes.[3] It has been supposed that this idea is based on the prevalence of communistic marriage.[4]

The Saint Tânsen.

10. Tânsen, the celebrated musician, is a sort of patron saint of dancing-girls. He was a native of Patna and a disciple of the famous Hari Dâs Gusâîn, of Bindraban. He went to the court of Akbar, became a Muhammadan,

---

[1] Blochmann, *Aîn-i-Akbari*, I, 173.

[2] Hardy, *Manual of Buddhism*, 244.

[3] Tawney, *Katha Sarit Sâgara*, I, 354; II, 621: *Dábistân*, II, 154.

[4] Darwin, *Descent of Man*, II, 361: Lubbock, *Origin of Civilisation*, 96: Wake, *Serpent Worship*, 149: Robertson Smith, *Kinship*, 143: Westermarck, *History of Human Marriage*, 80.

and is buried at Gwâlior. It is said that he used to listen to the men singing at the well and appropriate their melodies. His contemporary and rival Brij Baula was able, it is said, to split a rock with a single note. The story goes that he learnt his bass from the creaking of the flour-mill. It is believed that chewing the leaves of the tree over the grave of Tânsen gives an astonishing melody to the voice, and singing girls make pilgrimages there for this purpose.[1]

Distribution of castes of Prostitutes and Dancing-girls according to the Census of 1891.

District.	Hindu.	Musalmân.			Total.
		Tawâif.		Others.	
	Paturiya.	Bakariya.	Harkaya.		
Dehra Dûn . . .	...	...	...	11	11
Sahârunpur . . .	43	...	...	707	750
Muzaffarnagar . .	2	1	1	537	541
Meerut . . .	...	...	...	571	571
Bulandshahr . .	1	...	...	474	475
Aligarh . . .	4	...	4	250	258
Mathura . . .	...	3	...	87	90
Agra	2	...	105	272	379
Farrukhâbâd . .	182	236	...	1,036	1,454
Mainpuri . . .	...	...	26	500	526
Etâwah . . .	...	...	513	581	1,094
Etah . . .	...	...	...	1,080	1,080
Bareilly . . .	...	...	...	74	74
Bijnor . . .	...	...	...	260	260
Budâun . . .	98	...	...	591	689
Morâdâbâd . . .	[illegible]	...	...	211	219

[1] Bholanâth Chandra, *Travels*, II, 68, *sq.*: Sleeman, *Rambles*, II, 333, *sq.*: Cunningham, *Archæological Reports*, II, 370; XXI, 110.

Distribution of castes of Prostitutes and Dancing-girls according to the Census of 1891—continued.

DISTRICT.	HINDU.	MUSALMÂN.			TOTAL.
	Paturiya.	Tawâif.		Others.	
		Bakariya.	Hurkaya.		
Shâhjahânpur . .	59	...	...	593	652
Pilibhît . . .	...		...	90	90
Cawnpur . . .	106	...	7	943	1,056
Fatehpur . . .	18	18	...	479	515
Bânda . . .	75	...	...	89	164
Hamîrpur . . .	7	...	...	72	79
Allahâbâd . . .	159	...	...	360	519
Jhânsi . . .	...	...	...	61	61
Jâlaun . . .	11	...	6	103	120
Lalitpur . . .	...	...	...	9	9
Benares . . .	301	...	...	125	426
Mirzapur . . .	74	...	...	84	158
Jaunpur . . .	763	...	...	170	933
Ghâzipur . . .	807	...	...	854	1,661
Ballia. . . .	117	...	...	213	330
Gorakhpur . .	207	...	...	1,490	1,697
Basti	69	...	...	27	96
Azamgarh . . .	1,160	...	...	426	1,586
Kumaun . . .	63	...	...	...	63
Tarâi . . .	...	...	...	21	21
Lucknow . . .	21	22	...	567	610
Unâo . . .	21	9	...	335	365
Râê Bareli . . .	5	...	42	545	592
Sîtapur . . .	16	4	4	1,371	1,395

Distribution of castes of Prostitutes and Dancing-girls according to the Census of 1891—concluded.

District.	Hindu.	Musalmân.			Total.
	Paturiya.	Tawâif.		Others.	
		Bakariya.	Hurkaya.		
Hardoi . . .	7	...	...	1,801	1,808
Kheri . . .	...	...	...	850	850
Faizâbâd . . .	2	...	...	87	89
Gonda . . .	180	...	...	324	504
Bahrâich . . .	36	...	10	936	982
Sultânpur . . .	86	...	...	612	698
Partâbgarh . . .	...	...	...	395	395
Bârabanki . . .	...	...	...	684	684
Total .	4,710	293	718	21,958	27,679

Teli[1]—(Sanskrit *tailika, taila,* "oil expressed from sesamum, mustard, etc.,").—A large caste of pressers of oil and traders in various commodities. The caste is probably a functional group which Mr. Risley[2] thinks must have been recruited from the respectable class of Hindu society, because "oil is used by all Hindus for domestic and ceremonial purposes, and its manufacture could only be carried on by men whose social purity was beyond dispute." Whatever the case may be in Bengal, in Northern India there is no special idea of purity attached to the Teli; in fact it is probably not too much to say that the reverse is the fact. Mr. Ibbetson[3] says of the Panjâb:—"The Teli is of low social standing, perhaps about the same as that of the Julâha, with whom he is often associated, and he is hardly less turbulent and troublesome than the latter."

Tribal traditions.

2. The tribe seems to be singularly destitute of traditions of origin. In most of our Districts all they can say is that they are indigenous. The

[1] Based on enquiries at Mirzapur and notes by the Deputy Inspectors of Schools, Farrukhâbâd, Agra, Azamgarh, Basti.

[2] *Tribes and Castes*, II, 305.

[3] *Panjáb Ethnography*, paragraph 647.

sub-divisions with local names derive, of course, their origin from the places which supply their title. In Mirzapur they tell a story that there was once a man who had three sons and owned fifty-two *mahua* trees (*bassia latifolia*). When he became aged and infirm, he took his sons to the grove and told them to divide them among themselves. After some discussion they decided not to divide the trees, but the produce of them. One of them fell to collecting the leaves and he became a Bharbhûnja or grain-parcher, who still uses leaves in his oven; the second collected the flowers and corollas and, having distilled them, became a Kalwâr; the third collected the kernels (*koina*), crushed them and became a Teli.

Internal structure.

3. At the last census the Telis were classed in a number of endogamous sub-castes: Byâhut, who are so called because they do not allow widow marriage and marry virgin brides by the standard form (*byâh*); Jaiswâr, named from the old town of Jais in the Râê Bareli district; Jaunpuri, who trace their origin to Jaunpur; Kanaujiya to Kanauj; Mathuriya to Mathura; Râthaur, which is the name of a famous Râjput sept; Sribâstab from the ancient city of Srâvasti, now represented by the ruins of Sahet-Mahet in pargana Balrâmpur of the Gonda district; and Umarê, which is the name of one of the Banya sub-castes. It will be observed how largely local designations appear in this list. Besides these among the Muhammadan branch, we find the Bahlîm, Desi, Doâsna and Ekâsna. In Mirzapur we find the Kanaujiya, Sribâstava, Pachhiwâha or "Western;" Byâhuta, Bhainsaha, who carry goods on the male buffalo (*bhainsa*), Chachara, who are said to take their name from their fondness for the *chachar* (Sanskrit, *charchara*), the special song sung at the Holi festival; and the Turkiya or Muhammadan Teli. In Benares, according to Mr. Sherring,[1] the divisions are the Byâhutbans, the same as the Byâhuta mentioned above; the Kanaujiya; Jaunpuriya; Sribâstav; Banarasiya, or those of Benares, Jaiswâra; Lâhauri, from Lahore; and the Gulhariya and Gulhâni; of all of whom the Gulhâni are the lowest. The Jaunpuriya are said not to deal in oil but in pulse (*dâl*). In Farrukhâbâd we have the Râthaur, Parnâmi, Rethi, Jaiswâr, Sriwâr, Mathuriya, and Bhiân. In Basti we find the Biâhut, Jaunpuri, Kanaujiya, Turkiya, and Saithwâr, which last is a Kurmi sub-caste. In Pilibhît are the Purbiya or

---

[1] *Hindu Tribes and Castes*, I, 301.

"Eastern," Bhadauriya, which is a well-known Râjput sept, the Râthaur, Tilbhurjiya or parchers of sesamum. In Azamgarh the sub-castes are Jaunpuri, Byâhut, Kalaunjiya, which is possibly a corruption of Kanaujiya, Barbhaiya or "the greater brethren," Madhesiya or "dwellers in the middle land," Madhya-desa, which is, according to tradition, the country lying between the Himâlaya on the north, the Vindhya range on the south, Vinasama or Kurukshetra on the west, Prayâga or Allâhâbâd on the east; and Turk or the Musalmân Branch. In Agra we have the Râthaur, Chamâr Teli and Musalmân Teli. To the east of the Province again they are divided into the Pachpiriya or worshippers of the Pânchon Pîr, and the Mahabiriya or devotees of Mahâbîr. All these sub-castes are endogamous. In Azamgarh it is said that this is certainly the case with the Jaunpuri, Byâhut, and Barbhaiya; but that the Kalaunjiya and the Madhesiya sometimes intermarry. The census returns show 742 sections in the Hindu and 239 in the Muhammadan branch. Of these those of the greatest local importance are the Kaithiya of Mainpuri, the Parnâmi of Cawnpur, the Surahiya of Allahâbâd, the Bâtra of Jhânsi and Lalitpur, the Mâhur of Mirzapur, the Baraniya, Kaithiya, Mukeri and Parnâmi of Jaunpur, the Dakkhinâha and Jhijhautiya of Gorakhpur and Basti, the Bahrâichiya of Bahrâich, and the Makanpuri of Partâbgarh. To the east of the Province the rule of exogamy seems to be that a man cannot marry in his own family (*kul*) or in that of the maternal uncle or father's sister until at least three generations have passed. In Farrukhâbâd a man cannot marry a near relation or the descendant of a common ancestor or of a blood relation on the father's or mother's side as long as any relationship is remembered; he cannot marry two sisters at the same time, but he may marry the sister of his deceased wife.

Marriage customs.

4. Marriage customs of the Telis are of the usual respectable kind. All except the Byâhut, allow widow marriage. There are usually three forms of marriage: *Byâh, Shâdi, Charhaua* or *Charhéké,* when the marriage takes place according to the orthodox ritual at the house of the bride; *dola* when the ceremonies are done at the house of the bridegroom; and *dharauna* or *sagâi* for widows. Among the more respectable families the preference is for the marriage of a girl in infancy (*kunwâri*), and it is considered disreputable to keep a girl who has menstruated (*rajasthala, rojasula*) unmarried. To take the rules in Azamgarh

as an example, in *dharauna* or widow marriage, the binding portion of the rite is "foot worship" (*pâê-pûj*), when the father of the woman puts her hand in that of the bridegroom. In ordinary marriages the rite of *tilak* is performed twice, and if after the first the boy dies, the girl will not be regarded as a widow and can be married by the rite of *pâê-pûja*. The two occasions on which the *tilak* rite is performed are at betrothal (*mangani*) and at marriage. At betrothal the form is that the bride's father comes to the house of the bridegroom; at the appointed time he washes, first the right, and then the left foot of his future son-in-law, and throws some rice at his feet. Next, with the point of his thumb directed towards the boy's nose, he makes four lines, with curds, on his forehead; on the curd mark he sticks seven grains of rice, and touches the boy's forehead with the sacred *kusa* grass, water, curds, rice, and red sandalwood. During the *tilak* rite at marriage, if the bride be less than eleven years old, she is seated in the lap of her father; if above that age, on a leaf mat (*pattal*). After the *tilak* rite the girl's father puts her hand in that of her husband and lets some *kusa* grass, water, rice and money fall into his hand. A widow generally marries the younger brother of her late husband; but the levirate is not enfored, and the woman's right of choice is recognised. A wife can be divorced for adultery and a man for adultery with a woman of another caste. In both cases the sanction of the tribal council is essential.

Religion.

5. The Turkiya, Bahlîm, Desi, Doâsna and Ekâsna Telis are Muhammadans; the others are Hindus, but they seldom procure initiation into one of the standard sects. Their clan deities to the east of the Province are Ghâzi Miyân and other members of the quintette of the Pânchon Pîr, Hardiya or Hardaur Lâla, the godling of cholera, Mahâbîr and Mahâdeva. Ghâzi Miyân is worshipped with an offering of goats, fowls, rice, boiled with pulse (*khichari*), bread, garlands of flowers, a head dress (*muraith*), and a small loin cloth (*langot*). The other members of the Pânchon Pîr receive similar offerings. Bread, a Brâhmanical cord, and rose perfume (*'itr*) are offered to Mahâbîr and Mahâdeva. Hardiya receives, during cholera epidemics, a sacrifice of goats, fowls, and young pigs. In the Central Duâb a sacrifice of a goat or ram is made to Devi and to Shaikh Saddu, who is the women's godling. Any one can do the Devi sacrifice, but Shaikh Saddu is served by a Mujâwar. Among god-

lings of the aboriginal races they acknowledge Jakhai Deota, whose priest is a Dhânuk. They are served by Brâhmans of the usual officiant classes. They cremate their dead and perform the funeral rites according to the orthodox ritual.

Occupation and social status.

6. Their special business is the manufacture of oil, and in almost every bâzâr the Teli may be seen driving his little blind-folded ox round his oil mill. But the recent extension of the use of foreign mineral oils must be seriously interfering with his business. Medicinal oils are made by the Gandhi. The Teli usually makes at least three kinds of oil.[1] The first class includes linseed (*alsi, tísi*), mustard (*sarson*), poppy-seed (*dánaposta, khashkhash*), black mustard (*túya*) *mahua*, cocoanut (*gola náryal*), sesamum (*til*), *eruca sativa*, (*láhi*), safflower (*kusum*), *gehuán*, a wheat grass yielding grain, and the berries of the *ním* tree (*nímkauri*). These are all crushed and oil expressed from them in the ordinary mill (*kolhu*). Castor oil (*rendi ká tel*) forms a class in itself. The third class consists of some oils of a medicinal nature, such as that from the almond (*bádám*). Those who work the oil mill treat it as a sort of fetish and a representative of Mahâdeva, and worship it at the Dasahra festival. Many of them have taken to shopkeeping of various kinds, money-lending, dealing in grain, and agriculture. As a rule Telis will eat goat's flesh, mutton, fowls, and fish. Those of the Sribâstav sub-caste are said to eat pork. They will drink spirituous liquor. In Azamgarh the Barbhaiya sub-caste are said to be peculiar in refusing to wear any torn clothes, and if they cannot afford new clothes prefer to go partly unclothed. They are said to worship like Brâhmans. As has been already said, the social position of the Teli is not a high one. *Kahán Rája Bhoj, kahán Lakhu Teli?*—"What comparison is there between a real gentleman and a Teli upstart even if he be made of money?" *Teli kya jáné mushk ki sár?*—"What can a Teli know of the smell of musk?" The women say *Teli khasam kiya rukha kháwé*—" Marry a Teli and live on dry crusts." The Teli's ox is, of course, proverbial, *Teli ke bail ko ghar hi kos pachás*—" Though he stays at home the Teli's ox does his hundred miles," and *Teli ka bail* is the common term for the man who slaves for nothing.

[1] See Hoey, *Monograph*, 191, *sq.*

Distribution of Telis according to the Census of 1891.

Districts.	Hindus.									Muhammadans.					
	Byâhut.	Jaiswâr.	Jaunpuri.	Kanaujiya.	Mathuriya.	Râthaur.	Sribâstab.	Umarê.	Others.	Bâhlîm.	Desi.	Doâsna.	Ekâsna.	Others.	Total.
Dehra Dûn	437	212	...	...	...	...	...	...	90	157	...	...	...	2,668	3,564
Sahâranpur	1	91	...	...	...	...	...	...	248	573	4,048	4,276	1,434	37,438	48,109
Muzaffarnagar	...	...	...	...	...	...	...	...	8	50	326	8,550	...	3,358	12,292
Meerut	...	...	...	...	...	129	...	...	863	...	...	1,995	3,057	11,673	17,717
Bulandshahr	...	...	...	...	...	...	...	...	783	498	...	...	...	7,369	8,650
Aligarh	...	...	...	...	...	1,197	...	...	1,218	1,432	...	...	...	6,884	10,731
Mathura	...	...	...	...	...	659	...	...	1,274	...	...	...	...	4,427	6,360
Agra	...	...	...	4	...	7,204	1	...	1,417	...	...	...	...	4,513	13,139
Farrukhâbâd	15	...	...	88	32	14,743	83	...	260	...	...	...	...	...	15,221
Mainpuri	...	...	...	8	...	9,503	2,295	...	883	...	...	...	...	57	12,746
Etâwah	...	...	...	32	265	12,737	...	...	1,256	...	...	...	...	...	14,290

Etah	6	...	75	1	4,093	5,446	...	...	804	24	...	...	...	1,261	11,710
Bareilly	...	...	...	...	3,150	14,885	...	...	579	156	...	...	...	3,382	22,152
Bijnor	...	...	...	...	...	4	...	...	...	...	...	...	255	12,750	13,009
Budâun	...	...	...	...	3,773	6,958	...	...	211	369	21	...	...	3,703	15,035
Morâdâbâd	...	...	...	...	...	233	...	...	151	85	...	...	...	14,183	14,652
Shâhjahânpur	...	37	...	8	6	23,629	83	...	560	...	...	...	...	7	24,330
Pilibhît	2	69	37	64	2	10,450	...	...	608	500	2	...	...	343	12,077
Cawnpur	80	1,405	...	148	...	19,342	5,284	1,657	1,871	...	...	...	...	...	29,787
Fatehpur	40	118	...	15	...	...	11,557	278	1,148	...	...	...	...	5	13,161
Bânda	426	3	...	6	...	6	8,929	1,699	1,467	...	...	...	...	...	12,536
Hamîrpur	...	...	...	...	80	3,241	6,817	405	736	..	...	...	...	...	11,279
Allahâbâd	20,785	...	...	68	...	8	4,814	440	2,484	...	...	...	...	48	28,647
Jhânsi	...	6	...	...	...	753	751	...	7,536	...	...	...	...	4	9,050
Jâlaun	1,083	...	...	...	12	7,638	67	...	1,328	...	...	...	...	...	10,128
Lalitpur	...	...	...	...	...	...	...	...	6,963	...	...	...	...	...	6,963
Benares	15,645	...	1,273	1,077	...	...	...	...	2,455	...	...	...	...	...	20,450
Mirzapur	23,610	45	330	561	293	...	...	...	286	...	...	...	...	107	25,232

Distribution of Telis according to the Census of 1891—concluded.

District.	Hindus.									Muhammadans.					
	Byâhut.	Jaiswâr.	Jaunpuri.	Kanaujiya.	Mathuriya.	Râthaur.	Sribâstab.	Umarê.	Others.	Bahlîm.	Desi.	Doâsna.	Ekâsna.	Others.	Total.
Jaunpur	...	...	...	3,708	...	...	...	...	19,381	...	...	...	...	201	23,290
Ghâzipur	478	19	3,925	15,291	...	...	...	...	3,886	...	...	...	...	...	23,599
Ballia	45	...	259	23,987	...	...	...	...	254	...	...	...	...	...	24,545
Gorakhpur	1,072	440	24,040	54,462	...	...	47	...	6,056	245	...	...	...	1,437	87,799
Basti	22,282	438	6,469	1,425	...	...	...	...	2,934	1,847	...	...	...	4,930	40,325
Azamgarh	119	99	14,939	11,013	...	...	45	...	2,819	...	...	...	...	1,803	30,837
Tarâi	...	...	...	...	...	493	...	...	893	16	...	...	...	2,652	4,054
Lucknow	79	11,665	...	101	...	617	...	35	1,664	1,549	...	...	...	710	16,420
Unâo	1	10,529	1	26	44	9,005	...	...	812	...	...	...	...	...	20,418
Râe Bareli	...	13,133	17	204	...	...	...	...	8,217	27	...	...	...	174	21,772
Sîtapur	4	8,442	6	4,038	...	6,809	211	105	808	4,540	...	...	...	664	25,627

Hardoi . .	...	760	...	1	...	28,296	...	...	295	...	...	...	...	107	29,459
Kheri . .	...	5,604	...	2,524	...	9,857	1	...	73	733	...	...	...	187	18,979
Faizâbâd . .	4,432	1,523	8,812	236	...	...	191	...	478	1,396	...	...	...	925	17,993
Gonda . .	19,850	627	2,313	...	...	...	11	...	51	2,776	...	...	...	3,581	29,209
Bahrâich . .	4,931	5,433	107	10	...	229	...	1	2,177	3,079	...	...	...	5,096	21,063
Sultânpur . .	6,364	3,752	4,450	260	...	...	...	...	2,572	...	...	...	...	666	18,064
Partâbgarh .	11,202	31	402	65	...	...	...	...	3,885	...	..	...	...	6	15,591
Bârabanki .	...	9,939	...	4	...	...	...	...	758	4,604	...	...	...	6,665	21,970
TOTAL .	132,989	74,420	67,455	119,435	11,750	194,071	41,187	4,620	95,500	24,656	4,397	14,821	4,746	143,984	934,031

Thâru.[1]—A tribe which has its head-quarters in the Himâlayan Tarâi and colonies in the Gorakhpur Division and Northern Oudh. Mr. Nesfield, who has given an elaborate account of these people, says:—"To the east they extend about as far as the river Kusi, where they come in contact with the Mechas, a tribe similar to themselves in habits and features, and inhabiting that portion of the Tarâi which separates the plains of Bengal from the hills of Sikkhim. To the west they extend as far as the river Sârda, which flows between Kumaun and Nepâl. At this point they dovetail with another forest tribe similar to themselves in appearance and culture, the Bhuksas. The strictly Bhuksa country commences from the Gola or Kicha river, about thirty miles to the west of the Sârda, and extends westward as far as the Ganges, while a few straggling villages are to be found still further west as far as the Jumna. Between the Sârda and the Gola rivers there is a debateable tract, about thirty miles wide, in which both tribes occasionally reside. In one village at least, and probably in more, the inhabitants are the progeny of mixed parentage, although intermarriage between the tribes is not openly allowed by either."

Origin of the name.

2. Many attempts have been made to explain the origin of the Thâru.[2] Some of these are sufficiently absurd. Thus some derive it from *tahrê*, "they halted," after their alleged flight into the forest; others from *tarhua*, "wet," in allusion to the swampy nature of the tract in which they live. A Pandit told Mr. Carnegy that it was derived from *thal* (Sanskrit *sthala*, "firm ground"). They say themselves that they are Râjputs who ran away after the great fight at Hastinapur, and that their name means "Quaker," from *thatharâna*, "to tremble." Others say that the name simply means "residents of the Tarâi." Another suggestion is that it is derived from the Hindi *Athvâru*, "an eighth-day serf," a man who is bound to give his lord one day's labour in the week. "But," as Mr. Nesfield says, "this implies what is not true. The Thârus are remarkable

---

[1] Largely based on Mr. J. C. Nesfield's valuable article in the *Calcutta Review* (XXX-I) and the *Gospel in Gonda* by Rev. S. Knowles, with notes from M. Chhedi Lâl, Deputy Inspector, Schools, Gorakhpur; M. Mumtâz Ali Khân, Assistant Manager, Balrâmpur Estate, Gonda, and Bâbu Badari Nâth, Deputy Collector, Kheri.

[2] *Oudh Gazetteer*, II, 126; *North West Provinces Census Report*, 1867: I, 61; *North-West Provinces Gazetteer*, VI. 358; *Journal, Asiatic Society of Bengal* 1847, page 450; Carnegy, *Notes*, 8, Knowles, *loc. cit.*, 213.

for their indolence, aversion to service, and incapacity for sustained field labour, and they have never been in the position of serf to any landlord. Had this been the case, they would have sunk long ago into the ranks of Arakhs, Pâsis, Chamârs, Koris, and other Hindu castes of the lowest rank, who serve as field labourers or bond-slaves to landlords in the open plain, and have lost the free life of the forest which Thârus still enjoy."

3. A more probable attempt has been madè to connect it with some local root. Mr. Knowles says that it comes from a verb used by the hillmen, *thârna*, "to paddle about;" and hence Thâru means "a paddler." By another account *thâr* means "wine," and the name Thâru, or "wine bibber," was given them by one of the Kshatriya Râjas of the plains, who, when he invaded the hill country, was amazed at their drunken habits. "Another etymology," says Mr. Nesfield, "suggested is from *thâr*, which, in the colloquial language of the lowest classes, but not in the language of books, signifies, "forest;" and thus Thâru would mean "man of the forest," a name which correctly describes the status of the tribe. On the whole, however, it is safer not to search for any Hindi etymology, but to consider the name as sprung from the language of the tribe itself, which is now for the most part obsolete. An aboriginal name underived from any Sanskrit or neo-Sanskrit source is the fit appellative of an aboriginal, casteless and un-Brâhmanized tribe whose customs have been only slightly modified by contact with those of the Aryan invader."

Traditions of origin.

4. The origin of the Thârus has formed the subject of much controversy. One account is thus given by Dr. Buchanan:[1]—"The Gurkhas seem to have been soon expelled from Magadha by a people called Thâru, who are said to have descended from the hills and extended themselves over every part north of the Ghâghra at least. Of this people very numerous monuments are shown, and from these they would appear to have been an industrious, powerful race, as the number of great buildings in brick which they have left is very considerable. The Thârus, in fact, pretend to be the proper descendants of the Sun, and their having expelled the Gurkhas from their usurped estates, and their having descended for that pur-

[1] *Eastern India*, II, 341, *sq.*

pose from the hills, are not incompatible with that pretension. Their claims to rank are, however, treated with the utmost contempt, because they are an abomination to the Brâhmans, and indulge in all the impurities of eating and drinking." He goes on to say that they retain in their features strong marks of a Chinese or Tartar origin, although it must be confessed that these marks are somewhat softened, and that the faces of the men especially do not differ so much from those of the Hindus as those of a pure Chinese do. Still, however, a difference is observable even in the men, and in the women and children is very closely marked.

5. The tradition in East Oudh is that after the fall of the Buddhist dynasty of Kanauj, the Thârus descended from the hills and occupied Ajudhya. They dispossessed the Buddhists, called in Râja Sri Chandra, of Srinagar, in the hills about Badari Nâth, who drove back the Thârus, and, marching north, founded Chandravatipur, now known as Sahet-Mahet, or, as Mr. Hoey would call it, Set-Met or Srâvasti. Lassen, in his account of the later dynasty of Kanauj, describes an inscription which records that Sri Chandra Deva, the first of the great Râthaur Princes who came to the throne in 1072 A.D., was protector of the sacred places of Ajudhya and Kosala or Srâvasti.[1]

6. On the other hand they asserted to Mr. Knowles[2] that they were immigrants from the Dakkhin or the south country. In Bijnor they claim Chithor as their place of origin and refer to Jaymal and Patta. They say that they were driven out, apparently in the third siege of Chithor, by Akbar in 1567 A.D., and that they were originally Râjputs, who lost caste by using intoxicating liquor and rearing fowls. They never claim a Gurkha or hill origin. Interspersed with them are other tribes, generally called Thâru, but quite distinct, such as Gaharwâr, who also claim to be Râjputs. They never intermarry or eat with the Thârus, abstain from liquor, and never eat fowls. Others, again, as the Dangras, are looked down on as a lower caste by

---

[1] Mr. W. C. Benett, *Indian Antiquary*, II, 13, quoting Lassen: *Alterthumsk*, III, 751 Colebrooke, *Essays*, II, 286; *Asiatic Researches*, XV, 447, 457; *Journal Asiatic Society, Bengal*, X, 101.

[2] *Loc. cit.*, 209.

the Thârus.[1] Regarding the Chithor story, Mr. Nesfield says:—"Some Thârus know nothing about this tradition, and those who do are not able to tell you whether it was the sack by Alâuddîn (A.D. 1303), or that by Bahâdur Shâh (A.D. 1533), or that by Akbar (A.D. 1567). The story is absurd on the face of it; not the slightest allusion to Thârus in connection with any of these events is made by the Muhammadan historians. The fiction of having come from Rajputâna was invented by some of the clans merely to raise themselves in their own and their neighbour's estimation. There is scarcely a hunting tribe or caste in Upper India which has not set up a similar claim."[2]

6. He quotes another legend which centres round Raksha or Rikheswar, their patron saint or founder. "Both names are evidently corruptions of some obsolete Thâru word which has been toned down to suit the Hindi accent. According to the legend in vogue among the Thârus of Kheri, this deified founder was a son of the renowned aboriginal King, Râja Ben or Vena, whose name is still rife in many of the oldest cities of Upper India and Bihâr, as one who held the rank and title of Chakravartti or universal Emperor in the olden time. In Manu's Institutes[3] he is stigmatised as the first king who allowed a man to marry the wife of his deceased brother. According to Manu he died from the effects of his unbridled lusts. According to the Vishnu Purâna, he was beaten to death by a gang of saintly men armed with blades of holy grass, all of which had been consecrated with magic words. Benbans is still a title of several Dravidian tribes on the Vindhyan range. Rikheswar or Raksha was banished, it is said, from his father's court, and ordered, with his band of male followers, to seek for a new home in the north, from which they were never to return. Setting out on their wanderings, they took as their wives any women whom they could steal or capture on the road, and in this way the Thâru tribe was founded. It was not till they had reached the Sub-Himâlayan forest, in which they still dwell, that they decided to rest and settle. The soul of Raksha is still believed to hover among the people of his tribe, just as in ancient days he led them safely through the wide

[1] Mr. E. Colvin, *Census Report, North-West Provinces*, 1865, I, Appendix 60, *sqq*.

[2] *Loc. cit.*, 33.

[3] IX, 66.

wilderness into a new and distant settlement; so in the present day he is said to be the guardian and guide of men travelling on a distant journey. No Thâru ever sets out from his village for such a purpose without first propitiating him with gifts and promising him a sumptuous feast of flesh, milk, and wine on his return. His presence is represented by a mound of mud, with a stone fixed in the middle, and he delights in seeing the blood of a live capon dashed against this stone and to feel its blood trickling down the side. One peculiarity of this god is that he is deaf, an emblem of his antiquity; and hence vows and prayer are addressed to him in a stentorian tone of voice. The title Gurua, which is generally prefixed to his name, implies that during his residence on earth he was famous as a wizard or medicine man, and acquired through this means the kingship or leadership of his tribe."

Ethnical affinities of the Thârus.

8. Dr. Oldham [1] believes that the Thârus are Indian aborigines and certainly very different from the Tartar Highland races. That the tribe has suffered much admixture is quite certain. Mr. Nesfield [2] writes:—"Owing to the intermarriages which have taken place within the last two or three centuries between Thâru men and Nepâlese women the physiognomy of the Thâru tribe has acquired, in some instances, a slightly Mongolian cast, which shows itself chiefly, but not to a striking degree, in slanting eyes and high cheek bones. In other respects their physical characteristics are of the strictly Indian type. They have long, wavy hair, a dark, almost a black, complexion, and as much hair on the face and body as is usual with other natives of India. In stature, build, and gait they are distinctly Indian and not Mongolian; nor have they any traditions which connect their origin with Nepâl." One of Mr. Risley's [3] correspondents remarks on the scantiness of their beards, but this peculiarity may be due to crossing with Nepâlese or Mech. Mr. Knowles [4] says that "some of the women are very fair, and are good looking both in face and figure; though they generally partake of the Mongolian style of features. They prove themselves genuine

---

[1] *Nepâl*, 151.
[2] *Loc. cit.*, 37.
[3] *Tribes and Castes*, II, 313, note.
[4] *Loc. cit.*, 210.

daughters of Eve by their love of finery. They love to adorn themselves with heavy silver armlets, bracelets, anklets, nose-rings and necklaces of beads and many coloured shells. They wear their long black hair, not tied up in a knot, but rolled into a long horn behind. A more frequent application of water would make their bright yellow skins look more fair and healthy. Their toe and finger nails are nearly all destroyed from being so constantly soaked in water during the rice-sowing season."

9. The most probable explanation based on the available evidence seems to be that the Thârus are originally a Dravidian race who, by alliances with Nepâlese and other hill races, have acquired some degree of Mongolian physiognomy.

Internal organisation.

10. As might have been expected from the wandering habits of the Thârus and the varying influences to which they have been exposed, they tend to break up into a number of sub-tribes which are very intricate and not easily analysed. Those in Muhamdi of Kheri are said to be divided into three endogamous groups: Bâna, Batûr, and Malwariya; the last of whom take their name from Malwâra, a province of the Tarâi, lying east of Kanchanpur. In Gonda, according to Mr. Carnegy,[1] they have six endogamous groups: (a) Gurbans Katheriya, who are said to take their name from being of the race of Guru Rikheswar. They used to wear the Brâhmanical thread, but do not do so now. They drink spirits, eat flesh and fish, but not pork, and they employ washermen, barbers, and oil-pressers. They marry by the rites of *tilak* and *phaldân*; (b) Dingoriya or Dingariya, who rear pigs and poultry, shave themselves and wash their own clothes, using for this purpose the ashes of the *ásan* tree (*Terminalia alata tomentosa*). They remove dead cattle with their own hands, and are their own oil-pressers. They disregard all marriage ceremonies, and all that is necessary is for the friends to assemble, kill and eat a pig, and make the girl over to her husband. They will smoke, but will not eat with the Mânjhi Musahras; (c) Tharkomahra, who perform the same mean occupations and ceremonies as the Dingoriya, but in addition they make earthen vessels, and they smoke with none of the other sub-tribes; the name is a corruption of Thâru-

[1] *Notes*, 9, *sqq*.

Kumhâr; (*d*) the Mânjhi Musahra, who may be connected ethnically, as they are by function, with the Musahars of the Vindhyan plateau, who differ from the Dingariya in that they are fishermen and carry the litters of the Gurbans Katheriya, Dingariya, and Purabiya; (*e*) the Purabiya or "Eastern" drink spirits and eat flesh, cultivate land and employ washermen, barbers and also Chamârs, to remove dead cattle. They smoke with the Dingariya and marry like Gurbans Katheriya; (*f*) Dhaikar, who are mendicants and get fixed annual alms from the other five classes. They eat with the Dingariya, and worship a godling of their own, named Kharag.

11. According to Mr. Nesfield,[1] in Gorakhpur the Thârus divide themselves into two great sections: the Pachhami or "Western" and the Pûrabi or "Eastern;" but what or where the dividing line is to be found has not been stated. The "Western," it is said, call themselves Chhatris, and refuse to eat with the "Eastern." The "Eastern," again, divide themselves into the "Upper Eastern" (*Barka*) and the "Lower" (*Chhutka*). Among each of these again is a large number of smaller clans, some of the names of which are Dagwariya, Nawalpuriya, Marchaha, Kupaliha, Jogithâru, Kosithâru, Kawasiya, and Garhwariya.[2] A different account of the divisions and sub-divisions of the tribe is given in the Gonda district. There the tribe divides itself into two great sections: the Dingariya (who are the Dingoriya of Captain Thorburn) and the Kathariya, the first of which indulges in pork, and the second, according to their own statement, abstain from it. Other witnesses, however, deny that the Kathariya abstain from swine's flesh. As to the smaller sub-divisions into which both sections are sub-divided, there are such diversities of statement that it is impossible to get at the truth."

12. The Jugi Thârus, according to Mr. Knowles,[3] supply the Kanphatas or ear-pierced priests for the temple sacrifice at Tulasipur, as they are adepts in striking off by a single blow the heads of the goats and buffaloes brought as an offering to Devi. The two-fold division into Dangariya and Kathariya is also given

---

[1] *Loc. cit.*, 30, *sq.*
[2] *North-Western Provinces Gazetteer*, VI, 358.
[3] *Loc. cit.*, 116.

by Mr. Benett,[1] and is confirmed by a correspondent from the Gonda district, who does not, however, admit that the Dangariyas abstain from pork. The names of the sub-sections, according to another authority in the Gonda district, are Pûrabiya, Dangariya Kathariya, Amara, Tharjogi, Khuna, and Dingar. A correspondent from Kheri gives them as Gorhwaliya, Pachhihân or "Western," Malwariya, Dangariya, Suhaniya, and Râji, which last is usually regarded as a separate tribe. In Gorakhpur, besides the list already given, another enumeration as follows was furnished: Pachhâha (Barka, Chhutka), Kathariya, Dangariya, Khon, Khusiya, Marchaha, Kachla, Kanphata, Sarkohar, Nawalpuriha The Thârus of Kumaun gave another list which contains only five names: Thâr, Batta, Mahtam, Râwat, and Barwâik; the last three of which seem to depeud merely on status. The Thârus of Bhinga, on the edge of the Bahrâich district, gave another list containing seven names: Dangariya, Kathariya, Khond, Dakhar, Râji, Musahar, Bot. In another part of the Bahrâich district the names given were Kusmaha, Kathariya, Bantar, Dakhar, Dundwâr, Kachla, Rotar, and Jogi.

13. Another carefully prepared list comes from Balrâmpur in the Gonda district. It gives Dangwariya, Katheriya, Umra, Jogi, Dhaker, Pûrabiya, Batâr, Khusiya, Dhîmar, Unchdih, Kumhâr, Khûn, Rautâr, Detwâr, Kuchhila, Râjbatâr, Dhakwâl, Mandaha, Musahar, Dendwâr, Pradhân, Boksa. Of these it is said that the Dangwariya take their name from a place called Dang, which is somewhere in Nepâl; the Kathariya from a place called Kathâr in Deokhur. Of the Umra it is said that the name is a corruption of Dayamûr, "root of mercy," the title of the Kshatriya Chief who adopted the manners and customs of the Thârus and finally joined them. Of the Jogi Thârus the legend runs that a Sâdhu once kept a woman of the Thâru tribe as his mistress, and their descendants became known as Jogi Thâru. They still perform some of the rites of the Jogis. Thus, they bury their dead and erect over the grave a mound (*samâdh*). They eat and drink from the hands of the Dangwariya Thârus; but the Dangwariyas will not take food from their hands. This is rather like the relation of the Patâris and Mânjhis. Formerly it is said that they used to admit

[1] *Oudh Gazetteer*, III, 502.

to their clan a Dangwariya male who cohabited with one of their women or a Dangwariya woman who lived with one of their men. This custom has now ceased in British territory, but still prevails in the hills. The Dhaker are reported to be a branch of the Dangwariya. They are mendicants, who beg only from Thârus, and are endogamous. The Khûn are hardly found in British territory. They live by fishing and by attending sacred places, where they dive for and collect fragments of gold and coral which are thrown into the sacred stream with the ashes of the Hindu dead. The Pradhân are found in the direction of Hardwâr and are the same as the Mahton or Mahtam of the other lists. The Census returns show 73 sections of the tribe. Some of these are taken from Râjput septs or the names of other tribes, such as Bhagat, Gadariya, Jogi, Kathariya, Raghubansi, Râwat, and Râna; others are territorial, as Bijnauriya ("those of Bijnaur"), Jaunpuri, Kâshigauhân, Moṭipurha, Nawalpurha; most of them are, however, purely local titles, which must await wider knowledge of the geography of the Tarâi and its neighbourhood and the local patois of the tribe before their meaning can be ascertained.

14. The truth seems to be that the tribal organization of the Thârus is not well established and is constantly changing under the influence of the local surroundings, and that the landmarks between the Thârus and allied tribes, such as the Bhoksas and Râjis, are very uncertain. The extensive lists given by Mr. Risley from Bihâr contain some of the names which have been already enumerated, but it is fruitless to attempt to work out the analogies in detail.

Marriage customs.

15. Of the marriage customs of the Thârus, Mr. Nesfield writes:—"Until the nuptial ceremony has been completed, and the woman has become the recognised property of some individual man, she is regarded as the common property of the clan, and is treated accordingly; till then there is no restriction of intercourse. Even when the marriage knot has been tied, it is not very difficult to get it unloosed; for the contract is not binding for life, or invested with anything like a sacred character, as it is with the Hindus, and men can and do change their wives in a spirit of mutual accommodation.[1] It

---

[1] *Oudh Gazetteer*, III, 503; and see Letourneau, *Evolution of Marriage*, 52.

should be added, however, that so long as the contract between the man and woman lasts, the latter is as chaste and faithful as any wife could be." At the same time it should be stated that some of the Thârus repudiate the idea that pre-nuptial license or anything in the form of communal marriage is tolerated.

16. The usual age for marriage on the woman's part is about seventeen or eighteen, and a man usually makes his first marriage at about that age. The Bengal Thârus practise both infant and adult marriage and one sub-division of them are said to tolerate sexual intercourse before marriage.[1] There is no betrothal in infancy, except among some clans which have come more completely under the influence of Hinduism. According to Mr. Nesfield, "the marriage contract is arranged, not by the parties themselves, but by the fathers on either side; and the pair for whom the negotiation is made have no power either to choose or refuse. The father of the youth goes over to the village or clan in which the father of the young woman resides, and after making his proposals for the price to be paid for her, offers him a drink of wine, and if the present is accepted, the bargain is closed. The contract once made is faithfully kept by both parties. The price paid for the woman may be in cash or kind, and its value depends on the means of the purchaser or the attractiveness of the woman." In Bihâr [2] the bride-price is supposed to be nine rupees, but is liable to vary according to the means of the family. "The choice of the bride is limited by the rule of exogamy; in other words she must not be a blood relation to the husband chosen for her, nor of the same village, but of some outside village or clan. Wife capture is secretly practised to some extent among the Thârus. Thay have been known to carry off girls by stealth from the Bhuksa tribe conterminous with their own borders on the Sârda river, and from the Nepâlese tribes living on the outer spurs of the Himâlaya mountains; and this practice of getting wives from Nepâl will explain the slightly Mongolian cast of face which has now become rather common, though not universal, among the Thâru tribe. But though the fact of wife capture has become almost obsolete, the form is still preserved in the manner in which the bride is conducted to her new home. The father of the bridegroom never goes to take her away from her own clan or village

[1] Risley, *loc. cit.*, II, 314.
[2] *Ibid*, II, 314.

unless he is accompanied by a select bodyguard of fellow tribesmen. They enter the bride's house in the evening, eat and drink all they can get there in the way of pig, goat, wine, rice, and *ghi ;* and then carry her off on the following morning led by a band of men dancers, men singers, and men musicians, while the bride herself screams and cries as if she were being led off by violence. All this implies a demonstration of force, though no such thing as force is really anticipated or intended."

Marriage by capture.

17. It is needless to say that much the same fiction of capture is found in the marriage usages of other tribes as well as the Thârus. Thus, writing of the Eastern Districts of the Panjâb joining on to these Provinces, Mr. Ibbetson[1] says: "The strict rule of tribal exogamy which still binds all classes, both Hindu and Musalmân, excepting, however, the priests and traders, who observe only the prohibitions of the Sanskrit scriptures, especially the rule against marrying from neighbouring village, the formal nature of the wedding procession, which must be as far as possible mounted on horses, and in which males only may take part, the preparatory oiling of the bridegroom, the similar treatment of the bride being, perhaps, a later institution,—all point to marriage by capture. So does the use of the bloody hand at both villages. The marking all the turnings from the village gate to the bride's house may be a survival of a very common intermediate stage, where the bridegroom visits the bride by stealth. The rule that the procession must reach the girl's village after midday, must not enter the village, but remain outside in a place allotted to them, the fight between the girl's and boy's parties at the door of the bride's house, the rule that the girl shall wear nothing belonging to herself, the hiding of the girl from the boy's people at the wedding ceremony,—all point to marriage by capture. So does the rule by which the boy's party must not accept food at the hands of the girl's people after the wedding, and must pay for what they eat on the succeeding night, and the fiction by which the girl's father is compelled to ignore all payment of money by the bridegroom's friends. The bloody hand stamped on the shoulder of the boy's father by the girl's mother as he departs, and the custom which directs the girl to go off bewailing some one of her male relatives,

[1] *Panjâb Ethnography,* 184; and see McLennan, *Studies,* 33, *sqq.; Primitive Marriage,* 27, *sqq.*

who has lately died, saying 'Oh! my father is dead! 'Oh! my brother is dead' are very marked; as is the fight with sticks between the bride and bridegroom. Finally we have the rule that after the ceremonial goings and comings are over, the wife must never visit her father's house without his special leave, and the fact that the village into which his daughter is married is utterly tabooed for her father, her elder brother, and all her near elder relatives. They may not go into it, or even drink water from a well in that village, for it is shameful to take anything from one's daughter or her belongings. Even her more distant elder relations will not eat or drink from the house into which the girl is married, though they do not taboo the whole village. The boy's father can go to the girl's village by leave of her father, but not without. Similarly, all words denoting male relations by marriage are commonly used as terms of abuse, as, for instance, *susra, sâla, bahnoi, jamâi,* or father-in-law, wife's brother, sister's husband, and daughter's husband. Of these the first two are considered so offensive that they are seldom used in their ordinary sense." It is necessary to say that many of the conclusions of Mr. Ibbetson, as thus given, have been disputed.[1]

18. Among the Thârus, to complete the analogy to the old custom of wife capture, there is no celebration of nuptial ceremonies after the bride and bridegroom have come to their journey's end. As soon as they enter the house appointed for they are, *ipso facto,* man and wife. Mr. Risley [2] remarks that slight traces of the form of capture may perhaps be discerned in the ritual, but these are not very marked among the Thârus of Bihâr. "Brâhmans officiate as priests, and the brother-in-law of the bride usually takes a prominent part in the proceedings. In the Mardaniya and Chitwaniya sub-tribes the bridegroom's party, instead of being entertained by the bride's people, are expected to feast the latter for three days before the bride is produced. No second ceremony (*gauna*) is performed when the bride goes finally to live with her husband. When she is married as an adult, she goes to her husband at once, and in all cases it is deemed proper for her to spend one night at her husband's house immediately after marriage. On the occasion of this visit she and the relations who accompany her

---

[1] *Panjâb Census Report,* I, 336.
[2] *Loc. cit.,* II, 314, *sq.*

are entertained at a feast called *dulhi bhatáwan*, 'giving rice to the bride,' which celebrates her formal admission into the sept to which her husband belongs. If she is still an infant, she is taken back next day to her parents' house by her brother-in-law, and remains there until she has attained sexual maturity."

19. Among the Dangariyas of Gonda it is forbidden to introduce women of low castes, such as the Kori, Chamâr, or Musalmân; but if one of the sept can induce a woman of a caste higher than his own to live with him, the union is recognised, and children born of the pair are regarded as legitimate and enjoy full tribal rights.

20. In Gorakhpur the betrothal is arranged by neighbours and friends on both sides, and the pledge of the engagement is the sending of twelve cups (*tarahi*) of spirits by the father of the bridegroom to the house of the bride. When this is accepted the engagement is complete. There are three forms of marriage ceremony in vogue: the *Pachhiwáhán* or "Western," the *Purbiha* or "Eastern" and the *Bhoj* or "Banquet." The most respectable form, in which the rites are done at the house of the bride, whose father provides a suitable dowry, is known as *Pachhiwáhán*. In the *Purbiha* form no dowry is given. The *Bhoj* is the least respectable of all, and is only done by the very lowest members of the tribe. The binding portion of all three forms is the *sendúrbandhan*, when the youth applies vermilion (*sendúr*) to the parting (*máng*) of the girl's hair.

21. Thâru marriages are usually done in the early spring; but this is not essential, and they have not reached the stage when the rite cannot be done except on a lucky day selected by a Brâhman astrologer. Polygamy, divorce in the form of the expulsion from the house of the faithless wife with the approval of the council, widow marriage, and the levirate under the usual restrictions are all allowed. Divorced women can marry again like widows, and both classes are distinguished by the title *urari*, or "selected," from women who were married as virgins by the full ritual. The social status of a married widow or divorceé is, however, inferior to that of a regularly married wife; but for the purposes of succession both rank alike.

22. Of the Thâru birth rites Mr. Nesfield [1] writes:—"After the birth of a child the mother is not allowed to taste food or water for two days. On the

Birth rites.

[1] *Loc. cit.*, 16.

third day she is allowed to drink as much wine as she desires, and some is rubbed over her body. Thâru women assist each other at the time of childbirth. They are said to be very skilful in midwifery, and Chamâr women are not employed for such purposes as among Hindus. They have a form of lustral ceremony or baptism for the benefit of new-born babes. On the day of its birth the child is immersed in water, while the oldest man in the family pronounces over it certain auspicious words. After the immersion ceremony is over, the child is fumigated with fire and smoke; a tuft of dry *kâns* or *kusa* grass is dug out by the roots. After placing the head of a snake and the sting of a scorpion inside the tuft, they set it on fire, holding the flame as near as possible to the place where the child is lying. The ingredients taken from the snake and scorpion are intended to render the child proof for the remainder of his life against the attack of secret enemies of all kinds. An iron tool is kept in the room where the child sleeps to avert the Evil Eye. When the child is four or five months old, a name is selected for it, and this is bestowed before an assembly of friends by the oldest man in the household."

23. Among the more Hinduised Thârus of Gonda, a Chamârin is sometimes called in at births, and after six days her place is taken by the wife of the barber. All Thârus, except the Kathariyas, starve the mother after delivery, and she is not fed without a preparatory offering of *laddu* sweetmeats to Bhâgawati. On the twelfth day the birth pollution is removed by a bath. There is no trace of the couvade.

Adoption.

24. Among the Thârus if a man is childless, he adopts one of his nephews, in preference the son of his elder brother. He assembles the clansman and taking the boy in his lap, he puts his cap on his head, which signifies that he is his son. Among the Dangwariya sept in Gonda, when a man marries a widow he very often adopts her son by her first marriage, and the son thus adopted receives a larger share of the inheritance than the issue of the marriage with his mother.

Death customs.

25. Earth burial seems to have been the usual way in which the Thârus formerly disposed of their dead; but cremation is now taking its place, except in the case of those who die of cholera or small-pox; these are always interred.

"After cremation the ashes are scattered in the nearest river. Before, however, the corpse has been disposed of by either rite, it is usual to paint it with vermilion and expose it for one night on a mound outside the house. From this mound, as from a stronghold, the spirit of the dead is supposed to scare away wild animals from the crops.[1] Whether the body is buried or burnt, the ceremony is always performed on the southern side of the village, a notion probably borrowed from the Hindus, who consider that the north is the region commonly frequented by divine spirits, and the south by human souls.[2] The man who puts the first fire to the funeral pyre is considered to be unclean from having brought himself within dangerous reach of the contagion of death. He is therefore, kept at a distance for ten days after cremation, and compelled to live entirely alone. On the expiry of the tenth (or the thirteenth as some Thârus relate) the friends of the deceased meet at the house where he died, and after undergoing the ceremony of shaving, they hold a feast of the dead. The banquet prepared for this purpose consists of cooked flesh and wine, the scent and smoke of which are intended to refresh the departed soul; the solid parts, that is, the flesh and wine, themselves are consumed by the living." Mr. Nesfield[3] suggests that the funeral feast consumed by the relations developed into the feeding of Brâhmans, because while offerings to the dead should be made through fire, Manu[4] taught that "there is no difference between fire and a Brâhman," and that an oblation of food to such a holy man is "an offering in the fire of a sacerdotal mouth."

26. "In certain rare cases the burial rite is performed in a manner distinct from either of those already described. A man noted above his fellows for wisdom in counsel, bravery in the chase, or knowledge of the magical or medicinal arts, is buried under the floor of the house in which he was living before his spirit departed. The house thenceforth becomes a temple, and ceases to be used as a dwelling-place for man.[5] The soul of the dead becomes its

---

[1] With this compare Spencer, *Principles of Sociology*, I, 257, *sqq.*; Tylor, *Primitive Culture*, II, 150.

[2] Manu, *Institutes*, III, 206; for the situation of Yamapura or Yamasodana, see Monier-Williams, *Brâhmanism and Hinduism*, 290.

[3] Spencer, *loc. cit.*, I, 155, *sqq.*; Tylor, *loc. cit.*, II, 30.

[4] *Institutes*, III, 212, 91 : 168.

[5] Spencer, *loc cit.*, I, 251.

occupant, and it lives there to bless those whom it has left behind. At periods of three or six months after the death, the friends and neighbours of the deceased assemble round his grave or temple and make an effigy in clay, parts of which are painted in various colours, intended to reproduce the appearance of resuscitated life. His worshippers fall down weeping and wailing before the image, and place offerings of cooked flesh and wine at its feet. Presently, at a given signal, as soon as the soul of the dead is believed to have been propitiated by the scent of roast meat and the fumes of wine, they commence to dance and sing with every expression of joy; and the proceedings of the day are closed with consuming the solid parts of the offering."

27. According to another account from Gonda, the dead are cremated, except those who have died without heirs, and these are buried. The Jogi Thârus, as already stated, raise a mound (*samâdh*) over the graves of their dead. When a corpse is cremated, they bury the ashes on the spot or throw them into a neighbouring stream. Only a few, who are more completely Hinduised, carry the bones to the Ganges. When a person dies of pestilence, the body is buried for the time, and, when the plague is over, disinterred and cremated. They shave the hair of the corpse, cut the nails, bathe it, and rub it with *ubtan*, consisting of ground mustard mixed with turmeric and water. It is then carried on a cot to the cremation ground. The mourners take with them some pulse, rice, ghi, and some earthen vessels. Before the corpse is burnt, they make two fireplaces on which they place two vessels, in which each of the mourners, by turn, cooks some rice and pulse. Then the corpse is placed upon the pyre, and the chief mourner walks seven times round it and sets fire to it. On their return to the house of the deceased, his widow and children wash some copper pice in water and sprinkle it over the party of mourners. The relatives supply some spirits and the friends *sharbat*, which are mixed together and drunk by all present. The man who burns the pyre secludes himself ten days in the case of a dead man and nine days for a woman. The Kathariya and Dangwariya septs keep a lamp burning in the house for ten days after the death to give light to the ghost when it comes to visit its home. On the tenth day they feast their clansmen, and on the thirteenth Brâhmans. The other Thârus perform the rites in the ordinary Hindu way.

Religion.

28. The religion of the more primitive branches of the Thârus is based on a belief in ghosts and consists of little else; the Thârus of the plains are becoming rapidly Hinduised. The soul is believed to survive the body, wandering forth into space and frequenting the haunts of the living sometimes with malignant, sometimes with friendly, intentions. "One Thâru, on being questioned what became of the soul after death, gave an answer, which verifies, with remarkable closeness, the explanation of the ghost theory given by Dr. Tylor. He said that at the time of sleep his soul or second self leaves him and wanders about at will; and as he was not able to say where his soul goes to or what it does during the intervals of sleep, so he could not pretend to say what became of it after the final sleep of death had set in.[1]"

29. Mr. Knowles, whose knowledge of the beliefs of the Thârus is unique, writes[2]—"It was to be expected that this people would be very superstitious. The *bhûts* or demons lurking in the forest trees, especially the weird *semal* or cotton tree (*bombax heptaphylla*) and the *prets* or spirits of the dead lead there a very miserable life. When the last ray of light leaves the forest, and the darkness settles down upon their villages, all the Thâru men and women and children huddle together inside their fast-closed huts in mortal dread of these ghostly beings, more savage and cruel than the leopards, tigers, and bears that now prowl about for their prey. Only the terrible cry of "Fire" will bring these poor fear-stricken creatures to open their doors and remove the heavy barriers from their huts at night; and even in the day time, amid the hum of human life, the songs of the birds, and the lowing of the cattle no Thâru—man, woman or child—will ever venture along a forest line without casting a leaf, a branch, or a piece of old rag upon the Bansati formed at the entrance of the deep woods, to save themselves from the many diseases and accidents the goblins and malicious spirits of the forests can bring upon and cause them. The Bansati or 'good spirit' of the woods is a square space cut in the ground six feet by six covered with pine branches."

30. The Thâru patron saint Raksha or Rikheswar has been already mentioned. Mr. Risley[3] thinks that he is identical with the

---

[1] Nesfield, *loc. cit.*, 18, *sq.*; Tylor, *Primitive Culture*, I, 436, *sqq.*
[2] *Loc. cit.*, 214.
[3] *Ibid*, II, 315.

Rikhmun of the Musahar Bhuiyas. Malignant spirits "cause fever, ague, cough, dysentery, fainting, headache, madness, bad dreams, and pains of all sorts. In fact the Thârus have no conception of natural disease, and no belief in natural death, except what is faintly conceived to be the result of physical decay. Their state, therefore, would be one of utter helplessness, were it not for the reputed skill of medium men or sorcerors, who profess to have the power to control the spirits of the air, or to interpret their grievances or wants. In the Thâru language these men are called Bararar; but the titles of Guru, Gurua, Bhagat, Nyotya, Ojhait, all of which are borrowed from the Hindi, are now in common use, though even of these the last two are probably of aboriginal or non-Sanskritic origin. The power of the medicine man is tremendous. He has a host of liege spirits at his command. Not only can he expel a fiend from the body of a sufferer, but he can produce suffering or death by driving a malignant spirit into the body of his foe. In order to exorcise an evil spirit, he holds in his left hand some ashes of cowdung, or grains of mustard seed, or wild nuts, and after breathing some mystical virtue into them by the utterance of a spell, he causes the patient to eat them, or has them attached to his arm. One of the spells uttered at such times is as follows. It is addressed to Kâlika, the Thâru goddess of death and patroness of the magical arts :—

Gurhai Gur sair, Gur tantra mantra, Gur ;
Lakhai niranjan ; toku sohai phulka bhâr ;
Hamka sohai gun vidya kai bhâr ;
Yahân kai vidya nahîn,
Kâmru Kâm kai vidya ;
Jaisé vidya Kâmru Kâm kai lâgai, waisé vidya lâgai mor.

The language is that of bad and scarcely intelligible Hindi and may be rendered thus :—

"The Guru Kâlika is great; she is everything; she is magic by deeds (*tantra*); she is magic by words (*mantra*). She points out the way to relief. Thou, O Kâlika, deservest to be heaped with flowers! I too deserve to be heaped with secret wisdom, the wisdom of Kâmru Kâm, not the wisdom of the country. Whatever effect the knowledge of Kâmru Kâm produces, such effects let my knowledge produce also."

31. Mr. Knowles[1] says :— "Their religion is as simple as them-

[1] *Loc. cit.*, 212.

selves. A very primitive piece of wood in the shape of a Mahâdeva stone, near which is erected a long stick, with a bit of red cloth fastened to the top, is all they have as an object of worship; and I found a very few in a village pay any attention even to this. They have some idea of a Supreme Being they call Nârâyan, who gives them sunshine and rain and harvests; but they have no proper idea how this great, far-off Being is to be approached and worshipped. I found about five Thârus, who had taken to themselves the luxury of a Brâhman Gura from Balrâmpur, and who carried on *pûja* in the usual Hindu orthodox way."

32. "The goddess who presides over life and death, and whom the Thârus believe to be the supreme power in the universe, is Kâlika, one of the numerous forms of Devi, Durga or Kâli, at whose name all India trembles, especially the low tribes and the casteless tribes, among whom she originally sprung. One of her titles in Oudh is Sonmat or Sonwat, "the crescent headed;" Chândika Devi is the goddess of the Bhars, and her name means the same. Mari, the patron goddess of Kanjars, is also worshipped by them. She appears to be identical with Samai or Samaiya, who, according to Dr. Buchanan,[1] is a Thâru deity. Medicine men look to Kâlika as the special patroness of their art. To the fair sex she is the goddess of parturition, and her aid is specially invoked by women who have had no children. All classes combine to give her a periodical ovation, accompanied by much dancing, banqueting, and drinking of wine, about the middle of October. Thârus also take part in the huge animal sacrifice performed at the celebrated altar in Devi Pâtan, in the Gonda district. Such is her thirst for blood that at this time twenty buffaloes, two hundred and fifty goats, and two hundred and fifty pigs are slaughtered daily, for ten days continuously. The sacrifice is vicarious, the blood of the buffaloes, etc., being intended as a substitute for that of human victims. This loathsome festival is thronged with visitors from the plains of India and from the hills of Nepâl, Sikkhim and Bhutân."[2]

33. "Another deity revered by Thârus, and like Kâlika of indigenous or non-Aryan origin, is her consort Siva, known chiefly among Thârus by the name of Bhairava, 'The Terrible,' Thâkur, 'The Lord,' and amongst Hindus by that of Mahâdeva, 'The

---

[1] *Eastern India*, II, 389.
[2] Nesfield, *loc. cit.*, 27.

Great God.' He, like his spouse, is a god of destruction and thirst for blood. But he is chiefly worshipped by the Thârus as the author of reproduction, of which a stone lingam, as among Hindus, is made the symbol. It is more usual, however, for a Thâru to erect a mud mound in front of his house, and fix an upright pole in the centre, to represent tho presence of this phallic divinity. Nature worship among Thârus is represented by two deities of some importance. One is Madhu the god of intoxicating liquor, specially of the rice wine made by themselves. He represents the goddess Varunani, Varuni, Mada or Sura of Vaishnavism.[1] The other is Dharchandi, 'the patroness of cattle,' though her name would imply that she was at first intended to personate the Earth. Her shrine, like those of the deities already named, is a mound of clay. The mound dedicated to Dharchandi is studded with short wooden crosses, on which rice, pulse, and other produce of the fields are offered, and always on plates of leaf. Her shrine is so placed that all the cattle of the village, together with the swine, sheep, and goats, pass it on going out to graze, and repass it on their return. When the cattle sicken or die, larger and more valuable offerings are made. Neither of these deities is known or worshipped by other natives of Upper India." In Champâran, Kuân is worshipped as a village deity by casting sweetmeats down a well (*kuân*) and smearing vermilion on its rim.[2]

34. In Gonda, besides the worship of Mahâdeva and Bhâgawati, the Jogi Thârus worship a deified worthy known as Ratinâth. They have also minor village deities, known as Garar Bîr, Kâli, and Deohâr, or the collective village pantheon. Bhâgawati is worshipped on the tenth of Kuâr with a sacrifice of a pig or a fowl and with an offering of milk and wine. At the same time the brethren are fed on sweetmeat. If there are several Thâru families in a village, they will each feed the brethren on successive days. Those who are poor feed only one member of each family of the brethren. Mahâdeva is worshipped daily with an offering of sandal, washed rice (*achhat*), flowers, incense, a lighted lamp, and water. The worship of Garar Bîr and Kâli is done in the months of Jeth, Bhâdon, and Aghan. In the months of Jeth and Bhâdon the offering consists of a pig, goat, ram, fowl, wine, and milk. In Aghan they

---

[1] Monier-Williams, *Brâhmanism and Hinduism*, 108.
[2] Risley, *loc. cit.*, II, 316.

offer the *maguri* fish (*macropteronatus magur*), fowls, eggs, rats, wine, and milk. The above is the rule among the Dangwariya Thârus. The Kathariya offer a ram in Asârh, and in Aghan a mixture of new rice, *ghi*, and sugar. The offerings are consumed by the worshippers. The worship of these deities is often carried on by a general subscription among all the Thâru residents of the village.

35. In Gorakhpur their chief objects of worship are Mahâdeva and Bhawâni. They have also a crowd of minor godlings, such as Sâwan, Lutta, Mangan, the Jâk and Jâkni, who are field godlings; Brahm, a deified Brâhman ghost; Mari, the goddess of death, and Bâgheswari, the tiger goddess. Of the origin and attributes of these godlings they are quite ignorant. Sâwan, Lutta, and Mangan receive a sacrifice of a cock at the Naurâtri; Bâgheswari is worshiped through a Gurua or Ojha with an offering of rice-milk. After sowing the autumn crops, Jâk and Jâkni receive an offering of some oilcake and a chicken. At the same time a cock is offered to Mari. Brahm is worshipped at any time of sickness or other trouble with an oblation of milk.

Animal and plant worship.

36. Thârus hold three animals sacred above all others, and these they would deem it a sacrilege to destroy—the cow, the serpent, and the monkey,—of which the cow and monkey are probably adored through the example of their Hindu neighbours. The snake has a special service at the Nâgpanchami. The only tree to which they appear to show any particular respect is the *pîpal*.

Festivals.

37. In the spring Thârus observe the annual festival of fire, an observance "resembling, in many respects, the Holi of the Hindus, and known to Thârus themselves by this and no other name. A mound of earth is prepared, in the centre of which a pole is fixed in a vertical position, the phallic emblem of reproductive energy. Offerings of turmeric, hemp, *dhatûra*, and other pungent or odorous herbs are placed upon the pole and mound by the assembled people. Straw and stubble and sticks are then piled around the pole; and the oldest or most respected man in the assembly puts fire to it. After the bonfire has burnt itself out, they amuse themselves with dancing, playing the drum and cymbals, pelting each other with coloured powder, singing amorous songs, and cracking lascivious jokes. The evening is spent in feasting on roast meats and rice and drinking wine. The only difference between this and the Hindu form of the Holi is

that the same gods and demi-gods are not honoured in the one as in the other, and that the Thârus have retained the old phallic emblem, which among Hindus has gone entirely out of use." [1] As has been shown elsewhere,[2] this probably represents a more primitive form of the usage than that at present prevailing among Hindus. We have met a similar usage among the Dravidian tribes of Mirzapur, who burn the old year (*sambat jalâna*) in the form of a stake. In Gorakhpur, where the Thârus have come more completely under Brâhmanical influence, they observe all the ordinary Hindu festivals.

Social status and occupation.

38. Mr. Nesfield [3] has given an elaborate account of the social life of the Thârus. They live by hunting and fishing, gathering forest fruits and vegetables, grazing cows and buffaloes, making *ghi*, keeping pigs, fowls, and goats, and practising a rude form of agriculture. "As hunters they despise and shun such vermin as jackals, snakes, and lizards. The animals which they chiefly hunt are the wild boar, the deer, the antelope, and other large game in which their forests still abound. They also lay snares for the porcupine (*sahi*) and eat its flesh, which is considered to bear some resemblance to that of the pig. Sometimes, but only when they are pressed for food, they will eat field rats. They are fond of hares when they can catch them, and they are not averse to the flesh of the river tortoise. When the stock of meat happens to become larger than they can consume at once, their mode of preserving it is by cutting it into strips and drying it in the sun."

39. Mr. Knowles [4] remarks that though the men and boys go about almost in a nude state, with only a piece of cloth hung loose in front, held by a string fastened round the waist, yet the wives and daughters of the tribe are so well clothed that only the arms and feet are left exposed.

40. In Gonda they eat pork, and the flesh of deer and those cloven-footed animals which ordinary Hindus eat, fowls, fish, both scaled and scaleless, tortoises, rats and hares. They will not eat beef, or the flesh of the monkey, crocodile, snake, lizard, jackal, and

[1] Nesfield, *loc. cit.*, 30.
[2] *Introduction to Popular Religion and Folklore*, 391, *sq*.
[3] *Loc. cit.*, 3, *sqq*.
[4] *Loc. cit.*, 210.

other vermin. This is also the case in Gorakhpur; but here there seems to be an increasing tendency towards the restrictions in force among Râjputs, of whom they claim to form a branch. In Gonda all Thârus will smoke together. The Kusumha, Dahel, Lampochhna and Parpariya or Palpharaha septs eat *kachchi* and drink together. These will not eat with Kumhâr Jogi and Dhaker. But the latter will eat from the Kusumha. The Dangwariya and Katheriya will eat *pakki* together. The Brâhmans and Kshatriyas of the hills will not touch food from any Thâru; but they will drink water drawn by members of the Dangwariya sept. The Brâhmans of the plains will drink water drawn by the Katheriyas. Their chief fishing implements are the hook and line, the net and the funnel-shaped basket. They often poison the water and catch fish in this way. Their favourite root is a plant of the yam species, which grows freely at the foot of the hills. Wild rice, the flower of the *mahua* tree (*bassia latifolia*) and the fruit of the wild fig tree are gathered in their several seasons. Until recently they used to cultivate in a rude way by cutting and burning down the jungle, but now they cultivate the transplanted rice throughout the Tarâi, and they have a valuable source of food in the plantain which grows plentifully around their villages. Mr. Knowles[1] writes that "the rice which is not carefully taken out of the husk and is therefore all broken, is their principal food. They eat three times a day. At what answers to our breakfast they eat a meal of boiled rice; at what we call our tiffin they make a meal of boiled rice-water, and at our dinner time they make a more substantial meal of pulse and rice and the meat of any game they may have shot or caught in the jungle. But they never eat bread of any kind. Little wheat is grown and that for market. The first meal is called *kalwa* or *kalewa* (Sanskrit *kalya-varta*); the second *mingi* and the third *beri.*" The women do the largest part of the sowing, weeding and harvesting, while the men engage in hunting, fishing, etc., which they regard as the proper occupation of their sex. "The only kind of labour, which a Thâru will undertake, is that of elephant-driver to some Râja. Their skill as elephant-drivers is admitted everywhere; and latterly they have acquired the art of catching wild elephants from the forest and taming them for the Râja of Balrâmpur and other noblemen."

---

[1] *Loc. cit.*, 211.

Villages and houses.

41. Their villages, according to Mr. Knowles,[1] are from one to two miles distant from each other, and the houses are all made of wood or grass. The outside grass walls of each house are plastered over with red mud. They never use cowdung for this and other household purposes as is usual with the people outside the jungle; that they use only for manure. The cattle sheds are protected from beasts of prey by strong wooden palings. The wells in the village are kept from falling in by boards being let down and fastened together. The houses are large, cool and commodious, and generally raised on poles, like those of the Dyaks described by Mr. Wallace,[2] in order to protect the inmates from damp and malaria. They contain large jars of red clay in which food grain and seed rice are kept Dr. Buchanan [3] remarks that "the huts of the Thârus have straight ridges, and in general are much wider and longer than those of other natives. But one hut usually serves as the residence of a family, which in the southern parts of the District would have three or four huts round a yard. On one side of the hut is usually a garden, neatly fenced and containing tobacco, mustard and a few plantain trees. The Thârus keep cows, buffaloes, sheep, goats, fowls, and pigeons, and this live-stock occupies an open end of their hut separated from the dwelling apartments by a hurdle wall."

42. "Every little village," writes Mr. Nesfield [4] "is a self-governing community. Disputes are decided by a council of elders, and this is sometimes presided over by a headman who, in the Thâru language, was formerly called Barwâik, but who is now dubbed even by themselves with the ordinary Hindu title of Chaudhari. The office of headman is not hereditary. The man selected is one whose age, experience and knowledge of the magical and medicinal arts entitle him to more respect than the rest; and he acquires the status of headman by tacit consent and not by formal election. The decisions of the council or the headman are obeyed unreservedly; and there is no such thing known as a Thâru taking a fellow tribesman before a tribunal outside his own community. Litigation between Thârus and Hindus is equally unknown. Amongst themselves the Thârus are, for the most part, a peaceful and good-natured race,

---

[1] *Loc. cit.*, 211.
[2] *Malay archipelago*, 59.
[3] *Eastern India*, II, 40.
[4] *Loc. cit.*, 6, sq.

following without question, as if by a law of nature, the customs and maxims of their ancestors."

43. Their strongest form of oath is placing the hand on the lingam of Mahâdeva or on the shrine of Kâlika. "A less potent oath, and one evidently derived from the Hindus, is by holding water in the palm of the hand, the water being supposed to have come from the Ganges. When two persons accuse each other of some fault, and it is known that one or other must be guilty, resort is had to the floating test. The two disputants are flung simultaneously into deep water, and the one who rises first is declared guilty. Another kind of ordeal practised by them consists of throwing a coin into a bowl of boiling oil or boiling water, and thrusting in the arm to take it out. If the arm comes out unblistered the person is declared innocent."

Tools: industries.

44. "The tools and weapons used by the Thârus are not made by themselves. The share of the plough, the point of the spear, the blade of the axe or hatchet, and the blade of the hoe with which they dig the yam are procured from Lohârs. The recollection of stone weapons survives even in tradition. The curved knife (*khukhuri*) is procured from Nepâl. Their plough is of the same design as that used by Hindus, but more simple, for the upright pole (*jangha*), to which the oxen are attached is in the same piece of wood with the curved part to which the iron-share is fastened." They work in bamboo, reeds, and fibres, and make baskets, snares, nets, and similar appliances for hunting and fishing. A peculiar article of dress is the broad leaf umbrella worn over the head to keep off the sun and rain.

Dances.

45. They have a national dance performed by boys or men, never by girls or women. "A boy of fifteen or sixteen is dressed as a woman, and his partner beats a small drum suspended from the neck. The pair advance and retreat with a gliding motion, and represent with coarse fidelity the advances of the lover and the coyness of the maid. As they proceed they warm to the work; and I shall never forget the ecstatic but somewhat ludicrous rapture which shone in the face and spake in every limb of the drummer after two hours of the exercise and the infusion of a large amount of raw spirits. Every now and then the dancing gives place to a dramatic interlude, in which a dullard is made the butt of the rough and occasionally

obscene wit of the leading actor. These scenes were invariably the vehicle of satire, and the Brâhmans of the plains and Sir Jang Bahâdur of Nepâl were visited with unsparing ridicule." [1]

46. They make their principal intoxicating drinks from rice. This rice liquor is drunk more or less every day, and every member of the family—from the oldest to the youngest—drinks it. "They say by only thus drinking they can be kept alive in these forests, especially in the rains. The water in the village wells is certainly not fit to drink without some disinfecting process, and the Thârus themselves say that drinking it would kill a *desi* or person living outside the forest in a week. Of course they drink to excess on special occasions. Every now and then they have a big *nâch* or dance of a very degrading kind. In it they act a regular play in which there is a plot and a grand finale. A Nepâl prince who carries off a beautiful Thâru girl figures in it. The women take part in it, and I am told the curtain had better fall over the last act." [2]

Intoxicating drinks.

47. Like all secluded races the Thârus are notorious for witchcraft and in the plains, Thâruhat or "the Thâru country" is a synonym for witch land. "Every Thâru woman," says Mr. Knowles,[3] "after the marriageable age, is supposed by those who live outside the Thâru country to possess the *tona* or power of the Evil Eye to bewitch and enchant; so that she has the power to turn a *desi* or stranger into a wild animal or destroy him slowly by consumptive fever. This, I find, is one reason why all the natives outside the forest dread the Thârus and fear to live among them The forest officer has had the greatest difficulty in getting carpenters and masons to come out and build his house, because they were afraid of Thâru *tona*. The power of the Evil Eye displays itself in two forms : the major curse being known as *lohna*, which commences with violent wasting away, and results invariably in a rapid death. For the lesser (*bej*), recovery may be expected; it displays itself in a low fever accompanied with diarrhœa. The fever and dysentery of the Tarâi keep the superstition alive. Both men and animals are sup-

Sorcery and witchcraft.

---

[1] *Oudh Gazetteer*, III, 504.

[2] Knowles, *loc. cit.*, 212. It has been generally believed that the Thârus are proof against malaria : but the Bengal returns (*Census Report*, 173) shows that they are unusually short lived.

[3] *Loc. cit.*, 214.

posed to be subject to this malignant influence; but a handsome bachelor is considered the most likely victim. The souls of those who are thus affected remain for ever in the power of the enchantress, and when she dies she becomes a Bhukchm, a malignant demon, commanding a troop of the souls she has slain. Among the lower castes of Hindus, and especially the Kewats and Châis, whose traditional descent from the Kaivartas or Nishâdas stamps them as non-Aryan, are found individuals who possess the secret antidote to the fascination. At Pipra Ghât on the Râpti, between Utraula and Tulasipur, there is an especially famous exorcisor, who has a large school of pupils."[1]

Social life.

48. The only caste with whom the Thârus live on in intimate terms is that of the Banjâras. The honesty of the Thârus is proverbial. It is said that when a family flies into the hills they will always leave any arrears of rent that may be due tied up in a rag to the lintel of their deserted house. It is said that husband and wife never quarrel. "This is not," says Mr. Knowles,[2] "because the women are kept under; for they seem as free and independent in their movements as the men. A Thâru woman will look as straight at you when you speak of her as a European woman will. I noticed another good trait in the social character of these people. The parents seem as fond of the girls as of the boys, and make no degrading distinction as the natives of the plains do. The Thâru's word of endearment for his wife is *jâni*. He calls his daughter a *bâbu* and his son a *bhaiya*—"My love," "my lord," "my brother."

Distribution of Thârus according to the Census of 1891.

Districts.	Number.	Districts.	Number.
Bareilly	8	Tarâi	15,332
Pilibhît	46	Kheri	1,975
Gorakhpur	3,072	Gonda	2,475
Basti	208	Bahrâich	2,311
Kumaun	65		
		Total .	25,492

[1] *Oudh Gazetteer*, III, 503.
[2] *Loc. cit.*, 210.

Thathera[1]—(Probably derived from Sanskrit *tashta-kâra*, "one who polishes")—The caste of braziers and makers and sellers of brass and copper vessels. It is not easy to ascertain exactly the difference of function between the Kasera and Thathera. According to Mr. Nesfield:[2] "The Kasera's speciality lies in mixing the softer metals (zinc, copper, and tin), and moulding the alloy into various shapes, such as cups, bowls, plates, etc. The Thathera's art consists in polishing and engraving the utensils which the Kasera supplies." In the Panjâb it would seem that the Kasera is the capitalist dealer, while the Thathera is the skilled artizan.[3] But these functions seem to overlap, and in Mirzapur the term Thathera seems to be more generally applied to the craftsman who makes ornaments out of the alloy known as *phûl.*

Tradition of origin.

2. Curiously enough, there is, in Oudh, a widespread tradition that the Thatheras were lords of the land before the Râjput invasion.[4] Mr. McMinn hazards the speculation that the Thatheras of Oudh legend were Bhars; others say that they were Thârus. But all this is mere speculation, and we really know nothing as to the people who are referred to. The tribe in Mirzapur say that they came from Bengal some three or four generations ago, and they name a place called Nasîrganj in the Shâhâbâd District as their head quarters. In Lucknow they say that they were originally Kshatriyas, and they have the stock story that, when Parasurâma destroyed the Kshatriya race, one of their women, who was pregnant, was protected by a certain Kamandala Rishi, and that her offspring founded the caste of Thatheras. They add that their original home was a place called Ratanpur in the Dakkhin. In Benares, according to Mr. Sherring,[5] they wear the Brâhmanical thread and claim to hold a place intermediate between the Kshatriyas and Vaisyas. The caste is obviously purely occupational.

Internal organization.

3. The internal organization of the caste is very complex. At the last Census no less than three hundred and fourteen sub-castes were recorded, but

---

[1] Based on enquiries at Mirzapur and notes by M. Chhotê Lâl, Lucknow; Pandit Baldeo Prasâd, Deputy Collector, Cawnpur.

[2] *Brief View*, 29.

[3] Johnstone, *Monograph on Brass and Copper Ware*, 17.

[4] Elliott, *Chronicles of Unâo*, 25; *Oudh Gazetteer*, I, 22, 221, *sq.* 270, 275. *Hardoi Settlement Report*, 75, 85, 100, 165, 227.

[5] *Hindu Tribes*, I, 321.

it is at present impossible to say how many of these represent endogamous, and how many exogamous, groups. In Mirzapur there are two endogamous groups, Awadhiya or "those of Oudh," and Bhusantiya. In Lucknow the chief exogamous groups are Bhariya, Bangariya, Barwâr, Daundiya Kheriya, who take their name from the famous Bais Râjput stronghold on the Ganges, Gurha, Barhariya, Tusaha, Gulraha, Dandiya, Jarseth, and Lodh.

Exogamy.

4. The exogamous groups practise the usual rule which excludes the line of the paternal and maternal uncle and the paternal and maternal aunt for three or four generations, or until all knowledge of relationship is lost.

Marriage.

5. They marry in the orthodox way by the forms known as *byáh* or *charhaua* and *dola*. Widow marriage and the levirate are allowed under the usual restrictions.

Religion.

6. Some Thatheras are Saivas; but most of them are Vaishnavas. In Mirzapur they worship Mahâbîr, the Pânchon Pîr, and Devi in the form of Bhâgawati. Mâhabîr is worshipped in the months of Sâwan or Kuâr and on the birth of a child with an offering of sweetmeats, fried gram (*ghughuri*), bread, and the erection of a flag (*jhanda*) in his honour. The Pânchon Pîr are worshipped at marriages and at the festivals of the Diwâli and Khichari; at marriages with an offering of a head-dress (*maur*) and food, on the Diwâli with parched grain (*lái, chura*), and at the Khichari with *khichari* or rice boiled with pulse. They worship as a fetish the furnace (*bhatti*) in which the metal they work up is melted. In Lucknow their anvil (*niháí*) and hammer represent a deity known as Kalawati Kanya or "the skilful maiden." Their domestic ceremonies are superintended by a low class of Brâhmans, who, in Lucknow, are Tiwâris.

Social customs and status.

7. They drink spirits and eat goat's meat and mutton as well as fish. They eat *pakki* cooked by Brâhmans, Râjputs, and Halwâis; but *kachchi* only if cooked by one of their own caste. Banyas and all lower castes eat *pakki* cooked by them; but *kachchi* cooked by them is eaten only by Nâis and other castes of similar social standing.

Distribution of the Thatheras according to the Census of 1891.

Districts.	Hindus.	Musalmâns.	Total.
Dehra Dûn	9	...	9
Sahâranpur	71	17	88
Muzaffarnagar	91	252	343
Meerut	37	...	37
Bulandshahr	10	...	10
Aligarh	129	...	129
Mathura	347	...	347
Agra	133	...	133
Farrukhâbâd	304	...	304
Mainpuri	81	...	81
Etâwah	94	...	94
Etah	39	...	39
Bareilly	32	...	32
Bijnor	148	216	364
Budâun	31	...	31
Morâdâbâd	60	...	60
Shâhjahânpur	356	...	356
Pilibhît	29	...	29
Cawnpur	247	...	247
Fatehpur	492	...	492
Bânda	259	...	259
Hamîrpur	86	...	86
Allahâbâd	1,398	...	1,398
Jhânsi	546	...	546
Jâlaun	87	...	87
Lalitpur	137	...	137

Distribution of the Thatheras according to the Census of 1891—concluded.

Districts.	Hindus.	Musalmâns.	Total.
Benares	470	...	470
Mirzapur	143	...	143
Jaunpur	907	...	907
Ghâzipur	806	...	806
Ballia	414	...	414
Gorakhpur	1,631	...	1,631
Basti	1,605	...	1,605
Azamgarh	1,826	...	1,826
Tarâi	12	37	49
Lucknow	702	...	702
Unâo	1,233	...	1,233
Râê Bareli	129	...	129
Sîtapur	347	...	347
Hardoi	55	...	55
Kheri	777	...	777
Faizâbâd	354	...	354
Gonda	2,136	...	2,136
Bahrâich	533	...	533
Sultânpur	513	...	513
Partâbgarh	430	...	430
Bârabanki	547	...	547
Total	20,823	522	21,345

Thavai—(Sanskrit *sthapati*, "a master-builder").—The caste of masons and bricklayers. At the last Census they appear to have been included under Râj (*q. v.*). They are the Thavi of the Panjâb, who is a mason and bricklayer in the hills, and claims to have been originally a Brâhman, who was degraded because he took to working in stone. The caste is purely occupational and contains both Hindus and Muhammadans; the latter say that their first *ustâd* or teacher was Bâba Ibrahîm, or father Abraham. The Hindu branch say the same of Viswakarma, the architect of the gods. The Muhammadan branch worship their tools at the Id festival, and offer sweetmeat to them. The Hindu Thavais, when they commence work in the morning, say *Viswakarma ki jay ho*, "Glory to Viswakarma."

Tiyar, Tiar.—A Dravidian boating and fishing tribe in the Eastern Districts, sometimes classed as a sub-tribe of the Mallâh. The word is possibly derived from Sanskrit *tîvara*, "a hunter or fisherman." According to Mr. Risley's account [1] their customs on the whole correspond with those of the allied fishing and boating tribes. They are apparently the same as the so-called Teehurs of Oudh, who furnish one of the stock instances of communistic marriage. They are said to "live almost indiscriminately in large communities, and even when two people are regarded as married the tie is but nominal." [2] Though there may be considerable laxity of sexual intercourse among a people, the males of whom are compelled by their profession to leave the women for considerable intervals, the statement is perhaps exaggerated. The Tiyars also furnish one of the best modern cases of human sacrifice. The account given by Mr. Goad,[3] after describing how the bodies of two murdered men were found in 1865 in a hut in the Benares district, goes on to say:—"Two of the Tiyar caste had been down to Bengal in charge of some boats; when they returned they brought a letter addressed to the Tiyar caste calling on them to become vegetarians (*bhagat*); they were not to kill fish, nor eat them any more. This letter appears to have been circulated among the Tiyar caste in the Benares, Azamgarh, and Ghazipur districts, and which resulted in the above assemblage, on which occasion they acted a regular play by five men representing five deities,—Râm, Mahâbîr, Mahâdeo Senior (*sic.*), Zetbut (*sic.*), and Mahâdeo Junior (*sic.*)—that is to say, the three defendants—Beni, Pirthi Pâl, and Bassi represented the deities

---

[1] *Tribes and Castes, sqq.*, II, 328.

[2] Lubbock, *Origin of Civilisation* 89, quoting Watson and Kaye, *The People of India*, II, plate 85.

[3] Quoted by Dr. Chevers, *Medical Jurisprudence*, 406, *sqq.*, from Lewin's *Police Guide*, 205.

Râm, Mahâbîr, and Mahâdeo Junior, and the deceased Shiubharat and Râm Sewak, Mahâdeo Senior and Zetbut; and by the order of Râm, Mahâdeo Junior, and Mahâbîr slew Zetbut and Mahâdeo Senior, Râm having promised to bring them to life again. This appears to be a most curious case, as nothing of the kind has been heard of before. The actors in this affair are a low caste, and next to savages, so that it is difficult to get a proper meaning to the catastrophe."

2. The same is the name of a clan of Râjputs in Sultânpur. Mr. Millet[1] describes them as nearly an extinct race, who are said to have been at one time lords of Pargana Sultânpur. "They succeeded the Bhadaiyâns, the conquerors of the Bhars and were in turn overcome by the Bachgotis, whose star is at present in the ascendant. The order of succession is chronicled in the following doggerel lines :—

Bhar mâr Bhadaiyân :
Bhadaiyân mâr Tiyar :
Tiyar mâr Bachgoti.

The Tiyars gave their name to one of the old sub-divisions of the pargana, Tappa Tiyar, and this, perhaps, rather than the entire pargana, was the extent of their dominions. At present they have nothing more than a right of occupancy in a few acres in their own Tappa. Regarding the Tiyars very little is known. Mr. Carnegy[2] considers them to belong to the Solar race; they themselves say that they are descended from immigrants from Baiswâra, who received a grant of the Bhadaiyâns territory from the Râja of Benares. Mr. Millet suggests a connection between their name and the Tarâi or Tîrabhukti (Tirhût).

Tomar (Sanskrit *tomara*, "a club") **Tunwar.**—A famous sept of Râjputs. Though a sub-division of the Yadubansi the are usually reckoned as one of the thirty-six royal races. They furnished India with the dynasty of Vikramaditya. Delhi was rebuilt by Anangpâl Tomar in A.D. 731—736 and became his capital and that of several of his successors; but, according to General Cunningham,[3] there is reason to believe that subsequently the Tomar capital was removed to Kanauj, where it remained for several generations prior to the invasion of Mahmûd of Ghazni. Shortly after that the small town of Bâri, north of Lucknow, became the

---

[1] *Sultânpur Settlement Report*, 134, *sq.*
[2] *Notes*, 27.
[3] *Archæological Reports*, I, 141, *sqq.*; 283.

capital till about 1050 A.D., when the Tomars returned to Delhi before the growing power of the Râthaurs; and then Anangpâl, the Second, rebuilt the city and erected the Lâlkot There is an inscription of his on the iron pillar, dated 1052 A.D., and just a century after Anangpâl III was defeated by Visala Deva, Chauhân, in 1151-52 A.D. The history of the dynasty has been worked out with great detail by General Cunningham.

2. The Tomar dynasty of Gwâlior was founded by Bîr Sinh Deva, who was probably a member of the Delhi family, and, according to the annalists, declared his independence in the time of Alâ-ud-dîn Khilji; but there is a difficulty about the dates, and General Cunningham [1] believes that the rise of the Tomars must have taken place during the few troubled years that immediately preceded the invasion of Timûr. His successor, Dungar Sinh, who came to the throne in 1424, raised the kingdom to great prosperity and began the great rock sculptures. Their power reached its zenith in the reign of Mân Sinh, who succeeded in 1486 A.D., and the kingdom was finally destroyed by Ibrahîm Lodi in 1519 A.D., who captured the capital.

3. In these Provinces the present status of the clan does not correspond with the splendour of its traditions. The Janghâra of Budâun claim to be of this stock; but their genealogical lists do not substantiate their assertion. They fix their immigration in the time of Shahâb-ud-dîn (1202—1206 A.D.). In Morâdâbâd [2] they fix their settlement at Sambhal at 700 A.D., where it is said to have lasted till 1150 A.D., the time of the rise of the Chauhâns. The Bareilly clan claim to have entered the district under their leader Hansrâj, and expelled the Guâlas in 1388, and the Ahîrs and Bhîls between 1405 and 1570 A.D.[3] The Batola of Garhwâl claim to be another branch of the same stock.[4] In the Eastern Districts they are not considered to be of high rank, a fact which Dr. Buchanan [5] explains in his quaint way by alleging that the last princes of the race were "abominable heretics."

4. In Sîtapur they marry girls of the Gaur, Ahban, Bâchhal, or Janwâr septs.

---

[1] *Ibid*, II, 381, *sq*.
[2] *Settlement Report*, 8.
[3] *Settlement Report*, 224.
[4] Atkinson, *Himalâyan Gazetteer*, III, 276.
[5] *Eastern India*, II, 463.

Distribution of the Tomar Rájputs according to the Census of 1891.

Districts.	Hindus.	Muhammadans.	Total.
Sahâranpur	1,005	16	1,021
Muzaffarnagar	307	1,362	1,669
Meerut	391	...	391
Bulandshahr	482	3,344	3,826
Aligarh	1,436	...	1,436
Mathura	1,042	38	1,080
Agra	5,521	37	5,558
Farrukhâbâd	769	...	769
Mainpuri	2,976	2	2,978
Etâwah	2,128	15	2,143
Etah	2,265	57	2,322
Bareilly	29	...	29
Bijnor	67	207	269
Budâun	2,987	70	3,057
Morâdâbâd	1,201	107	1,308
Shâhjahânpur	989	...	989
Pilibhît	280	2	282
Cawnpur	958	...	958
Fatehpur	911	...	911
Banda	584	23	607
Hamîrpur	76	...	76
Allahâbâd	268	...	268
Jhânsi	270	...	270
Jâlaun	4	...	4
Lalitpur	184	...	184
Benares	157	...	157
Ghâzipur	2	5	7

Distribution of the Tomar Râjputs according to the Census of 1891—concld.

Districts.	Hindus.	Muhammadans.	Total.
Ballia	389	...	389
Gorakhpur	86	135	221
Basti	...	408	408
Azamgarh	1	171	172
Tarâi	158	...	158
Lucknow	105	3	108
Unâo	115	27	142
Raê Bareli	177	...	177
Sîtapur	1,882	1	1,883
Hardoi	1,227	...	1,227
Kheri	1,164	9	1,173
Faizâbâd	151	...	151
Bahrâich	29	...	29
Sultânpur	12	...	12
Partâbgarh	61	...	61
Bârabanki	69	...	69
Total	32,915	6,039	38,954

Turk (Sanskrit *turushka*), a term properly applied to the Mongolian Turkomâns of Turkistân. Sir H. Yule [1] shows that the distinction which we now make between Turk and Turkomân was popular as early as the twelfth century. On the Biloch frontier the word Turk is equivalent to Mughal, and it is often used by Hindus for any official of foreign birth. In the Panjâb even Hindu clerks of the Kâyasth caste are sometimes called by this name. The Dravidian tribes very often call any Muhammadan a Turk.

2. In these Provinces there is a large cultivating caste in the Tarâi known as Turk, and in Azamgarh the term is applied to a

[1] *Marco Polo*, I, 44.

section of the Koeris. Those in the north of Rohilkhand are described as a more manly people than the Naumuslim and appear to have come into the district at an early period with some of the Sayyid colonies.[1]

3. From a report received from the Râmpur State it appears that the Turks claim to be originally emigrants from Turkistân, whence they came in the train of the army of Shahâb-ud-dîn Ghori. They deny that they have ever admitted converts from Hinduism; but they are more Hindu in their customs than other Muhammadans. They marry early, earlier than even the many Hindu castes, and for the ceremonial shaving of their children prefer the month of Baisâkh. They care little about the seclusion of their women. They are endogamous, and if a Turk marries a woman of another Muhammadan tribe he is put out of caste. The women wear a peculiar dress, the scarf and drawers, which are generally of coarse cloth, being dyed blue and lined with red. The drawers are very loose above the knee and tight over the ankle. They have sections whose names are derived from local appellation and do not influence marriage. Their profession is agriculture.

Distribution of the Turks according to the Census of 1891.

Districts.	Number.	Districts.	Number.
Allahâbâd . . .	7	Tarâi	4,953
Gorakhpur . . .	7	Lucknow . . .	9
Garhwâl . . .	18	Rampur . . .	34,008
		Total .	39,002

[1] *Morâdâbâd Settlement Report*, 22; *Azamgarh Settlement Report*, 34.

U

Udâsi (Sanskrit *udas,* "to sit separate or apart from").—An order of Hindu ascetics who are said to have been founded by Sri Chand, the son of Nânak.[1] "The Udâsis were distasteful to the third Guru, Amar Dâs, who excommunicated the order; but it appears to have been revived by Bâba Gurditta, the son of the sixth Guru, Har Govind. Gurditta proclaimed his mission in the following manner: There was on a hill near Râwalpindi a Muhammadan faqîr called Budhan Shâh, to whom Bâba Nânak had entrusted some milk to be kept till his successor should come to claim it. This faqîr, seeing Gurditta approach, requested him to appear in the form of Bâba Nânak, and Gurditta having acquiesced, earned the title of Bâba and a claim to considerable sanctity. He lived mainly at Kirtârpur, but he died at Kiratpur, where there is a handsome shrine in his honour, built on an eminence commanding a fine view. At Kiratpur there is also a shrine known as Mânji Sâhib, where Bâba Gurditta is said to have discharged an arrow, which fell in the plain below at a place called Patâlpuri, long used as a burning ground for the Sodhis. Gurditta is said also to have been known merely as Bâbaji.

2. "The Udâsis are divided into four orders (called Dhuân, 'smoke,' from the fires round which they sit), named after four noted Udâsis, *viz.*, Phûl Sâhib, whose shrines are at Bahâdurpur and Chini Ghâti in the Hoshyârpur district; Bâba Hasana, whose shrine is at Charankaul, near Anandpur; Almast Sâhib, who is represented at Jagannâth and Naini Tâl; and Govind Sâhib, who is represented at Shikârpur in Sindh and at the Sangalwâla Gurudwâra in Amritsar. There are also sections called Bhagat Bhagwân and Sangat Sâhib, but it does not appear clearly whether these are separate sections or subordinate to, or identical with, some of the above. The Bhagat Bhagwâns are said to have a Gurudwâra at Patna. They are the followers of one Bhagat Gir of that city, who was converted by Dharm Chand, the grandson of Nânak.

3. "The Sangat Sâhibiya will not eat with others. They were founded by Bhâi Bhâlu, who, according to one version of the story, was a Jât merchant of the Mâlwa country; and, according to another,

---

[1] *Panjâb Census Report,* 151.

a carpenter of Amritsar. He was, while yet in darkness, a follower of Sultân, but was persuaded by Guru Govind Sinh to throw over the form of worship and adopt the name of Sangat Sâhib. Another legend ascribes the origin of the Sangat Sâhibiya to Bhâi Pheru. It is said that a large number of Jâts, carpenters, and Lohârs belong to this section. They have a Gurudwâra in the Lahore district, and the Brahmbhût Akhâra at Amritsar. Each sub-division of the Udâsis has a complete organization for collecting and spending money, and is presided over by a principal Mahant, called Sri Mahant, with subordinate Mahants under him.

4. "The Udâsis are recruited from all castes and will eat food from any Hindu. They are almost always celibates and are sometimes, though not usually, congregated in monasteries. They are generally found wandering to and fro from their sacred places, such as Amritsar, Dera Nânak, Kirtârpur, and the like. They are said to be numerous in Mâlwa and in Benares. In the Panjâb returns they appear strongly in Jâlandhar, Rohtak, and Fîrozpur. It is a mistake to say that they are not generally recognised as Sikhs; they pay special reverence to the Adi-granth, but also respect the Granth of Govind Sinh and attend the same shrines as the Sikhs generally. Their service consists of a ringing of bells and blare of instruments and waving of lights before the Adi-granth and the picture of Bâba Nânak. They are, however, by no means uniform in their customs. Some wear long hair, some wear matted locks, and others cut their hair. Some wear caste marks (*tilak*); others do not. Some burn the dead in the ordinary Hiudu way; some, after burning, erect monuments (*samâdh*); others apparently bury the dead. They are for the most part ascetics, but some are said to be engaged in ordinary secular pursuits. The ordinary dress of the ascetics is of a red colour, but a large section of them go entirely naked, except for the waist-cloth, and rub ashes over their bodies. These, like the naked sections of other orders, are known as Nangê; they pay special reverence to the ashes with which they smear their bodies and which are said to protect them equally from either extreme of temperature. Their most binding oath is on a ball of ashes.

5. "In Ludhiâna the Udâsis are mostly Jâts by origin, the disciple and successor (*chela*) being usually chosen from this tribe and are found to be in possession of the Dharmsâlas in Hindu villages, where they distribute food to such as come for it and read the Granth,

both of Bâba Nânak and of Guru Govind Sinh, though they do not attach much importance to the latter. The head of the college is called Mahant and the disciples *chelas*. They live in Sikh as well as in Hindu villages, and it is probably on this account that they do not quite neglect Guru Govind Sinh. They rarely marry; and if they do so, generally lose all influence, for the dharmsâla becomes a private residence closed to strangers. But in some few families it has always been the custom to marry, the endowments being large enough to support the family and maintain the institution; but the eldest son does not in this case succeed as a matter of course. A *chela* is chosen by the Mahant or by the family. If a Mahant whose predecessors have not married, should do so, he would lose all his weight with the people."

6. In these Provinces perhaps the most important Gurudwâra of the Udâsis is that at Dehra, which was built in 1669 A.D.[1] The Mahant is the richest man in the Dûn. His election from among the disciples (*chela*) of the last deceased Mahant was formerly guided by the Sikh chiefs of the Panjâb, a fee (*nazarâna*) of five hundred rupees being presented by the British Government at the installation with the complimentary gift in return of a pair of shawls. The distinctive head-dress of the sect worn by the high priest and his disciples is a cap of red cloth, shaped like a sugar loaf, worked over with coloured thread and adorned with a black silk fringe round the rim. Some of the more ignorant Udâsis have a legend in defiance of all chronology, that Gorakhnâth was the first disciple of the order, and was converted by Nânak. Once, they say, there was a contest between Nânak and Gorakhnâth which of them was the greater. To try his power Nânak assumed the form of a fish, and Gorakhnâth failed to catch him. But when Gorakhnâth took the shape of a mosquito, Nânak seized him. Then Gorakhnâth admitted his inferiority and became the disciple of Nânak. The form of initiation is that the Guru bathes the disciple and smears his body with ashes, and with the same substance makes a long and slightly curved mark on his forehead. Then the initiate washes the feet of the Guru and four of his senior disciples with water which he drinks. If he can afford it he then feasts the brethren. They will eat and drink from the hands of all but the lower class of

[1] Atkinson, *Himâlayan Gazetteer*, III, 197.

Hindus. They always repeat an invocation to the Creator in the words *Satya Srî Kartâr*; and they salute the brethren in the words *Gor lagâta hûn*—"I salute your feet." The use of intoxicants is strictly forbidden by the rules of order, but many use *gânja* and opium. Here they appear always to cremate their dead. Some of the ashes are occasionally kept, and a monument, which they call *jantri*, is erected over them.

Distribution of the Udâsis according to the Census of 1891.

DISTRICTS.	Number.	DISTRICTS.	Number.
Debra Dûn . . .	652	Hamîrpur . . .	1
Saharânpur . . .	357	Allahâbâd . . .	70
Muzaffarnagar . .	35	Jhânsi	6
Meerut . . .	158	Benares . . .	9
Bulandshahr . .	6	Mirzapur . . .	23
Aligarh . . .	2	Jaunpur . . .	33
Agra	10	Ghâzipur . . .	66
Farrukhâbâd . .	38	Ballia	227
Mainpuri . . .	11	Azamgarh . . .	12
Etâwah . . .	5	Garhwâl . . .	14
Etah	28	Tarâi	17
Bareilly . . .	64	Lucknow . . .	35
Bijnor . . .	105	Râê Bareli . . .	3
Budâun . . .	2	Sîtapur . . .	204
Morâdâbâd . . .	270	Kheri	46
Shâhjahânpur . .	3	Faizâbâd . .	58
Pilibhît . . .	64	Gonda	17
Cawnpur . . .	7	Bahrâich . . .	73
Fatehpur . . .	13	Sultânpur . . .	42
Bânda	5		
		TOTAL .	2,791
		Females . . .	770

Ujjaini.—A sept of Râjputs who take their name from the city of Ujjain, the Ozene of the Greeks. In Azamgarh [1] they can tell no more of their history than that they emigrated sixteen generations ago ; they once held the greater part of pargana Gopâlpur, but were obliged to give way to the Kausiks. In Cawnpur [2] they carry back their first settlement to the arrival from Ujjain of Sûr Sâh, a Panwâr Râjput, by invitation of his connection Jay Chand, of Kanauj, who invested him with the title of Râja of the Ujjainis. They are thus really of Panwâr origin. In Sultânpur [3] they are said to have succeeded the Bhars. It may be noted that some of the Bais and other Râjput septs in Oudh also claim their origin from Ujjain.

2. In Farrukhâbâd they claim to belong to the Garga *gotra* ; give girls to the Chandel, Bhadauriya, Kachhwâha, Chauhân, and Pramâr ; and marry their sons to the Chamar Gaur, Râthaur, Gaharwâr, and Sombansi. In Ballia their *gotra* is Saunak. They take wives from the Haihobansi, Barwâr, Nikumbh, Kinwâr, Raghubansi, Sengar, Sakarwâr, Chandel, Maharwâr, and Pachhtoriya. They give brides to the Bisen, Sirnet, Râjkumâr, Baghel, Bais, Kausik, Nâgbansi, Raghubansi, Chauhân, and Haihobansi.

Distribution of Ujjaini Râjputs according to the Census of 1891.

Districts.	Number.	Districts.	Number.
Farrukhâbâd . .	740	Basti	211
Mainpuri . . .	40	Azamgarh . . .	551
Etâwah . . .	121	Lucknow . . .	38
Shâhjahânpur . .	40	Unâo . . .	482
Cawnpur . . .	5	Sîtapur . . .	105
Hamîrpur . . .	3	Hardoi . . .	269
Allahâbâd . . .	5	Faizâbâd . . .	77
Benares . . .	157	Gonda . . .	15
Mirzapur . . .	4	Bahrâich . . .	19
Jaunpur . . .	19	Sultânpur . . .	207
Ghâzipur . . .	242	Partâbgarh . . .	4
Ballia . . .	775		
Gorakhpur . . .	457	Total .	4,586

[1] *Settlement Report*, 60.
[2] *Ibid*, 22, 25.
[3] *Oudh Gazetteer*, I, 25.

Ummar.—A sub-caste of Banyas found in considerable numbers, except in the Meerut, Agra, and Kumaun divisions. An attempt has been made to connect their name with that of the Umras, who are described by Colonel Tod as a branch of the Sodhas, and who gave their name to Umarkot. Those to the east say that they emigrated from the neighbourhood of Ajudhya about three generations ago. To the east they are divided into three endogamous groups—Til Ummar, Derh Ummar, and Dûsra, of which the last holds an inferior position. Widow marriage is not allowed. They agree in their customs with the Kasaundhan (*q. v.*). Their clan deities to the east of the Province are Mahâbîr, Mahâdeva, and Devi. To Mahâdeva and Mahâbîr they offer sweets, Brâhmanical cords, gram, and flowers on the twenty-eighth day of Sâwan. They worship Devi at the Naurâtri with offerings of cakes (*sohâri*), sweetmeats (*halwa*), and a burnt-offering of camphor. Their priests are Sarwariya Brâhmans.

Occupation and social life.

2. The Ummar are shopkeepers and usually sell provisions and tobacco. The use of meat and spirits is prohibited. Their priests, but not other Brâhmans, eat *pakki* prepared by them. Banyas eat *pakki* but not *kachchi* cooked by them. They will eat *pakki* cooked by Brâhmans and by other Banyas, but *kachchi* only if cooked by one of their own sub-caste.

Distribution of Ummar Banyas according to the Census of 1891.

DISTRICTS.	Number.	DISTRICTS.	Number.
Bulandshahr . . .	1	Pilibhît . . .	639
Mathura . . .	17	Cawnpur . . .	7,548
Agra . . .	35	Fatehpur . . .	2,972
Farrukhâbâd . .	883	Bânda . . .	622
Mainpuri . . .	1	Hamîrpur . . .	4,371
Etâwah . . .	168	Allahâbâd . . .	645
Bareilly . . .	61	Jhânsi . . .	1,178
Morâdâbâd . . .	1	Jâlaun . . .	302
Shâhjahânpur . .	1,752	Lalitpur . . .	1

Distribution of Ummar Banyas according to the Census of 1891—concld.

Districts.	Number.	Districts.	Number.
Benares . . .	424	Hardoi . . .	2,744
Mirzapur . . .	3,893	Kheri . . .	1,114
Jaunpur . . .	3,731	Faizâbâd . . .	14
Gorakhpur . . .	611	Gonda . . .	969
Basti . . .	537	Bahrâich . . .	1,447
Azamgarh . . .	270	Sultânpur . . .	216
Lucknow . . .	3,122	Partâbgarh . . .	2,934
Unâo . . .	812	Bârabanki . . .	1,655
Sîtapur . . .	823	Total .	46,513

Unâi, Unâya.—A sub-caste of Banyas chiefly found to the east of the Province. They take their name from their *dih* or place of origin, Unâo. To the east they have formed two endogamous groups: the Unâi and Unâwa Unâi, the latter of whom are held in higher estimation because they prohibit widow marriage. They are practically all Hindus, the Jainas being very few among them.

Distribution of Unâi Banyas according to the Census of 1891.

Districts.	Number.	Districts.	Number.
Farrukhâbâd . .	3	Râê Bareli . . .	1
Shâhjahânpur . .	27	Sîtapur . . .	2,268
Pilibhît . . .	284	Hardoi . . .	10
Cawnpur . . .	4	Kheri . . .	1,073
Benares . . .	38	Faizâbâd . . .	31
Jaunpur . . .	1,501	Gonda . . .	661
Gorakhpur . . .	4,657	Bahrâich . . .	2,966
Basti	241	Partâbgarh . . .	8
Azamgarh . . .	2	Bârabanki . . .	2,354
Lucknow . . .	1,766	Total .	17,895

Utkala.—A tribe of Brâhmans who take their name from Odra or Orissa, of whom a few are found in these Provinces. According to Mr. Beames[1]: "Tradition relates that all the original Brâhmans of Orissa were extinct at the time of the rise of the Gangavansa race of kings, but that ten thousand Brâhmans were induced to come from Kanauj and settled in Jaypur, the sacred city, on the Baitarani river. The date of this immigration is not stated, but the fact is probably historical, and may have been synchronous with the well-known introduction of Kanaujiya Brâhmans into the neighbouring province of Bengal by King Adisura in the tenth century. When the worship of the idol Jagannâth began to be revived at Puri, the Kings of Orissa induced many of the Jaypur Brâhmans to settle round the new temple and conduct the ceremonies. Thus there sprang up a division among the Brâhmans, those who settled in Puri being called the Dakkhinatiya Sreni, or Southern Class, and those who remained at Jaypur the Uttara Sreni, or Northern Class. The latter spread all over Northern Orissa. Many of the Southern Brâhmans are also found in Balasore, and the divisions of two classes are fairly represented in most parts of the district, though the Southern Class is less numerous than the Northern. The former are held in greater esteem for learning and purity of race than the latter."

2. The divisions of the Utkala Brâhmans are most extensive and intricate. As they are scantily represented in these Provinces, it will be sufficient to refer the reader to the lists given by Messrs. Sherring, Risley, and Dr. Wilson.[2]

Distribution of the Utkal Brâhmans according to the Census of 1891.

Districts.	Number.	Districts.	Number.
Sahâranpur	4	Fatehpur	3
Muzaffarnagar	1	Jâlaun	2
Mathura	26	Gorakhpur	6
Mainpuri	185	Lucknow	1
Bareilly	8	Sîtapur	1
Shâhjahânpur	11		
Cawnpur	2	Total	250

[1] Risley, *Tribes and Castes*, I, 160.
[2] *Hindu Tribes*, I, 73, *sq.*; *Indian Caste*, II, 222, *sq.*

V

Vallabhachârya, Gokulastha Gusâîn.—A sect who take their name from the great heresiarch Vallabhachârya, who was born in 1479 A.D., being the second son of Lakshman Bhat, a Talanga Brâhman of the Vishnu Swami Sampradaya. "By the accident of birth, though not by descent, he can be claimed as a native of Upper India, having been born at Champaranya, a wild solitude in the neighbourhood of Benares, whither his parents had travelled up from the South on a pilgrimage. Their stay in the holy city was cut short by a popular emeute, the result of religious intolerance; and the mother, who was little in a condition to encounter the distress and fatigue of so hasty a flight, prematurely gave birth on the way to an eight-months' child. Either from an exaggerated alarm as to their own peril, or as was afterwards said, from a sublime confidence in the promised protection of Heaven, they laid the babe under a tree and abandoned it. When some days had elapsed and their fears had subsided, they cautiously retraced their steps, and finding the child still alive and uninjured on the very spot where he had been left, they took him with them to Benares." By another form of the legend the scene of Vallabhachârya's miraculous deliverance is fixed at Chunâr, and the parents are said to have thrown the child into a well which is known as the Achâraj kûp, or "wonderful well." Hence the place is visited by large numbers of Vallabhachârya pilgrims, who have erected a temple there dedicated to Mahâ Prabhu. The slaughter of fish and other animals is specially prohibited within the sacred precincts and bathing in the sacred well is supposed to be a remedy for leprosy and barrenness in women.

Principles of the sect.

2. The sect has acquired rather disgraceful notoriety in connection with the famous Mahârâja libel case which was tried in Bombay in 1862. The proceedings of this remarkable trial have been reprinted in a book entitled "The History of the sect of the Mahârâjas of Vallabhachâryas in Western India," which gives a full account of their history, tenets, and religious practices. From this authority[1] we learn that a "Vallabhachâryan temple consists of three separate compartments. The central one is larger and more open than the

[1] Page 99, *sq.*

other two, being intended for the accommodation of the numerous worshippers who daily throng there. Of the remaining two, one is the residence of the Mahârâja, and the other is dedicated to the worship of the image of Krishna. The temples are numerous all over India, especially at Mathura and Brindaban. In Benares there are two very celebrated and wealthy temples, one of which is dedicated to Krishna under the name of Lâlji, and the other to the same god under the name of Purushottamji. Those of Jagannâth and Dwârika are also particularly venerated, but the most celebrated of all these establishments is that at Sri Nâthadwâra in Mewâr. The image is said to have transported itself thither from Mathura, when Aurangzeb ordered the temple it stood in to be destroyed. The present shrine is modern, but very richly endowed, and the high priest, a descendant of Gokulnâthji, is a man of great wealth and importance.

3. The image Thakurji, or the idol, in the different temples is either of stone or brass, and represents Krishna in various attitudes, corresponding to those which he is alleged to have assumed in the several periods of his earthly existence, either when performing uncommon feats and miracles, or living at particular places, or engaged in particularly interesting scenes. Each of these is worshipped under a different name; that of Sri Nâthji, being the most important and most honoured, is at Nâthadwâra. Krishna is here represented as a little boy in the act of supporting the mountain Govardhan on his little finger, to shelter his playmates from a heavy shower of rain which had overtaken them when at play. This image is always splendidly dressed, and richly decorated with ornaments, which are often of the value of several thousand pounds." For further particulars of the sect generally full information may be obtained in the authority from which this quotation has been made.

The Mathura Vallabhachârya.

4. Of the sect at Mathura Mr. Growse[1] writes:—"Unlike other Hindu sects, in which the religious teachers are usually unmarried, all the Gusâîns among the Vallabhachâryas are invariably family men and engage freely in secular pursuits. They are the Epicureans of the East, and are not ashamed to avow their belief that the ideal life consists rather in social enjoyment than in solitude and mortifica-

---

[1] *Mathura*, 261, *sqq*.

tion. Such a creed is naturally destructive of all self-restraint, even in matters where indulgence is by common consent held criminal; and the profligacy to which it has given rise is so notorious that the Mahârâja of Jaypur was moved to expel from his capital the ancient image of Gokul Chandrama, for which the sect entertained special veneration, and has further conceived such a prejudice against Vaishnavas in general, that all his subjects are compelled, before they appear in his presence, to mark their foreheads with the three horizontal lines that indicate a votary of Siva. However, as in many other forms of religion, and happily so in this case, practice is not always in accordance with doctrine. Though there may be much that is reprehensible in the inner life of the Gusâîns, it is not at Gokul obtruded on the public, and has never occasioned any open scandal, while the present head of the community, Gusâîn Parushottam Lâl, a descendant of Bitthalnâth's sixth son Jadunâth, deserves honourable mention for his exceptional liberality and enlightenment."

5. At all Vallabhachârya temples, the daily services are eight in number, *viz.*, 1st, Mangala, the morning levée, a little after sunrise when the god is taken from his couch and bathed; 2nd, Sringâra, an hour and a half later, when the god is attired in all his jewels and seated on his throne; 3rd, Gwâla, after an interval of about three-quarters of an hour, when the god is supposed to be starting to graze his cattle in the woods of Braj; 4th, Râj Bhog, the midday meal, which, after presentation is consumed by the priests and distributed among the votaries who have assisted at the ceremonies; 5th, Uttâpan, about 3 P.M., when the god awakes from his siesta; 6th, Bhog, the evening collation; 7th, Sandhya, the disrobing at sunset; and 8th, Sayan, the retiring to rest. Upon all these occasions the ritual concerns only the priests, and the lay worshipper is only a spectator, who evinces his reverence by any of the ordinary forms with which he would approach a human superior.

6. On the full moon of Asârh there is a curious annual ceremony for the purpose of ascertaining the agricultural prospects of the year. The priests place little packets of the ashes of different staples, after weighing them, in the sanctuary. The temple is then closed, but the night is spent in worship. In the morning the packets are examined. Should any of the packets have increased in weight, that particular article of produce will yield a good harvest; and should

they decrease, the harvest will be scanty in proportion to the decrease.

Distribution of the Gokulastha Gusâîns according to the Census of 1891.

DISTRICTS.	Number.	DISTRICTS.	Number.
Fatehpur . . .	1	Faizâbâd . . .	26
Gorakhpur . . .	3	TOTAL .	30

CASTE INDEX.

[The references are to paragraphs. The castes to which asterisks are attached are the subject of special articles.]

A

B

C

D

E

F

G

H

I

J

K

L

M

N

O

P

Q

R

S

T

U.

V

W

Y

Z

SUBJECT INDEX.[1]

A

[1] The references are to articles and paragraphs.

B

C

D

E

F

G

H

I

J

K

L

M

N

O

P

Q

R

S

T

U

V

W

Y

Z

THE TRIBES AND CASTES OF THE NORTH-WESTERN PROVINCES AND OUDH

THE TRIBES AND CASTES OF THE NORTH-WESTERN PROVINCES AND OUDH

W. CROOKE

IN FOUR VOLUMES
VOL. III

GYAN

Published by

Gyan Publishing House
5, Ansari Road
Daryaganj, New Delhi-110002
Phone: 011-47034999, 9811692060
E-mail: books@gyanbooks.com

Distribution Network
gyanbooks.com
India, USA, Canada, UK, Australia, France

ISBN : 978-81-212-4170-0 (Set)
ISBN : 978-81-212-4713-9 (HB)
First Published, Calcutta, 1896

2nd Impression 2020

Printed at: Gyan Press, Delhi.

The
Tribes and Castes of the North-Western Provinces and Oudh Vol. III
Author: W. Crooke

THE

TRIBES AND CASTES

OF THE

NORTH-WESTERN PROVINCES AND OUDH.

VOLUME III.

I

'Irâqi, Irâki, Rânki, Ranki, Râki.[1]—A sub-caste of Muhammadan Kalwârs. They profess to take their name from the country of 'Irâq, which is now divided into 'Irâq Ajami, or Persian Irâq, which is nearly coincident with ancient Media, and 'Irâq Arabi, or Arabian Irâq, on the lower course of the Tigris and Euphrates.[2] According to others the name is only a corruption of 'Araqi, from,' Araq "spirituous liquor." In Bihâr they are known as Kalâl, which is merely a variant of Kalwâr and the name by which the tribe are known in the Eastern Panjâb.[3] The word Kalâl is derived from the Sanskrit *kalyapâla*, *kalyâpâla*, *kalyapâlaka* or *kalyâpâlaka*,[4] meaning "a distiller." Some of the Rânkis profess to be the descendants of Persian immigrants, but there seems little doubt that they are little more than Kalwârs who have embraced Islâm. The professed Muhammadan members are said to call themselves Rânki, while others who call themselves Ranki occasionally for the sake of trade sink their Muhammadanism, and revert to the name of Kalwâr, which suits their Hindu customers better. The only difference between them is that Rankis fasten their coats in Hindu fashion to the left and Rânkis in Muhammadan fashion to the right. A Rânki wears a beard and uses a tinned water jar (*badhna*); the Ranki wears no beard and uses

---

[1] Based on local enquiries at Mirzapur, and a very complete note by Sayyid Khairuddîn Husain Khân, Excise Superintendent, Azamgarh.

[2] Irâq (Mesopotamia) means "a level country beside the banks of a river."—Burton, *Arabian Nights*. *Note 53rd Night.*

[3] Risley, *Tribes and Castes*, II., 196; Ibbetson, *Panjab Ethnography*, 335.

[4] Mr. Nesfield's suggestion to connect the word with the *Khairwâr* catechu-maker, and Mr. Risley's derivation from *kalwâla*, "one who works a machine," *Kal* (*loc. cit.* I., 385) are equally untenable.

a brass *lota*. The Rânkis in Mirzapur fix their head-quarters at a place called Belkhara, in the Partâbgarh District, whence they emigrated some forty years ago.

Traditions of origin.

2. Once upon a time, they say, a Muhammadan army passed Belkhara, and the soldiers seized a Kalwâr and made him a Muhammadan by force. His descendants are the present Rânkis. There seems little doubt that their conversion occurred in comparatively recent times. Those who have advanced in the belief in Islâm regard Hazrat Jilâni of Bâghdâd as their patron saint.

Tribal organization and marriage rules.

3. Those in Mirzapur certainly have a tribal council (*panchâyat*) which is said not to be the case in Azamgarh,[1] but as they have scattered about in small numbers it is not influential. The president, who is a hereditary officer, is called Chaudhari. Formerly, it is said, the council used to meet to settle trade questions, but now since their dispersion it has become a simple council which meets to settle charges of adultery, breach of caste rules, and the like. Illicit intercourse with a woman of another caste is punished by expulsion, and the offender is re-admitted on feeding the clan on meat boiled with rice (*pulâo*) and liquor. A few years ago the tribal council of the town Rânkis prescribed abstinence from spirits, but the scattered members of the tribe do not carry out this order. If a man seduce a woman of the caste he is obliged to marry her by the Nikâh form. If a woman intrigue with an outsider she is permanently expelled. Their rules of exogamy appear to be a sort of compromise between Hindu and Muhammadan rules. At the last census the Muhammadan Irâqis were recorded in fourteen sections :—Anfi, Angi, Bandi, Bata, Kaldâr, Panchambar, Quraishi, Rafki, Rângi or Rânki, Sâna, Shaikh, Sadîqi, and Zangi. But these do not appear to influence marriage. A man may not marry the daughter of his father's sister or of his own sister, but he can marry the daughter of his maternal uncle. They give daughters as brides into families with which they are already closely intermarried, but do not take wives from them. Polygamy is recognised. Women have considerable freedom before marriage, but after marriage are secluded until they have three or four children, when the restriction ceases. If a man seduce an unmarried girl, both are put out of caste until their respective

[1] Mr. J. R. Reid, *Settlement Report*, 36.

fathers give a tribal feast; and they are then married by the Nikâh form and admitted to caste. Girls are usually married at the age of ten and the boys at fifteen. The marriage is arranged by the brother-in-law of the boy's father. The consent of the parents is essential, and the parties have no freedom of choice. No bride price is paid. After the consummation of the marriage, the bride's father is expected to give something to the bridegroom's father by way of dowry: this becomes the property of the bride. No physical defect arising after marriage is sufficient to annul it, but this is not the case if any defect in either party which existed before marriage has been fraudulently concealed by the relations on either side. When a woman is proved to be habitually unchaste, she is divorced by the council, and a regular letter of divorcement is drawn up. The marriage of widows and divorced women with leave of the council is permitted, and their children rank equally with those of a regular marriage.[1]

Widow marriage and levirate.

4. Marriage of widows is performed by the Qâzi reading the *Nikâh* over both parties. The man gives the widow some jewels and a sheet, which she puts on. Her father is then expected to feast the clansmen, but if he cannot afford this, he gives them a drink of sharbat, and the ceremony is complete. Contrary to Muhammadan customs,[2] the levirate is permitted with the ordinary restriction that it is only the younger brother of her late husband who can take the widow to wife. If the right of the levirate be not claimed, she can marry outside the family of her late husband. In this case the children by her late husband remain in charge of his brother, and they will inherit their father's estate. The same rule applies in the case of the levirate, with this difference that the levir, in addition to being a trustee for his nephews, is, during their minority, entitled to the usufruct of their estate. There is no fiction of attributing the children of the levir to the mother's first husband.

Adoption.

5. A sonless man may adopt a son with the consent of his heirs. He may adopt his daughter's son. While an adopted son is alive, a second

[1] There appears to be no fixed rule that a divorced woman cannot marry within the period of *iddah*.—Hughes' *Dictionary of Islám*, 317.

[2] The only Muhammadan races among whom it appears to exist are the Afghâns.—Elphinstone, *Picture of the Kingdom of Cabul, I., 168*, quoted by Letourneau, *Evolution of Marriage*; 263; and the Biluchis, Westermarck, *History of Human Marriage*, 511, note.

not be adopted. A bachelor, a blind, impotent or lame man can adopt, but not an ascetic. A woman can adopt only by permission of her husband, and if a man adopt a son his widow cannot adopt again. But she can adopt if such adopted son dies, provided the property be the acquired property of her husband. A man can give his only or eldest son or brother to his brother for adoption. A girl may be adopted. The person, however, usually adopted is a nephew or son-in-law, but preference is given to a nephew. In default of a nephew on the male side or daughter's son or son-in-law, they adopt a sister's son. If the son adopted give shares to his brothers in the property of his adoptive father, he can also inherit from his natural father. But not unless the condition is fulfilled, or unless his natural father leave no other son. All this is, of course, contrary to Muhammadan law. "An adopted son or daughter of known descent has no right to inherit from his or her adoptive parents and their relatives—the filiation of this description being neither recommended nor recognized by Muhammadan law. Such son or daughter is, however, entitled to what may be given under a valid deed in gift or will. In this particular the Muhammadan agrees with the English and the Hindu with the Roman law."[1] If after adoption a natural son be born, he and the adopted son share equally. The custom of beena marriage prevails to some extent, and in this case the son-in-law living with his father-in-law acquires no rights of inheritance.

Succession.

6. A man's heirs are his sons, but the property is divided according to the number of mothers. A father cannot during his lifetime nominate particular son to take a larger share than that of the others. When an estate has been held jointly by a father and his sons, and is distributed among the sons on the father's decease, the sons will take all the joint estate, moveable or immoveable, ancestral or acquired. But any part of such estate which a particular son has acquired by succession from his maternal grandfather or father-in-law does not come under division. When there are no sons, but grandsons or great-grandsons, the shares are allotted according to the number of sons of the deceased. If a man die leaving a widow or widows, a daughter and daughters and brothers with their descendants, but no male lineal descendants within their generations, the inheritance

[1] *Tagore Law Lectures*, 1873, p. 124.

will devolve on the brothers; but the widow is entitled to maintenance. The widow, however, will inherit if her late husband lived apart from his brothers, and she can alienate by sale. But if she become unchaste, her husband's brethren will exclude her and take the property. A daughter never inherits from the father unless during his lifetime he assign her a share by deed; and she has no right to maintenance out of her father's estate. But by caste rules the brothers are held bound, out of love and affection, to support their sisters who are childless widows. If a man used to live separate from his brothers with his mother, and dies without a male lineal descendant, a widow, a daughter or daughter's son, the inheritance will devolve upon the mother. She has a life interest, and at her death the nearest agnate will inherit. It seems also agreed that when the inheritance passes to the associated brethren the owner may by will select a particular brother as his heir. When a wife dies holding property in her own right, the husband succeeds. The son of a widow who re-marries inherits from his father. The step-father supports him till he is twelve years old, after which he returns to his father's family. A man who retires from the world and joins a religious order loses his right to inherit or to retain his property, which passes to his heirs.

Birth ceremonies.

7. There is no ceremony during pregnancy. When parturition is difficult, the woman is given some water to drink on which a Maulavi has blown and over which he has recited some passages of the Qurân. The woman is delivered on the ground. After birth a Chamâin midwife is called in, who cuts the cord and buries it in the ground where the child is born. Over it a fire is kept lighting till the twelfth day. On the sixth day the midwife bathes the mother and child. On the twelfth day the whole house is whitewashed and plastered, and the earthen vessels replaced. On that day the mother and child are bathed by the barber's wife. Her feet are not dyed with lac, as is usual with Hindus. While she is being bathed her women friends sing. On that day, if the father can afford it, he feeds the clansmen on bread, rice, and parched gram. Some families who are extra strict consider the mother impure for forty days.

Circumcision.

8. A boy is circumcised (*Musalmâni karâna*) at the age of five or seven. The ceremony is done in the month of Ramzân or Barê Pîr. Sweet bread

and meat boiled with rice (*pulão*) are first offered to God with prayers, and then the barber making the boy stand facing the east performs the operation. Before and after the boy prays in a mosque. During the operation the boy is given a dose of ma'jûm composed of *bhang* and sugar. The wound is washed with a decoction of makoya (? sarsaparilla), oil of jasmine (*chameli*) or cocoanut, and a decoction of the leaves of the *nîm* tree is applied daily. The barber receives four annas as his remuneration and a pice or two from each of the friends present. After this the clansmen are feasted.

Marriage.

9. The marriage arrangements are made by the brother-in-law, or in default of him by some near relation of the boy's father. Then comes the betrothal (*mangani*). The marriage follows a year after. They have the *matmangar* ceremony as among low Hindus.[1] Some families set up a nuptial shed (*mânro*), and some do not. In the same way some anoint the bridegroom with turmeric and oil: others use only mustard oil. Before the procession starts the clansmen are entertained at a feast (*bhatwân*). Some offer on the wedding day sweet bread and other choice food to God and Muhammad, others do not. The bridegroom in a white or yellow dress is taken to his bride's house on horseback. When the procession reaches the bride's door, her relations advance a few paces to receive and then escort them to the place prepared for their reception. The Qâzi then reads the *Nikâh* first over the bridegroom and then over the bride, after which the friends are treated to sharbat and given a feast. Next morning the bride's father produces the dowry before the friends of the bridegroom, and after feasting them the bride is dismissed with her husband. Some follow the Hindu practice of plunging the marriage festoons (*bandarwâr*) into running water on the fourth day after the wedding. This form of marriage is called *shâdi* or *charhanwa*, in distinction with widow marriage, *sagâi*.

Burial.

10. The dead are buried in the usual Muhammadan way in a burial ground known as Harâwal, "the place of bones" (*hâr, haddi*). The body in the grave is covered with boards, over which leaves of the *palâs* (*butea frondosa*) are laid. After the funeral sharbat is distributed to clansmen. On the fourth day rice and *pulâo* are distributed to

[1] For this see *Bhuiya*, para. 14.

friends and beggars. In the same way, on the tenth day food is distributed in the name of the dead, and the clansmen are fed on the twentieth day, and again on the fortieth, while money, cloth and the articles used by the deceased are given to a Maulavi in the hope that the spirit will enjoy them in the land of the dead.[1] On the Shab-i-barât every year bread, meat, and the *halwa* sweetmeat are offered in the name of the dead.

Religion.

11. Rânkis are Muhammadans of the Sunni sect. Those resident in villages observe yearly the marriage of Ghâzi Miyân, and offer in his name sacrifices of goats, rams, and sweetmeats. They also worship the Hindu goddess Bhawâni. They make pilgrimages to the graves of martyrs (*sayyid,* a corruption of *shahîd*), and offer to them blood sacrifices and sweetmeats. Their festivals are the Îd, Baqrîd, marriage of Ghâzi Miyân, and Muharram. During the Muharram many of them get drunk. To protect children from evil spirits they put an amulet (*ta'awîz*), blessed by a Maulavi, round their necks. The ghosts of the dead are supposed to visit their friends in dreams naked and to bring disease. They observe the usual Hindu meeting and other omens.

Social life.

12. Women wear a number of silver rings in the ears and an ornament known as *patta,* nose-rings (*nathiya*), necklaces, wrist ornaments,(*chûri, dharkaua*), arm ornaments (*jaushan, bâzu*), anklets (*kara, pairi*). They swear by the form *Râmdohâi* and by the Vindhyabâsini Devi of Bindhâchal; those more under the influence of Islâm on water and the Qurân. They employ Ojhas in cases of demoniacal possession. The effects of the Evil-eye are removed by the incantations of a Muhammadan Faqîr. They will not eat pork and will not touch a Dom or Mehtar, or the wife of a younger brother. The more circumspect are teetotallers. Those who live in cities eat beef, but villagers do not. They will eat the flesh of the horse and camel, fowls and fish, but not alligators, snakes, lizards, or rats. The men eat apart and before the women. Before eating they say a grace,

---

[1] The practice of leaving articles for the use of the dead is common. See Parkman, *Jesuits in North America, Introduction*, para. 81. He quotes the *Times* of October 28th, 1865, describing the funeral rites of Lord Palmerston : "And as the words 'Dust to Dust, Ashes to Ashes,' were pronounced, the chief mourner, as a last precious offering to the dead, threw into the grave several diamond and gold rings."

bismillâh. They use opium, gânja, and tobacco freely. When a guest arrives the women seize his feet and weep. This is known as *bhentna.* Then they wash his feet and give him drink and tobacco. They salute in the Muhammadan form, *assalâmu 'âlaikam,* with the reply *Wâ 'alaikum assalâm.* No Hindu eats the leavings of their food except Doms and Mehtars. They will not eat food touched by a Dom, Chamâr, Dhobi or Mehtar.

13. They are generally petty shopkeepers, often selling pipes and tobacco and lending money. There is a colony of them in the town of Lâr in Gorakhpur, who are influential and thriving merchants, who deal largely in hides and ordinary country produce.

Occupation.

Distribution of the 'Irâqis according to the Census of 1891.

District.	Numbers.	District.	Numbers.
Sahâranpur	10	Gorakhpur	2,910
Muzaffarnagar	2	Basti	139
Meerut	28	Azamgarh	1,005
Agra	6	Tarâi	13
Farrukhâbâd	28	Unâo	42
Etah	3	Hardoi	36
Bareilly	1	Kheri	125
Allahâbâd	33	Faizâbâd	161
Jâlaun	55	Gonda	307
Benares	13	Bahrâich	332
Jaunpur	641	Sultânpur	1,141
Ghâzipur	2,079	Partâbgarh	7
Ballia	2,560	Total	11,677

J

Jâdon.—(Sanskrit *Yâdava*). A sept of Râjputs who claim their descent and name from Yadu, son of Yayâti, the fifth monarch of the Lunar dynasty. Colonel Tod calls them "the most illustrious of all the tribes of Ind"; but in the Panjâb their name has been overshadowed by the Bhatti, the title of their dominant branch in modern times. "The only Hindu descendants of the Yaduvansi at the present day are the Jâdons of the small state of Karauli to the west of the Chambal and at Sabalgarh or Jadonvati in the Gwâlior territory east of that river; but the Musalmâns of acknowledged Jâdon descent form a very large portion of the population of Eastern Râjputána, from Sohna and Alwar on the west to the Chambal on the east, and from the banks of the Jumna to Karauli and Sabalgarh on the south. These Jâdon Musalmâns are known as Khânzâdas and Meos. The Yaduvansi claim descent from Krishna. The first historical name is Dharma Pâla, 77th in descent from Krishna. His title Pâla has come down to the present Karauli Râjas. His date is about 800 A.D. His capital was Bayâna, from which his descendants were driven out by Muhammad Ghori and Kutb-ud-dîn Aibak who took Tahangarh in 1196 A.D. After this the Jâdon Râja retired to Karauli and thence across the Jumna to Sabalgarh, but eventually returned to Karauli."[1]

2. The tribe in these Provinces is now represented by the Râja of Awa in Pargana Jalesar of the Etah District, whose pedigree is, however, somewhat doubtful. The family in Jewar of Bulandshahr are known as Chhokarzâda, or descendants of a slave girl, and the inferior members of the tribe are called Bâgri, as a title of reproach.[2] The Barêsir of Agra are said to have been given this title, which corresponds to Bahâdur, by Akbar for their services at the siege of Chithor. They claim descent from Râja Tindpâl of Bayâna. The Jasâwat are another branch of immigrants to Agra from Jaysalmer and Jaypur. There appears to be no trace in these Provinces of the regular houses (*Kothri*) of Karauli—Hâdoti; Amargarh; Inâyati; Raontra; Bartûn; Hari Dâs; Mukund.[3] Some of the Jâdons, such as those in Mathura, allow widow marriage, and have hence

[1] Cunningham, *Archæological Reports,* XX., 5, sqq.
[2] Raja Lachhman Sinh, *Bulandshahr Memo.* 160, sq.
[3] *Karauli Gazetteer,* 46.

fallen in estimation. The Nâra are said to be descended from a barber woman (*nâyan*) as also the Bâgri clan about Bharatpur and Banda. Several of the Jât tribes are also said to be Jâdons and the Sinsinwâl of Bharatpur are predominant among them. The Ahar also call themselves Jâdons of inferior descent.

3. They hold the Ganges in particular veneration. They are now quiet and well-conducted, and it may be noted that their asserted forefathers, the Yâdava, are called Ahinsaka, or "inoffensive," in the Vêda.[1]

4. There is by one account a difference between the Jâdon and the Jâdonbansi, the latter being more respectable than the former. The Jâdons are said to be endogamous, while the Jâdonbansi ally themselves with the respectable Râjput septs; but this is, of course, denied by the wealthier members of the sept.

Distribution of the Jâdon and Jâdubansi Râjputs according to the Census of 1891.

DISTRICT.	Jâdon.	Jâdubansi.	TOTAL.
Sahâranpur	...	32	32
Muzaffarnagar	...	23	23
Meerut	...	264	264
Bulandshahr	11,316	250	11,566
Aligarh	...	31,905	31,905
Mathura	14,546	984	14,530
Agra	8,530	54	8,584
Farrukhâbâd	156	4	160
Mainpuri	1,348	55	1,403
Etâwah	832	...	832
Etah	11,015	190	11,205
Bareilly	...	446	446
Bijnor	...	23	23
Budaun	...	468	468

[1] Wilson, *Rig Veda*, I., 279.

Distribution of the Jâdon and Jâdubansi Râjputs according to the census of 1891.—contd.

District.	Jâdon.	Jâdubansi.	Total.
Morâdâbâd	...	21	21
Shâhjahânpur	...	19	19
Pilibhît	...	50	50
Cawnpur	596	11	607
Fatehpur	37	2	39
Hamîrpur	14	9	23
Allahâbâd	...	69	69
Jhânsi	28	30	58
Jâlaun	186	665	851
Lalitpur	4	...	4
Benares	...	3	3
Ghâzipur	2	1	3
Ballia	...	83	83
Azamgarh	...	19	19
Tarâi	...	2	2
Râê Bareli	...	16	16
Sîtapur	...	15	15
Hardoi	...	5	5
Kheri	...	73	73
Faizâbâd	...	3	3
Gonda	...	1	1
Sultânpur	...	13	13
Partâbgarh	...	32	32
Total	48,610	35,840	84,450

Jais.—A Râjput sept found in the Central Duâb, who claim to derive their name from the old town of Jais in the Râê Bareli District. In Mathura they say that they moved from Jais to Bikâner, and that their ancestor, Jas Râm, who first settled at Bhadanwâra after dispossessing the Kalârs, was a leper who had been cured of his disease by a pilgrimage to the sacred places at Braj; in acknowledgment of the divine favour, he constructed the Râm Tâl at Sunrakh and made his home there. The titles in the family are Kunwar for the elder and Bâbûji for the younger branch.[1] Sir H. M. Elliot remarks that their rank may be judged by the fact that they receive in marriage the daughters of Kachhwâha, Jaiswâr and Bâchhal Râjputs.[2]

Jaiswâr.—A sub-caste of Banyas with both a Hindu and a Jaina branch. Like so many sub-divisions of other tribes, they take their name from the old town of Jais in the Râê Bareli District. Sir H. M. Elliot notes[3] that "Qasba Jais is mentioned with distinction in the early Muhammadan authors, particularly in the Lutâif-i-Ashrafi, or record of the acts and opinions of Ashraf Jahângîr. On one occasion when this sainted person visited Jais it is stated that nearly three thousand pupils came out to pay their respects. In the Imperial Register also it is mentioned as the chief town of a large Pargana; and it may be questioned if it was not even at one time the seat of a subordinate Government, for in a book published at Leyden in 1631, *De Imperio Magni Mogolis sine India Vera*, the author, Jean de Laet, divides the empire into thirty-seven provinces, of which one is Zesswal or Jesswal; and as there is no other in his list which at all corresponds with Oudh, or any other place in its neighbourhood, we may, in want of more certain information, surmise that Jais may have been intended." But the place there mentioned is said to lie east of Patna and has been identified by a recent writer with Rangpur.[4] The ancient name of Jais was Udyânnagar, said to be derived from its founder the Saint Udalik Muni. It was a Bhar stronghold and was destroyed by Sayyid Sâlâr Masaud. It has been suggested that the original name of the place meant "garden" (Sans. *udyâna*), and that the modern name is only a Persian translation of this—*Jâê' Aish*—meaning either "place of delight" or "place of an army."

2. The Jaiswâr Banyas are strongest in Aligarh and Agra.

---

[1] Growse, *Mathura*, 420.

[2] *Supplementary Glossary*, s. v.

[3] *Supplemental Glossary*, s. v. *Jaiswâr*.

[4] *Calcutta Review*, 1870, p. 346; and see *Oudh Gazetteer*, II., 95; *Sultânpur Settlement Report*, 34, *sq*.

Distribution of Jaiswâr Banyas according to Census of 1891.

DISTRICTS.	Hindus.	Jainas.	TOTAL.
Bulandshahr	2	1	3
Aligarh	1,894	301	2,195
Mathura	116	41	157
Agra	710	3,312	4,02
Farrukhâbâd	6	...	6
Etah	24	265	289
Budaun	8	62	70
Morâdâbâd	...	3	3
Shâhjahânpur	3	...	3
Pilibhît	3	...	3
Cawnpur	10	...	10
Bânda	...	1	1
Allahâbâd	66	...	66
Lalitpur	...	30	30
Benares	33	...	33
Ghâzipur	68	...	68
Ballia	14	...	14
Gorakhpur	82	...	82
Azamgarh	130	...	130
Lucknow	17	...	17
Râê Bareli	7	...	7
Sîtapur	4	...	4
Bahrâich	4	...	4
TOTAL	3,201	4,046	7,247

Jaiswâr.—(Residents of the old town of Jais in the Râê Bareli District).—A sept of Râjputs. The term is really only another name for the Bhatti, or rather of one clan of the Bhatti tribe. The Bhatti are, however, considered of higher rank than the Jaiswâr, the latter having intermarried with spurious Râjputs. Many of them are now known as Gûjars. There is another sept in the Central Duâb known as Jais who do not appear in the returns of the last Census. They are said to have moved from Jais to Bikâner. In Mathura[1] they say that their ancestor was Jasrâm, who first settled at Bhadanwâra after dispossessing the Kalârs, and that he was a leper who had been cured by a pilgrimage to Braj. The titles of the family are Kunwar for the eldest, Bâbûji for the younger branch. Sir H. M. Elliot remarks that their rank may be judged by their receiving in marriage the daughters of the Kachhwâha, Jaiswâr and Bâchbal Râjputs. The rank of the sept is, however, not high, and they are said to give girls to the Bargala and Bâchhal, and to take girls from the Bargala.

Distribution of Jaiswâr Râjputs according to the Census of 1891.

District.	Number.	District.	Number.
Muzaffarnagar	5	Shâhjahânpur . . .	13
Meerut	131	Pilibhît	50
Bulandshahr . . .	1,235	Hamîrpur . . .	221
Aligarh	6	Allahâbâd . . .	29
Mathura	189	Jhânsi	968
Agra	15	Lalitpur . . .	1
Farrukhâbâd . . .	354	Gorakhpur . . .	33
Mainpuri	157	Azamgarh . . .	4
Etâwah	132	Lucknow . . .	38
Etah	168	Kheri	9
Bareilly	98	Faizâbâd . . .	10
Budaun	52	Bârabanki . . .	194
		Total .	4,112

[1] Growse, *Mathura*, 420.

JALÂLI.

Jalâli.—A class of Muhammadan Faqîrs who take their name from their founder Sayyid Jalâl-ud-dîn, who was a native of Bukhâra and a pupil of Bahâwal Haqq, the Sahrwardi saint of Multân, whose shrine is at Uchh in Bahâwalpur territory. "This teacher," says Mr. Maclagan,[1] "was himself a strict follower of the law, but his followers who call themselves Jalâlis are in many ways backsliders. They pay little attention to prayer. They use large quantities of *bhang*, and are given to eating snakes and scorpions. They shave their beards, moustaches and eye-brows, and wear only a small scalp-lock (*choti*) on the right side of the head. They are branded with a special mark on the right shoulder, wear glass armlets, have a woollen cord round their necks, a cloth on their heads, and are a vagabond set with no fixed dwelling-places. There is a section of the order known as the Chahl Tan, or 'Forty Bodies,' who are said to be derived from a luckless woman who, wishing to be a mother, swallowed forty philtres instead of one, and thus produced forty children in place of one only. The Jalâlis are said to be strong in Central Asia."

Distribution of the Jalâlis according to the Census of 1891.

DISTRICT.	Number.	DISTRICT.	Number.
Dehra Dûn	24	Pilibhît	17
Sahâranpur	421	Allahâbâd	36
Muzaffarnagar	596	Ghâzipur	10
Meerut	478	Gorakhpur	4
Bulandshahr	278	Basti	1
Farrukhâbâd	14	Azamgarh	536
Etâwah	6	Tarâi	34
Etah	43	Lucknow	33
Bareilly	319	Sîtapur	87
Bijnor	424	Bahrâich	48
Morâdâbâd	176	Bârabanki	128
Shâhjahânpur	58	TOTAL .	3,771

[1] *Panjâb Census Report*, 195 *sq.*

Jangama.—(Sanskrit *jangama*, "moving.")—A Saiva order, who are also called Linga-dhâri, because they wear a miniature lingam on the breast or arm. In the Panjâb they are regarded as a class of Jogis who wear brass flowers in their ears instead of the ordinary *mundra* earrings. It is said that when Siva at his marriage desired to give alms to the Brâhmans, no Brâhman appeared; the god thereupon tore open his leg (*janga, jangha*) and produced therefrom a man called Jangama, to whom he gave his alms. "These Jangamas are looked on as Brâhmans, and are said to correspond with the Lingâyats[1] of Central and Southern India. They dress and live like Jogis; they beg in the bâzârs, demanding a pice from every shop; they go about ringing bells, they carry peacock feathers in their hands and sing songs in praise of Siva." [2]

2. Of the sect in the hills Mr. Atkinson writes—"They acknowledge the spiritual supremacy of Bâsava (Vrishabha), who was minister of Bijjala Deva, Kalachûri Râja of Kalyâna, and murdered his master in 1135 A. D. Bâsava wrote the Bâsava Purâna, and his nephew the Channa Bâsava Purâna, which are still the great authorities of the sect. They style themselves Puritan followers of Siva under the form of a *linga*, and all others idolators. They say that they reverence the Vedas and the writings of Sankara Achârya, but they reject the Mahâbhârata, Râmâyana and Bhâgavata as the invention of Brâhmans. They consider both Sankara Achârya and Bâsava as emanations of Siva. Bâsava himself was a Siva Brâhman and devoted himself to the worship of Siva under the form of a *linga*, as the one god approachable by all. He denounced the Brâhmans as worshippers of many gods, goddesses, deified mortals, and even of cows, monkeys, rats and snakes. He set aside the Veda as the supreme authority, and taught that all human beings are equal, and hence men of all castes, and even women, can become spiritual guides to the Jangamas. Marriage is imperative with Brâhmans, but permissive only with the followers of Bâsava. Child marriage is unknown, and betrothal in childhood unnecessary. Polygamy is permissible with the leave of a childless wife. A widow is treated with respect and may marry again, though, while she is a widow, she may not retain the jacket, perfumes, paints, black glass armlets, nose and toe rings, which form the peculiar garb of the married

---

[1] Monier Williams, *Brahmanism and Hinduism*, 88.
[2] Maclagan, *Panjâb Census Report*, 116.

women. A Jangama always returns a woman's salutation, and only a breach of chastity can cause her to lose her position. They are also called Vîra Saiva, to distinguish them from the Arâdhya, another division of the worshippers of Bâsava, who call themselves descendants of Brâhmans and could not be induced to lay aside the Brâhmanical thread, the rite of assuming which requires the recital of the Gâyatri or hymn to the Sun. Hence the Jangamas regard this section as idolators and reject their assistance. Those who totally reject the assistance of Brâhmans are called Sâurânya and Visesha. The Sâmânya or ordinary Jangama may take wine and betel and may eat in any one's house, but can marry only in his own caste. The Visesha is the Guru or spiritual preceptor of the rest. The lesser vows are addressed to the *linga*, the Guru and the Jangama brother in the faith. The *linga* represents the deity, and the Guru he who breathes the sacred spell into the ear and makes the neophyte one with the deity; hence he is reverenced above the natural parents. The *lingas* in temples are fixed there and are hence called *Sthâvira*; the *lingas* of Bâsava are called *Jangama*, or "able to move about," and the followers Jangama or living incarnations of the *linga*. The Arâdhyas retain as much of the Brâhmanical ceremonial as possible; they look down on women and admit no proselytes. They call themselves Vaidika and say that the Jangams are Vedabahyas. The latter declare that every one has a right to read the Veda for himself, and that the Arâdhyas are poor blind leaders of the blind, who have wrested the Scriptures to the destruction of themselves and others. The Jangama worships Siva as Sadasiu, the form found in Kedâr, who is invisible, but pervades all nature. By him the *linga* is worshipped as a reliquary and brings no impure thought. He abhors Mâya or Kâli, who is one with Yona, and is opposed to licentiousness in morals and manners. He aims at release from earthly lusts by restraining the passions; he attends to the rules regarding funerals, marriage, and the placing of infants in the creed, and is, as a rule, decent, sober and devout. Burial is substituted for cremation, and Brâhmans are set aside as priests."[1]

3. The Jangamas in Benares, who call themselves Vîra Saiva or Lingadhâri, profess to be the followers of VîraBhadra, the son of Mahâdeva. In this sect are found Brâhmans, Kshatriyas, Vaisyas,

[1] *Himalayan Gazetteer*, II., 862, sqq.

and Sûdras, Sannyâsis, and Achâryas. Unlike other Hindu sects, it binds all its members in a bond of brotherhood. There are ascetic as well as house-keeping members. They will not eat or drink from the hands of other castes or sects, but they avoid Doms, Chamârs and similar menials, even if they belong to the sect. On the twelfth day after a child is born one of the house-keeping (*grihastha*) Jangamas comes and worships a miniature *linga* with an offering of sandal-wood (*chandan*), washed rice (*achchhat*), flowers, and incense, and ties the *linga* round the neck of the infant. This *linga* remains with the child all its life and even accompanies him to the grave. When the child is five years old the initiation rite is done in the following way:—A holy square (*chauk*) is made on which is placed a sacred water jar (*kalas*). The Guru or Mahant sits in the square and his feet are worshipped with an offering of sandal-wood, holy rice, flowers, a lamp and sweetmeats. The neophyte bathes and puts on a sheet of silk (*pitámbar*), or, in default of this, a wet loin cloth, and smears his forehead with ashes. The formula of initiation—*Om namah Sivay*—is whispered into his ear. After this, if the child is intended to live a worldly life, he is kept at home; if he is intended to be an ascetic, he is made over to the Mahant, who takes him to his monastery, and for a year or two teaches the rules of the Siva *linga* worship.

4. To make him a perfect Jangama he is initiated for a second time. A week or so before the day fixed for the ceremony the Guru sends an invitation to the other members of the sect, and a special invitation is sent to the Guru of another monastery asking him to attend with Siddheswara Deota. The Guru of every monastery has an image of this deity, which is made of ashes and is regarded as the family deity. When all are present, a square is made in which the Guru sits. The neophyte is shaved by a barber and after bathing and putting on a silken robe he sits before the Guru. The worship of Siddheswara is performed in the same way as the worship of the Guru at the first initiation, and the same *mantra* is whispered again into the ear of the lad, after which he prostrates himself three times before the Guru. A feast to the brethren follows, and the ceremony ends with the presentation of money and clothes to the Guru who has brought the image of Siddheswara. After this the lad is known as *kânaka ki murti*, or "the golden image," and a full disciple of his Guru.

5. The Guru may have as many disciples as he pleases, and from

among them he chooses his successor. When a disciple is appointed successor to the Guru he is called Pati, "Lord," or Chariti, "Minister." Sometimes one, sometimes two, persons hold these two posts. When he is appointed successor of the Guru, the worship of Siddheswara is performed as at his initiation. A burnt sacrifice (*homa*) is done and all the members present, following the Mahant who brings the image of Siddheswara, mark the forehead of the candidate and offer him costly presents, and all fall down on the ground before him.

6. Jangamas are generally wealthy people, and many of them own landed property. The worldly members of the sect marry in their own caste, but only with members of the sect. Their ceremonies are performed just like those of ordinary high-class Hindus. The mendicant members dress like Sannyâsis. Some wear long locks (*jata*); others shave their heads, beards, and moustaches. They wear clothes dyed in ochre and in the ears rings (*kundal*) of Rudrâksha beads. They have a miniature *linga* round the neck. The Mahant wears usually a turban dyed in ochre, and he never wears shoes, but sandals (*kharaun*). The worldly members may dress as they please; the only mark of their sect which they carry is a miniature *linga* in a small box of gold, silver, brass, or copper, which is tied in a piece of cloth on the neck or right wrist.

7. They bury their dead in the following way:—The corpse is washed and dressed in the clothes worn during life. Then the whole is smeared over with ashes and a necklace of Rudrâksha beads tied on it. It is then seated on a stool in a sitting posture and worshipped as a form of Mahâdeva with sandal, holy rice, flowers, etc.; songs are sung before it; texts of the Scriptures recited and musical instruments played. This goes on for a whole day or more, and large sums are spent in charity. The grave is dug from north to south and is two and a half yards in length and one and a half yards broad. On the north side steps are made, and on the southern side a small room is dug with a bricked arch for a doorway leading into the grave. The corpse, with loud cries of "*Mahâdeva, Mahâdeva,*" is brought into the side-room, seated on a sort of chair (*chauki*) and placed facing the north. It is worshipped with sandal-wood, holy rice, flowers, leaves of the *bel* tree and ashes. In this room are placed all the articles which an ascetic Jangama needs in his lifetime. The whole corpse is then covered with ashes and *bel* leaves. The room is then closed with a wooden door leaving the corpse inside and the grave is

filled up with earth. The only succeeding ceremonies are on the second and thirteenth day; on the second day the members of the sect are fed; on the thirteenth there is a second feast for members of the sect as well as for outsiders. Sayyadâna or "bed gifts," which correspond to the gifts made to a Mahâbrâhman at a Hindu funeral and intended for the use of the spirit in the other world, are among the Jangamas made to a member of the sect. Over the chamber in which the corpse is placed a mound (*samâdhi*) is raised, and on it is placed a *linga* of Mahâdeva, which is daily worshipped.

8. One of the chief duties of the members of the sect is to revere the Mahant like a deity. All orders issued by him must at any cost be obeyed. Whenever they meet him, whether the place be clean or foul, they must prostrate themselves before him. They have notning to do with Brâhmans in their religious or domestic ceremonies. Those who beg ask only for uncooked food. They beg in the name of Mahâdeva. All of them abstain from animal food and intoxicating liquor. They do not care to look on any one who does not wear a necklace of Rudrâksha beads; if they cannot wear these beads, they mark the forehead with ashes. Almost the whole day is spent in devotion, the result of which they believe will be ultimate absorption in Sankar or Mahâdeva. They are respectable people, and particularly object to any member of the sect doing immoral acts.

Distribution of the Jangamas according to the Census of 1891.

District.	Number.	District.	Number.
Dehra Dûn	2	Cawnpur	14
Muzaffarnagar	38	Lalitpur	31
Meerut	29	Gorakhpur	15
Bulandshahr	20	Basti	3
Aligarh	677	Râê Bareli	59
Agra	32		27
Mainpuri	17		
Etah		Total	964

Janghâra.—A large and somewhat turbulent sept of Râjputs chiefly found in Rohilkhand. Their name is said to mean "worsted in war" (*Jang-hâra*), which was derived from their defeat by Râja Hirand Pâl of Bayâna or Shahâb-ud-dîn Ghori. One tradition in Rohilkhand represents them as having dispossessed the Katheriyas. In Bareilly they say that when under Râo Mahrûp Sinh they first entered Bilâspur, they expelled the Ahîrs in 1405 A. D., and in 1570 Basant Sâh drove out the Banjâras and the Bhîls.[1] The Budaun legend is that they came under the leadership of a worthy named Dhappu Dhâm, whose pugnacity is recorded in the verse —

Nîché dharti, ûpar Râm ;
Bîch men laré Dhappu Dhâm.
" Below is earth, above is Râm ;
Between is fighting Dhappu Dhâm."

There are two divisions of them, the Bhûr or residents in the sandy tract, and the Tarâi, or men of the lowlands.

2. In Shâhjahânpur[2] they claim descent from the Tomar kings of Delhi, which they say they left in disgust at the accession of the Chauhâns. Five brothers led five different parties, and the youngest of the five crossed the Ganges and settled at Sambhal in the Morâdâbâd District. He had two sons, and one of them went to Bulandshahr. The other, Hansrâj, had three sons and they moved east from Sambhal. One settled on the high land east of the Râmganga, and from him are descended the Bhûr Janghâras ; of the other two, who were by a second marriage, one was the ancestor of the Tarâi Janghâras, now found in Bareilly and Shâhjahânpur, and the other of the Budaun clan. Some of the Bhûr Janghâras say that the ancestors of the Tarâi Janghâras were sons of a woman of the sept, and hence their descendants hold a lower rank. This account is not admitted by the Tarâi Janghâras, but the difference in rank is not denied. Their settlement may be placed in the fifteenth century, or nearly three hundred years later than their alleged emigration from Delhi, and their genealogical tables do not support their alleged Tomar descent. One of the tribes of the Barhai claim to belong to them. In the Central Duâb they are closely connected with the Chauhâns. The Tarâi branch permit widow marriage, which probably accounts for their lower social rank.

3. In Bareilly they are reported to take brides from the Bâchhal, Gaur, Sombansi, Râthaur, Tomar, Bhateli, Raikwâr, Panwâr, Bais,

---

[1] *Settlement Report*, 19.
[2] *Settlement Report*, 59.

Nikumbh, Dhâkrê, Chandel, Janwâr, and Gautam septs ; and to give brides to the Gautam, Chauhân, Katheriya, and Râthaur.

Distribution of the Janghâra Râjputs according to the Census of 1891.

District.	Number.	District.	Number.
Sahâranpur . . .	1	Morâdâbâd . . .	124
Meerut . . .	9	Shâjahânpur . . .	5,841
Bulandshahr . . .	831	Pilibhît	1,318
Mathura . . .	870	Tarâi	1
Agra . . .	176	Sîtapur . . .	53
Farrukhâbâd . .	137	Hardoi	513
Mainpuri . . .	41	Kheri	235
Etâwah . . .	5	Bahrâich . . .	1
Etah	401		
Bareilly . . .	5,163		
Budaun . . .	9,289	Total .	24,812

Jangra.—A small caste of dyers and cloth printers found in Bundelkhand. They trace their origin to the famous fortress of Rintimbûr in the Jaypur State, Râjputâna. They are found in large numbers in the native state of Lodi Fatehpur in Central India. They follow the customs of the higher class Hindus and prohibit widow marriage. A wife may be put away for misconduct and cannot marry again. The lowest caste from which they will eat *pakki* is the Nâi. They will eat *kachchi* only if cooked by a casteman or a Brâhman.

Janwâr.—A sept of Rajputs found principally in Oudh. Of them Sir C. Elliott[1] writes :—"After the taking of Kanauj and the expulsion of the Râthaurs, the earliest colonists were the Janwârs, who settled in Pargana Bângarmau. The Janwârs came from Ballabhgarh, near Delhi, and colonised twenty-four villages, which lie partly in the north-western corner of Pargana Bângarmau and partly in the Hardoi District. Sûraj and Dâsu were their leaders, but Sûraj would not stop here and went on to the country beyond the Ghâgra, where he founded the Ikona Râj, of which the Mahârâja of Balrâmpur, through the rebellion and extinction of the elder branch, is now the head. Dâsu, the younger

[1] *Chronicles of Unao*, 32, sqq.

brother, received the title of Râwat, and when his descendants divided their twenty-four villages into four portions (*taraf*), the eldest and principal branch was called the Rautâna *taraf*, or the Râwat branch. They received six villages and an equal share fell to each of the three younger branches, who are named after Lâl, Bhân, and Sîthu, their respective heads. These four branches have this peculiarity that the estate has always descended entire to the eldest son, and the cadets are provided for by receiving a few fields for cultivation at low rent rates. This is the only instance I know of the *gaddi* or entail principle existing in a small land-holding clan. One village has been given to the Chandels as the marriage portion of a Janwâr bride, and one or two have been alienated through debts and mortgages; but each of the four branches of the family still retains the majority of their original villages, and the eldest son holds the whole of the lands belonging to his branch.

2. "Whether it was this uncommon law of primogeniture that drove out the cadets, or whether a younger son entered the Delhi service and received the tract as a Jâgîr, is doubtful; but nine generations, or about two hundred and fifty years ago a large branch of these Janwârs settled in the Pargana of Fatehpur Chaurâsi, taking the lands from the aboriginal Thatheras or Lodhas. They are divided into three branches, two of which take their name from places—Thaktaya and Sarâi,—and the third, strangely enough, either from its original head, or, as the common story goes, from the murder by two of its chiefs of the eldest son of the oldest or Sarâi branch. It is called Markaha, or 'the murderous house.' But the elder branch kept up its superiority and completely subjugated the other two divisions of the family in the end."

The Janwârs of Bahrâich.

3. "The Janwârs relate that their ancestor Bariyár Sâh, a Sombansi chieftain of Pawagarh on the confines of Gujarât, had been worsted in a dispute with his father and brothers and was imprisoned by Sultân Ghiyâs-ud-dîn Balban of Delhi. He was released by Sultán Jalál-ud-dîn Firoz Khilji, and fearing to return to his own country, collected a band of followers and joined the Governor of Bahrâich, by whom he was sent against the Bhars and Thârus settled in forests between the Râpti and the hills. I have not been able to procure any exact date; but if the names of the Delhi Emperors are correctly given, that immigration occurred, like that of the Kalhans, at the commencement of the fourteenth century. The advance of the

Janwârs was hemmed in by dense forests, peopled only by small communities of the lower castes, and it was Mâdho Sinh, the seventh in descent from the original invader, who first penetrated close to the present town of Balrâmpur and expelled Khannu Chaudhari, a carpenter by caste, the head of the former society." [1]

Other Janwâr colonies.

4. In Sîtapur they fix their home in Gujarât and have a family tree extending to thirty-three generations and 1149 years. Another family are said to take their origin from the famous Janakpur in Mithila or Tirhût.[2] Mr. Carnegy believes that some of them are of Dikhit descent.[3] In Kheri they claim to have been originally Chauhâns, and their ancestor, Jamni Bhân, was granted in A. D. 1562 the post of Chaudhari with the right of collecting two pice per *bigha* on all the cultivated land in the district.

5. In Sîtapur they are reported to give brides to the Gaur and Tomar septs, while they usually take Bâchhal girls to wife. In Unâo they generally marry their daughters to Panwârs living across the Ganges, Dikhits and Jâdonbansis, and they take brides from the Chandel, Gaur, Chauhân or Raikwâr septs.

Distribution of the Janwâr Râjputs according to the Census of 1891.

DISTRICT.	Number.	DISTRICT.	Number.
Agra	22	Basti	317
Mainpuri	1	Azamgarh	2
Etâwah	26	Lucknow	2,902
Bijnor	15	Unâo	3,691
Morâdâbâd	194	Râê Bareli	1,449
Shâhjahânpur	245	Sîtapur	3,041
Pilibhît	15	Hardoi	2,440
Cawnpur	986	Kheri	973
Fatehpur	768	Gonda	827
Bânda	1,301	Bahrâich	1,477
Allahâbâd	3	Sultânpur	8
Jâlaun	127	Partâbgarh	17
Lalitpur	302	Bârabanki	826
Benares	2		
		TOTAL	21,977

[1] *Settlement Report*, 9.

[2] *Settlement Report*, 93, 99.

[3] *Notes*, 48.

Jât.[1]—An important agricultural tribe found chiefly in the western part of the Province in the Meerut and Rohilkhand Divisions and in smaller numbers in the Central Duâb.

Origin.

2. The traditions of the tribe do not throw much light on their origin. According to one story, at one time when Himâchal was performing a great sacrifice he invited all the gods to be present except his son-in-law Mahâdeva. His wife Pârvati heard of this from her husband, and was obliged to go alone. When she arrived she found that no seat and no share of the offerings had been allotted to her spouse; so she was wroth, and threw herself into the sacrificial fire, where she was consumed to ashes. When Mahâdeva heard of this he was consumed with anger, and untying his long hair (*jata*) dashed it on the ground. Instantly a powerful being arose and stood with folded hands before the god to do his bidding. Mahâdeva ordered him to go at once and destroy the sacrifice of Himâchal. He carried out the order and was named Vîrabhadra, from whom are descended the race of the Jâts, and they take their name from the matted hair (*jata*) of the lord Mahâdeva.

3. All the Jâts of these provinces have more or less vague traditions that they originally came from the Panjâb or Rajputâna. Thus in Mathura they assert that they originally migrated from Bayâna to Hissâr and thence made their way down the Jumna. In Bijnor they fix their original home at Dhâranagar, whence they came under the leadership of Râja Jagat Deva. Others in Bijnor refer their origin to Udaypur. By another account, when Muhammad Ghori conquered Chithor, two of the fugitives escaped, one in the direction of Nepâl, and the other wandering through Ajmer, Bikâner and Delhi arrived at Mîranpura, a village in the Muzaffarnagar District. Thence he came to Jhandapur, near Bijnor, and warred with the Kalâls, who then ruled the land. They overcame him and killed his whole family, except, as is the stock incident in many tribal legends, a pregnant woman who escaped to her father's house at Dhanaura in the Rohtak District, where she gave birth to a son named Dasanda Sinh. A musician took pity on the lad and brought him to the court of the Emperor at Delhi, who sent a force with him to Bijnor and restored him to his family estates.

---

[1] Based on information obtained at Sahâranpur and notes by Mr. P. J. Fagan, C. S.; M. Atma Râm, Head Master, High School, Mathura; Chaudhari Dhyân Sinh, Morâdâbâd; the Deputy Inspectors of Schools. Bijnor. Bulandshahr. Meerut.

4. An attempt has been made to trace the ethnological connections of the Jâts much further than this. Thus General Cunningham[1] identifies them with the Xanthii of Strabo and the Jatti of Pliny and Ptolemy, and fixes their parent country on the banks of the Oxus between Bactria, Hyrkania and Khorasmia. In this very position there was a fertile district irrigated from the Margus river, which Pliny calls Zotale or Yothale, which he believes to have been the original seat of the Jattii or Jâts. "Their course from the Oxus to the Indus may, perhaps, be dimly traced in the Xuthi of Dionysius of Samos and the Zuthi of Ptolemy, who occupied the Karmanian desert on the frontier of Drangiana. They may have been best known in early times by the general name of their horde as Abars instead of by their tribal name as Jâts. According to this view, the main body of the Jattii would have occupied the district of Abiria and the towns of Pardabathra and Bardaxema in Sindh, while the Panjâb was principally colonised by their brethren the Meds." On this Dr. Pritchard writes—"The supposition that the Jats or Jâts of the Indus are descendants of the Yuetschi does not appear altogether preposterous, but it is supported by no proof except the very trifling one of a slight resemblance of names. The physical characters of the Jâts are very different from those attributed to the Yuetschi and the kindred tribes by the writers cited by Klaproth and Abel Remusat, who say they are of sanguine complexions with blue eyes." Others have attempted to identify them with the Kshatriya tribe of the Jâtharas; but in opposition to this Mr. Growse[2] argues that their home is always placed in the south-east quarter, while it is certain that the Jâts came from the West. By another theory they are identified with the Jarttika, who with the Bahîka and Takka are said to have been the original inhabitants of the Panjâb. They were in the time of Justin known as Aratta, *i.e.*, Arashtra, or "people without a king," and are represented by the Adraistae of Arrian, who places them on the banks of the river Ravi.[3] According to Mr. Nesfield's theory,[4] the word Jât is nothing more than the modern Hindi pronunciation of Yadu or Jâdu, the tribe in which Krishna was born, which is now represented by the modern Jâdon Râjputs.

---

[1] *Archæological Reports*, II., 55.
[2] *Mathura*, 8.
[3] Cunningham, *Bhilsa Topes*, 89.
[4] *Brief View*, II., sq.

5. The opinion of the best Indian authorities seems to be gradually turning to the belief that the connection between Jâts and Râjputs is more intimate than was formerly supposed. Thus, writing of Hissâr, Mr. P. J. Fagan says :—" It would probably require a lifetime of careful study and comparison before we could reach any satisfactory decision in the question whether Jâts and Râjputs are identical, similar or distinct races. The popular native account of the matter is simple enough; the Jâts, in common with many of the other tribes, are, according to the common opinion of the country side, Râjputs who have fallen in the social scale by infringing the rules forbidding the marriage of widows, enforcing the seclusion of women, and the like. In regard to customs, religious and social, Jâts and Râjputs are very similar; whatever differences are apparent in the latter are the very grounds assigned for their lower social position. My opinion is that we cannot properly set aside the weight of common tradition on the point, and I think we must hold that within certain limitations Jâts and Râjputs were originally one race; but that, instead of the Râjput remaining stationary and the Jât falling in the social scale, it is the Râjput who has risen, while the Jât has remained stationary or risen only slightly." And he goes on to hazard the theory that of the two sub-divisions the Sivagotra represent the non-Aryan and the Kâsib or Kasyapa *gotra* the Aryan part of the tribe.

Connection of Jâts and Râjputs.

6. To much the same effect Mr. Ibbetson writes[1] :—" It may be that the original Jât and the original Râjput entered India at different periods in its history, though to my mind the term Râjput is an occupational rather than an ethnological expression. But if they do originally represent two separate waves of immigration, it is at least exceedingly probable both from their almost identical physique and facial character, and from the close communion which has always existed between them, that they belong to one and the same ethnic stock; while, whether this be so or not, it is almost certain that they have been for many centuries, and still are, so intermingled and so blended into one people that it is practically impossible to distinguish them as separate wholes. It is, indeed, more than probable that the process of fusion has not ended here, and that the people who thus in the main resulted from the blending

[1] *Panjâb Ethnography*, paras. 421, 422.

of the Jât and the Râjputs, if these two were ever distinct, is by no means free from foreign elements. We have seen how the Pathân people have assimilated Sayyids, Turks and Mughals, and how it was sufficient for a Jât tribe to retain its political independence and organisation in order to be admitted into the Biloch nation; we know how a character for sanctity and exclusiveness combined will in a few generations make a Quraish or a Sayyid; and it is almost certain that the joint Jât-Râjput stock contains not a few tribes of aboriginal descent, though it is probably in the main Aryo-Skythian, if Skythians be not Aryans. The Mân, Her and Bhûlar Jâts are known as *'asl* or 'original' Jâts, because they claim no Râjput ancestry, but are supposed to be descended from the hair (*jata*) of the aboriginal god Siva; the Jâts of the south-eastern divide themselves into two sections—Sivgotri, or of the family of Siva, and Kâsibgotri, who claim connection with the Râjputs; and the names of the ancestor Bar of the Sivgotris and of his son Barbara are the very words which the ancient Brâhmans give as the marks of the barbarian aborigines. Many of the Jât tribes in the Panjâb have customs which apparently point to non-Aryan origin, and a rich and almost virgin field for investigation is here open to the ethnologist.

7. "But whether Jâts and Râjputs were or were not originally distinct, and whatever aboriginal elements may have been affiliated to their society, I think that the two now form a common stock, the distinction between Jât and Râjput being social rather than ethnic. I believe that those families of that common stock whom the tide of fortune has raised to political importance have become Râjputs almost by mere virtue of their rise; and that their descendants have retained the title and its privileges on the condition, strictly enforced, of observing the rules by which the higher are distinguished from the lower castes in the Hindu scale of precedence, of preserving their purity of blood by refusing to marry with the families of lower social rank, of rigidly abstaining from widow marriage, and of refraining from degrading occupations. Those who transgressed these rules have fallen from their high position and ceased to be Râjputs; while such families as, attaining a dominant position in their territory, began to affect social exclusiveness and to observe the rules, have become not only Râjas, but Râjputs, or 'sons of Râjas.'"

8. In addition to all this there is good reason to suspect that the modern Jât race has become under the influence of infanticide

very much intermixed. From a recent Report[1] it would seem that Jâts are much addicted to purchasing girls of low caste and passing them off among their friends as genuine girls of the tribe and then marrying them. This, of course, much weakens the force of any available evidence from anthropometry in settling the ethnological affinities of the tribe.

Physical appearance.

9. Of the tribe in Râjputâna a competent observer, Dr. Brereton, writes[2] :—"In physique the Jâts are generally of fair height, but below the average of Râjputs or other castes. Their chest measurement and weight are in fair proportion to their height ; the extremities, especially the lower, are often disproportionate to their abnormal length. The women are of very strong physique, exceeding men in this respect, proportionately speaking. They are not remarkable for personal beauty, but some have very fine figures. They are most industrious and contented, work in the fields, etc., but are said to rule their husbands. The prevailing complexion is fair and the colour of the eyes dark ; the hair is dark, fine, and straight ; beard and moustaches scanty, and the former not usually worn. The crania are of tolerably fair size and shape, often elongated, altogether a lower type than the Brâhman skull. Their intellectual faculties are not brilliant, partaking more of shrewdness and cunning than ability. They are said to possess courage and fidelity, are industrious and persevering in their habits, and are of an agile and muscular frame."

9. In these Provinces the connection between Jâts and Râjputs is very generally asserted. Thus the Jâts of Agra consider themselves illegitimate descendants of the Yâdus of Bayâna, and have a tradition that their original home was Kandahar.[3] The Godha section claim descent from a Pramâr Thâkur, who came from Dhâr in the Dakkhin, and the Dangri section assert that they are descended from a Sisodiya Râjput of Chithor. "It is an undisputed fact," says a writer, who is himself a Râjput,[4] "that the Sinsiwâl Jâts of Bhartpur are the descendants of a Jâdon and the Thakurelê Jâts of a Chauhân ; similarly there are many Jât clans who have undeniably descended from Râjputs by women of inferior stocks. Râjput princes used to admit Jât and Gûjar women into

---

[1] *Infanticide Report, N. W. P.*, 1888, p. 2.

[2] *Rajputâna Gazetteer*, I., 162.

[3] Tod, *Annals*, II., 197, *Note*.

[4] Raja Lachhman Sinh, *Bulandshahr Memo.*, 171, sq.

their zanânas on account of their strength and graceful appearance. Some, however, do not claim Râjput descent, as the Poniya, who say that they sprung from the *jata* or matted hair of Mahâdeva at Mount Kailâsa. Hence these may be supposed of Getae descent; others refer their origin to Garh Gajni in the west, probably the Ghazni of Afghânistân. Poniya is also the name for a species of snake, and this connects them with the Nâgvansi or Takshak race. Colonel Tod in the Jaisalmer Annals shows that many of the clans are of Jâdon descent. The fact that Jâts practise widow marriage disproves the assertion that they used to intermarry with the Râjputs." This view of the case has been to some extent disproved by what has been already said.

Connection of Jâts and Gypsies.

10. It has been suggested that the Jâts were at least one of the elements out of which the Gypsy race was formed. The question is too large to be considered here;[1] but it may be noted that besides the evidence of language we have some indications of at least six westerly movements of the races of the North-Western Frontier, who are often collectively known as Jâts.[2] Thus we have a doubtful reference to a transplanting of Kerks, Sindhis, Kolis, Meds, and other West Indian tribes before the Christian era. Next we have the bringing of the Luris or Indian musicians to Persia by Bahrâm Gor about A. D. 450 and their subsequent dispersion. A body of Kerks, Sangars, and Jâts were deported from the Persian Gulf to Asia Minor. A body of Jâts is said to have been deported westward after the invasion of India by Mahmûd of Ghazni in 1025 A. D. The same results followed the conquests of the Seljuks in the twelfth century and those of Osmanli Turks in the fourteenth. Finally there was a movement westward at the close of the fourteenth century as the results of the ravages of Timûr.

Tribal organisation.

11. In these provinces the Jâts are divided into two great subdivisions, the Dê or Dhê and Helê in the Ganges-Jumna Duâb, which correspond to the Pachhâda and Deswâla of Delhi and Rohilkhand. General Cunningham,[3] assuming that the last two names mean "late" and

---

[1] On this see *Edinburgh Review*, July 1878; Burton, *Sindh*, 248 sq.; Dowson's Elliot, *History*, I., 397, sq.; Rawlinson, *Seventh Monarchy*, 298; MacRitchie, *Gypsies of India*, 339.

[2] See Authorities quoted, *Bombay Gazetteer*, XIII., 714.

[3] *Archæological Survey*, II., 57.

"aboriginal," concludes that the Pachhâda or Dhê Jâts were a comparatively recent colony. "This is confirmed by the known facts in the history of Bhartpur, which owes its rise to Chûraman Jât, who after the death of Aurangzeb migrated with his followers from the banks of the Indus." The Helê or Dhê are considered the superior of the Deswâla or Pachhâda, and they almost everywhere practise female infanticide. The two sub-divisions are usually asserted by Jâts themselves to be endogamous; but this is in some places at least not the case. According to Sir H. M. Elliot,[1] the Dhê have frequently no Jâga or genealogist as the Helê have. He asserts that they never intermarried till comparatively recent times, when the Balamgarh Râja married with the Kaothal family. Another good authority[2] states that "till very recently one division did not intermarry or mess with another; but now there is very little distinction between them in the Rohilkhand Districts, and in the Duâb too there have been instances, but comparatively few, of intermarriages. As a rule the Helê have no great objection to marry the daughters of the Dhê, but they hesitate to give them their own daughters. The Dhê observe certain domestic rites which are contrary to the rites of other Hindu castes, and this is quoted by the Helê as an indication of their low origin. One of these rites is that the Dhê bridegroom wears the veil (*sehra*), while the Helê, like the Râjputs and other high castes, wear the coronet (*maur*). The Dhê, however, eat from earthen vessels, which is more a Muhammadan than a Hindu custom. The Helê are old immigrants and the Dhê new-comers. In the Upper Duâb they speak of Hariyâna as their home."

12. In connection with this Mr. Ibbetson writes[3] :—"There is an extraordinary division of the Jâts of Delhi, Rohtak, and Karnâl, and, indeed, of the other land-owning castes, who have for the most part taken the one side or the other, into two factions known as Dehiya and Haulâniya. The Dehiyas are called after a Jât tribe of that name, with its head-quarters about Bhatgânw in Surpat, having originally come from Bawâna near Delhi. The Haulâniya faction is headed by the Ghatwâl or Malak Jâts, whose head-quarters are Dherka-Ahulâna in Gohâna, and who were, owing to their successful opposition to the Râjputs, the accepted heads of the Jâts

---

1 *Supplemental Glossary*, sv.
2 Râja Lachhman Sinh, *Bulandshahr Memo.*, 171, sq.
3 *Panjâb Ethnography*, *loc. cit.*

in those parts. Some one of the Emperors called them to assist him in coercing the Mandahâr Râjputs, and thus the old enmity was strengthened. The Dehiya Jâts, growing powerful, became jealous of the supremacy of the Ghatwâls, and joined the Mandahârs against them. Thus the country side was divided into two factions: the Gûjars and Tagas of the tract, the Jaglân Jâts of Thapa Naultha, and the Latmâr Jâts of Rohtak joining the Dehiyas, and the Huda Jâts of Rohtak and most of the Jâts of the tract, except the Jaglâns, joining the Haulâniyas. In the Mutiny, disturbances occurred in the Rohtak District between these two factions, and the Mandahârs of the Nardak ravaged the Haulâniyas in the south of the tract. The Jâts and Râjputs seem, independently of these divisions, to consider each other, tribally speaking, as natural enemies, and I have often been assured by Jâts, though I do not believe it, that they would not dare to go into a Râjput village at night."

13. The name Dhê has by some been connected with the famous race of the Dahae, whom Virgil[1] calls *indomitæ*. They are said to have lived in juxtaposition and alliance with the Massagetæ or Yuchi. The combined tribe forced the Sakas to the south, and they overcame the Græco-Bactrian Empire. Prof. Rawlinson[2] explains the name of the Dahae as meaning *rustici*. They were at one time spread over the whole country from the Caspian to the Persian Gulf and the Tigris; they are even mentioned in Scripture[3] among the Samarian colonists, being classed with the men of Babylon and Elam. Strabo groups them with the Sakas and Massagetæ as the great Skythian tribes of Inner Asia, North of Bactriana. Justin speaks of *Dahae qui inter Oxum et Jaxartem non procul a limine maris Caspii habitant*.[4]

14. Besides these two great divisions of Dhê and Helê, the Jâts are split up into a vast number of exogamous sections (*gotra, pâl*). The last Census in these Provinces records no less than 1,791 sections of the Hindu and 106 of the Muhammadan Jâts. Along the Western frontier the most powerful of these are the Ghatwâl, who are also called Malak, a title which they are said to have obtained as follows:—" In

Exogamous groups of Jâts.

[1] *Æneid*, VIII., 728.

[2] *Herodotus*, I., 413.

[3] *Ezra*, IV., 9.

[4] XII., 6; Beal, *Fah Hian*, 35, note; Rawlinson, *Herodotus*, III., 209; Wilson, *Ariana Antiqua*, 141, sq.

the old days of Râjput ascendancy the Râjputs would not allow the Jâts to cover their head with a turban, nor to wear any red clothes, nor to put a crown (*maur*) on the head of their bridegroom, or a jewel (*nath*) in the woman's nose. They also used to levy seignorial rights from virgin brides. Even to this day Râjputs will not allow inferior castes to wear red clothes or ample loin-cloths in their villages. The Ghatwâl obtained some success over the Râjputs, especially over the Mandahâras, and removed the obnoxious prohibition. They thus obtained the title of Malak or 'master,' and a red turban as their distinguishing mark, and to this day a Jât with a red turban is most probably a Ghatwâl." In Hissâr, according to Mr. Fagan, they claim to be descended from Siroha Râjputs and to have come from Garh Gajni, wherever that may be. They say that they originally settled in Rohtak, where they were under the heel of the Râjputs to such an extent that their women had to wear nose-rings of straw. The Jâts attacked and overcame the Kallanûr Râjputs in a dispute arising out of a marriage procession; but peace was made and both sides settled down. Subsequently the Râjputs invited the Ghatwâls to an entertainment and treacherously blew them up with gunpowder. One Ghatwâl woman, according to the stock legend, who was not present, was the sole survivor and escaped to Depâl near Hânsi. She happened to be pregnant, and her two sons founded the present sept.

15. Other powerful septs are the Jakhar, who are sprung from a Râjput tribe variously stated to be Chauhân and Udha. They take their title from an ancestor of that name. It is related of him that a Râja of Dwârika had a huge and heavy bow and arrow, and promised that whoever could lift it up should be raised in rank above a Râja. Jakhar attempted the task, but failed, and for shame left for his native country and settled in Bikâner. This story, puerile though it may seem, probably implies that the Jakhar became Jâts by degradation from the military caste of Râjputs.

16. The Sahrâwat, who take their name from Sahra, a son or grandson of Râja Anangpâl Tunwar, appear to have come originally from the neighbourhood of Delhi.

17. The Bhainiwâl, who claim to be Deswâli, appear to have been originally Chauhân Râjputs of Sâmbhar in Rajputâna, whence they spread into Hissâr through Bikâner.

18. The Deswâl must not be confounded with the Deswâli, which is a comprehensive name for all the Jât tribes dwelling in the

Hariyâna or Des of Hissâr and Rohtak. All these tribes were probably as closely connected with Rajputâna as are the present Bâgris, but the connection is more remote and less well remembered. The Deswâl, Dallâl, and Mân Jâts are all said to be related closely, being descended from one Dhanna Râo of Silauthi in Rohtak, by a Bargûjar Râjput woman, who had three sons, Dillê, Desal, and Mân, who gave their names to the three tribes of Dallâ, Deswâl, and Mân Jâts.

Septs in the North-West Provinces.

19. Beginning with the most Westerly Districts we find in Sahâranpur that the most powerful septs are the Deswâli, Pachhâdê, and Sinmâr; in Muzaffarnagar we have the Deswâli, Baliyân, Gauthiwâra, Rathê, Sarâwat, Bodlân, Jatarni, Kankhandi, Pachhâdê, Panwâr, and Rikhbans. The Census returns give as the only septs of local importance the Daswân, Gotwâla, Malua, and Maula of Muzaffarnagar.

20. All through these lists sub-castes and sections are inextricably mixed up. Thus in Meerut we have the Deswâli and Hela combined with the Chauhân, Dahuna, Daiha, Pachhâdê, and Tomar.

21. In Mathura, according to the last Census, the chief sections are the Barh, Khutel, Lathor, Chhokar, Churel, Gadar, Gauthwâra, Godhi, Maini, Panwâr, Phokha, Râwat, Sakarwâr, Sangeriyân, Sarâmat, Sinsinwâra and Thenwâr. The Nohwâr and Narwâr, who are so closely related as to be prohibited from intermarriage, are also a compact and powerful body. The former take their name from their original settlement in Noh of Jalesar Pargana, now included in the Etah District. Their position in the caste may be estimated from the fact that while they take their wives from the Pachahras and other clans of the South, they only give their daughters to the Sinsinwârs and other powerful clans of the West. They, of course, claim descent from Prithivi Râja; but coming to later times they say that their ancestor lived in Jartauli of Aligarh. They may have been driven from thence when Ibrahîm Lodi attacked Jartauli for rebellion.[1] He had two sons, one of whom, Rati Râo, colonised Noh, and the other Narwâr. The children of Rati Râo gave up Noh to their family priests and founded the villages of Bhenrai and Bajna, whence they spread over the Pargana. A descendant of the brother, who founded Narwâr, settled at Barauth, from whence have sprung the hamlets which now

[1] Dowson, Elliot, *History*, V., 104.

constitute separate villages. The Pachahras founded *ta'aluqa* Aira Khera of Mahâban and thence Dunetiya of Mât.[1]

22. The Aligarh Jâts trace their descent from Makkhan, who, at the end of the sixteenth or beginning of the seventeenth century, led a tribe of Thenwân Jâts from Rajputâna into the neighbourhood of Mursân. He there married a woman of the Khoken Jâts, who with the Brâhmans were the earliest settlers.[2] The Jâts of Eastern Aligarh are principally members of three great clans—the Khandiya in Tappal, the Thakurel in Hasangarh Pargana, and the Thenwân in Gori, Mursân, and Hâthras, and are of much more standing in the country. They date their arrival about 1046 A.D., when their ancestor Bikram Thâkur drove out the Janghâra Râjputs and Kalârs who inhabited the tract. The Khandiya Jâts of Tappal derive their name from the village of the same name in the Pargana and are of comparatively modern date.[3] Other important Aligarh clans are the Ahlâwat, Badhauniya, Bangar, Bharangar, Chang, Chhokar, Chaudhrai, Dagor, Dikkhit, Gandhor, Gûjar, Katheriya, Mahur, Pachhâda, Panwâr, Punriya, Râthaur, Sangwân, Sarâwat, and Tomar. Many of these are the names of well-known Râjput septs.

23. It is unnecessary to repeat the lists of names in the Census returns or to attempt any more detailed account of migrations and local history of these multitudinous septs.

24. These septs are, as has been said, exogamous, but there are all sorts of grades among them, and the rules of intermarriage are most intricate. If an ordinary Jât is asked about it, he merely says that he leaves all this to his family priest. As an illustration of this it may be noted that just across the border of these Provinces in the Rohtak District the Mundlâna and Ahulâna Jâts do not intermarry by reason of old feuds. The Goliya do not marry with the Dâgar or Solankhi, for while they were Brâhmans the latter were their clients (*jajmân*), and when they lost their caste, the former only of all Jâts would give them brides. The Deswâl do not intermarry with the Chaudharân, or Phogat, nor the Chîlar with the Chikâra, nor the Malak with the Dalâls of the Sampla Tahsîl, though they will intermarry with other Dalâls.[4]

---

[1] *Mathura Settlement Report*, 33, sq.
[2] *Settlement Report*, 25.
[3] *Ibid.*, 32, sq.
[4] *Settlement Report*, 65.

25. The Jâts have a tribal council known as *panchâyat* which is presided over by a headman, or Chaudhari, which deals with the usual cases of violation of caste rules and customs. The eldest son of a deceased Chaudhari takes his father's place, provided he is competent to discharge the duties of the post. The usual punishment is certain compulsory entertainments to the brethren. In Sahâranpur, at least, it seems to be the rule that if an unmarried girl intrigues with a low-caste man, she is permanently expelled; but if her lover be a man of higher caste than her own, the fault is forgiven on her relations providing a feast according to the award of the council.

Tribal council.

26. Polygamy is allowed, and all Jâts agree that polyandry is abominable. But there seems reason to believe that in some cases it prevails. In Rohtak[1] it is reported that "considering the obligations laid on them by religion to marry, an extraordinarily large number of Jâts remain bachelors. It is common enough to find instances in every pedigree table where the elder of a number of brothers only is married, or perhaps one or two; and though the people would never admit it, it is most probable that in such cases a modified system of polyandry does prevail." There appears to be no well-defined rule as to the payment of a price for either bride or bridegroom. Wherever brides are scarce owing to infanticide, there seems no doubt that girls are purchased; and when the relations of the bride are poor, the bride price takes the form of a contribution given by the friends of the youth to the relations of his bride to assist in defraying the cost of the wedding feast. Among the more well-to-do members of the tribe the tendency is towards the payment of a dowry with the bride. Widow marriage and the levirate are allowed; but here too there seems to be a movement in favour of insisting that if a widow marries again, her husband should be an outsider. The general rule seems to be that when there are no brothers of the late husband, the woman takes with her to her new home her children with any movable property she can secure, and the children of the first marriage are practically adopted and supported by their step-father; on the contrary, if the brothers of the first husband be alive, they take charge of their nephews and rear them until they come of age, receiving as their remuneration for the duty of guardian-

Marriage rules.

[1] *Settlement Report*, 62.

ship the usufruct of the property during the minority of their nephew.

27. In widow marriage the rites are very simple. When the barber and the family priest have arranged the match, a day is fixed on which the bridegroom with a few friends goes to the house of the bride. He remains there for the night, and next morning the woman puts on bangles and the other ornaments which she was obliged to discontinue when her first husband died. Most of these ornaments are generally presented by the bridegroom. When he brings home his wife, he is expected to give a dinner to his brethren. When a man goes to marry a widow, he wears white clothes, not red and yellow as is the rule in a regular marriage.

Domestic rites: Birth.

28. Among the Jâts of these Provinces there is little in the domestic ritual to distinguish them from orthodox Hindus. When a woman is about to be delivered, they wave over her head a rupee and a quarter with a vow of worshipping Devi if the result is successful. If the woman recovers, this money is spent in buying cakes and sweetmeats which are offered at the shrine of the goddess. When delivery is tedious, the patient is given water over which a Faqîr has breathed, or in which has been steeped the quadrangular rupee known as Châryâri, because it bears the names of the four companions (*châr yâr*) of the Prophet—Abubakr, Usmân, Umar, and Ali. In Sahâranpur the place of the midwife appears to be generally taken by a Qasâi woman. If a son is born, she gets a fee double of that for a girl, and Brâhman women are called in to sing songs of rejoicing. In delivery the mother is generally laid on a bed made of cakes of the dung of the sacred cow. The mother is bathed on the tenth day, and the whole house is plastered. On the twelfth day, the birth impurity is finally removed by a bath, and the menials are rewarded. Brâhmans and clansmen are fed, and the house is purified by a sprinkling of cow-dung and Ganges water. They do not perform the rite of *Annaprâsana,* or *Kanchhedan,* in the regular way; the noses and ears of children are bored whenever it may be convenient.

Adoption.

29. Adoption is allowed. There is no regular rite except the feasting of male friends and Brâhmans, while soaked gram is distributed among the women.

Marriage rites.

30. The marriage rites are performed among the Sahâranpur Jâts as follows:—The age for betrothal is between five and twelve. The girl's father

searches for a youth, and when he has found one, his Brâhman priest and barber are sent to make the arrangements. They compare the horoscopes and make certain that the family is of pure blood and not suffering under any social stigma. When this is settled, a rupee, known as *mangani*, is paid to the youth, and this settles the engagement. Two or three years after, when the boy has attained puberty, his father sends and enquires when he may come to fetch his bride. If the bride is nubile and her friends can afford the expense, the answer is *Byâh sajha lo*—"Set the wedding in train." If he is not ready, he makes no answer, and the phrase is *dhîl de dena.* The procession starts in the usual way; but it is characteristic of Jâts that the waving done for good luck over the pair is done with a copper coin of the Emperor Aurangzeb. On the day the bridegroom starts, a wedding pavilion is put up at his house, and nine Brâhmans are fed in the name of the Naugraha or nine planets. When the procession reaches the house of the bride, her mother comes out, and, after waving the part of her robe covering her breast over his head, touches it with her lips. This is known as the *sewal* rite. The binding part of the rite is the seven-fold circumambulation of the sacred fire by the pair with their garments knotted together.

Death rites.

31. The dead are cremated in the ordinary way. That night the chief mourner, who lit the pyre, places a cup of milk on a little platform of sticks in the road to the burning ground for the use of the ghost, and on the third day he hangs a pitcher of water to a *pîpal* tree, leaving a small hole in the vessel through which the water slowly drops for the refreshment of the spirit.

Religion.

32. Jâts are Hindus, Sikhs, and Muhammadans. In Sahâranpur, they, when Hindus, chiefly worship Mahâdeva and Devi, and a host of village godlings, ghosts and demons. Among local godlings the most important are Gûga, Lakhdâta, Pyârêji, and Randeo, of most of which some account has been given elsewhere.[1] In Mathura their favourite godlings are Dâûji and Girirâj; in Bijnor, Châmunda Devi is a sort of tribal goddess, and they also have much respect for what they call Gâêyon ka Devata or the "lord of cows." They also worship various Muhammadan saints, such as Zâhir Dîwân,

---

[1] *Introduction to Popular Religion*, 133.

Zainuddîn, and Shaikh Saddo.[1] In the direction of Rajputâna they have much respect for Mâta or the small-pox goddess; but the chief object of veneration of all the Western Jâts is Tejaji,[2] a sort of legendary hero, half deified, who is said to have died from snake-bite. The Jâts believe that if they are bitten by a snake, and tie a thread round the right foot while repeating the name of Tejaji, the poison will prove innocuous. His main temple is at Sarsara in Kishngarh. He is always represented as a man on horseback with a drawn sword, while a snake is biting his tongue. Nearly all the Western Jâts wear an amulet of silver with this device round their necks. In the Upper Ganges-Jumna Duâb three of the best known local godlings are Dharm Sinh, Sâvant Sinh, and Hazâri Sinh. Their priests are drawn from the menial tribes, such as the Mâli and Kahâr. All three are the deified ghosts of persons who have died in an unusual way or whose funeral obsequies were not duly performed. Their feast day is Sunday, and on certain occasions the godling sends his influence on his attendant (*sir par â jâta*). They then "play" (*khelna*), or move their heads about in a frantic way, answer questions, and give oracles. Sâvant Sinh appears only on the night of the Anant Chaudas feast, the fourteenth of the light half of Bhâdon; the other deities deliver oracles all through the year. They are propitiated by the feeding of Brâhmans and Jogis, with offerings of flowers and sweetmeats, and lamps lighted with ghi. Another deity is Bûrha Bâba, "the old master." He was a Gadariya, or shepherd, by caste, and was noted for his proficiency in Sanskrit. When he is not duly propitiated he brings ringworm (*ganj*) on children. Some people he afflicts with boils, but he is not very malevolent, and a small offering regularly made prevents him from doing much harm. At the last Census no less than 54,849 persons in the Western Districts declared themselves votaries of Bûrha Bâba. Jâts are also much addicted to ancestor worship and have many such shrines in their villages. In Karnâl, the Sandhu Jâts worship Kâla Mehar or Kâla Pîr, their ancestor, whose chief shrine is at Thâna Satra, in Siâlkot, the head-quarters of the Sandhus; the Halâwat Jâts worship a common ancestor called Saddu Deo. They are much afraid of the ghosts of the dead. Besides the regular *srâddha*, one mode of propitiating them is to pour some water at the root of a *pîpal* tree, and

[1] *Introduction to Popular Religion*, 129, 138.
[2] *Ibid*, 135.

distribute some cloth, cotton and sesame on a Saturday in alms. The Evil Eye is avoided by wearing a blue string round the neck, making a black mark on the forehead, waving red pepper, wheat chaff, salt, and mustard round the head of the patient, and then burning them on the family hearth.

Social customs.

33. Their oaths are on the Ganges, or a bottle of its water kept for this purpose, by some the godlings, such as Gûga, Tejaji or Dâûji, on their sons' heads or by touching an idol in a Hindu temple. They eat the same food as higher class Hindus, including wild pigs and fowls; they will not eat beef or pork. They name the deity Nârâyan, when they eat, and throw a little food on the ground. They salute each other in the form *Râm! Râm!* Sikhs use the phrase *Wâh Guru ki fateh.* They are not considered strict in the matter of eating, drinking, and smoking, and, though they profess not to drink spirits, the rule does not seem to be rigidly observed.

Character and occupation.

34. The Jât takes a high rank among the cultivating races of the Province. He is simply a slave to his farm, and this absorption in rigorous out-of-door work at all seasons has had its effect on his character and physique. He never dreams of taking any service, except in the army; he is thrifty to the verge of meanness, and industrious beyond comparison; if his crops fail, it is sheer hard luck. When he is not busy in his field, he lets out his cart for hire, or busies himself in collecting manure, which he manages with great care and skill. His fault is quarrelsomeness; and, in litigation, he never knows when he is beaten. In the life of the village he is a general butt, and is noted for his rustic, boorish ways. This is reflected in the proverbial wisdom of the countryside:—

Jangal Jât na chheriyé, hatti bîch Kirâr,
Bhûkha Turk na chheriyê, ho jâé jî ka jhâr—

"Meddle not with the Jât in the wilds, or the Kirâr at his mart, nor a hungry Turk; if you do, you will risk your life."

Kabit sohé Bhât ko,
Kheti sohé Jât ko—

"Songs suit a Bhât, and husbandry a Jât."

Jât mara tab jâniyé jab terahwîn guzar jâé—

"Never be sure a Jât is dead till the days of mourning for him are over."

Distribution of Jâts according to the Census of 1891.

Districts.	Hindu.	Musalmân.	Sikh.	TOTAL.
Dehra Dûn	285	7	71	363
Sahâranpur . . .	12,316	364	361	13,041
Muzaffarnagar . . .	71,848	8,792	326	80,966
Meerut	148,580	4,707	2,103	155,390
Bulandshahr . . .	54,290	58	20	54,368
Aligarh	80,585	...	51	80,636
Mathura	123,101	95	732	123,928
Agra	54,943	3	319	55,265
Farrukhâbâd . . .	240	4	6	250
Mainpuri	952	13	12	977
Etâwah	294	...	13	307
Etah	204	5	9	218
Bareilly	8,876	...	...	8,876
Bijnor	57,097	...	647	57,744
Budaun	4,649	27	...	4,676
Morâdâbâd	80,215	...	43	80,258
Shâhjahânpur . . .	383	...	7	390
Pilibhît	831	...	...	831
Cawnpur	589	...	6	595
Fatehpur	115	6	...	121
Bânda	5	1	15	21
Hamîrpur	45	...	1	46
Allahâbâd	564	41	...	605
Jhânsi	328	10	738	1,076
Jâlaun	102	...	1	103
Lalitpur	85	...	46	131

Distribution of Jâts according to the Census of 1891—concld.

Districts.	Hindu.	Musalmân.	Sikh.	Total.
Benares	55	6	24	85
Mirzapur	41	...	...	41
Jaunpur	85	...	...	85
Ghâzipur	8	...	8	16
Ballia	2	...	...	2
Gorakhpur	18	3	...	21
Basti	476	...	...	476
Azamgarh	4	...	...	4
Kumaun	6	...	...	6
Garhwâl	16	...	...	16
Tarâi	1,180	...	...	1,180
Lucknow	2,302	2	147	2,451
Unâo	92	...	...	92
Râê Bareli	...	1	42	43
Sîtapur	93	...	6	99
Hardoi	34	...	...	34
Kheri	793	4	18	815
Faizâbâd	45	3	138	186
Gonda	899	6	42	947
Bahrâich	79	18	88	185
Sultânpur	18	14	...	32
Partâbgarh . . .	7	...	11	18
Bârabanki	79	...	7	86
Total .	707,854	14,190	6,058	728,102

Distribution of the Chief Jât Sections.

	Sahâran-pur.	Muzaffar-nagar.	Meerut.	Buland-shahr.	Aligarh.	Mathura.	Agra.	Bareilly.	Bijnor.	Budaun.	Morâbâbâd.	Tarâi.	Gonda.
Ahlâwat	...	...	...	...	2,020	602	...	...	...	...	217	...	...
Aujiya	...	...	...	...	...	...	...	...	...	251	...	...	...
Aujlan	...	...	388	...	...	...	...	...	...	...	...	...	...
Autal	...	200	...	...	...	...	...	264	...	...	...	...	...
Baban	...	...	...	...	...	...	...	...	...	...	378	...	...
Bacharnè	...	...	...	...	...	6,705	...	...	...	...	...	...	...
Badhauniya	...	...	...	...	1,062	1,842	...	...	...	...	...	...	...
Baliyân	...	9,933	...	...	1,724	...	...	...	...	...	...	...	...
Bangar	...	...	...	...	1,029	923	...	...	...	...	...	...	...
Bhangiwâl	...	212	...	...	...	...	...	...	...	...	...	...	...
Bargûjar	...	...	...	...	783	...	...	...	...	...	...	...	...
Barh	...	...	...	...	...	22,627	8,503	...	...	...	...	...	...
Berhwâl	...	...	...	...	...	...	241	...	...	...	...	...	...

Distribution of the Chief Jât Sections—continued.

	Sahâranpur.	Muzaffarnagar.	Meerut.	Bulandshahr.	Aligarh.	Mathura.	Agra.	Bareilly.	Bijnor.	Budaun.	Morâdâbâd.	Tarâî.	Gonda.
Bhagotar	...	...	...	...	...	...	1,580	...	...	...	...	...	...
Bhâranagar	...	...	...	...	...	4,358	525	...	...	...	...	...	...
Bhatti	...	224	...	...	...	...	...	...	...	...	...	...	...
Bhîtwâns	...	...	...	...	481	...	...	...	...	...	...	...	...
Bhitwâr	...	...	...	...	...	234	...	...	...	...	...	...	...
Bodiyân	...	1,641	...	...	...	...	...	...	...	...	...	...	...
Bora	...	...	...	559	478	...	...	...	...	...	...	...	...
Chamer	...	...	...	...	287	1,368	9,508	...	...	...	...	...	...
Chandel	...	...	...	...	480	...	...	...	...	...	...	...	...
Chang	...	...	...	...	1,848	730	...	...	...	...	...	...	...
Chandhari	...	...	...	...	3,813	...	...	...	270	...	...	...	...
Chauhân	...	...	1,107	...	...	...	...	...	...	...	...	...	...
Chhokar	...	...	...	...	1,111	3,422	1,399	...	...	...	...	...	...

Chhuttan . . .	...	...	...	...	828	...	...	...	...	...	...	...	...
Churel . . .	...	...	...	...	373	1,459	1,441	...	...	...	...	...	...
Dagar . . .	...	...	...	7,130	...	...	...	...	...	...	...	...	...
Dagor . . .	...	...	...	...	4,727	475	1,057	...	...	...	...	...	...
Dahima . . .	...	...	...	1,541	...	...	...	...	...	...	...	...	...
Dahuna . . .	...	...	...	...	...	...	...	...	...	...	...	...	...
Daiha . . .	...	...	8,562	...	...	...	...	...	...	...	...	...	...
Dangiya . . .	...	...	...	...	...	...	...	...	...	...	217	...	...
Dangar . . .	...	...	...	...	...	...	...	...	...	...	...	...	...
Deswâli . . .	6,538	25,406	85,965	3,099	2,152	1,401	266	...	53,150	14,502	14,740	978	...
Dhâkra . . .	...	...	...	274	...	...	...	...	...	...	...	...	...
Dhana . . .	...	...	...	...	...	...	...	...	...	...	238	...	...
Ḍhanoi . . .	...	...	...	...	538	...	...	...	...	...	...	...	...
Dhârhiwâl . .	...	...	...	...	...	...	...	338	...	...	...	...	...
Dhelphora . .	...	...	230	...	...	...	...	...	...	...	...	...	...
Dhingar . . .	...	...	...	202	...	...	...	...	...	...	...	...	253
Dholiya . . .	...	...	...	...	370	...	...	...	...	...	...	...	...

Distribution of the Chief Jât Sections—continued.

	Sahâran-pur.	Muzaffar-nagar.	Meerut.	Buland-shahr.	Aligarh.	Mathura.	Agra.	Bareilly.	Bijnor.	Budaun.	Morâdâbâd.	Tarâi.	Gonda.
Dikhit . . .	...	...	...	...	2,899	...	...	...	...	...	...	...	...
Dusâdh . . .	...	...	...	...	...	620	...	...	...	...	...	...	...
Faujdâr . . .	...	...	...	...	...	631	...	...	...	...	...	...	...
Gadar . . .	...	...	...	...	...	2,070	...	...	...	...	...	...	...
Gaharwâr . .	...	...	...	...	...	...	602	...	...	...	...	...	...
Gahlot . . .	...	...	...	...	426	...	...	...	...	...	...	...	...
Gandawâl . .	...	929	...	...	...	...	...	...	...	...	...	...	...
Gandhar . . .	...	...	...	...	...	...	303	...	...	...	...	...	...
Gandhfla . . .	...	...	...	...	627	...	...	...	...	...	...	...	...
Gandhor . . .	...	...	...	...	2,468	...	...	...	...	...	...	...	...
Gangâs . . .	...	...	...	222	...	...	...	...	...	...	...	...	...
Ganthwârâ . .	...	11,476	...	...	...	1,205	1,976	...	...	...	...	...	...
Gaur . . .	...	...	...	...	247	...	...	...	...	...	...	...	...

Gillu . . .	...	...	...	...	...	...	...	367	...	...	...	...	...
Godara . . .	...	...	...	330	...	...	...	252	...	...	...	...	...
Godhi . . .	...	...	...	...	785	3,123	453	...	...	...	...	...	...
Goriya . . .	...	...	...	...	...	...	...	...	...	...	254	...	...
Gûgar . . .	...	...	...	...	24,013	...	...	...	...	...	...	...	...
Hela . . .	...	...	32,761	13,904	...	...	...	...	...	...	...	...	...
Henya . . .	...	...	...	...	...	...	1,567	...	...	...	...	...	...
Indauliya . .	...	...	...	...	...	237	1,876	...	...	...	...	...	...
Jaiawâr . . .	...	...	...	...	996	...	...	...	...	...	...	...	...
Jakhar . . .	...	...	...	...	...	...	...	...	...	...	415	...	...
Jatarni . . .	...	1,299	259	...	...	...	...	...	...	...	...	...	...
Jatu . . .	216	...	...	...	...	...	...	...	...	...	...	...	...
Kachhwâha . .	...	...	...	...	1,049	...	413	...	...	...	...	...	...
Kanchir . . .	...	...	...	...	1,116	229	...	...	...	...	...	...	...
Kankhandi . .	...	1,040	...	...	...	...	...	...	...	...	...	...	...
Katheriya . .	...	...	...	...	3,021	...	...	...	...	...	...	...	...
Khokhar . .	...	...	442	...	...	...	...	...	...	...	...	...	...

Distribution of the Chief Jât Sections—continued.

	Sahâran-pur.	Muzaffar-nagar.	Meerut.	Bulaud-shahr.	Aligarh.	Mathura.	Agra.	Bareilly.	Bijnor.	Budaun.	Morâdâbâd.	Tarâi.	Gonda.
Khubar . . .	...	...	...	...	198	1,524	1,191	...	...	...	...	...	...
Khunkhuniya . .	...	...	...	...	776	245	...	...	...	...	...	...	...
Khutel . . .	...	...	...	...	1,389	10,906	1,936	...	...	...	...	...	...
Kistwâr . . .	...	...	...	...	...	272	...	...	...	...	...	...	...
Koil . . .	...	...	...	...	592	...	...	...	...	...	...	...	...
Kunthal . . .	...	250	...	...	...	...	...	...	...	...	...	...	...
Lahiri . . .	...	...	...	303	...	...	...	...	...	...	...	...	...
Lathar . . .	...	...	...	320	...	8,974	...	...	...	...	...	...	...
Lohain . . .	...	...	...	...	...	...	...	257	...	...	...	...	...
Mahur . . .	...	...	...	...	4,523	513	1,033	...	...	...	...	...	...
Maini . . .	...	...	...	...	...	3,360	...	...	...	...	...	...	...
Mathuriya . .	...	...	...	...	400	...	...	...	...	...	...	...	...
Mohjit . . .	...	...	...	1,729	...	...	...	...	...	...	...	...	...

Mori . . .	...	...	...	...	...	...	645	...	...	...	...	...	...
Mûndhan . . .	...	...	...	...	...	...	...	...	911	...	...	...	...
Nohwâl . . .	...	...	...	1,594	...	...	1,051	...	...	...	...	...	...
Nanoliya . .	...	...	...	...	650	...	...	...	...	...	...	...	...
Pachhâdê . . .	1,343	1,157	1,121	...	3,287	814	184	2,105	1,908	28,516	28,267	...	...
Padhân . . .	330	...	...	...	...	...	...	...	...	...	...	...	...
Panwâr . . .	...	...	...	...	7,277	1,509	242	...	...	...	218	...	...
Parihâr . . .	...	...	...	...	...	...	498	...	...	...	...	...	...
Phokha . . .	...	...	...	...	...	1,228	...	...	...	...	...	...	...
Puâr . . .	...	1,528	311	1,888	...	...	...	...	...	...	...	...	...
Puniya . . .	...	...	...	306	...	393	298	...	...	...	...	...	...
Punriya . . .	...	...	...	...	3,254	...	...	...	...	...	...	...	...
Purbar . . .	...	469	...	...	1,345	1,661	...	...	...	...	...	...	...
Raikwâr . . .	...	...	...	...	385	397	...	...	...	...	...	...	...
Rajauriya . .	...	...	...	3,604	...	...	...	...	...	...	...	...	...
Râna . . .	...	...	...	...	1,302	902	828	...	...	...	...	...	...
Rânghar . . .	...	...	...	...	379	...	...	...	...	...	...	...	...

Distribution of the Chief Jât Sections—concluded.

	Sahâran-pur.	Muzaffar-nagar.	Meerut.	Buland-shahr.	Aligarh.	Mathura.	Agra.	Bareilly.	Bijnor.	Budaun.	Morâdâbâd.	Tarâi.	Gonda.
Râhtaur . . .	...	...	...	...	2,568	...	...	...	...	...	...	...	...
Râthi . . .	...	2,750	351	...	...	...	...	228	...	...	...	...	...
Râwat . . .	...	...	...	1,942	1,765	2,010	377	...	...	...	...	...	...
Rikhbans . .	...	927	...	...	...	...	...	...	...	...	...	...	...
Rora . . .	...	...	...	...	...	...	...	...	...	...	366	...	...
Saigal . . .	...	...	...	...	...	...	...	...	...	205	...	...	...
Sakarwâr . . .	...	...	...	...	1,119	3,596	1,589	...	...	...	...	...	...
Sakel . . .	...	...	...	...	...	...	...	...	273	...	...	...	...
Salaklain . . .	...	866	494	...	...	...	...	...	...	...	...	...	...
Sangeriyân . .	...	...	...	...	...	11,868	...	...	...	...	...	...	...
Sarâmat . . .	...	...	...	...	...	1,714	...	...	...	...	...	...	...
Sarâwat . . .	...	2,106	...	...	1,775	...	3,461	...	...	206	...	...	...
Sangwân . . .	...	...	...	718	5,194	...	...	...	...	...	...	...	...

Sidhu . . .	...	...	...	...	...	...	...	781	...	...	...	...	...
Sinmâr . . .	700	...	...	...	...	...	...	...	...	...	...	...	...
Sinsinwâr . .	...	...	218	3,618	5,325	4,219	3,013	292	...	...	...	...	...
Sohron . . .	...	...	...	...	...	476	...	...	...	...	...	...	...
Sugariyân . .	...	...	...	...	...	596	909	...	...	...	...	...	...
Thakurela . .	...	...	...	5,681	28,871	826	...	...	...	...	304	...	...
Thenwân . . .	...	...	...	...	7,365	3,524	...	...	...	...	...	...	...
Tomar . . .	...	...	4,283	...	6,967	578	...	...	...	...	...	...	...
Uriya . . .	...	...	...	...	1,720	...	...	...	...	...	...	...	...

Jati—(Sanskrit *Yati*, "one who has restrained his passions and abandoned the world").—A class of mendicant devotees who are the priests of the Jainas or Sarâogis. According to Mr. Sherring the term is applied also to those Gusâîns, Bairâgis, and Udâsis who practise celibacy; and another variety are akin to the Jogis; but the application of the term to any but the Jaina sect appears very unusual. The total strength of the Jainas in these Provinces, according to the returns of the last Census, was 84,785 persons, or 18 in 10,000 for the whole population. According to Mr. Baillie[1] "the sectarian divisions of the faith are little known to the majority of Jainas in these Provinces, to whom the Svetambara, though they have temples at Ajudhya and probably elsewhere, are practically unknown. The entries in the sect column were, therefore, in general the names of the principal Jinas—Adi Nâth, Ajit Nâth, Pâras Nâth, Mahavîra, or Nîm Nâth, or the word Sarâvgi, that by which a secular Jaina is distinguished from a Jati or member of an ascetic order. The total number of Svetambaras shown in the Province was 2,235. It may be assumed that the others are Digambaras. The Jaina lists show that the adherents of the religion are almost entirely Banyas: 83,976, out of the total 84,601, entered originally as Jaina in religion, being of that caste. The Agarwâla, Jaiswâr, Khandelwâl, Purwâr, Paliwâl and Oswâl sub-castes are the most important. Four hundred and fifty-one Râjputs appear, possibly converts, but more probably, as mostly shown, of the Jaiswâr sub-caste, really belonging to the trading community. There are thirty-two Brâhmans, Gaur being more numerously represented than any other sub-caste. Gaur Brâhmans, even though Hindus, are employed by Jainas as temple attendants, and sometimes join the faith of their patrons."

2. On the Jaina faith the remarks of Dr. J. Burgess[2] may be quoted:—"As their name implies, the Jainas are the followers of the Jinas, or 'vanquishers' of sins, men whom they believe to have obtained Nirvâna, or emancipation, from the continual changes of transmigration. With them 'life,' which they do not distinguish from 'soul' and its vehicle 'matter,' are both uncreated and imperishable, obeying eternal physical laws with which asceticism and religious ceremonial alone can interfere. Their ceremonial has, therefore, no real reference to a supreme personal God, and their

[1] *Census Report, North-Western Provinces*, 134.

[2] *Indian Antiquary* II., 14, *sqq*.

doctrine excludes his Providence. This at once points to their connection with the Buddhists; indeed there can be little doubt that they are an early heretical sect of the Hinayana school of that persuasion, and owed a part of their popularity, on the decline of the purer Bauddha doctrines, to their readier admission of the worship of some of the favourite Hindu divinities into their system and their retention of the tyranny of caste customs. But much of their phraseology is of Buddha origin; thus their laity are called Srâvakas—'hearers'—the same name as among the most ancient Buddhists is applied to those 'who practise the four realities and suppress the errors of thought and sight, without being able to emancipate themselves entirely from the influence of passion and prejudice,' but 'who, occupied wholly with their own salvation, pay no regard to that of other men.' Then the Buddha is constantly spoken of as the Jina, or 'vanquisher,' his exit from existence, like that of the Jaina Tîrthankaras, is his Nirvâna; both employ the Swâstika and Sâtya as a sacred symbol; the sacred language of the Buddhists is Mâgadhi, of the Jainas Arddha Mâgadhi; the temples of both sects are Chaityas; those who have attained perfection are Arhans; and Digambaras, or naked ascetics, were a Bauddha as well as a Jaina sect.[1] Further, the Jainas indicate South Bihâr as the scene of the life and labours of nearly all their Tîrthankaras, as it was of Sakya Sinha. Buddha is often called Mahâvîra, the name of the last Tîrthankara, whose father the Jainas call Siddharta, the 'establisher of faith,' the proper name of Buddha, and both are of the race of Ikshvâku; and Mahâvîra's wife was Yasoda, as Buddha's was Yasodhara. Moreover, Mahâvîra is said to have died at Pawa, in Bihâr, about 527 B.C.; and Gautama Buddha, between Pawa and Kusinâra, in 543 B.C. These coincidences with many analogies of doctrine and practice seem to indicate that the Jainas are of Bauddha origin."

3. "The leading and distinguishing doctrines of the Jainas are—the denial of the divine origin and authority of the Vedas; reverence for the Jinas who by their austerities acquired a position superior to that even of those Hindu gods whom they reverence; and the most extreme tenderness of animal life. Life is defined to be without beginning or end—endowed with attributes of its own, agent and destroyer, conscious, subtle, proportionate to the body it

---

[1] Hodgson *Illustrations of Buddhism*, 43, 213.

animates—diminishing with the gnat and expanding with the elephant; through sin it passes into animals or goes into hell; through virtue and vice combined it passes into men; and through the annihilation of both vice and virtue it obtains emancipation. The duties of a Yati, or ascetic, are ten—Patience, gentleness, integrity, disinterestedness, abstraction, mortification, truth, purity, poverty, and continence; and the Srâvakas add to their moral and religious code the practical worship of the Tîrthankaras and profound reverence for their more pious brethren. The moral obligations of the Jainas are summed up in their five *Mahâvrata*, which are almost identical with the *pancha sila* of the Bauddhas—Care not to injure life, truth, honesty, chastity, and the suppression of worldly desires. They enumerate four merits or *dharma*—Liberality, gentleness, piety, and penance; and three forms of restraint—Government of the tongue, of the mind, and of the person. Their minor instructions are, in many cases, trivial and ludicrous—such as, not to deal in soap, natron, indigo, and iron; not to eat in the open air after it begins to rain; nor in the dark, lest a fly should be swallowed; not to leave a liquid uncovered, lest an insect should be drowned; water to be thrice strained before it is drunk; and *vayukarma*, keeping out of the way of the wind, lest it should blow insects into the mouth.

4. "The Yatis, or priests, carry an *ugha*, or besom made of cotton thread, to sweep insects out of the way of harm as they enter the temples, or where they sit down, and a *mohomati*, or mouth cloth, to prevent insects entering the mouth while praying or washing the images. The proper objects of worship are the Jinas or Tîrthankaras, but they allow the existence of the Hindu gods and have admitted to a share of their worship such of them as they have connected with the tales of their saints. As, among the Bauddhas, Indra and Sukra is of frequent occurrence, the Jainas distinguishing two principal Indras—Sukra, regent of the north heaven, and Îsâna, regent of the south, besides many inferior ones; and images of Sarasvati and of Devi, or Bhawâni, are to be found in many of their temples. Nor are those of Hanumân, Bhairava, and Ganesa excluded from their sacred places. Besides, they have a pantheon of their own in which they reckon four classes of superhuman beings—Bhuvanapatis, Vyantaras, Jyotishkas, and Vaimanikas—comprising first the brood of the Asuras, Nâgas, Garuda, the Dikpâlas, etc., supposed to reside in the hells below the earth; secondly,

the Râkshasas, the Pisâchas, Bhûtas, Kinnaras, Gandharvas, etc., inhabiting mountains, forests, and lower air; thirdly, five orders of celestial luminarics; and, fourthly, gods of present and past Kalpas, of the former of which are those born in the heavens—Saudharma, Îsâna, Sanatkumâra, Mahendra, Brahma, Lâutaka, Sukra, Sahasrâra, Ânata, Pranâta, Arana, and Âchyata, etc. Each Jina, they say, has also a sort of familiar goddess of his own, called a Sâsanadevi, who executes his behests. These are perhaps analogous to the Sâktis, or Mâtris, of the Brâhmans; indeed among them we find Ambika, a name of Kaumâri, the Sâkti of Karttikeya and Chanda, and Mahâkâli, names of Bhawâni" [1].

5. The Jatis are divided into the real Jati, who wear white clothes, and the Sewara, who dresses in ochre-coloured garments. According to Mr. Sherring, the Sewaras walk about with head and feet bare, holding a red stick in the hand, and they carry with them a kind of brush made of peacocks' feathers, with which they sweep the ground before sitting down, lest they should injure a worm or an insect. Both these classes beg cooked food from the houses of Jainas or Sarâogis. By Hindus they are held in abomination and contempt, and are said to practise magic and witchcraft.

6. The last Census shows only 12 Jaina Faqîrs,—4 at Saharânpur, 1 at Muzaffarnagar, 1 at Mathura, 2 at Agra, 4 at Jalaun.

Jhamaiya.—A small sub-caste of Banyas who seem to be identical with, or an off-shoot from, the Bishnoi (*q.v.*), and to take their name from the tribal Saint Jhâmbaji. Until quite recently it is said they followed the Bishnoi custom of burying their dead. They now place them on a mat and fling them into a river [2].

Distribution of the Jhamaiya Banyas according to the Census of 1891.

Districts.	Number.
Farrukhâbâd	42
Etâwah	794
Cawnpur	1,250
Hamîrpur	2
Jhânsi	2
Allahâbâd	486
TOTAL	2,576

[1] The whole question of the origin of the Jainas is elaborately discussed in two papers by Professor Lassen: *Indian Antiquary* II., 193 *sqq.*, 258 *sqq.* Also see a paper by Mr. Thomas, *Ibid* VIII., 30 *sqq.*

[2] *Census Report North-West Provinces*, 1865, *Appendix* 88.

Jhijhotiya, Jajahutiya.—A branch of the Kanaujiya Brâhmans who take their name from the country of Jejâkasukti, which is mentioned in the Madanpur inscription. Of this General Cunningham writes[1]:—"The first point deserving of notice in these two short but precious records is the name of the country, Jejâkasukti, which is clearly the Jajâhuti of Abu Rihân. The meaning of the word is doubtful, but it was certainly the name of the country, as it is coupled with *desa*. I may add, also, that there are considerable numbers of Jajahutiya Brâhmans and Jajahutiya Banyas in the old country of the Chandels or Bundelkhand. I would identify Jajahuti with the district of Sandrabatis of Ptolemy, which contained four towns, named Tamasis, Empalathra, Kuropovina and Nandubandagar. Judging from the relative positions assigned to them by Ptolemy, I think that the first, which is to the North-East of Sandrabatis, may be Darsanda, the second Mahoba, the third Khajurâho, and the fourth, which is the most Westerly, Bhander." The Jami-ut-tawârikh of Rashîd-ud-dîn[2], quoting from Abu Rihân al Birûni, mentions the Kingdom of Jajhoti as containing the cities of Gwâlior and Kalinjar, and that its capital was at Khajurâho. The popular and incorrect explanation is that they are really Yajurhota Brâhmans, because, in making burnt offerings, they followed the rules of the Yajur Veda.

2. According to a list procured at Mirzapur their *gotras* are—Awasthi; Bhareriya Tivâri; Arjariya Kot; Gautamiya of Ladhpur; Patariya of Kannaura; Pâthak of Kalyânpur; Gangelê of Matayaya; Richhatiya of Kuba or Kunwa; Tivâri of Eji; Chaubê of Kachhaura; Nâyak of Pipari; Bâjpei of Binwârê; Dikshit of Panna; Kariya Misra; Sondelê Misra. The above fifteen *gotras* intermarry on equal terms. Below these are five, which are lower and give daughters to the higher fifteen, but are not given brides by them in return. These are—Sirsa; Soti; Sonakiya; Ranaiya; Bhonreli Dûbê. This list has little resemblance to that given by Mr. Sherring[3].

The Jhijhotiya Brâhmans have but an indifferent reputation.

---

[1] *Archæological Reports* X., 99; II., 413.
[2] Dowson's *Elliot* I., 54.
[3] *Hindu Castes* I., 56.

Distribution of the Jhijhotiya Brâhmans according to the Census of 1891.

Districts.	Number.	Districts.	Number.
Sahâranpur . . .	1	Jhânsi . . .	20,519
Agra	1	Jâlaun . . .	11,140
Etah	1	Lalitpur . . .	16,258
Bareilly	4	Ghâzipur . . .	132
Cawnpur	77	Gorakhpur . . .	3,184
Banda	734	Faizâbâd . . .	74
Hamîrpur . . .	19,497		
		TOTAL .	71,622

Jhojha.—A tribe of cultivators found hardly beyond Sahâranpur, Muzaffarnagar, and Bijnor. Of them, Sir H. M. Elliot writes [1]—"The word means literally 'the stomach' (Sanskrit *jarjara*, 'hollow'), and is the designation of an inferior class of Muhammadans. The Jhojhas of Pargana Baran of Bulandshahr represent themselves as converted Râthaurs, Chauhâns, and Tuars, but by others they are considered to be converted slaves of these tribes. In like manner those of Anupshahr are said to be the slaves of Mughals converted to Muhammadanism. They are despised by the Bargûjars and other converted Râjputs of the neighbourhood, with whom they are not suffered to intermarry; from which their servile origin may be fairly presumed. They are scattered over different parts of the Duâb and Rohilkhand, and are reported to be good cultivators.—Hence the proverb—

Jhojha hâli lekar, ghar baitho chaupar khel.

'Employ a Jhojha as a ploughman,
and you may sit at home and play backgammon.'

The complete list of their sections, as shown in the Census returns, shows that the tribe is of mixed origin. Thus, with Hindu names, like Banjâra, Benbans, Chaudhari, Chauhân, Desi, Deswâli, Kolipanwâr, Orh, Râjput, and Rori, we have later orthodox Muhammadan names, like Ghâzi, Ghori, Pathân, Shaikh and Sadîqi.

[1] *Supplementary Glossary s. v.*

"2. One of the chief causes of the value attached to their service is, that being Musalmâns, they are not restrained by Hindu observances of particular festivals. Thus, while Hindus are waiting for the Dithwan before they cut their sugarcane, the Jhojhas have already begun to press their cane and manufacture their sugar."

3. In Oudh, a branch of the tribe is said to have held Pargana Gopamau in Hardoi, and to have been conquered by the Gaur Râjputs. Mr. Butts thinks they were converted Bhars who yielded to the Muhammadans and embraced their faith. In Lucknow many forts are attributed to them, and they are considered to have been converted Bhars or Pâsis [1].

Distribution of the Jhojhas according to the Census of 1891.

Districts.	Number.	Districts.	Number.
Dehra Dûn . . .	21	Shâhjahânpur . .	8
Sahâranpur . . .	12,867	Pilibhît . . .	4
Muzaffarnagar. . .	7,477	Cawnpur . . .	3
Meerut	3	Tarâi	133
Bulandshahr . . .	21	Sîtapur . . .	26
Agra	3	Kheri	1
Farrukhâbâd . . .	11	Faizâbâd . . .	6
Etah	1	Bahrâich . . .	3
Bijnor	5,765	Partâbgarh . . .	464
Morâdâbâd . . .	30	Total .	26,847

Jogi—(Sanskrit *Yoga*, "union"). A "term properly applied to the followers of the Yoga, or Patanjala, school of philosophy, which, among other tenets, maintained the practicability, even in life, of acquiring entire command over elementary matter by means of certain ascetic practices. The practices consist chiefly of long continued suppressions of respiration; inhaling and exhaling the breath in a peculiar manner; of sitting in eighty-four different attitudes; of fixing the eyes on the top of the nose; and endeavouring, by force of mental abstraction, to effect a union between the

[1] *Hardoi Settlement Report, 155; Lucknow Settlement Report, 126.*

portion of vital spirit residing in the body and that which pervades all Nature, and is identical with Siva considered as the Supreme Being and source and essence of all Creation "[1].

Sub-divisions of Jogis.

2. The last Census divides the Jogis into the two main classes of Aughar and Gorakhpanthi. The real founder of the sect is said to have been that mysterious Saint Gorakhnâtha about whom so many wonderful tales are told, but whose personality and history are for the most part shrouded in legend and mystery. He is said to have had twelve disciples whose names are very uncertain, and there are several lists of them. One list is—Sat Nâth, Dharm Nâth, Kâya Nâth, Âdh Nâth, Mast Nâth, Abhapanthi, Kalepa, Dhajpanthi, Handibirang, Ramkê, Lachhmankê, Darya Nâth. According to another—Aipanthê, Ramkê, Bhartari, Sat Nâth, Kanibaki (disciples of Jâlandhar Nâth; of this branch are the Sapelas), Kapâl Muni, Lachhman Natesar, Ratan Nâth, Santokh Nâth, Dhajpanthi (followers of Hanumân), Man Nâth (followers of Râja Rasâlu). A third list gives—Sant Nâth, Râm Nâth, Abbang Nâth, Bharang Nâth, Dhar Nâth, Gangâi Nâth, Dhaja Nâth, Jâlandhar Nâth, Darpa Nâth, Kanak Nâth, Nîm Nâth, and Nâg Nâth[2]. The best known sub-divisions are the Aughar and the Kanphatas, of whom a separate account has been given. Mr. Maclagan suggests that "there are many things which point to a non-Hindu origin for the Jogis and Sannyâsis. The Hindu wears a scalp-lock, carries the sacred thread, burns his dead, and, generally speaking, abstains from flesh and wine. The Jogis too are remarkably prevalent in the Peshâwar and Kâbul direction, where Buddhism was once so strong. And the names of their twelve Nâths bear some resemblance with those of the Jaina Tîrthankaras. There are legends too which connect Gorakh Nâth in a special way with Nepâl, and the Panth of Jâlandhar Nâth is often termed Pânâth from the fact that its members in place of Nâth adopt after their names the termination *Pá*, which is the Tibetan epithet for our familiar *wála*."

Other Jogis.

3. Besides the respectable members of the sect who are contemplative ascetics, there are others who do not bear such a reputable character. Among these the Bhartari and Nandiya Jogis are Hindus, and the Bhaddar

---

[1] Wilson, *Essays I*, 206.
[2] Maclagan, *Panjâb Census Report*, 114.

very often Musalmâns. They wear a beard and a long sort of coat dyed with ochre which is called *gudri*. On the shoulders they carry an alms wallet (*jholi*) dyed in ochre, and a turban of the same colour. The Bhartari Jogis carry about with them a sort of fiddle (*sârangi*) and a stick called *bairâga*. They play on the fiddle and sing songs in honour of Bhartrihari, who is said to have been the brother of Râja Vikramaditya. His shrine is in the Chunâr Fort, and he passes part of the day there and the rest in Benares. They wear round their necks a necklace (*mâla*) of *rudrâksha* beads. The Bhaddari Jogis dress in very much the same way, but do not carry a fiddle. They tell fortunes by means of palmistry and exorcise ghosts and demons.

4. The Nandiya Jogis wear the same dress, but do not carry a fiddle. They lead about with them a deformed ox, an animal with five legs, or some other malformation. He is decorated with ochre coloured rags and cowry shells. They call him Nandi or the vehicle of Mahâdeva, and receive gifts of grain from pious Hindus, half of which they put into their wallet, and give the other half to the animal. They usually carry on a more profitable business than other kinds of beggars. The ox is trained to give a blessing to the benevolent by shaking its head and raising its leg when its master receives a gift. Some of the Jogis of this class carry about with them a brush which they wave over the heads of children afflicted with the Evil Eye. These people are hereditary beggars, and keep houses and families. The boys are initiated into the order at the time when the ceremonial shaving (*mûndan*) is carried out. Then the Guru makes over a ragged garment (*gudri*) to the neophyte, with a wallet and fiddle, the implements of his trade. The Guru often receives considerable sums of money for initiating a disciple. The mendicants of the order assemble at the time of initiation, and unless the candidate is a hereditary member of the order, his friends have to give seven dinners to the brethren. They beg from both Hindus and Musalmâns, but naturally Hindus are their chief supporters. They do not take cooked food as alms, not because they are particular in matters of eating, because they can take *kachchi* from a Chamâr or any caste not inferior to his. The alms they take are money or uncooked grain, and they will also take rags and old clothes. The Bhartari Jogis sing songs in honour of Bhartrihari, Râja Gopi Chand, and Mahâdeva. They also sing songs in honour of Daya Râm (*karkha*). The Bhaddari or Nandi Jogis hardly ever

sing; or, if they do sing, it is songs in honour of Mahâdeva. To the west of the province they sing songs to Zâhir Pir, or the love ballads of Hîra and Rânjha, or the adventures of Amar Singh Râthaur. They also work as tailors and silk-spinners, and have several *gotras* with Râjput names, such as Chauhân, Kachhwâha, Gahlot, etc. These all eat and intermarry with each other except in their own *gotra*.[1]

5. Many of these Jogis have a very indifferent reputation. They wander about and make themselves acquainted with the history and antecedents of any rich family which may have lost a near or important relative, and, personating the absentee, readily obtain access to the family, which results in a general plunder of the premises and the disappearance of the swindlers. They also pretend to change copper into gold, a power which they trace to one of their order in the time of the Sultân Altitmish. Some are professional poisoners; others pretend to deal in millstones and steal cattle.[2]

6. Marco Polo mentions the Jogis under the name of Chughi, and says "they are properly Abraiman (Brâhmans), but they form a religious order devoted to the idols. They are extremely long-lived, every one of them living to one hundred and fifty or two hundred years. They eat very little, but what they do eat is good, rice and milk chiefly. And these people make use of a very strange beverage; for they make a potion of sulphur and quicksilver mixed together, and this they drink twice every month. This they say gives them long life."

Bernier[3] mentions the same custom.

Distribution of the Jogis according to the Census of 1891.

Districts.	Aughar.	Gorakh-panthi.	Others.	Muhammadans.	Total.
Dehra Dûn	86	90	927	...	1,103
Sahâranpur . . .	...	...	13,713	21	13,734
Muzaffarnagar . . .	1,235	1,744	6,250	2,769	11,998
Meerut	1,646	1,612	8,729	1,142	13,129

[1] Râja Lachhman Sinh, *Bulandshahr Memo.* 188. *sqq.*

[2] *Report, Inspector-General Police, North-Western Provinces, 1867, p. 94: 1868, p. 5: 1869, pp. 121-125.*

[3] *Travels* II. 130.

Distribution of the Jogis according to the Census of 1891—contd.

DISTRICTS.	Aughar.	Gorakh-panthi.	Others.	Muham-madans.	TOTAL.
Bulandshahr	49	2	3,662	53	3,766
Aligarh	...	...	3,353	25	3,378
Mathura	...	...	...	128	128
Agra	32	48	2,165	758	3,003
Farrukhâbâd	...	...	219	68	287
Mainpuri	...	...	815	...	815
Etâwah	...	...	642	166	808
Etah	8	22	891	159	1,080
Bareilly	...	...	738	254	992
Bijnor	821	232	923	428	2,404
Budaun	15	...	850	14	879
Morâdâbâd	52	91	2,339	84	2,566
Shâhjahânpur	...	...	41	730	771
Pilibhît	16	...	227	3	246
Cawnpur	...	240	704	326	1,270
Fatehpur	...	129	1,016	56	1,201
Bânda	...	1	781	3	785
Hamîrpur	14	6	309	349	678
Allahâbâd	1	...	603	512	1,116
Jhânsi	2	180	1,260	3	1,445
Jâlaun	...	...	517	...	517
Lalitpur	...	...	308	...	308
Benares	186	226	7	...	419
Mirzapur	...	71	...	43	114
Jaunpur	...	...	116	940	1,056
Ghâzipur	9	30	133	5	177
Ballia	...	80	8	67	155

Distribution of the Jogis according to the Census of 1891—concld.

Districts.	Aughar.	Gorakh-panthi.	Others.	Muham-madans.	Total.
Gorakhpur	...	372	521	680	1,573
Basti	...	4,106	...	1,355	5,461
Azamgarh	7	...	5,757	470	6,234
Kumaun	5	3,031	...	...	3,036
Garhwâl	...	407	827	...	1,234
Tarâi	54	399	38	...	491
Lucknow	6	...	1,051	276	1,333
Unâo	1	...	25	372	398
Râê Bareli	...	...	26	296	322
Sîtapur	12	14	11	471	508
Hardoi	...	...	...	368	368
Kheri	...	...	331	202	533
Faizâbâd	...	...	24	711	735
Gonda	45	...	75	1,180	1,300
Bahrâich	15	...	5	391	411
Sultânpur	...	...	...	864	864
Partâbgarh	...	...	...	458	458
Bârabanki	...	...	...	393	393
Total	4,317	13,133	60,937	17,593	95,980

Johiya.—A sect of Râjputs, who, according to Sir H. M. Elliot,[1] "are by some authorities included among the thirty-six Royal races of India; by others they are considered a mere ramification of the Yadu Bhatti. In the gathering of the Râjputs to defend the Mori Prince of Chithor they are styled "Lords of Jangaldes," which included Hariyâna, Bhatner, and Nâgaur. There are, I believe, no Râjputs of this clan, except a very few in Khairagarh of Allahâbâd, and those in the Duâb, who form a Chaurâsi in the

[1] *Supplementary Glossary* S. V.

neighbourhood of Allahâbâd and Chail, and who are all converted to Muhammadanism. Colonel Tod considers the Johiyas to be totally extinct."

Joshi.[1]—A term applied to at least two very different classes of people. The proper term for the astrologer or astronomer, whose function is the preparation of horoscopes and the ascertaining of the lucky and unlucky influences which attach to particular times, is Jyotishi, which comes from the Sanskrit *Jyautishika* or "one skilled in astronomy and astrology." He is always a Brâhman, and though not holding a very high position, he is an indispensible personage in the village economy. From this Joshi is a corruption, and he, in the Plains at least, is a much less respectable practitioner. He is also known as Bhaddali from his eponymous ancestor, and Bhanreriya from his approximation to the Bhând or actor-singer caste. Bhaddali, who was a famous astrologer and the author of a well-known book on the subject known as Sagunâvali or "the interpretation of omens," is said to have been the son of the celebrated Varâha Mihira, who was one of the "nine gems" of the Court of Vikramaditya. He was the author of the Brihat Sanhita and Brihaj Jâtaka, and is said to have died in 587 A. D.

2. The birth of Bhaddali is told in this wise:—Varâha Mihira, after a life spent in the study of astrology, was on his return home. By his art he had discovered that, if he begot a son at a particular time, the child would be a profound adept in the science. On the road he was delayed and was obliged to halt at the house of a Dhobi, or, as some say, of an Ahîr. The master of the house was absent, but his lady was at home. The sage lamented to her that he was unable to meet his wife at the auspicious moment. She thought the opportunity too good to be lost for the production of a child with such a future. From their embraces she conceived, and the famous Bhaddali was the result. Next day Varâha Mihira reached home, and his wife also conceived and bore a son. Before she was delivered he gave her a ball, and told her when the child was born to throw the ball within the sacred circle in which he was engaged in the study of the stars. The result of his calculations was unfavourable, and he declared that he was not the father of the child which she bore to him. In his rage and grief he left his wife and child, and went and settled in a foreign land.

---

[1] Largely based on a note contributed by Pandit Janardan Dat Joshi, Deputy Collector, Bareilly.

3. The two boys grew up and both became adepts in astrology. After a time, when they were taunted about the uncertainty of their descent, they consulted the stars, and ascertaining that Varâha Mihira was their father, started in search of him. When after a long and weary march they reached a certain city, they found a great crowd assembled. An astrologer, who was their father, Varâha Mihira, had foretold that at a certain time and place a fish would drop from the sky. The King of the land and all his subjects were assembled to see the promised miracle. When the boys made their calculations they found that the fish would certainly drop from heaven, but not at the exact time and place foretold by the astrologer, their father. Their announcement turned out correct, and they were greatly applauded, while their father was brought to shame. In his surprise he asked them to explain his mistake. They informed him that he had not made allowance for the slight movement of the earth while the fish was falling from heaven, and they added that he also failed to take account of the time which the ball had taken to fly through the air when thrown by his wife before it fell in the sacred circle. Varâha Mihira was confounded, and now confident of the virtue of his wife, returned home with his sons. The son of the low caste woman being illegitimate was not allowed to become a proficient in Sanskrit literature, but confined his studies to Hindi, in which language he wrote the famous treatise on omens, to which reference has already been made. He then, before Râja Bhoj was born, foretold the glory to which he would attain; but Munja, the uncle of the young prince, in his jealousy had him exposed in the jungle, where he was rescued by a Brâhman, and lived to ascend the throne.

4. The Joshis of the Plains are followers of the Sâma Veda, while those of the hills follow the Yajur Veda. The best known *gotras* of the former are Bharadwâja, Pachrauliya; Sikrauriya; Urauriya; Kakara; Silâchar (Sila Achârya); or Silauta; Chhibari; and Pârâsara. But the Census returns, which include no less than 451 sections, lead to the conclusion that the Joshis, at least in the Plains, are a very mixed body. We have few of the regular Brâhmanical *gotras*, and many which suggest a lower origin or connection, such as Bâgri, Bais, Bâri, Barwâr, Chamargaur, Chauhân, Gautam, Raghubansi, Râjput, Sunâri, and Tuar; with local sections such as Aharwâr, Bhojpuriya, Gujarâti, Indauriya, Hardwâri, Kanaujiya, Magarwâr, Muazzamnagariya, Saksena, and Sri-

bâstam. They are entitled to receive only three kinds of offering (*dâna*)—those made to Sanîschara or Saturn, who is universally regarded as of evil omen, and those made to Râhu and Ketu, the demons who are the cause of eclipses. Gifts to Sanîschara are made only on a Saturday from morning to noon, and consist of an iron dish (*bâlti*), one *ser* and a quarter of *urad* pulse, five *chhâtanks* of vegetable oil, and a small sum of money. The gift to Râhu Deota includes seven kinds of grain, a knife or other iron cutting instrument, a goat, and a small piece of sapphire (*nîlum*). These are given to the Joshi on a Wednesday after the recital of appropriate verses (*mantra*). The offering to Ketu includes a lamb or sheep, oil, an iron vessel, a piece of green cloth, some coral, and emerald (*zummurud*), gold, and a small sum of money. This is given to the Joshi on a Friday night, just when one or two stars are visible; to use their own phrase, it should be done in the shade of stars. The little bits of gold and precious stones used in these offerings are sold by Sunârs at a half pice each, and of course only a very minute portion is given.

5. The *gotras* already named are exogamous; a son can be married in a *gotra* lower than that of his father; but with girls the rule of hypergamy prevails, and she must be married in a superior *gotra*, if possible to a Gangaputra boy. But on the other hand, a Gangaputra will never marry his daughter to a Joshi. When the bride is brought home (*gauna*), the members of the *gotra* assemble and drink milk boiled with rice and sugar. This is known as *dûdhabhâti*, and represents a sort of formal initiation of the bride in the family of her husband. From that time the members can eat *kachchi* cooked by her. It may be noted that among Brâhmans the bride cannot cook *kachchi* for her new family until she attains puberty, and until the rite following impregnation (*garbhadhâna*) is performed. The Khasiyas of Kumaun are still more particular, and will not eat from the hand of the bride until she bears children.

6. These Joshis of the plains are worshippers of godesses rather than of gods. Next to these their most favourite deity is Mahâbîr.

The Mârwâri Joshis.

7. The Mârwâri Joshis are Panch Gaur, and are divided into Adi Gaur; Jaypuri Gaur; Mâlavi Gaur and Gûjar Gaur or those of Jaypur, Mâlwa, and Gujarât. Some of them are found in Benares, and they, as well as

the Kumaun Joshis, are quite distinct from the common Joshis or the plains. In the case of the Gûjar Gaur Joshis, the term Joshi is a title and does not represent an actual caste.

The Kumaun Joshis.

8. Of these, Mr. Atkinson[1] writes:—"The Joshis, though hardly ranked as Brâhmans in the plains, have attained in the hills, by long prescription, a claim to be considered Brâhmans, and intermarry with Pants, Pânrês, Tiwâris, and others. They are by occupation astrologers and horoscope-makers, but large numbers now affect government service or agriculture." They have several *gotras*, of which the following account is given by Pandit Janardan Joshi. The Gârgya *gotra* are said to be descended from Sushanidhi, a Chaubê Brâhman, of Jhûsi, near Allahâbâd, who is said to have accompanied Râja Som Chand to Kumaun where he was appointed his Wazir. An absurd legend tells that these Joshis take their name from Jhûsi, their original home. They are divided into various local sections, such as those of Jhijar, Shilakhola, Digoli, Kotwâlgânw, etc., none of which intermarry. The Angiras *gotra* claim descent from Nathrâj Pânrê of Khor in Kanauj, who came to Kumaun on a pilgrimage to Badarinâth, and obtained employment as an astrologer, and the village of Siren in Katayûr free of revenue. From thence they spread over Kumaun, and continued for a long time to perform simply priestly functions, but in the troubles which arose on the accession of Trimal Chand in 1626 A.D., they succeeded in obtaining a share of State offices, and have never failed to be represented in Government service. Service and agriculture are the occupations of the division to the present day, and they claim the title of Dîwân. The Kausik *gotra* has a history of nineteen generations in Kumaun. They claim their origin from a place called Nadiya Santipur, whence they came and settled at Doti. Before their immigration they are alleged to have been Bâjpei Brâhmans. Of the other *gotras* Mr. Atkinson writes:—"The Joshis of the Upamanya *gotra* claim descent from a Misra Brâhman of Diptiya. They say that some of his descendants became Pânrês, and that those who devoted themselves to astrology became Joshis. Bîrbhadra of this *gotra* was the first of them to obtain any notoriety, but they have a great predilection for Government service and call themselves Dîwân They are also known as Dauya or Dhumya Joshis from their prin-

[1] *Himalayan Gazetteer*, III, 423 sq.

cipal village. The Joshis of the Bhâradvâja *gotra* make their ancestor come from Jhûsi near Allahâbâd, and he settled in the village of Silagânw, whence his descendants are called Silwâls. Those that live at Chînakhân and Darhyâl are called after these villages."

9. The poorer members of the Gangoli Joshis still practise astrology, as indeed do all. Mr. Atkinson adds—"there is no real evidence that they came from the plains; but if they did they are a remarkable example of a caste hardly considered as being on the outskirts even of Brâhmans in the plains, having attained to such a respectable position in the hills which they still maintain by the intelligence and energy of their representatives. For the last two centuries they have been the master movers in all intrigues, and have monopolised to a great extent all the valuable government appointments, and possess an influence second to none, and which has to be carefully adjusted by the administration."

Distribution of the Joshis according to the Census of 1891.

Districts.	Number.	Districts.	Number.
Dehra Dûn	168	Shâhjahânpur	1,558
Sahâranpur	797	Pilibhît	609
Muzaffarnagar	218	Cawnpur	809
Bulandshahr	900	Fatehpur	675
Aligarh	1,112	Bânda	185
Mathura	566	Hamîrpur	1,415
Agra	1,712	Allahâbâd	200
Farrukhâbâd	2,022	Jhânsi	1,177
Mainpuri	2,391	Jâlaun	1,239
Etâwah	2,278	Lalitpur	619
Etah	1,080	Benares	2
Bareilly	846	Jaunpur	98
Bijnor	1,975	Ghâzipur	85
Budaun	1,066	Gorakhpur	230
Morâdâbâd	1,265	Basti	158

Distribution of the Joshis according to the Census of 1891.
—contd.

Districts.	Number.	Districts.	Number.
Azamgarh . . .	185	Faizâbâd . . .	212
Tarâi	199	Gonda	178
Luckno . . .	974	Bahrâich . . .	589
Unâo	312	Sultânpur . . .	392
Râê Bareli . . .	295	Partâbgarh . . .	199
Sîtapur . . .	1,273	Bârabanki . . .	299
Hardoi	1,175		
Kheri	1,312	TOTAL .	35,049

Julâha, Jolâha—the Muhammadan weaving caste. It has been supposed that they represent some menial Hindu weaving caste who were converted wholesale to Islâm. On the other hand, it is possible that they may have grown up among the Muhammadan body. But there seems good reason to believe that they are an occupational caste recruited from diverse sources. Thus as Mr. Ibbetson remarks "we find Koli Julâhas, Chamâr Julâhas, Mochi Julâhas, Râmdâsi Julâhas, and so forth: and it is probable that after a few generations these men will drop the prefix which denotes their low origin and become Julâhas pure and simple[1]."

2. The Parsotiya Julâha of Rohilkhand is a Hindu and apparently only a variety of Kori. Julâhas at the last Census recorded themselves in 244 sections of the usual type. These seem to have no influence on marriage. Many of these suggest a connection with other tribes and sects, such as Bais, Banya, Bargûjar, Bhangi, Bhât, Bisen, Chamâr, Chauhân, Gaur, Koli, Râjput, Tamoli, Teli, Tomar. Others represent local settlements as Bahrâichiya, Chaurasiya, Faizâbâdi, Gangapâri, Haidarâbâdi, Hasanpuri, Kanaujiya, Kânhpuriya, Khairâbâdi, Mathuriya, Mirzapuri, Multâni, Purabiya, Sarwariya, Shahâbâdi and Uttarâha. Others again are of the regular Muhammadan type: Madâri, Muhammadi, Momin, Mughal, Pathân, Shaikh, Sadîqi and Sunni.

3. The word Julâha is of Persian origin (*julâh*, *julâha*, a

[1] *Panjâb Ethnography*, para. 612.

weaver, *jula julla*, a ball of thread). Julâhas generally object to the name and call themselves Mûmin or Momin or orthodox; Nûrbâf "weavers in white." Julâhas are very clannish and usually intermarry in families with whom they have been accustomed to eat and smoke for generations. They say they are the direct descendants of Adam, who, when Satan made him realise his nakedness, taught the art of weaving to his sons. They do not profess to admit outsiders into the caste, but this undoubtedly often occurs, and, as above stated, the caste is almost certainly recruited from persons who assume the name of Julâha as an occupational title.

4. They follow the Muhammadan rules of marriage and inheritance. They are particularly careful in forbidding the intermarriage of foster children. A man cannot have two sisters to wife at the same time.[1] Many of them in the villages revere the local gods, and some worship Mâta Bhawâni. They also pay great respect to the tombs of saints and martyrs. They offer food, sweets and cakes to the sainted dead at the festivals of the Îd and Shab-i-barât and offer to them goats and rams at the Bakrîd.

Occupation and social rules.

5. The business of the Julâha has sadly decreased in consequence of the introduction of foreign cloth. Many have now taken to cultivation and various forms of labour. The Julâha generally bears the character of being cowardly, pretentious, factious and bigoted. They took a leading part in the recent Benares riots and some of the worst outrages in the Mutiny were their work. In the villages the Julâha is looked on as a fool, and a butt of the agricultural classes who are always jeering at his ignorance of crops. "The Julâha's goat and given to viciousness" (*Julâhê ki chheri markahi*). "Eight weavers quarrelling over nine pipes" (*âth Julâha nau huqqa, jis par bhi thukkam thukka*). "The Julâha steals a reel of thread at a time, but God makes him lose all at once." (*Julâha churâvê nali nali, khuda churâvê ekke beri*). "The arrow of the weaver" (*Julâhê ka tîr*). "What the Kamboh wins the Julâha eats"

---

[1] Writing of Bengal, Mr. O'Donnel says: "Although in Bengal proper the Shaikh is usually a petty cultivator, he ranks above the Jolâha or weaver. In Eastern Bengal the Shaikh young man marries at about 21 years of age, and the Jolâha two years earlier; while the Jolâha girl is married at 11 years and the Shaikh girl a month or two over 12 years. Ten per cent. of the former under ten years of age are given in marriage and less than five of the latter. Much the same state of things exists in other parts of Bengal proper; but as noticed before, the age of wedlock is lower in Western Bengal, the local practice being probably influenced by Hindu example." *Census Report*, 210.

(*Jīte Kamboh khāe Julāha.*)[1] "If you were going to turn Muhammadan you might do so in a less disreputable place than a Julâha's house" (*Turk bhay to Julāhe ke ghar*). *Julāhe ki'aql gude men hoti hai.* "The Julâha's brains are in his backside." *Khet khāe gadha, maral jāe Julāha*—"The ass eats the crop and the Julâha gets thrashed." One proverb embodies a curious piece of folklore. *Julāha bhutiaile tīsi khet*—"The Julâha lost his way in a linseed field." A Julâha is supposed to have taken the linseed field covered with blue flowers for a river and tried to swim in it. As a parallel, Mr. Christian[1] quotes from Kingsley's "The Roman and the Teuton"—"A madness from God came over the Herules, and when they came to a field of flax, they took the blue flowers for water and spread out their arms to swim through and were all slaughtered defencelessly." He might have added that the same tale appears in No. 149 of Grimm's German Stories.

Distribution of the Julāhas according to the Census of 1891.

Districts.	Number.	Districts.	Number.
Dehra Dûn	1,349	Moradâbâd	32,401
Sahâranpur	40,071	Shâhjahânpur	18,102
Muzaffarnagar	23,296	Pilibhît	15,461
Meerut	25,685	Cawnpur	4,347
Bulandshahr	13,147	Fatehpur	2,636
Aligarh	3,056	Bânda	75
Mathura	36	Hamîrpur	389
Agra	1,271	Allahâbâd	39,944
Farrukhâbâd	4,334	Jhânsi	51
Mainpuri	1,326	Jâlaun	377
Etâwah	2,352	Lalitpur	2
Etah	4,203	Benares	22,496
Bareilly	42,654	Mirzapur	13,582
Bijnor	61,523	Jaunpur	22,307
Budaun	19,894	Ghâzipur	28,564

[1] *Behar Proverbs*, 137.

Distribution of the Julâhas according to the Census of 1891.
—contd.

Districts.	Number.	Districts.	Number.
Ballia	30,547	Hardoi . . .	10,053
Gorakhpur . . .	117,891	Kheri	20,127
Basti	30,050	Fâizabâd . . .	25,473
Azamgarh . . .	53,075	Gonda	16,654
Tarâi	12,665	Bahrâich . . .	18,285
Lucknow . . .	5,966	Sultânpur . . .	10,345
Unâo	3,221	Partâbgarh . . .	9,497
Râê Bareli . . .	4,117	Bârabanki . . .	30,182
Sîtapur . . .	36,652	TOTAL .	7,80,231

Jyotishi.—(Sanskrit *Jyantishika*, root *jyut*, "to shine on, to illuminate"), a class of Brâhmans who devote themselves to fortune-telling, astrology, and the construction of horoscopes. The preparation of a horoscope is necessary for every respectable Hindu boy; hence the trade is a large one and very lucrative. But the functions of the Jyotishi are not confined to the twice-born castes, and he is ready to predict events for any person, even of low estate who can afford to pay him. This is one of the chief methods by which the casteless tribes have been brought within the Brâhmanical fold; and as a tribe of this kind tends towards Brâhmanism the Baiga or devil priest, who is invariably drawn from the aboriginal races, is replaced by the Ojha and the Jyotishi who claim to be Brâhmans. The Jyotishi is not regarded with any particular respect, and he is, of course, generally a quack and impostor.

K

Kabîr Panthi.—A Hindu sect who are followers of the Saint Kabîr. His name is from an Arabic root meaning "great". The history of the saint is very uncertain. He is believed to have been born at Benares and adopted by a Muhammadan weaver. By one account he was miraculously conceived by the virgin widow of a Brâhman, and he lived partly at Benares and partly at Magar, in the Basti District, in the reign of Sikandar Shâh Lodi, between 1488 and 1512 A.D. Owing to his connection with the weaver caste, many Julâhas are fond of calling themselves Kabîr Bansi, or Kabîr Panthi, without much reference to the special doctrines associated with the name of Kabîr. Writing of the Panjâb, Mr. Maclagan[1] remarks that the connection between weaving and religion is as interesting as that between cobbling and irreligion in England. "There are some Musalmân tribes (the Khokhars, Chughattas and Chauhâns, for instance) who are found in many parts of the Province performing indifferently the functions of the weaver and the Mulla." Kabîr is said to have been a disciple of Râmanand, and from one point of view the Kabîr Panthis are merely Râmanandis who refuse to worship idols. Kabîr, as the legend of his death shows, was a product of both Hindu and Muhammadan influence. When he died at Magar the Hindus and Muhammadans disputed as to the disposal of his body. But while they were contending the saint himself appeared and told them to look under the sheet which covered his corpse, and then immediately disappeared. When they raised the sheet they found only a heap of flowers. Of these the Hindus took half and burned them at Benares, while the Muhammadans buried the remainder at Magar, where a cenotaph was raised over them, and the saint is worshipped in both places by the followers of the rival creeds.

2. On the principles of the sect Professor Wilson[2] writes:—"The Kabîr Panthis, in consequence of their master having been a reputed disciple of Râmanand and of their paying more respect to Vishnu than the other members of the Hindu triad, are always included among the Vaishnava sects and maintain, with most of them, the Râmâwats especially, a friendly intercourse and political

---

[1] *Panjâb Census Report*, 142.
[2] *Essays*, I, 74.

alliance. It is no part of their faith, however, to worship any Hindu deity, or to observe any of the rites or ceremonials of the Hindus, whether orthodox or schismatical. Such of their members as are living in the world conform outwardly to all the usages of their tribes and caste, and some of them pretend even to worship the usual divinities, though this is considered as going further than is justifiable. Those, however, who have abandoned the fetters of society abstain from all the ordinary practices, and address their homage chiefly in chanting hymns exclusively to the invisible Kabîr. They use no *mantra* or fixed form of salutation, they have no peculiar mode of dress, and some of them go nearly naked, without objecting, however, to clothe themselves when clothing is considered decent or respectful. The Mahants wear a small skull cap; the frontal marks, if worn, are usually those of the Vaishnava sects, or they make a streak with sandal or Gopichandan along the ridge of the nose; a necklace and rosary of Tulasi are also worn by them, but all these outward signs are considered of no importance, and the inward man is the only essential point to be attended to."

The writings of Kabîr.

3. It is perhaps more by his writings than by his actual teaching that the chief influence of Kabîr has been gained.[1] His doctrines and precepts are embodied in the Sukh-nidhân and the Adi-grantha of the Sikhs. Next to the Râmâyana of Tulasi Dâs there is perhaps no body of literature which is so popular among Hindus of Northern India as the Bîjak of Kabîr, and his verses and apothegms are ever on the lips of both Hindu and Musalmân.

4. The sect is open to both Hindus and Musalmâns, and perhaps in consequence of this it is not a favourite with men of high caste. Most of its adherents, in these Provinces at least, are drawn from the inferior castes, as the lower Banyas, Sunârs, Lohârs, Koiris, Koris, Kâchhis, Kumhârs, Barhais, Chamârs, and Julâhas. Among the weaving castes it is, as has been said already, extremely popular. There is no regular formula of initiation (*mantra*). The introduction of a neophyte is performed in this way. A piece of ground in the monastery or in the house of the candidate is carefully cleaned and plastered. In this is placed a pitcher full of water, in the mouth of which are fixed some mango twigs (*palâv*); on the pitcher

---

[1] On this see Grierson, *Modern Vernacular Literature*, 7.

a lamp is lighted with ghi and an offering is made consisting of sandal, holy rice (*achchat*), and flowers and incense is burned. A garland of flowers is placed round the neck of the pitcher and the core of a cocoa-nut with some *batâsha* sweetmeats is offered. Some camphor is burnt and the neophyte sits in the holy square before the Guru, who makes him say the words :—

Satya purusha ko swâns se hriday men japo.

"Repeat the name of the true being within you with breath." The disciple then with his joined hands thrice makes obeisance to the Guru and utters thrice the words, *Bandagi Sâhib !* "My service to the Master." This is the common form, but the ritual with the more learned Mahants is of an elaborate type After this the Guru teaches the disciple the Gâyatri or Morning Prayer and the Sandhya Sumiran or evening prayer. This Gâyatri is not the usual Hindu form—*Tat savitur varenyam bhargo devásya dhîmahi dhiya yo nah prachodayât.*—"Let us meditate on that excellent glory of the Divine Vivifying Sun; may he enlighten our understandings." The KabîrPanthi Gâyatri is a song (*bâni*) composed by Kabîr himself and runs as follows :—

Kabîr din duni darbesha dwâr salâmat lekha ;
Tum rund mund men pira ;
Tum phâka, phakkar phakira ;
Tum chalo kaun ki chál ;
Tum ramo kaun ki nál ;
Tum sarbangi sahjer men, tum ko wâr na pâr.
Sakal nirantar tum rano tumhâré gahar ganbhîr.
Khâli khalak mujh mâhîn yon Guru kahain Kabîr.
Satya nâm ki ârti nirmal bhaya sharîr.
Dharm Dâs loké chalé guru bahiyân milé Kabîr.

"The faith of Kabîr is double mendicancy ; only bowing to the door of God is taken into account. It is thou who feelest pain in the headless body. It is thou who livest in the starving mendicant. In whose footsteps canst thou walk ? In whose stream canst thou flow ? Thou art of all forms and hast neither beginning nor end. Thou art the beginning and thou art the end. Thou art the bank of all the rivers (religious sects). Thou pervadest the entire universe. Thou art deepest of all. Saith Kabîr "Without me (God) the Universe is empty ; it is I that fill the Universe. If you light the sacred lamp of truth your body will be free from darkness. Dharm Dâs (the slave of virtue) holds the hand of his religious guide Kabîr and ascends to heaven."

6. The Sandhya Sumiran or Evening Prayer is as follows :—

Sánjh bhae, din atháe, chakai dína roé.
Chal chakwa ohi deswán jahán diwas rain nahín hoé.
Rain ki bichhuri chakai aya mili prabhát.
Jo jan bichhuri nám ke páwai diwas nahín rát.
Binwat honkar jori ke, sunu guru kripa nidhán.
Daya gharíbi bandagi samâta shíl karár.
Eté gahané bhakta ke adi bhakti sringár.
Kewal nám kewal guru bâla pír Kabír.

"Evening has come and the sun has set. Then cries the Brâhmani duck. 'O mate of mine! Let us seek that land where there is no night nor day.' When the duck parts from her mate at night she meets him again at dawn; but he who parts with the True Name never finds it again either by night nor day. Generosity, humility, worship, the universal brotherhood of mankind, uniform observance of law, and morals—these are the ornaments of a devotee, and his decoration is the love of God. The True Name is the only religious guide, and his greatest prophet is Kabîr."

7. Besides these, the Guru teaches the disciple a number of hymns which he commits to memory, and sings morning and evening. The Guru visits his disciples once a year in the cold weather, and he and other mendicants of the sect are entertained by him for a couple of days. Every day the disciple washes the big toe of his Guru and drinks the water (*charanamrita*). When the Guru is leaving the disciple does obeisance, and makes him a present of money, clothes, vessels, etc., and salutes him with the words *Bandagi Sáhib*, thrice. As long as the Guru stays in his house the disciple joins the mendicants in singing songs morning and evening. When the disciple visits his Guru he is entertained by him, but gives him a present when he leaves. The Guru's influence over his disciple is altogether exercised in the interests of morality, and should he offend he is very sternly reprimanded by the Guru. One of the main principles of the sect is to submit everything in life to control of the Guru; at the same time Kabîr himself did not exact unquestioning obedience from his disciples, and encouraged them to investigate for themselves the truth of his advice and injunctions.

Distribution of the KabîrPanthis according to the Census of 1891.

District.	Number.	District.	Number.
Debra Dûn	34	Fatehpur . . .	9
Muzaffarnagar . .	6	Hamîrpur . . .	8
Bulandshahr . .	258	Allâhâbâd . . .	12
Aligarh	114	Jhânsi . . .	8
Agra	8	Jâlaun . . .	3
Farrukhâbâd . . .	2	Ghâzipur . . .	209
Bareilly . . .	15	Gorakhpur . . .	40
Bijnor	2	Basti . . .	8
Morâdâbâd . . .	36	Tarâi . . .	4
Shâhjahânpur . .	57	Lucknow . . .	16
Pilibhît . . .	72	Faizâbâd . . .	16
Cawnpur . . .	18		
		Total .	955

Kâchhi.[1]—The tribe of opium-growers and market gardeners. They represent in the west of the Province the Koiri and Kurmi of the eastern districts. Their name has been variously explained. Some connect it with the Sanskrit *kaksha*, "a flank or enclosure"; others with *karsha* "a furrow"; others again connect it with *kâchhna*, the term for collecting the opium from the capsules of the poppy, or with *kachhâr*, "the low rich alluvial land" which they usually cultivate. They claim, however, some connection with the Kachhwâha sept of Râjputs, who may have a totemistic relationship with the *kachhapa* or tortoise, as the Kurmi, with *kurma*, the turtle. They are also known in the extreme west of the Province as Nainaya, Sahnai, Bârahmâshi, or those who keep their lands under crops all the year round. Another name of the tribe is in some places Murâo, or growers of the radish (*mûli*);

[1] Mainly based on notes by E. Rose, Esq., C. S., Collector of Farrukhâbâd; Bâbu Sânwal Dâs, Deputy Collector, Hardoi; and the Deputy Inspector of Schools, Agra.

but in other parts of the country, as, for instance, in Râê Bareli, the two names are not quite identical. There the Murâo cultivates all kinds of vegetables, including turnips, onions and turmeric, which the Kâchhi does not. The tribe appears to be singularly devoid of local traditions. The Saksenas say they come from Sankisa and the Kanaujiyas from Kanauj, which they abandoned after the defeat of Jay Chand by Shahâbuddîn Ghori in 1193-94. In fact, some of them ascribe their origin to this sovereign and say that he gave the name to those of his servants who grew vegetables for his court. The tribe is most probably an offshoot of the great Kurmi race, and has divided from them owing to the special occupation which they practise.

Tribal organisation.

2. The Kâchhis are divided into a number of endogamous sub-castes, which vary from district to district. The Census returns divide the Kâchhis into 560 sub-castes, of which the most important are the Chithoriya, Churela, Hardiya, Kachhwâha, Kanaujiya, Patarita, and Saksena. Among those of local importance we find the Puniya of Bulandshahr; the Amariya and Purabiya of Agra; the Amariya and Nijakotiya of Mainpuri; the Parnâmi and Sakauriya of Etâwah; the Bhadauriya and Purabiya of Shâhjahânpur; the Baheniya and Murai of Cawnpur; the Baheniya, Dangarha, and Murai of Fatehpur; the Bhagta and Sakta of Allahâbâd; the Amariya and Parnâmi of Jâlaun; the Bhadauriya and Saloriya of Lalitpur; the Dhenkuliya and Thakuriya of Lucknow; the Chauhân, Kichar, Kusha, and Thakuriya of Râê Bareli; and the Dholakiya or "drummers" and Thakuriya of Unâo. In Farrukhâbâd, where the Kâchhis are very influential, we find five sub-castes, the Hardiya or growers of turmeric (*haldi*), the Saksena, who take their name from the famous Buddhist city of Sankisa on the borders of Farrukhâbâd, and Etah; the Piyâzi or growers of onions (*piyâz*); the Kachhwâya, and the Kanaujiya from Kanauj. In Râê Bareli they name seven endogamous sub-castes—the Kachhwâha, Koiri, Murai, "radish (*mûli*) grower," Kanaujiya, Haldiha, Kabariya or huckster, who in some of the large cities like Lucknow is a Mewafarosh or fruit seller, and the Bhemua. In Agra we find five sub-castes—the Kachhwâha, Chakchainiya or Chakseniya, the Hardainiya, Murâo, and Khariha. The Singrauriya take their name from the old town of Singraur, about twenty-five miles higher up the Ganges than Allâhâbâd. The Murâos again have divisions of their own. One list divides

them into the Hardiya, Rotiya, and Kachhwâya. These last are the most numerous sub-caste in Bulandshahr and claim descent from a mother of the Mâli tribe by a father of the clan of Kachhwâha Râjputs. In Râê Bareli they again give their sub castes as Brâhmaniya, Haldiha, Kanaujiya, Kâchhi, and Kurmi, and in Hardoi as Haldiya; Dhakauliya, who take their name from the well lever (*dhenkli*) which they use; the Kanaujiya, Kachhwâha, Saksena, Bhadauriya, who, like the Râjput clan of the same name, derive their title from the Pargana of Bhadâwar in the Agra District; Thakuriya, who claim descent from the Kachhwâha clan of Thâkurs; and the Munwâr, who trace their origin to some Muni or saint of olden days. As already stated, all these sub-castes, some of which are local some eponymous, and some purely occupational, are all endogamous. They are also characterised by some peculiarities. Thus in Agra the women of the Kachhwâha sub-caste wear a foot ornament called *gujari*, which is not allowed to others. In Farrukhâbâd the Saksena women similarly wear a special bangle known as *lutua* or *lakhota*, made of brass and lac, which is particularly large and heavy. This ornament is peculiar to them.

Tribal council.

3. Like all tribes on the same grade, they have an influential tribal council (*panchâyat*). In Farrukhâbâd the chairman is known as Mahtiya or Chaudhari and the council consists of a certain number of members selected for their respectability and intelligence; but when any special business is to be decided, the attendance of at least one member of each family resident within the local jurisdiction of the council is necessary. They have power to decide all private disputes; they can expel any member for debauchery or other offence contrary to tribal usage; and they can re-admit culprits to caste privileges on providing a feast to the caste, on feeding a certain number of Brâhmans, or undergoing other prescribed penance.

Rule of exogamy.

4. Within the sub-caste the rule of exogamy does not appear to be very accurately formulated. In Farrukhâbâd a man cannot have two sisters to wife at the same time, and he cannot marry in the family of his paternal aunt or uncle. Those who are more advanced show a tendency to adopt the regular Hindu rules of exogamy. In Agra they bar the family of the mother and grandmother on both sides. Among the Murâos of Hardoi a man does not marry his daughter in a family in which his own son or the son of a near

relative is married. This prohibition lasts for three or four generations, and the line of cousins is also barred. But the rule does not seem to be very definite, and each case is dealt with by the tribal council.

Marriage ceremonies.

5. Marriage ceremonies are of the usual type. In Farrukhâbâd they can be married at any age above seven, but the boy must be older than the girl. Elsewhere there is no fixed rule, and both infant and adult marriage prevails. There are the usual three standard types,—*Shâdi* or *Charhaua*, *Dola*, and *Dharauna*. In the first, all the ceremonies are conducted at the house of the bride, while those of *Dola* are done at the house of the bridegroom. In *Dola* the father of the bride comes to the house of the bridegroom with some clothes and ornament for his daughter on the marriage day, and washes and worships her feet and offers the presents. By *Dharauna* only widows are married, and the only ceremony is the giving of a feast to the clansmen. In the *Dola* marriage there is this much survival of marriage by capture, that the bride is taken away secretly at night. The offspring of *Dharauna* marriages, known as *Dharauniya* in Farrukhâbâd, inherit equally with children by a regular marriage. The levirate is permitted under the usual conditions, but is not compulsory on the widow. If she has very young children she usually takes them to her new home, and there they join the family of her second husband and lose all rights in their father's estate.

Birth ceremonies.

6. There is nothing special about the birth ceremonies. The *chhathi* or sixth day ceremony consists in the worship of the goddess Bihai, who whispers in the child's ear, and he smiles in his sleep if she speaks kindly and weeps if she reproves. In Farrukhâbâd the Hardiyas do not adopt formally; but a childless man keeps the son of his daughter or some other near relation as his heir. Among the other sub-castes the practice of adopting a near relation with the consent of the brethren notified at a tribal feast is becoming more common.

Disposal of the dead.

7. They burn the married and bury the unmarried dead. On the thirteenth day offerings of food and water are given to the manes. Brâhmans are fed and clothes and utensils are given to them for the soul in the other world. The son-in-law and daughter's son are also fed; this is perhaps a survival of the primitive rule of descent in the female

line. Similar offerings are also made at the anniversary of the death; but they do not perform the regular *Srâddha*.

Religion.

8. In Agra, if they can be said to follow any particular sect, they are Sâktas and their chief reverence is paid to Durga Devi, who is worshipped on the seventh day of the waning moon in the months of Chait and Âsârh, with offerings of cakes, sweetmeats, and money. These offerings are taken by a Gadhera, or donkey-keeping Kumhâr. If the day of the service fall on a Monday, Wednesday, or Friday it is considered very auspicious. This worship is done to the goddess in her form of Sîtala, who brings the small-pox. Another goddess, Birâhi, is also worshipped with an offering of cakes. Nâgar Sen is propitiated with cocoanuts, eggs, and red lead, which are given to him on a Friday and received by a Dhobin. He is one of the general disease godlings. Kuânwâla, "he of the well," is a sort of bogie who lies in wait for children and springs upon them when he finds them alone. To keep him quiet they pour water out of a goat-skin bag on Monday or Wednesday and lay a sweet ball (*laddu*) on the ground where two roads meet. Châmar is worshipped with cakes, sweets, incense, and red lead at the Holi and Diwâli, and sometimes on Mondays. His offerings are taken by one of the Mahaur Kolis, who are his priests. If he is not duly propitiated he stops the milk of cows and buffaloes. Lâl Mani is a household godling who receives cakes and sweets on a Monday; these are eaten by the worshipper and his family. Bhûmiya, the godling of the village site, also receives cakes and sweetmeats, which are taken by low caste beggars. Sayyid is much dreaded; people in trouble, and when there is sickness in the family, get a Musalmân Faqîr to offer some sweet cakes in his name. The Miyân of Amroha is propitiated in the same way. Sîtala and Kuânwâla are the special deities of women and children. When serious cases of disease or other misfortune occur, animal sacrifices are necessary. Devi Durga receives a young buffalo; Châmar, a ram; Nâgar Sen and Lâl Mani, a he-goat. The Devi sacrifice is done at the boundary of the village; those of other godlings at their special shrines. In Farrukhâbâd their chief reverence is paid to Madâr Sâhib of Makhanpur and to Sayyid Mard at some tomb in the village. They also pay special reverence to Bisâri or Visâli Devi, "the poisonous one," who has her shrine at Sankisa. She is supposed to inflict sore eyes on those who neglect her. Her priests can bring ophthalmia on whom they

please by lighting a fire and throwing hot coals on her image. When a person is thus afflicted he lays aside seven cowries, a piece of turmeric and charcoal, and an iron nail, as marking his vow to make a pilgrimage to her shrine. This is undertaken in the months of Chait, Âsârh, or Kuâr. The offering consists of a packet of betel, sweets, eight small cakes, and some cash. If he offers only a copper coin the offering is *kachchi*, or imperfect. If silver is given it is *pakki*, or perfect. The priests of her temple promise life-long immunity from sore eyes to those who make a "perfect" offering; those who make an "imperfect" offering are liable to a return of the disease. Those who cannot afford to make the regular pilgrimage go a mile or so in the direction of her temple and make the offering in a field which must be beyond the village boundary. This is known as *Âdha jatiya*, or "the half-pilgrimage." The Kâchhis of Râê Bareli specially worship a deity known as Brahma Gusâîn. To the west their priests are Kanaujiya or Bhaddari Brâhmans, the latter of whom are held in low estimation. Their chief festivals are the Holi and Diwâli; and though they do not pay much regard to other festivals, they perform the usual ceremonies.

Demonology and devil-possession.

9. They have the usual beliefs in demonology, and in their opinion most diseases are due to the influence of evil spirits. In such cases a sorcerer (*nauta*) is consulted, and he gives them a black thread (*ganda*) or some holy ashes (*bhabût*) as a specific. They dread the ghosts of the dead, who have a habit of appearing naked at night if proper donations of clothes are not given to Brâhmans at the obsequies. They believe in the Evil Eye, the effects of which are obviated by burning red pepper, salt, and bran in the house fire. The evil influence departs in the smoke and stench. Or they take secretly some straw from seven thatches, light it and put it into an earthen pot, which is placed upside down in a vessel of water and then waved seven times round the head of the patient. If the patient is really suffering from the Evil Eye the water rises in the upper pot and gives out a disgusting smell. When a woman is barren she tries to cut off some of the hair of a child of a large family or a shred from the mother's sheet. Hence barren women are watched, because this spell is very injurious to those on whom it is practised.

Taboos.

10. The Hardiya sub-caste will not grow sugarcane or chillies. They can give no explanation of this, except that it is not the custom. Those who have

taken the Bhagat vow will not eat with others; and it is only very close relations who will eat out of the same dish. The members of the different sub-castes will not eat together. Some will not eat the *baingan* or egg-plant in the month of Sâwan or fish or flesh in the fortnight sacred to the dead (*Kanâgat*). Men and women eat apart and children with both. When they eat some put a little food in the fire or give a morsel of bread to the cow. They observe the usual naming taboo. The younger members of the family do not call seniors by their names. A daughter-in-law will not call her father-in-law by his name, but will address him as *bhâi* "brother" or *bâpu* "father." A husband addresses his wife as the mother of so and so his son. A son calls his father *akka* or *chacha* "uncle."

Occupation.

11. The Kâchhis are one of the best tribes of agriculturists in the Province. They are quiet, industrious, well-behaved people, who devote themselves to the cultivation of the more valuable crops, such as vegetables, opium, sugarcane, turmeric, etc.

Distribution of Kâchhis according to the Census of 1891.

District.	Chithoriya.	Churela.	Hardiya.	Kachhwâha.	Kaithiya.	Kananjiya.	Patariha.	Saksena.	Others.	Total.
Dehra Dûn	...	...	43	81	...	...	...	202	14	340
Sahâranpur	...	...	...	...	...	...	...	...	108	108
Muzaffarnagar	...	...	...	8	...	...	...	...	17	25
Meerut	...	...	...	...	...	17	...	...	1,181	1,198
Bulandshahr	...	...	...	1,290	...	...	...	...	372	1,662
Aligarh	...	...	...	5,206	...	...	...	...	15,363	20,569
Mathura	...	3	6	3,192	...	...	...	18	1,590	4,809
Agra	...	...	14	43,523	...	2	30	1,760	5,329	50,658
Farrukhâbâd	16	...	619	16,535	265	1,924	5	47,683	548	67,595
Mainpuri	...	...	25	9,877	435	...	...	56,682	2,904	69,923
Etâwah	...	...	96	14,770	93	...	...	34,154	2,631	51,744
Etah	...	836	664	1,490	465	15	6,391	37,426	8,908	56,195

Bareilly	...	...	...	...	...	...	...	26	...	26
Bijnor	...	...	...	...	...	...	...	...	258	258
Morâdâbâd	...	...	...	...	...	..	...	3	229	232
Shâhjahânpur	...	...	3,899	18,163	...	1,280	...	9,765	2,059	35,166
Pilibhît	...	...	...	232	...	...	...	...	...	232
Cawnpur	...	...	100	28,425	...	2,600	...	871	15,297	47,293
Fatehpur	...	...	...	5,468	...	769	...	...	3,921	10,158
Bânda	...	...	10,909	11,270	...	205	...	...	136	22,520
Hamîrpur	...	...	5	30,768	...	...	3	...	625	31,401
Allahâbâd	...	...	...	18	...	27,186	174	10,119	562	38,059
Jhânsi	...	...	38	33,271	...	6	...	...	3,327	36,642
Jâlaun	...	...	20	23,702	...	...	...	...	3,503	27,225
Lalitpur	...	...	...	26,283	...	2	25	10	1,753	28,073
Ghâzipur	...	...	...	...	...	...	...	...	1	1
Gorakhpur	...	...	...	32	...	...	...	...	...	32
Tarâi	...	...	...	...	88	...	...	...	369	457
Lucknow	...	...	92	3,277	68	109	...	...	766	4,312

Distribution of Kâchhis according to the Census of 1891—contd.

District.	Chithoriya.	Churela.	Hardiya.	Kachhwâha.	Kaithiya.	Kanaujiya.	Patariha.	Saksena.	Others.	Total.
Unâo	...	...	...	4,728	...	7,656	...	...	19,521	31,905
Râê Bareli	...	...	4,059	1,481	...	217	...	...	2,861	8,618
Sîtapur	...	...	...	310	...	2	...	8	11	331
Hardoi	...	...	9,137	35,975	...	533	...	147	1,365	47,157
Kheri	...	...	2,224	6,006	...	71	...	...	79	8,380
Faizâbâd	...	...	...	...	...	...	...	...	6	6
Gonda	...	...	...	...	...	...	...	...	1	1
Bahrâich	...	...	9	...	...	...	...	...	3	12
Partâbgarh	...	...	...	...	...	44	...	...	...	44
Total	16	839	31,959	325,381	1,414	42,638	6,628	198,874	95,618	703,367

Kachhwâha.—An important Râjput sept. The popular etymology derives the name from the country of Kachh, but it is more probably connected with the Sanskrit *Kachhapa*, "relating to a tortoise," and may possibly be totemistic. The most important traditions of the sept are, of course, connected with the famous Jaypur branch.

"The accepted legend traces back their lineage to Kusa, the second son of Râma, who ruled at Ajudhya and is said to have emigrated thence to Rohtâs on the Son river, whence after several generations a second immigration brought Râja Nala westward across the Jumua to Narwar. And at Narwar the family or the sept established itself, until Dhola Râê founded the parent city of the present Jaypur State at Amber in A. D. 967. At the time the country round is said to have been all parcelled out among many petty chiefs, Râjputs of the Tuar dynasty which reigned at Delhi. After years of warfare and fluctuations of power, Dhola Râê and his Kachhwâhas are said to have absorbed and driven out the petty chiefs and to have at last founded a solid dominion with a substantial territory. The tribal sovereignty thus set up was originally known by the name of Dhûndar, from a celebrated sacred mount of that name on what is now the State's western frontier. Half a century later another chief, Hanuji, wrested Amber from the Mînas and consolidated his power, placing his head-quarters at Amber, which gave its name to the chiefship thenceforward until 1728 A. D., when the second Jay Sinh deserted it for Jaypur."[1]

Tribal organisation.

2. There are twelve chief Kachhwâha clans of which the most trustworthy list is that given by Colonel Tod. These are:—Chhattrabhujaut, Kalyânaut, Nathâwat, Balbhadraut, Khangaraut, Sultânaut, Pachhayanaut, Gugâwat, Khumbâni, Khumbhâwat, Siubaranpota, Banbîrpota. In addition to these four others are named—Rajâwat, Narûka, Bhankâwat, Parinmalot.

The Narwar and Gwâlior branch.

3. The sept in Narwar and Gwâlior became independent under Vajra Dâma, one of whose inscriptions is dated 977 A. D. His great grandson, Bhawâna Pâla, must have been reigning as an independent chief in 1021 A. D., when Mahmûd of Ghazni, in his march against Kalinjar, accepted the submission of the Râja of Gwâlior. The

[1] *Rajputâna Gazetteer*, II., 135.

Kachhwâhas continued to reign till 1129 A. D., when the last king of the race, Tejpâl or Tejkaran, lost his sovereignty through his love for the fair Maroni, whose beauty still affords a theme for the poetic skill of the bards. The Kachhwâhas of Gwâlior, Narwar, and Jaypur, all agree in the same story of the love-blind Dulha Râê, or the bridegroom prince, who was supplanted by his cousin or nephew, the Parihâr Chief Parâmal or Parâmarddi Deva.[1] The Kachhwâha dynasty of Amber obtained possession of Narwar through the marriage of their daughters with the Moghul Emperors of Delhi. The history of this dynasty commences with Râj Sinh, son of Bhîm Sinh, and grandson of Prithivi Râja, who reigned over Amber and Jaypur in the reign of Sikandar Lodi. Prithivi Râja is said to have had nineteen sons, of whom several succeeded to the throne. Râj Sinh was succeeded by his son Râmdâs. Fateh Sinh succeeded his father about 1610 A. D., but his son Amar Sinh lost Narwar in the reign of Shâhjahân, as all the members of his family declared in favour of his elder brother, Prince Khusru. Gwâlior is said to have been founded by a Kachhwâha Chief, Sûraj Sen, the petty Râja of Kuntalpuri or Kutwar. A list and history of the dynasty lasting from 925 to 1104 A. D. is given by General Cunningham. He considers the name of the clan to be derived from *kachhapa-ghâta* or tortoise-killers.[2]

The Kachhwâhas of the North-West Provinces.

4. In these Provinces the Kachhwâhas are pretty generally distributed except in the Eastern Districts. All, or nearly all, claim a Western origin from Amber or Jaypur; but the legends of their immigration are very contradictory. Thus in Faizâbâd they fix their arrival from Jaypur about six hundred years ago under Ranjît Sinh, who expelled the Bhars. In that district most of their proprietary rights have been absorbed by the Râjkumârs.[3]

Those in Sîtapur allege that they came from Jaypur in 1459 A. D. under Bahrâm Sinh and that they belonged to the Rajâwat clan, of which the present Mahârâja of Jaypur is the head[4]. In Mathura they are classed as Gaurua, which is a general term for septs degraded by widow marriage[5]. In Bulandshahr they allege

---

[1] Cunningham, *Archæological Reports*, II., 312.
[2] *Ibid.*, II., 317, *s. q.*
[3] *Settlement Report*, 156.
[4] *Settlmeent Report*, 93.
[5] Growse, *Mathura*, 376.

that their forefathers emigrated from Narwar to Amber and thence to the Ganges-Jumna Duâb.[1] The Etâwah and Jâlaun branch emigrated from Gwâlior and took possession of the tract of country which from them took its name of Kachhwâhagarh; or Kachhwâhiyagarh, which is now Pargana Mâdhogarh in the Jâlaun District.[2] The few Kachhwâhas in the Eastern Districts seem to have lost all traditions of connection with Rajputâna, and have invented a ridiculous legend that they sprang from the thigh of the mythic cow Kâmadhenu.[3]

Religion.

5. The Kuladevi or family deity of the Kachhwâhas in their original home is the Jamwâhi Mahâdevi, whose temple is in the gorge of the Bânganga river in Jaypur teritory, not far from the south-east corner of the Alwar State. "It was here that Dhola Râê, the founder of the present Jaypur State, and subsequently his son, are said to have received miraculous aid from Mahâdevi in contending with Mînas and Bargûjars. The sons of the Alwar Chief go in state to this temple to have the ceremony of tonsure performed. Sîta and Râma are, however, naturally the deities to whom most respect is paid by Narûkas and other Kachhwâhas, since they claim descent from Râma and Sîta, whose images are carried with the army both in Alwar and in Jaypur. Sri Krishna, too, as his birth-place, Mathura, is so near, is also much reverenced by the ruling family and upper class; and Baladeva, Sri Krishna's elder brother, is in high repute. *Jay Baldeoji* and *Jay Raghunâthji* are the commonest forms of salutation.[4]"

6. By one account they claim to belong to the Kasyapa, by another to the Manava *gotra*. In Sultânpur they take brides from the Tilokchandi Bais, the Chauhâns of Mainpuri, the Bhadauriya, Râthaur, Kánhpuriya and Bandhalgoti septs; in Aligarh from the Pundîr, Jais, and Bâchhal. In Sultânpur they give brides to the Ṭilokchandi Bais, Mainpuri Chauhâns, Bhadauriya, and Râthaur; in Aligarh to the Pundîr, Gahlot, Solankhi, Chauhân, Panwâr, Tomar, and Janghára.

---

[1] *Census Report, North-West Provinces*, 1865, I., App. 17.
[2] *Ibid., App.* 85.
[3] Buchanan, *Eastern India*, II., 460.
[4] *Rajputâna Gazetteer*, III., 212.

Distribution of the Kachhwâha Râjputs according to the Census of 1891.

District.	Numbers.	District.	Numbers.
Sahâranpur . . .	44	Jâlaun . . .	6,670
Muzaffarnagar . .	2,434	Lalitpur . . .	62
Meerut	2,228	Benares . . .	22
Bulandshahr . . .	421	Mirzapur . . .	1
Aligarh	1,056	Jaunpur . . .	16
Mathura	5,671	Ballia . . .	64
Agra	4,704	Gorakhpur . . .	39
Farrukhâbâd . . .	1,482	Basti	38
Mainpuri . . .	998	Azamgarh . . .	1,073
Etâwah	7,099	Tarâi	56
Etah	460	Lucknow . . .	175
Bareilly	342	Unâo	900
Bijnor	54	Râê Bareli . . .	1,196
Budâun . . .	244	Sîtapur . . .	794
Morâdâbâd . . .	397	Hardoi . . .	1,293
Shâhjahânpur . . .	341	Kheri	783
Pilibhît	130	Faizâbâd . . .	294
Cawnpur . . .	7,677	Gonda . . .	109
Fatehpur . . .	1,512	Bahrâich . . .	166
Bânda	654	Sultânpur . . .	1,628
Hamîrpur . . .	710	Partâbgarh . . .	359
Allahâbâd . . .	216	Bârabanki . . .	110
Jhânsi	564	TOTAL .	55,286

The Rajputâna Census of 1891 shows the Kachhwâhas to number 106,705.

Kadhera, Kadhâr.—(Possibly Sanskrit *Karsha-kâra*, "One who drags or ploughs.")—A caste shown in the last Census for the first time in considerable numbers in the Western Districts. Little seems to be known about them. It is reported from Unâo, which shows them in the largest numbers, that they are really a sub-caste of Mallâh, living chiefly in the riverine parts of the district and excellent cultivators in those regions subject to floods. They seem to have almost altogether given up their proper trade of boatmen. All those shown in the Census returns are Hindus. No less than five hundred and fifty-nine sub-castes are recorded. These seem to show that the caste is probably of very mixed origin, as the list contains the names of numerous well known tribes and sub-castes such as Bâgri, Baiswâr, Bâori, Bargûjar, Bâtham (Srivâstavya), Chauhân, Dâdupanthi, Dhânuk, Dhuna, Dusâdh, Gahlot, Gamela, Gaur, Gûjar, Jâdon, Jais, Kabîrbansi, Kâchhi, Kachhwâya, Kamângar, Kânhpuriya, Katiyâr, Korchamra, Lodha, Luniya, Mallâh, Mehtariya, Naddâf, Nânakshâhi, Nunera, Ojha, Pardesi, Pundîr, Râêdâs, Râj, Râjput, Rangsâz, Ror, Saîn, Saksena, Sânsiya, Saraswati, Soeri, Solankhi, Tamoli, and Tomar.

Distribution of Kadheras according to the Census of 1891.

District.	Numbers.	District.	Numbers.
Muzaffarnagar . .	54	Pilibhît . . .	19
Meerut	2,039	Cawnpur . . .	1,270
Bulandshahr . . .	3,857	Fatehpur . . .	73
Aligarh	6,901	Bânda . . .	219
Mathura . . .	2,881	Hamîrpur . . .	1,508
Agra	4,197	Allahâbâd . . .	3
Farrukhâbâd . . .	84	Jhânsi . . .	289
Mainpuri . . .	1,219	Jâlaun . . .	1,105
Etâwah	703	Lalitpur . . .	224
Etah	2,946	Tarâi	467
Bareilly	5	Unâo	13,947
Bijnor	336	Sîtapur . . .	14
Budâun	3,658	Hardoi . . .	332
Morâdâbâd . . .	3,094	Gonda . . .	8
Shâhjahânpur . . .	301	TOTAL .	51,753

Kahâr.[1]—(Sanskrit, *Skandha-kára,* "one who carries things on his shoulder"). A tribe who engage in cultivation, particularly in connection with growing water nuts, etc., in tanks, fishing, palanquin carrying, and domestic service. This variety of occupations renders a complete analysis of the tribe and its sub-castes very difficult. Kahârs are sometimes known as Mahṛa (Sanskrit *Mahila,* "a woman"), because they have the entry of the female apartments. Another name for them is Dhîmar (Sanskrit, *Dhívara,* "a fisherman"), though some of them profess to regard it as a honorific term from Sanskrit *dhi,* or "intellect, intelligence." When they are engaged in domestic service they are often known as Behara, which is probably a corruption of the English "bearer," rather than, as one theory would represent it to be, from the Sanskrit *Vyavahára,*[2] "business." Another name for them is Bhoi, which is a Southern Indian word (Telegu and Malayalam *boyi,* Tamil *bovî*). In the Konkan people of this class are known as Kahâr Bhui, which is the origin of the title "boy" applied by Europeans to their personal servant in Western India.[3] In parts of Bundelkhand they are known as Machhmâra, "fish killers" (Hindu *machhi-márna*), and in other places Singhâriya, because they cultivate the Singhâra nut or water caltrop (*trapa bispinosa*).

Tribal traditions.

2. According to the Brâhmanical genealogists the Kahâr is one of the mixed castes, descended from a Brâhman father and a Nishâda or Chandâla mother. Their appearance suggests a considerable admixture of what is called non-Aryan blood. Their occupation as servants in high caste families would perhaps in some cases improve the breed; and in Bengal, according to Mr. Risley,[4] "they admit into their community Brâhmans, Râjputs, Kâyasths, Kurmis, and children of Kahâr women by men of those castes on condition of performing certain religious ceremonies and giving a feast to the heads of the caste. Instances of men born in a higher caste applying for enrollment as Kahârs are probably rare, and occur only when the applicant has been turned out of his own caste for an intrigue with a Kahâr woman." The existence of this custom of admitting outsiders to the community is distinctly denied in these Provinces and does not appear to prevail.

---

[1] Based on enquiries at Mirzapur and notes by Munshi Karam Ahmad, Deputy Collector, Jhânsi, and the Deputy Inspectors, Pilibhit, Bareilly, Agra, Bijnor.

[2] By another account it is an abbreviation of the Uriya *dal behara,* "the leader of a band."

[3] See *Hobson-Jobson, s. v.*

[4] *Tribes and Castes,* I., 370.

3. The Dhuriya sub-caste describe their origin as follows:—"Mahâdeva and Pârvati were returning from the house of Himâchal, the father of Pârvati, with their luggage on their heads. Seeing his spouse wearied with the burden, Mahâdeva told her to look behind and hand over her burden to the two men who were following her. These were the two ancestors of the Dhuriya Kahârs, whom Mahâdeva formed out of a handful of dust (*dhûl*, *dhûr*)." The Bihâr Kahârs claim descent from Jarâsandha, King of Magadha. The legend is thus told by General Cunningham.[1] When Jarâsandha was king he built a tower on the Giriyak hill in Gaya as his sitting place (*baithak*); here he would sit and lave his feet in the waters of the Panchina below. Close to his sitting place was Bhagwân's garden, which in a year of drought was nearly destroyed. Bhagwân accordingly, after fruitless efforts to keep it flourishing, caused it to be proclaimed that he would grant his daughter and half his kingdom to him who should succeed in watering his garden plentifully with Ganges water in a single night. Chandrâwat, the leader of the Kahârs, at once came forward and undertook the task; first he built the great embankment to bring the waters of the Bâwan Ganga rivulet to the foot of the hill below the garden, and then began lifting it up to successive stages by means of the common native swing basket and rope. When the work was completed Bhagwân repented of his offer and the Pipar came forward and offered to assume the form of a cock and crow while Bhagwân was to urge the Kahârs to hasten their operations. The Kahârs, hearing the cock crow, believed that night was over, and fearing the vengeance of Bhagwân, fled to the banks of the Ganges at Mokâma. Bhagwân next day sent for the Kahârs to receive their wages, but not one of them was to be found. At last he induced some of them to return and gave each of them 3½ sers of grain. Ever since that period 3½ sers of grain has been the legitimate wages for a day's work to Kahârs, and to this day they can legally claim, and as a matter of fact, actually receive the value of this amount of grain for a day's work.

4. Another legend thus accounts for their not taking Brâhmans as their spiritual guides (*guru*). As told in Bareilly, it describes how the Saint Nârada Rishi one day went to Râma in search of a Guru. He was told that he would see his appointed Guru next

---

[1] *Archæological Reports*, VIII., 100.

morning. The first person he met next morning was a Dhîmar fisherman, with his net over his shoulder. So Nârada saluted him and addressed him as his Guru. But when he saw to what caste he belonged he said "How can I have a Kahâr as my spiritual guide?" Then the Kahâr cursed him with the curse that he should pass through eighty-four lakhs of lives before he attained heaven. Nârada was striken with fear and complained to Râma, who would not listen to his petition. So Nârada made eighty-four lakhs of pictures of animals, snakes, and insects on the ground and rolled his body over them by way of undergoing the required number of transmigrations. He then said to the Kahâr "Pardon me and consider yourself my Guru." From that day the Kahârs say that they are the Gurus of Brâhmans and will not take Brâhmans as their Gurus, but accept the services of Jogis instead.

Internal organisation.

5. At the last Census the Kahârs recorded themselves under fifteen sub-castes, besides a number of smaller groups which were not of sufficient numerical importance to warrant inclusion in the final returns. These sub-castes are Bathma, Bot, Dhînwar or Dhîmar, Dhuriya, Gharûk, Jaiswâr, Kamkar, Khawar, Mahar, Mallâh, Raikwâr, Rawâni, Singhariya, Turai. These illustrate the various elements out of which the present caste has been organised. Of these the Bâtham take their name from the city of Sravasti; the Bot are a well known hill tribe separately described; the origin of the Dhîmar and Dhuriya has been already given; the Gharûk, or "housemen," (*ghar*) supply many of our bearers; the Goriya are in some way according to their own explanation allied to the Gonr; the Jaiswâr take their name from the old town of Jais; the Kamkar have been described in a separate article; the etymology of Mahar has been already given. The Mallâh are a well known boating tribe and the Raikwâr a sept of Râjputs. In Mirzapur they name as usual seven endogamous sub-castes—Turâh; Bathawa; Dhuriya; Dhîmar; Rawâni or Ramâni; Kharwâr or Kharwâra; and Jaiswâr. In Bijnor they call themselves Dhanor and have five sub-castes—Narai, Pachhâdê or Western, Golê, Khâgi, and Dhanor. Of these the Golê are vagrants and wander about on the banks of rivers in search of fish, living in huts made of reeds (*sirki*). In Jhânsi they divide themselves into Raikwâr, Bathma, Dhuriya, Guriya, Noriya, Mallâh, and Turai, of which there are numerous *gotras* such as Imiliya, Ateriya, Munderiya, Dahariya, and Damrauniya. A

list from Lalitpur gives the sub-castes as Goriya, Dhuriya, Mâlavi, and Gotiya. In Bareilly again ten sub-castes are recorded—Turai or Turaiya, Bathma, Goriya or Guriya, Dhuriya, Thanesara, Mahâwar, Bota, Kîra, Khadwâra, and Chander, the last two of whom are out-castes. In Agra the Turai say they are the descendants of Machharnâth or Matsyendranâtha and that Tulasi was their mother. They are servants and carry palanquins and burdens on the bahangi or bamboo laid on their shoulders. They will not kill insects (kîra), and like them are the Raikwâr, Dhuriya, and Kharagwâr. The Singhariya take service; but their chief business is growing the singhâra nut. The Chandel and Bais will eat pork. In the Eastern Districts the Gonr are stone-cutters, drawers of water, bearers of palanquins, a duty which they share with the Musahar, and cultivators. One special business they carry on is collecting the singhâra nut from tanks. The Dhîmars, who correspond to the Jhînwar of the Western Districts and the Panjâb, work as boatmen and fishermen. With these are sometimes included the Châi, who are fishermen and practise petty theft. In the hills they reckon twelve sub-divisions, which, according to Mr. Atkinson, [1] are exogamous, though in this assertion he is probably mistaken. Of these the Rawâni, Ghanik, Gariya, Kharwâra, and Nâwar are litter bearers and act as scullions and attendants; the Bathma follow the same occupations and are also grain-parchers; the Dhîmar add to these the trade of fishermen; the Mallâh that of boatmen; the Turâha and Bot that of green grocers and cultivators; and the Bâri that of basket makers.

6. The detailed Census returns give 823 sections of the Hindu and 24 of the Muhammadan branch. Of these the locally most important are the Jaliyân of Dehra Dûn, the Deswâli, Dhaunchak and Gurwal of Sahâranpur; the Ballâi, Chauhân, Gahlot, Makhanpuriya, Noiban, Ronida, Sarmodhna, and Tomar of Bulandshahr: the Bhirgudi and Râwat of Aligarh; the Deswâli of Mathura; the Kadha and Mathuriya of Agra; the Bharsiya of Farrukhâbâd; the Khâgi, Mathuriya, Matiyawâr, and Pachhâdê of Mainpuri; the Bodalê and Khâgi of Bareilly; the Khâgi and Pachhâdê of Moradâbâd; the Sanauriya of Shâhjahânpur; the Nikhâd of Cawnpur; the Juriya and Kharê of Jhânsi; the Kachhwâha of Lalitpur; the Kanaujiya of Benares and Ballia; the Panwâr and Sâkta of Jaunpur; the Hardiha of Ghâzipur; the Jethwant of Gorakhpur;

[1] *Himalayan Gazetteer*, III., 540.

the Dakkhinaha and Sorahiya of Basti; the Gond and Kanaujiya of Azamgarh; the Bhond and Nikhâd of Lucknow; the Bhond and Khairpuriya of Unâo; the Bhond, Dina, Ghatwariya, Jethwant, Nikhâd, and Rautiya of Râe Bareli; the Jethwant of Sîtapur; the Gurunâtha and Jethwant of Hardoi; the Jethwant, Kharmorha, Luniya, Medha, Nikhâd, and Turkiya of Bahrâich; the Dutiya, Lakhauna, Nikhâd, and Paskauta of Sultânpur; the Paskauta or Pâsi kewats of Partâbgarh; the Bhond, Kharmona, Morha, Nathu and Nikhâd of Bârabanki. These details will give some idea of the intricacy of the organisation of the caste as at present constituted. Everywhere we find a tendency towards the formation of distinct endogamous groups whose connection with the original stock, if there ever was one, is shadowy in the extreme.

Tribal Council.

7. The rules regarding the Tribal Council may be illustrated by the customs of Dhîmars of the Jhânsi District. The council is called Panchâyat. All the caste people attend it, as well as the so-called Panch, who have been nominated at some previous meeting. They are the spokesmen of the assembly and carry on the enquiry into the case then pending, explain the facts to the assembly, take the verdict, and pronounce the final order. The functions of the Panchâyat are,—first, in case a widow re-marries, it is for them to assess the compensation which her second husband should give to the relatives of her deceased husband; 2ndly, in case a member commits some offence, *e.g.*, theft in his master's house, adultery, trespass, etc., it is for the council to excommunicate the offender; 3rdly, the *panchâyat* has to decide certain disputes about property. In Jhânsi there are twelve headmen (*mukhiya*) for the twelve quarters (*pura, muhalla*) of the city. In order to form what may be called a quorum, it is necessary that some or at least one of the chief men be present; otherwise the meeting must be postponed. When the judgment is over, the parties are obliged to draw up a regular agreement in accordance with it, and when the matter is one connected with property, this is written on stamped paper. Any disobedience is punished by excommunication and fine.

Marriage rules.

8. A man must marry within his sub-caste, but not in his own *gotra*. In Jhânsi, in addition to this, he may not marry the daughter of his uncle on the father's and mother's side, or of his father's or mother's sister. In most places, however, the simple rule is that a man does not

marry in any family as long as relationship is remembered. If after subsequent enquiry, in spite of all reasonable precaution on his part, such relationship be ascertained, it does not matter. Polygamy is recognised, but with certain restrictions. Thus in Jhânsi before a man can marry again he must obtain the permission of his first wife. If she refuses to give her consent, he can bring the case before the Council. They will go into the matter, and if he show sufficient cause, such as that his present wife is barren or diseased, they will authorise him to marry again, and, if necessary, to get rid of his first wife, should she persist in her opposition to his second marriage. Girls are, as a rule, unless they are orphans or their parents are very poor, married about the age of eight, before puberty; boys are usually married before fifteen. If there be more wives than one, the senior is known as *jethi*, and her juniors have to obey her in household matters. Concubinage is so far recognised that a man cannot keep a girl who has never been married. If he takes to himself a widow or the wife of another, he has to give a dinner to the caste and pay compensation to the relatives of the widow or to the aggrieved husband. In Jhânsi the fine for keeping a widow is ten rupees, and for living with the wife of another man sixty rupees. No bride price is paid for a virgin. A man will be permitted by the Council to put away his wife if she commits adultery or steals or misappropriates his property. When a woman is divorced in this way, she and her husband have to execute a deed of release (*fârigh-khatti*) on stamped paper. The children of all unions recognised as valid by tribal custom rank equally for purposes of inheritance.

Widow marriage.

9. Widow marriage is recognised; the only ceremony is the notification of the fact to the Council and the provision of a dinner and spirits for the clansmen. If the younger brother of the deceased husband is adult and unmarried, he, as a matter of course, takes over the widow. In this case the levir has the right to the custody of his nephews and nieces; but the children by each husband are heirs to the goods of their respective fathers.

Marriage ritual.

10. The marriage ritual is of the usual type. Poor people marry by the *dola* form, where all the ceremonies are done at the house of the bridegroom. In a regular marriage (*byâh, charhaua*) the binding part of the ceremony is the worshipping of the feet of the bridegroom (*pair pûja, pâuw pûja*) by the father of the bride.

11. The dead are cremated when adult; buried when unmarried or the victims of epidemic disease or snake-bite. The ordinary *srâddha* is done in their honour. As among many similar tribes, they have a special ceremony of purification in two special cases—(*a*) to remove what is called *hatya* or the guilt of killing a cow, ass, or cat, (*b*) to remove the taint of a person committing suicide on account of the acts of another. In such cases the offender is sent to the Ganges to bathe, and on his return has to feed the brethren. Kahârs are orthodox Hindus and worship most of the ordinary gods. They are seldom initiated into any of the regular Hindu sects. To the east of the Province they worship Bhairon, Mahâbir, Birtiya (who is vaguely regarded as a *bîr* or dangerous demon), and the Pânchonpîr, of whom Amina Sati in the form of Amina Bhawâni is most venerated. Bhairon, Mahâbir, Amina Bhawâni, and Birtiya are worshipped on the tenth lunar day of Kuâr. To Mahâbir are offered clothes, Brâhmanical cords (*janeo*), and garlands of flowers; to Bhairon a goat and a libation of wine with *bara* or cakes made of the *urad* pulse; Amina receives a young pig and a libation of wine. The Pânchonpîr are worshipped generally in the month of Jeth with various kinds of cakes, cucumber, and sharbat. In Jhânsi they worship all the ordinary Hindu gods, and in addition Sîtala, Hardaul Lâla, and Bhûmiya, the local deity of the hamlet. In this district in the worship of Devi they are said to combine in a curious way the Hindu and Muhammadan ritual. A Musalmân and a Khatîk accompany the Dhîmar to the shrine of Devi. The Musalmân pronounces the *Kalima* when the knife is plunged into the throat of the victim, the Khatîk cleans the carcase, and then the worshipper and his friends cook and eat the meat. In Jhânsi, when they cultivate the *singhâra* or water-nut they worship a local deity known as Siloman Bâba and his brother Mâdho Bâba with the sacrifice of a goat and libations of wine. If they cultivate melons, they worship these spirits as well as another named Ghatauriya Bâba. All these have platforms (*chauntra*) erected on the banks of rivers and tanks, and are believed to be the protectors of the crop. Kâlu Kahâr, whom the Dhîmars believe to be a deceased ancestor, is invoked by them when they go out fishing or commence to carry a palanquin. On the third day after a death, in Jhânsi, the kinsmen and relatives have themselves shaved and then bathe in a tank or river. In the evening all the people of the caste are

invited. This is called *Pun kâ bulâna* or "the invitation to the charitable act." An effigy of the dead man is made of straw and wood. All who attend touch its mouth five or seven times with a morsel of food prepared specially for the purpose. The effigy and the offerings are then laid by the roadside and the guests partake of the funeral feast.

Social customs.

12. Seven names are proposed for boys and five for girls; but the first name is used only for daily use and for ceremonial purposes. If a man's children die, the next baby is called some contemptuous name, such as Damru ("bought for a farthing"), Basora ("like one of the sweeper caste"). When they are sworn before the tribal council, they have to lift a vessel containing Ganges water and a leaf of the *tulasi* plant. When the water of an ordinary well is used for this purpose, it must be drawn by an unmarried girl, and she drops into it a little Ganges water and a leaf of the *tulasi* plant. Ordeals, especially that of the red-hot iron, were in use under the Marhatta Government in Jhânsi; but since the country was ceded to the British, the custom has been discontinued. They believe in the ordinary omens, and in cases of sickness the evil spirit is exercised by the Syâna or wizard. At the Akhtîj festival, held in the month of Baisâkh, the Jhânsi Dhîmars assemble at the temple of Devi near Pachkinya. The fair is attended by both sexes, and it is a favourite joke to try and make young married men and women break the taboo of mentioning the names of wife or husband. It is only the very young or inexperienced who allow themselves to be brought to ridicule in this way. When they are sowing melons, they select in particular the day on which the feast in honour of Bara Ganesa is held in the month of Mâgh. On the Akhtîj festival they take omens as to the character of the coming agricultural seasons in this way. They keep by them a pod which contains four grains of gram. Five jars (*ghaila*) are filled with water, and into four of them a grain of the gram is placed. Each represents one of the months of the rainy season—Âsârh, Sâwan, Bhâdon and Kuâr. Whichever swells up indicates that there will be abundant rain in the month which it represents. On this day of the Akhtîj they commence to plant out the sprouts of the water-nut, and during the planting, constant offerings are made to Siloman Bâba and Mâdho Bâba to prosper the crop.

Occupation and social status.

13. It will have been seen from the enumeration of the sub-castes that the occupations of the Kahâr are diverse. Of the Western Kahâr Mr. Ibbetson writes :—" He is the carrier, waterman, fisherman, and basket maker of the East of the Panjâb; he carries palanquins and all such burdens as are borne by a yoke on the shoulders; and he is specially concerned with water, insomuch that the cultivation of water-nuts and the netting of water-fowl are for the most part in his hands, and he is the well-sinker of the Province. He is a true village menial, receiving customary dues and performing customary service. In this capacity he supplies all the baskets needed by the cultivator, and brings water to the men in the fields at harvest time, to the houses where the women are secluded, and at weddings and other similar occasions. His social standing is in one respect high; for all will drink at his hands, but he is still a servant, though the highest of the class." As one correspondent remarks. " This caste is so low that they clean the vessels of almost all castes except menials like the Chamâr and Dhobi, and at the same time so high that, except Kanaujiya Brâhmans, all other castes eat *pakki* and drink water from their hands." This is one of the many puzzling inconsistencies which we constantly encounter in considering the social intercourse of the various castes. Those who are engaged in personal service consider themselves superior to those who perform menial occupations such as fishing, stone-cutting or bearing of burdens, and are more exacting in arranging the marriages of their daughters. They drink liquor and eat goat's flesh and mutton; some fowls and pork. Some, according to Mr. Risley, eat field rats. But in spite of this they have some curious prohibitions of their own. Thus a Kahâr engaged in personal service with a Brâhman, Râjput, Bâbhan, Kâyasth, or Agarwâla will only eat his master's leavings so long as he is himself unmarried. They are also particular to explain that their women may not wear nose-rings or have their foreheads tattooed. In Jhânsi, the rule about eating is said to be that they can eat *pakki* touched by, and sitting side by side with, a Nâi or Kâchhi, but not food cooked by a Nâi. The lowest caste with whom they will eat *kachchi* is the Ahîr, and they will smoke with any caste except a Bhangi. To the East Banyas will eat *pakki* cooked by them and Chamârs and other menials will eat *kachchi*. They will themselves eat *kachchi* cooked

by Brâhmans and Râjputs. A curious illustration of the respect in which the caste is held is the worship in the Western Districts of the Jhiwarni or female water-bearer at the Hoi festival, which takes place eight days before the Diwâli. After the house is plastered with cow-dung, figures of a litter (*doli*) and bearers are made on the walls with four or five colours, and to them offerings with incense, lights, and flowers are given. The legend runs that at the commencement of the Kaliyuga death, famine, and pestilence devastated the land, and, though the Brâhmans fasted and prayed on the seventh day of the dark fortnight of each month, there came no relief, and being disheartened, they were about to abandon their prayers, when a Jhiwarni sat in their midst and encouraged them to further efforts. As they prayed, Châmunda Devi appeared in the form of Kâli among them, with her head in her hands, and proclaimed that these evils were due to the wickedness of mankind and prescribed the observance of the Hoi festival. The reward of the Jhiwarni has since then been to be exalted to the chief place of honour at the festival. The story, no doubt, represents some primitive form of worship, the real motive and origin of which have now been forgotten.

Distribution of Kahârs according to the Census of 1891.

District.	Batham.	Bot.	Dhinwar.	Dhuriya.	Gharûk.	Goriya.	Jaiswâr.	Kamkar.	Khawar.	Mahar.	Mallâh.	Raikwâr.	Rawâni.	Singhariya.	Turai.	Others.	Muham-madans.	Total.
Dehra Dûn	39	64	...	27	62	56	...	...	15	1,926	...	...	...	...	...	1,379	8	3,576
Sahâranpur	...	1,922	...	6	964	898	5	...	...	32,600	...	...	...	...	...	9,047	...	45,442
Muzaffarnagar	...	...	1,176	...	...	...	...	...	86	42,933	...	...	...	...	131	2,330	37	46,693
Meerut	...	2,473	...	60	...	10	...	...	...	36,560	...	...	...	...	1,013	2,843	2	42,961
Bulandshahr	...	8	798	220	...	60	...	...	...	2,959	...	...	...	...	9,246	4,981	4	18,276
Aligarh	132	46	...	...	...	...	...	...	...	...	...	...	...	...	11,211	14,823	...	26,212
Mathura	890	...	...	2	...	...	...	...	...	22	...	...	...	1,399	66	3,149	...	5,528
Agra	2,946	...	665	26	8	88	...	...	3	25	...	5	46	83	4,371	1,877	...	10,143
Farrukhâbâd	24,253	...	...	31	...	1,860	...	...	...	...	...	...	2	...	2,631	564	10	29,351
Mainpuri	16,773	...	...	...	37	43	...	...	...	426	6	...	...	58	5,968	210	...	23,521
Etâwah	14,438	...	28	2	...	27	...	...	58	...	...	26	...	...	520	969	1	16,069
Etah	4,190	...	...	2,576	1	2	...	...	3	...	75	...	...	65	14,263	204	...	21,379
Bareilly	40,393	...	15	11	...	...	...	...	31	...	9	...	...	...	8,252	3,011	...	51,722
Bijnor	...	...	12,559	...	...	2,569	...	...	...	27	...	...	...	1,328	...	1,164	2,841	20,288
Budâun	22,393	...	...	10	856	...	...	...	...	...	...	...	...	...	16,545	395	...	40,199
Morâdâbâd	49	...	...	10	1,553	557	...	...	...	2,158	...	...	2	...	24,759	4,829	601	34,518

Shâhjahânpur .	37,983	9	...	364	1	768	1	...	...	...	...	...	3	...	...	715	...	20,044
Pilibhit . .	15,388	401	...	59	...	204	...	...	...	...	2	...	...	...	104	176	...	16,334
Cawnpur . .	6,407	4	84	7,163	28	1,865	1	...	10	3	...	220	64	...	163	4,860	...	20,822
Fatehpur . .	...	...	8	3,233	...	446	4	...	6	...	...	28	7	...	...	142	...	3,874
Bânda . . .	17	21	473	4,797	...	3	6	...	...	...	...	5,443	...	...	447	201	...	11,408
Hamîrpur . .	1	2	99	3,874	...	7	...	...	...	...	...	7,201	...	...	...	436	...	11,620
Allahâbâd . .	14	...	169	11,030	8	4,976	185	...	121	...	...	7	96	...	12	991	75	17,684
Jhânsi . . .	99	...	596	7	...	3	...	...	...	...	5	9,525	1	...	...	497	1	10,734
Jâlaun . . .	1,077	..	41	157	...	28	...	...	17	...	...	1,008	3	...	61	1,330	...	3,722
Lalitpur . .	...	...	...	...	...	3	...	...	...	...	...	5,772	3	...	...	1,088	...	6,866
Benares . .	...	...	1,373	248	...	526	3,043	...	7,262	...	...	...	719	...	...	2,274	76	15,521
Mirzapur . .	...	477	1,891	6,319	...	217	2,385	...	4,753	...	...	...	3,805	...	...	708	12	20,090
Jaunpur . .	...	...	4,097	13,531	..	1,538	...	...	4,702	...	...	...	...	...	28	2,771	378	27,522
Ghâzipur . .	...	...	1,198	87	2	939	1,146	1,994	11,881	...	...	...	1,264	...	7	3,362	...	21,880
Ballia . . .	...	...	1	...	...	1	...	16,545	116	...	...	...	...	...	...	4,663	...	21,226
Gorakhpur . .	...	10	791	35,892	1,027	4,150	111	19,053	215	...	...	...	162	...	3,466	7,640	5	72,522
Basti . . .	806	...	181	39,121	1,884	1,016	...	469	257	...	...	...	...	...	520	2,072	705	47,030
Azamgarh . .	...	...	2,151	27,019	...	1,993	2,293	1,574	2,464	...	...	...	2	...	229	3,287	358	41,370
Kumaun . .	...	...	...	...	...	...	...	...	...	...	...	...	...	...	...	44	...	44
Garhwâl . .	...	...	101	...	...	...	2	...	...	...	...	...	...	...	...	1,992	...	2,095

Distribution of Kahârs according to the Census of 1891—contd.

DISTRICT.	Batham.	Bot.	Dhinwar.	Dhuriya.	Gharûk.	Goriya.	Jaiswâr.	Kamkar.	Khawar.	Mahar.	Mallâh.	Raikwâr.	Rawâni.	Singhariya.	Turai.	Others.	Muham-madans.	TOTAL.
Tarâi . . .	1,980	9	4	3	...	...	...	...	...	189	...	...	...	36	2,775	477	414	5,887
Lucknow . .	374	1,392	102	10,412	1,235	214	...	...	217	10	...	3	39	2	4	3,673	518	18,193
Unâo . . .	399	434	...	2,502	...	4,516	...	...	...	...	56	...	8	188	...	3,600	...	11,703
Râê Bareli . .	315	912	73	2,538	8	4,222	...	...	...	...	...	...	420	...	...	3,090	22	11,910
Sitapur . . .	104	161	20	14,323	30	4,362	104	...	...	...	...	...	...	...	...	13,932	46	33,082
Hardoi . . .	6,468	...	...	...	...	17,310	...	...	...	...	...	...	...	...	...	5,004	...	28,801
Kheri . . .	3,651	2,468	311	15,702	548	7,326	3,727	...	...	20	328	...	...	...	283	128	...	34,477
Faizâbâd . .	...	...	...	25,460	728	7,065	...	...	384	...	...	...	...	...	...	3,735	28	37,400
Gonda . . .	...	5,569	1,335	12,825	25,866	9,386	...	19	124	...	...	...	...	...	...	264	72	55,460
Bahrâich . .	...	5,134	6,527	10,146	4,559	3,663	...	...	...	...	...	...	13	...	...	17,675	121	47,838
Sultanpur . .	...	...	...	14,381	1	1,677	...	...	892	...	...	...	...	...	...	7,267	460	28,678
Partâbgarh . .	...	...	48	7,410	...	2,747	...	...	405	...	...	...	4	...	...	247	123	10,984
Bârabanki . .	159	369	...	11,737	780	...	...	...	...	1,229	...	...	...	...	...	8,396	10	22,680
TOTAL .	201,738	21,885	36,865	283,321	40,186	87,350	13,513	39,653	33,922	121,087	481	29,238	6,673	3,157	107,075	158,807	6,928	11,91,379

Kâkan.—A sept of Râjputs found in the Eastern Districts. In Ghâzipur they say they came from Mhau Aldamau, in Faizâbâd, and expelled the Bhars. In Azamgarh they say they are descended from Mayûra Bhatta, the hero of the Bisen sept, and fix their original home at a place called Kapri Kedâr, somewhere in the west, and say that they overcame the Suiris. They had a Chaurâsi of eighty-four villages.[1] The curious effects of *kodo* (*paspalum frumentaceum*) have invested it with a degree of mystery, as it causes a sort of intoxication, and the Kâkan Râjputs are said to worship it as a divinity. They never cultivate or eat *kodo*, and the reason assigned, is that while under the influence of the grain, they were set upon by some of the neighbouring tribes and lost the greater part of their once extensive possessions.[2]

Kalhans.—A sept of Râjputs in Oudh, who are said to take their name from the fact that one of their early leaders used to pet a black swan (*kâla hansa*). This may perhaps have been the tribal totem. They are now represented by the Babbnipair family of Gonda, who are the only legitimate descendants of the old Kalhans Râjas of Khurâsa, whose kingdom extended from Hisâmpur in Bahrâich far into the Gorakhpur District.[3] Their leader, Sahaj Sinh, came at the head of a small force from the Narbada valley with one of the Tughlaq Emperors, and was deputed by him to bring into obedience the country between the Ghâgra and the hills. The ruler of the land was Ugrasen, the Dom, and as he dared to aspire to the hand of the daughter of the Râjput, they plied him and his followers with strong drink till they were insensible and then murdered them. The last of the race, Râja Achal Nârâyan Sinh, carried off, by force, the daughter of a Brâhman, Ratan Pânrê. He starved himself to death at the gate of the palace and cursed the family, except the descendants of the younger Râni, with ruin and blindness. He prayed to the river Sarju for vengeance on his oppressor, and in answer to his prayer, a wave from the river swept away the fort of the Râja.

2. The Kalhans do not rank with Râjputs of the bluest blood. In Râê Bareli[4] their sons marry the daughters of Chauhân (not those of Mainpuri) Bais and Amethiya girls. In Gonda they are reported

---

[1] Oldham, *Memo.*, I., 12; *Azamgarh Settlement Report*, 62.
[2] Elliot, *Supplemental Glossary*, *s.v. kodo*.
[3] *Oudh Gazetteer*, I., 88, *sqq*.
[4] *Settlement Report, Appendix C.*

to marry their daughters in the Bais, Bhadauriya, Chauhân, and Bisen septs, and to accept brides of the Bais, Bisen, Bandhalgoti and other fairly respectable septs.

Distribution of the Kalhans Râjputs according to the Census of 1891.

District.	Numbers.	District.	Numbers.
Sahâranpur . . .	8	Lucknow . . .	38
Meerut	3	Unâo . . .	6
Agra	5	Râê Bareli . .	88
Bareilly . . .	20	Sîtapur . . .	74
Morâdâbâd . . .	109	Hardoi . . .	2
Pilibhît	2	Kheri . . .	14
Cawnpur . . .	1	Faizâbâd . . .	273
Fatehpur . . .	8	Gonda . . .	14,586
Bânda	3	Bahrâich . . .	3,022
Allahâbâd . . .	2	Sultânpur . . .	48
Jhânsi	6	Partâbgarh . .	42
Gorakhpur . . .	492	Bârabanki . . .	1,293
Basti	3,611		
		Total .	23,756

Kâlupanthi.—A sept numbering 266,161 persons, chiefly found in the Meerut Division, and worshippers of Kâlu Kahâr, a low-caste godling, venerated chiefly by Chamârs, Sainis, Gadariyas, and other low castes.

Kalwâr.[1]—The distilling, liquor-selling, and trading caste. The name of the caste is certainly derived from Sanskrit *Kalyapâla, Kalyapâlaka,* "a distiller," and Mr. Risley's derivation from *Kalwâla,* "one who works a machine," is untenable. Mr. Nesfield regards the name as equivalent to Khairwâr or Kharwâr, "a maker

[1] Based on enquiries at Mirzapur and notes by Mr. A. B. Bruce, C. S., Ghâzipur, Munshi Bhagwân Dâs, Tahsildâr, Allahâbâd, Bâbu Badri Nâth, Deputy Collector, Kheri.

of catechu" (*khair*), and says that this "implies that the caste has sprung out of such tribes as the Châîn, Khairwâr, Musahar, etc., all of whom are skilled in making the intoxicating juice called catechu." But the latest authorities [1] give no support to the idea that catechu has any intoxicating properties; and, further, the physical appearance of the Kalwâr certainly approximates him more to the Banya than to the dark-skinned, broad-nosed Kharwâr. The caste is probably of occupational origin, and may be an offshoot from the Banya or other Vaisya tribes which has lost social position through its connection with the preparation and sale of intoxicating liquors. On this account he is known as Âbkâr.

2. The traditions of the caste do not give much help in deciding their ethnological affinities. To the east of the province they claim Kshatriya origin and call themselves Laukiya Chauhân, a term which they explain to be derived from Lauki, "the bottle gourd," the shell of which is said to have been used in early times to measure liquor. In Ghâzipur, they say that Râja Vena was killed by the Brâhmans for his impiety, and that when he was cremated, from his pyre sprang seven castes of whom the Kalwâr was one. In Oudh they say that Mahâdeva once rubbed the sweat off his body and formed a man out of it to whom he gave a cup of wine. He was the ancestor of the Kalwârs.

3. The comparatively low origin of the caste is shown by their possessing no real *gotra* system. Some of their priests say that the richer Kalwârs belong to the Kasyapa *gotra*; but this *gotra* is the general refuge of those who do not possess this form of tribal organization.

Internal structure.

4. At the last Census the Kalwârs were recorded in seven main endogamous sub-castes—Bâtham, who take their name from the old city of Srâvasti; Golherê; Jaiswâr, or "residents of the town of Jais;" Kanaujiya, "those of Kanauj;" Mahur; Purabiya; or "eastern"; and Sewara. The detailed Census lists give no less than 619 sub-castes of the Hindu and 12 of the Musalmân branch of the tribe. Of these those of most local importance are the Sant of Dehra-Dûn; the Chobdâr, Gond, and Tânk of Sahâranpur; the Chobdâr and Gond of Muzaffarnagar; the Mahur and Seohâra of Agra; the Gond and Tânk of Bijnor; the Dewat and Magaraha of Cawnpur;

[1] Watt's *Dictionary of Economic Products*, I., 42.

the Seohâra of Fatehpur, Bânda, Jâlaun, and Hamîrpur; the Chausaki and Râê of Jhânsi and Lalitpur; the Pachhwâha and Uttarâha of Mirzapur; the Byâhut and Charandha of Ballia; the Byâhut, Charandha, Dakkhinâha, Girdaha, Jaunpuri, Karandha, and Uttarâha of Gorakhpur; the Gurer of Râê Bareli, Bahrâich, and Lucknow; the Bihipuriha and Nagariha of Unâo; the Pachhwâha of Bahrâich. To the east of the province the highest in rank are the Byâhut, who rest their claims to respectability on their prohibition of widow marriage and take none but virgin brides (*byâhta*). The lowest of all are the Sûnri, who take their name from the Sanskrit *shundaka*, "a distiller" (*shunda*, "spirituous liquor"). Between these two are the Jaiswâr, who, as already stated, take their name from the old town of Jais. It is curious to observe that the Bengal Kalwârs have lost all recollection of their original head-quarters and have invented an eponymous ancestress, Jaisya, and a place called Jaispur, the exact locality of which they are unable to state, as their head-quarters.[1] Next come the Bhainswâr, who take their name from their business of carrying about goods on male buffaloes (*bhainsa*); the Gurer, whose name seems to come from Sanskrit *gudala*, "a spirituous liquor distilled from molassess" (*guda*); the Bhujkalaura, who, according to Mr. Sherring, [2] are a cross between the Bhunjas or grain-parchers and Kalwârs; the Bhojpuriya and Tânk, both of which appear to be local titles. Besides these are the Rânki or Irâqi or Kalâl, Kalâr, who are Muhammadans and are dealt with separately. It is curious, again, that these sub-castes are almost quite different from those prevailing in Bihâr, where Mr. Risley names the Banaudhiya, Byâhut, Bhojpuri, Deswâr or Ajudhyabâsi, Khalsa, and Kharidaha or "purchasers." A list from Ghâzipur gives Jaiswâr, Kharidaha, Byâhut, Sûnri, Gurer, Kalâr, and Rânchi or Rânki. From Allahâbâd we have Byâhut, Jaiswâr, Karaiya, Gurer, Sihor, Sûnri, and Rânki or Râki. In Agra we have the Mathuriya or "those of Mathura," who are also called Mahâjan and deal in corn, having given up the liquor trade altogether; Soharê, who may be the same as the Sûnri of the eastern distircts and distill and sell liquor; the Gulharê, who follow the same occupation; and the Sungha, who are said to be so called because they smell (*sungna*) spirits.

---

[1] Risley, *Tribes and Castes*, I., 385.

[2] *Hindu Tribes and Castes*, I., 303.

5. Again, in Bihâr the Kalwârs appear still to maintain an elaborate system of sections of the territorial type which give rise to a special rule of exogamy; but those further west in these provinces seem to have shed off their sections altogether, and the prohibition against intermarriage extends to members of their own family and that of cousins for three generations in the ascending line, or as long as any recollection of relationship exists. Marriage is also prohibited in a family in which a son or daughter may have been already married. In Ghâzipur the marriage law is that a man must marry in his own sub-caste and not with any ascertained relation of his father or mother. In all cases a Kalwâr may marry the younger sister of his late wife, but not her elder sister or two sisters at the same time.

The tribal council.

6. In Mirzapur, the tribal council (*panchâyat*) is presided over by a chairman (*chaudhari*), who is not a permanent official, but is selected at each meeting on grounds of respectability and aptitude for the discharge of his duties. The council deals with offences against morality and tribal usage, and the usual punishment for offences of this kind is a fine ranging from five to twenty-five rupees according to the means of the culprit, and two feasts to the brethren, one of *pakki* or cakes, etc., prepared with butter and meat, and the other *kachchi*, or ordinary bread, rice, pulse, vegetables, etc. In Allahâbâd there is no general council. Each sub-caste holds a meeting of the adult males to decide caste matters, and the penalty is a feast (*bhoj*) to the brethren; no money fines are imposed.

Marriage rules.

7. Polygamy is permitted, but in some of the sub-castes there seems to be an increasing tendency towards monogamy. Pre-nuptial immorality involves the excommunication of the girl offending. There is no regular bride price; but if the parents of the girl are poor, they sometimes receive aid in money from the friends of the bridegroom to carry out the wedding. To the east of the province the Byâhut sub-càste, who pretend to extra purity and will not eat animal food or drink spirits, usually marry their daughters in infancy; the others at the age of eight or ten; but among those who have acquired wealth there is a constant tendency to adopt infant marriage as being more respectable. Intertribal infidelity does not seem to be strictly reprobated; but a married woman detected in an intrigue can be expelled by permission of the council, and such a woman,

among some at least of the sub-castes, cannot be re-married by the *saḡâi* form; while among others it seems to be allowed on condition that she amends her conduct and that her friends feed the brethren. Except in the Byâhut sub-caste, widow marriage and the levirate are allowed; but the levirate is not compulsory on the widow. The only rite in widow marriage is that the man goes to the house of the widow with a suit of clothes and ornaments for her. He eats and drinks there and remains for the night. Next morning he brings his wife home and gives a dinner, by which his marriage is recognised.

Birth rites.

8. As a rule, there are no ceremonies during pregnancy; but in some families what is known as the *korapûri* rite is done, which simply consists in placing some cakes (*pûri*) in the lap of the expectant mother. In cases of difficult labour she is given some water to drink which has been blown over by a Pandit, or Ojha, and the other women of the house vow to worship Kâlika and the Pânchonpîr if the result be satisfactory. During the twelve-days period of birth impurity the mother is bathed thrice—on the third, sixth, and twelfth day. At the second and third bathing (*nahân*) the brethren, if possible, are entertained; and at the last bath the earthen pots in use in the house are replaced; the members of the family wear clean clothes and eat choice food. During her first bath the mother listens carefully for the voice of any human being; because in popular belief the character of the child will resemble that of the person whose voice is heard by the mother on this occasion. At the age of five or seven the child's ears are bored and the hair shaved at some recognised place of pilgrimage. This marks the introduction of the child into caste, and from that time the caste rules regarding food, etc., must be observed. This custom of dedication of the hair prevailed also among the Greeks. Pausanias describes the statue of a boy on the banks of the Cephissus dedicating his hair to that river.[1]

Marriage ceremonies.

9. The marriage ceremonies are of the orthodox type; but special attention is given to the betrothal, which is known as *barraksha* or *pyâla*, "the cup," because on this occasion the bride's father presents to the father of the bridegroom a cup with one or two rupees in it. They have the usual forms of marriage, the *charhaua* or respectable form,

[1] I., 37, and compare *Iliad*, XXIII., 135.

the *dola* where the rite is done at the house of the husband, and, lastly, the *hánkwa* or "driving," or the *pánwpúja*, "feet worship," which is the lowest of all. In the last case her father brings the girl to the house of the bridegroom, and gives him a present of one rupee or two annas. Then a vessel full of water is placed near the feet of the bridegroom, from which his father-in-law takes some water and sprinkles it upon his face. Then he makes a mark (*tíka*) with curds and rice upon the forehead of his son-in-law, telling him that as he is too poor to afford it, the rest of the ceremony must be done at a later time at the house of her husband.

Disposal of the dead.

10. The dead are cremated in the ordinary way. After the mourners' return home they make little cups of the leaves of the *ber* (*ziziphus jujuba*), fill them with spirits, and pour the contents on the ground. Those who are orthodox suspend a vessel of water (*ghant*) on a *pípal* tree for the use of the ghost during the ten days of the death rites. On the tenth day presents of vessels and the other goods of the deceased are made to the officiating Mahâbrâhman, and the chief mourner worships Gauri and Ganesa at home. They perform the *sráddha* in the orthodox way.

Religion.

11. The Kalwârs employ Brâhmans as priests, who seem to be received on an equality with those who officiate for the higher castes. To the east of the Province they chiefly worship Durga in the form of Kâlika the Pânchonpîr, Phûlmati Devi, Chausathi, and Hardiha or Har daul Lâla. Kâlika is worshipped on the first Monday in the month of Aghan with an offering of *bhang*, wine, molasses, and chaplets of flowers. The Pânchonpîr are worshipped in Sâwan with rice-milk, cakes, gram, and the sacrifice of a goat or ram. In Allahâbâd they have made an extraordinary conversion of the great saintly quintette of Islâm. According to them, they consist of Ghâzi Miyân, Parihâr, Athîlê or Hathîlê, Brahma Deota, and the Barê Purukh, who seems to be the personified ancestor of the tribe, "the old man" *par excellence*. Ghâzi Miyân is, according to their account, the martyred hero of Bahrâich; Parihâr, the son of the giant Râvana of the Râmâyana; Hathîlê, the sister's son of Ghâzi Miyân; Brahma Deota was a Brâhman who died as a follower of Ghâzi Miyân, whose spiritual guide was Barê Purukh,—a most wonderful jumble of all the mythologies. The other tribal deities are worshipped in the same way. They have, in Banjâri, a

sort of tribal goddess whose worship is carried out by general subscription. "Whether Madain, the god of wine," says Mr. Baillie,[1] "should be regarded as specially a low-caste god, or as belonging to the class of demons with whom he would be classed by most Hindus, is an open question. He is, though feared by Oudh Chamârs as far more terrible than any other god, little acknowledged as a special tutelary god, his worshippers being in general ashamed to admit that they regard him as their god, although they regard a false oath sworn by Madain as more certain to attract retribution than one by any other god in the pantheon. Madain, well known and well feared as he is, has, therefore, only 2,639 special worshippers."

12. The aonla tree is specially worshipped in the month of Kârttik by feeding Brâhmans and doing a fire offering (*homa*). They also revere the *nîm* and *pîpal* tree, the former of which is said to be the abode of Devi, and, as such, women bow as they pass it, while the *pîpal* is the home of Vasudeva and the other gods. They fast on Sundays in honour of Sûraj Deota, the sun god, and they pour wine on the ground in honour of Sâiri or Sâyari Devi, of whom they can give no account, except that she was the sister of the Yakshas. Each house has a family shrine at which the household gods are worshipped. This is specially done at child-birth, and among them the god most usually worshipped in his way is Ghâzi Miyân, whose symbol, an iron spear (*sâng*), is kept near his shrine. If Kalwârs are ever initiated into any of the regular sects, it is generally the Vaishnava or Nânakshâhi.

Festivals.

13. They observe the standard festivals, the Phagua or Holi, the Naurâtra of Chait, Ghâzi Miyân kâ byâh, the Dasahra, Kajali, Tîj, Nâgpanchami Kanhaiya-ji-ki-ashtami, Anant, Bijaya, Dasmi, Diwâli, Pyâla or worship of Kâlika in Pûs, Khichari, and Basant. They also join in the Muhammadan Muharram. The seat on which they sit in the liquor shop is regarded as a sort of a fetish, and to it a burnt offering (*homa*) is made.

Social customs.

14. The women of the caste have their hands tattooed; they wear a nose-ring (*nathiya*), ear ornaments (*utarana*), bangles (*kara, dharkaua*), arm ornaments (*bâzu, humel*), neck ornaments (*guriya, kantha*), forehead

[1] Census Report, North-Western Provinces, 220.

ornaments (*tíka, handi*), anklets (*páézeb, pairi*). Kalwârs swear on Ganges water, by touching the idol in a temple after bathing, on the heads of their sons, on the feet of a Brâhman, by placing the leaf of the *pípal* tree on their heads, and by standing in running water. They believe in magic and the Evil-eye; if a child is the victim of fascination, they make a Muhammadan faqîr blow over his head. They will not touch a Dhobi, Chamâr, or Bhangi, nor the wife of a younger brother or nephew. Yudhishthira, it is said, once saw the toe of his younger brother's wife, and when he went to heaven he found that her toe was in hell. A man (*samdhi*) will not touch the *samdhin* or mother of his son's wife or daughter's husband. A man will not mention his wife by name, nor a wife her husband. They eat the flesh of goats, sheep and deer, fowls and fish, and drink spirits often to excess. They will eat *pakki* cooked by Brâhmans, Kshatriyas, and Halwâis; they eat *kachchi* only if cooked by one of their own sub-caste or by their religious guide or Guru.

Occupation and social status.

15. Their occupation is distilling and selling spirituous liquor and dealing in money, grain, and various kinds of merchandise. Their connection with the liquor trade tends to lower them in popular estimation, and they hardly rank higher than the Teli. As money-lenders they are grasping and miserly. In dealing with the public excise contracts they are shrewd and enterprising and much given to combination. A popular proverb represents the Kalwâr's wife lamenting because such a quantity of good water which might be used for better purposes is flowing away in the Ganges—*Ganga bahi páé, Kalwárin chhâti pítê*; and another still more uncomplimentary says "If you have never seen a Thag, look at a publican"—*Thag na dekhé, dekhé Kalwâr.*

Distribution of the Kalwârs according to the Census of 1891.

District.	Bâtham.	Golcerê.	Jaiswâr.	Kananjiya.	Mahur.	Purabiya.	Sewara.	Others.	Muhammadans.	Total.
Dehra Dûn	...	...	121	...	...	...	...	951	...	1,072
Sahâranpur	...	...	15	...	...	...	...	1,949	119	2,083
Muzaffarnagar	...	...	...	...	...	2	...	1,601	90	1,693
Meerut	...	...	...	...	...	...	...	1,562	124	1,686
Bulandshahr	...	...	...	...	...	...	...	230	114	344
Aligarh	...	...	...	...	...	...	...	51	26	77
Mathura	...	...	7	1	74	...	67	334	27	510
Agra	...	140	...	163	924	...	1,011	1,006	...	3,244
Farrukhâbâd	547	218	13	...	...	...	...	306	...	1,084
Mainpuri	...	...	...	...	...	...	...	40	...	40
Etâwah	...	114	...	...	...	...	...	72	2	188
Etah	...	...	...	...	...	...	...	32	...	32
Bareilly	...	82	688	251	...	...	...	336	...	1,357

Bijnor . . .	...	...	...	...	...	...	...	1,053	415	1,468
Budâun . . .	...	...	...	...	...	...	...	34	...	34
Morâdâbâd . . .	...	...	...	...	...	...	...	406	419	825
Shâhjahânpur . .	3,052	2,232	366	117	...	51	...	653	...	6,471
Pilibhît . . .	239	151	1,499	14	...	243	...	81	...	2,227
Cawnpur . . .	124	1,217	5,727	...	...	75	...	2,895	6	10,044
Fatehpur . . .	2	42	1,695	...	...	...	...	2,130	...	3,869
Bânda . . .	...	155	1,954	...	...	...	...	4,079	...	6,188
Hamirpur . . .	...	...	40	1	...	3	...	3,039	...	3,083
Allahâbâd . . .	...	...	15,243	3	...	...	...	1,443	1	16,690
Jhânsi . . .	...	20	28	...	...	...	...	2,511	...	2,559
Jâlaun . . .	5	93	...	...	...	...	...	2,352	...	2,450
Lalitpur . . .	...	...	33	...	...	...	...	1,299	...	1,332
Benares . . .	...	12	14,225	125	...	217	...	3,277	...	17,856
Mirzapur . . .	...	...	14,576	1,393	...	214	...	436	...	15,619
Jaunpur . . .	...	249	16,843	...	...	...	...	863	...	17,955
Ghâzipur . . .	...	...	11,913	80	...	...	...	850	...	12,843

Distribution of the Kalwárs according to the Census of 1891—contd.

District.	Bâtham.	Golherê.	Jaiswâr.	Kananjiya.	Mahur.	Purabiya.	Sewara.	Others.	Muhammadans.	Total.
Ballia	...	...	3,090	111	...	...	...	9,669	...	12,870
Gorakhpur	...	...	35,795	147	...	...	...	12,032	2	47,976
Basti	...	...	12,192	81	...	...	...	1,292	...	13,565
Azamgarh	...	...	10,202	457	...	...	...	7,565	1	18,225
Garhwâl	...	...	...	...	...	...	...	7	...	7
Tarâi	...	...	...	...	...	...	...	22	66	88
Lucknow	176	495	3,502	3	...	130	...	1,472	...	5,778
Unâo	...	...	4,116	...	...	...	...	1,646	...	5,762
Râê Bareli	33	...	6,404	67	...	37	...	2,476	40	9,057
Sîtapur	2,020	99	6,421	...	...	...	...	1,024	...	9,564
Hardoi	4,552	1,923	1,452	7	...	...	...	271	...	8,205
Kheri	4,329	189	3,405	105	...	...	...	509	...	8,537
Faizâbâd	...	133	12,382	72	...	...	...	207	...	12,794

Gonda . . .	...	...	15,946	...	...	...	...	675	...	16,621
Bahrâich . . .	157	...	5,277	6	...	225	...	3,515	2	9,182
Sultânpur . . .	...	...	12,849	87	...	304	...	1,313	...	14,553
Partâbgarh . .	...	...	9,923	3	...	73	...	712	...	10,711
Bârabanki . .	40	...	7,890	193	...	...	...	960	...	9,083
Total .	15,276	7,564	235,822	3,487	998	1,574	1,078	81,238	1,454	348,491

Kamângar.—The maker of bows (*kamân*). A small occupational caste who have been apparently at the last Census included in one of the castes of wood-workers, such as Kadhera or Barhai. Closely alied to them are the Tîrgar or arrow-makers (*tîr*, an arrow), whose name is corrupted into Tîlgarh. They claim descent from Mârkandeya Rishi, who is said to have been the inventor of the art of archery. Their traditions centre round Ajudhya and a place called Isaya Balla in the Râê Bareli District. Some of the women of the Muhammadan Tîrgars act as midwives. They live by service and the making of bows and arrows, walking sticks, children's playthings and pipe stems (*nigâli*). Some do wood-painting; they work in wood, reeds, and bamboo, not in leather.

2. They eat mutton, goats' flesh, and fish; not beef, pork, or vermin. They will eat *pakki* cooked by Brâhmans, Râjputs, or Halwâis, and *kachchi* cooked by Brâhmans. Mr. Nesfield thinks they are an offshoot of the Dhânuks, but this is doubtful. The centre of the bow-making trade, which has now practically disappeared, used to be Tilhar in the Shâhjahânpur District, which was known as *kamân kâ shahr* or the city of bows.[1]

Kamboh.—An influential cultivating and land owning class found in the Meerut and Agra Divisions. The origin and ethnological affinities of the tribe have given rise to much speculation. In Jâlandhar the tradition is that "in A. D. 1654 the Panjâb was devastated by disastrous floods. To restore prosperity Jahângîr sent for Sher Shâh, a Sûbah, who took with him from the city of Sunam (possibly a mistake for Sohna in Gurgaun, a former stronghold of this tribe) Rattu and Achhra, the ancestors of the Kambohs. The latter he located near Chuniân in the Lahore District. The former settled in the neighbourhood of Tibba near Sultânpur in Kapurthala, and with his relations formed twelve villages which are still known as Bârah. Another derivation is from *wâra*, an enclosure. In Sikh times the Kambohs came from Kapurthala into Jâlandhar. The derivation of their name has not yet been ascertained. According to their account, they originally lived about Mathura and were Kshatriyas. When ParasuRâma was slaughtering the Kshatriyas, he found their ancestor Bhûp Râê armed and girt up for the fray. He, therefore, proposed slaying him; and on Rûp Râê's saying that he was not a Ksha-

---

[1] *Settlement Report*, 63.

triya, ParasuRâma replied that he was armed and redolent of the Kshatriyas (*kam bú hai; ya'ané teri bú Kshatriyonwâli hai*). Rûp Râê at once objected that he was not *qâim bú* (of any fixed odour) at all and so got off. He afterwards was known as Qaimbu, which gradually got changed into Kamboh. This ridiculous story is merely quoted on account of the bearing it may have on the traditions of some of the Bijnor Kambohs that they were of the same stock as the Khatris. The division into Qalami and Zamîndâr Kambohs—"of the pen" and "agricultural" Kambohs—is recognised. The latter only are found here. They are quiet, well-disposed people, good cultivators, and except that they pretend to be in distressed circumstances when there is nothing the matter with them, they have no bad qualities. They say they are divided into fifty-two clans; none of the names given of them is that of an important Arain clan. The names of these clans—Gorê Hândê, and Momi—are the same in both tribes. The Phillaur Kambohs, though few, have a history of their own. They were Sûrajbansi Râjputs, and came from Kâmrûp on the Brahmaputra to Delhi in the reign of Humayun (1530—1556). Thence one ancestor, Bodh Râê, migrated to the Lahore and another, Dalu Râê, to the Jâlandhar District. This tradition may have its origin in the achievements of Akbar's general, the Kamboh Shâhbâz Khân, who distinguished himself in Bengal and had nine thousand horse under his command when operating on the Brahmaputra. The Kambohs do not claim any relationship with the Arains. They practise widow marriage (*karewa*). Their women do not help in agricultural work, but bring out food to their relations in the field.[1]" In Montgomery, again, the Kambohs "claim descent from Râja Karan, but one of their ancestors had to fly to Kashmîr and married the daughter of a gardener to save his life. The Râja reproached him with contracting such a low alliance and said "*Tum ko kuchh bú khândâni kî nahîn hai? Tum kam-bú-wâlê ho*"—meaning there was no trace of high family in him; hence the name. Those in Montgomery divide themselves into Lamawâla Kamboh and Tappawâla Kamboh, *lamma* meaning west or the country about Multân. Tappa, they say, is the region between the Byâs and the Satlaj."[2]

---

[1] *Jálandhar Settlement Report*, 83 *sq*.
[2] *Montgomery Settlement Report*, 56.

2. The Muhammadan branch in these provinces connect their name with that of the old Kais Sovereigns of Persia. When the Kais, they say, lost the throne, they retired to India and called themselves Kai amboh or "the congregation of the Kais." There can, however, be very little doubt that, in name at least, they are the representatives of the Kambojas. They are regarded by Wilson as the people of Arachosia, and are always mentioned together with the north-west tribes, Yavanas, Sakas, and the like. They are famous for their horses, and in the Râmâyana they are said to be covered with golden lotuses, probably some ornament or embellishment of their dress. We have part of the name in the Cambistholi of Arrian, the two last syllables of which represent the Sanskrit *sthala*, "a place or district;" and the name denotes the dwellers in the Kamba or Kambis country.[1] Sâgara, it is said, would have destroyed them, but they appealed to Vasishtha, his family priest, and he ordered Sâgara to spare them, but he put distinguishing marks upon them. It is further noted that they spoke a language similar or akin to that of the Aryans.[2]

Real origin of the name.

3. The Kambohs of these provinces have probably entered it from the Panjâb. They are a hardy independent people and do not pay much deference to the leading castes. One authority calls them "a turbulent, crafty, stiff-necked race, and as such more akin to Afghâns than any of the meek Hindu races of the plains of India wherein they have been now settled for generations."[3] They are certainly not popular with their neighbours; and the proverb is familiar all over Northern India—*Yakê Afghân, doum Kamboh, seum badzât Kashmîri*—"the Afghân is the first, the Kamboh the second, and the Kashmîri the third rascal in the land." But this verse must, as Professor Blochmann[4] shows, be very modern; for during the reigns of Akbar and Jahângîr it was certainly a distinction to belong to this tribe, and in one version of it the three rogues are the Sindi, the Jât, and the Kashmîri.[5]

Character and occupation.

---

[1] Wilson, *Vishnu Purána*, 194; Rajendra Lâla Mitra, *The Yavanas of the Sanskrit writers; Journal Asiatic Society of Bengal*, 1874, 374, *sq.*
[2] Muir, *Ancient Sanskrit Texts*, II., 355.
[3] Rajendra Lâla Mitra, *Indo-Aryans*, II., 186.
[4] *Ain-i-Akbari*, I., 399.
[5] Lady Burton, *Arabian Nights*, IV., 92.

4 Their sections do not throw much light on their origin. Some are obviously designed to connect them with Râjputs, such as Chhatri, Jâdonbansi, Raghubansi, Râjput, and Sûrajbansi. Others are probably local, as Chaurâsi, Chaurâsi Goli, and Chaurâsi Kanha. Of the others, such as Bâwan and Bâwan Goli, Bel, Bendpâri, Chodsi, Dangan, Dewâsi, Dhaman, Dhani, Dholdhar, Gâdi, Ganaiti, Gatru, Hatthi, Kahoji, Kakli, Kalûri, Karai, Karâs, Karni, Khattâri, Lurkaji, Makotri Mal, Mûki, Murli, Rajwâni, Sankla, and Thapri, no intelligible account is forthcoming.

Distribution of the Kambohs according to the Census of 1891.

District.	Hindu.		Musalmân.	Total.
	Chaurasiya.	Others.		
Dehra Dûn	149	141	5	295
Sahâranpur	2,304	967	689	3,960
Muzaffarnagar	386	534	8	928
Meerut	...	760	480	1,240
Bulandshahr	...	...	11	11
Aligarh	...	...	38	38
Agra	...	...	1	1
Farrukhâbâd	...	...	67	67
Mainpuri	...	...	2	2
Etâwah	...	...	2	2
Etah	...	...	437	437
Bijnor	63	211	16	290
Budâun	...	...	11	11
Morâdabâd	...	308	294	602
Shâhjahânpur	...	...	19	19
Cawnpur	...	...	7	7
Fatehpur	...	...	62	62
Bânda	...	...	17	17
Hamîrpur	...	...	2	2
Allahâbâd	...	...	50	50

Distribution of the Kambohs according to the Census of 1891—contd.

District.	Hindu.		Musalmân.	Total.
	Chaurasiya.	Others.		
Jhânsi	...	...	24	24
Jâlaun	...	...	23	23
Ghâzipur	...	...	8	8
Gorakhpur	...	...	6	6
Basti	...	...	13	13
Tarâi	105	294	...	399
Lucknow	...	...	9	9
Sîtapur	...	...	10	10
Bahrâich	...	...	2	2
Bârabanki	...	...	9	9
Total	3,007	3,215	2,322	8,544

Kamkar.[1]—A tribe found chiefly in the Eastern districts, where they take service with Hindu masters. According to one theory, the word is derived from Sanskrit *Karma-kâra*, "a workman"; according to others it is connected with Sanskrit *Ka, Kam*, in the sense of "water," meaning "a water-drawer." Of the ethnological affinities of the caste little appears to be known. In Western Bengal the word Kamkar is a title of Kahârs,[2] and as the occupation and status of the two tribes are very similar, it is possible that they may be allied. In Basti they claim to be descended from the celebrated Jarâsandha, King of Magadha. The Kahârs, it may be noted, have a similar tradition—a fact which goes to confirm the connection of the tribes.

Marriage rules.

2. In Basti they have two endogamous sub-castes—the Chandwâr and Nikumbh. Their rule of exogamy excludes marriage with the daughter of the maternal uncle and the paternal and maternal aunt. Marriage

[1] Chiefly based on notes by W. H. O. N. Segrave, Esq., District Superintendent, Police, Basti.

[2] Sherring, *Tribes and Castes*, I., 339; Risley, *Tribes and Castes*, I., 395.

generally takes place at the age of twelve or thirteen. Polygamy is permitted, but they have seldom more than two wives. Polyandry is prohibited. The levirate is allowed, but is not compulsory on the widow. They have the usual marriage forms—*charhaua*, the respectable form; *dola* used by poor people; and *dharauna*, for widows. A wife can be divorced for infidelity, and she can be re-married by the *dharauna* form on payment of a fine in the shape of a feast to the clansmen.

Religion.

3. They are Hindus and may belong to the Saiva, Vaishnava or Sâkta sect, but they are seldom regularly initiated. They have Brâhmans for their religious guides. They worship Mahâdeva, Durga, and Kâli. Kâli is worshipped on Fridays, and Mahâdeva at the Sivarâtri. In their domestic ceremonies and ritual they follow the example of respectable Hindus.

Occupation.

4. Their special occupation is acting as domestic servants in the families of Râjas and rich Hindus, and they bear a good reputation for activity and fidelity. Some of them hold land as cultivators with and without rights of occupancy.

Social customs.

5. They drink spirits and eat the flesh of goats and deer and fish. They will use the leavings of their religious guide. They will not eat monkeys, cow meat, pork, crocodile, jackal, etc. Those who are Bhagats will not eat meat or drink spirits. They will eat *pakki* from the hands of Kahârs, Ahîrs and Châis. They will eat *kachchi* from the hands of Brâhmans and Kshatriyas. They will drink from the hands of Koris and Kahârs. They smoke only with their own clansmen.

For the distribution of the Kamkars see under *Kahâr*.

Kandêwâl; Kandêwâla.—A sub-caste of Banyas who take their name from their trade of dealing in cowdung fuel (*kanda*); which is an important industry in some of the larger towns. The Kandêwâl either purchases fuel from the neighbouring cultivators, or he takes a lease of the right to collect the manure at camping grounds and other places where oxen are kept. The caste is sometimes confounded with the Khandewâl (*q. v.*); but they appear to have no connection. They have not been separately recorded at the last Census.

Kanaujiya.—A small sub-caste of Banyas.

Distribution of the Kananjiya Banyas according to the Census of 1891.

District.	Number.	District.	Number.
Sahâranpur . . .	1	Benares . . .	36
Agra	1	Mirzapur . . .	55
Cawnpur . . .	8	Ghâzipur . . .	7
Fatehpur . . .	21	Gorakhpur . . .	83
Bânda	8	Azamgarh . . .	5
Allahâbâd . . .	122	Sîtapur. . . .	9
Jhânsi . . .	15	Bahrâich . . .	43
Jâlaun . . .	1	Sultânpur . . .	1
		Total .	416

Kanaujiya; Kanyakubja.—A local branch of Brâhmans, included in the Pancha Gauda. They take their name from the famous city of Kanauj, of which only a few ruins now remain in the Farrukhâbâd District. It is curious to remark the large number of sub-castes and sections of various tribes which derive their names from this great capital. "The vast empire," writes General Cunningham,[1] "which Harsha Vardhana raised during his long reign of forty-two years between A. D. 607 and 648 is described by Hwen Thsang as extending from the foot of the Kashmîr Hills to Assam, and from Nepâl to the Narbada river. He intimidated the Râja of Kashmîr into surrendering the tooth of Buddha, and his triumphal procession from Pataliputra to Kanauj was attended by no less than twenty tributary Râjas from Assam and Magadha on the east, to Jâlandhar on the west. In the plenitude of his power Harsha Vardhana invaded the countries to the south of the Narbada, where he was successfully opposed by Râja Pulakesi, and after many repulses was obliged to retire to his own kingdom. Kanauj was the capital of the Tomars down to the invasion of Mahmûd in A. D. 1021, immediately after

[1] *Archæological Reports*, I., 280.

the death and defeat of Râja Jaypâl. Shortly after that date the small town of Bâri to the north of Lucknow became the capital, until about 1050 A. D., when the Tomars retired to Delhi before the growing power of the Râthaurs. Once more Kanauj became the capital of a powerful kingdom, and the rival of Delhi both in extent and magnificence. Here Jaya Chandra, the last of the Râthaurs, celebrated the Aswamedha or "horse sacrifice"; and here in open day did Prithivi Râja, the daring chief of the Chauhâns, carry off the willing daughter of the Râthaur king in spite of the gallant resistance of the two Banâphar heroes, Alha and Udal. The fame of these two brothers, which is fully equal to that of Prithivi Râja himself, is still preserved in the songs and traditions of the people amongst the Chandels of Mahoba and the Râthaurs and Chandels of the Duâb. After the fall of Delhi in January 1191 A. D. Muhammad Ghori marched against Kanauj. Râja Jaya Chandra retired before him as far as Benares, where he made his last stand, but was defeated with great slaughter. The Râja escaped from the field; but was drowned in attempting to cross the Ganges. When his body was recovered by the conquerors, it was found that he had false teeth fixed with wires of gold. With Jaya Chandra ended the dynasty of the Râthaurs of the Duâb, and the wealth and importance of the far-famed capital of Kanauj."

Tribal organisation.

2. The tribal organisation of the Kanaujiya Brâhmans is very intricate. They are also known as Khatkul, (*shatakula*), or "those of the six clans." For these there is a mnemonic formula in use—*kâk, sâs, ubha*. *Kâ* expresses those who belong to the Kâtyâyana *gotra*; *ka* to the Kasyapa; *sá* Sandilya, *sa* Sankrita; *u* Upamanyu; *bha* Bhâradwâja. These members of the six clans are regarded as the true Kanaujiyas.

3. In their marriage rules these Khatkul Kanaujiyas have the following peculiarities. The children of a second wife can intermarry with the family of the first wife, provided the *gotra* is different, and they do not come within the other prohibited degrees. In marriage, again, what is known as the custom of *adla-badla* prevails; for instance, two men often exchange sisters in marriage. If a bride has been given to a family, the two families will not intermarry till the expiry of five generations. After this interval marriage is allowed. When a man of the Khatkul marries for the first time he takes his wife from the Khatkul; but he can-

not receive a second wife from them, and has, if he wishes to marry a second time, to marry in the lower grade or Panchâdari, described later on. The members of the Khatkul practise monogamy, and never marry a second time while the first wife is alive, whether she be barren or not.

The Panchâdari and Dhâkara Kanaujiyas.

4. Below the Khatkul come the Panchâdari and below them the Dhâkara. The former are said to have sprung originally from the Khatkul; but they emigrated to a distance at an early time, and have hence lost the status which their ancestors once enjoyed. The Panchâdari are of two kinds, the Sudha Panchâdari or "pure" Panchâdari, and secondly those who are degraded by association with the Dhâkara. The Dhâkara form the lowest grade of Kanaujiya, and have fallen in status, because they plough with their own hands and smoke. They usually marry among themselves; but sometimes they ally themselves with the poorer members of the Panchâdari group. The Panchâdari who intermarry with the Dhâkara do so only because they receive large sums for brides and are degraded by this connection and fall into the Dhâkara grade. There is a third kind of Panchâdari who rank even below the Dhâkara. They are called Bhulnihai ki Panchâdari. They too are said to have sprung originally from the Khatkul. They usually intermarry with their own group; if any of the higher grade families, for the sake of money, give them brides, they sink to their status.

The origin of the Bhulnihai Kanaujiyas.

5. The Bhulnihai Kanaujiyas are said to trace their origin to a bandit named Sîtal Prasâd Trivedi, who lived about a century ago. He, with a large body of followers, attacked the Nawâb of Lucknow, who appointed him Chakladâr. He was the son of Thâkur Prasâd, who was infatuated with the daughter of a butcher of Lucknow. She is said to have been one of the great beauties of the time. He purchased her for a large sum and took her to wife. By her he had three daughters. One day Sîtal Prasâd tauntingly said to his half-sisters, "Let me see what Mughal or Pathân I am to have as my brother-in-law!" When their mother heard the sneer she refused to eat, and when Thâkur Prasâd saw her in this state and learnt the cause of her grief, he said, "I will marry them into families higher than those into which the real sisters of Sîtal Prasâd have been married." So he sent the barber Phuljhâri and ordered him to find husbands for the girls.

6. Phuljhâri went and arranged their marriages among respectable families of Morâdâbâd, Kanauj, and Asani, which are the headquarters of the best Kanaujiyas. He betrothed one of the girls to a Misra of Morâdâbâd; a second to one of the Hira ke Bâjpei of Asani; the third to one of the Dîp ke Misra of Kanauj. When the girls were being married the relations of the husbands planned not to eat from the hands of the daughter of the butcher or her daughters. When they refused to eat with his wife and her daughters, Sîtal Prasâd threatened to blow them from his cannon, and they were obliged to give way. Since then the families who formed this connection have lost their former rank. The story is interesting, whatever be its truth, in connection with the remarks made in the article about Brâhmans, suggesting that some of the families are of mixed origin.

7. Among the Khatkul there is a section known as Bâla ke Sukla. They drink spirits and worship the goddess Chhinnamasta or Chhinnamastaka, the decapitated or headless form of Durga. They are considered one of the most respectable of the Khatkul, and their position is not lowered by their indulgence in wine. In fact the contrary is the case, and all the respectable Khatkul families intermarry with them. Bâla, after whom they are named, was a devoted worshipper of the goddess and never saluted anyone with a bow. Once a number of Kanaujiya Brâhmans made a plot to spit on him when he went to the Ganges to bathe. When he came out of his litter on the banks of the river they all spat at him. He sat down and laughingly said, "To be spat on by so many eminent Brâhmans is as good as a bath in Gangaji." So his enemies were ashamed and begged his pardon. Then he said, "The reason I bow to none is that my power is without limit, of which I will give you proof." So he bowed to a stone close by and it was broken into fragments. They were astonished, and bowing at his feet went their way.

8. There is another and similar division of Kanaujiya Brâhmans based on social status. The highest grade are known as Mahtur and are divided into Uttama or "highest," Madhyama or "middle," and Nikrishta or "debased." Lower than these are the Gohiya, who have similarly three grades—Uttama Madhyama, and Nikrishta. Lowest of all are the Dhâkara or "mongrel" already described. They have also the three grades of Uttama, Madhyama, and Nikrishta. These sections are endogamous as a

general rule. But poor families, as has already been said, lose status by selling brides to sections lower than themselves.

9. A list given below gives the classification as accurately as it can be ascertained :—

Mahtur Uttama.—Including the Bâjpei of Lucknow and Haura; the Misra of Parsu; the Tivâri of Chattu; the Pânrê of Khori; the Sukla of Fathâbâdi; the Pânrê of Gigâson; the Sukla of Bâla; the Dikshit of Srikant; the Awasthi of Madhu; the Misra of Bîr.

Mahtur Madhyama.—Bâjpei of Unchê Lucknow, Haura, Bisa; Misra of Majhgânw, Ankini, Kanauj; Sukla of Bâla; Pânrê of Khori; Misra of Parasu; Dikshit of Srikant; Sukla of Nabhel; Awasthi of Madhu, Prabhâkar; Misra of Sothiyâya, Bîr; Sukla of Chhangê; Pânrê of Gingâso; Tivâri of Chattu; Dikshit of Kangu, Bireswar.

Mahtur Nikrishta.—Bâjpei of Unchê Lucknow, Batesvar, Deva Sarma; Misra of Akini, Sothiyâya; Misra of Hemkar; Trivedi of Hari; Sukla of Peku, Keshu, Nabhel; Dûbê of Gharbas; Misra of Kanauj; Pânrê of Khori.

Gohiya Uttama.—Bâjpei of Dhanni, Târa; Sukla of Nayâya Bâghsa; Misra of Gopinâth Dhobiha; Sukla of Sandat; Pânrê of Lucknow; Bâjpei of Sinsarma, Pitha; Awasthi of Bare; Tivâri of Dama; Sukla of Nabhel; Dikshit of Bâbu; Misra of Kanauj; Pânrê of Khori and Dodarê.

Gohiya Madhyama.—Misra of Baijgânw, Badarka, Kanauj; Sukla of Nabhel, Bhandat; Awasthi of Gopâl; Misra of Gopinâth; Dûbê of Kapitânrê; Tivâri of Gopâl; Bâjpei of Kâsirâm, Manirâm; Bâjpei of Mathura Gopi; Misra of Banwâri.

Gohiya Nikrishta.—Misra of Pasikhera, Gopi, Lalkar; Sukla of Durgadâs, Nabhel; Bâjpei of Tirmal; Trivedi of Prayâg; Tivâri of Ghagh; Dikshit of Antêr; Sukla of Hari; Bâjpei of Gopi.

Dhâkara Uttama.—Agnihotri; Pâthaka; Chaubê; Upâdhyâya; Adharja.

Dhâkara Madhyama.—Sabarni; Thakuriha; Mairha; Râwat.

Occupation.

10. The Kanaujiya Brâhman, besides his priestly functions, takes readily to agriculture, soldiering, and service. He furnished and still furnishes many recruits to what used to be known as the Pânrê regiments, the numbers of which have been in recent years much reduced. He is less a stickler for his dignity than the Sarwariya, and

while the latter invariably does his farming through a ploughman the former may often be seen driving his plough himself. Both will stand on the harrow (*henga*) with which the clods are broken.

Distribution of Kanaujiya Brâhmans according to the Census of 1891.

District.	Number.	District.	Number.
Dehra Dûn . . .	372	Lalitpur . . .	742
Sahâranpur . . .	387	Benares . . .	8,104
Muzaffarnagar . .	111	Mirzapur . . .	9,499
Meerut . . .	1,003	Jaunpur . . .	1,845
Bulandshahr . .	329	Ghâzipur . . .	28,004
Aligarh . . .	942	Ballia	86,382
Mathura . . .	793	Gorakhpur . . .	4,406
Agra	2,663	Basti	2,177
Farrukhâbâd . .	67,025	Azamgarh . . .	1,593
Mainpuri . . .	10,092	Kumaun . . .	1,603
Etâwah . . .	51,910	Garhwâl . . .	497
Etah	1,220	Tarâi	1,413
Bareilly . . .	5,910	Lucknow . . .	39,428
Bijnor . . .	701	Unâo	120,301
Budâun . . .	1,043	Râê Bâreli . . .	83,284
Morâdâbâd . . .	915	Sîtapur	98,766
Shâhjahânpur . .	43,545	Hardoi . . .	110,358
Pilibhît . . .	11,823	Kheri	64,237
Cawnpur . . .	168,360	Faizâbâd . . .	2,965
Fatehpur . . .	60,553	Gonda	21,549
Bânda . . .	38,963	Bahrâich . . .	27,799
Hamîrpur . . .	24,269	Sultânpur . . .	3,260
Allahâbâd . . .	12,548	Partâbgarh . . .	587
Jhânsi . . .	2,119	Bârabanki . . .	57,083
Jâlaun . . .	20,185	Total .	1,303,348

Kându.[1]—(Sanskrit *Kandayika,* "a baker;" *Kandu,* "an iron cooking vessel.") A tribe usually classed, as at the last Census, as a sub-caste of Banyas. Mr. Risley treats them in Bengal as equivalent to Bharbhûnja, Bhujâri, and Gonr, and calls them "the grain-parching caste of Bihâr and Bengal, supposed to be descended from a Kahâr father and a Sûdra mother, and ranking among the mixed castes."[2] Writing of Gorakhpur, Dr. Buchanan says[3]:—"The Kândus are reckoned among the Vaisyas, although a great part of them are mere farmers, nor do their women parch grain; but many keep shops, and the term Vaisya here seems merely to imply merchant, and is almost unconnected with caste. The Kândus are considered on a level with the lower Banyas." Mr. Sherring seems to have thought them to be a sub-caste of Bharbhûnjas. In Ballia the name seems to be synonymous with the Halwâi. The fact appears to be that the Kându practises many allied occupations in connection with the preparation and selling of the minor articles of food, and his exact status is not very easily determined. In Bengal and Bihâr they have, according to Mr. Risley, ten sub-castes—Madhesiya; Magahiya; Bantariya or Bharbhûnja; Kanaujiya; Gonr; Koranch; Dhuriya; Rawâni; Ballamtiriya; and Thather or Thathera. In Ballia they name three sub-castes—Kanaujiya; Madhesiya or "residents of the middle kingdom" (*Madhyadesa*), who are also known as Guninâthi and Tanchara or Tachara. These again are divided into a number of sections (*mûl, kuri*), some of which are Khula, Ganga-pâni, Belwâr, Khopadiha, and Dahkaich, all of which are different from any in Mr. Risley's lists, and thus illustrate the remarkable fertility with which these sections are developed. In Mirzapur Madhesiya appears to be the only sub-caste except the Gonr. In Gorakhpur Dr. Buchanan found the Madhyadesiya, Kanaujiya, Gonr, and Chanchara.

2. There is also a certain difference of function between these sub-castes. In the Eastern Districts the Kanaujiya and Madhesiya seem chiefly to parch grain, while many of the Gonr, at least in Mirzapur, work at stone-cutting. Further east, according to Mr. Risley, the Madhesiya and Bantariya adhere strictly to their hereditary profession of parching grain and selling sweetmeats;

---

[1] Based on enquiries at Mirzapur and notes by Bâbu Padam Deonârâyan Sinh of Ballia and Munshi Râmsaran Dâs of Faizâbâd.

[2] *Tribes and Castes,* I., 414.

[3] *Eastern India,* II., 465.

the Kanaujiya sub-caste are said to make saltpetre; while the Madhesiya Guriya are cultivators, personal servants, and thatchers of houses; the Gonr cut and dress stones, sell sweetmeats, or act as personal servants in the houses of zamîndârs. Grain-parching, building mud walls, brick-laying, and thatching are the characteristic occupations of the Koranch, while the Dhuriya and Rawâni carry palanquins and make sweetmeats. All the sub-castes, or at any rate their women, practise grain-parching more or less; and the separation of each group from the main body seems to have been due either to geographical position or to the circumstance of the males of the group adopting other occupations in addition to their hereditary profession. The Dhuriya and Rawâni rank lowest of all, owing either to their having taken up the comparatively menial profession of palanquin-bearing, or to their being branches of the Kahâr caste, who went in for grain-parching and thus came to be associated with the Kândus. These two inter-marry with each other. All the other sub-castes are endogamous.

Rule of exogamy.

3. The rule of exogamy of the Kândus is thus stated in Ballia: they marry within their own sub-caste, but not within their own section (*mûl, kuri*); they do not marry in their own family, or in that of their maternal uncle, or in that of their father's maternal uncle. Some are more scrupulous still, and do not marry in the family of their mother's or grandfather's maternal uncle. They cannot marry the children of their mother's sister. They may marry two sisters; but the elder must be married before the younger. In Mirzapur they state the rule in this form: they do not marry in their own family, in the family of their maternal uncle and father's sister, till three generations have passed. According to Mr. Risley the rules of exogamy in Bihâr are not very well defined. In Faizâbâd they cannot marry within seven degrees on the father's and mother's side.

Marriage rules.

4. Marriage is both infant and adult, but the former is more respectable and more common. Sexual license before marriage is neither recognised nor tolerated. In Mirzapur they say that a man can take a second wife in the lifetime of the first, only with her consent; in Faizâbâd polygamy is allowed with a limit of three wives at the same time. Marriage is of the usual three forms—*charhaua* or *shâdi*, of which the binding part is the giving away of the bride (*kanyâdân*) by her father and the marking of the parting of her hair with red-lead

(*sindurdân*) by the bridegroom; the *dola* marriage, in which all the ceremonies are done at the house of the bridegroom, is used only by poor people; widows are married by the *sagâi* or *dharewa* form, in which the only ceremony is that the man applies red-lead to the parting of the woman's hair and feasts the clansmen. The levirate prevails under the usual condition that it is only the younger brother of the deceased who can take his widow. The woman can, however, marry an outsider, usually a widower, if she pleases. There is no regular tribal law of divorce; but a man can turn out his wife for infidelity; if her paramour be a man of another caste, she is permanently expelled; if he be a clansman, she can be restored to caste privileges on her parents paying a fine, which is spent on entertaining the tribal council.

Religion.

5. The Kândus are all Hindus: some are professedly Vaishnavas and some Sâktas; but few are regularly initiated into any sect. They regard themselves in Ballia as the descendants of a saint named Guninâth, and all fines for breaches of caste discipline are realised in his name. They do not appear to have any definite traditions regarding this worthy. Some of them worship the Pânchonpîr and two goddesses—Sati and Bandi Mâi. In Bihâr, according to Mr. Risley, "the Gonr sub-caste worship once a month a small silver image of Bandi Mâi; and on the tenth day of the Dasahara festival they wash the chisel, hammer and T-square, which they use for stone-cutting, and worship these tools with libations of butter. The Koranch also worship Bandi, but make her image of cloth, like a doll." In Ballia they also worship Mahâbîr and the sun godling—Sûraj Nârâyan. In Mirzapur some get themselves initiated into the Râmanandi and Kabîrpanthi sects, and worship in addition Chausati, the Pânchonpîr, Hanumân, Bhâgawati, and Singursâl. The worship of the Pânchonpîr is done in the usual way. To Hanumân they offer sweetmeats, sacred threads (*janeu*) and pieces of cloth on a Tuesday in the month of Sáwan. To Chausati they present flowers, cakes, sweets (*halwa*), and occasionally in time of trouble they sacrifice a young pig. To Singursâl they give two cakes, some *halwa* sweetmeat, and a young pig at the completion of a marriage and at the birth of a son.

Occupation.

6. As already said, their occupations are varied. In Faizâbâd they make sugar and sugar-candy, parch grain, and work as masons and agriculturists. In

Ballia they make and sell sweetmeats, parch grain, and go about the villages buying up corn, which they carry to market on oxen. They also keep grain and grocery shops. Some are landlords and some cultivators. In Mirzapur they deal in grain and flour, etc., make and sell sweetmeats, and act as money-changers. The Gonr sub-caste cut and sell stone.

Social rules.

7. Those who become initiated in one of the Vaishnava sects do not eat meat or drink spirits; those who are not initiated eat goat's flesh, mutton, and fish, and drink spirits. They will eat *kachchi* cooked by a Brâhman or clansman, and drink water from the hands of a Kahâr or Bâri. To the east of the Province they employ Sarwariya Brâhmans as their priests, and these are received on terms of equality by other Brâhmans.

Distribution of Kândus according to the Census of 1891.

DISTRICT.	Number.	DISTRICT.	Number.
Bulandshahr	1	Ghâzipur	24,585
Mathura	4	Ballia	35,935
Agra	27	Gorakhpur	49,715
Farrukhâbâd	2	Basti	11,460
Bareilly	3	Azamgarh	18,815
Cawnpur	28	Lucknow	31
Fatehpur	16	Hardoi	1
Bânda	3	Kheri	938
Jhânsi	1	Faizâbâd	8,857
Benares	4,155	Gonda	3,690
Mirzapur	1,002	Bahrâich	4,927
Jaunpur	4,741	Sultânpur	112
		TOTAL	169,049

Kanet.—A sept of Râjputs found in considerable numbers in Dehra Dûn. Of the Kanets Mr. Ibbetson writes:[1]—"The Kanets are the low caste cultivating class of all the Eastern Himalayas of the Panjâb and the Hills at their base, as far west as Kulu and the eastern portion of the Kângra District, throughout which tract they form a very large proportion of the total population. The country they inhabit is held or governed by Hill Râjputs of

[1] *Panjâb Ethnography*, 268.

pre-historic ancestry, the greater part of whom are far too proud to cultivate with their own hands, and who employ the Kanets as husbandmen. The Kanets claim to be of impure Râjput origin, but there is little doubt that they are really of aboriginal stock. The whole question of their origin is elaborately discussed by General Cunningham.[1] He identifies them with the Kunindas or Kulindas of the Sanskrit classics and of Ptolemy, and is of opinion that they belong to that great Khasa race which, before the Aryan invasion, occupied the whole sub-Himalayan tract from the Indus to the Brahmaputra, and which, driven up to the Hills by the advancing wave of immigration, now separates the Aryans of India from the Turanians of Tibet. But the Kanets are divided into two great tribes, the Khasiya and the Râo, and it is probable the Khasiyas are really descended from intercourse between the Aryan immigrants and the women of the Hills. The process by which the Khas tribe of Nepâl thus grew up is admirably described by Mr. Hodgson in his Essay on the military tribes of that country, which is quoted at some length by General Cunningham. The distinction between Khasiya and Râo is still sufficiently well marked —a Khasiya observes the period of impurity after the death of a relation prescribed for a twice-born man; the Râo that prescribed for an outcast. The Khasiya wears the sacred thread, while the Râo does not. But the distinction is apparently breaking down, at least in Kulu, where the two tribes freely eat together and intermarry, though the Khasiya, if asked, will deny the fact."

Kânhpuriya.—A Râjput sept in Oudh who were portions of the same wave of Hindu immigration as the Bais about the middle of the sixteenth Century. They trace their descent from the celebrated Rishi Bhâradwaja, and the birth of their eponymous hero Kânh is thus told[2]:—The Saint Suchh lived at Manikpur in the reign of Mânik Chand, whose only daughter he married. She appears in many legends, contracted many alliances, and by each transmitted the Râj and the Gaharwâr blood. By this marriage two sons were born, one of whom turned Brâhman and the other Chhatri. The Chhatri was Kânh, who married a Bais girl, abandoned Mânikpur, and founded the village of Kânhpur, on the road between Salon and Partâbgarh, whence the sept takes its name. The tribe deity of the clan is the Mahesa Râkshasa, or buffalo demon, to whom they offer one buffalo at every third Bijay Dasmîn feast, and another for every wedding

[1] *Archæological Reports*, XIV., 125, *sqq.*
[2] Benett, *Clans of Râê Bareli*, 9; *Oudh Gazetteer*, I., 56.

or birth which has occurred since the last sacrifice. The importance of this legend lies in the fact that all the leading tribes, of whose immigration there can be no doubt, retain distinct legends of their former home. Here it is admitted that the founder of the tribe in these parts was also the first of his people who was admitted into the Hindu caste system, as his father the Rishi and his anchorite ancestors were, of course, of no caste at all. By another account[1] the sept is sprung from one Chuchu Pânrê, who was a devotee of the Rishi Bhâradwaja at Allahâbâd. The great Gaharwâr Râja Mânik Chand had no sons, though he had tried to win one by marrying at his own expense the daughters of thousands of indignant Brâhmans. So at last he gave his adopted daughter, whom his Râni had picked up at the Mânikpur Ghât on the Ganges, to Chuchu Pânrê, and her son was Kânh, the founder of the sept. Their legend is also involved with that of the so-called Bhar Râjas Tiloki and Biloki, who, as has been shown in connection with the Bhars, had no historical existence.

2. In Sultânpur they are reported to take brides from the Bilkhariya, Tashaiya, Chandauriya, Kath Bais, Bhâlê Sultân, Raghubansi, Râjkumâr, Bachgoti, and Bandhalgoti; to give brides to the Tilokchandi Bais, Chauhâns of Mainpuri, Sûrajbansi of Mahul, Gautam of Nagar, and Bisen of Majhauli. They claim to belong to the Bhâradwaja *gotra*.

Distribution of the Kânhpuriya Râjputs according to the Census of 1891.

District.	Number.	District.	Number.
Dehra Dûn . . .	37	Azamgarh . . .	20
Sahâranpur . . .	2	Lucknow . . .	62
Farrukhâbâd . . .	5	Unâo . . .	72
Mainpuri . . .	8	Râê Bareli . . .	7,824
Etâwah . . .	4	Sîtapur . . .	94
Cawnpur . . .	70	Hardoi . . .	3
Bânda . . .	3	Kheri . . .	10
Allahâbâd . . .	517	Faizâbâd . . .	188
Lalitpur . . .	7	Bahrâich . . .	74
Benares . . .	36	Sultânpur . . .	4,515
Jaunpur . . .	383	Partâbgarh . . .	5,724
Gorakhpur . . .	73		
Basti . . .	1	Total .	19,734

[1] Carnegy, *Notes*, 40.

Kanjar.[1]—A name applied to an aggregate of vagrant tribes of a gypsy character, and probably Dravidian origin, which are found generally distributed throughout the Province. The name has been derived from the Sanskrit *kánana-chara*, in the sense of a "wanderer in the jungle;" but it is perhaps quite as likely that it does not come from any Aryan root. There can be little doubt that the Kanjars are a branch of the great nomadic race which includes the Sânsiya, Hâbûra, Beriya, Bhâtu and more distant kindred, such as the Nat, Banjâra, Baheliya. This appears to be clear from their sub-castes. One correspondent, giving the popular native idea of the affiliation of these gypsy tribes, classes them in twelve divisions :—

(*a*) Kuchbandiya, who make the *kúnch*, or brush used by weavers for cleaning thread, the *sirki* or roofing mat, dig the *khas-khas* grass used for making *tattis*, twist rope, hunt wolves, and catch vermin.

(*b*) Nat, who is a tumbler and gymnast, dances on a rope, or walks on stilts.

(*c*) Turkata, who takes his name from the *tur*, or weaver's brush, and is a quack doctor, and sells herbs and drugs, which he collects in the jungle.

(*d*) Beriya, who prostitutes his women and trains them to sing and dance.

(*e*) Beldâr, who wanders about and works at digging tanks and building mud walls.

(*f*) Chamarmangta, who cleans the wax out of ears, does cupping, and extracts carious teeth.

(*g*) Sânsiya, who begs and, when occasion serves, commits theft and dakâiti.

(*h*) Dom, who kills dogs, acts as a scavenger and executioner.

(*i*) Bhâtu, who lives by stealing and thieving cattle.

(*j*) Qalandar, who trains monkeys and bears to dance, and makes articles of tin for sale.

(*k*) Baheliya, who is a fowler and hunter.

(*l*) Jogi, who is a snake-charmer and blows the *tomri*, or gourd pipe.

It would perhaps be too much to say that the ethnological

---

[1] Based on enquiries at Mirzapur and notes by Bâbu J. G. Banerji, Râê Bareli, and the Deputy Inspectors of Schools, Agra, Shâhjahânpur, Budâun, Pilibhit, Bijnor, and in particular Munshi Maidayâl Sinh of Aligarh.

iden'ity of these tribes is fully established; but that they are all pretty much of the same social grade, and that they approximate to a large degree in occupation and function, is quite certain.

Tribal legends.

2. There is not much in their tribal legends, so far as they have been recorded, which throws light on their history or origin. They trace their descent to their deified ancestor Mâna, who is known as Mâna Guru, and his wife Nathiya Kanjarin, who used to live in the jungle, and made their living by hunting and plunder. Mandohar was the mother of Mâna, but further than this his origin is a blank. One story runs that Mâna once went to Delhi to practise his trade of a brush-maker. The Emperor of Delhi had at that time two famous wrestlers, Kallu and Mallu, who were the champions of the world. They were particularly noted for their skill in swinging the athletes' chain bow (*lezam*). Mâna happened to pass by and, taking the bow, plunged it so deep in the ground that no one could withdraw it. When the Emperor heard of this, he sent for Mâna and made him wrestle with his champions. He defeated them easily and was dismissed with a great reward.

Tribal organisation.

3. The tribal organisation of the Kanjars is, as might have been expected, complex. The last Census divides them into four main sub-castes—Jallâd or "executioners;" Kûnchband or "brush-makers;" Pattharkat or "stone-cutters," which, according to Mr. Nesfield, connects them with the Age of Stone; and Râchhband or "makers of the weaver's comb." All these divisions are thus purely occupational. Mr. Nesfield in his interesting account of the tribe[1] says that they profess to have seven clans, of whom five are well established, and four can be explained by their crafts—Maraiya or "worshippers of Mari;" Bhains, "buffalo-keepers;" Sankat, "stone-cutters" (the Pattharkat of the Census enumeration); Gohar, "catchers of the iguana" (*goh*); and Soda. The enumeration given by a correspondent from Aligarh seems to be the most accurate and complete. He divides them into two main branches—Kûnchband and Jallâd or Sûpwâla, "makers of sieves." Of the Kûnchband there are nine sections—Maraiya, "worshippers of Mari;" Bhains, "buffalo-men;" Sankat, "stone-cutters;" Soda; Kâra; Lakarhâr or "wood-men;" Goher, "iguana-catchers;" Sonra; and Untwâr or "camel-

[1] *Calcutta Review*, LXXVII., 368, *sqq.*

men." Most of these names are found in lists received from other parts of the Province. Thus from Etâwah we have Maraiya, Sonra, Sonrasen, Bhains, and Gohera; from Shâhjahânpur, Maraiya, Soda, Goher, Untwâr, Lohiya or "iron-men," and Lakarha or "wood-men;" from Mirzapur one list gives Kanaujiya, Sankat, Sonra, Bhanes, Maraiya, and Baid or "physician." Another gives Kanaujiya, Bhains, Son, Maraiya, Ekthauliya Bhains, and Khatâniya; a third shows Untwâr, Bhains, Kanaujiya, Sonra, who say they take their name from *soa*, dill or fennel, Maraiya, Sankat, and Barâriya or "immigrants from Barâr." From Agra we get a list which mixes up occupational names of allied castes—Kûnchband; Singiwâla or "cuppers by means of a cow horn (*singi*);" Kanghiwâla "comb-makers," who, when they become rich, call themselves Banjâra and deal in oxen; Kabûtarwâla or Brajbâsi, who are really rope-dancing Nats; Baddhik; Hâbûra; Nat; and Barua, who catch and exhibit snakes. In Bijnor there are two sections—the true Kanjars and the Adhela Kanjars, who are of mixed descent. It is significant that the Bhains section of Budâun have changed their name into Baiswâr, and are beginning to claim a connection with the Bais Râjputs. In short the caste is, at present, in a transitional stage and is breaking up into functional groups, as they gradually become settled and shed off their old gypsy habits and mode of life.

4. In Aligarh, again, we have another and quite separate subdivision, with whom the more respectable, or Kûnchband Kanjars, admit no connection. These Jallâd or Sûpwâla Kanjars have eleven sections—Dhobibans, "of washerman race;" Sirkiband, "makers of roof mats;" Jhijhotiya, who take their name from Jhijhoti, the old name for Bundelkhand; Chanâl or Chandâl, "outcasts;" Kedâr, probably from Kidârnâth; Ghamra, "lazy, stupid;" Mattu, "earthmen;" Ghussar, "intruders"; Bhâru, "carriers"; Pattari, "leafmen"; Bohat, "sowers." These are their own explanations, and must, of course, be accepted with caution. These people are said to speak a Panjâbi dialect, and they are, as we shall see, followers of Nânak. With them the Kûnchband Kanjars deny all connection.

5. The 106 section names of the Hindu and 6 of the Muhammadan branch recorded in the Census returns are of the ordinary type. Many of them suggest connection with other tribes, such as Bais, Banjâra, Bhangiwâla, Bind, Chauhân, Hâbûra, Jâdonbansi, Kachhwâha, Lâlbegi, Lodha, Luniya, Mewâti, Râjbansi, Râj-

kumâ:, Râjput, Râikwâra, Râmjani, Râthaur, Sûrajbansi, and Thâkur. Many, again, are of local origin, such as Agarwâl, Ajudhyabâsi, Allahâbâdi, Bâtham from Srâvasti as well as Sribâsta Bihârwâla, Bangâli, Gangwâr, Jaiswâr, Kanaujiya, Karnâtak, Mainpuriya, Nizâmâbâdi, Panjâbi, Saksena, Sarwariya. We find, again, many occupational titles, Jallâd, "executioner;" Kûnchbandh, "brush-maker;" Kusbandhiya, "collector of sacred grass;" Pahalwân, "athlete;" Pattharkat, "stone-cutter;" Phânswâr, "strangler;" Sapera, "snake-man;" and Sirkiwâla, "he that lives under a mat."

Marriage rules.

The two great Aligarh sub-castes, Kûnchband and Jallâd or Sûpwâla, are endogamous, and the sections are exogamous. All the sub-castes mentioned in the Agra and Bijnor lists are also endogamous. Among the exogamous sections there is also the additional law, which is not very clearly defined, which bars the marriage of near cognates. Among the more civilised Kanjars adult marriage appears to be the general rule. In Mirzapur they have a custom of what is known as "womb betrothal," in which two fathers engage their children still unborn; this is known as *pet manganiya.* Widow marriage and the levirate are both allowed, the latter under the usual restriction that the widow may marry the younger, not the elder, brother of her late husband.

Marriage ritual.

7. Writing of the vagrant branch of the tribe Mr. Nesfield says:—"Their marriage customs are quite distinct from those of Hindus. There is no betrothal in childhood; no selection of auspicious days; and no elaborate ceremonies or ritual. The father, or other near relatives of the youth, goes to the father of the girl, and after winning his favour with a pot of toddy, and gaining his consent to the marriage of his daughter, he seals the bargain with a gift of money or some tool or animal which Kanjars love. The girl selected is never a blood relation to the intended husband, and she is almost always of some other encampment or gang.[1] A few days after the bargain has been made the youth goes with his father and as many other men as he can collect, all in their best attire and armed with their best weapons, and demands the girl in tones which imply that he is ready to seize her by force if she is refused. The girl is always

[1] On this see Westermarck, *History of Human Marriage*, 332, *sqq.*

peacefully surrendered in virtue of the previous compact, and this demonstration of force is a mere form—a survival of the primitive world-wide custom of marriage by capture.[1] On the arrival of the Kanjar bride at the encampment of her intended mate, a few simple ceremonies are performed. A pole is fixed in a mound of earth, and on the top of the pole is tied a bunch of the *khaskhas* root, or anything else that may be equally fitted to serve as an emblem of the Kanjar industries. The bridegroom takes the girl by the hand, and leads her several times round the pole in the presence of the spectators. A sacrifice of roast pig or goat, with libations of toddy, is then offered to Mâna, as the ancestral hero of the tribe, and songs are sung in his honour. When this is finished, there is a general feast and dance, in which every one at last gets drunk. The father of the bride does not give away his daughter without a dowry. This consists in a patch of forest supposed to be his own, which becomes thenceforth the property of the bridegroom, so long as the encampment remains near the place or whenever it may return to it. No one without the bridegroom's consent will be authorised to use this piece of forest for hunting, trapping, digging roots of *khaskhas*, etc."[2]

8. A Kanjar marriage was thus described by a number of members of the tribe at Mirzapur :—As circumstances require, either the father of the girl or the boy arranges the match. They do not go on this mission themselves, but depute one of their relations. When the preliminary arrangements are complete, the fathers on both sides go and inspect the boy and girl to make sure that there is no physical defect in either. Next follows the betrothal, when the boy's father with two or three friends goes to the house of the bride and the two fathers embrace with the salutation *Rám ! Rám !* Then, contrary to the ordinary Hindu custom, the father of the youth pays for a dinner of pork, rice, pulse, and liquor for his companions and the friends of the bride. All of them then join in singing, and this constitutes the betrothal (*mangani*). Next morning the youth's father returns home with his friends, and then the marriage follows as soon as may be convenient.

9. The fathers on both sides get their village Brâhman to fix a lucky hour for commencing the preparations. One of the friends

---

[1] Westermarck, *History of Human Marriage*, 383, *sqq*.

[2] *Cf. Korwa*, para. 10.

conveys an invitation to the guests. When the youth's party goes to the girl's house, it is accompanied by all the women and children of the family—another violation of Hindu custom. There is no wave ceremony (*parachhan*) at the bride's door. When the party has arrived, the Brâhman is again asked to fix an auspicious hour for the marriage. Both the fathers each arrange a separate marriage shed before the house of the bride. These consist of four bamboos, one at each corner, with a bamboo and a plough beam set up in the centre, a wooden representation of parrots, and a vessel of water, over which are laid some mango leaves and *kusa* grass On the top of this they place a saucer full of *urad* pulse, and upon it a lamp is lighted. A grindstone and rice-pounder are also placed in the pavilion. The boy's father shoots an arrow into the air, and from the spot on which it falls the women bring some earth, which is placed in the shed, and not used, as among other castes, for making the fire-place on which the wedding dinner is cooked. When the lucky hour comes, the youth goes into the girl's pavilion, and the women of her family bring out the bride. The pair are bathed in the pavilion, and the girl is dressed in a white sheet, and the boy in a new suit, coat, turban, and drawers, all white. These clothes must be of unwashed cloth. The boy sits on a piece of *sirki* mat facing west, and the girl on another mat opposite him, facing east. He then rubs red-lead seven times on the parting of her hair and the bride's sister knots their clothes together, and they move round seven times, the youth in front, and the girl behind. This ceremony is generally done at such a late hour of night that none but the immediate friends of the parties are witnesses; it is considered very unlucky for a stranger to be present. Then his sister takes off the boy's marriage crown (*maur*) and places it in a sieve, which she lays in the shed, and all present are supposed to put a small contribution in it. Out of this liquor is purchased, and all present drink and sing until the morning.

10. Next morning the bride and bridegroom sit down and make cakes (*pûri*) together. The girl cooks those the boy kneads, and *vice versâ*. Each makes seven cakes in this way. Then the women of the family take the pair to worship Ganga Mâi, and the cakes which they have made are offered to her. When the Ganges is far off, any tank or stream answers for the worship. When this is done the pair return to the pavilion and gamble there. Some rings and cowries are put into a jar, and the boy and girl

plunge their hands in; whichever succeeds in getting the mos , will rule the other during their married life. They are then taken to the retiring room (*kohabar*), a rite which, as elsewhere explained, implies the immediate consummation of the marriage. The walls of this room are decorated with various marks, the significance of which is now lost. These marks the pair worship by rubbing them with a little ghi. Then the bride feeds her husband seven times with curds and molasses, and he does the same for her. They have nothing corresponding to the Hindu *gauna* ceremony. The bride is sent home at once with her husband. As she is going away her father gives her whatever dowry he can afford. All the marriage ceremonies are performed by the clansmen, and no Brâhman is employed. In Aligarh there is a curious ceremony which appears to be symbolical of marriage by capture. After the marriage, the pair are taken to a neighbouring tank and the bride strikes her husband with a small whip specially made of cloth for this purpose. In Aligarh the widow marriage rite takes a very simple form. There is no betrothal, and when the match is arranged, the brethren are assembled and the bride's father or some kinsman knots the clothes of the pair together and the bride is invested with a set of green glass bangles (*chûri*), which are provided by the person who ties the marriage knot. The Kûnchband Kanjars make the women on this occasion wear a loin-cloth (*dhoti*) and not a petticoat (*lahnga*), among the Jallâd or Sûpwâla Kanjars, on the contrary, the bangles for the bride are provided by the bridegroom, and he supplies the marriage feast; besides this, the Jallâd bride wears a petticoat and not a loin-cloth. At all their marriages the *gadaila* or digging implement with which they dig *khaskhas* and kill wolves or vermin is placed in the marriage pavilion during the ceremony. From Etah it is reported that when the match is finally arranged, the wedding day is fixed. The bride's father sends for the bridegroom when all the arrangements are complete. No Brâhmans are employed. First what is known as the *darwâza* or door rite is performed, most of which consists in the waving of a tray on which some milk, ghi, and a lamp are placed over the head of the youth by the mother of the girl. Then the *bhânwar* or circumambulation rite is done. This is always done by the sister of the bride, her husband, or daughter, in which we may possibly see a survival of the matriarchate.

Birth ceremonies.

11. The mother during delivery lies on the ground with her feet to the north and her head to the south. The sweeper midwife cuts the cord, and the mother is then attended by the women of her own family. No ceremonies are performed during pregnancy. Among the Kûnchband Kanjars, when a child is born, the brethren are assembled, and treacle and rice are distributed by the father. This is known as *bihâi*, and is intended as a propitiation of the goddess of that name who rules the fate of the infant. Then some old man of the family or some connection by marriage (*mân*) names the child. On the sixth day (*chhathi*) the women assemble and sing songs and dance in the room in which the child was born. At the dinner, which is usually given on this occasion, the males are fed on wheaten cakes and the women on rice. Among the Etah Kanjars the mother and child are bathed on the third day and the child is named by an old man of the tribe.

Death rites.

12. Speaking of the vagrant branch of the tribe Mr. Nesfield says—"There are three different modes in which Kanjars dispose of their dead—submersion in deep water by fastening a stone to the corpse, cremation, and burial. Each clan disposes of its dead according to its own hereditary and special rites. The first method is the least common; the next may have been borrowed from the Hindu rite, which was itself imported by the Aryan tribes from Persia; the last is the one most frequently practised as well as most highly esteemed. A man who has acted as a spirit medium to Mâna is invariably buried in the earth, to whatever clan he may have belonged. Mâna himself was so buried at Kâra (as some Kanjars relate) in the Allahâbâd District, not far from the Ganges, and facing the old fort of Mânikpur on the opposite bank. Three days after the corpse has been disposed of, there is a feast of vegetables and milk, but no meat; and a similar feast is held on the seventh day. A third banquet is afterwards given on any day which may be found convenient, and at the banquet flesh and wine are freely consumed. When both the parents of a man have died, a fourth feast is given in their joint honour. In all these feasts it is the soul of the dead which is fed, or meant to be fed, rather than the bodies of the living." In Mirzapur they invariably bury their dead. A cloth is spread over the corpse, and the brethren attend and drink spirits. Then it is removed to the grave. After the burial they bathe, eat molasses,

and come home. Beyond the distribution of spirits and molasses to the mourners by the relatives of the deceased, there is no feast on the day of the funeral. On the tenth day the brethren are fed and treated to liquor. No sacred balls (*pinda*) are offered, and no Brâhmans are entertained. On the anniversary of the death, the brethren are fed and treated to spirits. On this day one *pinda* is offered by the chief mourner. They observe the fortnight of the dead (*pitra-paksha*), not like ordinary Hindus on the first, but in the second fortnight of Kuâr, which Hindus call the "fortnight of the gods" (*deva-paksha*). In Aligarh they usually bury their dead, but sometimes expose the corpse in the jungle. In burial the corpse is laid with the feet to the north and the head to the south. It is first washed by the eldest male member of the family and shrouded in a white sheet. A bier is made of bamboos tied together with red thread (*kaláwa*), and four of the brethren take it to the burial ground. On the way, it is once laid on the ground and each man puts a little earth near the head of the corpse. This is known as the "stage" (*manzil*). After the grave is dug, the son of the deceased, or, in his absence, some other chief mourner, burns the left thumb of the dead man with fire, and then the body is interred. On returning, bread and sugar are served out to the mourners, and on the third day (*tíja*) they have a dinner of cakes and pulse. The Jallâd Kanjars dispose of their dead in the same way except that they do not burn the thumb of the corpse. The Kûnchband Kanjars offer water to the manes during the nine days of Kuâr, known as the Naurâtri; this the Jallâds do not do. In Etah they are in the intermediate stage between burial and cremation, and both practices prevail. Some bury only the unmarried dead. On the funeral day the brethren are fed, and also on the third and seventh, and on the anniversary. They have no *terahwín* or thirteenth day rite.

Religion

13. Writing of the vagrant Kanjars Mr. Nesfield says—"The religion of the Kanjars, so far as we have been able to learn, is quite what we should expect among a primitive and uncultivated people. It is a religion without idols, without temples, and without a priesthood. They live in constant dread of evil spirits, the souls of the departed, who are said to enter the bodies of the living as a punishment for past misdeeds or neglect of burial rites, and to produce most of the ills to which flesh is heir. In this creed they stand on

the same intellectual level with their more civilised kinsfolk, the Hindus, among whom it is universally believed that the air is peopled with *bhûts*, malignant spirits, who haunt grave-yards, lurk in trees, re-animate corpses, devour living men, or attack them with madness, epilepsy, cramp, etc. They have no belief in natural death, except as the effect of old age. All deaths, but those caused by natural decay or violence, are ascribed to the agency of evil spirits. The dead are buried five or six feet deep, lest a wild beast should tear up the carcase, and, by disturbing the body, send forth its attendant soul to vex and persecute the living. When a patient is possessed, they employ an exorcist or spirit medium, whom they call Nyotiya, to compel the spirit to declare what his grievance is, so that satisfaction may be given him, and he may thus be induced to leave his victim in peace. The spirit medium has power, they say, to transport the goblin into the body of some living person, and to make that person his mouth-piece for declaring its will.

14. "The man-god whom the Kanjars worship is Mâna, a name which does not appear in the lists of Hindu deities. He is something more than what Mitthu Bhukhiya is to the Banjâra, Manjha to the Riwâri, Alha and Udal to the Bundela, Râê Dâs to the Chamâr, Lâl Guru to the Bhangi or Nânak to the Sikh. Mâna is worshipped with more ceremony in the rainy season, when the tribe is less migratory, than in the dry months of the year. On such occasions, if sufficient notice is circulated, several encampments unite temporarily to pay honour to their common ancestor. No altar is raised, no image is erected. The worshippers collect near a tree, under which they sacrifice a pig, a goat, a sheep, a fowl, make an offering of roasted flesh and spirituous liquor. Formerly, it is said, they used to sacrifice a child, having first made it insensible with fermented palm-juice or toddy. They dance round the tree in honour of Mâna, and sing the customary songs in commemoration of his wisdom and deeds of valour." There is then a funeral feast at which most of the banqueters get drunk, and occasionally one of them declares himself to be under the special influence of the god and delivers oracles. The Kanjar goddesses are Mari, Parbha, and Bhuiyân. Mari, the goddess of death, is also known as Mahârâni Devi, and is supreme, and appears to be worshipped as the animating and sustaining principle of nature. Parbha or Prabha, meaning "light," is the goddess of health, and more particularly of the health

of cattle. She is also worshipped by Ahîrs and similar tribes. Bhuiyân, also known as Bhawâni, is the earth goddess.

15. In Mirzapur the Kanjars seem to depend most on the worship of their deceased ancestors. They say that their dead are more kindly than those of other low castes, because they do not require an annual worship, and are satisfied if at marriages and other festive occasions a leaf platter of food is placed on their graves. Their clan deities are Dhâmin Deva and Mâna, the Pahlwân or wrestler. The graves of these worthies, who are the deified ancestors of the tribe, are at Mânikpur, and there they make occasional pilgrimages, and offer the sacrifice of a pig and an oblation of spirits. They are very careful about the disposal of the offering. It is eaten in secresy and silence by the male worshippers, and no woman or stranger to the tribe is allowed to be present or share in the meal. In Mirzapur, like the Hindus around them, they also pay reverence to the Vindhyabâsini Devi of Bindhâchal, and have their children's heads shaved at her shrine. They also revere the Pânchonpîr with the sacrifice of a cock. In Aligarh the Kûnchband Kanjars call themselves Sâktas, and have a preference for the worship of Devi; while the Jallâd or Sûpwâla call themselves Nânakpanthis and worship Nânak Guru. At Bijaygarh in the Aligarh District the Kûnchband Kanjars have a platform (*chabûtra*) raised in honour of Mâna and Nathiya, the deified ancestors of the tribe. Their feast day is the sixth of the light half of Bhâdon, when they make an offering of spirits, one rupee four annas in cash, a young pig, and an *usar-sânda* lizard to these deities. They have another, whom they call Deota or "the godling." His shrine is at Dhanipur, close to Aligarh, and he is worshipped on a Sunday or Tuesday in the month of Asârh with an offering of cakes. Like many of the low castes in their neighbourhood, they also worship Jakhiya. His shrine is at Karas in the Aligarh District. His feast day is the sixth of the dark half of Mâgh, when a pig and some sweetmeats (*batâsha*) are offered to him. These are consumed by the worshippers themselves, a part being given to the Panda or sweeper priest who tends the shrine. The Jallâd or Sûpwâla Kanjars in the Aligarh District are Nânakshâhis, and make pilgrimages to his shrine at Amritsar. On the night of the Diwâli they cook the *halwa* sweetmeat and distribute it among their friends. Before they distribute it they cover the vessel with a cloth and offer it to Nânak with the words *Shukr hai tera ki baras din râzi khushi se guzra ; aur*

tujh se âgê ko yahi ummed hai—"Praise be to thee who has preserved us in happiness for a year! We hope the same favour in the future." They will not uncover the vessel till all its contents are distributed, because they believe that it increases by the supernatural power (*mâya*) of Guru Nânak. The priests of the Kûnchband Kanjars are their *mân* or relations on the female side, apparently a survival of the matriarchate; the priest of the Jallâds is called *masand*, which, according to one explanation, is a corruption of *masnad*, "the royal seat," and is selected for his knowledge of Gurmukhi. The offerings of the Kûnchband Kanjars are these—to Nathiya, a pig; to Mâna Guru, an *ûsar-sânda* lizard; to Devi, a goat; to Jakhiya, a pig; to Madâr, a fowl. The Jallâds give a goat to Nanak. The Kûnchbands sometimes offer the hair of an infant to Mâna.

Festivals.

16. The Kûnchband observe the Holi, Diwâli, Dasahra, and Janamashtami. At the Holi they drink, smoke *bhang* and *charas*, and sprinkle coloured powder about like Hindus. At the Diwâli they drink and gamble and their women make some figures on the walls of the house and at night offer boiled rice (*khîl*) and sweets (*batâsha*) to them. They have no special observance of the Dasahra and Janamashtami, except that they consider them to be holidays. On the ninth of the light half of Kuâr they make a present of food to the *mân* or relative on the female side who acts as their priest. This is done in the belief that the food thus offered passes through him to their deceased ancestors. They have a survival of grove worship in their worship of Nathiya, which is always done under some trees in which she is supposed to reside. The Jâllads make an offering to Kâli in the same way.

Demonology.

17. In cases of disease or trouble a Syâna or wizard is called in to settle the appropriate offering to the particular ghost which is the cause of the trouble. If a goat is to be offered its forehead is first marked with a *tîka*. The *imli* or tamarind tree is in particular believed to be the residence of the sacred dead. When the Kûnchband bury the dead they place a pice with the corpse as a viaticum; the Jallâds place two wheaten cakes with the same object. The technical name for this is *tosha*, which means "provisions for a journey." When a man is attacked by an evil spirit the Syâna first makes an offering to Devi, consisting of treacle, ghi, cloves, and incense, with some red-lead, which are

thrown into a fire (*agyári*). The Devi then "comes on the head" of the Syâna and he names the evil spirit who is afflicting the patient. Then a cup of spirits is placed under the head of the sick man and afterwards moved four times round his head (a process known as *utára* or "removing"), when it is drunk by the Syâna, who is supposed in this way to remove the evil influence from the patient. Finally he describes the sacrifice which it is advisable to offer. In some more serious cases the Syâna fills a saucer with cooked rice, some cloves, *batásha* sweetmeat and an egg, and places it where four roads meet; meanwhile the friends of the sick man sing and beat a brass tray over his head to scare the spirit. The disease is supposed to be communicated to some passer-by. The Churel or ghost of a woman who dies during her menses or at her confinement is much dreaded; children who die before the age of twelve return in the form of an evil spirit known as Masân. Those who die of snake-bite or any other form of unnatural death become an Aût, or a person for whom there is none to make the water oblation. All these have the same attributes, except Masân, which is dangerous only to children. The Kûnchband Kanjars offer water to the Pitri or sainted dead on the eight or ninth of the light half of Kuâr; this is done by the Jallâds on the Holi and Diwâli.

Totemism, omens, etc.

18. The Bhains and Untwâr sub-castes are probably of totemistic origin; these will not kill or eat the buffalo or camel respectively. They respect the *imli* or tamarind tree as the abode of spirits. The *khas* grass is a sort of tribal totem and it and the leaves of the mango are fixed upon the marriage shed. The Kûnchbands believe Saturday to be an unlucky day. The Jallâds have the same idea about Tuesday. As regards omens, a fox, tiger, wolf, *úsar-sánda* lizard, tortoise, and the *goh* lizard or the *sâras* crane are lucky if they cross the road from right to left; if from left to right it is an evil omen. So with a cat, jackal, or cobra passing from the right to the left. Their women do not wear a nose-ring; to the East they wear brass bangles (*máthi*) and heavy anklets (*pairi*). The Jallâd women do not wear any gold ornaments. Their chief oaths are to stand in a river up to the neck; the man who stays longest in the water is believed. They also swear on the Ganges and on the *pípal* tree, or by touching the head or arm of a son or other close relation. The Kûnchband Kanjars swear also by Mâna and Nathiya; the Jallâds by Guru Nânak. Some of them by the use of appropriate spells (*mantra*) obtain the

power of controlling evil spirits. These are recited at night in burial-grounds, and specially on the night of the Holi or Diwâli. On such occasions a burnt offering (*agyári*) is made with treacle, ghi, cloves, and incense.

Occupation and social status.

19. The Kanjars, in their occupations and mode of life, closely approximate to the European gypsy. Of the vagrant branch of the tribe Mr. Nesfield writes—"Their natural home is the forest, where they subsist by hunting wolves, hares, and any kind of animal they can kill or catch, by gathering such roots and vegetable products as require no cultivation, and by extracting juice from the palm tree, which, after it has become fermented, is the favourite beverage of almost all the wandering and low-caste tribes of India. They are clever at trapping birds and squirrels, and any other kind of vermin which chance may throw in their way, all of which they eat indiscriminately. They are never seen in groups of more than twenty or forty persons of all ages at a time, and the number is sometimes even less.[1] These little groups may unite sometimes for special and temporary objects; but large groups are never permanently formed. Among the Kanjars there are some groups or clans which make a habit of keeping within easy reach of towns and villages, while others seldom or never leave the forest. But even among the former it is not merely the proximity of settled communities which prevents the formation of larger groups. For even in wide forest tracts, where there is ample space and no impediment from higher races, the same law of petty, non-associative hordes prevails, and it would be a rare thing to find an encampment of more than, or even as many as, fifty persons."

20. "The arts of the Kanjar are making mats of the *sirki* reed baskets of wattled cane, fans of palm leaves, and rattles of plaited straw, the last of which are now sold to Hindu children as toys, though originally they were used by the Kanjars themselves (if we are to trust to the analogies of other backward races) as sacred and mysterious instruments. From the stalks of the *múnj* grass and from the roots of the *palása* tree they make ropes, which are sold or bartered to villagers in exchange for grain, milk, pigs, etc. They prepare the skins out of which drums are made, and sell them to Hindu musicians, though probably, as in the case of the rattle,

[1] On this see Spencer's *Principles of Sociology*, I., 432.

the drum was originally used by the Kanjars themselves and worshipped as a fetish : for even the Aryan tribes, who are said to have been far more advanced than the indigenous races, sung hymns in honour of the drum or *dundubhi* as if it were something sacred. They make plates of broad leaves which are ingeniously stitched together by the stalks ; and plates of this kind are very widely used by the inferior Indian castes and by confectioners and sellers of sweetmeats. The mats of *sirki* reed, with which they cover their own temporary sheds, are largely used by cart-drivers to protect their goods and themselves against rain. The toddy or juice of the palm tree, which they extract and ferment by methods of their own, and partly for their own use, finds a ready sale among low-caste Hindus in villages and market towns. They are among the chief stone-cutters of Upper India, especially in the manufacture of the grinding-stone, which is largely used. They gather the white wool-like fibre which grows in the pods of the *salmali* or Indian cotton tree, and twist it into thread for the use of weavers. In the manufacture of brushes for the cleaning of cotton yarn, they enjoy an almost entire monopoly, and another complete or almost complete monopoly enjoyed by Kanjars is the collection and sale of the roots of *khaskhas* grass, which are afterwards made up by others into door screens and used as refrigerators during the hottest months of the year. The roots of this wild grass, which grows in most abundance on the outskirts of forests or near the banks of rivers, are dug out of the earth by an instrument called *khanti*. The same implement serves as a dagger or short spear for killing wolves and jackals, as a tool for carving a secret entrance through the clay wall of a villager's hut in which a burglary is meditated, as a spade or hoe for digging snakes, field mice, lizards, etc., out of their holes, and edible roots out of the earth, and as a hatchet for chopping wood." Mr. Nesfield sees in these arts and industries the germs of many functions which have now become hereditary in the Baheliya, Bâri, Behna or Dhuniya, Chamâr, Kori, Kalwâr and others. But we know too little of the evolution of Indian handicrafts to accept such ingenious speculations with perfect confidence.

21. In his diet the Kanjar is catholic to a degree. He will eat almost anything, except beef, monkeys, crocodiles, and snakes. The Kûnchband Kanjar will not eat, drink or smoke with any caste but his own ; but he will eat *kachchi* cooked by a Chamâr. The Jallâds eat *kachchi*, drink and smoke with sweepers. To

quote Mr. Nesfield again—"Whatever a Kanjar kills, from a wolf to a reptile, he eats. The weapon with which they kill little birds is nothing but a pole pointed with a thin, sharp piece of iron. The man lies motionless on a patch of ground which he has first sprinkled with grain, and as the birds come hopping round him to pick up the grain, he fascinates one of them with the pole, by giving it a serpent-like motion, and then spikes it through the body. Kanjars seldom or never use the bow and arrow, but they use the pellet-bow, which requires much greater skill. The pellet is nothing but a little clay marble dried in the sun. With this they not infrequently shoot a bird flying. The *khanti* or short spear is merely used in close combat, but is thrown with almost unerring effect against wolves and jackals as they run. For catching a wolf in the earth they place a net and a light at one end of the hole and commence digging at the other end. The wolf, attracted by the light, runs into the net, and the Kanjar batters his head with a club and kills it."

22. At the same time many Kanjars are now taking to a more settled life: some are cultivators and field labourers; others live in towns and make door-screens, baskets, sieves, and the like, and some of them in this way have considerably raised their social status.

Kanjars are particularly careful to protect any member of the tribe from being assaulted without reason by another clansman or have his goods robbed. Such cases form the subject of a most elaborate enquiry. The tribal council sits at least fifteen days in succession, and the guilty person has to pay the whole cost of their entertainment. The offender is excommunicated until he pays a fine and the whole expenses of the proceedings. When, in Etah, a woman is accused of immorality, she is subjected to the ordeal of holding a hot iron weeding spud in her hand. If the skin is not burnt, she is acquitted.

Distribution of Kanjars according to the Census of 1881

DISTRICT.	Jallâd.	Kûnchband.	Pattharkat.	Râchhband.	Others.	Muhammadans.	TOTAL.
Dehra Dûn . . .	...	...	...	...	12	...	12
Sahâranpur . .	...	55	...	...	100	...	154
Muzaffarnagar . .	...	55	...	...	26	1	82

Distribution of Kanjars according to the Census of 1891—contd.

District.	Jallâd.	Kûnch-band.	Patt-harkat.	Râchh-band.	Others.	Muham-madans.	Total.
Meerut . .	...	...	...	...	497	...	497
Bulandshahr . . .	42	140	...	...	327	...	509
Aligarh . . .	...	...	...	...	806	...	806
Mathura . . .	...	53	9	...	220	...	282
Agra	...	355	...	...	559	1	915
Farrukhâbâd . .	33	92	...	...	310	5	440
Mainpuri . . .	...	206	...	...	252	1	459
Etâwah . . .	...	102	...	...	103	...	205
Etah	...	260	...	...	209	...	469
Bareilly . . .	228	...	...	...	141	...	369
Bijnor	...	...	...	...	205	...	205
Budâun . . .	...	61	...	...	372	...	433
Morâdâbâd . . .	28	...	...	...	545	...	573
Shâhjahânpur . .	...	71	...	34	170	...	275
Pilibhît . . .	23	83	...	...	167	141	414
Cawnpur . . .	48	1,234	...	3	477	...	1,762
Fatehpur . . .	...	143	...	...	370	...	513
Banda	...	321	...	...	...	...	321
Hamîrpur . . .	...	99	...	...	2	...	101
Allahâbâd . . .	...	51	4	...	192	25	272
Jhânsi	...	108	2	5	48	...	163
Jâlaun	...	100	...	15	36	...	151
Lalitpur . . .	...	...	66	5	...	...	71
Benares . . .	...	...	...	...	27	...	27
Mirzapur . . .	...	...	...	...	69	5	74
Jaunpur . . .	...	8	...	...	7	...	15
Ghâzipur . . .	...	60	...	...	21	...	81
Ballia	...	64	...	...	...	...	64

Distribution of Kanjars according to the Census of 1891—concld.

District.	Jallâd.	Kûnch-band.	Patt-harkat.	Râchh-band.	Others	Muham-madans.	Total.
Gorakhpur	...	87	85	...	201	...	373
Basti	...	...	417	...	848	...	1,265
Azamgarh	...	2	...	...	41	28	71
Tarâi	...	85	...	20	58	1	164
Lucknow	...	284	...	...	31	13	328
Unâo	...	35	...	...	138	...	173
Râê Bareli	...	43	30	...	10	..	83
Sîtapur	...	595	...	...	...	...	595
Hardoi	...	90	...	...	197	...	287
Kheri	...	424	...	...	251	...	675
Faizâbâd	...	73	...	...	54	...	127
Gonda	...	332	250	295	...	...	877
Bahrâich	...	542	103	67	831	...	1,543
Sultânpur	...	...	...	...	196	1	197
Partâbgarh	9	...	...	...	75	...	84
Bârabanki	...	104	55	...	115	35	309
Total	411	6,416	1,021	444	9,316	257	17,865

Kanphata (*kân*, "ear;" *phata*, "torn").—A class of Jogis, known also as Gorakhnâthi from the name of their founder or Darshani, because they wear a special earring. Of Gorakhnâth numerous legends are told. By one account he was a contemporary of the famous Bhartrihari, who is said to have been the brother of Vikramaditya. The Kanphatas themselves say that their sect existed before this world of ours came into existence. When Vishnu came out of the lotus at the creation of all things, Gorakhnâth was in Patâla or the lower regions. Vishnu, terrified at the waste of waters, went to Patâla, and implored the aid of Gorakhnâth, who, in pity for the deity, gave him a handful of ashes from his eternal fire (*dhuni*), and told him that if he sprinkled the dust over the water, he could create the world. It happened as he promised, and then Brahma, Vishnu and Siva became the first disciples of the Saint. By another story Bhartrihari happened to go into a forest where Gorakhnâth was practising austerities; but he knew not that the Saint was there. Soon after the disciples of Gorakhnâth met him and asked him to become a disciple of their master. He answered, "What do I care for Gorakhnâth? If he wishes to learn the ways of the Almighty, let him come and learn from me." Finally Gorakhnâth said to Bhartrihari—"If you give me a handful of patience (*santosh*), I will become your disciple." So Bhartrihari, in search of patience, came to the gods, but they could not supply it. At last he went to Vishnu, who said—"I cannot supply you with patience. If you want it you must go to Gorakhnâth who is the greatest of saints." Thus convinced, Bhartrihari accepted Gorakhnâth as his Guru.

Sub-divisions of the Kanphatas.

2. There are said to be twelve sections of the sect who take their name from the twelve disciples of Gorakhnâth, but none of them can even pretend to give a complete list of them. Ordinary Kanphatas know of only four: Brahma; Râma; Lakshmana and Kapilâni. A list from the Panjâb[1] gives them as follows:—Mathesri, founded by Lakshmana, a disciple of Gorakhnâth; Satnâth, who are said to follow Brahma, which is more than doubtful; Satnâth, said to be followers of Râma Chandra; Bhartrinâth, followers of Bhartrihari; Papankh; Kâmdhaj, of Dhrudhuwâra, near Jaypur; Hethjhauli, of Gorakhpur; Dhajpanth, said to be in Lanka or Ceylon; Chandbharag, in Kachh, near Dwârika; Dâs Gopâl in Jodhpur; Mastnâth, at Dhauli Momrhi, near Delhi; and Aryapanth, at Bor Bosan, near Kâbapîr Thaneswar.

The Western Kanphatas.

3. The seat of the Western Kanphatas is at Dhinodhar on the edge of the Ran of Cutch (Kachh). Of them we learn[2] that "the Dhinodhar monks, endowed by more than one of the Râos, are a rich body, living in a large, comfortably fortified and fenced monastery on a wooded knoll overlooking a little lake at the foot of Dhinodhar Hill, with temples, dwelling-houses, and the tombs of their headmen (*pîr*). Among the buildings, Dharmnâth's shrine, before which a lamp

---

[1] *Panjâb Notes and Queries*, II, 45.
[2] *Bombay Gazetteer*, V, 86: also see *ibid*, VIII., 155, sq.; 447.

always burns, is a prominent object. Except for their huge horn, agate or glass earrings, about 2¼ ounces in weight, which make their ear lobes ugly and almost painful to look at, the Kanphatas wear the ordinary Hindu dress, a coat and waist-cloth generally of a red ochre colour.[1] The head of the monastery is, on succession, invested by the Râo with a gold-bordered silk turban, a sacred woollen neck thread (*sheli*), a scanty waist-band, white waist-cloth, a red or brick-coloured scarf, and wooden pattens. His ornaments are very old and rich. The earrings, the same in shape as those worn by his disciples, are gilt and inlaid with gems. From his neck hangs a rhinoceros'-horn whistle, which it is one of his chief privileges to blow when he worships the gods. Their ordinary food is millets and pulse. Worshippers of Siva, they have a special ritual for their god, the head repeating a hymn in his honour on the second of every month. Their worship is a form of abstraction (*yoga*), the special tenets of their founder having long been forgotten. As they are bound to celibacy, the sect is kept up by recruiting. New-comers generally belong to one of two classes: orphans or the children of destitute persons who enter as boys, or lazy or disheartened men who are taken in sometimes at an advanced age. The novice starts as the disciple of some member of the sect, who becomes his spiritual guide (*guru*). On joining, his guide gives him a black woollen thread, tied round the neck with a *rudra* knot, from which hangs a two-inch horn or speaking-trumpet (*sringinâu*), and through it he is made to repeat the words *omkâr, upadesâ, adesa*, or the mystic *om*. His conduct is closely watched for eight months. Then, if he has behaved well, he is taken before the god Bhairava and has the cartilage of his ears slit by one of the devotees. In the slit a stick of *nîm* is stuck, and the wound cured by a dressing of *nîm* oil. When the ear is well again, agate, glass or bone rings are thrust into the slit, the hair, beard and mustaches are shaved, and by the guide the rule (*upadesa mantra*) of the sect—'Be wise, pious, and useful'—is whispered into the disciple's ear, and he is called by a new name ending in Nâth. He

[1] The appearance of the ears of many of the statues at Elephanta recalls the Arab traveller Sulaimâni's remark that the Balhara, perhaps the Selhara, king of the Konkan was prince of the men who have their ears pierced (Dowson's *Elliot*, I., 3). In 1583 the English traveller Fitch noticed that the ears of the women of Ormus were so stretched by the weight of their earrings that a man could put three of his fingers in the holes in the lobes (Harris *Voyages*, I., 207). See other references collected in *Bombay Gazetteer*, XIV., 83.

is now a regular devotee, repeating the name of the founder of the sect, serving his guide; and doing any duty he may be set to. Devotees of this sort are buried, and, on the twelfth day after death, a feast is given and alms distributed by the oldest disciple who succeeds to his guide's place. On the death of the head of the monastery the guides choose one of their number to succeed. The position of head is one of much local honour. The Râo invests him with a dress, pays him a visit, and is received by the holy man seated. In former times, when oppression was threatened, the Kanphatas, like the Bhâts and Chârans, used to commit *trâga* by sacrificing one of their number, so that the guilt of his blood might be on their oppressor's head."

4. In other parts of Bombay the rule of celibacy imposed upon the Mahant appears to be relaxed, and, failing issue, he is allowed to adopt a disciple who succeeds to his office. The special earrings worn by the sect are regarded as a sort of a fetish, and if once lost cannot be replaced. Sir G. Jacob notes a case where the companion of a Kanphata had been killed by outlaws and the abbot tried to persuade him to allow his wounded ear to be sewn up and a new earring supplied; he refused, saying that he would die with his brother, and he soon after died, and they were buried in the same grave. He also notes that "except that the cow is held sacred and the hog unclean, they eat freely of fish, flesh, and fowl. Travellers are freely received and fed, hospitality being part of their religion. Their religion otherwise appears to consist in worshipping their idol, morning and evening. The rest of the day is passed in amusement or in indolence, except at stated times for meals, when they meet together to feast with such strangers as wish to join them. Twice every day provisions are distributed to all who may ask for them. When the provisions are cooked, a servant of the abbot's goes to the bank of the Saraswati and calls twice with a loud voice—'Whoever is hungry, come, the abbot's table is spread. Whoever comes gets a meal."

The Kanphatas of the North-West Provinces and Oudh.

5. The chief seat of the Kanphatas of these Provinces is Gorakhpur, where they say Gorakhnâth was buried, and where his grave (*samâdhi*) is an object of veneration. Brâhmans, Vaisyas, Kshatriyas and Sûdras can all join the sect. The initiation is done in this way: The barber first shaves the head, beard, and mustache of the candidate. He is then seated before the Guru facing the

north, and the Guru puts round his neck a thread, known as *nád jáneu*, made of sheep's wool. To this is attached a small whistle (*nád*) made of deer's horn. Then the whole body of the neophyte is smeared with ashes. This constitutes the first initiation which entitles the disciple to begin to serve his religious guide. This is not done by the chief priest of a monastery, but by some of his mendicant disciples. When his Guru is satisfied with the conduct of the disciple after a period of probation, which lasts a half year or more, the second stage of the initiation comes off. The disciple bathes and puts on a narrow loin-cloth (*nigoti*), ties a string of *múnj* grass or a brass or iron chain round his waist, and smears his body with ashes. The upper part of his person he covers with a cloth (*anchala*) dyed in ochre.

Then he appears before two disciples of the head Guru, and they make him sit facing the north. One of them holds his hands and the other pierces the lobes of his ears with a knife. Two plugs (*kundal*) are placed in the gashes, and the treatment of the wounds occupies forty days, during which they are daily bathed with pure water. When a cure has been effected the next stage comes on. The neophyte bathes and assumes the *nád janeu* as before, and with his body smeared with ashes appears before the chief Guru. He puts in his ears rings (*kundali*) made of earthen-ware and weighing about a quarter of a pound. On this occasion the formula used is—*Om, soham*, "Om, that I am;" when the ears are being pierced the *mantra* is *Siva Gorakh*. Then the Guru distributes sweetmeats among the members of the sect present. This rite is known as *tyága* or "the abandonment of the world." Next follows the worship of the goddess Bâla Sundari, who is for the occasion represented by a twisted thread wick, which is fixed in a ball of dough and set alight. This is placed in a holy square made on the ground with lines of flour, and by it is placed a water jar (*kalas*). The light is worshipped with an offering of flowers, *halwa*-sweetmeat, cakes and a cocoanut. The cocoanut is split with a knife before being offered,—a rite which is an evident substitute for a human sacrifice. This worship of Bâla Sundari is annually performed. She is said to be merely a representation of Gorakhnâth; but the form of her worship seems to show that she is more probably some form of Kâli.

6. Kanphatas also worship Bhaironnâth on every Sunday and Tuesday. To him are offered cakes made of the *urad* pulse, known

as *bara*, flesh, wine, chaplets of flowers and *laddu* sweetmeats. These offerings are consumed by the worshippers.

7. The ordinary dress of the Kanphata consists of a girdle (*kardhan*) made of *mūnj* fibre, iron or brass, a narrow waist-cloth dyed in ochre. The body is smeared with ashes, the hair long and matted or wholly shaved, as well as the beard and mustache. He carries in his hand a cocoanut bowl (*khappar*), and wears an upper sheet dyed with ochre, a woollen sacred cord (*janeu*) round the waist, not as Brâhmans wear it over the shoulder, and to this is attached a deer-horn whistle (*nād*).

8. They live by begging and by selling a woollen string amulet (*ganda*), which is put round the necks of children to protect them from the Evil Eye. They beg only from Hindus, and use the cry *Alakh !* " The invisible one. " They take money as well as food. They will eat from the hands of Brâhmans, Kshatriyas, and the higher Vaisyas ; but not from the lower castes, from whose hands respectable Hindus will not eat. They eat meat, not beef or pork, and take intoxicants freely. They do not sing as they beg.

9. They bury their dead. The corpse is first bathed, and dressed in the usual garments of every-day life. The begging bowl (*khappar*) is filled with milk, and put in a wallet, which is hung on the shoulders of the corpse or laid by its side to serve as food for the spirit. If the dead man was the disciple of a Guru who possessed landed property, it is buried in a sitting posture with the head to the north ; if he be a disciple of a man without landed property it is thrown into a river. After the burial sweetmeats (*laddu*) are distributed among the mourners, and, on the third day, cakes, rice and milk are laid on the tomb (*samādh*), and the members of the sect eat them. There is no ceremonial impurity after death. A masonry monument is afterwards erected, and a (*lingam*) placed upon it. At this worship is done and periodical offerings are made.

The Kanphatas of the Hills.

10. In the Hills [1] the Kanphatas follow the Tantrika ritual which is distinguished for its licentiousness. Both the *linga* and *yoni* are worshipped by them, and they declare that it is unnecessary

---

[1] Atkinson, *Himalayan Gazetteer*, II., 865, *sq*. Wright, *History of Nepāl*, 140; 152.

to restrain the passions to arrive at release from metamorphosis. They are the great priests of the lower Sâkti form of Bhairava and even of the village gods. They eat flesh and drink wine and indulge in the orgies of the left-handed sect. Departing from the original idea of the female being only the personified energy of the male, she is made herself the entire manifestation, and, as in the case of Durga, receives personal worship to which that of the corresponding male deity is almost always subordinate. They trace their origin to Dharmanâtha, who is said to have been one of the twenty-two disciples of Machhendranâtha or Matsyendranâtha, among whom was Gorakhnâtha, one of the most celebrated of the nine *nâtha* or ascetics of ancient India. Dr. Buchanan [1] alleges that they are really the same as the Kapâlikas, who were so called because they used to drink out of human skulls (*kapâla*). Hiouen Thsang, and, before him, Varaha Mihira, who lived in the sixth century, show that they had a knowledge of this sect, who they allege were so called because they wore about their persons a death's-head, which they used as a drinking vessel.[2]

Distribution of the Kanphata or Gorakhnâthi Jogis according to the Census of 1891.

Districts.	Number.	Districts.	Number.
Dehra Dûn	90	Jhânsi	180
Muzaffarnagar	1,744	Benares	226
Meerut	1,612	Mirzapur	71
Bulandshahr	2	Ghâzipur	30
Agra	48	Ballia	80
Etah	22	Gorakhpur	372
Bijnor	232	Basti	4,106
Morâdâbâd	91	Kumaun	3,031
Cawnpur	240	Garhwâl	407
Fatehpur	129	Tarâi	399
Bandâ	1	Sîtapur	14
Hamîrpur	6	Total	13,133

[1] *Eastern India*, II., 484, *sq.*

[2] Barth, *Religions of India*, 214.

Kanyûri.—(Known also as Khandûri.)—A class of Hill Brâhmans who belong to the Saunaka *gotra* and Madhandhiniya *sâkha*. "They are so called after the parent village of Kanyûra in Pargana Chândpur. Though ranked as Brâhmans, they are called Pahâri or Hill Kâyasths, and carry on the duties of clerks. Their *gotra* is the same as that of the Râja of Garhwâl, who has several in his employ, and a few families exist in Dehra Dûn."[1]

Kapariya, Khapariya.[2]—A tribe of beggars and pedlars found in various parts of the Provinces, who have not been separately enumerated at the last census. There is some difference of opinion as to the proper spelling of the name. They call themselves Kapariya, which they say means "sellers of the old clothes" (*kapra*) which they get in alms. Another story is that they were created last of all the castes from the head (*kapâl*) of Siva and Pârvati, or from the perspiration that fell from their foreheads when they were wearied with the work of creation. Those who call them Khapariya adopt the skull legend and derive the name from *Khapar, Khappar*, which means either "a skull" or "the gourd cup" carried by mendicants.

Tribal organisation.

2. They have seven exogamous septs—Sirmaur, which they say means a "crown on the head" and is superior to the others; Chandel, who are so called because their ancestors lived among that tribe of Râjputs; Banchhor, who take this name because their ancestors abandoned their forest life; Gautam, who trace their origin to the Rishi Gotama; Samudraphen, whose ancestor was born from the foam of the sea; Chaudhari, whose forefathers lived among the Kurmis. The Fatehpur lists add Khetgariyâr and Patlê.

Exogamy.

3. No one can marry in his own sept and in addition the usual formula—*chachera, mamera, phuphera, mausera*,—which bars the line of the paternal uncle, maternal uncle, paternal aunt, and maternal aunt, is adopted.

Tribal council.

4. They have a tribal council (*panchâyat*) of which the chairman (*mukhiya*) is a hereditary officer. If the chairman be a minor, his nearest competent relation acts for him until he is fit to perform the duty. Offenders are usually punished with fine which ranges from one rupee and

---

[1] Atkinson, *Himalayan Gazetteer*, III., 270.

[2] Based on information collected at Mirzapur and notes by Munshi Gurdayâl Sinh, Deputy Inspector of Schools, Fatehpur.

a quarter to five rupees, and the money thus collected is spent in drinking.

Marriage.

5. The boy's father has to pay at least one hundred rupees to the father of the girl, and the marriage cannot be performed until this is paid. The age for betrothal is seven or eight and for marriage fifteen or sixteen. Infidelity is so far condoned that a woman is reprimanded three times before she is finally excommunicated for misconduct. Widow marriage and the levirate are both allowed, but there seems to be a tendency to reform about this, and some of the tribe at Mirzapur deny that they allow widows to re-marry. Concubinage is prohibited.

Birth.

6. There are no ceremonies during pregnancy; but on the day after the child is born a Brâhman astrologer is called in to decide whether the day of birth is lucky or not; but no regular horoscope is prepared. On the ninth day rice and pulse cakes (*bara*) are cooked and eaten only by the women and girls of the family and their friends. After the house is purified and the dirty clothes and old earthen vessels removed, the mother and infant are bathed at an auspicious time fixed by the Pandit. Then the mother sits in the court-yard or in the kitchen with a dish before her of the following food, in quantity sufficient for five women: boiled pulse (*dâl*), boiled rice (*bhât*), wheat cakes fried in butter (*pûri*), cakes of *urad* pulse (*bara*), large soft pulse cakes (*phulauri*), curry, curds, sweets (*batâsha*) and a plantain. These things are eaten by her five nearest relations, and afterwards the clansmen are fed. She cannot look after household affairs till the twelfth day, when she is again bathed and has to worship the village well. She bathes, puts on a garment dyed yellow with turmeric and goes to the nearest well, where she plasters a piece of ground, makes a burnt offering (*hom*), and offers to the well treacle, red-lead, ochre, butter and sugar. She then bows down to the well and prays for the welfare of her child, household and herself.

Marriage ceremonies.

7. Marriage ceremonies are of the usual high-class type. As the bride makes the first six circuits round the sacred fire she says: *Pahli bhaunriya jo phirai, bâba, abhûn tumhâr*—"While I make the first circuit I am still thine, O father!" This she says at each of the circuits till the last, when she says:—"*Sâtwân bhaunriya jo phirai, bâba, ab bhai parai*—"After making the seventh circuit, O father! now I belong

to another." These revolutions round the sacred fire form the binding part of the ceremony.

Disposal of the dead.

8. The more respectable members of the tribe burn their dead; poorer people only scorch the face of the corpse and throw it into some river. They very rarely take the ashes to the Ganges. The person who fired the pyre lives apart for nine days. On that day all the clansmen shave, and after bathing return to the house of the deceased, where the heir makes presents to the Mahâpâtras and feeds the clansmen. After three fortnights they again give a feast and place food for the dead outside the village. This is done again in the sixth and twelfth month. At the Pitrapaksha, or fortnight sacred to the dead, a Mâli woman spreads flowers at the door, and if they can afford it food is given to Brâhmans.

Religion.

9. Kapariyas are Hindus and worship Kâli, Durga, Parameswar and Mahâdeva. To Kâli-Durga they offer goats, cakes, pottage (*lapsi*) and spirits at the Naurâtra of Chait and Kuâr. To Mahâdeva and Parameswar they make no offering, but only do reverence to them. They reverence the *pîpal*, *tulasi* plant, and banyan (*bar*), if they have made a pilgrimage to Gaya.

Social rules.

10. Women who have lost children abstain from eating the egg-plant (*baingan*) until the child grows up. Then the father gives a feast, of which the egg-plant forms a part, and the mother shares in it. They will not eat food touched by a Bhangi, Dhobi, Chamâr, Muhammadan, Kumhâr, Teli, Darzi, Patwa, Koli, Mâli or Khatîk. They will eat *kachchi* and *pakki* from Brâhmans and Kshatriyas. To the east of the Province no caste except Chamârs and other menials will eat from their hands, and even Chamârs are now beginning to refuse to do so. The men wear their hair long, and both men and women wear round their necks the seeds of the *ghungchi* (*abrus precatorius*).

Occupation.

11. The men wander all over the country begging and selling ponies and goats. They have been suspected of illicit coining and passing bad money. The women do not beg or go to strange houses. Unmarried girls do not cover the head, and busy themselves milking the goats which they take about with them. At Fatehpur, their head-quarters, they do not cultivate. They say that when they were first created Siva

told them to sow gram, but in their ignorance they split each grain before sowing, and since then they have been ordered to live by begging. They are always on the move, except in the rains, and carry about small tents. On the whole they bear an indifferent character, and have been caught committing petty thefts and practising various forms of swindling.

Karnâta.—One of the local groups of Brâhmans included among the Pancha Drâvida. They are Brâhmans who inhabit the Karnâtak, or tract of country where the Canarese language is spoken. They are, of course, exotic in this part of India, and most of them are found in Benares, where they have a high reputation for piety and learning. Mr. Sherring's[1] informant divides them into eight sub-divisions—Haiga, Kwâta, Shivelri, Barginâra, Kandawa Karnâta, Maisûr Karnâta, and Sirnâd.

Distribution of Karnâta Brâhmans according to the Census of 1891.

District.	Number.
Mathura	24
Morâdâbâd	6
Benares	403
Kumaun	112
Tarâi	23
Faizâbâd	16
Total	584

Kasarwâni, Kasarbâni.—A sub-caste of Banyas found in considerable numbers in Allahâbâd, Mirzapur, Benares, Ballia, and Partâbgarh. They take their name from *Kânsya-kâra-vanij*, "a seller of brass vessels." To the east of the Province they have two endogamous sub-divisions—Purabiya or eastern and Pachhiwâha or western. Besides this they have a large number of sections. According to Mr. Risley[2] there are as many as ninety-six in Bihâr. "A man must not marry in his own section and must also

[1] *Hindu Castes*, I, 96.
[2] *Tribes and Castes*, I., 429.

observe the standard formula of prohibited degrees reckoned to the fifth generation in the descending line." To the east they say that they emigrated from Kara Mânikpur only some two or three generations ago. They practise infant marriage and cannot take a second wife in the life-time of the first without her consent. Widows can marry again by the *sagâi* form, and the levirate is recognised but not compulsory on the widow. They have no regular divorce, but a man can discard his wife for adultery.

2. Many of them are initiated into the Râmanandi sect, and to the east of the Province they specially worship the Pânchonpîr and Mahâbîr. Their family priests are Sarwariya Brâhmans. They are usually grocers, and sell flour, grain, salt, tobacco, and other articles of food. It is said that some, who are Pachpiriyas, eat meat, but the worshippers of Mahâbîr totally abstain from it. Brâhmans and Kshatriyas will not eat either *pakki* or *kachchi* cooked by them; other Banyas will eat *pakki* but not *kachchi*, and they will eat *kachchi* only if cooked by one of their own sub-castes. Kahârs and Nâis will eat *kachchi* cooked by them.

Distribution of Kasarwâni Banyas according to the census of 1891.

District.	Number.
Dehra Dûn	4
Sahâranpur	4
Farrukhâbâd	76
Mainpuri	1
Etâwah	146
Cawnpur	550
Fatehpur	1,231
Banda	3,441
Hamîrpur	1
Allahâbâd	34,036
Jhânsi	1

Distribution of Kasarwan Banyas according to the Census of 1891—continued.

DISTRICT.	Number.
Benares	5,936
Mirzapur	8,717
Jaunpur	805
Ghâzipur	1,141
Ballia	3,366
Gorakhpur	641
Basti	84
Azamgarh	47
Lucknow	683
Sîtapur	33
Faizâbâd	219
Gonda	123
Sultânpur	93
Partâbgarh	4,246
TOTAL	65,625

Kasaundhan.—(*Kânsa*, "bell metal"; *dhana*, "wealth.")—A sub-caste of Banyas found throughout the Province, except the Meerut, Agra, and Rohilkhand Divisions. According to the Benares tradition they have come there from Lucknow. In Benares they have two sections, the Purbiya or Purabiya or "eastern" and the Pachhaiyan or "western." In Mirzapur their sections are Khara or "faithful," who prohibit widow marriage, and the Dûsra or "second," who allow it. Those of the Khara section take wives from the Dûsra, but do not give them girls. The Dûsra are consequently obliged to find brides among themselves. They fix their head-quarters at Jaunpur, and say they emigrated to Mirzapur some two or three generations ago.

2. Marriage usually takes place at the age of five or six. The Dûsra section allow widow marriage according to the usual *sagâi* or *dharewa* form. A woman can be discarded for infidelity with the consent of the village council.

Marriage.

3. To the east of the Province they worship Mahâbîr and the Pânchonpîr. Sarwariya Brâhmans are their family priests. According to Dr. Buchanan,[1] in Gorakhpur and Bihâr their family priests are mostly Kanaujiya and Sakadwîpi Brâhmans, and they follow the Nânakpanthi sect. In Mirzapur they are usually Râmanandis.

Religion.

4. They make their living by money-changing (*sarrâfi*), dealing in grain and other articles of food and matting (*tât*).

Occupation.

5. They abstain from meat and spirits. They will eat *kachchi* prepared only by themselves. Their family priests, but not ordinary Brâhmans, eat *pakki* cooked by them. This is allowed to any other caste except Kshatriyas. Low castes such as Nâis and Kahârs eat *kachchi* cooked by them.

Social rules.

Distribution of Kasaundhan Banyas according to the census of 1891.

DISTRICT.	Number.
Debra Dûn	85
Bulandshahr	1
Farrukhâbâd	17
Bareilly	2
Budâun	50
Morâdâbâd	1
Shâhjahânpur	11
Fatehpur	483
Bânda	3,508

[1] *Eastern India*, I., 161.

Distribution of Kasaundhan Banyas according to the Census of 1891—contd.

DISTRICT.	Number.
Hamîrpur	611
Allahâbâd	268
Jhânsi	2
Benares	953
Mirzapur	164
Jaunpur	669
Ghâzipur	491
Gorakhpur	15,983
Basti	18,149
Azamgarh	346
Lucknow	2,014
Unâo	69
Râê Bare'i	4,842
Sîtapur	252
Kheri	86
Faizâbâd	12,122
Gonda	22,489
Bahrâich	4,645
Sultânpur	3,893
Partâbgarh	67
Bârabanki	5,468
TOTAL	97,741

Kasera.—(Sanskrit *kánsya kára*, "a worker in bell metal.")[1] The brass-founding caste. According to Mr. Risley,[2] they are

[1] But on the suffix *era* see Hœrnle, *Comparative Grammer of the Gaudian Languages*, para. 249, *sqq*.

[2] *Tribes and Castes*, I., 429.

"probably an offshoot from one of the higher mercantile castes, which was separated from the parent group by adopting this special profession. The fact that the Kaseras have a well-defined set of exogamous sections and pride themselves on their purity of descent seems to indicate that the caste is a homogeneous one, and is not, like many of the functional castes, a collection of men from several different groups held together merely by the bond of a common occupation." In Mirzapur, which is one of the head-quarters of the caste, they call themselves Kshatriyas, and assert that they were driven to adopt their present occupation when Parasurâma made a general massacre of the Kshatriya race.[1]

Internal structure.

2 In Benares they name seven endogamous sub-castes—Purbiya or Purbiha (Eastern), Pachhâwan or Pachhiwâhan (Western), Gorakhpuri (from Gorakhpur), Tânk (either connected with the Râjput clan of that name or, as Mr. Sherring supposes, from the principality of Tânk (Tonk), Tanchara, Bhariya, and Golar. Of these the Purbiya or Purabiya, Pachhiwâhan, and Golar are found in Mirzapur. The Purabiya and Pachhiwâhan sub-castes are divided into a number of exogamous sections (*al*). The following are the sections of the Purabiya in Mirzapur:—Baikata, Barwâr, Paigiha, Belkatha, Chorkat, Chûrîhâr, Ganreriya, Ghorcharha, Gurteliya, Hardiha, Kardhaniyator Mahobiya, Kharmarauriya, Lohâr, Mahobiya, Qalaigar, Tamaha, Teliya. The sections of the Pachhiwâhan are:—Bâri, Bapdahka, Berwâr, Belkata, Budhmaniya, Chilimâra, Chûrîhâra, Dhumel, Ghoraha, Ghamela, Ghumila, Hardiha, Jarseth, Jhamaiya, Katha, Khutaha, Koraiya, Mahalwâr, Paitiha, Rahilaha, Sirbhaiyân, Songar. The Golar are few in numbers in Mirzapur, and do not appear to have any well-recognized sections. They are a separate sub-caste of Kaseras who have been permanently excommunicated for some violation of caste rules and form an endogamous sub-caste of their own. These three sub-castes are endogamous and do not eat together. As to the origin of these sections—some are obviously the names of existing castes such as the Teliya, Lohâr, Ganreriya, Chûrîhâr, Qalaigar, and Bâri. Others like the Mahobiya and Kardhaniyator Mahobiya ("those who break the

---

[1] In Mirzapur they represent themselves as descended from the ancient Kshatriya Râjas—Tamar, Mordhuja, Tânchardhuja, and Haihaya. Mordhuja is possibly Moradhwaj (Cunningham, *Archæological Survey*, VI., 227; XVII., 98). Haihaya was the name of the Kala Chûri dynasty of Chedi (*ibid.*, IX., 77).

CHAMÂR.

waist string") are of local origin (from Mahoba in the Hamîrpur District). It illustrates the fertility with which these sections are produced that none in these Mirzapur lists correspond with those given by Mr. Risley for Bihâr.[1] In the hills the Kasera is represented by the Tamota or Tamta, who is a Dom. The complete lists show 53 sections of the usual type. Some are territorial such, as Ajhudhyabâsi, Brij, Jamnapâri, Jaunpuri, Kanaujiya, Mainpuriya, Pachhiwâhan, Purabiya; others are taken from tribes with which they imply some connection, such as Ahîrbansi, Chhatri, Paribais Chhatri, Tânk, and Sombansi. They practise a strict rule of exogamy. No man may marry a woman of his own section, and the tendency among the more respectable Kaseras appears to be to extend this prohibition so as to prevent not only persons of the same section from intermarrying, but to bar intermarriages between persons whose fathers, mothers, grandfathers and grandmothers belong to the same section. They have in addition a rule of exogamy based on geographical position. Thus the Mirzapur Kaseras intermarry only with those resident in Benares and Jaunpur, not with those of Bihar.

Marriage rules.

3. Infant marriage is the rule with all the more respectable Kaseras, but ordinary people marry their daughters at ten or twelve. Inter-tribal fornication in the cases of unmarried people or widows and widowers seems to be lightly regarded. The offenders are not excommunicated, only fined. In Bihar[2] it would seem that polygamy is allowed only if the first wife is barren: here, as far as can be ascertained, a man may marry as many wives as he can afford to keep. They have the ordinary forms of marriage,—*charhauwa,* the respectable form, and *dola,* used by poor people. Widows can marry by *sagâi,* but they profess this to be a modern institution. She may marry the younger brother of her late husband or an outsider as she pleases. A husband can put away his wife for adultery with a member of another caste, and a wife can leave her husband if he does not support her, or abandons his religion. Divorced women cannot re-marry within the tribe.

Religion.

4. Kaseras generally follow the Vaishnava or Nânakpanthi sect. Their clan deities are the Pânchonpîr, Durga, and Bandi Devi. The first are

---

[1] *Tribes and Castes*, II., *Appendix*, 71.
[2] Risley, *loc cit.*, I., 430.

worshipped in the month of Jeth on a Sunday or Wednesday, with offerings of pulse cakes (*phulauri*) and bread. Durga is worshipped on 15th Chait with an offering of cakes (*púri*), rice milk (*khír*), and sweetmeats. Bandi Devi is honoured with an offering of pepper and sugar dissolved in water (*mirchwán*) at the full moon of Sâwan. When a person recovers from small-pox a yellow cloth and some flowers are dedicated to Sitâla Mâta. All these offerings are, after dedication, consumed by the worshippers. Their priests are Tiwâri Brâhmans, who are received on terms of equality by other Brâhmans. The dead are cremated in the ordinary way, and balls (*pinda*) are offered to them on the 15th of any month which falls on a Wednesday, and also in the first fortnight of Kuâr. On such occasions uncooked grain (*sídha*) is given to Brâhmans. People who die in a distant land or who have died a violent death are thrown into running water and cremated in effigy, with the usual ceremonies, within six months of death.

Occupation and social status.

5. There is some difference of opinion as to their occupation. According to Mr. Nesfield[1]: "The Kasera's speciality lies in mixing the softer metals (zinc, copper, and tin) and moulding the alloy into various shapes, such as cups, bowls, plates, etc. The Thathera's art consists in polishing and engraving the utensils which the Kasera supplies." On the other hand Mr. Hoey[2] says that at Lucknow the manufacturer of brass vessels is called indifferently Thathera, Kasera, or Bhariya. In Mirzapur it appears that the name Kasera is confined to the moulder of vessels in brass or alloy and to the man who beats out trays out of metal sheets, while the Thathera makes and sells ornaments made of alloy (*phúl*). A workman akin to him is the Dhaliya or Dhalnewâla of Lucknow, who makes ornaments (*hansli, kara, tariya*) of zinc (*jasta*), others from pewter (*ránga*), and who moulds in lead moulds for other artizans.[3] The Kaseras pretend that they were originally landowners like the Kshatriyas. Kaseras all wear the sacred thread (*janeu*), and are very punctilious in matters of caste. They eat the flesh of goats and sheep and fish. They do not drink spirits. They eat *pakki* cooked

---

[1] *Brief View*, 29.

[2] *Monograph*, 198.

[3] *Ibid.*, 102. Dr. Buchanan (*Eastern India*, II., 260) says: "In some places these two professions are considered distinct, the makers and menders of vessels being called Kasera, and the makers of ornaments being called Thathera, but in others the terms are used as synonymous."

by all Brâhmans, Kshatriyas, and Vaisyas, except Kalwârs, Kâyasths, Nâis, Bâris, and Ahîrs. They eat *kachchi* cooked by their own tribesmen or priests. It is said that all Brâhmans, except Sarwariyas, will eat *pakki* cooked by them, and Nâis, Bâris and Kahârs eat *kachchi* prepared by them. A full account of the Kasera's craft will appear in the forthcoming Monograph on the brass metal trade of the Province and need not be repeated here.

Distribution of Kaseras according to the Census of 1891.

District.	Number.
Mathura	3
Cawnpur	14
Allahâbâd	43
Benares	1,697
Mirzapur	2,475
Jaunpur	174
Ghâzipur	7
Ballia	253
Gorakhpur	493
Basti	751
Azamgarh	141
Lucknow	114
Unâo	155
Râê Bareli	9
Sîtapur	67
Hardoi	8
Faizâbâd	57
Gonda	461
Bahrâich	319
Partâbgarh	32
Total	7,273

Kashmîri.—(Residents of Kashmîr.)—A small sub-caste of Banyas, found in small numbers in Bareilly and Pilibhît.

Kâsip.—(Sanskrit, *kashyapa*, "tortoise," which may have been the tribal totem.)—A sept of Râjputs most numerous in Shâhjahânpur, who are low in the social scale, though claiming to be an offshoot of the Kachhwâhas. Their tradition is that they are immigrants from Kashmîr, the Râja of which they claim as a member of the clan, and allege that he recently recognised the fact.[1] He is usually called a Dogra Râjput; but Dogar is only another name for Jammu, and Dogra is a general term for any Kashmîri Râjput.

Distribution of the Kâsip Râjputs according to the Census of 1891

District.	Number.
Muzaffarnagar	1
Bulandshahr	7
Mainpuri	17
Etah	1
Bareilly	125
Budâun	44
Shâhjahânpur	2,330
Pilibhît	178
Jhânsi	3
Azamgarh	1
Lucknow	8
Sîtapur	9
Hardoi	35
Kheri	180
Total	2,939

Kathak, Kathik.—(Sanskrit *kathika*, "a professional story-teller.")[2]—A caste of story-tellers, singers, and musicians.

[1] *Settlement Report*, 24: 59.

[2] Based on enquiries at Mirzapur, and a note by Munshi Bhagwân Dâs, Tahsîldâr, Allahâbâd.

2. According to one story they are really Gaur Brâhmans, who used originally to sing and dance in the temples of the gods, and a certain Muhammadan Emperor of Delhi once heard them and was so pleased with their skill that he ordered them in future to perform in public. Another story connects them with King Prithu, "who was son of Vena, son of Anga. He was the first king, and from him the earth received her name Prithivi. The Vishnu Purâna says that the Rishis 'inaugurated Vena monarch of the earth,' but he was wicked by nature and prohibited worship and sacrifices. Incensed at the decay of religion, pious sages beat Vena to death with blades of holy grass. In the absence of a king, robbery and anarchy arose, and the Munis, after consultation, proceeded to rub the thigh of the dead king in order to produce a son. There came forth a man like a charred log with flat face and extremely short. This man became a Nishâda, and with him came out the sins of the departed king. The Brâhmans then rubbed the right arm of the corpse and from it sprang the majestic Prithu, Vena's son, resplendent in body, glowing like the manifested Agni. At his birth all creatures rejoiced; and through the birth of this virtuous son, Vena, delivered from the hell called Put, ascended to heaven."[1] This monarch found that the art of the Udgatri, or chanter of the Vedic hymns, had fallen into disuse, so he performed a rite (*yaksha*) and out of the sacred fire-pits (*agni-kunda*) came out three men, Mâgadha, Sûta, and Bandijad, from the first of whom are descended the Kathaks, from the second the Bhâts, and from the third the Maithila Brâhmans.

Traditions of origin.

3. The Kathaks themselves profess to be divided into sixteen sections, which all seem to be of local origin and derived from the places which they used to occupy in former times. Of these the names of fifteen have been ascertained at Mirzapur :—Bhadohiya, from Pargana Bhadohi in the Mirzapur District; Mathapati, whose ancestors are said to have been heads of a monastery (*matha*); Mahuâri; Bhunsaiha; Gonraha, from Gonda; Usari; Mandik; Rajaipur; Matepur; Naikan; Jangali and Mangali, who are chiefly found in the direction of Azamgarh and Gorakhpur; Mohânw; Thakurahân; and Mâlik. Each of these again is divided into *gotras*, but of these it has been,

Tribal organisation.

[1] Dowson, *Classical Dictionary*, s. v.

in consequence of the general ignorance prevailing among the caste, impossible to procure a list. All they can say is that their *gotras* correspond with those of the Kanaujiya and Sarwariya Brâhmans. Their law of exogamy is the same as that of the Brâhmans, and a man cannot marry in his section or in his own *gotra* until at least seven generations have passed. In their marriage, birth and death ceremonies they follow the usages of Brâhmans. The complete Census returns give 378 section names of the usual type. Side by side with Brâhmanical terms such as Misr, Dikshit or Bhâradwâja, we find numerous others derived from those of well-known tribes, such as, Bâchal, Bagheli, Bais, Bargûjar, Bundel, Chauhân, Chhatri, Dhârhi, Dhobi, Gadariya, Gaharwâr, Gaur, Hurakiya, Jâdon, Kâyasth, Khatri, Koliya, Lodh, Mehtariya, Niyâriya, Panwâr, Paturiya, Raghubansi, Raikwâr, Râthaur, Râwat, Sengar, Sûrajbansi, and Tomra. Besides these are numerous purely local terms, such as Ajudhyabâsi, Bahâdurpuriya, Baksariya, Bishnpuriya, Dakkhinâha, Hasanapuri, Kanaujiya, Madhupuriya Mathurabâsi, Pachhwâhân, Purabiya, Sâranpuriya, Sarwariya.

Religion and social status.

4. Kathaks are popularly regarded by low-caste Hindus as equal to Brâhmans, and all castes, including Râjputs, salute them and beg a blessing. The only practical difference between them is that they cannot receive the gifts of piety (*dâna*) which are taken by Brâhmans. Widow marriage is prohibited. In addition to all the ordinary Hindu gods the Kathaks worship Ghâzi Miyân and offer to him sweet cakes (*pakwân*) in the months of Kuâr and Chait. They employ Brâhmans for ceremonial purposes, and such Brâhmans are received on terms of equality with other Brâhmans. They eat fish, goats, sheep, but, of course, not beef, and they do not drink. But while they hold a fairly respectable position, their business degrades them to some extent. Their women are secluded except on very special occasions, such as marriages in very high caste families; but the men are known as Bharuas or the attendants of the ordinary dancing girls, who are often prostitutes, and from this occupation many of them are believed to be negligent as regards the strict caste rules of eating, drinking, etc. They play on the small drum (*dhol*) and the cymbals (*majîra*), and they also act as the teachers of singing and dancing women whom they accompany to respectable houses at marriages and similar occasions and receive half their earnings. Their clan deity is the goddess Saraswati,

whom they worship at the Basant Panchami festival on the fifth day of Phâlgun with offerings of sweetmeats, flowers, burnt offerings (*homa*), and incense (*dhûpa*). On this occasion an image of Saraswati or Gauri is made of cowdung and worshipped. The Census returns show 5,311 worshippers of Saraswati. Mr. Baillie writes: "It is probable that these are due less to her position as a river goddess than to those attributes which she acquired as the patroness of the ceremonies performed on the margin of her holy waters, and subsequently as the inspirer of the hymns recited at these ceremonies. She is now known mainly as the goddess of speech and learning, the inventress of the Sanskrit language and patroness of arts and sciences."[1] Those who are less particular worship Mahâbir and the Panchonpir.

Distribution of Kathaks according to the Census of 1891.

District.	Number.
Farrukhâbâd	8
Hamîrpur	24
Jâlaun	24
Benares	100
Mirzapur	11
Jaunpur	53
Ghâzipur	25
Ballia	13
Gorakhpur	569
Basti	230
Azamgarh	215
Lucknow	32
Râê Bareli	210
Sîtapur	51
Hardoi	2

[1] *Census Report, North-West Provinces and Oudh*, 234; *Panjâb Census Report* 105; Monier Williams, *Hinduism and Brâhmanism*, 429.

Distribution of Kathaks according to the Census of 1891—contd.

District.	Number.
Faizâbâd	6
Babrâich	312
Partâbgarh	149
Total	2,034

Katheriya.—A sept of Râjputs confined to Rohilkhand and the Central Duâb. They derive their name from Kathehar, the old name of Eastern Rohilkhand, which again is supposed to be derived from *kather*, a brownish loam of a thirsty tenacious nature with a subjacent sandy stratum requiring copious rain for irrigation. Others with less probability connect the name with Katyûr in the Hills or Karttikeyapura. The country of Kathehar is now confined to the tract lying between the Râmganga, Sârda, and Khanaut rivers. The accounts vary as to the time they entered Rohilkhand. One story is that Bhîma Sena drove out the Ahîrs about the time that Prithivi Râja ruled at Delhi and Jay Chand at Kanauj. According to General Cunningham they did not invade the country till 1174 A.D., and their ancient capital was Lakhnaur.[1] They appear to be in some way connected with the Gaur sept, and one account represents that they expelled the Bâchhals; but, on the other hand, Mr. Moens denies that the Bâchhals ever held sway in Bareilly. In Shâhjahânpur[2] it is said that the Gaurs helped them against the Pathâns. The Morâdâbâd[3] tradition is that they were Sûrajbansis of Ajudhya, who were driven from thence when the Aryan invasion was temporarily pushed back by the aboriginal races, and that they came with real or pretended authority from the Muhammadans to seize the country occupied by the Ahars.

2. In Bareilly the Katheriyas take their wives from the Bais, Sombansi, Bargûjar, and Bhur Janghâra septs, and give girls to the Chauhân, Râthaur, Bhadauriya, and Chandel. In Farrukhâ-

[1] *Bareilly Settlement Report*, 21, *sq.*; *Archæological Reports*, I., 251, 356
[2] *Settlement Report*, 107, *sq.*
[3] *Settlement Report*, 9.

bâd they give their girls to the Bhadauriya, Kachhwâha, Chauhân, and Râthaur, and procure wives from the Chandel, Ujjaini, Gaharwâr, Jaiswâr, Nikumbh, Panwâr, and Bais.

Distribution of the Katheriya Râjputs according to the Census of 1891.

District.	Number.
Sahâranpur	2
Muzaffarnagar	7
Meerut	172
Bulandshahr	45
Aligarh	18
Agra	94
Farrukhâbâd	1,308
Mainpuri	796
Etâwah	143
Etah	3,042
Bareilly	6,708
Bijnor	24
Budâun	4,921
Morâdâbâd	8,145
Shâhjahânpur	9,031
Pilibhît	1,823
Allahâbâd	32
Ghâzipur	3
Tarâi	401
Sîtapur	219
Hardoi	280
Kheri	522
Bahrâich	16
Total	37,752

Kâthi.—A Râjput sept, some members of which are found in Bundelkhand. According to Professor Wilson,[1] the word Cathaei or Kattia is derived from Kshatta or Kshatriya. Colonel Tod[2] classes them among the thirty-six Royal races, and describes them as a most important tribe in the Western Peninsula, which has effected the change of the name from Saurâshtra to Kâthiawâr. "Of all its inhabitants the Kâthi retains most originality; his religion, his manners, and his looks are all decidedly Scythic." They have been identified with the Khatraioi of Ptolemy. "According to the Greek writers the people who held the territory comprised between the Hydraotes (Râvi) and the Hyphasis (Biyâs) were the Kathaioi, whose capital was Sangala. The Mahâbhârata and the Pâli Buddhist works speak of Sangala as the capital of the Madras, a powerful people also known as Bâhîka. Lassen, in order to account for the substitution of name, supposes that the mixture of the Madras with the inferior castes had led them to assume the name of Khatriyas (Kshatriya, the warrior caste) in token of their degradation, but this is by no means probable. The name is still found spread over an immense area from the Hindu Koh as far as Bengal, and from Nepâl to Gujarât, under forms slightly variant: Kâthi, Katti, Kathia, Khatri, Khetar, Kattaur, Kattair, Kattak, and others. One of these tribes, the Kâthi, issuing from the lower parts of the Panjâb, established themselves in Saurâshtra, and gave the name Kâthiavâd to the great peninsula of Gujarât." [3] Widow-burning is mentioned by Megasthenes as a peculiar custom of the Kathaei.[4]

2. The Kâthiawâr legend is that they were ordered to drive off the cattle of Virât. This, as Râjputs, they refused to do, and Karan struck his staff on the ground and produced out of the wood (Kâshtha) a man, who carried out his orders, whence their name. They worship the sun and use it as a symbol in all their deeds. "The symbol has much resemblance to a spider, the rays forming the legs, but that there may be no mistake underneath is always written, 'the witness of the holy sun.' Their contact with Hindus has gradually instilled into them some respect for the ordinary Hindu gods and for Brâhmans. They are exceedingly super-

---

[1] *Ariana Antiqua*, 197.
[2] *Annals*, I., 119 *sqq.*
[3] McCrindle, *Indian Antiquary*, XIII., 360.
[4] Bunbury, *Ancient Geography*, I., 563.

stitious and believe in omens, placing the greatest reliance on the call of a partridge to the left. At funeral ceremonies, instead of feeding crows, they feed plovers, and have a strong friendly feeling towards them. The Kâthis are exceedingly hospitable, and are always sociable and friendly. They are illiterate and indolent spending their time in gossip and social entertainments, and rarely troubling themselves about their affairs. They have adopted the Hindu feeling about the holiness of the cow, otherwise they are not particular about their food or liquor. The women are proverbially handsome and bear a high character. They are on a social equality with their husbands, and are treated as companions. A Kâthi seldom marries more than one wife, though they are not limited in this respect. Widow marriage is allowed, but it is seldom practised, except in the case of a husband dying and leaving a younger brother. In such cases the rule is peremptory that the younger brother must marry his brother's widow." [1]

3. One story about the Kâthi makes them out to have originated in Kurdistân, whence they were driven out by Tiglath Pilesar of Assyria about 1130 B. C. Abul Fazal, in the *Aîn-i-Akbari*, represents them as akin to the Ahîrs.

4. In the Panjâb the Kathiya claim to be Panwâr Râjputs.[2] They are described as "a handsome, sturdy race, and nearly all Jâts of the Great Râvi, do not allow their children of either sex to marry until they have attained the age of puberty, because, as they justly consider, too early marriages would be detrimental to the physique of the race." One account fixes their original home in Bikâner, whence they entered Gujarât. Another tradition is that they were driven out of the valley of the lower Ghaggar about the time of Timûr's invasion.

Kathiyâra.[3]—(Sanskrit *kâshtha kâra*, "a worker in wood.")—A small caste of bricklayers and carpenters, who were recorded in the Aligarh District in 1881, but have probably been included in the Râj or Barhai caste at the last Census. They have five exogamous sections—Kathar, Kokâs, Sakoriya, Hindoliya, and Hirnotiya. They marry outside their section and not in the section of their ancestors on the father's or mother's side, as long as any relationship is remembered, or in families to whom they have, within memory,

---

[1] *Bombay Gazetteer*, VIII., 122, *sqq.*

[2] Ibbetson, *Panjâb Ethnography*, para. 472.

[3] Chiefly based on a note by Munshi Maidayâl Sinh, Deputy Collector.

given a bride. They may marry two sisters, but not at the same time, nor the younger before the elder.

2. The legend told by the caste runs that Sîta, the deserted wife of Râma Chandra, was living in the forest with the Rishi Bhâradwaja. She had one son, Lava; and one day she happened to go to fetch water, taking the child with her. When Bhâradwaja returned in her absence, he missed the child, and blaming himself for his carelessness in allowing it to be taken away by a wild beast, he made another child in its image out of *kusa* grass. When Sîta returned with her baby in her arms she was surprised to see the other child; but she adopted it as her own, and from his origin he was called Kusa. At the contest of the Aswamedha he fought so hard (*kathara*) that his descendants were called Kathiyâra. They fix their original head-quarters at Sambhal in the Morâdâbâd District, and thence to Jalesar and Aligarh, about one hundred and fifty years ago. On account of their descent from *kusa*, they will not sleep on *kusa* grass, nor will they cut or use it; in other words, *kusa* grass was possibly a totem.

Legend of origin.

3. They practise adult marriage and sexual license before marriage is lightly regarded. Their marriage ceremonies are of the normal type. Widows marry by *karâo*. A wife can be divorced for adultery, with the permission of the tribal council, and she cannot be again married in the caste.

Marriage rules.

4. They worship the Miyân of Amroha or Jalesar, Zâhirpîr, and Jakhiya. Of Miyân they say that his name was Mîrân. He was an ordinary Faqîr at Amroha. One day he was rebuilding the wall of his hermitage (*takiya*), when he found an old lamp that belonged to the Jinn. When he took it home and lighted it the Jinn appeared and bowed down before him. One day he ordered the Jinn to bring him the daughter of the king of Rûm. He did so, and Mîrân was so pleased with her that he made the Jinn bring her every night. At last her father noticed that she was pale; so he got her to tell him what was going on. When the king heard the case he was wroth, and sent his own four Jinns to arrest Mîrân. When Mîrân heard of this he was afraid and asked his Jinn to protect him. They advised him to get into his water-vessel (*badhana*), and when the Jinns of the king of Rûm came they carried him off in the pot as he was. The king, when he heard of the magical power of Mîrân, was afraid to open the pot, and he

Religion.

had it buried in the hermitage which he used to occupy at Amroha. Mîrân implored his Jinn to release him, but they refused, on account of his iniquity, and he is there still and is widely worshipped.

5. Of Jakhiya the tale is thus told: There was once the wife of a Brâhman, who was taking food to her husband, when she was forced by a sweeper and became in child. She told her husband what had happened; he, believing her innocent, forgave her, and kept the matter secret. When her seventh month had passed, one day her husband beat her for some fault, and the child cried out against him from her womb. The Brâhman was stricken with fear and determined to kill the child. When the baby was born, in fear of his father, he took refuge in the pig-stye of a sweeper, and there his father killed him. As he was dying he implored Bhagwân that his next birth should be in some high-caste family. So he has since then been worshipped. He is also known by the name of Masân or the deity of the cremation ground. Children suffering from convulsions are taken to his shrine and most of them recover. The cure is attributed by some to the thaumaturgic power of the saint, and by others to the electrical effect of the peacock feathers with which the patient is fanned continuously for three days.

Social status and occupation.

6. They employ Sanâdh Brâhmans as their family priests. They do not perform the regular *sráddha*, but, during the fortnight sacred to the dead (*kanágat*) they usually feed a Brâhman or two, and do the same on the anniversary of a death in the family. They work as carpenters and bricklayers. The only meat they eat is mutton; they drink spirits, and those who abstain both from meat and wine are considered more respectable than the others. They will not eat, drink or smoke with any other caste but their own. They eat *kachchi* cooked by Brâhmans and *pakki* cooked by Ahîrs, Lodhas, Mâlis, and Kahârs.

Katiyâr.—A sept of Râjputs shown in insignificant numbers at the recent Census only in the Bulandshahr District. There is, however, a sept of the same name in the Hardoi District, who are said to have emigrated from Sonoriya near Gwâlior under Râja Deva Datta, about three hundred years ago. "His clan was then called Tomar. Family feuds led him to migrate from Sonoriya to Singhi Râmpur in the Farrukhâbâd District on the Ganges; thence he gradually fought his way westward. At Khasaura he sided with the Baihar Ahîrs, and crushed their rivals, the Dhânuks. Then, turning on the Baihars, he smote and spared not till they accepted his dominion. After establishing himself at Khasaura he drove out the Thatheras. A career of massacre earned for his sept the name Katiyâr or "slaughterers."[1]

Distribution of the Katiyâr Râjputs according to the Census of 1891.

District.	Number.
Bulandshahr	26
Total	26

Katwa, Katua.[2]— (*Kâtna,* "to spin thread)."—A small caste found at the last Census only in Azamgarh and Pilibhît, and sometimes classed as a sub-caste of the Kori. They have a tradition that they were originally Bais Râjputs, whose ancestors, having been imprisoned for resistance to authority, were released on the promise that they would follow a woman's occupation of spinning thread. They have the usual rule of exogamy which bars marriage with any relative as long as any recollection of previous marriage connection remains. Marriage should take place in infancy; but if, owing to poverty, it be deferred till after puberty of the girl, no incontinence is tolerated. Marriage follows the usual stages of *tilak* or betrothal, and the *pâé-pûja* or worshipping of the feet of the bridegroom by the father of the bride and the formal giving away (*kanyâdâna*).

Occupation and social status.

2. Some few of them work at spinning thread, but most of them keep grain shops and sell cloth and thread. They employ to the east of the Province Sarwariya Brâhmans as their family priests. They do not eat meat or drink spirits.

Distribution of Katwas according to the Census of 1891.

District.	Number.
Pilibhît	7
Azamgarh	302
Total . .	309

[1] *Settlement Report,* 173.

[2] From a note by Qâzi Khairuddin, Azamgarh.

Kausik.—A sept of Râjputs hardly found outside the Benares and Gorakhpur Divisions. According to some, the title is a mere nickname, meaning "squint-eyed" (Sanskrit *kusika*). They say themselves that they take their name from their eponymous ancestor, Kusika or Kusa, whom they identify with Viswamitra, the famous sage who was born a Kshatriya, but, by intense austerities, raised himself to be a Brâhman, and was finally promoted to be one of the seven great Rishis. His father, or as some say his son, was Gadhi, the reputed founder of Gadhipur, which is identified with the modern Ghâzipur. Many generations after came Râja Chandra Prakâsh, who had two sons, Râja Bhoj and Indradaman; the former became Râja of Dhâranagar, and the latter of Ghâzipur. The Dhuriyapâr family in Gorakhpur claim their name and descent from Râja Dhruv Chandra, who expelled the Bhars and occupied the present Dhuriyapâr Pargana. The town of Gopâlpur, from which the family takes its title, was founded by his successor, Râja Gopâl Chandra. The Ghâzipur branch select their religious guides (*guru*) from a sect of monotheists peculiar to Ghâzipur called Bheka Shâhi. The Gorakhpur branch hold a respectable rank, and intermarry with the Chandrabansi, Sûrajbansi, Baghel, Sirnet, and Chauhân septs.

2. From Ballia it is reported that they marry girls of the Haihobans, Ujjaini, Nikumbh, Kinwâr, Narwâni, Karchhuliya, Sengar, Barwâr, Bais, Barhiya, Bargaiyan, Raghubansi, Sûrajbansi, Pachhtoriya, Bisariha, Donwâr, and Palwâr septs; and to give brides to the Ujjaini, Haihobans, Bais, Raghubansi, Bisen, Sûrajbansi, Narwâni, Palwâr, Nikumbh, Sirnet, Râjkumâr, Durgbansi, Chauhân, and Baghel septs. Those in Azamgarh are said to take brides from the Barhiya, Gaharwâr, Dikshit, Kâkan, Gahlot, Bachgoti, Bais, and Chandel; and to give girls to the Sirnet, Bais, Râjkumâr, Panwâr, Chandrabansi, Gargbansi, and Raghubansi septs. They claim to belong to the Kausik *gotra*.

Distribution of the Kausik Râjputs according to the Census of 1891.

District.	Number.
Cawnpur	3
Allahâbâd	1

Distribution of the Kausik Râjputs according to the Census of 1891—contd.

District.	Number.
Jhânsî	69
Benares	171
Jaunpur	91
Ghâzipur	720
Ballia	4,998
Gorakhpur	7,115
Basti	980
Azamgarh	4,505
Râê Bareli	13
Faizâbâd	574
Bahrâich	4
Sultânpur	85
Partâbgarh	39
Total	19,368

Kâyasth, Kâyastha.[1]—The well-known writer class of Hindustan.—About the derivation of the term there is some difference of opinion. Mr. Colebrooke gives as the popular derivation the Sanskrit *kâya-sanstitah,* "staying at home," in reference to their sedentary habits. The caste themselves derive their name from *kâya-stha,* situated in the body, incorporate, with reference to the legend of their descent, which will be given further on.

Origin of the caste.

2. Like all people who are on their promotion the Kâyasths are particularly sensitive as to any imputations on the purity of their descent, and it is, from every point of view, useless to revive a troublesome

[1] Based on notes by Munshi Râm Saran Dâs, Faizâbâd; Pandit Baldeo Prasâd, Deputy Collector, Cawnpur; Munshi Ummed Lâl; The *Tawârîkh Qaum Kâyasth,* by Munshi Awadh Bihâri Lâl; and *Tawârîkh Gaur Kâyasth,* by Munshi Kishori Lâl.

controversy. Mr. Risley remarks that "the physical characters of the Bihâr Kâyasths (who are identical with those of these Provinces) afford some grounds for the belief that they may be of tolerably pure Aryan descent, though the group is doubtless a functional one recruited from all grades of the Aryan community." The case of the Kâyasths of Bengal is not so clear, though it is reported that the Kâyasths of Northern India have recently shown an inclination to admit them to full rights of communion. Of them Mr. Risley writes: "Putting tradition aside, and looking, on the one hand, to the physical type of the Kâyasths, and, on the other, to their remarkable intellectual attainments, it would seem that their claim to Aryan descent cannot be wholly rejected, though all attempts to lay down their genealogy precisely must necessarily be futile. It appears to be at least a plausible conjecture that they were a functional group, developed within the Aryan community, in response to the demand for an official and literary class, which must in course of time have arisen. This class would naturally have been recruited more largely from the peaceful Vaisyas and Sûdras than from the warlike Kshatriyas, while the Brâhmans would probably have held aloof from it altogether."

3. It is, of course, not difficult to do, as some advocates of a higher status for the caste than others are disposed to admit have done, to produce texts in support of their views; but it is obvious that the question cannot be settled by reference to writings, the authority of some of which is not quite free from suspicion. The matter is one of purely physical conformation, and, before it can be finally settled, the anthropometrical data must be much larger than they are at present. At the same time it may perhaps be said that most competent observers of the physical appearance of Kâyasths are not prepared to accept the conclusion of the writers of the Jatimâla and similar authorities, which deny wholly or partly their Aryan descent; and so far as the evidence from customs and manners goes, the result is the same.[1]

The tribal legends.

4. With this preface we may now go on to relate the legends of their origin given by the members of the caste themselves. One story tells that in the beginning of all things there were thirteen Yamas in

[1] Any one curious as regards this controversy may consult, on the one hand, the *Kayastha Ethnology* of Munshi Kâli Prasâd and Bâbu Guru Prasâd Sen's article in *Calcutta Review*, XCI., 156.

Yamapuri, the kingdom of the dead. The last of these was Chitra. In those days there were three men of the same name in a certain city. One was a Râja, the second a Brâhman, and the third a barber. When the time appointed for the Râja's life had expired, Yama sent his messengers (*dûta*) to bring his soul to Yamapuri. The messengers spared the Râja and brought the soul of the Brâhman and barber to Yama, who, when he consulted his register, found that a mistake had occurred. Brahma was grieved when he heard of this, and began to meditate how he could so arrange the affairs of Yamapuri so as to avoid similar mistakes in future. Up to that time there was no such thing as carnal birth; life was produced by the milk of the gods. While Brahma was thus reflecting, Vishnu appeared before him in his four-handed form. In one hand he held a pen, in the second the Vedas, in the third the *pâsa* or noose with which Yama catches the souls of the dead, in the fourth the *danda* or mace with which he punishes the wicked. Vishnu then spread his delusion over Brahma and he took him on his knee and said, "As you existed in my body unseen, I give you the name of Chitragupta and make you the fourteenth Yama." He then ordered Chitragupta to assume charge of Yamapuri and to stop mental creation and introduce the arrangement of carnal births. He added that he should, in future, worship Sûrya, Vishnu, Devi, Ganesa, and Siva, but that he (Brahma) was to be his personal god (*ishta-devata*). When the gods heard that mental creation was to cease, Dharma Sarma Rishi represented to Brahma that he wished to marry his daughter Irâvati to Chitragupta, and Manuji, the son of Sûrya, proposed to give him his daughter Sudakshina also. To this Brahma agreed, and the double marriage was performed. Irâvati bore to Chitragupta eight sons—Chârn, Suchâru, Chitraksha, Matiwân, Hanumân, Chitrachâru, Charuna, and Jitindriya; by Sudakshina he had four sons—Chitrabânu, Vibhânu, Viswabhânu, and Vrijbhânu. When Brahma saw the increase of the family of Chitragupta he was pleased and said, "My son! I have created from my arms the Kshatriyas, who will be lords of Mrityuloka, the world of death. I desire to make your sons Kshatriyas like them." But Chitragupta said, "Most of the Râjas of the world will fall into hell. I do not desire this fate for my sons. I pray thee to allot to them some other function." Brahma was pleased and answered, "Your sons shall wield the pen and not the sword. For four births shall they live in the world of death. Then, if they deserve it, they shall be removed to the heaven of the gods." So the sons of Chitragupta came down to this world of ours, and, when they had established their human race, they were readmitted into heaven.

5. So Chitragupta remains the recorder of Yama. A soul, when it quits the body, seeks its abode in the lower regions; there the recorder Chitragupta reads out its account from his register, called Agrasandhani, and the soul either joins the Pitri, or is sent for punishment to one of the twenty-one hells, or is re-born on earth in some other form. Dr. Muir[1] translates a description of Chitragupta from the Vrihannaradiya Purâna, which he describes as "tasteless and extravagant": "The dreadful Chitragupta, with a voice like that issuing from the clouds at the mundane dissolution, gleaming like a mountain of collyrium, terrible with lightning-like weapons, having thirty-two arms, as big as two *yojanas*, red-eyed, long-nosed, his face furnished with grinders and projecting teeth, his eyes resembling oblong ponds, bearing death and diseases." In the Padma Purâna we also read: "Brahma having remained in meditation for a while, there sprang from his whole body a male of godlike form bearing an inkpot and a pen. This being was named Chitragupta, and he was placed by Brahma near Dharmarâja to register the good and evil actions of all sentient beings. He was possessed of supernatural wisdom, and became the partaker of sacrifices offered to the gods and fire. It is for this that the twice-born always give him oblations from their food. As he sprang from the body of Brahma he is said to be of the Kâyastha class. His descendants are Kâyastha of numerous *gotras* on the face of the earth." And in the Bhavishya Purâna we read: "Thou art sprung from my (Brahma's) body; therefore thou shalt be styled Kâyastha. Thou shalt be known on the earth by the name of Chitragupta. O son, having obtained my positive commands, thou shalt be posted for ever in the kingdom of Dharmarâja for the discrimination of virtue and vice! Let the religious duties prescribed for the Kshatriya caste be followed by thee according to rule. O son, beget devout children on the face of the earth." At the last Census only 1,967 persons were recorded as worshippers of Chitragupta, which is explained by the fact that "Kâyasths are in general orthodox Saivas or Vaishnavas and worship Chitragupta with simply a

[1] *Ancient Sanskrit Texts*, V., 302, *note*.

somewhat greater degree of reverence than other castes use to the spirits of their ancestors".

Tribal organisation.

6. The Kâyasths are divided into twelve endogamous sub-castes. These are Srivâstavya or Sribâstab; Bhatnâgara or Bhatnâgar; Saksena; Amisht or Anvasta; Aithan; Asthâna; Bâlmîk or Vâlmîki; Mâthur; Sûryadhwaja or Sûrajdhwaj; Kulsreshta or Kulasreshta; Karan or Karana; Gauda or Gaur and Nigam, with a thirteenth known as Unâya or those of Unâo. These it may be convenient to consider separately.

The Srivâstavya or Sribâstab Kâyasths.

7. These are said to be descended from Bhânu, the son of Chitragupta. He is said to have emigrated to Kashmîr, where he became Râja of Srinagar, and thence obtained his name. On him was conferred the title of Râja-adhirâja by Chandragupta, the Râja of Magadha. By another account the name is derived from Srivatsa, "the favourite of the goddess of fortune," an epithet of Vishnu, whom they are said principally to worship. But there can be little doubt that the name is really territorial and derived from the ancient town of Srâvasti, now Sahet-Mahet, in the Gonda District. They, like the Gaur Kâyasths, have two sections Khara and Dûsra—which are also endogamous. About the explanation of these names opinions differ. Khara possibly represents the Sanskrit *sata* in the sense of "right" or "excellent"; while Dûsra implies an inferior grade. By one story those were named Khara who took up their residence at Ajudhya during the time of Râmchandra; while those who went and lived elsewhere were called Dûsra or "second rate." By an extraordinary feat of folk etymology some of the Oudh Kâyasths say that the twelve sub-castes married each the daughter of a deity (*deota*). On this the Râkshasas determined not to be outdone, and persuaded each of them to take a Râkshasa bride as well. The descendants of the deity became known as Deosra or Dûsra, and those of the demons Khara, which is supposed to be derived from Râkshasa.[1] A third story brings the date of the division down to the time of Akbar. At the Baqar 'Id he, as was the custom of his Court, ordered the flesh of the sacrificed goats to be distributed among his courtiers. Those who accepted the favour were known as Khara or "high-class"; those

[1] *Partâbgarh Settlement Report*, 61, *sq*.

who refused were called Dûsra or "second rate." One of them refused the gift with contumely, and was called Akhori, which is said to mean "one whose faith remained intact." By another story this word, which is the name of one of the Bengal sections, means "one who would not eat" the forbidden food. According to Mr. Sherring,[1] two other clans of this sub-caste, the Niplê Shabân and the Buddhi Shabân, are to be found in the Allahâbâd and Fatehpur Districts. The Sribâstab is by far the most numerous sub-caste of the Kâyasths of these Provinces.

The Bhatnâgar Kâyasths.

8. The Bhatnâgar sub-caste is supposed to be descended from Chitra, the son of Chitragupta. They are said to derive their name from their residence on the banks of the Bhat river, or at the old town of Bhatner, the fort of which is of some historical interest, having been at various times captured by Mahmûd of Ghazni, Taimûr, and Kamrân, the son of Humayun. Among them are two endogamous sections—Bhatnâgar Vaisya or Qadîm, the "real" or "ancient" Bhatnâgars, and the Gaur Bhatnâgari, who are, as will be seen in the account of that sub-caste, connected with the Gaur.

The Saksena Kâyasths.

9. According to the tribal tradition, the word Saksena is a corruption of the Sanskrit *Sakhi-sena* in the sense of "friend of the army," and was a title given to them by the Srivastâvya Râjas of Srinagar on account of their skill in war. But there can be no doubt that the name is really a territorial title derived from the old town of Sankisa in the Farrukhâbâd District. They have three endogamous sections—Khara and Dûsra, which agree with those of the Sribâstav sub-caste, and Kharua, which is said to mean "pure," and was conferred as a recognition of his honesty on one of their ancestors who was Treasurer to Kusa, one of the twin sons of Râma and Sîta. The name of this worthy is said to have been Sûrya Chandra or Soma Datta. By another story the Dûsra section took its name from the fact that they went with Humayun, the father of the Emperor Akbar, when he had to take refuge in Irân after his defeat by Shîr Shâh. They remained some sixteen years in exile with that monarch, and when they returned the "real" or Khara Saksena sub-caste refused to eat *kachchi* with them. It may be conjectured that the terms Khara and Dûsra really imply some

[1] *Hindu Tribes*, I., 309.

actual distinction of social rank and that the fission of the sub-caste into these two sections was the result of some internal quarrel about eating or some other social observance. The traditional ancestor of the Saksena sub-caste is Matimân, the son of Chitragupta.

The Amisht or Ambastha Kâyasths.

10. The Amisht or Anvasta or Ambastha sub-caste are by tradition the descendants of Hanumân, son of Chitragupta. They are said to have settled at the Girnâr Hill and to have taken their name from their worship of the goddess Ambaji or Amba Devi. There seems, however, to be some reason to suspect that they may be the representatives of the Ambastha race, the Ambastae of Arrian, who are traditionally descended from a Brâhman and a woman of the Vaisya tribe, and were noted for their skill in medicine. It may be noted that the practice of surgery is an occupation of some Kâyasths. At the town of Nagrâm, in the Lucknow District, there is a colony of Kâyasths, known as Kohhal, who are oculists and are held in great local repute. None of the Amisht sub-caste appear to be found in these Provinces; they are chiefly resident in Bengal.

The Ashthâna Kâyasths.

11. The Aithâna sub-caste are traditionally the descendants of Visvabhânu, son of Chitragupta. The legendary explanation of the name is that their ancestor once presented to Râja Banâr of Benares eight (*astha*) kinds of pearls—those of the snake, of the shell, of the bamboo, of the conch-shell, of the hog, of the elephant, and one that fell down with the rain from heaven. They have two endogamous sections which do not eat together—the Pûrabi or Mashriqi, "Eastern," who are found in Jaunpur and its neighbourhood, and the Maghribi or Pachhami, "Western," which are found in and about Lucknow.

The Vâlmîki Kâyasths.

12. The Vâlmîki or Bâlmîk sub-caste are said to be descended from Vibhânu or Vrijbhânu, the son of Chandragupta, who is said to have gained the name of Vâlmîki from his austerities. The name is supposed to be derived from the fact that he was so intensely devoted to meditation on God that he allowed the ants to form an ant-hill (*vâlmîka*) over him. They do not appear to have any legend connecting them with the famous Vâlmîki, the author of the Râmâyana. They have three endogamous sections—Mambâi, those of Bombay; Kachchhi those of Kachchh or Cutch; and Sorathi, those of Surat or Saurâshtra. They are not recorded at the recent Census in these Provinces.

13. The Mâthur sub-caste are said to be descended from Chăru, son of Chitragupta. They take their name from their settlement at Mathura. According to one account they have three endogamous sections—Dihlawi, "those from Delhi"; Kachchhi, from Kachchh or Cutch; and the Lachauli of Jodhpur. By another account the Lachauli or Jodhpur sect is called Panchauli, from a king of that country named Pancha.

The Mâthur Kâyasths.

14. The title of the Sûrajdhwaj or Sûryadhwaja Kâyasths means "one having the sun for his emblem." By their own story, they call themselves the descendants of Vibhânu, son of Chitragupta. The title of Sûryadhwaja is said to have been conferred on him by Râja Sura Sena of the race of Ikshwâku, because he helped him in performing a sacrifice. There is a more scandalous derivation of the name and origin of this sub-caste which is particularly irritating to Kâyasths and need not be repeated. They profess excessive purity and call themselves Sakadwîpi or Scythian Brâhmans.

The Sûryadhwaja Kâyasths.

15. The Kulsreshta or Kulasreshta (Sanskrit *kulasreshtin*, "well-born") claim to be descended from Jitindriya or Atindriya, the son of Chitragupta. The legend runs that he was the most amiable of all the sons of Chitragupta, and every year used to invite his brothers and, after drinking the water in which he washed their feet, to entertain them. This devotion to his brethren was counted unto him as righteousness. When his allotted space of life had passed, a messenger from Yamapuri came to him and said, "If you do not care to go to Heaven just now, some other arrangements will be made for you by your father Chitragupta." He replied that he preferred to go to Heaven at once, so a heavenly chariot (*rimâna*) came down for him and carried him first to the Agniloka Heaven, where he saw his father Chitragupta, who was pleased to see him, and, mounting on the same chariot, took him round all the Heavens. At last, when they reached Prajapati Loka, another chariot met them and carried them to Brahma Loka, where he was received into eternal happiness. Hence the honourable title conferred on his descendants. The Kulsreshta Kâyasths are divided into two endogamous sections, Bârah Khera, or "the twelve ancient village sites," and Chha Khera, or "the six sites." These do not eat *kachchi* together.

The Kulasreshta Kâyasths.

16. The Karan is a purely Bengal sub-caste. The name is applied to the indigenous writer class of Orissa, of whom a full account is given by Mr. Risley. The word, of course, is the Sanskrit *karana* (root *kri*, "to do"); but traditionally they take their name from some place named Karnâli on the Narbada. They have two endogamous sections—the Gayawâla or "those of Gaya," and the Tirhûtiya or Tirhûtwâl, who are residents of Tirhût.

The Karan Kâyasths.

17. The Gaur Kâyasths claim to derive their name from Gaur or Gauda, the old capital of Bengal, and say that the Sena dynasty was furnished from their sub-caste. Their primal ancestor, Bhâga Datta, is said to have fought in the war of the Mahâbhârata on the side of Duryodhana against Yudhishthira. Another famous king among them was Râja Lâla Sena. Among Kâyasths it is the custom at marriages for women to make an image of lamp-black, which they call Kâl Sen, and worship it with the family deity. According to one account this Kâl Sen really represents the famous Râja Lâl Sen. The last of the dynasty is called by them Râja Lakhmaniya, and to him the Brâhmans announced that a Turk or Musalmân, whose hands were long enough to touch his feet, would wrest the Kingdom of Bengal from him. At last Bakhtiyâr Khilji was found able to perform this feat, and he deposed the Gaur Kâyasth dynasty. After the conquest the Gaur Kâyasths learnt that some persons of the Bhatnâgar sub-caste were in the Muhammadan service, and the two bodies began to amalgamate, and some of the Gaur Kâyasths also took service with the foreigner. Finally, they adopted from the Bhatnâgars the Bâm Mârgi or left-hand worship and the veneration for Bhairava Chakra, and began to eat with them. So the Bhatnâgars invited the Gaurs to eat *kachchi* with them, and though there was no intermarriage between the two clans, the Bhatnâgars came and ate *kachchi* at the houses of the Gaurs; but when the Bhatnâgars invited the Gaurs to pay them the same compliment they refused. At this the Bhatnâgars took extreme offence, and when some of the Gaurs, who were friendly to them, did eat *kachchi* with them, their more scrupulous brethren excommunicated them. At that time Nasîruddîn was Emperor of Delhi, and he had both Gaur and Bhatnâgar Kâyasths in his service. When the Delhi branch of the Bhatnâgars heard of these events they determined to excom-

The Gauda or Gaur Kâyasths.

municate their Eastern brethren unless the Gaurs would agree to eat *kachchi* with them, and pressure was brought to bear by the Muhammadan Emperor to secure this object. In the end some Gaurs did eat with the Bhatnâgars, and were hence called Gaur Bhatnâgari ; while other more scrupulous Gaurs fled from Delhi in preference to eating with the Bhatnâgars. One of them was a woman far gone in pregnancy. She took refuge in the house of a Brâhman, and when her son was born and grew up the Brâhman married his daughter to him. The remaining Gaurs went to Budâun and settled there. Hearing of this, the Delhi Bhatnâgars again complained to the Emperor and he sent officers to bring the Budâun Gaurs and force them to eat with the Bhatnâgars. They implored the help of their Brâhman friends, and, in order to protect them, the Brâhmans invested them with the Brâhmanical cord, and when they were asked said that these Kâyasths were their brethren. The royal officers were not satisfied with this statement and forced the Brâhmans to eat with these Gaur Kâyasths on the same cooking-place (*chauka*). On this, to the great disgust of the Bhatnâgars, the Emperor dismissed their complaint, and in their anger the Bhatnâgars excommunicated their brethren; and thus there came to be two classes of Bhatnâgars—the Khâs or "real" Bhatnâgars, who had held no communion with the Gaurs, and the Gaur Bhatnâgars, who had eaten with them. And for the same reason there came to be four sections of the Gaurs—*first*, the real Gaurs, who held offices on the Bengal frontier, such as at Nizâmâbâd, Jaunpur, and other places; *secondly*, those who had eaten *kachchi* with the Bhatnâgars; *thirdly*, those who were admitted into communion by the Budâun Brâhmans; and *fourthly*, those who had admitted to caste rights the woman whose son was born in the Brâhman's house.

18. Then followed sundry internal quarrels, which appear not to be quite settled up to the present day. It is said that the third class of Gaurs above mentioned settled at Nizâmâbâd; with these the members of the third class would hold no connection, and appointed the Budâun Brâhmans to be their family priests. The Gaurs of the second class requested these Brâhmans to arrange to get them admitted to equal rights with their clients. This request was so far agreed to that they were admitted to communion; but the Gaurs of the fourth class refused to give them their daughters in marriage. After a time this difference is said to have

disappeared. Hearing of this the Gaurs of the first class, who were dispersed in various places cut off connection with those of Nizâmâbâd from those of the second class. But in time this quarrel was settled, and they are said now all to intermarry. But even now it would seem that occasional attempts are made to revive this old tribal quarrel. The sections above described are now known as Khara, Dûsra, Bangâla, Delhi Shimâli, and Budâuni.

19. It has seemed worth while to give what may be considered a prolix account of a petty caste disagreement. But the story is interesting from two points of view. In the first place, it illustrates the manner in which these tribal sections are being developed. It is on the basis of some insignificant disagreement about ceremonial, such as eating and drinking, etc., that so many of these endogamous groups are now developed and after a time recombine. The system of caste is, in fact, so far from being in a stable condition, that it is in a state of perpetual flux; and we may conjecture that it was from causes such as these in the remote past, of which we have no trustworthy records, that the endogamous groups, which we now call castes, were largely developed. *Secondly*, it is curious to consider the attitude which the Muhammadan Government adopted in dealing with a caste quarrel like this. Now-a-days we can hardly conceive the Government putting pressure on one body of people to admit another set to caste privileges; but this was not so in the olden time, and the influence of the ruling power in moulding the system of caste is a factor which cannot be ignored.

Marriage.

20. In the matter of intermarriage the Kâyasths follow the standard rule of exogamy based on the text of Yajnavalkya as expounded by the author of the Mitakshara, which bars marriage between *sapindas*, that is, who are within five degrees of affinity on the side of the mother and seven degrees on the side of the father. Among the sub-castes which still maintain the organisation of local groups or sections (*al*) marriage cannot take place between persons belonging to the same *al*; nor can a man marry a woman belonging to the *al* of his maternal grandfather or great-grandfather. A man cannot take two sisters to wife at the same time; but he may marry the younger sister of his deceased wife. Mr. Risley gives some examples of outsiders being admitted among the Kâyasths of Bengal; but such a custom is forbidden among the Kâyasths of these Provinces. Of

course if a member of the caste be expelled for misconduct and subsequently perform the expiatory ceremony (*prayâs-chitta*) he can be restored to caste rights. Adult marriage is the rule, and infant marriage the exception, among most of the Kâyasths. Sexual license before marriage is neither recognised nor tolerated, and the parents and other members of a girl thus offending would be promptly excommunicated. Polyandry is utterly prohibited, and polygamy, though allowed, is rarely resorted to unless the first wife be barren, in which case the stringent necessity of begetting male issue makes a second marriage permissible. Re-marriage of widows is absolutely prohibited, and should a widow be found unchaste, she and her relations are promptly put out of caste. There is no legalised divorce; but if a wife commit adultery, she is at once put out of caste, and she cannot eat or associate with any member of the community. Such women cannot, as a matter of course, marry again.

Marriage ceremony.

21. Kâyasths follow the highest form of the eight kinds of marriage recognised by Manu in his Institutes—that known as Brahma. The ceremony is performed according to the rules laid down in the Sanskrit treatise known as the Vivâha Paddhati, with Vedic formulas (*mantra*), as in the case of Brâhmans and the other twice-born classes. The essential and binding portions of the ceremony are the *nanyâdâna* or giving away of the girl by her father, the *panigrahana* or taking of the bride's hand by the bridegroom, *saptapadi* or seven-fold circumambulation of the sacred fire by the pair, and the *sindûrdâna* or application of red powder by the bridegroom to the parting of the hair of the bride. As a rule, too, every Kâyasth bridegroom must be invested with the sacred thread before, or at the time of, marriage.

22. The following account of a rural Kâyasth marriage in Oudh was prepared by a native correspondent for Mr. J. C. Nesfield, and may be quoted here. When a son or daughter is twelve years of age the father and other relations begin to make arrangements for their marriage. The father of the girl, or her brother, accompanied by a Pandit and a barber, go in search of a girl. They try, if possible, to secure a girl of higher rank and station than their own. When they have fixed upon a boy they call for his horoscope (*kundali*), and compare it with that of the girl, and consult a Pandit on the subject. This is known as *ganna*

ganana. If the horoscopes agree, negotiations as to the amount of the dowry proceed, and when this is settled, a day for the *barraksha*, or betrothal, is selected. On that day the father or brother of the girl with the Pandit and barber repair to the house of the boy, and make over to the boy a Brâhmanical cord and some money in proportion to the amount of the dowry which has been agreed on. Then the barber or Kahâr of the boy's family prepares some *sharbat*, which is given to the relatives, priest, and barber of the bride. After this they are entertained with tobacco, betel, and cardamoms. On this a day is fixed for the regular betrothal (*tilak*) and for the wedding. If the girl's home is near, her friends return at once; if not, they stay for the night. When they are leaving, the bridegroom's father gives the priest and barber of the girl a present, which is known as *bidâi.* When they return, the girl's father also consults a Pandit, to ascertain if the day fixed for the betrothal and marriage is auspicious. If the report of the Pandit is favourable, this date is finally fixed; if not, it is changed and a fresh date selected which will satisfy the Pandits on both sides.

23. It sometimes happens that the *tilak* and marriage do not come off for six months or a year from the date of the preliminary betrothal; and should either party be unable from any cause to make the necessary arrangements, it is again postponed. Up to this stage the engagement may be broken if either party be found to be affected with any physical defect such as blindness, dumbness, leprosy, or the like, or if, on further examination, any disagreement be found to exist in the horoscopes. The girl's father announces the day on which the *tilak* will be sent. At this time half the dowry arranged on is sent to the father of the boy. Half is given in cash and half in vessels and clothes, which usually consist of one large dish (*thâra*) of alloy (*phûl*) or silver, one turban, one bale of muslin or other embroidered cloth, four pieces of other cloth (*nainsukh, tanzeb*), one or five cocoanuts, some sandal wood, one handful of turmeric, seven betel-nuts covered with silver foil, two-and-a-half *panseris* or twelve-and-a-half sers of rice coloured with turmeric, some *dûb* grass, one or two annas worth of pice. Others, who can afford it, give richer gifts—horses, elephants, and the like. These things are collected by the father of the bride, and on the appointed day he invites his brethren, who are seated on a carpet and served with cardamoms; while the ladies are taken to the inner apartment and entertained in the same

way. Then on a platform (*chabûtra*) in the court-yard, which has been freshly plastered with cow-dung, the bride is seated and five women, whose husbands are alive, place the gifts on a large tray and lay them in her hands. This is then taken up by the Pandit and laid before the assembled brethren, while he recites auspicious verses. When the brethren approve of the gifts, the father of the girl, his priest, barber and Kahâr get ready to proceed to the house of the boy. Meanwhile the assembled women sing the following song:—

Pahilawa sayunwan dahi wa machhariya; he dulhé upran das pân;
Sagun bhal pâyon.
Hâthi charan dulhé hâthi charhi jân sasurâr;
Sagun bhal pâyon.
Hansi hansi puchhai dulhin dei dulhé kekari je banjhiya kokhi janmen?
Sagun bhal pâyon.
Maiya to hamri Kausalya dei, unahi ke je banjhiya kokhi janmen.
Sagun bhal pâyon.

"The first good omen is the curds and fish and the ten packets of betel on the bridegroom. I have got a good omen.

"O bridegroom! mount on an elephant and ride to the house of thy father-in-law. I have got a good omen.

"The bride laughing asks, 'From what barren mother wast thou born?' I have got a good omen.

"The boy answers—'My mother was Kausalya (mother of Râma). From her barren womb was I born.' I have got a good omen."

24. When the party of the bride reaches the house of the bridegroom, his barber washes their feet, first washing those of the priest. Then he serves round pipes, *sharbat*, cardamoms and betel. Meanwhile the boy's father has invited his brethren and friends. Betel and pipes are passed round and the girl's Pandit opens the presents before the company. Either on this day, or when the anointing begins, the *tilak* ceremony is performed. This is done as follows:—A platform is made in the court-yard and fresh plastered with cow-dung. On this is placed a wooden seat (*pîrha*) and under it some barley. On the seat the Pandit makes a holy square (*chauk*) with flour, and places a pitcher on the platform, near which is erected an image of Gauri made of cow-dung.

The pitcher represents Ganesa Deota. To the south-west of the pitcher the Pandit makes a representation of the nine planets (*nava-graha*). The boy is seated on the stool, and the Pandit makes him worship Gauri and Ganesa, and the nine planets. This done, the Pandit puts the dish containing the presents in the hands of the girl's brother, and he presents them to the bridegroom, while the Pandit recites appropriate verses. The boy takes the tray into the oratory (*deoghar*) sacred to the family god (*kula-devata*), and as he walks on, a woman pours a little water on the ground before him. This is known as *arghadána*. Money is distributed among the Brâhmans present and their wives, and the assembled women sing the following song:—

Sura gáé ké gobar main angna lipáya wa gajmoti chauk puráya-waré, lalanwán.

Gajmoti chauk purái ka subaran kalas dharáyi ké mánik diyana jaláuré, lalanwán.

Mánik jaláike chandan pírha dharáyware, lalanwán.

Ádhé pirhwa par baithé Rája Dasarath ke putwa, ádhé Janak ki dhiya ré, lalanwán.

Achhat dúb láiké dharé wa charan par Síya dekhi muskán.

Syám baran unki manhin na bháwai Rám chuman kaisé jáb wali.

Chuman charan sarúp Rám Hariwálé.

Báyen bar Rám, dahiné ang Síta, bích thaiyán Dhaurahar gir.

Ávan már Mahádeva baithi dhyán lagáiale.

Chuman charan sarúp Rám Hariwálé.

Ek sakhi uthi bolan lagi, "Sun sakhi bát hamár."

Wai triya alankit uhai, hamdhan kul unjiyár.

Chuman charan sarúp Rám Hariwálé.

"I plastered the court-yard with the dung of the sacred cow Surabhi. I made a square of large pearls.

"Making a square of large pearls, I placed in it a golden pitcher full of water.

"Placing the golden pitcher, I lighted the lamps of gems.

"Near it I placed the stool of sandal-wood.

"On half of it sits the son of Dasaratha, on the other half the daughter of Janaka.

"When we placed holy rice and sacred grass at their feet, Sîta smiled.

"The swarthy face pleaseth me not. How can I go and kiss him?

"Kiss the feet of Râma, who is personified as Krishna.

"Râma sits on the right and Sîta on the left, and betwixt them is Mount Dhawalagiri.

"There Mahâdeva sits and the ascetics absorbed in devotion.

"Kiss the feet of Râma, who is personified as Krishna.

"One maiden gets up and says—'Other women may be blamed, but I am the light of this blessed family.'

"Kiss the feet of Râma personified as Krishna."

25. The woman who pours water before the boy as he goes into the oratory sings as follows:—

Ari ari Saguni, ari ari Saguni, sagunwa lai áwa
Tuharé sagunwa ré tuharé sagunwa saguni hoya byáh.
Moré ké angana, moré ke angan chandan guchha rukhwa, teki tar
Rája Dasarath ke putwa sájai bárát.
Dekhab re máiya, dekhab re mái bába mor beohár.
Bahiyán le jhijhikoré chhinari ka putwa, túta motin ka hár.

"Come, goddess of good luck, come! It is by thy omens that the wedding will be completed.

"In my court-yard, in my court-yard the son of Raja Dasaratha arranges the procession.

"O mother! mother! see my arrangements.

"The son of the rake shook my arm and my necklace of pearls was broken."

26. Meanwhile the guests are entertained by the singing of a nautch girl and dinner is served. The second or third day those who have brought the *tilak* return home, and the priest and barber are suitably fed. Then they sing as follows:—

Suno, suno, Rám Chandra gári.
Sári sarit atlas ka lahnga, úpar naurang sári.
Bánh bijáyath, jaushan sohai úpar tariwan sári.
Itna pahini jab nikarin Kausalya chhindari ráur mohtári,
Upra sé uparhi ta bolai "Charhi áo hamári atári."
Suno, suno, Rám Chandra gári.
Sama Lála ki dulhin aisi bani jaisi Kanchanpur kaminiya;
hán, hán, Kanchanpur ki kaminiya.
Unké mángé ka sendur aiso bana jaisé Bhádon birbahutiya.

Unké máthe·kí bendi aisi bani jaisé Bhádon keri bijaliya.
Unké nain ka kájar aiso bano jaisé Sáwan ki ghata gheriya.
Unké dánton ki missi aisi bani jaisé Sáwan lanké bijuliya.
Unké angé ka jobanwa, aiso banyo jaisé anba lagé tikorwa.
Unki níbi ka gathiya aisi bani jaisé nebua galgalwa, hán, hán paké nibu galgalwa.
Samadhi ke bahini ka joban aiso bana, jaisi jhamra par ka taroia.
Rája mohé, bábu mohé aur Mughal Pathán.
Ghora daurâwat Phiringi mohé, jinki dhiri baniyân.
Muskini samadhi Lála tuhanka buláwen Díwánji Díwán salámat;
Kaun uhai taksír ji?
Uhai samadhin aparbal sowai Julahwa ke tírji.
Hansi hansi sej bichhai, kekar sé beniya doláwai ji;
Jab olrai lági samadhin chhindariya Julahwa ke áwai juri tab ji.
Jab karwat mángai, karwat mángai Julahwa jála risiyái ji.
Lauti re Julahwa, lauti re Julahwa, jatiya sé kihesi aját ji;
Hansi hansi puchhai Julahwa sé "Rám kaun uddam kai ke khaib ji.
Teri nariya ré bharangin, teri nariya ré bharangin, dhotiya binauri chauthán ji.
Chauthâné ki dhoti ré au malmal ka thán ji.
Pahiro tu samadhi Lála pahiro tu samadhi Lála, apni joiya ka prasád ji.

"O Râma! Listen to their jeers. The lady's sheet flows like a river. Her petticoat is of satin. Over it is a new robe. On her arm shines the band and armlet. Over her head is a fine sheet. When the coquettish mother of Râma comes out thus attired they call from the balcony, 'Come to my upper chamber.' O Râma listen to their jeers.

"The wife of the father-in-law is so decorated that she looks like a woman of the City of Gold. The parting of her hair is red as the lady-bird insect of Bhâdon. Her forehead spangles look like the lightning; the lamp-black on her eyes looks like the dark clouds in the month of Bhâdon; the black on her teeth is like the lightning in Sâwan; her breasts are like the swelling mangoes; her waist-knot is like the lime; her bosom is like the cucumber. The Râja, the Bâbu, the Mughal, and the Pathân are bewitched by her beauty; so are the Europeans who speak sweetly.

"O father-in-law, smile; Dîwânji (the bridegroom) is calling you. I salute you, Dîwânji. What fault have I committed? The mother-in-law loves the weaver. She smiles, spreads the couch, and fans him. As she was falling asleep the weaver was attacked with fever. When she wanted him to turn round he was wroth.

"Come back, weaver! Through thee I have lost my caste. How am I to live? I will fill thy shuttle and weave a cloth four pieces long. It will be of muslin, and the father-in-law will wear it round his loins as an offering from his spouse."

27. Meanwhile the fathers on both sides begin making preparations for the marriage. The bride's father collects grain and other supplies, and the father of the bridegroom gives earnest money (*sai*) to musicians and dancers, to the Mâli for the wedding crown (*maur*), to the Kahâr bearers, to the Bânsphor for a basket (*dâl*), to the Lohâr for the wedding bracelet (*kangan*), to the potter for vessels, to the Sunâr for the ear-ring (*bâla*), and cloths and jewelry for the wedding gift (*dâl*) are also prepared. Invitations are issued in the form of a letter written on paper dyed with turmeric (*pîli chitthi*), and are sent with a betel-nut by a Nâi or Bâri.

28. Next comes the Pachhorna ceremony. The women of the neighbourhood are invited by a woman of the Nâi or Bâri caste. When they arrive, the parting of their hair is marked with red-lead and oil, and some *urad* pulse is given to them, which they clean (*pachhorna*) in a winnowing fan. As they do this they sing as follows:—

Moré anganwa chandan gachha rukh, tehi tar sugwa sagun liyé thârh;

Pahil sagunwa ré suga—Ahîr ghar jâé; dahi ka dahenriya mandaua dhâi dei;

Dusaré sagunwa ré suga—Pandit gharé jâé, subh ka lagana mandaua dhâi dei;

Tîsaré sagunwa suga—Konharwa gharé jâé, subh ka kalaswa mandaua dhâi dei;

Chauthâ sagunwa suga—Kunderé gharé jâé, subh ka sindhurwa mandaua dhâi dei;

Pânchwân sagunwa suga—Bajajwa gharé jâé, subh ka chundariya mandaua dhâi dei;

Chhathwân sagunwa suga—Chûriharwa gharé jâé, subh ka jorwa mandaua dhâi dei.

Banai ai badari barasai lagi menh,
Bhîjan lâgé dulhâ dulhin jural saneh.

Dulha jo puchhai dulhin sê "Ek bát chalo, ham tum rachin dhamár."

"Kaisê main cháhun dulhê? Beiliya juri chhánh.
Baba kê angna rê prabhu sajan sab thárh."

"Kekarê gumanwa rê dhaniya birwa na kháu; Kekarê gumanwa dhaniya utara na dewa?
Bába ka gumanwa rê dhaniya dina dúi chár;
Hamrê rê gumanwa dhaniya janam siraya."

"In my court-yard is a sandal tree on which sits a parrot bearing good omens.

"First, the parrot goes to the Ahîr and brings his curd vessel, which is placed as a good omen in the marriage shed.

"Secondly, he goes to the Pandit and brings the news of the lucky time, which is a good omen.

"Thirdly, he goes to the potter and places the lucky pitcher in the shed, which is a good omen.

"Fourthly, he goes to the carpenter and brings the lucky red-lead box and places it in the shed, which is a good omen.

"Fifthly, he goes to the cloth merchant and brings the coloured sheet to the shed, which is a good omen.

"Sixthly, he goes to the bangle maker and brings the lucky bangles and places them in the marriage shed.

"The clouds collect, the rain begins to fall. The bride and bridegroom begin to get wet and are joined in love.

"Says the bride—'Come, let us go together and make a bower.' 'How can I go under the cold shade of the Bela flower?' 'In the court-yard of our grandfather the worthy elders are assembled.'

"'In whom dost thou trust that thou wilt not take the coriander?'

"'My master, I cannot answer for fear of my brother.'

"'You may trust in your grandfather for two or three days. After that you must trust in me all your life long.'"

The women who perform this ceremony are given each two-and-a-half sers of *urad* pulse.

29. Next comes the *matchhua* rite, which is done in the evening. All the women collect, and the barber's wife puts some grain in a sieve with five roots of turmeric, two betel-nuts, and a lighted lamp. All the women, headed by the barber's wife, holding the sieve, go to a tank to the east, north, or west of the village.

Before they start, the head woman of the family puts oil and red-lead in the parting of their hair. They take a large basketful of rice and pulse (*khichari*) to the tank, and sing the following song :—

Mewari wâri saguni âj banê.

Angna lipai rakheu ho. Mewari wâri saguni âj banê.
Chauki purâi rakheu ho. Mewari wâri saguni âj banê.
Kalsa dharai rakheu ho. Mewari wâri saguni âj banê.
Pírhwa dharai rakheu ho. Mewari wâri saguni âj banê.
Dulhin baithê rakheu ho. Mewari wâri saguni âj banê.

"The maidens give a good omen. Have the court-yard plastered. Have the holy square made. Have the sacred pitcher placed. Have the wooden stool arranged. Get the bride seated. The maidens give a good omen."

30. When they reach the tank the oldest woman of the family, wearing a yellow garment, plasters a piece of ground, and in it she places some turmeric and red-lead, and fixes an arrow within it. She also places five roots of turmeric, two betel-nuts, and five handsful of earth, with the winnowing fan containing the articles which they have brought with them. She burns some incense and lights a lamp. While this is being done a song which cannot be printed is sung. The food is distributed, and as they come home they sing :—

Thârhi pukârai mero yâr ; Mohna terê jiu dard na âwai.
Mohana kiti rupaiya teri châkari aur kitê takê tera roz ?
Thârhi pukârai, etc.
Mohana sau sau rupaiya meri châkari ; lâkh taka mera roz.
Thârhi pukârai, etc.
Mohana chhor Phirangiya ki châkari; Mohana chhor Paturiya ke sâth.
Thârhi pukârai, etc.
Dântan ke batisiya Mohana chhoro Mahobê ka pân.
Thârhi pukârai, etc.

"My dear, I stand and implore you, but your heart feels no pity for me. O Mohan ! how much is your pay and how much do you get daily ?" "I get a hundred rupees a month and a lakh of pice a day." "O Mohan ! give up the service of the European and the company of the dancing-girls. O Mohan ! give up the betel of Mahoba which colours your thirty-two teeth. O friend ! I stand and implore you."

31. When they return home, an unmarried girl, who brings a little earth from the tank, has a brass drinking vessel (*lotâ*) full of

water and a pestle moved round her head. A rice mortar is then placed on a plastered platform in the court-yard, and seven women whose husbands are alive pound rice in the mortar. While doing this they sing songs unfit for publication. Sometimes instead of rice *masûr* pulse is pounded, and the ceremony is known as *masûr chhâtna*. In connection with this is the rite known as *rora darna*, when seven women, as before, crush *urad* pulse in the family mill (*chakki*) The songs sung on this occasion are of the same description.

32. Then, according to which house the rite applies, the bride or bridegroom, as the case may be, is seated on a stool in the house, and seven women whose husbands are alive rub him or her with barley flour mixed with oil and turmeric. A song is also sung on this occasion, and when the rice and pulse has been distributed among them, the women sing the evening (*sandhya*) song, which is as follows :—

Khair supariya besahi mangâib debé Râja Dasarath hâth,
Âpan âpan dal sajé jé âwai bhal bidhi sâjé bârât.
Dhauté Naua ré dhaute, Bâriya dhâya ken khabar janâu ;
Ketik dal lawen Râja Dasarath sut jin dekhi rîndhon main bhât.
Ek lâkh hâthi, dûi lâkh ghora, tîn lâkh âyé sukhpâl.
Majhki palkiya Râja Dasarath sut âyé chaunr dhurai châriu pânw ;
Kahanwân bâjai damru sahnaiya, kahanwân sankh bisankh ?
Kahwân ke Râja put biâhan âwen ? Kahanwân uthai jhankâr ?
Awadh ke Râja put biâhan âwen, Janak uthain jhankâr.
Jai bârât mandwé tar utâri, tasu no parchhai dâmâd.
Kachhu parchhai, kachhu badan nihârai kâla bhanwar ré dâmâd.
Chummon main haradi, chummon rẹ lochan, chummon main bar ka lilâr.
Sûraj ki joti sé adhik nain sundar sânwalé baran Sri Râm.
Bhayal byâh charhal sir sendur nau lâkh daij thor.
Purba ka dandiya pachhu uhai bâba maiya ka dharai lagê ânsu.
Bhaûji ka jiyara anand bhai bâba nanad chalen sasurâr.
Jauné bât dhiya mori jaihen pipara ka pât khahrâi.
Koili sabad dhiya roati jaihen chhatya bihri mori jây.
Bât ka batohiya ghar kahab sandeswa maiya se kahab arthâi.
Majhi usariya mori gadiya bisari ge mori maiya dharihâi uthâi.

" 'I bought catechu and betel and handed them to Râja Dasarath. They have adorned their followers and the wedding party. O barber and Bâri! run and see how many men have come, and inform me, so that I may cook rice for them.' 'One lâkh elephants, two lâkhs of horses, and three lâkhs of palanquins have come.' In the middle palanquin is Râja Dasarath's son, over whom fans are being waved. Where is the drum being beaten and the trumpet and conch shell blown? What Râja has come to be married, and where does the music sound? The King of Oudh has come to be married. The music is in Mathura and the city of Janak. The procession reaches the house, and the door rite is being performed. Diamonds, rubies, gems, and garlands are presented. The procession comes under the marriage shed, and the mother of the bride moves a water vessel and a pestle over the head of her son-in-law. As she does the wave ceremony, she looks at the bridegroom, who is black as the large black bee. I kiss turmeric; I kiss the eyes and forehead of the bridegroom. Râma is as bright as the sun, black coloured though he be. The marriage is over, the parting of the bride's hair has been marked with vermilion. Nine lâkhs are her dowry. When the pole of the litter is turned, the mother weeps. The sister-in-law is pleased that her husband's sister is going to the house of her lover. The mother says—'The leaves rustle on the road as my daughter passes by. My daughter mourns as she goes like the cuckoo, and at this my heart is broken.' As she goes along, my daughter says to those she meets on the road—'Go tell my mother that I have forgotten my dolls in the middle portico, and that she must keep them safe.'"

33. This song is sung daily in the evening till the marriage day. When but two hours remain to dawn, seven women, whose husbands are alive, are called to wash the pounded *urad* pulse. As they wash it, they sing the song which is sung on the occasion of the *tilak*. The earth which has been brought by a virgin from the tank is used to make a fireplace, which is worshipped on the day when the anointing of the bride and bridegroom commences.

34. Next comes the wake (*rât juga*), which is performed on the fourth night before the wedding day. The invitations are sent round by the wife of the barber and the Bâri. Meanwhile cakes are made to the amount of two-and-a-half, five, seven, or ten maunds weight according to the circumstances of the family. Then the oven, which has been constructed of the sacred earth brought from the village tank, is worshipped in this way. It is first smeared with rice soaked in water and turmeric, and then a lamp is put

upon it, with a pice, a piece of turmeric, and some betel-nuts. Then seven women whose husbands are alive smear it with the rice and sing:—

Bhor bhayal bhinsâr chiraiya ek bolai
Jay jagâo kaun Râma jin ghar osari.
Na morê dhenu gâbhin na morê osari.
Kukuru ke sabad bhayal bhinsâr pathai deb kaun Râm âpan dhana,
Au apani main loni dhana dîkhê na deb parchhâi na deb.
Kânê kundal, garê moti mâl;
Kâhê keri tori chulhiya, kahê lagê uchakan?
Kaun charitra tori chulhiya; kaun Râni pûjai?
Sonen kari morê chulhiya, rûpê lage uchakan.
Ratan jaril mor chulhiya, to Jirbal Râni pûjai.

"The morn is about to dawn; go and wake so and so, whose turn it is. 'Neither is my cow in calf, nor is it my turn.' The morning breaks at cock crow. I shall send my son; I shall allow none to see my bridegroom, nor permit any one to do the wave ceremony over him. He has ear-rings in his ears and a string of gems round his neck. Of what is your oven made, and why is it lifted up? What quality does it possess, and what Râni does it worship? 'It is made of gold and it is raised up for its beauty. It is studded with gems and the Râni Jirbal worships it.'"

35. Next comes the *Til pûjna* ceremony, which in some families is done five, and in some two, days before the wedding. At this time the *kohabar*, or wedding symbol, is made either in three or five places in the house. It is usually made at both sides of a special room door, and also within the room itself. That inside the room is made with sixteen lumps (*piriya*) of cow-dung stuck on the wall. On the right side of the door are fixed three and on the left side four lumps of cow-dung. When this is being done, the following song is sung:—

Angna kai kohabar Mahâdeva chitra bichitra, bhîtara kai kohabar Mahâdeva likhlain banai.
Tehi baithi Mahâdeva dâsali sej.
Jata phailai Mahâdeva sûtain sâri rât;
O tisari sûto Mahâdeva jata bewa sikori.
Hamarê naiharwa kai chundari Mahâdeva dhumil jani hoya.
Etna suni Mahâdeva chali risiâya.
Bhîtara kai sejiya Mahâdeva angana le dânsain.

Jau ham hobai Mahádeva sada kai sohágin rimiki jimiki daiwa barsé sáré rát.
Kukuri lagái Mahádeva gorwári; apani gorwariya Gaura sútai hamen dewa.
Apani gorwariya Mahádeva sutani jo deb.
Deswa Mahádeva birahi kai likhwa na deb.

"Mahâdeva makes a wonderful *kohabar* mark in the court-yard, and I shall make it myself in the inner room. Sitting there, Mahâdeva spreads the couch. With his matted hair flowing he sleeps all night. O Mahâdeva! draw up thy matted hair that the garment given by my mother be not stained. Hearing this, Mahâdeva rises angrily. He brings the couch from the inner room and lays it in the court-yard. 'O Mahâdeva! if I am to be all my life married, the rain will fall pitter patter all night long.' Mahâdeva stands bending at the foot of the bed. 'O Gaura! let me sleep at the foot of thy bed.' 'O Mahâdeva! if I allow thee to sleep at the foot of my cot, thou wilt have no thought for those husbands who are away from their wives in the world.'"

The *kohabar* marks are made by the aunt or elder sister of the bride or bridegroom.

36. Next follows the rite of *kalas gothna*, or the smearing of the marriage pitcher. Seven women whose husbands are alive bathe and put on clean clothes. Their hair is oiled, the parting marked with vermilion, and their laps filled with barley. Then they smear a fresh earthen pitcher with cow-dung and stick lumps of the same substance all round it. On these grains of barley are sprinkled, and as they do this they sing:—

Ãdhê talwa men Nág chunai, ádhé Nágin chunai, tabhún na talwa suháwan kamal bina.
Ãdhê mandwa got baithê, ádhé gotin baithê, tabhún na mandwa suhawan ekré nand bina.
Awahu nand gusáin, mori thakuráin, baitho mánjh usáré, kalas mor gotho.
Jo main baithon, bhauji, jan baitháon, tín baran kai sadhi tinu ham lebai.
Bhaiya ka hásul ghorwa na bhatijwa kai mohar, bhauji, tohari bagar kai tilarwa tiniu ham lebai.
Na morai hásul ghorawa na bhatijwa kai mohar, na morai garkai tilariya moré kachhu nahin.

Ganuán kẽ natẽn Nauniya nanad mor lagai. Tu baitho mánjh usariya kalas mor gotho.

Angana sẽ bhaiya bhîtar gae, bhauji se mati karai. Deswa nikari ham jábai bahiniya ke káran.

Ao nanad gusáîn, mori thakuráin, baith mánjh úsar, kalas mor gotho.

Debon main hásul ghorawa, bhatijwa kai mohar, ápanê garê kai tilariya, morê gharê sab kuchh.

" 'The snake feeds in half the tank and his mate in the other half. Even then the tank has no beauty without the lotus. In half of the marriage shed sit the tribesmen and in the other half their wives. But even then the pavilion has no beauty without the husband's sister. O husband's sister! mistress of your passions, my mistress, sit in the midst of the pavilion.' 'O wife of my brother! if you ask me to sit here I agree, but three things you must give me—the horse of my brother with the gold chain round its neck, the gold coin my nephew wears, and you must present me with your three-strand gold chain.' 'No horse, nor gold coin, nor three-strand chain have I.' By village relationship the barber's wife is as my husband's sister, sit in the middle and smear the pitcher. The brother goes into the house and consults his wife. I shall quit my native land on account of my sister. O my husband's sister! mistress of passion, my own mistress, sit in the midst and smear the pitcher. 'I will give you the horse with the golden chain, the nephew's gold coin, and the three-strand chain round my neck.' "

37. After this the grandfather or uncle of the bride or bridegroom sits on a platform in the courtyard, which has been plastered with cow-dung, with the corners of their garments tied together. This is done, they bathe and put on clean clothes. They sit facing the east, and the worship of *Tel* is performed as follows: In a dish flowers, holy rice, *dúb* grass, betel, red lead, curds, and sweetmeats are placed. The Pandit makes an altar (*bedi*), and Gauri and Ganesa are worshipped, and after them the Nine Planets (*naugraha*) to whom the offering is made. Incense is burnt, and a lamp lighted with camphor. The barber then digs a hole in the ground, in which the worshippers fix a harrow (*henga*), and the earth is filled in round it. Then the worshipper makes seven marks on the harrow with powdered rice and oil, and binds a thread (*raksha*) round it and the sacred water pitcher (*kalsa*). Two wisps of grass are tied to the top

of it, and a lamp is lighted on each side. More wisps of grass are tied to the harrow, and on each a lighted lamp is fixed. The harrow is then worshipped, and garlands of flowers are tied round it. This worship is known as *Taran toran.* The offerings in this case are turmeric, washed rice, betel, and flowers. After this a shallow hole is dug on the right side of the house in which the *Kohabar* marks have been made, as already described, and the earth from the hole is laid on seven leaves of the plantain or *sāl* tree, which are worshipped with an offering of turmeric, clean rice, flowers, curds, incense, and lamps. The earth is formed into a rude representation of the deities who are worshipped. This is known as *Bastu pūja.* After this, they lay some shoots of the mango tree on the plantain and *sāl* leaves, and the hole is filled up and plastered over. The mango shoots are allowed to project just over the surface of the ground. To these worship is again done as before, and this is known as *Bansapti pūja,* or the worship of the forest goddess.

38. This done, they return to the platform and worship the gods. They go into the *Kohabar* room and do worship to the lumps of cow-dung fixed on the wall. This is known as *Nandâdi sapta mâtri pūja.* Then they put two earthen pots on the fire-place and tie threads (*raksha*) round them. Under them is placed some mango wood, but it is not lighted. They return to the *Kohabar* room, and again worship the sixteen lumps of cow-dung placed on the wall. To them is fixed a piece of new cloth dyed in turmeric. This is known as *Kumâr jâdi khodas mâtri pūja.* Next a small earthen vessel is covered with a new cloth dyed in turmeric, and the worshipper mentally repeats the names of his deceased relations up to the seventh generation, and drops a grain of rice at the name of each. The names of both male and female ancestors are repeated, and the hair of each pair of worshippers is tied together and upon it milk and *sharbat* is poured, so as to fall into the vessel into which the rice has been dropped.

39. When this is done, the bride or bridegroom, according to which family is performing the rite, is seated on a wooden stool (*pīrha*) on the platform, and under it barley or rice is scattered. Oil and turmeric are sprinkled with a wisp of grass on the images of Gauri and Ganesa, and the Pandit does the same for the bride or bridegroom, as the case may be. After this seven women whose husbands are alive rub oil and turmeric on the body of the bride or bridegroom, and sing a song, kissing the feet, knees, breast,

shoulders and forehead of the bride or bridegroom. Rice, pulse, and cakes are distributed, and songs are sung, and in the evening the friends are entertained.

40. Next the father's sister of the boy or girl is called. Her head is oiled and the parting marked with red-lead. A new earthen pot, to the outside of which lumps of cow-dung are fixed, is placed on the fire-place close to the platform near the harrow, and the sister of the father of the boy or girl parches twenty-five sers of paddy in it, and a song is sung. Flour, turmeric, and water are then mixed up in the same pot, and when it is taken off the fire-place the heads of seven women whose husbands are alive are decorated with oil and red-lead. These women proceed to make an image of Gauri. Thirty-five sers of rice flour are kneaded and mixed with sugar and fruits. Out of this are made the images of a male and female. Sometimes two pair of images are made, and the female image is dressed with women's ornaments and the male with those of a man.

41. After this, at the house of the bride, the rite of *Sohâg bândhna* is done. A box is filled with the trinkets, red-lead, etc., used by a woman who is not a widow. These are put in the box by seven women whose husbands are alive. That night, about two hours before dawn, the bride and her female friends take some rice and a red-lead box and go to the house of a Dhobin to ask for *sohâg*. She has her head smeared with oil and red-lead near the Dhobi's washing-tub (*nând*). The Dhobin sits facing the east, and the bride opposite her. The Dhobin covers the bride's head with her sheet, and marks the parting of her hair with red-lead, with the finger of her left hand. Then she rubs her own forehead against that of the bride, and the bride gives her the box of red-lead while a song is sung. Then they go in succession to the houses of seven women whose husbands are alive, and to each of them the bride gives a box of red-lead They return home just as the day dawns. A number of women who are not widows are invited and fed, and the bride sits before them on a wooden stool on the platform, under which rice is sprinkled. Behind her sits her mother, grandmother or aunt, who covers the bride's head with her sheet. A leaf platter is placed before the bride, and each of the women gives her *sohâg* or the symbol of married happiness in this way: Each woman puts in the bride's dish cakes (*pûri*), sugar, curds, two pice and a box of red-lead, and covers her head with her sheet. Each woman marks her

own head with red, and the bride does the same seven times, taking the colour from the heads of the married women. While this ceremony goes on the bride and the women fast. Then follows a general feast.

42. Meanwhile, at the house of the boy on the Bhatwân or day but one before the wedding, all the brethren are fed, and those who intend to accompany the procession have uncooked food served out to them. Dancing goes on at the door. On the morning of the wedding day the boy is anointed with turmeric and oil, and part of his head is shaved. Then he is made to stand on a plough yoke (*juâtha*), and the Nâi or Kahâr bathes him. The water thus used is received in an earthen pot, and his body is wiped with a cloth, which is the perquisite of the man who bathed him. A new loin-cloth is put on him, and the old one is given to the Nâi. His father's sister moves over his head mustard and salt to baffle the Evil-eye, and lights a lamp before him. He is then seated on a wooden stool, under which rice is sprinkled on the platform; the Nâi cuts his nails, while the Bâri holds an umbrella over his head. When the nail-cutting is over, the women give a present to the Nâi, who dyes the feet of the boy with lac (*mahâwar*). The tailor then dresses him in his wedding suit, and the Sunâr brings his ornaments. He puts the marriage bracelet (*kangan*) on his wrist. The Pandit marks his forehead with sandal-wood, and his father's sister marks his eyelids with lamp-black. Next the Mâli puts the marriage crown (*maur*) on his head, and all these persons are rewarded by the parents.

43. Next, the husband of the bridegroom's father's sister does the rite known as *Takri pherna*. He holds a thread and walks seven times round the boy. When the circuits are complete, the thread is broken. For this he receives a present. Then he pounds some rice, of which a little is tied in a red cloth round the wrist of the boy with the thread which has already been used in this ceremony. This done, the bridegroom comes out and gets into his palanquin, accompanied by his mother or grandmother. They are all carried round a well which has been duly married and music is played. While he goes round the well, his other female relations sit by turns in the palanquin, and each of them gives four pice to the Kahâr bearers. This ceremony is known as *Dera chapâwan*. Next the mother offers her breast to her son, and as the women return home the procession starts for the house of the bride.

44. That night again the women friends are invited, and a rice mortar is placed on the platform. On this the mother and grandmother sit, and on it is placed a pot full of barley flour and sweetmeats, and a lamp is lighted. A basket is put over all, and finally the food is distributed to seven women whose husbands are alive, and they sit round the pot and drum on it with sticks.

45. The actual marriage rite at the bride's house is of the normal type, and need not be described at length.

Religion.

46. Kâyasths are Hindus, but belong to various religious sects: some are Saivas, some Sâktas, some Vaishnavas. The first two predominate. Some few are Nânakshâhis, Kabîrpanthis or Achâris, or belong to the Arya Samâj. The fact of their belonging to different sects does not prevent them from associating freely as members of the same brotherhood. A man of the Vaishnava sect may marry a Sâkta woman, provided the rules of exogamy are observed, and after the marriage it will be optional for the woman to give up animal flesh and wine or to continue to use them, even though the husband as a Vaishnava be a vegetarian and total abstainer. Chitragupta, the progenitor of the caste, is worshipped by them daily, in places where a temple in his honour exists. In other places he is worshipped annually on the second day of the bright fortnight of the month Kârttik, which is known as the Yamadvitiya, Chitragupta being one of the fourteen Yamas. He is also worshipped on the second day of the dark fortnight of the month of Chait. The offerings to him consist of fruits, sweetmeats, and money, the last being appropriated by the Pujâri or Brâhman priest in charge of the temple. Worship is also done to the Kula devatas, or family gods, which are different in different families. The other deities worshipped are the same as those of the other higher Hindu castes. The chief among these are Durga, Jayanti, Lakshmi, Shambhari, Mahâdeva, Vishnu, Ganesa, Krishna, Râma, Ganga, Ananta, and Nârâyana. Brâhmans are employed for all religious rites, and are received on an equality with other Brâhmans. They are generally known by the titles of Purohit, Pâdha, Achârya, etc.

Social status and occupation.

47. Notwithstanding the jealousy with which they are regarded by their less astute neighbours, the social position of the caste is a high one. Those who do not belong to the Vaishnava sect usually eat meat. Those who are Sâktas drink intoxicating liquor, but it is believed that the move-

ment in favour of total abstinence has in recent years done much to reduce the drunkenness which formerly prevailed to a large extent. Those who are Vaishnavas are, of course, abstainers. The only meat they eat is mutton or goat's flesh, and in matters of food they are strictly orthodox. They cannot eat *kachchi* or *pakki* out of the same dish, or drink out of the same vessel of, or smoke out of the same *huqqa* with, members of any caste but their own. They will use the cocoanut pipe bowl (*nâriyal*) of any Kâyasth, but they cannot smoke out of the mouthpiece (*naicha*) of any one not belonging to their own sub-division. Suratwâla, or those who are illegitimate, cannot smoke with those of legitimate descent. All the sub-divisions may eat *pakki* together but not *kachchi*.

The occupation of the caste is in the main literary, and they have supplied many valuable officers of Government and members of the Bar and Educational Department. There are numerous Sanskrit terms indicating the present occupations of the caste such as Lekhaka, Lipakâra, Aksharjîvaka, Aksharachana, Aksharachuncha, Lipakâra, and Aksharachanchu ; but it is impossible to identify the present caste specially with any of these. While the higher members of the caste rank high in general repute, the village Lâla, who is very often an accountant, is in evil repute for his astuteness and chicanery.

Distribution of Kâyasths according to the Census of 1891.

District.	Asthâna.	Bengâli.	Bhatnâgar.	Gaur.	Kulsarisht.	Mâthur.	Nigam.	Saksena.	Sribâstab	Unâya.	Others.	Total.
Debra Dûn	1	...	174	...	...	41	...	55	83	...	7	361
Sahâranpur	...	...	1,129	...	...	61	...	369	177	...	318	2,054
Muzaffarnagar	6	2	684	...	9	56	...	96	120	5	123	1,101
Meerut	27	12	1,420	...	2	275	...	1,308	271	5	475	3,795
Bulandshahr	...	...	350	...	...	341	...	1,253	469	9	1,376	3,798
Aligarh	...	1	30	...	403	1,175	...	2,603	364	...	3,472	8,047
Mathura	66	1,206	130	2	1,114	376	19	1,359	912	23	293	5,500
Agra	535	4	884	...	2,176	724	3	2,875	3,373	15	127	10,716
Farrukhâbâd	5	36	105	5	·12	93	75	7,848	3,611	54	612	12,456
Mainpuri	...	2	59	1	1,613	88	...	4,786	1,577	51	105	8,282
Etâwah	...	93	80	...	217	41	273	3,336	3,608	80	332	8,260
Etah	4	5	64	1	2,015	56	1	5,728	344	4	53	8,275
Bareilly	28	9	537	...	...	156	...	15,804	1,076	...	15	17,625
Bijnor	3	...	2,591	...	...	418	...	502	153	2	70	3,739
Budâun	...	18	322	...	1	304	...	8,347	185	10	17	9,204
Morâdâbâd	...	26	3,253	...	11	1,459	...	5,367	702	2	378	11,198
Shâhjahânpur	47	...	244	...	16	70	...	7,572	3,629	..	95	11,603

Pilibhît	27	...	447	...	...	25	...	4,236	356	31	45	5,167
Cawnpur	18	121	29	...	204	118	862	1,179	10,043	2,692	262	15,528
Fatehpur	166	12	11	20	8	18	175	76	7,918	395	34	8,833
Bânda	...	47	12	...	...	41	82	248	6,381	1,471	1,367	9,649
Hamîrpur	18	...	131	...	...	47	22	2,375	3,442	1,342	22	7,400
Allahâbâd	86	430	94	2	...	35	5	666	19,283	66	659	21,326
Jhânsi	...	42	80	53	...	79	33	780	4,618	37	1,408	7,230
Jâlaun	27	1	53	...	374	...	117	1,314	4,713	389	543	7,531
Lalitpur	1	6	16	...	3	14	...	117	2,350	59	3	2,569
Benares	37	89	43	21	...	23	...	16	14,047	104	1,325	15,705
Mirzapur	54	4	4	1	...	1	...	400	12,382	10	41	12,897
Jaunpur	1,273	...	...	...	...	...	13	86	9,474	44	3,953	14,843
Ghâzipur	52	23	30	78	...	173	7	13	14,734	36	238	15,384
Ballia	...	69	10	40	...	...	...	18	14,750	...	78	14,965
Gorakhpur	159	42	61	88	...	9	3	74	24,865	4	4,405	29,710
Basti	129	15	...	16	...	...	...	171	20,807	...	...	21,136
Azamgarh	2,417	2	76	690	...	55	...	69	12,993	...	201	16,503
Kumaun	...	...	...	...	...	...	...	...	...	...	50	50

Distribution of Kâyasths according to the Census of 1891—continued.

District.	Asthâna.	Bengâli.	Bhatnâgar.	Gaur.	Kulsarisht.	Mâthur.	Nigam.	Saksena.	Sribâstab.	Unâya.	Others.	Total.
Garhwâl . . .	...	...	...	...	...	...	...	...	91	...	53	144
Tarâi	...	...	129	...	2	51	...	944	74	...	7	1,207
Lucknow . . .	100	208	67	49	1	247	858	2,716	11,003	1,620	551	17,420
Unâo	583	7	25	...	...	1	1,333	257	7,591	9[illegible]	13	10,744
Râê Bareli . . .	...	86	12	...	...	...	60	69	12,712	23	115	13,077
Sîtapur	433	22	162	29	...	6	33	1,686	10,862	172	15	13,420
Hardoi	2,073	1	15	...	...	420	17	861	6,491	57	...	9,935
Kheri	70	14	50	...	...	207	8	1,562	6,922	42	190	9,065
Faizâbâd . . .	1	...	78	101	...	18	4	305	15,627	81	10	16,225
Gonda	31	1	37	...	...	154	129	206	19,564	149	...	20,271
Bahrâich . . .	32	2	30	...	...	135	33	401	9,709	68	...	10,410
Sultânpur . . .	11	...	50	...	...	...	10	124	13,233	...	...	13,428
Partâbgarh . . .	13	...	47	...	...	6	1	75	9,264	5	265	9,676
Bàrabanki . . .	65	...	21	...	...	177	385	186	12,164	831	133	13,962
Total .	8,598	2,658	13,876	1,207	8,180	7,794	4,561	90,538	339,117	10,922	23,785	511,426

Kewat.—A caste of fishermen, boatmen, and cultivators. The analysis of the Kewats is rendered very difficult, because they merge on the one side into Binds and on the other into Mallâhs, and, as was the case at the recent Census, each is very often recorded as a sub-caste of the other. They are usually considered to be the modern representatives, at least in name, of the Kaivartas or Kevartas. Their name is generally derived from Sanskrit *ka*, "water," and *vritti*, "occupation," in the sense that they live on or by water. But Professor Lassen[1] asserts that the use of *ka* in this sense is extremely unusual in early Sanskrit, and that the true derivation is Kivarta, a corruption of Kimvarta, meaning "a person following a low or degrading occupation." "This," he adds, "would be in keeping with the pedigree assigned to the caste in Manu, where the Kaivarta, also known as Mârgava or Dâsa, is said to have been begotten by a Nishâda father from an Ayogavi mother, and to subsist by his labours in boats. On the other hand, the Brahma-Vaiyarta Purâna gives the Kaivarta a Kshatriya father and a Vaisya mother as far more distinguished parentage; for the Ayogavi, being born from a Sudra father and a Vaisya mother, is classed as *pratiloma*, 'begotten against the hair,' or in the inverse order of the precedence of the castes."

Tribal organisation.

2. As will be seen from the annexed figures, abstracted from the returns of the Census, a large number of the Kewats of the Eastern Districts have recorded themselves as a sub-caste of Mallâhs, and they are also obviously very closely mixed up with the Binds. This list gives their sub-castes as—Agarwâl, which is also the title of a sub-caste of Banyas; Bâtham from Srâvasti; Ghogh, who say they take their name from *ghonga*, "a cockle shell"; Jaiswâr, a common title for the sub-castes of various menial tribes; Kharbind or "pure Binds"; Kharot or "straw men"; Mallâh; Nikhâd or Nishâda. In Mirzapur they class themselves as Châi, Tiyar, Bathawa or Bathama, Sorahiya, Muriyâri, Bind or Kewat, and Goriya, which are connected with the Gonr grain-parchers and workers in stone. All these are endogamous, and their rule of exogamy follows the usual formula, *chachera, mamera, phuphera, mausera*, by which the line of the aunt and uncle on the paternal and maternal sides are barred as long as any recollection of relationship can be followed.

[1] Quoted by Risley, *Tribes and Castes*, I., 376.

Like the Mallâhs, they call themselves the descendants of Nishâda, who rowed Râma Chandra across the Ganges on his way to Prayâg or Allahâbâd, and they fix the scene of this occurrence at the Râmchaura Ghât over the Ganges near Bindhâchal in the Mirzapur District, which they regard as the head-quarters of the caste. The detailed Census lists give 296 names of the usual type. Their connection with other tribes is marked by names such as Bind, Châîn, Kharbind, Kharwâr, Koriya, Luniya, Mallâh, side by side with others, which express the rising pretensions of the more prosperous members of the tribes, as Dichhit, Gaur, Kachhwâha, Sombansi, and local names like Agarwâl, Aharwâr, Ajudhyabâsi, Kânhpuriya, Jaiswar, Magahiya, Mâthur, Pachhwâhan, Sarwariya, and Sribâstab.

Marriage.

3. Marriage takes place among them at the age of five or seven. Mr. Risley[1] notes the curious fact in Bihâr that "it is deemed of less importance that the bridegroom should be older than the bride, than that he should be taller. This point is of the first importance, and is ascertained by actual measurement. If the boy is shorter than the girl, or if his height is exactly the same as hers, it is believed that the union of the two would bring ill luck, and the match is at once broken off." The marriage ceremonies are of the ordinary character. A second wife cannot be taken during the life-time of the first unless he can show to the satisfaction of the council that she is barren or hopelessly diseased. Widows can marry by the *sagâi* form. She can marry her husband's younger brother, and she usually does so if he is a bachelor and of marriageable age. A man can expel his wife for adultery, but inter-tribal incontinence is very lightly regarded, and can be atoned by giving a feast. But if a woman is detected in an intrigue with a stranger, she is permanently expelled from caste. A wife can also, with the permission of the council, separate from her husband if he fail to support her.

Religion.

4. The Kewats are orthodox Hindus. To the east of the Province they worship Kâli, Bhâgawati, and their boat. Kâli is worshipped every second year with a sacrifice of goats and an offering of flowers. Mâhabîr gets some *laddu* sweetmeats on a Tuesday, and the river gets a few drops of milk on Sundays. When they return from a voyage they make a burnt offering to, and hang some flowers upon,

---

[1] *Loc. cit.*, I., 455.

their boat. If possible, they feed a few Brâhmans at the same time. Sarwariya Brâhmans officiate at their weddings and other ceremonies.

Occupation and social status.

5. The Bâtham Kewats pretend to extra purity, and are careful to conform to a higher standard of living than the ordinary members of the tribe, most of whom, unless they are Bhagats, eat all kinds of fish, and even, it is said, the tortoise and crocodile. They drink spirits, but will not eat beaf, pork, or fowls. They will eat *kachchi* cooked by no caste but their own; *pakki* cooked by Brâhmans, Kshatriyas, or Vaisyas. They rank on about the level of the Koiri or Teli. A Bihâr proverb quoted by Mr. Christian runs— *Nauwa Kewat chînhê jât; barka log kê chikkan bât*—"The barber and the boatman are the only people who recognise their caste-fellows; high-caste people are good only for talk."

Distribution of Kewats according to the Census of 1891, including Mallâh Kewats.

District.	Agârwâla.	Bâtham.	Ghogh.	Jaiswâr.	Kharbind.	Kharot.	Mallâh.	Mallâh Kewat.	Nikhâd.	Others.	Total.
Dehra Dûn	...	...	...	...	...	...	...	...	...	22	22
Sahâranpur	...	...	...	...	...	...	...	18	...	3	21
Muzaffarnagar	...	...	...	...	...	...	...	2	...	...	2
Meerut	...	...	...	...	...	...	...	51	...	...	51
Farrukhâbâd	...	...	...	...	...	...	...	1	...	...	1
Pilibhît	...	...	...	...	...	...	...	...	...	26	26
Cawnpur	...	...	...	...	...	...	...	...	...	8	8
Fatehpur	...	9,460	3,715	...	4	...	153	...	402	11,545	25,279
Bânda	148	8,273	11,615	...	23	...	56	...	56	2,464	22,535
Hamirpur	5,025	55	3,522	...	...	...	...	...	40	767	9,409
Allahâbâd	...	...	...	...	...	...	6	31,197	14	7	31,224
Jhânsi	291	...	...	...	...	...	...	...	...	6	297
Jâlaun	577	...	...	...	...	...	...	1	...	112	690
Benares	...	...	...	...	...	...	...	1,506	...	...	1,506
Mirzapur	...	...	...	...	...	...	...	46,085	...	...	46,085
Jaunpur	...	...	...	...	...	...	...	31,339	...	...	31,339
Ghâzipur	...	...	...	...	...	...	...	9	...	...	9
Ballia	...	...	...	...	...	...	...	136	...	...	136
Gorakhpur	...	...	...	...	62,417	29,543	897	16,554	7,415	31,114	147,940
Basti	...	...	...	...	30,927	...	...	355	2,537	2,840	36,659

District.	Agarwâla.	Bâtham.	Ghogh.	Jaiswâr.	Kharbind.	Kharot.	Kallâh.	Mallâh Mewat.	Nikhâd.	Others.	Total.
Azamgarh . .	...	...	...	...	14,227	2,069	...	647	...	2,697	19,640
Lucknow . .	...	...	...	...	159	...	...	88	...	3	250
Unâo . . .	...	...	...	...	254	...	...	...	...	870	1,124
Râê Bareli . .	...	...	...	...	...	...	...	96	...	...	96
Sîtapur . .	...	...	...	...	...	...	...	2	...	12	14
Hârdoi . . .	...	...	...	...	...	...	...	...	534	14	548
Kherî . . .	...	...	...	...	...	...	...	1,055	...	90	1,145
Faizâbâd . .	...	...	...	...	30,740	3,5[illegible]8	108	...	533	4,820	39,769
Gonda . . .	...	...	...	...	...	...	...	...	...	6,223	6,223
Bahrâich . .	...	...	...	43	403	...	...	...	61	1,359	1,866
Sultânpur . .	...	...	...	...	12,632	...	...	1	1	2,552	15,186
Partâbgarh . .	...	...	...	...	5,743	...	...	...	69	113	5,925
Bârabanki . .	...	...	...	...	...	...	...	170	...	...	170
Total .	6,041	17,788	18,752	43	157,529	35,180	1,220	129,313	11,662	67,667	345,195

Khâgi.[1]—An agricultural tribe found in Rohilkhand. One derivation of the word is from Sanskrit *Khadgika*, "a swordsman." According to the Budâun tradition they were originally Chauhân Thâkurs, who emigrated under their leaders Kanka and Mahesa from Ajmer in a season of a famine, about three hundred years ago, and settled at the town of Sahaswân in the Budâun District. Here they grew in importance, and were after a time appointed by the Emperor of Delhi Sûbahs or Governors, one of Sahaswân, and the other of the adjoining Pargana of Soron in the Etah District. They were required to pay a quarter of the revenue of these Parganas into the Delhi treasury, and this after a time they failed to do, the remittance being embezzled *en route* by one of their agents, a Musalmân, at Delhi. A punitive force was sent against them by the Emperor, and a battle ensued, in which both their leaders and a considerable number of their followers were killed. The widows of those killed, contrary to the custom of Thâkurs, remarried (which is known locally by the phrase *kâj karna*), and from this they are said to take the name of Khâgi. In Bareilly one tradition makes them the descendants of Râja Bhâgîratha, a descendant of Sâgara, whose austerities induced Siva to allow the Ganges to descend to the

[1] From notes by Mr. C. S. Delmerick, Opium Department, Budâun, and Pandit Janardan Dat Joshi, Deputy Collector, Bareilly.

earth for the purpose of bathing the ashes of Sâgara's sons, who had been consumed by the wrath of the sage Kapila. Hence their special reverence for the Ganges. By another account they are descended and derive their name from Râja Kharga, eighth in descent from Râja Sâgara. In their appearance, manners, and customs there is nothing to corroborate their claim to Râjput descent. There are two sites in Sahaswân which they point out as monuments of their former glory. One is a Khera or mound known locally as "the Old Fort," and the other a mango grove called Lakha Pera, or "the grove of the hundred thousand trees."

2. Their sub-divisions, shown to the number of 135 in the detailed Census lists, are of the usual type. Side by side with tribal names like Bais, Baiswâr, Banya, Banjâra, Chandeli, Chauhân, Dalera, Dhîmar, Gaurâhar, Kharluniya, Lodha, Raghubansi, Raikwâr, Râjput, Râthaur, Sainikhor, Sombansi, and Tomar, we find the usual local titles, such as Ajmeri, Amritpuriya, Chandpuriya, Jaiswâr, Jalâlpuriya, Mathuriya.

Manners and customs.

3. Their manners and customs are exactly the same as those of inferior Hindu tribes, such as the Lodha. They do not perform the regular *Srâddha*, but in the Kanâgat, or fortnight sacred to the manes of the dead, they do what may be called the minor *Srâddha* by feeding Brâhmans and offering sacred balls (*pinda*). They recognise widow marriage by the *Kâj* form and also the levirate. They worship the Ganges, Siva, Devi, and Ganesa, but are not initiated into any particular sect. Their priests are Sanâdhya Brâhmans, who hold a low rank in their tribe. In their demonology they follow closely the customs of the inferior Hindu tribes by whom they are surrounded. As a local godling they chiefly worship Bhûmiya. They will eat *pakki* with Kahârs; they eat *kachchi* with none but members of their own tribe, but they will eat *kachchi* prepared by Agarwâlas and no other class of Banyas. Some families refuse, according to general Hindu custom, to have the noses of their girls pierced or to allow them to wear nose-rings. For this they are unable to assign any reason. They do not hold land as zamîndârs, but they are excellent agriculturists, industrious, thrifty, and well-behaved.

4. For the distribution of the Khâgi, see under *Lodha*.

Khairwa.[1]—A small tribe of catechu-makers and cultivators found in Jhânsi. They do not appear under this name in the last

[1] Based on notes supplied through Mr. H. C. Ferard, C. S., Lalitpur.

Census. They take their name from the *Khair* tree (Sanskrit *Khadira*, the *acacia catechu*). They are admittedly a compound of various jungle tribes who have taken to this special occupation. They have some vague traditions that they once were lords of the country, and that their ancestor was a prince, who was defeated and driven into the jungles by his elder brother. They allege that their ancestors came into the Jhânsi District in the time of Râja Chhatar Sâl of Panna, who died in 1713 A. D. By another account they are an offshoot of the Sahariyas, with whom their *gotras* are said to be identical: this is far from improbable.

Marriage rules.

2. They do not marry in their own *gotra*, or in the family of their maternal uncle, father's sister, or mother's sister for six generations after the last intermarriage. They profess now to have abandoned the practice of introducing strangers into the caste. A second marriage is allowed only if the first wife be barren. Concubinage is tolerated. Pre-nuptial immorality is lightly regarded, provided the paramour of the girl is a member of the tribe; in this case the stigma is removed by a tribal feast. Marriage takes place between the age of seven and fifteen. The match is arranged by the father or maternal uncle of the boy. There is no freedom of choice allowed to the pair themselves. When the family of either party is considered less respectable than that of the other, a sum of money is paid to help the marriage expenses. This does not go to the parties themselves, but to the father, who spends it at the wedding. A wife can be turned out by her husband on proof of adultery. Such a woman can re-marry in the tribe by the *sagâi* form, if her friends give a feast to purify her. Children by any sort of marriage or connection which has been sanctioned and approved by the council share as heirs in the goods of their late father. Children by a father or of a woman of another caste are not admitted to tribal privileges. Widow marriage and the levirate under the usual restrictions are recognised, and it seems to be compulsory on the widow to marry the younger brother of her late husband if he be willing to take her. It is also said that the fiction prevails that the children of the levir are those of his late brother; if this be true, it is perhaps a solitary instance of this idea among castes like this.

Birth ceremonies.

3. When a woman is seven months pregnant a tribal feast is given by the father. A woman of the Basor tribe acts as midwife, and her place is taken

as nurse by the wife of the barber. On the tenth day is the *daswán*, when the mother is bathed and the clansmen fed. There is no trace of the couvade. Adoption is recognised when the child is formally accepted in the presence of the members of the council. Just before puberty the ears are bored and the ceremonial shaving (*múnran*) takes place.

Marriage ceremonies.

4. The betrothal is fixed by the payment of a rupee to the bridegroom ; his forehead is marked, and then the engagement cannot be broken. The binding part of the marriage ceremony is the *pheri*, or walking round the marriage shed. They perform the ceremony, such as it is, themselves, and do not employ Brâhmans.

Death ceremonies.

5. The adult dead are burnt near the village. The ashes are thrown into some neighbouring stream, and the bones reserved for removal to the Ganges. They do not employ Brâhmans at these ceremonies, and do not perform the *Sráddha*. The man who lighted the pyre is impure for eleven days, when he shaves, bathes, gives the funeral feast and some uncooked grain to a Brâhman.

Religion.

6. As already said, they do not accept the religious services of Brâhmans. They usually worship Devi with a sacrifice of goats or rams. Their holidays are the Râm Naumi, Janaki Naumi, Siva Râtri, Janamashtami, Deothân, Phagua or Holi, Diwâli, Dasahra, Sankrânt, and Nâgpanchami. The women have the Tîja as their festival. They have much fear of the ghosts of the dead, and lay out food and drink to propitiate them. But they have no time sacred to the worship of ancestors, whom they seem to regard as a sort of family guardians to be propitiated in times of sickness and other trouble. They believe in the usual meeting omens. When one or two children die in succession they give the next baby an opprobrious name. All of them have two names—one for ordinary use, and a second, which is kept secret, and used only for ceremonial purposes. They swear by taking a *lota* full of water on their heads, by standing in water, by going to the temple of Devi, and by putting fire on the palm of the right hand. They know little of magic and witchcraft. They are firm believers in demoniacal possession, and in cases of illness call in a sorcerer to drive off the evil spirit. They believe in dreams, which are interpreted by some old person of the tribe; dreams which appear towards the morning generally turn out true. Good-looking or

prosperous people are likely to be attacked by the Evil-eye; its effects are obviated by waving some salt and pepper round the head of the patient and then throwing them on the fire. They object to touch Chamârs, Bhangis, Koris, and Kumhârs.

Social customs.

7. They practise the usual taboos of avoiding eating at the house of a son-in-law and calling the wife or head of the family by name. They eat goats' meat and fish and drink spirits. They will not eat beef. At the commencement of a meal they dedicate a scrap of food to Devi. They use intoxicants, such as *bhang*, *gânja*, and opium. Their salutations are *Râm! Râm! Jay Krishna! Jay Râdha Krishna.* They eat and smoke only with clansmen.

Occupation.

8. Their occupation is making catechu from the wood of the *Khair* tree. In this they approximate to the Khairis of the Lower Himalayas, who are usually Doms, and to the Kathkâris of Bombay, who represent themselves as descended from the monkeys of the army of Râma. These people in Bombay now "subsist almost entirely by hunting; now that their more legitimate occupation of preparing catechu (*Kath*) has been interfered with, they habitually killand eat monkeys shooting them with bows and arrows. In order to approach within range they are obliged to have recourse to stratagem, as the monkeys at once recognise them in their ordinary costume. The ruse usually adopted is for one of the best shots to put on a woman's robe (*sâri*), under the ample folds of which he conceals his murderous weapons. Approaching the tree on which the monkeys are seated, the sportsman affects the utmost unconcern and busies himself with the innocent occupation of picking up twigs and leaves. Thus disarming suspicion, he is enabled to get a sufficiently close shot to render success a certainty." To illustrate the superstitious ideas connected with the manufacture of catechu, it may be noted that in Bombay "every year, on the day after the Holi, the *chûlha* ceremony takes place. In a trench, seven feet long by three and about three deep, *Khair* logs are carefully stacked and closely packed till they stand in a heap about two feet above ground. The pile is then set on fire and allowed to burn to the level of the ground. The village sweeper breaks a cocoanut, kills a couple of fowls, and sprinkles a little liquor near the pile. Then, after washing their feet, the sweeper and the village headman walk barefoot hurriedly across the fire. After this the strangers come to fulfil vows, and giving one anna

and a half cocoanut to the sweeper and the other half cocoanut to the head man, wash their feet and turning to the left walk over the pile the fire seems to cause none of them any pain." [1]

The same form of fire worship prevails among the Dusâdhs and similar tribes in the Eastern Districts of these Provinces. In Mirzapur the business of preparing catechu is almost entirely confined to the Bhuiyas and Bhuiyârs.

Khandelwâl, Khandelwâla.[2]—A sub-caste of Banyas, with a Hindu and Jaina branch, found principally in the Western Districts. They take their name from the town of Khandela, north of Jaypur, like the tribe of Brâhmans of the same name. Their tradition is that there were four brothers who were soldiers. One day they went out hunting and killed a favourite deer belonging to a hermit. He was about to destroy them by his curse, when they promised to abandon soldiering and hunting. From them the present Khandelwâls are descended. This is the sub-caste to which most of the celebrated Mathura Seths belong.

Internal organisation.

2. The Khandelwâls have seventy-two *gotras*, of which the following list was procured in Mirzapur:—Torawâl; Baraiya; Dhamani; Dhankaliya; Dangaich; Machhiwâl; Pabuwâl; Barhera; Batwara; Kulwal; Sanbhariya; Bail(1); Burhwaliya; Thakuriya; Kadâwat; Râwat; Jhâlâni; Saunkhiya; Nâtâni; Vais; Amairiya; Dân; Jasoriya; Gandhi; Katta; Kath; Kayathwâl; Kathoriya; Kilkiliya; Khunteta; Kharâwat; Jhaginiya; Tâmi; Tamoliya; Dusâdhu; Pitaliya; Bâjârghar; Bhukhmâra; Methi; Mânikbahora; Mamoriya; Sethi; Haldiha; Âkar; Ghiya; Babb; Bhagla; Pharsoiya; Pâtoda; Banwâri; Bhusar; Bargota; Meharwâl; Sahoriya; Atoriya; Mâli; Nârâyanwâl; Rajoriya; Bisaura; Harsoiya; Bharâriya; Sankhani; Bhuriya; Patoriya, Bawari, or Babari; Bâr; Mangrauriya; Pagwewa; Goliya; Chamariya; Bail (2); Tandwaiya. It would be useless to speculate on the meaning of these names: some are plainly connected in some way with other existing castes, some are local, and others occupational.

Marriage.

3. The prohibited degrees in marriage are the bridegroom's *gotra*, that of his maternal uncle, and those of the maternal uncle of his father and

[1] *Bombay Gazetteer*, X., 48; III., 310; and on the Catechu Industry, Watts *Dictionary of Economic Products*, I., 27, *sqq*.

[2] From enquiries at Mirzapur and a note by Bâbu Mûl Chand, Khandelwâl, Native Commissioner to His Highness the Mahârâja of Benares.

mother. Girls are usually married before the age of twelve. A man cannot marry a second wife during the lifetime of the first without her consent. Widow marriage is not permitted.

Religion.

4. They are usually initiated into the Vaishnava sect. Their *gurgharāna* or family of spiritual guides is the Sâdhubara of Jaypur. Their priests are Gaur Brâhmans. They are said to have either twenty-four or thirteen clan goddesses; but it has been found impossible to procure a complete list. The following eleven are named at Mirzapur:—Chawan; Nâgin; Baburi; Jiyan; Âtan; Kalyâni; Mukhta; Sakrâi Mâta; Tâmbi; Loha; and Jhalâi. One of these goddesses goes to three *gotras*. They are worshipped after child-birth and marriage and at the Naurâtra in the months of Chait and Kuâr. Nine kinds of sweetmeats are offered to them, *viz.*, *papari*, *gujhiya*, *pheni*, *doyatha*, *pua*, *ghughuri*, *kasar*, *khîr*, and *halwa*. Garlands of flowers and the fire sacrifice (*hom*) are also made as offerings.

Social rules.

5. The use of meat and spirits is prohibited in the sub-caste. They eat *kachchi* cooked only by Gaur Brâhmans and their own castemen. They eat *pakki* cooked by Agarwâlas, Oswâl, and Maheswari Banyas. Only Kahârs, Nâis, and lower castes will eat *kachchi* cooked by them.

Distribution of the Khandelwāl Banyas according to the Census of 1891.

DISTRICT.	Hindus.	Jainas.	TOTAL.
Sahâranpur	25	74	99
Muzaffarnagar	15	2	17
Meerut	238	40	278
Bulandshahr	1	...	1
Aligarh	232	...	232
Mathura	2,338	348	2,686
Agra	1,599	720	2,319
Farrukhâbâd	72	36	108
Mainpuri	122	...	122
Etâwah	506	...	606

Distribution of the Khandelwâl Banyas according to the Census of 1891—contd.

District.	Hindus.	Jainas.	Total.
Bareilly	6	...	6
Bijnor	52	113	165
Budâun	40	26	66
Morâdâbâd	250	566	816
Pilibhît	68	...	68
Cawnpur	...	11	11
Bânda	30	...	30
Allahâbâd	79	...	79
Benares	40	...	40
Mirzapur	27	...	27
Lucknow	20	43	63
Hardoi	18	...	18
Partâbgarh	8	...	8
Bârabanki	...	6	6
Total	5,886	1,985	7,871

Khandelwâl.—A local tribe of Brâhmans, who take their name from the town of Khandela in the Jaypur territory on the borders of Shaikhâwati. They claim to be a branch of the Adi Gauda or high class Gaur Brâhmans.

Distribution of Khandelwâl Brâhmans according to the Census of 1891.

District.	Numbers.	District.	Numbers.
Sahâranpur	30	Etah	7
Meerut	16	Budâun	43
Bulandshahr	9	Morâdâbâd	34
Mathura	199	Hamîrpur	5
Agra	2	Total	345

Khangâr,[1] **Khagâr.**—A tribe of thieves and village watchmen practically confined to Bundelkhand. They are also known as Râo Khangâr in relation to their alleged Râjput descent, or Râwat. When they hold the post of village watchmen, they are called Kotwâl or Kotwâr, "head policemen." There is much controversy as to the meaning of the name. According to some it is connected with the Hindi *Khankh*, Sanskrit *Karkara*, "withered or degraded." Others derive it from *Khadga*, "a sword."

Tribal legends.

2. The tradition of the caste is that they were formerly Râjputs of the Khagâr sept and were degraded. One tradition tells that they entered Bundelkhand from somewhere to the north of Kâlpi, and took service with the Bundela Râjputs. Their chief settlement was at Kurârgarh in the Bhîkamgarh State. They failed to pay their revenue, and by the orders of the Emperor Akbar, the Bundela Râja, with the help of some Gaharwâr Râjputs from Kâshi or Benares, destroyed them by giving them drugged wine to drink, and then massacred them. It is needless to say that this is a legend common to many of the degraded tribes, such as the Bhars and others. Their Râja at the time was Nâga Râja, and, after the massacre of his followers, he and his Râni escaped. He cut off half his mustache, and she took off half her jewelry, which they swore not to wear again until they wreaked their revenge on the Bundelas. By another legend only the Râni escaped the massacre of the tribe. She took refuge in a field of saffron (*kusum*), whence she was rescued by some Parihâr Râjputs, and bore a son, who was the ancestor of the present Khangârs. All this is, of course, mere folk-lore, and this escape of the pregnant mother is one of the stock incidents in the folk-tales. It is said that no Khangâr is, even to the present day, allowed to enter the fort of Kurâr, and that, in memory of the birth of their ancestor in the saffron field, no Khangâr will wear cloth dyed with saffron. Another legend runs that the Bundela Râja had a son by a Khangâr woman, who was called Baghel, and received Kurâr as his inheritance. His descendants are now known as Bimhar, and until lately they were not acknowledged by the Khangârs; this has been lately allowed after a tribal council. By another account they were the

[1] Based on notes by Mr. J. S. Meston, C.S., Settlement Officer, Jhânsi; Mr. W. Cockburn, Deputy Collector, Jâlaun; and M. Karam Ahmad, Deputy Collector, Jhânsi.

descendants of Râja Bijay Sinh of Gurnâl, and were exterminated by the Gaharwâr Râjputs from Kashi, because their Râja dared to propose to marry a Gaharwâr girl. This legend is also common to a number of tribes of the same social rank. They also say that one of the Bhadauriya Râjputs once married in their sept, and to this day that, whenever there is a marriage among the Bhadauriyas, the house-master sends for a Khangâr and marks his back with his hand steeped in turmeric before he pays the same mark of respect to his other guests. As a further mark of their Kshatriya descent, they say that they to this day give a sword as a marriage gift, as other Râjputs do. Further, whenever a new Bundela Râja of Datiya is enthroned, a model of the Kurâr fort and of the last Khangâr Râja is made in clay, which the Bundela breaks as part of the ceremony. Still another story tells that one of their Râjas once offered his head to Devi and the goddess replied, "Wash it" (*khangârna*). From this they were called Khangâr.

3. All these legends are an interesting example of a process which has undoubtedly gone towards the formation of many Râjput septs. That there is a large body of tradition in corroboration of the Râjput descent of the tribe is quite certain. It may also be assumed as true that the Khangârs were once lords of that part of the country; but when we examine their system of *gotras*, it seems plain that their claim to Râjput lineage cannot be accepted. They have, in fact, a well-developed totemistic series of *gotras* which marks them down at once to be of Dravidian origin.

Tribal organisation.

4. One list of these is as follows:—Sârdu; Bhârta; Parsaniya; Bisora; Hathgotiya; Maltiya; Kurariya; Ghorgotiya; Bilgotiya; Bijaniya; Bharda; Nâhargotiya; Nâggotiya; Kusumgotiya; and Bargotiya. Of these, the Sârdu are said to be the highest, and will not drink spirits, in memory of the catastrophe which fell upon the clan at the hands of the Bundelas. The Hathgotiya claim kindred with the elephant (*hâthi*), and at marriages mount the bridegroom on an elephant; the Ghorgotiya similarly respect the horse (*ghora*); the Nâhargotiya are of the kindred of the lion (*nâhar*); the Bargotiya with the *bar* or banyan tree, which they worship; the Nâggotiya with the *nâga* or serpent; and the Kusumgotiya with the safflower (*kusum*). Another list gives the Khargotiya and Sangotiya, who are connected in the same way with the grass (*khar*) and hemp plant (*san*). A third list gives as one of their *gotras* Basor, which is

the name of a Dom sub-caste; Nîmgotiya, sprung from the *nîm* tree; Gohiya from the *goh* or iguana; and Bâmhan Rautiya, who claim to be half Brâhmans and half Râjputs; and to these apparently totemistic names may be added from the Census lists—Chhachhûndar, "musk-rat"; Gajgoti, "the kindred of the elephant"; Hirangot, "the kindred of the deer"; Pipariya, "of the Pîpal tree." Besides this there is a tribal legend that they are the forefathers of the Arakhs, a distinctly Dravidian caste, who are said to be an offshoot from them. This totemistic tribal structure clearly shows their Dravidian origin, and disposes of their claim to Râjput descent. They are, in short, on the same level as the Benbans Râjputs, who are Kharwârs, and the Pâsi and Bhar tribes of Oudh, some of whom have almost certainly succeeded in establishing a fictitious Râjput connection. It was out of such elements doubtless that many of the Râjput tribes were formed, and in the case of the Khangârs it is only from the fact that they have as yet been unable to shed off their totemistic sections that we are able actually to ascertain their real origin. The lesson is a useful one in dealing with the pretensions of many now degraded tribes to a higher origin, and it would not be perhaps too much to say that while we have instances in plenty of tribes who have raised themselves in the social scale, it would be difficult to point to one undoubted instance of a tribe which, having once arrived at that stage of culture to enable them to assert the rank of Râjputs, ever fell back into the grade of landless labourers and thieves such as the Khangârs are at present.

Marriage rules.

5. The rule of exogamy is that a man does not marry in the *gotra* of his father or mother until three generations have passed, and they have the usual formula known as *dúdh bacháké*, or avoidance of blood relations, which is common to them and all ordinary Hindus, and is intended to reinforce the *gotra* law of exogamy and prevent intermarriage, which, without it, would still be possible. In their ceremonies there is a line drawn between the more respectable Khangârs, who ape a Râjput descent, and the Kotwâr or village watchman class, who retain many usages of a more primitive type. Thus, the higher class Khangârs profess to have only quite recently adopted the custom of widow marriage and the levirate, which is admittedly authorised among those of the lower class. Among the Nâhargotiyas the clothes of the bridegroom are dyed with turmeric, and with saffron among the other sections. The lower members of the

tribe employ no barber or Brâhman except for the actual ceremony, while among the higher class the preliminary negotiations and ceremony are performed in the orthodox way. The more respectable Khangârs are now prohibiting concubinage with women of other tribes, but a low-grade man may keep a concubine of a caste other than his own, provided it be of a grade superior to his own. A man cannot marry a second wife without the distinct leave of the first wife. At a marriage among respectable Khangârs the bridegroom is expected to send five rupees by the barber who arranges the match; the same sum when the *lagan* or fixing of the wedding day comes off. On the other hand, the father of the bridegroom receives a present of one rupee when he enters the village of the bride, ten rupees when he reaches her door; her mother gives him a rupee when he goes to her room after the marriage: besides which all the bride's relations are expected to give something. All the other ceremonies at a respectable wedding are of the normal character.

Birth rites.

6. The birth rites are of the usual kind. When a boy is born the mark of the Swâstika is made on the wall of the house, and on the thirteenth day a cow-dung Swâstika is made and taken to a tank, into which it is flung. *Laddu* (sweets made of rice) are distributed, which are known as *chhathi kâ chânwal*, or "the rice of the sixth day." There is no sign of the couvade, but it is contrary to etiquette for the father to talk about the birth of his child or to receive the congratulations of his friends. He leaves the grandfather of the child to receive and interview friends who call for this purpose.

Religion.

7. Khangârs are all Hindus, and by preference worshippers of Devi. In addition, they worship the sainted forefathers of the tribe, Nâga Bâba and Kaneriya Bâba. The worship of the latter seems to be confined to the lower section of the tribe. They also make periodical pilgrimages to Kurâr, the original home of the tribe, where they worship Gidwânsa Mâta, a tribal mother who has a shrine on the embankment of the lake. Each family among the lower class Khangârs makes a platform to Kaneriya Bâba at his house, and offers eggs and cocoanuts on the occasions of domestic ceremonies, such as birth or marriage. The worship is performed at night, and is kept secret: only members of the family can receive a share of offerings (*prasâd*). At marriages the women do the mysterious Mehra Pûja,

or woman worship, at which only members of the family on the paternal side are allowed to attend.

Tree worship.

8. Tree worship is very well developed among the tribe. The Rajauriya section worship the *gunj* tree (*abrus precatorius*) ; the Jacheriyas, the *jacher* tree ; the Sanauriyas, the *nandi* tree ; the Beliyas, the *bel* or *ægle marmelos ;* just as the Baguliyas worship the *bagula* or paddy-bird and the Magariyas the *magar* or alligator. All Khangârs worship the *anola* (*phyllanthus emblica*) on the ninth day of the waxing moon of Kârttik. The worship of the *bar* or banyan tree by the Bargotiya subdivision has been already referred to.

Social life and occupation.

9. Unlike the higher castes, they have a tribal council (*panchâyat*), with a president (*mukhiya*), who is appointed from time to time on the ground of fitness for the post. They have some connection with eunuchs. One of their women, they say, was once saved by an eunuch, and to this day eunuchs call Khangârs *bhânja* or sister's son. The higher class Khangârs will eat only the food which is permitted to Râjputs ; those of the lower sort no doubt eat jungle animals, and, it is said, various kinds of vermin ; but if they do so, they do not care to admit the fact. Their rules of eating are uncertain. According to one account they will eat *pakki* and *kachchi* with Kurmis ; according to another they will eat *kachchi* cooked by any Brâhman, Râjput, or Banya, and *pakki* from the hand of any one but a Chamâr, Dhobi, Mehtar, Kori, or Basor. They will not smoke with any caste but their own. The Nâi is said to be the highest caste which will eat *pakki* with them. The Kori will eat *kachchi* and Brâhmans will drink water drawn by them ; but it is not quite certain how far these rules apply to the whole caste, or only to the more respectable branch. The Khangârs are landless labourers, except in very few instances. They serve the Bundelas as servants, and as they have a very indifferent reputation, they are very often appointed village watchmen on the same principle that Pâsis very often hold the same position in Oudh and the Eastern Districts of the Province. Though not exactly a criminal tribe, they are prone to commit thefts and burglaries.

Distribution of Khangârs according to the Census of 1891.

District.	Bal.	Chikwa.	Mugda.	Others.	Total.
Mathura	...	...	...	188	188
Agra	...	...	...	6	6
Mainpuri	...	...	...	59	59
Etâwah	18	...	...	147	165
Bijnor	...	...	...	3	3
Cawnpur	364	...	...	126	490
Fatehpur	...	...	...	50	50
Bânda	319	...	...	146	465
Hamîrpur	2,372	...	...	6,428	8,800
Jhânsi	376	...	...	9,123	9,499
Jâlaun	810	...	...	6,869	7,679
Lalitpur	175	118	437	4,787	5,517
Total .	4,434	118	437	27,932	32,921

Khânzâda.[1]—(Descendants of the Khân; another and probably less correct explanation would make them out to be Khânazâd, or "descendants of a slave.")—A tribe who do not appear in the returns of the last Census, but who deserve mention. There appear to be two classes of people known in these Provinces by this name—those of the Western Districts and those of Oudh.

The Western Khânzâdas.

2. Of this tribe in Gurgâon Mr. Channing writes[2]:—"The Khanzâdas were a race who were formerly of much more importance than they are at present. They claim to have been formerly Jâdon Râjputs, and that their ancestors, Lakhana Pâla and Sumitra Pâla, who dwelt at Tahangarh in Bhartpur, were converted to Islâm in the reign of Fîroz Shâh (A. D. 1351 to 1388), who gave Lakhana Pâla the name of Nâhar Khân, and Sumitra Pâla that of Bahâdur Khân, and, in recognition of their high descent, called them Khânzâda, and

[1] Partly based on a note by M. Sayyid 'Ali Bahâdur, Deputy Collector, Partâbgarh.

[2] Gurgâon Settlement Report, 30.

made them bear rule in Mewât. There is no doubt that they were the ruling race in Mewât down to the time of Bâbar; since then they have gradually declined in importance, and now own only a few villages in this District. In Alwar, also, the Khânzâdas have fallen from their ancient rank, and now possess but few settlements. I have a suspicion that they are more intimately connected than they acknowledge with the Meos; but the Meo inhabitants of various villages profess to have been formerly Khânzâdas and to have become Meos by intermarriage. Their traditions, also, which point to Sarahta as their ancient home, agree, I think it will be found, with those of more than one class of Meos. If my supposition, that the Meos are converted Mînas, is correct, I am inclined to suspect that the Khânzâdas are the representatives of the noble class among the aboriginal population." General Cunningham writes:—"The Khânzâdas, who, for several centuries, were the rulers of Mewât, claim descent from the Jâdon Râja Tahan Pâla. When Muhammad Ghori captured Tahangarh, many of the Jâdon families dispersed and settled wherever they could find a home. One Chief, Tej Pâla, founded Tejâra, and Lakhana Pâla, one of his descendants, was the founder of the great family of the Khânzâdas. During the last two centuries, since the territory of Mewât has fallen into the hands of the Hindus of Alwar and Bhartpur, it has become the fashion to doubt the Jâdon descent of the Khânzâdas, and to suggest that the title is derived from Khânazâda, 'a slave.' But the term is Khânzâda, 'the offspring of a Khân,' and not Khânazâda, 'the offspring of a house, a slave.' But their claim to royal descent from the Hindu Râjas of the country is too well attested to be shaken by the mere guesses of their enemies." [1]

The Khânzâdas of Oudh.

3. Of the clan in Sultânpur the following account is given in the Settlement Report[2]:—"Jaychand Sinh was son of Jura Sinh, of the line of Râj Sâh, son of Baryâr Sâh (see *Bachgoti*). His son, Tilok Chand, was a contemporary of Bâbar, during one of whose Eastern expeditions he laid the foundation of the future greatness of his house. Either taken prisoner in battle or arrested as a refractory landholder, Tilok Chand fell a prisoner into Bâbar's hands. He was allowed to choose between the adoption of the faith of Islâm

---

[1] *Archæological Reports*, XX., 10, *sqq.*

[2] Page 142, *sqq.*

with immediate liberty, or adherence to his own religion with incarceration for an indefinite period. With many respectable precedents to guide him, he selected the former alternative, was received into Imperial favour, and called Tâtâr Khân. His sons, Barîd Khân and Jalâl Khân, adopted the title of Khânzâda from their father. This is the local tradition, and differs somewhat from the account given by Sir H. M. Elliot (s. v. *Bachgoti*), who says that the Khânzâdas must have been converted before the Mughal dynasty commenced, as we read of Bachgotis [with Musalmân names before that. Perhaps their conversion was indirectly connected with the turbulence in the reign of Sikandar Lodi. Hasan Khân, son of Bazîd Khân, gave his name to Hasanpur, now their head-quarters." The same writer goes on to give a full account of the family, which can be consulted by the curious.

The Khânzâdas of Partâbgarh.

4. The Khânzâdas of Partâbgarh include representatives of several Râjput septs—the Bisen, Râjkumâr, Bachgoti, Bhâlê Sultân, Sombansi, Bais, Kânhpuriya, Chauhân, Bilkhariya, Bharsyân; and there are others known as Madarakiya, Shaikh, and Khânzâda. Shaikhs and Khânzâdas are such as have acquired most of the Musalmân usages. The Bilkhariyas and Bhâlê Sultân Khânzâdas are endogamous; the other groups are exogamous. Daughters, by the rule of hypergamy, are married into higher groups than their own, and boys into those that are equal and inferior. Most of them have now taken to call themselves Shaikhs. They belong to the Sunni sect, but it is reported that some of their women worship Devi.

Kharâdi.—(*Kharrâd; Kharrât,* "a lathe.")—The caste of turners. They are probably closely allied to Barhai. The Kunera (*q. v.*) is another artificer of the same class, and like him is the Gargarasâz, who makes the stems of pipes (*huqqa*). The Kharâdi makes in his lathe the legs of beds (*chârpâi*), and in Benares and Ahraura, in the Mirzapur District, he makes the wooden toys which are so popular under the name of "Benares toys."

2. These are turned on the lathe and then laquered. A good account of the process will be found in the monograph on the wood manufacturers of the Panjâb by Mr. M. F. O. Dwyer, C. S. The Kharâdis are a very respectable class, and one of them is said never to be seen in jail. Those recorded at the last Census include the Hindu and Muhammadan branch. Probably many of the turners have been entered under some of the sub-castes of Barhai.

3. Of the seventeen sections of the Hindu and three of the Muhammadan branch, some, such as Bais, Kanha Thâkur, Kath Bais, illustrate the pretensions of the caste to Râjput origin: others, as Dhundiya Khera, Jaiswâr, Jamnapâri, and Mainpuri, are of local origin.

Distribution of the Kharâdis according to the Census of 1891.

District.	Hindus.	Musalmâns.	Total.
Sahâranpur	...	226	226
Muzaffarnagar	...	25	25
Farrukhâbâd	1	...	1
Etah	...	2	2
Bijnor	...	19	19
Budâun	...	5	5
Cawnpur	15	...	15
Fatehpur	41	...	41
Jâlaun	...	1	1
Benares	302	...	302
Gorakhpur	197	65	262
Basti	109	...	109
Râê Bareli	37	...	37
Sîtapur	1	6	7
Gonda	9	...	9
Bahrâich	...	27	27
Sultânpur	82	18	100
Partâbgarh	12	...	12
Bârabanki	...	4	4
Total	806	398	1,204

Kharot.—A caste shown in the returns of the last Census as containing 5,641 persons in the Basti District only. Mr. Baillie would class them with the Kewat sub-caste of the same name. But they are more probably identical with the sub-caste of Beldâr, under which article some reference has been made to them. The detailed Census returns give three sections—Dakkhinâha, or "Southern," Jaraut, and Mahuâr or "collectors of Mahua" (*bassia latifolia*).

Kharwâr.—A Dravidian landholding and cultivating tribe found in South Mirzapur. The differences in social position between various branches of the tribe render an analysis of it difficult. Some have attained a good position as landholders and claim a high social rank, while others are menials, hewers of wood and drawers of water for the superior tribes. That they are of Dravidian origin is clearly proved by their totemistic sept system. One account connects them closely with the Cheros.[1] The Santâl legend, again, runs :—"A wild goose coming from the great ocean lighted at Ahiri Pipri, and there laid two eggs. From these two eggs a male and female were produced, who were the parents of the Santâl race. From Ahiri Pipri [2] our progenitors migrated to Hara Dutti, and then they greatly increased and multiplied, and were called Kharwârs."[3] Again, we are told that the tribe now calling themselves Santâl were formerly called Kharwâr.[4] What the real origin of the name Kharwâr may be is not easily determined. The Kharwârs in South Lohârdaga, according to Mr. Risley, regard the *Khar* grass as their totem, and will not cut or injure it while it is growing.[5] He remarks : "The adoption of the *Khar* as a totem may, of course, be due merely to the consonance of names—a factor which plays an important part in the speculation of savages regarding their own descent. If, on the other hand, the case is one of genuine survival, it goes far to suggest the inference that the Kharwâr tribe of the present day may be merely an enlarged totem sept, which broke off from some larger group, and, in course of time, developed a separate constitution." On the other hand, the people themselves in Mirzapur seem to have no tradition of this *Khar* totem, and derive their name either from their occupation as makers of catechu (*Khair*) from the tree *acacia catechu* or to their emigration from some place called Khairagarh, regarding which there is

---

[1] Dalton, *Descriptive Ethnology*, 127.

[2] This Pipri is identified by Nesfield (*Calcutta Review*, LXXXVI., 11,) with an old Chero stronghold in the hills close to Chunâr in the Mirzapur District.

[3] Dalton, *Descriptive Ethnology*, 209.

[4] Dalton, *Descriptive Ethnology*, 210.

[5] *Tribes and Castes*, I., 474.

a great difference of opinion. If the Santâl tradition is to be accepted, Khairagarh is the place of that name [1] in the Hazâribâgh District ; but the Mirzapur tradition seems to point to some place of the name either to the South or West, in which case Khairagarh may be identified with the most important of the Chhattisgarh feudatory states,[2] or with the Pargana of that name in the Allahâbâd District. The tradition of a connection with the fort of Rohtâsgarh [3] appears to be unknown to the Mirzapur tribe, who represent themselves to be emigrants from Rîwa and Singrauli. Their tribal shrine is at a place called Kota in the Singrauli Pargana of Mirzapur, where there is a shrine of Juâlamukhi Devi, where most of them assemble for worship at the Râmnaumi festival in the month of Chait. They bring their Brâhmans from Singrauli and Pâlamau.

Internal organization.

2. The internal organization of the tribe varies in different parts of Mirzapur. Throughout they seem to have shed off the elaborate organization of totem septs which prevails in Bengal.[4] North of the river Son there are four exogamous and one endogamous sub-division. The four exogamous sub-divisions are—

(1) Sûrajbansi, who claim descent from the sun, like the corresponding Râjput tribe. It may be noted that the Bengal Birhors affirm that they and the Kharwârs are of the same race, descended from the Sun.[5] This sub-division is now in process of elevation to Râjput rank. This process is also going on in Bengal, where the Râjas of Râmgarh and Jashpur have nearly succeeded in obliterating their Turanian traits by successive intermarriages with Aryan families.[6]

(2) Duâlbandhi, these are the Duâlbandh of the Bengal lists.[7] They say that their name is derived from *duâl*, "a leather belt," because they were once soldiers.

3. Pâtbandhi, the Pâtbandh of the Bengal lists. They say they are so called because they were once very rich and wore silk (*pât*).

---

1 Dalton, *loc. cit.*, 211.

2 *Central Provinces Gazetteer*, 242.

3 Risley, *loc. cit.*, I., 472 ; Dalton, *loc. cit.*, 127.

4 Risley, *Tribes and Castes*, II., *Appendix*, 78, *sqq*.

5 Dalton, *Descriptive Ethnology*, 219.

6 *Ibid.*, 129. For examples of the same process at work in other Dravidian tribes, see Ball, *Jungle Life*, 117 ; Forsyth, *Highlands of Central India*, 8.

7 Risley, *loc. cit.*

(4) Benbansi; of the origin of the name there are two accounts: one is that *ben* means a bamboo, from which this sub-division is descended, and which some of them will not cut. Others derive it from Râja Ben or Vena, the early type of the insolent opponent of the religion established by the Rishis. This sub-division has made rapid strides to acquire the rank of Râjputs. The head of them is the Râja of Singrauli in Mirzapur, who calls himself a Benbansi Râjput. Up to a generation or two ago his family used, it is said, to shave their heads when deaths occurred among the Dudhi Kharwârs. Now he keeps Hindu priests, wears the Brâhmanical cord, and has succeeded in intermarrying with such a well-known Râjput tribe as the Chandels. These four sub-divisions are exogamous, and intermarry on terms of equality, though, as might be expected among the sub-divisions on their promotion to Râjput rank, the rule of hypergamy is advancing in favour.

(5) Khairaha, who are said to derive their name from the extraction of catechu (*kattha*) from the Khair tree (*acacia catechu*). This occupation is considered disreputable, and the members of this sub-division do not intermarry with the other four higher sub-divisions. In Dudhi, again, there are apparently only two sub-divisions—the Duâlbandhi and the Pâtbandhi—which are exogamous and intermarry on equal terms. In Singrauli they name seven exogamous sub-divisions—Pâtbandhi, Duâlbandhi, and Sûrajbansi, which have been already described. Besides these there are the Bhogta or Bhugta, which is one of the sub-divisions recognized in Bengal[1]; the Kharchurwa, who are makers of catechu and apparently identical with the Khairaha noted above; the Chikchikwa; and the Pradhân or "leader." This sub-division, like the Sûrajbansi, who now claim to be Râjputs, say that they originally belonged to that tribe, but suffered a temporary loss of respectability when they began to eat fowls and drink liquor. These abominations they have now discarded, and have been restored to their proper rank.

Physical appearance.

3. In appearance the more advanced members of the tribe are in strong contrast to the more primitive families. Some of the former have received some admixture of Hindu blood. The real Kharwârs Colonel Dalton

[1] Dalton, *loc. cit.*, 129; Risley, *loc. cit.*, II., *Appendix*, 78.

compares with the Santâls: "They are very dark, with pyramidal-shaped low noses, thick protuberant lips and cheek bones or zygomata, which project so as to make the temple hollow." A writer in the *Calcutta Review*[1] says of the tribe in Shâhâbâd:—"The hair of the Kharwâr is black and straight. The form of the face is more oval, and the nose and lips are thinner than is the case with the other hillmen, the Chero, who has more regular features, alone excepted. There is nothing peculiar in the skull, but a slight depression from the extremities to the eyes and downwards gives a height to the cheeks and a protrusion but closeness to the lips, imparting an expression of shyness, for which the Kharwâr is too well noted. The chest is rather narrow, the abdomen large, the limbs long and flat, the gait erect, but both fingers and toes disproportionally heavy." At the same time, in South Mirzapur, even people who have lived all their lives among these Dravidian races fail to identify them easily. All they can say with certainty is that the Majhwârs and Kharwârs are known by the breadth and coarseness of their noses, while the Bhuiyârs are known because they speak through their noses in a very marked way.

Tribal council.

4. In Pargana Dudhi there are three tribal councils, with their head-quarters at Gonda, Bajiya, and Bamhni, respectively. They sometimes take the title of Mânjhi (with the tribe of which name they have no connection) or Mahto. The president first makes private enquiries into cases brought to his notice, and, if he thinks it advisable, convokes a meeting of the general council. Every householder has a right to a seat on the council. No oath is administered, the witnesses being simply admonished to tell the truth. If the council disagree, a sub-committee or cabinet of five leading members, known as the Pachkûti, or "five families," is appointed to investigate, and whatever decision they arrive at, it is accepted by the general council. In Singrauli whoever pleases can call a meeting of the council, for whom he must provide sufficient food and liquor. The meeting is presided over by the headman (*gánwha*) of the village in which the meeting takes place. If the village headman does not happen to be a Kharwâr, another *gánwha* of the tribe is summoned from elsewhere. If the offender does not accept the order of the council, he is excommunicated (*lota báj kar dena*) until he submits, and he is then obliged to feed the brethren.

[1] LXIX., 356.

5. As already stated, the sub-divisions, except the Khairaha, are exogamous; but in order to bar close intermarriages, which are possible even with this prohibition, marriages within the family of the mother's brother (*mâmu*), father's sister's husband (*phûpha*), are prohibited for two or three generations, and the same rule applies to families into which a sister has been married. Differences in geographical position, wealth, or social position are not a bar to intermarriage; but marriages with families who carry on degrading occupation are prohibited. A man may marry as many wives as he can afford to purchase and maintain. They live in separate rooms in the same house. The senior wife is head of the household, and is treated with respect at social meetings. Concubinage is not allowed, and there is no trace of polyandry. Women enjoy considerable freedom both before and after marriage. Inter-tribal incontinence is lightly regarded, and an unmarried girl detected in an intrigue with a man of her tribe is restored to caste rights on her father giving a tribal feast. If her lover is of another caste, the expulsion is permanent. As in Bengal,[1] infant marriage prevails. The marriage age is from five to ten. Adult marriage is considered disgraceful. After the girl has been inspected by the boy's father, all subsequent arrangements are made by the brother of the boy's mother (*mâmu*). There are no professional match-makers, and the parties have no right of choice. The bride price is five rupees in cash, two to four sers of sweetmeats, and five maunds of rice and pulse. This is not a fixed amount, but is increased or decreased according to the circumstances of the parties. The bride price is understood to be spent by her father on the marriage feast.

Marriage rules.

6. A woman can be divorced for habitual infidelity, and a woman can leave her husband for the same reason, which must in both cases be proved to the satisfaction of the council. If a man ill-treats his wife, she runs away to her father's house, and the council then warn the husband to treat his wife better; in bad cases they fine him, and recognise the wife's right to refuse cohabitation. A divorced wife may marry again in the *sagâi* form. If the husband is impotent, and it is assumed that the marriage has not been consummated, the council divorce them, and give the bride leave to marry again in the regular

Divorce.

[1] Risley, *loc. cit.*, I., 475

form: in this case the new husband has to return the original bride price through her father.[1] Concubinage, as already stated, is prohibited, but illegitimate children, though assumed to belong to the father's tribe, are not admitted to caste privileges.

Widow marriage and the levirate.

7. The tribe is at present in a state of transition as regards widow marriage and the levirate. The more Hinduised Kharwârs, particularly those who aspire to Râjput rank, prohibit both.[2] But those of the more primitive type permit these arrangements. A noted ascetic, the Dûbiya Bâba, has recently led a crusade against both customs among the Mirzapur Kharwârs. Where widow marriage prevails, a man, whether already married or a bachelor, can take a widow into cohabitation, and when he announces the fact to the council, he has to give a feast. Children by such cohabitation are considered to rank lower than those born of a regular marriage, and in some families they receive only one-fourth share as compared with that of legitimate children.

Adoption.

8. The more Hinduised branches of the tribe are beginning to recognise the ordinary rules of Hindu adoption. Among those of a more primitive type, adoption does not depend on any religious theory, and it seems to be recognised that a sonless man can select one of his brother's sons as his heir, and the arrangement will be valid if it is sanctioned by the council.

Beena marriage.

9. The custom of beena[3] marriage (*gharjaiyán*) prevails. The son-in-law, while on probation, does field work, and receives maintenance, but has no claim to succeed to the property of his father-in-law.

Succession.

10. As regards succession, there is the same divergence between the more Hinduised members, who abide by the regular Hindu law, and the less advanced, who adhere to a vague tribal custom. Among them primogeniture is so far admitted that the eldest son receives, in excess of his younger brothers, one-twentieth of the cattle and one-tenth of the vessels and other household goods. With the exception of this, all joint property, whether ancestral or acquired, is divided equally

---

[1] On this see Westermarck, *History of Human Marriage*, 528, 534.

[2] In Bengal, too, the same variance of custom prevails. Risley, *Tribes and Castes*, II., 475.

[3] Lubbock, *Origin of Civilisation*, 78.

among the sons. If the widow remains at home, does not re-marry, and looks after her children, she has a life interest, which may cease on her expulsion for unchastity. Girls have no rights, except that of support out of love and affection, if they cannot get on with their husband, and have to return to the family home. If a widow, while pregnant, marries again, her child is attributed to the step-father. Only children at the breast accompany the widow on re-marriage, and the step-father is bound to support and get them married. If a man becomes an ascetic, he is regarded as civilly dead, and all his goods pass to his sons. The office of headman (*gânwha*) is hereditary, and if the eldest son of the deceased turn out incompetent, the council will appoint his younger brother in his stead.

Birth ceremonies.

11. The birth pollution lasts for six days. The Hinduised Kharwârs name the child when it is first fed on grain (*anna prâsana*) in the sixth month, and the name is fixed by the family priest (*purohit*), according to the asterism (*nakshatra*) of birth. The child's head is ceremonially shaved in the third, fifth, or seventh year at the temples of Kuâri Sobnâth on the Son, Juâlamukhi Devi, and Kota in Singrauli, or at the shrine of Vindhyabâsini Devi at Bindhâchal. At the same time the child's nails are cut: until this time the mother may bite off the child's nails, but not touch them with iron. Among the ruder Kharwârs, in cases of difficult parturition, the mother is given two-and-a-half leaves of the *mahua* (*bassia latifolia*) crushed in water. She is delivered on the ground facing the north, and if a son is born, while the Chamâin midwife is cutting the cord, the women of the family sing the song of rejoicing (*sohar*). On the sixth day the mother is bathed by her brother's wife (*bhaujâi*) or husband's sister (*nanad*), the latter of whom cleans and re-plasters the delivery room (*saur*), for which she receives a trifling present. Some families have a similar custom on the twelfth day (*barahi*). There is the usual survival of the couvade in the husband doing no work on the day his child is born and taking a mouthful of the cleansing draught which is given to the mother.

Marriage ceremonies.

12. The Mirzapur Kharwârs have retained some of the primitive or non-Aryan customs which those in Bengal have abandoned as far as marriage is concerned.[1] They, however, get the village Pandit to fix a lucky

[1] Dalton, *Descriptive Ethnology*, 130.

day for the betrothal (*mangani, barrekhi*), when the boy's father brings to the girl's house three or four jars filled with flour cakes (*pûa*) cooked in butter and five rupees in cash. It is the etiquette on this occasion that he should be accompanied by five of his clansmen, among whom the *mâmu*, or brother of his wife, who has arranged the marriage, takes a leading place.[1] The two fathers-in-law *in futuro* sit opposite each other, the boy's father puts the bride price into his platter and exchanges it for that of the bride's father. The platters are then filled with liquor and exchanged four times more. This constitutes the betrothal, and the boy's father and his friends sit down outside. One or two of the girl's friends bring them a goat, and it is the etiquette to say—"Although the girl's father cannot entertain you, he sends you this vegetable [2] (*chaurâi sâg*), which, we hope, you will honour us by accepting." To this the reply is—"My connection by marriage (*samdhi*) is good in every way." They then bring the goat back to the girl's father, who kills and cooks it with other food, and then invites them to the betrothal dinner saying—"I have provided the best in my power. Be pleased to accept it as an offering" (*prasâd kariyé*). After this, when the wedding day is fixed by the Pandit, the earth ceremony (*matmangar*) is done in both houses, the earth being dug by the Baiga, who is blindfolded while doing so. He takes up five handfuls of the earth and passes them over to five unmarried girls of the tribe, who carry it off in the folds of their sheets, and then bring it in five baskets to the marriage shed (*mânro*), which has five bamboos fixed in the centre. The girls make the earth into a stand for the sacred water jar (*kalsa*), over which is a saucer of barley with a lighted lamp. The Pandit next sprinkles some oil with a bunch of *dûb* grass over the bride or bridegroom, as the case may be, and then the women rub him or her all over with oil and turmeric. With this mixture on the boy and girl sleep for the night, and next day the bridegroom is bathed by the barber and the bride by the barber's wife, who cuts the nails and colours their feet with lac dye (*mahâwar*). The mother of the boy or girl and four other women relatives have their nails cut and their feet coloured at the same time. Before the procession starts, the boy's brother-in-law (*bahnoi*) brings him

---

[1] On this see *Majhwâr*, para. 14.

[2] The *chaurâi* or *chaulâi* is a common potherb (*amaranthus anardana*)—Watt, *Dictionary of Economic Products*, I., 210.

five times backwards and forwards to his mother, who sits on a rice mortar (*okhal*), and she seizes him by his loin-cloth and will not let him start until she gets a present. The bridegroom is carried in the procession in a large cot known as the ship (*jahâz*).[1] When they arrive at the bride's house the "door worship" (*duâr pûja*) is performed. The bridegroom sits in a square (*chauk*) made of flour, and the girl's father puts a mark (*tíka*) on her forehead with rice and curds, after which the Pandit says—"If you intend to give anything to your son-in-law, do so now," and he presents him with a calf, a loin-cloth, and two brass vessels (*lotá, thâli*). Then the bridegroom with his friends retires to the reception place (*janwânsa*), where some friends of the bride wash his feet (*pânw pakhârna*)[2] with those of his party. When the bridegroom comes to be married, there is a survival of marriage by capture in five boys blocking the way and preventing him from going in until they are paid five annas each. Here, again, he receives presents from the bride's father, and after this the clothes of the pair are knotted together, and they walk five times round the five bamboos fixed in the centre of the shed, one of which he marks with red-lead each time as he goes round. After which he marks the bride's head with red-lead in the usual way. The bride and bridegroom are then taken into the retiring room (*kohabar*), the walls of which are decorated with various figures by the younger sister of the bride. The most common mark is three converging lines like the top of Siva's trident. Then the bridegroom refuses to sit beside the bride until he gets a present, when the barber unknots the clothes of the married pair. In the centre of the marriage shed is placed a sort of totem consisting of images of parrots (*suga*), represented sitting on a tree made of the wood of the cotton tree (*semal*). After the marriage this is scrambled for, and the pieces are carried off as trophies by the unmarried boys of the tribe, while, in the retiring room, it is the rule for the bridegroom to mark the wall decorations with a splash of red-lead, and then five unmarried girls wash the feet of the bride and bridegroom, and will not let them go until they get a small present. Next morning is the *confarreatio*, when the bridegroom eats rice and pulse with the bride, and refuses to do so until he gets a tray (*thâli*) as his fee (*khichari khilâi*). After this

---

[1] See *Majhwâr*, para. 16. The same custom prevails among the Kurmis of Bengal. See Dalton, *Descriptive Ethnology*, 319.

[2] On the foot-washing ceremony see Campbell, *Notes*, 29.

a tray is passed round and every guest is expected to make a small contribution to cover the marriage expenses. The bride and bridegroom are then sent off together in the "ship litter" (*jahâz*). When she arrives at her husband's house, the bride holds on to the poles of the litter and refuses to dismount until her mother-in-law gives her a rupee. Then they go into the retiring room (*kohabar*), where the bride splashes red-lead on the wall decorations, and their clothes are again knotted and untied by five girls, who wash the feet of the pair. Next morning the bride comes into the marriage shed (*mânro*) with a tray, and all the friends present give a contribution in aid of expenses. The same day the bride and bridegroom take the two sacred jars and throw them into a neighbouring stream, bring them home filled with water, and worship the village shrine on the way. The binding part of the ceremony is the marking of the bride's hair with red-lead, but the Mirzapur tribe have discarded the Bengal custom of mixing it with blood,[1] while they retain the practice of emblematical tree marriage.

Death ceremonies.

13. The dying person is taken into the open air to die, and on the day of death the house court-yard is not swept. This is like the practice of the Congo negroes, who abstain for a whole year from sweeping the house, lest the dust should injure the delicate substance of the ghost.[2] Among the more Hinduised Kharwârs the dying man is made to touch a female calf, which is then given to a Brâhman, and some Ganges water and a leaf of the sacred *tulasi* (*ocymum sanctum*) are placed in his mouth. The corpse is cremated in the usual way. No implements are placed with the corpse. The chief mourner after cremation sweeps the ashes and bones together, and pours over them a libation of unboiled milk, barley, and sesamum, to support the soul in the next world.[3] After a person dies it is always necessary to watch a corpse lest demons should possess it. They tell a story about this. Once an unmarried girl of the tribe died, and her relatives went to fetch wood to cremate her. A demon got hold of the girl, and she was rescued only with the greatest difficulty. The death impurity lasts

---

[1] Risley, *Tribes and Castes*, I., 475.

[2] Tylor, *Primitive Culture*, I., 454.

[3] In Shâhâbâd, in Bengal, the chief mourner buries part of the bones near the pyre on the day after cremation, and in the following month of Kârttik takes them to the river Ganges or Durgâvati, where he dives deep into the water and commits them to the stream, *Calcutta Review*, LXIX., 363.

ten days, and ends with the shaving of the kinsmen and a feast given by the relatives of the deceased.

Ancestor worship.

14. On the tenth day after death, a goat is sacrificed in the name of the deceased, and during the days of mourning, food is regularly laid out for him[1] along the road by which the corpse was removed. Each house has a mud platform (*chaura*), which is supposed to be the abode of the family dead. They do the usual *sráddha* ceremony through a Brâhman.

Religion.

15. They call themselves Hindus, but they do not worship any of the usual Hindu gods, except the Sun (*sûraj*), to whom, as in Bengal, they appeal in times of trouble, and to whom the householder bows when he leaves his house in the morning. Their tribal deities are Juâlamukhi Devi of Kota and Râja Lâkhan. This Juâlamukhi Devi must not be confounded with the more famous Juâlamukhi Devi or Juâlamâi who has her shrine at Nagarkot in the Kângra Valley. The two Juâlamukhi Devis were recorded at the last Census as possessing 116,769 votaries. All they know of Lâkhan is that, as they believe from the similarity of name, he came from Lucknow. This deity has a curious history, for he is almost certainly identical with Lakhana Deva, the son of the famous Jaya Chandra of Kanauj, who apparently led the Hindus against the advancing Muhammadans.[2] Lâkhan is worshipped in the month of Sâwan in the house, at the same platform where the dead are propitiated, with the sacrifice of a goat and a burnt offering (*hom*). Juâlamukhi Devi is also worshipped in Sâwan. Other local deities are Mahâdeva, Râja Chandol,[3] and Mother Earth, which is usually reverenced in association with the collective village gods (*Dih, Dharti*) in the month of Baisâkh by the offering of a goat, which is sacrificed by the Baiga. In none of these offerings do the women share, except the senior wife, who takes part in the offerings to the sacred dead. The worship to Mahâdeva is done by a low class of Tiwâri Brâhmans, who also officiate at marriages. The south and west rooms of the house are those in which the family godlings (*deota*) reside, and no one will touch the threshhold of

---

[1] For other instances see Campbell, *Notes*, 2.

[2] There is a pillar in his honour at Belkhara, in the Mirzapur District. See Cunningham, *Archæological Reports*, XI., 129.

[3] For his worship see *Majhwâr*, para. 40.

these rooms with his foot. When the newly-married pair come home, Dulha Deva, the god of marriages, is worshipped near the family cooking-place. They feed a goat with rice and pulse, cut off its head with an axe, and say—"Take it, Dulha Deva, and be merciful to us!" Then they cook and eat the victim. On the day this worship is done, they remove the ashes out of the fireplace very carefully, without using a broom, and throw it away some distance from the house. If the ashes are dropped on the ground while being removed in this way, it is considered a very unlucky omen. No woman is allowed to be present at the worship of Dulha Deva.

16. The worship of Muchak Râni seems hardly to reach Mirzapur, but the following account by Mr. L. R. Forbes from his Palâmau Settlement Report may be quoted:—"The Kharwârs, like all the aboriginal tribes, are very superstitious, and people the jungles and hills with spirits and gnomes, to whom they offer sacrifice at certain times of the year. One of the most remarkable of these is called the Durgagiya Deota. This spirit rejoices in the name of Muchak Râni. She is Chamâin by caste and her home (*naihar*) is on a hill called Bûharaj; her priests are Baigas. All the Kharwârs regard her with great veneration, and offer up pigs and fowls to her several times during the year. Once a year, in the month of Aghan, what is called the *Karûj pûja* takes place in her honour. The ceremony is performed in the village threshing-floor, when a kind of bread (*pakwân*) and kids are offered up. Once in three years the ceremony of marrying the Râni is performed with great pomp. Early in the morning of the bridal day, both men and women assemble, with drums and horns, form themselves into procession, and ascend the hill, singing a wild song in honour of the bride and bridegroom. One of the party is constituted the priest, who is to perform the wedding ceremony. This man ascends the hill in front of the procession, shouting and dancing till he works himself into a frenzy. The procession halts at the mouth of a cave, which does, or is supposed to, exist on the top of the hill. The priest then enters the cave and returns, bringing with him the Râni, who is represented as a small oblong-shaped and smooth stone, daubed over with red-lead. After going through certain antics, a piece of *tasar* silk cloth is placed on the Râni's head, and a new sheet (*dohar*) is placed below her, the four corners being tied up in such a manner as to allow the Râni, who is now supposed to be seated n her bridal couch, to be slung on a bamboo, and carried like a

dooly or palanquin. The procession then descends the hill and halts under a *bar* tree till noon, when the marriage procession starts for the home of the bridegroom, who resides on the Kandi hill. On their arrival there, offerings, consisting of sweetened milk, two copper pice, and two bell-metal wristlets, are presented to the bride, who is taken out of her dooly and put into the cave in which the bridegroom—who, by the way, is of the Agariya caste—resides. This cave is supposed to be of immense depth, for the stone goes rolling down, striking the rocks as it falls, and all the people listen eagerly till the sound dies out, which they say it does not do for nearly half an hour. When all is silent, the people return rejoicing down the hill, and finish off the evening with a dance. The strangest part of the story is that the people believe that the caves on the two hills are connected, and that every third year the Râni returns to her father's house (*naihar*). They implicitly believe that the stone yearly produced is the same. The village Baigas could probably explain the mystery. In former times the marriage used to take place every year, but, on one occasion, on the morning succeeding the marriage ceremony, the Râni made her appearance in the Baiga's house. The Baiga himself was not present, but his wife, who was at home, was very indignant at this flightness on the part of the Râni, and the idea of her gallivanting about the country the morning after her marriage so shocked the Baigâin's sense of propriety, that she gave the Râni a good setting down, and called upon her to explain herself; and as she could give no satisfactory account of her conduct, she was punished by being married every three years, instead of yearly as before."[1]

Demonology and superstitions.

17. They have apparently abandoned the custom of triennial festivals.[2] Their great festival is in the month of Sâwan, when they dance the Karama dance and indulge in a good deal of rude debauchery. They will not name the pig, tree squirrel, hare, jackal, monkey, or bear in the morning: if they have to mention the pig, they call it *lamtot banaila*; the squirrel, *chikhura;* the hare, *chaugora* ("the footed one") and *patthar ghuswa* ("he that hides in the rocks"); the jackal, *sigo*; the red monkey, *pat mahari*; the bear, *jagariya*. They

[1] This is a very interesting account of a ceremony, which is evidently analogous to those described by Mr. Frazer in his *Golden Bough*, where the corn spirit is annually revived to secure a favourable harvest.

[2] Risley, *Tribes and Castes*, I., 475; Dalton, *Desriptive Ethnology*, 129.

have a great respect for the tiger, and when one is killed, they retire out of view and will not look on its dead body. They believe that if they join in hunting the animal, it will never show itself. On the feast of the Nâgpanchami they do not worship the snake, but smear the horns of the cattle with oil and give them salt. At the last Census 25,336 persons were recorded as Nâga worshippers. When a man has been killed by a tiger, his ghost is propitiated with an offering of a female goat or fowl, and a mud shrine (*baghaut*) is erected in his memory, and placed in charge of the Baiga. When the Sâmbhar stag eats the leaves of the *kahor* and *mâmar* trees, it is a sign of abundance of rain. Other signs of rain are when the throat of the chameleon (*girgit*) gets red, when the under-hairs of a buffalo's tail become scarlet, when the paddy-birds collect round the cattle as they graze, and when the peacocks cry. Witchcraft is firmly believed in. Witches often take the form of tigers. When the demons, who live in the *bahera* (*terminalia bellerica*) and the cotton tree (*semal*), are on the move, a little bird, called the *kúsat*, cries out and raises the alarm. They tell of a Kharwâr who once came on the snake goddess (*nâgin deota*) laying her eggs. When she saw him she came and rolled herself at his feet. The man asked what she wanted. She implored him to throw the eggs into a water hole. So he made a sort of litter of bamboos, and, putting all the eggs on it, went with the Nâgin to the water. The Nâgin plunged in. He was afraid to follow, but the Nâgin said—"Come on! Don't be afraid." When he went in, the water dried up, and he took the eggs to the resting-place of the Nâg. The man remained there eight days, and the Nâg entertained him royally. His relatives thought that a tiger had carried him off, and prepared to do the tenth-day ceremony for him. When the Nâg heard this he said—"Your people think you are dead; now ask whatever you want." The man asked for a brass pot (*batua*), a spoon (*karchhul*), and a pan (*kardhi*). These the Nâg gave him and let him go. When he came home he found his clansmen preparing to do his funeral ceremony. They asked him where he had been, but he never told any one till the day of his death.[1] They have a great respect for the sacred drum

---

[1] These stories of how a human being makes friends with the denizons of the water are common in folk-lore: for instance, Crofton Croker's tale of the "Soul Cages"; W. B. Yeats, *Fairy and Folk Tales of the Irish Peasantry*, 61; and "Jullanar of the Sea," Lane's *Arabian Nights*, III., 234. Nâgê, it may be noted, is a general term among the Mundas of Bengal for the minor deities or spirits who haunt the swampy lower levels of the terraced rice-fields. Dalton, *Descriptive Ethnology*, 188; Risley, *Tribes and Castes*, II., 103.

(*mândar*), which is used at the Karama festival. In some places it is even worshipped in the form of Mândar Devi, who has her shrine under a *mahua* tree (*bassia latifolia*). Demons of all sorts are much dreaded, and they are supposed especially to haunt cremation grounds and old wells and tanks, particularly those in which any one has been drowned. The *kumbhi* tree is believed to be specially infested in this way, and no one will walk under a tree of that species; but to walk under a mango tree is very lucky. On the 11th of the light half of Kârttik, special propitiation is done to malignant ghosts, and people drive iron nails into the head legs of their beds to keep them off. On the 11th Kârttik and at the Diwâli, a cock is offered in the cow-house and a young pig in the buffalo enclosure. Gaurâiya Deota is the godling of the cow-house, and to him are offered the earthen bowl (*gaurâiya*) of the tobacco pipe. Before the Holi fire is lit, a fire sacrifice (*hom*) is made under a cotton tree (*semal*), and its trunk is smeared with red-lead. The men are in the habit of using foul language to women not related to them from the Basant-panchami to the Holi. Fields are constantly injured by the thievish sprites, the *chor* and *chorni*, who are specially looked after by the Baiga. Like the Parahiyas (para. 14), they have a great respect for the goat, which they worship before they sacrifice it. Trees and animals they consider have souls like men. The only difference is that when the souls leave them, they do not go to Parameswar as those of men do. Beyond this they appear to have no tangible belief in a future world of rewards and punishments.

Social customs.

18. The women are tattooed in the style common to the Dravidian tribes;[1] there is no trace of a tribal tattoo. If they are not tattooed, they think Parameswar will brand them in the next world. The women wear heavy pewter anklets (*pairi*), glass bangles (*chûri*), and head necklaces. Their special oaths are taking a piece of hot iron in the hand, by the Ganges, putting their hands on their sons' heads, or touching a cow. These oaths are usually sworn in boundary disputes and caste quarrels, and the violation of them is believed to lead to poverty and death. They believe in the demoniacal theory of disease, and whenever a person is sick, an Ojha is called in. He puts some rice before the patient, who blows on it, gets into a

[1] For details see *Agariya*, para. 22.

state of ecstacy, and names the particular *Bhût* which has done the mischief. When he announces this, the patient also gets into a sort of fit and asks the *Bhût*, who answers by the Ojha, what offering he wants. They believe in the treatment of hysteria in girls by beating them with the sacred chain (*gurda*), which is in charge of the Baiga.[1]

Taboos.

19. They will not touch a woman during the pollution after parturition. A woman in her menses is kept in a separate room with another entrance, so that she can go in and out without passing through the court-yard.[2] They will not touch a Chamâr, Dharkâr, or Ghasiya, nor the maternal aunt of the wife (*mamiya sâs*), nor the wife of a younger brother. They will not mention by name their wives, father-in-law, mother-in-law, or younger brother's wife.[3]

Festivals.

20. Their great festival is in the middle of Bhâdon, when a leafy branch of the *karam* tree is cut, daubed with red-lead and butter, and fixed up in the court-yard. This marks, as among the Orâons,[4] the time for the transplanting of the rice. The women and men, dressed in gala clothes, place themselves into opposite rows. The national drum (*mândar*)[5] is beaten, when they advance and retreat, and finally dance round the branch in a circle. Sometimes, in the course of the performance, one of the men is seized with the divine afflatus, and murmurs some broken words, which are taken as an omen of the prospects of the coming harvest.[6] The deity connected with agriculture is Baghesar, the tiger lord, who is worshipped by the Baiga with the sacrifice of a white cock; and at the same time a white hen is offered to Âd Chandi Devi, who appears to be a Hinduised representative of Chando Omal, the moon divinity of the Mundas in Bengal.[7] At the last Census, 1,326 persons recorded themselves as worshippers of Chandi Devi, but she has her seat at the Chandi hill overhanging Hardwâr, and is apparently different from the Dravidian goddess of the same name. They surround the

---

1 On this see *Majhwâr*, para. 45.

2 On this see Frazer, *Golden Bough*, I., 238, *sqq*.

3 See Lubbock, *Origin of Civilisation*, II., 122.

4 Dalton, *Descriptive Ethnology*, 259.

5 There are numerous instances of the respect paid to the drum. In the Atharva Veda (Muir, *Sanskrit Texts*, V., 466) is a hymn to the sacred drum, and see Tylor, *Anthropology*, 293; *Calcutta Review*, LXXVII., 372.

6 See a good account of the observances in *Calcutta Review*, LXIX., 364, for Shâhâbâd.

7 See Dalton, *loc. cit.*, 186.

piled grain with a ring of cow-dung or charcoal, and put on the top of it a piece of cow-dung which is called *barhâwan* or "that which gives the increase." Until the grain is measured they will not leave an open basket near the pile, lest Bhûts should remove the grain. After it is measured they never touch it.[1] When they are sowing they take five handsful of grain from the sowing basket and pray to Dharti Mâta, the earth goddess, to be benignant. They keep this grain, grind it, and offer it to her at her regular festival in the month of Sâwan (September). When they eat they call on Paramesar, and throw a little of the food on the ground.[2]

Food.

21. They will not eat the meat of the cow, buffalo, monkey, horse, elephant, camel, donkey, alligator, lizard, or rat. Men and women eat apart. The children eat first, and the head of the household after them. They use liquor freely, and chew tobacco (*surti*). The use of liquor they consider wards off disease, but drunkenness is discreditable. They will eat food cooked in butter (*pakka khâna*) from the hands of Brâhmans, and will drink water from a Chero, but the better class are giving this up.

Local organisation.

22. They are very clannish and have a local organisation called *eka*, including the people of two or three villages, which meets to consider public matters; but this is becoming weakened.

Occupation and social status.

23. Most of them are cultivators; a few hold land. Their social position varies: the more Hinduised claim the rank of Râjputs, those of the more primitive type are on the same level as Cheros and Majhwârs.

Khasiya.—A sub-division of hill Brâhmans, who take their name from the ancient Khasa race. Of these Mr. Atkinson writes:[3] — "The lists give some two hundred and fifty septs of Khasiya Brâhmans, of whom the majority are cultivators and plough themselves. They worship sometimes Siva and Vishnu, but chiefly Bhairava, the more common forms of the Sâktis and the village deities. It would be useless to give a list of their names, which are chiefly derived from the villages in which they live. Some claim common origin with the Brâhmans of the plains; thus the Shâranis, Dobhâls, Gahtyâris, Kanyânis, and Garwâls say that

---

[1] See M. Conway, *Demonology*, II., 117.
[2] Tylor, *Primitive Culture*, II., 270.
[3] *Himalayan Gazetteer*, III., 428, *sqq*.

they were originally Tiwâris; the Mûnwâlis, that they were Chaubês; the Papanois, that they were Upretis of Doti; the Chaunâls, that they were Chaubês of Mathura, who settled in Mânili, in Kâli Kumâun, and took the title Pânrê and their present name on emigrating to Chauni; the Kuthâris call themselves Pants; the Ghushuris, Daurbas, Shanwâls, and Dhunilas call themselves Pânrês; the Laimdaris, Chavanrâls, Phuloriyas, Oliyas, Naniyâls, Chaudâsis, Dalakotis, Burhalakotis, Dhulâris, Dhurâtis, Pancholis, Baneriyas, Garmolas, Walauniyas, and Birariyas allege that they are Joshis; the Bânaris and Nainwâls, that they were Phulâri Brâhmans; the Kaphulis, Dhankolas, and Bhagwâls, that they were Bhatts of Doti; the Jâlis, Nakhyâls, Thapaliyas and Haribols, that they were Upâdhyas; the Bhanautiyas, that they were Gaurs; the Mashyâls, that they were Kanaujiyas; the Pâtasis, that they were Pâthaks; and the Baraniyas, that they came from Benares and were astrologers to the Râja. Septs named after villages, and who do not attempt to give any account of their origin, are the Kholiyas, Kunwâlas, Lweshâlis, Kaphariyas, Baithariyas, Mehalkhâniyas, Nainoliyas, Meltis, Tarâriyas, Hâtwals, Pokhariyas, Chhatguliyas, besides some one hundred and fifty others. They do not know either *sâkha* or *prâvara*, and often have little knowledge even of their *gotra*. The Kanseris worship Siva as Bibhândeswar, a name for which there are few temples. Akariyas derive their name from the fact that they were free from taxation (*a* "privative" and *kara*, "tax"). Balariyas belong to Purnagiri in Kâli Kumaun. Ghughutyâls are Râjputs of Ryûni, degraded from Brâhmans on account of an offence committed by their ancestor. Rasyârs say they were so called because they were Brâhman cooks (*rasoiya*) to Râjas. The Namgis supply Purohits to the Bhotiyas of Juhâr. The Phulrâis supplied flowers for worship at the Nanda Devi temple. The Ghaibhanariyas perform funeral ceremonies for people who die without heirs. Panerus are suppliers of drinking-water (*pâni*). The Dobhâls of Doba village are also called Jagariya or exorcists, and are authorities on the possession by devils, and are called in on such occasions. The Oliyas, on the other hand, avert the evil effects of hail-storms (*ola*), and in Kuâr wander about from village to village begging their dues, a measure of rice. The Chilakutis act as priests of the village god Saim, in Chaugarkha. Nearly ninety per cent. of the Brâhmans in Kumaun belong to the Khasiya race, and are so classed by the people themselves. A few of the better class worship the orthodox deities alone, but the great mass serve the Bhairavas, Bhûts, Bhûtinis, and are, to all intents and purposes, as much priests of non-Brahmanical deities, as their representatives further east who know not the name of Brâhman. They are a simple race, and not to be confounded with the Hill Pujâri or temple priest, or the Nâth ; but in times of rejoicing assume the functions of religious directors in the very simple ceremonies deemed necessary. The Khasiyas never tried to connect themselves with the plains till late years, when they see that such connections add to their personal dignity."

Khasiya.—A sept of hill Râjputs who represent the great Khasa race. In the Vishnu Purâna we find Khasa as the daughter of Daksha, wife of Kasyapa and mother of the Yakshas and Râkshasas. In the same compilation they appear under the name of Yaksha. They are mentioned in the Karna Parvan of the Mahâbhârata as living in the Panjâb between the Arattas and Vasatis. In the Vayu Purâna, the Khasas are named as one of the tribes which Sâgara would have destroyed had he not been restrained by Vasishtha; and in Manu they are reckoned as degraded Kshatriyas. They inhabited the part of Tibet immediately north of Garhwâl, and we have here a hint as to the origin of the celebrated fable told by Herodotus about the ants who throw the gold out of their burrows. In the Mahâbhârata the Khasas are specially mentioned among the Northern tribes who brought presents of *paipilika* gold, so called because it was collected by ants (*pipîlaka*). This would indicate that the Khasas were the carriers of Tibet gold dust. The same word occurs in various well-known geographical terms, such as Kashgâr, Hindukush, Kashmîr, and many others.[1] Even Bâbar had a very shrewd idea of this. "About these hills," he writes, "are other tribes of men. With all the investigation and enquiry I could make among the natives of Hindustân, I could get no sort of description or authentic information regarding them. All that I could learn was that the men of these hills were called Kas. It struck me that as the Hindustânis frequently confound *shîn* and *sîn*, and as Kashmîr is the chief, and indeed, as far as I have heard, the only city in these hills, it may have taken its name from that circumstance." [2]

---

[1] Atkinson, *Himalayan Gazetteer*, II., 375, *sqq.*
[2] Leyden, *Bâbar*, 313.

2. "The account," writes Mr. Atkinson, "that the Khasiyas of Kumaun give of themselves tallies in all respects with the indication from other sources. They always profess to be Râjputs, who have fallen from their once honourable position by the necessity of living in a country and in a climate where the strict observance of the ceremonial usages of their religion is impossible; and undoubtedly this statement is supported by all the facts, so far as we are acquainted with them, which have any bearing on the question. It has been sometimes, but hastily, assumed, apparently from analogous circumstances in Nepâl, that the Kumaun Khasiyas are a people of mixed Tibetan and Indian race. The Khasiyas of Nepâl may have been less exposed to Aryan influences throughout their successive wanderings, or may have been modified by admixture with Tibetan tribes. For, as we proceed eastward from the Kâli, we find conditions of climate, which, however unlike those of Tibet, must still be less antagonistic than those of the Western Himâlaya to the diffusion of a Mongolian race. But this admission does not affect the Khasiyas of Kumâun, who, in physiognomy and form, are as purely an Aryan race as any in the plains of Northern India. The language of the Khasiyas is a purely Hindi dialect both in its vocables and in its grammatical structure, and no signs of foreign admixture have hitherto been discovered in it. Supposed resemblances in feature between the Khasiyas and the neighbouring Tibetan tribes have helped to lead some to a conclusion different from that now given, but this resemblance has no real foundation in fact. The people of the plains, no doubt, differ greatly in appearance from those of the hills, but not more so than might be expected, when we consider the great difference in the physical conditions of the countries that they respectively inhabit, nor more than the Aryan races of the plains, owing to similar causes, differ amongst themselves. The moist climate of Lower Bengal, the comparatively dry heat of the North-Western Provinces, and the still drier climate of the Panjâb, with its great extremes of heat and cold, cause those physical changes in the inhabitants that are so remarkable and clearly recognisable by the most casual observer. If, to the effects of climate, we add the influence of the various races which have from time to time invaded India, we shall have reason to believe that much of the variations observed in the plains is due to circumstances which have been wanting in the hills. However this may be, this much is certain at least, that, at the present time, the Khasiyas of Kumaun

and Garhwâl are in all respect Hindus. They are so in language, religion, and customs, and all their feelings and prejudices are so strongly imbued with the peculiar spirit of Hinduism that, though their social habit and religious belief are often repugnant to the orthodox of that faith, it is impossible for any one who knows them to consider them other than Hindus. Year by year, with increasing communication with the plains, the hill Hindu is more and more assimilating his practice with that of his co-religionists in the plains, whilst to the North, the Tibetan Bhotiyas are becoming more observant of Hindu customs."

3. "In Garhwâl there are numerous sections of the Khasiyas named after the parent village (*thât*), and carrying its name wherever they go, such as Patwâl, which gives its name to Patwâlsyân; Kaphola, hence Kapholsyûn; Bagarwâl; Ambâna, who were Bhatts of Benares, but are here Râjputs; Ramola; Dânas, or Dânavas, representatives of the old tribe of that name; the Khandawâris, Durhyâls, Sanaulas, Dalanis, and Bukilas call themselves Râwats; Boras, Kairas, and Choriyas come from Kumaun. All of these are engaged in agriculture and petty trade, and none of them will call themselves Khasiya. All style themselves Râjputs and many say that they were settled in their present village before Brâhmans and Râjas came. They worship principally the village gods, care little for Brâhman aid in their domestic ceremonies, unless he be a Khasiya, do not wear the sacred thread (*janeu*), and on occasions of joy or sorrow, marriage or deaths, the house is simply purified by cow-dung and cow urine. The marriage or funeral ceremonies are short or long according to the purse of the employers. They intermarry with each other according to local rules peculiar in some respects to each tract."[1]

Khatîk.[2]—(Sanskrit, *Khattika*,[3] "a butcher or hunter.")—A cultivating, labouring, and vegetable-selling caste found all over the Province. They are no doubt very closely connected with the Pâsis, of whom they are sometimes classed as a sub-caste. Of the seven sub-castes enumerated by Mr. Sherring, two—Bauriya and Pâsi—may be excluded. Of the remaining five, two are territorial—

---

[1] Atkinson, *loc. cit.*, III., 276.

[2] Based principally on enquiries made at Mirzapur, and partially on a note by Nawab Muhammad Ali Khân of Bulandshahr.

[3] As an amusing instance of a folk etymology, a writer in North-Western Provinces. Census Report (1865), *Appendix* B, 42, derives the name from *khatka*—"rapping," because a man of this caste once had an intrigue with a married woman and used to rap at her door to gain admittance! Râja Lachhman Sinh derives it from "*ghât*," "to kill or watch." *Bulandshahr Memoir*, 185.

Ajudhyabâsi and Sunkhar. The Sunkhar are said to take their name from the town of Sonkh in Mathura. At the same time Sonkh does not appear[1] to possess any traditions of the caste, and their own legends point rather to Jaunpur and Oudh. The other three—Bakarqassâb or Qassâi are butchers, who sell and slaughter goats; the Chalan-mahrâo are workers in leather, especially using it for covering or lining; the Ghorcharâos are grooms. The Ajudhyabâsi sell fruit and vegetables and do general work for hire. All the sub-castes are endogamous.[2] In Mirzapur the sub-divisions are Ajudhyabâsi and Sunkhar, between whom the only difference is that the former eat beef and the latter abstain from it. To the West of the Province they have two endogamous sub-castes—Khara and Khalranga or leather dyers.[3] The last Census classifies them under the heads of Chauhân; Chik or Bakarqassâb; Kabâriya or Mewafarosh, "fruit-sellers"; Rajauriya, who probably take their name from the old Râjput Chauhân fort in the Etah District; and Sonkhar. The Kabâriya is often a sort of marine store-keeper, who buys all kinds of old rubbish (Hindi *kabâr*, Sanskrit *kapâla*). In Agra they have three sub-castes—Chik, Bûchar (our English "butcher"), and Sunkhar. There some of these Chiks make winnowing fans (*sûp*) and sieves (*chhalni*); the Bûchar sell goats' flesh and mutton, not beef; and the Sunkhar sell fruit and work as grooms. In Bulandshahr we have the Khara or "pure," Khallu or "hidemen," and Chik. The complete Census returns show no less than 816 sub-divisions of the Hindu and 7 of the Musalmân branch. Of these, those of the most local importance are the Bilwariya of Meerut, the Bargûjar, Chauhân, Chauseni, Khatri, and Sanwariya of Bulandshahr; the Gandhîla and Tomar of Aligarh; the Ajudhyabâsi and Khokhar of Allahâbâd; the Sengarwâr of Mirzapur; the Kanaujiya and Sagahiya of Gorakhpur; the Bandichhor of Basti; and the Tanbina of Lucknow.

Marriage rules.

2. In Bihâr they regulate their marriages by the standard formula, calculated to five generations in the descending line.[4] In Mirzapur they do not marry into the family of the maternal uncle, father's sister, and mother's sister for three generations, and in their own family they

---

[1] Growse, *Mathura*, 379.
[2] *Hindu Tribes and Castes*, I., 400.
[3] Râja Lachhman Sinh, *loc. cit.*, 185.
[4] Risley, *Tribes and Castes*, I., 477.

do not intermarry for four generations. The occupations considered disreputable in forming alliances are those of a butcher, shoemaker, or carter of manure. Monogamy is the rule of the caste and concubinage is prohibited. In Bihâr they practise infant marriage, marrying their daughters between the age of five and twelve years. In Mirzapur the age is eight or ten. The bride price is fixed at seven rupees. They have a powerful tribal council (*panchâyat*) under a hereditary president (*Chaudhari*). When he is appointed he has to present the council with a gallon of spirits. If a man abduct another man's wife, he is fined twenty-five rupees. This, which is also the rule among some of the cognate castes, is known by the special name of *pachîsi*. Besides this, he has to provide a dinner, consisting of boiled rice, pork, and three gallons of liquor. If an unmarried girl intrigue with a clansman, her parents are fined two gallons of liquor, and then they are re-admitted to caste; but the man has to give something more to buy liquor before the clansmen will smoke with him. Men or women caught intriguing with a stranger to the caste are permanently excommunicated. All money fines are spent on liquor. If the Chaudhari or any member abuse the caste as a body, he is put out of caste. In former times the orders of the Chaudhari used to be enforced by corporal chastisement, but this has now ceased, and a fine is imposed. A wife can be expelled if she is proved faithless, and she can put away her husband if he is impotent or abandons his religion. No separation is permitted without leave of the council.

Widow marrigae.

3. The levirate is permitted, but not enforced. A widow generally marries a widower. The only ceremony is that the pair are shut up in a dark room, and he rubs red-lead on the parting of her hair and puts a new suit of clothes and some ornaments on her. The clansmen are then treated to boiled rice, pork, and liquor, and next morning the bride is brought home. When she arrives the female relatives of her husband look in her face and give her a present (*munhdikhâi*)

Birth ceremonies.

4. The ceremonies at birth are as usual among menial castes. When the midwife cuts the navel string, she throws it outside the house, a fire is lighted near the mother, and some branches of the thorny *bel* (*ægle marmelos*) are hung to the house eaves to scare off ghosts. The birth pollution lasts for twelve days, and the husband does not cohabit with his wife for six months after her confinement.

5. Marriage is arranged by the father's sister's husband of the boy. The betrothal (*mangani*) is confirmed by the two fathers sitting together in a square in the court-yard of the bride's house. They exchange a leaf platter (*dauna*) full of liquor, drink it, and the bride's father receives one ser of rice and five pieces of turmeric. The clansmen feast and drink; next morning the bridegroom's father returns home and sends the bride price—seven rupees. Then follows the *matmangar* ceremony three days before the wedding. At this the drum of the Chamâr, who leads the procession of women as they go to dig the clay, is worshipped, and offerings are made at the village shrine (*deohâr*). The bridegroom's mother then smears his back with turmeric and barley flour, and the earth is brought home and put under the marriage shed, which is made of bamboo, with a bamboo in the centre. In the centre is the water jar (*kalsa*), which is smeared with cow-dung and decorated with red-lead and mango leaves. On the top is placed a saucer (*parai*) full of rice. The actual ceremony takes place towards morning. The bride's father's sister brings out the bride, and her father washes her's and the bridegroom's feet and drinks a little of the water. The bridegroom then rubs red-lead on the parting of her hair, and the pair walk five times round the central bamboo: at each revolution the bride's brother puts a little parched rice into a fan (*sûp*), which the bridegroom holds, and then scatters the rice on the ground. Next follows the usual ceremony of the *Kohabar*.[1] After the bride is brought home, her father-in-law-sister plunges the water jars and marriage festoons (*bandanwâr*) in a neighbouring stream or tank, and on her way home offers sweetmeats and a burnt-offering (*hom*) to the ghosts which inhabit the old *pîpal* and banyan trees in the village. The binding portion of the ceremony is the feet-washing and the rubbing of red-lead on the parting of the bride's hair.[2]

Marriage ceremonies.

6. The dead are cremated in the usual way. When the mourners return, a fire is kindled at the door of the dead man; on this a little oil is poured, and the mourners warm their feet in the smoke and then

Death ceremony.

---

[1] For which see *Majhwâr*, para. 18.

[2] Mr. Sherring says that, at the marriage ceremonies of Khatiks and Pâsis boys dress themselves in women's clothes and dance in public; but the Bhars do not observe this custom and make use of the drum and other instruments of music on such occasions which the others do not. *Hindu Tribes and Castes*, I., 400.

chew some *nîm* leaves; liquor is then served round. Food is regularly laid out for the dead during the days of mourning. On the ninth day the mourners shave their heads, and the barber makes ten lumps of milk and rice cooked together, which the chief mourner throws into a tank or stream in the name of the dead. In the evening a pig is sacrificed in the name of the deceased, and the clansmen consume the flesh with liquor. In the first fortnight of Kuâr, they offer lumps of boiled rice and milk to the dead, and lay out cakes, rice, milk, and flesh for the spirits. No Brâhman officiates, and his place is taken by the barber.

Religion.

7. The great deity of the tribe is Karâr Bîr, who has his shrine at Jaunpur.[1] In Mirzapur they say that he was an Ahîr by caste, who was killed by the Muhammadans, because he would not renounce his religion. Karâr Bîr was found to possess 31,408 worshippers at the last Census. He was a demon who inhabited the site of the present Jaunpur. Râmchandra attacked him, tore him to pieces, and left his trunk in the form of a shapeless mass of stone, which is now worshipped. The fort is known as Karârkot to Hindus, and the neighbouring quarters of the city as Karâra Muhalla. He is said to have left his name in that of the Karâkat Pargana of Jaunpur.

He is now represented by a black stone, which is supposed to have marvellous powers. He last displayed his influence when the British tried and failed to blow up part of the Jaunpur fort. His offering is a loaf, five-and-a-quarter sers of rice, a pitcher of liquor, and the *laddu* sweetmeat. They also worship the deified ghost of some unknown Brâhman known as Bâmat, Bâbhan or Brâhman Deva. This worship of a dead Brâhman under the name of Brahm is most popular. No less than 406,787 persons recorded themselves as votaries of Brahm at the last Census. Some of the more famous Brâhms are Ratan Pânrê and Harshu Pânrê.[2] His offering is a Brâhmanical thread (*janeu*), a pig, and a cup of liquor. He is said also to have been a martyr to the faith. Some worship Bhawâni and others Birtiya, who is, according to them, a demoness. Her votaries have a mud altar (*bedi*) in the house, and on it, in the full moon of Sâwan, they offer a young pig, and drop a mixture of pepper, sugar, and water (*mirchwân*) on her altar. They have the usual worship of Sîtala Mâi performed by women when small-pox

---

[1] *Archæological Reports,* XI., 104.

[2] For these worthies see *Introduction to Popular Religion and Folk-lore, 121, sq.*

prevails. The special time for worshipping Bhawâni is at the Naurâtra of Chait. Her offering is a pig, cakes (*pûri*), and sweetmeats (*halwa*). In Bulandshahr they worship the Ganges, Devi, and the Mîran Sâhib of Amroha. On feast days they offer liquor to the village gods (*deohâr.*) On the Pacheinyân festival they lay some milk and parched rice near the hole of a snake. Their festivals are the Khichari or Khincharwâr in Pûs, the Phagua in Chait, and the Kajari in Sâwan. On these days they drink liquor and offer some to the tribal deities. The ghosts of the dead, if not propitiated, appear in dreams and bring disease and death. Such cases are treated by the Ojha.

Social observances:

8. Women are tattooed on the arms. They wear no nose-rings nor glass bangles (*chûri*). They have ear-rings, armlets (*dharkaua*), and necklaces. Men swear on the heads of their sons and on Ganges water, in the form *Râm dohâi*. Some will not eat beef. They will not touch food touched by a Chamâr, Dom, Dharkâr, Musahar, Pâsi, or Dhobi; the last they consider the foulest of all. They will not touch the wife of a younger brother or a daughter's mother-in-law, and will not speak of a wife by her name. Men and women eat together, but not out of the same dish. They salute a daughter's father-in-law in the form *Râm Juhâré*, and others with the *pâélagi* and *asirbâd*. To the West of the Province they are considered next lowest to the Bhangi.[1] In the West of the Panjâb they are tanners and rank higher than those to the East, who are pig-keepers.[2] To the East of these Provinces they hold a very low rank: no one will drink water touched by them. They will eat food touched by the Nâo, Bâri, or Ahîr. Their chief occupations are keeping and selling pigs and selling vegetables and fruits, which they buy wholesale from Koiris. On the whole they bear a good character, and seldom come before the Courts.

Distribution of Khatîks according to the Census of 1891.

District	Hindus.						Muhammadans.	Total.
	Chauhân.	Chik :— Bakar-qassâb.	Kabâriya : Mewa-farosh.	Rajauriya.	Sonkhar.	Others.		
Dera Dûn . .	...	...	...	...	40	330	...	370
Sahâranpur .	...	...	...	...	...	2,522	...	2,522

[1] Râja Lachhman Sinh, *loc. cit.*, 185.
[2] Ibbetson, *Panjâb Ethnography*, para. 602.

DHARKÂR.

Distribution of Khatîks according to the Census of 1891—contd.

District.	Hindus.						Muhammadans.	Total.
	Chauhân.	Chik :—Bakarqassâb.	Kabâriya : Mewafarosh.	Rajauriya.	Sonkhar.	Others.		
Muzaffarnagar	23	9	36	9	...	2,751	...	2,828
Meerut	...	...	...	...	6,567	1,530	...	8,097
Bulandshahr	2,954	...	...	2,210	...	16,305	...	21,469
Aligarh	52	...	...	22,623	...	17,656	...	40,331
Mathura	56	153	17	1,725	...	3,353	1	5,305
Agra	70	1,821	54	174	38	3,830	...	3,987
Farrukhâbâd	...	...	...	...	10	950	17	977
Mainpuri	12	125	122	22	...	1,510	..	1,791
Etâwah	118	144	143	140	...	1,657	...	2,202
Etah	200	196	40	101	98	1,235	...	1,870
Bareilly	...	...	722	22	...	2,167	...	2,911
Bijnor	...	...	...	...	...	555	...	555
Budâun	1,102	...	...	234	36	2,430	...	3,802
Morâdâbâd	1	...	...	429	85	462	...	977
Shâhjahânpur	...	...	...	...	14	1,906	...	1,920
Pilibhît	...	...	...	...	...	1,463	...	1,463
Cawnpur	...	3	116	...	2,698	4,650	...	7,467
Fatehpur	...	...	...	...	3,347	4,194	6	7,547
Bânda	...	...	...	...	1,153	1,255	13	2,421
Hamîrpur	...	15	...	...	425	1,025	...	1,465
Allahâbâd	...	...	15	...	3,568	1,556	9	5,148
Jhânsi	...	47	104	5	10	1,105	12	1,283
Jâlaun	19	27	2	34	12	768	...	862
Lalitpur	18	82	...	...	...	273	...	373
Benares	...	...	...	...	4,305	1,424	16	5,745
Mirzapur	...	...	...	...	4,738	248	...	4,986
Jaunpur	...	...	...	...	3,100	132	...	3,232

Distribution of Khatîks according to the Census of 1891—concld.

District.	Hindus.						Muhammadans.	Total.
	Chauhân.	Chik :—Bakar-qassâb.	Kabâriya : Mewa-farosh.	Rajauriya.	Sonkhar.	Others.		
Ghâzipur	...	...	5	...	1,185	76	...	1,266
Ballia	...	...	...	...	...	32	...	32
Gorakhpur	...	...	3,352	...	1,826	4,714	1	9,893
Basti	...	...	...	...	5,300	956	...	6,256
Azamgarh	...	...	12	...	3,968	1,407	...	5,387
Kumaun	...	...	...	...	...	1	...	1
Garhwâl	...	...	...	...	...	9	...	9
Tarâi	...	...	...	22	...	96	187	305
Lucknow	...	131	837	...	727	1,780	...	3,477
Unâo	...	...	...	...	258	538	...	796
Râê Bareli	...	11	335	...	844	1,003	...	2,193
Sîtapur	...	...	...	...	99	59	...	158
Hardoi	...	...	...	...	...	36	...	36
Kheri	...	...	...	...	2	2	11	15
Faizâbâd	...	...	...	...	603	933	...	1,536
Gonda	...	...	...	...	9,287	582	...	9,869
Bahrâich	...	...	...	...	...	...	...	...
Sultânpur	...	...	...	...	1,049	499	...	1,548
Partâbgarh	...	...	...	...	286	218	15	519
Bârabanki	...	...	...	...	271	456	...	727
Total	4,625	2,764	5,912	27,750	55,949	92,639	290	189,929

Khatri.—(Sanskrit *Kshatriya.*)—A mercantile caste which has its origin in the Panjâb, but is found in considerable numbers throughout these Provinces.

2. One of the best accounts of the caste is that given by Sir G. Campbell in his paper on the "Ethnology of India" published in the "Journal

Sir G. Campbell's account of the caste.

of the Asiatic Society of Bengal" for 1866. He writes:— "Trade is their main occupation, but in fact they have broader and more distinguishing features. Besides monopolising the trade of the Panjâb and the greater part of Afghânistân and doing a good deal beyond these limits, they are in the Panjâb the chief civil administrators, and have almost all literate work in their hands. So far as the Sikhs have a priesthood, they are, moreover, the priests or Gurus of the Sikhs. Both Nânak and Govind were, and the Sodhis and Bedis of the present day are, Khatris. Thus, then, they are in the Panjâb, so far as ā more energetic race will permit them, all that Marhatta Brâhmans are in the Marhatta country, besides engrossing the trade, which the Marhatta Brâhmans have not. They are not usually military in their character, but quite capable of using the sword when necessary. Diwân Sâwan Mal, Governor of Multân, and his notorious successor Mûl Râj, and many of Ranjît Sinh's chief functionaries, were Khatris. Even under Muhammadan rulers in the West they have risen to high administrative posts. There is a record of a Khatri Dîwân of Badakshân or Kundûz, and, I believe, of a Khatri Governor of Peshâwar under the Afghâns. The Emperor Akbar's famous minister Todar Mal was a Khatri, and a relative of the man of undoubted energy, the great Commissariat contractor of Agra, Joti Prasâd, lately informed me that he also is a Khatri. Altogether there can be no doubt that these Khatris are one of the most acute, energetic, and remarkable races in India, though, in fact, except locally in the Panjâb, they are not much known to Europeans. The Khatris are staunch Hindus, and it is somewhat singular that while giving a religion and priests to the Sikhs, they themselves are comparatively seldom Sikhs. The Khatris are a very fine, fair, handsome race, and, as may be gathered from what I have already said, they are very generally educated.

3. "There is a large subordinate class of Khatris, somewhat lower but of equal mercantile energy, called Rors or Roras. The proper Khatris of higher grade will often deny all connection with them, or at least only admit that they have some sort of bastard kindred with Khatris; but I think there can be no doubt that they are ethnologically the same, and they are certainly mixed up with Khatris in their avocations. I shall treat the whole kindred as generally Khatris.

4. "Speaking of Khatris, then, thus broadly, they have, as I have said, the whole trade of the Panjâb and of most of Afghânistân. No village can get on without the Khatri, who keeps the accounts, does banking business, and buys and sells the grain. They seem, too, to get on with the people better than most traders and usurers of this kind. In Afghânistân, among a rough and alien people, the Khatris are, as a rule, confined to the position of humble dealers, shop-keepers, and money-lenders; but in that capacity the Pathâns seem to look on them as a kind of valuable animal, and a Pathân will steal another man's Khatri, not only for the sake of ransom, as is frequently done on the Peshâwar and Hazâra frontier, but also as he might steal a milch cow, or as Jews might, I dare say, be carried off in the Middle Ages, with a view to render them profitable.

5. "I do notknow the exact limits of Khatri occupation to the West, but certainly in all Eastern Afghânistân they seem to be just as much a part of the established community as they are in the Panjâb. They find their way far into Central Asia, but the further they get the more depressed and humiliating is their position. In Turkistân Vambery speaks of them with great contempt, as yellow-faced Hindus of a cowardly and sneaking character. Under Turkomân rule they could hardly be otherwise. They are the only Hindus known in Central Asia. In the Panjâb they are so numerous that they cannot all be rich and mercantile, and many of them hold land, cultivate, take service, and follow various avocations.

6. "The Khatris are altogether excluded from Brâhman Kashmîr. In the hills, however, the Kakkas, on the east bank of the Jahlam, are said to have been originally Khatris (they are a curiously handsome race), and in the interior of the Kângra Hills there is an interesting race of fine patriarchal-looking shepherds called Gaddis, most of whom are Khatris. Khatri traders are numerous in Delhi; are found in Agra, Lucknow, and Patna; and are well known in the Bara Bâzâr of Calcutta, though they are principally connected with Panjâb firms.

7. "The Khatris do not seem, as a rule, to reach the Western coast; in the Bombay market I cannot find that they have any considerable place. In Sindh, I find in Captain Burton's book an account of a race of pretended Kshatriyas, who are really Banyas of the Nânakshâhi (Sikh) faith, and who trade and have a large

share of public offices. They are evidently Khatris.[1] Ludhiâna is a large and thriving town of mercantile Khatris, with a numerous colony of Kashmîri shawl-weavers."

Tribal traditions.

8. The tribal tradition runs that when Parasu Râma, the sixth Avatâra of Vishnu, was engaged in subduing the Kshatriyas in the interest of the Brâhmans, of which caste he was a member, he violently caused the miscarriage of every pregnant woman he could find. Through fear some women who were pregnant took refuge with certain Brâhmans, and when their persecutor detected them their protectors saved their lives by declaring that they were Brâhmanis. In order to corroborate this assertion the Brâhmans ate food at the hands of the women. The children of these women were the progenitors of the present Khatris. It is said that these Brâhmans were of the Sâraswat tribe, and as a proof of their assertion the Khatris point to the fact of the Sâraswat Brâhmans still accepting food cooked by them. Another and more recent tradition is to the effect that up to the time of Alamgîr the Khatris did not abandon their old profession of soldiering; but when a large number of them were slain in the Dakkhin war, he felt pity on the condition of their widows, and proposed that they should be re-married. He summoned a council of the more respectable Khatris of Delhi, and proposed that they should adopt widow marriage. Their headmen Lallu and Jagdhar opposed the proposed reform, and the meeting was dissolved. Hence to this day *Lallu Jagdhar* is a term applied to a meeting which comes to no conclusion. The Emperor did not insist further on the adoption of the reform, but dismissed the Khatris from his military service; but gave them the duty of Dalâli or brokers, which is still their speciality. Another version of the story is that those who consented to the proposal of Alamgîr to adopt widow marriage are called the Bârahghar; those who dissented, Chârghar; and those who induced the Emperor to abandon the scheme Âdhaghar. The Rora are said to be those who, when questioned by the Râja of Gaya, and a great persecutor of the tribe, denied being Khatris.

Ethnological affinities of the Khatris.

9. About the ethnological affinities of the tribe there is much difference of opinion.[2] Mr. Ibbetson says that the validity of their claim to be

---

[1] For these Gujarât Khatris, see *Bombay Gazetteer*, V., 49.

[2] For some of the evidence on one side of the case a tract by the late Bâbu Harish Chandra of Benares may be consulted.

direct representatives of Kshatriyas[1] of Manu "is as doubtful as most other matters connected with the fourfold caste system." On the other hand, Mr. Nesfield thinks their claim to be valid, and adds that "the cause which detached the Khatri from the Kshatriya and shut out all possibility of a return to the ancestral caste was the establishment of a marriage union between fragments or clans drawn from several different sub-castes of Kshatriyas, between whom no connubial rights had hitherto existed, or from sub-castes of Kshatriyas mixed with Brâhmans. There is much reason to believe that Brâhmans as well as Kshatriyas have contributed to form the new caste of Khatri," and he goes on to allude to the fact, already referred to, that Sâraswat Brâhmans eat food at their hands. On the other hand, Mr. Risley[2] urges that the internal organisation of the caste "furnishes almost conclusive proof that they are descended from neither Brâhmans nor Kshatriyas, and that the theory connecting them with the latter tribe rests upon no firmer foundation than a resemblance of name, which, for all we know, may be purely accidental. Their features and complexion, indeed, entitle them to be ranked as Aryans of comparatively pure lineage, but among their numerous sections we find none of those territorial names which are characteristic of the Râjput septs. The section names of Khatris belong to quite a different type, and rather resemble those in vogue among the Oswâls and Agarwâlas. Were they descended from the same stock as the Râjputs, they must have had the same set of section names, and it is difficult to see why they should have abandoned them for less distinguished patronymics. In addition to their own sections, they have also the standard Brâhmanical *gotras*; but these have no influence upon marriage, and have clearly been borrowed, *honoris causâ*, from the Sâraswat Brâhmans, who serve them as priests. If, then, it is at all necessary to connect the Khatris with the ancient fourfold system of castes, the only group to which we can affiliate them is the Vaisyas. This conjecture is at least in keeping with the present occupations of the caste, and gets us out of the difficulty which led Sir G. Campbell to propound the doubtful theory that in the ordinary course of history the warlike conquerors of one age become the astute money-dealers of another. In truth, however, all specu-

---

[1] Punjâb Ethnography, para. 539.
[2] Tribes and Castes, I., 480.

lations which profess to connect existing castes with the four traditional castes are on the face of things futile and misleading. We do not know enough about these primitive groups to be able to apply to their internal structure that minute analysis which alone can determine their precise tribal affinities."

10. By another authority[1] an attempt has been made to connect the Khatris with the Jâts. It is urged that the *sehra* or veil, and not the *maur* or crown, is used in marriage among both races; that the Khatri women alone of Hindus wear shoes, though the custom down East is dying out and the only observance of it is the sending of a pair of shoes among the wedding presents of the bride. The Khatris deny that they ever had the custom of eating from vessels (*rikâbi khâna*) or that their women ever wore clothes of Muhammadan fashion (*turki kapra*), while the Pachhâda Jâts still openly practise both customs at marriage feasts. Again, there is a tradition that the Tagas were once Khatris, and expelled for drinking; the Tagas ridicule this, but the Khatris assert that it is the case. On the other hand, their connection with Jâts has been denied on the ground that no pious Brâhman eats food prepared[2] by a Jât, but most will if cooked by a Khatri. As Khatris mostly inhabit the Muhammadan capitals, Lahore, Delhi, Agra, Lucknow, etc., many Muslim customs, as wearing the *sâri* on marriage, the use of shoes by females, etc., have crept into their society as well as among Kâyasths, Agarwâlas, Oswâls, and other similar tribes, and Khatris and Kâyasths for the same reason use a greater number of Persian words in familiar language than other Hindus.

11. Another suggestion[3] is that their peculiar customs and modern immigration into these provinces indicate them to be one of the Hindu tribes which occupied the trans-Indus region at the time of Alexander's invasion, and an attempt has been made to identify them with the Xathri, who were recorded by the Greek historians to have been on the Chinâb when Alexander invaded the Panjâb.

12. On the whole, it seems quite clear from their physique and general appearance that the Khatris are of Aryan descent, and if we admit, which is probably the case, that the aggregate of tribes now known under the name of Râjput and Brâhman is of mixed

---

[1] *Indian Antiquary*, I., 269, *sq.* [2] *Ibid.*, II., 26, *sqq.*
[3] Râja Lachhman Sinh, *Bulandshahr Memo.*, 166.

origin, it is not difficult to imagine that the Khatris may have been an offshoot from one or the other, and Mr. Risley's argument based on the character of their sections does not seem conclusive. We know from numerous instances, such as the Benbans Râjputs of Mirzapur and some of the Oudh septs, that this internal structure is far from stable, and it may be true that the Khatris were once a higher race which accepted a lower status when they took to mercantile occupations.

Internal structure.

13. The internal structure of the Khatris is very intricate. At the last census of these provinces they recorded themselves in ten main sub-castes—Kakkar, Kapûr, Khanne, Lâhauri, Mohendra, Meherê, Rora, Seth, Surîn, and Tandan. The complete returns show 761 sub-divisions in which the endogamous sub-castes and exogamous sections are inextricably mixed together. To quote Mr. Ibbetson for the Panjâb branch of the caste:—"In recent times there has sprung up a system of social graduation in accordance with which certain Khatri tribes refuse to intermarry with any save a certain specified number of their fellow-tribes, and the distinctions thus created have been formulated in a set of names such as Dhâighar, 'he who only marries into two-and-a-half houses'; Chârzâti, 'he who marries into four tribes'; Chhahzâti, 'he who marries into six tribes'; and so on. This purely artificial and social classification has obscured the original tribal divisions of the caste; for Khatris of the same tribe may be in one part of the province Chârzâtis, and in another Bârahzâtis, and so forth. The returns then show three different kinds of divisions—first the four real tribal sections—Bunjâhi, Surîn, Bahri, and Khokhrân; then the four of the most important of the artificial divisions alluded to above Dhâighar, Chârzâti, Panjâti, and Chhahzâti; and finally six of the most important clans—Sodhi, Bedi, Kapûr, Khannê, Marhotra, and Seth. The origin of the division into the four sections called Bunjâhi, Surîn, Bahri, and Khokhrân, is said to have been that Alâ-ud-dîn Khilji attempted to impose widow marriage upon the Khatris. The Western Khatris resolved to resist the innovation, and sent a deputation of fifty-two (*bâwan*) of their members to represent their case in court; but the Eastern Khatris were afraid to sign the memorial. They were therefore called followers of Shara Ayîn, or the Muhammadan customs—hence Surîn; while the memorialists were called Bâwanjâti, from the number of the deputation or of the clans, respectively,

represented by the members of the deputation; hence Bunjâhi. The Khokhrân section is said to consist of the descendants of certain Khatris who joined the Kokhars in rebellion, and with whom the other Khatri families were afraid to intermarry; and the Bahri section, of the lineage of Mahr Chand, Khân Chand, and Kapûr Chand, three Khatris who went to Delhi in attendance upon one of Akbar's Râjput wives, and who, thus separated from the rest of the caste, married only within each other's families. But these are fables, for the same division into Bahri and Bunjâhi appears among the Brâhmans of the Western plains. The number of clans is enormous. The most important in point of social rank are the Marhotra or Mahra, the Khanna, the Kapûr, the Seth, the first three of which are said to be called after the names of the three men just mentioned, while Seth is a term now used for any rich banker. These four clans belong to the Bahri section of the caste, and constitute the Dhâighar and Chârzâti divisions, which stand highest of all in the social scale. The origin of the term Dhâighar lies in the fact that the families of that division exclude not only the father's clan but also such families of the mother's clan as are closely connected with her, and thus reduced the clans available for intermarriage to two-and-a-half. I should say that each division will take wives from one below it, though it will not give its daughters to it in marriage. The Bedi and Sodhi clans belong to the Bunjâhi tribe, and owe most of their influence and importance to the fact that Bâba Nânak belonged to the former and Guru Râm Dâs and Guru Har Govind to the latter. They are commonly said to be the descendants of these men, but this appears to be a mistake, the two clans dating from long before Bâba Nânak. The Sodhis played an important part during the Sikh rule. They claim descent from Sodhi Râê, son of Kal Râê, king of Lahore; and the Bedis from Kalpat Râê, brother of Kal Râê and king of Kasûr, who, being deprived of his kingdom by his nephew, studied the Vedas at Benares and was known as Vedi. The modern head-quarters of the Bedis is at Dera Nânak in Gurdâspur, where Bâba Nânak settled and died, and of the Sodhis at Ananpur in Hoshyârpur, which is also the centre of the Nihang devotees."

14. In Mirzapur the tribal arrangement is very intricate. They name five main sub-divisions, Dhâighar, Chârghar, Bârahghar, Bâwanghar, and Surativâl, who are lowest in rank. Each of these has four sections Meharhotra, Tandan, Kapûr, and Khannê.

These again are provided with sub-sections. Those of the Meharhotras are Lalwânê (Natkhol) and Kanauj kê Meharê; of the Tandan, Ranjît kâ Tandan, Pihâna kâ Tandan, and Billimâr Tandan; of the Kapûr, Kodokhânê Kapûr; and of the Khanna Nakhsikhana Khanna. The Dhâighar give their daughters only in marriage to members of their own sub-division and take wives from their own sub-divisions or from the Chârghar. If one of the Dhâighar marry in the Bârahghar he is degraded. The daughters of the Dhâighar are sometimes married in their own sub-divisions or to members of the Dhâighar. The males of the Chârghar take wives from the Bârahghar. There is thus a well-established rule of hypergamy in force in the tribe.

15. In Benares, according to Mr. Sherring[1] they are divided into two main branches—the Purbiya or "Eastern" and the Pachhainiya or "Western." The Pachhainiyas are divided into six sub-tribes, each of which has a number of clans (*gotra*). The Arhâighar or Chauzâti comprise the Khanna, Kapûr, Mehra, and Seth clans, whose *gotras* are for the first three Kausal and of the last Vatsa. They are the head of the Pachhainiya branch, and will marry their sons into any of the next four sub-tribes, though they will not permit Chhahzâti men to marry Chauzâti women. The second sub-tribe, the Chhahzâti, has six clans, Bahel, Dhanwân, Beri, Vij, Saigal, and Chopra. Of the third sub-tribe, the Panjzâti, Mr. Sherring does not give the clans. Of the fourth, the Bahri, there are, according to the same authority, twelve clans,—Upal, Dugal, Puri, Kochar, Nandê, Mahpê, Handê, Bhallê, Mangal, Badahrê, Sowâti, and Kulhar. All these clans intermarry. They also marry their daughters into the three preceding sub-tribes, but cannot receive their women in marriage. The fifth sub-tribe, Bâwanjâhi, has fifty-two clans which intermarry. The Bahri clan will receive their women in marriage, but will not give their own in return. Of the sixth sub-tribe, the Khokhrân, there are nine clans, who are—Kohali, Anad, Bhasirn, Chuadha, Sabrwâl, Suri, Sahani, Ghei, and Sethi. These nine clans intermarry, but Khokhrân are endogamous.

16. The divisions of the Khatris of Bengal are very similar. Mr. Risley names six sub-castes, Chârjâti, Panchjâti, Chhahjâti, Bârahjâti, Bahannajâti, and Piruwâl, each with a number of sections

---

[1] *Hindu Tribes*, I., 280, *sqq*.

which need not be detailed. He adds that the Chârjâti sub-caste "is again divided into Arhâighar and Chârghar, apparently hypergamous groups, the former of which is deemed superior to the latter. It seems probable that the first five sub-castes were originally hypergamous divisions, the order of precedence being that given above. Intermarriage between members of different sub-castes is not known at the present day, but it is considered right for a man to marry in his own group, and the sub-castes are practically endogamous. The Piruwâl sub-caste has always been endogamous."

Marriage.

17. Boys are married between the age of ten and twenty-five; but infant marriage is preferred. Girls are married between nine and fourteen. Polygamy is allowed, but there seems to be an increasing prejudice against it. Widow marriage is forbidden.

Religion.

18. Khatris are generally Vaishnavas or Nânakpanthis and their family priests are Sâraswat Brâhmans. Their domestic ceremonies are of the standard orthodox type.

Social status.

19. Khatris rank high among Hindus. Sâraswat Brâhmans eat *pakki* and *kachchi* with them; Banyas eat *pakki*; and Kahârs and similar castes eat *kachchi* cooked by them. They themselves eat *pakki* and *kachchi* cooked only by members of the caste or Sâraswat Brâhmans. Their women have a reputation for their beauty and fair complexion. A Bihâr proverb says—*Khatri sê gora pandu rogi, Kâyasth se chatur parbhogi*—"An albino only is fairer than a Khatri and an adulterer than a Kâyasth." Another runs—*Rûp na singâr, Khatrâni ki sâdh*—"Without beauty or ornaments she would be a Khatri woman."

Distribution of Khatris according to the Census of 1891.

District.	Kakkar.	Kapûr.	Khannê.	Lahori.	Mahendru.	Mehnê.	Rora.	Seth.	Surîn.	Tandan.	Others.	Total.
Dehra Dûn . . .	...	...	7	...	...	130	22	8	10	1	399	577
Sahâranpur . . .	...	103	48	...	...	54	547	32	30	23	1,584	2,421
Muzaffarnagar . .	3	33	42	...	...	22	890	18	...	...	260	1,268
Meerut	9	77	121	10	...	91	624	16	86	8	935	1,977
Bulandshahr . . .	6	...	6	...	...	1	...	3	22	...	577	615
Aligarh . . .	...	...	...	...	...	...	26	...	...	...	918	944
Mathura . . .	...	144	4	2	10	69	371	53	...	46	855	1,554
Agra	83	251	18	33	9	86	196	70	5	211	981	1,943
Farrukhâbâd . . .	6	154	9	...	...	260	164	24	...	698	80	1,395
Mainpuri . . .	17	11	27	...	...	7	...	1	129	...	28	220
Etâwah . . .	57	80	3	...	28	75	...	...	...	185	134	562
Etah	6	32	12	...	11	69	...	4	29	2	85	250
Bareilly . . .	12	243	589	8	...	316	69	154	14	299	793	2,497
Bijnor	570	34	...	...	...	36	...	...	313	...	22	945

Budâun	...	...	...	...	...	...	...	2	...	36	94	132
Morâdâbâd . . .	4	285	368	35	...	174	329	64	56	368	781	2,464
Shâhjahânpur . . .	2	221	7	11	11	211	26	262	7	307	412	1,477
Pilibhît	...	1	14	...	...	8	...	1	5	4	204	237
Cawnpur . . .	...	338	128	4	138	322	88	150	...	405	1,145	2,718
Fatehpur . . .	37	34	32	...	...	5	...	29	...	43	110	290
Bânda	13	9	40	...	...	...	...	9	17	9	33	130
Hamîrpur . . .	...	5	1	...	...	1	...	3	...	...	44	54
Allahâbâd . . .	2	54	16	...	...	29	...	21	...	77	3,155	3,354
Jhânsi	...	...	...	...	...	...	...	...	...	9	460	469
Jâlaun	7	23	23	...	...	52	3	5	7	8	184	312
Lalitpur . . .	3	1	...	...	2	209	...	...	...	...	44	259
Benares	...	273	1	...	...	173	2,024	502	136	122	1,054	4,285
Mirzapur . . .	...	...	...	...	...	185	...	...	...	458	13	656
Jaunpur . . .	...	2	...	...	...	...	...	...	...	...	290	292
Gorakhpur . .	1	2	4	...	...	16	...	62	5	12	86	188

Distribution of Khatris according to the Census of 1891—concld.

District.	Kakkar.	Kapûr.	Khannê.	Lahori.	Mahendru.	Mehnê.	Rora.	Seth.	Surîn.	Tandan.	Others.	Total.
Ballia	...	...	...	...	...	...	...	...	...	...	255	255
Basti	...	...	...	...	...	...	11	...	...	...	117	128
Azamgarh . . .	...	1	4	...	12	1	7	1	9	...	217	252
Kumâun . . .	...	...	...	...	...	...	...	...	...	...	46	46
Tarâi	...	...	...	...	...	...	...	...	...	...	389	389
Lucknow . . .	...	140	190	11	31	198	52	619	92	161	1,335	2,829
Unâo	25	...	7	...	...	13	15	...	...	145	147	352
Râê-Bareli . . .	8	...	1	...	...	2	...	...	11	...	117	139
Sîtapur	10	158	31	53	125	531	...	223	9	261	442	1,843
Hardoi	6	34	...	...	...	376	1	7	...	278	138	840
Kheri	8	55	1	...	7	176	39	...	...	64	188	538
Faizâbâd . . .	...	5	...	...	...	403	19	9	...	229	499	1,164
Gonda	...	41	10	...	...	31	...	...	...	41	137	260
Bahrâich . . .	8	2	53	...	...	50	1	14	...	...	476	604

Sultânpur . . .	...	...	...	...	...	...	...	...	9	...	247	256
Partâbgarh . . .	...	...	18	...	...	8	...	...	...	...	137	163
Bârabanki . . .	...	11	...	...	...	158	...	59	...	280	35	543
TOTAL .	903	2,857	1,835	167	384	4,548	5,524	2,425	1,001	4,790	20,682	45,116

Khawâs, Khawâss.—(Plural of *Khâs* "peculiar"; *Khâssa*, "distinguished people.")—A name specially applied to the offspring of slave girls, other than those of Brâhman origin, who have cohabited with the men of Nepâl. Their descendants along the Gorakhpur and Basti frontier are known by this special name.

Khichi.—A Râjput sept, a branch of the Chauhâns. In Lucknow they trace their origin to Raghugarh, near Narsinhgarh. Their old country is known as Khichwâra. In the Panjâb their traditions refer them to Ajmer, thence to Delhi, and from Delhi to the Satlaj, during the Mughal rule. In Oudh they have a ridiculous legend to account for their name. One of their sept was once distributing gold and silver in heaps as alms. "It is boiled rice and pulse" (*khichari*), said he And ever since they have been called Khichi.[1]

Khumra.—A tribe found chiefly in Rohilkhand, of whom little is known, save that their chief business appears to be cutting and exporting millstones (*chakki*), an indispensable article in every native household. They carry about these stones by stringing them on an axle through the central hole and dragging them along the road behind a buffalo. In these Provinces they are called Muhammadans. The complete Census returns give their sections as Bâhman, Dulha, Gori or Gaur, Hataiwâlê, Quraishi, Multâni, Nawabâr, Pachhawi, Pathân Najuri, Sadîqi, Tarâi, and Tayâr.

2. From the Râmpur State it is reported that they are low-class Muhammadans, whose occupation is making mats and fans. As regards religion, they are indifferent Muhammadans, and their women dress like Hindus. They resemble Julâhas in their manners and customs, and are converts to Islâm from one of the low Hindu tribes.

Distribution of Khumras according to the Census of 1891.

District.	Number.	District.	Number.
Sahâranpur	216	Tarâi	108
Muzaffarnagar	75	Lucknow	106
Meerut	350	Unâo	43
Bulandshahr	2	Sîtapur	168
Aligarh	4	Hardoi	8
Bareilly	555	Kheri	242
Bijnor	2,166	Bahrâich	180
Morâdâbâd	584	Bârabanki	187
Shâhjahânpur	149		
Pilibhît	55	Total	5,193

[1] *Lucknow Settlement Report*, LXXI; Ibbetson, *Panjâb Ethnography*, para. 449.

Kinwâr.—A sept of Râjputs in the Eastern Districts, numerous in Bhâgalpur, but of no standing in Gorakhpur. In Ghâzipur one division of the sept is Chhatri, another Bhuînhâr. They say that a Dikshit Râja, named Mân Dikshit, lived at a place called Manchhatra Asthân on the Jumna, and that his descendants established a kingdom at Padampur in the Karnâtic. By another account they came from a place named Karnât Padampur, which they believe to be near Delhi. Two cadets of the family took service, one with the Gaharwâr Râja of Benares, the other with one of the Gautam Bhuînhârs, who were at war, and each married a daughter of his patron. They derive their name from Dankin on the river of the same name, of which all they know is that it is somewhere to the South and was their early home.[1]

2. From Ballia it is reported that they take brides from the Barwâr, Narwâni, Nikumbh, Chandel, Ujjaini, Karchhuliya, Khâti, Pachhtoriya, and Sengar septs, and give brides to the Haihobans, Ujjaini, Narwâni, Nikumbh, Barwâr, Kausik, Raghubansi, Bisen, Chauhân, Palwâr, Sirnet, Râjkumâr, Sûrajbansi, Maunas, Bhrigbansi, Singhel, and Sengar septs.

Distribution of the Kinwâr Râjputs according to the Census of 1891.

District.	Number.	District.	Number.
Sahâranpur	16	Gorakhpur	680
Muzaffarnagar	1	Basti	528
Meerut	1	Azamgarh	95
Cawnpur	65	Kumaun	56
Allahâbâd	14	Tarâi	69
Jâlaun	164	Lucknow	12
Benares	19	Sîtapur	149
Mirzapur	6	Kheri	60
Jaunpur	30	Gonda	513
Ghâzipur	103	Bârabanki	177
Ballia	5,127	Total	7,885

[1] Buchanan, *Eastern India*, II., 463; Oldham, *Ghâzipur Memoir*, I., 61.

Kingriya, Kingariya, Kingriha.[1]—A tribe of dancers and singers found in some of the Eastern Districts. They do not appear in the returns of the last Census, and have perhaps been classed in some places with the Dhârhi, to whom they are probably akin. The name Kingariya is derived from the *Kingri*, a kind of two-stringed gourd lute, which they play. The name Panwariya, by which they are also known, appears to be derived from the Hindi *Pânwara*, "a carpet" (*pânw*, "a foot"), on which they sit when they perform. They are in habits and occupation very like the Garris of the Panjâb, who carry a zither-like instrument called a *King*.[2]

Tribal organisation.

2. In Mirzapur they name seven endogamous septs :—Kingariya or Kingariha, Banhkata, Jogi, Sewara, Khapariya, Atît, and Banhchariya. The Banhkatas appear to derive their name from their custom of cutting their arms (*bânh-kâtna*) in order to extort alms. They are also known as Kaparchirwa, or people who wound their heads with the same object. They carry an iron spike on which a number of little bells are hung. They rattle the bells as they beg from door to door, and if any one refuses alms they strike their arms or heads with the spike and draw blood. The Jogis are in no way connected with the regular ascetics of that name. They are professional beggars who dress in clothes coloured with ochre (*geru*) like the real Jogis. When they go on begging excursions they carry a rosary of *rudrâksha* beads, and a *sârangi* or fiddle, on which they play and sing songs in honour of Râja Bhartrihari, who is said to have been brother of Vikramaditya and to have abandoned his kingdom and become an ascetic. These people are really Sunni Muhammadans, who get themselves up as Hindu Jogis to deceive pious Hindus. The Sewaras, so called because they do service or attendance (*sewa*) to the gods, wear their hair long, and keep ponies and asses on which they carry their families and goods from one village to another in search of alms. The Khapariyas, who are possibly the same as the tribe of that name separately described, are said to derive their title from their habit of carrying about a human skull (*khapar*) in which they take alms. The Atîts get

---

[1] Based on enquiries at Mirzapur and a note by Bâbu Mûl Chand, Subordinate Judge, Family Domains of His Highness the Mahârâja of Benares.

[2] *Panjâb Census Report*, 1891, page 338.

themselves up like the Hindu beggars of that name (*q. v.*), carry *rudrâksha* beads, and cover their bodies with ashes. The Banhchariyas beg, but they have some other occupations as well. They make petty ornaments of pewter. Some keep snakes and scorpions, which they exhibit, and some go about with dancing monkeys. The tribe so called is thus made up of very diverse elements, and is obviously of very mixed origin, a considerable part of it being probably derived from the Nats and similar vagrant races. Their only tradition is that they are descended from Bâba Abbâs, by whom they possibly mean the paternal uncle of the Prophet; in Mirzapur they say that they came from some place in the West and settled at Bijaypur.

Tribal council.

3. They have a tribal council (*panchâyat*) under a headman (*chaudhari*), who is an hereditary permanent official.

Marriage.

4. They follow the Musalmân prohibited degrees, and the ceremony is the regular *nikâh*. They have a curious rule by which an unfaithful wife is, on a charge for adultery being established against her, fined three rupees ten annas, and has then liberty to go where she pleases. Widow marriage and the levirate are allowed. When a betrothal is arranged the father of the boy pays two-and-a-half annas to the father of the girl. This makes the engagement binding. A date is then fixed with the consent of both parties, and on that day the boy's father goes to the house of the bride with some clothes and molasses. He presents these things to the girl, and her father pays in return two rupees, and the matter is settled. If either party after this breaks the engagement, he has to pay a fine of five rupees, and is awarded five blows of a shoe in presence of the council.

Purification.

5. After child-birth the mother is impure for one month and twenty-five days. During the first twelve days she is bathed thrice—on the sixth, tenth and twelfth. Then the thirteenth day ceremony (*terhîn*) is performed, and after a month and twenty-five days elapse she is again bathed, and then becomes pure. After menstruation a woman is impure for four days, and is then purified by bathing. After a funeral they are impure for forty days. In the interval a feast is given on the third day (*tîja*).

6. They are Muhammadans of the Sunni sect and venerate Ghâzi Miyân; some also make an occasional sacrifice to Kâli Bhawâni. The latter is worshipped in the house kitchen in the month of Sâwan with an offering of cakes (*pūri*) and sweetmeats (*halwa*). They offer food to the spirits of the dead during the Muharram. They employ Brâhmans to give them the omens at marriages and other important occasions. Their regular priests, who perform the marriage service, are drawn from the Dafâli caste. Their great festivals are the Îd, Baqarîd, and Shabirât.

Religion.

7. They will not eat or drink with a Dhobi, Dom, Chamâr, Bhangi, or Pâsi. They drink spirits and eat the flesh of cloven-footed animals, fish, and fowls; they will not eat the flesh of monkeys, beef, pork, whole-footed animals, snakes, jackals, crocodiles, or vermin. There is, however, a tendency in recent times to restrict the use of liquor, and now in Mirzapur if a man drinks he is fined five annas before he is allowed to take his seat in the tribal council. They use *gānja* and *bhang* like Hindu begging tribes. The women wear a sheet (*sâri*), a bodice (*jhūla*), and put red-lead on the parting of the hair, like Hindu wives. In their ears they wear rings of iron or silver, nose-rings, necklaces, bangles of glass, and anklets. The men wear the loin-cloth (*dhoti*) and jacket (*mirzâi*) like Hindus, and let their beards grow. When they go begging they carry an alms bag (*jhori*), dress like Hindu Faqîrs, and carry their musical instruments with them—the *tumba* or gourd drum and the *kingri*—from which they take their name. They attend the houses of rich Hindus and Muhammadans when a son is born and sing the *sohar* or song of rejoicing. Generally they wander about from house to house begging and singing. A few cultivate, but in a careless, unthrifty fashion.

Social rules.

Kirâr.—A caste which has been separately recorded at the last Census, but which is usually treated as a sept of Râjputs. In Aligarh,[1] where they appear in the largest numbers, though numbered among Râjputs, they are considered of very inferior rank. In Mainpuri,[2] where also they are numerous, they claim to be a branch of the Mathura Jâdons, and say that their ancestor Kun-

---

[1] *Settlement Report*, 32.
[2] *Mainpuri Settlement Report*, 20.

war Pâl invaded the country about five centuries ago and conquered the fort of Kirarwa, now Karera, where they settled, and were named after it. But the process was evidently different, and Kirarwa was so called from Kirârgânw, the village of the Kirârs. They have been identified with the Kirâtas, who, according to Manu, with other Dasyu tribes, became Vrishala, or outcast, from the extinction of sacred rites and from having no intercourse with Brâhmans.[1] Of them Mr. Atkinson[2] says:—"There is every reason to suppose that the Nâgas, Kirâtas, and Khasas entered India by the same route as the Aryas, and that the Kirâtas were the first to arrive, then the Nâgas, and then the Khasas. The earliest notice regarding the Kirâtas brings them as far westward as the Jumna in the first century. Local tradition in Nepâl gives them an eastern extension to Bhutân, and at a very early date they held the Nepâl valley. Twenty-nine names[3] of kings of this race are given in the local history of Nepâl. We have collected the names of fourteen rulers attributed to the Khasa race in Kâli Kumaun, which are so similar in character that there can be little doubt of a close connection between them. Indeed the community in manners and religion between the different divisions of the snake-worshipping tribes would alone show a common origin, and will also explain how they all insensibly blend with each other. In the list of peoples given in the Vishnu Purâna[4] we have already seen that the Kirâtas or Kirâtis are said to have occupied the country to the East of Bharata, as the Yavanas dwelt in the West. In the Mahâbhârata we find them to occur with the Jangalas (or 'dwellers in thickets'), Kuruvarnakas (or 'dwellers in the Kuru jungles'), and Barbaras in one place, and again we have the 'Kirâtas, Tamasas, and Kirâtas Sudestas, and people near the mount called Yamuna.' All these indications[5] agree with the position already arrived at on the Upper Jumna and Ganges. The Tamasas are the people of the Tons or 'dark river,' so called from the effects of the forests on its banks, and itself an affluent of the Yamuna or Jumna. The Kirâtas are also joined with the Sakas and Savaras as Dasyus,[6] and in the Râmâyana they are described as 'with sharp-pointed hair-

---

[1] X., 43, 44; Muir, *Ancient Sanskrit Texts*, I., 482, *sqq*.
[2] *Himalayan Gazetteer*, II., 363.
[3] Wright, *Nepâl*, 89, 106, 312.
[4] Wilson, VII, 30.
[5] *Ibid.*, 171, 176, 187.
[6] Muir, *loc. cit*, II., 365, 491.

knots, gold-coloured, and pleasant to behold.' It was as a Kirâta that Rudra appeared to Arjuna in the valley of the Ganges. The local annals of Nepâl ascribe to the Kirâtas a dynasty, that ruled in the valley for ten thousand years in Dwaparayuga, where also there was a celebrated settlement of the Nâgas, and after expelling an Ahîr family, they continued in the valley, and were rulers of Nepâl when Asoka visited it in the third century before Christ. We are further told that they lived previously to the East, but that they were removed tō Suprabha (Thânkot), to the West of the valley, before establishing themselves in Nepâl.[1]

"The Kirâtas are now a short, flat-faced people, powerfully built, and are Buddhist by religion. From Dr. Campbell we learn that on the frontier between Sikkhim and Nepâl they are regarded as generically one with the Limbus. According to him, the subdivisions of the tracts inhabited by the Limbus are two in number—Kirântdes, extending from the Dûd Kosi to the Arun river east, and the Limbudes from the Arun to the Konki. Using the tribal name Limbu in its extended sense, we have the Hung and Râê divisions, the first of which carries us back to the Hunas and the Hingu of the Markandeya Purâna. This identification is strengthened by the marked Mongolian features of the people, who, owing to their isolated position, have had but little intercourse with Aryans or Aryanised tribes, and preserve the original type intact. We cannot be wrong in assigning these Kirântis to the Kirâtas, of whom we have recorded so much, but they have no connection in appearance, language, or religion with any important section of the people now inhabitants of the tract between the Tons and the Sârda."

2. The connection between any of these races and the present Kirârs of the Central Ganges-Jumna Duâb is only pure speculation.

3. Their sections do not throw much light on their origin, except that the occurrence among them of the names of other Râjput septs may tend to show that their claim to Râjput origin is unfounded. Thus we have the Dhâkara, Jâdon, Jâdonbansi, Jasâwat, Râwat, and Sengar, combined with local terms such as Maheshpuriya, Mathuriya, and Sherpuriya.

---

[1] Wright, *Nepâl*, 89, 106, 110, 312; *Journal, Asiatic Society, Bengal*, 1849, pages 733, 766; 1856, 456.

Distribution of Kirârs according to the Census of 1891.

District.	Number.	District.	Number.
Aligarh	10,364	Morâdâbâd . . .	144
Agra	1,554	Pilibhît	3
Mainpuri . . .	5,900	Jhânsi	374
Etah	6	Jâlaun	18
		Total .	18,363

Kisân.[1]—(Sanskrit *krishâna*, "a ploughman.")—A caste of cultivators found chiefly in the Central Ganges-Jumna Duâb. They are undoubtedly very closely allied to the Kurmi, Koeri, and Kâchhi. In Farrukhâbâd they are sometimes known as Kisân Mahur, and in the Oudh as Mahatiya (*mahto*, "a leader"). There are, according to the last Census, nine endogamous sub-castes:—Bâtham (named from Srâvasti); Gadhara, or donkey-men; Hardiya, or growers of turmeric (*haldi*); Jariya; Khâgi; Lodha; Patariya or Patariha; and Saksena, which take their name from the old town of Sankisa in the Farrukhâbâd District. There is a tradition in Hardoi that they were once extensive owners of the soil.[2]

Marriage rules.

2. A man must marry within his own sub-caste; a man does not give his daughter in marriage in a family where his son has been already married. Persons descended from a common ancestor do not intermarry for three or four generations. A man cannot marry the children or grandchildren of his sister or daughter. Two sisters may be married one after the other, but not at the same time, and the elder must be married before the younger. Marriage is both infant and adult, and sexual license before marriage is not tolerated. Polygamy is allowed, but is very rare, and only allowed when the first wife is barren. There are the usual three forms of marriage—that by the revolution, (*bhanwar*) round the sacred fire, which is the most respectable form;

---

[1] Chiefly based on notes received through Mr. E. Rose, C.S., and Bâbu Sânwal Dâs, Deputy Collector.

[2] *Settlement Report*, 198.

the *dola* marriage, where all the ceremonies are done at the house of the bridegroom; lastly, there is the *dharauna* form for widows. The levirate is permitted, but not enforced, and, as usual, the widow can marry the younger, not the elder, brother of her late husband. A man can put away his wife for adultery, and all he has to do is to notify the fact to the tribal council.

Religion and social customs.

3. Kisâns are all Hindus and worship the ordinary gods. They venerate in addition the Miyân of Amroha as their patron saint. Goats and sheep are offered to Devi and Miyân on a Monday or Friday; the worshipper and his family consume the meat, while a share is given to the Faqîrs and Dhânuks, who tend the shrine. During the month of Kuâr offerings of water and sacred balls (*pinda*) are made to the sainted dead. If a man dies without a son, his nearest relative makes the offering. The ordinary *Srâddha* is performed at the anniversary of the death. The Kisâns eat the flesh of sheep and goats and fish; they will not eat, drink, or smoke with any other caste. Most of them are cultivators and a few field-labourers. They are a respectable, industrious people, and many of them practise the higher forms of agriculture, growing crops, such as sugarcane, tobacco, vegetables, etc.

4. The Khâgi,[1] who are nearly all found in Budâun, claim to be Chauhân Râjputs; but it is needless to say that their assertion is disputed. According to the tribal legend two brothers, by name Kanka and Mahesa, Chauhân Râjputs, with a few followers, left Ajmer in a year of famine and settled at Sahaswân in the Budâun District. Here they grew in importance, and were after a time raised by the Emperor of Delhi to the post of Sûbah or Governor. One of them ruled Sahaswân and the other the Pargana of Soron, in the Etah District. The terms on which they held these offices was that they should pay a quarter of the revenue collected into the Imperial treasury. This after a time they failed to do, a remittance which they sent to Delhi in charge of a Musalmân being embezzled by him. A punitive force was sent against them by the Emperor, and both the brothers with a considerable number of their followers were killed. Now the widows of the men who were killed, contrary to the custom of the tribe, married again, and such connections being locally known as *Kâj*, they came to be called Khâgi! There are two sites at Sahaswân, which they point to as monuments of their former

[1] Based on a note by Mr. C. S. Delmerick.

glory : one is a mound (*Khera*) known as "the old fort," and the other a mango grove called Lakha Pera, or "the grove of one hundred thousand trees." The Khâgis are excellent agriculturists, industrious, thrifty, and well-behaved. Another explanation of their name is that it means "swordman" (Sanskrit, *Khadga*).

Distribution of Kisâns according to the Census of 1891.

DISTRICT.	Bâtham.	Gadhara.	Hardiya.	Jaroya.	Khâgi.	Lodha.	Patariha.	Rajauriya.	Saksena.	Others.	TOTAL.
Farrukhâbâd	6,241	3,240	222	25,045	...	1,293	53,094	...	...	1,418	90,553
Mainpuri	...	...	...	...	...	...	...	...	...	5	5
Bareilly	...	...	...	129	...	2,613	47,889	...	1,549	11,053	63,133
Budâun	...	...	...	...	584	...	3,188	...	771	16,793	21,336
Morâdâbâd	...	...	...	...	...	...	15	342	...	289	646
Shâhjahânpur	58,368	...	...	...	16	...	22,585	...	...	3,456	84,425
Pilibhît	10,265	...	...	...	...	...	41,139	26	7	3,769	55,206
Cawnpur	...	...	...	...	...	...	...	...	...	9	9
Hamîrpur	...	...	...	...	...	...	...	...	...	1	1
Tarâi	16	...	...	...	...	...	2,456	560	...	351	3,383
Sitapur	...	...	...	...	...	...	...	...	...	4	4
Hardoi	20,763	...	...	...	...	...	8,822	...	...	4,850	34,435
Kheri	4,592	...	...	...	...	...	3,503	...	...	3,514	11,609
Partâbgarh	...	...	...	...	...	...	...	...	...	10	10
TOTAL	100,245	3,240	222	25,174	600	3,806	182,691	928	2,327	45,522	364,755

Koiri, Koeri.[1]—(Perhaps from Sanskrit *krishi kâri*, "cultivating." Mr. Nesfield's idea that the name implies that they are civilised Kols is not probable.)—They are undoubtedly closely allied to the Kurmis, with whom, according to Dr. Wise, in Bengal, they drink, but do not eat, while the Kurmis attend their marriages and partake of the feast.[2] Colonel Dalton believes them to be the descendants of the earliest Aryan colonists in Bengal.[3] It is possible that they may have some non-Aryan affinities, but how far this may be the case is at present very doubtful. Their only

[1] Based principally on a note by Pandit Bhân Pratâp Tiwâri, of Chunâr.
[2] Risley, *Tribes and Castes*, I., 500.
[3] *Descriptive Ethnology*, 317, *sq*.

tradition, which is common to many of the gardening tribes, is that they were created by Siva to tend the raddish (*mûli*) (whence the title of Murâo, which is sometimes applied to them), and to work in the sacred garden of Benares.

Internal structure.

2. They are divided into a number of endogamous sub-castes, the titles of which vary in different districts. Some of these sub-castes are of local origin:—Sarwariya (from Sarjupâr, "country beyond the river Sarju"); Prayâgha (from Prayâg or Allahâbâd); Kanaujiya or Kanaujiha (from Kanauj); Illahâbâdi (from Allahâbâd); Brijbâsi ("residents of Brij, Braj, or Mathura"); Purbiha ("Eastern"); Dakkhinâha ("Southern"); Banarasiya ("from Benares"); Magahi or Magahiya ("from Magadha"). There are again the Kachhwâha, which assert connection with the Râjput clan of that name; the Narâigana; the Torikoriya, who appear to take their name from cultivating the *turai* or *taroi*, the *cucumis acutangulus*; the Hardiha or Hardiya, who take their name from the turmeric plant (*haldi*, *hardi*); the Bardawâr or "bullock men": the Bhaktiya or "vegetarians" (*bhagat*), who wear a necklace made of the beads of the sacred *tulasi* and do not use meat, fish, and spirituous liquor, and offer no blood sacrifices (*baldân*); the Sakatiya, who are said to derive their name from their preference for the Sâkta ritual; and the Kori, who must not be confounded, as Mr. Sherring does, with the weaver class of the same name. It illustrates the fertility with which these sub-castes are developed that only two of the sub-castes in these provinces, the Kanaujiya and the Magahiya, agree with those enumerated by Mr. Risley in Bihâr. Of the 140 sub-divisions enumerated in the complete Census lists a large number are of local origin, such as Ajudhyabâsi, Audhiya, Azamgarhiya, Bhîmpuriya, Brijbâsi, Dakkhinâha, Desi, Jaiswâr, Jaunpuriya, Kanaujiya, Madhesiya, Rajauriya, Saksena, and Sarwariya. Others are the names of other well-known castes, as Bairâgi, Baiswâr, Hurakiya, Râthaur, and Sûrajbansi.

Marriage rules.

3. The sub-castes practise exogamy according to the standard formula, which prevents intermarriage with the families of the maternal uncle and paternal and maternal aunt within three generations. Within the sub-caste, again, they have a sort of phatria or brotherhood, known as *chatâi*, from the mat on which the council assembles. Thus, in Mirzapur there are fourteen *chatâi* of the Sakatiya sub-caste, each of which has

a headman (*chaudhari*) of its own; and unless he gives permission the members of another *chatâi* are not permitted to join in discussion on caste matters. But this organization seems to have only this connection with marriage that they generally choose their brides locally out of the *chatâi* to which they are attached, but the *chatâi* is not endogamous: at marriages, too, only the members of the particular *chatâi* are invited, and this acts as a check on expenditure. The marriage invitations are issued by the Chaudhari, each of whom keeps a tribal mat and a tribal cauldron (*panchâyati tât, panchâyati handa*). These are purchased out of the fines imposed on offending members, and are used at all marriage and funeral ceremonies within the *chatâi*. The mat is spread at the door of the person at whose house the meeting is held, and the cauldron is filled with water for the refreshment of the guests. At all meetings the house-owner has to provide two annas for tobaco and two annas for the pay of the barber who circulates the invitations. When the council assembles, the person who proposes a marriage stands in the middle with his hands folded and says—"I wish to marry my son or daughter. What is the opinion of the Panch?" He then names the family and *chatâi* of the person with whom he proposed the marriage. When the council gives its approval a Brâhman is called in who makes the calculation known as *râsbarg*, to ascertain if the omens are propitious. When this is settled, the Chaudhari sends for the parents on both sides and sanctions the alliance.

Marriage ceremonies.

4. On this the boy's father gives four pice and the girl's father two pice to the Brâhman, and the two fathers-in-law smoke together. This is known as *taka uthâoni*, or the "lifting of the copper coin." The marriage ceremony is usually in the *dola* form. When the lucky time for the betrothal (*tilak*) is fixed, the girl's father brings an eight annas piece, a handful of rice, five pieces of betelnut, five roots of turmeric, and some *dûb* grass to the boy's house. Before some of the clansmen he marks the boy's forehead with curds, on which some grains of holy rice (*achhat*) are stuck, and gives him the presents he has brought. Then the marriage date (*lagan*) is fixed by the Brâhman, and singing (*gît gauna*) begins in both houses, and is followed by the *matmangara*, common to all the lower castes to the East of the Province. On the day fixed the boy's father, accompanied by some clansmen and a litter (*dola*) and bearers, goes to the girl's house. For her he brings a white sheet and loin-cloth (*châdar, dhoti*), and

a white loin-cloth for her mother. The clansmen are assembled, and with the salutation *Râm! Râm!* sit and smoke together and then eat. Meanwhile the women sing songs, usually of a very obscene character. Next morning her mother dresses the girl in her new sheet and loin-cloth, in the folds of which (*khoinchha*) she puts pice to the value of one anna, a handful of rice, and a ball (*piriya*) of coarse sugar. The marriage is usually performed after the pair arrive at puberty. Then the bride is sent off in the litter to her husband's house. When the litter arrives at the boy's house, it is rested on the ground outside. Some curds are placed in a saucer (*daheri*), and some pepper and sugar are mixed in water, and the whole poured on tho ground as on offering to Dharti Mâta, the earth goddess. This offering is called *Mirchwân* (*mirch*, "pepper"). Then her husband's sister (*nanad*) takes the bride out of the litter, and receives as her perquisite the money which had been placed by her mother in the folds of the bride's loin-cloth.

5. On that day the bride is fed on cakes (*pûri*) and rice milk (*khîr*) sweetened with coarse sugar. Then the Brâhman fixes an auspicious time for the anointing (*tel hardi*). Some of the clansmen erect a nuptial shed (*mânro*), and the Brâhman makes the pair sit down on stools. He reads only a few verses of the regular service and rubs them on the forehead, arms, and legs with a bunch of *dûb* grass soaked in oil and turmeric. Next comes the *bhatwân*, when the guests are entertained on boiled rice and pulse. On the day of the marriage the bride's father appears with his family priest (*purohit*), barber, and some of his clansmen. He brings with him a set of brass vessels (*lota, thâli*), a stool (*pîrha*), a yellow loin-cloth (*piari dhoti*) for the bride, and a yellow upper sheet (*kanhâwar*) and a yellow loin-cloth for the bridegroom. He stays outside, at some distance from the boy's house. At the actual marriage he is allowed to stand near the door—obvious survivals of marriage by capture. The boy goes into the marriage shed and puts on the clothes brought by his father-in-law and a coat (*jâma*), a turban (*pagri*), and a nuptial crown (*maur*), provided by his own family. He sits facing the east on the stool which his father-in-law brought with him. Then the barber's wife brings out the girl and seats her on a leaf mat (*patari*) to his left, and ties her loin-cloth to his upper sheet. Then the bride's father washes the feet of his son-in-law, and putting the bride's hand into that of the bridegroom places on them a lump of wheat dough on which an eight-anna piece is

stuck. Over this the girl's brother pours some water, and this constitutes the giving away (*kanyâdân*) of the bride. Then the Brâhman recites a verse known as the song of prosperity (*sumangali*), which runs—"O Bhagwân and Vishnu, may the marriage be lucky ! O Garuda, vehicle of Vishnu, be auspicious ! O Vishnu, with eyes like the lotus, be auspicious ! O Hari, you are the incarnation of prosperity !" Then the bride's father gives the vessels to the bridegroom, who takes some red lead in his hands and makes a dedication to Gauri and Ganesa, whose images are made in cowdung. Then some cloths are spread round to conceal them from view, and the boy takes five pinches of red-lead and applies it to the parting of the girl's hair. After this they march five times round the pavilion, the bridegroom leading the way and the bride following. Then the barber's wife takes them both into the retiring room (*kohabar*), the walls of which are decorated with five streaks of a mixture known as *aipan*. The bride and bridegroom fold their hands, and the latter takes off his bridal crown (*maur*) and places it at the foot of the wall where the marks have been made. On that day the girl's father fasts—a survival of marriage by capture. The clansmen are entertained that evening. Next morning comes the ceremony of "sugar and curds" (*gurdahi*). The bridegroom's father feeds the bride's father with sugar and curds, and receives a present of eight annas. In the evening the girl's father with his clansmen goes to the bridegroom's house and eats there. When he has done eating, he presents eight annas to his daughter's father-in-law.

6. On the third day the bride's father takes her home on foot, and on the fourth day is the regular departure (*gauna*). The bridegroom goes with a litter and bearers, his barber, and some clansmen to the bride's house. As is the usual custom, his father does not accompany him, because it is believed that if he hears his daughter-in-law weeping as she leaves her parents, his son will die. That night they are entertained by the bride's relations, and next morning bring her home. When her litter approaches the house of her husband, the ceremonies of *daheri* and *mirchwân*, as already described, are repeated, and her mother-in-law, taking the bride out of the litter, escorts her into the house, feeds her on cakes (*pûri*) and rice milk (*bakhîr*), and presents her with four annas for the privilege of looking at her face (*munh dikhâi*). In the evening the women of the clan are entertained, and the men eat after them. This

custom appears to be a speciality of the Koiris. The Brâhman receives two rupees and four annas as the marriage fees (*byâh kâ neg*). A wife can be divorced by the tribal council for infidelity.[1]

Birth ceremonies.

7. The umbilical cord is cut by the midwife (*Chamâin*), and a fire (*pasanghi*) is lighted over it. This fire is intended to protect the child from the evil spirit Jamhua, the terror of Indian mothers.[2] A lamp lit with castor oil is also burnt in the room for twelve days. They have the usual sixth (*chhathi*) and twelfth day ceremony (*barahi*). On the latter occasion they have what is called the "nail-cutting" ceremony (*nakh kataiya*). The women of the neighbourhood collect and rub their bodies with oil and turmeric, and going to the house contribute each an anna and receive a little caudle (*suthauri*) in exchange. This is done when a son is born.

Death ceremonies.

8. The dead are cremated in the usual way. On the thirteenth day after death they make the mourning oblation (*khorasi ka pinda*), and distribute dry grain to Brâhmans. The only *mantra* used is *Pitr rupi Janardhana*— "Vishnu is present in the form of your ancestors." They have no ceremony at six months or a year after death.

Religion.

9. Whenever Koiris follow any of the recognised sects, it is usually the Vaishnava. Those of the Bhakta sub-caste initiate their children as Bhagats or vegetarians at a very early age. They are specially devoted to the worship of the Pânchonpîr and Mahâbîr, and the followers of these two deities do not intermarry. Mahâbîr is worshipped on Tuesday in the month of Sâwan with an offering of sweetmeats (*laddu*), a Brâhmanical cord (*janeu*), and a burnt offering of barley, butter, and sugar. On tenth light half of Sâwan, tenth light half of Kuâr, and first dark half of Chait they worship the Pânchonpîr with offerings of crushed grain and cakes. At the Naurâtra of Chait and Kuâr, milk and rice are cooked and made into long cakes (*phur*), which are offered at the house shrine (*dinkari*), a lamp is kept lighting for nine days, garlands of flowers

---

[1] *Sagâi* wives, *i.e.*, widows married in accordance with the custom of *sagâi* prevailing among the Koiris and other low castes of Bihâr, are so far the legal wives of their husbands as to justify the punishment of persons committing adultery with them.—*Bissurâm Koiri* versus *The Empress*, III, *Calcutta Law Reports*, 410.

[2] Jamhua appears to be a form of Yama, the god of death. It is really infantile lockjaw caused by careless cutting of the cord.

are offered, and incense is burnt. During this festival they meet at the house shrine, and some member of the family generally becomes possessed by the deity and falls into a state of religious ecstacy, in the course of which he utters what are taken for prophecies.

10. As among many of the middle class Hindus, when a man eats with a person who has offended against the rules of caste (*kupadi*), or intrigues with a woman of another caste, or uses unseemly language to the tribal council, he is excommunicated, until he has a recitation at his house of what is known as the Katha Satnârâyan. This among the Koiris and the tribal feast which accompanies it costs about twenty-five rupees. The offender has to fast all day; in the evening he bathes and employs a Brâhman to do the Satnârâyan worship. The Sâlagrâma, or ammonitic pebble representing Vishnu, is washed in a compound of five ingredients (*panchamrit*) made of curds, milk, butter, honey, and sugar, and is then bathed in Ganges water. If any one is invited to hear the recitation and fails to attend, it is believed that he will die or fall into trouble. Every spectator brings with him a garland of flowers, some sweetmeats (*batâsha*), and money, which are the perquisite of the officiating Brâhman. After the recitation is over, the Brâhman performs the *ârti* ceremony by burning some camphor over the Sâlagrâma, in the smoke of which all rub their hands, touch their foreheads, and give a copper coin to the officiating Brâhman. There are five parts (*adhya*) in the *katha*, and at the end of each the conch shell (*sankh*) is blown, and a bell is rung. At the close a burnt offering (*hom*) is done and each one receives a little portion of the offering (*prasâd*) laid before the Sâlagrâma. This offering is called *panjîri*, and consists of wheat, flour, and sugar. If he does not take it with him, he falls into misfortune. At the next tribal meeting the offending person receives some of the *panjîri* and *panchamrit*, and is restored to caste privileges.

Occupation and social status.

11. Koiris are excellent cultivators, and generally devote themselves to growing the more valuable crops, such as opium, tobacco, garden vegetables, etc. They maintain a fairly high standard of social purity. Among the sub-castes in the east of the province only the Prayâgaha drink spirits. The Bhakta sub-caste do not eat flesh; the others eat mutton, goat's flesh, and fish. The Prayâgahas eat *pakki* cooked by Brâhmans, but the others do not eat even *pakki*, except when cooked by their own caste-fellows. Brâhmans drink water from their

hands. and low castes, such as Dhobis and Chamârs, eat both *pakki* and *kachchi* cooked by them. They never accept personal service, and are a thriving, industrious, well-conducted class.

Kol.—A Dravidian tribe found in considerable numbers along the Vindhya Kaimûr plateau. There is considerable difference of opinion as to the meaning of the name. *Kola* in Sanskrit means "a hog"; and, according to some, the tribal designation is simply a term of contempt applied by the Aryans to the aborigines. According to Herr Jellinghause,[1] the word means "pig-killer." According to others, like the tribal terms Ho and Orâon, it is derived from the Mundâri *Ho, Horé*, or *Horo*, which means "a man."[2] The change of *r* to *l* is familiar and needs no illustration, while in explanation of the conversion of *h* into *k* we may cite *hon*, the Mundâri for "child," which in Korwa becomes *kon*, and *koro* the Muâsi form of *horo*, "a man."[3] It may be added that the Khariyas of Chota Nâgpur call the Mundas Kora, a name closely approaching Kol.[4] The name Mundâri or Munda, which is the usual title of the tribe in Chota Nâgpur, does not appear to be known in the North-Western Provinces. According to Mr. Risley, this term is of Sanskrit origin (*munda*), and is a titular or functional designation used by the members of the tribe as well as by outsiders, much in the same way as the Santâls call themselves Mânjhi, the Bhûmij, Sardâr, and the Khambu of the Dârjîling hills, Jimdâr. Colonel Dalton[5] tentatively connects it with *mon* or *mân*, the Assamese term for the Burmese. Others, again, take the term Munda to mean "the shaven people (Sanskrit, *munda*). A sept of Baigas in the Central Provinces are called Mundiya, as it is alleged, because their heads are shaved with the exception of a single lock.[6]

---

1 Risley, *Tribes and Castes*, II., 101.

2 Dalton, *Descriptive Ethnology*, 178.

3 In Kâthiawâr the Kolis derived their name from *kol*, a boat, seafaring being a distinctive occupation of Kolis, or, as Dr. Wilson alleges, Koli means a "clansman" (*Bombay Gazetteer*, VIII., 140). In the Dakkhin the word Koli is said to mean "clansman," from *kul*, a clan, as opposed to *Kunbi*, "the family man," from *kutumb*, "a family." The mystic Brâhmanic origin of the Kolis is that they are the same as the Kirâta of the Purânas, who are said to be descendants of Nishâda, who was born from the arm of Vena, a king of the sun race. The Kolis claim descent from Vâlmîki, the compiler of the *Râmâyana*.—Mackintosh, *Transactions, Bombay Geographical Society*, I., 201, 202, quoted in *Bombay Gazetteer*, XVII., 193; also see a curious dissertation on the subject in Oppert, *Original Inhabitants of Bharatavarsa*, 121, *sqq*.

4 Risley, *loc. cit.*, II., 101.

5 *Loc. cit.*, 119.

6 *Central Provinces Gazetteer*, 279.

KOL.

2. Among the Mundâris of Lohârdaga, who are certainly identical with the Kols of Mirzapur, Colonel Dalton[1] describes the males as averaging five feet five or six inches in height:—"In features they exhibit much variety, and, I think, in a great many families, there is a considerable admixture of Aryan blood. Many have high noses and oval faces, and young girls are at times met with who have delicate and regular features, finely chiselled straight noses, and perfectly formed mouths and chins. The eyes, however, are seldom so large, so bright and gazelle-like as those of pure Hindu maidens, but I have met strongly marked Mongolian features, and some are dark and coarse like the Santâls. In colour they vary greatly, the copper tints being about the most common. Eyes dark-brown, hair black, straight or wavy, and rather fine, worn long by males and females, but the former shave the forehead. Both men and women are noticeable for their fine erect carriage and long free stride."[2] In Mirzapur there is a curious belief prevalent that no pure Kol woman has any hair on the pubes. Mahâdeva, so the story goes, once caught a Kol girl and parched some gram on that part of her person, on which ever after hair refused to grow.[3] The Mirzapur Kols are a very dark race, but their features are hardly so coarse as those of the Mânjhis or Kharwârs.

Appearance.

3. According to one legend, Yayâti, the fifth king of the Lunar race, divided his empire among his five sons. The offspring of his son Turvasu, according to the Harivansa, settled in the South, and the tenth generation from him inclusive, consisting of four brothers, Pândya, Korala, Chola, and Kola, divided the empire they had inherited. The descendants of Kola were the present Kols.[4] The Munda myth, as recorded by Colonel

Traditions of origin.

---

[1] *Loc. cit.*, 190. The Bengal statistics show the curious fact that the Bhûmij and Kol, who are the first in the rank of fecundity in Orissa, are at the bottom of the scale in Chota Nâgpur. The great tribe of Larka Kols in Sinhbhûm marries less than any race in the Lower Provinces, there being in every 100 males between 15 and 40 years of age as many as 55 unmarried men, and in a similar female population 49 unmarried women. This is due to the pre-nuptial infidelity of the Dravidian woman, which enables the men to postpone marriage till they are well advanced in age and desire to found homes for their old age (*Census Report*, 175, 189).

[2] *Loc. cit.*, 190.

[3] De indigenis Tanembaris et Timorlaonis, dum loquitur Riedel, adulescentes et puellas dicit saepe consulto abradere pilos pubis nullâ aliâ mente, nisi ut illæ partes alteri sexui magis conspicuæ fiant.—Westermarck, *History of Human Marriage*, 201.

[4] Colonel Wilford, *Asiatic Researches*, IX., 91. *sq.*, quoted by Dalton, *Ethnology*, 161; Elliot, *Glossary*, s. v. *Cole.*

Tickell,[1] tells how the self-existent primeval deities Otê Borâm and Sing Bonga created a boy and girl, and put them together in a cave to people the world, and finding them to be too innocent to give hope of progeny, he instructed them in the art of making rice beer, which inflames the passions, and, in course of time, they had twelve sons and twelve daughters. As is usual in myths of the class, the children were divided into pairs, and Sing Bonga set before them various kinds of food for them to choose from before starting in the world. The fate of their descendants depended on their choice. "Thus the first and second pair took bullocks' and buffalos' flesh, and they originated the Kols (Hos) and the Bhûmij (Matkum); the next took of the vegetables only, and are the progenitors of the Brâhmans and Chhatris; others took goats and fish, and from them are the Sûdras; one pair took shell-fish, and became Bhuiyas; two pairs took pigs and became Santâls. One pair got nothing, seeing which the first pair gave them of their superfluity, and from the pair thus provided sprung the Ghâsis, who toil not, but live by preying on others." This legend, by identifying the Kols with the kindred Dravidian races, must be much closer to the truth than the Brâhmanical story, which would make them akin to the Râjputs. The Kols of Mirzapur state that they are emigrants from a place called Kiutali, in the territories of the Bardi Râja in the Rîwa State. They name one Nânhu as their ancestor, and, like the Musahars (*q. v.* para. 2), have a tribal temple at Pipri, near Chunâr, where is the shrine of Birmha Devi, the goddess of the shrine. She must be worshipped either in the months of Chait or Kuâr with a fire sacrifice (*hom*), and the offering of a goat or lamb. Their other tribal deity is Râja Lâkhan or Lakhana Deva.[2] Like many of the kindred tribes, they have legends of a kingdom in the Gangetic valley, whence they were expelled by the Savaras, and retired into the hill-country to the South. What is now Saktîsgarh in the hill-country above Chunâr was formerly called Kolâna, and the Pargana of Kol Asla in Benares still bears their name.

Tribal organisation.

4. The Kols in the North-Western Provinces seem to have shed off the elaborate system of totemistic septs which are found among the Mundas of

---

[1] *Asiatic Researches*, IX., 797; Dalton, *loc. cit.*, 185.

[2] For whom, see para. 16.

Bengal.[1] They are divided into a number of endogamous septs, such as the Rautiya or Rautel (Râwat, Sanskrit *Râjputra*, "a prince"). They are also known as Dahait or villagers, and have another sub-division, the Mahtiyân (*mahto*, "a leader"), with whom they intermarry on equal terms; Thakuriya (Thâkur, "a lord"); Banaj; Pahariya, or "mountaineers"; Barwâr, "descendants of the fig tree"; Bin, who may be the same as the Binds; Harwariya, "ploughmen"; Rajwariya, who may take their name from the Bengal Rajwârs[2]; and Hanriyânwa or "people of the cooking pot" (*hânri*), which is also a sub-sept of the Murmu Santâls.[3] Some Kols also name as one of their septs the Chero, who are now regarded as a distinct tribe, but have clearly parted from the parent stock in comparatively recent times.

Tribal council.

5. They have a tribal council (*panchâyat*), at which only the heads of families have a seat.[4] The council decides questions regarding marriage and morality. There is no special time for meeting, but these questions are considered when the brethren assemble at marriages and funeral feasts. The office of the headman (*chaudhari*) is hereditary.[5] All offences are reported to the headman, who, if he thinks the matter worth enquiry, calls in a few of the brethren, consults them, but does not necessarily follow their advice, and then issues his order. The usual punishment is a cash fine, which is spent in feeding the clansmen. In serious offences, the culprit is put out of caste, sometimes for a considerable period, and only restored on feeding the brotherhood. Any resistance to the order of the headman is dealt with very severely. If the headman happen to be a minor, one of his kinsmen is nominated to perform his duties until he comes of age.

Marriage rules.

6. The septs (*kuri*) are endogamous, and they do not intermarry as long as any relationship between the parties is remembered, or into the family of the maternal grandfather (*nâna*) or father's sister (*phûa*). The negotiations are commenced by the father of the bridegroom, who, when he approves of

---

[1] Risley, *Tribes and Castes*, II, *Appendix*, 102. *sq. q*.

[2] Risley, *loc. cit.*, II., 192; Dalton, *loc. cit.*, 326.

[3] Risley, *loc. cit.*, I., 313.

[4] This contempt for persons unmarried is common among similar people; Westermarck, *History of Human Marriage*, 137.

[5] This corresponds to the Munda Parha system of the Mundas. Dalton, *loc. cit.* 168.

the girl, makes over to her father one-and-quarter rupees to clench the engagement. Like most Hindus, they will not marry in the dark fortnight of the month.[1] They generally marry in the months of Mâgh, Phâlgun, Baisâkh, and Jeth, and have the usual prejudice against Pûs and Chait, which are prohibited (*kharwâns*) for this purpose. After the bride comes to her husband's house, she is not allowed to cook for the family until a village astrologer fixes an auspicious time. This is known as the *khichari* or meal of boiled rice and pulse. All the bridegroom's friends eat the food cooked by her, and give her a present known as "the dowry" (*daija*). Kols profess a prejudice against polygamy, but this is a counsel of perfection, and most of them who can afford it marry more wives than one. Women are worked so hard that the first wife often selects her husband's second partner: the wives very seldom quarrel among themselves, and in a Kol family there is very little of the wrangling, wife-beating, and nose-cutting which goes on in ordinary Hindu households.[2] As a matter of fact every man and woman is married. The only bachelors are those who are so miserably poor as to be unable to pay the bride-price, and the only unmarried woman is one who suffers from blindness, leprosy, or some incurable disease; and in the same way all widows are married to some one or other. Her relations in fact insist, like the parents of Penelope,[3] on this being done. Concubinage with a woman outside the tribe is forbidden; but a man may cohabit with any woman of the tribe, provided he gives a feast to the tribesmen, and her children rank as heirs with those of a regular marriage. Sexual intercourse with an unmarried girl is tolerated, as in the case with the Bengal Mundas,[4] but if she is detected in an intrigue with an outsider, she is expelled from the tribe. Infant marriages are not customary, except among the more Hinduised branches of the tribe; but to keep a girl unmarried after she attains the age of puberty involves disgrace to her parents.[5] While the parents of both parties are alive, the assent of them to the marriage is considered

---

[1] On this see Westermarck, *History of Human Marriage*, 424.

[2] Westermarck, *loc. cit.*, 495, *sq.*; for nose-cutting, *ibid.*, 122; on hard labour as a cause of polygamy, Letourneau, *Evolution of Marriage*, 123.

[3] *Odyssey*, XIX., 158, and see the instances collected by Westermarck, 134, *sqq.*; 438, *sq.*

[4] Risley, *Tribes and Castes*, II., 102; Westermarck, *loc. cit.*, 364.

[5] See instances in Westermarck, *loc. cit.*, 136.

essential; and if the father and mother are dead, their power of veto and arranging the marriage devolves on the paternal uncle or elder brother of the boy or girl. As a rule, the parties themselves have very little to say to the matter.[1] The relatives on each side examine the bride and bridegroom so carefully that no physical defects can escape detection: if between betrothal and marriage one party turn out to be leprous, crippled, blind, or impotent, the marriage can be broken off; but when once married, such defects are not a ground for the annulment of the marriage. Among the Kols of Mirzapur there appear to be no tradition of polyandry or of the custom of the *jus primæ noctis;* but the latter certainly existed in a modified form in comparatively recent times in Rîwa and Palâmau. It is said that the Râja used to make tours in his dominions and visit those of his subjects who had pretty daughters. There was a special phrase for such visits (*bijay karna,* "to conquer, enjoy"), and he used often to give a village to a girl who pleased him. Such villages are to this day known as *Bijâya gânw.*

Divorce.

7. There is no regular form of divorce. A husband or wife can be separated for habitual infidelity or for eating food not permitted to the caste. But divorces for infidelity are uncommon, as the matter must be proved to the satisfaction of the tribal council by the evidence of actual witnesses, and proof of general repute or suspicion will not be accepted. Women who have children are very seldom divorced, unless the evidence against them is absolutely overwhelming.[2] If a woman is divorced for adultery with a stranger to the tribe, she is permanently expelled, and cannot be re-married in the tribe; but this is not the case with divorce for offences against caste rules regarding food, in which case, if her friends care to satisfy the tribesmen by a feast, she can be restored to caste and re-married. Divorced women often form connections with males of the tribe in secret, or live apart from their friends by labour or begging, or become Muhammadans and drift into cities as prostitutes. But prostitution in the tribe is unknown, and married women have generally a better character than Hindus of the same social grade. A seducer of a married woman is often

---

[1] On this see Westermarck, *loc cit.*, 219, 221.

[2] See cases collected by Westermarck, *loc. cit.*, 525.

forced by the council to repay the marriage expenses to her husband.[1] Men feel shame, it is said, in bringing about their babies in their arms in the presence of their father or uncle; and if two brothers live together, they generally each carry about the child of the other. This can hardly be anything but a survival of the system of female kinship.[2] This is further proved by the fact that many of the quarrels between husband and wife result from this practice, the refusal of the husband to take his own children in his arms being looked upon by the mother as an imputation on her character. Children of a concubine of the tribe are, as already stated, recognised as legitimate. Children by a strange woman follow the caste of the father,[3] but are not admitted to rights of commensality and marriage. It is understood, however, that in the next generation the prohibition is removed. Such people marry among themselves, and a class of half-breeds, known as *ardhel*, is occasionally found. But tribal discipline is so strong that such cases are uncommon.

Widow marriage.

8. So far from any prohibition extending to widow marrage, it is considered right and proper that marriageable widows should be married, and the only restriction is that it is understood that she should not make a fresh alliance until a year after her husband's death.[4] When a woman becomes a widow she takes off the toe-rings (*angûtha*), and does not put them on until she marries again. She also washes the red lead out of the parting of her hair. The levirate is permitted, under the usual restriction, that a widow can marry only the younger, not the elder, brother of her late husband. In fact, it is the duty of the levir to take her over,[5] and it is only on his refusal that she can ally herself with a stranger, who, in most cases, is a widower. The widow, if she remains unmarried, has a right to maintenance; but if she marries again she loses all rights

---

[1] This is the case with the Bengal Mundas also.—Dalton, *Ethnology*, 194.

[2] Lubbock, *Origin of Civilisation*, 145, *sqq*. The taking up of the child in the arms of the father was by the Romans an admission of paternity, and they had a special term—*suscipio*—for the practice.

[3] Westermarck, *loc. cit.*, 102.

[4] Westermarck, *loc. cit.*, 128.

[5] As among the Gonds—Forsyth, *Highlands of Central India*, 158. Mr. O'Donnell, *Census Report*, 186, remarks that the smaller number of widows among the Dravidian tribes is not due to their re-marrying more often than Hindus, but simply to virgin marriages being made so very much later in life, with the necessary result that widows are absolutely fewer at twenty years of age.

in her husband's estate, and her children remain with their paternal uncle, who acts as trustee of their property till they come of age, when, if they are sons, they inherit ; if daughters, the estate goes to the associated brethren. The children of a second marriage have no claim to the first husband's property, and there is no fiction by which they are supposed to be the issue of the first husband. There are no traditions of *sati* among the Kols and allied tribes.

Adoption.

9. The Mirzapur Kols profess to have an elaborate series of rules on the subject of adoption ; but it is almost certain that most of these have been borrowed from their Hindu neighbours. The more primitive basis of the practice among them seems to be that a sonless man can adopt his brother's son, and that this is done without any religious sentiment in connection with the *srāddha*. They say that if a man have a son or grandson he cannot adopt; that he need not consult his heirs ; that he may adopt his daughter's son ; that he can adopt, if his son adopts another faith or has committed such an offence against tribal rules as to be beyond forgiveness by the council ; that, while an adopted son is alive, a second cannot be adopted ; that a bachelor, a blind or impotent man, can adopt, but not a person who adopts a religious life (*Sādhu*, *faqīr*) ; that a woman cannot adopt as long as the younger brother of her husband (*dewar*), her husband's elder brother (*bhasur*), or her husband's father (*sasur*) are alive, nor can she adopt at all except under the death-bed instructions of her husband. The eldest or only son of a man may be adopted, and the person adopted should be of the same family (*kul*) as the adopter. But if a suitable relation cannot be found, a boy may be selected from any sept (*kuri*) except that of the Rautel. A boy adopted loses all rights to the property of his natural father, unless the latter die without heirs.

Succession.

10 A man's heirs are his sons, and they inherit equally, except that the eldest son gets something (such as a bullock, a brass vessel, etc.) in excess of the others.[1] It is, however, an understood rule that the inheritance is not divided among the sons until the youngest comes of age, and the feeling seems to be in favour of maintaining the union of the

---

[1] On the rights of the eldest son, see Westermarck, *loc. cit.*, 100.

associated brethren. Daughters have no rights, except to maintenance, if they cannot agree with their husbands and are obliged to return to their father's house. There seems to be no custom, as among the Bengal Mundas, by which unmarried sisters are divided among the brothers.[1] The sons share equally, no matter how many mothers there may be ; nor is the rank of the mother taken into account in deciding the right to succession. A sister or her children have no right to succeed. If a widow who has a child at the breast re-marries, she takes it to her new husband, who is understood to be bound to support it till, if a girl, she marries, or a son, till he is able to support himself. It is said that if a man becomes a *sâdhu* or ascetic he can take away his personal goods, but loses his rights of inheritance. Such cases are, however, so uncommon that it can be hardly said that any definite rule prevails.

Relationship.

11. Besides persons descended from a common male ancestor, members of those families from which brides are taken, or into which daughters are married, are considered relations, and the relations of the wife are held to be relations of the husband. The following scheme of relationship applies to all the kindred tribes except the Mânjhis, who are more closely allied to the Gonds, than the surrounding races.

---

[1] Dalton, *Ethnology*, 201, *sq*.

A.—Relations through the Father, whether of man or woman.

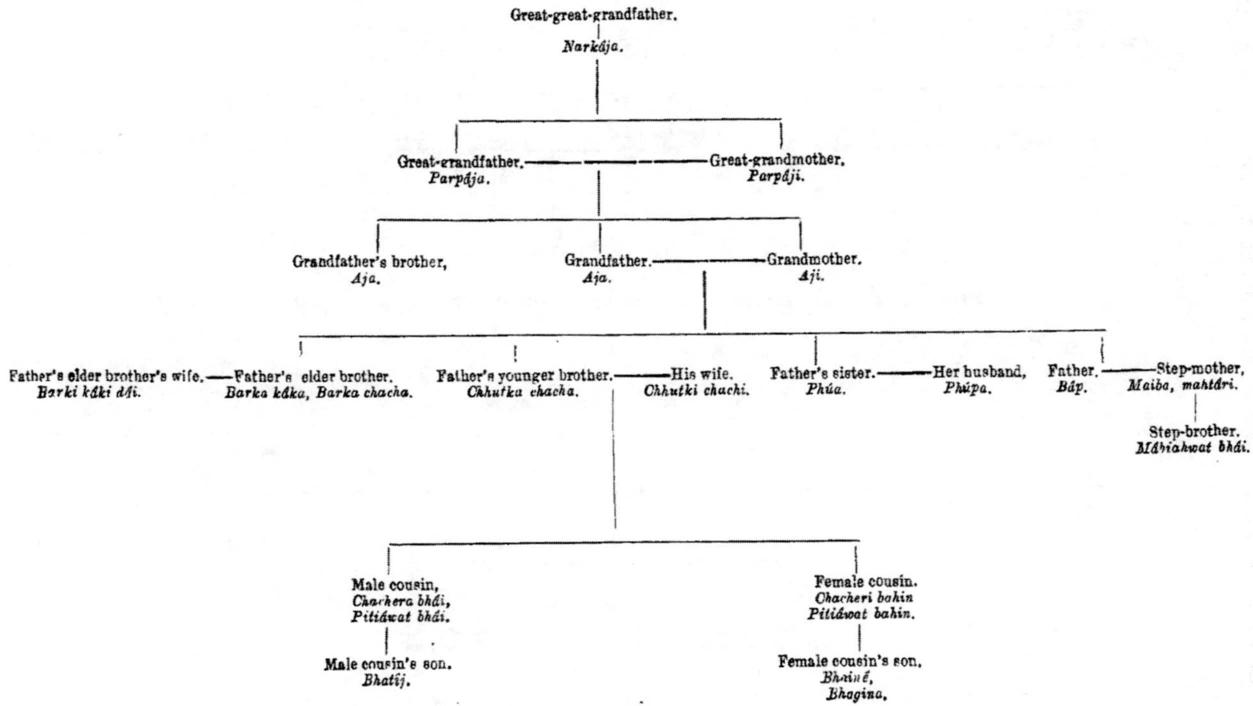

B.—Relations through the Mother, whether of man or woman.

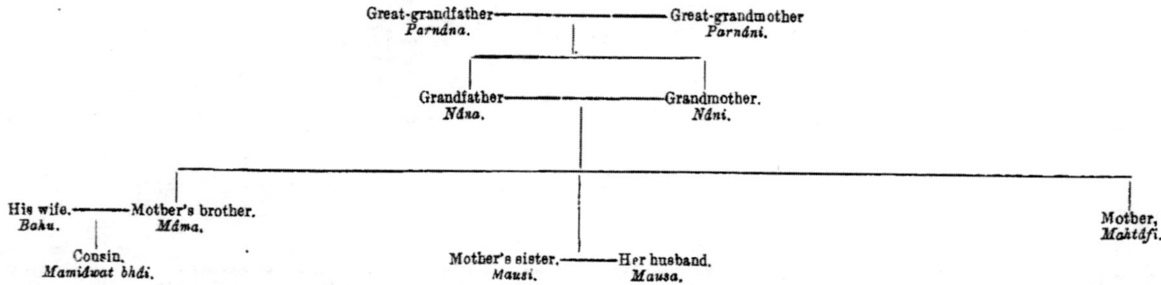

C.—Relations through the Brother and Sister, whether of man or woman.

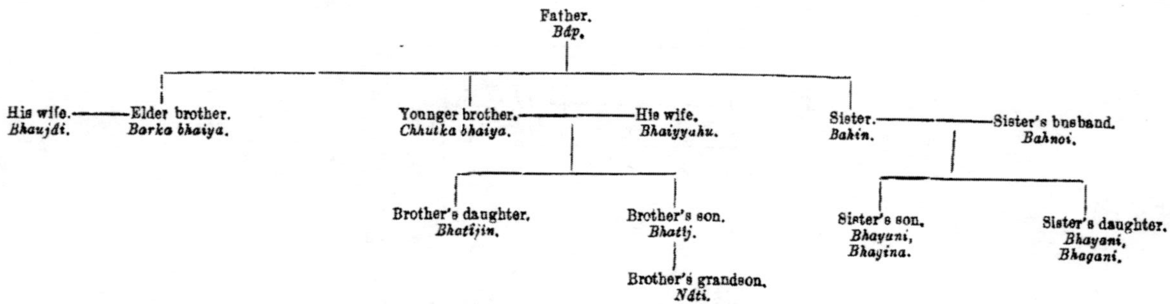

D (1).—*Relations through the Wife of a man.*

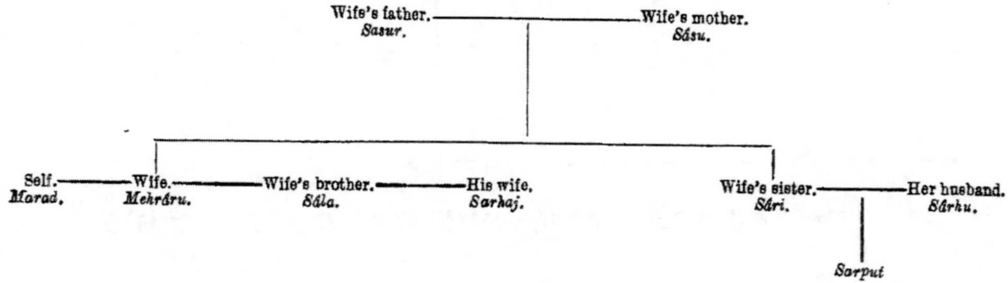

D (2).—*Relations through the Husband of a woman.*

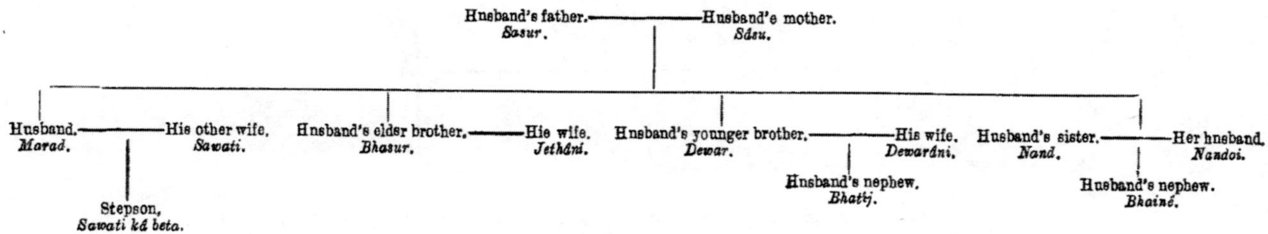

E (1).—Relations through the Son, whether of a man or woman.

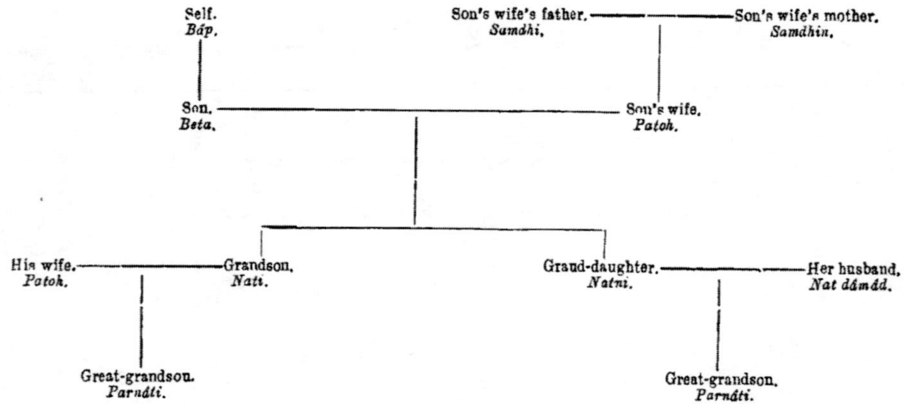

E (2).—Relations through the Daughter, whether of a man or woman.

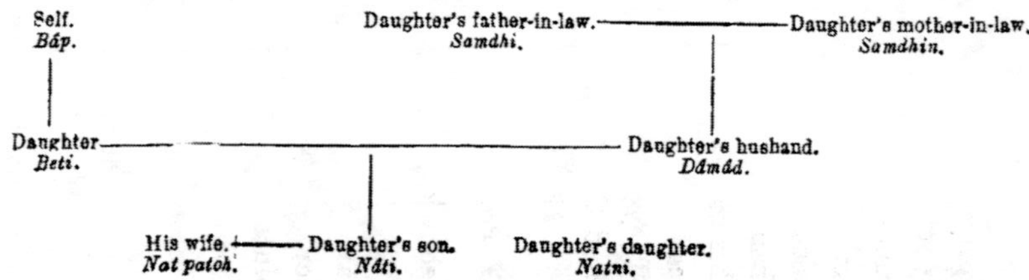

The family in which the father's sister (*phúa*) is married is *phuphuáwar;* where a sister is married, *bahiniáwar;* the grandmother's family, *ajiáwar;* the mother's family, *naniáwar;* where one is married, *sasurár;* the family in which a son or daughter is married, *samdhiyán*. The father is called *bábu, dáda, káka;* his father's elder brother, *chacha;* his younger brother, *kakka;* father's father, *bába:* elder brother, *bhaiyya;* elder sister, *dîdi, bahin;* father's mother, *barki mái;* elder paternal uncle's wife, *barki káki;* younger paternal uncle's wife, *chhutki káki;* elder brother's wife, *bhauji;* younger brother's wife, *dulaiya;* son's wife, *dulaiya;* maternal uncle's wife, *mámi;* mother's mother, *náni;* mother's sister, *máosi;* mother's father, *nána;* wife's father, *mahto;* brother-in-law's elder sister, *jethsar;* brother-in-law's younger sister, *sári;* sister's husband, *bahnoi;* his father, *mahto*. A man calls his wife "mother of his son"—*Rám ki mái*, "Mother of my son Râma."[1] When they call a friend they say *bhaiyya*, "brother," or *ár* (*yár*), "friend." They remember genealogies up to the third or fourth generation, and the names of women up to that of their grandmother.

Pregnancy and birth.

12. They observe the usual taboo for five days in the case of menstrual women. There is no ceremony during pregnancy. When a boy is born, a song of rejoicing (*sohar*) is sung by the women of the clan. It is etiquette that the child should be born in the house of the father as an admission of paternity.[2] When the child is born, the cord is cut and buried in the room, and over it a fire is lit in an earthen pot, into which a bit of iron is put as a protection against evil spirits which may assail mother and child.[3] There is an elementary form of the couvade in the theory that the husband is impure, as well as his wife, sits apart and cooks for her, and receives a sip of the purifying draught which is administered to her. Among the more advanced Kols the woman is regarded as impure up to the twelfth day, when the barber's wife comes, bathes mother and child, and removes the foul clothes. Among the more primitive Kols a Dhobi is not employed, and the cleaning of the clothes is done by the mother herself, or some other woman in the family. The child is usually named in the sixth month, when it is first fed on grain (*anna*

---

[1] On this see Westermarck, *loc. cit.*, 378.
[2] See Westermarck, *loc. cit.*, 105.
[3] Tylor, *Primitive Culture*, II, 195.

prâsana, pâsni). They do not seem to have any form of ordeal in selecting the name,[1] but the child is generally named after some deceased ancestor, whose spirit is supposed to be embodied in the infant. The husband does not cohabit with his wife until the child is weaned, for about nine months after her confinement.

Marriage.

13. After the match is arranged, there is a regular form of betrothal, in which in some places part of the bride-price is paid in advance.[2] The bride-price is low, five rupees in cash, a loin-cloth (*dhoti*), and five measures (*paseri*) of paddy. This is much lower than among the Bengal Mundas, where the extravagance of the bride-price has become a serious obstacle to marriage.[3] Among the Kols of Mirzapur the moderation of the bride-price encourages marriage and promotes tribal morality.[4] Before the marriage they do the ceremony of the lucky earth (*matmangara*),[5] which is brought home by the barber's wife and made into a platform, on which the wedding jar (*kalsa*) is placed. The pavilion (*mânro*) is erected at both houses on the fifth day before the wedding. The poles are of the wood of the *sâl* tree (*shorea robusta*), and it is roofed with bamboos. Inside are placed the marriage jar, images of parrots (*suga*) made out of the wood of the cotton tree (*semal*), and an iron spike is fixed in the ground in the centre. The bride and bridegroom are carefully anointed for five days—the former by her sister-in-law (*nanad*) and the latter by his sister. The bridal party, on arriving at the bride's village, presents an offering of money, cloves, betel, etc., to the village headman, which may possibly be a relic of the commutation of the *jus primæ noctis* already described, but is more probably one of the ordinary dues levied by the landlord from his tenants. In return, he is expected to give wood, the use of a horse or cart, or other assistance to the marriage. The more advanced Kols have a ceremony of the usual Hindu type. The bride and bridegroom worship Gauri and Ganpati. The bridegroom sits on a stool, and the bride's father pours water on his hands, with which the boy washes his feet. The Pandit reads the usual verses; but among the more primitive Kols, no Pandit is called in, and the sister's son of the bridegroom performs

---

[1] As among the Bengal Mundas.—Dalton, *loc. cit.*, 191.
[2] For betrothal among kindred races, see Westermarck, *loc. cit.*, 224.
[3] Ball, *Jungle Life*, 479; Dalton, *Ethnology*, 192.
[4] On this see Westermarck, *loc. cit.*, 133.
[5] See *Bhuiya*, para. 14.

the ceremony.[1] While the women sing the song of rejoicing (*gítmangar*), the bridegroom rubs red-lead on the parting of the bride's hair, and this is the binding part of the ceremony. This is clearly a survival of the original blood covenant.

14. Next the pair are led into the retiring room (*kohabar*), where rude jokes are played on the bridegroom by the women of the bride's family. One form of this is to say—"This rice pestle (*lorha*) is your bride's father, and this lamp (*chirâgh*) is your bride's mother." On this the boy breaks the lamp with the pestle. The whole ceremony appears to be a survival of the primitive custom of the immediate consummation of the marriage after the wedding.[2] Then follows the wedding feast, which is an important part of the ceremony among all primitive races,[3] and after this is the regular *confarreatio* (*khichari*) of bride and bridegroom, in which the latter refuses to share until he gets a present from the girl's father.[4] This is the regular form of marriage called *sindúrdân*, so called from the red lead (*sindúr*) which the bridegroom applies to the parting of the bride's hair. Besides this there is the *dola* form, where the bride is brought to her husband's house and the marriage performed with a much less elaborate ritual. Two other forms are also recognised—the *gandharap*,[5] or marriage by mutual consent of the parties, and the *udhâr*, or marriage by abduction. These terms are of course due to the Brâhman priests of the tribe, but the forms are primitive. These marriages are so far prohibited that in the former a fine of three rupees, and in the latter four rupees, is levied, and then, after a tribal feast, the wife is recognised and her children are legitimate.

15. The dying person is taken outside the house and laid on the ground.[6] The Mírzapur Kols have quite abandoned the primitive form of funeral rites in force among their Munda brethren in Bengal,[7] and they do not erect the curious *menhirs* or monuments which are described

Death ceremonies.

---

[1] This is the usual custom among the Kolarian races of Bihâr.—Dalton, *loc. cit.*, 63.

[2] The rite in its primitive form is maintained among the Bengal Mundas.—Dalton, *loc. cit.*, 194.

[3] Westermarck, *loc. cit.*, 418.

[4] Westermarck, *loc. cit.*, 419, 427.

[5] For the real Gandharva marriage see Manu, III., 26.

[6] Tylor, *Primitive Culture*, I. 453.

[7] For this see Dalton, *Ethnology*, 202.

by Dr. Ball.[1] People dying of small-pox and cholera are always thrown into a river. Children who die while being nursed by their mothers are buried, and among the less Hinduised branches of the tribe the body is taken into any convenient place in the jungle and burnt in a very perfunctory way by the relatives, without any special ritual or the services of any funeral priest. The more Hinduised Kols north of the river Son cremate the body in the way common to low-caste Hindus. After cremation the way home is led by the chief mourner, who is protected by the companions, who follow him, from the spirit of the dead. On arriving at the house of the deceased, each of the mourners chews a small piece of pepper pod, which he spits out, and then, after rinsing his mouth and washing his hands, returns home.[2] From that time till the next evening the tribesmen fast, and then assemble and eat together. This feast is known as the "milk" feast (*dúdh*); and the chief mourner who lit the pyre plants in the ground a few blades of the sacred *kusa* grass near some water, and on this, as a dwelling-place for the wandering ghost, the tribesmen pour water daily after bathing. The man who fixes the pyre goes about with a brass vessel (*lota*) and a piece of iron in his hand as a preservative against ghosts. They do not hang a vessel (*ghant*) on a *pípal* tree, and have no regular *sráddha* ceremony; but on the tenth day some of the more Hinduised Kols give a little grain to a Brâhman. Like the Bengal Mundas,[3] they lay some ashes on the floor of the house. On the night of a death, and if, in the morning, a mark like the foot of a fowl is found in it, they conclude that the spirit of the deceased has quitted his former abode.[4]

Ancestor worship.

16. Whenever there is a tribal feast, a fowl is offered to the spirits of the dead and a little liquor is poured on the ground. The victim is con-

---

[1] *Jungle Life*, 64, 162, 347; and Dalton, *loc. cit.*, 203.

[2] This perhaps represents the leaf of the bitter *ním* tree, which is used in the same way by Hindus.

[3] Dalton, *loc. cit.*, 205.

[4] "Every night for one moon two old men went to the grave about dusk and carefully swept all round it; each morning for the same period they visited it to see if there were any tracks of the dead man on the swept space."—Brough Smith, *Aborigines of Victoria*, I., 119. "After a death has taken place in a family the straw or chaff from the bed of the departed is taken into an open space and burned. Among its ashes the survivors look for a footprint, and that member of the family whose foot fits the impression will be the next to die."—Henderson, *Folklore of the Northern Countries*, 51.

sumed by the worshippers, who also make a fire offering (*hom*) with butter and coarse sugar. When the offering is made they say—"Do not injure us or our children." They do not make any special offering to the dead at funerals or cremations, but they fear them greatly. Such ghosts appear in dreams and trouble those who do not duly propitiate them. They appear in the form of the night-mare, sit on the chest, squeeze the throat, or suck the blood like the vampire.[1] These ghosts most usually appear at the Naurâtra in the months of Chait and Kuâr. Persons who have died in an unnatural or unusual way, such as by drowning or snake-bite, are specially propitiated, and this department is in charge of the village Baiga, who fixes down these wandering vicious spirits in a special shrine (*thân*) under a tree, where, when any trouble visits the village, he offers a fowl, which he eats himself, and makes an oblation (*tapauni*) of spirits.

17. The Mirzapur Kols appear to have lost all recollection of Sing Bonga, the Sun god, revered by the Mundas of Bengal—"a beneficent but somewhat inactive deity, who concerns himself little with human affairs, and leaves the details of the executive government of the world to the gods in charge of particular branches or departments of nature."[2] In Mirzapur the Kol bows before Sûraj Nârâyan the Sun god, when he leaves his house in the morning, but does not seem to venerate him more than all Hindus do. There is a regular sect of Sauras, or worshippers of Sûrya, the Sun god, who numbered at the last Census 41,904 persons. These are quite distinct from the ordinary domestic worship of the sun. The Kol worships demons and sprites (*bhût, pret*), whom he greatly fears, and the souls of the dead—those of women being propitiated by women and those of men by men. He also worships the aggregate of the local gods (*dih, deohâr*) through the village Baiga. Besides these there are several special Kol deities. Of these the chief is Gansâm, who is usually identified with Bara Deo,[3] "the great god." Gansâm, who is certainly a non-Aryan deity, is now becoming gradually admitted into the Brâhmanic pantheon as Ghanasyâma, "the dark-blue rain cloud," which has become on epithet of Krishna. The current explanation

Religion.

---

[1] Tylor, *Primitive Culture*, II., 189, 191.

[2] Risley, *Tribes and Castes*, II., 103; Dalton, *Ethnology*, 186, sq.

[3] Bara Deo is a well-known deity of the Gonds.—*Central Provinces Gazetteer* 104.

that Gansâm is a debased survival of an Aryan nature god is much less probable than that after a Sanskrit etymology has been discovered for his name, this deity is becoming recognised by Hindus.[1] Gansâm is worshipped by the Baiga in a rude hut outside the village, inside which is a mud platform (*chaura, baithak*), on which the deity rests when so disposed. A red flag marks his temple. He is the protector of crops, and is propitiated by the Baiga with the sacrifice of a fowl, goat, or young pig, with an oblation of liquor, in the month of Kârttik, when the transplanted rice is ripening. He very often too resides in a *nîm* tree, and near his shrine is generally a rude stone representing Devi, some vague manifestation of the female principle in nature.

18. Râja Lâkhan is a godling of another type. He is a deified mortal, Râja Lakhana Deva, the son of the great Râja Jay Chandra of Kanauj, who was killed by Shahâbuddîn Ghori in 1194 A. D.[2] The dominions of Lakhana Deva must have reached close to the Kol country, as there is a pillar with an inscription in his honour at Belkhara near Chunâr.[3] There is reason to believe that he led a campaign against the Muhammadan invaders, and this is perhaps the cause of his deification. Now nothing is known of him, except that, by an obvious folk etymology, he is said to have a shrine somewhere near Lucknow. Besides these there are several minor deities, such as Rakhsel and Phûlmati Devi, who are the local guardians of men and cattle, and are little more than village gods of a somewhat higher rank than the undescribed aggregate of divinities who reside in the village shrine. The Nâg or snake-god is worshipped at the Nâgpanchami. The Baghaut or tiger-ghost, Bansapti Mâta, the goddess of the jungle, Chithariya Bîr, "the hero of tatters," who lives in a tree on which rags are hung, and many similar deities of forest and mountain are respected, particularly when disease attacks men and animals. On this occasion the usual ceremony of the scapegoat (*chalâwa*) is managed by the Baiga. Brâhmans of an inferior type are occasionally called in, and are even paid to eat cakes (*pûri*) in the houses of the more Hinduised Kols. The house-god is Dulha Deo, the bridegroom god, who is specially revered by women and at mar-

---

[1] A similar instance is Siva in his form as Bhairava, who is a direct adaptation of the non-Aryan Bhairon.

[2] See Elphinstone, *History of India*, 365.

[3] Cunningham, *Archæological Reports*, XI., 129.

riages with the bloodless sacrifice of cakes and milk. To the souls of the dead the house-master occasionally offers a fowl, ram, or goats, which is then eaten by the family.

Festivals.

19. They appear in Mirzapur to have abandoned the regular tribal festivals of the Mundas.[1] They now observe the usual Hindu festivals of the Naurâtra in the first nine days of the light half of Chait and Kuâr; the Phagua on the first of Chait; the Khichari in the end of Pûs; and the Nâgpanchami.[2] On the fifth of the light half of Sâwan, at the Naurâtra they fast; at the Phagua drink liquor and eat good food; at the Khichari they eat rice and pulse (*khichari*) and give some to Brâhmans; at the Nâgpanchami they offer milk and parched rice at the hole of some snake; at the Naurâtra they get into an ecstatic state (*abhuâna*), and some one falls into a frenzy and screams out oracles. The spirits of the dead reside in a special mud platform erected in the south room of the house. Dulha Deo has his abode in the cook-room. The women also pay particular honour to a deity called Bâsdeo, who resides in a *pîpal* tree. This is really Vasu-deva, which is an adaptation of the Hindu cult of Krishna. The axe and sickle are looked on as a kind of fetish: no one will spit on them or defile them, and they are kept in a place safe from injury.

Omens.

20. They have the usual meeting, sneezing, twitching omens, and their regard for lucky days and directions is the same as those of the other Dravidian races.

Oaths.

21. They swear by putting the hand on the axe or sickle, by the religious preceptor (*guru*), by the Ganges. by taking up the shoe of a Brâhman—"May my children die if I lie," is the usual form.

Dreams.

22. Dreams are believed to indicate the future, and in particular imply the dissatisfaction of the sainted dead when they are neglected. The oldest man in the family interprets them. The only way to ward off evil dreams is to propitiate the souls of the dead.

Amulets.

23. All disease is due to demoniacal influence, and the Ojha is called in to define the offended demon, and present suitable offerings. The Evil-eye

---

[1] For which see Risley, *loc. cit.*, II., 104.

[2] According to Dalton, *Ethnology*, 177, there are no traces of snake worship among the Kols, except in the name of the rainbow (*lûrbeng*), which means "serpent." There are, however, Nâgbansis and Nâgesars allied to them.

is avoided by amulets, particularly the soap-nut, which bursts when the glance falls on them.

Taboos.

24. They revere the cow and buffalo, and will not injure them Every hair on a cow's body is a godling (*deota*), and he who kills a cow offends as many godlings as there are hairs on its body. They appear to have almost entirely lost the prejudice against the use of milk which is common to other Kolarian races.[1] They will not eat food touched by a Dhobi, Chamâr, Dom, Dharkâr, Dusâdh, Kharwâr, Majhwâr, Panka, Agariya, Ghasiya, Chero, or Bhuiyâr. They have an especial abhorrence for Dharkârs, whom they consider particularly polluted. Children are not allowed to join in any worship, and it is only the head wife who does worship to the ancestors or Dulha Deo. A man will not touch his younger brother's wife, the mother-in-law of his son or daughter, nor his wife's elder sister.[2] They will not call by name their wives, nor the wife of a younger brother, nor the mother-in-law of their son or daughter. Nor will they name their religious teachers (*guru*). They prefer not to name the dead. Certain villages, where murders have occurred or where misers or bad characters live, are tabooed in the morning. So in the morning they will not speak of death or beasts of prey. When they have to mention an unlucky place or persons, they point in that direction and say the first letter of the name. If they have to speak of an elephant in the morning they call him *dantihawa*, "he with the teeth," the tiger, *panjahawa*, "he with the claws," and so on.

Agricultural ceremonies.

25. The best day for commencing agricultural operations is Friday. They do not plough on the Nâgpanchami. They do the Kûnrmundan ceremony with an offering to the local gods when sowing is over.[3] Fields should be ploughed five times for luck. Before sowing they sacrifice to "the goddess of verdure," Hariyâri, Hariyari, or Hariyâi Mâi. She is worshipped by breaking up some cloves in a brass vessel (*lota*), which are mixed with water and poured on the ground. If cloves are not procurable, a simple stream of water is poured on the ground in honour of the goddess.

---

[1] Dalton, *Ethnology*, 190.

[2] On this see Lubbock, *Origin of Civilisation*, II., *sqq*.

[3] This perhaps corresponds to the Damurai of the Bengal Mundas.—Dalton, *loc. cit.*, 198.

Social rules.

26. They eat the flesh of pigs, fowls, and all kinds of fish. They will not eat the flesh of cows, horses, donkeys, camels, elephants, alligators, snakes, lizards (*bistuiya*), or jackals. They certainly do not eat carrion, as appears to be the case in Sinhbûm.[1] They do not eat meat during the fortnight sacred to the manes of the dead (*pitrpaksha*): women are not allowed to eat pork, and have their meals separate from the men.[2] Liquor and tobacco are freely used, and oblations of spirits are made to the godlings. The women are treated fairly well, and little quarrelling goes on among them, but it is doubtful if there is much affection between husband and wife, though the contrary has been asserted.[3] They have the fondness for children which is characteristic of most primitive races.[4] The senior wife is honoured and respected. Youngers salute elders with the *päêlagi* form, and the answer is *jiyo nîkê raho*—"may you live and thrive." To strangers they *salâm*. When guests arrive they are saluted, and the wife washes his feet and gives him a tobacco pipe. If any woman in the family is connected with the guest by blood, she seizes him round the waist and weeps, and then provides him with food with the elders of the family. It is the custom for a guest to bring with him some parched grain for the children of his host. The lowest caste who will accept food from their hands is the Kurmi. They only use pipes smoked by Kols. Only Doms, Dharkârs, and Chamârs drink water from their vessels. They wear the scalp-lock, but never shave the beard and mustache, except in mourning. They have a special kind of music known as *koljhari*.

Occupation.

27. Most Kols are ploughmen; a few have land of their own. The usual wages of a Kol ploughman are two sers of grain *per diem*, and a leaf umbrella (*chhopi, kholâur*), a blanket, and a rupee-and-a-half in cash *per annum*. They also get some special food at the festivals of the Dasahra, Kûnrmundan and Pachheinyân on 20th Sâwan. They also get a *bîgha* of land free of rent. This is known as *kola, koliya*. The village landlord takes two days' forced labour in the year from

1 Ball, *Jungle Life*, 159.
2 For similar restrictions among savages see Lubbock, *Origin of Civilisation*, 447.
3 Jellinghause quoted by Westermarck, *History of Human Marriage*, 358.
4 Spencer, *Principles of Sociology*, I., 66.

all ploughmen, one for ploughing and the other for thatching his house. The more primitive Kols practise the system of cultivation by burning (*dahya*) down the jungle.

Kori.[1]—The Hindu weaver caste. Their name has been derived from that of the Kol caste, of whom they have by some been assumed to be an offshoot. In Sanskrit, *kaulika,* in the sense of "ancestral," has also come to mean "a weaver." According to their own story, the Saint Kabîr was one day going to bathe in the Ganges, and met a Brâhman girl who saluted him. He said in reply—"May God give you a son." She objected that she was a virgin and unmarried; but he answered that his word could not fail. So she immediately got a blister on her hand, out of which a boy was born. She was ashamed and left the child on the banks of the river, where a heifer that had never calved gave him milk, and he was adopted by a weaver who taught him his trade. He got his name because he was born of a virgin (*kuâri*) or of a girl untouched by man (*kori*). Hence the verse popular among them—

Kori korê kalas kê, nirgun kâ jâya ;
Kâya dhânkê apni bhava sâgar âya.

"Born of an undefiled jar, of him free from passion, he lowers his body and enters the ocean of existence."

They are probably an occupational caste derived from various sources.

Internal structure.

2. At the last Census the Koris were recorded in a large number of principal sub-castes :—Aharwâr, taking their name from the old town of Ahâr in the Bulandshahr District; Bais, the name of a well-known Râjput sept; Ballâi; Bhadauriya, which is also another Râjput sept; Bhainhar; Bunkar (*bunna,* "to weave"); Dhaman; Jaiswâr, from the town of Jais in the Râê Bareli District; Jatua, who say they have some connection with the Jâts or were born direct from the matted hair (*jata*) of Siva; Juriya; Kabîrbansi, called after Kabîr, the forefather of the caste; Kaithiya, who spring from the Kâyasths; Kamariha or Kamariya; Kanaujiya, from Kanauj; Katua; Korchamra, who spring from Chamârs; Kushta; Mahurê; Odh or Orh; Parsutiya (Sanskrit, *prasava,* "procreation"); Sakarwâr,

---

[1] Based on enquiries at Mirzapur and notes by Munshi Râm Saran Dâs, Faizâbâd; Munshi Râm Sahây, Teacher, Tahsîli School, Mahoba, Hamîrpur; Munshi Mai Dâyâl Sinh, Deputy Collector, Shâhjahânpur; and Munshi Gopâl Prasâd, Nâib Tahsîldâr, Phaphûnd, Etâwah.

or those from Fatehpur Sikri; Sankhwâr. There are many other sub-castes spread over the province. Thus in Shâhjâhânpur we find Jaiswâr, Kanaujiya, Kachhwâr, Manwâr, Gangapâri, or "those from beyond the Ganges, Banswâr, Baiswâr, Katyâr, Patra, Gujarâti, Khatiya, and Chapar. In Hamîrpur are the Kutar, Kamariha, Jaiswâr, Sakhwâr, Dhiman, and Sunwâni. In Bijnor those who practise the occupation of applying leeches on patients are called Jonkiyâra (*jonk*, "a leech"). In Etâwah are the Mahur, Sakhwâr, Bhandauliya, and Chandauliya. In Mirzapur they class themselves as Chamâr-Kori who follow the usages of Chamârs and the Kori who connect themselves with Kahârs. Here they say that they are emigrants from Udaypur. The Juriya or Joriya of Faizâbâd claim to be Brâhmans and immigrants from a place called Katwi in the Jaunpur District. They admit Brâhmans, Kshatriyas, Vaisyas, Ahîrs, Kurmis, Murâos, and similar people into their caste. This generally occurs when they have contracted illicit intercourse with women of the tribe. They are worshippers of Mahâbîr and Bhâgawati, to whom they offer sacrifices of sheep and goats. Formerly they used only to weave in silk; now they make cotton cloths and do masonry. The Koris have been extraordinarily fertile in the development of sub-divisions. The complete Census lists contain no less than 1,040 names.

Manners and customs.

3. In their manners and customs Koris agree very closely with the Chamârs and people of a similar social grade, which it is unnecessary to repeat. In Hamîrpur, they are reported to have a special form of introducing the bride into her husband's house. The oldest man of the household prepares some cakes fried in butter, known as *mâên*, and offers them with the sacrifice of a pig to a local godling known as Baltai. Then comes the *nihâran* ceremony, when three wheaten cakes are baked, which the newly-married pair tread under foot, and are then allowed to enter the house. There are regular marriage brokers in Hamîrpur, each of whom receives a pair of loin-cloths (*dhoti*) contributed by the parents of the pair at betrothal, marriage, and the coming home of the bride, should she not have arrived at puberty when the wedding takes place. In most cases, however, the marriage is arranged by the sister's husband of the boy—apparently a survival of the matriarchate. A woman married by the *Karâo* ceremony is not allowed to enter her husband's house in the day-time; she must do so secretly and at night. Hence of such marriages the

proverb runs—*Kála munh, andhiyárê pákh,* "with a black face and in the dark fortnight of the month." A widow cannot re-marry by the *Karáo* form until at least the thirteen days of mourning for her late husband are over. Authorities differ as to whether they admit outsiders into the caste. A correspondent from Etâwah asserts that it is a well-known fact that they admit Brâhmans, Râjputs, Banyas, Kâyasths, Ahîrs, Gadariyas, Kâchhis, Kahârs, Bhurjis, Barhais, Khâtis, and Kurmis into their community, but draw the line at Chamârs, Telis, Dhobis, and Bâris, as well as sweepers and Dhânuks. This is said not to take place in other districts. The same correspondent also asserts that in Etâwah it is well ascertained that in the levirate the widow is allowed to marry the elder as well the younger brother of her late husband. This, if correct, is very remarkable, as it is totally opposed to the usage of all other castes of the same social status.

Religion.

4. The Koris are all Hindus. In Faizâbâd they are said to follow the Râêdâsi or Sivanârâyani sect, of which some account has been given in connection with Chamârs. In Bijnor they are Kabîrpanthis. This is also the case in Hamîrpur, where their religious ceremonies are performed by the daughter's husband, another relic of the matriarchate. To the West they also worship Zâhirpîr and the Miyân of Amroha and Jalesar, and to the East the Pânchonpîr and Sîtala Mâta.

Occupation and social status.

5. The status of the Kori is very low. In Mirzapur it is said that Brâhmans will drink water from the hands of the Kahâr Koris, but not from the Chamâr Koris. Only Dhobis and Chamârs will eat *kachchi* or *pakki* cooked by the latter; Koris will, to the East, eat *kachchi* cooked by Brâhmans and Kshatriyas and *pakki* prepared by all Vaisyas, except Kalwârs. Their occupation is weaving coarse country cloth, but some take to service and field labour or hold land as tenants. Kushta or Koshta, one of their sub-castes, is the general name for a weaver in the Dakkhin.[1]

[1] *Bombay Gazetteer,* XVII, 112, *sqq.*

Distribution of the Koris according to the Census of 1891.

District.	Aharwâr.	Bais.	Ballai.	Bhadauriya.	Bhainhar.	Bunkar.	Dhaman.	Jaiswâr.	Jatua.	Juriya.	Kabirbansi.	Kaithiya.	Kamariha.	Kanaujiya.	Katua.	Korchamra.	Kushta.	Mahure.	Odh.	Parautiya.	Sakarwâr.	Sankhwâr.	Others.	Total.
Dehra Dûn	...	...	...	...	...	...	...	24	...	...	393	...	...	...	...	...	...	...	41	...	...	...	3,986	4,444
Sahâranpur	...	...	...	...	...	...	36	143	...	...	3,077	...	...	114	...	451	...	...	...	...	...	...	13,659	17,480
Muzaffarnagar	...	...	...	...	...	...	...	6	...	...	3,330	...	...	...	...	...	...	...	...	...	...	...	8,483	11,819
Meerut	...	...	...	...	...	...	...	...	...	...	408	...	...	...	...	...	...	...	936	...	...	...	160	1,504
Bulandshahr	...	...	...	...	...	...	...	3	...	...	1,701	...	...	...	...	...	...	...	5,876	...	...	...	16,715	24,295
Aligarh	...	...	...	...	...	...	...	...	...	...	573	...	...	...	...	..	...	7,485	2,966	...	...	...	21,324	32,348
Mathura	...	...	730	...	...	...	3	2	14	...	240	14	...	5	...	...	18	15,698	763	...	181	263	1,921	19,852
Agra	8	275	14	1,133	...	...	26	114	...	...	36	6	...	2	...	...	...	21,720	15	...	323	6,677	2,596	32,945
Farrukhâbâd	324	...	...	...	...	...	78	341	690	...	369	...	2,871	110	...	406	...	594	5	113	245	5,958	3,309	15,413
Mainpuri	...	12	...	1,086	...	...	...	31	64	...	79	...	1,219	...	...	10	...	732	...	...	6	9,859	1,187	14,235
Etâwah	640	...	...	...	...	...	...	96	...	...	114	1,964	3,521	36	...	64	...	506	1	996	3,539	9,407	2,333	23,217
Etah	...	...	...	...	...	...	7	70	...	...	377	942	339	...	...	30	...	4,433	86	1,173	...	3,182	1,598	12,237
Bareilly	...	...	...	...	4	...	...	...	...	...	395	...	...	1,013	...	43	109	...	...	3,885	...	411	42,829	48,689
Bijnor	...	...	...	...	90	...	...	...	...	...	...	...	...	...	...	...	...	...	...	...	...	...	7,565	7,655
Budaun	...	...	...	...	...	...	3	...	...	...	6,103	1,004	...	...	...	...	...	1,057	...	...	...	184	4,584	12,935
Morâdâbâd	...	...	...	...	1,156	...	...	22	...	...	1,203	...	...	...	...	...	...	...	60	...	...	...	3,353	5,794
Shâhjahânpur	...	...	...	...	...	...	608	712	50	7	179	469	136	887	...	4	...	29	...	363	684	7,486	8,777	20,391

Distribution of the Koris according to the Census of 1891—continued.

District.	Aharwār.	Bais.	Ballai.	Bhadauriya.	Bhainhar.	Bunkar.	Dhaman.	Jaiswār.	Jatua.	Juriya.	Kabīrbansi.	Kaithiya.	Kamariha.	Kanaujiya.	Katua.	Korchamra.	Kushta.	Mahure.	Odh.	Parsutiya.	Sakarwār.	Sankhwār.	Others.	Total.
Pilibhît	...	...	...	...	...	...	1,543	615	145	...	500	31	1	35	7	...	378	...	...	394	1,408	515	2,681	8,253
Cawnpur	2,330	...	...	...	...	...	3,755	1,002	...	...	199	...	20,489	81	...	68	66	177	...	374	...	842	14,620	44,003
Fatehpur	...	...	...	...	...	...	6,471	3,921	...	...	148	...	...	2	...	...	...	...	...	...	...	12	9,929	20,483
Bânda	55	...	...	...	...	...	520	13	...	...	525	...	...	17	...	3	485	...	...	...	2,443	...	23,719	27,780
Hamîrpur	7,548	...	...	...	...	...	...	6	...	...	29	...	616	1	...	...	89	25	...	67	2	4,090	14,806	27,279
Allahâbâd	...	...	...	...	...	...	5	5,042	...	1,397	15	...	...	...	...	...	30	...	...	...	...	...	12,938	19,427
Jhânsi	21,899	...	...	...	...	612	8	108	...	...	125	...	2	...	...	...	889	203	2	22	36	2,106	1,473	27,485
Jâlaun	12,266	...	...	...	...	...	...	...	...	...	95	...	9	...	...	...	161	...	...	424	...	7,980	1,554	22,489
Lalitpur	1,070	...	...	...	...	6,905	51	...	...	...	158	...	...	...	...	...	...	30	...	...	1	21	2,138	10,374
Benares	...	...	...	...	...	...	...	...	...	...	...	...	...	...	...	...	146	...	...	...	...	...	...	146
Mirzapur	...	...	...	...	...	...	...	1	...	...	...	...	...	...	...	...	...	...	...	...	...	...	27	28
Ghâzipur	...	...	...	...	...	...	...	...	...	...	...	...	...	...	...	...	...	...	...	...	...	...	57	57
Gorakhpur	...	...	...	...	...	...	...	...	...	...	...	...	...	...	...	...	...	...	...	150	...	...	937	1,087
Basti	...	...	...	...	...	...	...	...	...	670	...	...	...	...	...	...	...	...	...	31	...	...	1,590	2,291
Azamgarh	...	...	...	...	...	...	...	...	...	...	...	...	...	...	302	...	...	...	...	...	...	...	379	681
Garhwâl	...	...	...	...	...	...	...	...	...	...	...	...	...	...	...	...	...	...	...	...	...	...	3	3
Tarâi	...	...	...	...	425	...	...	...	...	...	3	...	...	...	...	...	...	18	...	...	...	...	531	977
Lucknow	...	...	...	...	...	...	12,996	219	...	...	50	28	...	...	...	2	...	29	...	111	164	...	6,073	19,672

Unáo	...	...	...	...	...	...	10,575	57	...	...	4	...	...	123	...	...	...	...	...	136	5	...	11,750	22,650
Râê Bareli	...	...	...	...	...	...	27,883	5,468	...	1,591	...	190	...	293	...	18	...	...	...	...	...	...	2,014	37,457
Sitapur	...	...	...	...	...	...	2,802	68	...	...	11	1,821	...	...	...	17	...	3,835	...	718	...	149	1,964	11,385
Hardoi	...	...	...	...	...	...	...	22	...	...	...	3,527	...	14	...	...	...	...	...	...	163	5,157	3,616	12,499
Kheri	...	...	...	...	2	...	6,601	477	50	...	...	3,304	...	182	...	...	...	770	...	...	969	...	7,265	19,620
Faizâbâd	...	576	...	...	...	...	15,461	702	...	8,721	...	...	...	...	...	...	184	...	...	...	...	...	16,131	36,775
Gonda	...	...	...	...	...	...	27,986	...	...	...	...	...	...	...	...	...	...	...	...	...	...	...	115,827	143,813
Bahrâich	...	...	...	...	...	...	9,360	34	...	12	...	...	...	...	...	68	...	...	...	...	89	...	42,449	52,002
Sultânpur	...	...	...	...	...	69	12,281	2,463	...	...	...	...	...	...	...	1,111	19	...	...	...	...	...	4,328	20,271
Bârabanki	...	14	...	...	6	...	24,290	...	...	...	...	...	...	...	...	...	...	...	...	...	...	...	1,099	25,409
TOTAL	46,140	877	744	2,219	1,683	7,586	163,349	21,782	1,013	7,398	20,439	13,300	29,203	2,915	309	2,285	2,674	57,341	10,751	8,957	10,258	64,299	444,227	919,649

Kormangta.—A Hindu religious order, so-called because they are said to beg only from members of the Kori tribe (*Kori mángna*). We have similarly the Chamar-mangta, who beg from Chamârs, and the Pasmangta from Pâsis. The Census shows them only in Oudh.

Distribution of the Kormangtas according to the Census of 1891.

District.	Number.
Unâo	82
Râê Bareli	223
Bârabanki	582
Total	887
Males	439
Females	448

Korwa.—A Dravidian tribe found in the part of Mirzapur south of the river Son and along the frontier of Sarguja. They assert that they have emigrated from Sarguja within the last two or three generations. They appear to be the aborigines of Sarguja, Jashpur, and Palâmau, and this "claim is in some measure borne out by the fact that the priests who propitiate the local spirits are always selected from this tribe."[1] Among the offshoots of the original tribe now residing in Mirzapur there appears to be no trace of the singular legend that they are descended from the scare-crows set up to frighten wild animals by the first men who raised crops in Sarguja, which were animated by the great spirit to save his votaries the trouble of continually making new ones.[2] There seems little doubt that they are in name and origin closely connected with the Kûrs, whose name Mr. Hislop connects with Kol, and describes as "found on the Mahâdeva hills and westward in the forest on the Tâpti and Narbada until they come in contact with the Bhîls. On the Mahâdeva hills, where they have been much influenced by the Hindus, they prefer the name of Muâsi, the origin of which I have not been able to ascertain, unless it be that the word is derived from the *mahua* tree."[3] Like the Kûrs, the Korwas of

---

[1] Risley, *Tribes and Castes*, I., 511.

[2] Dalton, *Descriptive Ethnology*, 226; Risley, *loc. cit.*, II., 511; Driver, *Journal Asiatic Society of Bengal*, 1891, page 25.

[3] *Papers*, 25. A scattered tribe with a very similar name, Mahwaiya, are found in some of the jungles in Pargana Barhar of Mirzapur and seem now to be disappearing by amalgamation with the Kols.

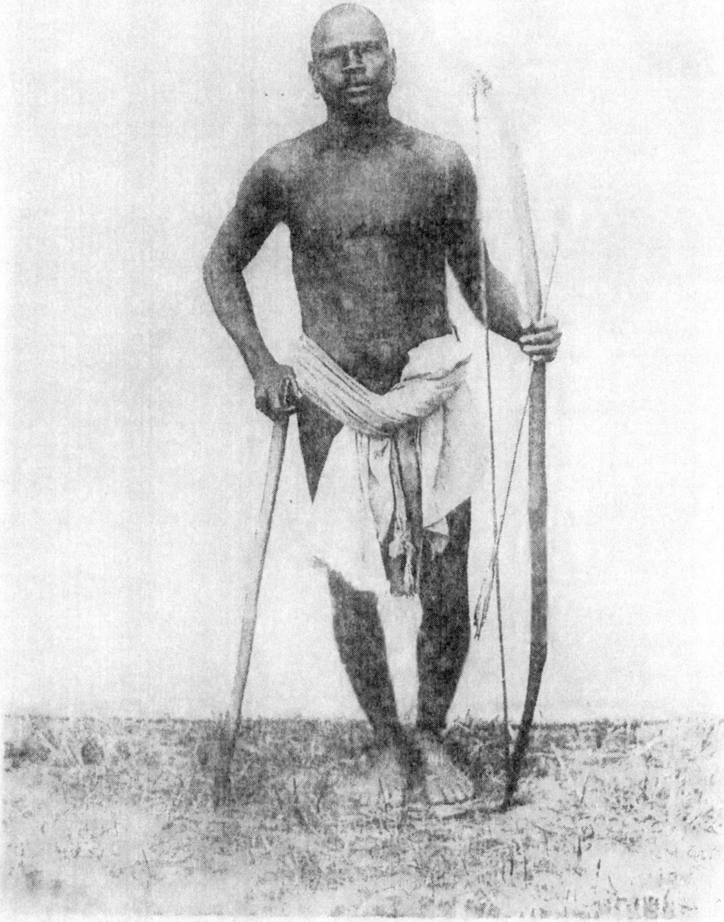

KORWA.

Chota Nâgpur have some traditions connecting them with the Mahâdeva hills as the first seat of their race.[1] The word Korwa seems to be another form of Kol. Herr Jellinghause interprets the word Kol to mean "pig-killer,"[2] but the better opinion seems to be that it is a variant for *horo*, the Mundâri for "man." The Khariyas of Chota Nâgpur call the Mundas Kora—a name closely approaching Kol.[3]

Tribal organization.

2. No trace can be found in Mirzapur of the sub-tribes of Agariya Korwa, Dand Korwa, Dih Korwa, and Pahariya Korwa found in Bengal,[4] nor of the Birhor and Kisân Korwas mentioned by Mr. Driver.[5] There is, again, no trace of the interesting series of totemistic sub. divisions recorded from Rânchi by Mr. Risley.[6] The Mirzapur tribe say that there are two sub-tribes, Korwa and Korâku, both of whom are mentioned by Colonel Dalton.[7] The former live in Pargana Dudhi, the flat country north of the Sarguja plateau, and the latter in the Sarguja hills. The former have almost abandoned the use of the bow and arrow, which is said to be habitually used by the latter. Among themselves the Mirzapur Korwas call the males Korâku and the women Koriku.

Appearance.

3. Colonel Dalton's description applies very well to the Mirzapur tribe. He describes them as "short of stature and dark-brown in complexion, strongly built and active, with good muscular development, but, as appeared to me, disproportionately short-legged. The average height of twenty Sarguja Korwas whom I measured was five feet three inches, and of their women four feet nine inches only. In feature the characteristic types are not very prominent: a breadth of face from the lateral projection of the zygomatic arches and narrowness of forehead are the most remarkable traits: the nose, chin, and mouth are better formed than we generally find them among the rude tribes of the Dravidian stock; and, notwithstanding the scare-crow tradition, the Korwas are, as a rule, better looking than the Gonds and Orâons. The males, I noticed, were more hirsute than

---

[1] Driver, *loc. cit.*, 24.
[2] *Kola* in Sanskrit means "a hog."
[3] Risley, *loc. cit.*, II., 101.
[4] Risley, *loc. cit.*, I., 512.
[5] *Loc. cit.*, page 25.
[6] *Loc. cit.*, *Appendix*, 83.
[7] *Descriptive Ethnology*, 230, 231.

the generality of their cognates, many of them cultivating beards or rather not interfering with their spontaneous growth, for in truth in their toilettes there is nothing like cultivation. They are as utterly ungroomed as the wildest animals. The neglected back hair grows in matted tails which fall behind like badly frayed ropes or is massed in a chignon of gigantic proportions, as preposterous as any that the present tactless period has produced, sticking out behind sometimes a foot from the back of the head. The women appear ground down by the hard work imposed upon them, stunted in growth, black, ugly, and wretchedly clad, some having only a few dirty rags tied round their persons, and in other respects untidy and unclean."[1] Dr. Ball noticed particularly "the unkempt condition of their matted locks of hair, in which they commonly hitch the shafts of their arrows."[2]

Tribal organization.

4. They have a tribal council (*bhaiyâri*), in which, degraded as they are, they are superior to the Cyclopes Homer's type of "a froward and lawless folk."[3] This is summoned by invitation (*neota*) when necessary. It is presided over by a permanent hereditary president (*pradhân*). The leader of all the Korwas in Mirzapur is Somchand Korwa of Bisrâmpur in Pargana Dudhi. Every adult male has a right to sit on the council, which deals with cases of adultery, etc. Only clansmen are accepted as witnesses. No one is sworn. The sentence is usually to give a feast, and if any offender disobeys the order, he is excommunicated and remains outcaste until he obeys.

Marriage rules.

5. There are in Mirzapur no exogamous sub-divisions. The family of the mother's brother (*mâmu*) and that of the father's sister's husband (*phûpha*) are barred: and when a family lives together the members do not intermarry within four or five degrees.[4] As a rule, they have only one wife and do not indulge in concubinage or polyandry. The marriage age is twelve for males and ten for girls. The marriage is usually arranged by the brother-in-law (*bahnoi*) of the

---

[1] *Descriptive Ethnology*, 226.

[2] *Jungle Life*, 661.

[3] *Odyssey*, IX., 112.

[4] In Chota Nâgpur, according to Mr. Driver, "Korwas are divided into several families, each of which is known by its *gotra*, and no two people of the same *gotra* are allowed to marry."—*Journal Asiatic Society of Bengal*, 1891, page 26.

bridegroom. The bridegroom has, however, generally a voice in the matter. There are many runaway marriages. In selecting a wife working capabilities are more regarded than beauty. The bride-price is five rupees and one or two maunds of rice. After the betrothal the appearance of any physical defects is not a ground for breaking off the match, nor are idiocy, lunacy, impotence, or mutilation a sufficient cause.

Divorce.

6. Sufficient grounds for divorce are eating from the hands of, or intriguing with, a Dom, Chamâr, or Dharkâr. The only ceremony is the announcement of the fact before the council; but the council will put a man out of caste if he maltreats his wife, and she can complain against him to the council and get him fined. A divorced woman cannot re-marry.

Widow marriage.

7. Widows may be married again by the *sagâi* form. They generally marry widowers, and it seems unusual for a bachelor to take a widow to wife. The man has to give the relations of the widow a rupee and a quarter and then takes the woman home. The levirate is permitted under the usual restriction that it is only the younger brother of the husband who can take his widow: and if he chooses to claim her she cannot marry an outsider. If she have a child at the breast, she takes it with her to her new husband. Older children remain with their paternal uncle.

Relationship.

8. The family into which his son marries or into which his daughter is married are relations. They call a father *apa*; grandfather, *tatang*; great-grandfather, *dâdi*; a son is *hopon*; a grandson, *kurin*; a great-grandson, *bahotu*. The following is their system of relationship:—

A.—Relations through the Father, whether of man or woman.

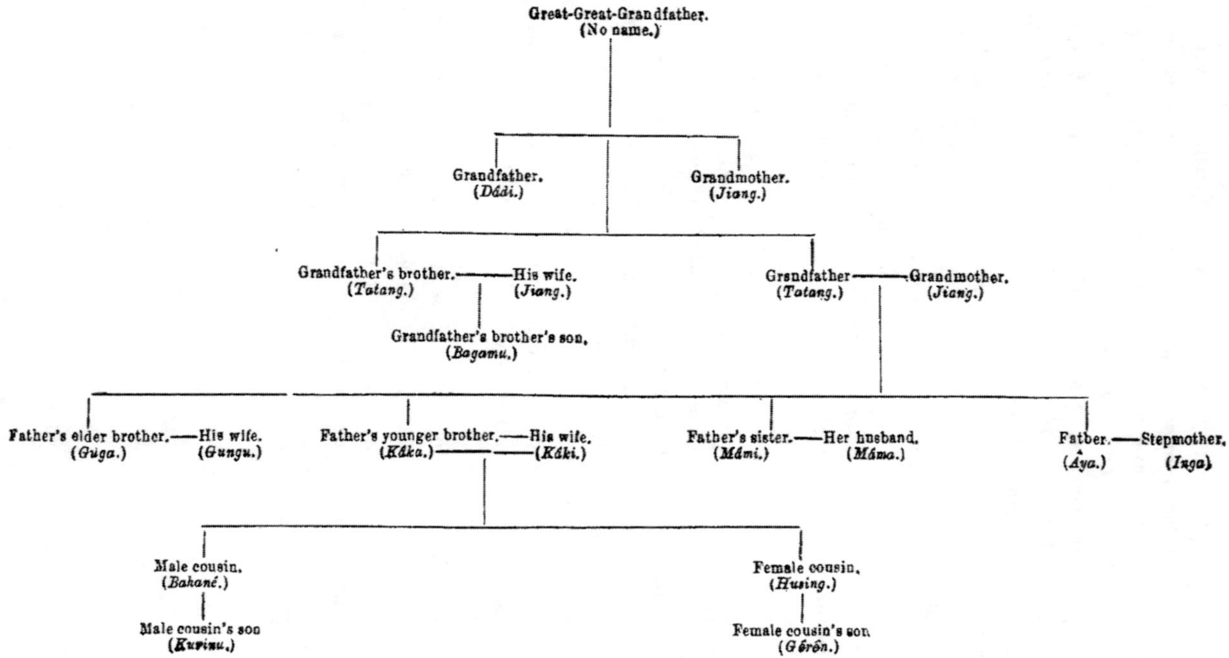

This group is called *Jiat.*

B.—Relations through the Mother, whether of man or woman.

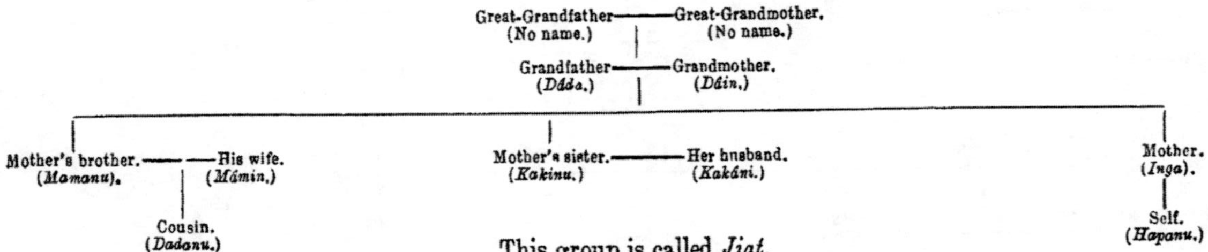

This group is called *Jiat.*

C.—Relations through the Brother and Sister, whether of man or woman.

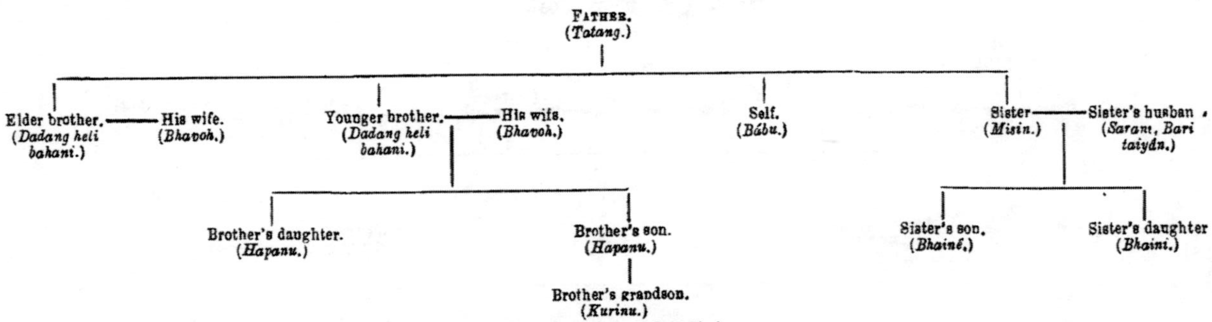

This group is called *Misinu.*

D.—Relations through the wife of a man.

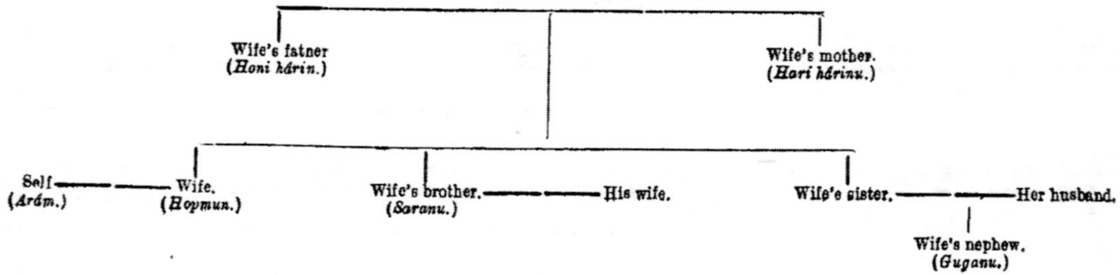

This group is called *Sasurál.*

E (1).—Relations through the Son, whether of man or woman.

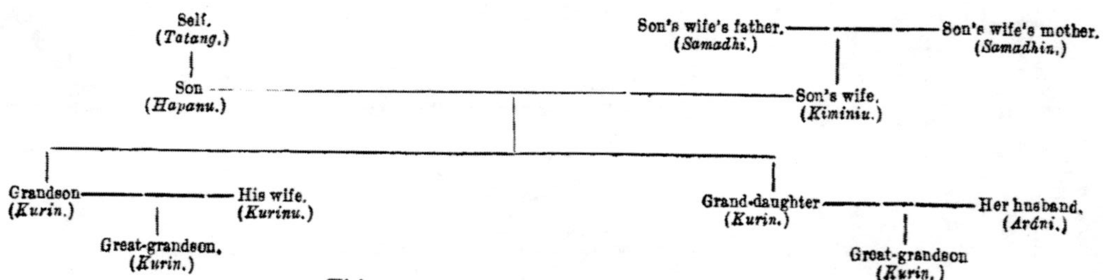

This group is called *Samdhimán.*

E (2).—Relations through the Daughter, whether of man or woman.

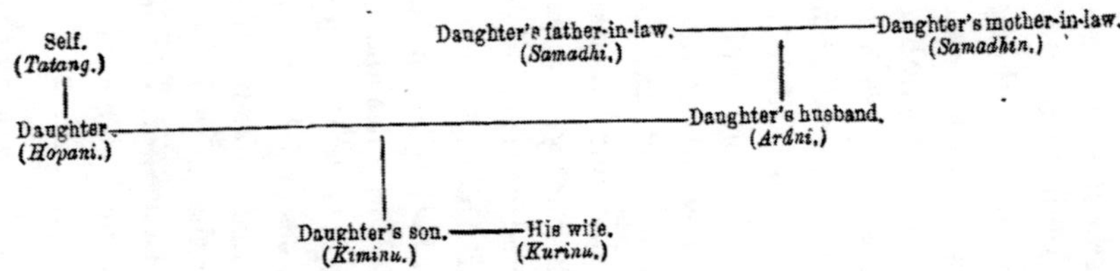

This group is called *Samadhinu.*

This is not the place to attempt systematic analysis of these records of relationship, It may merely be noticed that there is no term for a great-grandfather or great-grandmother ; that the names for the grandmother and grandfather's brother's wife are the same; that the term for the father's younger brother and his wife are purely Hindi, as is the case with the wife of the younger brother, sister's son, sister's daughter, and for the father and mother of the son's wife. This illustrates the vagueness of the marriage tie among these people.[1] Among themselves they call the sister *aya ;* their own wife, *Bâbu kai inga ;* elder brother's wife *bhavoh ;* mother's brother, *mâma ;* mother's father, *tatang ;* sister's husband *taiyân ;* wife's brother, *saranu ;* father's sister's husband, *mâma ;* father's sister, *mâmi ;* a woman's father-in-law *bûrha* ("old man") ; wife's sister's husband, *saddhu ;* wife's brother's son, *dangeru* ; son's wife, *bâi ;* son's or daughter's son, *kurin.*

Birth ceremonies.

9. The woman is delivered sitting on the ground. Some old woman of the tribe cuts the cord with a sickle, and throws it outside the house. The Chamâin midwife is not employed. The moment the child is born a fire is lit in the house and kept burning for twelve days. The husband does not enter the delivery room for five days. On the sixth day the old woman bathes the mother and child, and two or three of the clan are fed on pulse and rice. The woman's clothes are washed, and she goes back to the delivery room (*saur*). On the twelfth day the mother goes and bathes in a stream, washes her clothes, and comes home and cooks for the family. On the twelfth day the child is named by the father or grandfather, and is generally called after some deceased ancestor, who is understood from a dream to be re-born in the baby.[2] There appears to be no trace of the

---

[1] For a discussion of the system of nomenclature see McLennan, *Studies in Ancient History and the Patriarchal Theory ;* Morgan, *Systems of Consanguinity, passim ;* Starcke, *Primitive Family, Chapter* V. ; Lubbock, *Origin of Civilization, Chapter* IV.

[2] Mr. Driver notes in Chota Nâgpur that children are named a month after they are born. "They are only named after their grandparents, when the mother dreams of a visit from the said ancestors. If a girl is to be born, the woman dreams that either her own or her husband's mother came with an offering of *târpât* earrings or beads ; but if a boy is expected she dreams that either her own or her husband's father came with an offering of a *dibi* or *batua* (small brass pots for eating out of). The child is then called its grandparent's embodiment (*ântar*) and is named after the said ancestor. A big feast is always given at a christening. Boys are preferred to girls."—*Journal Asiatic Society of Bengal,* 1891, *page* 28.

couvade. These people have the intense fear of pollution from the menstrual or parturition discharge which is characteristic of all primitive races.[1]

Marriage customs.

10. The boy's father goes and inspects the girl: when he approves of her, the maternal uncle (*mâmu*) of the boy completes the negotiations. If the girl's father approves of the proposal, he feeds the envoy. On the marriage day, which is fixed by mutual arrangement, the bridegroom goes to the bride's house with some of his relations. Once the procession starts, neither party can withdraw from the match; and if either object, he is forced to consent by an order from the council. At the marriage the oldest man present calls the bride and says to her—"We have made you over to the son of so and so. You must never leave him, no matter what trouble you undergo. Don't disgrace your family by an intrigue with a man of another caste." After this exhortation the bridegroom rubs red lead on the girl's head. This is the binding portion of the ceremony. After this the clansmen are fed on goat's flesh and rice, and next day the bridegroom brings the bride home and feasts his clansmen. There is no trace of the professional match-maker, the best man and the bridesmaids, and the knotting of the garments of the pair which are part of the ritual in Chota Nâgpur.[2] When a girl is married a piece of jungle is assigned her as a hunting ground where she can dig roots and collect wild fruits. No one else dares to interfere with her domain, and the right is strictly enforced by the council.[3]

Mr. Campbell (*Notes* 4) remarks:—"Another ground for the belief in the return of ancestors was the likeness of children to the dead. The Konkan Kunbis, and even Brâhmans, believe that the dead ancestors sometimes come in children, and so in many cases children are named after their grandfathers or grandmothers. Among Gûjarât Musalmâns, if a child is naughty or peevish, its mother or nurse says—'Its kind has come on its head.' It is the belief of the Khonds that an ancestor comes back in a child (Macpherson, 56). Among the American Indians when a man dies the medium puts his hands on the head of one of the mourners, and the spirit of the dead enters him, ready to appear in his next offspring (Bancroft, III., 517). Among the Laplanders of Europe an ancestral spirit tells the mother that he has come into the child, and to call the child by his name.—Tylor, *Primitive Culture*, II. 4."

[1] Frazer, *Golden Bough*, II., 238, *sq*.

[2] Driver, *Journal Asiatic Society of Bengal*, 1891, *page* 27.

[3] See similar cases in Lubbock, *Origin of Civilization*, 455, and compare *Bhar*, para. 10.

11. The dying person is taken into the open air before death.[1]

Death customs.

The tribe is in a transition stage between burial and cremation.[2] Some families practise one form and some the latter. Those that bury the dead have regular tribal, or family, burial-grounds. Even among those who cremate the dead, young children and those who die of epidemic diseases are buried. When they cremate, they take the corpse to a place north-east of the village. It is laid on its back, with the feet to the south. Wood is piled over it, and the son of the deceased, or if he has no son, his brother or other male next of kin, walks five times round the pyre with a grass torch and fires it. When it is well alight they leave it, bathe, and return home. Next day the chief mourner goes to the pyre and collects the ashes. Then a message is sent round to the effect that the funeral ceremony (*khoiya, khaur*) will take place on a certain day. The clansmen collect and shave themselves.[3] A barber is not employed. Then they wash their clothes and have a feast at the house of the deceased. From that day all are pure. They have, as far as can be ascertained, no ceremony to propitiate the spirits of the dead. When they burn or bury a corpse, they place with it the ornaments, clothes of the deceased, and an axe, none of which are broken. These are to be the support of the deceased in the after world, but as to any abode of happiness or retribution they have no idea. All they know is that the spirit goes to Paramesar, but this is the case with the souls of trees and animals as well as men.

12. They do not even pretend to be Hindus, and have no connection with the Bráhmans.

Religion and superstitions.

They worship as their tribal god Râja Chandol in the month of February (Phâlgun) with an offering of a cock, some red lead (*sendúr*), and flowers. This offering is made by the Baiga, many of whom are found in the tribe.[4] They are much beset by malignant ghosts (*bhút*), particularly those of strange villages, who are excluded by the Baiga, who goes round the village circuit once a year dropping a little liquor as he walks, and thus forming a magic

---

[1] Tylor, *Primitive Culture*, I., 453.

[2] There is a good note on this fact among the Greeks in Blackie's *Iliad* on VII., 328.

[3] On this ceremonial shaving after a death compare Homer, *Iliad*, XXIII., 135; *Odyssey*, IV., 198.

[4] This is also the case with the Bengal Division of the tribe, Dalton, *Ethnology*, 130, 221. For the worship of Râja Chandol, see *Majhwâr, para.* 40.

line over whch foreign ghosts are unable to cross. When the Baiga is a drunken rascal, as is often the case, this performance takes a considerable time, and the heavy charges for liquor are received badly by his parishioners. When Bhûts attack people and bring disease, particularly fainting or epileptic fits, an Ojha is called in to exorcise the Bhût, or if the patient is a young woman, she is taken to a local shrine and thrashed by the Baiga with his heavy iron magic chain (*gurda*).[1] There is hardly any trace of ancestor worship, except in times of extreme sickness, when a Korwa will sacrifice a goat in the name of his late father or mother. They do not consider any more remote ancestors deserving of any propitiation. When they make an offering of food to the dead they throw a morsel on the ground. They do not appeal to any deity when eating. They believe in the local gods (*dih*) which live in the tree over the village shrine (*mánrar*). They respect the house and will not bathe inside it. They will not touch the threshold on entering or coming out. When there is small-pox or cholera in a Korwa village, the Baiga makes a daily burnt offering with sugar and butter. When cholera appears, he goes to the village gods and says—"If you remove this pestilence, we will do extra worship to you." In cases of fever, which are regarded as of demoniacal origin, the Baiga prays to the local gods and prescribes a decoction of various jungle roots for the patient. Thursday and Friday are their lucky days, and the north and east the auspicious quarters of the sky. When a snake hisses rain is near; when the bees swarm it is an omen of good rain, but when they abandon their hive famine may be expected. Their only oath is to swear by their mothers, and this is the strongest oath which a Korwa can take. A man will not touch the wife of his younger brother or his sister. They sow, if possible, on the first Friday in Asârh. At sowing time the Baiga first makes an offering of butter and molasses in his field, and he is paid to make a similar offering at the village shrine (*mánrar*). They count the new year from the beginning of February (Phâlgun), when they give the Baiga a sieve full of grain, a contribution known as *kharwan*.

Food and social customs.

13. They will not eat the flesh of the snake, tiger, hyæna, jackal, iguana, tortoise, house lizard, and similar animals. Among birds they do not eat the

[1] See *Majhwár, para.* 45.

vulture. They will not eat locusts. They will eat the flesh of the bear, monkey, pig, ox, buffalo, and all kinds of deer. They also on occasions eat carrion. They use liquor, hemp, and tobacco as intoxicants, but not *gānja*. Liquor they believe keeps off malaria. Most of their food is, however, jungle products, such as the *mahuā* (*Bassia latifolia*), the *piyār* (*Buchanaria latifolia*), the *tend* (*Diospyros ebenum*), *sarai* (*Boswellia thurifera*), *ber* (*Ægle marmelos*). They also eat a number of seeds, leaves, stems, roots, and fungi, some of which are bitter or poisonous and require special treatment to make them wholesome.[1] Roots are dug with a special instrument called a *khanta* or "digger," which every Korwa carries.[2] It consists of a stick, on the end of which is fastened a long iron spike. They procure what they want in the way of food by exchanging forest products, such as *bahera* (*myrobalan*), lac, silk cocoons, and various jungle dyes and seeds. The young salute the elders by *pāélagi* or bending the left hand on the hollow of the right elbow: the right hand is then lifted up to the face with the word *pāélagi*, "I touch your feet," in reply to which the senior says "*Jiyo pūta!*" "Live long, my son!" They are considered so degraded that they will eat and smoke with Doms. clothes of both sexes are disgracefully scanty. But the women wear brass rings (*churla*) on the arms and pewter anklets (*pairi*). A few have now taken to working as ploughmen, but as a rule they pick up their living as best they can in the jungle and practically do no cultivation. The women are worked hard and roughly used at times. The tribe certainly does not do any iron work, as would seem to be the case in Bengal.[3] They are very expert in the use of the axe (*tāngi, bhalua*), and some can shoot fairly well at short distances with the bow and arrow. They are also expert in making fire by the friction of two pieces of dry bamboos. They smoke tobacco out of leaf pipes made of the leaves of the *sāl* (*Shorea robusta*).[4] The Korwas, on the whole, are much the most primitive and miserable tribe to be found in these Provinces.

---

[1] A full list of jungle products used by the Dravidian tribes is given by Dr. Ball in *Jungle Life*, 695 *sqq*.

[2] This is exactly like the *gadahla* or *gahdal* which Mr. Nesfield, *Calcutta Review*, LXXXVI, 23, describes as the distinctive weapon of the Musahars, *q.v.*

[3] Risley, *Tribes and Castes*, I. 512.

[4] Of some of these pipes recently sent to the Pitt Rivers Museum, Oxford, Mr. Balfour writes that he smoked one nine times, and that it drew excellently and was little burnt.

KUMHÂR.

Kotwâr.—(*Kotwál*, "the keeper of a castle.")—A small tribe containing only 97 persons recorded at the last Census only in the Mirzapur District. In Bengal the term is applied to a special tribe of village watchmen.[1] In the Central Provinces it is the name of one of the sections of the Halba Gonds.[2] In Mirzapur the name is only an occupational term applied to the Pankas (*q. v.*), in relation to their duty as watchmen.

Kunera, Kundera.—(Sanskrit *kunda-kára*, "a bowl-maker.")—A caste of village turners found along the Rîwa border in the Mirzapur District. Their business is making on the lathe the stems of tobacco pipes (*huqqa*) out of the wood of the acacia catechu (*Khair*). They are evidently closely allied to the Kharâdi (*q. v.*). They do not appear in the Census lists. They say that they were originally Bais Râjputs, and were driven by the tyranny of some conqueror to take to their present occupation. They are endogamous and say that they do not intermarry with a family with whom they have a previous connection by marriage until eight generations have passed or all knowledge of the connection has disappeared.

Kumhâr, Kumbhâr.—To the east of the Province, *Kohár*; *Konhár*.[3] (Sanskrit *kumbha-kára*, "a maker of jars.")—The caste of potters. There are various traditions of their origin. According to the Brâhma-vaivarta Purâna they are born of a Vaisya woman by a Brâhman father; the Parâsara Sanhita makes the father a Mâlakâra or gardener and the mother a Chamâr; while the Parâsara Padhati holds that the ancestor of the caste was begotten of a Teli woman by a Pattikâra or weaver of silk cloth. Sir Monier Williams, again, in his Sanskrit Dictionary describes them as the offspring of a Kshatriya woman by a Brâhman.[4] As a matter of fact, this respectable lineage is claimed by only one sub-caste, the Chauhâniya Misr. According to a Bengal story, a water jar was wanted at the marriage of Siva, and as no one knew how to make one, the god took a bead from his necklace and created a potter out of it; while with a second he made a woman, who became the potter's wife. By a legend current in these Provinces

---

[1] Risley, *Tribes and Castes*, I., 515.

[2] Hewitt, *Ráêpur Settlement Report*, 36.

[3] Based on enquiries at Mirzapur and notes by Munshi Sayyad Ali, Bahâdur, Deputy Collector, Partâbgarh, and Mr. W. H. O'N. Segrave, District Superintendent, Police, Basti.

[4] Risley, *Tribes and Castes*, I., 518.

the progenitor of the caste was one Kopa Bhagat, a Rishi, who was ordered by Parameswar to make earthen vessels. One day he put some vessels into his kiln, and it so happened that in one of them a cat had given birth to kittens. In those days it used to take a full year to make earthen pots; but by the prayers of the saint the pots were baked in a single day, and the kittens came out safe and sound. This happened on the Sakat chauth or birth-day of Ganesa; and since then, in honour of this event, Kumhârs will not load their kilns on that day. This Kopa Bhagat is said to have lived at Jagannâth, and hence Kumhârs regard it as their head-quarters. Another account is that in old days people used to work up the clay for pots with their spittle, and Parameswar, deeming this unclean, revealed the secret of the wheel. That the trade is an ancient one is shown by the fact that earthen vessels are mentioned in the Rig Veda.[1]

Internal structure.

2. The Kumhârs of these Provinces are divided into a number of endogamous sub-castes. The last Census enumeration classes them under the main heads of Bardiya or Bardiha, Bardhiya or Bardhiha, "those who convey their clay on oxen" (*barda, bardha*); Chakbais, or "the Bais of the wheel" (*châk*), who claim kindred with the famous Râjput sept of that name; the Gadherê who carry their clay on asses (*gadhê*); the Gola who make round (*gol*) vessels, or who, according to another account, are of impure blood; the Kanaujiya from Kanauj; Kasgar or Kûzagar, "makers of goblets" (*kas, kûza*), who are usually Muhammadans; Mahar; and Mathuriya, "those from Mathura." This, however, does not exhaust the catalogue. Thus, in Mirzapur we find, in addition to the Bardiha or Bardhiha, the Kanaujiya and the Gadhilaha or Gadhaiya already referred to; the Suariha or Suariya, who keep pigs (*sûar*) and are the lowest of all; the Churiha or Churiya, who are so-called because their women wear glass bangles (*chûri*), instead of the ordinary metal bracelet (*mâthi*); and the Athariya or Âthariha, who are said to be so-called because they use vessels of the shape of the Muhammadan *sahnaki*, of which the local name is *athâri*. In Benares Mr. Sherring adds the Hatheliya, who take their name from the handle (*hatheli*) with which the wheel is turned; the Kastora, who are the same as the Kasgar and

---

[1] Rajendralâla Mitra, *Indo-Aryans*, I., 274.

make water goblets (*surâhi*), cups, plates, tobacco pipe bowls of the *madâri* shape, and the ordinary pipe bowl (*chilam*); and the Chauhâniya Misr, who claim descent from Chauhân Râjputs and Misr Brâhmans. In the Central Duâb we find, in addition to the Mathuriya and Gola, who work by wheel, the Parodiya, who are moulders of toys. In Partâbgarh are found the Bardiya, the Purbiya or Purabiya or "Easterns," the Agarwâla, who follow the name of the well-known Banya sub-caste, and the Pahâriya or hill men. In Basti are the Dakkhinâha or "Southerns," the Chamariya, who have something to say to Chamârs, the Bardiha, the Kanaujiya, the Tikuliya, who make the forehead spangles (*tikuli*) worn by women, and the Kasgar. In Agra are the Bardhiya and Gadhwâr, which latter corresponds to the Gadhaiya already mentioned. The complete lists give no less than 773 sub-divisions of the Hindu and 52 of the Muhammadan branch. Those of most local importance are the Badalna and Mehra of Sahâranpur; the Baheliya, Baresra, Bharatdûâri, and Desi of Bulandshahr; the Bidaniya and Chakhri of Agra; the Dilliwâl of Bareilly; the Baheliya of Budâun; the Gaur of Morâdâbâd; the Gadhila of Shâhjahânpur; the Bakhri, Chakhri, and Pundîr of Bânda; the Kasauncha of Jaunpur; the Ajudhyabâsi, Belkhariya, Dakkhinâha, Desi, and Sarwariya of Gorakhpur; the Birhariya and Dakkhinâha of Basti; the Bahrâichiya and Daryâbâdi of Bahrâich; and the Râmpuriya of Gonda.

Marriage rules.

3. All these sub-castes are endogamous. Their rules of exogamy do not appear to be very strictly defined. To the East they generally follow the standard formula—*chachera, mamera, phuphera, mausera,* which bars the line of the paternal and maternal aunt and uncle as long as any recollection of relationship prevails. From Bareilly it is reported that they marry in their own sub-caste, but not in the families of relatives or strangers. In other places, again, this clannish habit of the Kumhârs is noticed, and it would seem that there is a tendency to marry in the families of neighbours and acquaintances. There is no trace, as far as can be ascertained, of the exogamous, totemistic sections found by Mr. Risley in Bengal. They generally practise monogamy; but a second wife may be taken with the permission of the tribal council if the first be barren. Marriage is both infant and adult, the former being invariably adopted by any one who can afford it. The actual ceremony is

performed in the way common to the castes of the same grade which has been already described. The respectable form is *byâh* or *charhaua,* the second *dola,* and the *sagâi* or *kâj* or *karâo* for widows. Widow marriage and the levirate are allowed on the usual conditions.

Domestic ceremonies.

4. The ceremonies at birth and death present no feature of interest. Those who are Hindus cremate, and those who are Muhammadans bury their dead. When a man wishes to separate from his wife or *vice versâ,* they appear before the council, and whichever desires a separation, breaks a tile before the other with his or her foot.

Religion.

5. The Kumhârs are mostly Hindus, but are seldom initiated into any of the recognised sects. To the east of the province their deities are the Pânchonpîr, Bhawâni, the village godlings (*deohâr*), and Hardiya or Hardiha. He who is properly the deity who presides over cholera, Hardaul or Hardaur Lâla, has become among them a household godling with much the same functions as the Dulha Deo of the Dravidian races. He is worshipped in the months of Kârttik and Baisâkh in the light fortnight with an offering of a pair of loin-cloths (*dhoti*) dyed with turmeric, two saucers full of rice with a piece of coarse sugar in each, some betel and areca nut (*pân supâri*), catechu (*khair*), cardamoms (*ilâchi*), and cloves (*laung*). The worshipper puts on the loin-cloths and his family eat the offering. Nearly every house has some sort of family shrine dedicated to this deity. The Pânchonpîr receive an offering of cakes (*pûri*) and sweetmeats (*halwa*) on the tenth day of the months Kuâr and Baisâkh. They are also, when sickness or other serious trouble comes, propitiated by the sacrifice of a goat, of which the head goes to the Dafâli or hedge priest and the rest of the meat is cooked then and there and eaten by the worshipper and his relations and friends. A young pig, cakes (*pûri*), and sweetmeats (*halwa*) constitute the offering to Bhawâni, and she also receives by deputy through the worshipper, who himself wears it in her honour, a coloured loin-cloth at the Naurâtra of Chait. Brâhmans do little for them, except fixing the lucky days for marriages and the commencement of other business, and their place at marriages and cremations is taken by the family barber. But, as in most of these tribes who hold rather a low rank in the social scale, there is a tendency to secure, if possible, a rise in the world, and this can be most easily

done by shedding off low customs like widow marriage and the like, and accepting the services of a Brâhman priest. Hardly any have as yet risen to the performance of a regular *srâddha;* but some of them offer sacred balls (*pinda*) and pour water on the ground in honour of the sainted dead in the holy fortnight (*pitra paksha*) of Kuâr. When a child is born, during a small-pox epidemic and in the month of Chait, women worship Sîtala or Mâta. The Kumhârs are, as the keepers of Sîtala's vehicle, the donkey, much addicted to this worship. They also, as we have seen in the case of the Agarwâla Banyas, bring their donkeys for use in the marriage ceremony. The potter's wheel (*châk*) is looked on by them as a sort of fetish, and is worshipped as a representation either of Krishna or of Prajapati, being the emblem of reproduction. In many places Kopa Bhagat, the tribal saint, is worshipped under the title of Barê Parukh, or "the great old man." This worship is mostly done by women, and his offering consists of bread, rice, and some *urad* pulse. In Basti they have a collection of local deities—Samai, Devi, Kâli, the village godlings (*dih*), Bhawâni, Chamariya, Korhaniya, and the Pânchonpîr. Samai is a jungle goddess like Bansapti Mâi, who is worshipped with blood sacrifices. At the last Census 37,584 recorded themselves as her worshippers. All these, except the Pânchonpîr, are worshipped with sacrifices of pigs, goats, and buffaloes, and with cakes, betel, and flowers. They are generally worshipped at the Naurâtra or the nine days of the waxing moon in the month of Kuâr. The objects of worship are consumed by the worshipper and his relations and friends. All the above-mentioned things are offered to the Pânchonpîr, except the pigs. They employ Brâhmans only in the worship of Kâli when a fire offering (*homa*) is made to the goddess.

Occupation and social status.

6. A very complete and interesting account of the Panjâb Kumhârs and their industries has been given in the "Monograph on the pottery and glass industries" of that Province compiled by Mr. C. J. Halifax, C S. The Kumhâr of the plains is represented in Garhwâl by the Pajai, some of whom come from the plain country, but some of whom are indigenous HandKiya or vessel-making (*hânri-karna*) Doms. In the Panjâb he is more often called Gumiyâr. Mr. Ibbetson describes him as "true village menial, receiving customary dues, in exchange for which he supplies all earthen vessels needed for household use, and the earthenware pots used in the Persian

wheel, wherever that form of well gear is in vogue. He also, alone of all the Panjâb castes, keeps donkeys, and it is his business to carry grain within the village area, and to bring to the village grain bought elsewhere by his clients for seed or food. But he will not carry grain out of the village without payment. He is the petty carrier of the villages and towns, in which latter he is employed to carry dust, manure, fuel, bricks, and the like. His social standing is very low, far below that of the Lohâr and not very much above that of the Chamâr; for his hereditary association with that impure beast, the donkey, the animal sacred to Sîtala, the small-pox goddess, pollutes him, as also his readiness to carry manure and sweepings. He is also the brick-burner of the Panjâb, and he alone understands the working of kilns, and it is in the burning of pots and bricks that he comes in contact with manure, which constitutes his fuel." As he cannot make pots during the rainy season, he is obliged to take to some other form of day labour, such as working as a carrier, plasterer, etc. At the same time it must be remembered that he deals only with the purer forms of manure, such as cowdung, road sweepings, and the like, and has no connection with ordure. In some of our towns such as Lucknow, Chunâr, and Azamgarh, he makes various kinds of ornamental pottery, toys, images of the gods, and the like. Only the Suariya sub-caste keep pigs and eat pork. The others eat mutton and goat flesh and all fish, except the river shark (*gûnch*). In these Provinces their social status is very low. One reason assigned for this is that he is a kind of butcher, because he cuts the throats of his pots as he takes them from his wheel. "Had they cut human throats," drily remarks Dr. Buchanan, "they would probably have attained a higher station." They profess not to eat food cooked by any caste but themselves; but this rule does not apply to the women and children. In the villages many have taken to agricultural work. Mr. Halifax calculates that in the Panjâb only one-third or one-fourth of the Kumhârs actually work at the pottery trade, and the proportion is probably not much higher in these Provinces. They are a quiet, respectable, industrious people, and seldom come before our courts.

Distribution of Kumhârs according to the Census of 1891.

District.	Bardiha.	Chakbais.	Gaderi.	Gola.	Kanaujiya.	Kasgar.	Mahar.	Mathuriya.	Others.	Muhammadans.	Total.
Dehra Dûn	14	1	...	435	...	...	...	...	874	...	1,324
Sahâranpur	1,886	...	...	..	...	94	6,625	...	5,904	936	15,445
Muzaffarnagar	...	...	...	8,548	3	58	4,329	...	954	1,148	15,040
Meerut	...	...	...	22,909	...	869	562	...	2.277	1,111	27,728
Bulandshahr	...	...	...	4,214	...	319	45	30	11,679	591	16,878
Aligarh	...	...	244	4,491	...	...	...	...	11,742	42	16,519
Mathura	...	...	511	7,114	...	...	190	191	2,795	5	10,806
Agra	1,256	3,972	5,568	3,476	...	...	10	132	1,724	...	16,138
Farrukhâbâd	7,169	214	91	288	11	...	83	41	135	1	8,033
Mainpuri	4,269	...	3,835	415	...	...	203	3	1,726	18	10,469
Etâwah	9,597	345	312	11	5	3	...	...	614	121	11,008
Etah	...	40	1,632	7,090	...	...	...	297	1,430	37	10,526

Distribution of Kumhârs according to the Census of 1891—continued.

District.	Bardiha.	Chakbais.	Gaderi.	Gola.	Kanaujiya.	Kasgar.	Mahar.	Mathuriya.	Others.	Muhammadans.	Total.
Bareilly	131	...	100	7,454	...	...	...	1,602	1,289	57	10,633
Bijnor	...	...	...	3,768	...	40	7,255	...	557	2,550	14,170
Budâun	67	...	...	6,960	655	28	...	107	3,610	40	11,467
Morâdâbâd	...	...	...	20,108	...	6	393	392	2,307	467	23,673
Shâhjahânpur	7,626	65	...	834	23	12	27	70	1,325	1	9,983
Pilibhît	3,881	...	155	667	...	56	...	...	708	115	5,582
Cawnpur	7,947	6,227	...	...	38	4	...	7	850	...	15,073
Fatehpur	2,040	7,339	...	...	38	...	...	...	555	50	10,022
Bânda	309	16,130	19	11	2	...	...	...	2,626	...	19,097
Hamîrpur	848	4,854	11	...	...	...	...	...	10,768	...	16,481
Allahâbâd	16,121	1,686	...	...	4,565	85	...	...	3,468	117	26,042
Jhânsi	3,733	...	2,179	...	...	...	...	...	898	...	6,810
Jâlaun	6,627	30	654	...	...	13	...	54	889	...	8,213

Lalitpur	3,143	...	47	...	...	...	...	...	371	...	3,615
Benares	...	...	...	...	14,282	...	...	...	2,144	...	16,426
Mirzapur	...	...	...	...	18,512	...	...	...	786	...	19,298
Jaunpur	1,848	332	...	...	23,110	...	...	...	1,742	...	27,032
Ghâzipur	145	...	...	...	15,830	...	...	...	195	29	16,199
Ballia	...	...	...	...	10,227	...	...	...	1,487	...	11,714
Gorakhpur	3,913	18	...	...	39,759	...	76	...	12,505	76	56,347
Basti	29,910	1,391	...	...	...	18	...	...	5,402	...	36,721
Azamgarh	...	133	...	...	31,170	...	...	...	1,256	11	32,560
Kumaun	...	...	...	...	...	...	...	...	1	...	1
Garhwâl	...	...	...	...	...	...	...	...	34	...	34
Tarâi	...	...	...	1,706	...	...	37	...	66	254	2,063
Lucknow	4,801	2,071	...	...	144	...	2	24	943	655	8,640
Unâo	5,666	1,604	...	...	14	...	...	...	3,533	82	10,899
Râê Bareli	9,021	3,019	...	...	30	...	...	...	995	330	13,395
Sîtapur	8,103	1,341	...	...	31	...	...	17	296	104	9,892
Hardoi	8,627	1,350	...	...	424	...	...	...	381	3	10,785

Distribution of Kumhârs according to the Census of 1891—concluded.

District.	Bardiba.	Chakbais.	Gaderi.	Gola.	Kanaujiya.	Kasgar.	Mahar.	Mathuriya.	Others.	Muhammadans.	Total.
Kheri	7,295	331	...	...	...	...	...	...	46	16	7,688
Faizâbâd	12,710	1,280	...	...	7,824	65	...	...	1,010	97	22,986
Gonda	15,458	321	...	...	...	...	...	...	2,048	244	18,071
Bahrâich	5,060	259	...	...	10	...	20	...	5,204	238	10,791
Sultânpur	12,107	1,528	...	...	2,026	...	...	...	1,831	138	17,630
Partâbgarh	9,612	823	...	...	228	...	...	...	789	...	11,522
Bârabanki	6,870	221	...	...	155	...	...	...	3,764	505	11,515
Total	217,810	56,995	15,358	100,499	169,116	1,670	19,857	2,967	118,533	10,189	712,994

Kunjra.—(Sanskrit *kunj*, "a bower, an arbour".)—The caste of greengrocers, who sell country vegetables and fruits. They are also known as Mewa-farosh, Sabz-farosh, or Sabzi-farosh. In Lucknow[1] the castes who usually deal in country vegetables and fruits are Kunjras, Kabâris, or Kabariyas (who more generally correspond to our marine store dealers and are dealers in all kinds of second-hand rubbish) and Khatîks. "These persons buy vegetables daily in the marts (*mandi*), to which they are brought by Murâos, Kâchhis, and others who are occupied in market gardening. They buy country fruit in the various seasons in the same way. Others buy up produce of fields, sugarcane, potatoes, onions, and other vegetables, store onions, potatoes, and other tubers for seed and for sale when the market is dear." Others deal in fruit imported by Kâbuli merchants. The Kunjra is returned in that name only in the east of the Panjâb, and probably in other parts of the Province it is more usual to call him Arain or Bâghbân.[2] In some parts of Bengal the term Kunjra is used in an abusive sense, and they call themselves Mewa-farosh, Sabz-farosh, or Bepâri.

Tribal organisation and marriage rules.

2. In Mirzapur they have two endogamous local sub-divisions—the Kalkatiya, "those of Calcutta," and the Mirzapuriya. The complete Census returns show 94 sections of the normal type—some local, as Gorakhpuri, Jaiswâra, Jaunpuriya, Kashmîri, Kolapuri, Purabiya, Sarwariya, Uttarâha; others occupational, as Bâghwân, "gardeners," Kabariya, "general dealers," Mewa-farosh, "fruit sellers," Sabzi-farosh "greengrocers," Tambâkuwâla, "tobacco men"; others are derived from well-known castes, as Bhûinhâri, Chauhân, Kahariya, Lodhi, Mehtariya, Râjput. They appear to be broken up into groups which habitually eat and smoke together, and with these they intermarry. Their rule of exogamy is that they will not marry any one with whom a direct relationship can be traced, but the recollection does not go beyond two or three generations. They can marry the daughter of a maternal uncle, but not of a father's sister. All marriages are made among families residing in the same locality. Polygamy is allowed, and a man may marry two sisters; but in the case of second marriages in the lifetime of the first wife, the permission of the tribal council must be obtained. Marriage usually

[1] Hoey, *Monograph on Trades and Manufacture*, 149, *sq.*
[2] Ibbetson, *Panjâb Ethnography*, 301.

takes place at the age of twelve or fourteen. The regular form of marriage is known as *charhauwa*, of which the binding portion is the recital of the Muhammadan *sharah*. Widows can marry by the *sagâi* form, and the levirate generally prevails. Divorce of the husband by the wife is practically unknown: a man may divorce his wife by leave of the council for unchastity. If her paramour be a member of another tribe, she is permanently excluded from caste: if of her own tribe, she can re-marry by the *sagâi* form.

Religion.

3. Kunjras are Muhammadans of the Sunni sect. Their clan deities are Ghâzi Miyân and the Pânchon-pîr. To the former they offer sweetmeats and garlands of flowers on the first Sunday in the month of Jeth; and to the latter the fruit of the *mahua* (*Bassia latifolia*), sweetmeats, and *sharbat*. They bury their dead in the recognised Imâmbâra. On the day of the 'Îd they offer vermicelli (*senwâi*, *siwaiyân*) and milk, and on the Shab-i-bârât *halwa* sweetmeats and bread to the souls of the dead.

Social status.

4. In the cities their women have an equivocal reputation, as the better looking girls who sit in the shops are said to use considerable freedom of manners to attract customers. They drink liquor and eat beef, mutton, goat's flesh, fowls, and fish. They will not eat the leavings of any other caste. They eat and smoke with all Muhammadans except Mehtars. Doms alone will eat food touched by them. Some now practise cultivating like the Kâchhi and Koeri tribes, with whom they are very closely allied, and are an industrious, well-conducted class of people.

Kurmi, Kunbi.[1]—A very important cultivating caste widely distributed throughout the Province. Various derivations have been proposed for the name. Some take it to be derived from Sanskrit *kutumba*, "family," others from Sanskrit *krishi*, "cultivation"; others from *kurma*, the tortoise incarnation of Vishnu, either because it supports the earth or because it is worshipped by this and some of the allied agricultural castes, or because it may have been the tribal totem. The Western Kurmis have a vague tradition that they are descended from, and named after, the Kauravas of the great Mahâbhârata war.[2] Recently some Kurmis in these

---

[1] Based on enquiries at Mirzapur and notes by Munshi Bâsdeo Sahây, Head Master, High School, Farrukhâbâd; Mr. W. H. O' N. Segrave, District Superintendent, Police, Basti; Pandit Baldeo Prasâd, Deputy Collector, Cawnpur.

[2] Dr. Oppert connects them with the Dravidian Kurumbas or Kudumbas. (*Original Inhabitants of Bharatavarsa*, 261.)

Provinces have claimed Brâhmanical origin and the right of investiture with the sacred cord.

Origin of the caste.

2. Regarding the origin of the tribe there has been considerable discussion. At least in these Provinces they have no tangible traditions which are of any service in ascertaining the origin of the caste. Dr. Buchanan asserts a connection between the Gorakhpur Thârus and the Kurmis,[1] but this rests on no satisfactory evidence. Colonel Dalton[2] regards the Kurmis of Bihâr as some of the earliest of the Aryan colonists of Bengal, a brown tawny-coloured people, of average height, well-proportioned, rather lightly framed, and with a fair amount of good looks. They show well-shaped heads and high features, less refined than Brâhmans, less martial than Râjputs, of humbler mien even than the Goâlas ; but, except when they have obviously intermixed with aborigines, they are unquestionably Aryan in looks. Grey eyes and brownish hair are sometimes met with among them. The women have usually small and well-formed hands and feet.

3. On this Mr. Risley[3] comments :—"The foregoing description clearly refers only to the Kurmis of Bihâr, who are on the whole a fine-looking race, though perhaps hardly so Aryan in appearance as Colonel Dalton seeks to make out. The caste bearing the same name in Chota Nâgpur and Orissa belongs to an entirely different type. Short, sturdy, and of very dark complexion, these Kurmis closely resemble in feature the Dravidian tribes around them. In Manbhûm and the north of Orissa it is difficult to distinguish a Kurmi from a Bhûmij or a Santâl, and the latter tribe, who are more particular about food than is commonly supposed, will eat boiled rice prepared by Kurmis, and, according to one tradition, regard them as half brethren of their own, sprung from the same father, who begot Kurmis on the elder and the Santâls on the younger of two sisters. The question then arises—Are these Kurmis a degraded branch of the Kurmis of Bihâr and Upper India, or

---

[1] *Eastern India*, II., 469.

[2] *Descriptive Ethnology*, 320.

[3] *Tribes and Castes of Bengal*, I., 529. On the other hand, Mr. O'Donnell writes :—"The statistics indicate very clearly, when read along with the similar figures for Bihâr, the ethnic origin of the Bauri, Dom, Dusâdh, Rajwâr, Koeri, and Kurmi. They are Dravidians of the full blood, with a small admixture of Mongoloid affinities in both Bihâr and Western Bengal. It is very doubtful if they have been in any way affected by contact with the Aryan."—*Census Report*, 175.

should they be treated as a separate caste formed out of Dravidian elements and owing their name to the accident of their having devoted themselves exclusively to cultivation? Colonel Dalton does not distinctly commit himself to either view; but it is clear from his account of the caste that he was conscious of the difficulty, and was on the whole inclined to dispose of it by the hypothesis of degradation. This theory, however, fails entirely to account for either the remarkably uniform type of the Chota Nâgpur Kurmis or for their totemistic usages. The latter point, however, appears to have been unknown to Colonel Dalton, and might possibly have induced him to change his opinion. Three hypotheses seem to be more or less tenable—(1) that the class Kurmi is made up of two distinct stocks, the one Aryan and the other Dravidian; (2) that the entire group comes of an Aryan stock, the type of which has been modified to a varying extent by mixture of blood and vicissitudes of occupation; (3) that the entire group was originally Dravidian, but that those portions of it which lay in the way of the Aryan invasion were refined by intercourse with the immigrants, while those settled in remote parts of the country preserved their primitive type."

4. The question can be settled only by the evidence of anthropometry, which has hardly advanced sufficiently to enable the matter to be settled. Most observers in these Provinces will be inclined to believe with Mr. Risley that the signs of so-called Aryan origin in the Kurmis are not so clear as Colonel Dalton found to be the case in Bihâr. But with a tribe so widely spread, and so exposed to varied influence, as the Kurmi, such a divergence in physical type is only to be expected. On the whole, perhaps it is safest, for the present to regard them as an occupational caste from which has, at various times, diverged a series of kindred castes, such as the Koeri, Kâchhi, Saini, Mâli, and others connected with the higher forms of husbandry.

Internal structure.

5. At the last Census the Kurmis were enumerated in eleven main endogamous bodies or sub-castes—Baiswâr; Bardiha ("bullock-men"—*bard, bardh*, "an ox"); Gangapâri ("residents beyond the Ganges"); Gujarâti ("residents of Gûjarât"); Jaiswâr ("residents of the old town of Jais in the Râê Bareli District"); Kanaujiya ("residents of Kanauj"); Kharêbind or "pure" Binds, which is a well-known division of the Bind tribe; Patariha, or Patthariha, "stone men"; Rârh; Sainthwâr or Saithwâr, who appear to take their name from

the *sentha* (*Saccharum sara*), a sort of reed grass, from the stalks of which chairs and stools are made; Singraur, who assert some connection with the Pargana of Singrauli in the Mirzapur District. Besides these, there is in the Azamgarh District the caste of Mals, who are apparently closely allied to the Kurmis. In Mirzapur we have the Jaiswâr; Chanau or Chananu; Patanwâr or "residents of Patna"; Sandhauwa or "washers of hemp" (*san-dhona*); the Patthariya, or workers in, and sellers of, stone, and the Athariya. In Farrukhâbâd are found the Kanaujiya; Kathiyâr; Gangwâr or Gangapâri; Jaiswâr; Sachân; and Bota. In Râê Bareli are the Kanaujiya; Gûjarâti; Chhappariya ("makers of thatches"); Patthariya; Khapribandh or "tilers"; Lakariya, "workers in wood," and Jaiswâr. In Gorakhpur are found the Patanwâr; Saithwâr, whom Dr. Buchanan identifies with the Ajudhiyas of Bihâr, who claim there to be of the highest dignity and the purest blood and are usually cultivators, while in Bengal they often enlist in the native army or serve as constables;[1] the Chanau; Dhelphora or "clod-breakers" (*dhela-phorna*); Sankatwa or Sankata, "hemp-weavers" (*san-kâtna*); and Audhiya of Ajudhya. In Cawnpur are the Sachân; Katwâr; Umrân; Bhandâri, "store-keepers"; Kanaujiya; and Patariya or Patthariya. In Kheri their sub-castes are Kanaujiya; Thakuriya; Kachhwâha; Haridwâra; Manwa; Jaiswâr; and Kori. The strongest sub-caste in Oudh is the Jaiswâr, who trace their origin to Kanauj, whence they say they were driven five hundred years ago by famine. In Gorakhpur they are divided into Kanaujiya; Bâhmaniya; Goyit; and Jaruhâr. In Râê Bareli the Kharêbind sub-caste is in some way closely connected with the Bais Râjputs. The sub-castes in Azamgarh[2] are Audhiya; Dhilphora or Dhelphora; Jaiswâr; Sankata; Sainthwâr; and Mal, who consider themselves superior, and regarding them it is said *Banal Mal, bigaral Kunbi*—"When the Mal thrives, the Kunbi fails." Mr. Sherring[3] gives their sub-castes in Benares—Kanaujiya; Hardiya or "growers of turmeric" (*hardi*); Illahâbâdi, "residents of Allahâbâd"; Brajbâsi, from Braj or Mathura; Kori, which is the name of a distinct tribe; Purbiha or Purbiya, "those of the East"; and Dakkhinâha, "those from the South."

---

[1] Risley, *loc. cit.*
[2] *Settlement Report*, 33.
[3] *Hindu Castes*, I., 326.

6. The complete census lists give 1,488 sub-divisions, of which those locally most important are the Gaharwâr, Kathiyâr, and Lohât of Farrukhâbâd; the Jâdon, Jadua and Kathiyâr of Bareilly; the Jâdon of Pilibhît; the Katwâr, Sunwân, and Uttarâha of Cawnpur; the Andhâr, Karjwa, Sahjan, Singraul, Uttarâha, and Uttam of Fatehpur; the Bargaiyân, Chandel, Chandpurha, and Chandrâwal of Bânda; the Simmal and Usrehti of Hamîrpur; the Chandel, Chandaur, Chandrâwal, Jariya, Jhamaiya, Karjwa, Sakarwâr, and Singraul of Allahâbâd; the Usrehti of Jhânsi; the Bhukarsi, Mahesri, and Usrehti of Jâlaun; the Usrehti of Lalitpur; the Uttarâha of Benares; the Gondal of Mirzapur; the Jhura of Ghâzipur; the Dhelaphor of Ballia; the Akrethiya, Audhiya, Bathma, Birtiya, Chandaur, Dhelaphor, Naipâli and Tarmala of Gorakhpur; the Samsoil of Basti; the Dhelaphor, Dhindhwâr, and Uttarâha of Azamgarh; the Jâdon of the Tarâi; the Bhûr of Râê Bareli; the Bâchhal, Gangwâr, and Kutwâr of Sîtapur; the Mewâr and Sankhwâr of Kheri; the Samâna and Samsoil of Gonda; the Khawâs of Bahrâich; the Birtiya of Sultânpur; and the Chaudhari, Kairâti, and Râwat of Bârabanki.

7. Their immigration to Cawnpur[1] must have followed that of the Thâkurs and Maliks because they occupied most inferior lands. One branch of them is called Jhamaiya, after a Faqîr, Jhâmbaji, who, about five hundred years ago, attracted persons of various castes, Banyas, Ahîrs, Kurmis, etc., to become his followers. As these partook of his food, they were expelled from their own caste. Many of their customs are more Musalmân than Hindu, *e.g.*, till seventy years ago they buried and did not burn their dead; certain mosques are attributed to them, and they marry among themselves, having regard only to nearness of relationship. There is a shrine in Maswânpur, Pargana Jajmau, where one of their notables is worshipped, more, it is said, with Musalmân than Hindu rites. They are curiously reticent about their origin and customs.

Marriage rules.

8. There appears to be no trace in these Provinces of the elaborate system of totemistic sections which are found in Chota Nâgpur. In Bihâr, according to Mr. Risley, "the section names are titular, and the tendency is to discard the primitive rule of exogamy in favour of

---

[1] *Settlement Report*, 26, *sqq.*

the more modern system of reckoning prohibited degrees by the formula of certain prohibited sections (*mûl*). Where the section rule is in force, it is usually held that a man may not marry a woman of his own section, or of the sections to which his mother and his paternal and maternal grandmothers belonged. These facts tell in favour of the theory that all Kurmis are derived from a Dravidian stock; for if the Bihâr Kurmis had been originally Aryans, they could have had no motive for discarding their original section-names; whereas a Dravidian tribe, intimately associated with Aryans and subjected to Aryan influences, would certainly be anxious to cast off totemistic designations, which would serve only as a badge of social inferiority. It should be observed, moreover, that even in Bihâr the Kurmis have not risen high enough to establish a claim to use the Brâhmanical *gotras*, and have had to content themselves with a titular series of names; while in Bengal they are excluded, on the ground of their Dravidian descent, from the group of castes from whose hands a Brâhman can take water." To the east of these Provinces the Kurmis practise a law of exogamy, under which marriage is prohibited with the family of the maternal uncle for five generations; with the family of the father's sister for the same number of generations; in their own family (*kul*) for as long as they can remember relationship. As in many of the castes of the same social grade, there is a strong prejudice against entering into a marriage engagement with a family with whom there has been no previous alliance or connection. From Farrukhâbâd it is stated that marriages still take place between the Kathiyâr and Bota sections, and that the rule of exogamy is that a man must not marry a blood relation on the father's or mother's side. In Cawnpur the rule is said to be that a man cannot marry in a family which is known to have a common ancestor with him; nor in the family of his father's sister or mother's brother; he cannot marry two sisters at the same time, but he may marry the sister of his deceased wife.

9. Polygamy is allowed, and practically a man may have as many wives as he can afford to keep; but there seems to be an increasing prejudice against the practice, and among some of the sub-castes there appears to be an advancing tendency to the adoption of the rule that a man should not marry again while his first wife is alive unless she is barren or incurably diseased. There is a preference for infant marriage where the parents can afford it, and

in any case it is considered disgraceful to keep a girl unmarried after she has become nubile. There is no regular system of paying for either the bride or bridegroom; but it is understood that her parents should give the bride a dowry to the best of their ability. A faithless wife can be divorced with the assent of the brethren, and, indeed, when adultery is notorious, it is incumbent on the husband to put her away. To the east of the Province at least a clear distinction is drawn between an immoral connection with a clansman and a stranger. In the former case, the divorced wife may marry again in the tribe by the *sagâi* form; in the latter case re-marriage in the tribe is forbidden. Widow marriage and the optional levirate, under the usual restriction that the elder brother of the late husband is barred, generally prevails; but even here there seems to be a progressing change in practice; to the East it seems to be generally allowed; of the Farrukhâbâd sub-castes the Kathiyârs and Gangwârs allow it; the Kanaujiyas have almost entirely put a stop to it; and a movement for its prohibition is in progress among the Kathiyârs. If the widow marry an outsider, the children and the property of the deceased husband pass to his brothers, who act as guardians of the children and provide for them out of their father's estate; but if the widow have a baby in arms, she usually takes it away to her new home, and there it passes into the family of her second husband.

Marriage ceremonies.

10. There is nothing very peculiar in the marriage ritual. In Bihâr they have a curious custom of tree marriage, of which Mr. Risley has given a full account; in these Provinces the only trace of this seems to be the rule that if the astrological signs portend that the bride may probably be left a widow, she is married to a *pípal* tree before the regular ceremony comes off. In the marriage of virgin brides (*shâdi, byâh, charhaua*) the binding parts of the ceremony are the worshipping of the feet of the bridegroom by the father of the bride (*pânw pûja*); the giving away of the bride (*kanyâdân*); the applying of red lead to the forehead of the girl (*sendûrdân*).

Birth and death.

11. The Kurmis seem to be particularly sensitive regarding the birth pollution. The mother is regarded as impure for fifteen days after parturition, and, as among the lower castes, though the usual sixth and twelfth day ceremonies (*chhathi, barahi*) are performed, she is still not allowed for some days to cook and join her family. When they adopt, a

brother's son is generally selected, and the only observance is the formal announcement of the fact at a tribal feast. They cremate their married dead, and bury the corpses of children and those who die of any epidemic disease. The death ritual is of the orthodox type, and they perform the *srâddha.* To the east of the Province some go to Gaya for this purpose.

Religion.

12. In religion they follow the rule of other Hindu castes of similar social standing. To the East their ceremonies are performed by Brâhmans of the Sarwariya tribe; further West by the Kanaujiyas. To the East they worship Mahâbîr, Thâkurji, Sîtala. Mahâbîr is worshipped on a Tuesday in Baisâkh or Sâwan with sweetmeats (*laddu*), sweet bread (*rot*), gram (*ghughuri*), a Brâhmanical cord (*janeu*), and a piece of cloth dyed with turmeric. Thâkurji is worshipped in an oratory (*deoghar*) attached to each house in the latter half of the month of Kârttik. They offer to him rice, treacle, and a cloth dyed with turmeric, all of which are used by the worshippers. He also receives flowers and garlands. Sîtala is worshipped on the seventh day of Asârh with an offering of cakes (*pûri*) and the *halwa* sweetmeat. In the Western Districts some few of them accept the *Guru mantra* or formula of initimation given by the spiritual preceptor. In Gorakhpur the household deity is Surdhir, who is worshipped by women in the month of Sâwan with the sacrifice of a young pig and rice boiled in milk (*khîr*). He is apparently the same as Sânwar or Kunwar Dhir, who, according to the last Census Report, is closely connected with the Pânch-Pîr and worshipped with the assistance of a Dafâli. In Basti they worship Mahâbîr and a household godling, Bâbi Pîr. The offerings to the former are received by Brâhmans, Gusâîns, and Mâlis and those of the latter by Muhammadan faqîrs. In Cawnpur they appear to be chiefly worshippers of Devi.

Social rules.

13. Their social status is respectable. They will not eat *kachchi* even if cooked by a Brâhman who is not their Guru. The same rule applies to *pakki.* Some local Brâhmans will eat *pakki* from their hands, and the same is the case with respectable Kshatriyas. All other castes eat *pakki* from their hands without hesitation. In Farrukhâbâd it is reported that they will eat *pakki* from the hands of Kâyasths, *kachchi* of Brâhmans; they will drink from the vessels of Banyas, but will smoke only with members of their own caste. Râjputs will eat

pakki from them, and Nâis and Mâlis their *kachchi*, while the latter will drink water from their vessels. In Oudh [1] they have traditions of having been land-owners before the Râjput conquest, and Mr. Butts remarks that the same is the case in Lucknow, where "they do not seem to have been a low-caste tribe. They worshipped Mahâdeva. In the village of Gadiya he is still worshipped under the name of Kurmiyâni Nâth, or 'Lord of the Kurmi race,' and of late years a small temple has been erected in his honour. In the village of Tîka is a tank at which, it is said, the Kurmi women used to commit *sàti.*" They very generally object to sow pepper and similar vegetables, which they regard to be the business of Kâchhis and Koeris. Many of them are Bhagats and will not eat meat or drink spirits; but some eat goat's flesh, mutton, and fish. They have a prejudice against eating the turnip.

Occupation.

14. They are about the most industrious and hard-working agricultural tribe in the Province. The industry of his wife has passed into a proverb—

Bhali jât Kurmin, khurpi hâth,
Khet nirâwê apan pî kê sâth.

"A good lot is the Kurmi woman; she takes her spud and weeds the field with her lord."

Her interest in the welfare of the crop is expressed by—

Ek pân jo barsê Swâti,
Kurmin pahirê sonê ki pâti.

"If only one shower fall in the asterism of Swâti, the Kurmi woman wears rings of gold."

At the same time he is in popular belief untrustworthy, and a Bihâr proverb quoted by Mr. Christian says—

Patthal par jo jâmê ghurmi,
Tabahûn nân âpan hokhê Kurmi.

"The tender creeper *ghurmi* will sooner grow into the stone than the Kurmi be true to you."

---

[1] *Sîtapur Settlement Report,* 73; *Lucknow Settlement Report,* 138.

Distribution of the Kurmis according to the Census of 1891.

District.	Baiswâr.	Bardiha.	Gangapârî.	Gûjarâti.	Jaiswâr.	Kanaujiya.	Kharêbind.	Patariha.	Rârh.	Sainthwâr.	Singraur.	Others.	Total.
Dehra Dûn	...	...	...	340	40	...	...	...	...	...	...	999	1,379
Sahâranpur	...	...	...	4	158	...	...	22	...	...	...	287	471
Muzaffarnargar	...	...	...	2	39	39	...	1	...	...	...	106	187
Meerut	...	...	...	...	...	...	...	111	...	...	...	2,242	2,353
Aligarh	...	...	...	...	...	...	...	...	...	...	...	67	67
Mathura	...	...	...	...	32	1	...	...	...	2	...	139	174
Agra	330	...	...	...	7	...	...	...	...	...	...	489	826
Farrukhâbâd	...	...	8,131	...	113	5,530	...	...	...	...	...	15,261	29,035
Mainpuri	...	...	...	...	16	152	...	...	...	...	...	149	317
Etâwah	...	...	225	...	59	1,641	...	...	...	...	...	249	2,174
Etah	...	...	...	...	...	...	...	...	...	...	...	21	21
Bareilly	...	...	60,717	...	...	10,157	...	...	...	...	...	16,436	87,310

Distribution of the Kurmis according to the Census of 1891—continued.

District.	Baiswâr.	Bardiha.	Gangapâri.	Gûjarâti.	Jaiswâr.	Kanaujiya.	Kharêbind.	Patariha.	Bârh.	Sainthwâr.	Singraur.	Others.	Total.
Bijnor	...	...	3	...	144	...	...	...	...	...	...	77	224
Budâun	...	...	6	...	...	5,851	...	...	...	...	...	517	6,374
Morâdâbâd	...	...	83	...	25	11	...	5	...	...	...	205	329
Shâhjahanpur	8	1	12,123	2	77	13,888	...	1	...	...	12	599	26,711
Pilibhît	...	2	42,328	...	1,758	2,114	9	56	...	...	...	2,066	48,333
Cawnpur	14	...	7	...	304	1,955	...	1,771	...	...	5	39,464	43,520
Fatehpur	...	...	...	...	77	11,140	...	...	...	...	1,032	28,049	40,298
Bânda	...	...	...	...	26	342	...	4	...	...	5,567	27,102	33,041
Hamîrpur	1	...	...	...	...	18	...	...	...	...	5	3,235	3,259
Allahâbâd	...	...	...	...	1,559	291	1,494	93,089	...	...	18,101	36,492	151,026
Jhansi	...	...	...	...	30	12	...	...	...	...	1	12,180	12,223
Jâlaun	...	12	...	...	32	14	...	101	...	...	...	15,406	15,565
Lalitpur	...	46	154	...	43	...	...	...	...	...	...	6,165	6,408

Benares . .	...	329	...	...	2,158	105	...	...	...	...	...	89,734	92,326
Mirzapur . .	2,757	360	...	...	40,147	57	...	16,249	...	...	975	7,459	68,004
Jaunpur . .	513	...	...	437	3,094	...	...	44,068	...	...	...	985	49,097
Ghâzipur . .	...	...	...	...	8,178	262	...	4	...	...	...	1,873	10,317
Ballia . .	...	...	...	...	7,757	439	1,146	...	...	...	...	2,200	11,542
Gorakhpur . .	...	...	...	1,946	49,773	464	442	14,563	...	98,626	...	35,787	201,601
Basti . .	...	...	...	15,927	122,813	...	...	5,292	...	...	...	3,685	147,717
Azamgarh . .	...	...	...	832	3,674	761	...	2,850	...	294	...	29,428	37,839
Tarâi . .	...	...	3,668	...	4	3	...	...	...	...	...	2,375	6,050
Lucknow . .	1,001	365	...	456	16,606	4,006	...	...	...	...	99	1,085	23,618
Unâo . .	...	...	...	...	365	11,101	...	...	...	...	...	6,318	17,784
Râê Bareli .	194	2,990	2	15,170	12,453	3,601	100	1,183	...	...	636	9,335	45,664
Sîtapur . .	56	2,427	...	58	58,361	10,291	...	...	...	...	...	14,460	85,653
Hardoi . .	...	...	...	...	...	1,400	...	...	...	...	...	17,728	19,128
Kheri . .	33,807	...	...	268	3,686	31,476	...	...	...	...	...	11,787	81,024
Faizâbâd . .	...	...	...	11,713	58,610	...	...	...	1	...	...	3,824	74.148
Gonda . .	...	...	...	2,031	90,820	...	...	3,558	...	...	...	21,789	118,198

Distribution of the Kurmis according to the Census of 1891—concluded.

District.	Baiswâr.	Bardiha.	Gangapâri.	Gûjarâti.	Jaiswâr.	Kanaujiya.	Kharêbind.	Patariha.	Rârh.	Sainthwâr.	Singraur.	Others.	Total.
Bahrâich . .	11	...	...	45,580	41,463	...	...	53	3,006	...	...	5,125	95,238
Sultânpur . .	...	83	...	...	26,825	243	7,501	793	...	...	...	4,478	39,923
Partâbgarh .	...	...	...	...	2,403	...	12,639	51,197	...	...	...	43,999	110,238
Bârabanki .	59,968	...	...	439	95,486	...	...	...	...	...	...	3,030	158,923
Total .	98,660	6,615	127,447	95,205	649,215	117,365	23,331	234,971	3,007	98,922	26,433	524,486	2,005,657

Kurwâr.—A sub-caste of Banyas found only in Etah and the Districts of the Rohilkhand Division.

Distribution of the Kurwâr Banyas according to the Census of 1891.

District.	Number.	District.	Number.
Etah	1,954	Morâdâbâd . . .	7
Bareilly	471	Pilibhît . . .	22
Budâon . . .	4,436	Sîtapur . . .	14
		Total .	6,904

Kûta, Kûtamâli.—A small caste found only in Bijnor, Morâdâbâd, Gorakhpur, and Bahrâich. They seem to take their name from *kûtna, malna,* "to pound," as their occupation is husking rice.

Distribution of the Kûtas according to the Census of 1891.

District.	Number.	District.	Number.
Bijnor	139	Gorakhpur . . .	530
Morâdâbâd . . .	3,009	Bahrâich . . .	351
		Total .	4,029

L

Lakhera (*lâh ; lâkh ;* Sanskrit *laksha-kâru,* " worker in lac ") the caste which makes bangles and other articles of lac.—Of these Mr. Baillie[1] writes : "Entries for persons shown as of the caste of Lakhera, Kancher, Manihâr, Chûrihâr, and Potgar, appeared with such irregularity from different districts, that it was considered necessary to make enquiry on the subject. The result was that Lakheras and Kanchers have been combined ; but Manihârs, though probably identical, kept separate. The accounts given by members of the caste of their origin are very various and sometimes ingenious. One account is that, like the Patwas, with whom they are connected, they were originally Kâyasths. According to another account they were made from the dirt washed from Pârvati before her mariage with Siva, created by the god to make bangles for his wife, and hence called Deobansi. Again, it is stated, they were created by Krishna to make bangles for the Gopis. The most elaborate account of their origin given is that they were originally Yaduvansi Râjputs, who assisted the Kurus to make a fort of lac, in which the Pândavas were to be treacherously burned. For this treachery they were degraded and compelled eternally to work in lac or glass. They are in status ordinary low caste Hindus, permitting widow marriage and divorce, drinking wine, but not eating pork. They make forehead spangles (*tikuli*) as well as lac and glass bangles." In Bihâr they are known as Lahera or Laheri, and Mr. Risley gives an account of them.[2]

Distribution of Lakheras according to the Census of 1891.

DISTRICTS.	Numbers.	DISTRICTS.	Numbers.
Muzaffarnagar . .	1	Farrukhâbâd	31
Bulandshahr . . .	1	Mainpuri	24
Mathura . . .	58	Etâwah	182
Agra	90	Etah	7

[1] *Census Report, North Western Provinces,* 1,321.

[2] *Tribes and Castes.*

Distribution of Lakheras according to the Census of 1891—concld.

Districts.	Numbers.	Districts.	Numbers.
Bareilly . . .	57	Benares . .	143
Morâdâbâd . . .	1	Ghâzipur . . .	1
Cawnpur . . .	55	Gorakhpur . . .	577
Bânda	111	Basti	87
Hamîrpur . . .	303	Râê Bareli . . .	223
Jhânsi	430	Gonda	348
Jâlaun	374	Bahrâich . . .	161
Lalitpur . . .	242	Bârabanki . . .	281
		Total .	3,678

Lâlkhâni,[1]—a sept of Muhammadan Râjputs, who take their name from Lâl Khân, their chief.—The Census returns obviously underrate their numbers. They claim descent from Kunwar Pratâp Sinh, a Bargûjar Thâkur of Rajor in Rajputâna, who joined Prithivi Râja of Delhi in his expedition against Mahoba. On his way thither, he assisted the Dor Râja of Koil, or Aligarh, in reducing a rebellion of the Mînas, and marrying the Râja's daughter, received as his dowry one hundred and fifty villages near Pahâsu in Bulandshahr. The eleventh in descent from Pratâp Sinh was Lâl Sinh, who, though a Hindu, received from the Emperor Akbar the title of Khân, whence the name Lâlkhâni, by which the family is ordinarily designated. It was his grandson, Itimâd Râê, in the reign of Aurangzeb, who first embraced Muhammadanism. The seventh in descent from Itimâd Râê was Nâhar Ali Khân, who, with his nephew Dûndê Khân, held the fort of Kumona in Bulandshahr against the English, and thus forfeited his estate, which was conferred on his relative Mardân Ali Khân. The chief families of the sept have their head-quarters at Chitâri, Pahâsu, and Dharmpur, all in the Bulandshahr District. The family, in commemoration of their descent, retain the Hindu titles of Kunvar and Thakurâni, and have hitherto, in their marriage and other social customs, observed

[1] Growse, *Mathura*, 19.

many old Hindu usages. The tendency of the present generation, and particularly of the Chitâri family, is rather to affect an ultra-rigid Muhammadanism.

2. They are often called Naumuslim, which is a general term for all recently converted Hindus. The customs of Naumuslim Thâkurs are a curious mixture of the Hindu and Muhammadan, as they intermarry only with Thâkurs similarly situated, maintaining the relative precedence of caste as among Thâkurs, and being generally called by well-known Thâkur-names. But their dead are buried; they are married by Qâzi, and they observe Muhammadan customs at birth, marriage, and death. They cannot, as a rule, recite the prayers or perform the orthodox obeisances (*sijda*). At the same time they worship Devi to avert small-pox, and keep up their friendly intercourse with their old caste brethren in domestic ceremonies; eating, however, apart from them.[1]

Distribution of the Lâlkhânis according to the Census of 1891.

Districts.	Numbers.	Districts.	Numbers.
Sahâranpur	2	Farrukhâbâd	8
Muzaffarnagar	170	Mainpuri	2
Bulandshahr	3	Morâdâbâd	81
Aligarh	127	Jhânsi	1
Mathura	2	Lucknow	9
Agra	42	Sîtapur	1
		Total	448

Lautamiya:—a Râjput clan found in Pargana Duâba of Ballia; they are a sturdy, independent race, and addicted to frays and feuds of a serious character. Their origin is doubtful, and they do not hold a high rank among Râjputs. Many of them used to be closely associated with the gangs of Dusâdh robbers for whom the Pargana was famous.[2]

[1] *Cawnpur Settlement Report*, 26.
[2] Oldham, *Ghâzipur Memo.*, I., 59.

Lodha[1] an agricultural and labouring caste very widely distributed through the North-West Provinces and Oudh.—Various derivations have been suggested for the name, such as Sanskrit *lodhra,* the bark of the tree *Symplocos racemosa,* used in dyeing; Sanskrit *lubdhaka,* "a hunter;" Hindi *launda, londa,* "a clod." Of the tribe in the Bulandshahr District, Râja Lachhman Sinh[2] writes:—"From their short stature and uncouth appearance, as well as from their want of a tradition showing their immigration from other parts, they appear to be a mixed class proceeding from aboriginal and Aryan parents. They call themselves the ancient inhabitants of the district, and we know from the Purânas that, among the forest tribes, there was one variously called Sodh, Bodh, Lodh, and Rodh. We also know that there was a large forest along and below Delhi on the Jumna. These may be the descendants of these foresters. In the districts below Agra they are considered so low, that no one of high caste drinks water touched by them; but such is not the case in the districts above Agra. Below Agra, they work chiefly as boatmen." Under the name of Lodhi they are found widely spread throughout the Central Provinces; in some places they have a reputation for turbulence and defiance of the law; they seem all to be comparatively recent immigrants from the direction of Bundelkhand. In Jhânsi they say that Narwâr was the original seat of the tribe after their immigration from Ludhiâna in the Panjâb, and that they came thence to Bundelkhand about a thousand years ago. In Lalitpur[3] also they claim kinship with the hill Lodhis of Central India, call themselves Thâkur, and are described as turbulent and ill-disposed. In Agra they are known as Pariya, which is the name of one of their sub-castes, or Purabiya, "Eastern," because they call themselves Bais Râjputs and immigrants from Dundiya Khera or Ajudhya. In Hamîrpur they call themselves Kurmi, Jariya, Mahâlodhi or Tandaiya. They were early settlers in Oudh[4] prior to the Râjput invasion, and were sufficiently powerful to offer a stern resistance to the invaders. They may possibly be an off-shoot from the great Kurmi tribe and

---

[1] Based on information supplied by the Deputy Inspector of schools, Agra; Bâbu Ishan Chandar Banarji, Râê Bareli; M. Râm Sahay, Tahsili School Mahoba, Hamîrpur.

[2] *Bulandshahr Memo.* 182, sq.

[3] *Gazetteer, North Western Provinces, I.,* 331.

[4] *Chronicles of Undo,* 25.

it is certain that physically they are more allied to the lower or so-called aboriginal section of the population than to any of the higher castes.

Internal organisation.

2. The Lodhas are divided into a large number of endogamous sub-castes. Among these, at the recent Census, were enumerated the Bhosiya or Bhusiya, "Chaff men" (*bhûsa*, "chaff"); the Jaiswâr, who take their name from the old town of Jais in the Râê Bareli District; Jariya; Khâgi who have been dealt with separately; Mathuriya "those from Mathura;" Patariha; Saksena from Sankisa in the Farrukhâbâd District; and Singraur. In Agra we find the Jariya; Patariya or Patariha; the Mathuriya; and the Antarvedi, "the inhabitants of Antarveda" (*antar*, "between," *vedi*, "a piece of flat ground prepared for sacrifice,") which was an old name for the Lower Duâb or the country lying between Etâwah and Allahâbâd, but is sometimes applied to the whole of the Ganges-Jumna Duâb. The women of the Jariya sub-caste wear bangles of lac and bore their noses, both of which practices are prohibited to those of the Patariya sub-caste. In Unâo they are sometimes known as Patariya after the sub-caste of that name, and they have three sub-castes:—Patariya, Jariya, and Kathariya, who probably take their name from Kathehar, the old name of Rohilkhand. The complete Census returns name 515 sub-divisions of the normal type. Of these, those locally of most importance are the Katâri and Mahra of Bulandshahr; the Mahuriya of Aligarh; the Bhagîrathi and Tarwariya of Mathura; the Sankhwâr of Mainpuri; the Dilliwâl and Purabiya of Pilibhît; the Sengar of Fatehpur; the Mohan and Mahur of Hamîrpur; the Barwariya and Mahâlodha of Jhânsi; the Bhadauriya and Sanaurhiya of Lalitpur; the Khâgi and Khargbansi of the Tarâi; the Bâtham of Unâo; and the Binaunân of Bahrâich.

Marriage rules.

3. All these sub-castes are endogamous. Their rule of exogamy is not very clearly stated; but it would seem that they avoid intermarriage with near relations, both in the paternal and maternal lines, and will not give a bride to a family into which one of their youths has intermarried within the period of ordinary memory.

Domestic ceremonies.

4. Their domestic ceremonies are of the normal type. Widow marriage and the levirate under the usual restrictions are permitted. Divorce is allowed

in case of adultery proved to the satisfaction of the tribal council; but for the first offence, the erring wife is merely reprimanded. Divorced women are not allowed to marry again within the caste. The betrothal is settled by the mutual exchange of presents between the two families. There is no bride price; but it is understood that the bride is provided with a dowry. In Unâo the betrothal is called Takahai, because the father of the bride puts two pice (*taka*) in the hands of the bridegroom and this settles the match. In Râê Bareli, on his marriage day, the boy eats a dish, called *lakhani*, made of rice and *urad* pulse, with the other boys of his own caste.

Religion.

5. They are all Hindus. In Agra Devi is their tribal goddess, but they also worship Râmchandra,[1] Kuânwâla, or the well godling, and Jakhaiya. Kuânwâla has a brick temple with three doors in front, and inside a miniature well, in which are placed two images. Cakes of wheat flour, boiled rice, milk, sweetmeats, and flowers are thrown into the well as an offering, and water is poured on the ground before the temple. The women dance and play on rude tambourines made of brass cups (*katora*). This worship is done in the month of Asârh. There is a famous shrine in honour of Jakbaiya in the village of Pendhat or Paindhat in the Mainpuri District. "There is no fixed day, but the latter fortnight of Mâgh or Asârh are chosen for these meetings (*jât*) on a Sunday. The story runs that during the war between Prithivi Râja and Jay Chand of Kanauj, an Ahîr was bringing his wife from home, and with him were a Brâhman and a low caste man, a Bhangi or a Dhânuk. The three men joined in the fight and were killed. The Bhangi fell first, and the other two fell at some distance from him. Even when dead their headless trunks (*dúnd*) continued the fight. The Bhangi became a Bhût, or malignant ghost, under the name of Jakhaiya, and the place where he fell is called Jakhaiya to this day. Droves of pigs are grazed here, and at the time of the great gathering the swine-herds will kill one of them for a trifle and let the blood flow on the spot. At the other place, where the Brâhman and Ahîr fell, there is a temple, and cocoanuts and the like are offered. People come in thousands from the surrounding districts, even from Farrukhâbâd, which touches the opposite side of the district,

---

[1] At the last Census 1,099,111 persons were recorded as worshippers of Râm-Chandra.

and pay their devotions here. The great object of the journey is to obtain offspring and have an easy child-birth.

"The worship is said also to have a good influence on the winter rains (*mahâwat*)"[1]

6. Another saint, worshipped by the Lodhas of Agra, is Sayyid Mohsin Khân, whose tomb is in the town of Ihtimâdpur. Lamps, filled with ghi, sweets, and flowers are offered to him, and the offerings are taken by the Musalmân Faqîrs who attend the tomb. In most of their villages they have a temple of Devi, to whom offerings are made of goats, sweetmeats, and a fire sacrifice. This worship is performed at night and in times of trouble. Kuânwâla and Jakhaiya are the special deities who guard children.

7. In Unâo they worship Brahma Deo, and the Miyân of Amroha and Jalesar, with offerings of boiled rice and cakes, the produce of the last harvest, in the months of Kuâr, Aghan, and Chait. When a son is born, this offering is made on a larger scale. The Faqîr, who officiates, receives a fee of eight annas and the greater part of the offerings. In Hamîrpur they worship Gusâîn, "the Lord;" they prepare both *pakki* and *kachchi* food for the occasion and offer a goat.

Social status and occupation.

8. As we have already seen, their social position to some extent varies in different parts of the province. In Agra they will eat *kachchi* only from the hands of a casteman or Brâhman. They will eat *pakki* from the hands of Halwâis; will smoke only with a man of their caste; and will take water from a Banya. Sanâdhya Brâhmans eat *pakki* from their hands; and Koris, Chamârs, Kahârs, Gadariyas, and the like will eat *kachchi*. In Hamîrpur they drink liquor, and eat pork, goat's flesh, fish, fowls, and eggs. All through the Province they are tenants and field-labourers, and are considered to be good agriculturists, with a special aptitude for growing rice.

---

[1] *Gazetteer, North Western Provinces*, IV, 748.

Distribution of Lodhas according to the Census of 1891.

Districts.	Bhosiya.	Jaiswâr.	Jariya.	Khâgi.	Mathuriya.	Patariha.	Saksena.	Singraur.	Others.	Total.
Dehra Dûn	...	...	678	...	...	2,001	...	...	277	2,956
Sahâranpur	7	10	1,246	...	992	43	...	...	484	2,782
Muzaffarnagar	...	27	64	...	16	35	...	...	1,200	1,342
Meerut	...	...	1,093	...	...	2,705	...	...	3,788	7,586
Bulandshahr	191	...	...	...	23,107	1	...	...	21,958	45,257
Aligarh	...	...	1,047	...	6,558	...	...	...	31,192	38,797
Mathura	20	...	62	...	6	72	...	...	2,509	2,669
Agra	...	...	1,006	...	15,833	4,829	...	...	1,551	23,219
Farrukhâbâd	...	...	272	...	270	1,306	...	...	267	2,115
Mainpuri	...	...	61	262	16,278	29,682	7,361	...	801	54,445
Etâwah	...	...	29,123	...	3,951	5,169	...	...	1,311	39,554
Etah	...	...	...	667	24,308	51,465	1,258	...	2,218	79,916

Bareilly	...	...	4,078	...	...	...	...	...	976	5,054
Bijnor	...	4	...	41	...	146	...	...	51	242
Budâun	...	...	4	...	4,767	966	...	...	72	5,809
Morâdâbâd	...	...	83	...	10,748	...	...	29	1,058	1,918
Shâhjahânpur	...	5	1,996	...	...	671	...	...	826	3,498
Pilibhît	...	...	23,137	...	81	...	...	...	12,974	36,192
Cawnpur	...	92	42,383	...	84	241	...	299	1,898	44,997
Fatehpur	...	...	34,559	...	...	90	...	11,160	1,511	47,320
Bânda	...	...	6,838	...	...	13	...	9,829	1,369	18,049
Hamîrpur	...	...	758	...	...	...	...	14	55,948	56,720
Allahâbâd	...	...	11,761	...	...	...	...	1,967	589	14,317
Jhânsi	...	...	13,490	...	...	88	...	...	13,182	26,760
Jâlaun	...	...	4,186	...	11	...	...	...	7,362	11,569
Lalitpur	783	...	15,759	...	...	61	...	...	12,103	28,706
Benares	...	6	...	...	...	...	...	...	14	20
Jaunpur	...	...	276	...	...	...	...	3	...	279
Gorakhpur	...	11	1,702	...	...	2	...	...	623	2,338

Distribution of Lodhas according to the Census of 1891—concluded.

Districts.	Bhosiya.	Jaiswâr.	Jariya.	Khâgi.	Mathuriya.	Patariha.	Saksena.	Singraur.	Others.	Total.
Basti	...	...	20,755	...	...	...	...	...	2,375	23,130
Garhwâl	...	...	...	...	...	...	...	...	16	16
Tarâi	...	...	2	...	1,716	658	...	...	1,982	4,358
Lucknow	...	...	43,168	...	24	870	...	...	9,935	53,997
Unâo	...	...	77,814	...	350	9,010	...	...	451	87,625
Râê Bareli	..	235	48,349	...	...	1,189	...	...	14,463	64,236
Sîtapur	...	...	30,518	...	...	10,389	...	...	366	41,273
Hardoi	...	...	5,281	...	...	206	...	...	1,026	6,513
Kheri	..	...	13,856	...	...	19,256	...	...	1,377	34,489
Faizâbâd	...	...	323	...	677	...	...	...	420	1,420
Gonda	...	...	9,613	...	208	127	...	...	6	9,954
Bahrâich	...	...	35,953	...	...	1,097	...	...	7,153	44,203

Sultânpur	...	...	7,326	...	...	...	...	...	43	7,369
Partâbgarh	...	...	628	...	...	...	...	...	98	726
Bâra Banki	...	...	24,193	...	...	10,673	...	...	622	35,488
TOTAL .	1,001	390	513,441	970	109,985	153,061	8,619	23,301	218,445	1,029,213

Lohâr[1] (Sanskrit *lauha-kára*, "a worker in iron," the blacksmith caste.—As Professor Schrader[2] has shown, the Indo-Germanic names for the smith have a threefold origin. They are derived either from words designating metals or metal collectively, such as the Hindi Lohâr and the Greek Chalkeus or Sidereus; or, secondly, from verbals which mean "hewing"; or, thirdly, substantives with the general meaning of "worker," "artificer," are specialised down to the narrower meaning of "smith." Such is the Sanskrit Karmakâra, "a blacksmith," which really means "workman" *par excellence*. It has been suggested that the Lohâr is ethnically connected with the Dravidian Agariya, or iron smelter, who has been separately described; and the evidence from Bengal to some extent corroborates this view.[3] But the Mirzapur Agariya does no blacksmith's work: all he does is to smelt the iron and work it up into rough ingots, which are afterwards converted into axe heads and agricultural implements by the Lohâr, who is admittedly a recent immigrant into the hill country, and utterly repudiates any connection with the iron-smelter of the jungles. The internal organization of the caste suggests that it is formed of many different elements, and is, in the main, of occupational origin.

Legendary origin.

2. Practically all Lohârs trace their origin to Visvakarma, who is the later representative of the Vedic Twashtri, the architect and handicraftsman of the gods, "the fashioner of all ornaments, the most eminent of artizans, who formed the celestial chariots of the deities, on whose craft men subsist, and whom, a great and immortal god, they continually worship."[4] One tradition tells that Visvakarma was a Brâhman and married the daughter of an Ahîr, who was in her previous birth a dancing-girl of the gods. By her he had nine sons, who became the ancestors of various artizan castes, such as the Lohâr, Barhai, Sunâr, Kasera, etc. By another tradition they are the offspring of a Brâhman from a Sûdra woman. Many of the Western Lohârs fix their original home at Mithila, whence they

---

[1] Based on enquiries made at Mirzapur and notes by M. Bâsdeo Sahay, Head Master, High School, Farrukhâbâd; the Deputy Commissioner, Sultânpur; the Deputy Inspector of Schools, Dehra Dûn.

[2] *Prehistoric Antiquities*, 154.

[3] Risley, *Tribes and Castes*, II, 22.

[4] Dowson, *Classical Dictionary*, s. v.

say they emigrated to Mathura with Sri Krishna. At the last Census, 18,805 persons, chiefly Barhais and Lohârs, recorded themselves as worshippers of Biskarma or Visvakarma.

The wandering blacksmiths.

3. Occasional camps of these most interesting people are to be met with in the districts of the Meerut Division. They wander about with small carts and pack animals, and, being more expert than the ordinary village Lohâr, their services are in demand for the making of tools for carpenters. weavers, and other craftsmen. They are known in the Panjâb as Gadiya or those "who have carts" (*gâdi, gâri*). Mr. Ibbetson [1] says that they come up from Rajputâna and the North-Western Provinces, but their real country is the Dakkhin. In the Panjâb they travel about with their families and implements in carts from village to village, doing the finer kinds of iron-work which are beyond the capacity of the village artizan. Of the same people Mr. Balfour [2] writes that they are called in Dakkhini Ghisâri, in Marhatti Lohâr, but call themselves Târêmûk. They worship Khandoba. Their marriages are conducted in the Hindu manner, but intoxicating drinks are largely used. They have earned a great name for gallantry, and it is very usual to hear of the rough Târêmûk levanting with another man's wife. On the occasion of a birth they sacrifice in the name of Satvâi. They burn the bodies of the married people and lay the ashes by a river's side; but the unmarried dead are buried, and for three days after the funeral food is carried to the grave, though they draw no augury of the state of the soul of the deceased from any animal eating the food. In the Dakkhin [3] this class of wandering blacksmiths are called Saiqalgar or knife grinders or Ghisâra or grinders (Hindi *ghisâna*, "to rub"). They wander about grinding knives and tools. "They are wiry men with black skins, high cheek bones, and thick lips. Latterly they have taken to shaving the head, but some keep the Hindu top-knot. Since their conversion to Islâm most men wear the beard. The women dress their hair rather oddly, plaiting each tress in a separate band." They make nails and tongs, and the women blow the bellows, and collect scraps of iron in towns as materials for their husbands' anvils.

---

[1] *Panjâb Ethnography*, para. 624.

[2] *Journal, Asiatic Society of Bengal, Vol.* XIII, No. 145.

[3] *Bombay Gazetteer*, XVI, 82.

Though never pressed for food, they lead a hand-to-mouth life, always ready to spend what they earn in food and drink. They say they are sprung from Visvakarma,[1] the framer of the universe, who brought out of fire, the anvil, the bellows, the sledge, and the small hammer. He taught them how to make Vishnu's discus, arrow, trident, horse-shoes, sword, and war chariot. When these were prepared and approved by their master, the caste came to be called Ghisâdi, and were told to make various tools and weapons of war. They are strong, dark, dirty, drunken, hot-tempered, and hardworking. In Ahmadnagar [2] "early marriage, polygamy, and widow marriage are allowed and practised, and polyandry is unknown. The women mark their brows with sandal paste when they bathe. On the fifth day after the birth of a child, an image of Satvâi is worshipped in Kunbi fashion, and the child is named and cradled on the seventh and ninth by female friends and relations, who are asked to dine at the house. The mother keeps her room and is held impure for forty days. On the day before the marriage the "god pleasing" (*devkârya*) is performed, when their marriage guardian (*devak*), the leaves of the mango, *ficus glomerata, Syzigium Jamolanum, Prosopis spicigera*, and *Calatropis gigantea*, are laid in a dining dish with a sword on them and taken to the temple of the village Mâruti, with music, and a band of friends, by two married pairs—one from the bride's and the other from the bridegroom's,—whose skirts are tied together. They are then again brought back and laid before the house gods until the ceremony is ended. The family gods are worshipped with the customary offerings, a goat or a sheep is slain in their name, and the caste people are feasted. All the rites connected with marriage, before and after the guardian worship, are the same as among local Kunbis, and the caste people are treated to a dinner at the house of the pair, or uncooked food is sent to their houses. When a girl comes of age, she sits apart for four days, and is bathed on the fifth, when her female friends and relations meet at the house, dress her in a new robe and boddice, and fill her lap with rice and a cocoanut. They mourn their dead twelve days, burying the unmarried and burning the married after the Kunbi custom. The son, or chief mourner, gets his face clean shaven, except the eye-brows on the

---

[1] *Bombay Gazetteer*, XX, 101.

[2] *Ibid*, XVII, 98.

tenth or twelfth, without requiring the services of a Brâhman priest, and, on the tenth, treats the caste people to a dinner of stuffed cakes and rice with split pulse. The death day is marked by a "Mind rite" (*srâddha*), and the dead are remembered in all Souls' fortnight in the dark half of Bhâdon, on the day which corresponds with the death day. They are bound together by a strong caste feeling, and settle social disputes at meetings of castemen. Breaches of rules are punished by fines, which generally take the form of caste feasts, and a free pardon is granted to those who submit."

It has seemed worth while to collect so much information about these people, because they probably represent the most primitive form of workers in iron, and are thus closely allied in function, if not in race, to the European Gipsy, whose chief occupation is that of the farrier and tinker.

The Lohârs of the North Western Provinces and Oudh. Internal organization.

4. The Lohârs of these Provinces include both a Hindu and a Muhammadan branch, of which the former is far more numerous than the latter. At the last Census the Hindu Lohârs were divided into nine main sub-castes :—Ajudhyabâsi, or "residents of Ajudhya;" Visvakarma, who take their name from their eponymous ancestor; Dhaman; Kanaujiya, from Kanauj; Lâhauri, from Lahore; Mahul; Mathuriya, "those from Mathura;" Ojha, or those professing a Brâhmanical origin, the word being probably derived from the Sanskrit *Upâdhyâya*, "a teacher;" and Râwat, which comes from the Sanskrit *Râjdûta*, "royal messenger." But this does not exhaust the catalogue of sub-castes. Thus, we find at Mirzapur, besides the Kanaujiya, the Mauliha or Mauliya, who are said to derive their name from the country of Malwa, and to be identical with the Mahauliya of Benares and the Mahul of the Census lists. Mr. Sherring names in addition the Sribâstava, who take their name from the old city of Sravasti : the Malik; the Banarasiya, "those of Benares;" the Chaurâsiya who, are perhaps called after Tappa Chaurâsi in the Mirzapur District; Purabiya or "Eastern;" Maghaiya or Magahiya, those of Magadh; Sinar and Mathuriya who derive their name from Mathura. In the Central Duâb their divisions are Tumariya, who assert some connection with Tomar Râjputs; Jholiya or "wearers of the wallet" (*jholi*); Gurhâbâdi; Logvarsha or Laungbarsa; and Siyâhmaliya, or "workers in black iron." Akin to these are the

Palauta of Bijnor and the Kachhlohiya, or "workers in unpurified iron," of Morâdâbâd. The complete Census returns show 736 sub-divisions of the Hindu and 114 of the Musalmân branch. Of these those locally most important are the Deswâli of Sahâranpur: the Lotê of Muzaffarnagar and Meerut; the Sengar of Jhânsi: the Gotiya of Lalitpur, the Byâhut, Gorê and Uttarâha of Ballia; the Basdiha, Byâhut, Dakkhinâha, Malik, Uttarâha of Gorakhpur; the Dakkhinâha of Basti: and the Gamela of Sîtapur.

The Ojha Lohâr or Barhai.

5. One sub-caste known almost indifferently as Ojha Barhai or Lohâr is almost entirely confined to the Central Duâb. They often call themselves Maithal or Mathuriya Ojha. The word Ojha, as has been already remarked, is probably a corruption of the Sanskrit Upâdhyâya "a teacher." They allege that they were brought to Mathura by Sri Krishna from Mithila. They claim to be of Brâhman descent and have provided themselves with a number of the ordinary Brâhmanical *gotras*:—Bharadwâja; Vasishtha; Gautam; Kasyapa; Sandilya; Vatsa, etc. These are all derived from the names of various Rishis from whom they claim descent. In Farrukhâbâd and its suburbs they are divided into some twenty-four groups (*thok*) each of which has a headman (*chaudhari*) of its own, to whom all social questions are referred. If the matter is not very particular, he calls a meeting of his group and settles it according to the opinion of the majority. In weightier cases members of the other groups are also invited to attend. Their rule of exogamy is in an uncertain condition. Properly speaking no man should marry in his own *gotra* according to the usual Brâhmanical formula; but as a matter of fact, few of them know to which *gotra* they belong and they simply use the ordinary rule which prohibits intermarriage between blood relations on the paternal and maternal sides. Polygamy is allowed, polyandry prohibited. Girls are married between five and fourteen years of age. A man may expel his wife for proved immorality, but this is no ground for a woman leaving her husband. Divorced wives and widows may re-marry by the *dharauna* form. In widow marriage there is no regular ceremony; but the man who takes a widow to live with him has to undergo some sort of expiation, such as bathing in the Ganges, feeding the brotherhood and distributing alms to

Brâhmans. The levirate is allowed under the usual restrictions, but is not compulsory.

6. No ceremonies are performed during pregnancy. On an auspicious day, generally on the third day after her confinement, the ceremony of *latadhoba* is performed when one lock of her hair is washed. This is followed by the *bâhar nikalna* when she leaves the confinement room for the first time. As a safeguard against demoniacal influences when she brings out the baby in her arms, an arrow is held in its hand by its maternal uncle who, as in other castes of the same social grade, bears an important part in these domestic ceremonies, probably a survival of the matriarchate. On the sixth day (*chhathi*) the mother and child are bathed again. On this occasion the goddess Bihi or Bihai Mâta, whose name is probably a corruption of the Sanskrit *Vidhi*, "Fate," is worshipped as the protector of the child. As soon as the child is born she is installed in the house and a representation of her is made on the wall with ghi. On the sixth day she is dismissed after being duly honoured with an offering of cakes, flowers, etc. As she is regarded as influencing the destiny of the child, on the day of her worship the baby is dressed in its best clothes so as to ensure it a prosperous life. Then the whole house is purified; a fire sacrifice is made; the family gods are worshipped; the child is named and food is distributed to Brâhmans. When they adopt, a regular deed of adoption is drawn up and the fact is notified to the brethren by a distribution of cocoanuts and sweets.

7. Marriage in the regular form is solemnised according to the standard Brâhmanical form; poor people, however, marry by *dola*, when the bridegroom's father goes to the house of the girl, brings her home and goes through the ceremonies at his own house. There is in the ceremony a survival of marriage by capture. A representation of a fish is made of flour and is hung by a string which the bride holds in her hand. She will not enter the house until the boy succeeds in piercing it with an arrow, which the bride tries to prevent by moving it about as he aims at it.

8. The death ceremonies are of the normal type and the usual Srâddha is performed. The birth pollution lasts for ten days; that of menstruation for seven days; that after a death for thirteen days. Their tribal deity is Durga. They also in the month of Mâgh make pilgrimages to the shrine of Shâh Madâr. The

offerings, consisting of sweetmeats (*revari*) flowers and pice are taken by the guardians (*khâdim*) of the tomb. Shaikh Saddu is the guardian of women and children. When a birth or marriage occurs in a family he is worshipped on a Saturday. The women fast and in the evening a Mujâwar is sent for; a sacred square (*chauka*) is made with cow-dung and offerings consisting of a he-goat, cakes, curry and rice are made. The Mujâwar pronounces the Fâtiha and takes away the offerings. A local godling known as Deota is also worshipped. Pilgrimages to his temple are undertaken in the month of Mâgh. The offerings to him consist of a cocoa-nut, a loin cloth and some pice. The marriage ceremonies commence with ancestor worship. Figures representing them are made on a wall with yellow clay and a lamp placed on a sieve laid on an earthen pot is kept burning near the place. Sweetmeats and other dainties prepared for the marriage feast are first offered to the sainted dead, and every important ceremony commences with an offering to them. This ancestor worship is confined to women. Snakes are also worshipped by women on the feast of the Nâgpanchami; if this worship be neglected, it is believed that some member of the family will be bitten. The *bargad* tree (*ficus Indica*) is also worshipped on the fifteenth of the month of Chait. Women whose husbands are alive fast up to noon and do not eat any salt that day. When they go to a *bargad* tree they make offerings of some grain, flowers and a lighted lamp and then go round it seven times holding in their hands a thread of cotton which thus becomes wound round the trunk. The Sun is worshipped on Sunday, a fast is kept and the offerings are made at noon. On this occasion no salt is eaten. The Moon is worshipped on the festival of the Ganesa Chaturthi or Ganesa's fourth. Rice and curds are given to the family priest, offerings are made to the Moon and then the worshipper breaks his fast. Offerings are made to fire daily when the family take their meals. They believe in the Evil Eye which is obviated by burning in the presence of the person affected a strip of cloth his exact height which has been soaked in oil; or a blue thread of the same length is tied round a stone and thrown into the fire; or pepper pods, wheat bran and salt are passed round his head and burnt.

9. They eat meat, goat flesh and mutton, fowls and fish. They use all the ordinary intoxicants; but excess is reprobated. They will eat *pakki* from the hands of Agarwâla Banyas, and *kachchi* from Kanaujiya Brâhmans. They will drink water from the vessels of these two castes, but will smoke the huqqah of none

but a member of their own caste. Gaur Brâhmans will eat their *pakki*; none but members of the caste and the lowest menials will eat their *kachchi*.

Ordinary Lohârs.

10. Besides these Lohârs who claim a Brâhmanical origin, there are large bodies of them which make no such pretensions. In the Hills many of them appear to be members of the great Dom race and from Pargana Jaunsar Bâwar in Dehra Dûn it is reported that the fraternal or family form of polyandry prevails amongst them and that a woman may have as many as five so-called husbands at a time. This custom, it is hardly necessary to say, does not prevail among those residing in the plains. To the East of the Province they marry their daughters at the age of eleven or twelve; there is, however, an increasing tendency in favour of infant marriage and the richer a man is the earlier he is expected to marry his daughter. Anti-nuptial infidelity is not seriously regarded, provided that it be inter-tribal, and is punished by a fine payable to the tribal council and a certain amount of feasting of the brethren. A man can marry as many wives as he pleases, or can afford to support; but few marry more than one wife unless the first be barren or hopelessly diseased. Widows may marry in the *sagâi* or *kâj* form and the levirate, though permitted, is not compulsory on the widow and is restricted by the usual rule, that it is only the younger who can marry the widow of his elder brother. The children of such unions rank equally with the offspring of virgin brides for purposes of inheritance. Adultery is not severely dealt with, provided it be not habitual or become an open scandal: for the first offence the erring wife is admonished by the council. A repetition of the offence leads to her formal repudiation and such a divorced woman may re-marry in the tribe by the *sagâi* form, provided her paramour has not been a member of a menial caste. In Oudh there is an apparent survival of marriage by capture in the custom by which the women of the bride's household throw packets of betel and handfuls of barley at the bridegroom as he enters the house. They have also a sort of ordeal to ascertain the prospects of married life. A necklace is thrown into a bowl of water and the married pair scramble for it; whichever succeeds in holding it rules the other.

Religion.

11. They profess to be Vaishnavas, but few of them are regularly initiated. To the East their clan deities are Mâhâbîr and the Pânchon Pîr, with the tribal founder Visvakarma. The Pânchon Pîr are

worshipped on a Sunday or Wednesday in the months of Sâwan, Kuâr, Baisâkh or Jeth, with an offering of rice milk (*khîr*), cakes (*pûri*) and garlands of flowers. They worship Mahâbîr in the same months on a Tuesday or Saturday with an offering of sweetmeats (*laddu*) and sweet bread (*rot*). They are ministered in their religious ceremonies by a low class of Sarwariya Brâhmans. They worship their implements as fetishes, the seat represents Mahâdeva and the anvil Devi. At this worship of the anvil they invite the clansmen on an auspicious day and then wash the anvil and offer before it what is called *agiyâri* by burning sweet-scented wood before it. This is done only when the anvil is first made, and the ceremony ends with a distribution of sweetmeats among the guests. In Dehra Dûn they worship Kâli, Aghor Nâth, and Narasinha Deo. The worshippers of Narasinha, the man lion *avatâra* of Vishnu, numbered at the last Census 164,555 throughout the Province. They are specially worshipped when epidemic disease prevails with sacrifices of goats and pouring a little spirits near the shrine. In Farrukhâbâd they have a household godling named Kurehna, who is worshipped at marriages, child-birth, and death. The worship is a purely household one.

Occupation and social status.

12. The occupation of the blacksmith is no doubt very ancient in India. He is mentioned in the Rig Veda,[1] but though Indian steel was prized even among the ancient Greeks, "in literary monuments iron can not be traced with certainty before the end of the Vedic period when the oldest names of the metal occur."[2] The country Lohâr is a true village menial. He makes and repairs the agricultural implements of his constituents and receives contributions of grain at harvest time. Thus, in Bareilly he gets from 7½ to 12 *sers* of rice or *kodon* millet in the autumn and barley or oats in spring per plough. He also gets 2½ *sers* of new grain per plough at each harvest as *niboni* and one sheaf per plough which is known as *phiri*. He also gets two for each sugar mill, two *sers* of coarse sugar per field of sugarcane, and his share of the thirteenth jar of cane juice which is divided among the workmen. In Sultânpur he receives one and a half *panseri* or measures of five village *sers* at the autumn, and sheaves representing 2½ *sers* of grain in the spring harvest. In the cities they have greatly improved their position and rank as *mistri*

---

[1] Wilson, *Rig Veda Intro.*, XL.
[2] Schrader, *loc cit*, 204.

or "master" workman. They make carriages and other articles of European style, shoes for horses and keep ironmongers' shops, selling cooking utensils (*tawa, karáhi*), axes, knives, chains, nails, screws and the like. Such a trader is often known as Luhiya or Lohiya. In these Provinces the Lohâr appears to enjoy a social position rather superior to that of his brethren in the Panjâb. There, according to Mr. Ibbetson "his social position is low even for a menial, and he is classed as an impure caste, in so far that Jâts and others of similar standing will have no social communion with him, though not as an outcaste like the scavenger. His impurity, like that of the barber, washerman, and dyer, springs solely from the nature of his employment; perhaps because it is a dirty one, but more probably, because black is a colour of evil omen, though on the other hand iron has powerful virtue as a charm against the Evil Eye. It is not improbable that the necessity under which he labours of using bellows made of cow hide may have something to do with his impurity." This feeling of contempt for the blacksmith is not modern. In the Purânas the Karmakâra or smith is classed as one of the polluted tribes, and according to Manu[1] iron is one of the commodities which a Brâhman or Kshatriya, obliged to subsist by the acts of a Vaisya, must avoid. It is at least possible that some of the disrepute attaching to the smith may be connected with his association with the vagrant, gipsy tribes of which evidence has been already given. This feeling of impurity is not so much felt in the East of the Province. In Bihâr[2] they are said to rank with Koiris and Kurmis, and Brâhmans take water from their hands. In the Eastern Districts their women are reported to be chaste. There they drink spirits and eat the flesh of goats, sheep and deer, as well as fish. They do not eat meat of other kinds. They will take *pakki* from Brâhmans, Râjputs and members of the trading castes, except Telis and Kalwârs. They eat *kachchi* cooked by their own castemen or by their religious teachers and spiritual guides. They smoke only with their own tribe. Râjputs of the inferior septs, traders, and all menials will eat *pakki* cooked by them. Bâris, Chamârs and other low castes eat *kachchi* cooked by them. They are, on the whole, quiet, respectable, and little given to crime, except that they will occasionally make the chisel (*sabari*) used by the professional burglar.

---

[1] *Institutes* X.88.
[2] Risley, *loc cit*, II. 24.

Distribution of Lohârs according to the Census of 1891.

DISTRICTS.	Ajudhya-bâsi.	Visva-karma.	Dhamau.	Kanau-jiya.	Lâhori.	Mahul.	Mathu-riya.	Ojha.	Râwat.	Others.	Muham-madans.	TOTAL.
Dehra Dûn	...	...	469	199	...	...	87	...	...	1,946	123	2,824
Sahâranpur	...	...	2,321	60	9	...	67	...	...	4,633	3,814	10,904
Muzaffarnagar	...	10	379	...	...	...	...	...	...	4,197	5,630	10,206
Meerut	...	...	...	...	...	...	...	...	...	6,267	14,928	21,195
Bulandshahr	...	...	...	..	...	...	74	...	71	1,530	8,558	10,233
Aligarh	...	...	...	...	...	..	...	...	311	1,129	2,862	4,302
Mathura	2	...	32	...	...	27	380	141	10	2,402	76	3,070
Agra	21	...	...	...	...	6	380	1,687	...	945	59	3,098
Farrukhâbâd	114	...	...	...	...	382	11,353	978	...	368	...	13,195
Mainpuri	293	...	...	...	...	...	667	2,325	...	223	..	3,508
Etâwah	504	...	...	...	...	476	3,474	1,079	...	1,897	...	7,430
Etah	15	...	...	...	...	20	687	199	...	229	2,839	3,989
Bareilly	...	...	...	...	247	...	5,491	222	...	196	4,707	10,863
Bijnor	...	...	171	...	164	...	...	...	...	77	4,353	4,765

Budâun . . .	...	...	...	...	...	...	1,717	11	...	260	5,031	7,019
Morâdâbâd . . .	...	...	...	...	57	2	114	...	...	281	11,118	11,572
Shâhjahânpur . .	...	...	...	...	19	7	11,348	50	...	258	1	11,683
Pilibhît . . .	...	...	...	2	12	...	8,100	...	...	184	303	8,601
Cawnpur . . .	277	...	...	38	...	16,229	700	108	...	726	...	18,078
Fatehpur . . .	198	...	...	...	...	10,975	13	31	...	1,042	...	12,259
Bânda . . .	17	6	...	...	...	6,857	...	...	6	455	...	7,341
Hamîrpur . . .	25	...	...	...	...	6,848	27	...	...	769	...	7,669
Allahâbâd . . .	...	87	...	3,277	...	26,747	...	...	...	688	...	30,799
Jhânsi . . .	12	...	...	25	...	667	741	33	...	2,993	...	4,471
Jâlaun . . .	...	4	...	...	...	1,029	770	...	...	2,934	...	4,677
Lalitpur . . .	26	...	...	...	...	69	697	...	...	2,919	...	3,711
Benares . . .	...	344	...	18,365	...	...	...	...	...	2,386	...	21,095
Mirzapur . . .	...	666	...	23,951	...	54	...	...	...	366	...	25,037
Jaunpur . . .	...	1,885	...	22,371	...	3,343	...	...	...	1,423	...	29,022
Ghâzipur . . .	...	140	...	15,953	...	4,261	...	...	71	2,378	...	22,803

Distribution of Lohârs according to the Census of 1891—concluded.

Districts.	Ajudhyabâsi.	Visvakarma.	Dhaman.	Kanaujiya.	Lâhori.	Mahul.	Mathuriya.	Ojha.	Râwat.	Others.	Muhammadans.	Total.
Ballia	...	...	...	3,009	...	4,410	...	...	...	10,224	...	17,643
Gorakhpur	29	7	...	25,587	...	1,845	698	...	...	26,517	...	54,683
Basti	...	...	...	4,385	...	14,365	...	...	...	2,717	...	21,467
Azamgarh	...	879	...	25,717	...	...	...	...	...	3,628	...	30,224
Tarâi	...	...	...	...	126	...	283	...	...	543	1,740	2,692
Lucknow	...	...	...	52	...	4,620	94	93	...	586	5	5,450
Unâo	48	...	...	19	...	7,737	37	...	...	882	...	8,723
Râê Bareli	...	...	...	6	...	8,772	1	...	...	1,245	...	10,024
Sîtapur	31	...	...	84	...	7,368	403	...	...	2,787	...	10,673
Hardoi	...	...	...	...	...	3,996	6,872	...	...	65	...	10,933
Kheri	3	...	...	5	...	6,087	3,246	...	...	379	1	9,721
Faizâbâd	...	730	...	4,268	...	6,305	...	...	...	1,838	...	13,141
Gonda	...	...	...	15	...	13,031	...	...	...	11	30	13,087

Bahrâich . . .	1	4	...	23	...	7,759	...	...	...	837	26	8,650
Sultânpur . . .	...	707	...	1,389	...	7,134	...	...	...	2,793	...	12,023
Bâra Banki . . .	...	...	...	1	...	8,429	...	...	...	305	...	8,735
TOTAL .	1,616	5,516	3,372	148,801	634	197,088	58,461	6,957	1,456	102,009	66,204	592,114

Lohiya (*loha*, "iron") a sub-caste of Banyas found principally in the Eastern Districts of the province. They have a tradition that they derive their name from their place of origin—a certain Lohiya Ban or forest, but they are clearly an occupational sub-caste and take their name from dealing in iron, though they now add to this other forms of trade and even agriculture. Some are Vaishnavas and some Jainas.

Distribution of Lohiya Banyas according to the Census of 1891.

DISTRICTS.	Hindus.	Jainas.	TOTAL.
Sahâranpur	7	...	7
Meerut	1,457	...	1,457
Bulandshahr	134	...	134
Mathura	8	...	8
Agra	7	19	26
Etah	4	37	41
Bareilly	40	...	40
Bijnor	819	49	868
Budâun	61	...	61
Bânda	33	...	33
Hamîrpur	8	...	8
Jaunpur	2	...	2
Gorakhpur	6	...	6
Tarâi	52	...	52
TOTAL	2,638	105	2,743

Lorha, a caste of rope makers, shown only in the Sahâranpur District, where they aggregate 2,622 persons. They are probably from their occupation menials and allied either to the gipsy Kanjars or to the Doms and Dharkârs.

Luniya, Nuniya,[1] a caste believed to be in a large measure of Dravidian origin, engaged in cultivation, saltpetre making, and

[1] Based on notes collected at Mirzapur and reports from the Superintendents Ethnographical Enquiries, Azamgarh, Sultânpur.

various kinds of earthwork. They take their name from the Sanskrit *lavana* "the moist", which first occurs as a name for sea salt in the Atharvan Veda. In the oldest prose salt is known as Saindhava or "coming from the Indus."[1] The salt sold in Bâzârs is Sâmbhar which comes from the salt marshes of Râjputâna at Sâmbhar, Dindwâra and Panchhbhadra; Panjâb rock salt is known as *Khâri non, Sendha, Lâhauri non,* or *Kâla non*; sea salt is *Samudri non.*

Traditions of origin.

2. The Audhiya sub-caste has a tradition that they are descended from an ascetic named Bidur Bhagat "who broke his fast on salt earth, and being thereby disqualified for the higher life of meditation was condemned by Râmchandra to betake himself to the manufacture of saltpetre."[2] Who this Bidur Bhagat was, the Luniyas of these Provinces are unable to say. He may possibly be identical with Vidura, the younger brother of Dhritarâshtra and Pându, who were all three sons of Vyâsa, but only the latter two by the two widows of Vichitavirya. When Vyâsa wanted a third son, the elder widow sent him one of her slave girls, and this girl became the mother of Vidura, who is sometimes called a Kshatriya and is one of the wisest characters in the Mahâbhârata, always ready with good advice both for his nephews, the Pândavas, and for his brother Dhritarâshtra. Another tradition common all through the Province asserts that they are Chauhân Râjputs of the Vatsya *gotra.* Their original home is said to have been Sambhalgarh, which appears to be identical with Sambhal in the Morâdâbâd District. The city was besieged by a Muhammadan king who was anxious to take the lovely Princess Padmâvati to wife. On the city being captured she took refuge in the house of the family Bhât. All the women of the family were paraded before the conqueror who recognised Padmâvati, but the Bhât insisted that she was his daughter, and to prove the assertion was forced to eat with her. So she was saved from the Muhammadan, and the Râja, her father, promised that his descendants would pay forever a tithe of their substance to the family of the faithful Bhât. Their descendants are said still to give certain dues to Bhâts. Another Mirzapur tradition makes the Bind, Luniya, Kewat, and Musahar tribes the descendants of a

---

[1] Schrader, *Prehistoric Antiquities,* 318.

[2] Risley, *Tribes and Castes,* II, 135.

creature who was produced by the Rishis from the thigh of Râja Vena; after this they produced Râja Prithivi from his body. In Azamgarh they say that they are the descendants of a certain Râja Sena who was a king in their original seat of power, Morâdâbâd. The Sultânpur tradition tells that during the war of the Mahâbhârata a boy was born of a Sûdra mother and a Kshatriya father, and was appointed by Yudhishthira to level his camp and gained his name because, in the course of his excavations, he came across a bed of salt. These traditions throw little light on their origin. It seems quite certain that they are connected with tribes of undoubted Dravidian affinities like the Kewat and Bind, and Mr. Risley hazards the conjecture that the Binds may be the modern representatives of an aboriginal tribe from which the Luniyas have branched off as saltpetre makers, and the Beldârs as earth workers. He adds that the hunting and fishing proclivities of the Binds seem to suggest that they are the oldest of the three, while the Bengal totemistic sections of the Luniyas stamp them as Dravidian. On the whole, perhaps the safest theory of their origin may be to define them as an occupational caste which has sprung from one or other of the local non-Aryan races.

Internal structure.

3. The internal structure of the caste in these Provinces is far from clear. It rather looks as if they were still in a transition stage, and that the endogamous sub-castes were as yet not completely organised. The last Census classes them under the heads of Ajudhyabâsi; or "residents of Ajudhya;" Bachgoti or "descendants of the sage Vatsa;" Bhagîrathi the descendants of the sage Bhâgîratha; Chauhân, the largest of all, who have, as we have seen, a tradition of Râjput descent; Deorâj and Golê. In Mirzapur they keep these divisions in the back ground and have a system of local sub-divisions known as *dih*, each taking its name from the parent village. Some of these are the Ninaur, Surahan, Hand, Kotakbai, and Jhusi-Arail, the last of which appear to take their name from two old towns in the Allahâbâd District situated on the Ganges and Jumna respectively. Those who have a common *dih* do not intermarry; and they have an additional law of exogamy which prohibits marriage in the family of the maternal uncle and aunt as long as relationship is remembered and recognised, which in their caste is within two or three generations. Another statement of the law of exogamy is that a man cannot marry in the family of his mother,

father, father's sister, in his own *gotra*, or with the elder sister of his wife. Another story again in Mirzapur is that the endogamous sub-castes are Luniya; Mallâh; Kewat; Kuchbandhiya; Bind; Paśkewata and Musahar. Mr. Sherring[1] gives an additional set of sub-castes in Benares :—Chauhân; Audhiya, who come from Oudh and make saltpetre; Musahar, who are palanquin bearers; Bind, who are servants; Bhuînhâr, "occupiers of land;" Lodha, field labourers; Paramtâri, none of whom are found in Benares, but reside in the country further west; Dasaundhiya, who may perhaps be connected with the tribal tradition of the union between Luniyas and Bhâts, and Bujâr. Another list from Mirzapur gives the endogamous sub-castes as Bachgotra Chauhân, who wear the sacred cord (*janeû*) and trace their origin to Sambhal; inferior Bachgotra Chauhâns who do not wear the cord; Bhuînhâr; Bin or Bind; Pachkauta or Pachkewata, who are allied to the Kewats; Lodha and Musahar. A list from Sultânpur gives them as Jaiswâr, Chaurasiya, Chauhân, Satkaha, Rautâr, and Mahto, all of which are endogamous. These are in a great measure different from the sub-castes of Bihâr[2] :—Awadhiya or Ayodhyabâsi, who are perhaps identical with the Audhiya of these Provinces, Bhojpuriya; Kharâont; Magaiya; Orh; Pachhainya; Chauhân and Semarwâr with their totemistic sections which the Luniyas of the North-Western Provinces appear quite to have shed off. In addition to all this the Luniyas of these provinces recognise two great divisions, the Pachhainya or "Western" and the Purbiya or Purabiya, the "Eastern" branch. The complete Census returns show 808 sub-divisions, of which those locally most important are the Bhagawati of Mainpuri; the Semarwâr or "cotton tree people" of Ghâzipur and Ballia; the Khairpuriya, Karot, and Semarwâr of Gorakhpur: the Semarwâr of Azamgarh: the Khemkarani of Râê Bareli, the Bagulah of Hardoi; the Mahton and Sankat of Sultânpur; the Bhagotiya, Khemkarani and Mangarha of Partâbgarh. According to Mr. Sherring the Bachgotra sub-caste, who do not wear the sacred cord, will in Benares give their daughters to the Bhuînhâr Luniyas, but not sons to their daughters. This, if correct, goes to show, as before suggested, that the endogamous sub-castes are not only of comparatively recent formation, but are even still in process of elimination.

---

[1] *Hindu Tribes and Castes* I. 348.
[2] Risley, *loc. cit*, II. 135.

4. Whereas in Bihâr adult marriages are considered unfashionable, if not disreputable, in the Eastern Districts of these Provinces, marriage takes place when the parties attain puberty, at the age of ten or twelve. In Sultânpur, however, they usually marry at the age of seven and, as in all the castes of a similar social grade, there seems to be an increasing tendency towards infant marriage. Infidelity prior to marriage, provided the offence be committed within the tribe, is lightly regarded. Polygamy is recognised and polyandry regarded with a feeling of horror. Marriage follows the usual form of *shâdi* or *charhaua* when the bridegroom goes to the bride's house, marries her there, and brings her home in procession, the binding part of the ceremony being the worshipping of the feet of the bridegroom (*pairpûja, pânwpûja*) by the father of the bride; *dola*, where the bride is brought home quietly, and any ceremony performed is done at the house of the bridegroom; and thirdly, *sagâi* for widows. In the latter case she very often marries the younger brother of her late husband, but she is free to marry an outsider if her brother-in-law be already married, and the levirate is not enforced. A man can turn out his wife for infidelity, and she can with the permission of the tribal council leave him if he does not provide for her or is proved to be impotent. All divorces must be sanctioned by the tribal council, and a divorced woman can marry again by the *sagâi* form, provided she has not gone wrong with a man of another caste, in which case she is permanently expelled from caste.

Marriage rules.

5. Luniyas do not become initiated into any of the recognised Hindu sects. To the east of the province their deities are Mahâbîr and the Pânchonpîr. To the former, the offerings consist of moist gram fried in butter or oil (*ghughuri*) and sweetmeats, and they are made on the tenth day of Jeth. To the Pânchonpîr are presented fowls, goats and pigs, and pulse cakes cooked in oil or butter (*malîda*) and rice milk (*khîr*). This offering is made on some Tuesday in the month of Sâwan. Some of them prescribe a special offering for each of this quintette of saints; for Subhân some sweets and a castrated goat (*khassi*); for Ghâzi Miyân sweets and a goat; for Bâba Barahna a delicacy known as *tosha* made of wheat flour, sugar and clarified butter; for Palihâr liquor and a cock; for Amina Sati a cloth (*palâû*) with a red border; for Bîbi Fâtima sweets.[1] She

Religion.

---

[1] For the Pânchpir worship, see Mr. R. Greeven's *Heroes Five*, and *Introduction to Popular Religion and Folklore*, 129.

is particularly worshipped by women. These offerings are shared between a Faqîr and the family of the worshipper. In Azamgarh they worship Mahâbîr with an offering of sweets on a Tuesday. Though they are Hindus, they worship Muhammad and the Imâm Sâhib, who represents the martyrs Hasan and Husain; they consider Amina Sati to have been the mother of the Prophet—a curious mixture of belief in the saints of Islâm among a purely Hindu tribe. In Sultânpur their deities are Agwân and Kul Deo, which is properly a term applied by Hindus to their family god. To Agwân they offer in the month of Aghan rice and *urad* pulse, and in the month of Phâlgun cakes, all of which are consumed by the worshippers themselves. To Kul Deo the offering consists of parched gram flour (*satua*) and the egg plant (*bhanta, baingan*) These are offered in Baisâkh, and in Kuâr he receives cucumbers (*turoi, kakari*). They offer water and sacred balls (*pindu*) to the sainted dead on the Somwati Amâwas, or when the new moon falls on a Monday and at the fortnight of the dead (*pitrapaksha*) in the month of Kuâr, on the last day of which they distribute uncooked food (*sîdha*) to Brâhmans.

Occupation.

6. Prior to the Râjput immigration into Oudh, they appear to have held considerable landed property.[1] Now their main occupation is making saltpetre, but they do earthwork and act as agricultural labourers and cultivate land. They drink liquor and eat goat's flesh and mutton. Those who worship the Pânchonpîr also eat pork. They will not eat food cooked by an outsider. All classes of Hindus drink water touched by them; but none but Doms and Chamârs will eat food cooked by them. They will also be seen in the commencement of the cold season digging field rats out of their holes in the rice fields, and these they kill and eat with the contents of their underground granaries. In Bihâr Mr. Risley notes that "they think little of Bhagats, who practise small forms of asceticism by abstaining from certain kinds of food and drink, and I am informed that very few Bhagats are found among them." Their women have a good reputation for chastity, and they are on the whole fairly industrious, respectable people, who are more adventurous in emigrating with their families than their neighbours. They will collect on a railway or other large work and take contracts for earthwork. The men dig and the women and children carry off the clay in baskets. They seldom come before the Courts except in connection with violation of the Government salt monopoly.

---

[1] Elliott, *Chronicles of Unâo*, 25.

Distribution of Luniyas according to the Census of 1891.

DISTRICTS.	Ajudhya-bâsi.	Bachgoti.	Bhagirathi.	Chauhân.	Deorâj.	Golê.	Others.	TOTAL.
Dehra Dûn	...	...	...	140	...	6	47	193
Sahâranpnr	...	...	...	260	...	...	98	358
Muzaffarnagar	...	...	...	...	...	...	30	30
Bulandshahr	...	...	...	30	...	...	164	194
Mathura	...	...	...	28	...	402	77	507
Agra	...	...	...	36	...	55	174	265
Mainpuri	...	...	...	149	...	698	1,436	2,283
Etâwah	...	...	...	566	...	518	1,356	2,440
Etah	...	...	...	52	...	1,335	1,203	2,590
Bareilly	...	...	...	...	...	...	36	36
Budâun	...	...	...	1,223	...	260	422	1,905

Morâdâbâd	...	...	...	...	...	39	...	39
Shâhjahânpur	...	...	...	1,269	...	259	758	2,286
Pilibhît	...	...	...	883	...	...	224	1,107
Cawnpur	...	96	2,021	201	10	142	1,033	3,503
Fatehpur	170	35	...	1,852	320	...	2,790	5,167
Bânda	445	...	...	222	20	24	199	910
Hamîrpur	1	...	...	...	...	...	74	75
Allahâbâd	447	37	...	5,246	52	...	3,255	9,037
Jhânsi	42	...	...	33	...	97	20	192
Jâlaun	...	6	...	...	...	...	...	6
Lalitpur	...	...	...	1	...	...	3	4
Benares	395	7,038	...	6,288	...	...	2,614	16,335
Mirzapur	...	4,618	...	6,898	...	...	404	11,920
Jaunpur	...	...	...	13,472	...	...	6,920	20,392
Ghâzipur	856	16,794	...	1,303	...	...	2,208	21,161
Ballia	2,112	4,199	...	...	...	...	16,063	22,374

Distribution of Luniyas according to the Census of 1891—concluded.

Districts.	Ajudhya-bâsi.	Bachgoti.	Bhagîrathi.	Chauhân.	Deorâj.	Golê.	Others.	Total.
Gorakhpur	2,117	30,150	...	11,313	30	...	26,309	69,919
Basti	84	3,405	...	18,049	...	...	210	21,748
Azamgarh	476	47,105	...	7,880	...	...	4,336	59,797
Lucknow	722	385	484	1,038	21	...	765	3,415
Unâo	64	47	489	12	48	...	2,261	2,921
Râê Bareli	...	...	...	253	726	...	6,959	7,938
Sîtapur	295	...	293	9,159	...	...	602	10.349
Hardoi	...	15	8	...	...	...	2,564	2,587
Kheri	623	...	...	12,750	...	...	650	14,023
Faizâbâd	148	4,677	...	6,782	...	...	284	11,891
Gonda	...	...	...	22,471	...	...	516	22,987

Bahrâich	690	117	37	13,471	...	...	6,383	20,698
Sultânpur	...	677	...	4,047	153	...	5,758	10,635
Partâbgarh	208	...	...	1,117	1,462	...	10,017	12,892
Bâra Banki	104	...	...	15,163	...	88	441	15,708
GRAND TOTAL	9,999	119,401	3,332	163,657	2,842	3,923	109,663	412,817

M

Madâri; Madariya[1]—One of the Beshara or unorthodox orders of Muhammadan Faqîrs who take their name from the famous saint Zinda Shâh Madâr of Makanpur or Makhanpur in the Cawnpur District. There are, according to the usual computation, four sacred personages—Châr Tan or Châr Pîr, *viz.*, Muhammad the Prophet; his friend Ali; Ali's eldest son Imâm Husain and Hasan Basari. Khwâja Hasan Basari had two disciples, Khwâja Habîb Ajami and Khwâja Abdul Wâhid Qâd. From these were sprung the fourteen Sûfi Khânwâdas or sections. Of these, nine groups were sprung from Khwâja Habîb Ajami, *viz.*, the Habibiya, founded by two brothers Mubârak and Muhammad; Tafûriya, founded by Tafûr bin Isa, who is better known by his other name Bayazîd Bustâmi; the Kharkhiya, founded by Shaikh Marûf Khârkhi, Khârkh being a quarter (*muhalla*) of Bâghdâd; Siqtiya, founded by Khwâja Sri Siqti; the Junediya by Juned Bâghdâdi; the Gozrûniya, by Abu Ishâq of Gozrûn; the Tusiya by Alâ-ud-dîn of Tûs; the Firdosiya by Shaikh Najm-ud-dîn Kulera and the Sahrwardiya by Abu Najîb Sahrwardi. The remaining five sects of the Sûfis were founded by the disciples of Khwâja Abdul Wâhid Qâd, *viz.*, the Zadiya, founded by the five sons of Abdulla bin Ouf; the Ayâziya by Khwâja Fazl-bin Ayây; the Hubariya by Shaikh Hubara Basari; the Adhaniya by Sultân Ibrahîm bin Adhan, and the Chishtiya by Abu Ishâq of Chist, a village in Khurasân.[2]

2. But as a matter of fact the Madâris of Northern India have no real connection with these genuine Sûfi sects, because their founder Shâh Badi-ud-dîn Madâr neither had any disciples nor was he himself a disciple of any of the genuine Sûfi sects. The fact seems to be that the Indian Madâris were established in imitation of the Hindu Jogis and Sannyâsis and their professed division of fourteen sections is based on that of these Hindu ascetics. Like Hindu Faqîrs they apply ashes (*bhabhût*) to their bodies, wear iron chains round the head and neck, and carry a black flag and turban. They seldom pray or keep fasts, and use *bhang* freely as a beverage.

---

[1] Based on notes by M. Mahadeva Prasâd, Head master, Zilla School, Pilibhit: M. Hâji Rashid Khân, Mirzapur.

[2] *Latâif Ashrafi*, Delhi Ed. 343: *Dabistân ul Mazâhib*, Bombay. Ed 169.

3. The following account of Shâh Madâr was given by the present manager of the shrine at Makanpur.—" Shâh Madâr had fourteen hundred assistants (*Khalîfa*) but no daughter. He adopted Sayyid Abu Muhammad Khwâja Irghawân, Sayyid Abu Turâb Khwâja Mansûr, and Sayyid Abul Hasan Khwâja Taipur. These persons were his nephews. He brought them from the town of Junâr in the Province of Halab and settled at Makanpur in the Cawnpur District where he died and was buried. The descendants of Sayyid Abu Muhammad Khwâja Irghawân were always noted for their learning and piety. Besides those whom he adopted he also brought with him Sayyid Muhammad Jamâl-ud-dîn Janman Janti, who is usually called Jamanjati and is buried at Hilsa near Azîmâbâd. He also brought with him his younger brother Sayyid Ahmad from Bâghdâd. Both these were the nephews of saint Ghaus-ul-Azam and he made them his assistants. With Jamanjati came two other brothers Mîr Shahâb-ud-dîn and Mîr Rukn-ud-dîn, who were also nephews of Ghaus-ul-Azam. Their tombs are at Shaikhpur Dharmsâla in the Cawnpur District, about two miles north of Makhanpur. Jamanjati was also noted for his piety and learning and thousands of persons benefited by him. His followers are known as Dîwâna; numbers of these are still in Hindustân and are called Malang. Among the assistants of Shâh Madâr, Qâzi Mahmûd, son of Qâzi Hamíd, whose tomb is at Kantut in Nawâbganj, Bârabanki, was a great worker of miracles, and his followers are called Talibân. Bâba Kapûr's name was Abdul Ghafûr. His tomb is in Gwalior, and he was an assistant of Qâzi Hamîd and Qâzi Mazhar Qala Sher. His tomb is at Mâwar in the Cawnpur District. Qâzi Shahâb-ud-dîn Shamsumar was a famous learned man in the time of Sultan Ibrahîm Sharqi of Jaunpur. Another Khalîfa of this family was known as Parkâl-i-âtish, and he was buried at Baragân. These four, *viz.*, Abu Muhammad, Jamanjati, Qâzi Mazhar, Qâzi Mahmûd were the most distinguished of all the Khalîfas in the time of Tâj Mahmûd. The greater part of the Dargâh at Makanpur was built in the time of Shahâb-ud-dîn Shâhjahân, Emperor of Delhi. Finally, Sayyid Tamîz-ud-dîn was a noted man in this family. The descendants of Sayyid Abu Turâb and Sayyid Abul Hasan are known as Khâdim. The family of Qâzi Mazhar are known as Ashiqân or "lovers." Other famous tombs of members of the sect are those of Mufti Sayyid Sada Jahân at Jaunpur; Maulâna Hisâmuddin at Jaunpur; Mîr Muiz Husain at Bihâr; Shams Nabi at Lucknow; Abdul

Malik at Bahrâich ; Sayyid Ajmal at Allahâbâd ; Shaikh Muhammad Jhanda at Budâun ; Sayyid Ahmad at Khuluaban; Sayyid Muhammad at Kâlpi ; Shâh Dâta at Bareilly ; Maulâna Sayyid Râji at Delhi. The date of the death of Shâh Madâr is 17 Jamâdi-ul-awwal 838 Hijri."

4. According to the best authorities[1] Shâh Madâr came to Makanpur in the reign of Ibrahîm Shâh Sharqi of Jaunpur. But the local legends would bring him to the time of Prithivi Râja of Delhi. Many wonderful legends are told of him. He is said to have had an interview with Shâh Muîn-ud-dîn Chishti from whom he demanded a place to live in. On this the Khwâja sent to the Shâh a cup of water full to the brim, by which he meant that there was no place available for his accommodation. The Shâh in reply placed a rose in the cup, implying that he would be a rose among the general body of Faqîrs. On this the Khwâja appointed as his residence the site of Makanpur which was then occupied by a demon named Makna Deo. Him the Shâh expelled and the place was called by his name.

5. Another legend tells that he used to practise the art of keeping in his breath (*habs dam*) which is still common among various classes of ascetics. At last he was supposed to be dead and his disciples carried him to his burial. But he sat up and called out that he was alive in the words *Dam dâram* and they replied *Dam madâr*, "Do not breathe." Whereupon he really died and was buried ; but he has since appeared from time to time in many places. By another story it was the Prophet Muhammad himself who gave him the power of retention of breath (*habs dam*) and hence arose his longevity, as the number of his respirations was diminished at pleasure. So he is said to have reached the age of 383 years when he died, and some say that he is still alive and so he is named Zinda Shâh Madâr. His devotees are said never to be scorched by fire and to be secure against the poison of venomous snakes and scorpions, the bites of which they have power to cure. Women who enter his shrine are said to be taken with violent pains as if they were being burnt alive, some of them leap into fire and trample it down with the cry *Dam Madâr ! Dam Madâr !* Mrs. Mîr Hasan Ali[2] tells a story of a party of drunken revellers who trespassed in his tomb, one of them became

---

[1] Cunningham, *Archæological Reports*, XVII, 102, sq.

[2] *Observations on the Musalmâns of India*, II, 321, sq.

insensible and died. Dr. Herklots[1] describes the rite of Dhammâl Kûdna. They kindle a large heap of charcoal, and having sent for the Shâh Madâr Faqîrs, offer them a present. The latter perform Fâtiha, sprinkle sandal on the fire, and the chief of the band first jumps into it, calling out *Dam Madâr!* then the rest of them follow him and calling out *Dam Madâr! Dam Madâr!* tread out the fire. After that they have the feet of these Faqîrs washed with milk and sandal, and on examination of the probable injury, find that not a hair has been singed; and that they are as they were at first. They then throw garlands of flowers around their necks, offer them *sharbat*, food, etc. Some having vowed a black cow sacrifice it in the name of Shâh Badi-ud-dîn and distribute it in charity among Faqîrs. In some places they set up a standard (*alam*) in the name of Zinda Shâh Madâr and erect a black flag and perform his festival (*'urs*) and sit up and read his praises, have illuminations and perform religious vigils. This standard is left all the year in its original position and never removed as those of the Muharram are.

6. Some of the Madâris are family men (*takyadâr*) and lead a settled life; the Malangs lead a wandering life. Some have rent-free lands (*mu'âfi*) and cultivate or live by daily labour or by begging. Others, who are perhaps different from the true Madâris, go about with performing bears or monkeys or snakes and are jugglers and eaters of fire. They are wild looking people and rather resemble Nats and their vagrant brethren.

7. General Cunningham quotes one of the songs current at Makanpur, which is interesting in connection with what has been stated above.

Nahîn Salon, Kâré, Hilsé,
Nahîn Jât Bihâr, nahîn jât Bukhâré,
Ajmeré, Muner ko kaun gané?
Ali aur hen Pîr anek barâré.
Jot akhandit, Mangal mandit, Shiu Pandit kavirâj pukâré.
Jâpar rîjhat hen kartâr,
So ânat duâr, Madâr, tihâré.

"Who goes to Salon (the tomb of Pîr Muhammad) Karra (the tomb of Shaikh Karrak), or Hilsa (the tomb of Jaman Shâh Madâri) ? Who goes to Bihâr (the tomb of Shâh Makhdûm) or

---

[1] *Qanûn i Islâm*, 158.

Bukhâra ? Who cares for Ajmer (the tomb of Muîn-ud-dîn Chishti) or Munér (the tomb of Sharf-ud-dîn Muneri) when a greater saint is here ? A brilliant light and a holy delight—so says Siva Pandit the poet—for he whom the Maker chooses to favour comes to the shrine of Madâr."

Distribution of the Madâris according to the Census of 1891.

DISTRICTS.	Number.	DISTRICTS.	Number.
Dehra Dûn . . .	106	Jhânsi . . .	50
Sahâranpur . . .	4,571	Lalitpur . . .	33
Muzaffarnagar . .	2,391	Benares . . .	207
Bulandshahr . . .	2,235	Jaunpur . . .	1,917
Aligarh . . .	4,860	Ghâzipur . . .	1,273
Mathura . . .	2,787	Ballia . . .	515
Agra	520	Gorakhpur . . .	4,488
Farrukhâbâd . .	1,702	Basti	13,083
Mainpuri . . .	2,022	Azamgarh . . .	3,864
Etâwah . . .	2,626	Tarâi	2,216
Etah	4,491	Lucknow . . .	2,816
Bareilly . . .	8,944	Unâo	3,936
Bijnor	6,970	Râê Bareli . . .	1,273
Budâun . . .	7,241	Sîtapur . . .	5,671
Morâdâbâd . . .	7,474	Hardoi . . .	6,716
Shâhjahânpur . .	2,234	Kheri	4,529
Pilibhît . . .	2,510	Faizâbâd . . .	2,206
Cawnpur . . .	2,046	Gonda	10,277
Fatehpur . . .	2,428	Bahrâich . . .	5,651
Bânda	275	Sultânpur . . .	928
Hamîrpur . . .	87	Partâbgarh . . .	985
Allahâbâd . . .	3,990	Barâbanki . . .	3,518
		TOTAL .	148,662

Mahâbrâhman[1]—"Great Brâhman", a term used in ridicule or contempt for the class of Brâhmans who receive the funeral gifts. He is also known as Mahâpâtra or "prime minister," and Kantaha or Kataha, "snappish." In Gorakhpur, according to Dr. Buchanan,[2] they are called Karataha or "Brâhmans, like crows, that ..., who follow carcasses."

2. Of their origin there is no satisfactory account; but it may be reasonably suspected from their appearance and functions that they are an occupational tribe of some menial origin who were introduced into Brâhmanism. They, of course, claim to be real Brâhmans, and the comparatively small number of them recorded at the last Census is almost certainly due to their repugnance to the use of the contemptuous term by which they are commonly known. They have simply recorded themselves as Brâhmans without further distinction. By one account they are descended from Drona Achârya, the instructor in the military arts of both the Kaurava and Pândava princes. Hence, in Bombay and Rajputâna, they are usually known as Achârja or Achârya. By another story when Dasaratha died there was no son present to perform the funeral rites. So a Brâhman took charge of the corpse till Bhârata arrived who did the ceremony and then gave the clothes of the king to the Brâhman as a reward. The Brâhman objected to receive the gift, but was induced to do so on the advice of Vasishtha. When Râma came and heard what had happened he blessed the Brâhman and told him that no one could complete the death rites of his father unless he worshipped this Brâhman and his descendants on the eleventh day after the death. By another account again, the Brâhmans and Kshatriyas once met together to decide who should receive the various kinds of gifts (*dâna*). Those families who agreed to accept the funeral offerings were cut off from other Brâhmans and have been degraded ever since.

3. Every tribe of Brâhmans, the Gaur, Kanaujiya, Sarwariya, and so on, have each their own Mahâpâtras. They follow the ordinary Brâhmanical *gotras*. Thus in Gorakhpur the Mahâpâtras of Pargana Dhuriyapâr belong to the Sândilya *gotra*, one of the three highest classes of Brâhmans. All grades of people accept them as

---

[1] Based on notes by M. Ramsaran Dâs, Faizabad: M. Mahadeva Prasâd, Headmaster, Zilla School, Pilibhit: and Pandit Râmgharib Chaubê.

[2] *Eastern India*, II, 497.

MAHÂBRÂHMAN.

their funeral priests. Mahâpâtras are endogamous and avoid their own *gotra* and the same prohibited degrees in marriage as ordinary Brâhmans. They have their parish or circle of constituents (*jajmâni*) like the ordinary Purohits. They themselves employ Brâhman priests; but are always regarded with some contempt.

4. The special function of the Mahâbrâhman is the receiving of the funeral offerings, consisting of the clothes, jewelry, furniture, and other things belonging to the dead man. By his vicariously wearing and using these the theory is that the soul is provided with necessaries and luxuries in the next world. Hence, it is needless to say, the Mahâbrâhman from his association with death, is regarded as an ill-omened personage. No Hindu will mention his name in the morning before breakfast; in the Panjâb he rides on an ass, people are very chary about meeting them on the road, and when an official is receiving petitions the voice of a Mahâbrâhman answering his name makes all those in his neighbourhood give way and draw in their skirts. It is chaff against him that he watches the mortuary register for the death of a rich Mahâjan.

Distribution of the Mahâbrâhmans according to the Census of 1891.

DISTRICTS.	Achârj.	Kanaujiya.	Sarwariya.	Others.	TOTAL.
Dehra Dûn . .	...	...	...	59	59
Sahâranpur . .	673	...	...	193	866
Muzaffarnagar . .	426	...	...	219	645
Bulandshahr . .	350	...	...	246	596
Aligarh . . .	...	...	...	39	39
Mathura . . .	...	...	...	204	204
Agra	...	...	...	63	63
Farrukhâbad . .	...	...	...	22	22
Mainpuri . . .	...	...	...	129	129
Etâwah . . .	...	...	...	92	92
Etah	...	...	...	9	9
Bareilly . . .	...	12	...	121	133

Distribution of the Mahâbrâhmans according to the Census of 1891—contd.

DISTRICTS.	Achârj.	Kanaujiya.	Sarwariya.	Others.	TOTAL.
Bijnor	309	...	...	...	309
Budâun	...	...	...	230	230
Morâdâbâd	3	...	...	559	562
Shâhjahânpur	15	...	...	291	306
Pilibhît	300	29	...	64	393
Cawnpur	...	...	...	30	30
Fatehpur	...	...	...	39	39
Bânda	...	120	85	216	421
Hamîrpur	...	...	...	4	4
Allahâbâd	...	...	25	4	29
Benares	...	...	...	704	704
Mirzapur	...	...	...	199	199
Jaunpur	...	...	...	359	359
Ghâzipur	...	...	...	2,188	2,188
Ballia	...	...	...	3,261	3,261
Gorakhpur	...	...	559	868	1,427
Basti	...	...	...	153	153
Azamgarh	...	26	1,025	329	1,380
Tarâi	...	...	...	11	11
Lucknow	6	159	1	112	278
Unâo	...	98	...	52	150
Râê Bareli	...	...	...	414	414
Sîtapur	710	2	...	236	948
Hardoi	...	...	...	531	531
Kheri	224	73	...	97	394
Faizâbâd	...	...	...	219	219
Gonda	...	...	...	204	204

Distribution of the Mahâbrâhmans according to the Census of 1891—concld.

Districts.	Achârj.	Kanaujiya.	Sarwariya.	Others.	Total.
Bahrâich . . .	...	...	3	477	480
Sultânpur . . .	...	...	606	51	657
Partâbgarh . . .	...	...	485	...	485
Bârabanki . . .	...	38	83	86	207
Total	3,016	557	2,872	13,384	19,829

Mahâjan (*mahá*, "great;" *jan* Sanskrit *jana*, "man") a term generally applied to the higher class of banker and money lender, a title of a sub-caste of Banyas. Those in Etah are said to be descended from a Mahâjan and a Dhobi woman. The higher sub-castes of Banyas will not in consequence drink from their vessels. They are believed to have originally come from Mathura. They have *gotras*—Mâhur, Gulahri, Tînwâla, Kalâr, and Satwâla. The Tînwâla and Kalâr take liquor shops.

Distribution of Mahâjans according to the Census of 1891.

Districts.	Number.	Districts.	Number.
Bulandshahr . .	303	Budâun	13,140
Aligarh . . .	6,024	Morâdâbâd	57
Agra . . .	722	Shâhjahânpur . .	9,142
Farrukhâbâd . .	15,988	Pilibhît	642
Mainpuri . . .	15,995	Cawnpur	1
Etâwah . . .	11,293	Jâlaun	18
Etah	14,841	Tarâi . . .	272
Bareilly . . .	2,769	Kheri	2
		Total .	91,214

Mahârâshtra—"The great country," a local group of Brâhmans who occupy what is known as the Marhâta country. It is to be remarked that in some of the Purânas the form used is Mallarâshtra and its name has been interpreted as "the country of the Mahârs," a tribe of outcastes still found there. They have been identified with the Porauuroi of Ptolemy. Their principal settlement in these provinces is at Benares where they hold a very high rank for learning and theology. Dr. Wilson,[1] who gives a very full account of them, treats them under the heads of Desashtha; Kon[illegible]nastha; Karhâda, about whom there is a curious tradition of human sacrifice; Kânva; Madhyandina, who are perhaps referred to in Arrian;[2] Pâdhya; Devarukha; Palâsa; Kîrvanta; Tirgula; Javala; Abhîra; Sâvasa; Hasta; Kunda; Rânda Golika; Brâhman Jais; Sopâra; Khisti; Husaini; Kalanki; Shenavi.

Distribution of Mahârâshtra Brâhmans according to the Census of 1891.

Districts.	Number.	Districts.	Number.
Sahâranpur . . .	9	Fatehpur	4
Muzaffarnagar . .	20	Bânda	118
Bulandshahr . .	3	Hamîrpur . . .	75
Aligarh . . .	5	Allahâbâd . . .	1
Mathura . . .	100	Jhânsi	211
Agra	141	Jâlaun	559
Farrukhâbâd . .	8	Lalitpur . . .	1
Mainpuri . . .	68	Benares . . .	2,253
Etâwah . . .	4	Ghâzipur . .	71
Bareilly . . .	4	Gorakhpur . .	13
Bijnor . . .	11	Basti	8
Budâun . . .	13	Kumaun . . .	242
Morâdâbâd . . .	39	Garhwâl	62
Shâhjahânpur . .	43	Tarâi	175
Pilibhît . . .	2	Lucknow . . .	3
Cawnpur . . .	329	Gonda	5
		Total .	4,600

[1] *Indian Caste*, II, 17, sqq.

[2] McCrindle, *Megasthenes and Arrian*, 186; Max Müller, *Ancient Sanskrit Literature*, 333, 106: Weber, *History of Indian Literature*, 106: Oppert, *Original inhabitants of Bharatavarsa*, 22.

Mahesri, Maheswari[1] (*Mahesa*, "the great lord," an epithet of Siva) a sub-caste of Banyas found chiefly in the Western Districts. The Mahesris of these Provinces connect their origin with a place called Didwâna in the Jeypur State. By one form of the legend Sujât Sen, Râja of Khandela in Jaypur, had no son. The Pandits directed him to go into the forest and told him that by digging under a certain tree he would find an image of Mahâdeva, and that then he would have a son. The Râja did as he was told, and finding the image requested Mahâdeva to give him a son. The god granted his prayer, and while his heir was still a boy the Râja died. One day the prince went to hunt in the forest and there came upon a party of Rishis engaged in their austerities. There was a tank close by where the prince and his followers washed their weapons; whereupon the water became as red as blood. The Rishis believed that the prince and his followers were Râkshasas; so to prevent them from doing any harm they built a fort of iron round them. This fort stands to the present day and is known as Lohâgarh or "the iron fort." Immediately out of the fort came a voice saying "Strike! Strike!" (*mâr! mâr!*). The Râja went to see what this voice meant and when the Rishis saw him they cursed him and his seventy-two followers, and they were turned into stone. When the Rânis heard of the fate of the prince they started for Lohâgarh intending to become Sati with him. But when they had erected the funeral pyre and were about to mount it, Siva appeared and gratified at their devotion, stopped the sacrifice. Then he turned the stones into men again, and told them to give up the profession of arms and take to trade. After that the Râja became their tribal bard (Bhât or Jâga) and from his followers were formed the seventy-two *gotras* of the Maheswaris. By another form of the story the prince tried to force his way into the sacred ground in order to witness a sacrifice which the Rishis were about to perform, when they were turned into stone and revived by Siva at the intercession of Pârvati. They got the name of Maheswari because they were brought to life by Mahesa or Siva.

Internal structure.

2. It has been found impossible to procure a full list of the seventy-two *gotras* in these provinces. The following list has been prepared from two

---

[1] Based on enquiries at Mirzapur, and a note by the Deputy Inspector of Schools, Pilibhit.

imperfect lists, one from Mirzapur, the other from Pilibhît:—Ajmeri; Augar; Bahari; Baldua; Bângar or Bânghar; Baryal; Begi; Bhandâri; Bhutra; Bihâni; Binnâni; Chandak; Chitlângya; Dâga; Dammâri; Daurâni; Dhut; Heriya; Jagu; Jharkat; Kabara; Kallâni; Kankani; Karnâni; Khânsat; Khokhata; Khyalya; Kothâri; Laddha; Lakhautiya; Lohiya; Mal; Malpânrê; Mâlu; Mantri; Marada; Marudharân; Mundhara; Natharin; Nishkalank; Partâni; Parwâl; Pûndpâliya; Râthi; Sâbu; Sadhara; Saudhâni; Shikchi; Somâni; Soni; Tapariya; Tosaniwâl; Totala.

Religion and customs.

3. Maheswaris are very careful in the observance of all Hindu customs. They are very often initiated into the Vallabha Samprâdaya. Their priests are Gaur Brâhmans who come from the country of their origin. Gaur Brâhmans will eat *kachchi* and *pakki* from their hands and so will Agarwâlas. Maheswaris are noted for their charity and the regard they pay to Brâhmans and ascetics. They partake of no food without dedicating some of it to Krishnaji.

The western branch.

4. Among the Maheswaris of Rajputâna there is a remarkable custom connected with marriage. The bride's maternal uncle, on the bridegroom entering the house of the bride, catches her up in his arms and takes her round the bridegroom seven times.[1] In Bombay[2] the Meshri Vânyas are divided into Modhs who take their name from Modhera in Parântij; Dasa and Vîsa Goghua; Dasa and Vîsa Adâliya and Dasa and Vîsa Mandâliya. The Dasa and Vîsa Goghua and the Dasa and Vîsa Adâliya intermarry in Kachh and Kâthiawâr. They are very careful to visit the shrine of their family goddess Bhadrârika at Modhera. Though they claim the right to do so, all do not wear the sacred thread. Widow marriage is forbidden and polygamy is practised only when the first wife proves barren. At marriages, except among the Mandâliyas, Modh bridegrooms wear the sword. The proper Maheswaris claim descent from Nagor in Thar. They chiefly deal in clarified butter, oil, sugar and molasses. Vaishnavas by name, but with goddesses as their family guardians, their hereditary priests are Pâliwâl Brâhmans, though of late some Pokarnas have by purchase secured their patronage. Practising neither polygamy nor widow marriage, they are peculiar in not

---

[1] *Rajputâna Gazetteer*, II, 251.
[2] *Bombay Gazetteer*, V, 50, sq.

allowing their women to join the marriage party that goes to fetch the bride.

Distribution of Maheswari Banyas by the Census, 1891.

Districts.	Number.	Districts.	Number.
Sahâranpur . . .	247	Bânda . . .	16
Muzaffarnagar . .	737	Hamîrpur . . .	62
Meerut	1,066	Jhânsi . . .	152
Bulandshahr . . .	597	Jâlaun . . .	148
Aligarh	2,040	Lalitpur . . .	19
Mathura . . .	733	Benares . . .	225
Agra	490	Mirzapur . . .	76
Farrukhâbâd . . .	11	Ghâzipur . .	21
Etâwah . . .	603	Azamgarh . . .	38
Etah	549	Tarâi	120
Bareilly . . .	249	Unâo	15
Budâun . . .	265	Kheri	15
Morâdâbâd . . .	493	Faizâbâd . . .	2
Cawnpur . . .	21	Sultânpur . . .	6
Fatehpur . . .	4	Total .	9,010

Mahror.—A Râjput sept in Oudh, who by one account were originally Kahârs, and their name is said to have been changed from Mahra to Mahror by Tilok Chand.[1]

Mâhur.—A sub-caste of Banyas principally found in the Western Districts. Of the Mâhuri of Behâr who are probably identical with them, Mr. Risley[2] says that they "occupy nearly the same rank as Agarwâlas in social estimation. Like the Sikhs, the Mâhuris strictly prohibit the use of tobacco, and a man detected smoking would be expelled from the community. Another peculiar usage is that marriages are always celebrated at the bridegroom's house, and not at the bride's. Trade and money lending are the

[1] Elliott, *Chronicles of Unâo*, 62 : *Oudh Gazetteer*, III, 227, 550.
[2] *Tribes and Castes*, II, 44.

proper occupations of the Mâhuri. Some of them have acquired substantial tenures and set up as landlords."

Distribution of Mâhurs according to the Census of 1891.

Districts.	Number.	Districts.	Number.
Sahâranpur . . .	6	Hamîrpur . . .	12
Muzaffarnagar . .	2	Allahâbâd . . .	2
Meerut	12	Jhânsi . . .	126
Bulandshahr . .	289	Jâlaun	139
Aligarh . .	961	Lalitpur . . .	1
Mathura . . .	1,063	Benares . .	22
Agra	6,374	Ghâzipur . . .	3
Etâwah . . .	14	Tarâi	20
Etah . . .	37	Lucknow . . .	1
Bareilly . . .	3,463	Unâo	64
Budâun . . .	16	Râê Bareli . . .	9
Morâdâbâd . . .	1,664	Sîtapur . . .	176
Shâhjahânpur . .	1,148	Hardoi . . .	281
Pilibhît . . .	1,135	Kheri	407
Cawnpur . . .	27	Bahrâich . . .	5
Fatehpur . .	2	Total .	17,482

Maithila.—A local tribe of Brâhmans who take their name from Mithila, the kingdom of Janaka, father of Sîta, and now comprising the modern Districts of Sâran, Muzaffarpur, Darbangah Puraniya, and part of Nepâl.

2. Of this branch of Brâhmans Mr. Risley writes [1] :—" The Maithila or Tirhûtiya Brâhmans rank among the Pancha Gaur. Dr. Wilson, following Mr. Colebrooke, observes that fewer distinctions are recognised among the Maithila Brâhmans than among any other of the great divisions of Brâhmans in India. This statement needs to be qualified. It is true that the Maithila have no endogamous

[1] *Tribes and Castes*, I, 158.

divisions, but their exogamous groups are peculiarly numerous and complex, and they have a complete hypergamous system. For the latter purpose the caste is divided into five groups—Srotiya or Sotê, Jog, Panjibaddh, Nâgar, and Jaiwâr, which take rank in this order. A man of the Srotiya group may take a wife from the lower groups and is usually paid a considerable sum of money for doing so; but he loses in social estimation by the match, and the children of such unions, though higher than the class from which their mothers came, are nevertheless not deemed to be socially equal to the members of their father's class. The same rule applies to the other classes in descending order; each may take wives from the group below it. The principle of this rule is the same as that followed by Manu in laying down the matrimonial relations of the four original castes, and in its earliest form it seems to have gone the full length of forbidding a woman of a higher group to marry a man of a lower group. It is important, however, to notice that in Bihâr the rule is now much less stringent and rigid than in Bengal. Although it is admitted to be the right thing for a girl to marry within her own group or in a higher group, it is not absolutely obligatory for her to do so, and cases do occur in which a girl of a higher class marries a man of a lower class in consideration of a substantial bride-price being paid to her parents. The comparative laxity of Bihâr practice in this respect may be due partly to the character of the people, and partly to the fact that caste observances in that part of the country have never been laid down by a superior authority, such as Ballâl Sen, but have been settled by the people themselves at regular meetings held with that object. It is well known that the leading members of the Maithila sub-caste with their Pandits, their genealogists, and their marriage brokers, come together in many places in Tirhût for the purpose of settling disputed questions of caste custom and of arranging marriages. A community which has five hypergamous classes and a double series of exogamous groups, one based on locality and the other on mythical ancestry, and at the same time attaches great importance to purity of blood, may well find it necessary to take stock of its arrangements from time to time and to see whether the rules are being obeyed.

3. "Among the Maithila Brâhmans of Bihâr, as among the Kulins of Bengal, the bride-price familiar to students of early tradition has given place to the bridegroom-price, which hypergamy tends necessarily to develop. Polygamy, formerly characteristic of the

Bengal Kulin, is practised in Bihâr in much the same form by the Bikauwa or 'vendor', a class of Maithila Brâhmans who derive their name from the practice of selling themselves, or more rarely their minor sons, to the daughters of the lower groups of the series given above. Usually the Bikauwas belong to the Jog and Panji-baddh classes, and comparatively few of them are found among the Srotiya and Nâgar groups. Some have as many as forty or fifty wives, who live with their own parents and are visited at intervals by their husbands. Bikauwa Brâhmans who have married into the lower classes are not received on equal terms by the members of their own class, but the women whom they marry consider themselves raised by the alliance. The price paid for a Bikauwa varies according to the class to which he belongs and the means of the family of the girl whom he is to marry. It may be as little as twenty rupees; it has been known to rise as high as six thousand rupees."

4. The Census shows that the males bear a considerable disproportion to the females—815 to 515—though, of course, they do not practise infanticide.

Distribution of Maithila Brâhmans according to the Census of 1891.

Districts.	Number.	Districts.	Number.
Sahâranpur	4	Allahâbâd	14
Muzaffarnagar	6	Jhânsi	69
Bulandshahr	11	Benares	203
Aligarh	127	Ghâzipur	20
Mathura	239	Gorakhpur	171
Agra	49	Basti	100
Mainpuri	62	Garhwâl	14
Etah	61	Tarâi	10
Bareilly	29	Lucknow	2
Shâhjahânpur	11	Sitapur	18
Cawnpur	13	Bahrâich	11
Fatehpur	18	Sultânpur	34
Bânda	33	Bârabanki	1
		Total	1,330

MAJHWÂR.

Majhwâr, Mânjhi, Gond Majhwâr, an aboriginal tribe of Dravidian origin found in the hill country of South Mirzapur.—The word Mânjhi or Majhwâr (Sanskrit *madhya* = "in the middle, midmost") means "leader" or "headman," and is commonly used among the Santâls and Mundas in this sense.[1] The name Gond, according to Mr. Hislop,[2] is the same word as Khând, and Kondu in Telegu meaning "mountain," the term Gond is equivalent to "hill people."

Appearance.

2. Their appearance is of the ordinary Gond type. They answer to the description given by Captain Forsyth[3] of the aborigines of the Central Indian Highlands:—"Entirely naked, with the exception of a very dingy, and often terribly scanty, strip of cloth round the middle, there was no difficulty in detecting the points that mark the aborigines. They were all of low stature, the Korkus perhaps averaging an inch or two higher than the Gonds, who seldom exceed 5 feet 2 inches: the colour, generally, a very dark brown, almost black in many individuals, though never reaching the sooty blackness of the Negro. Among the Gonds a lighter brown tint was not uncommon. In features both races are almost identical: the face being flat, forehead low, nose flat on the bridge, with open protuberant nostrils; lips heavy and large, but the jaw usually well formed and not prominent like that of the Negro, the hair on the face generally very scanty, but made up for by a bushy shock of straight black hair. In form they are generally well made, muscular about the shoulders and thighs, with lean, sinewy forearm and lower leg. The expression of face is rather stolid though good humoured. Some of the younger men might almost be called handsome—of the thin pattern,—but the elders have generally a coarse, weather-beaten aspect, which is not attractive. All the men present carried little axes, without which they never stir into the forest, and many had spears besides." This fairly represents the Mirzapur Mânjhis, who have broader heads and coarser-made noses than the Kols or Pankas. Among the Mânjhis, the nose is particularly wide at the base and narrows to a pointed tip. Their height is rather greater than that of the Central Indian

---

[1] Dalton, *Descriptive Ethnology*, 208; Risley, *Tribes and Castes of Bengal*, II, 101; Ball, *Jungle Life*, 24. The Mânjhis do not appear in the last Census list and were possibly classed as Gonds or Kharwârs—they number 16,202 in Dudhi, 2,787 in Agori, and 2,316 in Singrawli of the Mirzapur District.

[2] *Papers relating to Aboriginal Tribes*, 4.

[3] *Highlands of Central India*, 125.

Gonds. The average is about 5 feet 4 inches, but some are as much as 5 feet 5 inches. Like other savages[1] they fail to appreciate, what is in our eyes, the higher type of Aryan beauty. The clothing of the Mirzapur Mânjhis is much superior in amount and quality to that of the Central Indian Gonds.

Tribal organization.

3. The Mânjhis of South Mirzapur are divided into five exogamous sub-divisions, each of which includes a number of totemistic septs. Each of these endogamous sub-divisions is named from the leading sept. They say that there was once a Gond who had five sons, from whom these sub-divisions are descended. Many of these sub-divisions and septs can be identified with those now existing among the Gonds and other Dravidian races. The five exogamous sub-divisions are Poiya, Tekâm or Tekma, Marâi, Oika or Waika, and Olku. The Poiya, which is a sept of the Bengal Gonds,[2] includes five sections: Markâm, Poiya, Kusro, Neti, and Sirso. The Poiya are said to take their name from the *pawai* tree, out of a leaf of which they believe themselves to have been born, and which they will not cut or burn. The Kusro is also a Gondi sept in Bengal and the Central Provinces.[3] The Markâm is also a sub-division of the Agariyas. The word means "a tortoise," which this sept will nôt kill or eat. It also appears among the Gonds of the Central Provinces.[4] The other septs of this sub-division have not been identified, but are probably both Gondi and of totemestic origin. The second sub-division includes the Tekâm or Tekma, Marpachi, Netâm, Posâm, Kariyâm, Sindrâm, Korâm, Oima, Dadâichi, Koâichi, Ulangwati, and Kârgoti. Many of these are both Gondi and totemistic, as will, probably on further enquiry in the Central Indian hills, be found to be the case with all. Thus Tekâm is a Gond sept.[5] Marpachi is possibly equivalent to the Narpachi of Mr. Hislop.[6] Netâm or Naitâm is a Gond sept derived from a word meaning "tortoise," which is the totem.[7] Posâm is possibly derived from

---

[1] Westermarck, *History of Human Marriage*, 257.

[2] Risley, *Tribes and Castes*, II, *App.* 54.

[3] Risley *Tribes and Castes*, II, *App.* 54; Hislop, *Papers*, *App.* p. ii.

[4] Hislop, *Papers*, *App.* ii; *Central Provinces Gazetteer*, 273.

[5] Hislop, *Papers*, *App.* ii; *Central Provinces Gazetteer*, 138, 273.

[6] *Loc cit.*

[7] *Central Provinces Gazetteer*, 139; Risley, *Tribes and Castes*, II, *App.* 54; Hislop, *loc cit.*

the Gond *pussi* or "cat," and is a sept among the Mundas of Bengal.[1] Similarly, the Sindrâm apparently take their name from *Sindri*, "a lizard," which is recorded as a Kolami word in Mr. Hislop's vocabularies. Dadâichi is possibly equivalent to the Dadave of Mr. Hislop's list.[2] Koâichi is probably the Kowa or Kawâchi of the Central Provinces,[3] and may be connected with Koa, a "silk cocoon," which gives its name to one of the Munda septs.[4] In the third or Marâi sub-division the septs are Soiyâm or Soima, Sarotiya, Pandaru, Karpê, Kussenga, Purkela, Masrâm, Armor, Arpatti, and Kârpatti. Many of these, and probably all, are both Gondi and totemistic. Thus Marâi reminds us of the Marâni or Marâwi Gond sub-divisions in the Central Provinces, as well as of the tribe of Mâri Gonds, and may be connected with the Gondi Mâra, "a tree," which appears in Mr. Hislop's vocabulary.[5] Sarota, again, is a Gond sept.[6] Soiyâm or Soima, a title possibly connected with the Suiya bird, which is held in high respect and used as a predictor of omens by all these allied races, is a sept of Râj Gonds in the Central Provinces and among the Kharwârs, Bediyas, and Mundas of Bengal.[7] Again, Pandarâm, a Central Provinces Gond sept, and Pânru, a totemistic Lohâr sept in Chota Nâgpur, remind us of the Pandaru of the Mânjhis.[8] Karsenga, Masrâm, and Armor must also be closely connected with the Gond septs of Kursenga, Mesrâm, and Armor.[9] In the fourth or Waika sub-division the septs are nine in number: Waika, Korâm, Armu, Pâwalê, Chîchâm, Walariya, Otê, Urrê, and Salâm. Of these the Korâm, Waika, Armu, Pâwale, Chîchâm, Otê, Urrê, and Salâm are undoubtedly analogous to the Kolâm, Wuika, Chichain, Watti, Wurê, and Salâm of the Central Provinces Gonds.[10] The Korâm sept again appears among the Gonds of Sarguja and Uriâr among the Bengal Kharwârs.[11] In the fifth and last sub-division the septs are Olku, Portê, Kôrcho, Kâmro, Sumer, Jaitha, and Sâhjad.

---

[1] Risley, *loc. cit.* Pussi is apparently our English Pussy.
[2] *Loc. cit.*, 4.
[3] *Central Provinces Gazetteer*, 138, 139.
[4] Risley, *loc. cit.*, II, 106.
[5] *Central Provinces Gazetteer*, 137, 138, 139; Hislop, *Papers*, 7.
[6] Hislop, *loc. cit.*, *App.* I; *Central Provinces Gazetteer*, 273.
[7] *Central Provinces Gazetteer*, 139; Risley *loc. cit.*, II, *App.* 8 : 79, *App.* 108.
[8] Hislop, *loc. cit.*, *App.* II; Risley, *loc. cit.*, II, *App.* 95.
[9] *Central Provinces Gazetteer*, 137, 138, 139, 273. Armor appears to give its name, to the town of Armori in the Chânda District.
[10] *Gazetteer*, 273, 137, 138, 139; Hislop, 10, 11, *App.*; 46, *App.* ii.
[11] Dalton, *Ethnology*, 278; Risley, *loc. cit.*, II, 79.

Of these Korcho is certainly a Gond sept,[1] and Portê is most probably identical with the Purthi of the Hos and the Porti of the Mundas, among whom it is said to mean a crocodile.[2] The septs of Sumer, Jaitha, and Sâhjad would appear to mark Hindu influence, if they respectively imply a connection with the holy mountain of Meru, the Hindu Jetha or "superior," and Sâhjaddi or "the descendants of the banker."

4. A large number of these totemistic septs still retain traditions of emigration from the Western hills from Jabalpur and the head-waters of the Son and Narbada rivers. They represent themselves as having come from a series of forts (*garh*), which can be recognised along the line of the Western Vindhyan and Kaimûr ranges. Thus, they are agreed that of the five brothers, Marâi was the greatest and ruled in Mandlagarh or Mandla, which was a noted Gond fortress.[3] So the Marpachi came from Sârangarh in Sambalpur; the Netâm from Sonagarh, which may be Sonagâon, in Wardha; the Sarota from Gârhagarh, which is possibly Garha, in Jabalpur; the Korcho from Phuljhargarh in Sambalpur; the Urrê from Jhanjhnagargarh, of which Jhânsigarh, or the fort of Jhânsi, is a variant; the Oima from Maruagarh, which may be Mâru, in Bilâspur; the Portê from Râêgarh in Sambalpur; the Poiya from Patnagarh in Sambalpur; the Kariyâm from Khairagarh in Chhattîsgarh; the Posâm from Ujjaingarh in Gwâlior; the Tekâm from Lânjigarh in Bâlaghât; and the Armu from Chândagarh, the head-quarters of the district of that name. Search has hitherto failed to identify Bilârogarh, the head-quarters of the Korâm, Dantagarh of the Markâm, Moharagarh of the Kusro, Chinwilgarh of the Armor, and Saidagarh of the Arpatti; but they are all doubtless to be found somewhere along the Western hills in Rîwa or the Central Provinces.

Traditions.

5. Besides the evidence from the names of the septs, there is ample proof that the basis of the tribal organization is totemistic. Thus they have a legend that the five ancestors of the sub-divisions once crossed a river on the way to a feast, and three of them returned on a raft. Meanwhile the river rose, and the other two brothers were unable to cross, when a tortoise (*kachhua*) took them up on its back and ferried

Totemism.

---

[1] *Central Provinces Gazetteer*, 273.

[2] Dalton, *loc. cit.*, 189; Risley, *loc. cit.*, II, 107.

[3] *Central Provinces Gazetteer*, 191, 286; Dalton, *loc. cit.*, 275.

them over. These two men were the ancestors of the Poiya and Tekâm sub-divisions, which to this day worship the tortoise, and will not injure or kill it.

Emigration.

6. They fix the date of their emigration into the Mirzapur Parganas of Dudhi and Singrauli, and the native state of Sarguja, at about ten generations ago. They maintain their connection with their native land by occasional pilgrimages to shrines at Sâranggarh and Maruagarh. They have a legend that when Râmchandra broke the famous bow at the court of Janaka, King of Videha, in Mithila, its pieces fell in four places, to the site of one of which, on the banks of the Narbada, they still resort for pilgrimage. The Gond connection is again kept up by the common worship of the national deities Bûrha Deo or Ningo, and his attendant Bâghiya. They say that there is a temple and images of these tribal gods at their place of pilgrimage on the Narbada. Here, in the land of their wanderings, Ningo resides, either in the common village shrine (*Deohâr*), or in some ancient *sâl* tree, which no Mânjhi will cut or injure.

Rules of exogamy.

7. The totemistic septs already named are exogamous. No one can marry in his own sept or *Kuri*, but it is obvious that this rule fails to prevent the marriage of near of kin, and so the more advanced members of the tribe have begun to reinforce it with the standard formula—*chachera, mamera, phuphera, mausera*, which bars the line of the paternal uncle, maternal uncle, paternal aunt, and maternal aunt: but the more primitive Mânjhis adhere to the old Gond rule[1] by which first-cousins, provided they are not the offspring of two sisters, by preference intermarry, and it is a taunt against them that, in defiance of Hindu custom, a man is not debarred from joking (*dillagi*) with the daughter of his own daughter.

Hypergamy.

8. Hypergamy so far prevails that the Poiya sept will not intermarry or eat with the Sarota, whom they consider inferior to themselves. They explain this by a curious legend which recalls the time when the tribe lived by hunting. A man of the Poiya sept had a hound which he prized so much that he used to feed it every day out of a new earthen vessel. One day a man of the Sarota sept asked him for

---

[1] For this rule among the real Gonds see *Central Provinces Gazetteer*, 276; Forsyth, *Highlands of Central India*, 158. The custom is referred to by Westermark *History of Human Marriage*, 297, and Lubbock, *Origin of Civilisation*, 144.

the loan of the dog, and when the animal was put in his charge, contrary to the injunctions of its master, he fed it upon scraps, and the animal went mad. The Poiya was so angry that he seized the Sarota, and, harnessing him to a plough, made him drag it through a field. Since then the Poiyas have taken an oath not to eat with or intermarry with a Sarota, because they are no better than oxen.

Tribal council.

9. They have a tribal council (*panchâyat*) at which every householder has a seat. This assembles on occasions when the brotherhood collect for marriages or funerals. When any caste matter, such as cases regarding marriage, adultery, eating with inferior castes, etc., has to be decided, the meeting is convened through the Patâri or tribal priest. At each meeting the oldest or most respectable member present is appointed chairman (*sarpanch* or *gânwha*). Offences against morality are punished by excommunication, which may be for as long as twelve years. Restoration to caste can only be effected by feeding the clansmen on goat's flesh and rice. The number of dinners to be given depends on the gravity of the offence. Disobedience to the orders of the council involves summary excommunication, and the offender has to pay a money fine in addition to giving a tribal dinner. Young men, if convicted of an offence, receive a shoe-beating under sentence of the caste tribunal. Witnesses in the case must belong to the caste. No oath is administered, but perjury before the council involves excommunication. When a man keeps an unmarried woman, or a woman intrigues with an unmarried man, the penalty of excommunication is rigidly enforced, and they can be restored only on payment of the fine and providing a dinner for the clansmen. In such cases if a man, through poverty or wilfulness, refuses to accept the orders of the council, and illegitimate children are born to him, their parents are unable to get them married in the tribe. In order to avoid this, the children often themselves pay the tribal fine and get their parents married in their old age. The marriage ceremony is performed in the usual way, they are restored to caste, and their children can be married in the tribe. If the illegitimate child happen to be a daughter, she of course cannot find the cost of getting her parents married and restored to caste. But her father's brother, or his son, is permitted to take her into his family and get her married in the regular way. She then obtains full rank in the tribe, but she is not allowed to visit her parents or eat in their house.

10. As long as the conditions of exogamy are observed, variations in social position, distance of residence, or differences in religious practice or occupation are not a bar to marriage. But it is essential that they should generally observe the same religion. They have not the distinct survivals of marriage by capture as found among the regular Gonds;[1] but connected with this is a special ceremony of *confarreatio*, by which the bride is not allowed to enter the house of her husband until he and she sit outside and join in eating rice milk, and boiled rice. As with the regular Gonds, monogamy is the general rule;[2] and, among ordinary people, only one wife is taken, unless she happens to be barren, when, as is usual among savage races,[3] a second woman is taken in marriage. But there is, among the better class of Mânjhis, no prejudice against polygamy; in fact it is considered respectable. The women do considerable field or other work, and hence their services are valued. There is a man at present in Dudhi who has seven wives. When there are more wives than one, they always live amicably together, because the more wives a man has the easier they get through the severe labour which falls to their lot.[4] The rights of the senior wife are always respected: she rules the household, and is treated with consideration at social meetings. Concubines are allowed in some places, but the general feeling is against the practice. Polyandry is absolutely forbidden, and even the idea is considered most repulsive. Unmarried girls are allowed considerable liberty, and tend cattle, and run about the village, and visit the houses of clansmen. Intertribal immorality is lightly punished. The father of the girl or her paramour, if he can afford it, has to pay a fine of two maunds of *kodo* millet and a feed of boiled rice and goat's flesh to the clansmen. Then the girl is made over by a sort of informal marriage to her lover, and both are admitted to full caste rights. But, if she is detected in an intrigue with a man of another caste, she is permanently excommunicated, and she can go and live with her paramour as his concubine if his tribesmen will allow it, or settle down apart from her family, and make her living as best she can.

Marriage.

---

[1] Hislop, *loc. cit.*, 11.
[2] *Central Provinces Gazetteer*, 106, 278.
[3] Westermark, *loc. cit.*, 488.
[4] On this see Westermark, *loc. cit.*, 491, 492, 495, 496; Letourneau, *Evolution of Marriage*, 130, *sq.*; Spencer, *Principles of Sociology*, I, 657.

Marriage preliminaries.

11. It is characteristic of the Mânjhis, like all Gonds,[1] that infant marriage is not the rule. Like all savages, maturity comes at an early age.[2] The usual age is sixteen for males and twelve for girls. There is no trace of the Gond custom of taking omens to determine the expediency of a match.[3] The negotiations are carried out by the Patâri, or tribal priest, and by preference the moonlight fortnight of the month is selected for the purpose. After the Patâri has selected the girl, the bridegroom's friends visit her house, and inspect her carefully to satisfy themselves that she has no mental or bodily defect. The consent of the parents on both sides is essential, and it is only in very exceptional cases that the parties exercise any right of choice.

Beena marriage.

12. When the bridegroom is poor, the arrangement sometimes takes the form of what is known to Ethnologists as the Beena marriage, in which the bridegroom serves her father a certain number of years for his bride. This is known as "the son-in-law-at-home" (*ghar-jaiyân*). The practice is very common among Gonds and the allied tribes like the Kurkus.[4] While undergoing his period of probation, the youth is carefully excluded from the society of his future bride and lives in an outhouse apart from the family. The practice, which necessarily implies poverty on both sides, involves some social discredit. But, so far as it exists in combination with intertribal license, it tends to check polygamy.[5]

Betrothal.

13. When the preliminary marriage arrangements are complete, the bridegroom's friends take some cakes (*pûri*) to the bride's house. The clansmen resident in the village are summoned. Then the two fathers put their hands together, and a leaf platter (*dauna*) full of liquor [6] is placed into the hands of each: these vessels they exchange, and then get

---

[1] Hislop, *loc. cit.*, 3.

[2] Spencer, *Principles of Sociology*, I, 51.

[3] Hislop, *loc. cit.*, 13.

[4] Hislop, *loc. cit.*, 26; *Central Provinces Gazetteer*, 49, 277; Dalton, *Ethnology*, 41, 47; Sherring, *Castes*, II, 302.

[5] On this see Westermark, *loc. cit.*, 493.

[6] The same custom prevails among the Bhils of the Western hills. When the bride price is settled, the father of the boy makes a cup of leaves of the Dhâk tree, placing it on the top of the *ghara* of liquor, and puts inside it two annas' worth of copper coin. The girl's brother, or some other relation, then takes the coin and turns the cup of leaves upside down. The betrothal is then complete, and nothing remains but to drink the liquor, which is done on the spot.—*Rajputána Gazetteer*, I, 118.

up and bow to each other and say "Hail, marriage connection!" (*Samdhi juhâr!*). Then the clansmen present consume the cakes and liquor, and the betrothal is finally settled.

Position of the maternal uncle.

14. It is an interesting feature in Mânjhi weddings, possibly connected with descent in the female line, that the maternal uncle of the bride presents her before marriage with a suit of clothes. Similarly the bridegroom's maternal uncle gives him a money present. These gifts are known by the special name of "dowry" (*daija*). When the marriage is over, the boy's father gives his son's maternal uncle a present: among poor people, a calf is given; among rich people a buffalo. He gives nothing to the maternal uncle of the bride. This present is known as the "dismissal gift" (*bidâi*).

The bride price.

15. It is characteristic of all Gonds that the bride is purchased, and the price consists of such things as are necessary for feeding the guests invited to the marriage.[1] Among the Mânjhis of Mirzapur, the price paid by the boy's father to the father of the girl consists of three maunds of rice, a goat, and two loin-cloths, or sheets (*dhoti, sâri*): one for the bride, and one for her mother. He also sends an earthen pot (*kunda*) full of cakes (*pûri*), and five rupees in cash: this sum, it is understood, will be expended in purchasing cooking vessels, which are to be given as a dowry by her father to the bride.

The marriage procession.

16. The bridegroom, when he starts to fetch his bride goes dressed in white clothes; coloured garments are forbidden. Before he starts, his mother does the *parachhan*, or "wave ceremony," by moving over his head a rice-pounder and a tray containing a lighted lamp, in order to bring good luck. Before the procession starts, his mother sits down and suckles the boy at her breast. This is apparently a symbolical recognition of maternity.[2] The bridegroom should be conveyed in the procession either on horseback or in a large cot litter known as "the ship" (*jahâz*). Not long ago a Mânjhi in South Mirzapur was excommunicated because he had his son taken to be married in a palanquin (*pâlki*). When the procession arrives at the girl's village they are escorted to their halting-place (*janwânsa*), which is generally an enclosed space

---

[1] Hislop *loc. cit.*, 18; *Central Provinces Gazetteer*, 186.

[2] The same custom prevails among other races in case of adoption.—Lubbock *Origin of Civilization*, 97.

surrounded with bamboo hurdles, under some trees in the neighbourhood. From there the bridegroom's father sends the bride a silver necklet (*hansuli*) and armlet (*bâzu*), which she wears at the marriage.

Marriage by capture.

17. On the day they arrive, the bridegroom's party are not fed,—a reminiscense of marriage by capture. Another indication of this is that when the bride and bridegroom are taken to the retiring-room (*kohabar*) after the marriage, the door is blocked by the wife of the bride's brother, who will not admit them until she receives a present. The marriage ceremony takes place in a nuptial shed (*mânro*) erected in the courtyard of the bride's house, where the ceremony, such as it is, is performed by the Patâri, or tribal priest. The Baiga, or aboriginal devil priest, has the special duty of planting the first pole of the marriage shed. Brâhmans have nothing to do with the business, except that in some of the more advanced families they are now asked to fix the lucky time (*sa'at*). The post of the best man is taken by the sister's husband of the bridegroom, who is known as the *lokana*, or "looker on." His business is to lift the boy off the cot on which he sits in state and place him on the marriage litter. He has also to see that he is provided with a black bead and a silver necklace round his neck, to save him from the Evil eye. Meanwhile, after the arrival of the bridegroom's procession, the Patâri makes a square (*chauk*) in the courtyard with lines of barley flour, and when the lucky moment arrives, the bridegroom and his friends march in with songs and beating of drums. In the centre of the square the boy's father solemnly plants a spear, an obvious survival of marriage by capture. The best man then escorts the bridegroom into the enclosure, waving a fan over his head, to guard him from the spirits of evil, which are particularly dangerous at such an important crisis in the life of the boy. Here the girl's female relations bar his entry and will not admit him until they receive a present. The bride is then brought out from the inner room, and they both sit, facing East, on rude mats made of the leaves of the *sâl* tree (*shorea robusta*). The best man fastens the clothes of the pair in a knot, inside which are tied up a copper pice and a piece of betel-nut, This done, the Patâri makes the pair revolve five times round the spear in the course of the sun, the bridegroom marching in front, followed by the bride, who rests her hands on his shoulders. After this the girl is formally made over by a rude *kanyâdân* ceremony

to the bridegroom's father. Her father asks: "Will you receive her?" and the answer is: "I have received her with pleasure." On this both the fathers-in-law (*samdhi*) embrace. Next the pair are again seated on the mats, and the bridegroom's drinking-vessel is placed before the bride and her's before him. Each drinks out of the cup of the other. Then the boy's father presents a new suit of clothes to each of the senior women of the bride's family, and her mother or grandmother washes the feet of the married pair, and makes a mark on the spear with some rice and curds, which are subsequently offered to Sûraj Nârâyan. Next she marks the foreheads of the pair with curds and rice, and the same ceremony is repeated by the father of the bride; after which the bridegroom smears the nose, forehead, and hair parting of the girl with red lead (*sindur*), and this is the binding part of the ceremony. The bride's father on this presents the bridegroom with a cow calf.

Ceremony of the kohabar.

18. After marriage the married pair are taken into an inner room known as the *kohabar*, the walls of which are decorated with rude figures of birds and animals, which were once probably tribal totems, but the meaning of the custom has now been forgotten. This ceremony points to the original habit of immediate consummation of marriage, as even now appears to be the habit among ruder allied tribes like the Orâons.[1] Now-a-days, among the Mânjhis, all that is done is that the bride and bridegroom eat together, the boy's crown (*maur*) is removed, and he has to submit to a number of coarse practical jokes on the part of the female relations of the bride. This over, the bridegroom retires and joins his friends outside the village. The marriage always takes place at night, and next day the bridegroom and his friends are summoned to the marriage feast. The invitation is conveyed by the Patâri, who takes a brass vessel (*lota*), containing a little rice, water, and a mango leaf, to the halting-place of the procession. He stands with the *lota* in his hand before the bridegroom's father, and humbly asks him to come to the feast.

---

[1] Dalton, *Ethnology*, 253. The ceremony forms the subject of a good Bihâr proverb:—*Manrwa men koi bât na pûchhe, kohabar dulaha ki chachi*: "No one speaks to her in the nuptial shed (where all have egress), but she claims the treatment of the bridegroom's aunt in the *kohabar* (where only the near relatives of the bride and bridegroom are allowed)."— Christian, *Bihar Proverbs*, 40.

The acceptance of the invitation is notified by his touching the *lota* with his hand. After this the invitation is conveyed in the same way to the relations and clansmen constituting the bridegroom's party. As they go to the bride's house, they are accompanied by a Chamâr or Ghasiya beating a drum. When they sit down to eat, the bridegroom and best man refuse to touch the food until the bride's father gives them a present.

The bringing home of the bride.

19. Next day they return home. If, as is usually the case, the bride is nubile, she goes home at once with her husband; if she is not nubile, there is a second *gauna* ceremony in the third or fifth year after the marriage. As she is being dismissed with her husband, the Patâri repeats some verses; and *pân* and betel are distributed. When she arrives at her husband's house, his mother and female relatives wave over her head a brass tray containing a lighted lamp. On this tray, round the lamp, are placed little balls of flour and cowdung. They also wave over her head the churn stick (*mathni*). In this ceremony the lamp is usually made of iron, as a protection against evil spirits. After this, the bride enters the house, and the women sing songs of joy. She and her husband are next rubbed with oil and turmeric, and they are made to walk round the central pole of the marriage shed (which is erected at the house of the bridegroom as well as at that of the bride) five times. Near it are placed some pieces of iron to ward off evil spirits, and a jar full of water as an emblem of prosperity. There also is prepared a retiring-room (*kohabar*), into which the married pair are taken, and given curds and coarse sugar to eat. Next, the bridegroom's mother and her women friends go to some neighbouring tank, which is pointed out by the village Baiga. There they collect some earth in the folds of their loin-cloths, and, bringing it home in a basket, put it in the marriage shed, near where the spear is fixed up. This is known as "the lucky earth" (*matmangara*).[1] On this they place two jars (*ghara*) full of water. Near these is placed a vessel containing a mixture of oil and turmeric. The bridegroom is then bathed by the women, and his body is touched five times with oil and turmeric. Up to this time the bride and

---

[1] Among other menial castes the "lucky earth" seems to be collected because from it the fireplace (*chûlha*), on which the wedding east is cooked, is made.

bridegroom wear white clothes: these are now replaced by coloured garments. The clothes of the pair are knotted together again, and they walk round the spear five times as before. The bridegroom's father and mother mark the foreheads of the pair with curds and rice flour, and the bride washes the feet of her father-in-law in token of submission to him: in return for this, he gives her a present (*neochhâwar*). Then the father of the bridegroom calls out in the presence of the clansmen: "I have now done my duty in getting them married. Let them work for their living. If they respect me, let them give me a drink of water in my old age. I have done my duty."

20. Then follow two ceremonies which are understood to bring good luck to the married pair. They sit down side by side, and five little piles of dry rice are placed on a currystone. The bridegroom grasps the bride's foot and with it knocks down each of the piles, one after the other. This is known as *Kuri dhakelwâna*. The people explain it to mean that the bride is now mistress of the house.[1] Then follows a curious emblematical ceremony. A wooden measure, which usually contains about two pounds, is filled with rice. The bride and bridegroom hold their hands open under it, the boy's hands above and the girl's below: the rice is then gradually poured into their hands from the measure. It is then collected and replaced, and if the measure fail again to hold all the rice, it is a lucky omen.

Final ceremonies.

This is, of course, generally arranged by the simple precaution of crushing the rice down into the measure as it is being filled before the ceremony.[2] When these ceremonies are concluded, the bride and some of the women take the sacred water-pot (*kalsa*) and convey it to a neighbouring stream, into which it is thrown.

21. Next follows the worship of Dulha Deo, the Gond god of marriages. He is the deified bridegroom: his legends are now vague and uncertain, but in all of them there is an echo of some terrible tragedy of the olden time which has deeply impressed these primitive races. A bride and bridegroom on their way home are said to

Dulha Deo, the god of marriage.

---

[1] A similar ceremony is described by Dalton (*Ethnology*, 234) among the Kurs or Muâsis.

[2] This custom of weighing is observed by the Kurkus of Hoshangâbâd, who use it as an omen to determine the prospects of the harvest.—C. A. Elliott, *Settlement Report*, p. 257.

have been killed by lightning, or in some other sensational way, and the bridegroom now lives in the stars and has become a god of the household and marriages. The time for his worship is in the middle of summer. He has no shrine, but some *sâl* tree (*shorea robusta*) in the jungle is marked out by the Baiga as his habitation, and at its foot a goat is sacrificed in his honour. Whenever this tree falls, the Baiga sits there for some time and works himself up into a state of religious frenzy, when he walks blindly on and touches another tree which replaces the ancient shrine. At marriages, two short sticks of *sâl* wood are fixed in the ground beneath the marriage shed. On these the Patâri puts the wooden rice-measure which has been used in the ceremony already described. After the marriage is over, the sticks are taken up and fixed in the floor of the family cookhouse, where they are kept with the similar sticks used in all previous marriages in the family, and worshipped at all subsequent marriages in honour of Dulha Deo.

The ceremony of *confarreatio.*

22. After the bride is formally introduced into the family of her husband, she remains there for five days, and then returns home to her father, returning to her husband after such an interval as may be found convenient.[1] When she first comes to her husband, the clansmen assemble, and a ceremony analogous to the *confarreatio* of the Romans is carried out. She first touches all the family cooking-vessels, and cooks for the tribesmen.

Binding portion of the ceremony of marriage.

23. The binding part of the marriage ceremony is understood to be the marking of the foreheads of the pair by the parents of the bridegroom. After the betrothal, the engagement may be annulled; but once this mark (*tîka*) is made, the marriage is irrevocable. This, the regular form of the marriage, is known as *charhauwa*, or the "offering," because the bride is offered to the bridegroom by her father.

Widow marriage.

24. Widow marriage by the form known as *sagâi* is freely allowed. The levirate is practised under the usual restriction that the younger brother has the first claim to the widow of his elder brother, but the elder

---

[1] This may be a survival of the general custom by which the bride and bridegroom are debarred from intercourse and obliged to meet secretly for some time after marriage. See instances given by Lubbock, *Origin of Civilization*, 81; Westermark, *History of Human Marriage*, 151.

brother cannot take the widow of his younger brother.[1] If the younger brother does not care to marry the widow, she can be married by an outsider, and, as a rule, all widows, except those suffering from any serious physical or mental defect, are married again either to their brother-in-law or to a stranger. In the levirate the only ceremony is the announcement of the fact to the clansmen and a feast to the near relations, if the parties can afford it. When a stranger desires to take over a widow, he sends to her friends one or two maunds of rice, a thread bracelet (*pahaunchi*), a pair of ear ornaments made of palm leaf (*tarki*), and one or two sheets. The woman is dressed in these, and in the presence of the clansmen each pours some sesamum oil over the head of the other. He then brings her home and gives a tribal feast. An outsider marrying a widow has to pay back to the younger brother of the deceased husband the sum of twelve rupees, which is supposed to be equivalent of the bride price originally paid for her. This, or some smaller sum proportionate to the means of the widow's second husband, is always awarded by the tribal council.

Divorce.

25. There is no legal rule of divorce. After a marriage is once performed, no physical defects in either party are sufficient to annul it: but if it turns out that the bridegroom is insane, or impotent, the marriage is annulled, and the bride is married again to one of his brothers, if such an arrangement is possible. But if the parties before marriage are aware of any defect in either, the marriage must be maintained. Grounds for divorce are adultery or absolutely final excommunication from caste of either party. It is said that it used to be the custom that if a woman was deserted by her husband for a year, she could remarry;[2] but if such was the custom formerly, the people deny that it is recognised at present. But no divorce is permitted without an enquiry and order of the tribal council. They profess that a divorced wife cannot re-marry, but that a divorced man is allowed to marry again after giving a tribal feast. But cases to the contrary have been quoted, and it would appear that the restriction on a divorced wife re-marrying is comparatively

[1] This is also a rule among the regular Gonds.—*Central Provinces Gazetteer*, 278; Forsyth, *Highlands of Central India*, 150; Dr. Westermark, *History of Human Marriage*, 510, *sqq.*, gives strong grounds for disputing the theory that the levirate is a survival of polyandry.

[2] For other instances of this see Letourneau, *Evolution of Marriage*, 237.

modern. The real tribal rule seems to have been that the man who took the widow in *sagâi* was obliged to return the bride price.[1]

Succession.

26. The children of recognised wives, which include offspring of the levirate and widows re-married according to caste custom, succeed equally to the goods of the father. No division takes place as long as the father lives and, as a rule, they continue to live together, the tendency being to form large united households.[2] At the same time the sons appear to have the right on the death of their father to claim their shares of the cattle and moveables; and set up for themselves. In a country where land is of little value and houses easily built, these give rise to no difficulty. Illegitimate children have no rights, but the tribal council generally awards them something out of their father's goods. Whether legitimate or illegitimate, children follow the caste of the father, but the illegitimate children are not allowed to eat with the clansmen. They appear generally to emigrate, or, if they remain at home, only intermarry with persons in the same rank as themselves. If a widow with children marry again, they remain with the friends of their father. If she marry outside the family of her late husband, she loses all rights to his estate, and her sons by him succeed. In this case the sons by both fathers are considered joint and equal heirs to the property of both. All, in any case, the widow can claim, is maintenance, and she has no power of making away with any property. In the case of the levirate, there is no fiction that the children by the second are those of the first husband: in fact, the theory of the value of a son from a religious point of view seems to be only very dimly understood.

Primogeniture.

27. If a man die, leaving a widow or widows, a son or sons, a daughter or daughters, brothers and other relations, the son or sons succeed to the estate of their father. The elder son gets something in excess, generally about ten per cent. in cattle and household goods, but there is no fixed rule. The inheritance is divided, not according to the number of wives, but of sons, and no regard is paid to the fact that one widow may be of better family than the others. The father cannot in his lifetime select any particular son to have a larger

---

[1] In Greece, in such cases, it was the lady's father who returned the bride price.—*Odyssey*, VIII, 318.

[2] This is the Kândh custom according to some authorities.—Dalton, *Ethnology*, 294.

share than the others: and the question whether one son may be better off than the others, or may have received a larger dowry with his wife is not considered.

The associated brethren.

28. In default of sons only, the brethren who have lived in association with the deceased are entitled to succeed. The sons of a deceased son or deceased associated brother succeed equally to the share which would have fallen to their father. If the brothers succeed they must maintain the widow. A concubine gets only what her paramour may have given her in his lifetime.

The rights of the widow.

29. If a man has died in a state of exclusion from caste his widow succeeds and his brothers have no rights. A widow's right to maintenance depends on her continuing chaste; and if she offends they are at liberty to turn her out.

The rights of daughters.

30. Girls have no right of inheritance, but are entitled to maintenance until marriage, and to have their wedding expenses paid out of the estate of their father.

Posthumous sons.

31. Posthumous sons have no rights unless the pregnancy of the wife has been acknowledged by the husband during his life.

Ascetics.

32. If a man abandons the world and becomes an ascetic he loses his right to inherit; his wife and sons, and in default of them his associated brethren, succeed to his property.

Succession to office.

33. Succession to any office, such as that of village headman, falls to the eldest son of the late incumbent: but if he prove unfit some other member of the family is selected to fill his place.

Adoption.

34. The tribe profess to maintain elaborate rules on the subject of adoption: but it is doubtful how far this is due to Hindu influence. The idea of adoption from a religious point of view in connection with the *sráddha* seems hardly to exist.[1] It is said that only a sonless man can adopt,[2] and that the consent of his collateral heirs is not needed. But he cannot adopt if his daughter's son is alive. If a man's son

---

[1] On this, see J. D. Mayne, *Hindu Law*, p. 87.

[2] *Ibid*, 89.

is permanently excluded from caste he can adopt one of his brother's sons. He cannot adopt a second time while the son first adopted is alive. A bachelor, a blind man, a cripple, a widower, or one who becomes an ascetic cannot adopt.[1] Nor can a woman adopt: a childless widow with property in her own right may give her goods to her kinsmen, but cannot adopt. But cases have been known in which a childless widow [2] has been allowed to adopt her brother's son with the consent of all the heirs. But it is settled that in any case a widow cannot adopt if a son already adopted by her late husband is in existence: and if a son thus adopted die, the widow cannot adopt unless her husband before his death have given her distinct authority to do so. A man cannot give his eldest or his only son to another to adopt:[3] but if he have a brother living apart, he can permit him to be adopted by another. There is no age fixed for adoption, but the boy must be unmarried. Girls cannot be adopted. As a matter of fact, a boy not a relation is never adopted, and the preference is always given to a nephew or first cousin on the male side,[4] and it is generally admitted that the adopter and the adopted son should be of the same sept (*kuri*). This excludes the son of a sister who necessarily follows the sept of his father. The only exception to this is the case of a daughter's son who is sometimes, but very rarely adopted.[5] As illustrating the vagueness of the conception of adoption, it appears to be tribal custom that the adopted son inherits both from his adoptive and his natural father. If a man have a son after he has adopted a boy, both share equally. As regards the special case of *gharjaiyân* or Beena marriage, this only takes place among poor people where they are unable to afford a regular marriage.

The period of probation is three years, and during this time the boy does house and field work, and is entitled to clothes and maintenance from his father-in-law in future. The girl to whom he is to be married gives him food and water, and, at least nominally, sexual intercourse between the pair is prohibited. After the three years' probation is over the girl's father gets them married at his own expense. After the marriage they can set up for themselves or continue to live with the bride's father who has no further

---

[1] On this, see J. D. Mayne, *Hindu Law*, p. 90.
[2] *Ibid*, p. 94.
[3] *Ibid*, p. 120.
[4] *Ibid*, p. 112.
[5] They would be excluded by Hindu Law, *ibid*, p. 113.

right to claim work from his son-in-law, and he on the other hand has no claim to succeed to his father-in-law's estate. In cases of adoption there is no special ceremony except the announcement of the fact to the assembled clansmen.

Relationship.

35. Besides agnates all cognates, that is to say, those families into which girls are given in marriage or whence brides are taken, are considered elations. These consist of the father-in-law (*sasur*), the wife's brother (*sála*). A man calls his brother-in-law (*sála*) *bábu*: close friends not related to him he calls *bhái* or *bábu*. They remember the names of male ancestors up to the third or fourth generation, and those of women up to the great grand-mother. They recognise a connection with persons born in the same village who are known as *ganwa bhái*.

Birth Ceremonies.

36. They have no observances during the pregnancy of the mother: she is not allowed to eat white grain, and gets only light food. The woman is delivered on the ground facing East. The after-birth is taken away secretly and buried.[1] When the parturition is difficult the midwife (*Chamáin*) hangs a piece of a jungle root, the name of which is kept secret by women, round her neck and fastens it with a bit of untwisted thread. Another device for the same purpose is to crush two and-a-half leaves of the *mahua* (*Bassia latifolia*) in water and make the woman drink it. The moment the child is born a bit of two jungle plants called *chitáwar* and *chináwar* is hung round its neck to keep off ghosts (*bhút*). The woman is kept isolated in a special room (*saunr*) where she is attended by the midwife.[2] The child is not left alone for a year after its birth, and some one always sits near it to ward off the attacks of ghosts, and with the same object some iron implement such as a sickle (*hansua*) or a betel cutter (*saranta*) is kept near the child's head. They say that iron is the weapon of Durga Devi and keeps off ghosts. For the same reason a fire is kept lighted over the place in which the umbilical cord (*nár*) is buried by the midwife in the delivery room. This is maintained as long as the woman remains in seclusion.

---

[1] A tomb was raised over the after-birth of Aurangzeb at Dohad in the Panch Mahâls. *Bombay Gazetteer*, III, 312.

[2] See the cases of this quoted by Westermark, *History of Human Marriage*, 485; and compare Frazer, *Golden Bough*, II, 238 sqq., Wallace, *Malay Archipelago*, 167.

It is considered improper that the child should be born elsewhere than in the house of the father. On the sixth day is the *chhathi* at which the mother and child are bathed.[1]

On the twelfth day is the *barahi* when the head of the child is shaved [2] and at the same time all the near clansmen shave their heads. On this day the dirty clothes are given to the Dhobi to wash, and the mother and all her relations, male and female, put on clean clothes. The mother and child are bathed and at this final bath the mother is rubbed with a mixture of oil and turmeric and is then finally pure and joins the family. On the sixth day there is no regular feast, only some of the female relations and friends who live close by are entertained. On the twelfth day the clansmen are fed and liquor is distributed : the earthen cooking vessels of the household are thrown away and replaced : the *karama* or tribal song and dance is performed and the sister of the child's father or the elder sister of the baby washes out and replasters the delivery room, for which she receives a present known as *neochhâwar*.[3]

Couvade.

37. There is a survival of the custom of couvade to this extent that when after delivery the woman is given a cleaning draught of ginger, turmeric, and molasses, the father has to take a drink of it first.[4]

Death ceremonies.

38. Like many other savage races the Mânjhis take the dying person into the open air so that there may be nothing to stop the egress of the departing

---

[1] The *chhathi* appears to represent among the true Gonds the time at which the base of the umbilical cord which is carefully buried dries up and falls off.—Hislop, *Papers*, App. IV. As among Hindus the *barahi* or twelfth day ceremony represents the time at which infants generally suffer from infantile lock-jaw which is caused by the cutting of the cord with a blunt, coarse weapon and the neglect of sanitary precautions. This disease is known as *jamhua* (the visit of Yama, the god of death or *ghugghua* from *ghuggha*, the owl, which is supposed to grip the child by the throat and stop its breathing.

[2] Child tonsure is a rite among the Santâls, and appears to be the only compulsory ceremony up to marriage. Dalton, *Ethnology*, 214.

[3] Among the real Gonds the woman remains apart for thirteen days after delivery : on the fifth day the female neighbours are feasted, and on the twelfth day male friends are entertained : on the thirteenth the purification is ended by giving a dinner to both parties. The child is named a month or two after. Among some tribes, however, the mother is isolated for a month, during which no one touches her and, unless there are grown up daughters, she is bound to cook for herself. But this is not general. Hislop, *Papers*, 5, 18, App. IV.

[4] This is a custom among a Madras tribe the Koravas : see Tylor, *Primitive Culture*, I, 84. On the custom generally, consult Lubbock, *Origin of Civilisation*, 15 *sqq*. : Letourneau, *Evolution of Marriage*, 316 *sqq*.

soul.[1] Like the Korkus,[2] they are in the transition stage between burial and cremation. People who die of small-pox and are supposed to be thus directly under the influence of the goddess Sîtala are buried, and so are children up to the age of about seven, unless they have been already married, in which case they are usually cremated.

The dying person is fed with a little rice and curds, and a small piece of silver is put into the mouth as a viaticum.[3] The Patâri priest admonishes his spirit to quickly leave the body of clay and depart to the next world. In the case of burial the grave is dug north and south in which direction the body is laid,[4] head upwards, tied up in a shroud. The grave is dug by the relatives, each of whom throws a little earth on the corpse. A cremation is carried out in the ordinary way at a regular cremation ground (*marghat*). If the deceased was an old man, a bludgeon (*lâthi*) and an earthen pot (*mitiya*) are left near the pyre. An axe is sometimes placed in the same way in order that the spirit may make its living in the next world. Near the pyre of an old woman are placed with the same object a grass spud (*khurpa*) and a stick and the wooden stand (*tehri*) on which the house water-pots are placed. These articles are not broken as is the case with other savage tribes.[5] The body is laid on the pyre, feet south and head north, and wood is piled over it. The pyre is fired by the nearest relative, the son or brother of the deceased. He lights a wisp of grass, walks five times round the pyre, and after applying the torch to the mouth of the corpse sets fire to the wood. One of the relatives brings home a lighted brand from the pyre which he gives to the female relations of the deceased. Each of them then steps once backwards and forwards over the brand. This is understood to imply that though the women folk did not go to the cremation ground they have shared in the obsequies. After this the women are considered impure and do not go into the house until they have bathed in the nearest stream. The male mourners, after the pyre is well alight, rub themselves with a mixture of oil and turmeric and

---

[1] Tylor, *Primitive Culture*, I, 453.

[2] *Central Provinces Gazetteer*, 49 : Forsyth, *Highlands of Central India*, 155.

[3] Tylor, *loc. cit.*, I, 494.

[4] The regular Gond custom seems to be the reverse of this.—*Central Provinces Gazetteer*, 278.

[5] Lubbock, *Origin of Civilisation*, 37 : Spencer, *Principles of Sociology*, I, 184.

butter. Most of them before cremation shave the head of the corpse and rub it with oil and turmeric before it is taken out for cremation. But the head shaving is not universal. If the deceased have died of a contagious disease, like cholera, the Baiga goes ahead of the funeral procession with a chicken in his hands, which he lets loose in the direction of some other village as a scape-goat to remove the infection. None but some other most experienced Baiga dares to touch or consume the scape-goat. When they take such a corpse to be cremated they also sprinkle sesamum on the ground as they go on, to prevent the return of the ghost.[1] After the cremation is over with the same object they sprinkle sesamum on the funeral pyre. Next day they sweep up the ashes and collect the bones for conveyance to the Ganges when an opportunity occurs. When the mourners after completing the obsequies return to the house of the deceased no food is cooked there, but is sent from the house of a daughter or sister of the deceased. After eating, the clansmen return home. On the third day all the earthen vessels are replaced and the barber shaves the heads of all the male relations.[2] On the fourth day the clansmen are fed and eat with the persons who fired the pyre. On the tenth day is the *daswân* when the Patâri priest sings a song in honour of the dead man and with other presents takes the clothes and vessels of the deceased as his representative, like the Hindu Mahâbrâhman, in the belief that these things will be passed on for the use of the deceased, in the world of the dead. On this day the clansmen shave their heads, beards and mustaches, reserving the scalp lock. After a feast to the brethren the death impurity is over.[3]

Propitiation of the sainted dead.

39. On the night of the cremation food is laid out on the road taken by the funeral procession, along which it is believed the spirit of the dead man returns. When a child is born the Patâri is asked which of the deceased ancestors has been re-embodied in the child and when the Patâri announces the name this is given to the child. In the same way if a calf is born and will not drink milk they call in an Ojha who says "Your father has been re-born in this calf." It is then taken great care of and not worked in the plough.

---

[1] Tylor, *Primitive Culture*, I, 126: Lubbock, *Origin of Civilisation*, 234.
[2] *Odyssey*, IV, 197: Spencer, *Sociology*, I, 164.
[3] Among the real Gonds the death impurity lasts only one day. Hislop, *Papers* 19.

The calf is not branded as with Hindus. They do not erect monuments to the dead as the Gonds do.[1] Whenever a son or daughter is married a fowl and some liquor are offered to deceased ancestors, and on the tenth day after a death the Patâri offers a burnt sacrifice (*hom*) in the courtyard in honour of the dead. They do not perform the annual death ceremony (*barsi*) or release male calves in honour of the dead: but some of the more wealthy Mânjhis are already approximating to Hindu custom in this respect.

40. The religious affairs of the caste are managed by the Patâri who corresponds to the Pradhâna[2] of the regular Gonds and performs the functions of Hindu Brâhman and Mahâbrâhman. As with the Gonds the Patâri does not seem to become defiled if a dog or cat dies in his house.[3] Some of the more advanced Mânjhis worship Mahâdeva who is admittedly the representative of the Gond deity Bara Deo and like him has an ox for his vehicle. Bara Deo is also known as Ningo Bâghiya or Bûrha Deo. Lingo or Lingal is a sort of prophet among the Gonds.[4] This deity is worshipped by the Patâri on his periodical visits to his constituents when he goes about rattling a number of iron rings fixed on a stick. He takes alms only from Mânjhis. They also worship the collective local gods in the form of a male deity Dih, and a female Deohârin. In honour of them small images of elephants, horses, etc., are placed under a *sâl* tree. Many of these shrines are by the more advanced Mânjhis identified with those of Devi. In this is placed a water vessel (*kalsa*) and over it is set up a red flag on a pole. The seat of the deity is represented by a little platform of mud on which offerings are made and fire sacrifices (*hom*) done. The sacrifices to these local gods are done by the Baiga who cuts off the head of a goat or chicken with an axe, holding the victim facing east opposite the shrine. To the sainted dead no blood offerings are made. To them are offered small round cakes which must be made by the wife of the eldest son.[5] These are offered in the cookhouse which

Religion.

---

[1] Hislop, *loc. cit.*, page 19.

[2] See Hislop, *loc. cit.*, 19.

[3] Hislop, *loc. cit.*, 5 *sq.*

[4] The name according to Hislop is of Gond origin; sometimes Bhân, Gondi for "devotee," is affixed to his name and sometimes Pariâr, which means "saint." Hislop, *Papers*, App. 8. The name as Forsyth remarks (*Highlands of Central India*, 188) probably represents the phallic nature of the worship. Bâghiya marks his connection with the tiger (*bâgh*); Bara or Bûrha means "great" or "ancient."

[5] Campbell, *Notes*, I.

represents the abode of the sainted dead. If she is unable from illness or any other cause to cook the whole number required, she makes one or two and the rest are cooked by the women of the family junior to herself. They hang up in their houses as charms to keep off disease the bones of pigs or the heads of monkeys which they hold in a certain degree of respect. When they are eating they mention the earth goddess in the Hinduised form of Sîtarâm and throw a little food on the ground.[1] On holidays the only grain they eat is *sáwán* (*panicum frumentaceum*) paddy and wheat. There is a special prohibition against using the small millet (*mijhari*) on holidays, and it is only very poor people who eat it. When milking a cow they utter no spell, but pour a little milk on the ground from the first teat they touch. They think it very unlucky to let salt fall on the ground, and will not pass it from hand to hand as they eat it. The sacrifice to the local female deity now identified with Devi is a female goat which has never borne a kid. Liquor is poured on the ground in honour of Gansâm who is a noted deity of the Kols. Women are not allowed to join in the worship of the *deohâr* or local gods, nor to consume any part of the offering.[2] On Sunday they make vows to Sûraj Deota, the Sun god, and pray to him to bless their occupations. On that day they eat only once and abstain from salt. The ceremony ends with a fire offering (*hom*) which is offered in the courtyard by the house owner.[3]

Ghost worship.

41. They do not worship all ghosts (*bhût*), but they believe that all disease is due to them. In such cases an Ojha is called in and he gets into a state of ecstacy (*khelna, abhuána*) and finally proclaims the special *bhût* which requires propitiation. Then they give a female goat, a fowl, some liquor and a piece of yellow cloth to the Ojha who offers them to the *bhût* and then appropriates them himself. Their theory of mountains is that they were rained down from heaven by Paramesar, and hence people are careful about going up mountains which are the abode of evil spirits. Many of these mountain ghosts are related. Thus, Turkin, a deified Muhammadan female ghost,

---

1 Spencer, *Sociology*, I, 259.

2 Spencer, *loc. cit.*, I, 229.

3 The Gonds worship the Sun as Rayetâl.—Hislop, *Papers*, App. 49 : also see *Central Provinces Gazetteer*, 49 : Forsyth, *Highlands of Central India*, 154 : Lubbock, *Origin of Civilisation*, 317.

who lives on the Jungail hill south of the Son, and Barwat, a male ghost, who lives on the Aunri hill, are sister and brother and rule all the mountain ghosts in that part of the country. When people ascend these haunted mountains they take the precaution of throwing some dry rice and flowers at the foot. They then clasp their hands and implore the local ghosts not to harm them. There is a stream called Sukandar, a tributary of the Kanhar on the Sarguja frontier, in which is a deep water hole supposed to be of unknown depth. In the middle of this is a mound on which is a *kurlu* tree. When ghosts become troublesome the Ojha searches for a piece of deer horn in the jungle and this he hammers with a stone into the tree and thus shuts up the ghost. The tree is covered with hundreds of such pieces of horn. The suppliant has to offer a water-pot (*lota*) and tray (*thâli*) under the tree. Only great Ojhas venture near the place, and when they do they tread very cautiously so as not to disturb the *bhûts*. The stones round the pool are very slippery, and it is supposed that the *bhûts* push in unwary visitors and drown them.[1] It is in this hole that the ruler of all the *bhûts* abides, and he allows no strange *bhûts* to enter it. In the same pool, however, live the snake god and his wife—the Nâg and Nâgin. To them are offered a red goat, a red fowl, and ten cakes (*pûri*). These offerings are made by any one afflicted by *bhûts*, and the service is performed by the village Baiga. There is another river named the Kurso in Sarguja which is also infested by these water *bhûts*. To these the Baiga does sacrifice that there may be good rain, productive harvests, and that epidemics may not visit his village. In the same stream lives a kind of demon known as Jata Rohini; the water hole in which he lives abounds in fish, and the Baiga catches one of them with his hands and offers it to the Deo. If any one but a Baiga dare to take a fish from here the Deo pushes him in and drowns him. No one dares to drink from there. If any one ventures to do so the water bubbles up and drowns him.

42. In Sarguja there are two noted caves—one on the Marcha, and the other on the Banka hill. In the former lives a male deity called Mahâdâni Deo. None dares to enter the cave. Now and then a white horse is seen near this cave, and his dung has been found there; but when any one approaches the place he disappears. This

[1] Spencer, *Sociology*, I, 219.

hill grows a quantity of wild pepper (*marcha*) whence its name, and this is brought home by the Mânjhis and used as a spell against disease. Not even a Baiga dares to enter the cave of Mahâdâni Deo. All he ventures to do is to sacrifice a he-goat in the neighbourhood in his honour. In the Banka hill is a cave in which a demon of the Dâno species lives. Her name is unknown, but she brings pain and disease and is of a very violent temper. To appease her the Baiga offers a black and white cock at the foot of the hill and makes a fire offering (*hom*) with molasses and butter. This done, he sprinkles some holy rice (*achhat*) in the direction of her cave which no one dares to enter. When she is angry a voice is heard from the hill saying "Beware! Beware!" (*khabardâr! khabardâr!*) and this is very often followed by an epidemic of cholera. Any one who approaches the neighbourhood of her cave is seized with diarrhoea.

43. There was once an Ahîr named Bachhrâj Kunwar. His leg was cut off in a fight with some Râja and he died. He has become a vicious ghost (*bîr*) and is now worshipped as a godling (*deota*). He now lives on the Ahlor hill in Sarguja, where his petrified body may still be seen, and the Mânjhis go there to worship him. His offering is a black goat, and this offering is specially made when a prayer to him has been answered. The Baiga does the sacrifice. The wife of this Bachhrâj Kunwar lives on the Jhoba hill in Sarguja. No one but a Baiga dares to ascend the hill, and even the Râja of Sarguja, when he visits the neighbourhood, sacrifices a black goat. Mânjhis believe that if these two deities are duly propitiated they can give anything they need. Similarly, on the Mânra hill in Pargana Singrauli lives a demon known as Darrapât Deo. No one dares to ascend the hill. Even Ojhas when they go there sacrifice a goat at the base. To illustrate the mixture of Hinduism with these aboriginal beliefs, it is said that when Râwana abducted Sîta he kept her for some time on this hill, and to this day on the summit may be seen her litter (*pâlki*) turned into stone.

44. Another deity of the same kind is Râja Chandol, whose shrine is on the Gonra hill in Pargana Dudhi under a *pîpal* tree. He is apparently the same as Chandor a deity of the Bengal Mundas [1] who appears to be the same as Chando Omol or Chanala, the moon,

---

[1] Risley, *Tribes and Castes*, II, 103.

worshipped by women as the wife of Singbonga and the mother of the stars.[1] Similar deities known as Mirga Râni and Koti Râni live on the Chainpur hill in Pargana Dudhi. Pât Deo is the deity of the Kaimûr hills in Sarguja, and he has a colleague Sonaich Deo who lives on the Baunra Bûnda hill. One local tradition of the Mânjhis makes Râja Chandol a Chauhân Chhatri from Rîwa. Like him is Bariyâr Sâh, who is said to have been a Rakhsel Chhatri and a Râja of Sarguja. He came to hunt in this part of the country when it was all jungle and took up his residence at Mahuli. He was killed by Bhaiyya Sâh, the ruler of Nagar Untâri, and his Râni became Sati in his honour: since then he and his Râni have been worshipped.

Sacred dances.

45. The sacred dance of the tribe is the *karama* which is performed round a branch of the *karam* tree (*anthocephalus cadamba*) set up in the courtyard of the house. The men and women stand in opposite lines and advance and retreat to the music of the sacred drum (*mândar*). Songs are sung, generally of a very gross nature, and the ceremony is the occasion for much drinking and dissolute conduct.

Pilgrimages.

46. Some of the richer Mânjhis go on the ordinary Hindu pilgrimages to Benares, Prayâg, the shrine of Vindhyabâsini Devi at Bindhâchal, etc. They also go to bathe in the Son which is known as Son Bhadra Mahârâj, "the fortunate great king." They visit a special shrine near his source at Amarkantak. The days for bathing are at eclipses and on the *khichari* festival on the last day of Pûs (January). Bathing is meritorious only on the north bank, which is known as that of Kâshi (Benares).

The tribal priests.

47. Brâhmans are employed by them only for the purpose of fixing lucky days at marriages, etc. The Patâris have been already mentioned. An account of them will be found in the special article referring to them. They worship Ningo Bâghiya and the other regular tribal gods. The Baigas who in the Central Provinces form a special tribe,[2] worship only the village gods and the village goddess, now generally identified with the Hindu Devi.

---

[1] Dalton, *Ethnology*, 186.

[2] Forsyth, *Highlands of Central India*, 373 sq.

48. Contrary to Hindu practice the Mânjhis yoke cows in the plough. They have a triennial festival in honour of Ningo Bâghiya at which according to a common Gond practice they sacrifice calves.[1] To Ningo Bâghiya some pillars are erected which are known as *deo kòthâr* or the "deity's store-house." On the third day of Baisâkh they pour water out of a *lota* on the pillar of Ningo Bâghiya, and sprinkle it with grains of sacred rice (*achhat*) after the sacrifice of a kid (*halwâna*). After this they cook and offer cakes which the Patâri and all the members of the household consume. Among Hindu festivals they recognise the Dasahara on the tenth bright half of Kuâr, the Anant Chaudas on the fourteenth bright half of Bhâdon and the Phagua or Holi on the full moon of Phâlgun. The women's festivals are the third light half of Bhâdon, the sixth and eleventh light half of Kârttik. The Til Sankrânt in Pûs is also observed. On the Sankrânt, or conjunction, in Baisâkh is the Satuân when people eat *sattu* or parched gram flour. Like other Hindus they do not eat mangoes before that date. On the third light half of Bhâdon the women fast, and on the eleventh is the main Karama[2] festival which is generally a drunken orgy. On this day every one dances the karama and drinks liquor, while the women fast. This day ends all agricultural contracts, such as partnership in cultivation, lending of ploughs, etc. On that day they eat the karami, which is a sort of weed found in tanks and streams. They also observe the Rakshabandhan or Salono on the last day of Sâwan, but with this peculiarity that there is no special date for tying on the wristlets of coloured string because Brâhmans are so few in number. They wander about the country during the whole of the following month and tie on the amulets as they arrive at each village. The Brâhman receives for this service some pice and grain which is in addition to the ordinary dues (*kharwan*) which he receives in the form of a sieve (*sûp*) full of grain at each harvest. Mânjhis are liberal in distributing dues of this kind, and in addition to the Brâhman, the Patâri, Nâu, Dhobi, the village messenger (*Kotwâr*), usually a

Festivals.

---

[1] On cow sacrifice among the Gonds, see Hislop, *Papers*, 19, 22.

[2] The Karama among more Hinduised menial tribes is replaced by the Jhûmar dance in which the women go round in a circle with joined hands, *sab milké jhûmar paré, thûthi kahié hamahûn.* "When all are dancing the Jhûmar the handless woman says 'Shall I join in'"? Christian, *Behâr Proverbs*, 51.

Panika by caste, and even in some places Musalmân faqîrs receive the same allowance. Some at the *pitra paksha,* or fifteen days sacred to the worship of the sainted dead, in the month of Kuâr offer the sacred ball (*pinda*) through the Patâri, and shave on the tenth day. There is not, as is the custom among many of the allied tribes, any festival at which youths and girls mix and arrange marriages. The women's festival on the third light half of Bhâdon is confined to married women, and is not shared in by girls or widows.

Women also observe the Jiutiya festival on the 9th of Kuâr.[1] On this day married women fast with the special object of securing long life (*jîv,* whence the festival takes its name) and prosperity to their mothers-in-law and sons. They have a special phrase when a man escapes a great danger, such as an attack from a tiger—*Tuhâr mâi khar Jiutiya kîhan.* "Your mother went through such a rigid fast at the Jiutiya that she did not even brush her teeth." The date of this festival appears to differ in various places. In Bengal it appears to be celebrated on 15th Assin and in Bihâr on 8th dark half of Kârttik. The object in all places seems to be the same, that married women by fasting invoke good luck and long life on their relations.[2]

Fetishism.

49. One fetish peculiar to the Mânjhis and allied Dravidian tribes is the *gurda* or chain fetish. This is an iron chain about 2½ feet long and 7 lbs. in weight, with an iron knot at the end. It is generally accompanied by a leather strip of the same length. This is in charge of the Baiga, and is kept hung up in the shed dedicated to the local deities (*deohâr*). It is treated with great respect and a genuine specimen can be obtained only with great difficulty.

When girls become hysterical they are taken to the shrine and there beaten by the Baiga with his chain, which is understood to embody the local divinity, until the devil leaves them. The treatment is said to succeed at once. It may be noted that this chain under the name of Sâkla Pen has among the regular Gonds become an actual divinity.[3] In the hot weather the local female deity identified with Devi wanders about the air in the middle of the day

---

[1] This, according to Hislop, *Papers,* App. II, is performed in Sâwan.

[2] Risley, *Tribes and Castes,* II, 190 : Grierson, *Behár Peasant Life,* 402.

[3] Sâkla (Hindi *Sánkar,* Sanskrit *Shrinkala,*) means "a chain." See Hislop, *Papers,* App. 47 : *Central Provinces Gazetteer,* 275.

in her chariot (*rath*); and if in that season of the year a child goes out dressed in red clothes the deity rides on it, and the child becomes insensible and can be cured only by the incantations of the Baiga. This is probably a popular way of explaining the effects of sunstroke.[1] One function of the Baiga is forming a sacred line with liquor round the village which foreign ghosts are unable to cross.[2] The belief in ghostly lights which appear to mislead the traveller at night is widespread. As already stated, the mud platform in the Baiga's shrine is supposed to be the residence of the local deities, and he sometimes in addition raises a special Brahm chaura which is a platform in honour of some Brâhman who has died by an unusual or untimely death. On Brahm worship Mr. Baillie writes—"The names classified in the list of Brahms are almost innumerable. The information about them varies from a full and circumstantial account like that given for Ratan Pânrê or which might be given for Harirâm, the Râj Brahm of the Basti District, down to that derived from the name only, the Brâhmanical character of which was taken to show that the particular Bâba referred to was a Brahm. The total number of Brahm worshippers according to the census statements was 406,787, large numbers of whom belong to the Râjput caste the members of which are most likely to incur persecution from a murdered or injured Brahm. The forms of death selected by suicide Brâhmans are diversified in the extreme. Of all I have heard the most horrible and most likely to impress the imagination of the persons against whom it was intended was that of a Brâhman in the Partâbgarh District, who when turned out of his land, to avenge himself, gathered a heap of cow-dung in the centre of one of the fields and lay down on it until he was eaten by worms. This happened sixty years ago, but his fields still stand a waste of jungle grass in the middle of rich cultivated lands, and neither Hindu nor Muhammadan will put a hand to a plough to till them. Whether Brahms are to be classed among malevolent or benificent spirits is a question which would probably be answered differently by different worshippers. Those families to whose account a Brahm's death is due would probably regard him as malevolent, but elsewhere a benificent interest is taken by Brahms in human affairs. Ratan Pânrê is said to be the tutelary deity of many Gonda

---

[1] For similar ideas, see Tylor, *Primitive Culture*, I, 293.

[2] For this, see Tylor, *loc. cit*, I, 454.

villages.[1]" Though they secretly sacrifice cows, they still so far reverence the animal as to bow to it on 15th Kârttik, when they give salt to the animals and oil their horns.[2]

50. The worship of the souls of the dead is, as already stated, in an elementary stage. It is only the more advanced Mânjhis who worship them during the Pitrapaksha in Kuâr, and many now get the Brâhman, and not the Patâri, to offer up the sacred ball (*pinda*) in their honour. When a man is asleep or insensible they believe that the soul is wandering abroad and returns to the body only on recovery of consciousness.[3] Dreams are sometimes true and sometimes false, but it is in this way alone that the spirits of the dead manifest themselves and their appearance is dreaded because it implies that they have not received their due propitiation, and then they bring disease and death.[4] This is particularly the case with the ghost of a Baiga or of his wife. They must be propitiated by the offering of a young pig. This Baiga ghost becomes ruler of all the village ghosts, and his wife queen of all the local Churels or ghosts of women who die within the period of child-bed impurity.

Totems.

51. The sword is a recognised Mânjhi totem. When women pass a *pîpal* tree they bow and veil their faces. No Mânjhi will cut a large tree or any tree which adjoins the special *sál* tree in which the local deity resides.

Omens.

52. The science of omens is widely recognised. When the female jackal (*phenkârin*) howls on the night the foundations of a house are laid the site is abandoned as unlucky. Meeting a hare is a very unlucky omen with them and all the allied tribes.[5] The sudden or unaccountable fall of a tree in front of a person undertaking a journey is also unlucky. The call of the *suiya* bird on the right is a good meeting omen: on the left the reverse; a tiger meeting a traveller is lucky, but stumbling on starting on a journey is ominous. If a jackal cross from right to left or a female *sâmbhar* deer appear in front the journey is abandoned. The langûr baboon

---

[1] *Census Report, North-Western Provinces*, 214: For Ratan Pânrê, see *Introduction to Popular Religion and Folklore*, 122.

[2] This corresponds to the Pola ceremony of the Gonds, for which see Hislop, *Papers*, App. III.

[3] Tylor, *Primitive Culture*, I, 436.

[4] Tylor, *loc. cit.*, II, III.

[5] The modern mythologists of course identify the hare with the Moon. De Gubernatis, *Zoological Mythology*, II, 81.

barking in front is lucky, and when this occurs they clasp their hands and salute the animal.

Taboos.

53. After a Mânjhi is initiated by his preceptor (*guru*) he is warned by him not to eat a particular fruit. This is very generally that of the *bargad* or banyan and is known as *guruchhorni*. Boys, and occasionally girls, have the *râs* name or that determined by astrological considerations fixed by the Pandit, but this is kept secret and they are called by another name.[1] They will not eat the flesh of the cow or the domestic pig, snakes, lizards, crocodiles, or rats. The disuse of beef is comparatively modern, and is based on religious considerations derived from their Hindu neighbours. They will not touch a Dom, Chamâr, Dhobi, or Dharkâr, and they particularly object to the presence of Doms in their villages. The women are not allowed to join in the tribal worship of Ningo Bâghiya, whom they hesitate to name and generally call Bûrha Deo or the "old god." A man will not call his wife by her name. If she has a son he calls her "mother of so and so." A man may not speak to his younger brother's wife or the mother of his son's wife or of his daughter's husband (*samdhin*). A wife may not call her father-in-law by his name.[2] In the morning no one will speak of a donkey, of quarrelling, or death. They have the usual euphemisms in speaking of more dangerous animals, unlucky villages, or disreputable or miserly people. A woman while in her menses is under a rigid taboo, sits and eats apart, and engages in no household duties.[3]

Oaths.

54. Their tribal oaths are touching a broad-sword,[4] touching the feet of a Brâhman, holding a cow's tail, touching Ganges water. They believe that anyone who forswears himself becomes poor and loses his children. Another form of oath occasionally employed is to stand in a pool of water or to walk through fire. These latter oaths are principally used in enquiries before the tribal council.

Witchcraft.

55. Witches are numerous, and feared, and are both male and female. They are detested by the Patâri priests, who use all their efforts to expel

---

[1] On this, see Lubbock, *Origin of Civilisation*, 243.

[2] On these prohibitions arising out of relationships, see Letourneau, *Evolution of Marriage*, 290 : Lubbock, *Origin of Civilisation*, II.

[3] Frazer, *Golden Bough*, II, 238 *sqq*.

[4] The Kanwars of the Central Provinces worship the broad-sword as an emblem of power under the name of Jhâra Khand or Jhagra Khand.—*Central Provinces Gazetteer*, 107.

them from the village. Witches are able to cause sickness and death. A suspected witch is caught, beaten with castor-oil rods,[1] and called on to withdraw her spells. Another plan is to put her standing in water, and to prick her on the breast, tongue, and thigh, with five or six needles tied together. The blood is mixed with rice, which she is made to swallow. The effect of this is that she forgets her unrighteous spells. The ordeal is efficacious only if performed by running water. It is considered possible to injure an enemy by feeding a goat on grain and then sacrificing it in his name before Mahâdâni or some of the other vicious godlings. There are numerous devices to check epidemics. When cholera begins, the elders of the village, with the Ojha, or wizard, feed a black fowl with grain, and drive it beyond the village boundaries, ordering it at the same time to take the disease away with it. If a resident of another village finds the fowl and eats it, cholera comes into his village. Hence, when disease is about, people are very cautious about meddling with stray fowls. When these animals are sent off, a little oil, red lead, and a woman's forehead spangle are usually fastened to its head. When such an animal appears in a village, it is taken to the shrine of the local god and sacrificed there, or in some cases they merely bow before it at the shrine and quietly pass it on to some other village. The original cost of the animal used as a scapegoat is defrayed by public subscription. This arrangement of sending out a scapegoat (*chalauwa*) is common all over the country.[2] Another method of keeping off disease is to hang little miniature cots (*chârpâi*) on the tree over the village shrine. When people are supposed to be under the dominion of a *bhût*, the Ojha is consulted, gets into a state of ecstacy, and names the particular ghost.[3] At exorcisms of this kind it is dangerous for outsiders to be present, as a wandering *bhût* may possess you, and this is perhaps one reason why it is so difficult to learn much of the proceedings of the Ojha.[4] In some cases, as already stated, persons, possessed by a *bhût*, are beaten with the sacred chain (*gurda*) of the Baiga. Another plan is to burn strong smelling substances near the patient in order to drive out the *bhût*. The resin (*dhûp*) extracted from the *sâl* tree is very commonly used for this purpose.

[1] These correspond in their efficacy to the Rowan of Scotland.—W. Henderson, *Folklore of the Northern Counties*, 224; Conway, *Demonology and Devil Lore*, I, 126.

[2] On Scapegoats, see Conway, *Demonology and Devil Lore*, II, 131, 169, 187.

[3] Tylor, *Primitive Culture*, I, 127, 439.

[4] *Ibid*, II, 135.

The office of the Ojha is considered respectable. Noted Ojhas take pupils on payment and instruct them in the craft. It principally consists in the knowledge of a number of hocus-pocus spells (*mantra*), which are used in sudden disease, snake and scorpion bite, and the like.

Dreams.

56. Dreams are valuable as announcing that dead ancestors, who alone appear in this way, need propitiation. They are interpreted by the oldest and most experienced member of the family. When spirits appear in dreams it is usual to promise to make an offering of cakes, molasses, and butter, which is generally effectual.

Evil Eye.

57. They believe in the influence of the Evil Eye (*nazar*). People born on a Saturday have the power of casting it, and it can be avoided by the passes (*jharna*) of an Ojha. They have the usual means of baffling the Evil Eye by hanging beads, nuts, cowries, etc., round the necks of children ; by hanging up a blackened tile in fields or on the roofs of houses ; and by driving iron pins into the door frame. Witches, and people who cast the Evil Eye, are believed to wander about at night with an evil effect. They touch people while they are asleep and beset them. They cut and carry off locks of their hair, and thus acquire an influence over them. Divination is an art unknown to the tribe, and is done for them by Brâhmans.

Agricultural beliefs.

58. On the third light half of Baisâkh, they take omens of the season, and make five furrows in the field with a plough. On that day they sow a little *sâwân* millet, generally five handfuls. When they begin cultivation, they take the plough five times round the field, and sow five handfuls of seed grain. That day they eat specially good food. They do not commence sowing until the Baiga sets the example ; and so with manuring. The Baiga throws down five baskets of manure and then every one does the same. They interpret the cry of the cuckoo (*papiha*) as an omen of heavy rain. When the tree lizard (*girgit*) becomes red, and the skin on a buffalo's tail scarlet, and when buffalo urine dries up at once on the ground, it is a sign of immediate rain. A rainbow in the evening marks the cessation of the rains : when it shows in the morning, rain will be abundant. When the honey in the nests of the jungle bee coagulates, and when there is frost in spring, the autumn rains will be heavy. When the crop is ripe, the Baiga cuts five handfuls, and harvest begins. There

is no special worship, but on that day the Baiga gets a meal of rice and pulse. Some, however, make an offering to the village gods. Cutting begins on Monday, Wednesday, or Friday. Saturday is a very unlucky day for beginning any field work. There appears no trace of the custom of rushing at the last uncut portion of the field and carrying the grain home with special ceremonies.[1] But when the new grain is ripe, the first five handfuls cut are taken home, crushed, and offered to Ningo Bâghiya. The special guardian deity of crops is known as the "Green lady"—Hariyeri or Hariyâri Devi. She is worshipped with a fire offering (*hom*) in the field at sowing and harvest time. Another of these field godlings is Chordeva, the field thief. He has a wife known as Chordevi, and both are sometimes known as Chor and Chorni. Like the Jâk and Jâkni,[2] they live in different but adjoining villages, and the Chor robs threshing floors to support his wife. Hence, if you see one village thriving and its neighbour ruined, you may know that the Chorni lives in the former and the Chor in the latter. These field thieves are kept in order by the Ojha and Baiga.[3] *Bhûts* are also in the habit of robbing threshing floors until the grain is measured. In order to counteract them, a sacred circle is made round the corn heap, and baskets are never allowed to remain mouth upwards.

Food.

59. In addition to the food taboos already noted, they will not eat flesh during the fortnight devoted to the souls of the dead (*pitra-paksha*), and when a man returns from a pilgrimage he abstains for a time from meat and fish. The children eat first and the eldest last, men and women eat apart. As they eat, they throw a little food and water on the ground in the name of Paramesar. They use hemp (*gânja*), liquor and tobacco. Liquor is offered to the local god (*Deohâr*), but not to Ningo Bâghiya. They believe that using hemp (*gânja*) keeps off itch and malaria; and that the use of liquor wards off malaria. Drunkenness is considered disreputable.

Salutation.

60. Equals salute one another in the form known as *pâélagi.* Elders receive the *pâélagi* and give a blessing (*asîs*) in return. They do *pâélagi* to clansmen and *salâm* to strangers. In the presence of superiors

---

[1] See Frazer, *Golden Bough*, Chap. III.

[2] For which see *Introduction to Popular Religion*, 234.

[3] Among the Orâons, Chordeva has become an evil spirit, which, in the form of a cat, injures pregnant women.— Dalton, *Ethnology*, 251.

some stand on one leg, take off their shoes or turbans, and *salám.* Connections by marriage (*Samdhi*) use the salutation *Juhár,* "may you live long!" An elder gives a blessing to a younger in the form *níkéraho:* "may you be prosperous!" They salute by putting the left hand under the right elbow and raising the right hand to the level of the forehead. Women on meeting embrace each other and weep.[1] When a man meets his mother, or grandmother, he touches her feet and says *Páélagi dái:* "I touch your feet mother!" She kisses him on the lips and cheeks and says *Jiyo putra:* "Live, my son!"

Status of women.

61. Women are, as a rule, well treated. They say that a house is empty (*súna*) without a woman in it. The wife, and especially the senior wife, if there are more than one, is mistress in household affairs, and she is consulted about marriage alliances and other important business. But women are considered much inferior to men, and a wife cannot sit on a cot in the presence of her husband: she eats after him and walks behind him on the road. But quarrelling and wrangling are certainly not so common among them as with ordinary low caste Hindus.[2] Some men, however, ill-treat their wives, and cases of suicide and the escape of young wives to their parents' home are not uncommon. The tribal council punishes misconduct of this kind. In any case a woman has to take bad language from her husband in silence or stand the risk of a beating.

Old people, visitors, strangers.

62. Old people are respected and supported. The Mânjhis are very hospitable, especially to clansmen, and often incur debt in consequence of this. When a guest comes, even if they have to borrow, they arrange a performance of the Karama for him and supply him with liquor. They assist relations on occasions of mourning and rejoicing. There is a good deal of clan feeling amongst them, and if a tribesman is injured by a stranger, they, though generally a very peaceable people, are ready to turn out with their bludgeons to assist him. They very seldom appear as plaintiffs or defendants in court, and violent crimes against person and property are practically unknown among them.

---

[1] This was the way in which Penelope welcomed Telemachus.—*Odyssey,* XVII, 38. And see the whole subject discussed by Darwin, *Expression of the Emotions,* p., 216, *sq.*

[2] This has also been noticed in the case of the Gonds.—*Central Provinces Gazetteer,* 35.

63. One division of Ahîrs, the Kaunrâi, will eat food and drink water touched by them. Doms will eat their leavings. They will eat food cooked in butter (*pakki*), only if cooked by themselves or by Brâhmans. They pride themselves on abstaining from the use of beef and pork.

Social status.

64. The women are tattooed. They say that if they are not tattooed, Paramesar will pitch them out of heaven.[1] Nearly all the men among the Mânjhis, as well as the allied tribes of the Chero, Panika, and Parahiya wear little brass or gold rings in the lobe of the ear.[2] Some wear their silver bangles on both wrists. Some Mânjhi men wear iron rings, made of three folds of wire, on the little finger and thumb of the right hand: some wear a broad brass amulet (*bâzu*) on the upper part of the left arm. A few wear silver images of Sîtala with the figure embossed and gilt. Some again have a thin double necklace of small purple beads, with a larger white glass bead strung between the others, every three or four inches apart. Some again wear a broad brass ring with a thin iron wire ring beside it on the first finger of the right hand. The better class wear the ordinary Hindu jacket (*mirzâi*) and loin-cloth (*dhoti*); but the clothing of the poorer men is very scanty and consists merely of a small loin-rag (*bhagai*), and a scrap of cloth tied round the head, while the hair hangs behind uncut and unkempt. The Mânjhi women all wear heavy pewter anklets (*pairi*). These are usually terribly heavy and cumbrous and give them a peculiar heavy stumbling gait.[3] Women of the Poiya sept wear another form of anklet like the *gorahra* of the Hindus. They are not allowed to wear yellow clothes nor glass bangles (*chûri*), and, even if married do not apply red lead to the parting of the hair, as ordinary low caste Hindu women do. They go so far as not to allow a woman of another caste into the dwelling-house or cow-shed, if she wears yellow clothes or a forehead spangle (*tikuli*). Mânjhi women must keep the head bare, and are not allowed to draw the sheet over it.

Clothes, jewelry, tattooing.

---

[1] Lubbock, *Origin of Civilization*, 374. For the custom of tattooing among these tribes, see *Agariya*, para. 22.

[2] The Mariya Gonds have the upper part of the lobe pierced and ornamented with small earrings of brass or iron.—*Central Provinces Gazetteer*, 35; Hislop, *Papers*, 11.

[3] These heavy anklets are a favourite subject of rural satire—*Bâhar pudwai tîn ser kê neura, gharê sûp na daura*: "outside she boasts of her anklets weighing three sers and has not at home even a grain sieve and basket."—Christian, *Proverbs of Behâr*, 34.

This rule is relaxed only for old women in cold or wet weather.[1] The women have a way of enveloping their lower limbs in the loin-cloth so tightly, that when they sit down on the ground they have to spread out their legs. They, also, contrary to the custom of all ordinary Hindu women, wear a sort of inner garment, like a man s *langoti*, which is known as *bhagua*. This is made specially for them by the weavers of the Panika tribe, who charge fancy prices for it. It is ornamented along the edges with red stripes. Women keep this a secret, and are very unwilling to speak of it or give a specimen. They also wear a specially warm heavily woven upper sheet of cotton known as *darab*, which has an ornamented border. This may be worn by other castes, but it is a special Mânjhi dress.

Morality.

65. Though there is a good deal of tribal license, both before and after marriage, the women are generally considered to be good wives. Prostitution or polyandry is unknown among them.

Occupation.

66. They work as cultivators and ploughmen and cultivate at lower rates than their Hindu neighbours. Their special form of cultivation used to be the *dahya*, by which a patch of jungle was periodically burnt down and seeds scattered in the ashes.[2] This is now being gradually abandoned. The first crop sown on newly cleared land is generally the small sesamum (*tilli*). They are, as is usual with half-civilised races,[3] lazy and inefficient cultivators.

Mal.—(Sanskrit *Malla*, "a wrestler"),[4] a sub-division of the Kurmi tribe almost altogether confined to the Azamgarh District.—A reference to them will be found under the head of Bisen Râjputs. They regard themselves as descended through a Kurmi concubine from the Rishi Mayûra Bhatta, who, after leaving Gorakhpur settled at Kankradih, on the banks of the Sarju, in Pargana Nathupur of the Azamgarh District. The present Mals of Kankradih claim to hold under a grant from Harsha Varddhana, King of Kanauj. The Mals are exogamous and intermarry with

---

[1] This is the rule also with the Santâls.—Dalton, *Ethnology*, 217.

[2] On this, see *Gazetteer, Central Provinces*, 280; Hislop, *Papers*, 2; Forsyth, *Highlands of Central India*, 102.

[3] See instances collected by Spencer, *Principles of Sociology*, I, 59.

[4] Dr. Oppert suggests that most of these tribal names of which the first syllable is Mal, such as Malla, Mala, Malava, Malaya, etc., are derived from the Gauda-Dravidian root Mala in the sense of "mountain."—*Original Inhabitants of Bharatavarsa*, 13.

the Sainthwâr Kurmis of Gorakhpur, who take the title of Nâgbansi or "of the seed of the dragon." Monogamy is the rule and concubinage is prohibited. Marriage is generally adult. Widow marriage is prohibited.

2.. Some are Vaishnavas and others Saivas. They specially worship Kâli and the Dih, the aggregate of the village godlings. In their ceremonies they agree with the Kurmis, of whom, in spite of their legend of aristocratic descent, they are admittedly a subdivision.

Malang: a class of Muhammadan Faqîrs who are usually regarded as a branch of the Madâri (*q. v.*). They call themselves specially followers of Jaman Jati, who was a disciple of Shâh Madâr—According to Dr. Herklots [1] "their dress is the same as that of the Muharram Malang Faqîrs, except that they wear the hair of the head very full, or it is matted and formed into a knot behind. Sometimes they wear some kind of cloth round the knot. Some of them tie round the waist a chain or thick rope and wear a very small loin-cloth. Wherever they sit down they burn the *dhûni* (fire) and sometimes rub the ashes over their bodies." Mr. Maclagan [2] says that in the Panjâb "the term is generally applied in a more general way to any unattached religious beggar who drinks *bhang* or smokes *charas* in excess, wears nothing but a loin-cloth, and keeps fire always near him. The Malangs are said to wear the hair on the head very full, or it is matted and tied into a knot behind. The shrine of Jhangi Shâh Khâki, in the Pasrûr Tahsîl of the Siâlkot District, is frequented by Malangs."

2. At the last Census they appear to have been included among the Madâris.

Mâlavi: a division of Brâhmans who take their name from being emigrants from Mâlwa.—Of them Sir J. Malcolm writes :[3] "Besides the various tribes of Brâhmans from the Dakkhin, there are no less than eighty-four sects in Central India ; but almost all these trace, or pretend to trace, the emigration of their ancestors, and that at no distant period, from neighbouring countries. The six sects, or Chhanâti tribe of Brâhmans, alone claim the Province of Mâlwa as their native country, and even they refer back to a period of twenty or thirty generations, when their ancestors came into it ; but they still

---

[1] *Qânûn-i-Islâm*, 192; and see the article *Dîwâna, supra.*
[2] *Panjâb Census Report*, 197.
[3] *Central India*, II, 122.

have a pride in being termed Mâlwa Brâhmans, which to the rest would be a reproach." Of the origin of the Mâlwa Brâhmans in this part of the country nothing very certain is known. Mr. Sherring[1] suspects that they are akin to their neighbours the Gujarâti Brâhmans. They have a legend that one of the kings of Mâlwa endeavoured to make all the Brâhmans of that Province eat *kachchi* and *pakki* together, and that, on their objecting, he confined them in a double-storied house. At night they saw the people of the place worshipping a local godling named Pânrê Bâba, and on this the Brâhmans vowed to worship the deity themselves if he saved them from their trouble. The Bâba got the doors unlocked, and they all fled to Benares. Some of their brethren who remained behind obeyed the orders of the king, and since then the branch in this part of the country have given up all connection with them.

Tribal organisation.

2. The Mâlavi Brâhmans are divided into thirteen-and-a-half *gotras*, which, with their titles, are as follows—Bhâradwâja, Chaubê Parâsara, Dûbê, Angiras Chaubê, Bhârgava Chaubê. All these are Rigvedis. Sândilya, Dûbê, Kâsapa Chaubê, Kautsa Dûbê—these are Yajurvedis—Vatsa, Vyâs, Gautam, Tivâri, Lohita Tivâri, and Kaundinya—who are Samavedis. Lastly come the Katyâyana, Pâthakand, the Maitreya, or half *gotra*, both of which are Samavedis. They follow the usual Brâhmanical rules of intermarriage. Their chief religious functions appear to be acting as family priests of the Mathura Chaubês. Many of them live by secular occupations, such as trading, doing clerk's work, and general service, and they are in fact more of a trading than a priestly class. The Mâlavi Brâhmans do not hold a high reputation in the Eastern part of the Province, and are generally regarded as tricky and quarrelsome.

Mâli[2] (Sanskrit *mâlika*, "a garland-maker,") a caste whose primary occupation is gardening and providing flowers for use in Hindu worship.—The caste is a purely occupational one, and there is good reason to suppose that the Mâli is closely allied to the Kurmi, Koiri, and Kâchhi, the two last of whom engage in the finer kind of culture which resembles that of the regular Mâli. At the same time the caste cannot be a very ancient one. "Generally speaking

---

[1] *Hindu Tribes*, I, 104, *sq*.

[2] Based on enquiries at Mirzapur and notes by Bâbu Âtma Râm, Head-master, High School, Mathura; M. Baldeo Sahây, Head-master, High School, Fatehgarh; M. Bhagwati Dayâl Sinh, Tahsildar, Chhibramau, Farrukhâbâd.

it may be said that flowers have scarcely a place in the Veda. Wreaths of flowers, of course, are used as decorations, but the separate flowers and their beauty are not yet appreciated. That lesson was first learned later by the Hindu when surrounded by another flora. Amongst the Homeric Greeks, too, in spite of their extensive gardening, and their different names for different flowers, not a trace of horticulture is yet to be found." [1]

Tribal legends.

2. One story of the origin of the caste is that one day Pârvati was plucking flowers in her garden, when a thorn pierced her finger. She complained to Siva, who took a particle of sandalwood from his head, or by another account a d op of his perspiration, and on this Pârvati wiped the blood from her wounded finger, and thus the first Mâli was created. According to the Bengal legend as told by Mr. Risley, they trace their descent from the garland-maker attached to the household of Râja Kans at Mathura Krishna asked him one day for a gar and of flowers, and he at once gave it. "On being told to fasten it with a string, he, for want of any other, took off his Brâhmanical cord and tied it; on which Krishna most ungenerously rebuked him for his simplicity in parting with it, and announced that in future he would be ranked among the Sûdras."

Internal organisation.

3. According to the returns of the last Census the Mâlis are divided into eight principal endogamous sub-castes: Barhauliya, Baheniya, Bhâgîrathi, Dilliwâl or Dehliwâl, Golê, Kapri, whose speciality is making the crowns, ornaments, etc., used in Hindu marriage processions, Kanaujiya, and Phûlmâli. The complete Census returns record 853 sub-divisions, among which those of most local importance are the Deswâli of Sahâranpur; the Panwâr and Samri of Bulandshahr; the Bahliyân, Bhanolê, Bhawâni, Bhomiyân, Khatri, Mohur, Meghiyân, Mulâna, and Pemaniyân of Morâdâbâd; the Râj-puriya and Tholiya of Basti; the Kota of the Tarâi. In Farrukhâbâd we also find the Kachhmâli, who claim kinship with the Kâchhis; Khatiya, who are said to owe their name to their constant use of manure (*khât*), and the Hardiya or growers of turmeric (*haldi*). In Agra are found the Mathur or "residents of Mathura," who are the same as the Phûlmâli or "flower" Mâli, work only as gardeners, and forbid widow mar-

[1] Schrader, *Prehistoric Antiquities*, 121.

riage; the Mewâti, or "those from Mewât," who allow widow marriage; and the Dilwâri, or Delhi branch, who permit widow marriage, and work at drawing gold and silver wire. In Mathura are found the Phûlmâli, Surâb, Hardiya, Saini, Golê and Kâchhi; of which the Saini and Kâchhi are usually treated as separate castes, and have been so recorded at the last enumeration. The sub-castes of the Mâlis and Sainis also disclose a strong resemblance. These sub-castes are endogamous and are each divided into a number of *gotras*, a fairly complete list of which no member of the caste can pretend to supply. The rule of exogamy is thus stated at Mathura: A man can marry within his own sub-caste, subject to the condition that the bride is not of the same *gotra* as that of the bridegroom, his mother, and grandmother. He can marry two sisters, but the second wife must be younger than the first. Marriage is usually infant if the parties can afford it, but the marriage of poor adult males is not uncommon. Widows and divorced wives can re-marry by the *sagâi* or *dharîcha* form, and the levirate is permitted under the usual conditions, but is not compulsory on the woman.

Religion.

4. In Mathura they are Sâktas and worship Devi as their tribal deity. In Farrukhâbâd they have a tribal godling named Kurehna, to whom they make offerings of he-goats, rams, and sweetmeats at marriages and at the birth of a male child. These offerings are made in the house with closed doors, and no member of another caste is allowed to be present. The offerings are eaten by the family, and whatever is left is immediately buried with great precautions against any one seeing the performance. In Dehra Dûn they are worshippers of Kâli Devi, Aghornâth, and Narasinha Deva. To the East of the Province they worship Kâli and Mahâkâli, and the Pânchonpîr in the manner common to castes of the same social grade.

Occupation.

5. The primary occupation of the Mâli is gardening and he is employed by private persons, or grows flowers and vegetables in his own land for sale. In the larger towns there is a considerable trade in flowers, which are used at marriages and other festivities, and bought to be offered at the daily worship of the gods. Some are again used for the manufacture of essences, of which the rose-water made in large quantities at Ghâzipur and Fatehgarh is a good example. The regular distiller of these essences is the Gandhi, who buys flowers

from Mâlis. There is also a wholesale dealer in flowers called Gulfarosh or "rose seller," who purchases flowers in large quantities and supplies orders for important marriages, etc. The Mâli again provides the nuptial crown (*maur*) for the bridegroom. He has another special function, as the village priest of Sîtala, and when an epidemic of small-pox rages in a village, a general subscription is raised, out of which the Mâli does the necessary worship to Kâli and Sîtala. He also inoculates children, and is thus a constant opponent to our vaccinators. In this capacity he is known as Darshaniya (*darshan*, "seeing, worshipping"). In the same way he is sometimes employed as a sort of hedge priest to the village godlings and minor gods when the services of a Brâhman or Sanyâsi are not available.

Social rank.

6. The rank of the Mâli is fairly respectable. They eat goat's flesh and mutton, but not beef, and drink liquor. In Farrukhâbâd they will eat *pakki* of Kâyasths; *kachchi* of Lohârs and Sunârs; and drink water with the same. Nâis and Kahârs will eat *pakki* from them, and Kahârs will eat their *kachchi*. The Mâli is a well-known figure in the folktales. The hero is often his son, or is protected by the gardener and his wife. One popular verse runs—

Mâli châhê barasna; Dhobi châhê dhûp; Sâhu châhê bolna; chor châhê chup.

"The gardener prays for rain; the washerman for sunshine; the banker loves a chat; and the thief quiet."

Distribution of Mâlis according to the Census of 1891.

DISTRICTS.	Barh-auliya.	Bahen-iya.	Bhâgi-rathi.	Dilli-wâl.	Golê.	Kapri.	Kanau-jiya.	Phûl-mâli.	Others.	TOTAL.
Dehra Dûn	...	10	110	...	270	...	5	146	233	774
Sahâranpur	...	3,619	7,803	1,718	11,814	54	117	172	5,704	31,001
Muzaffarnagar	...	483	4,831	...	852	109	1	278	883	7,437
Meerut	...	2,312	5,069	...	...	1	...	466	9,572	17,420
Bulandshahr	...	...	...	...	...	...	...	826	10,239	11,065
Aligarh	...	...	...	...	...	...	...	1,936	1,334	3,270
Mathura	...	...	...	2	5	...	...	5,524	1,561	7,092
Agra	...	...	...	...	...	...	6	291	...	729
Farrukhâbâd	45	...	...	...	...	...	330	2,391	927	3,693
Mainpuri	4	...	...	...	...	...	...	724	384	1,112
Etâwah	...	...	...	...	...	...	16	543	277	836
Etah	69	10	...	...	14	...	...	433	256	782
Bareilly	30	...	...	64	...	89	51	2,638	352	3,224

Bijnor	...	...	...	...	...	...	...	594	247	841
Budâun	256	...	...	24	...	...	2	1,055	983	2,320
Morâdâbâd	252	43,211	5,195	...	117	...	30	3,241	19,094	71,140
Shâhjahânpur	20	8	...	13	...	...	352	1,067	183	1,643
Pîlibhît	13	...	...	71	...	...	66	564	210	924
Cawnpur	225	...	...	...	17	...	431	2,880	2,511	6,064
Fatehpur	761	...	...	...	...	...	88	1,153	1,759	3,761
Bânda	153	...	...	...	...	...	...	1,468	288	1,909
Hamîrpur	...	...	...	...	...	...	3	1,722	333	2,058
Allahâbâd	1,325	...	...	...	...	...	...	592	1,771	3,688
Jhânsi	...	...	...	...	...	...	...	427	168	595
Jâlaun	...	...	...	...	...	...	...	567	174	741
Lalitpur	...	...	...	...	...	...	...	579	54	633
Benares	940	...	...	...	...	...	87	125	770	1,922
Mirzapur	1,044	...	...	...	...	...	...	...	876	1,920
Jaunpur	1,340	...	...	...	...	...	...	28	638	2,006
Ghâzipur	183	...	...	...	...	...	442	90	358	1,073

Distribution of Mâlis according to the Census of 1891—concluded.

DISTRICTS.	Barh-auliya.	Bahen-iya.	Bhâgi-rathi.	Dilli-wâl.	Golê.	Kapri.	Kanau-jiya.	Phûl-mâli.	Others.	TOTAL.
Ballia	...	...	...	...	...	...	682	642	480	1,804
Gorakhpur	394	...	...	...	...	...	505	1,540	2,341	4,780
Basti	1,106	...	...	...	...	...	...	395	1,173	2,674
Azamgarh	303	...	...	...	...	...	292	187	865	1,647
Garhwâl	...	...	...	...	...	...	...	...	36	36
Tarâi	...	10	1,912	...	12	...	...	247	4,215	6,396
Lucknow	141	...	...	32	...	...	122	1,426	1,963	3,684
Unâo	...	...	...	...	31	...	129	3,656	2,996	6,812
Râê Bareli	490	...	...	...	...	...	74	2,915	1,651	5,130
Sitapur	...	...	...	18	...	...	298	370	1,188	1,874
Hardoi	...	...	...	...	...	...	153	2,144	778	3,075
Kheri	...	...	...	9	...	...	22	575	228	834
Faizâbâd	1,682	...	...	...	...	...	...	145	450	2,277

Gonda	...	...	...	...	...	...	...	4,091	376	4.467
Bahrâich	188	...	...	...	..	...	24	216	950	1,378
Sultânpur	328	...	...	...	...	...	...	429	268	1.025
Partâbgarh	174	...	...	...	...	...	...	579	1,462	2 215
Bârabanki	577	...	...	...	...	...	79	2,177	965	3,798
TOTAL	12,043	49,663	24,920	1,951	13,132	253	4,407	54,254	22.479	245,876

Malkâna, Malakâna (*mâlik*, "a ruler").—A sept of Muhammadan Râjputs, chiefly found in Agra and Mathura. Originally they were mostly Jais and Gaurua Thâkurs who have been converted to Islâm by the sword, but still retain many Hindu customs and are known by Hindu names. They are classed among the Naumuslim.[1]

Distribution of the Malkânas according to the Census of 1891.

Districts.	Number.
Mathura	1,000
Agra	4,546
Mainpuri	27
Etah	28
Total .	5,601

Mallâh[2] (Arabic *mallah*, "to be salt," or, according to others, "to move its wings as a bird")—a general term including various boating and fishing tribes. The term is no doubt purely occupational, and, being of Arabic origin, must have been introduced in comparatively recent times. But in spite of the doubts expressed by Mr. Risley,[3] it seems beyond question that in Northern India, at least, there is a definite social group, including a number of endogamous tribes, of which various lists are given, which are collected under the general term Mallâh. The group includes a number of diverse elements, and it is this fact which makes an ethnological analysis of them so intricate and perplexing. By other tribes they are known as Mallâh, Kewat, Dhîmar, Karbak, Nikhâd, Kachhwâha, Mânjhi, Kumbhilak or Jâlak. They are very generally known as Mallâh or Mânjhi, but the latter is more properly the designation of the steersman of the boat, so called because he sits in the middle (*madhya*). They must be carefully distinguished from the Dravidian Mânjhis.

[1] *Mathura Settlement Report*, 35.

[2] Based on enquiries at Mirzapur and notes by Mr. W. Cockburn, Deputy Collector, Jâlaun; M. Udit Nârâyan Lâl, Ghâzipur; M. Bhagwân Dâs, Allahâbâd.

[3] *Tribes and Castes*, II, 64.

MALLÂH.

2. Most Mallâhs represent themselves as descended from the Nishâda, a mountain tribe of the Vindhya range. Though this country is famous as the kingdom of Nala, it does not appear exactly where it was situated. It may be concluded that it was not far from Vidharba (Bihâr), as that was the kingdom of Damayanti, and from the directions given by Nala to Damayanti, it seems to be near the Vindhya mountains, and roads led from it across the Raksha mountain to Avanti and the South as well as to Vidharba and Kosala. It may also be noted that a colony of the same people lived at Sringavera on the Ganges, a day's march above its junction with the Ganges, and their king is described in the Râmâyana as having treated Râma and Sîta with kindness in their wanderings.[1] The Bâthma or Sribâstav Mallâhs have a tradition that they were originally Srivâstava Kâyasths, and lived at some place called Srinagar in the hills, and were driven from there, because they refused to give one of their girls to the king of that country. The ancestor of the Mallâhs of the Ganges valley in the Eastern districts of the Provinces is said to have steered the boat in which Râm Chandra crossed the river on his way to Chitrakût during his banishment, and is said to have settled at the village of Râm Chaura, where there is now a ferry across the Ganges about twenty miles above Allahâbâd. The head-quarters of the Mirzapur Mallâhs is at Sirsa on the Tons, in the Allahâbâd District, close to where that river joins the Ganges. In Benares they have a tradition that "Râma, being pleased with the head of the caste, gave him a horse, on which he placed a bridle, not on the head, but, in his ignorance, on the tail. Hence the custom, it is stated, of having the helm at the stern of a boat instead of in front."[2]

Traditions of origin.

3. As might be expected in the case of a tribe which is of occupational origin and made up of various elements, the lists of endogamous sub-tribes are very indefinite. In the last Census these are given as Agarwâla; Bâthma (which appears to be a corruption of Srivâstava and to be derived from the old city of Sravâsti, the present Sahet Mahet of the Gonda District, which gives its title to so many sub-castes of

Tribal organization.

---

[1] Wilson, *Vishnu Purâna*, 190; *Theatre of the Hindus, Uttara Râma Charitra*, I 300.

[2] Sherring, *Hindu Tribes*, I, 347.

other tribes); Châîn, which is said to be derived from Charva, which was the title of a tribe supposed to be descended from an outcaste Vaisya; Dhuriya; Kewat; Kharêbind; Nikhâd, who take their name from their Nishâda ancestor; and the Surahiya. The complete returns give 625-sub-divisions of the Hindu and 22 of the Musalmân branch, of which those of the most local importance are the Chaudhariya of Aligarh; the Balliya of Mathura; the Jarya of Agra, Mainpuri, and Etâwah; the Bhok of Cawnpur; the Nathu of Allahâbâd; the Bhârmarê of Benares; the Tiyar of Ghâzipur; the Kulwant of Ballia; the Gonriya and Kalwant of Gorakhpur; the Dhelphora, Mahohar, Sonhâr, and Turaiha of Basti; the Bhontiya and Machhar of Garhwâl; the Râjghatiya of Lucknow and Bâṛabanki; the Dhâr of Unâo; the Kharautiya of Faizâbad; the Jalchhatri and Khas of Sultânpur. A list collected at Mirzapur gives the usual seven sub-castes—Muriya or Muriyâri; Bâthawa or Badhariya; Châi, Châîn or Chaini; Guriya or Goriya; Tiyar; and Surahiya or Sorahiya. So far this agrees with Mr. Sherring's list from Benares. The Mirzapur list adds Bind, and the Benares list Pandûbi or "one who dives in water;" Kulwat or Kulwant, "one of gentle birth;" and Kewat. An Allahâbâd list gives Bâthmi or Bathwa; Châîn; Ghogh; Tiyar; Goriya; Sorahiya, and Sribâthawa Some of these, such as the Bind, Kharêbind, and Kewat, have been separately enumerated at the last Census, and it is convenient to treat them as distinct endogamous groups; but the so-called classification of the Mallâhs as a caste is quite sufficient to show that it is nothing more than an occupational aggregate made up of very divergent elements.

Marriage rules.

4. All the sub-castes described above are strictly endogamous and will not eat or smoke together. They have, as a rule, no general tribal council; but the local groups hold meetings (*panchâyat*) of their own, consisting of as many adult males as can be brought together. They deal only with matters of caste discipline, and their orders are enforced by excommunication. Restoration is secured by giving a feast (*bhojan*) to the castemen. To the East of the Province, where they are most numerous, they appear to be in the transitional stage between infant and adult marriage;—the former being preferred by those families who have risen to a more respectable social position. Pre-nuptial infidelity is said to be reprobated but a clear distinction is drawn between an amour with a tribes-

man or an outsider. The latter involves summary excommunication of the girl and her relations; but it may be condoned by a tribal feast, and then the girl can be married in the caste. Their law of exogamy is not very clearly defined. In Allahâbâd it appears that the descendants of a common ancestor are not allowed to intermarry; but with such people who have no professional genealogists, the recollection of relationship lasts seldom more than three or at the most four generations, and after this cousins freely intermarry. The marriage in the regular form (*charhauwa*) runs through the regular stages—the inspection of the bride and bridegroom by the relations on both sides; the comparison of horoscopes (*râsbarg*); the dressing of the bride in clothes supplied by the bridegroom, which is known as the "marking down" of the girl (*larki kâ chhenkua*); the reciprocal present to the bridegroom (*bar chhekani*); the fixing by the village Pandit of an auspicious moment (*sâvat sa' at*) for the commencement of the anointing (*tel ablauni*) of the boy and girl; the sending to the friend on both sides of the marriage invitation (*lagan pattra*), which is tied with a red and yellow string (*kalâwa*) and contains inside a little rice and turmeric, all of which the bridegroom lays on the household shrine; the starting of the procession (*bârât*); the worship of Gancsa (*Ganeshji ki pûja*); the cooking of food for the family godling (*deota kâ neota*); the cooking of an offering of food for the sainted dead (*pitr kâ neota*); the ceremonial purchase of parched grain (*lâwa*), which is sprinkled on the hair as they revolve round the marriage shed; the waving ceremony (*parachhan*), done over the head of the bridegroom to scare evil spirits and bring good luck; the return of the procession to the halting-place (*janwânsa*) assigned to them outside the village; the actual ceremony, where the bride is brought out by the barber's wife and seated to the right of the boy; the tying of their clothes in a knot (*gathbandhan*); the five circumambulations (*bhaunri*) round the marriage shed; the marking of the parting of the bride's hair with red lead (*sindurdân*); the pouring over the pair of the parched grain by the bride's brother into a fan (*beni*) held by her; the visit to the retiring-room (*kohabar*), where the bridegroom's marriage crown (*maur*) is removed and he is fed on curds and sugar and freely chaffed by the female relations of the bride; the ceremonial *confarreatio* or feeding of the married pair on rice and pulse (*khichari*); the return of the bride, if she be nubile, to the house of her husband; the worship of the Ganges (*Gangaji ki pûja*);

the untying of the marriage bracelet (*kangan utárna*); the drowning of the marriage jar (*kalsa, bandanwár, dubána*). All these ceremonies have been more or less fully described in connection with other castes.

Widow marriage.

5. Widow marriage (*sagái, dharauna, baithki*) is permitted, and the levirate, under the usual limitations, is allowed; in fact the latter has the preference, and if there be a younger brother of the deceased husband who is unmarried and of a suitable age, the widow is generally married to him. The ceremony, such as it is, consists merely in the dressing of the woman in a suit of clothes and ornaments provided by the bridegroom. This is always done in secret at night in a dark room, apparently the element of secresy in the ceremonial being intended to propitiate the offended spirit of the dead husband. The parents of a virgin widow can dispose of her in marriage without the leave of the relatives of her late husband; but if the girl have lived with her first husband, his rélatives have a right to a voice in the subsequent disposal of her, and in many cases insist on being repaid the expenses of the first marriage by the friends of the second husband. A man can take a widow (*sagái*) while his first wife is alive; but he is understood to do this only in case his first wife is barren, or if, as is often the case, she desires to secure a helpmate for household work. But, as a rule, it is only widowers who take a widow in marriage by the *sagái* form. As Mallâhs often leave their wives and go away for considerable periods on voyages up and down the Ganges or Jumna, the women are left much to themselves, with the result that the standard of female morality is not high, and intertribal *liasons* are not seriously regarded. This can be atoned for by a tribal feast, and, as among most of the castes of a similar social rank, the tribal council requires substantial evidence, generally nothing short of the direct evidence of eye-witnesses will be accepted as sufficient. Habitual infidelity is regarded as sufficient grounds for a husband discarding his wife with the leave of the tribal council, and, though there is some difference of practice, it seems to be admitted that women discarded in this way may, if they show a tendency to reform their morals, be re-married within the tribe by the *sagái* form.

Domestic ceremonies.

6. Their domestic ceremonies are of the normal type. There are no ceremonies during pregnancy. The Chamârin midwife attends for six days, when, if the

baby be a boy, the usual *chhathi* ceremony is performed. In the case of girls, this is done on the eighth day, when the mother is regarded as pure, and a Pandit is called in, who selects the religious name (*râs ka nâm*), while the parents themselves select a name to be used for ordinary purposes. Children under eight years of age, or those who are unmarried, are buried; others are cremated in the usual way. For a male ten holy balls are offered on the tenth day, and for a woman nine on the ninth day. These are offered by the funeral priest (*Mahâpâtr, Mahâbrâhman*). On the anniversary (*barsi*), twelve balls are offered. They have a special *pinda* offering for the sonless dead. A few who are in good circumstances go to Gaya to perform the Srâddha, and they do the usual Nârâyani-bal ceremony for those who die away from home.

Religion.

7. To the East of the Province their tribal deities are Mahâdeva, Kâli, Bhâgawati, Mahâbîr, Ganga Mâi, Mahâlakshmi, Mahâsâraswati, the village godlings (*dih*), and the personification of the cremation ground in the form of Ghât or Masân. As household deities they have the Pânchon Pîr. Kâli and Bhâgawati are worshipped every second year with the sacrifice of a goat and the offering of chaplets of flowers. Mahâbîr receives sweetmeats on Sundays. Milk is poured as an offering to the Ganges before starting on a journey. The Pânchon Pîr are worshipped on a platform in the house with garlands of flowers, rice and pulse, sweetmeats (*laddu*) and sweet cakes (*rot*). Over this is poured a mixture of sugar and pepper dissolved in water and known as *mirchwân*, and the offering is finally consumed by the worshippers. In Bundelkhand they have a godling known as Ghatoi Bâba, who is probably connected with the cremation ground as already mentioned. A platform is made on the bank of a river under a tree, and a ram is sacrificed in his honour on the Dasahra or the tenth of the light half of Kuâr. The worshippers divide the offering among themselves. They have now come to regard Ghatoi Bâba as the ancestor of the tribe. All along the Ganges they worship the water godling Barun, who is the representative of the Vedic Varuna, the god of the sky. Further up the Ganges they worship specially Parihâr and Ghâzi Miyân, two of the quintette of the Pânchon Pîr, and make pilgrimages to Bahrâich and the other cenotaphs for that purpose. Their demonology is that common to all the lower races. The offering made through the Ojha, Bhagta, or Syâna to evil spirits is

technically known as *basandar*. To the East of the Province the demon known as Birtiya Bîr is worshipped in times of sickness or other trouble. A Khatîk brings a young pig and sacrifices it for them in the name of the demon. When a person recovers from small-pox, he offers sweets to Sîtala Mâi. When starting on a voyage they offer a burnt offering (*hom*) and garlands of flowers to their boat.

Occupation and social status.

8. The business of the caste is managing boats and fishing. Those who are well off own boats of their own and employ poorer members of the tribe to work for them. The women of the Goriya caste are said to have an indifferent character as compared with others. In the East of the Province the members of the Bâthawa sub-caste eat only the flesh of sheep, goats, deer and all kinds of fish, except the Gangetic porpoise (*sûs*), the *sekchi* and the crocodile. The others eat all kinds of fish and the tortoise. In Ghâzipur they are reported to eat the flesh of goats, pork, fish, tortoise, and rats; but not beef, monkeys, snakes, lizards, or the leavings of other people. In Allahâbâd they will eat *pakki* cooked at their own cooking place by a Brâhman, and with water supplied by themselves; but they will not eat *kachchi* cooked by a Brâhman, or even *pakki* if not cooked at their own fireplace. There is good evidence that many of the river dakâities committed in Bengal are the work of Mallâhs of these Provinces. Dr. Buchanan [1] writes: "Of late years the merchants, not only of Gorakhpur, but everywhere I have observed on the Ganges and its branches, have suffered very heavy losses from the carelessness and dissipation of the boatmen, who have become totally unmanageable. They have discovered the very great difficulty, if not impossibility, of obtaining legal redress against people who have nothing, who are paid in advance, and who can in general escape from justice by moving from place to place with the first boat that sails. There is great reason to suspect that the owners of the boat, or at least the Mânjhi who works for them, connive at the tricks of the men, and taking the full hire allow a part of the crew to desert, giving them a trifle, and keeping the remainder to themselves. The owners of the boats are totally careless about keeping the goods, and the composure with which I have seen the boatman sitting, while the

---

[1] *Eastern India*, II, 578.

merchant was tearing his hair and his property going to ruin, was truly astonishing." Much of this has, of course, ceased, since the introduction of the railway system has considerably reduced the river traffic. But even now Mallâhs bear an indifferent reputation as regards their dealings with their employers.

9. The Châi and Sorahiya sub-castes are so different from ordinary Mallâhs that they have been described in separate articles.

Distribution of Malláhs according to the Census of 1891.

Districts.	Agarwâla.	Bâthma.	Châin.	Dhuriya.	Kewat.	Kharê-bind.	Nikhâd.	Sorahiya.	Others.	Muham-madans.	Total.
Dehra Dûn	...	44	...	...	...	3	...	...	109	...	156
Sahâranpur	...	...	...	...	18	...	...	...	318	718	1,054
Muzaffarnagar	...	...	...	...	2	...	...	...	81	486	569
Meerut	...	...	...	...	51	...	...	...	967	1,212	2,230
Bulandshahr	14	104	...	...	...	...	...	...	1,596	42	1,756
Aligarh	...	87	...	...	...	...	...	...	2,402	...	2,489
Mathura	10	25	...	...	...	...	...	1	4,838	134	5,008
Agra	...	18	9	...	...	...	...	...	24,935	...	24,962
Farrukhâbâd	149	238	...	...	1	...	...	...	59	253	700
Mainpuri	1,422	116	...	...	...	...	101	...	1,567	...	3,206
Etâwah	1,603	483	534	...	...	...	4	...	1,323	...	3,947
Etah	...	...	...	...	...	...	...	...	10	73	83
Bareilly	...	...	...	...	...	...	45	...	65	...	110

Bijnor	...	...	...	...	...	...	...	...	96	16	112
Budâun	...	466	...	...	...	...	...	...	35	26	527
Morâdâbâd	...	4	...	...	...	...	123	...	865	28	1,020
Shâhjahânpur	...	...	...	...	...	...	6	...	612	378	996
Pilibhît	...	...	...	...	...	...	790	...	46	...	836
Cawnpur	6,332	2,839	156	...	...	...	92	...	7,445	40	16,904
Fatehpur	...	1,244	...	...	...	...	1	...	13	...	1,258
Bânda	1	...	...	...	...	...	...	...	...	...	1
Hamîrpur	1	...	...	...	...	...	...	...	2	...	3
Allahâbâd	34	13,480	1,588	...	31,197	1	222	...	1,201	...	47,723
Jhânsi	1,835	9	...	...	...	...	...	...	26	...	1,870
Jâlaun	1,878	2	398	...	1	...	...	...	293	...	2,572
Lalitpur	...	...	...	...	...	...	1	...	2	...	3
Benares	...	...	6,589	...	1,506	...	548	...	1,611	...	10,254
Mirzapur	...	208	12,438	...	46,085	...	507	...	326	...	59,564
Jaunpur	...	...	11,845	...	31,339	...	467	...	538	...	44,189
Ghâzipur	...	122	12,431	...	9	...	...	935	1,198	...	14,695

Distribution of Mallâhs according to the Census of 1891—concluded.

DISTRICTS.	Agarwâla.	Bâthma.	Chaîn.	Dhuriya.	Kewat.	Kharê-bind.	Nikhâd.	Sorahiya.	Others.	Muham-madans.	TOTAL.
Ballia	...	...	3,298	...	136	...	...	8,561	2,944	...	14,939
Gorakhpur	...	...	14,692	...	16,554	155	213	5,360	15,907	204	53,085
Basti	...	...	2,056	...	355	...	1,376	369	6,810	...	10,966
Azamgarh	...	...	4,177	...	647	...	222	6,159	2,242	12	13,459
Tarâi	...	...	...	...	...	...	...	...	14	...	14
Lucknow	...	70	498	...	88	177	297	...	1,357	1	2,488
Unâo	...	...	...	2,462	...	...	6	...	13	...	2,481
Râê-Bareli	...	104	...	...	96	...	125	...	625	...	950
Sîtapur	...	...	...	...	2	...	...	...	5	...	7
Hardoi	...	...	...	63	...	...	...	...	...	...	63
Kheri	...	3,153	...	...	1,055	...	...	...	680	...	4,888
Faizâbâd	...	...	1,268	...	...	...	...	109	247	...	1,624
Gonda	...	...	...	...	...	...	...	...	202	4	206

Bahrâich	...	...	...	...	...	...	...	...	14	...	14
Sultânpur	...	...	6,070	...	1	405	651	...	3,984	...	11,111
Partâbgarh	...	...	233	...	...	...	21	...	299	2	555
Bârabanki	...	...	466	...	170	...	1,159	...	1,576	...	3,371
TOTAL .	13,279	22,816	78,746	2,525	129,313	741	6,967	21,494	89,498	3,629	369,008

Malûkdâsi.—A religious order who have not been separately enumerated at the last Census. According to Professor Wilson[1] they are a sub-division of the Râmanandi Vaishnavas, and the succession of the leaders of the sect is said to be—Râmanand, Âsanand, Krishna Dâs, Kîl, Malûk Dâs, making the last, consequently, contemporary with the author of the Bhakta Mâla, and placing him in the reign of Akbar. But Professor Wilson is of opinion that Malûk Dâs was contemporary with Aurangzeb: "The modifications of the Vaishnava doctrines introduced by Malûk Dâs appear to have been little more than the name of the teacher, and a shorter streak of red upon the forehead; in one respect indeed there is an important distinction between these and the Râmanandi ascetics, and the teachers of the Malûkdâsis appear to be of the secular order (*grihastha*), or householders, while the others are all cenobites; the doctrines are however, essentially the same; Vishnu or Râma is the object of their practical devotion and their principles partake of the spirit of quietism, which pervades these sects. Their chief authority is the Bhâgavad Gîta, and they read some small Sanskrit tracts containing the praise of Râma; they have also some Hindi Sâkhis and Vishnupadas attributed to their founder, as also a work in the same language, entitled the Dasratan. The followers of this sect are said to be numerous in particular districts, especially among the trading and servile classes, to the former of which the founder belonged. A verse attributed to Malûk Dâs is proverbial:—

Ajgar karê na châkari, panchhi karê na kâm;
Dâs Malûka yon kahê;
Sab kâ dâta Râm:
'The snake performs no service,
The bird discharges no duty;
Malûk Dâs declares—
Râm is the giver of all.'[1]

2. "The principal establishment of the Malûkdâsis is at Kara Mânikpur, the birthplace of the founder, and still occupied by his descendants. There is a temple dedicated to Râmchandra; the *gaddi* or pillow of the sect is here, and the actual pillow originally used by Malûk Dâs is said to be still preserved. Besides this establishment there are other six Maths belonging to this sect at Allahâ-

---

[1] *Essays*, I, 100 *sq.*; Growse, *Mathura*, 212.

bâd, Benares, Brindaban, Ajudhya, Lucknow, which is modern, having been founded by Gomati Dâs under the patronage of Asaf-ud-daula, and Jagganâth, which last is of great repute, as rendered sacred by the death of Malûk Dâs."

Mandahâr.—A sept of Râjputs found mainly in the Muzaffarnagar and Sahâranpur Districts. They are also found in the neighbouring parts of the Panjâb. They are said to have come from Ajudhya to Jînd, driving the Chandel and Brâ Râjputs, who occupied the tract, into the Siwâliks and across the Ghaggar, respectively. They then fixed their capital in Kalâyit in Patiâla, with minor centres at Safîdon in Jînd and Asandh in Karnâl. They lie more or less between the Tunwar and Chauhân of the tract. But they have in more recent times spread down below the Chauhân into the Jumna River of the Karnâl District, with Gharaunda as a local centre. They were settled in these parts before the advent of the Chauhân, and were chastised at Samâna in Patiâla by Firoz Shâh. The Mandahâr, Kandahâr, Bargûjar, Sankarwâl, and Panihâr Râjputs are said to be descended from Lawa, a son of Râmchandra, and claim, therefore, to be solar Râjputs; and in Karnâl at least they do not intermarry.[1]

Mandârkiya.—A Râjput sept in Oudh who claim to be of Sombansi origin. They say that the name is derived from Sanskrit *Mandala*, "a circuit," the dominions of their founder Krishna Sinh. They more probably take their name from Mandar Sâh, who was one of the ancestors of the sept. Some of them are Hindus and some Muhammadans; the latter are said to have been converted to Islâm in the time of Shîr Shâh. But the change of religion has not bettered their condition, as the family is in the last stage of decay.[2]

Manihâr (Sanskrit *mani*, "a precious stone," *kâra*, "maker:") workers in glass and tin foil.—They are often confounded with the Chûrihâr, and in some places they appear to practise the same occupation: but their special business is to make and apply the pewter foil (*panni*), which is used in ornamenting bangles of a superior class.[3] There is both a Hindu and Musalmân branch, of whom the latter are much in excess. They are Sunnis and particularly respect the Pânchon Pîr and Ghâzi Miyân, whom they worship on

---

1 Ibbetson, *Panjâb Ethnography*, 238.
2 *Sultânpur Settlement Report*, 179; *Oudh Gazetteer*, III, 462.
3 See Hoey, *Monograph*, 147, *sq.*

the first Sunday in the month of Jeth with rich cakes (*malída*), rice and milk (*khír*), flowers and *sharbat*. They offer food to the sainted dead at the Shabibârât.

2. The complete Census returns show nineteen sub-divisions of the Hindu and one hundred and thirty of the Muhammadan branch. The Hindu sub-divisions are: Ajudhyabâsi, Angarkha, Baiswâr, Bankarwâr, Bargûjar, Chauhân, Hâriya, Jagarhâr, Juriya, Khatwâs, Lokheri, Manihâr, Mathuriya, Râmanandi, Regwa, Sâgar, Sanâwar, Sîsgar, and Tanbara. The Muhammadan sections are of various origin. Some are derived from other well known castes or septs, such as Bâchhal, Baheliya, Banjâra, Chandeli, Darzi, Ghosi, Kâchhiyana, Kalawant, Khatri, Kunjra, Mukeri, Murai, Panwâr, Qalandar, Râjput, Râwat, Raikwâr: local, as Alapuriya, Alampuriya, Bahrâich, Bâtham, Bishnpuriya, Dakkhinâha, Deswâl, Dilliwâl, Jaiswâr, Kanaujiya, Purabiya, Rikhpuriya, Sarwariya: or occupational, as Jauhari, "jewellers," Lakarha, "workers in wood," Lakhiya, "workers in lac."

Distribution of Manihârs according to the Census of 1891.

DISTRICTS.	Hindus.	Musalmâns.	TOTAL.
Dehra Dûn	...	3	3
Sahâranpur	31	1,098	1,129
Muzaffarnagar	1	711	712
Meerut	290	2,045	2,335
Bulandshahr	118	1,133	1,251
Aligarh	4	2,692	2,696
Mathura	74	1,169	1,243
Agra	41	2,018	2,059
Farrukhâbâd	...	1,528	1,528
Mainpuri	1	1,032	1,033
Etâwah	...	1,062	1,062
Etah	...	1,738	1,738
Bareilly	88	2,070	2,158
Bijnor	...	2,083	2,083

Distribution of the Manihârs according to the Census of 1891—contd.

DISTRICTS.	Hindus.	Musalmâns.	TOTAL.
Budâun	3	1,909	1,912
Morâdâbâd	112	2,549	2,661
Shâhjahânpur	...	2,994	2,994
Pilibhît	...	1,282	1,282
Cawnpur	...	2,438	2,438
Fatehpur	...	1,038	1,038
Bânda	26	103	129
Hamîrpur	...	361	361
Allahâbâd	...	1,985	1,985
Jhânsi	3	63	66
Jâlaun	...	415	415
Lalitpur	18	1	19
Benares	1	...	1
Mirzapur	...	11	11
Jaunpur	...	665	665
Ghâzipur	2	...	
Gorakhpur	6	994	1,000
Basti	670	256	926
Azamgarh	16	62	78
Garhwâl	40	51	91
Tarâi	...	479	479
Lucknow	31	1,651	1,682
Unâo	...	1,530	1,530
Râê Bareli	...	2,572	2,572
Sîtapur	...	2,430	2,430
Hardoi	...	2,855	2,855
Kheri	...	2,608	2,608
Faizâbâd	...	1,316	1,316

Distribution of the Manihârs according to the Census of 1891—concld.

DISTRICTS.	Hindus.	Musalmâns	TOTAL.
Gonda	8	4,078	4,086
Bahrâich	...	4,375	4,375
Sultânpur	...	1,453	1,453
Partâbgarh	...	153	153
Bârabanki	...	2,554	2,554
TOTAL	1,584	65,613	67,197

Mârwâr.—A sept of Râjputs who are said to have come from Mârwâr to Ghâzipur at the same time as the Punwârs of Ujjain. They are a manly race, but do not show any marked sign of Aryan origin.[1]

Mârwâri[2] (a resident of Mârwâr): a term which appears to bear two meanings,—the aggregate of Banyas who have emigrated to these Provinces from Rajputâna and its neighbourhood, including a number of sub-castes, such as Agarwâlas, Oswâls, and Maheswaris, who are to a large extent Jainas; secondly, a true sub-caste of the name.—It would seem that at the last Census the Jaina Mârwâris recorded themselves under their special sub-castes, and it is only the Hindu branch which has been separately entered under the name of Mârwâri.

The Western Mârwâris.

2. The following account of the sub-caste in Bombay deserves quotation:[3] "Of these classes of money-lenders, the Mârwâri Srâvaks are by far the most numerous and successful. So completely, indeed, have these foreigners in the rural parts of the Surat District monopolised the business of bankers and usurers, that in the villages south of the Tapti, Mârwâri is the common term in use for a money-lender. No information has been received as to when and from where these Mârwâri Srâvaks have come into the Surat District. But, as

[1] Oldham, *Ghâzipur Memo.*, I, 63.

[2] Based on information collected at Mirzapur and a note by M. Mahâdev Prasâd, Head Master, High School, Pilibhît.

[3] *Bombay Gazetteer*, II, 187, *sq.*

money-lenders of this class are not found north of the Tapti, the common opinion that they have worked their way north from the Dakkhin through the Thâna District may perhaps be correct. Though as aliens in race and religion, and related to them by the least amiable of ties, the Mârwâri money-lender bears among the people of the Surat District a character of unscrupulous greed and dishonesty; towards strangers of his own caste, he would seem to show much sympathy and active kindliness. Arriving in Surat without money or education, the Mârwâri Srâvak is taken in hand by his caste fellows, fed by them, set to work, and in his leisure hours taught to write and keep accounts. With this help in starting, the immigrant, who is frugal, temperate, and hardworking, soon puts together a small sum of ready money. From this amount, by advancing to the poorest classes sums seldom exceeding R5, his capital has in a few years increased to R2,000 or R3,000. With these savings he returns to Mârwâr, and at this stage of his life he generally marries. Practising economy even in his native land, the Mârwâri brings back with him to the village, where he formerly had dealings, enough ready money to enable him to start as a trader. His shop once opened, he settles in the village, leaving it only when forced by urgent reasons to visit Mârwâr, or, because—an event which seldom happens—he has become a bankrupt. Except hamlets chiefly inhabited by aboriginal tribes, almost every village in Surat has its Mârwâri shop-keeper and money-lender."

3. "In the larger villages, with enough trade to support more than one shop, the Mârwâri keeps but little grain in stock. In smaller and outlying villages, where he is the only trader, the Mârwâri starts as a general dealer, offering for sale, in addition to grain, spices, salt, sugar, oil, cloth, and bracelets of brass. The settler is now a member of the community of Mârwâri shop-keepers and money-lenders. This body has a social life, distinct from that of the villagers, with whom its members have dealings. Though the families of the different sub-divisions of the Mârwâri money-lenders do not intermarry, they are connected by many ties. In the event of the death of one of their number, the members of his caste from the neighbouring villages meet together to attend his funeral. Before the anniversary of the death has come round, his near relations, arriving from Mârwâr, unite with the other members in giving an entertainment to the Mârwâri community. As the

number of guests is small, and as all are possessed with the love of economy, the expenditure on such entertainments is, unlike the cost of a funeral feast among Gujarât Srâvaks, moderate.

4. "Almost all Mârwâris of this class are Srâvaks, or followers of the Jaina religion, and in the largest of a group of villages a temple of Pârasnâth is generally to be found. To meet the expense attending the maintenance of worship the settler devotes a fixed portion of his gains. At the same time he subscribes to a provident fund for the help of the widow and children of any member of his community who may die leaving his family in straitened circumstances. When a Mârwâri shop-keeper dies young, until his son is of age, the widow, with the help of a confidential clerk, generally manages the business. In such cases, it is said, the shop-keepers of neighbouring villages are of much help to the widow, giving her advice as to the conduct of the business, aiding her in keeping her accounts, and in recovering her outstanding debts.

5. "Connected by such ties as these, a community of interest is said to prevail among the Surat Mârwâris, and there would seem to be less of that competition of capital, which, in the districts of Northern Gujarât, helps the debtor to play off the Vânya creditor against his rival the Srâvak money-lender. Settled in one of the best houses of the village, with a good store of cattle and grain, spoken of by all with respect as the Seth or 'master,' and seldom without some family of debtors bound to perform any service he may stand in need of, the village money-lender, though he seldom becomes a large capitalist, lives in a state of comparative comfort." More information as to the methods of Mârwâri money-lending will be found in the report of the Deccan Commission.[1]

The Mârwâris of the North-Western Provinces.

6. The Mârwâris of Mirzapur are divided into nine exogamous sub-divisions:—Singhâniya; Gûndaka; Sarrâf; Sarâogi; Jhujhunwala; Bajauriya, Khemka; Bazâz Bartya. Each of these sub-divisions has one hundred and seventy-two sections. The rule of exogamy is that a man must not marry in his sub-division, in the section of his maternal uncle, in the section of his mother's maternal uncle, in the section of his grandfather's maternal uncle, in the section of his grandmother's maternal uncle, in the section of his mother's, grand-

[1] P. 11, *sq*.

father's and grandmother's maternal uncle. Girls are usually not married till they come to puberty or ten years old. Widow marriage is prohibited.

Birth ceremonies.

7. In the eighth month of pregnancy, the ceremony of *athmâsa utârana* is performed. Eight kinds of sweetmeats are placed in eight leaf platters (*dauna*), and an old woman of the tribe or family waves them round the head of the expectant mother. The sweetmeats are then sent to the houses of the relations of the family. When the child is born, a Chamârin is called in, who cuts the cord and buries it at the entrance of the room in which the confinement took place. Then a curious ceremony follows :

The brother-in-law (*bahnoi*) or sister's husband of the father of the baby touches the place where the cord was buried, and receives in cash or a piece of jewelry as a present. A Pandit is then called in who makes a note of the exact time of birth, on which he bases his calculation of the horoscope (*Janampattri*). On the fifth day the mother washes her hands and feet and puts on a new garment. For five days she is fed on a compound of ginger, treacle, dill (*ajwâin*), and other spices. From the sixth day she gets ordinary food. The Chamârin attends for five days, and after that her place is taken by the barber's wife and other servants of the family. When a month has passed, the mother is bathed and some water is poured out as offering to the Sun. Then the mother takes the child in her arms and goes to worship the Ganges, if it be near at hand. The offering to Ganga Mâi is some grain and sweets (*batâsha*) with flowers and sandalwood. When she returns home, she distributes among her friends some grain and sweets. On that day, before the Ganges is worshipped, the whole house is plastered and all the earthen vessels are replaced, and the mother and baby are dressed in new clothes. When the child is six months old, the *anna-prâsana* ceremony is done by giving the child some rice-milk at an auspicious time named by the Pandit. Next follows the ceremonial shaving (*mûnran*), for which no special time is fixed. Poor people take the child to the temple of some neighbouring goddess and have it shaven there; but rich Mârwâris go to the temple of Sati Mâta at Fatehpur in Mârwâr. The mother takes the child in her arms, bathes, offers a sheet to Sati Mâta, and then walks five times round the temple. After this the child is shaved by one of the barbers attached to the shrine. Only the top-knot (*choti*) is left uncut. After they return home, a dinner is given to the clansmen. Boys have the ears and girls the nose pierced (*kanchhedan, nakh-chhedan*), but no regular time is fixed for this. When it is to be done, the family priest worships the goddess Lohsani for five days with an offering of *kasar*, a particular kind of sweetmeat (*laddu*) made of parched rice and sesamum mixed with treacle. When the auspicious hour arrives, the goldsmith is called, and he bores the ears or nose of the child, who is given a *laddu* to eat during the operation.

Marriage ceremonies.

8. The marriage ceremonies begin with the betrothal ceremony (*sagâi*). First of all the bride's father sends for the horoscope of the bridegroom, and has that of his daughter compared with it by his Pandit. When the result of the comparison proves satisfactory, the fact is communicated to the father of the bridegroom, who sends to the bride by his sister, or, in default of her, by a Brâhmani, some red powder (*rori*) and some rice dyed in turmeric. The bearer marks the bride's forehead with the powder and sprinkles the rice over her. Her mother puts a rupee in the dish in which the rice and powder were brought, and this is taken to the mother of the boy. In return, the bride sends a dish of sweets (*laddu*) to the bridegroom. His mother procures some more *laddus*, and mixing the whole together sends them round to the friends of the family. The phrase for this is *sagâi kâ laddu bântna*. Next the friends of the boy send some clothes and ornaments for the bride, and for this some money is sent by her father. These ceremonies usually take place when the boy and girl are under the age of eight.

Marriage preliminaries.

9. When a girl is between nine and ten, the marriage day is fixed, after consultation with the Pandit. Ten days before the appointed day, the ceremony of *har-dat* is performed. The women arrange the sacred marriage jar (*kalsa*) in the house and sing songs before it. Beside it is made an image of Ganesa, the god of luck, and the boy is made to worship him and the jar, and to distribute money to Brâhmans. The same ritual is carried out also in the house of the girl. Every day in both houses sweets are made and distributed among friends. Three days before the marriage day comes the *telwân*, when turmeric and oil are mixed in four earthenware saucers and the mothers of the bride and bridegroom anoint them with it. Before the anointing begins, the

unguent is offered to Ganesa. After the mothers have done the anointing, it is repeated by seven married women whose husbands are alive. Every day, up to the marriage, Ganesa is worshipped and every day the bride and bridegroom are anointed.

The procession.

10. Two days prior to the marriage, the boy's father feeds his clansmen, and on the last day before the wedding the *banauri* ceremony is done. Some powdered henna (*mendhi*) is put on the hand of the boy, and he is made to mount a mare, on which he rides to the house of the bride. Her father and his friends receive him at the door and mark his forehead with red powder. Each of them presents him with a rupee and a cocoanut, while the women of the family sing songs of rejoicing. Then the boy returns home. On the marriage day a cloth is hung up and held at each corner by a man. In the centre is placed an earthen cup, with a hole in the bottom, in which is placed a thread made of cocoa fibre. The boy is made to sit under the cloth, and, after he is rubbed with turmeric and oil, he worships Ganesa. The cloth is then tied to a peg in the house; this ceremony is called *manda*. After this Brâhmans are fed. In the evening his mother rubs the boy with oil and turmeric from head to foot, seven married women of the caste whose husbands are alive do the same. This is called *tel utárna*. He is then bathed and dressed in his marriage dress and ornaments, and the family priest marks his forehead with red powder and puts on his marriage crown. He is then mounted on an ass as a propitiation to Sîtala, and the animal is fed on *múng* pulse. The mother then offers her breast to her son, while she covers his head with the part of the sheet which conceals her bosom. The owner of the ass receives a sheet and a rupee, and the forehead of the animal is marked with red powder and turmeric. The boy then dismounts from the ass and mounts a horse. Here the mother, as before, offers her breast to her son. As he prepares to ride away, his sister holds back the horse by the bridle and will not let him go until she receives a present. Then a man holds an umbrella over the boy and fans him with a yak's tail, and a girl marks the horse behind him with some mustard (*sarson*) and salt as preservatives against the Evil Eye. With the same object his elder brother's wife or some other female relation puts lampblack on his eyes.

The arrival of the bridegroom.

11. After all this he sets out with his party (*bárát*) for the house of the bride, accompanied with music and fireworks. He rides round the town or

village in procession, and finally reaches the door of the bride. Over the door are erected some rude representations of birds, etc. (*toran*), which the bridegroom strikes with the branch of a *nim* tree —an obvious symbol of the opposition which he may expect in taking away the bride. This done, his future mother-in-law comes out and waves a lamp over his head as a spell against demoniacal influence. The party then retire to the place (*janwânsa*) arranged for their reception. On the marriage day the nuptial shed (*mânro*) is erected at the house of the bride. A long pole, dyed with ochre, is set up in the courtyard; near it is laid some sand, and on it a pitcher of water. This done, Brâhmans are fed and baskets of sweetmeats are placed near at hand, which the bride distributes to the assembled Brâhmans. She is then made to worship Gauri and Ganesa. After this, she, accompanied by the other women of the family, goes to the village potter's house and worships his wheel (*châk*) as a symbol of fertility. When they are coming home, the potter's wife accompanies them, bearing on her head two pitchers—one small and the other large—with the necks decorated with gold tinsel. In these, water is sent for the refreshment of the bridegroom and his friends. The bride is then bathed and dressed in a white sheet with a red cloth over her head. Next a sort of platform is made of sand in the courtyard, and at each corner a peg is fixed, to each of which a stick is tied. In the centre a fire is lighted of mango wood. This platform is known as *chauri*.

The marriage ritual.

12. When the bridegroom arrives he is seated on a sort of chair under the shed and the bride sits on his left. The corners of their garments are knotted together, and they are made to worship Gauri and Ganesa. This done, the ceremony of *hathlewa* is performed. For this a ball of flour, turmeric, and henna is made, and this is placed in the hand of the bride. Over this the bridegroom lays his hand, and the pair are made to walk four or seven times round the platform, while the Brâhman recites verses and makes a fire sacrifice (*hom*). When he has completed this, he receives his fee (*dakshina*). Next the bride and bridegroom go into an inner room and worship what is known as the *thâpa*. This is a series of marks on the wall which have already been made by the women of the house with red powder (*rori*). Before these the bridegroom is made to recite some verses, and the bride's mother gives him a present. This over, the bridegroom rejoins his friends.

13. Next day the women of the tribe plait the hair of the bride and put some fruit into the sheet covering her bosom. Each woman gives her a present of money or ornaments. That day the bridegroom with his friends is entertained at the house of the bride, and the father of the bridegroom distributes sweetmeats among the relatives and friends of the bride.

The second day.

14. Next day the procession returns to the house of the bridegroom. Before they start the bride's father gives what he can afford by way of dowry, such as vessels, clothes, etc. Then the married pair take their seats in the same palanquin and return home. When they reach the house, the bridegroom walks in followed by the bride. When they come into the courtyard, seven dishes are placed in succession before them, which the bridegroom pushes away with the sword which he wears all through the marriage festivities. Then his father takes up the bridegroom in his lap and her mother-in-law does the same for the bride. Next the Ganges and Sîtala Mâta are worshipped, and the marriage bracelets (*kangan*) worn by the bride and bridegroom are put in a dish full of water, and the bride and bridegroom have a struggle to see which of them will take them out first. This is known as "the gambling" (*júa khelna*).

The return.

15. A dying person is brought out of the house and laid on a piece of ground plastered with cowdung. Then the *pancha-ratana*, consisting of gold *tulasi* leaves, curds, pearls, and Ganges water are placed in his mouth. After death a sacred ball (*pinda*) is offered in his name and the corpse is laid on the pyre. The remaining funeral and purificatory ceremonies are performed in the orthodox Hindu fashion.

Funeral ceremonies.

Distribution of Márwári Banyas according to the Census of 1891.

DISTRICTS.	Number.	DISTRICTS.	Number.
Agra	2	Shâhjahânpur	289
Farrukhâbâd	72	Cawnpur	14
Etâwah	2	Jhânsi	6

Distribution of Mârwâri Banyas according to the Census of 1891 —concld.

Districts.	Number.	Districts.	Number.
Jâlaun	21	Unâo	4
Benares . . .	21	Sîtapur . . .	14
Mirzapur . . .	32	Gonda . . .	15
Jaunpur . . .	8	Bahrâich . . .	11
Ghâzipur . . .	3	Sultânpur . . .	1
Gorakhpur . . .	164	Partâbgarh . . .	2
Azamgarh . . .	11		
Lucknow . . .	28	Total .	720

Mâthur.—A sub-caste of Banyas; so called because they believe their native place to be Mathura.

Distribution of Mâthur Banyas according to the Census of 1891.

Districts.	Number.	Districts.	Number.
Meerut	16	Allahâbâd . . .	2
Mathura	171	Mirzapur	1
Agra	9,953	Lucknow	3
Farrukhâbâd . . .	4	Unâo	5
Mainpuri . . .	10	Sîtapur	3
Etâwah	98	Hardoi	3
Etah	133	Gonda	7
Budâun	32	Partâbgarh . . .	300
Morâdâbâd . . .	10		
Cawnpur	41	Total .	10,792

Mauhâr.—A Râjput sept in Bânda, who say they are emigrants from Sambhal in Morâdâbâd. They claim Chauhân descent, and say that they separated from the parent stock on account of some breach of caste rules.[1]

Meo, Mewâti, Mîna, Mîna Meo.[2]—A famous tribe who, though fairly numerous in the Provinces, are still foreigners to it. The word Mewâti means a resident of the land of Mewât, the name of which has been derived from the Sanskrit *mîna-vati*, "abounding in fish." The similarity of names and the legend of Sasibadani, as well as the fact that the sections of both tribes closely agree, has led to the general belief that the Mînas and Meos, who are classed as distinct in their native home Rajputâna, are really of common origin. This famous tribal legend is thus told by General Cunningham.[3] "The Mirâsis are the bards and singers of the Meos at all their marriages and festivals. At a marriage feast the most popular song is the love story of Darya Khân Meo and Sasibadani Mîni. The scene of most Meo legends is laid at Ajângarh, an old fort in the hills, only four miles to the west of Kamân. Todar Mal, who was the landlord of Ajângarh, used to repeat the following verse:—

Pânch pahâr ke râjahi,
Aur pûro tero dal,
Âdhê Akbar Bâdshâh,
Âdhê Pahat Todar Mal:

"In the kingdom of the five hills, with its force complete, half is the Emperor Akbar's and half Pahat Todar Mal's."

This saying was repeated to Akbar, who sent for Todar Mal and demanded why he made himself equal to the Emperor. The Meo replied: "As I am zamîndâr of the five hills, half the produce belongs to me and half to your Majesty." Akbar was so pleased with the reply that he gave Todar Mal a rent-free grant, with rank in his army. It happened afterwards that Todar Mal was sent on an expedition with Bâda Râo, Mîna. The latter took the Meo to his house, where they drank wine together and became friends. Then Todar Mal said to the Mîna: "My wife will shortly give birth to a child; if a girl, I will give her in marriage to your son; if a boy, he will marry your daughter." Todar Mal's wife gave birth to a son, who was named Darya Khân, and Bâda Râo's wife gave birth to a daughter, who was named Sasibadani or 'moon-like body,' or 'moon face.'

---

[1] *Gazetteer, North-Western Provinces*, I, 101, 160.
[2] Partly based on note by Bâbu Âtma Râm, Head Master, High School, Mathura.
[3] *Archæological Report*, XX, 22, *sqq*.

When the children reached ten years of age Bâda Râo sent the signs of betrothal (*tîka*) to Darya Khân, the son of Todar, and after a year a marriage party started from Ajângarh with several hundreds of Meos for the village of Bâda Râo. When the bridegroom reached the house, he struck the ornament (*toran*) over the door (according to custom) by making his horse leap; for otherwise being a boy he could not have reached it. The marriage ceremony was thus complete; but as the Mînas wished the Meos to eat flesh with them, as well as to drink wine, the Meos pretended that the Emperor of Delhi's troops had attacked their village and so the whole marriage party retired, leaving Sasibadani in her father's house.

2. "When the girl grew older she sent a letter to Darya Khân, but it was unfortunately given to Todar Mal, who beat the messenger. A second letter was afterwards safely delivered to Darya Khân, who at once mounted his horse and started for the Mîna village. As he approached, a woman, who was carrying a basket of cowdung (*hail*), saw him and throwing down her basket rushed off at once to Sasibadani, to whom she said: *Beti Bâda Râo ki sunyon mhâri ter, Awat dekho Malko, main ne adbhar dâri hail*: 'O Bâda Râo's daughter, listen to my word; I saw the Malik coming and threw down my basket of cowdung half way.' Darya Khân was kindly received by his father-in-law, and the two sat down and drank freely. But when the Mîna pressed his son-in-law to eat some roasted meat, Darya Khân struck him a blow on the mouth and knocked out two of his teeth. Then all the Mînas drew their swords and would have killed Darya Khân at once, but Bâda Râo's son interposed and took him inside the house to his sister Sasibadani. At night Darya Khân fled with Sasibadani, and was pursued by the Mînas. But he reached his uncle's house in safety, when the Mînas dropped the pursuit." This story of Darya Khân Meo and Sasibadani Mîni is a very popular one, and their song is sung at every new marriage by their Mirâsis or bards. One result of this affair has been the discontinuance of marriages between the Meos and the Mînas, which had previously been common.

3. "Whatever truth there may be in the above story, the people generally refer to it as the cause of the discontinuance of marriages between the tribes. The acknowledgment of the previous intermarriage seems to offer rather a strong proof that the Meos must

have been a cognate race with the Mînas, holding the same social position—higher perhaps than the Ahîr and other agricultural classes, but decidedly below the Râjputs, from whom they claim descent. I am inclined, therefore, to agree with Major Powlett that the Meos and Mînas may have had a common origin. I have a suspicion that they may be the descendants of the Megallæ, mentioned by Pliny, who dwelt along the Indus and the Jumna, apparently bordering on the Jumna. As the name is spelt Mewara as well as Mev, I think that Akbar must have revived the old form which gives a very near approach to Megallæ."

Internal organization.

4. Whatever their connection with the Mînas may be, the Meos themselves pretend to Râjput descent and name thirteen clans (*pâl*) and fifty-two *gotras*; but Mr. Channing[1] writes that no two enumerations of the Pâls that he has seen correspond precisely, and curiously enough the fifty-two *gotras* include the Pâls, and are not, as would at first appear, in addition to them. What the exact relationship of the Pâl to the *gotra* may be cannot be ascertained without much more local enquiry in Rajputâna. It is possible that the system of exogamy practised in the tribe may be in a stage of transition, which indeed is not wonderful, considering the various elements out of which the caste is evidently made up. As Sir A. Lyall[2] writes: "It is a Cave of Adullam that has stood open for centuries. With them a captured woman is solemnly admitted by a form of adoption into one circle of affinity, in order that she may be lawfully married into another, a fiction which looks very like the survival of a custom that may once have been universal among all classes at a more elastic stage of their growth; for it enables the circles of affinity within a tribe to increase and multiply their numbers without a break, while at the same time it satisfies the conditions of lawful intermarriage." The following is General Cunningham's[3] enumeration of the Meo Pâls: Five Jâdon clans—Chhirkilât, Dalât, Demrot, Nâi, Pundelot; five Tomar clans—Balot, Darwâr, Kalesa, Lundavât, Rattâvat; one Kachhwâha clan—Dingâl; one Bargûjar clan—Singâl. Besides these there is one miscellaneous or half-blood clan—Palâkra. Mr. Channing's enumeration is somewhat different—

[1] Ibbetson, *Panjáb Ethnography*, section 478.
[2] *Asiatic Studies*, 162.
[3] *Archæological Reports*, XX, 23.

Balant; Ratâwat; Darwâl; Landâwat; Chirklot; Dimrot; Dulot; Nâi; Tunglot; Dahugâl; Singâl; Kalesa or Kalsakhi. The complete Census returns give ninety-seven sub-divisions of the Meo or Hindu and three hundred and forty-seven of the Mewâti or Musalmân branch. The Hindu branch have annexed various Râjput septs, such as Bargûjar, Hara, Janwâr, Kânhpuriya, Raghubansi, Râwat, and Tomar. The names of the Musalmân sections illustrate the composite nature of the caste. We find Râjput sept names, such as Bargûjar, Chandela, Chauhân, Gahlot, Jâdon, Kachhwâha, Rathauriya, side by side with Bhât, Dakaut, Gadariya, Ghosi, Gûjar, Guâl, Julâha, Kabariya, Kori, Nâi, and Rangrez: besides local terms, such as Audhiya, Ismâîlpuriya, Khairâbâdi, Malakpuriya, Mirzapuriya, and Sultânpuriya.

The Meos of Rajputâna.

5. The best available account of the Rajputâna branch of the tribe is that by Major Powlett:[1] "The Meos are numerically the first race in the Alwar State, and the agricultural portion of them is considerably more than double any other class of cultivators except Chamârs. They occupy about half the territory, and the portion they dwell in occupies the north and east. They are divided into fifty-two clans, of which the twelve largest are called *pâl* and the smaller *gotra*. These clans contend much with each other, but the members of a clan sometimes unite to assist one of their number when in danger of being crushed by a fine, or to recover a village lost to the clan by want of thrift. The Meos, for they no doubt are often included under the term Mewâti, were, during the Muhammadan period of power, always notorious for their turbulence and predatory habits; however, since their complete subjection by Bakhtâwar Sinh and Banni Sinh, who broke up the large turbulent villages into a number of smaller hamlets, they have become generally well behaved; but they return to their former habits when opportunity offers. In 1857 they assembled, burnt State ricks, carried off cattle, etc., but did not succeed in plundering town or village in Alwar. In British territory they plundered Fîrozpur and other villages, and when a British force came to restore order many were hanged.

6. "Though Meos claim to be of Râjput origin, there are grounds for believing that many spring from the same stock as the Mînas. However, it is probable enough that apostate Râjputs and bastard sons of Râjputs founded many of the clans as legends tell.

[1] *Rajputâna Gazetteer*, III, 200.

The Meos are now all Musalmâns in name; but their village deities are the same as those of the Hindus, and they keep several Hindu festiv ls. Thus, the Holi is with Meos a season of rough play, and is considered as important a festival as the Muharram, 'Id, or Shab-i-bârât; and they likewise observe the Janam Ashtami, Dasahra, and Diwâli. They often keep Brâhman priests to write the note (*pîli chitthi*) fixing the date of marriage. They call themselves by Hindu names, with the exception of Râm; and Sinh is a frequent affix, though not so common as Khân. On the Amâwas, or monthly conjunction of the sun and moon, the Meos, in common with Hindu Ahîrs, Gûjars, etc., cease from labour; and when they make a well, the first proceeding is to erect a platform (*chabûtra*) to Bhaironji or Hanumân. However, when plunder was to be obtained, they have shown little respect for Hindu shrines or temples; and when the sanctity of a threatened place has been urged, the retort has been—*Tum to deo ; ham Meo*—'You may be a god, but I am a Meo.' As regards their own religion, Meos are very ignorant. Few know the *Kalima*, and fewer still the regular prayers, the seasons of which they entirely neglect. This, however, applies only to Alwar territory; in British, the effect of the schools is to make them more observant of religious duties. Indeed, in Alwar, at certain places where there are mosques, religious observances are better maintained, and some know the *Kalima*, say their prayers, and would like a school.

7. "Meos do not marry in their own clan (*pâl*), but are lax about forming connections with women of other castes, whose children they receive into the Meo community. On marriage, two hundred rupees is considered a respectable sum to spend, that is to say, one hundred and thirty on betrothal (*sagâi*) and seventy on marriage. They sometimes dower their daughters handsomely, and sometimes make money by them. Indeed they often say that they have sold their daughters to pay their debts. As already stated, Brâhmans take part in the formalities preceding a marriage, but the ceremony itself is performed by the Qâzi, who receives a fee of about R1-4 and eight sers of rice. The rite of circumcision is performed by the village barber and the village Faqîr, who also guards a new grave for some days till the ground has become too hard to disturb. As agriculturists, Meos are inferior to their Hindu neighbours. The point in which they chiefly fail is in working their wells, for which they lack patience. Their women, whom

they do not seclude will, it is said, do more field work than the men; indeed women are often found at work when the men are lying down. Like the women of low Hindu castes, they tattoo their bodies—a practice disapproved by Musalmâns in general. Meos are generally poor and live badly. They have no scruples about getting drunk when opportunity offers. The men wear the loin and waist cloth (*dhoti, kamari*), and not drawers (*pâëjâma*). Their dress is in fact Hindu. The men often wear gold ornaments, but the women are seldom or never allowed to have them."

8. Sir J. Malcom[1] says that it is hard to say whether the Meos of Central India are Hindus or Muhammadans. They partake of both religions and are the most desperate rogues in India. Though they are stigmatised as robbers and assassins, they are admitted to be faithful and courageous guards and servants. Their chiefs invariably took the lead in robberies on a large scale. Colonel Hervey[2] says that the Mînas of Upper Rajputâna are Hindus of the straitest sect, and not only do Hindus of every denomination, high and low, but all Thâkurs, Jâts, and Ahîrs will even partake of food which has been prepared by them. Brâhmans and Banyas alone refrain from eating their food and drinking their water. They will however drink water which has been drawn by a Mîna, but not put it into any drinking utensil. They never intermarry in their mother's *gotra* except after a remove of four generations. The installation of the Mahârâja of Jaypur is not considered complete until the ceremony of fixing the mark of sovereignty (*tilak*) is performed by the headmen of the two leading sub-divisions. They guard the Mahârâja's harem, and are the constituted watchmen of the State. They do not, however, mix with the Parihâr Mînas inhabiting Khairwâra, who eat the flesh of young buffaloes. In the Western Panjâb, Mr. J. Wilson[3] says that they erect in their villages the standard of Sayyid Masâud. The erection of these is the privilege of a body of Shaikhs, who are known as mosque attendants (*mujâwir*), and have divided the Meo villages among them. Each man annually sets up a standard in each village of his own circle, receiving one rupee from the village for so doing, and appropriating all offerings made by the people. The usual offering is a

---

[1] *Central India*, II, 175.
[2] *Indian Antiquary*, III, 85, *sq*.
[3] *Ibid*, VIII, 209.

HARISCHANDI.

sort of sweetmeat made of bread crumbs, *ghi*, and sugar, which is called *malida*; this is brought by the worshippers and put in the hand of the attendant Mujâwir; he places it at the foot of the standard, reciting the blessing (*Al-ham-du-illah*), while the worshipper makes an obeisance. The Khânzâdas, who are closely connected with the Meos, have the same ceremony. According to General Cunningham,[1] they reverence the local deities of the Hindus, such as Bhaiyya, a platform with white stones placed upon it, who is also called Bhûmiya, Châhund, or Khera Deo. He thinks that the custom of tattooing, common among the women, points to a connection with the lower classes of Hindus, and perhaps also with the aboriginal Mînas, rather than to any relationship with the Râjputs. They may, however, have been Râjputs on the side of the fathers, while the mothers preserved the customs of the lower races to which they belonged. He also describes the lavish waste with which they perform the ceremony of the funeral feast, which is called *shakkarâna* from the quantity of sugar consumed by the guests.

The tribe in the North-Western Provinces and Oudh.

9. The last Census classes them under three heads: the Meo and Mîna, who are all Hindus; and the Mewâti, who are all Muhammadans. There is a legend current that the two sons of Râja Jaswant had once, in the course of a hunting excursion, caught and brought in two wild cows. Their friends taking pity on the calves, which were left deserted in the jungle, taxed the princes with their irreligious conduct; upon which their father turned them out of his palace. One of them turned a freebooter and directed his course to Jamundes, or the country between the Ganges and the Jumna; after making a great booty in slaves and goods, he returned to his native place, Mewât, which he continued to govern in the name of his father. He had, however, lost the orthodoxy of his Hindu faith by leading a dissolute life and forming connections with women of different creeds and castes during the period while he roamed about as a freebooter. From him the present Mewâtis are said to be descended. Another legend[2] derives the name Meo from the word *maheo*, which they use in driving their cattle; and a third story[3] says that when a majority of

---

[1] *Archæological Reports*, XX, 22, *sq*.
[2] Raja Lachhman Sinh, *Bulandshahr Memo.*, 183, *sq*.
[3] Tod, *Annals*, II, 387.

the tribe were converted to Islâm, the remainder, who preserved their faith, were termed Amîna Meo or "pure Meos," whence the name Mîna. Again, according to Colonel Tod, Maina means the unmixed class, while Mîna is applied to the mixed tribe, of which they reckon twelve communities (*pâl*) descended from Râjput blood, *e.g.*, Chauhân; Tuar; Jâdon; Parihâr; Kachhwâha; Solanki; Sânkla; Gahlot, etc. The word *pâl*, according to the same authority, means a "defile in a valley suitable for cultivation and defence." In Cawnpur,[1] the Mînas call themselves Thâkurs, and adopt the clan names of Chandel and Chauhân; but they are despised by real Thâkurs. In the Central Duâb, they are reported to worship a deified ancestor named Jagat Deo in the form of a rude clay image, to which cakes are offered. They disclaim all connection with the regular Mewâtis and call themselves Râjputs: but they are endogamous and marry usually in the exchange form: a man giving his sister in marriage to his wife's brother. As a mark of distinction from the regular Meos, some call themselves Meh.

10. The Muhammadan branch, who are usually known as Mewâti, claim to have been originally Jâdons and members of other Râjput septs of Mewât, who were converted to Islâm by Alâ-ud-dîn Ghori. They are said to be immigrants from Alwar, Bhartpur, and Gurgâon. Their settlement in Mathura is dated, in the reign of Râo Sindhia of Gwâlior, about a hundred years ago. They follow the law of exogamy prevailing among the Hindu branch but, in other respects, are regulated by the rules of Islâm. They allow widow marriage by the *dharîcha* form. The betrothal is settled by the bride's father sending from one to five rupees by his barber and friends; this is laid in the lap of the boy in the presence of the assembled brethren, and by its acceptance the betrothal is confirmed. Their birth and death ceremonies are of the normal Muhammadan type.

Occupation.

11. At present nearly all of them are cultivators and day-labourers. In the Ganges-Jumna Duâb, they have been a thorn in the side of successive rulers since the dawn of history. We first hear of them when, at the instigation of Prithivi Râj of Delhi, they were expelled from the Upper Duâb by the Râjputs of the Bargûjar, Bhatti, Chokar,

[1] *Settlement Report*, 18.

Jâdon, and Gahlot septs. In the early Muhammadan era they again broke out and gave constant trouble, until they were brought under subjection by Ghayâs-ud-dîn Balban.[1] Zia-ud-dîn Barni[2] describes their misconduct in the neighbourhood of Delhi. Mubârak Shâh waged an unsuccessful campaign against them, but finally defeated them in 1425 A.D.[3] They again broke out three years later, and the war went on till 1432 A.D.,[4] when they were at last coerced. Bâbar, on his arrival at Agra, describes their leader Râja Hasan Khân as "the chief agitator in all these confusions and insurrections."[5] Farishta[6] describes two terrible slaughters of turbulent Mewâtis by Imâm-ud-dîn, Wazîr of Nasîr-ud-dîn Mahmûd, in 1259 A.D., and again by Balban in 1265. In the Mutiny, they and the Gûjars of the Upper Duâb were notorious for their turbulence, and seriously impeded the operations against Delhi. The popular idea of them is quite in unison with their history: *Pahlé lât, pichhé bât ; Dekhi tori Mewât ; pahli gâli, pîchhé bât* are common proverbs, which mean that, in dealing with a Mewâti, you had better kick or abuse him before you do business with him; their niggardliness is recorded by *Meo beti jab dé, jab okhal i bhar rupaya rakhvâle*: "the Meo will not give his daughter in marriage till he gets a mortar full of silver;" his blood-thirstiness—*Meo ka pût barah baras men badla leta hai*: "the Meo's brat takes his revenge when he is twelve years old;" his toughness—*Meo mara jab jâniye, jab tîja ho jâé*: "Never be sure that a Meo is dead till you see the third-day funeral ceremony performed."

Distribution of the Meos according to the Census of 1891.

Districts.	Hindus.			Muhammadan.	Total.
	Meo.	Mîna.	Others.	Mewâti.	
Dehra Dûn . . .	...	...	...	51	51
Sahâranpur . . .	...	...	...	1,944	1,944

[1] Râjâ Lachhman Sinh, *loc. cit.*, 183, *sq.*
[2] Dowson's *Elliot*, III, 103.
[3] *Ibid*, IV, 60, *sq.*
[4] *Ibid*, IV, 75.
[5] *Ibid*, IV, 263.
[6] Briggs, *Farishta*, I, 244, 256.

Distribution of the Meos according to the Census of 1891—contd.

Districts.	Hindus.			Muhammadan.	Total.
	Meo.	Mîna.	Others.	Mewâti.	
Muzaffarnagar	22	...	22	1,093	1,137
Meerut	2	1	1	5,190	5,194
Bulandshahr	2,807	2,795	12	2,723	13,337
Aligarh	346	254	92	5,345	6,037
Mathura	594	429	165	4,179	5,367
Agra	599	590	9	2,724	3,922
Farrukhâbâd	...	...	...	231	231
Mainpuri	15	15	...	247	277
Etâwah	...	...	...	1,505	1,505
Etah	6	6	...	1,048	1,060
Bareilly	...	...	...	10,044	10,044
Bijnor	1,832	...	1,382	356	3,120
Budâun	2,092	2,092	...	890	5,074
Morâdâbâd	1,659	1,488	171	2,095	5,413
Shâhjahânpur	19	...	19	679	717
Pilibhît	...	...	...	2,248	2,248
Cawnpur	...	...	...	474	474
Fatehpur	...	...	...	345	345
Bânda	...	...	...	66	66
Hamîrpur	...	...	...	15	15
Allahâbâd	...	...	...	1,250	1,250
Jhânsi	...	...	...	91	91
Jâlaun	...	...	...	62	62
Lalitpur	1	...	1	32	34
Benares	18	18	...	193	229
Mirzapur	...	...	...	103	103
Jaunpur	600	600	...	1	1,201

Distribution of the Meos according to the Census of 1891—concld.

Districts.	Hindus.			Muhammadan.	Total.
	Meo.	Mina.	Others.	Mewâti.	
Ghâzipur	...	...	...	30	30
Ballia	...	...	...	141	141
Gorakhpur	...	...	...	207	207
Basti	...	...	...	16	16
Azamgarh	...	...	...	207	207
Tarâi	480	467	13	2,533	3,493
Lucknow	...	...	...	1,934	1,934
Unâo	...	...	...	1,121	1,121
Râê Bareli	...	...	...	401	401
Sîtapur	...	...	...	331	331
Hardoi	...	...	...	124	124
Kheri	...	...	...	685	685
Faizâbâd	...	...	...	252	252
Gonda	...	...	...	518	518
Bahrâich	...	...	...	870	870
Sultânpur	...	...	...	462	462
Partâbgarh	...	...	...	116	116
Bârabanki	...	...	...	160	160
Total	10,642	8,755	1,887	60,352	81,616

GRAND TOTAL		
	HINDUS	21,284
	MUHAMMADANS	60,332
		81,616

Milki.[1]—A Muhammadan tribe in some of the Eastern districts and parts of Oudh who are not recorded separately in the last Census. In Unâo, they are landholders and field labourers. In Azamgarh, they are regarded as the aristocracy of the Muhammadan

[1] Based on a note by M. Chhutan Lâl, Deputy Collector, Unâo.

community, and are so called because their ancestors were the class to whom principally revenue grants (*milk*) were given under the Muhammadan rule. They are the class with whom we are most brought in contact, for they hold a good deal of landed property and from among them come many of our native officials and lawyers, the tribe in this respect occupying among Muhammadans the position that Kâyasths do among Hindus. They are, as a rule, inclined to indolence, and are wanting in practicality. Their neighbours do not put much trust in their generosity or straightforwardness. There is a popular proverb—

Milki kâ janê parâê dil ki ?
Paithê duâr niklê khirki :

"What does a Milki know of the feelings of another ?
He comes in by the door and out by the window."[1]

They are, as a rule, wanting in enthusiasm for their creed. Some are Shiahs and some Sunnis, and their lives are regulated by the orthodox rules of Islâm.

Mirâsi, Dom Mirâsi, Dûm Mirâsi.—A caste of singers, minstrels and genealogists. They are obviously an offshoot of the great Dom tribe, and at the last Census appear to have been classed among the Muhammadan Doms. The word Mirâsi is derived from the Arabic *Mirâs*, "inheritance," in the sense that the members of this caste are a sort of hereditary bards or minstrels to the lower tribes, as the Bhât is to the Râjputs. They are also known as Pakhâwaji, from the *Pakhâwaj* or timbrel which they play ; Kalawant, "possessed of art or skill" (*kala*); Qawwâl, "one who speaks fluently, a professional story-teller." They sometimes abbreviate the word Mirâsi into Mîr, as if they were Sayyids. They are seemingly closely akin to the Dhârhi, and the Muhammadan Mirâsis and Dhârhis appear to intermarry and eat together.

2. The Mirâsi has two functions—the men are musicians, story-tellers, and genealogists ; the women dance and sing, but they are said to perform only in the presence of women, and are reputed chaste. A writer in the *Calcutta Review*[2] gives an amusing account of the Mirâsi :—

"The Mirâsi is a perfect Autolycus at weddings and other functions among the Jâts, and again at the 'solid funerals,' in which the Râjput takes his pleasure sadly, as becomes a gentleman. One often meets him on a raw-boned steed, its tail dyed in the fashion to a ' air, and a pair of kettle-drums strapped across its withers wh'' ; the tails of a new pink turban, the fresh spoil of some magnan-ir ous client, stream in the March breeze behind the bard and genealogist. These 'beggars on horseback' absorb a most inordinate share of the farmer's gains, and help him, if recklessly disposed, in a variety of ways along the road proverbially open to the *nouveau riche* of all societies. For generations back the lords of Dig and Bhartpur were hardly recognised as even yeomen; but seventy years of peace and comparative plenty have trebled the demand for pedigrees as well as other luxuries." Writing of the Panjâb, Mr. Ibbetson says: "The position of the Mirâsi, as of all the minstrel castes, is exceedingly low; but he attends at weddings and similar occasions to recite genealogies. Moreover, there are grades even among Mirâsis. The out-caste tribes have their Mirâsis, who, though they do not eat with their clients, and merely render them professional service, are considered impure by the Mirâsis of the higher castes. The Mirâsi is generally a hereditary servant, like the Bhât, and is notorious for his exactions, which he makes under the threat of lampooning the ancestors of him from whom he demands fees."

3. The instruments of the Mirâsi are generally the small drum (*dholak*), the cymbals (*majîra*), and the gourd lute (*kingri*). They are said to have been converted to Islâm in response to an invitation from the poet Amîr Khusru, who lived in the reign of Alâ-ud-dîn Khilji (1295 A. D.). The most famous of them in recent times was Râji-ud-daula, who ruled the Court of Oudh. Another was 'Ali Bakhsh who married a European woman, and whose daughter married Nasîr-ud-dîn Haidar. The current proverbs illustrate the unfavourable view of the Dom Mirâsi: *Dom, Banya, Posti—tînon beîmân:* "The Dom, Banya, and opium-eater are all three rogues;" *Dom doli, Pâthak piyâda:* "The Dom in a litter and the Brâhman priest on foot;" *Munh lagâi Domni bâl bachhê samet âê:* "Encourage the singing woman, and she will come with all her brats;" *Bâp Dom aur Dom hi dâda; Kahê miyân? main shurfa zâda!* "His father was a bard, and so was his grandfather; but he says, 'Sir! My family is noble!'"

Mochi (Sanskrit *mochika*)—the cobbler and shoemaker class. They are properly an occupational sub-caste of Chamâr. There appear to be two kinds of Mochis: one, who make and cobble shoes are real Chamârs; those who make saddles and harness call themselves Sribâstab Kâyasths, with whom they intermarry and agree in manners and customs. They do not appear to know anythi g of the Bengal tradition of their origin, which is thus told by Mr. Risley:[1] "One of the Prajapati or mind-born sons of Brahma w. in the habit of providing the flesh of cows and clarified butter as a burnt offering (*ahuti*) to the gods. It was then the custom to eat a portion of sacrifice. restore the victim to life, and drive it into the for. On this occasion the Prajapati failed to resuscitate the sacrificial animal, owing to his wife, who was pregnant at the time, having clandestinely made away with a portion. Alarmed at this, he summoned all the other Prajapatis, and they sought by divination to discover the cause of the failure. At last they ascertained what had happened, and as a punishment the wife was cursed and expelled their society. The child which she bore was the first Mochi or tanner, and from that time forth mankind, being deprived of reanimating cattle slaughtered for food, the pious abandoned the practice of killing kine altogether. Another story is that Muchirâm, the ancestor of the caste, was born from the sweat of Brahma while dancing. He chanced to offend the irritable sage Durvâsa, who sent a pretty Brâhman widow to allure him into a breach of chastity. Muchirâm accosted the widow as mother and refused to have anything to do with her; but Durvâsa used the miraculous powers he had acquired by penance to render the widow pregnant, so that the innocent Muchirâm was made an outcaste on suspicion. From her twin sons descended the two main sub-castes of the Bengal Mochis." The Bengal Mochi evidently corresponds more to our Chamâr than Mochi. In Bengal he tans hides like the Chamâr, but will only cure those of the cow, goat, buffalo, and deer.

2. Lucknow and Cawnpur are the great centres of the shoe-making trade. A full account of the Lucknow shoe industry has been given by Mr. Hoey.[2] A common proverb runs—*Mochi mochi laren phaté râj ke jîn:* "When saddlers squabble the Râja's saddle gets torn," *i. e.,* "Too many cooks spoil the broth."

3. The Census returns show 150 sub-divisions of the Hindu and 27 of the Musalmân branch. We find, as usual, many names taken from those of other castes and septs, such as Bâgri, Bais, Bargûjar. Barwâr, Basoriya, Dhuna, Gaur, Gidhiya, Jâdon, Janwâr,

---

[1] Tribes and Castes III, 1895.

Jât, Kachhwâha, Kâyasth, Kori, Râjput, Ramosiya, Sakarwâr, Tomar: with local groups, such as Agarwâl, Allahâbâdi Bhojpuriya, Chaurasiya, Dilliwâl, Gujaratiya, Jaiswâr, Kanaujiya, Saksena, Shirâ' ., Sribâstab.

Distribution of Mochis according to the Census of 1891.

Districts.	Hindus.			Musalmâns.	Total.
	Sribâstab.	Others.	Total.		
Dehra Dûn . . .	...	92	92	...	92
Sahâranpur . . .	...	582	582	227	809
Muzaffarnagar . .	...	214	214	101	315
Meerut	...	180	180	67	247
Bulandshahr . . .	...	87	87	6	93
Aligarh	...	123	123	...	123
Mathura . . .	...	65	65	1	66
Agra	10	360	370	12	382
Farrukhâbâd . . .	151	343	494	20	514
Mainpuri . . .	...	69	69	1	70
Etâwah	18	261	279	21	300
Etah	61	100	161	2	163
Bareilly	...	169	169	...	169
Bijnor	...	...	...	294	294
Budâun	...	34	34	...	34
Morâdâbâd . . .	2	149	151	42	193
Shâhjahânpur . . .	73	85	158	34	192
Pilibhît	22	52	74	45	119
Cawnpur	40	1,116	1,156	36	1,192
Fatehpur	50	117	167	11	178
Bânda . . .	39	159	198	...	198
Hamîrpur	61	98	159	2	161

Distribution of Mochis according to the Census of 1891—concld.

Districts.	Hindus.			Musal-mâns.	Total.
	Sribâstab.	Others.	Total.		
Allahâbâd	17	560	577	19	59
Jhânsi	115	...	115	3	118
Jâlaun	14	118	132	3	135
Lalitpur	...	56	56	...	56
Benares	8	43	51	67	118
Mirzapur	102	23	125	...	125
Jaunpur	...	14	14	126	140
Ghâzipur	...	...	...	63	63
Ballia	...	...	...	123	123
Gorakhpur	59	29	88	261	349
Basti	...	...	...	322	322
Azamgarh	...	4	4	124	128
Kumaun	...	115	115	...	115
Garhwâl	...	...	...	...	...
Tarâi	...	10	10	...	10
Lucknow	...	570	570	569	1,139
Unâo	28	32	60	...	60
Râê Bareli	18	91	109	152	261
Sîtapur	162	129	291	5	296
Hardoi	45	101	146	25	171
Kheri	106	...	106	1	107
Fâizâbâd	31	49	80	184	264
Gonda		9	9	155	164
Bahrâich	51	118	169	66	235
Sultânpur	...	64	64	342	406
Partâbgarh	...	38	38	93	131
Bârabanki	...	108	108	47	155
Total	1,283	6,736	8,019	3,672	11,691

G. I. C. P. O.—No. 17 S. to G. N. W. P —22-5-96.—500.